Contract Cases and Materials

Robert Clark
&
Blanaid Clarke

GILL & MACMILLAN

Gill & Macmillan Ltd
Goldenbridge
Dublin 8
with associated companies throughout the world
www.gillmacmillan.ie

© Robert Clark and Blanaid Clarke 1994

0 7171 2196 8

Design and print origination by
Carrigboy Typesetting Services
Printed in Malaysia

A catalogue record is available for this book from the British Library.

Contents

Preface

As law teachers charged with the task of instructing undergraduate students for whom contract law is a central element in the curriculum we have long felt the need for a collection of cases and materials which would give these students ready access to primary sources in this area. We hope that this casebook will provide teachers and students with much of the case-law and the academic commentary needed to give Irish students competence in what can be a difficult and complex area of law.

The materials compiled here are intended as a course book rather than a collection of indigenous Irish material. While acknowledging that a casebook restricted to Irish materials may be a worthy and justifiable tool (e.g. *McMahon and Binchy on Torts*), we prefer an intensive and comprehensive work that draws upon pertinent material from other jurisdictions. In the area of contract, many key issues are not covered in modern Irish case-law, and we believe that students should be aware of the nature of these issues and their potential solutions, even if the solutions presented are from other jurisdictions. This approach provides Irish students with a comparative analysis of common law contract law and with the opportunity to contrast competing approaches to universal problems.

While Irish contract law tends to follow the pattern set by the English common law there have always been points of divergence from, and differences in emphasis to, that jurisdiction. Irish law on unconscionability and the Statute of Frauds, for example, even prior to 1922, was often at different stages of development to the relevant English law. On the former, the wonderful judgment of Gavan Duffy J. in *Grealish v. Murphy* [1946] IR 35 stands both as a profound analysis of aspects of Irish law and society and as a literary gem. More recently, the development of promissory estoppel and legitimate expectation through *Webb* shows how judicial ingenuity in the area of contract continues to play an important cultural and historical role. In the main, we have set out the law in a way which, we hope, will enable the student to extract the conceptual and doctrinal lessons from the primary source.

The casebook is longer than we had planned and the problem was always rather what to discard than what to keep. Drawing on our experience of teaching in university law schools, we edited or omitted areas that are either shunned or are educationally incoherent (e.g. gaming contracts and infant contracts). Areas that we regard as of immense practical and academic interest were treated comprehensively (e.g. exemption clauses and damages). We hope that this selection process has not rendered the book too unbalanced.

The extracts are not laid out in a common format. Some judgments and some law reports include footnotes while others include references in the text. In general we have adhered to the layout of the primary source although we have tried to avoid duplication of references in order to preserve space. For similar reasons some footnotes have been omitted or abridged from certain primary materials. We accept responsibility for errors and omissions. We would be happy to hear from readers who wish to point these out or to castigate us for any infelicities detected in the book!

Robert Clark   Blanaid Clarke
Mount Merrion   Los Angeles

3 September 1994

Acknowledgments

For permission to use copyright material, grateful acknowledgment is made to the following:

Blackwell Publications for extracts from the *Modern Law Review*;

Butterworths (Australia) for extracts from the *Victoria Law Reports*;

Butterworths (UK) for extracts from the *All England Law Reports*;

Canada Law Book Inc. for extracts from the *Dominian Law Report*;

Carswell for extracts from the *British Columbia Law Reports*;

Clarendon Press for extracts from *Consideration: A Restatement* by P.S. Atiyah and *Remedies for Breach of Contract* by G.H. Treitel;

Columbia Law Review for extracts from the *Columbia Law Review*;

The Incorporated Council of Law Reporting for England and Wales for the use of case extracts from the *Weekly Law Reports*, *Queen's Bench*, *King's Bench*, *Appeal Courts*, *Industrial Case Reports*, all part of their series of English Law Reports;

The Incorporated Council of Law Reporting for Ireland for extracts from the *Irish Reports*;

The Incorporated Council of Law Reporting for Northern Ireland for extracts from the *Northern Ireland Law Reports*;

The Law Book Company Ltd for extracts from the *Commonwealth Law Reports* (Australia);

McGill-Queen's University Press for extracts from the *McGill-Queen's Law Journal*;

The Roundhall Press for extracts from the *Irish Law Reports Monthly* and the *Irish Law Times Journal*;

Sweet & Maxwell Ltd for the use of case extracts from the *Fleet Street Reports* (FSR), extracts from *Damages* by McGregor, *Exemption Clauses* by David Yates and *Contract Law in Ireland* by Robert Clark;

University of Queensland Press for extracts from *Consideration Reconsidered* by K.C.T. Sutton;

Yale University Press for extracts from the *Yale Law Journal*;

The Publishers, despite their best efforts, were unable to trace the remaining copyright holders. They will, however, make the usual and appropriate arrangements with any who contact them.

Table of Cases

Cases in italics are cited only.

Table of Statutes and Regulations

EC/EU

US

Chapter One

Introduction to the Law of Contract

SECTION ONE—CONTRACT IN EARLY SOCIETIES

Max Weber, in his classic study, *On Law in Economy and Society* (ed. Rheinstein, New York: Clarion 1954) sought to develop the jurisprudential character of legal rights and privileges, one of which he identified as the legal privilege which grants a person the freedom to regulate relations with others by acts of volition or free will:

. . .

. . . Freedom of contract, for example, exists exactly to the extent to which such autonomy is recognised by the legal order. There exists, of course, an intimate connection between the expansion of the market and the expanding measure of contractual freedom or, in other words, the scope of arrangements which are guaranteed as valid by the legal order or, in again different terms, the relative significance within the total legal order of those rules which authorise such transactional dispositions. In an economy where self-sufficiency prevails and exchange is lacking, the function of the law will naturally be otherwise: it will mainly define and delimit a person's non-economic relations and privileges with regard to other persons in accordance, not with economic considerations, but with the person's origin, education, or social status.

Section 2. Development of Freedom of Contract—'Status Contracts' and 'Purposive Contracts'—The Historical Origin of the Purposive Contracts
   1. 'Freedom' in the legal sense means the possession of rights, actual and potential, which, however, in a marketless community naturally do not rest predominantly upon legal transactions but rather directly upon the prescriptive and prohibitory propositions of the law itself. Exchange, on the other hand, is, within the framework of a legal order, a 'legal transaction', *viz.* the acquisition, the transfer, the relinquishment, or the fulfilment of a legal claim. With every extension of the market, these legal transactions become more numerous and more complex. However, in no legal order is freedom of contract unlimited in the sense that the law would place its guaranty of coercion at the disposal of all and every agreement regardless of its terms. A legal order can indeed be characterised by the agreements which it does or does not enforce. In this respect a decisive influence is exercised by diverse interest groups, which varies in accordance with differences in the economic structure. In an increasingly expanding market, those who have market interests constitute the most important group. Their influence predominates in determining which legal transactions the law should regulate by means of power granting norms.
   That extensive contractual freedom which generally obtains today has, of course, not always existed; and even where freedom of contract did exist, it did not always prevail in the spheres in which it prevails today. Freedom of contract once existed indeed in spheres in which it is no longer prevalent or in which it is far less prevalent than it used to be. We shall survey the main stages of development in the following brief sketch.

1

In contrast to the older law, the most essential feature of modern substantive law, especially private law, is the greatly increased significance of legal *transactions*, particularly *contracts*, as a source of claims guaranteed by legal coercion. So very characteristic is this feature of private law that one can *a potiori* designate the contemporary type of society, to the extent that private law obtains, as a 'contractual' one.

Weber went on to examine certain legal phenomena that could be described as contract related, such as inheritance dispositions, public appointments by governments, and certain social arrangements within primitive societies which could loosely be described as contractual. These led Weber to conclude that a 'contract', in the sense of a voluntary agreement constituting the legal foundation of claims and obligations, has been widely diffused even in the earliest stages of legal history. He continued to develop this theme by examining the role of contract as an economic tool.

. . . however, the farther we go back in legal history, the less significant becomes contract as a device of economic acquisition in fields other than the law of the family and inheritance. The situation is vastly different today. The present day significance of contract is primarily the result of the high degree to which our economic system is market-oriented and of the role played by money. The increased importance of the private law contract in general is thus the legal reflex of the market orientation of our economy. But contracts characteristic of a market economy are completely different from those contracts which in the spheres of public and family law once played a greater role than they do today. In accordance with this fundamental transformation of the general character of the voluntary agreement we shall call the more primitive type 'status contract' and that which is peculiar to the exchange or market economy 'purposive contract'.

The distinction is based on the fact that all those primitive contracts by which political or other personal associations, permanent or temporary, or family relations are created involve, substantially, a change in what may be called the total legal situation (the universal position) and the social status of the persons involved. To have this effect these contracts were originally either straightforward magical acts or at least acts having a magical significance. For a long time their symbolism retained traces of that character, and the majority of these contracts are 'fraternisation contracts'. By means of such a contract a person was to become somebody's child, father, wife, brother, master, slave, kin, comrade-in-arms, protector, client, follower, vassal, subject, friend, or, quite generally, comrade. To 'fraternise' with another person did not, however, mean that a certain performance of the contract, contributing to the attainment of some specific object, was reciprocally guaranteed or expected. Nor did it mean that the making of a promise to another would, as we might put it, have ushered in a new orientation in the relationship between the parties. The contract rather meant that the person would 'become' something different in quality (or status) from the quality he possessed before. For unless a person voluntarily assumed that new quality, his future conduct in his new role could hardly be believed to be possible at all. Each party must thus make a new 'soul' enter his body. At a rather late stage the symbolism required the mixing and imbibing of blood or spittle or the creation of a new soul by some animistic process or by some other magical rite.

One whose thinking is embedded in magic cannot imagine any other than a magical guaranty for the parties to conform, in their total behaviour, to the intention of the 'fraternisation' they contracted. But as the notion of the divinity gradually replaces animism, it is found necessary to place each party under the dominion of a supernatural power, which power constitutes not only their collective protection but also jointly and severally threatens them in case of antifraternal conduct. The *oath*, which originally appears as a person's conditional self-surrender to evil magical forces, subsequently assumes the character of a conditional self-curse, calling for the divine wrath to strike. Thus the oath remains even in later times one of the most universal forms of all fraternisation pacts. But its use is not so limited.

In contrast to the true magical forms of fraternisation, the oath is also technically suited to serve as a guaranty for purposive contracts, i.e. contracts neither affecting the status of the parties nor giving rise to new qualities of comradeship but aiming solely, as, for instance, barter, at some specific (especially economic) performance or result. This type of contract, however, does not appear in the most primitive society. In earliest times, *barter*, the archetype of all merely instrumental contracts, would seem to have been a general phenomenon among the comrades of an economic or political community only in the non-economic sphere, particularly as barter of women between exogamous sibs whose members seem to confront each other in the strange dual role of being partly comrades and partly strangers. In the state of exogamy barter appears also as an act of fraternisation; however much the woman may be regarded as a mere object, there will rarely be missing the concurrent idea of a change of status to be brought about by magical means. The peculiar duality in the relations between the exogamously cartelised sibs, created by the rise of regulated exogamy, may perhaps help to explain a much discussed phenomenon, namely, the phenomenon that certain formalities were sometimes required for the marriage with a concubine while the marriage with the legitimate wife might be entered into without any formalities. It may be that the latter remained formless because it was the original and pre-exogamous type of marriage, while barter in pre-exogamous times did not yet have anything to do with fraternisation. It is more plausible, however, that fixed contractual formalities were necessitated by the need for special arrangements regarding the economic security of the concubine who lacked the generally fixed economic status of the legitimate wife.

Economic barter was always confined to transactions with persons who were not members of one's own 'house', especially with outsiders in the sense of non-kinsmen, non-'brothers'; in short, non-comrades. For precisely this reason barter also lacked in the form of 'silent' trade any trace of magical formalism. Only gradually did it acquire religious protection through the law of the market. Such protection, however, would not arise as a set of settled forms until a belief in gods had taken its place alongside those magical conceptions which had provided appropriate means of direct guaranty only for status contracts. Occasionally it would also happen that a barter transaction might be placed under the guaranty of the status contract through some special act of fraternisation or some equivalent. This would not generally happen, however, unless land were involved. Normally, barter enjoyed practically no guaranty, and the conception was non-existent that barter could mean the assumption of an 'obligation' which would not be the product of a natural or artificial all-inclusive fraternal relationship. As a result, barter at first took effect exclusively as a set of two simultaneous and reciprocal acts of immediate delivery of possession. Possession, however, is protected by the claim for vengeance on, and expiation by, the thief. Thus, the kind of 'legal protection' accorded to barter was not the protection of an obligation, but of possession. Where, at a later time, the obligation of warranty of title came to develop at all, it was protected only indirectly in the form of an action for theft against the seller who lacked title.

Formal legal construction of barter does not begin until certain goods, especially metals, have acquired a monetary function, i.e. where sale has arisen. This development does not depend upon the existence of chartal or even state money, but, as shown especially in Roman law, on mere pensatory means of payment. The transactions *per aes et libram* constitute one of the two original forms of legal transaction in ancient Roman *ius civile*. In the domain of Roman urban developments this form of cash purchase acquired an almost universal function for the most diverse classes of private legal transactions, regardless of whether they involved questions of family or inheritance law or of exchange proper. The agreements of fraternisation as well as other forms of status contract were oriented toward the total social status of the individual and his integration into an association comprehending his total personality. This form of contract with its all-inclusive rights and duties and the special attitudinal qualities based thereon thus appears in contrast to the money contract, which, as a specific, quantitatively delimited, qualityless, abstract, and usually economically conditioned agreement, represents the archetype of 'coercing contract' (*Zwangskontrakt*). The money contract, as such a coercing contract of ethical indifference, was the appropriate means for the elimination of the magical and sacramental elements from legal transactions and for the secularisation of the law. In Roman law, for example, the civil marriage form of *coemptio* thus came to confront the sacred marriage form of *confarreatio*. The money contract was, it is true, not the only suitable means, but it was the most suitable. Indeed, as a specific cash transaction it was of a rather conservative nature since, originally at least, it was completely devoid of any promissory elements oriented towards the future. For the effect of this transaction, too, was solely to provide secure possession as well as a guaranty that the goods were properly acquired; however, at any rate originally, the transaction did not constitute a guaranty that the promises involved in it would be fulfilled.

The concept of obligation through contract was entirely alien to primitive law; it knew but one form of obligation and claim, *viz.* that arising *ex delicto*. The amount of the claim of an injured party was rigorously fixed by the practice of composition and its attendant conventions. The *wergilt* debt as set by the judge was the most ancient true debt and all other forms of obligation have derived from it. Conversely it can be said that only such actions were cognisable by the courts as arose from an obligation. As regards disputes between members of different kinship groups, no formal procedure existed for the restitution of chattels or the surrender of immovables. Every complaint was necessarily based upon the argument that the defendant had personally done the plaintiff a wrong which would have to be expiated. Hence there was no place for an action *ex contractu* or for the recovery of a chattel or a piece of land or for actions to determine personal status.

The importance of contract in early Irish society is examined by Professor Neil McLeod in his book, *Early Irish Contract Law* (Sydney: Centre for Celtic Studies 1993) Professor McLeod focused his attention on early Irish manuscripts in order to produce a statement of contractual principles to be found in seventh and eighth century Brehon law:

Early Irish law recognised the exchange of *féich*, 'obligations', as the basis of contract. The name given to each party to a contract, *féchem*, is itself an acknowledgment of the dominant role of such obligations in defining the contract relationship.

Berrad Airechta §49: Cid ara n-eperr féchem? Ní ansae, arindí dliges nó dligther de; ar is féchem cechtar n-aí.

Why is it that a contracting party (*féchem*) is so called? It is not difficult [to say], because of the fact that he is entitled to [something] or that [it] is owed from him; for each of them is a contracting party.

The obligation accepted by each contracting party is to render *folud*, 'consideration', to the other. The acceptance of this obligation in turn creates an entitlement (*dliged*) to the counter-consideration (*frithfolud*) promised by the other party.

In order to facilitate the enforcement of contracts, certain formal requirements are laid down in the laws; in particular the appointment of witnesses and sureties. The use of writing was limited and it was assumed that contracts would normally be made orally rather than in writing. In early Irish law there is no inherent distinction between the word *cor*, 'contract', and the fuller term *cor bél*, 'spoken contract'. In everyday usage *cor* had a wide range of meanings ('putting', 'throwing', 'casting') and *bél*, 'of the lips', simply indicated that the 'arrangement' meant was a contractual one.

In modern law, writing serves an important function in evidencing the terms of a contract. Early Irish law solved such problems of evidence by formally requiring the appointment of witnesses who were specifically charged with noting, and preserving in their memories, the terms of the agreement. The technical term of a contractual witness was *roach*, though often the more general term *fíadu*, 'eye-witness', is used in the law texts.

Under the canon law of the early Irish church, however, contracts were required to be in writing. While such a requirement did not spread to the secular law, the latter did accommodate church practice by recognising the validity of such written evidence as to the terms of a contract. Documents of this kind are referred to in the laws as *scríbend déodae*, 'holy writing', in acknowledgment of their ecclesiastical origin. But the use of writing was not a substitute for the appointment of witnesses; they were still required, as the canon law of the *Collectio Canonum Hibernensis* itself points out. While the native law accommodated the use of writing, a contract which had not yet been performed was unenforceable without witnesses.

As we shall see, the following passage neatly defines the role of sureties and witnesses in early Irish law.

Berrad Airechta §63: Báeth nech nad mbí naidm, na ráth, na fíadnaise fri cach cundrath fri forgell cuimne . . . Fir n-ambechtae cor cen ráith, cen fíadna, cen naidm. Ar is naidm do-boing, ráth gellas, fíadnaise con-oí la folta fíachu.

Senseless [is] anyone [for] whom there is not enforcing surety, nor paying surety, nor witnessing in regard to every bargain for the testimony of remembrance . . . An unprovable truth [is] a contract without a paying surety, without witnesses, without an enforcing surety. For in addition to considerations and obligations, it is the enforcing surety who exacts, paying surety who pledges, and the witnessing which preserves.

The institution of suretyship as a means of enforcing contracts was founded on the strength of personal bonds (of kinship and of patronage, for example). The sureties appointed by a party to a contract promised to safeguard the performance of the agreement much as a parent might guarantee a child's hire-purchase obligations today. The functional basis of suretyship was twofold. First, because of his superior social standing, the surety was more vulnerable to public disgrace, or more able to pay, than the party he secured. Second, the surety was in a better position to ensure adherence to the contract than the other party to it. The surety was often in the position of master in regard to the party whose contract he secured: a father would guarantee the contracts of his son, a lord those of his clients, an abbot the contracts of his-monastic subordinates, a teacher those of his apprentices.

There were three types of surety invoked to support contracts. The first was the *naidm* (or *macc*), the 'enforcing surety'. The *naidm* promised on his honour that the party who had invoked him would not default on his duties under the contract, and that if he tried to the surety would force him to fulfil them. The *naidm* was entitled to use any means necessary to extract payment from the defaulter who had invoked him. Usually this meant the distraint of his cattle, but he could seize the defaulter himself, and even kill him without legal penalty. The *naidm* not only extracted the amount owed to the other party; he was, in addition, entitled to be paid his own honour-price as compensation for the injury to his honour caused by the default. Because of his status, the *naidm*'s honour-price would often be quite large and would in any event be at least as large as the original debt under the contract. Taken together with the close relationship that existed between the enforcing surety and the party he represented, the pressures on the latter to observe the contract are obvious enough. In addition, an enforcing surety who failed to compel compliance with the contract lost his honour, since he had pledged on his honour that he would ensure the contract was performed. To lose one's honour was to lose one's rights and position in society.

Most contractual obligations were secured by the appointment of both an enforcing surety (*naidm*) and a paying surety (*ráth*). The *ráth* was a 'paying surety' who guaranteed that he would make good from his own resources the debts of the party he represented, should that prove necessary. But he was only liable to do so if the efforts of the enforcing surety failed. In such cases the *ráth*, too, was entitled to his honour-price and to recover, with interest, the amount he had paid to satisfy the claims of the creditor.

A third type of surety, less well attested in regard to contracts, was the *aitire* or 'hostage-surety'. This type of surety may have been invoked when the parties to a contract were themselves of such high status that persons able to undertake the duty of forcing them to fulfil their respective obligations were not readily available. On the other hand, the hostage-surety is found being invoked where the breach of a contract would give rise to a right to exact physical retribution; namely in a contract to avoid a blood-feud and provide sick-maintenance for injuries inflicted by the party invoking the hostage-surety:

> Críth Gablach ll. 52–3: Tongair fri corp — anmain, — do-tét aitire ar fer feras in fuil, i córus n-othruso, i mboin.

> There is a swearing by body and soul, and |a man| offers himself as hostage-surety for the man who caused the bloodshed, in accordance with the system of sick-maintenance, in exchange for a cow.

If the obligations of 'the man who caused the bloodshed' were not met, the hostage-surety would become a ready target for the pursuit of the blood feud.

Upon default, the hostage had to submit himself to the aggrieved party. The defaulter had ten days to ransom the hostage by paying the amount due (including a surcharge for default). After the ten-day period the hostage was forfeit. His liberty and life were technically at the disposal of the party to whom he had given himself up. But he could redeem himself by paying over an amount equal to the valuation of a human body at Irish law (7 *cumals* = 21 milking cows). The hostage was entitled to recover this payment and his honour-price from the defaulter, who remained liable on the contract itself.

It appears that witnesses and sureties were entitled to be paid a fee for being invoked in support of a contract . . .

. . .

In general then, a contract was unenforceable if it was not supported by sureties. This is not to say that it was void, only that no action could be taken to compel its performance. A contract once executed was not rescindable merely because sureties had not been appointed; as we shall see, the law specifically contemplates that there may have been no sureties when it comes to deal with actions for defects in consideration paid.

Indeed, where a contract involved the instantaneous exchange of consideration by both sides, there would be little need for sureties. The size of fees commanded by sureties and witnesses may also have ruled them out in many minor contracts of a more promissory nature.

Furthermore, the rule that sureties ought to be invoked was only a general one to which there was quite an extensive list of exceptions.

Coibnes Uisci Thairidne §§6–7: Ar dí-chenglaither cach cor cen ráith la Féniu. Inge secht n-uasalchuru nadat assai do thaithbiuch neoch ma ro-látar . . .

For every contract without a paying surety is rendered non-binding according to Irish law. Except seven noble contracts which are not easy to dissolve if they have been made . . .

These exceptional contracts may be compared with the seven contracts made 'without an enforcing surety, without a paying surety' in *Heptad* 25. As usual, the 'heptads' are merely illustrative rather than exhaustive of their subject matter, as is shown by the fact that they only partially overlap and also by the much longer list given in *Berrad Airechta* §§1–15 and §34. The contracts covered in these sources consist mainly of service contracts, namely contracts of clientship, contracts to secure the care of the aged, contracts of fosterage and education, payments for the services of poets, lawyers and doctors, contracts for the services and craftsmen and contracts with messengers.

. . .

Berrad Airechta §§1, 5 and 6, *Coibnes Uisci Thairidne* §7 and *Heptad* 25 also state that alms and offerings to the church need not be secured by sureties. There are some grounds for arguing that these payments to the church should be seen as being in exchange for its services in much the same way as the *tuillem bathais*, 'baptism fee', mentioned in *Berrad Airechta* §1. *Córus Béscnai* tries to rationalise the church's rights to offerings, tithes and first fruits as being balanced by the laity's rights to baptism, communion, requiem, and mass. Note that *Berrad Airechta* §§5 and 6 make it clear that offerings are not inviolable if the church to whom they are given has so strayed from orthodoxy in its religious functions as to no longer fit the definition of a church. But this appeal to the analogy of contracts for specific services as a rationale for the validity of unsecured offerings must in reality be seen as a legal fiction. That a church to whom an offering is made continues to function as it has always intended to function hardly amounts to consideration by way of the provision of services. (Note that *Córus Béscnai* elsewhere justifies such payments to the church rather on the basis that they are necessary to avert cosmic disorder.) In pragmatic terms at least, these payments are unilateral gifts to the church. Their inviolability is significant in that they cut across the interests of the donor's kin, and under ecclesiastical pressure appear to have been allowed in such a way that the donor need not turn to his kin either for permission or for the provision of sureties.

Most other promises of gifts are treated in early Irish law as normal contracts which must be secured by sureties in order to be enforceable. In modern law a contract only exists where it can be shown that each party has given consideration, i.e. (a promise of) something valuable, to the other. This modern definition of a contract cannot extend to gratuitous payments. Something quite different is the case in early Irish law. The explanation of the inclusion of gifts as contracts has as its starting-point a principle of law common to both ancient and modern Irish law. While both parties give 'something of value' to support their rights under the contract, it is not necessary for consideration to be evenly balanced. Modern law is only interested in the existence, not in the adequacy, of consideration. Consideration may be inadequate or minute, so long as it is tangible. But in early Irish law this principle was taken to its logical extreme: it was acknowledged that in some cases consideration may not be very one-sided but that it might even be totally so. In such cases the beneficiary, by doing what he has promised to do—namely nothing—easily 'fulfils' his obligations under the agreement and thereby creates an entitlement to the consideration promised him.

. . .

While an executed gift could not be reversed for want of consideration, not all gratuitous promises were binding as contracts. Except in the case of gifts to the church, the promise of a gift would need to be supported by sureties if it were to be enforceable. And all contracts were required to be made before formally appointed witnesses.

Sir Henry Maine, *Ancient Law* (Boston: Beacon (1864) (1963))

. . . The movement of the progressive societies has been uniform in one respect. Through all its course it has been distinguished by the gradual dissolution of family dependency, and the growth of individual obligation in its place. The individual is steadily substituted for the family, as the unit of which civil laws take account. The advance has been accomplished at varying rates of celerity, and there are societies not absolutely stationary in which the collapse of the ancient organisation can only be perceived by careful study of the phenomena they present. But, whatever its pace, the change has not been subject to reaction or recoil, and apparent retardations will be found to have been occasioned through the absorption of archaic ideas and customs from some entirely foreign source. Nor is it difficult to see what is the tie between man and man which replaces by degrees those forms of reciprocity in rights and duties which have their origin in the family. It is contract. Starting, as from one terminus of history, from a condition of society in which all the relations of persons are summed up in the relations of family, we seem to have steadily moved towards a phase of social order in which all these relations arise from the free agreement of individuals. In Western Europe the progress achieved in this direction has been considerable.

The word status may be usefully employed to construct a formula expressing the law of progress thus indicated, which, whatever be its value, seems to me to be sufficiently ascertained. All the forms of status taken notice of in the law of persons were derived from, and to some extent are still coloured by, the powers and privileges anciently residing in the family. If then we employ status, agreeably with the usage of the best writers, to signify these personal conditions only, and avoid applying the term to such conditions as are the immediate or remote result of agreement, we may say that the movement of the progressive societies has hitherto been a movement *from status to contract.*'

Note

The development of the law of contract in Ireland under the influence of English law was shaped by a number of factors, the most significant of which were the expansion of the King's Courts over the private affairs of individuals, the standardisation of pleadings and remedies through the writ system, and the inevitable reaction against the inflexibility that resulted by virtue of equitable jurisdiction and equitable remedies. In English feudal society many of the areas that are seen as contractual now were conceived to be part of the law of tenure, a part of the law of real property. Actions in the King's Courts to protect such rights began to be possible if the right had been ceded by way of a formal instrument—a deed. The cause of action used to protect and vindicate such rights were actions in covenant and debt. Such deeds were used in relation to agreements to convey property, or grant a lease for years, although in the later mediaeval period the action in covenant could be used in proceedings relating to any non-observance of the terms of any deed under seal.

The enforceability of simple contracts however, as distinct from contracts by specialty (verbal agreements as distinct from contracts under seal) evolved very slowly over the centuries. Actions in debt began to be entertained by the courts if the plaintiff, for example, had performed his part of the contract but the defendant had not. By the fifteenth century the limitations found in the writ system made it necessary to develop delictual or tortious causes of action if a wholly unperformed contract, broken by the defendant, could be capable of redress in the King's Courts. By forging an action from the action for trespass on the case and action in deceit, informal mutual promises could be enforceable, as where a doctor promised to cure a horse but did so negligently, thereby occasioning the death of the horse. The assumption of a duty by express or implied promise thus evolved into the action *in assumpsit*, available in cases of *misfeasance*, or a failure to correctly perform an assumed obligation. This action was, however, not available in cases of complete non-performance (*non feasance*) until 1602 when the Court of Exchequer Chamber decided *Slade's* case (1602) 4 Co. Rep. 91a. *Slade's* case marks the erosion of the older forms of action in covenant, debt and account, and the evolution of the principle that 'every contract executory imparts into itself an *assumpsit*, for when one agrees to pay money or to deliver anything, thereby he assumes or promises to pay or deliver it.'

For additional reading see Simpson, A *History of the Common Law of Contract* (OUP 1975); Holdsworth, *History of English Law*, vol. III, ch. 3; Jackson (1937) 53 LQR 525.

SECTION TWO—THE CAUSES OF ACTION

A. CONTRACT AND TORT

The fact that contract emerged from the law of tort and the law of property does not mean that the causes of action are broadly concentric. In many respects the law of tort, in particular the law relating to negligence and actionable misrepresentation, seeks to achieve quite distinct goals. The law relating to third party liability, the recoverability of non-economic loss and remoteness of damage, to mention just three elements, will produce different results depending on whether liability is established in contract or tort.

Finlay v Murtagh [1979] IR 249 SC

Henchy J.:

When a client complains that he has suffered loss because his solicitor has failed to show due care in the performance of his duty as solicitor, does the client's cause of action lie in contract or in the tort of the negligence? Or has he a choice? That is the problem presented in this appeal. The plaintiff client has founded his claim against the defendant solicitor in negligence, his case being (and it has not been denied) that the defendant did not, within the period fixed by the statute of limitations, bring an action for damages for personal injuries sustained by the plaintiff as a result of the alleged negligence of a third party. The plaintiff has served notice of trial against the defendant before a judge sitting with a jury, which he would be entitled to do if his cause of action lies, as has been pleaded, in tort. But the defendant contends that the cause of action is breach of contract, that is to say that it is founded on a breach of the implied term in the contract that he would carry out his duties as solicitor with due professional care and skill. If the defendant is correct in that contention, the notice of trial should have been for a judge sitting without a jury. So the defendant has moved in the High Court for an order setting aside the notice of trial which was served. Mr Justice D'Arcy refused to make that order as he held that the plaintiff's action lies in the tort of negligence. It is from that refusal that the present appeal has been brought by the defendant.

There has been no decision of this court on the point at issue but we have been referred to three decisions of the High Court. In *McGrath v Kiely*[1] the client sued his solicitor for negligence and, alternatively, for breach of contract in failing to show due professional care in the preparation of an action for damages for personal injuries. The claim was pursued in court as one for breach of contract and no effort was made to pursue the claim in negligence. The parties agreed to treat the solicitor's default as a breach of contract. Therefore, that case throws no light on the present problem.

The second case, *Liston v Munster and Leinster Bank*,[2] was an action by the personal representative of a customer of the bank against the bank for damages for negligence, for conversion, and for money had and received. The issue being whether the entire cause of action arose out of a contract, in which case notice of trial by a judge without a jury would be appropriate, or whether it lay partly in tort, in which case the notice of trial that had been served specifying trial by a judge with a jury would have been correct. In holding that the claim was partly for breach of contract and partly for conversion, O'Byrne J. applied the following test which had been laid down by Greer L.J. in *Jarvis v Moy, Davies, Smith, Vandervell & Co.*[3] at 405 of the report:

The distinction in the modern view, for this purpose, between contract and tort may be put thus: where the breach of duty alleged arises out of a liability independently of the personal obligation undertaken by contract, it is tort, and it may be tort even though there may happen to be a contract between the parties, if the duty in fact arises independently of that contract. Breach of contract occurs where that which is complained of is a breach of duty arising out of the obligations undertaken by the contract.

The third High Court case to which we were referred is *Somers v Erskine*.[4] There the question was whether an action commenced by a client against a solicitor for negligence, and sought to be continued against the solicitor's personal representative, had abated with the solicitor's death as an action in tort, or whether it survived his death as an action in contract. In an unreserved judgment Maguire P. applied the same test as was applied by O'Byrne J. in *Liston v Munster and Leinster Bank*, and held that the client's claim was essentially one in contract rather than in tort and that, therefore, the claim had survived the solicitor's death. In my opinion, the conclusion that an action by a client against a solicitor for damages for breach of his professional duty of care is necessarily and exclusively one in contract is incompatible with modern developments in the law of torts and should be overruled. In my view, the conclusion there reached does not follow from a correct application of the test laid down by Greer L.J. in the *Jarvis* case.

The claim made by the plaintiff in the *Jarvis* case was one by a client against stockbrokers 'for damages for breach of contract arising out of the defendants' relationship with the plaintiff as stockbrokers and client.' Therefore, it is clear that the action was one for breach of contract, at least in form. But the particulars given in the writ show that the substance of the complaint was that the stockbrokers had departed from the specific instructions given by the client. Therefore, the cause of action arose from the breach of a particular binding provision created by the parties, and not from any general obligation of care arising from the relationship of stockbroker and client. The nub of the matter was that the stockbrokers had defaulted on a special personal obligation which was imposed by the contract. They could not have been made liable otherwise than in contract and the court held correctly that the claim was 'founded on contract' in the words of the statute which was being applied.

The test adumbrated by Greer L.J., which commended itself to O'Byrne J. in *Liston v Munster and Leinster Bank* and to Maguire P. in *Somers v Erskine*, correctly draws a distinction between a claim arising out of an obligation deriving from, and owing its existence to, a personal obligation undertaken pursuant to a contract (in which case it is an action in contract) and a claim arising out of a liability created independently of a contract and not deriving from any special obligation imposed by a contract (in which case an action lies in tort). The action in tort derives from an obligation which is imposed by the general law and is applicable to all persons in a certain relationship to each other. The action in contract is founded on the special law which was created by a contract and which was designed to fit the particular relationship of that contract. As I understand it, therefore, the test propounded by Greer L.J. does not support the conclusion reached by Maguire P. that, because the contract of retainer implies a duty of professional care and skill and because a default in that duty has occurred, the cause of action lies exclusively in contract.

It has to be conceded that for over a hundred years there has been a divergence of judicial opinion as to whether a client who has engaged a solicitor to act for him, and who claims that the solicitor failed to show due professional care and skill, may sue in tort or whether he is confined to an action in contract. In *Somers v Erskine* (and in some

English cases) it was held that the sole cause of action was the solicitor's failure to observe the implied term in the contract of retainer that he would show due professional skill and care. It is undeniable that the client is entitled to sue in contract for breach of that implied term. But it does not follow that the client, because there is privity of contract between him and the solicitor and because he may sue the solicitor for breach of the contract, is debarred from suing also for the tort of negligence. Since the decision of the House of Lords in *Hedley Byrne & Co. Ltd v Heller & Partners Ltd*[5] and the cases following in its wake, it is clear that, whether a contractual relationship exists or not, once the circumstances are such that a defendant undertakes to show professional care and skill towards a person who may be expected to rely on such care and skill and who does so rely, then if he has been damnified by such default that person may sue the defendant in the tort of negligence for failure to show such care and skill. For the purpose of such an action, the existence of a contract is merely an incident of the relationship. If, on the one side, there is a proximity of relationship creating a general duty and, on the other, a reliance on that duty, it matters not whether the parties are bound together in contract. For instance, if the defendant in the present case had not been retained for reward but had merely volunteered his services to the plaintiff, his liability in negligence would be the same as if he was to be paid for his services. The coincidence that the defendant's conduct amounts to a breach of contract cannot affect either the duty of care or the common law liability for its breach, for it is the general relationship, and not any particular manifestation such as a contract, that gives rise to the tortious liability in such a case: see per Lord Devlin in the *Hedley Byrne* case at 530 of the report.

A comprehensive survey of the law governing the liability of a solicitor to his client in negligence is to be found in the judgment of Oliver J. in *Midland Bank v Hett, Stubbs & Kemp*,[6] in which it was held that the solicitor's liability in tort exists independently of any liability in contract. That conclusion, which was reached at first instance and with which I agree, may be said to be reinforced by *dicta* in the judgments of the Court of Appeal in *Batty v Metropolitan Realisations Ltd*[7] and *Photo Production Ltd v Securicor Ltd*.[8]

On a consideration of those cases and of the authorities mentioned in them, I am satisfied that the general duty of care created by the relationship of solicitor and client entitles the client to sue in negligence if he has suffered damage because of the solicitor's failure to show due professional care and skill, notwithstanding that the client could sue alternatively in contract for breach of the implied term in the contract of retainer that the solicitor will deal with the matter in hand with due professional care and skill. The solicitor's liability in tort under the general duty of care extends not only to a client for rewards, but to any person for whom the solicitor undertakes to act professionally without reward, and also to those (such as beneficiaries under a will, persons entitled under an intestacy, or those entitled to benefits in circumstances such as a claim in respect of a fatal injury) with whom he has made no arrangement to act but who, as he knows or ought to know, will be relying on his professional care and skill. For the same default there should be the same cause of action. If others are entitled to sue in tort for the solicitor's want of care, so also should the client; that is so unless the solicitor's default arises not from a breach of the general duty of care arising from the relationship but from a breach of a particular and special term of the contract in respect of which the solicitor would not be liable if the contract had not contained such a term. Thus, if the client's instructions were that the solicitor was to issue proceedings within a specified time, or to close a sale by a particular date or, generally, to do or not to do some act, and the solicitor defaulted in that respect, any resulting right of action which the client might have would be in contract only unless the act or default complained of falls within the general duty of care owed by the solicitor.

The modern law of tort shows that the existence of a contractual relationship which impliedly deals with a particular act or omission is not, in itself, sufficient to rule out an action in tort in respect of that act or omission. For instance, in *Northern Bank Finance Corp. Ltd v Charlton*[9] it was unanimously held by this court that a customer of a bank can sue the bank for the tort of deceit where the deceit arises from fraudulent misrepresentation made by the bank in the course of carrying out the contract between the bank and the customer. The existence of a contract, for the breach of which he could have sued, did not oust the customer's cause of action in tort.

Therefore, I conclude that where, as in the instant case, the client's complaint is that he has been damnified by the solicitor's default in his general duty of care, the client is entitled to sue in negligence as well as for breach of contract. In the plaintiff's statement of claim, after reciting his accident and his retainer of the defendant as the solicitor to prosecute his claim for damages in respect of it, the plaintiff pleads that the defendant 'negligently failed to issue proceedings on behalf of the plaintiff in respect of the accident aforesaid within the time limited by the Statute of Limitations 1957.' That was intended to be, and is, a claim in negligence. Such being the case, by virtue of the provision of s. 94 of the Courts of Justice Act 1924, as amended, the plaintiff was entitled to serve notice of a trial by a judge and jury. Mr Justice D'Arcy was correct in refusing to set aside the notice of trial so served. I would dismiss this appeal.

Griffin J.:

On 10 March 1970, the plaintiff was injured in the course of his employment whilst he was engaged in lagging pipes at a factory premises in Cork. In May 1970, he retained the defendant as his solicitor to act for him in the prosecution of a claim for damages for negligence arising out of the accident. Proceedings were not issued on behalf of the plaintiff within the time limited by the Statute of Limitations 1957, with the result that the plaintiff's claims against his employer and against the occupier of the factory are now statute barred. The plaintiff instituted proceedings against the defendant claiming damages for the negligence of the defendant in his conduct, as the plaintiff's solicitor, of business undertaken by the defendant on behalf of the plaintiff. In his defence the defendant has not denied his liability to the plaintiff, so that the only issue to be tried is that of damages.

The plaintiff served notice of a trial with a jury, and the defendant applied to the High Court to have the notice to trial set aside. The application was dismissed by Mr Justice D'Arcy. The defendant has now appealed to this court and the nett issue for determination on the appeal is whether the action should be tried before a judge and jury or before a judge sitting without a jury.

A solicitor holds himself out to the client who has retained him as being possessed of adequate skill, knowledge and learning for the purpose of carrying out all business that he undertakes on behalf of his client. Once he has been retained to pursue a claim for damages for personal injuries, it is the duty of the solicitor to prepare and prosecute the claim with due professional skill and care. Therefore, he is liable to the client in damages if loss and damage are caused to the client owing to the want of such skill and care on the part of the solicitor as he ought to have exercised.

[Counsel], for the defendant, contends that the duty owed by a solicitor to his client under his retainer is a duty which arises *solely* from the contract and excludes any general duty in tort; he submits that this action is one founded upon contract, in which event the plaintiff would not be entitled to have the action tried by a jury. [Counsel], for the plaintiff, submits that, apart from the duty which arises from contract, there is a general duty to exercise skill and care on the part of the solicitor, for breach of which he would be liable in tort if damage is suffered by the client as a result of the want of such skill and care. He submits that, as one claiming damages for negligence, this action is properly a claim in tort, in which case the plaintiff is entitled as of right to have the action tried before a judge and jury pursuant to s. 94 of the Courts of Justice Act 1924, as amended.

There is abundant, if somewhat conflicting, authority on the question in England, and in argument we were referred also to two Irish cases in which the question arose.

In *Groom v Crocker*[10] the Court of Appeal in England had to consider whether the mutual rights and duties of a solicitor and his client were regulated by the contract of employment alone, and whether the solicitor was liable in tort. It was there held that the contract of employment regulated the relationship and that the solicitor was not liable in tort. In the course of his judgment, Sir Wilfred Greene M.R. said at 205 of the report: 'In my opinion, the cause of action is in contract and not in tort. The duty of the appellants was to conduct the case properly on behalf of the respondent as their client ... The relationship of solicitor and client is a contractual one: *Davies v Lock;*[11] *Bean v Wade.*[12] It was by virtue of that relationship that the duty arose, and it had no existence apart from the relationship.'

Scott L.J. at p. 222, having set out the duty of a solicitor, said that the tie between the solicitor and the client is contractual and that no action lies in tort for the breach of such duties. MacKinnon L.J. put the position succinctly at 229 where he said: 'I am clear that this is a claim for damages for breach of contract . . .'

After that unanimous decision of the Court of Appeal, it was generally accepted in England, at least until very recently, that the liability of a solicitor to his client was contractual only and that he could not be sued in tort either in the alternative or cumulatively. The case has been almost universally followed and applied there since it was decided; see, for example, *Bailey v Bullock;*[13] and Hodson and Parker L.JJ. at pp. 447 and 481 respectively of the report of *Hall v Meyrick;*[14] *Cook v Swinfen.*[15] At 510 of the report of *Clark v Kirby-Smith*[16] Plowman J. said: 'A line of cases going back for nearly 150 years shows, I think, that the client's cause of action is in contract and not in tort: see, for example, *Howell v Young*[17] and *Groom v Crocker'*. In *Heywood v Wellers*[18] James L.J. said at 461 of the report: 'It is well known and settled law that an action by a client against a solicitor alleging negligence in the conduct of the client's affairs is an action for breach of contract: *Groom v Crocker.*' However, in that case Lord Denning did say at 459 that *Groom v Crocker* might have to be reconsidered, and in *Esso Petroleum v Mardon*[19] at 819 of the report he 'ventured to suggest' that that case, and cases which relied on it, are in conflict with other decisions of high authority which were not cited in them—decisions which show that, in the case of a professional man, the duty to use reasonable care arises not only in contract but is also imposed by the law apart from contract and is, therefore, actionable in tort; it is comparable to the duty of reasonable care which is owed by a master to his servant or vice versa; it can be put either in contract or in tort. In *Midland Bank v Hett, Stubbs & Kemp*, on which the plaintiff relied strongly, Oliver J., in a judgment in which he examined exhaustively all the leading cases on the subject of a solicitor's liability, held that a solicitor was liable in tort quite independently of any contractual liability.

In *Somers v Erskine* the client sued his solicitor for damages for negligence in the discharge of his professional duty to the client. The solicitor died after the action was commenced and one of the issues which then arose was whether or not the cause of action had survived against his executrix. It was held by Maguire P. that the action was in substance founded in contract and that, in considering whether an action is founded on contract or on tort, the court must look not merely at the form of the pleadings but at the substance of the action and decide whether it is founded on contract or tort. He adopted and applied the following passage from the judgment of Greer L.J. in *Jarvis v Moy, Davies, Smith, Vandervell and Co.* (a claim against a stockbroker) at 405 of the report:

> The distinction in the modern view, for this purpose, between contract and tort may be put thus: where the breach of duty alleged arises out of a liability independently of the personal obligation undertaken by contract, it is tort, and it may be tort even though there may happen to be a contract between the parties, if the duty in fact arises independently of that contract. Breach of contract occurs where that which is complained of is a breach of duty arising out of the obligations undertaken by the contract.

That passage had been accepted and approved by O'Byrne J. in *Liston v Munster and Leinster Bank*. Applying that test, the learned president held that the substance of the client's claim was the breach of a duty arising out of an obligation created by contract, and said that he found it difficult to dissociate that duty from the contract. Counsel for the defendant in that case had urged that the duty which was alleged to have been broken was merely the ordinary common law duty, the breach of which constituted negligence, i.e. the duty to take reasonable care in the particular circumstances; but the president held that the duty arose out of a contractual obligation only.

I have had the advantage of reading in advance the judgment of Mr Justice Henchy and I agree with him that Maguire P. did not correctly apply the test laid down by Greer L.J. in the *Jarvis* case. I agree with the analysis made by Mr Justice Henchy of the passage quoted from the judgment of Lord Justice Greer.

The only other Irish case cited in argument was *McGrath v Kiely* in which the client sued a surgeon and a solicitor, founding her claim for damages on both negligence and breach of contract. In the course of the hearing before Mr Justice Henchy it was conceded on behalf of the client that the liability sought to be imposed on each of the defendants arose *ex contractu*, so that the question of the liability of the defendants in tort was not argued and did not fall to be decided.

In *Somers v Erskine*, the learned president was not prepared to accept that, in the case of a solicitor, there was a general duty to use reasonable care imposed by the law quite apart from contract. He took the view that because there was a contractual relationship between the solicitor and the client, and a liability in contract for breach of the duty owed to the client, there was no duty in tort. Counsel for the defendant had cited the passage in *Bevan on Negligence* (4th ed.) p. 1384 that states: 'A solicitor is liable for negligence both in contract and in tort. He is liable in contract where he fails to do some specific act to which he has bound himself. He is liable in tort where, having accepted a retainer, he fails in the performance of any duty which the relation of solicitor and client as defined by the retainer imposes on him.' Authorities to support that proposition were not cited; if they had been cited, it is likely that the president would have come to a different conclusion. The law is concisely and clearly summed up in a few sentences in the well known passage in the speech of Viscount Haldane L.C. in *Nocton v Ashburton*[20] at 956 of the report: 'My Lords, the solicitor contracts with his client to be skilful and careful. For failure to perform his obligation he may be made liable at law in contract or even in tort, for negligence in breach of a duty imposed on him.' See also what was said by Tindal C.J. in *Boorman v Brown*[21] in the Court of Exchequer Chamber at 525 of the report and by Lord Campbell in the House of Lords at 44 of the report of the appeal. It is to be noted that these cases also were not cited in *Groom v Crocker*, or in the cases which followed it, and that the failure to do so led to the criticism of these cases by Lord Denning in *Esso Petroleum v Mardon*. In my opinion, the President was wrong in holding that the liability of the solicitor to the client was solely in contract. *Somers v Erskine* should not be followed.

Quite apart from the fact that *Somers v Erskine* was decided without the citation of relevant authorities and on an incorrect application of the test laid down by Greer L.J. in the *Jarvis* case, the decision is inconsistent with developments in the law of tort since the case was decided. It is now settled law that whenever a person possessed of a special knowledge or skill undertakes, quite irrespective of contract, to apply that skill for the assistance of another person who relies on such skill, a duty of care will arise: see the speech of Lord Morris of Borth-y-Gest at 502 of the report of *Hedley Byrne and Co. Ltd v Heller & Partners Ltd.* At 538 of the report Lord Pearce said: 'In terms of proximity one might say that they are in particularly close proximity to those who, as they know, are relying on their skill and care although the proximity is not contractual.' See also Lord Hodson at 510 and Lord Devlin at 530 of the report. Where damage has been suffered as a result of want of such skill and care, an action in tort lies against such person, and this applies whether a contractual relationship exists or not. This doctrine applies to such professional persons as solicitors, doctors, dentists, architects and accountants. Although in the *Hedley Byrne* case the aim was in respect of a non-contractual relationship, the statements of the Law Lords were general statements of principle, and it is clear from their speeches that they did not in any way mean to limit the general principle and that their statements were not to be confined to voluntary or non-contractual situations.

Therefore, where a solicitor is retained by a client to carry out legal business (such as litigation) on his behalf, a general relationship is established, and 'Where there is a general relationship of this sort, it is unnecessary to do more than prove its existence and the duty follows' per Lord Devlin at 530 of the report of the *Hedley Byrne* case. If, therefore, loss and damage is caused to a client owing to the want of such care and skill on the part of a solicitor as he ought to have exercised, there is liability in tort even though there would also be a liability in contract. Even if the relationship between the solicitor and the client was a non-contractual or voluntary one, the same liability in tort would follow.

In my opinion it is both reasonable and fair that, if the issues of fact are such that he would be entitled to succeed either in contract or in tort, the plaintiff should be entitled to pursue either or both remedies; there can be nothing wrong in permitting the plaintiff, who is the injured party, to elect or choose the remedy which to him appears to be that which will be most suitable and likely to attract the more favourable result.

In my judgment, the plaintiff in the instant case has a good cause of action in tort as well as in contract and is entitled to sue in respect of either or both remedies since he has suffered loss and damage as a result of the negligence of the defendant, as the plaintiff's solicitor, in failing to institute proceedings within the time limited by the Statute of Limitations 1957. Accordingly, the plaintiff is entitled as of right to have his action tried before a judge and jury, and Mr Justice D'Arcy was correct in so deciding. Accordingly, I would dismiss this appeal.

[1.] [1965] IR 497	[8.] [1978] 1 WLR 856	[15.] [1967] 1 WLR 457
[2.] [1940] IR 77	[9.] [1979] IR 149	[16.] [1964] Ch. 506
[3.] [1936] 1 KB 399	[10.] [1939] 1 KB 194	[17.] (1826) 5 B & C 259
[4.] [1943] IR 348	[11.] (1844) 3 LT (OS) 125	[18.] [1976] QB 446
[5.] [1964] AC 465	[12.] (1885) 2 TLR 157	[19.] [1976] QB 801
[6.] [1979] Ch. 384	[13.] [1950] 2 All ER 1167	[20.] [1914] AC 932
[7.] [1978] QB 554	[14.] [1957] 2 QB 455	[21.] (1842) 3 QB 511; (1844) 11 Cl. & Fin. 1

(O'Higgins C.J. and Kenny J. agreed.)

Note

1. The major losses experienced by members of Lloyds (names) during the late 1980s have been the subject of substantial litigation in England in 1993 and 1994. The names have sought compensation from underwriting agents alleging that these agents owed a duty of care in tort, and certain implied contractual duties, to the names in relation to the carrying out of their underwriting duties with care and skill.

In *Arbuthnott and Others v Fagan and Fettrim Underwriting Agencies Ltd and Others* TLR 26 July 1994, the House of Lords considered whether the names were owed concurrent duties in contract and tort and concluded that such duties, as a matter of principle, could subsist in the light of earlier cases that suggested that if liability was possible in tort and contract, the plaintiff should pursue his action in contract only.

Giving judgment for the House, Lord Goff rejected the view that there was any sound basis for a rule which confined the plaintiff to one cause of action only. Lord Goff observed that while the result may be untidy:

given that the tortious duty was imposed by the general law and the contractual duty was attributable to the will of the parties, it was not objectionable that the claimant might be entitled to take advantage of the remedy which was most advantageous to him, subject only to ascertaining whether the tortious duty was so inconsistent with the applicable contract that, in accordance with ordinary principle, the parties must be taken to have agreed that the tortious remedy was to be limited or excluded.

2. In cases of concurrent liability the plaintiff has a very good reason to seek to establish these alternative causes of action. Sometimes the alternative cause of action lengthens the period for which recovery of damages is possible or it revives an otherwise invalid cause of action. What happened in the *Arbuthnott* litigation as a result of their Lordships' decision?

3. For the importance of concurrent liability in damages, see, *inter alia*, the *O'Hanrahan* decision at p. 987 below.

B. Contract and Restitution

Beresford v Kennedy (1887) 21 ILTR 17

Beresford owned lands which adjoined the defendant's farmlands. The defendant's land was the subject of a boycott and fences and gates had not been maintained. The plaintiff's cattle wandered onto the defendant's land where they were seized by the local rate collector, the defendants owing some £25 in overdue rates. In order to obtain the release of his cattle the plaintiff paid the rates of £25 and then sued the defendants for this amount as being money paid for their use. The County Court Judge gave judgment in favour of the plaintiff saying it would be monstrous if the defendants could avoid payment of their lawful taxes as a result of a trifling trespass. The defendants appealed.

Andrews J.:

I am greatly indebted to the counsel on both sides for the assistance they have given me. It is not necessary for me to decide whether or not there was a deliberate act of trespass, on the part of the plaintiff Beresford, in driving his cattle on to defendants' land; but it was admitted by his counsel, that plaintiff's cattle were undoubtedly trespassing on defendants' land when they were seized, as they lawfully might be, by the collectors, the Miss Kennedys being the occupiers of the land, under the provisions of the Poor Rate and Grand Jury Acts. In all the cases in the books there has been something to create a privity between the parties in a case like this, and even if *England v Marsden* were not followed, I have enough materials to decide the case.

In *Exall v Partridge*, and that class of cases, the property seized was lawfully on the premises of the defendant, and there is no authority in the books to show that where property is unlawfully on defendants' premises, the wrongdoer can recover against the defendant, though, as I said, I don't hold that the trespass was wilful; but there is, in the facts before me, nothing from which there can be implied any request by defendant for the payment of the debt by plaintiff. I will not rely on *England v Marsden*, as I think that decision went too far; but I have carefully considered *Edmunds v Wallingford and Re Bishop*, and I can find nothing in them to warrant me in deciding in favour of the plaintiff, and, therefore, though I regret that I have to differ from the County Court Judge. I am obliged to reverse his decision, with costs; but I give defendants no costs of the hearing in the court below, as the case was one of much difficulty and importance.

Decree reversed.

C. CONTRACT AND PROMISSORY LIABILITY

The charitable subscriptions cases

Governors of Dalhousie College *v* Boutilier [1934] 3 DLR 593

Crocket J. gave judgment for the Supreme Court of Canada:

This appeal concerns a claim which was filed in the Probate Court for the County of Halifax, Nova Scotia, in the year 1931, by the appellant college against the respondent estate for $5,000, stated as having been 'subscribed to Dalhousie Campaign Fund (1920)', and attested by an affidavit of the college bursar, in which it was alleged that the stated amount was justly and truly owing to the college corporation.

The subscription, upon which the claim was founded, was obtained from the deceased on 4 June 1920, in the course of a canvass which was being conducted by a committee, known as the Dalhousie College Campaign Committee, for the raising of a fund to increase the general resources and usefulness of the institution and was in the following terms:

> For the purpose of enabling Dalhousie College to maintain and improve the efficiency of its teaching, to construct new buildings and otherwise to keep pace with the growing need of its constituency and in consideration of the subscription of others, I promise to pay to the Treasurer of Dalhousie College the sum of Five Thousand Dollars, payment as follows: Terms of payment as per letter from Mr Boutilier. A. 399.
> Name: Arthur Boutilier.

So far as the record discloses the subscription was not accompanied or followed by any letter from the deceased as to the terms of payment. He died on 29 October 1928, without making any payment on account. It appears that some time after he signed the subscription form he met with severe financial reverses which prevented him from honouring his pledge. That he desired and hoped to be able to do so is evidenced by a brief letter addressed by him to the President of the University on 12 April 1926, in reply to a communication from the latter, calling his attention to the subscription and the fact that no payments had been made upon it. The deceased's letter, acknowledging receipt of the president's communication, states: 'In reply I desire to advise that I have kept my promise to you in mind. As you are probably aware, since making my promise I suffered some rather severe reverses but I expect before too long to be able to redeem my pledge.'

. . .

There is, of course, no doubt that the deceased's subscription can be sustained as a binding promise only upon one basis, *viz.* as a contract, supported by a good and sufficient consideration. The whole controversy between the parties is as to whether such a consideration is to be found, either in the subscription paper itself or in the circumstances as disclosed by the evidence.

So far as the signed subscription itself is concerned, it is contended in behalf of the appellant that it shows upon its face a good and sufficient consideration for the deceased's promise in its statement that it was given in consideration of the subscription of others. As to this, it is first to be observed that the statement of such a consideration in the subscription paper is insufficient to support the promise if, in point of law, the subscriptions of others could not provide a valid consideration therefor. I concur in the opinion of Chisholm C.J., that the fact that others had signed separate subscription papers for the same common object or were expected so to do does not of itself constitute a legal consideration. Although there have been some cases in the United States in which a contrary opinion has been expressed, these decisions have been rejected as unsound in principle both by the Supreme Court of Massachusetts and the Court of Appeals of the State of New York. See *Cottage Street M. E. Church v Kendall* (1877), 121 Mass. 528; *Hamilton College v Stewart* (1848), 1 NY 581, and *Albany Presbyterian Church v Cooper* (1889), 112 NY 517. In the last mentioned case the defendant's intestate subscribed a paper with a number of others, by the terms of which they 'in consideration of one dollar' to each of them paid 'and of the agreements of each other' severally promised and agreed to and with the plaintiff's trustees to pay to said trustees the sums severally subscribed for the purpose of paying off a mortgage debt on the church edifice on the condition that the sum of $45,000 in the aggregate should be subscribed and paid in for such purpose within one year. The Court of Appeals held that it must reject the consideration, because it had no basis in fact, and the mutual promise between the subscribers, because there was no privity of contract between the plaintiff church and the various subscribers.

A perusal of the reasons for judgment of the Appeal Court of Manitoba, as delivered by Cameron J., in *Sargent v Nicholson*, already referred to, shows that that court also rejected the contention that it was a sufficient consideration that others were led to subscribe by the subscription of the defendant. In fact Cameron J.'s opinion quotes with approval a passage from the opinion of Gray C.J., in *Cottage St. M. E. Church v Kendall* that such a proposition appeared to the Massachusetts Supreme Court to be 'inconsistent with elementary principles'. The decision of the Appeal Court of British Columbia in *YMCA v Rankin* fully adopted the opinion of Cameron J., in *Sargent v Nicholson*, and is certainly no authority for the acceptance of other subscriptions as a binding consideration in such a case as the present one.

The doctrine of mutual promises was also put forward on the argument as a ground upon which the deceased's promise might be held to be binding. It was suggested that the statement in the subscription of the purpose for which it was made, *viz*.: 'of enabling Dalhousie College to maintain and improve the efficiency of its teaching, to construct new buildings and otherwise to keep pace with the growing need of its constituency' constituted an implied request on the part of the deceased to apply the promised subscription to this object and that the acceptance by the college of his promise created a contract between them, the consideration for the promise of the deceased to pay the money being the promise of the college to apply it to the purpose stated.

I cannot think that any such construction can fairly be placed upon the subscription paper and its acceptance by the college. It certainly contains no express request to the college either 'to maintain and improve the efficiency of its teaching' or 'to construct new buildings and otherwise to keep pace with the growing need of its constituency', but simply states that the promise to pay the $5,000 is made for the purpose of enabling the college to do so, leaving it perfectly free to pursue what had always been its aims in whatever manner its governors should choose. No statement is made as to the amount intended to be raised for all or any of the purposes stated. No buildings of any kind are described. The construction of new buildings is merely indicated as a means of the college keeping pace with the growing need of its constituency and apparently to be undertaken as and when the governors should in their unfettered discretion decide the erection of any one or more buildings for any purpose was necessary or desirable.

It seems to me difficult to conceive that, had the deceased actually paid the promised money, he could have safely relied upon the mere acceptance of his own promise, couched in such vague and uncertain terms regarding its purpose as the foundation of any action against the college corporation.

So far as I can discover, there is no English or Canadian case in which it has been authoritatively decided that a reciprocal promise on the part of the promisee may be implied from the mere fact of the acceptance by the promisee of such a subscription paper from the hands of the promisor to do the thing for which the subscription is promised. There is no doubt, of course, that an express agreement by the promisee to do certain acts in return for a subscription is a sufficient consideration for the promise of the subscriber. There may, too, be circumstances proved by evidence, outside the subscription paper itself, from which such a reciprocal promise on the part of the promisee may well be implied, but I have not been able to find any English or Canadian case where it has actually been so decided in the absence of proof that the subscriber has himself either expressly requested the promisee to undertake some definite project or personally taken such a part in connection with the projected enterprise that such a request might be inferred therefrom.

. . .

. . . the English decisions, give no countenance to the principle applied in *Sargent v Nicholson* and *YMCA v Rankin* and in the earlier American cases, as is so pointedly illustrated by the judgments of Pearson J., in *Re Hudson, Creed v Henderson* (1885), 33 WR 819, and Eve J., in *Re Cory, Kinnaird v Cory* (1912), 29 TLR 18. The headnote in *Re Hudson* states:

> A. verbally promised to give £20,000 to the Jubilee Fund of the Congregational Union, and also filled up and signed a blank form of promise not addressed to anyone, but headed 'Congregational Union of England and Wales Jubilee Fund', whereby he promised to give £20,000, in five equal annual instalments of £4,000 each, for the liquidation of chapel debts. A. paid three instalments of £4,000 to the

fund within three years from the date of his promise, and then died, leaving the remaining two instalments unpaid and unprovided for.

The Congregational Union claimed £8,000 from A.'s executors, on the ground that they had been led by A.'s promise to contribute larger sums to churches than they would otherwise have done; that money had been given and promised by other persons in consequence of A.'s promise; that grants from the Jubilee Fund had been promised to cases recommended by A.; and that churches to which promises had been made by the committee, and the committee themselves, had incurred liabilities in consequence of A.'s promise.

His Lordship held (33 WR, at p. 821) there was no consideration for the promise. 'There really is,' he said, 'in this matter, nothing whatever in the shape of a consideration which could form a contract between the parties.'

And he added:

I am bound to say that this is an attempt to turn a charity into something very different from a charity. I think it ought to fail, and I think it does fail. I do not know to what extent a contrary decision might open a new form of posthumous charity. Posthumous charity is already bad enough, and it is quite sufficiently protected by law without establishing a new principle which would extend the doctrine in its favour far more than it has been extended or ought to be extended.

In the *Cory* case a gift of 1,000 guineas was promised to a YMCA for the purpose of building a memorial hall. The sum required was £150,000, of which £85,000 had been promised or was available. The committee in charge decided not to commit themselves until they saw that their efforts to raise the whole fund were likely to prove successful. The testator, whose estate it was sought to charge, promised the 1,000 guineas and subsequently the committee felt justified in entering into a building contract,which they alleged they were largely induced to enter into by the testator's promise. Eve J., held there was no contractual obligation between the parties and therefore no legal debt due from the estate.

. . .

To hold otherwise would be to hold that a naked, voluntary promise may be converted into a binding legal contract by the subsequent action of the promisee alone without the consent, express or implied, of the promisor. There is no evidence here which in any way involves the deceased in the carrying out of the work for which the promised subscription was made other than the signing of the subscription paper itself.

. . .

The appeal, I think, should be dismissed with costs.

Contractual liability and conditional promises—'subject to contract' promises

Lowis v Wilson [1948] IR 347

By a document signed on 12 July 1948, the plaintiff, Muriel Lowis, Talbot Lodge, Blackrock, County Dublin, agreed to purchase from the defendant, James H. Wilson, Girley, Kells, County Meath, part of the lands of Girley, containing 76 acres, 2 roods, 30 perches, or thereabouts, statute measure, being the lands the subject of Folio No. 6959, County of Meath, held in fee simple subject to the revised annuity of £26, payable to the Irish Land Commission, for the sum of £6,000, together with five per cent auction fees, and to pay a deposit of £1,500 to the auctioneers on the signing of the agreement and the balance of the purchase money on 1 December 1948. The document contained a clause stating that 'this agreement is subject to the preparation of a formal contract to be prepared by W. O. Armstrong, Solicitor for the vendor, Kells, County Meath.' The defendant agreed to discharge all rent, rates and taxes up to 1 December 1948, upon which date possession was to be given to the plaintiff.

At the time of the signing of the said document, the plaintiff paid to the solicitor for the defendant, two sums, £1,500 and £300, respectively, representing the deposit and auction fees. Subsequently, the solicitor for the defendant drafted a formal contract for the sale of the lands and submitted it to the plaintiff for her approval. After negotiations between the parties the plaintiff intimated that she was not disposed to proceed with the purchase and, on 31 July 1948, her solicitor wrote to the solicitor for the defendant so informing him and requesting the return of the sums of £1,500 and £300 already paid as deposit and auction fees, respectively. In correspondence between the parties subsequently the plaintiff claimed that she had not entered into any binding contract for the purchase of the lands, on the ground that the document of 12 July 1948, was not a binding contract, but was merely an agreement for the preparation of a formal contract of sale; for the defendant it was contended that the document of 12 July 1948, was a binding contract for the sale of the lands, notwithstanding that it was a preliminary contract.

The defendant having failed to return the said sums of £1,500 and £300, as requested, the plaintiff by summary summons instituted proceedings for the return of the sum of £1,800.

Dixon J.:

If I had to deal with this matter on the basis of the principle stated (at p. 645) in *Chinnock v Marchioness of Ely*[1] and referred to, at p. 32, in *Winn v Bull*[2] and in later cases, I would have had some difficulty in deciding as to the proper application of this principle in the present case. It seems to me that it might have been arguable that the principle was not properly applied in all of the cases cited; but I have not now to consider any argument of that kind. [Counsel for the defendant's] argument was confined to a different question, possibly for the reason that the weight of all the cases from *Winn v Bull* onwards is that similar wording to that here was held to have had the effect of preventing an agreement, although it contained sufficient to satisfy the Statute of Frauds, from being a binding and enforceable agreement.

The reasons given in those cases were that the agreement was intended to be subject to the parties entering into a further agreement, and it was only when such further agreement had been entered into that the parties would have arrived at a firm and enforceable contract.

The progressive tendency in those cases in favour of regarding the original agreement as merely conditional culminated in *Chillingworth v Esche*.[3] In that case the position was put by two of the judges as being that, if an agreement to sell 'subject to contract' is entered into, it is not binding unless there are circumstances which would have the effect of inducing a court to take the opposite view. Although this statement of the position arrived at may represent a departure from, or advance on, the principle as originally formulated, the weight of authority would possibly have compelled me to adopt it.

I hold against the contention advanced by [counsel for the defendant], *viz.* that the document here was a final binding contract, subject to a condition which must be strictly and literally interpreted against the purchaser and that, on such interpretation, the condition has been fulfilled. That point is not dealt with in any of the cases referred to in the argument. Those cases dealt with the point whether the original agreement was a concluded one or merely an agreement to enter into an agreement.

The contention is that I am here dealing with a binding agreement subject to a condition subsequent for the 'preparation of a formal contract'. If that is a condition, then it may be divided into two parts, the first part being the preparation of the formal contract and the second part, that it should be prepared by the solicitor named. [Counsel for the defendant] says that this means what it says, viz. the preparation of a contract and that this condition has been fulfilled. I do not take the view that this is the meaning of the condition. It seems to me that the condition contemplates the completion between the parties of a contract and in that respect the use of the word, 'contract', is of importance. [The solicitor] could prepare a draft of a proposed contract, but he could not prepare a 'contract' as that would depend on the agreement of both parties evidenced by their signing or sealing the document.

I think that in view of the whole context of the agreement it is impossible to give it such a strictly literal meaning as [counsel for the defendant] contends for. In my view, the word, 'preparation', is used in a different sense to the words, 'to be prepared', unless the latter words are superfluous; and a literal interpretation would make the provision a futile and purposeless one. On the suggested interpretation I cannot see how either the condition or its fulfilment would advance the transaction in any way. There would, on such a view, be no necessity for the solicitor to do anything more than draft the document, and I refuse to accept the construction that the parties agreed to such an apparent futility.

I hold that the agreement comes into the category of the cases already cited, that is to say, that it is a contract to enter into a contract. It is a case where the parties had agreed up to a point, but were not fully agreed, and where the expression of their full agreement was to be embodied in a formal document. If my view is right, then it follows that the agreement is not enforceable and never was, and that the plaintiff has paid £1,800 without consideration and is entitled to recover that sum.

1. 4 De G. J. & S. 638.
2. 7 ChD 29.
3. [1924] 1 Ch. 97.

SECTION THREE—CONTRACT AND THE JUDICIAL PROCESS

Corbin, 'Conditions in the Law of Contract' (1919) 28 Yale LJ 739 at 740–1.

Interpretation and Construction of Contracts

The law of contract deals with those legal relations that arise because of mutual expressions of assent. The parties have expressed their intentions in words, or in other conduct that can be translated into words. The notion is not at all uncommon that legal relations called contractual cannot exist unless the parties intended them to exist, and that the sole function of the courts, therefore, is one of interpretation: What was the intention of the parties? This notion is far from correct. In almost all cases of contract, legal relations will exist, from the very moment of acceptance, that one or both of the parties never consciously expected would exist, and therefore cannot be said to have intended. Furthermore, the life history of any single contract may cover a long period of time, and new facts will occur after acceptance of the offer—facts that may gravely affect the existing legal relations and yet may have been utterly unforeseen by the parties. Many of these uncontemplated legal relations are invariably described as contractual. Therefore it appears that a necessary function of the courts is to determine the unintended legal relations as well as the intended ones.

The first step in this judicial process is the merely historical one of determining what the operative facts were. What did the parties say and do? What words did they use? Did they execute a document? This historical determination is made possible by evidence.

The next step is one of interpretation. In taking this step the court may put to itself two questions: first, what was the actual state of mind of the contracting parties, their meaning and intention at the time they said the words or performed the other acts to be interpreted; second, what meaning do the words and acts of the parties now express to a reasonable and disinterested third party? It is only in exceptional cases that these questions will be consciously considered by a court; usually the process of interpretation will involve rapid and unconscious shifts from the one aspect to the other.

Frequently the only way to arrive at an answer to the first question is to answer the second; in other cases the two may both be susceptible of answer and the two answers may not agree. If the actual intention of the parties is not the same as the meaning that is now conveyed to a reasonable man, it is the latter that will more often prevail. If, however, the parties clearly had a common meaning and intention, it will control irrespective of what a third person would have understood.

Often, however, the court cannot solve the problem before it by mere interpretation. The court's problem is to determine the jural relations of the parties as they are now; and these relations depend upon facts, both contemporaneous with the acceptance and subsequent thereto, which were not known or anticipated by the parties and as to which they made no provision that is capable of either sort of interpretation. The question now is, not what is the meaning of word, but what does the welfare of society require in view of these unknown or unanticipated circumstances? To answer this question the court must resort to general rules of law even though they were unknown by the parties, to rules of fairness and morality, to the prevailing *mores* of the time and place. This process may be called one of judicial construction. The line separating mere interpretation from *judicial construction*, although logically quite clear, will always be practically indistinct and difficult of determination, especially because the courts so frequently construct under the guise of mere interpretation.

Note

Corbin was not setting forward a view of the judicial process that characterised the essential nature of contract litigation as being mechanical in nature, rather he was emphasising the need to recognise that judicial techniques may be limited. The objectives behind the judicial process may differ.

As Duncan Kennedy wrote in 'Form and Substance in Private Law Adjudication' (1975) 89 Harv L Rev 1685 (footnotes omitted):

. . . The substantive and formal conflict in private law cannot be reduced to disagreement about how to apply some neutral calculus that will 'maximise the total satisfaction of human wants'. The opposed rhetorical modes lawyers use reflect a deeper level of contradiction. At this deeper level we are divided among ourselves and also within ourselves between irreconcilable visions of humanity, and society, and between radically different aspirations for our common future.

Considerations of space allow us to give just two examples of how perceptions may differ.

A. ETHICAL TENSIONS IN CONTRACT LAW

Terry, 'Unconscionable Contracts in NSW' (1982) 10 Aust B L Rev 311 at 313–6. (Footnotes omitted.)

Freedom and Sanctity of Contract

> If there is one thing which more than another public policy requires it is that men of full age and competent understanding shall have the utmost liberty of contracting, and that their contracts when entered into freely and voluntarily shall be held sacred and shall be enforced by the Courts of Justice. Therefore you have this paramount public policy to consider—that you are not lightly to interfere with freedom of contract.

Sir George Jessell's statement of the principles of freedom of contract and sanctity of contract—that subject to the restraint of legality the parties are free to negotiate their contracts on their own terms and the terms mutually agreed upon will be enforced by the courts without interference on the ground of fairness—expresses the fundamental and underlying assumption of the law of contract. These principles offer little scope for relieving a party from the burden of an oppressive contract. Although it has been suggested that 'there is the vigilance of the common law which, while allowing freedom of contract, watches to see that it is not abused' there is weightier authority against a public policy placing the ideal of contractual fairness above the need for stability, certainty and predictability which the classical theory emphasises. Despite a 'mosaic of decisions' in which relief from unconscionable contracts has been granted in particular cases, the principles of freedom and sanctity have survived the vast economic and social changes of the last century more or less intact and still represent the cornerstone of the law of contract. That the classical theory is alive and well in Australia is readily illustrated by the recent decision of the High Court of Australia in *South Australia Rlys Commissioner v Egan*. Menzies J. regarded the contract as 'so outrageous that it is surprising that any contractor would undertake work for the Railways Commissioner upon its terms . . . '. His Honour commented that it was 'perhaps the most wordy, obscure and oppressive contract that I have ever come across . . . ' from which 'not one oppressive provision which could have been found was omitted . . . '. the High Court made it clear that such provisions found little favour in modern eyes but nevertheless held that it was required to give legal effect to the provisions and was 'not to be deflected from that course because they appear unfair and one-sided'.

Criticism of the Classical Theory

The principles of freedom of contract and sanctity of contract developed in the context of a market place very different from that of today. The classical theory was ideally suited to both the practical and the theoretical requirements of the time. Freedom of contract was a realistic approach to the unsophisticated market place of the nineteenth century and a policy of non-interference with contracts was in accordance with the prevailing philosophy of *laissez-faire*. However, the incredible social and economic changes since that time have rendered the application of the classical theory in its full vigour inappropriate. Freedom of contract is distorted in the market place by inequality of bargaining power and the common law and statutory inroads into the sanctity of contracts have recognised this fact.

The assumption underlying freedom of contract—that 'contracts are based always on mutual agreement and [arise] out of free choice unhampered by external control or interference'—is no longer valid. Advancing business technology, increasingly sophisticated marketing techniques, the growth of a massive credit industry and a tendency to bigger business all erode the consumer's influence in contracting. In particular, the widespread use of standard form contracts has restricted the consumer's freedom to negotiate the terms of a contract. Standard form contracts are the inevitable by-product of a standardised mass-production society and have distinct and undoubted virtues that are discussed later in this article. Nevertheless, they are often used to exploit and abuse superior bargaining power. In A. *Schroeder Music Publishing Co. Ltd v Macaulay* Lord Diplock expressed strong disapproval of standard form contracts containing terms which have not been the subject of negotiation but have been 'dictated' by the party whose superior bargaining power enables him to say: 'If you want these goods or services at all, these are the only terms on which they are obtainable. Take it or leave it.' The market place of today is characterised by inequality of bargaining power. Where there is gross disparity of bargaining power, as in the vast majority of consumer contracts, there is little actual freedom to negotiate terms and the party with superior bargaining power can impose the terms on the weaker party.

If freedom of contract does not exist in practice, a rigid adherence to sanctity of contract perpetrates a 'pathetic contrast' between the textbook approach to contract and the commercial reality. The principle of sanctity of contract follows from that of freedom of contract: contracts should be enforced by the courts no matter what their terms or effects because the parties have only themselves to blame if the contract was harsh or otherwise unsatisfactory. When freedom to contract does not represent the reality of the market place, sanctity of contract is no longer a logical conclusion. To suggest that the judiciary has not been aware of the pathetic contrast between the theory underlying the law of contract and its distortion in the real world, is to do the judges a grave injustice. For many years equity has protected those who are particularly susceptible to exploitation because of a special disadvantage such as illness, ignorance, impaired faculties, financial need or inexperience, but the categories where relief has been granted are isolated and exceptional and the jurisdiction is confined within narrow limits.

The equitable jurisdiction to grant relief from unconscionable contracts has depended [more] on a narrow allegation of misconduct than abuse of superior bargaining power. Nevertheless Lord Denning M.R. in *Lloyd's Bank Ltd v Bundy* regarded 'inequality of bargaining power' as the 'single thread' linking the exceptional equitable categories:

> Gathering all together, I would suggest that through all these instances there runs a single thread. They rest on 'inequality of bargaining power'. By virtue of it, the English law gives relief to one who, without independent advice, enters into a contract upon terms which are very unfair or transfers property for a consideration which is grossly inadequate, when his bargaining power is grievously impaired by reason of his own needs or desires, or by his own ignorance or infirmity, coupled with undue influences or pressures brought to bear on him by or for the benefit of the other. When I use the word 'undue' I do not mean to suggest that the principle depends on proof of any wrongdoing.

Lord Denning's proposition has received support in later cases and may one day be seen as the first step in the development of an abuse of bargaining power principle of general applications, but at this stage it has not matured into a principle of general application and, having regard to the support that sanctity of contract received from the High Court in *South Australian Rlys Commissioner v Egan*, its assimilation into Australian common law is not a strong possibility in the near future.

The common law's failure to develop an unconscionability doctrine of general application does not mean that sanctity of contract is inviolate. The courts pay lip service to the notion of absolute freedom of contract, yet relief from unfair or oppressive agreements is widely and frequently given by surreptitious means. The Peden Report was critical of the manner in which the courts have responded to changing needs and expectations in the community: they have 'developed a number of devices to subvert the doctrine of sanctity of contract in order to do justice in individual cases'. These devices may achieve justice in an individual case but do not make a frontal attack on the root cause of the problem and 'present a multitude of individual decisions which fail to accumulate experience or authority in marking out the minimal requirements of fairness'. The recognition that 'unfairness' is the basis of these individual decisions is, in the view of many commentators, an essential step in the development of the law and it is unfortunate that Lord Denning's principle of general application has not received wider support.

Although the common law developments '[fall] short of any quantum leap in doctrine' they have, in effect, subverted the principle of sanctity of contract by surreptitious means in response to the commercial reality of the modern market place. The legislature has also recognised that a rigid policy of non-interference in contractual rights and obligations is no longer appropriate. The mass of consumer protection legislation testifies to the fact that *caveat venditor* rather than *caveat emptor* is the appropriate description of the market place today. The regulations of the contents of consumer contracts is a necessary and proper function of a responsible legislature.

B. Contract and Economic Theory

Kronman and Posner, *The Economics of Contract Law* (Boston: Little, Brown & Co. 1979) 1–7. (Footnote omitted.)

The law of contracts regulates, among other kinds of transactions, the purchase and sale of goods (including real estate) and services. Since buying and selling—and related transactions, such as leasing and borrowing, which are also governed by contract law—are quintessentially economic activities, it would seem that economics should have something useful to say to students of contract law. For example, economics may be able to tell us why people make contracts and how contract law can facilitate the operation of markets. And to the extent that contract doctrines reflect judicial efforts, whether deliberate or unconscious, to achieve efficiency, economics may help toward an understanding of the meaning of the doctrines and their appropriate limits.

. . .

The fundamental economic principle with which we begin is that if voluntary exchanges are permitted—if, in other words, a market is allowed to operate—resources will gravitate toward their most valuable uses. If A owns a good that is worth only $100 to him but $150 to B, both will be made better off by an exchange of A's good for B's money at any price between $100 and $150; and if they realise this, they will make the exchange. By making both of them better off, the exchange will also increase the wealth of the society (of which they are members), assuming the exchange does not reduce the welfare of non-parties more than it increases A's and B's welfare. Before the exchange—which, let us say, takes place at a price of $125—A had a good worth $100 to him and B had $125 in cash, a total of $225. After the exchange, A has $125 in cash and B has a good worth $150 to him, a total of $275. The exchange has increased the wealth of society by $50 (ignoring, as we' have done, any possible third party effects).

The principle is the same whether we are speaking of the purchase of a string of pearls, a lawyer's time, a machine for making shoes, or an ingot of aluminum. The existence of a market—a locus of opportunities for mutually advantageous exchanges—facilitates the allocation of the good or service in question to the use in which it is most valuable, thereby maximising the wealth of society.

This conclusion may be questioned on various grounds. For example, it may be argued that since 'value' in this analysis is measured by willingness to pay, which in turn is affected by the distribution of income and wealth (one cannot offer to buy a good without having money or the means to obtain it), the maximisation of value cannot be regarded as an uncontroversially proper goal for society to pursue.
. . .

The principle that voluntary exchange should be freely permitted in order to maximise value is frequently summarised in the concept (or slogan) of 'freedom of contract'. This is something of a misnomer, for the concept of *contract* typically plays an insignificant role in elucidations and critiques of the principle of voluntary exchange. Many value-maximising exchanges occur without contracts, or with contracts so rudimentary or transitory as to have little interest for economists studying the phenomenon of voluntary exchange. If A buys the *Chicago Tribune* from B, a news vendor, paying 20¢ for it on the spot, this is a value-maximising exchange; but it would be pretentious to speak of a contract between A and B, though technically there is one (if a section of the paper is missing, A can probably rescind the contract and get his 20¢ back). One can talk about the principle or system of voluntary exchange for quite some time before it becomes necessary to consider the role of contracts and contract law in facilitating the process.

In the newspaper example, the exchange is virtually (though not completely) instantaneous; and this provides a clue to the role of contracts in the process of voluntary exchange. It is true that, although money and good cross at the same moment, the actual *use* of the good—the reading of the newspaper—occurs after the exchange and takes some time; so really the process of exchange is not complete until the paper has been opened and inspected. Only then can the buyer be satisfied that he got what he paid for (that no pages are missing or illegible, etc.). Still, the time required to complete the exchange in the newspaper example is quite short. Where the time is long, contracts and contract law become important.

Suppose that A promises to build a house for B, construction to take six months to complete and B to pay either periodically or on completion. With construction so time-consuming, there is a significant likelihood that something will occur to frustrate the exchange—insolvency, changes in the price of inputs, labour troubles, etc. Nor is A's performance complete when construction of the house is finished. A durable good like a house by definition yields services to the purchaser over a period of time, a long one in the case of a house; and it is these services rather than the physical structure itself that the purchaser is hoping to acquire. If the house wears out long before the purchaser reasonably believed it would, the exchange will be effectively thwarted long after nominal completion of performance by the promisor.

Economists have pointed out that the cost of an undertaking tends to be inversely related to the time allowed for completion. Stated differently, it is costly to accelerate completion of a time-consuming task. It would also be costly to make goods less durable in order to compress the period in which the full exchange of the goods could be completed. These observations suggest that a system of contract rights, and not merely one of property rights, may be necessary to minimise the costs of production in a market system.

Thus far we have been attempting to elucidate the concept of a contract and explain its economic significance. We have said nothing about the economic function of contract *law*. Its basic function is to provide a sanction for reneging, which, in the absence of sanctions, is sometimes tempting where the parties' performance is not simultaneous. During the process of an extended exchange, a point may be reached where it is in the interest (though perhaps only the very narrow, short-run interest) of one of the parties to terminate performance. If A agrees to build a house for B and B pays him in advance, A can make himself better off, at least if loss of reputation (which, depending on A's particular situation, may be unimportant to him) is ignored, by pocketing B's money and not building the house. The problem arises because the non-simultaneous character of the exchange offers one of the parties a strategic advantage which he can use to obtain a transfer payment that utterly vitiates the advantages of the contract to the other party. Clearly, if such conduct were permitted, people would be reluctant to enter into contracts and the process of economic exchange would be retarded.

A non-instantaneous or extended exchange creates not only strategic opportunities that parties might try to exploit in the absence of legal sanction, but also uncertainty with regard to the conditions under which performance will occur. This uncertainty exposes the parties to the risk that the costs and benefits of their exchange will turn out to be different from what they expected. An important function of contract law is to enforce the parties' agreed-upon allocation of risk.

A related function is to reduce the costs of the exchange process by supplying a standard set of risk-allocation terms for use by contracting parties. Many substantive rules of contract law are simply specifications of the consequences of some contingency for which the contract makes no express provision. If the parties are satisfied with the way in which the rule allocates the risk of that contingency, they have no need to incur the expense of writing their own risk-allocation rule into the contract.

Besides (1) imposing costs on people who try to exploit the other party to the contract by refusing to abide by its terms and (2) providing a stock of standard contractual provisions, the law of contracts (3) imposes costs on, and thereby discourages, *careless* behaviour in the contracting process—behaviour that unnecessarily increases the costs of the process itself. Suppose A promises to give B a boat if B stops smoking, B complies with this condition (at some cost to himself), but A refuses to give him the boat. A proves that B misunderstood him—he never meant to promise him a boat. B in turn proves that he was reasonably induced by A's words and conduct to believe that A had indeed promised him the boat. If we believe that A did not in fact intend such a promise, then enforcement of the promise cannot be justified as necessary to prevent frustration of a value-maximising exchange; there is no basis for presuming that an exchange will make the parties better off if one of them never intended to make it. But we may still want to enforce the contract in order to give people in A's position an incentive to avoid carelessly inducing others to incur costs in reliance on the existence of a contract. This problem may seem to belong to the law of torts rather than contracts, since enforcement serves not to promote a mutually beneficial exchange but instead to deter careless behaviour. But enforcement does promote the contractual process by discouraging a costly form of carelessness that would tend to impede it.

The foregoing discussion suggests a resolution along economic lines of the old dispute in contract law over whether the basis of contract formation is a 'subjective' or 'objective' one—whether the law requires an actual meeting of minds or whether it is enough that the parties use words or conduct that would signify agreement to an impartial observer. Only a contract that involves an actual meeting of minds satisfies the economist's definition of a value-maximising exchange; but the economist allows a place for rules designed to prevent people from misleading others into thinking they have a contract with them; hence both the subjective and objective theories have a place in contract law.

The discussion to this point has emphasised the economic role of contract and has outlined the economic functions of contract law. It is, however, one thing to show that contract law *could* promote economic efficiency and another thing to prove that it *does*. A number of scholars in recent years have claimed that the common law, including the law of contracts, has an implicit economic logic—the purpose, or in any event the effect, of many common law doctrines is, they believe, to increase economic efficiency. One of the points emphasised by those sceptical of this theory is the implausibility of supposing that judges have been able to work out the economics of legal obligations and liabilities correctly. To be sure, one observes business firms behaving 'correctly' from an economic standpoint (i.e. maximising profits by equating marginal revenue to marginal cost) without being conscious of, or at least articulate about, what they are doing. But this can be explained by the competitive process: firms that do not maximise profits will be unable to attract capital from competing demanders and so will eventually be driven out of business. The survivors, the firms we observe, are those that pursue, whether unwittingly or deliberately, profit-maximising strategies. But it is unclear what the mechanism is that drives judges to discover and apply correct microeconomic principles.

In the case of contract law, however, a competitive mechanism is at hand to explain why the rules of contract law might be expected to be generally efficient. As we have seen, many rules of contract law are designed simply to supply contract terms where the parties have not done so expressly. If prospective contracting parties do not like the terms supplied by contract law, normally they are free to supplant them with their own express terms. The parties will prefer efficient terms because those are the terms that minimise the costs of the transaction to them, and accordingly the tendency will be to contract around any inefficient rules of contract law. The efficient rules will survive; the inefficient will be progressively ignored and eventually forgotten.

This competitive or evolutionary process is reinforced by two other factors. The first is the willingness of the courts to honour the parties' designation of the law to be applied to resolve any dispute arising from a contract between them. The second is the right of contracting parties to agree to submit any disputes arising out of the contract to a private arbitrator. Because of these factors, courts that apply inefficient rules of contract law will tend to lose cases to tribunals that apply efficient rules. Even if a court system does not 'mind' losing contract business, one will observe a body of cases heavily concentrated in tribunals that apply efficient rules.

The foregoing discussion does not, of course, prove that the rules of contract law are efficient; it simply makes the idea a bit less shocking. It should be noted, however, that the relevance of economics to contract law does not depend on proving that the logic of that law is economics. Since efficiency is an important value in our society (we need not decide here how important), a critique of contract law based on efficiency is a potentially powerful tool of legal reform.

Chapter Two

Formation of a Contract

INTRODUCTION

The process whereby a contract is agreed is not standardised or uniform. The most straightforward transactions, such as buying a newspaper or contracting to travel to work in the morning by bus are in theory governed by the same rules on formation as the most complex share or property transaction. The parties, and the courts, must be able to decide when the preliminary inquiries as to terms have ended and when one party at least has been prepared, like the Earl of Kildare, to 'chance his arm' and make an offer. The courts must also try and guarantee some parity of fairness by negativing the prejudice this can induce, hence the counter-offer rule and perhaps judicial sensitivity on lock-out agreements. The rules governing acceptances are also designed to preclude unfair practices, such as the 'silence deemed acceptance' rule which is viewed with hostility by the courts and the Oireachtas. The acceptance rules must also provide practical and fair methods of determining whether, when and where the contract was concluded, while being consistent with the intentions of each party.

While the principle of private autonomy suggests that each party should be free to determine how long the negotiations should last, the cases suggest some constraints may be placed on 'free will'. Negotiations cannot be expected to go on forever, and the rules which decide whether an offer can be accepted or not impose limits. Conversely, the rules also allow concluded 'contracts' to be unravelled—the subject to contract cases—when commercial expediency and practice deems this appropriate, even though the results in individual cases can be patently unjust.

SECTION ONE—OFFER

An offer is 'a clear and unambiguous statement of the terms upon which the offeror is willing to contract, should the person or persons to whom the offer is addressed decide to accept.'

R. Clark, *Contract Law in Ireland* (3rd ed. London: Sweet & Maxwell, 1992)

Bridget Tansey v The College of Occupational Therapists Ltd (HC) 27 August 1986, unrep. (1983/3591P)

The plaintiff applied for admission to St Joseph's College, an independent college, to take a preparation course for the defendant's diploma examinations.

She was granted a place in a course commencing in October 1978. The defendants published a manual providing details of the examination and stating that two retakes of each part of the examination were allowed. In April 1978 the defendants decided to amend their regulations and allow the students only one automatic retake. An erratum slip to this effect was included in only some of the copies of the manual handed out to new students in Autumn 1978. A notice of the amendment was dispatched by the defendants to St Joseph's in May 1978 and remained on the notice boards throughout 1978 and 1979. The amendment was also pointed out to students throughout the course. The plaintiff failed psychiatry in 1981 and again in the retake. An application to be allowed a second retake was denied.

Murphy J.:

The proceedings herein are based solely on the alleged contractual right of the plaintiff to two automatic retakes of each part of the defendants' examinations.

In these circumstances the case on behalf of the plaintiff is pleaded and argued as follows:

First, it is contended that the relationship between the plaintiff and the defendants is founded upon a contract which confers legally enforceable rights on the plaintiff. As the agreement (if any) between the plaintiff and the defendants related to the admission of the plaintiff to the course of studies approved by the defendants rather than the regulation of the conduct of students subsequent to their admission the matter is one—or so the plaintiff would contend—of general law and not a domestic matter which might, in the case of an appropriate institution, be dealt with by a visitor. The case of *Casson and Another and the University of Aston in Birmingham* |1983| 1 All ER 88 was cited as persuasive authority in support of this proposition.

Secondly, that the contract was made in the month of November 1978 by the plaintiff offering herself as a student for the defendants' diploma course and the defendants by their agents, St Joseph's College, and their officials handing to the plaintiff the defendants' manual for the course.

Thirdly, that the acceptance of the plaintiff's offer was on the terms and conditions and subject to the regulations contained in the manual actually handed to the plaintiff and did not include any alterations thereof which were not at the time brought to her attention.

Fourthly, that the plaintiff was not given that degree of notice of the amendment contained in the circular pinned to the college notice board which would be appropriate having regard to the nature of that condition. It was contended that the alteration was in the nature of a restrictive condition and accordingly that clear notice thereof should have been given to the plaintiff.

Fifthly, that the contract having been made by the acceptance of the plaintiff as a student no alteration in the terms of that contract could be made without the plaintiff's consent and that any notice or advice purporting to make such a change was ineffective (see *Olley and Malborough Court Ltd* |1949| 1 KBD 532).

Sixthly, that the plaintiff was entitled to damages for breach of contract which would reflect the income which she might have earned had she been permitted to resit her examination in psychiatry, duly passed it and then practised as an occupational therapist as against the income which she did in fact earn as a Montessori teacher notwithstanding the doubt which must exist as to whether she would indeed have succeeded in the examination. In support of that proposition reliance was placed on the decision of the late Mr Justice Dixon in *Hawkins and Rogers* |1951| IR 48.

On behalf of the defendants it was accepted that there was a contractual relationship between them and the plaintiff but only insofar as it related to the setting and correcting of individual examinations. It was the defendants' contention that such contracts arose and arose only as and when the plaintiff applied in writing to the defendants to sit the various exams constituting the diploma course and on the acceptance of those applications by the defendants. The defendants also accepted that there was a contract between the plaintiff and St Joseph's College for the provision of training and tuition. In particular the defendants contend that no contract was entered into between the plaintiff and the defendants in the year 1978. On their behalf it was said that they made no offer to the plaintiff and received no offer from her. Less still was one accepted. It was emphasised that the defendants did not know of the existence of the plaintiff at any time before she applied in 1979 to sit her Group I examination. To the argument that St Joseph's College acted as the agents of the defendants it was pointed out that the evidence made it clear that St Joseph's College was an autonomous body which exercised their own discretion as to what students they would take in and indeed their own judgment as to what students might expel [sic].

I am unable to accept that a contract between the defendants and the plaintiff came into existence at the time, in the manner or on the terms for which the plaintiff contends as aforesaid. One would like to think that a student in the plaintiff's position would have some guarantee that significant changes would not be made in the structure of the course which she was pursuing or the fundamental regulations governing it after she had embarked thereon. No doubt to some extent this is achieved by the sense of responsibility actually displayed by the defendants in the present case and hopefully exercised by similar bodies in other cases.

Contractual obligations derive from agreement made between two or more parties under which one promises or undertakes with the other the performance of some action. Ordinarily the existence of an agreement presupposes an offer by one party to perform the action on certain terms and the acceptance of that offer by the other. Logical analysis would suggest that the offer must be communicated to the person for whom it is intended and in turn his acceptance must likewise be communicated to the offerer. In the absence of such communication, whether expressed or implied, there would not be that meeting of minds which is implicit in the concept of any agreement. It must be recognised, however, that the innumerable authorities dealing with the law of contract and academic analyses of those decisions over many years reveal refinements of this analysis and apparent exceptions to it. Nevertheless, it seems to me that the case made on behalf of the plaintiff must be examined with a view to identifying the offer and acceptance constituting the alleged agreement.

The celebrated case of *Carlill and Carbolic Smoke Ball Co.* [1893] 1 QBD 256 is authority for the propositions first that an offer may be made to the world at large even though a contract can only be made with identified persons. Secondly that such an offer may be accepted by the performance of a particular condition prescribed in the offer and thirdly that as notification of acceptance is required for the benefit of the person who makes the offer he may, if he thinks it desirable to do so, dispense with such notice. Accordingly one could envisage circumstances in which an examining body might communicate to the public at large the terms in which they were offering a series of examinations and expressly or by implication inviting interested persons to accept that offer by undertaking a specified course of study. However that is not the present case. The plaintiff was not aware of any offer made by the defendants prior to the commencement of her studies and accordingly her application to St Joseph's and their admission of her as a student could not constitute acceptance of any offer by the defendants herein. Even if the position were otherwise this approach would be of no avail to the plaintiff—as her counsel fully recognised—because the terms and conditions on offer from the defendants at that time provided only for one automatic retake of failed examinations. Again it would not be sufficient for the plaintiff to argue that on her admission as a student of St Joseph's that the defendants thereby accepted an offer from her simply to take the exams which they proffered. To succeed in this case the plaintiff must establish the existence of a contract which incorporates the particular provision entitling her as of right to a second repeat of her examinations. In the circumstances of the present case it has to be contended either that the plaintiff should be seen as making an offer to take the defendants' course on such terms as they would prescribe and that the defendants accepted that offer by permitting or authorising St Joseph's College as their agents to hand to the plaintiff the manual containing the terms prescribed herein or, alternatively, that the presentation of the manual by St Joseph's to the plaintiff constituted an offer and that some conduct by the plaintiff—perhaps continuing with her course of studies—constituted acceptance of that offer. Counsel on behalf of the plaintiff did not pursue the second of these alternatives recognising, no doubt, the difficulty in establishing any action which could be interpreted as acceptance.

There are two formidable difficulties to be overcome in establishing the case on which the plaintiff does rely. First, it is difficult to conceive of an acceptance which would itself prescribe conditions. Ordinarily a communication in the course of negotiations leading to a contract which contains conditions not previously agreed by the party to whom the communication is addressed will fall to be treated as a new or counter offer rather than an acceptance. Secondly the plaintiff's argument was criticised on the basis that if the offer permitted the defendants to establish the terms, conditions or regulations governing the contract that there was no justification for assuming that these provisions would not be subject to alteration. However perhaps the best way of presenting the defendants' counter argument is to say that the plaintiff did not prescribe the production of the manual as the means of accepting any offer made by her and there is no internal evidence in this manual and nothing in the conduct of the officials of St Joseph's College by whom it was distributed to suggest that the circulation of the manual amongst the students was intended to constitute acceptance of a contract either by St Joseph's College or by the defendants. I believe that this objection to the plaintiff's argument is well founded. The manual contains for the greater part a large body of information in relation to the medical and surgical conditions relevant to the study of occupational therapy. The information with regard to examinations is obviously important but there is nothing in its presentation to suggest that the communication of this information by the officials of a recognised college should constitute acceptance of an offer by potential students.

I am not to be taken as laying down any principle that conditions or regulations made by an examining body—be it the defendants or any such body—could not be made part of a legally binding contract. Indeed it is possible that a successful argument could have been made to the effect that the amended rules of the defendants did form part of such a contract. All that can be said in relation to the present case is that the plaintiff has not proved that the plaintiff offered or the defendants accepted any offer by the plaintiff to take the diploma course on terms which included and included only the regulations contained in the unamended 1977 manual.

In these circumstances it seems to me—not without some regret—that the plaintiff's claim must fail.

Note

It is important to distinguish 'an offer' from other separate and distinct situations where a party makes a statement which resembles an offer, but which is not capable of being 'accepted', nor of giving rise to contractual obligations should the party to whom it is made assent to the terms of the statement.

A. INVITATION TO TREAT

The Minister for Industry and Commerce *v* Pim Bros Ltd [1966] IR 154

The defendants displayed an advertisement attached to a coat indicating that the cash price of the coat was 24 guineas and that the weekly payments in respect thereof were 5s 10d.

The plaintiff claimed that this advertisement did not comply with certain provisions of the Hire-Purchase and Credit Sale (Advertising) Order 1961 in relation to 'goods offered or available for sale by way of hire-purchase or credit-sale agreement', and brought a prosecution against the defendant under that order.

The District Justice found that the placing of the notice on the coat did not constitute an advertisement relating to goods offered for sale by hire-purchase or credit-sale agreement. It was rather an offer to treat for the sale of goods, with an indication that unspecified credit facilities would be available to a purchaser. He was however, unable to say whether it was an advertisement relating to goods 'available for sale'. The District Justice referred this question by way of a case stated for the opinion of the High Court.

Davitt P.:

If the advertisement was one relating to goods available for sale, whether by way of hire-purchase agreement or by way of credit-sale agreement, it would be one to which the Order applies; but it would comply with the provisions of the Order in as much as it includes a statement of the price at which the coat could be purchased for cash. What the defendants were really charged with was displaying an advertisement relating to goods offered for sale, by way of hire-purchase agreement or credit-sale agreement, which failed to include certain statements required by the Order. Before one could determine whether the advertisement related to goods *offered* for sale by way of hire-purchase agreement or to goods offered for sale by way of credit-sale agreement one would have to decide whether it related to goods offered for sale at all; in other words, whether the advertisement constituted an offer by the defendants to sell the coat. In one sense it could be described as an offer to sell. In popular terms the coat could properly be said to be on offer to the public. In the strictly legal sense, however, the advertisement was merely a statement of the cash price at which the defendants were prepared to sell the goods, with an indication that certain credit facilities, the exact nature of which were unspecified, would be available. This would not constitute an offer to sell which could be made a contract of sale by acceptance: *Harvey v Facey*.[1] This appears to have been the view taken by the learned District Justice and to be the real ground of his decision to dismiss. If the expression, 'offered for sale', in Article 6(1) of the Order is to be construed in the strict legal sense, then the learned District Justice was clearly correct in his decision. In my opinion, it should be so construed. Apart from any other consideration the distinction made in the Order between advertise-ments relating to goods offered for sale and goods available for sale, a distinction which does not appear in the relevant sections of the statute, indicates, to my mind, that the expression, 'offered for sale', as used in the Order should be construed in its strict legal sense. In the case of Case Stated No. 118 it was essential to prove that the coat was offered for sale in this sense. The learned District Justice was not satisfied that this had been established; and in my opinion he was correct in the view he took.

1. [1893] AC 552.

Note

In most cases an advertisement will be deemed to constitute 'an invitation to treat'. An exception to this is 'a unilateral contract' which is an offer intended to be legally binding (see p. 48).

B. A Declaration of Intention

Wilson *v* Belfast Corporation (1921) 55 ILTR 205

The defendants passed a resolution on 5 August 1914 agreeing to pay half wages to employees who joined the Defence Forces. This resolution was published in the press without the defendants' authority. At a further meeting on 23 September the defendants passed a second resolution limiting the offer to persons already in the council's service on 5 August. Subsequent to this second resolution Wilson entered the defendants' service and five months later joined the army. He notified the defendant of his claim to half pay. Wilson was later killed in action.

His widow and child later sued to recover the amount claimed to be due as half pay from the date of enlistment to the date of death.

The case came before the Irish Court of Appeal on appeal from the King's Bench Division.

O'Connor L.J.:

The wording of the committee's resolution of 5 August is not material. The plaintiff's case must be based on the council's resolution of 1 September. The court below decid-ed that that resolution referred only to persons in the employment of the corporation at the time, and I am of the same opinion. The resolution of 1 October put the matter beyond all doubt by limiting its application to those persons who were in the corpor-ation's service on 5 August. Wilson entered their employment three months later than the alleged contract. I say there was no such contract. Even if the original resolution embraced his class there was no contract. Was there an offer? Was it meant to be an offer? There was no intention to make the resolution an offer. Of necessity, it had to be public. Neither was there any communication. The reporter puts the resolution into the press: its publication is not authorised by the corporation, and could not be prevented by them. Before Wilson joined the army a new resolution had been passed. Even if he saw the first resolution, and did not see the second, it makes no difference to him. He had no right to assume that the corporation's resolutions are unalterable: they may change from day to day. Therefore, no contract at all was made. Apart from contract, there could be no valid claim under the statute.

Note

Compare this case to **Joseph P. Billings v Arnott & Co. Ltd (1945) 80 ILTR 50 (HC)**. In this case the defendants posted a notice offering any of their employees who joined the Defence Forces one half of their salaries up to the sum of £2 per week. The plaintiff, an employee, informed the defendants that he intended to accept this offer. He was told that this would not be possible as another employee from his department had already joined and he could not be spared. Despite this the plaintiff joined the Defence Forces. The plaintiff later sued for salary due for three and a half years on foot of the notice.

Maguire J. in the High Court:

There was an inducement to the employees to join the Defence Forces. The notice I find is unconditional, with no reservation to allow a refusal to release any employee. I cannot take the view that it was a mere declaration of intention. It is a clear expression of what the company would do. Acceptance was then completed when the plaintiff joined the Defence Forces and intimated his intention of so doing on 16 August 1940. On that view a contract was completed under which defendants undertook to pay plaintiff the allowance. There was no provision in the notice published that the managing director had power to decide to whom the allowance was to be paid. I am satisfied that the money claimed is due and accordingly I give judgment for the plaintiff for the sum claimed, with costs.

C. STEPS IN A NEGOTIATION

Boyers & Co. v D. & R. Duke [1904] 2 IR 617

The plaintiffs, drapers, wrote to the defendants, linen manufacturers, asking for their lowest quotation for a quantity of canvas. The defendants replied stating their lowest price. The plaintiffs subsequently sent in an order at this price. On discovering that a clerical error had resulted in an excessively low quotation, the defendants refused to supply at the original price. The plaintiffs sued for breach of contract.

Lord O'Brien L.C.J:

The short question in this case is, whether these letters or documents which passed between the plaintiffs and the defendants constitute a completed contract—whether they amount to an offer and an acceptance of the offer, or to a quotation and an order? If they amount to the former, they constitute a contract; if to the latter, that is to say to a quotation and order, they do not constitute a contract. The action in which the question arises was brought by the plaintiffs against the defendants for alleged breach of contract for the supply of canvas. The controversy arises, as I have said, upon the construction of the documents. My brother Wright, who tried the case, held that they did not constitute a completed contract, and we are of opinion he was right in so holding.

What, then, are these documents? The first is dated 23 February 1904, from the plaintiffs to the defendants, and is in the following terms: 'Please give us your lowest quotation for 3000 yards of canvas, $32^1/_2$ inches wide, to the enclosed sample, or near, and your shortest time for delivery, and oblige,' &c. Now, this is expressly a request for a quotation. The reply is dated 24 February 1904, and is as follows: 'We enclose sample, No. B 3932, nearest we have to match yours, also enclosed. Lowest price, $32^1/_2$ inches wide, is $4^5/_8$d per yard, 36 inches measure. Delivery of 3000 yards in 5/6 weeks.' This, in my opinion, amounts only to a quotation. Certainly quantity, price, and time of delivery are stated, but I think it is nothing more than a statement of their ability to turn out the subject-matter at a certain price at a certain time, and not an offer to sell it at the price, and to deliver it within the time, mentioned. It amounted to nothing more, in my opinion, than a quotation in reply to a request for one.

Now comes the third and last letter, which is said by the plaintiffs to be an acceptance of an offer to sell on certain terms. It is dated 3 March. I shall read it: 'Messrs D. & R. Duke, Brechin, NB Gents, Please get made for us 3000 yards of canvas, $32^1/_2$ inches wide, as per your quotation, 24 February, at $4^5/_8$d per yard; deliver same as quickly as possible. Also please quote us for same, 52 inches wide, for quantity of about 20,000 yards annually. As we have not had the pleasure of doing business with you before, we give you as reference Messrs Baxter, Brothers, Dundee; Messrs Richards, Ltd, Aberdeen. Canvas No. B 3932. (Signed) Boyers & Co. Also please quote us for canvas to sample enclosed, 52 inches, and oblige, B. & Co.'

Is this an acceptance of an offer, or an order? In my opinion it is not the acceptance of an offer, because the letter to which it was a reply was a quotation and not an offer.

This letter is nothing more than it purports to be, namely, an order based on a quotation. The words are: 'Please get made for us 3000 yards of canvas, $32^1/_2$ inches wide, as per your *quotation*, 24 February.' The first letter, that is to say, the letter of 23 February, asked for a *quotation*; the letter of the twenty fourth sent what was asked for; and the plaintiffs' letter of 3 March expressly refers to the letter of the twenty fourth, as 'per your quotation, 24 February.'

Light is also thrown upon the true character of the letter of 3 March by the giving of references as therein, which is certainly far more compatible with the giving of an order, or offer to purchase, than with a completed contract. The words 'as quickly as possible' in the letter of 3 March would perhaps point to an uncompleted contract, but I think this criticism is so minute that much weight is not to be attached to it.

We are of opinion that my brother Wright's view was correct, and that judgment should be for the defendants.

Madden J.:

The defendants in this case were asked for a 'quotation'. Now the word 'quotation' is capable of different meanings according to the connection in which it is used, but there is a common idea underlying them all, that of notation or enumeration. The things quoted may be passages in an author, the prices of specific articles, or the terms upon which work is to be done. In the case before us both parties agree that the documents before us must be read and construed, giving the words the ordinary meaning which they bear in the English language, having regard to the subject matter to which they relate; for neither party has contended that evidence should have been taken as to the use of the word 'quotation' in mercantile transactions.

A quotation might be so expressed as to amount to an offer to provide a definite article, or to do a certain work, at a defined price. But the ideas of a quotation, and of an offer to sell, are radically different. The difference is well illustrated by the case of *Harvey v Facey*.[1] There, to a telegram in these terms, 'Will you sell us B. H. P.? Telegraph lowest cash price', the answer was returned, 'Lowest price for B. H. P., £900.' The inquirer telegraphed, 'We agree to buy B. H. P. for £900 asked by you.' An exceptionally strong judicial committee of the Privy Council, in a judgment delivered by Lord Morris, held that the statement, or quotation, of the lowest price at which a definite thing will be sold, does not import an offer to sell.

The principle on which this case was decided applies with a greater force to mercantile transactions than to an application for a statement of the price of a single parcel of land. It is a matter of common knowledge that quotations of prices are scattered broadcast among possible customers. Business could not be carried on if each recipient of a priced catalogue offering a desirable article—say a rare book—at an attractive price, were in a position to create a contract of sale by writing that he would buy at the price mentioned. The catalogue has probably reached many collectors. The order of one only can be honoured. Has each of the others who write for the book a right of action? Wholesale dealers have not in stock an unlimited supply of the articles the prices of which they quote to the public at large. This stock usually bears some proportion to the orders which they may reasonably expect to receive. Transactions of the kind under consideration are intelligible and business-like, if we bear in mind the distinction between a quotation, submitted as the basis of a possible order, and an offer to sell which, if accepted, creates a contract, for the breach of which damages may be recovered.

These observations seem to apply with special force to a quotation furnished by a manufacturer, in the position of the defendants, stating the terms on which he is prepared to work, as to price and time for completion. He may receive and comply with many applications for quotations on the same day. If his reply in each case can be turned into a contract by acceptance, his looms might be burdened with an amount of work which would render it impossible for him to meet his engagements. In my opinion, a merchant, dealer, or manufacturer, by furnishing a quotation invites an offer which will be honoured or not according to the exigencies of his business. A quotation based on current prices usually holds good for a limited time. But it remains a quotation, on the basis of which an offer will not be entertained after a certain date. I have arrived at this conclusion irrespective of the terms of the letter of 3 March, as to which I will only say that it suggests to my mind that the writer knew well that he was giving an order, not accepting an offer for sale.

[1] |1893| AC 552.

(Gibson J. also held that no concluded contract existed.)

D. AUCTION SITUATIONS

Special rules regulate auction situations both at common law and under Statute.

Sale of Goods Act 1893 *s.* 58(2)

58. (2) In the case of a sale by auction:
(1) Where goods are put up for sale by auction in lots, each lot is *prima facie* deemed to be the subject of a separate contract of sale:

(2) A sale by auction is complete when the auctioneer announces its completion by the fall of the hammer, or in other customary manner. Until such announcement is made any bidder may retract his bid:

(3) Where a sale by auction is not notified to be subject to a right to bid on behalf of the seller, it shall not be lawful for the seller to bid himself or to employ any person to bid at such sale, or for the auctioneer knowingly to take any bid from the seller or any such person: Any sale contravening this rule may be treated as fraudulent by the buyer:

(4) A sale by auction may be notified to be subject to a reserve or upset price, and a right to bid may also be reserved expressly by or on behalf of the seller.

Where a right to bid is expressly reserved, but not otherwise, the seller, or any one person on his behalf, may bid at the auction.

Warlow v Harrison (1859) 1 E & E 309

Martin B.:

The defendant and a Mr Bretherton are auctioneers in partnership at Birmingham, where they have a repository for the sale of horses. In June 1858, they advertised a sale by auction at the repository. The advertisement contained, amongst other entries of horses to be sold, as follows. 'The three following horses, the property of a gentleman, *without reserve.*' One of these was a mare called Janet Pride. The plaintiff attended the sale, and bid sixty guineas for her: another person immediately bid sixty-one guineas; this person was Mr Henderson, the owner of the mare. The plaintiff, having been informed that the last bidder was the owner, declined to bid further; and thereupon the defendant knocked down the mare to Mr Henderson for sixty one guineas, and entered his name as purchaser in the sale book, which contained the names of the animals to be sold at the sale, and the names of the proprietors. The plaintiff went at once into the auctioneer's office, and saw Mr Bretherton and Mr Henderson, and claimed the mare from Mr Bretherton as being the highest *bona fide* bidder, the mare being advertised to be sold without reserve. Mr Henderson said, 'I bought her in; and you shall not have her: I gave £130 for the mare; and it is not likely I am going to sell her for sixty three.' On the same day, the plaintiff tendered to the defendant £63, in sovereigns, as the price of the mare, and demanded her. The defendant refused to receive the money or deliver the mare, stating that he had knocked her down to the highest bidder, and he could not interfere in the matter. There was evidence that the plaintiff had notice that the following were amongst the conditions of the sale:

1. The highest bidder to be the buyer; and, if any dispute arise between two or more bidders before the lot is returned into the stables, the lot so disputed shall be put up again, or the auctioneer may declare the purchaser.

3. The purchaser, being declared, must immediately give in his name and address, with (if required) a deposit of five shillings in the pound on account of his purchase, and pay the remainder before such lot or lots are delivered.

8. Any lot ordered for this sale, and sold by private contract by the owner, or advertised without reserve and bought by the owner, to be liable to the usual commission of 5 per cent.

. . .

. . . Upon the facts of the case, it seems to us that the plaintiff is entitled to recover. In a sale by auction there are three parties, *viz.* the owner of the property to be sold, the auctioneer, and the portion of the public who attend to bid, which of course includes the highest bidder. In this, as in most cases of sales by auction, the owner's name was not disclosed: he was a concealed principal. The name of the auctioneers, of whom the defendant was one, alone was published; and the sale was announced by them to be 'without reserve'. This, according to all the cases both at law and equity, means that neither the vendor nor any person in his behalf shall bid at the auction, and that the property shall be sold to the highest bidder, whether the sum bid be equivalent to the real value or not; *Thornett v Haines*.[1] We cannot distinguish the case of an auctioneer putting up property for sale upon such a condition from the case of the loser of property offering a reward, or that of a railway company publishing a time table stating the times when, and the places to which, the trains run. It has been decided that the person giving the information advertised for, or a passenger taking a ticket, may sue as upon a contract with him; *Denton v Great Northern Rly Co*.[2] Upon the same principle, it seems to us that the highest *bona fide* bidder at an auction may sue the auctioneer as upon a contract that the sale shall be without reserve. We think the auctioneer who puts the property up for sale upon such a condition pledges himself that the sale shall be without reserve; or, in other words, contracts that it shall be so; and that this contract is made with the highest *bona fide* bidder; and, in case of a breach of it, that he has a right of action against the auctioneer. The case is not at all affected by s. 17 of the Statute of Frauds, which relates only to direct sales, and not to contracts relating to or connected with them. Neither does it seem to us material whether the owner, or person on his behalf, bid with the knowledge or privity of the auctioneer. We think the auctioneer has contracted that the sale shall be without reserve; and that the contract is broken upon a bid being made by or on behalf of the owner, whether it be during the time when the property is under the hammer, or it be the last bid upon which the article is knocked down; in either case the sale is not 'without reserve', and the contract of the auctioneer is broken. We entertain no doubt that the owner may, at any time before the contract is legally complete, interfere and revoke the auctioneer's authority: but he does so at his peril; and, if the auctioneer has contracted any liability in consequence of his employment and the subsequent revocation or conduct of the owner, he is entitled to be indemnified.

We do not think the conditions of sale stated in the case (assuming the plaintiff to be taken to have had notice of them) affect it. As to the first, Mr. Henderson could not be the buyer: he was the owner; and, if it were material, there is ample evidence that the defendant knew him to be so: indeed we think he ought not to have taken his bid, but to have refused it; . . .

[1] 15 M & W 367.
[2] 5 E & B 860.

Tully *v* The Irish Land Commission (1961) 97 ILTR 174

The defendants advertised that a certain piece of property would be sold at public auction. Clause 2 of the conditions of sale stated that: 'the highest bidder shall be the purchaser and if any dispute arises as to any bidding the property shall be again put up for sale at the last undisputed bidding. There will be a reserve price and the Irish Land Commission,the vendors or their agents shall be at liberty to bid. . . . ' Clause 3 provided that the purchaser should pay a deposit to the auctioneer immediately after the sale and subscribe his name and address to the memorandum of agreement.

The plaintiff arranged that a friend (Mr J. Farrell) would bid on his behalf. The property was knocked down at the auction to a Mr Draddy who signed the memorandum attached to the conditions of sale. A dispute then arose as to which party had made the final bid. The plaintiff demanded that the auctioneer put the property up for sale again. The auctioneer refused and the plaintiff sued for breach of clause 2 of the contract, and claimed an injunction to prevent the defendants vesting the property in Mr Draddy.

Kenny J.:

The first matter argued has been whether the conditions of sale and the bidding at the auction were capable of constituting a contract between the plaintiff, bidding through his agent, and the Irish Land Commission that the property would be put up for sale again if there was any dispute about the last bidding. It has been contended by counsel for the Irish Land Commission and for Mr Draddy that clauses 2 and 3 of the conditions of sale and the bidding at the auction were not capable of constituting a contract between the plaintiff and the Irish Land Commission and that the words 'the highest bidder shall be the purchaser and if any dispute arises as to any bidding the property shall be again put up for sale at the last undisputed bidding' were not an offer and had no legal effect.

I think that clauses 2 and 3 of the conditions of sale were an offer which could be accepted by bidding at the auction and that they could constitute a contract between the Irish Land Commission and the highest bidder at the auction; this view seems to me to be in accord with legal principle and to be supported by the better authorities. Counsel have cited the views of some eminent writers of text books to establish that this view is incorrect; the passages cited shew some confusion between the two contracts which may be involved. When property is put up for sale, and is sold, a memorandum is signed by the purchaser, there is a contract for the sale of the property to the person who has signed the memorandum. The clauses of the conditions of sale which relate to what may happen before the purchaser signs the memorandum are capable of being an offer in connection with a different contract, a contract to which the Statute of Frauds does not apply and which may be accepted by bidding at the auction.

All the witnesses who gave evidence said that the conditions of sale were read before the bidding began; the bidding was clearly made on the terms of and by reference to them. When giving evidence, the plaintiff admitted that he did not attend the auction because of the conditions of sale, and he said that he would have gone in any event. It was argued by counsel for the Irish Land Commission that the plaintiff could not rely on the conditions of sale as an offer as he did not attend the auction because of them. But the conditions of sale were read before the bidding began and the biddings were made by reference to them and they were capable of being an offer.

It has also been argued that clause 2 of the conditions could not constitute an offer because the offeror (the vendor) cannot know the person who has accepted the bid and with whom the contract is made. This contention ignores the many cases in which it has been held that a person who had performed conditions published by another has thereby accepted the offer made by the publication even though his identity was not known. There is a contract when the conditions of a competition are published and somebody complies with the terms which entitles them to a prize. In most cases there is no difficulty about ascertaining the person who was the highest bidder and I do not see any ground, in principle, why it should be held that these conditions and the bidding at the auction were not capable of creating a contract between the Irish Land Commission and the person who made the highest bid. When conditions of sale are read, those relating to the conduct of the auction (such as clause 2) amount to an offer and the bidding is an acceptance. It has been suggested that this view leads to absurdity as it would have the result that the vendors were making an offer to everybody in this country but the offer which is made by the reading of the conditions of sale and the making of bids is an offer made by the owner of the lands who puts them up for sale to those who attend the auction and bid. The view that these conditions were capable of being an offer gets support from the fact that the conditions of sale were prepared by the Irish Land Commission who now argue that clause 2 of these conditions was without legal effect. If words are without legal effect they should not be inserted in conditions of sale. Words such as this appear in the conditions of sale for most of the public auctions in this country and are to be found in all the recognised books of precedents in conveyancing matters. I do not view with favour an argument by those who have drafted legal documents that the words used are without legal effect.

This conclusion seems to me to be supported by all the better authorities. [Counsel for the plaintiff] based his case on the decision of the Court of Exchequer Chamber in *Warlow v Harrison* (1858) 1 E & E 295, also reported at 29 LJ (QB) 14.

But the matter had been considered before then by Lord Cottenham L.C. in *Robinson v Wall* (1847) 2 Ph. 372. In that case property was put up for sale by auction without reserve and was sold; it was subsequently discovered that the vendor had arranged with a friend that bids would be made to raise the price. The purchaser then brought proceedings to be relieved from his contract. Lord Cottenham decided that the purchaser was entitled to succeed as a number of fictitious bids had been made. In the course of his judgment he said:

Now, that a sale by auction, announced to be without reserve, where there has been a bidding on the part of the vendor for the purpose of keeping up the price, cannot be enforced against the purchaser, was decided by Sir John Leach in the case of *Meadows v Tanner* 5 Madd. 34. Although that was the only case referred to, and the only one that I am aware of in which this particular question has arisen and been decided, it depends in fact upon the same principle as that numerous class of cases in which questions have been raised as to the effect of employing puffers at a sale. They all turn upon this, whether the course pursued by the vendor is or is not in violation of the contract which he enters into with the public as to the mode in which he offers the property for sale; and, in any case in which it is clear that the course pursued has not been consistent with that contract, a court of equity will treat the sale as contrary to good faith on the part of the vendor, and will refuse to enforce it.

There being, then, no doubt upon the law, the only question is whether that which took place in this case was or was not a violation of the contract proposed to the public, namely, that the property should be sold 'without reserve' . . . When a property is offered for sale without reserve, the meaning, and the only meaning that can be attached to it, is, that, of the bidders—the public—who choose to attend the sale, whoever bids the highest shall be the purchaser; that the biddings shall be left to themselves, and that there shall be no bidding on the part of the vendor. And it is not without reserve, the biddings are not left free from the interference of the vendor, if any means or contrivance, it matters not what, be resorted to for the purpose of preventing the effect of open competition. I consider, therefore, the term 'without reserve' to exclude any interference on the part of the vendor (or, which is the same thing, of those who come in under the vendor), which can, under any possible circumstances affect the right of the highest bidder to have the property knocked down to him, and *that*, without reference to the amount to which that highest bidding shall go.

It seems to me that the judgment of the Lord Chancellor assumes that the publication of the conditions to the public and the making of bids are together capable of constituting a contract.

A similar view was taken in *Warlow v Harrison* (1858) 1 E & E 309 by Martin B., Watson B. and Byles J. The judgment of Martin B. contains the following passage at p. 316:

> Upon the facts of the case, it seems to us that the plaintiff is entitled to recover. In a sale by auction there are three parties, *viz.* the owner of the property to be sold, the auctioneer, and the portion of the public who attend to bid, which of course includes the highest bidder. In this, as in most cases of sales by auction, the owner's name was not disclosed; he was a concealed principal. The name of the auctioneers, of whom the defendant was one, alone was published; and the sale was announced by him to be 'without reserve'. This, according to all the cases both at law and equity, means that neither the vendor nor the person on his behalf shall bid at the auction, and that the property shall be sold to the highest bidder, whether the sum bid be equivalent to the real value or not; *Thornell v Haines* 15 M & W 367. We cannot distinguish the case of an auctioneer putting up property for sale upon such a condition from the case of the loser of property offering a reward, or that of a railway company publishing a time-table stating the times when, and the places to which, the trains run. It has been decided that the person giving the information advertised for, or a passenger taking a ticket, may sue as upon a contract with him; *Denton v Great Northern Rly Co.* 5 E & B 860. Upon the same principle, it seems to us that the highest *bona fide* bidder at any auction may sue the auctioneer as upon a contract that the sale shall be without reserve. We think the auctioneer who puts up a property for sale upon such a condition pledges himself that the sale shall be without reserve; or, in other words, contracts that it shall be so; and that this contract is made with the highest *bona fide* bidder; and, in case of a breach of it, that he has a right of action against the auctioneer. The case is not at all affected by s. 17 of the Statute of Frauds, which relates only to direct sales, and not to contracts relating to or connected with them. Neither does it seem to us material whether the owner, or person on his behalf, bid with the knowledge or privity of the auctioneer. We think the auctioneer has contracted that the sale shall be without reserve; and that the contract is broken upon a bid being made by or on behalf of the owner, whether it be during the time when the property is under the hammer, or it be the last bid upon which the article is knocked down; in either case the sale is not 'without reserve', and the contract of the auctioneer is broken.

It has been strenuously argued that the other two judges, Bramwell B. and Willes J. did not agree with the judgment of Martin B. The judgment of Willes J. in *Warlow v Harrison* (1858) 1 E & E 309 at p. 318 was 'My brother Bramwell and myself do not dissent from the judgment which has been pronounced. But we prefer to rest our decision, as to the amendment, upon the ground that the defendant undertook to have, and yet there was evidence that he had not, authority to sell without reserve. The result is the same.' Words have lost their meaning if the judgment of Willes J. means that Bramwell B., and he dissented from the judgment of Martin B.

In *In re Agra & Masterman's Bank Ex parte Asiatic Banking Corp.* (1867) 2 Ch App 391 a declaration of the Court of Appeal in Chancery, Lord Cairns referred to *Warlow v Harrison* with approval.

In the well known *Carlill v Carbolic Smoke Ball Co.* [1893] 1 QB 256 Bowen L.J., said at p. 268:

> It was also said that the contract is made with all the world—that is, with everybody; and that you cannot contract with everybody. It is not a contract made with

all the world. There is the fallacy of the argument. It is an offer made to all the world; and why should not an offer be made to all the world which is to ripen into a contract with anybody who comes forward and performs the condition? It is an offer to become liable to any one who, before it is retracted, performed the condition, and, although the offer is made to the world, the contract is made with that limited portion of the public who come forward and perform the condition on the faith of the advertisement. It is not like cases in which you offer to negotiate, or you issue advertisements that you have got a stock of books to sell, or houses to let, in which case there is no offer to be bound by any contract. Such advertisements are offers to negotiate, offers to receive offers—offers to chaffer, as, I think, some learned judge in one of the cases has said. If this is an offer to be bound, then it is a contract the moment the person fulfils the condition. That seems to me to be sense . . .

In *Johnston v Boyes* [1899] 2 Ch. 73, the plaintiff sent his agent to bid at the auction and the agent who was the highest bidder was not allowed to sign the contract. The plaintiff then brought an action claiming damages for breach of the contract arising out of the clause in the conditions of sale that its highest bidder should be the purchaser. The judgment of Cozens Hardy J. contains the following passage:

> The plaintiff complains that by the defendants' direction Mr Johnston was not allowed to sign the contract, and the property was sold to some one else for £4,950, and the plaintiff claims damages on this footing. In point of law I think such an action can be maintained. A vendor who offers property for sale by auction on the terms of printed conditions can be made liable to a member of the public who accepts the offer if those conditions be violated; see W*arlow v Harrison* 1 E & E 295 and the recent case of *Carlill v Carbolic Smoke Ball Co.* [1893] 1 QB 256. Nor do I think that the Statute of Frauds would afford any defence to such an action. The plaintiff is not suing on a contract to purchase land; she is suing simply because her agent, in breach of the first and second conditions of sale, was not allowed to sign a contract which would have resulted in her becoming the purchaser of the land. I think this conclusion results from the decision of the Exchequer Chamber in W*arlow v Harrison* 1 E & E 317.

The cases which have been cited as authorities for the view that clause 2 of the conditions of sale in this case is not an offer capable of being accepted are not decisions to this effect. . . .

I am therefore of opinion that clauses 2 and 3 of these conditions were an offer which could be accepted so as to create a contractual relation and that there was a contract between the Irish Land Commission and the highest bidder at the auction, the contract being that the highest bidder should be the purchaser and that if any dispute arose as to any bidding the property would be put up for sale at the last undisputed bidding.

The next matter argues related to the time when a sale takes place where there is a public auction; it was submitted that the contractual obligation to put the property up for sale at the last undisputed bidding ended when the property had been knocked down to the purchaser. I think that the conditions of sale showed that the sale took place when the property was knocked down by the auctioneer. Clause 3 provided 'the purchaser shall immediately after the sale pay to the auctioneer a deposit of £25 per cent [sic] on the amount of the purchase money and there pay to the auctioneer his fees on the said price' and it contained a provision for signature of the memorandum.

As these matters were to be done 'immediately after the sale' the sale must have taken place before any of them were done and it follows, I think, that the sale took place when the property was knocked down to the highest bidder provided that the offer was over the reserve price. The contract for sale which comes into existence when the property is knocked down may not be enforceable because of the provisions of the Statute of Frauds but the absence of the memorandum in writing does not prevent a valid contract coming into existence. I respectfully agree with the judgment of Romer J. On *Philips v Butler* [1945] Ch. 358 in which the following passage appears:

> At a sale by auction a contract comes into being when the hammer falls, but neither party can enforce it unless some memorandum or note thereof is in . . . writing, and signed by the party to be charged or by some other person thereunto by him lawfully authorised as s. 40 sub-s. 1 requires. The only function of the memorandum is to provide evidence, which does not affect the terms of the contract but simply makes it enforceable. I cannot see any logical ground for suggesting that an auctioneer's authority to sign a memorandum on his vendor's behalf arises, not as soon as the contract subsists, but only when it has been partly performed by the purchaser's paying a deposit as part of the purchase price. On the decided cases, the auctioneer's authority to sign on the purchaser's—and, if necessary, the vendor's—behalf, arises as soon as the contract is concluded, and is an irrevocable authority.

A contract is therefore concluded when property is knocked down either by using the traditional 'hammer' or, as in this case, by giving some indication to the public attending the auction that the property has been sold. On that construction of the conditions of sale the contract made between the Irish Land Commission and the highest bidder was that if any dispute arose as to any bidding before the property was knocked down, the property would be again put up for sale at the last undisputed bidding. In this case the auctioneer held the property at the last bidding for nearly five minutes and then knocked it down to Mr Draddy. The dispute as to the person who made the last bidding first arose after the property had been knocked down to Mr Draddy; In my opinion the plaintiff's claim fails on this ground as there was not any breach of contract by the Irish Land Commission.

(Kenny J. accepted as a question of fact that Mr Farrell did not make any bid, believing the other bid to be spurious and hoping to acquire the property afterwards for a lower price.)

Note

It is common to find that an auctioneer may have standard conditions of sale which state that a bid, once made, may not be withdrawn (see *Tully's* case itself). Is this binding?

Are there circumstances in which the bidder, as an offeror, is free to withdraw the offer prior to the hammer falling?

Should 'without reserve' sales be treated differently?

E. TENDERS

When an advertisement is placed seeking to invite tenders from prospective contractors—suppliers of goods or services over a period of time perhaps—the advertisement is normally an invitation to treat. The tender form, while prepared in most cases by the person seeking the response of prospective contractors, is normally an offer which can be accepted or rejected. *Spencer v Harding* (1870) LR 5 CP 561.

The Commissioner of Public Works document *Tender for Works* is typical.

FILE NO. ..../...../........
OPENED BY ....on ..../...../19.....

COMMISSIONERS OF PUBLIC WORKS

TENDER FOR WORKS

to be Carried Out

at.. Co. ....

    I the undersigned do hereby propose to the Commissioners of Public Works to execute the works shown on the drawings and described in the Specification, which I have examined, and to find and provide all labour, materials and plant, and do all work incidental and necessary thereto subject to the Conditions of Contract appended hereto for the sum of †...pounds...
.... And do hereby agree should this Tender be accepted to observe and be bound by the said Conditions of Contract.

£

Dated this .... day of ...., 19.....
Contractor's Name in full ....and
full Signature ....
Postal Address ....
....Co. ....

The Secretary, Commissioners of Public Works,
        Dublin 2.

It is essential **(1) that the name of the Works be stated on the envelope; (2) that the tender be signed by the person who submits it, and (3) that a detailed estimate priced fully in accordance with the specification be furnished on pages 3 and 4** at the time of tendering**.**

TENDER ACCEPTED

Date ....19 .... Authorised Officer.

Form C33 (B74/33/1/37)   **Page 1**

F. Unilateral Contracts

Contracts may be either unilateral or bilateral. A bilateral contract is one where both parties to the contract are obliged to perform mutual duties.

In contrast, a unilateral contract is a contract which involves performance on one side making obligatory the promise of the other side. The outstanding obligation is thus all on one side. It may constitute an offer of an act in return for a promise, or the offer of a promise in return for an act. For example 'I will help you with your mortgage repayments, if you leave the house to me in your will.' In this case the offeror acts and the offeree makes the promise. Alternatively the offeror makes the promise and the offeree acts in the following example 'I will promise to give you £10 if you carry my bags to the hotel.' Thus such contracts are often called 'if' contracts.

Such an offer may be made to the world at large. In *Carlill v Carbolic Smoke Ball Co.* [1893] 1 QB 256 Bowen J. noted: 'It is an offer to become liable to anyone who, before it is retracted, performs the condition, and, although the offer is made to the world, the contract is made with the limited portion of the public who come forward and perform the condition on the faith of the advertisement.'

Wilson v Belfast Corporation and *Billings v Arnott & Co. Ltd* (pp 36–7 above) are the leading decisions on unilateral contracts in Irish law.

Kennedy *v* London Express Newspapers [1931] IR 532

On 1 January 1929 the defendants advertised in their newspaper a free accident insurance scheme for the benefit of 'registered readers'. Any sum payable was to be paid by The General Accident Fire and Life Assurance Corporation Limited. To qualify as a registered reader a person had to be a postal subscriber to the paper or be registered in the books of the defendants as having placed a daily order with a registered newspaper and be receiving it daily. The conditions provided *inter alia* that any dispute arising in relation to the insurance should be referred to arbitration.

On 1 January 1930 the advertisement of the scheme was repeated for the year 1930. This advertisement stated that there was no need for readers already registered to re-register. It also noted that arbitration would occur in London.

The plaintiff's wife, who was a registered reader in 1929 was killed in an accident in 1930 and the plaintiff claimed £100 under the insurance scheme. A dispute arose as to whether the plaintiff's wife had actually been in daily receipt of the paper prior to her death.

The plaintiff brought an action claiming the £100. The defendants applied to the High Court for an order to stay such proceedings on the grounds that the dispute between the plaintiff and the company is a dispute which must be submitted to arbitration. When this order was refused the defendants appealed to the Supreme Court. One of the questions the court had to decide was what law governed the contract and in particular what law regulated the arbitration proceedings.

Kennedy C.J.:

It would have been open to the parties to agree in express terms that the contract and the arbitration be governed as to interpretation, legal effect, and procedure by a particular law or body of laws, but they did not do so, and as we have consequently to determine the question, which is, by what law the parties *intended* the contract to be governed; *Hamlyn & Co. v Talisker Distillery*;[1] *Spurrier v La Cloche*,[2] and many other authorities. The first and most important clues to the intention of the parties are generally the *locus contractus* and the *locus solutionis*. In January 1929, the offer contained in the newspaper was accepted by the placing of the order for delivery of the paper with the local newsagent in Clonmel and the posting in Clonmel of the coupon registration form. In January 1930, the offer contained in the newspaper was accepted by renewing or continuing the order with the local newsagent in Clonmel for daily delivery of the paper. Unquestionably the contract was in each case made in the Saorstát. The contract was to be performed by the payment of certain pecuniary 'Benefits' in certain contingencies to Mrs Kennedy, whose registered address was in the Saorstát, or to her legal personal representatives. Therefore we have in the present case—unlike *Hamlyn & Co. v Talisker Distillery*—the important fact of the concurrence of the *lex loci contractus* and the *lex loci solutionis*. If we turn now to the arbitration clause itself, and look at it first as it stood in the 1929 contract, we will not find anything to indicate an intention to oust the law of the Saorstát and apply the law of England, as there was in the arbitration clauses in *Hamlyn & Co. v Talisker Distillery*, and *Spurrier v La Cloche*. On the contrary, the position resembles greatly that in *Lowden v Accident Insurance Co.*,[3] where the clause was held by Palles C.B. to be elastic, and to admit the proper laws of the place of the contract. The introduction of the words 'in London' in the 1930 contract had the effect of prescribing the place where the arbitration was to be held, but not of altering the law applicable. The contract is, in my opinion, governed by the law of the Saorstát, and is within the forum of the Saorstát, and the 'statutory provisions for the time being in force applicable thereto' (Condition (*n*)) are the provisions of the Irish Common Law Procedure Acts relating to arbitration; *Lowden v Accident Insurance Co.*, though the contract requires that the arbitration be actually held in London i.e. that the arbitrators shall sit there.

[1] |1894| AC 202.   [2] |1902| AC 446.   [3] 43 ILTR 277.

(The court decided to grant the stay to allow the dispute be determined by an award in an arbitration to be held in London according to the Irish statutes applicable to the arbitration.)

Note

It was noted in this case that neither the assurance corporation nor the newspaper company had issued a policy to Mrs Kennedy. Indeed it was admitted that the company were not legally in a position to issue such an insurance policy to anyone. Thus privity between the assurance corporation and Mrs Kennedy only existed because of the correspondence with the English solicitors admitting the existence of insurance cover by the corporation.

SECTION TWO—ACCEPTANCE

'Acceptance may be defined as a final and unequivocal expression of
agreement to the terms of an offer.' Clark (op.cit.)

A valid acceptance has two constituent parts. Firstly, the fact of agreement
must be proved. Such agreement may be inferred from the conduct of the
parties or from the strict observance of the express terms. Secondly, the
fact of acceptance must be communicated to the offeror.

A. FACT OF ACCEPTANCE

An acceptance must be an unqualified acceptance of the terms of the offer.
If the original terms in the offer are varied substantially it may be viewed
as a counter offer. Such a counter offer may be accepted in turn by the
original offeror. It also has the effect of rendering the original offer incapable of being accepted.

Counter offer

Titus L. Swan *v* Miller, Son and Torrance, Ltd [1919] IR 151

The defendants were the owners of a premises held under a 999 year lease,
and subject to the yearly rent of £50. Hamilton, acting as their agent,
entered into negotiations to sell their leasehold interest in the premises.
On 17 November Crotty, the plaintiff's agent, telegraphed Hamilton offering
£4,750 for the premises. Upon being informed of this the defendants wrote
to and telegraphed Hamilton to accept £4,750 plus £50 ground rent. On 20
November Hamilton wrote to the defendants informing them that the
plaintiff visited him that day 'to say he had bought Henry's factory at
£4,750, plus £50 ground rent'. On the same day Hamilton wrote to Crotty
notifying him that he had received the offer and had advised the defendants
to accept it. The plaintiff then sent the defendants a formal proposal to
purchase the premises for £4,750 subject to the yearly ground rent of £50
and providing for the payment of a deposit. On 22 November the defendants
wrote to Hamilton stating that 'as the details of the agreement are not in
any sense satisfactory as to payment and as to the present tenant' the
plaintiff's offer was declined and they had decided to sell to Henry, the
existing tenant.

The plaintiff sued for specific performance of the contract.

At first instance Ross J. held that the parties were in accord and a
binding agreement had been reached which met the requirements of the
Statute of Frauds. The defendants appealed to the Court of Appeal.

Sir J. Campbell C.:

In this state of facts the defendants contend first, that there was no concluded
agreement, that they and the plaintiff were never *ad idem*, as they were selling a non-
existing under-lease subject to a rent of £50, and the plaintiff was buying an existing

lease at that rent; and second, that there was no memorandum in writing signed by them or their authorised agent sufficient to satisfy the Statute of Frauds.

In my opinion their first contention wholly fails, as the idea of an under-lease was known only to themselves and Hamilton and was apparently never communicated either to Crotty or the plaintiff, or made in any sense a term of the contract. Hamilton as Ross J. states in his report, was admitted to have been authorised by the defendants as their agent to sell this property; and on the evidence I think it is clear that his agreement with Crotty was for the sale of these premises under an existing lease for a term of 999 years, subject to a rent of £50. Their second contention as to the absence of a sufficient memorandum in writing is a more serious matter. They put it in this way. Plaintiff's telegram of 17 November was, they argue, on the authority of *Hughes v Parker*,[1] an offer to purchase the fee simple at the price of £4,750, while Hamilton's acceptance was of something different by reason of the addition of a new term, the £50 rent. Counsel for the plaintiff have argued that this is immaterial, inasmuch as the documents establish that the liability of the purchaser for this rent was common knowledge, the subject matter of the bargain being, on the statements of both parties to it, premises held under a lease for 999 years, subject to a rent of £50. Being satisfied as I am that this contention is true in fact, I regret that I am unable to give effect to it by reason of the requirements of the Statute of Frauds, as in my opinion if the court is coerced to treat the lease as the subject matter for sale, the omission of any date for the commencement of this lease is a fatal objection.

The case for the plaintiff has, however, been presented in argument before us in an alternative way. His counsel admit that the defendants are right in contending, on the authority of *Hughes v Parker*, that plaintiffs' telegram of 17 November was in law an offer for the fee simple; but they say that on the same principle defendants' telegram of acceptance, followed by Hamilton's letter to Crotty of the same date communicating this acceptance, though vitiated as an acceptance by the introduction of a new term, was in law an offer to sell the premises in fee simple for £4,750, plus a perpetual charge or rent of £50, or, at the lowest, was an offer to sell all their interest in the property on the terms indicated: see *Bower v Cooper*;[2] that this offer became a binding contract once it was accepted, even verbally, by the plaintiff, and constitutes a sufficient memorandum in writing, signed by the party to be charged, entitling the plaintiff to specific performance on the part of the defendants by their conveying to him the interest which they in fact possess in the premises.

It is well settled that in contracts for the sale of lands where the vendor's estate turns out to be of a lower degree than that agreed to be sold, a willing purchaser is entitled to a decree for specific performance with compensation; and, though counsel for the defendants suggested that this doctrine is confined to cases where compensation is claimed, I think it certain that it has an *a fortiori* application where a willing purchaser is prepared to accept the actual estate of his vendor, and waives his claim to compensation.

It was assumed by counsel on both sides that a vendor who, in purporting to accept the purchaser's offer, introduces a new term into the proposed contract is, in law and in fact, making a counter offer, which the purchaser by accepting may convert into a contract; and this is stated to be the law in *Halsbury's Laws of England*, vol. vii, p. 350, para. 720. See *Lucas v James*[3] and *Honeyman v Marryat*.[4] In *Canning v Farquhar*[5] Lindley L.J. says that where a proposal for insurance does not state the premium to be paid, but is accepted by the company who state the premium, it amounts to a counter offer by them, binding as a contract when the premium is paid. If, therefore, this telegram of 19 November, from defendants to Hamilton, and his letter of same date to Crotty, constituted, as I am of opinion they did, a counter offer, it remains to consider whether it was accepted by the plaintiff. I should myself have thought that the conduct of the parties, plaintiff and defendants, as evidenced by their acts and correspondence from 19 to 23 |November|, inclusive, was abundantly sufficient to justify the inference that plaintiff, to the knowledge of the defendants, had accepted their counter offer of 19 November. Plaintiff begins his letter to them of 20 November with the words, 'I propose to purchase,' &c., and, read in the light of the previous correspondence, I think this letter should fairly be construed as suggesting the details for completion of a previous contract, while the defendants themselves by their letters to Hamilton of 22 and 23 November treat it as containing '*the details of the agreement*', and utilise it for what they aptly describe as an excuse for repudiation.

Ronan L.J.:

Assuming that there was a fresh offer on 19 November, containing a new term as to the £50 ground rent, is there any legal evidence of an acceptance of that offer between 19 and 22 November, when the defendants repudiated the entire transaction? The Lord Chancellor has suggested that the letter of 20 November from Swan to the defendants—a letter which was not relied upon as proof of an acceptance, and which is subsequent to all the documents specified in the declaration in the decree—could be taken as an acceptance of the offer of the nineteenth. What is this letter? 'I propose to purchase from you the premises known as No. 10 Maxwell St,' &c.; and then follow the terms of the proposal. I am unable to see how this letter can possibly be regarded as an acceptance of a former proposal. The letter of 22 November from the defendants to Hamilton refers to this letter of the twentieth, and states, 'As the details of the agreement are not in any sense satisfactory as to payment . . . we definitely decline offer,' &c. What are these details? They are obviously the details of the proposal contained in the letter of the twentieth, formal proposal. In other words, there was an offer on certain terms made by the letter of the twentieth, and that offer was declined by the letter of the twenty second.

I come now to the question of the agent's letter. What has to be proved by the plaintiff in this case is the actual acceptance of an offer communicated to the defendants prior to the date of the repudiation of the twenty second. We are, I think, now agreed that there was no binding agreement constituted by the documents mentioned in the declaration in the decree. What is the effect of the letter of 20 November, written by the agent, Hamilton, to his principal, Miller? 'Mr Swan . . . called with me to-day to say he had bought Henry's factory at £4,750, plus £50 ground rent, and thanking me for the information I had given him, and asking me to arrange with Mr Henry to see through the factory before he signed the agreement,' &c. Is that anything more than a narrative of something that had occurred in the past? '. . . to say he had bought . . . ' He thought that the original telegram and the reply formed a contract. That is the obvious meaning of it. It is not that he came to tell him that there was no contract up to then, but that he had received a fresh offer, which he had accepted. That is not the true construction of the letter. It is simply a narrative of what had taken place, and no more. But even if the letter went further, if it amounted to this, that Swan had called on him that day, and said that he had accepted the offer contained in the letter of 19 November, in my opinion that would be no proof of the fact of such acceptance.

O'Connor L.J.:

In the first place, on the face of the documents themselves there is no unconditional acceptance. The offer was £4,750 simpliciter; the alleged acceptance was £4,750 plus £50 annual ground rent. That is a vital difference. But then, it is said, by going behind the documents and looking at what passed verbally between the parties, we can find that they always understood that there was to be a rent of £50; and by thus forging out of verbal communications certain missing links, a chain can be produced that will stand the strain of the Statute of Frauds.

With great respect for the judgment of Mr Justice Ross, I cannot think the well-known principle whereby resort may sometimes be had to verbal communications to explain or supplement the written documents can help in this case. It is true that where a written contract for the sale of property refers to and identifies a certain thing, recourse can be had to verbal testimony to see what that thing is. A familiar example is where the writing refers to 'my interest' in named premises, or some such phrase; it is permissible to find out *aliunde* what 'my interest' is; *id certum est quod certum reddi potest*. But in this case, on reference to the evidence, we find that the parties were not *ad idem* at all. There was nothing certain between them, and therefore nothing could be made certain by referring to what passed verbally between them. If the real intention of the parties was to sell an existing leasehold interest, it may be—I do not so lay it down— that we could look at the lease to see what the leasehold was. Mr Crotty of course thought he was buying an existing leasehold; but he was wrong, for the defendants only meant to sell and offered to sell a derivative term, the commencement as well as the duration of which remained to be fixed. For this reason, I think the attempt to supplement the documents in the method suggested fails.

Alternatively, however, the plaintiff relies on a point not pleaded by him; and we are told, not argued or even thought of at the trial. It is this. The plaintiff says that Mr Hamilton's letter of 19 November 1917, constituted a fresh offer; that it was verbally accepted by Mr Swan himself, as appears by Mr Hamilton's letter to Mr Miller of 20 November; and that, a verbal acceptance being sufficient, the contract was concluded by the verbal acceptance.

For the reasons which I have already stated, the letter of 19 November—omitting any reference to the commencement or duration of the term proposed to be carved out—is not in my opinion a good memorandum to satisfy the Statute of Frauds. But then, we are invited to look at the document as embodying an offer to sell the fee subject to a rent of £50, and the plaintiff says he is willing to take a long term without compensation, in lieu of the fee. True, where an offer is made simply to sell without more, that *prima facie* means the fee. But the presumption that it means the fee entirely disappears where the facts show that it was not meant to sell the fee. Further, this point fails also for want of proof. The verbal acceptance relied on was from Swan to Hamilton. Neither of these witnesses was asked a word about it.

It is argued that the letter from Hamilton to Miller of 20 November is proof of the verbal acceptance relied on. In the first place, in my opinion, it does not, fairly construed, bear the interpretation sought to be put upon it. I think the letter refers not to a purported or intended acceptance by Swan, but to a mere statement by Swan that he was the principal for whom Crotty was acting in the purchase, which Swan looked upon as already concluded by the correspondence.

In the second place, I do not think that the letter is admissible as evidence of the fact to be proved. The fact to be proved is the verbal acceptance alleged to have taken place in an interview between Swan and Hamilton. The letter is a narrative of what took place at that interview. The interview could have been proved by calling and examining, on oath at the trial, Swan and Hamilton or anyone else who was present at it. What a person present at an interview says to somebody else, on another occasion, as to what took place at the interview is hearsay and, *prima facie*, at any rate, not evidence thereof.

1. 8 M & W 244. 3. 7 Hare 410. 5. 16 QBD 727.
2. 2 Hare 408. 4. 21 Beav 14.

Note

In *Stevenson, Jacques & Co. v McLean* (1880) 5 QBD 346 the defendant offered to sell iron at '40s nett cash per ton'. The plaintiffs sent a telegraph asking 'Please wire whether you would accept 40s for delivery over two months, or if not longest limit you would give'. As they received no reply they accepted the offer to sell at 40s cash. Meanwhile the defendant sold the iron to a third party. The plaintiffs were awarded damages for breach of contract as the court held that the plaintiffs had not made a counter offer but rather 'a mere enquiry, which should have been answered and not treated as a rejection of the offer'.

Wheeler & Co. Ltd *v* John Jeffrey & Co. [1921] IR 395

The defendants, a firm of Scottish brewers entered into negotiations with the plaintiffs, aerated water manufacturers and exporters operating in Belfast. On 20 May 1911 the defendants wrote appointing the plaintiffs sole agents for their beers for the West Coast of Africa. Following further correspondence the plaintiffs wrote on 10 June 'We will agree to carry on your agency as from 1 July next on the terms and conditions specified in our joint correspondence.' Up to this time the date of commencement had not been mentioned. On 12 June the defendants wrote acknowledging this letter.

The plaintiffs later sued for breach of contract and the question arose as to whether leave to issue and serve a writ out of the jurisdiction ought to be given to the plaintiffs.

The Kings Bench Division held that leave should be given as the contract was made or entered into in Ireland.

Sir J. Campbell C. (Court of Appeal):

We are all of opinion that the judgment of Pim J. cannot be allowed to stand. The facts are not in dispute. They turn upon correspondence between Scotch brewers and a firm of mineral water manufacturers in Belfast, and the purport of that correspondence was to endeavour to arrive at terms under which the Belfast firm would act as agents for the sale of the brewers' beers in West Africa. The parties appear to have come to terms rather quickly, but ultimately, on 10 June 1911, Wheeler & Co. wrote to Jeffrey & Co.: 'Under the circumstances we think your attitude is a reasonable one, and we will agree to carry on your agency as from 1 July next on the terms and conditions specified in our joint correspondence.' If they had left out the words 'as from 1 July next', and had simply agreed to carry on the agency on the terms specified in the joint correspondence, the question then would have been what was a reasonable time in connection with the starting of the agency; and if the parties did not agree upon that, it would have to be determined by the court. In reply to Messrs Wheeler's letter Messrs Jeffrey & Co. wrote: 'We are in receipt of your favour of 10 inst., and note with pleasure that you are agreeable to carry on the agency for our Lager, Pilsener, and Munich beers for West Africa as from the 1 prox. on the terms and conditions stipulated in our joint correspondence.'

It is said that that was not an acceptance of the offer that the agency was to start from 1 July; that it was merely a notification in reference to an already completed agreement. I think it is impossible to construe it in that way, because it is admitted that it would have been open to Messrs Jeffrey to have said, 'No, we cannot agree; 1 July would not suit us.' And if it was open to them to reject, was it not a new and material term of the contract? The acceptance of that new and material term was by letter written in Scotland; and in these circumstances the order of Powell J., giving liberty to the plaintiffs to issue a writ for service out of the jurisdiction, cannot be allowed to stand.

(Ronan and O'Connor L.JJ. concurred.)

Note

Rule 1 of Order XI of the Rules of the Supreme Court (Ir), 1905 governed the basis upon which a court could order service out of the Irish jurisdiction. Rule 1 of Order XI enumerated the cases in which such an order may be made and the enumeration was exhaustive. In this case the plaintiff relied on case (f) which was applicable where the contract which is sought to be enforced in the action was made, or entered into within the jurisdiction. Case (g) dealt with the situation where the contract was breached within the jurisdiction.

Thomas Brennan v William Lockyer and Others [1932] IR 100

Plaintiff claimed full benefit alleged to be due him in accordance with his membership of the Union of Post Office Workers Mutual Benefit Society (MBS). He stated that he had joined this union in 1909 and that 'all the transactions in respect of which the action was being brought' arose in Ireland. Leave to serve out of the jurisdiction was granted by the trial judge. The defendants appealed to the High Court. At this stage evidence was adduced to show that the Union of Post Office Workers MBS did not come into existence until 1919. In actual fact the plaintiff had joined a union called the Postmen's Federation in 1909 and in 1919 this union amalgamated with two other unions to form the Union of Post Office Workers. On 27 March 1909 a form was sent by two members of the Postmen's Federation to the Postmen's Federation MBS proposing the plaintiff for enrolment. The plaintiff was elected on 29 March and a certificate of enrolment was sent to the plaintiff. In the High Court Johnston J. refused to discharge the previous order holding that the receipt of the certificate of membership in Dublin by the plaintiff completed the contract.

The defendant appealed to the Supreme Court.

Fitzgibbon J.:

So far as the plaintiff's claim is grounded upon the original contract between himself and the Mutual Benefit Society attached to the Postmen's Federation, the plaintiff has certainly failed to satisfy me that it was entered into within the jurisdiction of the Irish courts. In March 1909, the plaintiff was already a member of the Dublin Parcels Branch of the Postmen's Federation. On 27 March 1909, at his request, a proposal and certificate in the following form, signed by another member of the federation and the Federation Secretary, was transmitted to the: Management Committee, in London, of the Mutual Benefit Society.

27837. Postmen's Federation Mutual Benefit Society.

We, the undersigned, hereby certify that Thomas Brennan, whom we propose for enrolment in the A and B Class of the MBS, is a member of the Dublin Parcels Branch of the Postmen's Federation, and is to the best of our belief in good health and was thirty one years of age last birthday.

Proposers | Member: John McGirt.
| Federation Secretary: J. Hoare.

In the event of my death before retirement, I, Thomas Brennan, a member of the above Society, nominate my wife, Sarah Brennan, to receive all benefits that may be due on my behalf from this Society.

> Signature: Thomas Brennan
> MBS Secretary: J. Hoare
> Date: 29 March 1909.

Full name as well as relationship to be given.
The Federation Secretary signs the top part, and the MBS Secretary the bottom part of this form.
The nomination of Sarah Brennan was made under a rule which empowered *members* to 'nominate any person to receive all benefits in the event of death, mental affliction, or other contingencies, on a form provided for that purpose, and forward it to the Central Secretary, a copy of which the member should retain.'

The only date upon this form is 29 March 1909. The plaintiff was in fact elected and enrolled as a member of the society on 27 March, and on 27 March he signed another document in the following terms:

4397. 27837.

Postmen's Federation Mutual Benefit Society.
(Widower's Branch.)

I, Thomas Brennan, a member of the Dublin Parcels Branch of the PFMBS, wish to propose my wife, Mrs Sarah Brennan, as a member of the above Branch, whose age was thirty years last birthday, and is, to the best of my belief, in good health.

Signatures | Proposer: Thomas Brennan.
| Branch Secretary: J. Hoare.

> Date, 27 March 1909.
> Wife's name in full.

It appears that this proposal was transmitted by the plaintiff along with the proposal signed by McGirt and Hoare, and was received and acted upon by the Management Committee on 27 March, as upon that date Thomas Brennan and his wife, Sarah Brennan, were elected and enrolled as members of the Mutual Benefit Society.

A free certificate of membership was, in accordance with the rules, sent by the secretary from London to Dublin, and it has been contended that the contract of membership was not complete until this had been communicated to the plaintiff, and that as he received it in Dublin, the contract of membership was entered into in Dublin when he received the certificate.

In my opinion, upon the true construction of the documents and the conduct of the parties that contention cannot be sustained.

There is, says Sir Frederick Pollock,[1] a material distinction, though it is not fully recognised in the language of our authorities, between the acceptance of an offer which asks for a promise, and of an offer which asks for an act, as the condition of the offer becoming a promise. When the acceptance is to consist of a promise, it must be communicated to the proposer. But when the acceptance is to consist of an act—as despatching goods ordered by post—it seems that no further communication of the acceptance is necessary than the performance of the proposed act, or at any rate the proposer may dispense with express communication, and an intention to dispense with it may be somewhat readily inferred from the nature of the transaction.

In the present case the plaintiff requested McGirt and Hoare to propose him 'for enrolment'. In the same document, reciting that he was already a member of the MBS, which he could not be until after the election and enrolment, he nominated his wife to receive all benefits, etc., and on the same day, by a separate document, again reciting that he was a member of the MBS, and purporting to exercise a privilege confined to members, he proposed his wife as a member of the branch.

These actions are in my opinion wholly inconsistent with an intention or belief on his part that he was not to become a member or possess any of the rights or privileges of membership unless and until the fact of his election had been communicated to him. If he had expressly said, 'I ask you to act on my request, and I waive all necessity for communication', there is no doubt that immediately upon enrolment he would have become a member of the benefit society, and in my opinion the nomination, and still more clearly the proposal for membership, of his wife, indicate a plain intention on his part to exercise the rights of membership at the earliest possible moment, and to dispense with any necessity for communicating his election to himself as a condition of his becoming a member. The rules of the society make liability to payment of levies depend upon the date of enrolment. 'All new members shall pay every levy announced after the date of their enrolment', and in my opinion a proposer who asked to be enrolled could not legally resist payment of a levy, announced after the date upon which he had in fact been enrolled, upon the ground that the fact of his enrolment had not come to his knowledge. It has been proved that Thomas Brennan was enrolled a member of the MBS upon 29 March, upon the proposal of McGirt, a member, and Hoare, the secretary, and that his wife, Sarah, was, upon the proposal of himself as a member and Hoare as secretary, enrolled as a member upon the same day. In my opinion the contract of membership was completed in London by the act of the management committee in accepting and acting upon the proposal of Thomas Brennan.

I agree with the view of the Chief Justice that the total lack of candour in the affidavit upon which leave to issue the summons was obtained by the plaintiff *ex parte* from O'Byrne J. would justify the court in setting aside the order which he was induced to grant.

I am also of opinion that there is no sufficient evidence of any contract between the plaintiff and the actual defendants to these proceedings, and if the full fact had been placed before O'Byrne J. I think it most improbable that he would have given leave to issue the summons.

[1] Pollock's *Principles of Contract*, (9th ed.), 36.

(Kennedy C.J. and Murnaghan J. concurred.)

Battle of the Forms

Due to the prevalence of printed form contracts in modern business a problem described as 'the battle of the forms' has arisen. This involves one party writing to another offering to contract on the terms set out in a printed form. The other party responds purporting to accept on the terms set out in a second printed form. Often in the course of negotiations a series of forms will pass in this way between the parties. Finally when a dispute arises as to the terms agreed, both parties claim to have contracted on the basis of their own printed forms.

Butler Machine Tool Co. Ltd *v* Ex-Cell-O Corp. (England) Ltd [1979] 1 WLR 401

Lord Denning M.R.:

This case is a 'battle of forms.' The plaintiffs, the Butler Machine Tool Co. Ltd, suppliers of a machine, on 23 May 1969, quoted a price for a machine tool of £75,535. Delivery was to be given in ten months. On the back of the quotation there were terms and conditions. One of them was a price variation clause. It provided for an increase in the price if there was an increase in the costs and so forth. The machine tool was not delivered until November 1970. By that time costs had increased so much that the sellers claimed an additional sum of £2,892 as due to them under the price variation clause.

The defendant buyers, Ex-Cell–O Corp. (England) Ltd, rejected the excess charge. They relied on their own terms and conditions. They said: 'We did not accept the sellers' quotation as it was. We gave an order for self-same machine at the self-same price, but on the back of our order we had our own terms and conditions. Our terms and conditions did not contain any price variation clause.'

The judge held that the price variation clause in the sellers' form continued through the whole dealing and so the sellers were entitled to rely upon it. He was clearly influenced by a passage in *Anson's Law of Contract*, (24th ed. 1975), 37 and 38, of which the editor is Professor Guest; and also by Treitel, *The Law of Contract*, (4th ed. 1975), 15. The judge said that the sellers did all that was necessary and reasonable to bring the price variation clause to the notice of the buyers. He thought that the buyers would not 'browse over the conditions' of the sellers; and then, by printed words in their (the buyers') document, trap the sellers into a fixed price contract.

I am afraid that I cannot agree with the suggestion that the buyers 'trapped' the sellers in any way. Neither party called any oral evidence before the judge. The case was decided on the documents alone. I propose therefore to go through them.

On 23 May 1969, the sellers offered to deliver one 'Butler' double column plane-miller for the total price of £75,535. Delivery ten months (subject to confirmation at time of ordering) other terms and conditions are on the reverse of this quotation. On the back there were sixteen conditions in small print starting with this general condition: 'All orders are accepted only upon and subject to the terms set out in our quotation and the following conditions. These terms and conditions shall prevail over any terms and conditions in the buyer's order.' Clause 3 was the price variation clause. It said: 'Prices are based on present day costs of manufacture and design and having regard to the delivery quoted and uncertainty as to the cost of labour, materials etc. during the period of manufacture, we regret that we have no alternative but to make it a condition of acceptance of order that goods will be charged at prices ruling upon date of delivery.'

The buyers replied on 27 May 1969, giving an order in these words: 'Please supply on terms and conditions as below and overleaf.' Below there was a list of the goods ordered, but there were differences from the quotation of the sellers in these respects: (i) there was an additional item for the cost of installation, £3,100 and (ii) there was a different delivery date: instead of ten months, it was 10–11 months.

Overleaf there were different terms as to the cost of carriage: in that it was to be paid to the delivery address of the buyers: whereas the sellers' terms were ex ware-house. There were different terms as to the right to cancel for late delivery. The buyers in their conditions reserved the right to cancel if delivery was not made by the agreed date: whereas the sellers in their conditions said that cancellation of order due to late delivery would not be accepted.

On the foot of the buyers' order there was a tear-off slip headed: 'Acknowledgment: Please sign and return to Ex-Cell-O. We accept your order on the terms and conditions stated thereon—and undertake to deliver by—Date—signed.' In that slip the delivery date and signature were left blank ready to be filled in by the sellers. On 5 June 1969, the sellers wrote this letter to the buyers: 'We have pleasure in acknowledging receipt of your official order dated 27 May covering the supply of one Butler Double Column Plane-Miller. This being delivered in accordance with our revised quotation of 23 May for delivery in 10/11 months, i.e. March/April 1970. We return herewith duly completed your acknowledgment of order form.' They enclosed the acknowledgment form duly filled in with the delivery date March/April 1970 and signed by the Butler Machine Tool Co.

No doubt a contract was then concluded. But on what terms? The sellers rely on their general conditions and on their last letter which said 'in accordance with our revised quotation of 23 May' (which had on the back the price variation clause). The buyers rely on the acknowledgement signed by the sellers which accepted the buyer's order 'on the terms and conditions stated thereon' (which did not include a price variation clause).

If those documents are analysed in our traditional method, the result would seem to me to be this: the quotation of 23 May 1969, was an offer by the sellers to the buyers containing the terms and conditions on the back. The order of 27 May 1969, purported to be an acceptance of that offer in that it was for the same machine at the same price, but it contained such additions as to cost of installation, date of delivery and so forth that it was in law a rejection of the offer and constituted a counter offer. That is clear from Hyde v Wrench (1840) 3 Beav 334. As Megaw J. said in Trollope & Colls Ltd v Atomic Power Constructions Ltd |1963| 1 WLR 333, 337: ' . . . the counter offer kills the original offer'. The letter of the sellers of 5 June 1969, was an acceptance of that counter offer, as is shown by the acknowledgment which the sellers signed and returned to the buyers. The reference to the quotation of 23 May referred only to the price and identity of the machine.

To go on with the facts of the case. The important thing is that the sellers did not keep the contractual date of delivery which was March/April 1970. The machine was ready about September 1970 but by that time the buyers' production schedule had to be re-arranged as they could not accept delivery until November 1970. Meanwhile the sellers had invoked the price increase clause. They sought to charge the buyers an increase due to the rise in costs between 27 May 1969 (when the order was given), and 1 April 1970 (when the machine ought to have been delivered). It came to £2,892. The buyers rejected the claim. The judge held that the sellers were entitled to the sum of £2,892 under the price variation clause. He did not apply the traditional method of analysis by way of offer and counter offer. He said that in the quotation of 23 May 1969, 'one finds the price variation clause appearing under a most emphatic heading stating that it is a term or condition that is to prevail.' So he held that it did prevail.

I have much sympathy with the judge's approach to this case. In many of these cases our traditional analysis of offer, counter offer, rejection, acceptance and so forth is out of date. This was observed by Lord Wilberforce in *New Zealand Shipping Co. Ltd v* A. M. *Satterthwaite & Co. Ltd* |1975| AC 154, 167. The better way is to look at all the documents passing between the parties—and glean from them, or from the conduct of the parties, whether they have reached agreement on all material points—even though there may be differences between the forms and conditions printed on the back of them. As Lord Cairns said in B*rogden v Metropolitan Rly Co.* (1877) 2 App Cas 666, 672: ' . . . there may be a *consensus* between the parties far short of a complete mode of expressing it, and that *consensus* may be discovered from letters or from other documents of an imperfect and incomplete description: . . . ' Applying this guide, it will be found that in most cases when there is a 'battle of forms', there is a contract as soon as the last of the forms is sent and received without objection being taken to it. That is well observed in *Benjamin's Sale of Goods*, (9th ed. 1974), 84. The difficulty is to decide which form, or which part of which form, is a term or condition of the contract. In some cases the battle is won by the man who fires the last shot. He is the man who puts forward the latest terms and conditions: and, if they are not objected to by the other party, he may be taken to have agreed to them. Such was *British Road Services Ltd v Arthur* V. *Crutchley & Co. Ltd* |1968| 1 Lloyd's Rep. 271, 281–282, per Lord Pearson; and the illustration given by Professor Guest in *Anson's Law of Contract*, (24th ed.), 37, 38 when he says that 'the terms of the contract consist of the terms of the offer subject to the modifications contained in the acceptance'. In some cases the battle is won by the man who gets the blow in first. If he offers to sell at a named price on the terms and conditions stated on the back: and the buyer orders the goods purporting to accept the offer—on an order form with his own different terms and conditions on the back—then if the difference is so material that it would affect the price, the buyer ought not to be allowed to take advantage of the difference unless he draws it specifically to the attention of the seller. There are yet other cases where the battle depends on the shots fired on both sides. There is a concluded contract but the forms vary. The terms and conditions of both parties are to be construed together. If they can be reconciled so as to give a harmonious result, all well and good. If differences are irreconcilable—so that they are mutually contradictory—then the conflicting terms may have to be scrapped and replaced by a reasonable implication.

In the present case the judge thought that the sellers in their original quotation got their blow in first: especially by the provision that 'these terms and conditions shall prevail over any terms and conditions in the buyer's order'. It was so emphatic that the price variation clause continued through all the subsequent dealings and that the buyers must be taken to have agreed to it. I can understand that point of view. But I think that the documents have to be considered as a whole. And, as a matter of construction, I think the acknowledgment of 5 June 1969, is the decisive document. It makes it clear that the contract was on the buyers' terms and not on the sellers' terms: and the buyers' terms did not include a price variation clause.

(Lawton and Bridge L.JJ. concurred.)

Buchanan t/a Warnocks v Brook Walker and Co. Ltd [1988] NI 116

The defendant contracted to supply cloth to the plaintiff. In an action for breach of contract arising from a dispute over the cloth the defendant attempted to rely on a jurisdiction clause which stated that the parties agreed to submit to the jurisdiction of the English courts. The plaintiff contended that this clause did not form part of the contract.

Carswell J.:

. . .

Although Lord Denning M.R. in *Butler Machine Tool Co. Ltd v Ex-Cell-O Corp. (England) Ltd* [1979] 1 All ER 965, 968 departed from the traditional analysis of offer and acceptance in a case of a complicated exchange of documents, I consider with respect that it is preferable to adhere to it where possible, as the other members of the court felt able to do. In my view the present case admits of such analysis. When the original order was sent on 29 September 1986 for twenty pieces, the colour had still to be decided, so that a material term remained to be agreed. The defendant on 3 October 1986 sent an order confirmation No. 716, containing some fresh terms, and on the principles set out in *Hyde v Wrench* (1840) 3 Beav 334 that document constituted a counter offer. It was not, however, immediately capable of final acceptance, since the choice of colour was still outstanding. The plaintiff wrote on 11 December 1986 asking for lab. dye samples to match an enclosed sample, and stating that he required 1000–1500 metres of cloth, which was rather more than twenty pieces. When the samples were sent, he wrote on 14 January 1987 accepting colour 6303 and placing an order for 1500 metres of HB quality cloth in dye shade 6303. The defendant replied on 21 January 1987 by a document entitled 'Confirmation of colouring instruction' No. 1293, for seventeen pieces of HB cloth in the colour blue 6303 at £6.35 per metre, and sent an additional order confirmation No. 879 for six pieces, which brought the total up to 1500 metres. In offer and acceptance terms I consider that the plaintiff's order of 14 January 1987 was an acceptance of the defendant's offer to supply twenty pieces on the terms contained in its order confirmation No. 716, plus the additional term now agreed of the colour. It was also an offer to purchase an extra quantity of cloth to make the total amount up to 1500 metres, which the plaintiff accepted by order confirmation No. 879. I do not consider that the fact the 'Confirmation of colouring instruction' document referring to seventeen pieces instead of twenty affects the analysis of agreement which I have set out.

The issue therefore is whether the plaintiff is to be taken to have agreed to accept the jurisdiction clause set out in the order confirmation documents. The defendant's case is that in sending the order confirmation No. 716 it propounded a number of terms set out on the reverse of the document, and that in finally placing the order on 14 January 1987 the plaintiff must be taken to have accepted those terms. In regard to the extra pieces ordered, the plaintiff must be taken to have offered to purchase them on the same terms as the original twenty pieces, so that when the defendant accepted the offer all those terms, including the jurisdiction clause, became part of the contract. Whether the plaintiff is to be taken to have accepted the terms set out on the back of the order confirmation document is to be decided by considering whether the defendant did what was reasonably sufficient to give the plaintiff notice of those terms. In my judgment it did so. The order confirmation No. 716 contained on its face the statement that the order was subject to the conditions of sale on the back of the form. The sentence does not appear to have been emphasised or highlighted, but it was plain enough to be seen and not obscured by other matters of detail. This was a commercial document, containing a number of details of the order, and it was envisaged and intended that it should be read with care and checked by the recipient. That fact alone takes it out of the category of consumer contracts, where a customer might not ordinarily be expected to read the fine print on a ticket. The plaintiff did not at any stage raise any objection to the terms, for the simple reason, according to his affidavit, that he did not read them. I consider, nevertheless, that the defendant was entitled to and did assume on the facts of the case that the plaintiff accepted the terms contained in the order confirmation. I hold therefore that the jurisdiction clause formed part of the contract of sale and purchase of the cloth.

G. Percy Trentham Ltd v Archital Luxfer Ltd and Others [1993] 1 Lloyd's Rep. 25

The plaintiffs, building contractors, sued the first defendants for breach of contract to manufacture and supply windows. They claimed that the windows were defective. The defendants denied the existence of binding contracts between them.

Steyn L.J.:

. . .

It is necessary to consider the basis of the judge's decision that Trentham proved the formation of two valid sub-contracts. It is common ground that as between Trentham and Archital no integrated written sub-contracts ever came into existence. There was no orderly negotiation of terms. Rather the picture is one of the parties, jockeying for advantage, inching towards finalisation of the transaction. The case bears some superficial resemblance to cases that have become known as 'battle of the forms' cases where each party seeks to impose his standard conditions on the other in correspondence without there ever being any express resolution of that issue. In such cases it is usually common ground that there is a contract but the issue is what set of standard conditions, if any, is applicable. Here the issue is one of contract formation. Moreover, the present case is different in the sense that Trentham's case was that the sub-contracts came into existence not simply by an exchange of correspondence but partly by reason of written exchanges, partly by oral discussions and partly by performance of the transactions. It will be necessary to trace the dealings between the parties, taking into account the judge's findings.

. . .

Before I turn to the facts it is important to consider briefly the approach to be adopted to the issue of contract formation in this case. It seems to me that four matters are of importance. The first is the fact that English law generally adopts an objective theory of contract formation. That means that in practice our law generally ignores the subjective expectations and the unexpressed mental reservations of the parties. Instead the governing criterion is the reasonable expectations of honest men. And in the present case that means that the yardstick is the reasonable expectations of sensible businessmen. Secondly, it is true that the coincidence of offer and acceptance will in the vast majority of cases represent the mechanism of contract formation. It is so in the case of a contract alleged to have been made by an exchange of correspondence. But it is not necessarily so in the case of a contract alleged to have come into existence during and as a result of performance. See Brogden v Metropolitan Rly (1877) 2 AC 666; New Zealand Shipping Co. Ltd v A.M. Satterthwaite & Co. Ltd [1974] 1 Lloyd's Rep. 534 at p. 539, col. 1; [1975] AC 154 at p. 167 D-E; Gibson v Manchester City Council [1979] 1 WLR 294. The third matter is the impact of the fact that the transaction is executed rather than executory. It is a consideration of the first importance on a number of levels. See British Bank for Foreign Trade Ltd v Novinex, [1949] 1 KB 628, at p. 630. The fact that the transaction was performed on both sides will often make it unrealistic to argue that there was no intention to enter into legal relations. It will often make it difficult to submit that the contract is void for vagueness or uncertainty. Specifically, the fact that the transaction is executed makes it easier to imply a term resolving any uncertainty, or, alternatively, it may make it possible to treat a matter not finalised in negotiations as inessential. In this case fully executed transactions are under consideration. Clearly, similar considerations may sometimes be relevant in partly executed transactions. Fourthly, if a contract only comes into existence during and as a result of performance of the transaction it will frequently be possible to hold that the contract impliedly and retrospectively covers pre-contractual performance. See *Trollope & Colls Ltd v Atomic Power Construction Ltd* [1963] 1 WLR 333.

The story starts on 12 January 1984 when Archital submitted four alternative quotations for phase 1 window works to Trentham. Discussions followed. On 24 January 1984 Archital substituted a revised offer in respect of one of the earlier quotations at a revised price of the order of £140,000. The offer was conditional on the incorporation of Archital's standard conditions or the so-called blue form. Trentham was not prepared to accept this offer but made a counter offer contained in Order No. 8235 dated 30 January 1984. This counter offer stipulated the work and price described in Archital's revised offer but was conditional on the incorporation of Trentham's standard terms of sub-contract. Moreover, the order was expressed to be: ' . . . subject to (a) Form of sub-contract being entered into . . . [and] (b) the signing and immediate return of the attached acknowledgment slip.' Neither of these formalities for acceptance was ever completed. The counter offer was subject to measurement and/or adjustment on completion. By an addendum dated 1 February 1984 this last stipulation was deleted and it was made clear that it was a lump sum contract. That was the offer which was open for acceptance by Archital from 1 February 1984. On 2 February 1984 the main contract for phase 1 was concluded.

On 10 February 1984 Archital responded by letter to Trentham's counter offer as revised on 1 February 1984. Archital confirmed that 'we have entered the contract into our Drawing Office Programme'. In the context, the judge held, one should read 'contract' as meaning 'project'. Two obstacles remained. First Archital's letter stated that at the meeting which led to Trentham's counter offer: ' . . . it was confirmed that the sub-contracts would be in the Blue Form of sub-contract.' In other words, Archital thought that there had been agreement to use Archital's preferred standard terms and conditions. Secondly, Archital said that they would not be able to comply with a programme with a commencement date of 14 May.

On 17 February 1984 Trentham's regional office at Rainham sent a reminder to Archital. It stated: 'Our order is subject to the signing and immediate return of the Acknowledgment slip as stated in the order form.' Negotiations then continued between Mr Chapple, on behalf of Trentham, and Mr Hazell, on behalf of Archital.

On 17 February Trentham's site office wrote to Archital as follows: 'We confirm our contract period is very short and that it is essential that you make every effort to meet the dates agreed with your Mr Rogers. We also confirm that you have already commenced working drawings, that you have sufficient information to enable you to proceed with your drawings, and that further details will be forwarded to you to enable you to complete your drawings as soon as possible.' The judge inferred that between 10 and 17 February 1984 Mr Chapple had agreed the programme with Mr Rogers, although in terms which were not proved before the judge. The appellants submit that there was no evidence on which to base this finding, and that the letter referred to a discussion which took place before 10 February. Having regard to the terms of the letters of 10 and 17 February I regard it as more probable than not that the judge's inference was right. It follows that one obstacle to the conclusion of a contract was removed.

That left the problem of Archital's request for the use of their preferred standard conditions. Mr Hazell reiterated this preference in a letter dated 24 February 1984. This letter reads as follows:

> Thank you for your letter dated 16 February 1984, we note your comments but our query was in connection with the sub-contract document.
>
> We wish the sub-contract to be carried out under the terms and conditions of the Standard Blue Form of Sub-Contract as agreed at the meeting attended by our Mr Rogers.
>
> Please confirm that we are to return your own form and that the Blue Form will be forwarded to us.

In this letter, and in a letter of the same date from Archital to Trentham's Rainham office, Archital described their reaction as a 'query'. Archital thought that Trentham had accepted Archital's request. Contrary to the submission of the appellant's counsel, I take the view that the judge was entitled to conclude that the letter of 24 February was not a rejection of the counter offer as revised on 10 February. This construction is reinforced by the letter of 9 March 1984 from Archital to Trentham which shows that the issue as to the standard conditions had been resolved.

The judge pointed out that there were now three matters to be considered: (i) payment procedure; (ii) insurance of unfixed goods; and (iii) disputes procedure. The judge found as a fact that the payment procedure had been agreed by 24 February and that the letter merely confirmed the position. In any event, from this time regular stage payments were made 'on the basis of the timetable provided in the Grey Form'. These findings are not challenged. But it is important to note that by 9 March Archital had already commenced the work and that from about this time Trentham made regular stage payments.

The second matter relates to Archital's request that Trentham should pay the cost of insuring unfixed goods which remained the property of Archital. Trentham did not agree to bear these costs. But the judge made the following findings of fact: 'Archital nevertheless delivered such goods to the site at its own risk. In accepting such risk, they accepted that in this respect the provisions of PGT's main contract should apply to their relationship with PGT in performing work at Southwood.'

This finding of fact is challenged on the ground that there was no evidence to support it. I disagree. By a letter of 23 March 1984 Trentham refused to accept these costs. Trentham described the risk as minimal. On 2 April 1984 Archital wrote to say that they were asking brokers for a quotation, and that they would write again. They failed to mention the matter again. Instead they continued to deliver goods to the site, to perform work and to receive stage payments. In these circumstances I am satisfied that there was sufficient evidence to support the judge's finding of fact. This obstacle to the conclusion of a contract was removed in April 1984.

The third matter to be considered is the lack of agreement on dispute resolution. The judge held that agreement on dispute resolution was not essential to the conclusion of the contract: the parties were content to treat it as a matter for further agreement after the conclusion of the contract. It was plainly not an essential matter as far as Trentham was concerned. Archital described their point of view as based on company policy. Nevertheless the letter describes Archital's concern about the identity of the adjudicator and stakeholder as a 'query'. This supports the view that Archital was also content to treat a dispute resolution mechanism as a non-essential matter. This ruling is criticised on the basis that there is no evidence to support it. I disagree. The judge's inference was reasonable and legitimate. In any event the parties subsequently agreed on the adjudicator and stakeholder. It is conceded that there was agreement on the stakeholder. By letter dated 22 April 1984 Archital said in respect of phase 2 that they took it that Trentham agreed to the same adjudicator and stakeholder 'as agreed for that contract' (i.e. phase 1). That is retrospectant evidence showing earlier agreement on the identity of both the adjudicator and stakeholder. It is true that Mr Steer, who testified on behalf of Trentham, was unaware of this agreement but he was not directly involved in the negotiations. It is also fair to add that the judge could not identify the adjudicator. On behalf of Archital it is submitted that there was no evidence to support the judge's finding of fact. That submission is wrong: there was strong evidence to support his finding.

The judge also found that Trentham delivered to Archital four separate orders for additional work in phase 1 all ' . . . subject to the conditions and terms of the original order'. These supplementary orders were accepted and executed by Archital, and Trentham made appropriate additional payments. Moreover, the judge pointed out that in the context of exchanges about phase 2, Archital offered to perform the work on the basis that the terms and conditions would be 'as for the original contract'.

The judge's conclusion was as follows:

I therefore conclude that Mr Chapple modified the terms of PGT's offer contained in their Order dated 30 January, in his telephone conversation with mr Hazell on 9 March, and that those terms were accepted on behalf of Archital by the letter dated the same day. If such acceptance is to be construed as being subject to the resolution of the issues of insurance and of the disputes procedure, rather than, as I think, those 'queries' being left for subsequent agreement, those matters were, in fact, duly resolved in the following months. At least from that point, Archital accepted PGT's modified offer by their conduct in carrying out the sub-contract work, and applying for and accepting payment on the agreed terms.

. . .

In a case where the transaction was fully performed the argument that there was no evidence upon which the judge could find that a contract was proved is implausible. A contract can be concluded by conduct. Thus in *Brogden v Metropolitan Rly*, the House of Lords concluded in a case where the parties had acted in accordance with an unsigned draft agreement for the delivery of consignments of coal that there was a contract on the basis of the draft. That inference was drawn from the performance in accordance with the terms of the draft agreement. In 1992 we ought not to yield to Victorian times in realism about the practical application of rules of contract formation. The argument that there was insufficient evidence to support a finding that a contract was concluded is wrong. But, in deference to counsel's submissions, I would go further.

One must not lose sight of the commercial character of the transaction. It involved the carrying out of work on one side in return for payment by the other side, the performance by both sides being subject to agreed qualifying stipulations. In the negotiations and during the performance of phase 1 of the work all obstacles to the formation of a contract were removed. It is not a case where there was a continuing stipulation that a contract would only come into existence if a written agreement was concluded. Plainly the parties intended to enter into binding contractual relations. The only question is whether they succeeded in doing so. The contemporary exchanges, and the carrying out of what was agreed in those exchanges support the view that there was a course of dealing which on Trentham's side created a right to performance of the work by Archital, and on Archital's side it created a right to be paid on an agreed basis. What the parties did in respect of phase 1 is only explicable on the basis of what they had agreed in respect of phase 1. The judge analysed the matter in terms of offer and acceptance. I agree with his conclusion. But I am, in any event, satisfied that in this fully executed transaction a contract came into existence during performance even if it cannot be precisely analysed in terms of offer and acceptance. And it does not matter that a contract came into existence after part of the work had been carried out and paid for. The conclusion must be that when the contract came into existence it impliedly governed pre-contractual performance. I would therefore hold that a binding contract was concluded in respect of phase 1.

(Gibson and Neill L.JJ. agreed.)

B. COMMUNICATION OF ACCEPTANCE

An acceptance is not effective until it is brought to the attention of the offerer by the offeree or any person authorised to convey this information.

A clause in the offer stating that silence will be deemed to be acceptance would not be enforced by an English or Irish court.

Sale of Goods and Supply of Services Act 1980. S. 47:

47. (1) Where:

> (a) unsolicited goods are sent to a person with a view in his acquiring them and are received by him, and
> (b) the recipient has neither agreed to acquire nor agreed to return them.

and either:

> (i) during the period of six months following the date of receipt of the goods the sender did not take possession of them and the recipient did not unreasonably refuse to permit the sender to do so, or
> (ii) not less than 30 days before the expiration of that period the recipient gave notice to the sender and during the following 30 days the sender did not take possession of the goods and the recipient did not unreasonably refuse to permit the sender to do so.

then the recipient may treat the goods as if they were an unconditional gift to him and any right of the sender to the goods shall be extinguished.

. . .

> (5) In this section:

'acquire' includes hire,

'send' includes deliver,

'sender' includes any person on whose behalf or with whose consent the goods are sent and any other person claiming through or under the sender or any such person.

'unsolicited' means, in relation to goods sent to any person, that they are sent without any prior request by him or on his behalf.

In *Russell & Baird Ltd v Hoban* [1922] 2 IR 159 the plaintiffs sent a contract note to the defendant, a prospective purchaser of oatmeal with whom they had

had discussions. The note concluded with the words 'If this sale note be retained beyond three days after this date, it will be held to have been accepted by the buyer.' Ronan L.J. held that 'No man can impose such conditions upon another. The document is conclusive evidence against the parties who sent it, that it was an offer which required acceptance'.

General Rule

The general rule states that acceptance must be communicated to the offeror.

Entores *v* Miles Far East [1955] 2 QB 327

The plaintiffs, an English company, sent a message by telex from London to the defendants in Amsterdam offering to purchase a quantity of steel cathodes. The defendants accepted this offer by telex from Amsterdam. The plaintiffs applied to serve notice of a writ out of jurisdiction claiming damages for breach of a contract made in England.

Denning L.J.:

When a contract is made by post it is clear law throughout the common law countries that the acceptance is complete as soon as the letter is put into the post box, and that is the place where the contract is made. But there is no clear rule about contracts made by telephone or by telex. Communications by these means are virtually instantaneous and stand on a different footing.

The problem can only be solved by going in stages. Let me first consider a case where two people make a contract by word of mouth in the presence of one another. Suppose, for instance, that I shout an offer to a man across a river or a courtyard but I do not hear his reply because it is drowned by an aircraft flying overhead. There is no contract at that moment. If he wishes to make a contract, he must wait till the aircraft is gone and then shout back his acceptance so that I can hear what he says. Not until I have his answer am I bound. . . .

Now take a case where two people make a contract by telephone. Suppose, for instance, that I make an offer to a man by telephone and, in the middle of his reply, the line goes 'dead' so that I do not hear his words of acceptance. There is no contract at that moment. The other man may not know the precise moment when the line failed. But he will know that the telephone conversation was abruptly broken off: because people usually say something to signify the end of the conversation. If he wishes to make a contract, he must therefore get through again so as to make sure that I heard. Suppose next, that the line does not go dead, but it is nevertheless so indistinct that I do not catch what he says and I ask him to repeat it. He then repeats it and I hear his acceptance. The contract is made, not on the first time when I do not hear, but only the second time when I do hear. If he does not repeat it, there is no contract. The contract is only complete when I have his answer accepting the offer.

Lastly, take the telex. Suppose a clerk in a London office taps out on the teleprinter an offer which is immediately recorded on a teleprinter in a Manchester office, and a clerk at that end taps out an acceptance. If the line goes dead in the middle of the sentence of acceptance, the teleprinter motor will stop. There is then obviously no contract. The clerk at Manchester must get through again and send his complete sentence. But it may happen that the line does not go dead, yet the message does not get through to London. Thus the clerk at Manchester may tap out his message of acceptance and it will not be recorded in London because the ink at the London end fails, or something of that kind. In that case, the Manchester clerk will not know of the failure but the London clerk will know of it and will immediately send back a message 'not receiving'. Then, when the fault is rectified, the Manchester clerk will repeat his message. Only then is there a contract. If he does not repeat it, there is no contract. It is not until his message is received that the contract is complete.

In all the instances I have taken so far, the man who sends the message of acceptance knows that he has not been received or he has reason to know it. So he must repeat it. But, suppose that he does not know that his message did not get home. He thinks it has. This may happen if the listener on the telephone does not catch the words of acceptance, but nevertheless does not trouble to ask for them to be repeated: or the ink on the teleprinter fails at the receiving end, but the clerk does not ask for the message to be repeated: so that the man who sends an acceptance reasonably believes that his message has been received. The offeror in such circumstances is clearly bound, because he will be estopped from saying that he did not receive the message of acceptance. It is his own fault that he did not get it. But if there should be a case where the offeror without any fault on his part does not receive the message of acceptance—yet the sender of it reasonably believes it has got home when it has not—then I think there is no contract.

My conclusion is, that the rule about instantaneous communications between the parties is different from the rule about the post. The contract is only complete when the acceptance is received by the offeror: and the contract is made at the place where the acceptance is received.

. . .

Applying the principles which I have stated, I think that the contract in this case was made in London where the acceptance was received. It was, therefore, a proper case for service out of the jurisdiction.

(Birkett and Parker L.JJ. concurred.)

Brinkibon Ltd v Stahag Stahl und Stahlwarenhandelsgesellschaft mbH [1983] 2 AC 34

Lord Wilberforce:

The general rule, it is hardly necessary to state, is that a contract is formed *when* acceptance of an offer is communicated by the offeree to the offeror. And if it is necessary to determine *where* a contract is formed (as to which I have already commented) it appears logical that this should be at the place where acceptance is communicated to the offeror. In the common case of contracts, whether oral or in writing *inter praesentes*, there is no difficulty; and again logic demands that even where there is not mutual presence at the same place and at the same time, if communication is instantaneous, for example by telephone or radio communication, the same result should follow.

Then there is the case—very common—of communication at a distance, to meet which the so called 'postal rule' has developed. I need not trace its history: it has firmly been in the law at least since *Adams v Lindsell* (1818) 1 B & Ald 681. The rationale for it, if left somewhat obscure by Lord Ellenborough C.J., has since been well explained. Mellish L.J. in In re *Imperial Land Co. of Marseilles* (Harris' case) (1872) LR 7 Ch App 587, 594 ascribed it to the extraordinary and mischievous consequences which would follow if it were held that an offer might be revoked at any time until the letter accepting it had been actually received: and its foundation in convenience was restated by Thesiger L.J. in *Household Fire and Carriage Accident Insurance Co. Ltd v Grant* (1879) 4 Ex D 216, 223. In these cases too it seems logical to say that the place, as well as the time, of acceptance should be *where (as when)* the acceptance is put into the charge of the post office.

In this situation, with a general rule covering instantaneous communication *inter praesentes*, or at a distance, with an exception applying to non-instantaneous communication at a distance, how should communications by telex be categorised? In *Entores Ltd v Miles Far East Corp.* |1955| 2 QB 327 the Court of Appeal classified them with instantaneous communications. Their ruling, which has passed into the textbooks, including *Williston on Contracts*, (3rd ed. 1957), appears not to have caused either adverse comment, or any difficulty to business men. I would accept it as a general rule. Where the condition of simultaneity is met, and where it appears to be within the mutual intention of the parties that contractual exchanges should take place in this way, I think it a sound rule, but not necessarily a universal rule.

Since 1955 the use of telex communication has been greatly expanded, and there are many variants on it. The senders and recipients may not be the principals to the contemplated contract. They may be servants or agents with limited authority. The message may not reach, or be intended to reach, the designated recipient immediately: messages may be sent out of office hours, or at night, with the intention, or upon the assumption, that they will be read at a later time. There may be some error or default at the recipient's end which prevents receipt at the time contemplated and believed in by the sender. The message may have been sent and/or received through machines operated by third persons. And many other variations may occur. No universal rule can cover all such cases: they must be resolved by reference to the intentions of the parties, by sound business practice and in some cases by a judgment where the risks should lie: see *Household Fire and Carriage Accident Insurance Co. Ltd v Grant*, 4 Ex D 216, 227 per Baggallay L.J. and *Henthorn v Fraser* |1892| 2 Ch. 27 per Lord Herschell.

(Lord Brandon delivered a concurring judgment and Russell and Bridge L.JJ. agreed.)

Lord Fraser:

. . . I have reached the opinion that, on balance, an acceptance sent by telex directly from the acceptor's office to the offeror's office should be treated as if it were an instantaneous communication between principals, like a telephone conversation. One reason is that the decision to that effect in *Entores v Miles Far East Corp.* |1955| 2 QB 327 seems to have worked without leading to serious difficulty or complaint from the business community. Secondly, once the message has been received on the offeror's telex machine, it is not unreasonable to treat it as delivered to the principal offeror, because it is his responsibility to arrange for prompt handling of messages within his own office. Thirdly, a party (the acceptor) who tries to send a message by telex can generally tell if his message has not been received on the other party's (the offeror's) machine, whereas the offeror, of course, will not know if an unsuccessful attempt has been made to send an acceptance to him. It is therefore convenient that the acceptor, being in the better position, should have the responsibility of ensuring that his message is received. For these reasons I think it is right that in the ordinary simple case, such as I take this to be, the general rule and not the postal rule should apply. But I agree with both my noble and learned friends that the general rule will not cover all the many variations that may occur with telex messages.

Kelly v Cruise Catering Ltd & Another (HC) 5 July 1994, unrep.

Blayney J.:

This is an appeal by the defendants against an order of Geoghegan J. refusing to discharge an *ex parte* order made under O. 11 of the Rules of the Superior Courts giving liberty to the plaintiff to serve on the defendants out of the jurisdiction a plenary summons claiming damages for breach of contract.

The plaintiff was injured in an accident which occurred on 23 October 1991 when he was working as a waiter/butler on board a ship, the Royal Viking Sun, of which the second-named defendant is the owner. The plaintiff was employed on the ship on foot of a written contract of employment made between the first-named defendant, as agent for the ship, and the plaintiff. It is alleged by the plaintiff that as a result of the breach of the defendants' contractual duty to him he was caused to fall when carrying a tray down a stairway in the ship. The accident occurred on the high seas when the ship was between Cozumel, Mexico, and Galveston, Texas. Immediately after the accident the plaintiff was treated by the ship's doctor and then by a doctor in Louisiana before he returned to Ireland.

The first-named defendant is a Bahamas corporation, and the second-named defendant is a company incorporated under the laws of Norway and has its central management there. The ship is registered in Nassau, in the Bahamas.

Geoghegan J. held that the plaintiff's contract of employment with the first-named defendant had been made within the jurisdiction and, accordingly, the defendants had been properly served under O. 11(1)(e)(i) which permits service out of the jurisdiction of an originating summons in an action brought, *inter alia*, to recover damages in respect of a contract 'made within the jurisdiction'. . . .

The place where the contract was made

The facts concerning the execution of the contract were not in dispute. It was signed in triplicate for and on behalf of the first-named defendant in Oslo on 15 October 1991 and was sent to the plaintiff on the same date with a covering letter. It was signed by the plaintiff in Dublin on 23 October 1991 and returned by him by post to Oslo. The covering letter had detailed instructions on the reverse side but these, unfortunately, were not in evidence. However, I think it is reasonable to assume that the plaintiff would have kept one of the three copies of the contract and returned the other two to Oslo. It is certainly common case that a copy of the contract duly signed was returned to Oslo.

It is clear on these facts that the contract was made by post so that the well settled rule as enunciated by Denning L.J. in *Entores LD v Miles Far East Corp.* 1955 22 QB 327, at 332, applies: 'When a contract is made by post it is clear law throughout the common law countries that the acceptance is complete as soon as the letter is put into the post box, and that is the place where the contract is made.' Accordingly, the plaintiffs' acceptance was complete when, in Dublin, he posted the signed contract to the first defendant and where the signed contract was posted, which was Dublin, was the place where the contract was made.

It was contended by counsel for the first-named defendant that this rule could on occasion cause injustice. It was possible, for example, that the acceptance might by lost in the post and in such cases it might be unjust to hold a party to a contract when he had never received the acceptance. That is no doubt correct but it is not a relevant consideration in the present case where the signed contract was received by the first-named defendant. There are no circumstances here calling for any divergence from the well established rule.

It was also contended that the implication from the form of the 'employee attestation' at the end of the contract was that there was to be no binding contract until the contract was returned to Oslo. The 'employee attestation' is as follows:

> I, the undersigned employee, declare that I have read and understood the terms of this agreement and that no oral promises or other agreements have been made to me and that I cannot claim and am not entitled to any additional benefits of any kind whatsoever except those provided in this agreement. I declare that the application for employment, previously filled out and signed, is true and correct in every respect and that, as part of my employment agreement, I agree to abide by the conditions set forth in the ship's articles and by such company rules and regulations as are in effect from time to time.
>
> I also certify that I have received the 'welcome aboard' booklet from the employer, and agree that I will abide by these terms and conditions.

I have carefully considered the terms of this attestation and I am unable to find in them any indication that they were intended to postpone the conclusion of the contract to a date later than that specified in the well settled rule. I am satisfied that they did not prevent the contract from becoming immediately effective once the signed contract was put in the post addressed to the first-named defendant in Oslo.

I would accordingly endorse the decision of the learned High Court judge that the contract was made in Dublin.

Postal Rule

The postal rule is an exception to this general rule. If an acceptance is posted, unless otherwise stated, it becomes valid from the date of posting.

Dooley *v* Egan (1938) 72 ILTR 155

Meredith J.:

This action was brought to recover the sum of £26 12s 0d alleged to be due for work and labour done and material supplied by the plaintiff at defendant's order. The Indorsement of Claim in the Civil Bill alleges that the contract which the plaintiff seeks to enforce was made in Dublin. The defendant company in their defence, besides disputing the claim, pleaded that the contract was not made in Dublin and that the Circuit Court in Dublin had no jurisdiction to hear the case under the provisions of s. 52 of the Courts of Justice Act, 1924.

This preliminary issue of jurisdiction was argued before Judge Shannon, who by order dated 23 March 1938, ordered that the action be struck out on the ground that the contract sued upon was not made within the jurisdiction. From this order the plaintiff has appealed.

The defendant company carry on business in Cork as traders in and distributors of medical and surgical instruments and hospital equipment. It appears that in June 1937, the defendant company received enquiries as to their ability to supply medical instrument cabinets of the type described in the *Surgical Manufacturer Company's Catalogue*. The defendant company then made enquiries by a postcard, which is not forthcoming, as to the ability of the plaintiff to supply them, the defendant company, as distributors, with the articles specified under the title in the catalogue and in reply to this enquiry they received a quotation in the form of a letter dated 22 June 1937. The terms of this letter are important and are as follows:

John Dooley,
General Sheet Metal Works,
Garville Avenue, Rathgar, Dublin,
22 June 1937.

Messrs. T. L. Egan and Co. Ltd,
9 Lavitt's Quay,
Cork.

Quotation.

Dear Sir(s),

I thank you for your esteemed enquiry of the 18 inst. and I have much pleasure in submitting my quotation as follows:

Description.	Price.
Six Sterilising Drums as per Specification supplied	£3 17 6 each less 25%
One Instrument Cabinet similar to No. B9558 in the Surgical Manufacturer Company's Catalogue	£18 0 0 less 25%

Awaiting the favour of your valued order and assuring you of my best attention at all times,

I am, dear Sir(s),
Yours faithfully,
John G. Dooley.

Delivery 3–4 weeks. Terms Nett M/A.

All quotations for Copper, Monel Metal, Stainless Steel, Tin and Brass Goods are given subject to Market Fluctuations without notice. All quotations are for immediate acceptance only and are subject to change without notice. The delivery of all orders accepted by me shall be contingent upon strikes, fires, accidents, delays of carriers and other causes unavoidable or beyond my control. I will not be responsible for damages due to any delays whatever. Clerical errors are subject to correction. Orders accepted by me cannot be countermanded without my consent and upon terms which will indemnify me against all loss.

The sentence in the letter 'All quotations are made for immediate acceptance only and are subject to change without notice' is important and was largely dealt with in the argument. To this letter the defendant company replied immediately by letter dated 24 June in which they said:

'We enclose herewith order for two cabinets and trust that you can let us have delivery as soon as possible, if possible around 23 to 28 July. We have to cancel order for sterilising drum at the moment as we have to submit another quotation.

Thanking you,
Yours faithfully,
T. L. Egan and Co. Ltd
C. Egan, Secretary'

The Order referred to is in a printed form headed:

T.L. Egan and Co. Ltd,
Surgical Instruments, Appliances, Dressings, etc.,
9 Lavitt's Quay,
Cork, 24 June 1937.'

It is directed to the plaintiff and simply specifies: '2 Instrument Cabinets similar to No. B9558, Surgical Manufacturing Company's catalogue at £18 0 0 each less 25%. C.E.' To this the plaintiff replied by letter dated 25 June 1937, which I will read later.

The whole question at issue is whether the letter of 22 June was an offer which defendant company accepted by their letter of 24 June, or the latter letter was an offer to purchase, which was accepted by the plaintiff's letter of 26 June. The plaintiff argued that this quotation of 22 June was not really an offer, but only a statement of terms on which the party was ready to discuss the question of sale. I was referred to the case of *Boyers v Duke*, |1905| 2 IR, 617. In the argument a good deal was made out of the sentence in the 'Quotation': 'All quotations are made for immediate acceptance only and are subject to change without notice.' The interpretation that I put upon that was this 'quotation' was an offer subject to immediate acceptance; but that if it were not accepted immediately it became subject to contingencies which made it vague and if it was not accepted immediately the decision in |1905| 2 IR at 617 would apply. But assuming that it is definite as to one instrument cabinet and one only then I do not regard it as indefinite in any way unless indeed it might be argued that these contingencies as to strikes might make it indefinite. I will therefore take this 'Quotation' to be a definite offer. The question then arises as to whether this offer was definitely accepted by the defendant's order of 24 June accepting two instrument cabinets. I think that matter may be disposed of by looking at it in the same way as the Court of Appeal looked at the case of *Wheeler v Jeffrey*, |1921| 2 IR at 395.

Let us suppose that when plaintiff got the order for two cabinets he had replied 'I have only quoted for one. I have one nearly ready. It is part of a large number I had made for another order and I have no difficulty in supplying one at the price quoted and within the time specified, but as labour conditions have changed and prices are different I am unable to supply two.' If the plaintiff had replied in this way the other party could say: 'But I want two cabinets, and as you say you can only supply one I'll enquire elsewhere.' Under those circumstances the application for two could not be regarded as the acceptance of the offer.

In this case subsequent correspondence showed that it did not matter to the plaintiff whether he supplied one or two; but those circumstances cannot affect the construction of the correspondence. Accordingly I hold that the order of 24 June was not an unqualified acceptance, but another offer which was accepted by the plaintiff's letter of 25 June which said:

Dear Sirs,

I thank you for your valued order of the 24 inst., for two Instrument Cabinets, and have great pleasure in placing the work in hands immediately and shall let you have delivery as soon as possible. Again thanking you for your esteemed order and assuring you of our best attention at all times.

I am,
Yours faithfully,
John G. Dooley.

Therefore I am of opinion that this letter from Dublin was the acceptance of the offer and that therefore the contract was made in Dublin. The Circuit Court judge decided that he had no jurisdiction. I reverse his Order of 23 March 1938, as I find he had jurisdiction, as the contract was made in Dublin.

Note

The justification for the postal rule was explained in *Adams v Lindsell* (1818) 1 B & Ald 681 where the court said that if the rule did not exist no contract could ever be completed by post. If the offeror was not bound until the acceptance was received, then the offeree should not be bound until he had received notification that the offeror had received his acceptance and assented to it. And so it might continue *ad infinitum*.

Sanderson *v* Cunningham and Others [1919] 2 IR 234

The plaintiff claimed £500 upon a policy of insurance, dated 28 June 1916, by which the defendants insured the plaintiff against damages and costs arising from accidents to motor vehicles belonging to the plaintiff . . . Messrs Coyle & Co., insurance brokers, Dublin, forwarded to the defendants a proposal for the insurance of nine motor vehicles. The policy issued by the defendants contained a number of conditions which were not in the proposal, and of which the plaintiff had no knowledge until he received the policy from Coyle & Co. The plaintiff accepted the policy subject to the conditions on which it was issued.

On behalf of the defendants an affidavit was filed stating that the proposal was forwarded to the Dreadnought Motor Policies, through whom it was ultimately submitted to the defendants, the underwriters; and in due course the policy was prepared in London, signed by the underwriters there, and sent through the Dreadnought Motor Policies to Messrs Coyle & Co. The policy contained on the front of it the following note, printed in red ink: 'The assured is requested to read the policy, and if incorrect to return it at once to the agents as under, to whom all communications referring to this insurance should be addressed.' On 16 June 1916, Messrs Coyle & Co. wrote to the manager of the Dreadnought Underwriters asking to have the date from which the insurance was to run altered from 17 May to 17 June. The policy, with this alteration, was returned in completed form. Previously to 28 June 1916, the plaintiff had full knowledge of all the conditions in the completed policy; and, subject to the one alteration referred to, the policy was approved of by him.

The King's Bench Division (Dodd and Gordon JJ.) held that the policy ultimately sent to the plaintiff contained new terms not included in the proposal, and, on the facts before them, that the acceptance was in this country; and gave leave to issue and serve the writ out of the jurisdiction. From this decision the defendants appealed.

. . .

Sir J. Campbell C.:

The sole and only question for decision in this case is whether, upon its facts, the contract of insurance was completed in London or in Dublin; and the answer to this question must largely depend on the nature and extent of the authority of Coyle & Co., the insurance agents or brokers, who effected the insurance on behalf of the plaintiff.

We are all of opinion, differing in this respect from the judges in the King's Bench Division, upon the affidavits and correspondence in the case, that Coyle & Co. had full authority from the plaintiff to negotiate for and effect on his behalf the contract contained in the particular policy sued on. We are also satisfied that the proposal was for a specific policy, known to Coyle & Co. as a Dreadnought motor policy, which to their knowledge would contain the conditions usual in a policy of this description, and, in the absence of any evidence or suggestion that the conditions of the policy in question were in any respect unusual in this sense, we must hold that plaintiff, through his authorised agents, received the precise form of policy for which he had bargained. We cannot, therefore, accept the view upon which the King's Bench Division acted in holding that the proposal was for a Dreadnought policy which was to contain no conditions, or that the insertion of the usual conditions of such a policy required an opportunity for the inspection of the document by the plaintiff, or his authorised agents in Dublin, before the contract could be treated as complete. If the plaintiff, or Coyle & Co., upon receipt of the policy, had objected to it on the ground that the conditions, in whole or in part, were not usual in a policy of this particular description, it would have been open to them to repudiate it at their risk in the event of it being subsequently found that the conditions were in fact only such as were usual; but this consideration cannot affect the question as to the venue in which the contract was completed.

Further, we are of opinion that in the circumstances of this case this contention on behalf of the plaintiff wholly fails upon another ground, because it appears from the correspondence that when the original policy was executed by the defendants, and received in Dublin by Coyle & Co., as the agents for the plaintiff, it was returned by them with a request for one alteration only, namely, a correction in the description in the policy of the particular vehicles to be insured. No objection whatever was taken at that time by Coyle & Co. to the conditions, which were in print, and were presumably the usual conditions in a Dreadnought policy; but the defendants, instead of returning it with the desired alteration, executed a fresh policy, which was precisely the same as the other in every respect, save as to the amended description.

These facts seem coercive as to the knowledge of Coyle & Co. that they had received a policy which agreed in form and effect with that for which they had proposed; and if it is the fact, as alleged on the part of the plaintiff, that this fresh policy was never seen by him, I think his acts, in subsequently refunding to Coyle & Co. the premium which, as their agents, they had paid on their account to the defendants, and in bringing this present claim upon foot of the policy, are coercive to the conclusion that Coyle & Co. had the fullest authority from him to complete the transaction.

It is always possible that a presumed acceptance of an offer may introduce a new term into the contract proposed, but the argument on behalf of the plaintiff would seem to lead to this, that in every contract the person who makes the offer is entitled by law to a reasonable interval in order to enable him to determine whether the acceptance is in fact in strict compliance with the offer, and that consequently the contract can never legally be complete until he has been afforded such an opportunity—a contention which is directly in conflict with the principles which determine the completion of the contract in all cases of an offer, followed by an unqualified acceptance. In this case we are of opinion that when the defendants executed the fresh policy and forwarded it from London to the authorised agents of the plaintiff, they both in fact and in law accepted the precise proposal that had been made to them, and consequently completed the contract. The contract was complete at the latest when, by forwarding the policy from London to Coyle & Co. in Dublin, they thereby communicated their acceptance of the proposal to the agents of the plaintiff, and as this was done in London we must reverse the order appealed from, and discharge the order for service of the writ outside the jurisdiction, with costs both here and below.

(Ronan and O'Connor L.JJ. concurred.)

Note

O'Connor L.J. pointed out in his judgment that the situation might have been different if the agents had instructions from England not to deliver the policy (which would be the usual way of indicating acceptance of the proposal) until the premium was paid. In such a case, he noted, it might be argued that the payment of the premium and not the signing of the policy, concluded the bargain.

A *Caveat*

The postal rule is not, however, a universal rule.

Holwell Securities *v* Hughes [1974] 1 WLR 155

On 19 October 1971 the defendant agreed to grant the plaintiffs a six month option to purchase certain freehold property. The terms of the agreement stated that the option would be exercisable 'by notice in writing to' the defendant. On 14 April 1972, just prior to expiry of the six month period, the plaintiffs' solicitors sent a letter to the defendant's solicitors and a separate letter to the defendant purporting to exercise the option.The second letter was never delivered. The plaintiffs sued for specific performance of the sale agreement, claiming that they had validly exercised the option.

Lawton L.J.:

The issue in this appeal was clear. Did the plaintiffs exercise an option to purchase the premises known as 571, High Road, Wembley, by posting a letter to the defendant which he never received? The answer to this problem can be reached by two paths: the short one and the roundabout one. Both, in my judgment, are satisfactory but the roundabout one has some paths leading off it which can lead the traveller after legal truth astray. The plaintiffs, I think, took one of these paths.

I propose in this judgment to start by taking the short path and then to survey the other. It is a truism of the law relating to options that the grantee must comply strictly with the conditions stipulated for exercise: in *Hare v Nicholl* [1966] 2 QB 130. It follows that the first task of the court is to find out what was stipulated: the instrument of grant has to be construed. It is a formal document which must have been drafted by someone familiar with conveyancing practice. From its lay-out and content it is likely to have been based on a precedent in the *Encyclopaedia of Forms and Precedents*. It follows, so it seems to me, that the words and phrases in it should be given precise meanings whenever possible and that words which are in common use amongst conveyancers should be construed in the way they use such words.

The material parts of the option clause are as follows: 'The said option shall be exercisable by notice in writing to the intending vendor at any time within six months from the date hereof . . .'. In my judgment, the phrase 'notice in writing' is of importance in this context. Conveyancers are familiar with it and frequently use it. It occurs in many sections of the Law of Property Act 1925; for examples, see ss 36 (2), 136, 146 and 196. In the option clause under consideration the draftsman used the phrase in connection with the exercise of the option but in other parts of the agreement he was content to use such phrases as 'agreed in writing' (see clause 4) and 'if required in writing' (see clause 8 (a)). Should any inference be drawn from the use of the word 'notice'? In my judgment, yes. Its derivation is from the Latin word for knowing. A notice is a means of making something known. The *Shorter Oxford English Dictionary* gives as the primary meanings of the word: 'Intimation, information, intelligence, warning, . . . Formal intimation or warning of something.' If a notice is to be of any value it must be an intimation to someone. A notice which cannot impinge on anyone's mind is not functioning as such.

Now in this case the 'notice in writing' was to be one 'to the intending vendor'. It was to be an intimation to him that the grantee had exercised the option; he was the one who was to be fixed with the information contained in the writing. He never was, because the letter carrying the information went astray. The plaintiffs were unable to do what the agreement said they were to do, namely, fix the defendant with knowledge that they had decided to buy his property. If this construction of the option clause is correct, there is no room for the application of any rule of law relating to the acceptance of offers by posting letters since the option agreement stipulated what had to be done to exercise the option. On this ground alone I would dismiss the appeal.

I turn now to what I have called the roundabout path to the same result. |Counsel| on behalf of the plaintiffs submitted that the option was exercised when the letter was posted, as the rule relating to the acceptance of offers by post did apply. The foundation of his argument was that the parties to this agreement must have contemplated that the option might be, and probably would be, exercised by means of a letter sent through the post. I agree. This, submitted |counsel|, was enough to bring the rule into operation. I do not agree. In *Henthorn v Fraser* |1892| 2 Ch. 27, Lord Herschell stated the rule as follows, at p. 33: 'Where the circumstances are such that it must have been within the contemplation of the parties that, according to the ordinary usages of mankind, the post might be used as a means of communicating the acceptance of an offer, the acceptance is complete as soon as it is posted.'

It was applied by Farwell J. in *Bruner v Moore* |1904| 1 Ch. 305 to an option to purchase patent rights. The option agreement, which was in writing, was silent as to the manner in which it was to be exercised. The grantee purported to do so by a letter and a telegram.

Does the rule apply in *all* cases where one party makes an offer which both he and the person with whom he was dealing must have expected the post to be used as a means of accepting it? In my judgment, it does not. First, it does not apply when the express terms of the offer specify that the acceptance must reach the offeror. The public nowadays are familiar with this exception to the general rule through their handling of football pool coupons. Secondly, it probably does not operate if its application would produce manifest inconvenience and absurdity. This is the opinion set out in Cheshire and Fifoot, *Law of Contract*, (3rd ed. 1952), 43. It was the opinion of Lord Bramwell as is seen by his judgment in *British & American Telegraph Co. v Colson* (1871) LR 6 Exch. 108, and his opinion is worthy of consideration even though the decision in that case was overruled by this court in *Household Fire and Carriage Accident Insurance Co. v Grant* (1879) 4 Ex D 216. The illustrations of inconvenience and absurdity which Lord Bramwell gave are as apt today as they were then. Is a stockbroker who is holding shares to the orders of his client liable in damages because he did not sell in a falling market in accordance with the instructions in a letter which was posted but never received? Before the passing of the Law Reform (Miscellaneous Provisions) Act 1970 (which abolished actions for breach of promise of marriage), would a young soldier ordered overseas have been bound in contract to marry a girl to whom he had proposed by letter, asking her to let him have an answer before he left and she had replied affirmatively in good time but the letter had never reached him? In my judgment, the factors of inconvenience and absurdity are but illustrations of a wider principle, namely, that the rule does not apply if, having regard to all the circumstances, including the nature of the subject matter under consideration, the negotiating parties cannot have intended that there should be a binding agreement until the party accepting an offer or exercising an option had in fact communicated the acceptance or exercise to the other. In my judgment, when this principle is applied to the facts of this case it becomes clear that the parties cannot have intended that the posting of a letter should constitute the exercise of the option.

The option agreement was one to which s. 196 of the Law of Property Act 1925 applied: see sub-s. (5), which is in these terms: 'The provisions of this section shall extend to notices required to be served by any instrument affecting property executed or coming into operation after the commencement of this Act unless a contrary intention appears.' The option agreement was an instrument affecting property. A notice in writing had to be given to exercise the option. Giving a notice means the same as serving a notice: see *In re* 88, *Berkeley Road*, N.W. 9 |1971| Ch. 648. The object of this subsection was to enable conveyancers to omit from instruments affecting property stipulations as to the giving of notices if they were prepared to accept the statutory ones. As there was nothing in the option agreement to a contrary effect, the statutory stipulations applied in this case. S. 196 (4) is in these terms:

> Any notice required or authorised by this Act to be served shall also be sufficiently served, if it is sent by post in a registered letter addressed to the lessee, lessor, mortgagee, mortgagor, or other person to be served, by name, at the aforesaid place of abode or business, office, or counting-house, and if that letter is not returned through the post office undelivered; and that service shall be deemed to be made at the time at which the registered letter would in the ordinary course be delivered.

The object of this subsection, as also of sub-s. (3), is to specify circumstances in which proof of actual knowledge may be dispensed with. This follows from the use of the phrase 'any notice . . . shall also be sufficiently served . . . '. If |counsel's| submissions are well founded, a letter sent by ordinary post the evening before the option expired would have amounted to an exercise of it; but a registered letter posted at the same time and arriving in the ordinary course of post, which would have been after the expiration of the option, would not have been an exercise. The parties to the option agreement cannot have intended any such absurd result to follow. When the provisions of s. 196 (4) are read into the agreement, as they have to be, the only reasonable inference is that the parties intended that the vendor should be fixed with actual knowledge of the exercise of the option save in the circumstances envisaged in the subsection. This, in my judgment, was enough to exclude the rule.

I would dismiss the appeal.

(Russell and Buckley L.JJ. agreed.)

Prescribed Method of Acceptance

In *Holwell Securities v Hughes* |1974| 1 All ER 161 the Court of Appeal held that because the prescribed method of acceptance had not been followed the acceptance was invalid. In some cases however, the courts take the view that even if a method is apparently prescribed e.g. signature on an acceptance form, an equally efficacious method of acceptance may suffice. So, in *Staunton v St Laurence's Hospital Board and Ireland and the Attorney General* (HC) 31 July 1987, unrep. (1985/2383P) the plaintiff was held to have validly accepted an offer of employment by way of a verbal response, notwithstanding that the offer included an attached form of acceptance. It is generally necessary to find that the method of acceptance selected by the offeree is not prejudicial to the interests of the offeror, otherwise the prescribed method will prevail (see *Walker v Glass* p. 80 below).

SECTION THREE—TERMINATION OF AN OFFER

A. REVOCATION

Since *Payne v Cave* (1789) 3 Term Rep. 148 it has been established that an offeror is entitled to revoke an offer at any time up until the offer has been accepted. To be effective however this revocation must be brought to the attention of the offeree.

The Guardians of the Navan Union *v* McLoughlin (1855) 4 ICLR 451

The plaintiffs placed an advertisement seeking tenders for the supply of certain articles. The defendant sent in a tender which was later accepted by the plaintiffs at a meeting of the Board of Guardians. Before the defendant was formally informed of his success, he learned from a third party that the plaintiffs were in debt and unlikely to be in a position to pay their suppliers. The defendant thus sent a letter to the plaintiffs stating that he had been informed that his tender was successful but demanding monthly payment of his bill. As he received no reply he refused to perform the contract.

The plaintiffs sued for damages for breach of contract.

Monahan C.J.:

The principal question in this case is, whether there has been a mutually binding contract? And in order to determine that question it is necessary to consider what is the true construction, first of the advertisement, and next of the tender and acceptance. The 1 & 2 Vic., c. 26 (Poor-law Act), provides that advertisements shall be inserted in certain newspapers, and that, as soon as tenders are accepted, written contracts shall be entered into, and that if the board think fit they may require bonds to be entered into by the contractors, with approved sureties. First then, what is the meaning of this advertisement? It declares 'Two solvent sureties will be required for the due performance of each contract; and the names and addresses of those proposed must be inserted in each tender. All bonds to be perfected on or before 29 September 1853, otherwise the contract to be null and void.' Does that mean that together with the tender the party should send the names of the sureties for the due performance of the written contract?

It is impossible to hold that there is any difference between this case and *The Guardians of the Hull Union v Petch*.[1] The only distinction which can be taken is this—that in the latter case there was a postscript to the advertisement, stating that 'all contractors would have to sign a written contract after acceptance of the tenders.' We think that, without any such postscript, that is really the meaning of the advertisement in the present case, for it plainly takes a distinction between the tender and the contract. The case of *The Guardians of the Hull Union v Petch* was almost stronger than the present; for although there was in that case a notification that the persons whose tenders were accepted would be obliged to enter into written contracts, nevertheless that requirement might have been dispensed with. The form of tender there was: 'Gentlemen, I propose to supply your house with meat, according to advertisement, for the ensuing three months, at six pence per pound;' and the acceptance was expressed in the following terms: 'Sir, I am directed by the guardians of the poor of this town, to inform you that you have been appointed butcher to this corporation,' &c. Therefore, if that was a contract, there was a complete acceptance; but the judgment of the court was, that 'the tender was only a proposal for a contract.' So we are of opinion that even if, in the present case, the acceptance had been formally signified to the party, still we could not on principle distinguish it from *The Guardians of the Hull Union v Petch*. But even if that case had never been decided, the other cases that have been cited establish that where there are written communications between parties, it is not enough for one of them to accept the other's proposal in his own mind or in his own office, but he must by some act, binding on himself, communicate his acceptance to the other party. Here there was no such communication, and therefore no such acceptance as would bind the defendant, who had consequently a right to retract.

The case of *Dunlop v Higgins*[2] went on this principle, that the putting of the letter into the post-office was an acceptance by the party, for he had put it out of his own power to retract. Therefore, although perhaps the justice of the case might require that there should be a verdict against the defendant, still, according to the law, the verdict must be set aside. Accordingly, the cause shown must be disallowed.

[1.]   24 LJ N. S. Ex 23.
[2.]   12 Jurist, 295.

Note

Why is it not relevant that the defendant was aware at the time of the revocation that the plaintiff had accepted the tender offer?

Compare this to the situation in *Dickinson v Dodds* (1876) 2 ChD 463. In that case the defendant offered to sell property to the plaintiff. Before the plaintiff could accept he learned that the defendant had agreed to sell the property to another party. The plaintiff later attempted to accept the offer. The Court of Appeal declared the offer to be no longer capable of acceptance.

Aubrey David Walker *v* Allan Glass [1979] NI 129

The plaintiff entered into negotiations with the defendant to buy property owned by the defendant. The negotiations culminated in the defendant sending the plaintiff an offer on 27 February. This offer stated that the purchase price was £400,000 and the offer was to remain open until 13 March. Furthermore it specified that unless the acceptance form annexed to the offer was delivered to the defendant's solicitors together with a deposit of £40,000 before 5 p.m. on 13 March the offer would be deemed to have been withdrawn. The plaintiff signed the acceptance on 2 March and telephoned the defendant's solicitors to inform them of this fact. Later that day the plaintiff was informed by the defendant's solicitors that the offer was withdrawn. This fact was confirmed by a letter and telegram sent that same day. On 12 March the plaintiff left the signed acceptance form and the deposit with the defendant's solicitors.

The plaintiff sued for specific performance.

Lowry L.C.J.:

I start with the following propositions:

(1) An offer may be withdrawn at any time before it has been accepted. Provided no consideration has been given by the offeree, this is so even where the offer (as in this case) was expressed to be kept open for a specified period:

Routledge v Grant (1828) 4 Bing. 653; 130 ER 920
Dickinson v Dodds (1876) 2 ChD 463.

(2) If the offeror prescribes a particular mode of acceptance, no contract is created unless the offer is accepted in that mode or in a way which is a beneficial to the offeror:

Chitty on Contract 24th ed. vol. 1, 38, para. 74;
Manchester Diocesan Council v Commercial and General Investments Ltd [1969] 3 All ER 1593.

(3) Revocation of an offer is not effective on the posting of a letter of revocation or the dispatch of a telegram, but only when the offeree receives notice of the revocation:

Henthorn v Fraser [1892] 2 Ch. 27.

In this case the question is whether the reference to delivery of the plaintiff's completed acceptance to the defendant's solicitors at their office together with £40,000 by way of deposit before 5 o'clock p.m. on 13 March 1979 merely conveyed the information that the defendant's offer should be deemed to have been withdrawn (without the need to withdraw it expressly) if these acts were not performed by the stated time or, on the other hand, prescribed a particular mode of acceptance. The plaintiff's counsel concede that, if the second view is correct, the plaintiff did not 'accept' the offer in a way which was as beneficial to the offeror as the prescribed mode.

The defendant, however, concedes that the delivery of a cheque on 12 March was as good as a payment in cash. There is also a third view, advanced on behalf of the plaintiff, namely that the need for payment by 13 March of a deposit of £40,000 (or such payment and also a signed acceptance) was an implied term of the contract.

On the first view there would be no need for a signed acceptance or a deposit by the offeree: the plaintiff could simply have telephoned his acceptance to Mr Murphy and the defendant, having made an offer in writing, would thereupon have become contractually bound to the plaintiff right up to the completion date (30 April 1979) and indeed up to such date (if later) as became the vital date when time was made of the essence. In the meantime, the defendant would have had no remedy against the plaintiff for non-performance and could not have withdrawn his offer before 13 March or had it deemed to be withdrawn thereafter. Nor could the defendant have insisted on a signed acceptance or a deposit at any time.

In face of the wording of the defendant's offer, one could not accept the proposition that he was not prescribing a mode of acceptance, because the consequences to the defendant of having his offer accepted by telephone would be unthinkable. The first view thus yields such an unlikely result that the plaintiff's counsel did not seriously support it. Instead, recognising that a signed acceptance was needed in order to put the parties on level terms and that a deposit would certainly be required by the vendor, he espoused the third view—that a deposit and probably a signed acceptance were required by necessary implication, but he argued that these requirements were satisfied, because there was evidence (if I believed it) that the acceptance of the offer was signed on 1 March and communicated to Mr Murphy on 1, or alternatively 2 March and it was agreed that the deposit was paid on 12 March. In other words, although the payment of the deposit by 13 March could be regarded as essential, the plaintiff, by writing and orally communicating his acceptance before the defendant withdrew, effectively froze the position (and thereby prevented the defendant from effectively withdrawing his offer) and then concluded the bargain by paying the deposit on 12 March (except for which payment the offer would have been deemed by 5.30 p.m. on 13 March to have been withdrawn).

The danger of this line from the plaintiff's point of view is that it concedes that a signed acceptance and payment of a £40,000 deposit are required, and thereby causes these two acts to assume the form of a prescribed mode of acceptance, but |counsel for the plaintiff| contends that the defendant was bound by the plaintiff's performance of one of the acts on 1 or 2 March, so that he could not withdraw his offer and had to give the plaintiff the chance to pay the £40,000 deposit at any time up to 5.30 p.m. on 13 March. He also makes the point that a purchaser who tells a vendor that he has signed the vendor's offer makes it possible for the vendor to give secondary evidence of the purchaser's having signed, if the signed offer is not produced by the purchaser at the trial of an action brought on the contract by the vendor. The practical difficulty, however, is that, in an action brought by the vendor, he (or his witness) might not be believed when he testifies that the purchaser had orally communicated the information that he had signed the offer.

The third view, as I have called it, ingeniously fits the facts, or alleged facts, in this case but I do not consider it to be sound. If the signing of the offer by the purchaser and the payment of a deposit constitute a prescribed mode of acceptance, one is driven to read the exact words by which the prescribed mode is expressed. They are found in the following sentence:

> This offer shall remain open for acceptance until 13 March 1979 and if the acceptance annexed hereto duly completed by purchaser shall not be delivered to Messrs Murphy, Irwin & Co., Solicitors for the vendor at their office at 14 Victoria Street, Ballymoney, together with £40,000 by way of deposit before 5 o'clock p.m. on said date, this offer shall be deemed to have been withdrawn, and in this respect time shall be of the essence.

The form of the acceptance annexed to the offer is:

> I hereby accept the above offer and:
>
> (a) Tender herewith £40,000 for deposit,
> (b) Agree to complete the purchase in accordance with the annexed conditions.
>
> Dated this   day of   1979
> . . . .

(The typed line is obviously meant to accommodate the purchaser's signature and that is the use to which it was in fact put.)

This means that the written and signed acceptance was to be delivered to Mr Murphy's office and to be accompanied by a deposit of £40,000. The close association of a signed acceptance and payment of a deposit in *both* the offer *and* the form of acceptance is, in my view an important pointer to the meaning of the contract. I now come back to the question whether what was done by 2 March was as beneficial to the offeror as the prescribed mode of acceptance and was sufficient to prevent effective revocation of the offer by the defendant. I consider that the answer to both questions is 'No'.

In the first place, as I have already stated, an oral communication to the vendor by a purchaser, saying that the latter has signed, does not put the vendor in as good a position as if the signed acceptance had been delivered to his solicitor. And in the second place, signature of the acceptance by the purchaser unaccompanied by payment of the deposit is not a complete performance of the prescribed mode of acceptance and does not put the vendor in as good a position as he demanded: if the purchaser does not go through with the contract a vendor who has not received the deposit is obviously in a worse position than a vendor who has received one. Indeed, |counsel for the plaintiff| frankly said that, if the written offer embodies a prescribed mode of acceptance, the vendor had not received as beneficial an acceptance as he demanded. In short, there is no good reason why the defendant here should have become and remained contractually bound from 1 to 12 March without having received a deposit from the plaintiff.

The defendant expressly withdrew his offer before he had received a written and signed acceptance and the deposit and in my opinion he was entitled to do so.

Accordingly I find, in favour of the defendant, that no binding contract existed before withdrawal of his offer.

Note

In a unilateral contract there is no acceptance of the contract until the offeree has fully performed the act required. For example: I offer a person £70 if he works for me for five hours. This contract is only complete when the offeree accepts which he only does by working a full five hours. If the offeree works for four hours and I do not prevent him continuing, he has not fully performed and thus he has not accepted the contract. Therefore I am entitled to revoke my offer. In *Daulia v Four Millbank Nominees Ltd* |1978| 2 All ER 557 Goff L.J. stated:

Whilst I think the true view of a unilateral contract must in general be that the offeror is entitled to require full performance of the condition which he has imposed and short of that he is not bound, that must be subject to one important qualification, which stems from the fact that there must be an implied obligation on the part of the offeror not to prevent the condition becoming satisfied, which obligation it seems to me must arise as soon as the offeree starts to perform. Until the offeror can revoke the whole thing, but once the offeree has embarked on performance it is too late for the offeror to revoke his offer.

In *O'Connor v Sorohan* |1933| IR 591 the Irish Supreme Court followed *Offord v Davies* (1862) 12 CB (NS) 748 on this point. There is however, no recent Irish decision on this issue.

B. REJECTION

An offer will be terminated once it is rejected by the offeree. A counter offer by the original offeree will be viewed as a rejection of the original offer.

C. Lapse of Time

Martin A. Commane *v* Johanna Walsh (HC) 3 May 1983, unrep.

By a standard form memorandum of agreement the plaintiff agreed to buy property from the defendant for £60,000. The property comprised three parcels of land which when described in the memorandum amounted to a total area of 51 acres 3 roods. However the final sentence of the memorandum noted that the total area being sold was 54.2 acres. The special conditions noted that 'No requisition or objection shall be raised as to the accuracy of the area in sale and purchaser shall be deemed to have inspected the property prior to completion of the contract.'

The vendor then wrote to say that due to a title problem with one of the parcels of land he suggested closing the sale in relation to the remaining two parcels and apportioning the purchase money accordingly.

In July the purchaser complained that the total acreage did not amount to 54.2 acres, and the vendor replied in August referring them to the Special Conditions. At some stage during the summer the purchaser entered on the land to cut and bale hay which was stored on the land. On 18 September he wrote to the vendors demanding completion on or before 19 October. On 30 September the vendors wrote back purporting to accept the offer previously made to complete the transfer of two parcels of the property. This was rejected by the purchaser on 1 October. Since the vendor was unable to establish title to one of the portions the purchaser wrote on 20 October demanding the return of his deposit.

O'Hanlon J.:

I feel, however, that I should also consider whether . . . the agreement was validly rescinded because of unreasonable delay on the part of the vendor in completing the transfer of the lands.

I have no hesitation in finding that the vendor and her solicitors were extremely dilatory in the way the sale was dealt with between May and October 1981, but the correspondence does not suggest that the delay was a source of great annoyance or upset to the purchaser at the time. The offer was made in the month of May to close the sale in respect of the greater part of the lands, leaving over until later the transfer of the small parcel in Folio 13155, and this offer was never formally withdrawn until after the vendor's solicitors had written on 30 September 1981, expressing the vendor's willingness to put through the sale in this manner. The offer when made remained open until it was withdrawn, or until it would be unreasonable to hold the purchaser to it any longer because of the length of time which had elapsed without acceptance. What is a reasonable time is a question of fact depending on the circumstances of each particular case. See, *Ramsgate Hotel Co. v Montefiore*, (1866) LR 1 Ex 109. In the present case, because of the rather casual approach adopted by both parties to the time for closing of the sale, and their early agreement that they would have to proceed on the basis of a good deal of delay in straightening out the title to Folio 13155, I would regard the offer to deal separately with this parcel of land as remaining open into the month of September 1981, and I do not consider that the letter of 19 September 1981, should be regarded as a revocation of the offer.

In this situation the vendor was willing to comply with her obligations under the Agreement for Sale, as varied by the special terms later arranged about Folio 13155, within the time which the purchaser sought to make of the essence of the contract. I think it very likely that the purchaser would have consented to the sale going through on this basis had he not become involved in a dispute about the acreage, when he asserted a claim which he was unable to enforce.

Consequently, if the matter had to be determined under the general law as to delay on completion and the entitlement of a purchaser in such circumstances to withdraw from his bargain, I would again hold that the contract had not been validly rescinded having regard to all the circumstances of the present case. The plaintiff's claim accordingly stands refused.

Lynch *v* St Vincent's Hospital (HC) 31 July 1987, unrep.

Costello J.:

In 1977 the Minister for Health had established a working party to examine a report, *inter alia*, on the form of contract to be entered into between consultants and their employing authorities, health boards and public voluntary hospitals. The working party produced an interim report which proposed a number of far-reaching new arrangements which were to apply to all new appointments. As to existing appointments it recommended that each consultant would have the option for a two year period [of retaining an] appointment on its existing terms or [entering] into the common contract. On 7 February 1983 St Vincent's financial controller sent a letter to Mr Lynch which stated:

> I enclose copies of common contracts.
> When you have perused the documents you could call to Sr Mary Magdalen's office to sign the same (if you so decide) and get her to countersign. One copy plus additional documents to be retained by yourself and one copy by the hospital.

I will call the document sent to Mr Lynch on 7 February the 'February document' and examine its contents in greater detail later. There are however two points about it which can be noted now. It was addressed to Mr Lynch in the hospital (not to his home address). And there was a blank space left in para. 6.2 which dealt with the service commitment which Mr Lynch was to give to St Vincent's. It is clear why this crucial point was left blank. Just at this time the hospital had written to the Comhairle suggesting that Mr Lynch's commitment should be changed from six to twenty one hours. When a copy of the common contract was sent to him formal approval of this change had not been obtained. Until the matter had been satisfactorily resolved it was obviously considered desirable not to specify what commitment should be provided for in Mr Lynch's contract.

Mr Lynch did not then sign the February draft. He was aware that he had a two year period in which to consider the position and like other consultants he took his time before committing himself to the new arrangements.

St Vincent's sent Mr Lynch a second copy of the common contract. This was produced at the hearing and has considerable bearing on the parties' legal rights. It is undated and Mr Lynch has been unable to find any covering letter by which it was sent and none exists in the hospital's files. It is addressed to him at his home address in Killiney and is obviously a freshly completed draft (and not a copy of the February document) because the words 'Thoracic Surgeon' have been typed in block capitals whereas they were typed in lower case in the February document. Most significantly it had completed para. 6.2 (which had been left blank in the February document) by inserting in type the figures '21' as the service commitment which Mr Lynch was required to give under the contract. But although the document is undated I think it is probable that it was sent to Mr Lynch in the month of September 1983 and I will call it the 'September document'. It will be recalled that in September 1983 agreement had been reached between the federated group and St Vincent's as to how Mr Lynch's service commitment should be divided between the two groups of hospitals and that on 9 September St Vincent's had written to the Department and to the Comhairle indicating its agreement to a service commitment of twenty one hours. It is probable that the September document was sent about that time to Mr Lynch. On 11 November the financial controller wrote to Mr Lynch asking him to call as soon as possible to sign the common contract, and on 12 December the Secretary/Manager wrote asking Mr Lynch 'to sign the contract as it now stands—seven sessions for SVH and four for Baggot Street'. This correspondence is of assistance not only in dating the September document but also as showing that St Vincent's was prepared to enter into a common contract with Mr Lynch which provided for a twenty-one hour commitment to St Vincent's even though the Comhairle had not formerly notified its approval of the 'restructuring' of the original appointment. Their confidence that they could do so sprang from the fact that they had been directed to prepare the common contracts with their consultants in accordance with the actual times their consultants were working in their hospital.

About this time the federated group had also sent a common contract to Mr Lynch which contained a service commitment of four sessions to the group's hospitals. He had signed neither contract on 16 January 1984 when he had resigned from Baggot Street.

Mr Lynch's acceptance of the common contract

Mr Lynch was aware in November 1984 that time was running out and that he would have to exercise the option by the end of the year if he wished to enter into the common contract with St Vincent's Hospital. He wrote on 15 November to the chairman of the Comhairle in an attempt to have his position clarified and shortly afterwards to St Vincent's and to the Federated Dublin Voluntary Hospitals. The replies he received were unsatisfactory and so he decided to seek legal advice. Before he did so, however, he was forwarded by St Vincent's Hospital (without any covering letter) a copy of a circular sent by the Department of Health to hospital authorities dated 23 November 1984. It was in the following terms:

> I am directed by the Minister to refer to previous correspondence regarding the introduction of the Common Contract for Consultant Medical Staff.
>
> Your attention is drawn to the terms of s. 9 of the Interim Report of the Working Party on the Common Contract and the option contained therein. The final option date in relation to all consultants shall be 31 December 1984.
>
> I am also to remind you that as and from 1 January 1984 all contracts entered into, except in the case of consultants holding teaching appointments shall be operative from a current date, i.e. the date of implementation of each individual contract (as per the Department's Circular S152/1 of 12 January 1984).

As a result of the advice he obtained he searched for the documents which he had at home relating to his appointment and found a portion of the September document (whose existence he had overlooked). He inserted in the February document the twenty one hour service commitment specified in the September document and signed it and delivered it to the hospital with an accompanying letter dated 29 December 1984 which reads as follows:

> I refer to the letter of 7 February 1983 offering me an appointment as consultant in Thoracic surgery in St Vincent's Hospital. I also refer to the copy of the memorandum from the Dept of Health addressed to the CEO of each Health Board and the Secretary/Manager of each voluntary hospital dated 23 November 1984 which you kindly sent me recently. I note that under the terms of that memorandum the final option date as mentioned in para. 9 of the Interim Report of the Working Party on the Common Contract is fixed as 31 December 1984.
>
> Having considered the matter I now give you notice that I accept the appointment offered by you, in the terms therein stated and in accordance with the Working Party Report and I enclose herewith the form of acceptance duly completed.
>
> I shall draw your attention to the fact that through what appears to be a clerical error the actual number of hours per week to be devoted to eligible patients (para. 6.2) appears to have been omitted from your letter of 7 February 1983. However in a somewhat similar though undated letter (copy enclosed) the number of hours was set out at twenty one per week and I have therefore inserted that figure. If the hospital wish to increase that figure I would have no objection.

To ascertain whether this brought into existence a new contract between him and the hospital it is necessary to consider in some detail the terms of the February document. The document sent to Mr Lynch on 9 February 1983 began by stating:

> You are hereby offered an appointment of consultant in Thoracic Surgery under St Vincent's Hospital Board of Management from 1 January 1983 subject to the terms and conditions specified in this contract and in the documents stated to be appended thereto: these jointly being the contract documents.

And para. 2 stated:

> If you agree to accept the appointment on the terms indicated, you should sign the form of acceptance at the foot of this document and return it to the Secretary/Manager, St Vincent's Hospital. A copy of the contract documents is attached and should be retained for future reference.

Details of terms of appointment then followed and after a space left for the signature of someone acting on behalf of St Vincent's Hospital the last paragraph of the document read:

> *Acceptance* (do not detach)
>
> I hereby accept the appointment offered above by Secretary/Manager St Vincent's Hospital, Board of Management on the terms and subject to the conditions of appointment referred to and I undertake to commence my duties with St Vincent's Hospital, Board of Management on 1 January 1983.

The contract which was then sent for signature was, however, not complete. S. 6 was headed 'Service Commitment and Rights of Consultant'. Its first paragraph (6.1) stated that the type of appointment offered by the contract had been regulated by the Comhairle in the manner following. And para. 6.2 read:

> On the basis of the provisions of para. 6.1 the scheduled service commitment of this appointment in respect of eligible patients shall be . . . hours per week.

Quite clearly Mr Lynch could not have entered into the common contract on receipt of the document as it did not contain a crucial term (the service commitment to be given under the contract).

I will now consider the legal effect of Mr Lynch's signature to the February document and his letter of 29 December 1984.

(a) It is pleaded in para. 4 of the defence that the offer made on 7 February 1983 was for appointment of the plaintiff on the basis of his working two sessions within the defendant's hospital but subject to its being previously structured by Comhairle na n-Ospidéal. This is incorrect. The service commitment was left open in the document because, as I have already pointed out, negotiations were in train with the Comhairle and the federated group on the subject.

(b) It is pleaded in para. 4 of the defence that the defendants could not offer any appointment for the plaintiff's commitment to sessions in excess of those structured by Comhairle na n-Ospidéal. This is not a correct interpretation of the legal position. As I have already pointed out there was nothing in the Health Act, 1970 or elsewhere which prohibited by law the hospital from amending Mr Lynch's existing service commitment even though it resulted in a service commitment different to that specified by the Comhairle when it originally regulated the appointment. Furthermore, it will be recalled that the hospital was prepared to enter into the contract with the amended service commitment in November and December 1983 even though it had not been formally sanctioned by the Comhairle at that time.

(c) It is pleaded in para. 5 of the defence that the plaintiff did not accept the offer made on 7 February 1983 but made a counter offer which could not be lawfully accepted by the defendants. This is not correct. In the light of the September document (which completed the space which had been left blank in para. 6.2 of the February document) Mr Lynch was entitled to regard the hospital as having offered him a contract which contained a service commitment of twenty one hours, a point which is reinforced by the letter from the hospital of 12 December 1983 requesting him to sign the common contract 'as it now stands—seven sessions for SVH'. By filling in this figure in the February document the plaintiff was not making a counter offer; he was merely inserting in the document the terms offered to him by the hospital. For reasons already stated by doing so and by signing the document he was not creating an illegal contract.

(d) Mr Lynch of course knew that the hospital was in correspondence with the Comhairle about the variation of the term of his original appointment relating to his service commitment to St Vincent's Hospital. But when the September document was sent and a completed offer made to enter into the common contract with Mr Lynch on the basis of a twenty one hour service commitment this offer was not made conditional on its terms being approved by the Comhairle, a point amply illustrated by the letter of 12 December 1983.

(e) Mr Lynch had originally entered into two separate contracts at the time of his appointment to the staff of St Vincent's Hospital and the staff of Baggot Street Hospital. His resignation from the staff of Baggot Street Hospital had no effect on his contract with St Vincent's Hospital. At that time a completed offer of a new contract had been made by St Vincent's Hospital. It was never revoked. Indeed the transmission to Mr Lynch of the Departmental circular of 23 November 1984 confirmed the existence of the offer. It has been stated in evidence that the transmission to him of the circular was due to an oversight. But even if this is so Mr Lynch was entitled to treat it as confirmation that the offer of the common contract still stood.

(f) The offer of the common contract by St Vincent's Hospital was not made conditional upon Mr Lynch entering into a similar contract with the Federated Dublin Voluntary Hospitals. The common contract could have contained a clause to the effect that in the case of joint appointments its validity depended on the execution of a common contract with each of the hospitals involved in the joint appointment. But it did not and the offer made by St Vincent's Hospital was not qualified in any way.

(g) The contract document was not signed by someone on behalf of the hospital. But such signature was not necessary in order to create a contractual relationship between the parties. The hospital had clearly offered to enter into the contract with the plaintiff. The terms of the offer were complete. And the hospital made it clear that it would regard itself as bound by the contract once it was signed by Mr Lynch.

(h) Finally, it was submitted that the February document was merely a contract sent for approval and not for signature and that an acceptance of a draft offer cannot operate to conclude a contract. I agree that the offer made in February 1983 was incomplete, but that does not mean that it can be regarded as a draft sent for approval—its terms expressly provide that signature of the document would amount to acceptance of the appointment on the terms of the document. A completed offer was made by the transmission of the September document to Mr Lynch.

I conclude therefore that Mr Lynch's signature to the document which he delivered to the hospital on 29 December 1984 was effective to create a binding contract between him and the hospital on the terms contained in that document and he is accordingly entitled to a declaration that he has lawfully and validly accepted an offer of employment made by the defendants for an appointment as consultant in thoracic surgery with a commitment in respect of eligible patients of twenty one hours per week.

Note

This case illustrates the fact that where contractual relations already exist a new offer may be capable of acceptance for a considerable period of time. Note how the court declined to interpret Lynch's responses as a counter offer.

D. DEATH

In re Whelan deceased, Dodd v Whelan [1897] 1 IR 575

Whelan guaranteed the current account of the firm Whelan & Maher. Although Whelan died in April 1895 no notice of his death was given to the bank. In November 1895 the bank manager learned of Whelan's death in a casual conversation. However the account was not closed until 1 January 1896.

The bank later claimed on foot of the guarantee for the balances due to them by the firm. The executors of Whelan's estate disputed their liability to any portion of the claim relating to advances after Whelan's death, or alternatively to the portion of the claim relating to advances made since the bank had knowledge of his death.

V.C.:

I do not think that, having regard to the decision of the Court of Exchequer in *Bradbury v Morgan*,[1] and the cases which have followed it, I can hold that the mere fact of the death of the guarantor, unknown to the creditor, terminated the operation of the guarantee. But the question arises whether mere knowledge of the death has that operation without formal notice being given by the executors to determine the guarantee. The nature of such guarantees and the right to determine them was carefully considered by Bowen J., in the case of *Coulthart v Clementson*,[2] an action which was tried by him on circuit, when he reserved the case for his further consideration. It was argued before him subsequently, and he again took time for consideration, so that the questions there raised were fully deliberated on by that eminent judge, and his opinion is entitled to great weight. He put the case as one of contract, and refers to the decision of the Court of Common Pleas in *Offord v Davies*,[3] and held that it was established by authority that such continuing guarantees can be withdrawn on notice during the lifetime of the guarantor, and that a limitation to that effect must be read, so to speak, into the contract. He then proceeded to consider the question of what is to happen on the death of the guarantor, and asks if the guarantee is then to become irrevocable and to go on for ever? He replies, and I think conclusively, that such a consequence of the death would be absurd. In this conclusion I entirely agree. He then proceeds to consider what notice should be deemed sufficient, and asks must the executor give special notice that the guarantee is withdrawn, or is it not enough that the creditor should be warned of the death of the guarantor and the devolution of his estate to others, and holds that, in the absence of special option to the personal representative to continue the guarantee, the notice of the death of the testator and of the existence of a will is constructive notice of the determination of the guarantee as to future advances. These words cannot be limited to cases where a will exists, and are *a fortiori* applicable to cases of intestacy, for such an option could only be given by a will, and if no will exists no such option can exist. In the absence of express authority from the deceased, whether he dies intestate or makes a will not giving such option, it would be equally outside the duty of the executor or of the administrator, as the case may be, to continue the course of dealing. Knowledge of the death therefore is, as considered by Bowen J., sufficient to put the creditor on inquiry whether there is any testamentary authority before making further advances. Nor is there any hardship upon or injustice to the creditor in so holding. His knowledge of the death should be enough to require him to hold his hand, and ascertain whether or not there is any option given to the personal representatives of the guarantor to continue the course of dealing, or rather to enter into a new contract of suretyship. The decision in *Coulthart v Clementson* is clear, that in case no such option exists, the course of dealing is determined by knowledge of the death.

The opinion of Mellish L.J., in *Harriss v Fawcett*,[4] a case referred to, not on this part of the question, by Bowen J., in *Coulthart v Clementson*, is quite in accordance with his views.

The case of *Coulthart v Clementson*, was commented on by Romer J., in *In re Silvester*;[5] but I cannot regard the *dicta* of the learned judge as sufficient to displace the decision of Bowen J., which was not appealed from and which I am prepared to follow. Of course, in the case of express provisions in the contract of guarantee, effect must be given to them, according to the true construction of the instrument; but there is not, in my opinion, anything in this letter of guarantee bearing upon the present question.

I therefore hold that advances made by the bank subsequent to their having knowledge of the death of the testator are not covered by the guarantee, but that those made prior to this were so covered.

1. 1 H & C 249.
2. 5 QBD 42.
3. 12 CB (NS) 748.

4. LR 8 Ch App 866.
5. [1895] 1 Ch. 573.

Note

The death of the offeree before the offer has been accepted renders the offer incapable of being accepted. This is clear from *Reynolds v Atherton* (1921) 125 LT 690.

SECTION FOUR—CERTAINTY

An agreement which is either vague or incomplete will not constitute a legally binding contract.

An agreement may be vague because it contains terms which are illusory, that is, lack promissory content, or are discretionary in nature, or are capable of interpretation in more than one way. Alternatively, agreement may not have been reached on certain important points.

Electricity Supply Board *v* Newman (1933) 67 ILTR 124

The defendant, Newman, entered into a contract with Dublin Corporation on 8 January 1927, which was in the following form: 'I, the undersigned, do hereby agree to indemnify the Dublin Corporation against any loss it may sustain by reason of the default of Mrs Betta Waddington, of No. 5 Lower Ormond Quay, in discharging the accounts for electricity supplied to her for a period not exceeding nine months at any time,' and was signed by the defendant.
. . .

During the period October 1929, to June 1930, electricity was supplied by the Electricity Supply Board to Mrs Betta Waddington at four different premises (all within the area of supply of the former Dublin Corporation undertaking), *viz.* at 5 Lower Ormond Quay, to the amount of £10 8s 6d, 6 Lower Ormond Quay to the amount of £6 15s 10d, 87 Marlborough Street to the amount of £9 6s 9d, and 108 St Stephen's Green to the amount of 16s 4d. Default in payment having been made by Mrs Waddington, the plaintiffs sued Newman, the defendant, on foot of his contract of indemnity for the total sum of £27 7s 5d due by Mrs Waddington in respect of all four premises.
. . .

Judge Davitt held that the contract on the face of it was ambiguous, the word 'accounts' being capable of meaning either the periodic accounts in respect of the electricity supply to one set of premises or accounts due in respect of the supply to a number of premises. Accordingly, he had admitted oral evidence to explain the meaning of the contract. On the evidence of the defendant, he was satisfied that, in signing the contract, the defendant had had no intention of giving a 'drag-net' indemnity which would cover the supply of electricity to Mrs Waddington at any premises and any number of premises which she might occupy. He was satisfied that the contract of indemnity was intended to apply only to the periodic accounts for the supply of current to Mrs Waddington at the premises No. 5 Lower Ormond Quay alone, . . .

Provincial Bank of Ireland, Ltd *v* Donnell (1932) 67 ILTR 142

The defendant gave the plaintiffs a guarantee expressed to be made 'in consideration of advances heretofore made or that may hereafter be made from time to time' by the plaintiffs to the defendant's husband. When the defendant's husband defaulted on his payments the plaintiffs sued the defendant for refusing to reimburse them under the guarantee.

Andrews L.J.:

The question then remains as to whether the consideration is made valuable by the reference to 'advances that may hereafter be made from time to time by the bank.' It is clear that an agreement by the plaintiff for a future advance to a third person is a sufficient consideration for the defendant's promise to be answerable for the payment to the plaintiffs of past and future debts of such third person. It is clear, however, that where, as in the present case, there is no agreement binding on the plaintiffs to make the advances, and no advances are in fact made, the guarantee fails for want of consideration.

Best L.J.:

The guarantee can, in my opinion, only be construed as an indication on the part of the plaintiffs that they might make further advances to the debtor, but there was no agreement binding them to do so and if, as is the case here, no advance was in fact made, the undertaking of the defendant fails for want of consideration and judgment should be in her favour.

Note

In this case the court also decided that as the plaintiffs had not threatened the defendant's husband with proceedings, there was no question of forebearance to sue which would have constituted good consideration. (See pp 146–150 below.)

Central Meats *v* Carney (1944) 10 Ir Jur Rep 34

Overend J.:

This action must be dismissed. The plaintiffs' claim is for an injunction restraining the defendant from supplying or selling, without the consent of the plaintiffs, cattle or meat to any person other than the plaintiffs in breach, as they allege, of the terms of a contract concluded between the plaintiffs, the defendant, and others on 28 September last. The present motion which in terms merely seeks an interlocutory injunction, is to be treated, by the wish of the parties, as the trial of the action. I have no pleadings before me other than the originating Summons and the Notice of Motion.

Para. 3 of Haskin's affidavit says that the contract between the parties is contained in five letters therein set out, and no other evidence has been given of the making of the alleged contract. The question is: Is there in existence an enforceable contract between the parties?

The first of these five letters is dated 25 September 1943, and is from Dublin Boned Meat, Ltd., to the plaintiffs. This letter was apparently written after a discussion between the parties, and it merely set out an outline of the proposition which they had been discussing, but does not constitute an offer.

From its terms it will be seen that Dublin Boned Meat Ltd, were proposing to 'guarantee to supply the plaintiffs with all the cattle which they obtain for canning purposes.' This seems to me to be a very vague term. No number of cattle is stated, and the proposal is subject to the parties coming to agreement as to two matters namely: alterations in price and an alteration in an insurance scheme.

This was followed by a second letter of 28 September from Dublin Boned Meat Ltd, to the plaintiffs. This letter provides that the cattle should be handled by Dublin Boned Meat Ltd, as agents for Irish Meat Suppliers Ltd, and for the plaintiffs, the killing of the beasts to be the responsibility of Dublin Boned Meat Ltd and that when the meat is boned and weighed the price is to be 10d per lb. This price is to be stabilised at that figure so far as possible, and in case any adjustment should be necessary Mr Staunton, one of the directors of Dublin Boned Meat Ltd, is to arbitrate. It is not clear, however, whether Staunton is to determine the necessity for any adjustment or merely the price to be fixed on adjustment.

Then comes the material clause by which the directors of Dublin Boned Meat Ltd, 'individually and collectively' agree to supply as many cattle as possible to the plaintiffs, and 'guarantee on no account to supply meat to any other Dublin or provincial canner without the consent of Central Meat Products and Irish Meat Suppliers'.

This would mean, no doubt, as many cattle as could be supplied, but there is nothing specific about the number, or the price, or the quality, and in my opinion, in the absence of these essential details, this letter cannot be regarded as a final offer.

In addition, it is important to note that the capacity of the plaintiffs to purchase cattle is limited by law as a result of a Government quota.

A third letter, bearing the same date and written by the plaintiffs to Dublin Boned Meat Ltd, is relied upon as an acceptance of the offer said to be contained in one or both of the preceding letters. The proposal for the supply of boned meat already made, however, related only to the companies concerned and not to any individual director, and accordingly this third letter of the 28 September, in which the plaintiffs merely accepted 'in principle' the proposals made to them, making that limited acceptance itself subject to conditions, was tantamount to a refusal to accept the offer, and was hardly even a counter offer. It was little more than an invitation to further discussions.

Then came the joint letter of the same date signed by all of the directors of Dublin Boned Meat Ltd, except Mr Flynn, which reiterates the proposals already outlined in the earlier letters. But this very document, which is relied upon by the plaintiffs as constituting an acceptance and thereby completing the contract, shows that there was no proposal for the supply of boned meat made at any time by any of the individual directors as such. This letter which is on the company's notepaper clearly does not establish an agreement by each of the signatories personally to be bound to the plaintiffs in the terms of the proposals set out in the long letter written earlier on the same day to which I have referred.

Accordingly in my opinion there is here no contract capable of enforcement at law between the plaintiffs and the defendant. The action accordingly must be dismissed with costs.

A. SUBJECT TO CONTRACT

It is common for agreements for the sale of land by private treaty to contain the term 'subject to contract'. Often parties will wish to ensure that the agreement will not be binding until a formal contract is signed by both parties. For example in the event of a higher offer being made to the vendor the latter would wish to be at liberty to accept. Much debate has occurred both in England and Ireland as to the precise effect of this phrase.

Thompson & Son Ltd *v* The King [1920] 2 IR 365

Following prolonged negotiations for the sale of a munitions factory in Waterford the defendants telegrammed the plaintiffs stating 'Will accept subject contract [*sic*] £24,200 . . .'. The plaintiffs replied by telegraph accepting the defendants' offer. When negotiations later broke down the plaintiffs sought specific performance of the contract.

Gibson J.:

The relevant principles of law are clear. The only difficulty in each case is as to their application. Where an offer and acceptance are made subject to a subsequent formal contract, if such contract is a condition or term which until performed keeps the agreement in suspense, the offer and acceptance have no contractual force. On the other hand, if all the terms are agreed on, and a formal contract is only contemplated as putting the terms in legal shape, the agreement is effectual before and irrespective of such formal contract. Where there is correspondence in the course of which it is alleged that a contract has been created, the whole correspondence should be read; but if it appears that a final agreement was come to at any stage, subsequent attempts to introduce new and varied terms must be disregarded. Subsequent letters, however, debating as to terms already discussed, may be material in considering whether there is any previous concluded bargain.

. . .

Did this expression 'subject contract' defer contractual obligation till a formal contract was settled, accepted, and executed; or does it mean that the purchase terms having been fully and finally settled, a further contract was only contemplated for the purpose of putting the bargain into legal shape, without substantial additions or alteration? I adopt the former construction. Considering the position of the minister and the limited company, the novel and somewhat loose character of the proposed bargain, the letters of 26 April and 8 May, the extreme brevity of the offer telegram, and the place in which, on the forefront of the telegram, the words occur, the expression conveys an essential condition without performance of which the proposed contract is incomplete. The telegram looks back to the letter of 26 April, which interprets it.

3. Taking the whole correspondence, telegrams, and draft in its original and amended form comprehensively together, I arrive at the conclusion of fact that there was no complete and binding contract.

Note

It is ironic that Gibson J. noted in this case that the law on this subject was settled and the only question with which he had to deal was its application.

Mulhall *v* Haren [1981] IR 364

An oral agreement was concluded between the plaintiffs and an auctioneer authorised by the defendants to sell their family home. The plaintiffs' solicitor later wrote to the auctioneer requesting a contract 'as the sale is subject to contract'. When the defendants refused to proceed with the sale the plaintiffs instituted an action claiming specific performance of the sale agreement.

Keane J.:

Had this question arisen prior to the decision of the English Court of Appeal in *Law v Jones*,[1] it would have been possible to resolve it with comparative ease. Indeed, I venture to think that, prior to that decision, very few members of either branch of the legal profession in England or Ireland would have thought that a writing which expressly stated that a sale of property was 'subject to contract' could constitute a memorandum or note sufficient to satisfy the Statute of Frauds. I believe that the same view would have been taken of a letter from a solicitor which formed part of a chain of correspondence commencing with a letter containing the 'subject to contract' stipulation. A series of authorities in both jurisdictions (commencing with *Winn v Bull*[2]) had established beyond serious doubt the principle that an oral agreement for the sale of the land which was stated to be 'subject to contract' was not enforceable. As a result, it had become a common practice for solicitors, who were acting for parties who had entered into such oral agreements, to commence the correspondence with a letter stating that the sale was 'subject to contract'. Their reasons for doing so were twofold. In the first place, they were conscious of the danger of committing their clients to an open contract for the sale of land by writing a letter which provided the necessary writing to satisfy the statute, a danger which was of particular significance having regard to the complexity of the law of real property. In the second place, they were alive to the possibility that disputes might arise as to the actual terms of the concluded bargain which could only result in expensive litigation.

But while this practice was common, it was by no means universal. Occasions arose, perhaps particularly in the sale of registered land, when the title was so abundantly clear as greatly to reduce the dangers to either party of an open title. There were also occasions on which solicitors, mindful of the fact that their clients had secured good bargains, avoided the use of the phrase 'subject to contract'. In such cases, however, the solicitors frequently used language which indicated that the parties contemplated the execution of a formal agreement. Thus, a solicitor initiating the correspondence, while not stating that the sale was 'subject to contract', might use some expression such as 'please let us have draft contract for approval'. In cases where a dispute arose as to whether, in such circumstances, an enforceable contract existed, the court had to undertake an enquiry as to what was the intention of the parties and, in particular, what was the significance of the fact that they contemplated the execution of a formal agreement. These cases must be carefully distinguished from the cases in which the documents stated that the sale was 'subject to contract'. They are fully reviewed in the judgment of Mr Justice Kenny in *Law v Robert Roberts & Co.*,[3] which was unanimously upheld by the Supreme Court on appeal. They are also reviewed in detail in the judgment delivered by Mr Justice Costello on 28 July 1977, in *Arnold v Veale*[4] (No. 3242P) where the judge was at pains to draw the distinction between the two lines of authority.

One of the earliest statements of the principle that the use of the phrase 'subject to contract' normally indicates that neither party to an arrangement intends to be bound by the terms of the arrangement until they are embodied in a form of contract is to be found in *Winn v Bull*. In that case, the defendant agreed with the plaintiff to take a lease of a house for a certain term at a certain rent 'subject to the preparation and approval of a formal contract.' No other contract was ever entered into between the parties. At p. 30 of the report Jessel M.R. said:

> Now with regard to the construction of letters which are relied upon as constituting a contract, I have always thought that the authorities are too favourable to specific performance. When a man agrees to buy an estate, there are a great many more stipulations wanted than a mere agreement to buy the estate and the amount of purchase money that is to be paid. What is called an open contract was formerly a most perilous thing, and even now, notwithstanding the provisions of a recent Act of Parliament—the Vendor and Purchaser Act, 1874—no prudent man who has an estate to sell would sign a contract of that kind, but would stipulate that certain conditions should be inserted for his protection. When, therefore, you see a stipulation as to a formal agreement put into a contract, you may say it was not put in for nothing, but to protect the vendor against that very thing. Indeed, notwithstanding protective conditions, the vendor has not unfrequently to allow a deduction from the purchase money to induce the purchaser not to press requisitions which the law allows him to make. All this shews that contracts for purchase of lands should contain something more than can be found in the short and meagre form of an ordinary letter.

At p. 32 Jessel M.R. said:

> It comes, therefore, to this, that where you have a proposal or agreement made in writing expressed to be subject to a formal contract being prepared, it means what it says; it is subject to and is dependent upon a formal contract being prepared. When it is not expressly stated to be subject to a formal contract it becomes a question of construction, whether the parties intended that the terms agreed on should merely be put into form, or whether they should be subject to a new agreement the terms of which are not expressed in detail. The result is, that I must hold that there is no binding contract in this case, and there must therefore be judgment for the defendant.

The latter passage was cited by Molony C.J. in the leading Irish case: *Thompson v The King*.[5] In that case, the words used were 'subject contract' and it was held that the agreement came within that might be called the 'subject to contract' line of authorities as distinct from the line of authorities applied in *Law v Robert Roberts & Co*. Accordingly, the agreement was held to be unenforceable. Gibson J. put the matter thus at p. 390 of the report: '2. Did the expression "subject contract" defer contractual obligation till a formal contract was settled, accepted, and executed; or does it mean that the purchase terms having been fully and finally settled, a further contract was only contemplated for the purpose of putting the bargain into legal shape, without substantial additions or alterations? I adopt the former construction.'

In *Lowis v Wilson*[6] an attempt was made to distinguish *Winn v Bull* on the ground that the agreement signed by Lowis, the plaintiff purchaser, stated that it was 'subject to the preparation of a formal contract to be prepared by W. O. Armstrong, Solicitor for the vendor . . . ' Dixon J. rejected the submissions that this rendered the case distinguishable from *Winn v Bull*. Recently, in *In re Hibernian Transport Cos Ltd*[7] Mr Justice Walsh said at p. 202 of the report: ' . . . in the ordinary course of events an agreement for the sale or purchase of land subject to contract means nothing more than an agreement to enter into a contract for the sale of land and, as such, it is not enforceable as if it were a contract.' It is right to say that this observation of the learned judge was probably *obiter*, but it is nonetheless noteworthy that no other member of the full Supreme Court who agreed with his judgment on the principal issue expressed any dissent from his view on this matter.

The same principle was applied in England in a number of cases subsequent to *Winn v Bull*: see *Sante Fé Land Co. Ltd v Forestal Land Co. Ltd*;[8] *Coope v Rideout*;[9] *Chillingworth v Esche*;[10] *Locket v Norman-Wright*;[11] *Keppel v Wheeler*;[12] *Raingold v Bromley*;[13] *George Trollope & Sons v Martyn Bros*[14]—that case was disapproved of by the House of Lords in *Luxor (Eastbourne) Ltd v Cooper*,[15] but not on this 'subject to contract' point—*Spottiswoode, Ballantyne & Co. v Doreen Appliances Ltd*[16] (per Lord Greene M.R. at p. 35) and *D'Silva v Lister House Ltd*.[17] It was also the view of a particularly strong Court of Appeal (consisting of Lord Greene M.R., Cohen and Asquith L.JJ.) in *Eccles v Bryant & Pollock*.[18] In this latter case, indeed, it was made clear that, in England at all events, where parties enter into an agreement for the sale of real property 'subject to contract', the contract is not complete until the parties have exchanged their copies in accordance with ordinary conveyancing practice in that country. Accordingly, in that case, even though the vendor's solicitors had signed the contract, it was held that the fact that no exchange of contracts had taken place was sufficient to prevent an enforceable contract from coming into being. In this country, however, the practice of exchanging contracts is not so universally followed as in England, at all events outside Dublin, as is borne out by the evidence of, [the solicitor for the plaintiffs]. Subject to this qualification, however, the law in both jurisdictions on this topic was the same and, until recent years, was settled, in my view, by this massive body of authority beyond any serious doubt.

But while the law on this topic had the advantages of reasonable certainty, it was also capable of producing results which appeared harsh and unjust. The extraordinary volatile market in land which developed in England and Ireland during the 1970s also led to a practice as unattractive as its name which is 'gazumping'. A vendor of land who had shaken hands on a deal frequently found himself with a substantially more attractive offer for the property within days, or even hours. There were many vendors who, whatever the temptations, refused to resile from bargains freely entered into, whether they were legally enforceable or not. But there were also some who either accepted the higher offer or went back to their original purchaser and attempted to squeeze more money out of him. Where no shadow of a memorandum in writing existed, even the most resourceful of lawyers or courts were powerless to redress such inequities unless, indeed, the doctrine of part performance could be successfully invoked. But where anything which could conceivably be regarded as a memorandum existed, considerable ingenuity was naturally expended upon bringing about the downfall of the 'gazumper'. It was perhaps to be expected that, in this context, some attempt would be made to dislodge the well entrenched 'subject to contract' rule.

The first bridgehead was effected in *Griffiths v Young*.[19]

. . .

It was argued on behalf of the plaintiff that the phrase 'subject to contract' was not a term of the contract but merely referred to a 'suspensive condition' which had been subsequently waived and could, accordingly, be ignored for the purpose of determining whether there was a sufficient memorandum or note of the agreement actually concluded. Widgery L.J., as he then was, thought the point a difficult one; but he appears to have accepted the general principle that a memorandum which, on its face, asserted that agreement had not been reached, could not be a memorandum for the purpose of s. 40. He accepted the submission made on behalf of the plaintiff that this principle had no application where the only defect in the memorandum was a reference to a 'suspensive provision' which had subsequently been waived. The other members of the court (Russell and Cross L.JJ.) came to the same conclusion, but neither of them appear to have experienced the same difficulty which troubled Widgery L.J. They were both satisfied that the subsequent oral waiver of the 'suspensive condition' cured any defect in the memorandum.

The far-reaching implications of the decision in *Griffiths v Young* soon became apparent when *Law v Jones* came before the same court—this time composed of Russell, Buckley and Orr L.JJ.

. . .

So far as the applicable law is concerned, the crucial passage from the judgment of Buckley L.J. appears at p. 124 of the report: 'But it is not, in my judgment, necessary that the note or memorandum should acknowledge the existence of a contract. It is not the fact of agreement but the terms agreed upon that must be found recorded in writing.'

. . .

In the words of Lord Denning M.R. at p. 159 of the report of *Tiverton Ltd v Wearwell Ltd*,[20] the decision in *Law v Jones* 'sounded an alarm bell' in the offices of every solicitor in England. I recall the decision being greeted with equal consternation in Ireland. In England, it prompted a leading article in the Solicitor's Journal (117 Sol J 293) and a lengthy correspondence from solicitors in the same periodical. The earliest possible opportunity was taken of questioning the correctness of the decision. The appeal from the order of Goulding J. in *Tiverton Ltd v Wearwell Ltd* was heard by the Court of Appeal (Lord Denning M.R., Stamp and Scarman L.JJ.) as a matter of urgency within a few months.

In the *Tiverton* case the plaintiffs orally agreed on 4 July 1973, on a sale of a property in Stepney to the defendants for £190,000. All the terms of the contract were agreed. Each side agreed to instruct their solicitors to confirm the sale. The purchasers' solicitors wrote on the same day to the vendors' solicitors as follows:

Empire House

We understand that you act for the vendor in respect of the proposed sale of the above-mentioned property to our clients Wearwell Ltd at £190,000 leasehold subject to contract. We look forward to receiving the draft contract for approval together with copy of the lease at an early date.

On the next day the vendors wrote to the purchasers as follows: 'This is to confirm my telephone conversation with you this morning when you agreed that the completion of the purchase of the property can take place as soon as possible.'

On 9 July the vendors' solicitors wrote to the purchasers' solicitors: 'We refer to your letter dated 4 July, upon which we have taken our client's instructions. We now send you draft contract for approval, together with a spare copy for your use, together with a copy of the lease dated 30 October 1934, and photocopy entries on our client's land certificate. We await hearing from you.'

On 19 July the vendors' solicitors wrote to the purchasers' solicitors saying that they understood that the matter was not proceeding any further. The purchasers' solicitors thereupon registered a caution at the Land Registry to prevent any dealings with the property by the vendors. The vendors thereupon issued proceedings claiming a declaration that there was no valid and enforceable contract, and asking for an order that the registration of the caution be vacated. Goulding J. ordered that the caution be cancelled and the purchasers appealed to the Court of Appeal. The appeal was specially expedited because of the importance of the point.

Lord Denning, after a detailed review of the authorities, summed up his view of the law as follows at p. 160 of the report: 'I cannot myself see any difference between a writing which—(i) denies there was any contract; (ii) does not admit there was any contract; (iii) says that the parties are in negotiation; or (iv) says that there was an agreement 'subject to contract', for that comes to the same thing. The reason why none of those writings satisfies the statute is because none of them contains any recognition or admission of the existence of a contract.' He thought that *Griffiths v Young* could be distinguished. In his view, however, *Law v Jones* was not capable of being distinguished; it was wrongly decided and should be overruled. In the course of his judgment, Lord Denning expressed his disagreement with the view of Buckley L.J. that authority for the proposition that the writing need not recognise the existence of a contract was to be found in a series of decisions dealing with offers in writing which were accepted by the other party by word of mouth or by conduct. He pointed out at p. 158 of the report that these were decisions of common law courts which did not recognise the doctrine of part performance and were, accordingly, necessary to meet the justice of the individual cases. It was accordingly held that a proposal made in writing but accepted verbally was capable of constituting a sufficient memorandum or note: see *Reuss v Picksley*.[21] But Denning M.R. also cited a passage from the judgment of Bowen L.J. in *In re New Eberhardt Co.*[22] in which he said that *Reuss v Picksley* had pushed the literal construction of the Statute of Frauds 'to a limit beyond which it would perhaps be not easy to go.'

At p. 162 of the report of the *Tiverton* case Stamp L.J. posed the question for decision as being ' . . . whether it is the law of England that a note or memorandum can satisfy the statute if, when read alone or with other documents which can properly be read with it, he who has signed it does not thereby recognise the existence of the contract upon which the other party seeks to make him liable.' He went on to say that the letter of 9 July 1973, whether read in isolation or together with the letter to which it was a reply, did not recognise the existence of a contract made orally on 4 July or any contract. While he does not say so in so many words, I think it is an inescapable inference that it was the use of the phrase 'proposed sale . . . subject to contract' in the letter of 4 July which rendered that letter incapable of being read as recognising the existence of a contract. Having gone on to consider the authorities in detail, at p. 168 of the report he summarised his view as follows: 'I consider that prior to the year 1970 it had been recognised by authorities binding upon this court (*viz. Buxton v Rust*[23] and *Thirkell v Cambi*[24]) that to satisfy the requirements of the statute there must be in the note or memorandum of the contract upon which the action is brought something to indicate that the party signing it thereby acknowledges or recognises the existence of the contract.' He also dealt with the 'offer' cases and said that they did not assist the defendants since those cases proceeded on the basis that a proposal in writing, though prior in time, could be a memorandum or note of a contract brought into being by the oral acceptance. He said that in such cases the court, in so holding, was accepting that the memorandum must recognise the contract on which the party charged is sued.

At p. 165 of the report of the *Tiverton* case Stamp L.J. quoted the succinct observation of Bowen L.J. in *In re Hoyle; Hoyle v Hoyle*[25] that the court, in determining whether a document is a sufficient memorandum, is not 'in quest of the intention of the parties, but only of evidence under the hand of one of the parties to the contract that he has entered into it.' At p. 167 he also pointed out that in *Buxton v Rust* (which was not cited to the court in *Law v Jones*) Willes J. and Lush J. both clearly indicated that, in their view, it was necessary that the letters relied on should constitute a recognition of the contract sued upon. At p. 170 he closely analysed the passage from *Chinnock v Ely*,[26] on which Buckley L.J. had placed reliance, and concluded that it did not support the inferences drawn from it by Buckley L.J. He went on to express his view that *Griffiths v Young*, in so far as it decides the contrary, was in conflict with the earlier decisions to which he had referred in his judgment. Although accepting that *Law v Jones* was plainly in conflict with the view of the law which he considered had been established by the earlier authorities, he did not consider that the court had jurisdiction to overrule it and simply preferred to follow the earlier authorities.

Scarman L.J. agreed with Stamp L.J. In the result, the appeal in the Tiverton case was dismissed. Leave to appeal to the House of Lords was granted but the appeal, so far as I can ascertain, was never pursued.

There are two features of the Tiverton case which are of cardinal importance. In the first place, it proceeded on the assumption that the evidence would establish, if the issue had to be resolved, that there was a concluded oral agreement for the sale of the property. In the second place, the letter containing the words 'subject to contract' was written by the solicitors for the purchasers, i.e. the party who was seeking to enforce the oral agreement. The letter which was relied on as a memorandum did not contain those words, but it formed part of the same chain of correspondence. In its major features, accordingly, that case is indistinguishable from the present case.

Since the other members of the court did not share the view of Lord Denning that the Court of Appeal in England had jurisdiction to overrule its earlier decisions, the position in theory in England is that there are at least two conflicting decisions of the Court of Appeal and that the law in that jurisdiction cannot be regarded as certain beyond doubt. However, I think that it is more sensible to regard the forceful judgments of Lord Denning and Stamp L.J. as representing the view of the law generally now held in England.

. . .

It appears to me that the wording of s. 2 of the Statute of 1695 plainly envisages a writing which is evidence of a contract entered into by the party sought to be charged, and that this is not met by a writing which uses language inconsistent with the existence of a concluded contract. It also appears to me that a long line of authorities has clearly established that the use of the words 'subject to contract' is inconsistent with the existence of a concluded agreement, save in the most exceptional cases.

The post–1970 Irish decisions commence with Arnold v Veale. That, as I have already indicated, was not a 'subject to contract' case when it was heard and decided by Mr Justice Costello. However, prior to the hearing of the defendant's appeal, a letter came to light written by the plaintiff to the defendant's auctioneer; in the course of that letter it was stated that certain matters remained to be agreed and that the sale was 'subject to contract'. The Supreme Court (the Chief Justice, Mr Justice Kenny and Mr Justice Parke) allowed the appeal. The main judgment of the Supreme Court was delivered ex tempore by Mr Justice Kenny and there is no written judgment available. However, it is clear from the judgment of Mr Justice Costello in the High Court that he found that there was a concluded oral agreement for the sale of the property. I appeared as counsel on the hearing of the appeal in the Supreme Court and my recollection is that it was not sought to disturb any finding of fact made by Mr Justice Costello and that the argument advanced on behalf of the defendant was that, in view of the plaintiff's letter to which I have referred, the correspondence could not constitute a sufficient memorandum to satisfy the requirements of the Statute of 1695. Accordingly, I take that decision as accepting, at least by implication, the principle that the writing relied on must acknowledge the existence of a concluded contract.

The next decision to which reference must be made is Kelly v Park Hall School.[27] In that case the trial judge (Mr Justice Hamilton) found that there was a concluded oral contract for the sale of the land. Two documents were relied upon as constituting a sufficient memorandum. The first was a letter dated 19 December 1977, from the auctioneers acting on behalf of the defendant vendors to the vendors' property adviser in the following terms·

Hall School—Lands at Rere

Dear Michael,

Further to our telephone conversation this morning, I confirm that we have agreed terms, subject to contract, for the sale of these lands to Mr Paddy Kelly of Berkeley Homes Ltd who were purchasers of the front lands. The principal terms to be included in the contract for sale are as follows:

> Proposed purchaser: Hickey, Beauchamp, Kirwan & O'Reilly (in trust).
> Proposed price: £175,000.

A non-refundable deposit of £35,000 to be paid on exchange of contracts, the balance to be paid not later than six months thereafter with interest at twelve per cent from the contract date until the closing date. I am sending a copy of this letter to Mr Haugh of A. & L. Goodbody and perhaps you could kindly confirm instructions to him on behalf of the Committee.

The second writing relied on was a letter from the defendants' solicitors to the plaintiffs' solicitors dated 13 January 1978, which enclosed a draft contract and concluded with the following sentence: 'On the instructions of our clients, this offer remains open for acceptance by your clients for a period of seven days only from the date of this letter and we are instructed that, if the contract is not back with us within the said period of time, duly executed, the offer is deemed to be withdrawn.' In the High Court Mr Justice Hamilton held that this latter document was a sufficient memorandum, since it enclosed a draft contract containing all the material terms. On appeal to the Supreme Court (Mr Justice Henchy, Mr Justice Kenny and Mr Justice Parke) it was held that the letter from the auctioneers dated 19 December 1977, was a sufficient memorandum, and the appeal was dismissed. Mr Justice Henchy said at p. 352 of the report:

> The case hangs on whether the letter of 19 December 1977, which I have quoted, constitutes a sufficient memorandum for the purpose of the Statute of Frauds. In my opinion it does. It *contains not only all the essential terms of the contract but also a recognition that a contract had been made*. It says: ' . . . we have agreed terms, subject to contract . . .' Since the judge, having heard oral evidence, held that the oral agreement recorded in the letter was a completed agreement in the sense that nothing further was left to be negotiated, the words 'we have agreed terms, subject to contract' must be taken to mean that a contract had been made, subject to its being formalised in writing. Therefore, it constitutes a sufficient memorandum.

The words which I have reproduced in italics appear to indicate an acceptance by Mr Justice Henchy of the proposition that the memorandum must recognise the existence of a concluded contract. Moreover, if the situation were otherwise, I consider it inevitable that the Supreme Court in that case would have expressed their disapproval of the decision in the *Tiverton* case. It is noteworthy that Mr Justice Henchy appears not to have shared the view of the High Court judge that the letter of 13 January 1978, was a sufficient memorandum—presumably because he did not consider that that letter recognised the existence of a concluded contract. I am fortified in arriving at this conclusion on the effect of the decision in the *Park Hall* case by the fact that a similar view of its effect was taken by Mr Justice Hamilton in *McInerney Properties Ltd v Roper*.[28]

While the decision in the *Park Hall* case seems to have proceeded on the basis that the memorandum must contain a recognition that a contract has been made, it might on first reading appear to lend support to the proposition that the words 'subject to contract' are not inconsistent with the existence of a concluded contract. If that were the effect of the decision, it would mean that the Supreme Court, by necessary implication, was disapproving of the decision in the *Tiverton* case and, also by implication, was overruling or disapproving of the long line of authority on the 'subject to contract' topic to which I have already referred. I doubt very much whether the Supreme Court intended to disapprove of the decision in the *Tiverton* case or to disturb the authorities in question. Had that been their intention, I think it would have been made clear in the judgment of Mr Justice Henchy. It may be significant that the plaintiff in the *Park Hall* case had already purchased the adjoining lands of the defendant and that, therefore, the title to the property being sold had been fully investigated by the plaintiff, so that the necessity for a formal contract had been significantly reduced. The actual wording used ('we have agreed terms, subject to contract') was also treated as being of importance. I think that the *Park Hall* case should properly be regarded as a special one decided on particular facts which do not arise in the present case and, as such, to be more akin to the *St Saviour's* case[29] . . .

The next case is *Casey v Irish Intercontinental Bank*.[30] In that case also the High Court found that there had been a concluded oral contract for the sale of the lands and that, as in the *Tiverton* case, the oral agreement had not been made expressly 'subject to contract'. However, the writing relied on as a memorandum, so far as material, was in the following terms: 'I, Patrick Casey, Gurrane House, Donoughmore, agree to purchase Park House and lands for £110,000 subject to contract and title. I agree to pay £25,250 as deposit.' Mr Justice Costello found in favour of the plaintiff. I believe that he did so in a written judgment but, as the text is not available in the Central Office, I cannot say what his reasons were for arriving at this conclusion. On appeal his decision was upheld by the Supreme Court (Mr Justice Henchy, Mr Justice Kenny and Mr Justice Parke). The main judgment in the Supreme Court (with which the other two judges agreed) was delivered by Mr Justice Kenny. The greater part of that judgment is taken up with a point which does not arise in the present case. The only reference to the fact that the writing relied on had used the phrase 'subject to contract and title' is in the following passage from the judgment of Mr Justice Kenny at p. 368 of the report:

> The words 'subject to contract and title' were not introduced into the transaction until 2 February when an oral contract for sale had already been made. Even if the reference to the contract and title is regarded as being incorporated in the contract, it does not make the execution of a contract a term of the agreement or a condition precedent to any contractual liability arising. I have already discussed this matter in the judgment which I gave, when I was a judge of the High Court, in *Law v Robert Roberts & Co*. That decision was affirmed by the Supreme Court and I do not intend to repeat what I said there.

Before preparing this judgment I read with the utmost care the judgment delivered by Mr Justice Kenny in *Law v Robert Roberts & Co*. In none of the letters to which reference is made in the statement of facts taken from that judgment (and appearing at pp 293–6 of the report) does the phrase 'subject to contract' or 'subject to contract and title' appear. Not merely are the letters in that case perfectly consistent with the existence of a concluded contract, but they go further. In his letter of 7 November 1960, Mr Hamilton, who was the auctioneer acting on behalf of the defendant vendors, said: 'We confirm herewith that acting on the instructions of our clients, Messrs Robert Roberts, we have accepted your offer of £4,750 and fees at 2½ per cent for the above property . . .'. *Law v Robert Roberts & Co*. is in no sense a decision on the meaning of the words 'subject to contract'. Nor is it an authority on the question as to whether a writing which does not acknowledge the existence of a concluded contract can be a sufficient memorandum. As the letter of 7 November 1960 (and the other letters referred to in the judgment) recognised in the plainest terms the existence of a concluded contract, that question did not arise. In these circumstances, I confess to finding some difficulty in understanding the reference to the *Roberts* case in the above passage from the judgment of Mr Justice Kenny in *Casey's* case.

In the course of argument counsel suggested that Mr Justice Kenny, in delivering judgment in *Casey's* case, must have overlooked the fact that the *Roberts* case was not an authority on the 'subject to contract' issue. Whether that be so or not, I must apply the law as stated by the Supreme Court. If this passage has the effect contended for by counsel for the plaintiffs, then, however that conclusion may have been arrived at, I am bound to apply the principle of law laid down. But it is stretching credibility too far for me to suppose that in this brief passage Mr Justice Kenny intended to overrule *Winn v Bull* and the other pre–1921 decisions on the 'subject to contract' point, *Thompson v The King* and *Lewis v Wilson*; and to express his disapproval of the numerous English authorities since 1921 on the same topic, culminating in the *Tiverton* case. Since *Casey's* case has not yet been reported, I do not know what arguments may have been advanced or what concessions made in the course of argument on either side. In these circumstances, I have come to the conclusion that I should not treat the decision as laying down any general principle of the nature contended for by counsel for the plaintiffs.

The last Irish case is *McInerney Properties Ltd v Roper*. In this case again the High Court (Mr Justice Hamilton) found as a fact that there was a concluded oral contract for the sale of the land. The writings relied on by the plaintiff as constituting a sufficient memorandum were two letters (each being headed 'subject to contract') dated 23 March and 17 April 1978, from the defendant's solicitors, and a draft contract which, it was claimed, was incorporated therewith. Mr Justice Hamilton, having considered the authorities and, in particular, *Law v Jones*, the *Tiverton* case and the *Park Hall* case, came to the conclusion that the letters were a sufficient memorandum. He summarised his conclusion as to the effect of the *Tiverton* case as follows: 'Consequently, it appears to me that the decision in *Tiverton Estates Ltd v Wearwell Ltd* was based not on the fact that the words "subject to contract" were used but that the writings sought to be relied upon as a sufficient note or memorandum did not contain an admission or a recognition that a contract had in fact been entered into.' That is a view which, with respect, I do not share. On the contrary, it seems to me that Lord Denning was at pains to emphasise that it was precisely the use of the words 'subject to contract' which prevented the writings from constituting an acknowledgement of the existence of a contract.

From this analysis of the authorities, I think that the following conclusions emerge:

1. A memorandum or note cannot satisfy the Statute of Frauds if, when it is read alone or with other documents which can properly be read with it, it does not contain a recognition, express or implied, of the existence of the oral contract sought to be enforced.

2. A letter, which expressly states that a transaction is 'subject to contract' cannot be a sufficient note or memorandum, since the use of those words is normally inconsistent with the existence of a concluded contract. It is only in certain rare and exceptional circumstances such as arose in *Kelly v Park Hall School* and *Michael Richards Properties v St Saviour's Parish* that the words 'subject to contract' can be treated as being of no effect.

3. In applying the two foregoing principles, it is immaterial whether the writing relied on itself contains the words 'subject to contract' or is part of a chain of correspon-

dence initiated by a letter which makes it clear that any oral agreement already arrived at is 'subject to contract'.

It seems to me that the application of those principles to the present case is sufficient to dispose of the contention that the letters referred to can be treated as a sufficient note or memorandum.

. . .

I indicated at an earlier stage of this judgment that there may indeed be cases in which a solicitor may feel that it is positively advantageous to his client to commit him to an open contract. I am far from saying that in such cases the solicitor is in any sense acting in dereliction of his duty to his client. But in the everyday case of a sale of property, where the parties have shaken hands on price but trust their respective solicitors to do everything that is necessary to protect them against all the traps and pitfalls that still beset the completion of sales of real property, a solicitor, in my view, is acting fully within the scope of his authority by making it clear in his initial letter that any oral agreement already concluded must be treated as 'subject to contract'. In so doing, he protects his client from the consequences of entering into an open contract. In the words of Lord Denning in the *Tiverton* case at pp 159–160 of the report, he does it 'in the confidence that it protects his client. It means that the client is not bound by what has taken place in conversation. The reason is that, for over a hundred years, the courts have held that the effect of the words "subject to contract" is that the matter remains in negotiation until a formal contract is executed . . .'.

That seems to me to be both good law and good sense. Its practical application is indeed well illustrated by the present case. I have already said that the oral agreement in this case was plainly unconditional. The parties did not expressly say that their oral agreement was 'subject to contract'. Nor did they say that it was subject to the plaintiffs obtaining the loan finance that they needed in order to complete the transaction; but [the solicitor for the plaintiffs] refrained from sending the formal contract back to the defendants' solicitors signed by his clients until such time as he was satisfied that they were in funds to complete the transaction. I have not the slightest doubt that the plaintiffs would have been appalled if, as a result of an unguarded letter written by [their solicitor] in the early stages of the transaction, they found themselves faced with serious financial consequences because, for some unforeseen reason, the offer of loan finance was suddenly withdrawn. If the plaintiffs' case is well founded, it would mean that, in those circumstances, they would have had no answer to a decree for specific performance in circumstances where they would not have had the finance to complete the transaction. The reason why the plaintiffs did not expressly say to [the solicitor for the defendants], or the defendants, that they regarded their oral agreement as subject to the obtaining of the necessary finance is obvious; they relied, as generations of house purchasers have relied, on the good sense and experience of their solicitors to protect them. If the submission made on behalf of the plaintiffs is well founded, it means that persons entering into property transactions of this nature have been deprived of a very important protection. For the reasons I have already given, I do not think that the *Park Hall* case and *Casey's* case would support so far-reaching a proposition. In so far as the proposition is supported by *Law v Jones* and *McInerney Properties Ltd v Roper*, I must respectfully decline to follow those decisions.

I should add that solicitors in search of guidance on this topic could not do better, in my view, than to follow the advice given in *Wylie's Irish Conveyancing Law* (Professional Books, 1978), the authority of which is, of course, substantially enhanced by the fact that the consultant editor for the Republic of Ireland is Mr Justice Kenny. At para. 9.047 on p.

364 Mr Wylie has this to say: 'Thirdly, if explicit instructions have not been obtained, the greatest care should be taken in dealing with all correspondence relating to the transaction. If it is intended that the matter should be regarded as still subject to negotiation, i.e. in the pre-contract stage, this should be stated expressly in the correspondence, perhaps, *all* correspondence, e.g. by entering a note that the matter is still "subject to contract".' And he adds in a footnote: 'This will probably be enough to prevent the correspondence from being regarded as a sufficient memorandum, i.e. by denying the existence of an agreement . . . ' In this case, I think that [the solicitor for the plaintiffs] achieved precisely that result by his prudence in making it clear in the initial letters that he wrote that the matter was still 'subject to contract'. I am satisfied that the use of those words was sufficient to prevent any subsequent letter in that correspondence from being a valid memorandum or note for the purpose of the Statute of Frauds.

There is another feature of the writing relied upon which is also fatal, in my view, to its validity as a memorandum or note for the purpose of the statute. It is clear that the writing must contain *all* the material terms of the oral agreement: *Hawkins v Price*[31] and per Lord Denning at p. 161 of the *Tiverton* case. In this case the letter from the defendants' solicitors dated 15 August 1978, expressly stated that the date for handing over possession remained to be agreed between the parties. In other words, one of the material terms was still in negotiation. Whether that statement correctly reflected the terms of the oral agreement is *nihil ad rem*; the fact remains that the writing relied upon expressly states that the closing date—a material item—remained to be agreed. There was, of course, no reference to the closing date in the other letters.

One cannot help feeling considerable sympathy for the plaintiffs in this case; but sympathy cannot determine the legal rights of the parties. I must apply the law as it appears to me to have been stated by courts of the highest authority in this country and in England. It follows that I must dismiss the plaintiffs' claim for specific performance.

[1] [1974] Ch. 112.	[11] [1925] Ch. 56.	[21] (1866) LR 1 Exch. 342.
[2] (1877) 7 ChD 29.	[12] [1927] 1 KB 577.	[22] (1889) 43 ChD 118.
[3] [1964] IR 292.	[13] [1931] 2 Ch. 307.	[23] (1872) LR 7 Exch. 279.
[4] [1979] IR 342n.	[14] [1934] 2 KB 436.	[24] [1919] 2 KB 590.
[5] [1920] 2 IR 365.	[15] [1941] AC 108.	[25] [1893] 1 Ch. 84.
[6] [1949] IR 347.	[16] [1942] 2 KB 32.	[26] (1865) 4 De G.J. & Sm. 638.
[7] [1972] IR 190.	[17] [1971] Ch. 17.	[27] [1979] IR 340
[8] (1910) 26 TLR 534.	[18] [1948] Ch. 93.	[28] (HC 31 July 1979).
[9] [1921] 1 Ch. 291.	[19] [1970] Ch. 675.	[29] [1973] 3 All ER 416.
[10] [1924] 1 Ch. 97.	[20] [1975] Ch. 146.	[30] [1979] IR 364.
		[31] [1947] Ch. 645.

Note

During the course of the arguments the plaintiffs claimed that the words 'subject to contract' had been inserted by their solicitor without their authority. Keane J. held however that the solicitor had implied authority to include this phrase. Although a solicitor may not alter the terms of an oral agreement already entered into by a client ('the unauthorised variation theory'), or indulge in further negotiations, he is bound to 'embody the bargain already concluded in a formal contract which gives his client the maximum protection consistent with the bargain'.

Boyle *v* Lee & Goyns [1992] ILRM 65

The facts

The plaintiff Eoin Boyle was a person who had experience of purchasing property and developing it. He was purchasing these premises as an investment property, the premises being let in a number of separate flats to separate tenants. His allegation was that the negotiations with regard to the purchase of the property took place orally between him and a Mr McManus who was a member of the staff of Lisney & Son, the auctioneers, and that as a result of those negotiations an agreement was reached for the sale by the defendants of the property to Mr Boyle for the sum of £90,000.

On the evidence of Mr Boyle, he was aware that the development which had so far taken place in the premises had not got full planning permission and was prepared to waive any difficulty in that context. He was also prepared to accept whatever the nature of the tenancies were and to buy subject to them on a representation made by Mr McManus that none of them were protected tenancies. With regard to the question of a deposit, he stated, at question 66, as follows:

Q. Now did the question of a deposit ever arise, was the question of a deposit ever suggested to you?
A. I asked Mr McManus was it necessary to go ahead and give him a deposit there and then, and he said no, it was not. If he had looked for a deposit I would have given it to him there and then; but he said that that was a matter that would be dealt with between the solicitors, that that would be caught up in the terms of the contract and the like later on, that was part of the formalities afterwards.

Further, dealing with the same topic and the question of a closing date, the evidence of Mr Boyle at questions 70 and 71 was as follows:

Q. But there was no agreement on the amount of the deposit?
A. No, there was no agreement on the amount of the deposit.
Q. No, and neither was any agreement as to when the sale would close?
A. There was no specific date mentioned because it was apparent to both Mr McManus and myself that I was very anxious to close the sale as soon as possible . . .

It is not in dispute on the evidence that there had been a series of offers rejected by Mr McManus on behalf of the vendors and that subsequently when the offer of £90,000 was finally made by the plaintiff that Mr McManus got the express authority of his clients to accept that figure. It was further not in dispute that at some time immediately prior to 8 July 1988 the plaintiff had satisfied himself as to the structural condition of the premises by the inspection of an architect and had arranged the entire finance for the immediate purchase of the premises.

On 8 July 1988 Mr McManus wrote to Mr Patrick J. Walsh, solicitor for the vendors, in the following terms:

Re: Mrs Maura Lee & Mrs E.N. Goyns, Premises 32 Elgin Road, Dublin 4

Dear Mr Walsh,

We refer to the recent negotiations in connection with the above property. I now write to confirm that we have received instructions from the vendors to accept an offer of IR£90,000 subject to contract. I would be obliged if you would prepare, and forward the contract which should incorporate the following agreed terms.

Proposed purchasers: Eoin Boyle & Susan Boyle, 165 Rathgar Road, Dublin 6.
Proposed purchase price: IR£90,000 subject to contract.
Proposed purchaser's solicitors: Patrick Clyne, Martin E. Marron & Co.
    10 Northumberland Road, Dublin 4.
Contents: Contents of the apartments are included in the sale price.
Tenants: The property is being sold subject to, and with the benefits of the tenants.
Closing date: As soon as legal formalities can be completed.

I am sending a copy of this letter to Mrs Lee and Mrs Goyns for their information. In the meantime, you will appreciate that this letter is for information purposes only, and does not by itself, constitute part of a binding contract. I trust that the sale will proceed smoothly and satisfactorily and if I can assist you further at this stage, please let me know.

Yours sincerely,

Mr McManus had given evidence at the hearing in the High Court, firstly, that it was a fixed policy of the firm of auctioneers to which he belonged not to purport to bind any client with regard to the sale of a property by any writing made by a member of the firm and that it was for that reason and in accordance with that policy and his instructions that he inserted the phrase 'subject to contract' in two separate places in the letter of 8 July 1988. He stated that he believed he must have conveyed to Mr Boyle the fact that their negotiations were subject to contract, but he could not affirmatively state that he had used that particular expression. With regard to the question of a deposit, he had also given evidence that it was a fixed policy of his firm not under any circumstances to accept or fix the amount of a deposit in any sale in which they were dealing and that it was for that reason that he informed the plaintiff that that would have to be arranged between the solicitors. He maintained that at all stages he did not intend to bind the vendors. He did not purport to say that the vendors had in any way forbidden him to bind them, and agreed that on the same date as he wrote to Mr Walsh the letter which has just been quoted, he wrote to each of the vendors an identical letter in the following terms:

Re: 32 Elgin Road, Ballsbridge, Dublin 4

I enclose for your information a copy of the letter which I have this day sent to your solicitor, Mr Patrick J. Walsh, in connection with the sale of your above property.

The survey has been carried out by the bank for the purchaser, and I would expect that the sale would now proceed without undue delay. I will keep you informed as to progress.

Yours sincerely.

The vendors did not pursue the sale of the premises any further with this purchaser, and no further documentation or facts arise which are relevant to this claim.
. . .

Issues argued

By order of 24 April 1989 made by Costello J., it was *inter alia* directed that certain issues should be tried between the parties so as to determine the motion then before the court. Those issues which were to be argued were as follows, when finally agreed between the parties.

(a) Whether prior to 8 July 1988 there was a concluded oral agreement between the plaintiff as purchaser and the defendants as vendors for the sale by the defendants to the plaintiff of the premises No. 32 Elgin Road in the City of Dublin, at the price of £90,000. On that issue the learned trial judge found the answer to be *yes*.
(b) If there was such a concluded oral agreement, what were the other terms thereof? The answer made by Barrington J. in his order of 30 June 1989 to that question was as follows:

    (i) The vendors were Mrs Lee and Mrs Goyns.
    (ii) The premises were 32 Elgin Road in the City of Dublin.
    (iii) The purchasers were Eoin Boyle and Susan Boyle.
    (iv) The purchase price was £90,000.
    (v) The sale was to include the contents of the apartments.
    (vi) The property was being sold subject to and with the benefit of the tenants.
    (vii) The closing date was to be as soon as the legal formalities were completed.

(c) If there was such a concluded oral agreement, whether there was sufficient note or memorandum of the said oral agreement to satisfy the Statute of Frauds (Ireland) 1695, contained in the letter dated 8 July 1988 from Lisney & Son to P. J. Walsh & Co., and to that issue the learned trial judge made the answer *yes*.

. . .

Grounds of the appeal

The defendants appeal to this court on two grounds.

(a) That the learned trial judge misdirected himself in law and on the facts in holding that the evidence supported or was capable of supporting a finding that prior to 8 July 1988 there was a concluded oral agreement for the sale of the premises at £90,000.
(b) That the learned trial judge erred in law in holding that the letter dated 8 July 1988 from Mr McManus to Messrs P. J. Walsh & Co. constituted a sufficient note or memorandum of an oral agreement to satisfy the Statute of Frauds 1695.

Finlay C.J.:

In the course of his judgment the learned trial judge stated that he believed both of the witnesses to be honest and candid in their evidence. His findings on the question as to whether an oral contract for sale had been made, and completely made, between the plaintiff and Mr McManus is based not, therefore, on the acceptance of the truth of one witness and the rejection of the truth or accuracy of another, but rather on inferences which he drew from the evidence. In particular, his finding that the failure of the parties to reach any agreement on the question of a deposit was irrelevant since it was of no importance in the contract, is a mixed finding of law and fact.

In my view, this finding was in error. The amount of a deposit to be made, even if a purchaser is willing to make a deposit of the appropriate amount, or the usual amount then experienced in transactions in Dublin, is too important a part of a contract for the sale of land in the large sum of £90,000 to be omitted from a concluded and complete oral agreement unless the parties in such an agreement had agreed that no deposit would be paid. In this case the evidence irresistibly leads to the conclusion that both Mr Boyle and Mr McManus agreed that there had to be a deposit, but left it over to be agreed between the solicitors when the formal contract was being settled as to its amount and form. In my view, that evidence, which was not in contest, must lead to a conclusion that there was not a complete contract made orally between Mr Boyle and Mr McManus before 8 July 1988.

That conclusion would determine this appeal, but since both parties have made the most careful and detailed submissions to this court on the legal questions arising with regard to the sufficiency of the note or memorandum, consisting of the letter written by Mr McManus to Mr Walsh, and since the submissions so made raise in question the meaning and effect of previous decisions of this court, I am satisfied that I should express a view on the questions thus raised.

Adequacy of the note or memorandum

S. 2 of the Irish Statute of Frauds of 1695, in so far as its provisions are relevant to the issues in this action, is as follows:

> . . . no action shall be brought whereby to charge . . . any person . . . upon any contract or sale of lands, tenements or hereditaments, or any interest in or concerning them, . . . unless the agreement upon which such action shall be brought, or some memorandum or note thereof shall be in writing and signed by the party to be charged therewith, or some other person thereunto by him lawfully authorised.

I have carefully considered this section, and leaving aside for the moment the strength or weakness of contending decisions, it appears clear that the section required that the *agreement* with which the person concerned was to be charged, had either to be in writing and signed by the party to be charged, or to be evidenced by some memorandum or note in writing, signed by the party to be charged. This must, it seems to me, inevitably lead to the conclusion that such of the decisions as speak of the necessity for the terms to be evidenced by a note or memorandum, or for the important terms, or necessary terms, to be so evidenced are, strictly speaking, incorrect.

It is obvious that in certain instances a total recital of all the necessary ingredients of a contract for the sale of land, that is to say, the names of the purchaser and the vendor, the exact description of the property and such other terms as would be considered essential, namely, the price, deposit, closing date, resume of the title, etc., could without any other expression indicating an acknowledgment of a binding or completed contract, necessarily imply the existence of such a contract.

Where, however, on the other hand, a document which contains a recital of certain terms, obviously relevant to a purchase and sale of land, purports to deny the existence of a completed or concluded contract, or makes use of expressions specially adapted to exclude the existence of a completed or concluded contract, it does not seem to me that as a matter of first principle the terms of s. 2 of the Act of 1695 could be complied with.

The argument largely put against this strict interpretation, which is, of course, an acceptance of the broad statement of principle to which I have already referred, and which is contained in the judgment of Keane J. in *Mulhall v Haren*, is that a party to an orally concluded agreement which is complete and intended to be complete, should not be permitted by the unilateral insertion into a note or memorandum in writing which he makes of the terms of that agreement, of a denial of it, or of a provision such as the phrase 'subject to contract' which is inconsistent with it, to escape on his own behalf or on behalf of this principal, from the enforcement of the contract.

To advance that argument is, of course, attractive but, in my view, it necessarily involves the precise mischief which the Statute of Frauds of 1695 was intended to avoid, and that is that it invites the court to amend by deletion, or by ignoring one of its terms, the note or memorandum relied upon by the plaintiff and signed by the defendant, such amendment or deletion depending on the finding by the court on oral evidence as to what was the agreement between the parties.

Such a principle clearly puts the oral evidence as superseding the only written evidence that is available. In broad terms, it is the clearest possible purpose of the Statute of Frauds 1695 to put the written evidence as dominant and superseding any oral evidence.

It is possible, without much difficulty, to see on consideration of the cases to which we have been referred, that the many instances which occurred of the making of contracts orally for the sale of land the existence of which and the complete nature of which is not even denied in subsequent litigation, has led courts to view with considerable disfavour the defence of non-enforceability due to a want of sufficient note or memorandum under the Statute of Frauds. It does not seem to me, however, that it can be justified, having regard to the obligation of the courts in the implementation of a plain statutory provision, to introduce into the interpretation of s. 2 of the Act of 1695 clauses or provisos which are not consistent with its plain meaning. Furthermore, all one's experience of the massive losses and inconvenience which can be suffered by prospective purchasers or vendors of land from non-completion of what they believe to be a contract, and the subsequent delays and difficulties arising from complicated litigation concerning it, indicates that the requirements of justice are that the law applicable to the formation of contracts for the purchase of land should be as certain as it is possible to make it. In modern times, probably the most important legal transaction a great number of people make in their lifetimes is the purchase or sale of their home. The avoidance of doubt and, therefore, the avoidance of litigation concerning such a transaction must be a well worthwhile social objective, as far as the law is concerned. To that end, certainty in the question of what is or is not a sufficient note or memorandum is a desirable aim. In my view, the very definite statement that a note or memorandum of a contract made orally is not sufficient to satisfy the Statute of Frauds unless it directly or by very necessary implication recognises, not only the terms to be enforced, but also the existence of a concluded contract between the parties, and the corresponding principle that no such note or memorandum which contains any term or expression, such as 'subject to contract' can be sufficient, even if it can be established by oral evidence that such term or expression did not form part of the originally orally concluded agreement achieves that certainty. The existence of such a rule or provision would not, in my view, allow for the 'exceptional cases' mentioned by Keane J. in the decision in *Mulhall v Haren*.

The decision in *Kelly v Park Hall School Ltd*, in so far as it appears to amend by deletion the note or memorandum in writing, signed on behalf of the vendor, by reference to the evidence of the oral agreements which had previously been arrived at between the parties, with great reluctance, is not a decision which I think this court can and should follow.

Similar considerations may, it seems to me, apply to the decision of this court in *Casey v Irish Intercontinental Bank*, though a decision on the validity of the concept of oral waiver of a suspensory condition in the writings which were part of the formation of the contract, is not a question at issue in this case. I would, therefore, allow this appeal . . .

(Hederman J. concurred.)

McCarthy J.:

It is a feature of property transactions in Ireland that they are often made with a minimum of formality, the circumstances, including the venue, of such bargains not being always conducive to the 'dusty purlieus of the law' (see Tennyson, In *Memoriam,* lxxxix). If parties are agreed on the terms which they regard as essential, it is not for others to evaluate with a different result. Mr Boyle was prepared to accept the tenancies; so what did it matter to Mr McManus? Mr Boyle offered a substantial deposit but Mr McManus said that that was a matter that would be dealt with between the solicitors and there would have been no problem about it. So also, both parties were anxious to close the sale and that would have been taken care of by the solicitors. As Mr Boyle said, (Q. 76) 'What he in fact said was, we had done a deal, and the solicitors would have to take care of the formalities.' The fact that one party says that there had been a deal would not make it so, if it were not in fact so. Equally, the fact that someone believes that no deal has been done would not make that necessarily so. In my view, Barrington J. was entitled to come to the conclusion that the parties had done a deal, the formalities to be cleared up by the solicitors. It may have been a highly informal deal; it may have omitted a variety of details that would be high in a lawyer's list of priorities, and Mr McManus may well have thought that there was no enforceable deal, but, in my judgment, there was a deal that contained all that the parties deemed essential. Mr McManus' caution, however, was to prove valuable.

The Statute of Frauds

The statute of 1695 (7 Will. III. c. XII) provides, so far as relevant:

> No action shall be brought whereby to charge any person upon any contract or sale of land, tenements, or hereditaments, or any interest in or concerning them unless the agreement upon which such action shall be brought, or some memorandum or note thereof, shall be in writing, and signed by the party to be charged therewith, or some other person thereunto by him lawfully authorised.

There was similar wording in the English Statute of Frauds 1677; in the three centuries since, this simple provision has provided the feedstock for a vast display of legal semantics, both academic and judicial. The Act as passed called for 'prevention of many fraudulent practices which are commonly endeavoured to be upheld by perjury and subornation of perjury.' It did not always have this desirable effect; genuine bargains could not be enforced because of the absence of the note or memorandum or some inadequacy in it. The section came to be construed as liberally as possible—seeking to 'find' the necessary evidence once the bargain was proved until, as appears to me to be the case, a note or memorandum which necessarily denied the existence of a bargain became itself evidence to support its enforcement. In my judgment, that is what happened here. Mr McManus wrote a letter to his client's solicitors, sending a copy to each of his clients, the vendors, recounting his instructions to accept the offer of £90,000 'subject to contract', a phrase repeated in the context of the proposed purchase price. He went on to say 'in the meantime, you will appreciate that this letter is for information purposes only, and does not by itself, constitute part of the binding contract.' It identified the agreed terms including price, 'the benefits of the tenants |sic|' and a closing date such as I have instanced. It made no reference to a deposit, because there was no agreement as to deposit save that there might be one. Mr McManus had no intention of evidencing an agreement; it was contrary to the fixed policy of his firm. If the letter to the solicitors is to be held to provide the required compliance with s. 2 of the statute, it means that the note itself has to be disregarded wherever it conflicts with the findings of fact made in respect of the oral agreement, and yet be used as the necessary evidence to support an action to enforce that agreement. In short, it means that the words 'subject to contract' do not mean what they say. In *Mulhall v Haren*, Keane J. made an exhaustive analysis of the Irish and English case law and concluded that *Tiverton Estates Ltd v Wearwell Ltd* correctly represented the law of England and should be followed unless it had been disapproved of in Ireland. He said:

> it appears to me that the wording of s. 2 of the statute of 1695 plainly envisages a writing which is evidence of a contract entered into by the party sought to be charged, and that this is not met by a writing which uses language inconsistent with the existence of a concluded contract. It also appears to me that a long line of authorities has clearly established that the use of the words 'subject to contract' is inconsistent with the existence of a concluded agreement, save in the most exceptional cases.

In *Mulhall*, Keane J. sought to distinguish *Kelly v Park Hall School* and *Casey v Irish Intercontinental Bank*, the one as being a special case decided on particular facts and the other as not laying down any general principle in support of using a 'subject to contract' note as sufficient for the statute. I find it difficult so to distinguish these two cases. No particular set of facts surrounding the making of the contract itself can relieve a plaintiff from giving the necessary evidence in writing; I find it impossible not to read *Casey's* case as other than holding that the words 'subject to contract' in the memorandum did not mean what they said. It follows that in my view neither case should be followed. It may well be thought that this rigidity of construction will result in genuine bargains not being enforced and that a court should, as I believe it has in the past 'to do a great right, do a little wrong' (see *Merchant of Venice*, IV i, 215). It is reasonable to assume that the writing requirement is well known to owners and buyers of land; Portia's rule of construction is the preferred alternative.

Conclusion

It follows that part of the deal between the parties was that the deal itself was subject to contract; in that sense, the deal was incomplete. As I understand it, the law does not recognise as enforceable a contract to enter into a contract. In any event, whatever be the exact nature of the deal, the terms of Mr McManus' letter cannot be used to meet the requirements of the Statute of Frauds.

I would allow the appeal, set aside the order of the High Court, and answer the questions posed in the manner set out in the judgment of the Chief Justice; and dismiss the action.

O'Flaherty J.:

During the hearing of the appeal, we have had the benefit of elaborate arguments by both sides on the concept of 'subject to contract'. This incantation has no talismanic property.

Before examining this phrase at all, it is necessary to go back to the rudiments of the law of contract and find out whether there was an offer and acceptance and an intention to create legal relations. That there was an agreement on price, offer and acceptance, there is no doubt. But beyond that, in my judgment, there was much to be sorted out. For a start, the matter of the tenancies was not resolved. It was easy for Mr Boyle to say at the trial that he was prepared to take the property subject to the tenancies whatever kind they were—but one of his answers suggested that he might have had to engage in litigation because of what he felt was a misrepresentation in relation to a tenant who had, in effect, a six-year tenancy. It is common case that Mr McManus left him under the impression that they were all short tenancies, meaning thereby not more than one year. Then, there was no closing date agreed. Mr McManus expressly declined to take a deposit believing that that was a matter proper to be put into the formal contract. So, it appears to me, that there was no *consensus ad idem*. There was, at the most, an agreement to agree. Further, Mr McManus's disposition was that he did not regard himself as an agent to bind his principals. He was their agent to get the best price that he could for the house and to conclude an agreement in honour to sell it at that price, but, prudently, as I believe, he did not think that he should be involved any further. I am puzzled as to how anyone can be anyone else's agent without taking on expressly the burden of such agency. (I leave aside special cases where through operation of law an agency may arise). I use the word 'burden' advisedly because, to take this case, there was so much that could have gone wrong with this sale if one were to assume that what passed between Mr Boyle and Mr McManus amounted to an agreement. I am leaving aside the Statute of Frauds point for the moment and I am prepared to assume that the agreement was capable of being proved. To what was Mr McManus exposing his firm? He certainly had not found out enough about the tenancies either to safeguard himself or bind Mr Boyle. The planning situation was another potential nightmare. In a word, if Mr McManus had truly bound his principals in the circumstances of this case, he was very likely preparing a bed of nails for himself and his firm and would open up the prospect of being sued in negligence by both his principals and by Mr Boyle.

On this aspect of the case, therefore, I reach the conclusion that there was no binding contract entered into between Mr Boyle and Mr McManus. The matter was subject to a formal contract being drawn up and, in any event, all the essential terms of the agreement had not been finalised.

Further, in the chronology which I have so far sketched, there was no enforceable agreement because there was nothing in writing.

. . .

And so I turn to a consideration of the 'subject to contract' cases. The phrase is used twice in the letter of 8 July and, in addition, Mr McManus made clear that the letter was written for information purposes only and did not by itself constitute part of a binding contract.

I cannot conceive of any language that could more clearly express the denial of the existence of a binding contract short of saying: 'Existence of contract denied'.

The historic purpose of the phrase 'subject to contract' or some similar phrase, was to keep negotiations in train and to allow either party to resile from the agreement made. That was the position for over a hundred years until in the 1970s property prices both in England and here became volatile. This led to the practice of 'gazumping' and since it is regarded as an odious thing, in the spirit of examining anything that may be said in defence of it, I put forward the views of Farrand, *Contract and Conveyance* (4th ed. 1980) 17:

> This established ability to resile led eventually to the imaginatively named and much maligned sub-practice of 'gazumping' i.e. of potential vendors increasing the agreed price of property (especially houses) sold 'subject to contract' and the ignominy seems to extend also to selling at an increased price to a different purchaser. The original prospective purchaser will nowadays have a tendency to flaunt his disappointment and indignation, for one thing he will likely enough have been hit in the pocket (e.g. surveyor's fees) and for another he may not be willing or able to pay more. Is the potential vendor to be blamed? It is true that most solicitors and many clients will say that they regard an agreement 'subject to contract' as morally, if not legally, binding (see, e.g. *Pimms Ltd v Tallow Chandlers in the City of London* |1964| 2 QB 547 at p. 552). Yet much more worthy of notice is Sachs J.'s penetrating judgment on:
>
>> this hybrid type of 'subject to contract' transaction which is so often referred to as a gentleman's agreement but which experience shows is only too often a transaction in which each side hopes the other will act like a gentleman and neither intends so to act if it is against his material interests (*Goding v Frazer* |1967| 1 WLR 286, at p. 293).

And, for example, the duty of trustees to sell only at the best price reasonably obtainable will override commercial morality, i.e. on receiving a higher offer before exchange, they must 'gazump'. This is subject, of course, to the dictates of proper prudence which would permit trustees to pray in aid the common sense rule underlying the old proverb: 'A bird in the hand is worth two in the bush' (per Wynn-Parry J., in *Buttle v Sunders* |1950| 2 All ER 193 at p. 195). Nevertheless, the current state of the housing market must surely lead even common prudence to speak in almost all cases for the better price.

The foundation case on this topic is *Chinnock v Marchioness of Ely* (1865) 4 De G. J. & S. 638. The facts of that case bear a certain resemblance to the facts of the present case in that the Marchioness of Ely had purchased a house which was the subject of very special conditions of sale and she was advised by her solicitor that she could not sell with safety without the sale being subject to the same or similar stipulations. The estate agent was so instructed and kept strictly to his instructions and made clear that he was not entitled to enter a binding agreement on behalf of his principal. But then after a certain hiatus in negotiations the vendor's solicitor wrote a letter to the plaintiff as follows at p. 644:

> We have been instructed by the Marchioness of Ely to proceed with the sale to you of these premises. The draft contract is being prepared, and will be forwarded to you for approval in a few days.

The submission made was that these words were a clear recognition of the fact that there had been a complete sale to the plaintiff and, at all events, amounted to a distinct acceptance of the terms stated by the plaintiff. Lord Westbury L.C. said that the words 'we are instructed to go on' were written with reference to the fact that the former proceedings had been interrupted by a temporary change of purpose on the part of the marchioness, but whether the words are taken in the one sense or the other, they cannot be severed from the rest of the letter, which describes the manner in which the sale was to be proceeded with, namely, by the preparation of a draft contract, which should be forwarded to the plaintiff for approval. Lord Westbury L.C. said at pp 645–6:

> I entirely accept the doctrine contended for by the plaintiff's counsel . . . that if there had been a final agreement, and the terms of it are evidenced in a manner to satisfy the Statute of Frauds, the agreement shall be binding although the parties may have declared that the writing is to serve only as instructions for a formal agreement, or although it may be an express term that a formal agreement shall be prepared and signed by the parties. As soon as the fact is established of the final mutual assent of the parties to certain terms, and those terms are evidenced by any writing signed by the party to be charged or his agent lawfully authorised, there exist all the materials, which this court requires, to make a legally binding contract.
>
> But if to a proposal or offer an assent be given subject to a provision as to a contract, then the stipulation as to the contract is a term of the assent, and there is no agreement independent of this stipulation.

That decision was followed in *Winn v Bull* (1877) 7 ChD 29. The agreement in that case was made 'subject to the preparation and approval of a formal contract'. Jessel M.R. said at pp 30–31:

> I am of the opinion there is no contract. I take it the principle is clear. If in the case of a proposed sale or lease of an estate two persons agree to all the terms and say, 'We will have the terms put into form', then all the terms being put into writing and agreed to, there is a contract.
>
> If two persons agree in writing that up to a certain point the terms shall be the terms of the contract, but that the minor terms shall be submitted to a solicitor, and shall be such as are approved of by him, then there is no contract, because all the terms have not been settled.
>
> Now with regard to the construction of letters which are relied upon as constituting a contract, I have always thought that the authorities are too favourable to specific performance. When a man agrees to buy an estate, there are a great many more stipulations wanted than a mere agreement to buy the estate and the amount of purchase money that is to be paid. What is called an open contract was formerly a most perilous thing, and even now, notwithstanding the provisions of a recent Act of Parliament—the Vendor and Purchaser Act 1874—no prudent man who has an estate to sell would sign a contract of that kind, but would stipulate that certain conditions should be inserted for his protection. When, therefore, you see a stipulation as to a formal agreement put into a contract, you may say it was put in for nothing, but to protect the vendor against that very thing. Indeed, notwithstanding protective conditions, the vendor has not unfrequently to allow a deduction from the purchase money to induce the purchaser not to press requisitions which the law allows him to make.
>
> All this shows that contracts for purchase of lands should contain something more than can be found in the short and meagre form of an ordinary letter.

In the House of Lords decision of *Rossiter v Miller* (1878) 3 App Cas 1124 Lord Cairns L.C. at p. 1139 said in relation to Lord Westbury's judgment:

. . . I entirely acquiesce in what he says, that if you find, not an unqualified acceptance of a contract, but an acceptance subject to the condition that an agreement is to be prepared and agreed upon between the parties, and until that condition is fulfilled no contract is to arise, then undoubtedly you cannot, upon a correspondence of that kind, find a concluded contract.

Now it is important to recall, I think, that most of these 'subject to contract' cases deal with correspondence passing *inter partes*. We have not that here. All that we have here is a letter sent by the estate agent to the clients' solicitor informing him, in broad outline, what had been agreed, but making clear that no *binding agreement* had been entered into.

Conclusions

In the circumstances, I do not think it necessary to traverse the ground that was so ably covered by Keane J. in the course of his judgment in *Mulhall v Haren*. While I appreciate that it would be possible to confine my judgment within a narrow ambit, out of deference to the elaborate arguments that were advanced before us, I feel I should give my conclusions as fully as possible. They are:

(1) The letter of 8 July 1988 does not satisfy the Statute of Frauds in that it makes clear that while there has been a measure of agreement reached, matters remain in a state of suspension pending the execution of a formal contract; in other words the negotiations have not been concluded. In addition, as I have already pointed out, the letter did not contain all the terms that the parties intended should be part of their bargain and which they intended would find expression in the formal contract.

(2) In order to satisfy the Statute of Frauds, the actual contract must be in writing or there must be some memorandum or note thereof. The agreement must be one where there is an intention to create legal relations and the writing must contain all the essential terms which had been agreed.

(3) The expression 'subject to contract' or 'subject to a formal contract being drawn up' or the like is *prima facie* a strong declaration that a concluded agreement does not exist. I would hold that there must be cogent evidence of a contrary intention before such a phrase is put to one side. I would equate it to 'existence of contract denied'. In this regard, the decisions of this Court in *Kelly v Park Hall School* and *Casey v Irish Intercontinental Bank* must be regarded as exceptional and confined to the peculiar facts found in each case and as properly confined to the era in which they were decided. I do not regard them as reversing the principles laid down in the nineteenth century decisions to which I have referred.

(4) Even if an oral agreement is concluded, and it is not itself made 'subject to contract' or the like nevertheless if the initiating correspondence thereafter contains that or a similar phrase, this involves that there is not a recognition, express or implied, of the existence of an oral agreement in the sense of one meant to be a binding contract.

(5) The 'written offer accepted orally' position is anomalous but is explained, I think, by the fact that once there is an oral acceptance of a written offer it is at that moment that a contract comes into existence and, therefore, the note or memorandum becomes relevant. See *Colgrave v Upcot* 5 Vin Abr 527 and *Reuss v Picksley* (1886) LR 1 Ex 342 and the discussion of this topic in the cases of *Law v Jones* |1974| Ch. 112; *Tiverton Estates Ltd v Wearwell Ltd* |1975| Ch. 146 and *Daulia Ltd v Four Millbank Nominees Ltd* |1978| 2 WLR 621. See, too, *Mulhall v Haren* p. 383 et seq.

. . .

In the circumstances, I would answer the questions posed: that there was no concluded oral agreement in the month of July 1988, and, even if there were, that the memorandum or note thereof relied upon is not sufficient to satisfy the Statute of Frauds.

I would allow the appeal.

Egan J.:

It is submitted that certain terms remained outstanding and these would include the closing date, the deposit and final details in relation to the tenancies. It should be emphasised that I am now dealing only with the question as to whether or not there was a concluded oral agreement. The wording of the memorandum dated 8 July 1988 is irrelevant in relation to this question. I will deal with the terms which are alleged to be 'outstanding':

1. *The tenancies*

It is abundantly clear on the evidence that the plaintiff agreed to accept the tenancies as they stood even though he knew that they did not conform with the planning permission.

2. *The closing date*

The learned trial judge was satisfied on the evidence that the closing date was to be 'as speedily as the legal formalities have been completed' and that it did not appear in the circumstances of the case to be a term of any real significance. It has long been established that where no time for performance is agreed the law implies an undertaking by each party to perform his part of the contract within a time which is reasonable having regard to the circumstances of the case: *Simpson v Hughes* (1896) 66 LJ Ch. 143.

Words such as 'as soon as possible' would also be construed by reference to what would be reasonable in the circumstances: *Hydraulic Engineering Co. Ltd v McHaffie Goslett & Co.* (1878) 4 QBD 670 (CA).

It is clear, therefore, that words which mean 'as speedily as the legal formalities have been completed' are not so uncertain in their meaning as to negative the existence of an oral agreement.

3. *The deposit*

In regard to this the learned trial judge stated that it was 'obvious that Mr Boyle was at all times prepared to pay a deposit, even a substantial deposit, had it been accepted from him and there was no problem in relation to the deposit'.

Again, in my view, the absence of specific agreement in relation to the payment of a deposit or the amount thereof does not negative the existence of an oral agreement. It is usual to have a deposit in the case of sales of land but it is not essential in law. In any event, having regard to the construction put on the evidence by the learned trial judge, it would be unrealistic to hold that failure to pinpoint a specific rate or sum for a deposit would, in the circumstances of this case, oblige the court to rule that there was no oral agreement.

Having regard to the foregoing matters, therefore, I am satisfied that the learned trial judge was justified in his finding that there had been a concluded oral agreement.

4. *The Statute of Frauds*

S. 2 provides that 'no action shall be brought to charge any person upon any contract or sale of lands, tenements or hereditaments, or any interest in or concerning them, unless the agreement upon which such action shall be brought, or some memorandum or note thereof, shall be in writing, and signed by the party to be charged therewith, or some other person thereunto by him lawfully authorised'.

The agreement itself need not be in writing. A 'note or memorandum' of it is sufficient, provided that it contains all the material terms of the contract. The circumstances of each case need to be examined to discover if any individual term has been deemed material by the parties; and, if so, it must be included in the memorandum: *Hawkins v Price* [1947] Ch. 645; *Schott v Bradley* [1971] Ch. 850.

Can it be said that all material terms of the oral agreement were included in the letter of 8 July 1988? The closing date is described as 'as soon as legal formalities can be completed' and this represents fairly what was agreed to. There is no mention of the requirement of a deposit but, there was no definite parol agreement and, in the circumstances of this case, the parties did not regard the question of a deposit as being of any significant or necessary materiality: see *Black v Kavanagh* (1974) 108 ILTR 91.

A more serious matter arises in relation to the tenancies. The evidence disclosed that there was a breach of planning permission and that it was a continuing breach. Mr Boyle gave evidence to the effect that he would accept the tenancies as they stood, even though there was a breach. In my opinion, this was an important and material term. It meant that if the sale went through he could be compelled by the Corporation to take steps to remedy the breach and that these steps might be difficult and costly. He was prepared to face up to this position but there was nothing in the note or memorandum to exonerate the vendors from any liability towards the purchasers in this event. For this reason alone, I hold that the note or memorandum was not sufficient to satisfy the requirements of the statute.

Having regard to the foregoing, it is not strictly necessary for me to deal with the legal effect of the words 'subject to contract' which are included twice in the memorandum relied upon and also the sentence which reads: 'In the meantime you will appreciate that this letter is for information purposes only and does not by itself constitute part of a binding contract'. Nothing could be clearer than the intention of the writer and the meaning, in particular, of the sentence quoted. Is this an answer to the problem in the sense of meaning that there can be no binding contract until a formal contract is entered into? It is consistent with the plain view of one of the parties but not necessarily of the other party. If the words are to be construed with reference to the parol agreement it could be argued that a finding to the effect that there had been a concluded agreement should mean that one party could not unilaterally negative the existence of such agreement. It has been held that the court, in determining whether a document is a sufficient memorandum is not 'in quest of the intention of the parties, but only of evidence under the hand of one of the parties to it, that he has entered into it': *In re Hoyle* [1893] 1 Ch. 84.

In England the balance of authority suggests that any alleged memorandum which purports to deny the existence of a contract cannot constitute a sufficient note or memorandum for the purpose of the Statute of Frauds, even though the parties themselves have actually reached a concluded agreement and parol evidence can be produced to prove this: *Tiverton Estates Ltd v Wearwell Ltd* [1975] Ch. 146.

The entire history of the law in relation to the expression 'subject to contract' was reviewed exhaustively by Keane J. in *Mulhall v Haren* [1981] IR 364 in which he held *inter alia* that a letter which expressly states that a transaction is 'subject to contract' cannot be a sufficient note or memorandum, since the use of those words is normally inconsistent with the existence of a concluded contract. He held that it was only in certain rare and exceptional circumstances such as arose in *Kelly v Park Hall School Ltd* [1979] IR 340 and *Michael Richards Properties Ltd v Corporation of Wardens of St Saviour's Parish*

[1975] 3 All ER 416 that the words 'subject to contract' could be treated as being of no effect. It is true that the *Park Hall* decision was that of the Supreme Court but the qualification or explanation of it given by Keane J. was subsequently accepted by Henchy J. in *McCarthy v O'Neill* [1981] ILRM 443 when he impliedly approved of the decision in *Mulhall v Haren*. I similarly approve.

I would allow the appeal and would answer the questions as follows:

(a) Yes.
(b) As found by the learned trial judge.
(c) No.

Note

In England as a result of the Law of Property (Miscellaneous Provisions) Act 1989 all contracts for the sale of land must be made in writing. A memorandum will no longer suffice: see *Record v Bell* [1991] 4 All ER 471.

B. IF THE PHRASE 'SUBJECT TO CONTRACT' IS NOT USED

Silver Wraith Ltd *v* Siuicre Eireann cpt (HC) 8 June 1989, unrep.

In the course of negotiating a lease, a series of letters passed between the parties.

Keane J.:

. . .

It then becomes of crucial importance from the court's point of view to see whether those letters establish a concluded and binding agreement. It is for that reason that much of the cross-examination on both sides was directed to the contents of those two letters; and in their closing submissions counsel directed much of their observations to what was contained in those letters.

I commence with the letter of 30 June 1986 addressed to Mr Murray from Mr Gray, which says: 'Further to your correspondence and subsequent discussions . . . the following terms are acceptable subject to full lease being agreed.' Now, what was intended to be conveyed by the phrase 'subject to full lease being agreed' and what did Mr Murray for his part understand by it? If one leaves the legalities aside for the moment, I think that any lay person reading that correspondence would not have much difficulty in inferring from the phrase that Mr Gray was seeking to convey to his opposite number in these discussions that, while he was proceeding to set out terms which he (Mr Gray) understood were acceptable to both of them, he was conveying that in the normal course of events, if the parties were *ad idem* on the main features of the lease (the rent, the length of the term and when the term was to commence) the matter should go to their respective solicitors; that a full lease containing all the covenants and conditions that might be appropriate in such a lease would then be drawn up, considered by their solicitors, possibly amended between them and that eventually from discussions between the solicitors an agreed lease which both parties were prepared to execute would emerge. Mr Gray was seeking to convey to Mr Murray that until that time his principals would not in any contractual sense be bound. That, I think, was what, without any knowledge of the various decisions relating to the equivalent phrase, a lay person of common sense and experience of business affairs would suppose Mr Gray intended to convey. In saying that I am assuming that any person reading the correspondence would have the same knowledge that I have of the context and background against which those letters were written.

This was not somebody offering to give a letting of a furnished bedsitting room. This was an officer of a large public company, a semi-State body, who was dealing with the lease of an extremely important and valuable property in a very commanding and prestigious situation in the most exclusive business area of Dublin. And in my view it would be extraordinary if a person in Mr Gray's position would have felt himself at liberty to incorporate all the final and concluded details of a lease of this property in this form and then treat anything that was done thereafter as a pure formality because the parties were fully contractually bound. I would find that an astonishing proposition and I think that most people reading the letter without any particular detailed knowledge of the legal background to this particular area of the law would have got that impression.

It is important to distinguish two matters here. What one is now concerned with is whether there was a concluded agreement between the parties and not whether there was a sufficient note or memorandum of the agreement to satisfy the Statute of Frauds because that only becomes relevant if there is a concluded agreement in the first place. So that in considering what inference one should draw from the phrase 'subject to full lease being agreed', at this stage one is not considering whether it would be fatal to the existence of a note or memorandum. The point is: What does it suggest in relation to the contracting state of mind, as it were, of the parties?

In that context there is a second matter which is of importance. The phrase used must be carefully distinguished from the phrase 'subject to contract' which is dealt with in the authorities here and in England. Those authorities have been concerned with situations where parties, usually lay parties or estate agents, had settled the terms of a purchase of property and then went to their solicitors and asked them to carry through the sale; and the solicitors, conscious of the fact that it might be dangerous for their clients to be bound by a purely oral contract, would write to their opposite number a letter headed 'subject to contract' and go on to say: 'We confirm the sale of this property etc.'.

Now, even in those circumstances it has sometimes been held that that is sufficient to prevent a sufficient note or memorandum to come into existence to satisfy the Statute of Frauds. But if one looks at the authorities, one finds that in those cases there had been a complete agreement, that the parties to the transaction had not in mind anything at all about it being subject to contract. It was their solicitors who subsequently put the phrase into the correspondence.

However, in this situation it is totally different. If these letters reflect (as I said at the outset, it is virtually agreed that they do) the actual state of mind of the parties at the time, then the coming into existence of a full lease is unquestionably a condition of the agreement and there is no question here of the phrase being subsequently inserted by a party in order to protect himself from an agreement already arrived at. That, I think, is the only inference that can be drawn from the use by Mr Gray in his letter of the phrase 'subject to full lease being agreed' because Mr Gray is the person concerned; he is a layman; he is not a solicitor coming into a deal which has already been concluded between others and saying: 'Well, I must protect these people because they have entered into an oral agreement. I will ensure that no note or memorandum comes into existence by heading the letter "subject to contract".' Here is a lay person writing his understanding of the situation as he sees it and he uses this phrase which in my opinion is only consistent with an intention to ensure that a contractual liability does not arise until a full lease has been agreed. That seems to me to be the weight that has to be attached to those words.

But it is by no means the end of the matter. Mr Gray then goes on to set out the terms which he says are acceptable. I do not have to read them out in detail. It is clear that they deal with what would be the central points in any lease—the rent, the term and when it is to commence.

I entirely accept counsel's submissions, supported by substantial authority, that the commencement date of the lease was specified not directly but inferentially in a memorandum that would satisfy the essential ingredients of an agreement for a lease.

One matter that is not included in the letter, of course, for the good reason that Mr Gray did not know it, is the identity of the lessee. But it is sufficient to say that the rent, the term, the commencement of the term—the important matters in any tenancy agreement or lease—were set out as ones which he was prepared to accept.

Now, if one leaves aside those introductory words 'subject to full lease being agreed'; if one assumes that those words were not there and if the case made on behalf of the plaintiff were correct, that letter demanded a one-line reply: 'We agree. Send the documents to our solicitors.' The letter one gets in reply is: 'Thank you for your letter dated 30 June . . . my comments are as follows: . . . .' The comments were quite unnecessary. If the plaintiff's case is correct, a simple statement in reply was required: 'I agree'. Mr Murray then goes on to pick out items with which he agrees, items 1, 2 and 3. Mr Murray says he agreed to item 4, but I think he has inserted qualifications which are very important because he and Mr Gray were probably thinking along roughly the same lines. They used the phrase 'full planning permission' by which they both meant a planning permission which would not be vulnerable to third party appeal but one which had been granted following notification of a decision so that there could be no appeal, or one granted on appeal by An Board Pleanala. I think that is what they meant. However, I do not attach much weight to that clause except to say that its actual tenor is not particularly consistent with the existence of a concluded agreement between the parties. Again, if there was then a concluded agreement between the parties, all Mr Gray had to say was 'I agree'. End of story.

However, in item 5 of his letter Mr Murray goes on to refer to Mr Gray's stipulation that there should be a deposit of three months' rent on signing the lease. He says that it is not normal practice for three months' rent to be paid in advance on signing the lease because 'you raised personal guarantees with me'. What was meant by that? What could be meant by it except that Mr Murray reasonably considered that he was still in negotiation with Mr Gray. Mr Murray was not accepting what Mr Gray said and there was no reason why he should. Mr Gray was putting forward a term in his letter of this alleged agreement that a deposit was required as well as three months' rent in advance, a term which Mr Murray considered unacceptable. Mr Murray was entitled to consider the term unacceptable but the fact that he did consider it unacceptable is inconsistent with the existence of any concluded agreement between the parties. Mr Murray also adds in his letter: 'particularly bearing in mind . . . personal guarantees with me', which is of considerable significance.

That evidence relates to the fact that there was continuing uncertainty as to who exactly was to be the lessee of this property assuming that this deal went through. This matter was of substantial importance to the lessor (the defendant in this case) and, again, it serves to distinguish this case from the 'subject to contract' cases referred to in the course of the argument. Those 'subject to contract' cases are invariably cases where the parties are selling property. Of course, once a person who is selling property has got his money that is the end of it as far as he is concerned. He could not care less who he has sold it to or what the purchaser does with the property.

Totally different considerations arise in the case of a lease. There the landlord is very much concerned with who his tenant is and very much concerned with solvency. The more valuable the property the more exposed the landlord is to comment or criticism. If the lessor is a public body or a semi-State body, it is most important that it should know who the lessee is. In this case the earlier correspondence indicated that Mr Murray might be dealing on his own behalf. There was then an indication of a Mr Les Sutton coming in and then an indication of a company called South Frederick Holdings Limited. Then at some later stage, without notification to the landlord, another company was brought into the picture and that company was the present Plaintiff, Silver Wraith Limited. It was perfectly obvious that Mr Gray was very concerned as to the nature of the lessee. I accept what Mr Gray said in relation to this matter and I do not think that he was seriously challenged about it. The lessee was certainly going to be a company and there would be a question as to who the shareholders were and what was the paid up capital of the company. And if the defendant was still not one hundred per cent happy with the proposed company, there could well be a question of personal guarantees. The correspondence shows that all these matters were up in the air: that there had been no finality. In my view, that, again, is fatal to the existence of any concluded agreement between the parties.

In those circumstances, therefore, it seems to me that the plaintiff's case fails *in limine*, as it were, because the plaintiff failed to establish the existence of a concluded and binding agreement between the parties. . . .

Note

Compare this to Irish *Mainport Holdings Ltd v Crosshaven Sailing Centre Ltd* (HC) 14 October 1980, unrep.

Lark Developments *v* The Right Honourable the Lord Mayor Aldermen and Burgesses of the City of Dublin (HC) 10 February 1993, unrep.

The plaintiffs entered into negotiations to buy property from the defendants. On 3 May 1989 the defendants wrote a letter to the plaintiffs identifying the parties, the subject matter, the price, and setting out the terms and time scales in detail. This letter was marked 'Without Prejudice'. The plaintiffs replied two days later describing the property in the same terms and stating 'I confirm our acceptance of the terms and conditions as stated in your letter'. On 15 June the defendants wrote to the plaintiffs informing them that the City Council had approved of the terms for the disposal of the properties. Later when the defendants refused to complete the sale the plaintiffs sued for specific performance.

Murphy J.:

The primary issue between the parties was whether on the receipt of that notification dated 14 June 1989 by the plaintiffs on the following day, 15 June 1989, there was a concluded agreement between the parties for the sale and purchase of the two sites hereinbefore described.

Whilst counsel on behalf of both parties sought to establish from the evidence given in court or from an analysis of the correspondence between the parties the belief or absence of belief as to the existence of a valid binding contract by one or other of the parties or their advisers, it does not seem to me that such evidence or indeed the conduct of the parties subsequent to the action could be of decisive importance in establishing whether or not, as of 15 June 1989, there was in force a valid binding contract.

Having regard to the fact that the correspondence identifies the parties, the subject matter, the price, and sets out terms and time scales in the detail which has been quoted above it would seem more appropriate to ask why it is said that no contract was concluded rather than analyse the arguments in favour of the existence of a contract.

Counsel on behalf of the defendants drew attention in particular to clauses 2 and 11 of the letter dated 3 May 1989. Clause 2 begins with the words 'The sale shall be by way of contract'. It was asserted that this was a clear and express reference to a contract for sale envisaged by the parties and, it was said, that there was no concluded bargain between the parties until a contract for sale in the usual legal form was executed by or on behalf of each of the parties. It was said that this argument was reinforced by clause 11 which, the defendants say, contains two distinct propositions, first 'That the above terms shall not constitute or be deemed to constitute a contract' and secondly '(that the above terms) are subject to the necessary approvals and consents being obtained'. It is argued that there was to be a contract between the parties and that the terms of 3 May did not constitute that contract.

There are other features of the letter of 3 May which might assist in justifying the inference that the parties intended the transaction between them should be enshrined in and subject to a further and more formal document. If nothing else one might expect a substantial and complex transaction of this nature to be scrutinised by legal advisers on behalf of both parties. There is an express reference in clauses 4 and 5 to the granting by the defendants of a building licence to the plaintiffs on foot of which the works were to be completed. The scheme was not a simple, or at any rate ordinary, transaction for the sale and purchase of land: the defendants were intent upon securing the erection of premises of a particular quality on these sites in the inner city within a particular time frame and these works were to be the subject matter of a building licence. Again it might be assumed that the parties would wish to suspend legal obligations until agreement was reached as to the precise terms of such documentation. An express reference is made in clause 8 of the terms to the 'Standard Law Society Conditions of Sale'. This reference, particularly the fact that those conditions required to be 'suitably amended', would lend some support to the argument that the parties intended the execution of a further document and that agreement upon the terms thereof and its execution was a condition precedent to any contractual obligation.

On behalf of the plaintiffs it was argued that clause 11 of the 'May' terms merely precluded those terms from being converted into a contract for sale by the purported acceptance thereof by the plaintiffs. They were being outlined as the terms (or, more correctly, the amended terms) on which the defendants would entertain an offer from the plaintiffs and it was only when an offer made (or confirmed) by the plaintiffs on those terms was duly approved and sanctioned that a contract would come into being. Essentially the plaintiffs say that there are not two distinct provisions in clause 11 but that the second part explains or reinforces the earlier part, that is to say, that no contract should be deemed to exist unless and until the necessary approvals had been obtained.

It is then said that clause 11 as so interpreted is entirely consistent with clause 2 which does indeed say that the sale should be by way of contract with a deposit of twenty per cent of the disposal price being paid within twenty eight days of notification to the proposed purchaser of the issuing of 'the approval of the City Council to the disposal'. This, it is said, confirms that an effective binding contract arises when the approval of the City Council was granted and communicated.

A building licence agreement was drafted, approved and executed by both parties in relation to the premises 21/26 North Great George's Street and this document was handed into court. It was not suggested, however, by either party that the preparation of this document was contentious in any way or that its terms required any negotiations between the parties. Again a separate contract for the sale of the premises 21/26 North Great George's Street was executed and bears date 26 March 1990. That contract is based on the *Incorporated Law Society of Ireland General Conditions of Sale* (1988 ed.). The particulars and tenure of the property comprised in the 1990 contract are very similar to but not quite identical with the particulars and tenure as described in the 1989 documents. Perhaps the most significant distinction between the two is that the 1990 contract refers to five particular documents of title which were not referred to in the earlier documentation. On the other hand the plaintiffs rely on the fact that the defendants were bound to procure themselves to be registered in the Registry of Deeds as the owners of the property and furthermore they would have been liable (or so the plaintiffs contend) to damages if they failed to make title in accordance with the provisions of the 1989 documents.

Perhaps the most significant feature of the 1990 contract is that the special conditions contained therein repeat precisely the timetable and material conditions contained in the earlier documentation. In many of the cases where it is contended that an informal agreement for the sale and purchase of land is conditional upon the execution of a formal document to be prepared and approved by lawyers on behalf of the parties, counsel on their behalf speculate as to the terms upon which prudent advisers would insist upon incorporating in the later document for the protection of their clients. In the present case the actual existence of a formal document renders such speculation unnecessary. It would seem clear that neither of the parties saw any necessity for the inclusion of any conditions other than the special terms already incorporated in the 1989 agreement in addition to the standard terms provided by the Incorporated Law Society precedent. In those circumstances the plaintiffs contend that a valid binding contract had come into existence by the communication to them on 15 June of the consent of the City Council to the disposal of the property. Alternatively the plaintiffs say that if a subsequent contract was required, it was a mere reduction of agreed terms to an appropriate form (see *Rossiter v Miller* 3 App Cas 1124 at 1151 and *Law & Another v Robert Roberts & Co.* [1964] IR 292 at 303).

Whilst the matter is not free of doubt, on balance I take the view that the communication by the defendants to the plaintiffs on 15 June 1989 of the decision of the City Council, at its meeting on 12 June 1989, to approve of the terms for the disposal of the two sites at North Great George's Street to the plaintiffs constituted the acceptance by the defendants of the offer which the plaintiffs had made by their acceptance, on 5 May 1989, of the revised terms and conditions propounded by the defendants in their letter of 3 May. The fact that the defendants stated that 'formal notification of this approval' would be issued by the law agent in due course did not postpone or suspend in any way the communication of the decision made by the defendants and its operation as an acceptance of the plaintiffs' offer. In reaching this decision it seems to me that the most important single fact is the timetable set out in the 1989 transaction which was expressed to operate from the notification to the plaintiffs of the issuing of the approval of the City Council to the disposal. That being so it is difficult to see how the parties could have intended to negotiate the terms of any other controversial document. The dates for payment of monies; the application for planning permission; the delivery of a building licence and indeed the period within which the buildings could be built were intended to run from the date which, as it transpired, was 15 June 1989 and a subsequent agreement could do no more and indeed the document as drafted did not attempt to do more than to repeat this provision. Indeed the 1990 agreement in that regard demonstrates the unreality of an additional agreement.

(In the circumstances Murphy J. stated damages would be a more suitable remedy.)

Contracts to make a Contract

In *Guardians of Kells Union v Smith* (1917) 52 ILTR 65 the plaintiffs invited tenders for the weekly supply of meat. The advertisement stated that the accepted contractor would have to execute a contract under seal with the plaintiffs before a certain date. The defendants' tender was successful but the plaintiffs purported to withdraw the tender and refused to supply the meat. The defendants sued for damages for breach of contract. The court awarded nominal damages to the plaintiffs for a breach of a contract to enter into the formal contract.

Hillas & Co. Ltd v Arcos Ltd (1932) 147 LT 503

Lord Wright (*obiter*):

There is no bargain except to negotiate, and negotiations may be fruitless and end without a contract ensuing; yet even then, in strict theory, there is a contract (if there is good consideration) to negotiate, though in the event of repudiation by one party the damages may be nominal, unless the jury thinks that the opportunity to negotiate was of some appreciable value to the injured party.

Courtney & Fairbairn Ltd v Tolaini Brothers (Hotels) Ltd [1975] 1 All ER 716

Lord Denning:

That tentative opinion by Lord Wright does not seem to me to be well founded. If the law does not recognise a contract to enter into a contract (when there is a fundamental term yet to be agreed) it seems to me it cannot recognise a contract to negotiate. The reason is because it is too uncertain to have any binding force. No court could estimate the damages because no one can tell whether the negotiations would be successful or would fall through; or if successful, what the result would be. It seems to me that a contract to negotiate, like a contract to enter into a contract, is not a contract known to the law. . . . I think we must apply the general principle that when there is a fundamental matter left undecided and to be the subject of negotiation, there is no contract.

The Court of Appeal determined that a contract to negotiate a building contract even though supported by consideration, lacked sufficient certainty to be legally binding.

Note

An agreement to make reasonable endeavours would appear to be binding.

Rooney v Byrne [1933] IR 609

O'Byrne J.:

This action arises out of a contract, dated 24 April 1931, for the sale of a house and premises. The consideration for such sale to the plaintiff was expressed to be the sum of £400, and the contract, which is in the form of a proposal and acceptance, then states: 'I now lodge the sum of £50 in the hands of your agents, Messrs Towers & Co., 11 Lower Abbey Street, being portion of such purchase money, and will pay the balance on the completion of the purchase.' There is a further stipulation in the contract that 'This proposal is subject to me getting an advance on the property.'

The first question for determination arises out of the last mentioned stipulation. It is argued that this proposal must be taken at its face value and that it makes the contract conditional on an advance being in fact obtained. In my opinion the stipulation means something more than that. We have to consider what was in the minds of the parties at the time the contract was signed. It is fairly clear that, in the contemplation of the parties, the purchaser would require to get an advance for the purpose of providing the purchase money, and the object was to provide that, in the event of his failing to get such an advance, the contract also failed. But in my opinion it was equally contemplated that the purchaser should make an effort to secure the advance. [Counsel] contends that it was competent for the purchaser to elect whether he would get an advance or not, and that, if he elected not to do so, the contract failed, even though he could get such an advance on reasonable terms. That, in my opinion, was not the intention of the parties. In my view the purchaser was bound to make reasonable efforts to secure the necessary advance, and, if he failed after such reasonable efforts to secure an advance on reasonable terms, the contract was then at an end.

Note

In *Cadbury Ireland Ltd v Kerry Co-op Creameries* [1982] ILRM 77 Barrington J. noted that a particular clause was not binding because it involved at best 'a commitment to enter into honest negotiations'. However, in *Bula Ltd & Others v Tara Mines Ltd* [1987] IR 95 Murphy J. noted that despite the decisions in *Courtney & Fairbairn v Tolaini Brothers (Hotels) Ltd* and *Cadbury Ireland Ltd v Kerry Co-op Creameries* consideration still had to be given to the observations of Lord Wright in *Hillas & Co. Ltd v Arcos Ltd*.

Pagnan SpA. v Feed Products Ltd [1987] 2 Lloyd's Rep. 601

The plaintiffs and defendants through an intermediary broker (Mr Pagnossin) entered into negotiations for the sale and purchase of corn pellets. On 1 February, following many telephone and telex exchanges, Mr Pagnossin sent telexes to both parties stating 'We confirm the following business today concluded through our intermediary' and setting out certain terms of the contract. The following day the defendants sent the plaintiffs a telex setting out the contract terms, not all of which corresponded with the previous telex. Certain of these terms proved unacceptable to the buyers and negotiations took place up to 8 February to sort out the differences. However on 9 March Mr Pagnossin forwarded from the defendants the formal contract documents containing certain of the unacceptable terms. The plaintiffs claimed that no binding contract existed.

The trial judge determined that a binding contract was formed on 1 February.

Lloyd L.J.:

As to the law, the principles to be derived from the authorities, some of which I have already mentioned, can be summarised as follows:

(1) In order to determine whether a contract has been concluded in the course of correspondence, one must first look to the correspondence as a whole (see *Hussey v
Horne-Payne* (1879) 4 App Cas 311).

(2) Even if the parties have reached agreement on all the terms of the proposed
contract, nevertheless they may intend that the contract shall not become binding
until some further condition has been fulfilled. That is the ordinary 'subject to
contract' case.

(3) Alternatively, they may intend that the contract shall not become binding until
some further term or terms have been agreed; see *Love and Stewart v Instone* (1917)
33 TLR 475, where the parties failed to agree the intended strike clause, and *Hussey
v Horne-Payne*, where Lord Selborne said at p. 323:

> . . . The observation has often been made, that a contract established by letters
> may sometimes bind parties who, when they wrote those letters, did not imagine
> that they were finally settling the terms of the agreement by which they were to be
> bound; and it appears to me that no such contract ought to be held established,
> even by letters which would otherwise be sufficient for the purpose, if it is clear,
> upon the facts, that there were other conditions of the intended contract, beyond
> and besides those expressed in the letters, which were still in a state of negotiation
> only, *and without the settlement of which the parties had no idea of concluding any agreement.*
> [My emphasis].

(4) Conversely, the parties may intend to be bound forthwith even though there are
further terms still to be agreed or some further formality to be fulfilled (see *Love
and Stewart v Instone* per Lord Loreburn at p. 476).

(5) If the parties fail to reach agreement on such further terms, the existing contract is
not invalidated unless the failure to reach agreement on such further terms
renders the contract as a whole unworkable or void for uncertainty.

(6) It is sometimes said that the parties must agree on the essential terms and that it
is only matters of detail which can be left over. This may be misleading, since the
word 'essential' in that context is ambiguous. If by 'essential' one means a term
without which the contract cannot be enforced then the statement is true: the law
cannot enforce an incomplete contract. If by 'essential' one means a term which
the parties have agreed to be essential for the formation of a binding contract,
then the statement is tautologous. If by 'essential' one means only a term which
the court regards as important as opposed to a term which the court regards as
less important or a matter of detail, the statement is untrue. It is for the parties to
decide whether they wish to be bound and, if so, by what terms, whether important
or unimportant. It is the parties who are, in the memorable phrase coined by the
judge, 'the masters of their contractual fate'. Of course the more important the
term is the less likely it is that the parties will have left it for future decision. But
there is no legal obstacle which stands in the way of the parties agreeing to be
bound now while deferring important matters to be agreed later. It happens every
day when parties enter into so-called 'heads of agreement'. [Counsel for the
plaintiffs] submits that that is a special case, but I do not think it is.

[Counsel for the plaintiffs] relied heavily on the fact that the judge described the terms
on which the parties had not yet agreed as 'terms of economic significance to these
buyers'. If I am right in the propositions I have stated, and in particular propositions
(4) and (6), the fact that the terms yet to be agreed were of economic significance
would not prevent a contract coming into existence forthwith if that is what the parties
intended. So I can find no error of law in the judge's approach.

Was the judge right to draw the inference which he did as to the parties' intentions? The matters upon which the judge relied are set out at p. 611 *ante*. I will not repeat them now. Among the more important are the following:

(1) Mr Pagnan told Mr Pagnossin on 1 February to book the business.
(2) Mr Pagnossin sent a confirmatory telex the same day referring to the business as:

'. . . having been concluded through our intermediary.'

(3) Neither party raised any objection to the confirmatory telex.
(4) The plaintiffs thereafter headed their telexes 'Contract 1 February 1982'.
(5) There was no communication of any kind between 8 February, when the defendants agreed the loading rate, and 9 March, when Mr Pagnossin despatched the documents.
(6) The plaintiffs did not then react as one would have expected if there had been no question of a binding contract.

[Counsel for the plaintiffs] argued that the parties' reactions are as irrelevant as their beliefs. I agree of course that the test is objective and the reactions of the parties are not conclusive. But I cannot accept that they are irrelevant. As to the other matters relied on by the judge, some of the more important of which I have mentioned, [Counsel for the plaintiffs] submitted that the judge gave them altogether too much weight. As for the gap between 8 February and 9 March, [Counsel] said that there could be several explanations. To choose one rather than another would be mere speculation.

I cannot accept those submissions. The judge regarded the matters to which I have referred as being: '. . . very strong indications that the parties intended to, and did, make a binding contract on 1 February.'

In my view he was right. Indeed the only indication the other way is that the parties continued with their negotiations after the confirmatory telex of 1 February. But that is not really an indication at all. Once one accepts that the parties are in law capable of making what I will call an interim agreement, it was only to be expected that they would continue negotiating the terms that remained without delay. This is what they did. In my view the judge drew the right inference as to the parties' intentions.

. . .

For the reasons I have given I would dismiss the appeal.

(Stocker and O'Connor L.JJ. concurred.)

Note

1. In *Queensland Electricity Generating Board v New Hope Collieries Pty Ltd* [1989] 1 Lloyd's Rep. 205 the Privy Council implied an obligation 'to make reasonable endeavours' to agree the appropriate terms.
2. In *Coal Cliff Collieries Pty Ltd v Sijehama Pty Ltd* (1991) 24 NSWLR 1, while the New South Wales Court of Appeal noted that the law will not enforce an agreement to agree, the majority of the court expressly rejected the view that every promise to negotiate in good faith is unenforceable. The majority agreed with Lord Wright's speech in *Hillas* 'that provided that there was consideration for the promise, in some circumstances a promise to negotiate in good faith will be enforceable depending on its precise terms.'

3. Restatement (2d) of Contract s. 205 [1981] states: 'Every contract imposes upon each party a duty of good faith and fair dealing in its performance and enforcement'.

In *Channel Home Centers, Grace Retail v Grossman* 795 F.2d 291 (3rd Cir. 1986) the US Court of Appeal noted:

Although no Pennsylvania court has considered whether an agreement to negotiate in good faith may meet these conditions, the jurisdictions that have considered the issue have held that such an agreement, if otherwise meeting the requisites of a contract, is an enforceable contract. See, e.g., *Thompson v Liquichimica of America, Inc.*, 481 F.Supp. 365, 366 (E.D.N.Y.1979); ('Unlike an agreement to agree, which does not constitute a closed proposition, an agreement to use best efforts [or to negotiate in good faith] is a closed proposition, discrete and actionable.'); *accord Repro-system, B.V. v SCM Corp.*, 727 F2d 257, 264 (2d Cir. 1984); *Chase v Consolidated Foods Corp.*, 744 F.2d 566, 571, (7th Cir. 1984).
. . .
. . . We are satisfied that Pennsylvania would follow this rule. . . .

Agreements to negotiate are often accompanied by lock-out agreements. Whereas the former involves a positive duty to negotiate with the other party, the latter involves a prohibition on negotiating with any third party or parties.

Walford and Others *v* Miles and Others [1992] 2 WLR 174

The respondents entered into discussions with the appellants with a view to selling their beneficial interest in a company and its business premises. On 17 March the appellants orally agreed to provide a 'comfort letter' in return for the respondents agreeing to break off negotiations with any third party, and to deal with the appellants exclusively. The comfort letter was dispatched and a draft share-purchase agreement was sent to the respondents, but the respondents decided not to proceed with negotiations and later sold to a third party. The appellants sued for breach of contract. The trial judge found that the oral agreement of 17 March was a separate and collateral agreement which the respondents had repudiated. On appeal the Court of Appeal held that the collateral agreement was merely an agreement to negotiate and was thus unenforceable. The appellants appealed to the House of Lords.

Lord Ackner:

The pleaded case

The Walfords relied upon an oral agreement, collateral to the negotiations which were proceeding to purchase the company and the land it occupied 'subject to contract'. The consideration for this oral agreement was twofold—firstly the Walfords agreeing to continue the negotiations and not to withdraw and secondly, their providing the comfort letter from their bankers in the terms requested.

For this consideration it was alleged in para. 5 of the statement of claim as follows: '. . . the first defendant on behalf of himself and the second defendant would terminate negotiations with any third party on consideration of any alternative with a view to concluding an agreement with the plaintiffs and further that even if he received a satisfactory proposal from any third party prior to the close of business on 25 March 1987, he would not deal with that third party or give further consideration to any alternative.'

As thus pleaded, the agreement purported to be what is known as a 'lock-out' agreement, providing the plaintiffs with an exclusive opportunity to try and come to terms with the defendants, but without expressly providing any duration for such an opportunity.

For reasons which will become apparent hereafter, it was decided to amend this paragraph by the following addition: 'It was a term of the said collateral agreement necessarily to be implied to give business efficacy thereto that, so long as they continued to desire to sell the said property and shares, the first defendant on behalf of himself and the second defendant would continue to negotiate in good faith with the plaintiff.'

Thus the statement of claim alleged that, not only were the defendants 'locked-out' for some unspecified time from dealing with any third party, but were 'locked-in' to dealing with the plaintiffs, also for an unspecified period.

. . .

In the Court of Appeal, by a majority (Dillon and Stocker L.JJ.) the appeal was allowed (save to the extent of the award of the damages for misrepresentation) on the grounds that the agreement alleged was no more than an agreement to negotiate and was therefore unenforceable. Bingham L.J. who dissented, would have held that the agreement was enforceable on the ground that it could be construed as an agreement by the Miles not to deal with any party other than the Walfords and not to entertain any alternative proposal.

The validity of the agreement alleged in para. 5 of the statement of claim as amended

The justification for the implied term in para. 5 of the amended statement of claim was that in order to give the collateral agreement 'business efficacy', Mr Miles was obliged to 'continue to negotiate in good faith'. It was submitted to the Court of Appeal and initially to your Lordships that this collateral agreement could not be made to work, unless there was a positive duty imposed upon Mr Miles to negotiate. It was of course conceded that the agreement made no specific provision for the period it was to last. It was however contended, albeit not pleaded, that the obligation to negotiate would endure for a reasonable time, and that such time was the time which was reasonably necessary to reach a binding agreement. It was however accepted that such period of time would not end when negotiations had ceased, because all such negotiations were conducted expressly under the umbrella of 'subject to contract'. The agreement alleged would thus be valueless if the alleged obligation to negotiate ended when negotiations as to the terms of the 'subject to contract' agreement had ended, since at that stage the Miles would have been entitled at their whim to refuse to sign any contract.

Apart from the absence of any term as to the duration of the collateral agreement, it contained no provision for the Miles to determine the negotiations, albeit that such a provision was essential. It was contended by [counsel for the appellants] that a term was to be implied giving the Miles a right to determine the negotiations, but only if they had 'a proper reason.' However in order to determine whether a given reason was a proper one, he accepted that the test was not an objective one—would a hypothetical reasonable person consider the reason a reasonable one? The test was a subjective one—did the Miles honestly believe in the reason which they gave for the termination of the negotiations? Thus they could be quite irrational, so long as they behaved honestly.

|Counsel for the appellants| accepted that as the law now stands and has stood for approaching twenty years, an agreement to negotiate is not recognised as an enforceable contract. This was first decided in terms in *Courtney and Fairbairn Ltd v Tolaini Brothers (Hotels) Ltd* |1975| 1 WLR 297, where Lord Denning M.R. said, at pp 301–302:

> If the law does not recognise a contract to enter into a contract (when there is a fundamental term yet to be agreed) it seems to me it cannot recognise a contract to negotiate. The reason is because it is too uncertain to have any binding force . . . It seems to me that a contract to negotiate, like a contract to enter into a contract, is not a contract known to the law . . . I think we must apply the general principle that where there is a fundamental matter left undecided and to be the subject of negotiation, there is no contract.

In that case, at p. 302b, Lord Denning M.R. rejected as not well founded (and Lord Diplock expressly concurred with this rejection), the dictum of Lord Wright in *Hillas & Co. Ltd v Arcos Ltd* (1932) 147 LT 503, 515: 'There is then no bargain except to negotiate, and negotiations may be fruitless and end without any contract ensuing; yet even then, in strict theory, there is a contract (if there is good consideration) to negotiate, though in the event of repudiation by one party the damages may be nominal, unless a jury think that the opportunity to negotiate was of some appreciable value to the injured party.'

The decision in *Courtney's* case |1975| 1 WLR 297 was followed by the Court of Appeal in *Mallozzi v Carapelli S.p.a.* |1976| 1 Lloyd's Rep. 407. In that case Kerr J. |1975| 1 Lloyd's Rep. 229 had applied the dictum of Lord Wright in *Hillas & Co. Ltd v Arcos Ltd*, 147 LT 503 before the *Courtney* case had been decided and held that there was an obligation on the parties at least to negotiate *bona fide* with a view to trying to reach an agreement. In that case a contract for the sale of grain contained a clause which provided: 'C.i.f. free out one safe port west coast Italy—excluding Genoa. First or second port to be agreed between sellers and buyers on the ship passing the Straits of Gilbraltar.' The Court of Appeal however held that it was impossible to say that the provision in the contract was legally enforceable, or that there was any legally binding obligation to negotiate.

The decision that an agreement to negotiate cannot constitute a legally enforceable contract has been followed at first instance in a number of relatively recent cases: *Albion Sugar Co. Ltd v Williams Tankers Ltd* |1977| 2 Lloyd's Rep. 457; *Scandinavian Trading Tanker Co. A.B. v Flota Petrolera Ecuatoriana* |1981| 2 Lloyd's Rep. 425; *Trees Ltd v Cripps* (1983) 267 EG 596; *Nile Co. for the Export of Agricultural Crops v H. & J. M. Bennett (Commodities) Ltd* |1986| 1 Lloyd's Rep. 555; *Voest Apline Intertrading GmbH v Chevron International Oil Co. Ltd* |1987| 2 Lloyd's Rep. 547; and *Star Steamship Society v Beogradska Plovidba* |1988| 2 Lloyd's Rep. 583.

In the Court of Appeal and before your Lordships |counsel for the appellants| submitted that the *Courtney* and the *Mallozzi* cases were distinguishable from the present case, because that which was referred to negotiation with a view to agreement in those cases was an existing difference between the parties. In the present case, so it was contended, by the end of the telephone conversation on 17 March there was no existing difference. Every point that had been raised for discussion had been agreed. However this submission overlooked that what had been 'agreed' on the telephone on 17 March was 'subject to contract'. Therefore the parties were still in negotiation even in relation to those matters. Further, there were many other matters which had still to be considered and agreed.

Before your Lordships it was sought to argue that the decision in *Courtney's* case
[1975] 1 WLR 297 was wrong. Although the cases in the United States did not speak
with one voice your Lordships' attention was drawn to the decision of the United States'
Court of Appeal, Third Circuit, in *Channel Home Centers, Division of Grace Retail Corp. v
Grossman* (1986) 795 F. 2d 291 as being 'the clearest example' of the American cases in
the appellants' favour. That case raised the issue whether an agreement to negotiate
in good faith, if supported by consideration, is an enforceable contract. I do not find
the decision of any assistance. While accepting that an agreement to agree is not an
enforceable contract, the Court of Appeal appears to have proceeded on the basis that
an agreement to negotiate in good faith is synonymous with an agreement to use best
endeavours and as the latter is enforceable, so is the former. This appears to me, with
respect, to be an unsustainable proposition. The reason why an agreement to negotiate, like an agreement to agree, is unenforceable, is simply because it lacks the
necessary certainty. The same does not apply to an agreement to use best endeavours.
This uncertainty is demonstrated in the instant case by the provision which it is said
has to be implied in the agreement for the determination of the negotiations. How can
a court be expected to decide whether, *subjectively*, a proper reason existed for the termination of negotiations? The answer suggested depends upon whether the negotiations
have been determined 'in good faith'. However the concept of a duty to carry on negotiations in good faith is inherently repugnant to the adversarial position of the parties
when involved in negotiations. Each party to the negotiations is entitled to pursue his
(or her) own interest, so long as he avoids making misrepresentations. To advance
that interest he must be entitled, if he thinks it appropriate, to threaten to withdraw
from further negotiations or to withdraw in fact, in the hope that the opposite party
may seek to reopen the negotiations by offering him improved terms. [Counsel for the
appellants], of course, accepts that the agreement upon which he relies does not
contain a duty to complete the negotiations. But that still leaves the vital question—
how is a vendor ever to know that he is entitled to withdraw from further negotiations?
How is the court to police such an 'agreement'? A duty to negotiate in good faith is as
unworkable in practice as it is inherently inconsistent with the position of a negotiating
party. It is here that the uncertainty lies. In my judgment, while negotiations are in
existence either party is entitled to withdraw from those negotiations, at any time and
for any reason. There can be thus no obligation to continue to negotiate until there is a
'proper reason' to withdraw. Accordingly a bare agreement to negotiate has no legal
content.

The validity of the agreement as originally pleaded in the statement of claim

Para. 5 of the statement of claim, as unamended, followed the terms of the oral
agreement as recorded in the penultimate paragraph of the letter of 18 March. It
alleged that for good consideration (and this certainly covered the provision by the
plaintiffs of the 'comfort letter') Mr Miles on behalf of himself and his wife agreed that
they: 'would terminate negotiations with any third party or consideration of any
alternative with a view to concluding an agreement with the plaintiffs and, further, that
even if he received the satisfactory proposal from any third party prior to the close of
business on 20 March 1987 he would not deal with that third party or give further
consideration to any alternative.'

Despite the insistence by [counsel] upon the implied term pleaded in the amendment involving the obligation to negotiate, Bingham L.J., in his dissenting judgment,
considered that that obligation could be severed from the agreement. He concluded
that the agreement, as originally pleaded was a valid and enforceable agreement and

entitled the Walfords to recover whatever damages they could establish resulted in law from its repudiation.

Before considering the basis of Bingham L.J.'s judgment, I believe it helpful to make these observations about a so-called 'lock-out' agreement. There is clearly no reason in the English contract law why A, for good consideration, should not achieve an enforceable agreement whereby B, agrees for a specified period of time, not to negotiate with anyone except A in relation to the sale of his property. There are often good commercial reasons why A should desire to obtain such an agreement from B. B's property, which A contemplates purchasing, may be such as to require the expend- iture of not inconsiderable time and money before A is in a position to assess what he is prepared to offer for its purchase or whether he wishes to make any offer at all. A may well consider that he is not prepared to run the risk of expending such time and money unless there is a worthwhile prospect, should he desire to make an offer to purchase, of B, not only then still owning the property, but of being prepared to consider his offer. A may wish to guard against the risk that, while he is investigating the wisdom of offering to buy B's property, B may have already disposed of it or, alternatively, may be so advanced in negotiations with a third party as to be unwilling or for all practical purposes unable, to negotiate with A. But I stress that this is a negative agreement—B by agreeing not to negotiate for this fixed period with a third party, locks himself out of such negotiations. He has in no legal sense locked himself into negotiations with A. What A has achieved is an exclusive opportunity, for a fixed period, to try and come to terms with B, an opportunity for which he has, unless he makes his agreement under seal, to give good consideration. I therefore cannot accept |counsel's| proposition, which was the essential reason for his amending para. 5 of the statement of claim by the addition of the implied term, that without a positive oblig- ation on B to negotiate with A, the lock-out agreement would be futile.

The agreement alleged in para. 5 of the unamended statement of claim contains the essential characteristics of a basic valid lock-out agreement, save one. It does not specify for how long it is to last. Bingham L.J. sought to cure this deficiency by holding that the obligation upon Mr Miles and his wife not to deal with other parties should continue to bind them 'for such time as is reasonable in all the circumstances.' He said: 'the time would end once the parties acting in good faith had found themselves unable to come to mutually acceptable terms . . . the defendants could not . . . bring the reasonable time to an end by procuring a bogus impasse, since that would involve a breach of the duty of reasonable good faith which parties such as these must, I think, be taken to owe to each other.' However, as Bingham L.J. recognised, such a duty, if it existed, would indirectly impose upon the Miles a duty to negotiate in good faith. Such a duty, for the reasons which I have given above, cannot be imposed. That it should have been thought necessary to assert such a duty helps to explain the reason behind the amendment to para. 5 and the insistence of |counsel| that without the implied term, the agreement, as originally pleaded, was unworkable—unworkable because there was no way of determining for how long the Miles were locked out from negotiating with any third party.

(Goff, Jauncey and Browne-Wilkinson L.JJ. concurred.)

Note

See Neill, 'A Key to Lockout Agreements' Vol. 108 LQR 405 and Davenport, 'Lockout Agreements' Vol. 107 LQR 366.

Pitt *v* PHH Asset Management Ltd [1993] 4 All ER 961

The defendant orally agreed to sell property to the plaintiff for £200,000 and not to consider any third party offers provided the plaintiff exchanged contracts within two weeks of receipt of the draft contract. Eight days later when the plaintiff was ready to exchange contracts, the defendant announced that he had been offered £210,000 for the property by a third party. When the plaintiff refused to match this price, the defendant sold the property to the third party. The plaintiff sued for breach of contract.

Gibson L.J.:

It seems to me that what was agreed was a lock-out agreement. In *Walford v Miles* [1992] 1 All ER 453 at 461, [1992] 2 AC 128 at 139 Lord Ackner said: 'There is clearly no reason in English contract law why A, for good consideration, should not achieve an enforceable agreement whereby B agrees for a specified period of time not to negotiate with anyone except A in relation to the sale of his property.' He identified the negative element in such an agreement as being the characteristic of a lock-out agreement: ' . . . B, by agreeing not to negotiate for this fixed period with a third party, locks himself *into* negotiations with A. What A has achieved is an exclusive opportunity, for a fixed period, to try and come to terms with B, an opportunity for which he has, unless he makes his agreement under seal, to give good consideration.' (Lord Ackner's emphasis)

In the present case it was not incumbent on the defendant to proffer a contract. It did not bind itself to do so, but once it did it was bound in my judgment by the terms of the lock-out agreement for the fourteen day period that followed. . . .

(Mann L.J. agreed.)

Bingham M.R.:

For very many people their first and closest contact with the law is when they come to buy or sell a house. They frequently find it a profoundly depressing and frustrating experience. The vendor puts his house on the market. He receives an offer which is probably less than his asking price. He agonises over whether to accept or hold out for more. He decides to accept, perhaps after negotiating some increase. A deal is struck. Hands are shaken. The vendor celebrates, relaxes, makes plans for his own move and takes his house off the market. The he hears that the purchaser who was formerly pleading with him to accept his offer has decided not to proceed. No explanation is given, no apology made. The vendor has to embark on the whole dreary process of putting his house on the market all over again.

For the purchaser the process is, if anything, worse. After a series of futile visits to unsuitable houses he eventually finds the house of his dreams. He makes an offer, perhaps at the asking price, perhaps at what the agent tells him the vendor is likely to accept. The offer is accepted. A deal is done. The purchaser instructs solicitors to act. He perhaps commissions an architect to plan alterations. He makes arrangements to borrow money. He puts his own house on the market. He makes arrangements to move. He then learns that the vendor has decided to sell to someone else, perhaps for the price already offered and accepted, perhaps for an increased price achieved by a covert, unofficial auction. Again, no explanation, no apology. The vendor is able to indulge his self-interest, even his whims, without exposing himself to any legal penalty.

The reasons why purchaser and vendor can act in this apparently unprincipled manner are to be found in two legal rules of long standing: first, the rule that contracts for the sale and purchase of land must be evidenced (or now made) in writing; secondly, the rule that terms agreed subject to contract do not give rise to a binding contract. These rules are deeply imbedded in statute and authority. They make possible the behaviour I have described, but the validity and merits of those rules are not, and could not be, the subject of challenge in this appeal.

For the purchaser there is, however, one means of protection: to make an independent agreement by which the vendor agrees for a clear specified period not to deal with anyone other than that purchaser. The effect is to give that purchaser a clear run for the period in question. The vendor does not agree to sell to that purchaser—such an agreement would be covered by s. 2 of the 1989 Act—but he does give a negative undertaking that he will not for the given period deal with anyone else. That, I am quite satisfied, is what happened here, as the judge rightly held. The vendor and the prospective purchaser made what has come to be called a 'lock-out agreement'. That was a contract binding on them both. The vendor broke it. He is liable to the prospective purchaser for damages which remain to be assessed. . . .

Chapter Three

Contract as a Promised Exchange

INTRODUCTION

Because the common law system of contract (save in cases where a promise is recorded under seal) has not imposed general requirements that promises be recorded in writing, or surrounded by other so-called requirements of form, the common law has not been able to easily filter out promises that are contractual from other kinds of transaction, such as a gift promise. As we saw in Chapter 1, the classical means of doing this was through the evolution of consideration. (*Governors of Dalhousie College v Boutilier*, p. 18 above.) What precisely is meant by consideration remains a matter of controversy, with scholars arguing about the differences between equitable and common law perspectives as well as the internal features—promise *per se*, reliance, or exchange? The orthodox view is that the exchange, or bargain theory, passed into the literature, and judicial utterances, as the paradigm, in the late nineteenth century, although even then the exceptions found in the case-law made this model neither a universal, nor a reliable, basis for predicting enforceability. Both practical commercial expediency, and underlying considerations of fairness, allow us to point to several lines of case-law that undermine the bargain theory, so much so that the American scholar, Charles Fried, (himself a moral philosopher who advocates a modified moral obligation theory) has remarked that the holes in the bargain theory are so pronounced that moral obligation is as consistent a theory as bargain: *Contract as Promise* (Boston: Harvard U.P. 1981).

While Fried's observation is no doubt given somewhat tongue-in-cheek, it is correct to point out the tensions that confront the orthodox view of contract as bargain. In Ireland, the recent cases on promissory estoppel and legitimate expectation make it clear that contract is only one way in which a promise, or a reasonably based belief or anticipated benefit, will be given legal substance by the judiciary.

SECTION ONE—BARGAIN

Atiyah, P. S., 'Consideration: A Restatement', *Essays on Contract* (Oxford: Clarendon Press, 1986)

1. *The Nature and Purposes of Consideration*

. . .

The truth is that the courts have never set out to create a doctrine of consideration. They have been concerned with the much more practical problem of deciding in the

course of litigation whether a particular promise in a particular case should be enforced. Since it is unthinkable that any legal system could enforce *all* promises it has always been necessary for the courts to decide which promises they would enforce. When the courts found a sufficient reason for enforcing a promise they enforced it; and when they found that for one reason or another it was undesirable to enforce a promise, they did not enforce it. It seems highly probable that when the courts first used the word 'consideration' they meant no more than that there was a 'reason' for the enforcement of a promise. If the consideration was 'good', this meant that the court found sufficient reason for enforcing the promise. All this is not to suggest that the law was ever unprincipled, or that judges ever decided cases according to personal or idiosyncratic views of what promises it was desirable to enforce. As always in the common law, it was the collective view of the judges, based largely on the conditions and moral values of the community, which prevailed over a period of time. The doctrine of precedent, then as now, was always available as an aid to the courts in deciding what promises to enforce.
. . .

At a relatively early date it was established that the courts would enforce a promise if another promise or an act was given in return for it; and also that they would not normally enforce a promise if it was merely intended as a gift with no return of any kind. In the first class of case it came therefore to be said that there was good consideration; there were good reasons for enforcing the promise. In the second class there was no such reason, and therefore no consideration. But it also became clear from a very early time that the whole law could not be reduced to such very simple terms. There were some cases in which a promise was given in return for another promise or an act, in which for one reason or another it was felt unjust or inexpedient that the promise should be enforced. Such cases could be, and sometimes were explained by saying that there was no consideration for the promise; but as the nineteenth century wore on, an alternative approach began to manifest itself. This was to say that there was good consideration (though perhaps the word 'good' would more usually be omitted) but that nevertheless the promise was unenforceable for other reasons, for example, because it had been extorted by duress, or fraud, or because it was illegal. The last type of case was often dealt with by saying that the consideration was unlawful; a judge who formulated his reasons in this way would perhaps, if pressed, have said that there was no 'good' consideration.
. . .

More recently still, this alternative approach has hardened so that courts now find nothing inconsistent in holding that there is consideration for a promise, but nevertheless refusing to enforce it because the transaction is illegal. This approach also manifests itself in the relatively modern device of refusing to enforce a promise on the ground that the promisor did not 'intend' to create legal relations by his promise. Where this is done (as it usually is) in a case where there is no express disavowal of the intent to create legal relations, it appears to be merely a legal justification for refusing to enforce a promise which the courts think, for one reason or another, it is unjust or impolitic to enforce. There seems no doubt that a hundred years ago the courts would have dealt with these problems in terms of consideration.
. . .

This change of approach is symptomatic of the change which has developed in the way lawyers think about consideration. It is no longer thought that consideration is a compendious word simply indicating whether there are good reasons for enforcing a promise; it is widely assumed that consideration is a technical requirement of the law which has little or nothing to do with the justice or desirability of enforcing a promise.

Modern lawyers thus see nothing incongruous in asserting that a promise made for good consideration should nevertheless not be enforced.
. . .

Exactly the same development has taken place with regard to those promises which are not normally enforced, that is the promise to make a gift with no return of any kind. Since the courts first decided that such promises were not enforceable, it came to be asserted that gratuitous promises were promises given without consideration. But in course of time, occasions arose when the courts found that there were sometimes very good reasons for enforcing gratuitous promises in certain cases, and they accordingly enforced them. When cases of this kind arose during the first part of the nineteenth century the natural approach of the courts was to say that there *was* consideration— which at that time seems merely to have meant that there were good reasons for enforcing the promise. But here again, as lawyers began to treat consideration as a 'doctrine' whose content was a set of fixed and rigid rules tailored to the typical case, these cases came to seem anomalous. It therefore became fashionable to deny that there was consideration; and yet such promises were and still are quite often enforced. Modern lawyers are thus forced to say that some promises may be enforceable even though there is no consideration for them.

However, this last proposition is one which lawyers have been much more reluctant to accept than the one previously discussed, that is that even promises supported by consideration may sometimes be unenforceable. There has seemed to be something almost akin to heresy in admitting that a promise may be enforced without consideration. This is fully borne out by the initial reactions to the High Trees[1] case which was originally looked on with great scepticism by the legal profession as an instance of Lord Denning's advanced and 'unsound' views.[2] But this is by no means the only instance of gratuitous promises being enforced by the courts. As will be seen below, many gratuitous promises are enforced by the courts, if the word 'gratuitous' is understood to mean a promise to make a gift, but the difference between most of these instances and the High Trees decision is that in the older cases it was traditionally asserted that there was in fact consideration.
. . .

As will be apparent from the above discussion, there has gradually been a hardening of the attitude of the English common lawyer to the whole notion of consideration. From being merely a reason for the enforcement of a promise (or possibly a reason for the creation or recognition of an obligation), it has come to be regarded as a technical doctrine which has little to do with the justice or desirability of enforcing a promise, or recognising obligations. Thus a promise for consideration may be unenforceable; and a promise without consideration may be enforceable. Interwoven with this development has been another which has also played a large part in leading to the conventional view of the law at the present day. This has been the persistent and apparently compulsive desire of lawyers to concentrate on the typical contractual promise and to draw conclusions of universal validity from that typical case. Thus, because it is often (or indeed usually) a good reason for enforcing a promise that the promisor has received a counter promise in return, lawyers appear to have convinced themselves that a wholly executory contract should always be enforceable, and that a counter promise is necessarily a benefit or a detriment, even before any performance or reliance. Because most contracts are bargains, lawyers have steadfastly refused to recognise the evidence under their very eyes, that courts often enforce promises which are not bargains, and that they do so for reasons of justice and good policy. Because a promise to make a gift is not usually recognised as a sufficient reason for its enforcement, lawyers have refused to acknowledge that in some circumstances it is particularly desirable to enforce a gratuitous promise and that the courts in fact do so. Because in most circumstances the consideration must in practice be supplied by the promisee, it was deduced (and even on one occasion stated by the House of Lords) that consideration must always move from the promisee; yet the courts in fact sometimes enforce promises in which the real ground for enforcing the promise is something done by a third party.

[1.] [1974] KB 130.   [2.] See e.g. Bennion, 'Want of Consideration' (1953), 16 MLR 441; Gordon [1963] Camb. LJ 222.

Defining Consideration

K.C.T. Sutton, *Consideration Reconsidered*, (University of Queensland Press 1974) ch. 2. (Footnotes abridged.)

Consideration and the Bargain Concept

The usual definition of consideration given by text writers and one which has received judicial approval on numerous occasions is that propounded by Lush J. in *Currie v Misa*.[1] 'A valuable consideration in the sense of the law may consist either in some right, interest, profit, or benefit accruing to the one party, or some forbearance, detriment, loss or responsibility given suffered or undertaken by the other.' The definition was itself based on a statement in Comyn's *Digest*,[2] which in turn relied upon cases decided at the close of the eighteenth century. However, the notion of defining consideration in terms of benefit or detriment goes back to at least 1588[3] and was explicable, as Ames has pointed out,[4] by the rise of the actions of *assumpsit* and *indebitatus assumpsit*.

But if the view put forward earlier is correct, and the doctrine of consideration is bound up with the concept of bargain which was inherent in it from the beginning, then the definition suggested by Lush J. is defective in that it does not emphasise this element. It is significant that Halsbury, in defining consideration, took the definition propounded in *Currie v Misa* but added the words 'at his [i.e. the promisor's] request' at the end, thus indicating that the detriment suffered by the promisee must be at the other party's behest.[5] It was this notion of reciprocity that suggested to some writers that the essence of consideration lay in the possible benefit or value to the promisor of what was given or promised in return, rather than the notion of detriment or burden to the promisee; but the answer to this view is that, if the doctrine of consideration is to be identified with the concept of bargain, any benefit to the promisor must necessarily be matched with a corresponding detriment to the promisee—with the one exception where the situation deals with the performance of a pre-existing contractual duty as in the *Shadwell v Shadwell* type of case.[6]

After the eighteenth century flirtation with notions of moral obligation and the like, the Victorian era saw a return to the orthodox view that the common law theory of enforcing simple contracts was one of giving effect to bargains.[7] Consideration came to be thought of as the price or agreed exchange for the promise, and increasing emphasis was laid on the necessity for an exchange reciprocally induced as an essential element. Hence, throughout the nineteenth century and persisting into the twentieth century, there is a hardening of the juristic attitude, with insistence being increasingly given to the notion of consideration as the price in return for which the promise is made.[8] Pollock in his *Contracts*[9] wrote that 'an act or forbearance of one party, or the promise thereof, is the price for which the promise of the other is bought, and the promise thus given for value is enforceable', and his description was adopted by Lord Dunedin in *Dunlop Pneumatic Tyre Co. Ltd v Selfridge & Co. Ltd*[10] and by the English Law Revision Committee in their report on the doctrine of consideration in 1937.[11]

When Holmes published *The Common Law* in 1881, he concluded that the same thing might be a consideration or not, according as it was dealt with by the parties. In his view, while consideration must not be confounded with motive, a consideration must still be given or accepted as the motive or inducement of the promise, and the promise must be made and accepted as the conventional motive or inducement for furnishing the consideration. The root of the whole matter lay in the relation of reciprocal conventional inducement, each for the other, between consideration and promise.[12] As Chief Justice of the Supreme Judicial Court of Massachusetts, Holmes declined to apply the 'reciprocal conventional inducement' theory rigorously in *Martin v Meles*[13] (which would have meant holding the promisor not bound by his promise) comforting himself with the reflection that 'courts have gone [to] very great lengths in discovering the implication of such an equivalence, sometimes perhaps even having found it in matters which would seem to be no more than conditions or natural consequences of the promise'.[14]

However, two years later, in delivering the opinion of the United States Supreme Court in *Wisconsin & Michigan Co. v Powers*[15] his Honour felt himself able to apply his 'conventional inducement' test to defeat the claim of the plaintiff company which had begun construction of a railway in reliance on a statute exempting any person who built such railway from taxation for ten years. The statute was later repealed and the plaintiff argued that the repealing Act was unconstitutional as impairing a contractual obligation. Holmes J. held that, while the building of the railway was a sufficient detriment to constitute consideration if other elements were present, yet in the absence of the element of conventional inducement the plaintiff's argument failed.

This case is somewhat reminiscent of the decision of the High Court of Australia in *Australian Woolen Mills Pty Ltd v Commonwealth*[16] where the plaintiff's claim, based on the existence of a contract between it and the defendant, was rejected on the ground that there was no such contract as alleged. The plaintiff relied on a statement by the Commonwealth Government that a subsidy would be paid to manufacturers of wool purchased and used for local manufacture, as a result of which it bought large quantities of wool and received certain subsidies. The claim was for subsidies payable in terms of the arrangement.

The High Court of Australia embraced the bargain theory of consideration with the comment that 'between the statement or announcement, which is put forward as an offer capable of acceptance by the doing of an act, and the act which is put forward as the executed consideration for the alleged promise, there must subsist, so to speak, the relation of a *quid pro quo*'.[17] Their Honours went on to endorse the proposition that the presence or absence of an implied request to do the act was a useful test for determining whether there was a true offer and acceptance or whether the offer was made to induce the doing of the act. In the result, the plaintiff's claim failed as there was no offer, no implied request that wool be bought, and no suggestion that promise of payment and purchase of wool were related so that one was consideration for the other.

It may be remarked at this point that it is a central thesis of this study that a rigorous application of the bargain theory, of the 'reciprocal conventional inducement' notion of consideration, would result in many decisions being found to be outside it. Street recognised this fact. He adopted Holmes' views but pointed out that while academic writers had embraced the bargain theory of consideration, its supremacy in the courts had never been complete. An element might be treated as consideration although the parties had not done so. The fact that the parties did not happen to treat an act of detriment as a consideration in a particular case was not conclusive that the act was not good consideration to support the promise.[18]

Corbin looked at another facet of the problem when he wrote that there were far too many decisions enforcing a promise where the only consideration was action by the promise in reliance on the promise, for the remarks of Holmes J. to be accepted without reserve.[19] Another American jurist, Langdell, likewise felt the difficulty of reconciling the bargain theory with its exceptions, but the exceptions he was concerned about were those bargains which the law did not regard as such and did not enforce. He defined consideration as the thing given or done by the promisee in exchange for the promise, and then had to enumerate a list of things which, if done by the promisee in exchange for the promise, would not be consideration therefore.[20] Finally, it should be noted that the American *Restatement of Contracts* first published in 1932, adopted the bargain theory of consideration,[21] but then felt constrained to introduce a new class of informal contracts which could not be brought within its framework.[22]

A thin veneer of rationalisation is usually given to the bargain theory by saying that certain acts given in exchange for a promise do not amount to consideration because they are of no value in the eye of the law. It was of course early realised that not every exchange could amount to consideration, and the test was evolved of according validity only to those exchanges which could be said to amount to a benefit to the promisor or a detriment to the promisee. In the prevailing climate of analytical historical juristic thinking in the nineteenth century, the theory became established that only an exchange which was a detriment to the promisee would be recognised by the law. Detriment to the promisee was the significant feature of consideration. The fact that the promisor received a benefit was merely incidental to the prime requirement of a bargained-for detriment to the promisee. This theory had the inestimable advantage that it met the demands of historical derivation from the action of *assumpsit*.

As a result, at the beginning of the twentieth century the view was widespread that the universal test of consideration was detriment to the promisee, and that the notion of benefit to the promisor was irrelevant and was a misconception due to the mistake of applying to *assumpsit* ideas which belonged exclusively to debt. There might be a benefit to the promisor and yet no consideration, as where the benefit did not come from the promisee, while on the other hand, detriment to the promisee was the all-embracing test.[23] However, this view was not accepted without question, and there were not wanting protagonists for the view that benefit to the promisor should be retained as an alternative test of consideration,[24] attention being drawn to the *Shadwell v Shadwell* type of case where there was said to be a benefit to the promisor without a corresponding detriment to the promisee in his right to have performed the pre-existing contractual duty owed by the promisee to a third party.

1. (1875) LR 10 Ex 153, 162.   2. 5th ed. (1822), vol. 1, 294.
3. See Coke *arguendo* in *Stone v Wythipol* (1588) Cro. Eliz. 126, and *Greenleaf v Barker* (1591) Cro. Eliz. 193.
4. 'The History of Assumpsit' in (1888) 2 Harv LR 1, 17.
5. *Laws of England*, (2nd ed., ed. Hailsham 1932), vol. 7, 136.
6. (1860) 9 CBNS 159; 142 ER 62.
7. Sharp, 'Pacta Sunt Servanda' in (1941) 41 Col LR 783.
8. See e.g. Langdell, *Summary of Contracts*, s. 45.
9. See e.g. 8th ed., 175.
10. |1915| AC 847, 855.
11. Cmd. 5449, s. 17, 12.
12. See pp 289–95. See also Langdell, *Summary of Contracts*, ss. 66–8; and *Fire Insurance Assn. v Wickham* (1891) 141 US 564, 579; *McGovern v New York* (1923) 138 NE 26 (CANY); *Foster v Dawber* (1851) 6 Ex. 839, 849–50.
13. (1901) 60 NE 397.
14. Ibid. at p. 398.   15. (1903) 191 US 379, 386.

16. (1953–54) 92 CLR 424.
17. Ibid. at pp 456–7.
18. *Foundations of Legal Liability* (1901),
    vol. 2, 71, 81 et seq.
19. 'Does a Pre-existing Duty Defeat
    Consideration?' in (1918) 27 Yale LJ 362.
20. *Summary of Contracts*, ss 45 and 54.

21. S. 75.
22. Ss 85–90.
23. See Langdell, *Summary of Contracts*, s. 64.
24. See e.g. Bennett, 'Is Mere Gain to a
    Promisor a Good Consideration for His
    Promise?' in (1896) 10 Harv LR 257.

Note

'A valuable consideration, in the sense of the law, may consist in some right, interest, profit, or benefit, accruing to the one party, or some forbearance, detriment, loss, or responsibility, given, suffered or undertaken by the other.' Per Lush J. in *Currie v Misa* (1875) LR 10 Ex 153

Despite the emphasis on benefit and detriment as indicators of a bargain there have been promises held enforceable in spite of the fact that there was no obvious detriment to the promisee.

A. PAST CONSIDERATION

Consideration may be executed or executory but it may not be past.

Pao On v Lau Yiu Long [1980] AC 614

The plaintiffs owned shares in a private company, Shing On, whose principal asset was a building under construction. The defendants were major shareholders in a public company, Fu Chip, which wished to acquire the building. It was agreed that the plaintiffs would transfer their shares to Fu Chip in return for shares in Fu Chip. At the defendants' request the plaintiffs agreed not to sell their Fu Chip shares for one year. Later the defendants gave the plaintiffs a guarantee in which they promised to indemnify the plaintiffs against any loss sustained if the Fu Chip share price fell during that period. When the share price fell the defendants refused to indemnify them claiming *inter alia* that there was no consideration for their promise.

This litigation took place before the courts of Hong Kong and was under appeal to the Privy Council.

Lord Scarman:

. . .

The Board agrees with [counsel for the plaintiffs'] submission that the consideration expressly stated in the written guarantee is sufficient in law to support the defendants' promise of indemnity. An act done before the giving of a promise to make a payment or to confer some other benefit can sometimes be consideration for the promise. The act must have been done at the promisors' request: the parties must have understood that the act was to be remunerated either by a payment or the conferment of some other benefit: and payment, or the conferment of a benefit, must have been legally enforceable had it been promised in advance. All three features are present in this case. The promise given to Fu Chip under the main agreement not to sell the shares for a year was at the first defendant's request. The parties understood at the time of the main agreement that the restriction on selling must be compensated for by the benefit of a guarantee against a drop in price: and such a guarantee would be legally enforceable. The agreed cancellation of the subsidiary agreement left, as the parties knew, the plaintiffs unprotected in a respect in which at the time of the main agreement all were agreed they should be protected.

|Counsel's| submission is based on *Lampleigh v Brathwait* (1615) Hobart 105. In that case the judges said, at p. 106: 'First . . . a meer voluntary courtesie will not have a consideration to uphold an assumpsit. But if that courtesie were moved by a suit or request of the party that gives the assumpsit, it will bind, for the promise, though it follows, yet it is not naked, but couples itself with the suit before, and the merits of the party procured by that suit, which is the difference.' The modern statement of the law is in the judgment of Bowen L.J. in *In re Casey's Patents* |1892| 1 Ch. 104, 115–116; Bowen L.J. said:

> Even if it were true, as some scientific students of law believe, that a past service cannot support a future promise, you must look at the document and see if the promise cannot receive a proper effect in some other way. Now, the fact of a past service raises an implication that at the time it was rendered it was to be paid for, and, if it was a service which was to be paid for, when you get in the subsequent document a promise to pay, that promise may be treated either as an admission which evidences or as a positive bargain which fixes the amount of that reasonable remuneration on the faith of which the service was originally rendered. So that here for past services there is ample justification for the promise to give the third share.

Conferring a benefit is, of course, an equivalent to payment: see *Chitty on Contracts*, (24th ed. 1977), vol. 1, para. 154.

|Counsel| for the defendants, does not dispute the existence of the rule but challenges its application to the facts of this case. He submits that it is not a necessary inference or implication from the terms of the written guarantee that any benefit or protection was to be given to the plaintiffs for their acceptance of the restriction on selling their shares. Their Lordships agree that the mere existence or recital of a prior request is not sufficient in itself to convert what is *prima facie* past consideration into sufficient consideration in law to support a promise: as they have indicated, it is only the first of three necessary preconditions. As for the second of those preconditions, whether the act done at the request of the promisor raises an implication of promised remuneration or other return is simply one of the construction of the words of the contract in the circumstances of its making. Once it is recognised, as the Board considers it inevitably must be, that the expressed consideration includes a reference to the plaintiffs' promise not to sell the shares before 30 April 1974—a promise to be performed in the future, though given in the past—it is not possible to treat the defendants' promise of indemnity as independent of the plaintiffs' antecedent promise, given at the first defendant's request, not to sell. The promise of indemnity was given because at the time of the main agreement the parties intended that the first defendant should confer upon the plaintiffs the benefit of his protection against a fall in price. When the subsidiary agreement was cancelled, all were well aware that the plaintiffs were still to have the benefit of his protection as consideration for the restriction on selling. It matters not whether the indemnity thus given be regarded as the best evidence of the benefit intended to be conferred in return for the promise not to sell, or as the positive bargain which fixes the benefit on the faith of which the promise was given—though where, as here, the subject is a written contract, the better analysis is probably

that of the 'positive bargain'. Their Lordships, therefore, accept the submission that the contract itself states a valid consideration for the promise of indemnity.

B. SUFFICIENCY

Once consideration has been proven to exist a court will not evaluate the comparative value of the promise given and the promise or act given in return. For this reason it is said the courts will not enquire as to the adequacy of consideration.

'The adequacy of consideration is for the parties to consider at the time of making the agreement not for the court when it is sought to be enforced.' Per Blackburn J. in *Bolton v Madden* (1873) LR 90 355

'Once there is consideration, its adequacy in this sort of case is irrelevant to its validity and enforceability.' Per Ellis J., in *Kennedy v Kennedy* (HC) 12 January 1984, unrep.

Consideration must however be 'sufficient' i.e. it must be something which is of value in the eyes of the law.

O'Neill v Murphy [1936] NI 16

The plaintiff sued for fees due for the performance of certain architectural and building work for the defendants. The defendants claimed that they had performed certain agreed services in return in the nature of prayers for the benefit of the plaintiff and his family. The court had to decide *inter alia* whether there was sufficient consideration in law for the alleged agreement.

Andrews L.J.:

. . .

In the first place the defendants have not satisfied me that the consideration relied upon in support of the alleged agreement is sufficient in law for that purpose. At the time that the plaintiff wrote the letter of 14 September 1926, to Father Murphy, a sum of £935 5s 0d, was due to him. In that letter he said: 'Now I think I will be well paid for anything I did if you can arrange with the Mother General to have daily prayers offered up for myself and family together with Mrs O'Neill and my brother J. K.' To this the Reverend Mothers replied on 18 September: 'The remuneration you ask for your gigantic work is indeed freely given. Daily prayers will be offered in every house of the Order for your intentions as a most generous benefactor.' A cheque for £200 was enclosed, which the plaintiff was asked to accept as a little favour and as a very small appreciation of the plaintiff's great work and generosity.

Now it is elementary law, which comes down to us from the Roman jurists, that to constitute an enforceable contract not under seal, there must be a good and valid consideration; and, whilst it is clear that courts will not interfere with the exercise of free will and judgment of the parties by inquiring into the adequacy of consideration, it is necessary that it should be sufficient in law. Thus, neither a mere voluntary courtesy nor some act already executed will suffice. So, too, a promise by a creditor to accept less than the full amount of his undisputed debt is not legally binding upon him. Such promise cannot be relied upon as a legal satisfaction, for there is no consideration for the relinquishment of the balance of the debt. *Cumber v Wane*,[1] and *Pinnel's case*,[2] are landmarks which are too firmly fixed in our law to be shaken; and, whilst it is true that the addition of some benefit or even of a legal possibility of benefit to a creditor will render the consideration sufficient to support an agreement, such benefit must, as pointed out by Lord Selborne in *Foakes v Beer*,[3] be an independent benefit of a kind which might in law be a good and valuable consideration for any other sort of agreement not under seal.

Now, whilst expressly disclaiming any opinion which might be construed as in the slightest degree derogatory of the real value and efficacy of prayer, I can only say that no case cited to us or which I have found, can properly be relied upon as an authority for the proposition that a mere promise by one person to say prayers or to cause prayers to be said for another amounts in law to a good and valuable consideration for a contract not under seal. If such be the law it should be laid down by our highest judicial tribunal—the House of Lords.

[1]. 1 Sm. LC (13th ed.) 373.   [2]. 5 Co. Rep. 117 (a).   [3]. 9 AC 605, 614.

(Best L.J. decided the case on other grounds and thus found it unnecessary to deal with the issue of consideration.)

C. COMPROMISE OF A CLAIM

Bryan O'Donnell *v* Michael J. O'Sullivan (1913) 47 ILTR 253

Palles L.C.B:

. . .

The action was brought on foot of a promissory note, and there is an admission here that this promissory note was given in respect of betting transactions. I have here the original document that shows the consideration for the £65. 'O'Donnell v O'Sullivan, £137 10s. I hereby consent to pay you £75—£10 in cash and promissory note for £65— in full payment of above. M. J. O'Sullivan, Hospital.' It is said that under these circumstance this is a good agreement for a compromise. This was an action which both parties knew could not succeed. The settlement of that is not good consideration for a compromise. I take it that it is settled law that unless there is a reasonable claim which is *bona fide* intended to be pursued, the settlement of that claim cannot be good consideration for a compromise. It lay then on the plaintiff to come forward and show that he had a reasonable claim against the defendant, and although this sum of £75 is in full payment of a gambling debt of £137 10s, that notwithstanding that there was new consideration for the agreement to pay the £75, and, to use the language of some of the cases, it was 'not to be taken as £75 on account of above, but for a sum equal to above.' He must come forward and prove that, in order to show that there is anything substantial in the nature of the compromise. If not, there was nothing to compromise. I doubt even if the new consideration would be sufficient, if part of the consideration was, as I think it was, this gambling debt of £137 10s, because that consideration is not made void, but illegal, and according to my recollection if part of the consideration is illegal it taints the whole. But my judgment is based on this, that the sum sued for is clearly for a gambling debt, and in order to make the agreement for a compromise a good contract there must be a reasonable claim *bona fide* intended to be pursued.

D. FORBEARANCE TO SUE AS CONSIDERATION

Fullerton *v* Provincial Bank of Ireland [1903] AC 309

. . .

In the spring of 1895 Colonel Stevenson having overdrawn his account with the Provincial Bank of Ireland was asked by the bank to reduce the debt. He wrote several letters to the manager in which he said that he was buying an estate and when he received the conveyance he would deposit the deed as a security for the overdraft. In July 1895, he deposited the conveyance with the bank. In July 1896, he executed a mortgage of the estate in favour of the appellants. This mortgage was registered in the Dublin registry of deeds by the appellants without notice of the prior charge. Colonel Stevenson afterwards sold the estate under the Irish Land Purchase Acts, and it became necessary to decide the priorities of the above two incumbrances.

Lord Macnaghten:

. . .

The other point on which the learned Solicitor General relied was that there was no proof of consideration. The promise, he said, if it was a definite promise, was *nudum pactum*—no doubt, he said, Colonel Stevenson had overdrawn his account, but there was no stipulation for forbearance for any definite time.

My Lords, this point seems to me to be settled by authority. In such a case as this it is not necessary that there should be an arrangement for forbearance for any definite or particular time. It is quite enough if you can infer from the surrounding circumstances that there was an implied request for forebearance for a time, and that forbearance for a reasonable time was in fact extended to the person who asked for it. That proposition seems to me to be established by the case of *Alliance Bank v Broom*,[1] to which my noble and learned friend Lord Lindley referred yesterday, and other cases, among which I may mention *Oldershaw v King*,[2] with the observations on that case and the case in Drewry and Smale, by Bowen L.J. in *Miles v New Zealand Alford Estate Co.*,[3] and I may add that the proposition seems to be good sense.

Lord Davey:

. . .

There can be no possible doubt that this promise was accepted by Mr Stuart on the part of the bank, but it is said that there was no consideration for it. Now in the letter of 18 May (that is the second letter) Colonel Stevenson writes to this effect, addressing Mr Stuart, 'All you require is a little patience and my account will be put on a satisfactory basis.' I think this means, 'Exercise patience and some forebearance and I will give you the required security and thus put my account in order.' The bank did exercise patience, and gave some forbearance by not demanding, as they might have done, immediate payment of the debt, and by giving Colonel Stevenson the required time to effect the security. I think that such forbearance in fact, although there was no agreement by the bank to forbear suing Colonel Stevenson for any definite period, was sufficient consideration to support his promise to give the security, on the principle stated by Kindersley V.C. in *Alliance Bank v Broom*. The Vice Chancellor's judgment in that case was quoted with approval by Lord Bowen in *Miles v New Zealand Alford Estate Co.*[4] as laying down a sound principle. In the case before Lord Bowen the question was whether a guarantee which had been given by the promoter of a company at a general meeting of the shareholders to guarantee a dividend of a certain amount for a certain time on the shares was given with or without consideration, and in referring to the case before him Lord Bowen said, after quoting the Vice Chancellor's judgment:

So it will be sufficient here that the directors did forbear, if their forbearance was at the request expressed or implied of the guarantor and in consequence of his guarantee being given, and it seems to me there is no sort of necessity to discover language of any particular form, or writing of any particular character, embodying the resolution of the directors. We must treat the thing in a business way and draw an inference of fact as to what the real nature of the transaction was as between business men.

My Lords, that seems to me to be directly applicable to the present question. There can be no doubt that the forbearance was given in this case, and I think it is a just inference of fact that it was given at the request of Colonel Stevenson in consequence of his undertaking to secure the account and place it on what he describes as a satisfactory basis.

[1.] (1864) 2 Dr & S 289.
[2.] (1857) 2 H & N 517.
[3.] (1886) 32 ChD 289.
[4.] Ibid. 266, 290.

(Shand and Lindley L.JJ. agreed on this issue.)

Provincial Bank of Ireland Ltd *v* Donnell (1932) 67 ILTR 142
(Facts on p. 92.)

Andrews L.J.:

In these circumstances the real defence urged before us by counsel for the defendant was that as the guarantee was not under seal it must, like other simple contracts, be supported by a valuable consideration. The mere existence of a debt is not sufficient to support the surety's promise to the creditor. A past or executed consideration, unless moved at the defendant's request, is not binding without some new consideration. It is true that an agreement by a creditor that he will forbear to sue the principal debtor for a past debt is a sufficient consideration for a person becoming a surety for the debt. So also is actual forebearance at the request, express or implied, of the defendant. But it is only by such agreement for forbearance or by actual forbearance to sue that a past consideration may be relied upon as a valuable consideration which will support the guarantee. It was to bring the present case within this principle that plaintiffs' counsel argued that the true meaning of the opening words of the guarantee sued upon is 'in consideration of your not suing my husband for advances already made to him.' The first difficulty, however, in upholding this construction is that, although such forbearance might have been easily expressed, this has not been done; and I am unable to put a forced and unnatural construction upon words which are in no way ambiguous merely to make the guarantee binding and enforceable by action. One ought to be slow in implying consideration in favour of the bank, whose document this guarantee is, especially when one remembers that when the guarantee was signed they did not stand to the defendant in the relationship of creditor and debtor.

The construction contended for becomes all the more difficult when it is remembered that as the Lord Chief Justice finds 'there was no talk about any agreement not to sue;' and, finally, the grammatical difficulties which arise from the reference to the past advances being immediately followed in the same sentence by a reference to the future advances compel me to reject the plaintiffs' contention without any hesitation. I leave the argument in reference to the consideration afforded by past advances by merely saying that if, apart from agreement, there was in fact a forbearance to sue there is not a particle of evidence to show, as is necessary, that such forbearance resulted from any request, express or implied, on the part of the defendant.

(Best L.J. concurred.)

The Commodity Broking Co. Ltd v Fergus Meehan [1985] IR 12

The defendant was the sole beneficial owner of the entire shareholding of Pistola Investments Ltd, a company which was heavily indebted to the plaintiff. In the course of a meeting between the two parties the defendant intimated that the company was insolvent and agreed to personally pay off this debt by instalments. When the defendant defaulted in his payments, the plaintiff sued for breach of contract. The defendant pleaded an absence of consideration.

Barron J. (HC):

. . .

The consideration relied upon by the plaintiff is that it forbore to sue the company. In the *Alliance Bank Ltd v Broom* (1864) 2 Dr and Sm 289 the defendant who was a customer of the plaintiff bank was asked to give security for money which he owed to the bank. He agreed to hypothecate certain goods in favour of the bank. When he failed to do so, the bank sought to enforce his promise, which he pleaded was given without consideration. He failed in this plea. It was held that he had by implication asked the bank to forbear and that he had received a sufficient degree of forbearance to amount to consideration for his promise. The Vice Chancellor Sir D.R.E. Kindersley said at p. 292:

> It appears to me that, when the plaintiffs demanded payment of their debt, and, in consequence of that application the defendant agreed to give certain security, although there was no promise on the part of the plaintiffs to abstain for any certain time from suing for the debt, the effect was, that the plaintiffs did in effect give, and the defendant received, the benefit of some degree of forbearance; not, indeed, for any definite time, but, at all events, some extent of forbearance. If, on the application for security being made, the defendant had refused to give any security at all, the consequence certainly would have been that the creditor would have demanded payment of the debt, and have taken steps to enforce it. It is very true that, at any time after the promise, the creditor might have insisted on payment of his debt, and have brought an action; but the circumstances necessarily involve the benefit to the debtor of a certain amount of forbearance, which he would not have derived if he had not made the agreement.

In *Miles v New Zealand Alford Estate Co.* (1886) 32 ChD 266 a director and shareholder had sold certain property to the company. At a general meeting, several shareholders complained that the company had overpaid for the property. To still such criticisms, it was agreed that the company should pay a minimum dividend and that in any year in which it was not earned the vendor would make up the difference. He was subsequently sued on this agreement and it was contended that forbearance by the company to bring proceedings in relation to the sale was a sufficient consideration to make the agreement binding. Cotton L.J. at p. 283 in considering the proofs to establish consideration said:

> Now, what I understand to be the law is this, that if there is in fact a serious claim honestly made, the abandonment of the claim is a good 'consideration' for a contract; and if that is the law, what we really have to now consider is whether in the present case there is any evidence on which the court ought to find that there was a serious claim in fact made, and whether a contract to abandon that claim was the consideration for this letter of guarantee.

Having considered the evidence he said at p. 285:

> The conclusion at which I have arrived is, that there is no evidence on which we ought to rely that there was in fact a claim intended to be made against Grant (the vendor), and, in my opinion, on the evidence before us, we ought not to arrive at the conclusion that there was ever intended to be any contract by the company, much less that there was in fact any contract binding the company that that claim should not be prosecuted, and should be given up.

Fry L.J. accepted the same test and took the view that there was no intention by the company to abandon its claim. At p. 300 he said:

> I think the true result of the evidence is to show that there was an expectation in the mind of Mr Grant that if he gave this document no proceedings would be taken against him, that there was an expectation in the minds of many of those who were present, if they got this dividend they would take no proceedings; but it appears to me it is not right or competent for the court to turn an expectation into a contract, and that is what I think we should do if we gave effect to this as a valid contract.

Bowen L.J. dissented. He regarded consideration as being any forbearance to sue as a result of the express or implied request of the promissor. He regarded the decision of the trial judge 'as finding that proceedings had been threatened, that Mr Grant knew that they had been threatened, that he gave the guarantee in order to put an end to them, and that the proceedings were dropped in consequence of his giving that undertaking.' He regarded this as a finding that there has been consideration and in doing so he expressly followed *Alliance Bank Ltd v Broom*. The majority view that there should be an actual agreement to abandon threatened proceedings before there can be good consideration was not followed in later cases.

On similar facts, *Alliance Bank v Broom* was approved by the House of Lords in *Fullerton v Provincial Bank of Ireland* |1903| AC 309. In the same case, the judgment of Bowen L.J. in *Miles v New Zealand Alford Estate Co.* was cited with approval by Lord Davey at p. 316.

In *Combe v Combe* |1955| 1 All ER 767 the court had to consider whether there was consideration for a promise by a husband to pay permanent maintenance to his wife upon the dissolution of their marriage. The wife was not paid and after several years sued on the promise. It was held that there was no consideration since she had been entitled at all times to apply to the court for maintenance and such right would have been unaffected by her husband's promise. Accordingly there had been no request to forbear. At p. 771 Denning L.J. said: 'I cannot find any evidence of any intention by the husband that the wife should forbear from applying to the court for maintenance, or, in other words, any request by the husband, express or implied, that the wife should so forbear. Her forbearance was not intended by him, nor was it done at his request. It was, therefore, no consideration.'

In the same case Asquith L.J. said at p. 774: 'Finally, I do not think an actual forbearance, as opposed to an agreement to forbear to approach the court, is a good consideration unless it proceeds from a request, express or implied, on the part of the promissor. If not moved by such a request, the forbearance is not in respect of the promise.'

In my view, these cases establish that the better view is that where a request express or implied to forbear from bringing proceedings induces such forbearance this amounts to good consideration. It is not necessary as the majority decided in *Miles v New Zealand Alford Estate Co.* that there should be an actual agreement not to sue.

The reality of the present case it that when the company was unable to meet its calls the plaintiff took steps to protect itself. So far as the plaintiff was concerned, the company was almost certainly unable to pay. Accordingly, every effort was made to ensure that a promise could be obtained from the defendant that he would pay instead. In the course of events, I can find no implied request by the defendant not to sue the company nor clearly any express request. Nor can I find that the defendant's promise to pay influenced the plaintiff's decision not to sue the company. The plaintiff did not deliberately refrain from suing the company. Had it seemed to it a sensible course to adopt, it would have done so. Its reason for not doing so was not the defendant's promise to pay, but the realisation that it would be a fruitless exercise. If it had been deliberately misled by the defendant, either as to the solvency of the company or into not suing the company by reason of the payments made, the matter might have been otherwise. But there is no evidence to suggest any such calculated conduct on the part of the defendant nor is such a case made. Reluctantly I must hold that no consideration was given for the defendant's promise.

In the circumstances the plaintiff's claim must be dismissed.

E. CONSIDERATION MUST MOVE FROM THE PROMISEE

In *Tweddle v Atkinson* (1861) 1 B & Sm 393 Crompton J. stated that 'the consideration must move from the party entitled to sue upon the contract; it would be a monstrous proposition to say that a person was a party to the contract, for the purpose of suing upon it for his own advantage and not a party to it for the purpose of being sued.'

McCoubray v Thompson (1868) 2 IRCL 226

Galwey owned a farm valued at £196 which he wished to divide equally between the plaintiff and the defendant. It was agreed that the farm would be transferred to the defendant who in turn promised to pay the plaintiff £98. Although the farm was transferred the defendant refused to pay the plaintiff claiming (a) that no promise was alleged to have been paid (b) that no promise could be implied and (c) that no consideration moved from the plaintiff to support an express or implied promise by the defendant.

Monahan C.J.

. . .

The demurrer in this case must be allowed; no express promise is made to the plaintiff; and if a promise is to be implied, it would appear to be rather to A. Galwey, from whom the consideration moved. It is true that in the note to *Lampleigh v Braithwait* in *Smith's Leading Cases*, p. 142, it is stated that if the plaintiff have intervened in the agreement it is sufficient; but on examining *Tipper v Bicknell*,[1] and the other cases which [counsel] has cited in support of that proposition, it will be found that in each of them something was done by the plaintiff, that some part of the consideration moved from him.

[1.] 3 Bing. NC 710.

Barry *v* Barry (1891) 28 LR (Ir.) 45

O'Brien J:

In this case the facts were that a farmer had two sons; and upon the marriage of one of them (the defendant), part of his farm, with part of his stock, was assigned to two persons in trust for the son. All the family lived together upon the lands till the father's death. By his will, taking no notice of the settlement, he bequeathed the whole lands to the same son, and bound him to pay certain legacies to his other children, amongst the rest £20 to the plaintiff. The terms of the will are considered sufficient either to create a charge of the legacies upon the farm or to amount to a gift of the lands upon the condition of paying them. The executors named in the will who were the same persons to whom the lands were assigned in trust by the settlement, some time after the death of the father, went to the son, and in the presence of the plaintiff asked him whether he would possess the lands and pay the legacies, which I would take to mean nothing more than whether he would prefer to take half the farm under his settlement, or the whole with the charges upon it. At that time the will was not proved. Afterwards the plaintiff asked the defendant to pay him, and he promised to pay him £12, after a certain fair where he would have cattle to sell. Upon these facts an action was brought by the plaintiff for the £20, in the form of an account stated; but it was assumed to be the question whether the plaintiff was entitled to recover upon the facts in any state of pleading in a common law action. Upon the trial evidence was given, which was admitted against the judge's own opinion, of a conversation in the lifetime of the testator, the effect of which was that the defendant agreed, if the farm and whole stock were left to him, to pay the sums to the other members of the family which were afterwards given by the legacies. But as this evidence could not be used to make a will without writing, or to affect the terms of the will, or to make a condition or charge which was not found in the will itself, so I consider it was not legally relevant, as direct evidence, though very material on cross-examination, to prove the promise afterwards made, or even to establish the nature of the possession of the farm by the defendant. Upon the question of law it was contended that there was no contract or consideration on which an action at law could be maintained at all, on the ground that there was no legal consideration at all, or that the plaintiff was a stranger to it.

I consider *Tweddle v Atkinson*,[1] and the other cases cited, really do not touch the point at all. But I am of opinion, if a person has a legacy upon land, and requires the devisee to pay it, and he promises to do so, that there is a consideration on which he can subject himself to liability in an action at law, and that that consideration is properly in the nature of forbearance, the person having the right and the power to enforce, as the plaintiff had, by means of a proceeding against the land or the assets, and it not being necessary, in my view, that the power should be actually used or referred to. There is another ground of consideration on which the plaintiff's claim was put. The assent of the executors to the defendant's possession of the whole of the lands was required, and without a positive act upon their part he was a trespasser. He must be presumed in law, therefore, to have taken possession by means of that positive act, and to that act the plaintiff was a party. In other words he was allowed by the executors, with the plaintiff's consent, to go into possession of property against which the plaintiff had a specific right, and the possession of the assets for a time however short was a benefit in law to the defendant, and might mean the whole loss of the plaintiff's remedy. The statement that he would 'possess' the lands might merely mean that the defendant would elect to take under the will, as against the settlement, but that, with his subsequent promises to pay, was evidence for the jury of a personal contract. For these reasons I consider that we do not, for the sake of honesty, trench upon any rule of law—nor are much affected as to anything but substantial right—in holding that the plaintiff was entitled to judgment.

Gibson J.:

. . .

In my opinion, apart from the fact of the defendant asking and getting time for payment, of which there was evidence, but which was not left to or found by the jury, the contract shows a valid consideration moving from the plaintiff, and is enforceable in law. The defendant got an advantage to which he was not entitled; and the plaintiff—who could have objected—might have been damnified by the defendant being then let into possession, and being enabled, with the consent of the executors, to deal with and dispose of the property bequeathed.

[1.] 1 B & S 393.

(Holmes J. concurred.)

Note

1. How does this case accord with the decision in *McCoubray v Thompson*?
2. It has been suggested that in the case of joint promisees, only one of the promisees needs to provide consideration. See *McEvoy v The Belfast Banking Co. Ltd*, p. 663 below.

F. PERFORMANCE OF EXISTING DUTIES

Performance of an existing duty imposed by a contract with a third party is good consideration.

Pao On v Lau Yiu Long [1980] AC 614
(Facts on p. 142.)

Lord Scarman:

. . .

The extrinsic evidence in this case shows that the consideration for the promise of indemnity, while it included the cancellation of the subsidiary agreement, was primarily the promise given by the plaintiffs to the defendants, to perform their contract with Fu Chip, which included the undertaking not to sell sixty per cent of the shares allotted to them before 30 April 1974. Thus the real consideration for the indemnity was the promise to perform, or the performance of, the plaintiffs' pre-existing contractual obligations to Fu Chip.

. . .

Their Lordships do not doubt that a promise to perform, or the performance of, a pre-existing contractual obligation to a third party can be valid consideration. In *New Zealand Shipping Co. Ltd v A. M. Satterthwaite & Co. Ltd (The Eurymedon)* [[1975] AC 154; [1974] 1 Lloyd's Rep 534], the rule and the reason for the rule were stated: 'An agreement to do an act which the promisor is under an existing obligation to a third party to do, may quite well amount to valid consideration . . . the promisee obtains the benefit of a direct obligation. . . . This proposition is illustrated and supported by

Scotson v Pegg (1861) 6 H & N 295 which their Lordships consider to be good law.'
Unless, therefore the guarantee was void as having been made for an illegal consideration or voidable on the ground of economic duress, the extrinsic evidence establishes
that it was supported by valid consideration.

Performance of an existing duty imposed by a contract with the promisor
or imposed by law is only good consideration if something more than is
required is undertaken.

Williams *v* Williams [1957] 1 WLR 148

Following his desertion by his wife, a husband agreed to support her and
pay her weekly maintenance. The wife later sued for sums due under this
agreement.

Denning L.J.:
. . .

The husband relies on the fact that his wife deserted him. If there had been a
separation by consent, he agrees that the agreement would have been enforceable. In
that case the husband would still be under a duty to maintain, and the sum of 30s a
week would be assumed to be a quantification of a reasonable sum for her maintenance having regard to her own earning capacity. The ascertainment of a specific sum in
place of an unascertained sum has always been held to be good consideration. So long
as circumstances remained unchanged, it would be treated by the courts as binding on
her and she could not recover more from him: see *National Assistance Board v Parkes*.[1] But
in the present case the husband says that, as the wife deserted him, he was under no
obligation to maintain her and she was not entitled to pledge his credit in any way.
Clause 2 therefore gives him nothing and is valueless to him. The husband says that
Goodinson v Goodinson[2] is distinguishable because there was no finding in that case that
the wife was in desertion, and moreover the wife promised to maintain the child as
well as herself.
    Now I agree that, in promising to maintain herself whilst she was in desertion, the
wife was only promising to do that which she was already bound to do. Nevertheless,
a promise to perform an existing duty is, I think, sufficient consideration to support a
promise, so long as there is nothing in the transaction which is contrary to the public
interest. Suppose that this agreement had never been made, and the wife had made
no promise to maintain herself and did not do so. She might then have sought and
received public assistance or have pledged her husband's credit with tradesmen: in
which case the National Assistance Board might have summoned him before the
magistrates, or the tradesmen might have sued him in the County Court. It is true that
he would have an answer to those claims because she was in desertion, but nevertheless he would be put to all the trouble, worry and expense of defending himself
against them. By paying her 30s a week and taking this promise from her that she will
maintain herself and will not pledge his credit, he has an added safeguard to protect
himself from all this worry, trouble and expense. That is a benefit to him which is good
consideration for his promise to pay maintenance. That was the view which appealed
to the County Court judge: and I must say that it appeals to me also.
    There is another ground on which good consideration can be found. Although the
wife was in desertion, nevertheless it must be remembered that desertion is never
irrevocable. It was open to her to come back at any time. Her right to maintenance was

not lost by the desertion. It was only suspended. If she made a genuine offer to return which he rejected, she would have been entitled to maintenance from him. She could apply to the magistrates or the High Court for an order in her favour. If she did so, however, whilst this agreement was in force, the 30s would be regarded as *prima facie* the correct figure. It is a benefit to the husband for it to be so regarded, and that is sufficient consideration to support his promise.

. . . I would dismiss the appeal accordingly.

1. [1955] 2 QB 506; [1955] 3 WLR 347; [1955] 3 All ER 1.
2. [1954] 2 QB 118; [1954] 2 WLR 1121; [1954] 2 All ER 255.

(Hodson and Morris L.JJ. both dismissed the appeal on the grounds that the desertion acted only to suspend the wife's right to maintenance.)

James McKerring *v* The Minister for Agriculture [1989] ILRM 82

The plaintiff farmer applied for grant payments under the tuberculosis and brucellosis eradication schemes. The defendant refused payment, claiming firstly that the plaintiff had not complied with the necessary conditions of the schemes, and secondly that payment was made on a purely *ex gratia* basis, not as a matter of legal obligation.

O'Hanlon J.:
. . .

As to whether the payment made is *ex gratia* or contractual, it is significant that the Permit Document, which is put forward as the written embodiment for the terms of the scheme, does not contain the words *ex gratia* but on the contrary contains a number of expressions more consistent with a promise to pay if certain conditions are fulfilled.
. . .

The conditions and provisions all convey to me the impression of a promise to pay, if they are duly complied with. It was not contended on behalf of the minister that there was no consideration flowing from the reactor-owner to the minister which would suffice to support a contractual relationship between the two parties, and it appears to me that there is sufficient consideration involved in strict compliance with all the conditions, even though some of them may be a matter of legal obligation as well.

Accordingly, I am not prepared to accept the second line of defence put forward on behalf of the minister . . .

(O'Hanlon J. found however that the plaintiff by his failure to comply with the conditions of the scheme had disentitled himself to grant payments.)

SECTION TWO—EXCEPTIONS TO BARGAIN

Atiyah (op. cit.). (Footnotes abridged.)

Consideration and Bargains

The third proposition which forms a central part of the orthodox doctrine is that the law enforces only bargains; that all contracts are bargains;[1] that consideration is not an artificial or accidental requirement of the law, but merely a recognition of the law's concern with bargains;[2] and that accordingly nothing can be consideration which is not regarded as such by the parties;[3] consideration, in short, is the 'price' of the promise.[4] It is my contention that this part of the orthodox doctrine, simply does not represent the law.

Before I consider the validity of the orthodox view it seems necessary to devote some consideration to an examination of what precisely is meant by a bargain. English writers and judges who make frequent reference to the concept of a bargain always appear to assume that the meaning of the concept is self-evident. I cannot recollect ever having seen any discussion in English legal literature of what precisely is meant by the concept. The American Restatement, Second (§3) defines a bargain as 'an agreement to exchange promises or to exchange a promise for a performance or to exchange performances', but Corbin adopts a narrower definition for the purposes of his great work. He regards a bargain as involving not merely an exchange, but an exchange of equivalents.[5] I think that Corbin's definition is nearer to the meaning of the term in ordinary usage, but whichever definition is adopted, I suggest that there are many contracts recognised and enforced by the courts which do not involve a bargain in either of these senses. I will refer to the Restatement's definition as the wider sense, and Corbin's as the narrower sense of the term. Both agree that the essential element of a bargain is that there should be an *exchange* of promise for promise, or promise for act. The consideration must be given *in return for* the promise. Now it cannot be doubted that most contracts are bargains, both in the narrow sense and the wide sense; but once again one sees here the apparent compulsion to generalise from the typical case. Because bargains are the most common form of contract, it is simply assumed, without examination of the evidence, that all contracts are bargains. Let us now examine the evidence, which in this context consists of the actual decisions of the courts. Naturally, there are more cases which do not fit the narrower sense than the wider sense.

Nominal consideration

A promise given for nominal consideration is perhaps a bargain in the wide sense, but not in the narrow sense. I doubt if the ordinary person would call such a contract a bargain which is one reason why the narrow definition of the term seems more accurate.

Collateral contracts

A collateral contract is sometimes a bargain in the wide sense, and perhaps arguably even in the narrow sense. For example, if a car dealer says to a prospective buyer, 'If you enter into a hire-purchase agreement to acquire this car from the X Finance Co., I promise to repair the brakes', or 'I warrant that the brakes are in good order', this is arguably a bargain even in the narrow sense. But even here it seems to stretch the meaning of the term to say that here is an exchange of *equivalents*, and I would prefer to regard this as a bargain only in the wider sense. But it must be recognised that there are a large number of collateral contracts which cannot possibly be regarded as bargains in either the narrow or the wide sense. An auctioneer promises to sell goods without reserve; this promise is enforceable by the highest bidder, his bid being treated as a sufficient consideration for the promise.[6] There is clearly no bargain here in any sense of the word; the auctioneer does not *exchange* his promise for the bid; the bid merely follows the promise in natural reliance thereon. Orthodox lawyers have indeed looked askance at the decision holding the auctioneer's promise binding,[7] but if we rid ourselves of the preconceived assumption that all considerations must fall within some predetermined pattern, is there any reason for doubting the decision? Orthodoxy finds difficulty in the decision because the consideration found in that case does not fit the typical pattern. But let us rephrase the issue facing the court in that case, and ask: Is there a sufficient reason for enforcing the auctioneer's promise? Can there be any doubt that the court's answer was correct?

. . .

Bailments without reward

A asks B to lend him a chattel for purposes of his own; B complies. A expressly or impliedly promises to return the chattel. This promise is undoubtedly enforceable, and a sufficient consideration (or reason) for enforcing the promise is the mere fact that B has voluntarily handed over his property to A for A's benefit.[8] There is plainly no bargain. Here again, it is sometimes argued that such cases are not 'genuinely' contractual. If the bailee damages the goods he is liable in tort, and therefore there is no need to invoke the law of contracts. This is true, but there may sometimes be situations where it is necessary to rely on the bailee's promise. For example, the bailee may promise to return the chattel on a specified date, and may return it late. No action would lie in tort for this, but it can hardly be doubted that an action would lie on the promise, and that there is good reason (or consideration) for such an action.

Conditional gift promises

A whole range of cases in which promises are enforced though there is no bargain is to be found in those cases in which the courts have enforced conditional gift promises. This group of cases may come as a surprise to the orthodox lawyer because orthodoxy insists that a promise to make a gift is not enforceable as a contract at all. The fact that the promise is conditional does not, according to orthodox doctrine, render the promise enforceable; and it is in fact necessary to distinguish very carefully between a conditional gift promise and a contractual promise. Nevertheless, the fact is that many such contracts have been enforced; or have been refused enforcement only on other grounds than absence of consideration.

One type of case in which a conditional gift promise may be enforced is exemplified by *Wyatt v Kreglinger*.[9] The plaintiff retires from the defendant's employment and the defendant promises to pay him a pension in consideration of a promise by the plaintiff not to compete or otherwise damage the defendant's interests. These promises are exchanged, but they are certainly not exchanged as equivalents; there is therefore a bargain in the wide sense, but none in the narrow sense. It is true that in this particular case there was considerable doubt about the enforceability of the contract, and the decision indeed went against the plaintiff on the ground (which was later much criticised) that the consideration was in restraint of trade. But this is not surprising. By 1933 orthodoxy had acquired such strength with regard to the doctrine of consideration that even the judges sometimes found difficulty in enforcing a promise in flat defiance of orthodox doctrine. It is of course pretty plain that the real reason (or consideration) for enforcing such a promise is the plaintiff's past services but it is also part of the orthodox doctrine that past consideration is bad.

In other similar cases, orthodoxy seems to have been defied by the courts with less difficulty. For example, there are cases in which a person has desired to make a gift of a house to another, and has persuaded the donee to enter into a contract to buy the property from a third party on the strength of a definite promise that he will himself pay the price. Such promises have been enforced,[10] though they are plainly gift promises, and there is equally plainly no bargain in any sense of the term. Perhaps the courts have felt less difficulty about such a case because the promisee clearly incurs a detriment in reliance on the promise by entering into the contract to purchase and pay for the property. Orthodoxy thereby seems to be complied with in so far as detriment is present; but orthodoxy is not complied with inasmuch as no bargain is involved.

Then there is the well-known line of cases beginning with *Dillwyn v Llewellyn*,[11] and continuing up to the present day through *Inwards v Baker*[12] to *Pascoe v Turner*[13] and many similar cases, in which a person promises another to give him some land, and allows the promisee to build a property on the land in reliance on the promise.[14] Here again (need one repeat it?) there is plainly no bargain. It is true that here also orthodoxy has caused the courts and commentators some uncomfortable moments. The promise in such a case is so obviously a promise to make a gift that the orthodox lawyer is unwilling to believe the evidence in front of him when he sees that the courts actually enforce such promises. Explanations are therefore put forward to show that the cases are not really contractual. Perhaps they are based on some 'equity';[15] perhaps they are based on estoppel of some kind or another;[16] perhaps the promise was not really enforced, but the courts were merely concerned to prevent unjust enrichment[17] (though this does not explain why—at least in some cases—the promisee gets the land as well as the house). Thus, for instance, we find Professor Allan criticising Lord Westbury for not making it clear in his judgment in *Dillwyn v Llewellyn* 'whether the right of the plaintiff was contractual in nature or whether it was a right bestowed *ex aequo et bono* by the court to compel completion of a gift'.[18] This criticism would have been unintelligible to Lord Westbury, who would probably have replied that of course the plaintiff's right was both. It was the right to enforce a promise (and to that extent contractual) because in the particular circumstances there was good reason (or consideration—and Lord Westbury uses this word in his judgment) to enforce the promise although it was a promise to make a gift. Professor Allan's criticism is only intelligible to the modern lawyer because orthodoxy appears to require a distinction to be drawn between a contractual promise and a promise to make a gift.

Another similar case—though admittedly an isolated decision—is *Re Soames*,[19] where a promise to make a gift to a school was enforced on the ground that the school governors had entered into various commitments in reliance on her promise, which the promisor must have anticipated. Once again, an enforceable promise though no bargain.

. . . The belief that all contracts are bargains has been unconscionably long in dying—indeed, it may be premature to say that it is dying even now, but it is certainly time that it was buried.

[1.] See e.g. Cheshire and Fifoot, *Law of Contract* (10th ed. by M. P. Furmston, 1981), 60–61.

[2.] See Hamson's well known article in 54 LQR 233.

[3.] A proposition stated by Holmes, *The Common Law*, 292.

[4.] Pollock's definition, adopted by Lord Dunedin in *Dunlop v Selfridge* [1915] AC at p. 855.

[5.] Op. cit., vol. i §10.

[6.] *Warlow v Harrison* (1859) 1 E & E 309.

[7.] See Slade, 68 LQR 238; cf. Gower, ibid., 457, and Slade's reply, 69 LQR 21.

[8.] *Bainbridge v Firmstone* (1838) 8 Ad & E 743.

[9.] [1933] 1 KB 793.

[10.] *Crosbie v M'Doual* (1806) 13 Ves Jr 148.

[11.] (1862) 4 De G F & J 517.

[12.] [1965] 2 QB 29.

[13.] [1979] 1 WLR 431.

[14.] See the analysis by S. Moriarty, 'Licences and Land Law: Legal Principles and Public Policy', 100 LQR 376 (1984).
[15.] Lord Denning in *Inwards v Baker*, at p. 37.
[16.] Maudsley, 81 LQR 183 (1965).
[17.] Treitel, *Contract*, 105–8.
[18.] 79 LQR 238, 241 (1963).
[19.] (1897) 13 TLR 439; cf. *Re Hudson* (1885) 54 LJ Ch. 811 which is to more orthodox tastes.

Saunders v Cramer (1842) 5 Ir Eq R 12

In anticipation of a marriage between her granddaughter and the plaintiff, a grandmother stated her intention to leave upon her death £2,000 and a house to her granddaughter. The grandmother died shortly after her granddaughter and the plaintiff married and the plaintiff claimed to be entitled to the £2,000 and the property. The Lord Chancellor held that the plaintiff's marriage was 'the most valuable of all considerations' for the contract.

Note

The Lord Chancellor also held that the marriage constituted 'solemn acceptance' of the grandmother's offer.

Shadwell v Shadwell (1860) 9 CB (ns) 159

An uncle wrote to his nephew as follows: 'I am glad to hear of your intended marriage with Ellen Nicholl; and, as I promised to assist you at starting, I am happy to tell you that I will pay to you £150 yearly during my life and until your annual income derived from your profession of a chancery barrister shall amount to 600 guineas; of which your own admission will be the only evidence that I shall receive or require.' The nephew sued his uncle's executors for arrears of the annuity, claiming that as consideration for his uncle's promise he had married Ellen Nicholl.

Erle C.J.:

The question raised by the demurrer to the replication to the fourth plea is, whether there is a consideration which will support the action on the promise to pay the annuity of £150 per annum.

. . .

The circumstances are, that the plaintiff had made an engagement to marry one Ellen Nicholl, that his uncle had promised to assist him at starting—by which, as I understand the words, he meant on commencing his married life. Then the letter containing the promise declared on is sent, to specify what that assistance would be, namely, £150 per annum during the uncle's life, and until the plaintiff's professional income should be acknowledged by him to exceed 600 guineas per annum; and the declaration avers, that the plaintiff, relying on this promise, without any revocation on the part of the uncle, did marry Ellen Nicholl.

Now, do these facts shew that the promise was in consideration either of a loss to be sustained by the plaintiff or a benefit to be derived from the plaintiff to the uncle, at his, the uncle's request? My answer is in the affirmative.

First, do these facts shew a loss sustained by the plaintiff at his uncle's request? When I answer this in the affirmative, I am aware that a man's marriage with the woman of his choice is in one sense a boon, and in that sense the reverse of a loss: yet, as between the plaintiff and the party promising to supply an income to support the marriage, it may well be also a loss. The plaintiff may have made a most material change in his position, and induced the object of his affection to do the same, and may have incurred pecuniary liabilities resulting in embarrassments which would be in every sense a loss if the income which had been promised should be withheld; and, if the promise was made in order to induce the parties to marry, the promise so made would be in legal effect a request to marry.

Secondly, do these facts shew a benefit derived from the plaintiff to the uncle, at his request? In answering again in the affirmative, I am at liberty to consider the relation in which the parties stood and the interest in the settlement of his nephew which the uncle declares. The marriage primarily affects the parties thereto; but in a secondary degree it may be an object of interest to a near relative, and in that sense a benefit to him. This benefit is also derived from the plaintiff at the uncle's request. If the promise of the annuity was intended as an inducement to the marriage, and the averment that the plaintiff, relying on the promise, married, is an averment that the promise was one inducement to the marriage, this is the consideration averred in the declaration; and it appears to me to be expressed in the letter, construed with the surrounding circumstances.

No case shewing a strong analogy to the present was cited: but the importance of enforcing promises which have been made to induce parties to marry has been often recognised; and the cases cited, of *Montefiori v Montefiori* 1 W Bl 363, and *Bold v Hutchinson* 20 Beavan 250, are examples. I do not feel it necessary to advert to the numerous authorities referred to in the learned arguments addressed to us, because the decision turns upon the question of fact, whether the consideration for the promise is proved as pleaded. I think it is; and therefore my judgment on the first demurrer is for the plaintiff.

The second demurrer raises the question whether the plaintiff's continuance at the bar was made a condition precedent to the right to the annuity. I think not. The uncle promises to continue the annuity until the professional income exceeds the sum mentioned. I find no stipulation that the annuity shall cease if professional diligence ceases—no limitation except a defeasance in case of an amount of income from the other source. If the prospect of success at the bar had failed, a continuance to attend the courts might be an unreasonable expense. My judgment on this demurrer is also for the plaintiff.

The above is the judgment of my brother Keating and myself.

Byles J.:

I am of opinion that the defendant is entitled to the judgment of the court on the demurrer. . .

. . .

The inquiry therefore narrows itself to this question—does the letter itself disclose any consideration for the promise? The consideration relied on by the plaintiff's counsel being the subsequent marriage of the plaintiff. I think the letter discloses no consideration. It is in these words: '11 August 1838. Gray's Inn. My dear Lancey—I am glad to hear of your intended marriage with Ellen Nicholl; and, as I promised to assist you at starting, I am happy to tell you that I will pay to you £150 yearly during my life and until your annual income derived from your profession of a chancery barrister shall amount to 600 guineas; of which your own admission will be the only evidence that I shall receive or require. Your ever affectionate uncle, Charles Shadwell.'

It is by no means clear that the words 'at starting' mean 'on marriage with Ellen Nicholl', or with any one else. The more natural meaning seems to me to be, 'at starting in the profession'; for, it will be observed that these words are used by testator in reciting a prior promise made when the testator had not heard of the proposed marriage with Ellen Nicholl, or, so far as appears, heard of any proposed marriage. This construction is fortified by the consideration that the annuity is not in terms made to begin from the marriage, but, as it should seem, from the date of the letter: neither is it in terms made defeasible if Ellen Nicholl should die before marriage.

But, even on the assumption that the words 'at starting' mean on marriage, I still think that no consideration appears, sufficient to sustain the promise. . . .

Note

1. It seems clear here that there is no element of a bargain in this case. Yet Erle C.J. went to great lengths to identify consideration in order to render the promise enforceable.
2. Under the Family Law Act 1981 it is no longer possible to sue for breach of a promise to marry.

M'Evoy v Moore (1902) 36 ILTR 99

. . .

The plaintiff was requested by the defendant's head groom, without the knowledge of the defendant, to go to the defendant's residence and do work as a stableman. Nothing was said as to wages or period of employment. The plaintiff worked in the defendant's stable for some weeks, and was seen at work by the defendant on several occasions. He then brought the present Civil Bill for wages. Barton J. held that when defendant's head groom employed plaintiff to do work for defendant, it might reasonably be presumed that he professed to do so on behalf of defendant, and although there was no contract as to time or rate of wages, an implied contract by the defendant to pay the plaintiff at the ordinary rate of wages arose by reason of the defendant having allowed the plaintiff to continue working for him after he became aware plaintiff was doing so.

Williams v Roffey Bros & Nicholls (Contractors) Ltd [1990] 1 All ER 512

Glidewell L.J.:

The facts

The plaintiff is a carpenter. The defendants are building contractors who in September 1985 had entered into a contract with Shepherd's Bush Housing Association Ltd to refurbish a block of flats called Twynholm Mansions, Lillie Road, London SW6. The defendants were the main contractors for the works. There are twenty eight flats in Twynholm Mansions, but the work of refurbishment was to be carried out in twenty seven of the flats.

The defendants engaged the plaintiff to carry out the carpentry work in the refurbishment of the twenty seven flats, including work to the structure of the roof. Originally, the plaintiff was engaged on three separate sub-contracts, but these were all superseded by a sub-contract in writing made on 21 January 1986 by which the plaintiff undertook to provide the labour for the carpentry work to the roof of the block and for the first and second fix carpentry work required in each of the twenty seven flats for a total price of £20,000.

The judge found that, though there was no express term providing for payment to be made in stages, the contract of 21 January 1986 was subject to an implied term that the defendants would make interim payments to the plaintiff, related to the amount of work done, at reasonable intervals.

The plaintiff and his men began work on 10 October 1985. The judge found that by 9 April 1986 the plaintiff had completed the work to the roof, had carried out the first fix to all twenty seven flats and had substantially completed the second fix to nine flats. By this date the defendants had made interim payments totalling £16,200.

It is common ground that by the end of March 1986 the plaintiff was in financial difficulty. The judge found that there were two reasons for this, namely: (i) that the agreed price of £20,000 was too low to enable the plaintiff to operate satisfactorily and at a profit. Mr Cottrell, a surveyor employed by the defendants, said in evidence that a reasonable price for the works would have been £23,783; (ii) that the plaintiff failed to supervise his workmen adequately.

The defendants, as they made clear, were concerned lest the plaintiff did not complete the carpentry work on time. The main contract contained a penalty clause. The judge found that on 9 April 1986 the defendants promised to pay the plaintiff the further sum of £10,300, in addition to the £20,000, to be paid at the rate of £575 for each flat in which the carpentry work was completed.

The plaintiff and his men continued work on the flats until the end of May 1986. By that date the defendants, after their promise on 9 April 1986, had made only one further payment of £1,500. At the end of May the plaintiff ceased work on the flats . . . the defendants engaged other carpenters to complete the work, but in the result incurred one week's time penalty in their contract with the building owners.
. . .

Was there consideration for the defendants' promise made on 9 April 1986 to pay an additional price at the rate of £575 per completed flat?

The judge made the following findings of fact which are relevant to this issue. (i) The sub-contract price agreed was too low to enable the plaintiff to operate satisfactorily and at a profit. Mr Cottrell, the defendants' surveyor, agreed that this was so. (ii) Mr Roffey, the managing director of the defendants, was persuaded by Mr Cottrell that the defendants should pay a bonus to the plaintiff. The figure agreed at the meeting on 9 April 1986 was £10,300.

The judge quoted and accepted the evidence of Mr Cottrell to the effect that a main contractor who agrees too low a price with a sub-contractor is acting contrary to his own interests. He will never get the job finished without paying more money.

The judge therefore concluded: 'In my view where the original sub-contract price is too low, and the parties subsequently agree that the additional moneys shall be paid to the sub-contractor, this agreement is in the interests of both parties. This is what happened in the present case, and in my opinion the agreement of 9 April 1986 does not fail for lack of consideration.' In his address to us counsel for the defendants outlined the benefits to the defendants which arose from their agreement to pay the additional £10,300 as (i) seeking to ensure that the plaintiff continued work and did not stop in breach of the sub-contract, (ii) avoiding the penalty for delay and (iii) avoiding the trouble and expense of engaging other people to complete the carpentry work.

However, counsel submits that, though the defendants may have derived, or hoped to derive, practical benefits from their agreement to pay the 'bonus', they derived no benefit in law, since the plaintiff was promising to do no more than he was already bound to do by his sub-contract, i.e. continue with the carpentry work and complete it on time. Thus there was no consideration for the agreement.

Counsel for the defendants relies on the principle of law which, traditionally, is based on the decision in *Stilk v Myrick* (1809) 2 Camp. 317, 170 ER 1168. That was a decision at first instance of Lord Ellenborough C.J. On a voyage to the Baltic, two seamen deserted. The captain agreed with the rest of the crew that if they worked the ship back to London without the two seamen being replaced, he would divide between them the pay which would have been due to the two deserters. On arrival at London this extra pay was refused, and the plaintiff's action to recover his extra pay was dismissed. Counsel for the defendant argued that such an agreement was contrary to public policy, but Lord Ellenborough C.J.'s judgment (as reported in Campbell's Reports) was based on lack of consideration. It reads:

> I think *Harris v Watson* ((1791) Peake 102, |1755–1802| All ER Rep 493) was rightly decided; but I doubt whether the ground of public policy, upon which Lord Kenyon is stated to have proceeded, be the true principle on which the decision is to be supported. Here, I say the agreement is void for want of consideration. There was no consideration for the ulterior pay promised to the mariners who remained with the ship. Before they sailed from London they had undertaken to do all they could under the emergencies of the voyage. They had sold all their services till the voyage should be completed. If they had been at liberty to quit the vessel at *Cronstadt*, the case would have been quite different; or if the captain had capriciously discharged the two men who were wanting, the others might not have been compellable to take the whole duty upon themselves, and their agreeing to do so might have been a sufficient consideration for the promise of an advance of wages. But the desertion of a part of the crew is to be considered an emergency of the voyage as much as their death; and those who remain are bound by the terms of their original contract to exert themselves to the utmost to bring the ship in safety to her destined port. Therefore, without looking to the policy of this agreement, I think it is void for want of consideration, and that the plaintiff can only recover at the rate of £5 a month.

In *North Ocean Shipping Co. Ltd v Hyundai Construction Co. Ltd, The Atlantic Baron* |1978| 3 All ER 1170, |1979| QB 705 Mocatta J. regarded the general principle of the decision in *Stilk v Myrick* as still being good law. He referred to two earlier decisions of this court, dealing with wholly different subjects, in which Denning L.J. sought to escape from the confines of the rule, but was not accompanied in this attempt by the other members of the court.

In *Ward v Byham* |1956| 2 All ER 318, |1956| 1 WLR 496 the plaintiff and the defendant lived together unmarried for five years, during which time the plaintiff bore their child. After the parties ended their relationship, the defendant promised to pay the plaintiff £1 per week to maintain the child, provided that she was well looked after and happy. The defendant paid this sum for some months, but ceased to pay when the plaintiff married another man. On her suing for the amount due at £1 per week, he pleaded that there was no consideration for his agreement to pay for the plaintiff to maintain her child, since she was obliged by law to do so: see s. 42 of the National Assistance Act 1948. The County Court judge upheld the plaintiff mother's claim, and this court dismissed the defendant's appeal.

Denning L.J. said:

> I approach the case, therefore, on the footing that, in looking after the child, the mother is only doing what she is legally bound to do. Even so, I think that there

was sufficient consideration to support the promise. I have always thought that a promise to perform an existing duty, or the performance of it, should be regarded as good consideration, because it is a benefit to the person to whom it is given. Take this very case. It is as much a benefit for the father to have the child looked after by the mother as by a neighbour. If he gets the benefit for which he stipulated, he ought to honour his promise, and he ought not to avoid it by saying that the mother was herself under a duty to maintain the child. I regard the father's promise in this case as what is sometimes called a unilateral contract, a promise in return for an act, a promise by the father to pay £1 a week in return for the mother's looking after the child. Once the mother embarked on the task of looking after the child, there was a binding contract. So long as she looked after the child, she would be entitled to £1 a week. The case seems to me to be within the decision of *Hicks v Gregory* ((1849) 8 CB 378, 137 ER 556) on which the judge relied. I would dismiss the appeal.

However, Morris L.J. put it rather differently. He said:

Counsel for the father submits that there was a duty on the mother to support the child, that no affiliation proceedings were in prospect or were contemplated, and that the effect of the arrangement that followed the letter was that the father was merely agreeing to pay a bounty to the mother. It seems to me that the terms of the letter negative those submissions, for the father says: 'providing you can prove that [the child] will be well looked after and happy and also that she is allowed to decide for herself whether or not she wishes to come and live with you.' The father goes on to say that the child is then well and happy and looking much stronger than ever before. 'If you decide what to do let me know as soon as possible'. It seems to me, therefore, that the father was saying, in effect: Irrespective of what may be the strict legal position, what I am asking is that you shall prove that the child will be well looked after and happy, and also that you must agree that the child is to be allowed to decide for herself whether or not she wishes to come and live with you. If those conditions were fulfilled the father was agreeable to pay. On those terms, which in fact became operative, the father agreed to pay £1 a week. In my judgment, there was ample consideration there to be found for his promise, which I think was binding.

Parker L.J. agreed. As I read the judgment of Morris L.J., he and Parker L.J. held that, though in maintaining the child the plaintiff was doing no more than she was obliged to do by law, nevertheless her promise that the child would be well looked after and happy was a practical benefit to the father, which amounted to consideration for his promise.

In *Williams v Williams* [1957] 1 All ER 305, [1957] 1 WLR 148, a wife left her husband, and he promised to make her a weekly payment for her maintenance. On his failing to honour his promise, the wife claimed the arrears of payment, but her husband pleaded that, since the wife was guilty of desertion she was bound to maintain herself, and thus there was no consideration for his promise. Denning L.J. reiterated his view that: 'a promise to perform an existing duty is, I think, sufficient consideration to support a promise, so long as there is nothing in the transaction which is contrary to the public interest.'

However, the other members of the court (Hodson and Morris L.JJ.) declined to agree with this expression of view, though agreeing with Denning L.J. in finding that there was consideration because the wife's desertion might not have been permanent, and thus there was a benefit to the husband. . . .

There is, however, [a] legal concept of relatively recent development which is relevant, namely that of economic duress. Clearly, if a sub-contractor has agreed to undertake work at a fixed price, and before he has completed the work declines to continue with it unless the contractor agrees to pay an increased price, the sub-contractor may be held guilty of securing the contractor's promise by taking unfair advantage of the difficulties he will cause if he does not complete the work. In such a case an agreement to pay an increased price may well be voidable because it was entered into under duress. Thus this concept may provide another answer in law to the question of policy which has troubled the courts since before *Stilk v Myrick*, and no doubt led at the date of that decision to a rigid adherence to the doctrine of consideration.

This possible application of the concept of economic duress was referred to by Lord Scarman, delivering the judgment of the Judicial Committee of the Privy Council in *Pao On v Lau Yiu* |1979| 3 All ER 65 at 76, |1980| AC 614 at 632. He said:

> Their Lordships do not doubt that a promise to perform, or the performance of, a pre-existing contractual obligation to a third party can be valid consideration. In *New Zealand Shipping Co. Ltd v A M Satterthwaite & Co. Ltd* |1974| 1 All ER 1015 at 1021, |1975| AC 154 at 168 the rule and the reason for the rule were stated as follows: 'An agreement to do an act which the promisor is under an existing obligation to a third party to do, may quite well amount to valid consideration: . . . the promisee obtains the benefit of a direct obligation . . . This proposition is illustrated and supported by *Scotson v Pegg* (1861) 6 H & N 295, 158 ER 121 which their Lordships consider to be good law.' Unless, therefore, the guarantee was void as having been made for an illegal consideration or voidable on the ground of economic duress, the extrinsic evidence establishes that it was supported by valid consideration. Counsel for the defendants submits that the consideration is illegal as being against public policy. He submits that to secure a party's promise by a threat of repudiation of a pre-existing contractual obligation owed to another can be, and in the circumstances of this case was, an abuse of a dominant bargaining position and so contrary to public policy . . . This submission found favour with the majority in the Court of Appeal. Their Lordships, however, consider it misconceived. . . .

It is true that *Pao On v Lau Yiu* is a case of a tripartite relationship, i.e. a promise by A to perform a pre-existing contractual obligation owed to B, in return for a promise of payment by C. But Lord Scarman's words seem to me to be of general application, equally applicable to a promise made by one of the original two parties to a contract.

Accordingly, following the view of the majority in *Ward v Byham* and of the whole court in *Williams v Williams* and that of the Privy Council in *Pao On v Lau Yiu* the present state of the law on this subject can be expressed in the following proposition: (i) if A has entered into a contract with B to do work for, or to supply goods or services to, B in return for payment by B and (ii) at some stage before A has completely performed his obligations under the contract B has reason to doubt whether A will, or will be able to, complete his side of the bargain and (iii) B thereupon promises A an additional payment in return for A's promise to perform his contractual obligations on time and (iv) as a result of giving his promise B obtains in practice a benefit, or obviates a dis-benefit, and (v) B's promise is not given as a result of economic duress or fraud on the part of A, then (vi) the benefit to B is capable of being consideration for B's promise, so that the promise will be legally binding.

As I have said, counsel for the defendants accepts that in the present case by promising to pay the extra £10,300 the defendants secured benefits. There is no finding, and no suggestion, that in this case the promise was given as a result of fraud or duress.

If it be objected that the propositions above contravene the principle in *Stilk v Myrick*, I answer that in my view they do not: they refine and limit the application of that principle, but they leave the principle unscathed, e.g. where B secures no benefit by his promise. It is not in my view surprising that a principle enunciated in relation to the rigours of seafaring life during the Napoleonic wars should be subjected during the succeeding 180 years to a process of refinement and limitation in its application in the present day.

It is therefore my opinion that on his findings of fact in the present case, the judge was entitled to hold, as he did, that the defendants' promise to pay the extra £10,300 was supported by valuable consideration, and thus constituted an enforceable agreement.

As a subsidiary argument, counsel for the defendants submits that on the facts of the present case the consideration, even if otherwise good, did not 'move from the promisee'. This submission is based on the principle illustrated in the decision in *Tweddle v Atkinson* (1861) 1 B & S 393, [1861–73] All ER 369.

My understanding of the meaning of the requirement that 'consideration must move from the promisee' is that such consideration must be provided by the promisee, or arise out of his contractual relationship with the promisor. It is consideration provided by somebody else, not a party to the contract, which does not 'move from the promisee'. This was the situation in *Tweddle v Atkinson*, but it is, of course, not the situation in the present case. Here the benefits to the defendants arose out of their agreement of 9 April 1986 with the plaintiff, the promisee. In this respect I would adopt the following passage from *Chitty on Contracts* (25th ed., 1983) para. 173, and refer to the authorities there cited: 'The requirement that consideration must move from the promisee is most generally satisfied where some detriment is suffered by him: e.g. where he parts with money or goods, or renders services, in exchange for the promise. But the requirement may equally well be satisfied where the promisee confers a benefit on the promisor without *in fact* suffering any detriment.' (*Chitty's* emphasis.) That is the situation in this case.

I repeat, therefore, my opinion that the judge was, as a matter of law, entitled to hold that there was valid consideration to support the agreement under which the defendants promised to pay an additional £10,300 at the rate of £575 per flat.

For these reasons I would dismiss this appeal.

Russell L.J.:

. . . In the late twentieth century I do not believe that the rigid approach to the concept of consideration to be found in *Stilk v Myrick* is either necessary or desirable. Consideration there must still be but in my judgment the courts nowadays should be more ready to find its existence so as to reflect the intention of the parties to the contract where the bargaining powers are not unequal and where the finding of consideration reflects the true intention of the parties.

What was the true intention of the parties when they arrived at the agreement pleaded by the defendants in para. 5 of the amended defence? The plaintiff had got into financial difficulties. The defendants, through their employee Mr Cottrell, recognised that the price that had been agreed originally with the plaintiff was less than what Mr Cottrell himself regarded as a reasonable price. There was a desire on Mr Cottrell's part to retain the services of the plaintiff so that the work could be completed without the need to employ another sub-contractor. There was further a need to replace what had hitherto been a haphazard method of payment by a more formalised scheme involving the payment of a specified sum on the completion of each flat. These were all advantages accruing to the defendants which can fairly be said to have been in consideration of their undertaking to pay the additional £10,300. True it was that the plaintiff did not undertake to do any work additional to that which he had originally undertaken to do but the terms on which he was to carry out the work were varied and, in my judgment, that variation was supported by consideration which a pragmatic approach to the true relationship between the parties readily demonstrates.

For my part I wish to make it plain that I do not base my judgment on any reservation as to the correctness of the law long ago enunciated in *Stilk v Myrick*. A gratuitous promise, pure and simple, remains unenforceable unless given under seal. But where, as in this case, a party undertakes to make a payment because by so doing it will gain an advantage arising out of the continuing relationship with the promisee the new bargain will not fail for want of consideration. As I read the judgment of the assistant recorder this was his true ratio on that part of the case wherein the absence of consideration was raised in argument. For the reasons that I have endeavoured to outline, I think that the assistant recorder came to a correct conclusion and I too would dismiss this appeal.

Purchas L.J.:

...

In my judgment, therefore, the rule in *Stilk v Myrick* remains valid as a matter of principle, namely that a contract not under seal must be supported by consideration. Thus, where the agreement on which reliance is placed provides that an extra payment is to be made for work to be done by the payee which he is already obliged to perform, then unless some other consideration is detected to support the agreement to pay the extra sum that agreement will not be enforceable. *Harris v Watson* and *Stilk v Myrick* involved circumstances of a very special nature, namely the extraordinary conditions existing at the turn of the eighteenth century under which seamen had to serve their contracts of employment on the high seas. There were strong public policy grounds at that time to protect the master and owners of a ship from being held to ransom by disaffected crews. Thus, the decision that the promise to pay extra wages even in the circumstances established in those cases was not supported by consideration is readily understandable. Of course, conditions today on the high seas have changed dramatically and it is at least questionable, counsel for the plaintiff submitted, whether these cases might not well have been decided differently if they were tried today. The modern cases tend to depend more on the defence of duress in a commercial context rather than lack of consideration for the second agreement. In the present case, the question of duress does not arise. The initiative in coming to the agreement of 9 April came from Mr Cottrell and not from the plaintiff. It would not, therefore, lie in the defendants' mouth to assert a defence of duress. Nevertheless, the court is more ready in the presence of this defence being available in the commercial context to look for mutual advantages which would amount to sufficient consideration to support the second agreement under which the extra money is paid. Although the passage cited below from the speech of Lord Hailsham L.C. in *Woodhouse AC Israel Cocoa Ltd SA v Nigerian Produce Marketing Co. Ltd* [1972] 2 All ER 271 at 282, [1972] AC 741 at 757–758 was strictly *obiter dicta* I respectfully adopt it as an indication of the approach to be made in modern times. The case involved an agreement to vary the currency in which the buyer's obligation should be met, which was subsequently affected by a depreciation in the currency involved. The case was decided on an issue of estoppel but Lord Hailsham L.C. commented on the other issue, namely the variation of the original contract in the following terms:

> If the exchange letter was not variation, I believe it was nothing. The [buyers] asked for a variation in the mode of discharge of a contract of sale. If the proposal meant what they claimed, and was accepted and acted on, I venture to think that the

[vendors] would have been bound by their acceptance at least until they gave reasonable notice to terminate, and I imagine that a modern court would have found no difficulty in discovering consideration for such a promise. Businessmen know their own business best even when they appear to grant an indulgence, and in the present case I do not think that there would have been insuperable difficulty in spelling out consideration from the earlier correspondence.

. . . The question must be posed: what consideration has moved from the plaintiff to support the promise to pay the extra £10,300 added to the lump sum provision? In the particular circumstances which I have outlined above, there was clearly a commercial advantage to both sides from a pragmatic point of view in reaching the agreement of 9 April. The defendants were on risk that as a result of the bargain they had struck the plaintiff would not or indeed possibly could not comply with his existing obligations without further finance. As a result of the agreement the defendants secured their position commercially. There was, however, no obligation added to the contractual duties imposed on the plaintiff under the original contract. *Prima facie* this would appear to be a classic *Stilk v Myrick* case. It was, however, open to the plaintiff to be in deliberate breach of the contract in order to 'cut his losses' commercially. In normal circumstances the suggestion that a contracting party can rely on his own breach to establish consideration is distinctly unattractive. In many cases it obviously would be and if there was any element of duress brought on the other contracting party under the modern development of this branch of the law the proposed breaker of the contract would not benefit. With some hesitation and comforted by the passage from the speech of Lord Hailsham L.C., to which I have referred, I consider that the modern approach to the question of consideration would be that where there were benefits derived by each party to a contract of variation even though one party did not suffer a detriment this would not be fatal to the establishing of sufficient consideration to support the agreement. If both parties benefit from an agreement it is not necessary that each also suffers a detriment. In my judgment, on the facts as found by the judge, he was entitled to reach the conclusion that consideration existed and in those circumstances I would not disturb that finding. . . .

A. Phang, 'Consideration at the Crossroads' (1991) 107 LQR 21

. . .

The second issue concerns (or, rather, questions) the very need for the doctrine of consideration in the first place. While the dispensation with the concept of legal benefit or detriment in *Williams v Roffey Bros* is desirable inasmuch as the concept entails 'an error of logic', serving, at any rate in bilateral contracts, to pull itself up by, as it were, its own bootstraps (see Goodhart, citing Corbin's views, in (1956) 72 LQR 490 at p. 492), it is submitted that the very doctrine itself needs re-examination, even in the formation of contract. It is, especially now that factual benefit and detriment have come to the fore, far too malleable. Further, despite the rejection of Lord Mansfield's gallant attempts at instituting a doctrine of 'moral' consideration, it looks very much as if we are back on the path towards it (witness, e.g. the reliance by the court in *Williams v Roffey Bros* on the judgments of the majority in *Ward v Byham* [1956] 1 WLR 496, the reasoning of which is not only vague, but, on one interpretation, also comes close to the borderline of 'moral' consideration).

In *The Alev*, Hobhouse J. observed ([1989] 1 Lloyd's Rep. 138 at p. 147): 'Now that there is a properly developed doctrine of . . . economic duress, there is no warrant for the court to fail to recognise the existence of some consideration even though it may be insignificant and even though there may have been no mutual bargain in any realistic use of that phrase.' A similar approach was adopted by Russell L.J. and Purchas L.J. in *Williams v Roffey Bros* (see |1990| 2 WLR 1153 at pp 1168 and 1170). Quite apart from the difficulties with economic duress mentioned earlier, this endorsement of technical consideration leads to at least one major problem. The doctrine would not aid in distinguishing between seriously intended agreements and gift arrangements, simply because (to paraphrase from para. 20 of the Law Revision Committee Report of 1937 (Cmd. 5449)) the well established rule that consideration need not be adequate entails the consequence that merely technical consideration will be enough, although the resulting transaction would, in substance, be a gift. Finally, the decisions of the courts, while true to the technicalities of the doctrine, often disregard business realities that could probably have been characterised as factual benefits or detriments had the court concerned been minded to do so.

Given the problems indicated above, it is submitted that serious thought ought to be given by both the legislature and the courts to a reappraisal of the doctrine of consideration. Complete abolition (advocated by Lord Wright as far back as 1936: see 49 Harv L Rev 1225) may be difficult to achieve except in the context of codification. The Law Commission could, perhaps, reconsider the 1937 proposal of the Law Revision Committee to the effect that consideration is merely evidence of a serious intention to contract, with the result that it should not be required where the promise itself is in writing. There are, of course, difficulties with that part of the proposal which emphasises the significance of writing. The experience in the US in this regard has not been altogether happy (see, e.g. von Mehren, (1959) 72 Harv L Rev 1009 at p. 1055). It has also been argued that writing can be just as casual and, consequently, produce just as unjust results as enforceable oral promises (see Patterson, (1958) 58 Col L Rev 929 at pp 958 and 963), although it is submitted that a process of education of the public could be initiated should this alternative criterion of writing be introduced. This proposed reform raises, in the final analysis, policy questions that are more appropriately within the province of Parliament.

It is suggested that, in the meantime, however, the courts ought to supplement the defects of consideration by a bolder development of the doctrine of promissory estoppel: indeed, there are signs that they are already moving towards doing so. This doctrine is grounded in the equitable rationale of unconscionability, and there is no reason in principle why it should not be employed even where to do so would incidentally override the rather technical requirements of consideration. Such an approach finds support in at least two first instance judgments: that of Oliver J. in *Taylors Fashions Ltd v Liverpool Victoria Trustees Co. Ltd* |1982| QB 133, especially at pp 151–152; and that of Robert Goff J. in *Amalgamated Investment & Pty Co. Ltd v Texas Commerce International Bank Ltd* |1982| QB 84, especially at pp 106–108 (although this liberal approach was limited by the Court of Appeal to the notion of 'estoppel by convention'). Indeed, in *Williams v Roffey Bros* itself, both Glidewell L.J. and Russell L.J. referred to a possible argument based upon promissory estoppel. The law relating to promissory estoppel has become more prominent since the recent High Court of Australia decision of *Waltons Stores (Interstate) Ltd v Maher*, (1988) 164 CLR 387—which, if accepted, gives the doctrine the effect of sword as well. There is no logical reason why promissory estoppel should not, if carefully developed, become a viable supplement to consideration. It need not, however, necessarily supersede consideration altogether; it is significant to note, in the context, that in the *Waltons Stores* case, at least one judge (Brennan J., at pp 423–4) indicated that given the various requirements of promissory estoppel, ' ... the concern that a general application of the principle of equitable estoppel would make non-contractual promises enforceable as contractual promises can be allayed.'

Note

See Adams & Brownsword, 'Contract, Consideration and the Critical Path', (1990) Vol. 53 MLR 536, where the authors argue that *Roffey Bros* decision is significant because it signals that the courts, in deciding whether or not to enforce a promise, may be guided less by technical questions of consideration than by questions of fairness, reasonableness and commercial utility.

SECTION THREE—ESTOPPEL

The doctrine as stated in *Pinnel's* case (5 Rep. 117 a) is 'that payment of a lesser sum on the day in satisfaction of a greater cannot be any satisfaction for the whole, because it appears to the judges, that by no possibility a lesser sum can be a satisfaction to the plaintiff for a greater sum.' This principle was affirmed by the House of Lords in *Foakes v Beer* [1884] 9 AC 605 where the court expressed the view that though the rule may be unwise it was too well established to overturn.

The Mayor, Aldermen and Burgesses of the Borough of Drogheda v Rev. Edward Fairtlough (1858) 8 ICLR 98

In 1820 the plaintiffs leased property to the defendant for a term of ninety nine years at a rent of £11 9s 8d. In 1842 in consideration of a fine and of the surrender of the original lease a new lease was granted with a reduced rent of £5 6s. This was paid until 1854 when the plaintiffs sued for arrears of rent calculated at the original rate from 1842 until 1854.

Lefroy C.J.:

. . .

. . . There are two grounds, therefore, upon which the defendant relies—either the old lease is not in existence, or, if it is in existence, then the rent under it has been paid and discharged. Accordingly, the defence alleges that, from the time of the granting of the new lease, payments were made under it from 1841 to 1854, *de anno in annum*, of the rent of £5 6s 0d, thereby reserved; and it alleges further, that the payments so made were made and received in satisfaction of the greater rent reserved by the old lease of 1820; in other words, that the rent of £5 6s 0d, paid annually under the new lease, was a satisfaction of the rent of £11 9s 8d, reserved under the old lease; and, in order to introduce matters material to the question, they say that the corporation repudiated the new lease during that period, and called upon the defendants to pay the rent under the old lease, which they refused to do, and that, that proceeding placed the parties in a position which made it desirable that they should come to an arrangement for their mutual accommodation, and that they did accordingly come to an arrangement, upon the one hand to pay, and, upon the other, to receive the less rent in discharge and satisfaction of the greater. Now, these matters are introduced for the obvious purpose of meeting the principle of the common law, which is, that payment merely of a less sum, when it is what we may call a parol payment or payment in fact, and not a payment in pursuance of a contract by deed, cannot, by the common law, be deemed to be any satisfaction whatsoever of a greater liquidated sum; but the law will allow the payment of a smaller sum to be a satisfaction of a greater liquidated sum, if there be, along with the payment of the smaller sum, any collateral advantage, however small, attending the transactions. Well then, the defence insisted upon is this: first, that it was agreed to pay and receive this less sum in satisfaction and discharge of the greater; and, secondly, that there was a consideration for that agreement, and, consequently, that the defence is good. The plaintiffs reply, as it was important for them to do, traversing the fact that the payments were made under any such agreement as alleged, and saying that, although in fact payments were made, yet they were not made or received in order to discharge or satisfy the greater rent; . . .

. . .

But, I must further observe, what is the consideration which the corporation received for this agreement? They received a less rent; but, upon the other hand, the tenant was allowed to keep in his pocket the balance of the greater rent. The arrangement may have been for their mutual advantage; but unquestionably no peculiar advantage whatsoever resulted to the corporation. There is no consideration for this alleged agreement; and even if there were a consideration—if a consideration could have been worked out of the circumstances, that consideration should have appeared upon the face of the agreement; for the rule of law is inflexible, that the consideration for an agreement must appear upon the face of the agreement, either expressly or by necessary inference, wherever, under the Statute of Frauds, an agreement is required to be in writing. Now, there is no consideration here, express or implied. The corporation, it is said, was to be at liberty to impeach the new lease; but they did not require a reservation for that purpose; the law gave them all they could desire; the law which annulled all acts done by the former corporation after a particular period (during which period the lease of 1842 was made) also rendered that lease a nullity, and deprived it of any existence capable of confirmation. There is, therefore, an utter failure both of evidence of the contract, and also of evidence of the consideration for it, to remove the rule of the common law, that payment of a less sum cannot be a satisfaction of a greater liquidated sum, unless there is some further advantage accompanying the payment, and that advantage must be a reasonable one, and must appear upon the face of the agreement.

Note

In the Law Revision Committee's Sixth Interim Report (Cmd. 5449) the abolition of the Rule in *Pinnel's* case was recommended.

The doctrine of estoppel acts as a qualification to this rule.

A. Traditional Estoppel

Traditional estoppel or estoppel by representation involves one party making a representation of fact to another party which is acted upon by that other party to its detriment. In such a case the first party is estopped from denying the truth of the representation.

M'Neill v Millen & Co. Ltd [1907] IR 328

The plaintiff left his car to be repaired in the defendant's garage. He informed the defendants of his intention to take out an insurance policy to cover his car against fire. The defendants said that this would be unnecessary as they had themselves insured his car. As a result of this statement the plaintiff refrained from insuring the car. When the car was destroyed by a fire in the garage it materialised that the car was not insured. The plaintiff sued for damages.

Lord O'Brien L.C.J.:

. . .

Now, putting out of consideration the earlier questions submitted to the jury, I apply myself to findings 4, 5 and 6. Number 4 is this—'Did the defendants represent to the plaintiff that the motor car was insured *for him*?' I emphasise the expression 'for him'; it seems to have been deliberately inserted by the Lord Chief Baron. *Answer:* 'Yes.' No. 5. 'Was such representation made negligently, carelessly, and without due and proper care?' *Answer:* 'Yes.' No. 6. 'Was it by reason of such representation that the plaintiff refrained from insuring the said car?' *Answer:* 'Yes.' These are the material questions. What do they amount to? That there was a representation made that a certain stage of things existed in point of fact—*viz.* that the motor car was, in fact, insured *for him*, a distinction which is important, having regard to Lord Cranworth's judgment in *Jorden v Money*;[1] distinguishing the previous decisions. It was not a case of mere promise or statement of intention; it was a representation of a matter as actually existing.

I think it was the duty of the defendants in this business transaction to take reasonable care that the statement they made, that the car was insured, was true; and I am of opinion that, inasmuch as they did not discharge their duty in this respect, the action can be sustained on the fourth and fifth findings: see Lord Esher's statement of the law in *Seton v Lafone*.[2] This cause of action would rest on a breach of duty—the negligent omission to see that their statements, made in the course of business, in a business transaction, were well founded. This would be a cause of action irrespective of estoppel; but I own I prefer to rest my judgment on the ground of estoppel. . . . and what is meant by the estoppel in this case is that the defendants were, having regard to the findings of the jury, estopped from denying that the evidence established the plaintiff's claim, as put forward in this amended paragraph. This is the way Lord Bowen, in the case cited (*Low v Bouverie*[3]), dealt with the topic of estoppel, as to estoppel not being in itself a cause of action, but merely a rule of evidence. On this question of estoppel all the findings of the jury are relevant, especially the sixth, to which, perhaps, an additional degree of importance should be attached; but I omit no one finding. The sixth finding is a finding that the representation made was the efficient cause, the *causa causans* of his not having insured himself. You have, then, in these findings a representation of fact plainly intended to be acted upon, as you have the representation in fact acted upon.

The leading case on this subject is *Freeman v Cooke*,[4] and it is there laid down that 'whatever a man's real meaning may be, if he so conducts himself that a reasonable man would take the representation to be true, and believe that it was meant that he should act upon it, and did act upon it as true, the party making the representation would be equally precluded from contesting its truth.' A host of other cases proceeded on the same lines; but there is a case which seems to be of considerable importance, *Carr v The London and North Western Rly Co.*[5]—of importance because this doctrine of estoppel or representation was gone into at great length. In that case the plaintiff received notice from the defendant railway company that they had three parcels of goods in their possession consigned to him. Thereupon, he instructed his broker to sell the three parcels. The three parcels were sold, and rent and charges due upon them were paid by the broker to the railway company. Only two parcels were, in fact, delivered to the railway company, and they discovered this two days after they had given the original notification to the plaintiff, but they did not correct the original advice, by stating that only two parcels had been in fact received, until after the sale and the payment of their charges. The plaintiff had to make good to his vendees the difference between the price of the third parcel and the price of the goods which they had to buy in substitution for it. It was held that the railway company were not estopped from showing that the goods had never reached their hands, and that they were not liable to the plaintiff for the difference.

In this case you have the very thing which was not in *Carr v London & North Western Rly Co.*, because you have here established that the efficient cause of his not insuring was the representation made by the defendants. Now, in *Carr v London & North Western Rly Co.* the court discussed at great length estoppel, and they laid down a number of propositions, amongst others this—'Another recognised proposition seems to be, that, if a man, either in express terms or by conduct, makes a representation to another of the existence of a certain state of facts which he intends to be acted upon in a certain way, and it be acted upon in that way in the belief of the existence of such a state of facts, to the damage of him who so believes and acts, the first is estopped from denying the existence of such a state of facts.' This is applicable to this case. A representation was made that the car was in fact insured for the benefit of the plaintiff, that there was a policy, portion of which had been placed opposite his car, and which in fact insured the money for him. It is clear that the person who made the representation intended it to be acted upon, and it was in fact acted upon, for, so to speak, the manner of acting was refraining from acting—refraining from insuring. The defendants must make good the representation that the insurance which existed was an insurance for the plaintiff's benefit, and that the money to be paid under it would be available for the plaintiff.

Madden J.:

I concur with the Lord Chief Justice in holding that the defendants are estopped from denying that the motor car was not only insured, but insured for the plaintiff. The defendants' counsel have contended that estoppel is not sufficient to support the plaintiff's action. Estoppel, they say, is only a rule of evidence, and cannot of itself be the foundation of an action. The thing the defendants are estopped from denying is, they contend, *nudum pactum*, inasmuch as they were not bound to insure the car for the plaintiff. I am not to be taken as deciding that there was no consideration for the insuring of the car, having regard to the agreement between the parties. But the answers of the jury to the fifth and sixth questions render it unnecessary to consider that question. The defendants may not have been under a legal obligation to insure the car. But there was, in my opinion, a duty cast upon them to take reasonable care that a statement made in the course of business, likely from its nature to affect conduct, was in accordance with fact. In the words of Lord Esher, M.R.: 'If a man, in the course of business, volunteers to make a statement on which it is probable that, in the course of business, another will act, there is a duty which arises towards the person to whom he makes that statement. There is clearly a duty not to state a thing which is false to his knowledge, and further than that, I think there is a duty to take reasonable care that the statement shall be correct': *Seton v Lafone*. The jury have found that the representation that the car was insured for the plaintiff was made negligently, carelessly, and without due and proper care, and further that it was by reason of such representation that the plaintiff refrained from insuring his car. The fact that the plaintiff has, as a consequence of the representation, altered his position to his loss, brings into operation the principle of representation. The defendants are bound to make good the representation thus acted upon, apart from any consideration in regard to the original action of the defendants in insuring the car.

1. 5 HL Cas 185.   4. 2 Ex. 654.
2. 19 QBD at p. 72.   5. LR 10 CP 307.
3. [1891] 3 Ch. at p. 105.

(Wright J. concurred.)

The defendant's appeal to the Court of Appeal was dismissed. However, the Court of Appeal stated that the ground of legal liability was contract.

B. PROMISSORY ESTOPPEL

Central London Pty Trust Ltd v High Trees House Ltd [1947] KB 130

In 1937 the plaintiffs leased to the defendants (a subsidiary of the plaintiffs) a block of flats for a term of ninety nine years at a ground rent of £2,500. In early 1940 owing to war conditions only a few of the flats were let and the plaintiffs agreed that the ground rent for the premises would be reduced to £1,250 as from the commencement of the lease. By the beginning of 1945 all the flats were let. In September 1945, the plaintiffs wrote to the defendants claiming that rent was payable at the rate of £2,500 and, subsequently in order to determine the legal position, they initiated friendly proceedings in which they claimed the difference between rent at the rate of £2,500 and £1,250 for the last two quarters of 1945. By their defence the defendants claimed that the agreement for the rent reduction operated during the whole term of the lease and, as alternatives, that the plaintiffs were estopped from demanding rent at the higher rate or had waived their right to do so.

Denning J.:

If I were to consider this matter without regard to recent developments in the law, there is no doubt that had the plaintiffs claimed it, they would have been entitled to recover ground rent at the rate of £2,500 a year from the beginning of the term, since the lease under which it was payable was a lease under seal which, according to the old common law, could not be varied by an agreement by parol (whether in writing or not), but only by deed. Equity, however stepped in, and said that if there has been a variation of a deed by a simple contract (which in the case of a lease required to be in writing would have to be evidenced by writing), the courts may give effect to it as is shown in *Berry v Berry*.[1] That equitable doctrine, however, could hardly apply in the present case because the variation here might be said to have been made without consideration. With regard to estoppel, the representation made in relation to reducing the rent, was not a representation of an existing fact. It was a representation, in effect, as to the future, namely, that payment of the rent would not be enforced at the full rate but only at the reduced rate. Such a representation would not give rise to an estoppel, because, as was said in *Jorden v Money*,[2] a representation as to the future must be embodied as a contract or be nothing.

But what is the position in view of developments in the law in recent years? The law has not been standing still since *Jorden v Money*. There has been a series of decisions over the last fifty years which, although they are said to be cases of estoppel are not really such. They are cases in which a promise was made which was intended to create legal relations and which, to the knowledge of the person making the promise, was going to be acted on by the person to whom it was made, and which was in fact so acted on. In such cases the courts have said that the promise must be honoured. The cases to which I particularly desire to refer are: *Fenner v Blake*,[3] *In re Wickham*,[4] *Re William Porter & Co. Ltd*[5] and *Buttery v Pickard*.[6] As I have said they are not cases of estoppel in the strict sense. They are really promises—promises intended to be binding, intended to be acted on, and in fact acted on. *Jorden v Money* can be distinguished, because there the promisor made it clear that she did not intend to be legally bound, whereas in the cases to which I refer the proper inference was that the promisor did intend to be bound. In each case the court held the promise to be binding on the party making it, even though under the old common law it might be difficult to find any consideration for it. The courts have not gone so far as to give a cause of action in damages for the breach of such a promise, but they have refused to allow the party making it to act inconsistently with it. It is in that sense, and that sense only, that such a promise gives rise to an estoppel. The decisions are a natural result of the fusion of law and equity: for the cases of *Hughes v Metropolitan Rly Co.*,[7] *Birmingham and District Land Co. v London & North Western Rly Co.*[8] and *Salisbury (Marquess) v Gilmore*,[9] afford a sufficient basis for saying that a party would not be allowed in equity to go back on such a promise. In my opinion, the time has now come for the validity of such a promise to be recognised. The logical consequence, no doubt is that a promise to accept a smaller sum in discharge of a larger sum, if acted upon, is binding notwithstanding the absence of consideration: and if the fusion of law and equity leads to this result, so much the better. That aspect was not considered in *Foakes v Beer*.[10] At this time of day however, when law and equity have been joined together for over seventy years, principles must be reconsidered in the light of their combined effect. It is to be noticed that in the Sixth Interim Report of the Law Revision Committee, paras 35, 40, it is recommended that such a promise as that to which I have referred, should be enforceable in law even though no consideration for it has been given by the promisee. It seems to me that, to the extent I have mentioned, that result has now been achieved by the decisions of the courts.

I am satisfied that a promise such as that to which I have referred is binding and the only question remaining for my consideration is the scope of the promise in the present case. I am satisfied on all the evidence that the promise here was that the ground rent should be reduced to £1,250 a year as a temporary expedient while the block of flats was not fully, or substantially fully let, owing to the conditions prevailing. That means that the reduction in the rent applied throughout the years down to the end of 1944, but early in 1945 it is plain that the flats were fully let, and, indeed the rents received from them (many of them not being affected by the Rent Restrictions Acts), were increased beyond the figure at which it was originally contemplated that they would be let. At all events the rent from them must have been very considerable. I find that the conditions prevailing at the time when the reduction in rent was made, had completely passed away by the early months of 1945. I am satisfied that the promise was understood by all parties only to apply under the conditions prevailing at the time when it was made, namely, when the flats were only partially let, and that it did not extend any further than that. When the flats became fully let, early in 1945, the reduction ceased to apply.

In those circumstances, under the law as I hold it, it seems to me that rent is payable at the full rate for the quarters ending 29 September and 25 December 1945.

If the case had been one of estoppel, it might be said that in any event the estoppel would cease when the conditions to which the representation applied came to an end, or it also might be said that it would only come to an end on notice. In either case it is only a way of ascertaining what is the scope of the representation. I prefer to apply the principle that a promise intended to be binding, intended to be acted on and in fact acted on, is binding so far as its terms properly apply. Here it was binding as covering the period down to the early part of 1945, and as from that time full rent is payable.

I therefore give judgment for the plaintiff company for the amount claimed.

1. [1929] 2 KB 316.
2. (1854) 5 HLC 185.
3. [1900] 1 QB 426.
4. (1917) 34 TLR 158.
5. [1937] 2 All ER 361.
6. [1946] WN 25.
7. (1877) 2 App Cas 439, 448.
8. (1888) 40 ChD 268, 286.
9. [1942] 2 KB 38, 51.
10. (1884) 9 App Cas 605.

The doctrine of promissory estoppel is limited in the sense that it is essentially defensive in nature.

Combe *v* Combe [1951] 1 All ER 767

Following their divorce the defendant agreed to make the plaintiff an allowance of £100 a year. The defendant did not make any of the agreed payments, but the plaintiff did not apply to the court for an order for permanent maintenance. It was proved as a matter of fact that the plaintiff earned more than the defendant. Nearly seven years later the plaintiff sued for arrears.

Denning L.J.:

. . .

Byrne J. held that the first three quarterly instalments of £25 were barred by the Limitation Act, 1939, but he gave judgment for £600 in respect of the instalments which accrued within the six years before the action was brought. He held, on the authority of *Gaisberg v Storr*,[1] that there was no consideration for the husband's promise to pay his wife £100, but, nevertheless, he held that the promise was enforceable on the principle stated in *Central London Pty Trust Ltd v High Trees House Ltd*[2] and *Robertson v Minister of Pensions*,[3] because it was an unequivocal acceptance of liability, intended to be binding, intended to be acted on, and, in fact, acted on.

Much as I am inclined to favour the principle of the *High Trees* case, it is important that it should not be stretched too far lest it should be endangered. It does not create new causes of action where none existed before. It only prevents a party from insisting on his strict legal rights when it would be unjust to allow him to do so, having regard to the dealings which have taken place between the parties. That is the way it was put in the case in the House of Lords which first stated the principle—*Hughes v Metropolitan Rly Co.*[4]—and in the case in the Court of Appeal which enlarged it—*Birmingham and District Land Co. v London & North Western Rly Co.*[5] It is also implicit in all the modern cases in which the principle has been developed. Sometimes it is a plaintiff who is not allowed to insist on his strict legal rights. Thus, a creditor is not allowed to enforce a debt which he has deliberately agreed to waive if the debtor has carried on business or in some other way changed his position in reliance on the waiver: *Re Porter (William) & Co. Ltd*,[6] *Buttery v Pickard*,[7] *Central London Pty Trust Ltd v High Trees House Ltd, Ledingham v Bermejo Estancia Co. Ltd, Agar v Bermejo Estancia Co. Ltd.*[8] A landlord who has told his tenant that he can live in his cottage rent free for the rest of his life is not allowed to go back on it if the tenant stays in the house on that footing: *Foster v Robinson*.[9]

Sometimes it is a defendant who is not allowed to insist on his strict legal rights. His conduct may be such as to debar him from relying on some condition, denying some allegation, or taking some other point in answer to the claim. Thus, a government department, who had accepted a disease as due to war service, were not allowed afterwards to say it was not, when the soldier, in reliance on the assurance, had abstained from getting further evidence about it: *Roberston v Minister of Pensions*. A buyer who had waived the contract date for delivery was not allowed afterwards to set up the stipulated time as an answer to the seller: *Charles Rickards Ltd v Oppenheim*.[10] A tenant who had encroached on an adjoining building, asserting that it was comprised in the lease, was not allowed afterwards to say that it was not included in the lease: J. F. *Perrott & Co. Ltd v Cohen*.[11] A tenant who had lived in a house rent free by permission of his landlord, thereby asserting that his original tenancy had ended, was not afterwards allowed to say that his original tenancy continued: *Foster v Robinson*. In none of these cases was the defendant sued on the promise, assurance, or assertion as a cause of action in itself. He was sued for some other cause, for example, a pension or a breach of contract, or possession, and the promise, assurance, or assertion only played a supplementary role, though, no doubt, an important one. That is, I think, its true function. It may be part of a cause of action, but not a cause of action in itself. The principle, as I understand it, is that where one party has, by his words or conduct, made to the other a promise or assurance which was intended to affect the legal relations between them and to be acted on accordingly, then, once the other party has taken him at his word and acted on it, the one who gave the promise or assurance cannot afterwards be allowed to revert to the previous legal relations as if no such promise or assurance had been made by him, but he must accept their legal relations subject to the qualification which he himself has so introduced, even though it is not supported in point of law by any consideration, but only by his word.

Seeing that the principle never stands alone as giving a cause of action in itself, it can never do away with the necessity of consideration when that is an essential part of the cause of action. The doctrine of consideration is too firmly fixed to be overthrown by a side-wind. Its ill effects have been largely mitigated of late, but it still remains a cardinal necessity of the formation of a contract, although not of its modification or discharge. I fear that it was my failure to make this clear in *Central London Pty Trust Ltd v High Trees House Ltd* which misled Byrne J. in the present case. He held that the wife could sue on the husband's promise as a separate and independent cause of action by itself, although, as he held, there was no consideration for it. That is not correct. The wife can only enforce the promise if there was consideration for it. That is, therefore, the real question in the case: Was there sufficient consideration to support the promise?

If it were suggested that, in return for the husband's promise, the wife expressly or impliedly promised to forbear from applying to the court for maintenance—that is, a promise in return for a promise—there would clearly be no consideration because the wife's promise would not be binding on her and, therefore, would be worth nothing. Notwithstanding her promise, she could always apply to the divorce court for mainten-ance—perhaps, only with leave—but nevertheless she could apply. No agreement by her could take away that right: *Hyman v Hyman*,[12] as interpreted by this court in *Gaisberg v Storr*. There was, however, clearly no promise by the wife, express or implied, to forbear from applying to the court. All that happened was that she did, in fact, forbear—that is, she did an act in return for a promise. Is that sufficient consideration? Unilateral promises of this kind have long been enforced so long as the act or forbearance is done on the faith of the promise and at the request of the promisor, express or implied. The act done is then in itself sufficient consideration for the promise, even though it arises *ex post facto*, as Parker J. pointed out in *Wigan v English and Scottish Law Life Assurance Assoc.*[13] ([1909] 1 Ch. 298). If the findings of Byrne J. are accepted, they are sufficient to bring this principle into play. His finding that the husband's promise was intended to be binding, intended to be acted on, and was, in fact, acted on—although expressed to be a finding on the principle of the *High Trees House* case—is equivalent to a finding that there was consideration within this long settled rule, because it comes to the same thing expressed in different words: see *Oliver v Davis*.[14] My difficulty, however, is to accept the findings of Byrne J. that the promise was 'intended to be acted on'. I cannot find any evidence of any intention by the husband that the wife should forbear from applying to the court for maintenance, or, in other words, any request by the husband, express or implied, that the wife should so forbear. He left her to apply, if she wished to do so. She did not do so, and I am not surprised, because it is very unlikely that the divorce court would have made any order in her favour, since she had a bigger income than her husband. Her forbearance was not intended by him, nor was it done at his request. It was, therefore, no consideration.

Birkett L.J.:

. . .

. . . I think the description which was given by counsel for the husband in this court, namely, that the doctrine there enunciated was, so to speak, a doctrine which would enable a person to use it as a shield and not as a sword, is a very vivid way of stating what, I think, is the principle underlying both those cases. Denning J. in *Central London Pty Trust Ltd v High Trees House Ltd* concluded his judgment with these words ([1947] KB 136): 'I prefer to apply the principle that a promise intended to be binding, intended to be acted on and in fact acted on, is binding so far as its terms properly apply.' If a husband who had entered into an agreement of this kind was to try to take advantage of it, I think the doctrine would then apply, but, so far as the wife is concerned, her right to apply to the court for maintenance is still, theoretically, in full force. . . .

Asquith L.J.:

The learned judge decided that while the husband's promise was unsupported by any valid consideration, yet the principle in *Central London Pty Trust Ltd v High Trees House Ltd* entitled the wife to succeed. It is unnecessary to express any view as to the correctness of the decision in the *High Trees* case, although I certainly must not be taken to be questioning it. I would, however, remark in passing that it seems to me a complete misconception to suppose that it struck at the roots of the doctrine of consideration. Assuming, without deciding, that it is good law, I do not think it helps the wife at all. What that case decides is that when a promise is given which (i) is intended to create legal relations, (ii) is intended to be acted on by the promisee, and (iii) is, in fact, so acted on, the promisor cannot bring an action against the promisee which involves the repudiation of his promise or is inconsistent with it. It does not, as I read it, decide that a promisee can sue on the promise. Denning J. expressly states the contrary.

. . .

Finally, I do not think an actual forbearance, as opposed to an agreement to forbear to approach the court, is a good consideration unless it proceeds from a request, express or implied, on the part of the promisor.

1. [1949] 2 All ER 411; [1950] 1 KB 107; 2nd Digest. Supp.
2. [1947] KB 130; [1947] LJR 77; 175 LT 332; 2nd Digest Supp.
3. [1948] 2 All ER 767; [1949] 1 KB 227; [1949] LJR 323; 2nd Digest Supp.

[4.] (1877), 2 App Cas 439; 46 LJQB 583; 36 LT 932; 42 JP 421; 21 Digest 310, 1137.
[5.] (1888), 40 ChD 268; 60 LT 527; 11 Digest 214, 990.
[6.] [1937] 2 All ER 361; Digest Supp.
[7.] (1946), 174 LT 144; 2nd Digest Supp.
[8.] [1947] 1 All ER 749; 2nd Digest Supp.
[9.] [1950] 2 All ER 342; [1951] 1 KB 149.
[10.] [1950] 1 All ER 420; [1950] 1 KB 616.
[11.] [1950] 2 All ER 939.
[12.] [1929] AC 601; 98 LJP 81; 141 LT 329; 93 JP 209; Digest Supp.
[13.] [1909] 1 Ch. 291; 78 LJ Ch. 120; 100 LT 34; 12 Digest 212, 1701.
[14.] [1949] 2 All ER 353; [1949] 2 KB 727; [1949] LJR 1661; 2nd Digest Supp.

Note

1. In which of the following two examples will Bill be able to rely on the doctrine of promissory estoppel?

    A. Sara promises to give Bill money to allow him buy computer software. Bill orders the software and Sara refuses to pay him. Bill sues her.

    B. Bill enters into a contract to supply computer software to Sara. Under the contract Bill must deliver the goods before 1 May. Sara tells Bill that as she has no immediate need for them he may deliver them at his convenience. Bill delivers the goods in April. Sara refuses to pay for them and Bill sues her.

2. Atiyah suggests in *Essays on Contract* that the *Combe* case decided only that an act or forbearance which naturally and foreseeably follows from, and in reliance on, a promise is not a consideration for the enforcement of the promise where the justice of the case does not require that it should be.

    Do you agree with this view?

The Revenue Commissioners *v* Moroney [1972] IR 372

In order to avoid estate duty at a later stage the defendants' father agreed to transfer his licensed business to the defendants. The transfer took place by way of a sale of the property to the defendants for £16,000. None of this money was ever paid nor did any of the parties to the transaction expect that it would be paid. The plaintiffs later claimed that part of the £16,000 was an asset of the father and that duty was thus payable on it.

Kenny J. (HC):
. . .

The liability for estate duty seems to me to depend upon whether the parent would have been successful in an action brought by him against his sons immediately after the deed was executed for any part of the £16,000.
. . .

    In the course of the hearing I asked whether the sons could succeed on a plea that the parent was estopped from claiming any part of the 'purchase' money. Counsel for the defendants did not show any enthusiasm for this point and so I did not have the advantage of hearing counsel for the plaintiffs on it. Despite this, I think that in an action by the parent against the sons they would succeed on what is now called promissory estoppel.

This doctrine first appeared in *Hughes v Metropolitan Rly Co.*[1] which was a claim that a lease be forfeited on the ground that the lessee was in breach of a covenant to effect certain required repairs within six months from the date on which the lessee received from the lessor a notice specifying the defects. The landlord gave notice of the breaches on 22 October 1874, and the tenant's solicitors wrote that the repairs would be commenced immediately but that they proposed to postpone them until they heard whether the landlord wished to purchase the tenant's interest. The landlord's solicitors replied asking whether the tenant was the owner of other adjoining property and was willing to give immediate possession of it and stating that, when they had this information, their client would consider whether he would acquire the tenant's interest. The attempt to negotiate a settlement broke down on 31 December and the question in the case was whether the six months ran from that date or from 22 October, for the repairs had been carried out within the period of six months from 31 December. The case was decided before the law was altered by s. 14 of the Conveyancing Act, 1881. In the course of his speech the Lord Chancellor, Lord Cairns, said at p. 448 of the report:

> . . . it is the first principle upon which all courts of equity proceed, that if parties who have entered into definite and distinct terms involving certain legal results— certain penalties or legal forfeiture—afterwards by their own act or with their own consent enter upon a course of negotiation which has the effect of leading one of the parties to suppose that the strict rights arising under the contract will not be enforced, or will be kept in suspense, or held in abeyance, the person who otherwise might have enforced those rights will not be allowed to enforce them where it would be inequitable having regard to the dealings which have thus taken place between the parties.

Lord Justice Bowen in *Birmingham & District Land Co. v London & North Western Rly Co.*[2] showed that the principle was not confined to forfeiture cases but was of general application; at p. 286 of the report he said: ' . . . if persons who have contractual rights against others induce by their conduct those against whom they have such rights to believe that such rights will either not be enforced or will be kept in suspense or abeyance for some particular time, those persons will not be allowed by a court of equity to enforce the rights until such time has elapsed, without at all events placing the parties in the same position as they were before.'

The doctrine got little attention in the textbooks until it was revived in striking fashion by Mr Justice Denning (as he then was) in *Central London Pty Trust Ltd v High Trees House Ltd.*[3] . . . In *Combe v Combe*[4] the same judge said that the doctrine 'only prevents a party from insisting upon his strict legal rights, when it would be unjust to allow him to enforce them, having regard to the dealings which have taken place between the parties.' These cases were discussed by Viscount Simonds in *Tool Metal Manufacturing Co. Ltd v Tungsten Electric Co. Ltd*[5] in which he said at p. 764 that the gist of the equity lies in the fact that one party has by his conduct led the other to alter his position; this aspect was emphasised by Mr Justice McVeigh in *Morrow v Carty;*[6] see also *Cullen v Cullen*[7] and *Inwards v Baker.*[8]

In *Ajayi v R. T. Briscoe (Nig.) Ltd*[9] the advice of the Privy Council, given by Lord Hodson, was that the doctrine is confined to cases where the representation relates to existing contractual rights. At p. 1330 of the report Lord Hodson said:

Their Lordships are of opinion that the principle of law as defined by Bowen L.J. has been confirmed by the House of Lords in the case of *Tool Metal Manufacturing Co. Ltd v Tungsten Electric Co. Ltd* where the authorities were reviewed and no encouragement was given to the view that the principle was capable of extension so as to create rights in the promisee for which he had given no consideration. The principle, which has been described as quasi estoppel and perhaps more aptly as promissory estoppel, is that when one party to a contract in the absence of fresh consideration agrees not to enforce his rights an equity will be raised in favour of the other party. This equity is, however, subject to the qualifications (1) that the other party has altered his position, (2) that the promissor can resile from his promise on giving reasonable notice, which need not be a formal notice, giving the promisee a reasonable opportunity of resuming his position, (3) the promise only becomes final and irrevocable if the promisee cannot resume his position.

This, if correct, would conclude this case in favour of the plaintiffs as any promissory estoppel arises here because the parent before the deed was signed represented by his conduct and by what he said to his sons that he would not require payment of any part of the 'purchase' price. Until the deed was signed, there were no legal relations to be effected.

In my view there is no reason in principle why the doctrine of promissory estoppel should be confined to cases where the representation related to existing contractual rights. It includes cases where there is a representation by one person to another that rights which will come into existence under a contract to be entered into will not be enforced. This is the way in which the doctrine is stated at p. 627 of *Snell's Principles of Equity* (26th ed. 1966) which has the considerable authority of having had Mr Megarry (as he then was) as one of its co-editors: 'Where by his words or conduct one party to a transaction makes to the other a promise or assurance which is intended to affect the legal relations between them, and the other party acts upon it, altering his position to his detriment, the party making the promise or assurance will not be permitted to act inconsistently with it.' It seems to me that the parent represented to his sons that he would never seek payment of any part of the consideration of £16,000 and that they acted on this by signing the assignment. Each of them altered his position to his detriment because by signing each took on a legal liability to pay two thirds of the consideration which they would not otherwise have assumed. Although they got the benefit of the interest in the joint tenancy, it seems to me to be probable that if they had refused to sign the deed in the form in which it was they would have got this without payment. The assumption of the legal liability created by the deed was in my opinion sufficient to raise the equity against the parent and the representation has become final because the sons cannot be restored to their original position unless the view is taken that there never was a debt. This equity does not affect the rights of other parties who would be entitled to rely on the deed, but this does not assist the plaintiffs. Their claim can succeed only if the parent would have succeeded in a claim against his sons.

In my view the plaintiffs' claim fails because the parent would not have got judgment against the sons for any part of the 'purchase' price if he had sued them for it.

1. (1877) 2 App Cas 439.   6. |1957| NI 174, 181.
2. (1888) 40 ChD 268.   7. |1962| IR 268, 292.
3. |1947| KB 130.   8. |1965| 2 QB 29.
4. |1951| 2 KB 215, 219.   9. |1964| 1 WLR 1326.
5. |1955| 1 WLR 761.

Note

1. The plaintiffs appealed to the Supreme Court. There the court held that the evidence established that the defendants were never indebted at any time to their father in respect of the £16,000. As the doctrine of promissory estoppel arises only when there is liability in law to pay the money, it was deemed unnecessary to express any view on the applicability of the doctrine.
2. Evidence that the £16,000 was never intended to be paid was admitted despite the Parol Evidence Rule. This was because the rule does not apply to the statement of the consideration in the deed because 'the statement of the consideration forms no part of the terms of the deed, but is only a statement contained in the deed of an antecedent fact'.
3. The defendants' counsel argued that if the father had sued the sons could have successfully counterclaimed for rectification. This argument did not succeed because 'the court could have rectified the deed only if there was a mutual mistake so that the deed did not express the transaction between the parties or if there was fraud by the parent because he, knowing that there was a mistake and that his sons did not realise this, allowed them to execute the deed in the form in which it was.' Furthermore, 'a deed cannot be rectified because it has consequences which the parties did not foresee if the transaction which they intended finds expression in the document which it sought to rectify.'

In *Keegan & Roberts Ltd v Comhairle Chontae Atha Cliath* (HC) 12 March 1981, unrep. Ellis J. applied the test set out in *Woodhouse AC Israel Cocoa Ltd S.A. v Nigerian Produce Marketing Co. Ltd* [1972] AC 741 that to be effective 'an estoppel has to be clear and unequivocal and be understood in the sense required as a question of construction in all the surrounding circumstances'.

In *Folens and Co. Ltd v The Minister for Education, Ireland and the Attorney General* [1984] ILRM 265 McWilliam J. made it clear that in order to claim promissory estoppel there should be 'a definite commitment or representation'.

Chartered Trust Ireland Ltd *v* Thomas Healy and John Commins (HC) 10 December 1985, unrep.

The first defendant agreed to acquire a lorry from Fleming, who unknown to the first defendant, had illegally imported it into this jurisdiction passing it off as another lorry which had a proper and valid registration here. The purchase was financed by the plaintiffs under a hire-purchase agreement. Fleming furnished the plaintiffs with an invoice from a Mr Commins. It subsequently materialised that this invoice had been obtained illicitly. The first defendant used this lorry for one year before handing it back to Fleming to regularise a tax problem. Fleming disappeared with the lorry and the first defendant later ceased paying the hire purchase instalments. The plaintiffs sued for the balance due on foot of the agreement.

Barron J.:

. . .

The defendant's defence to the plaintiff's claim is that the hire purchase agreement was not made in compliance with the provisions of the Hire-Purchase Act 1946. Secondly, the defendant maintains that since he did not receive the vehicle set out in the hire purchase agreement that the entire was a nullity and that he is entitled to damages from the plaintiff for his failure to deliver to him the correct vehicle. He then counterclaims for all the sums paid on foot of the agreement since he says that he got no consideration for the sums paid. In defence to this counterclaim the plaintiffs say that the defendant is estopped from making this allegation. They then say that if he is entitled to claim damages from them that they are entitled to an indemnity from John Commins. John Commins' defence to this claim for an indemnity is that he knew nothing at all about the transaction, and is not responsible for the action of his secretary who wrote out the invoice since it was done to his prejudice.

The first question to be determined is whether or not there was a valid hire purchase agreement. The arrangements for the purchase of the lorry were made by the plaintiff with either Fleming or his agent. Whichever it was, it is clear that the latter was aware that the lorry which he had for sale was not the lorry registered under the number 889 OZA. Such person was also aware that the plaintiff did not know this and was entering into the contract to purchase the lorry in the mistaken belief that it was. I am also satisfied that such person must have known that the plaintiff would not have entered into such a contract if it had been aware of the mistake it was making. In my view, the mistake made by the plaintiff to the knowledge of Fleming or his agent was such that the contract became null and void. In the result, the plaintiff never became the owner of the lorry delivered to the defendant. It follows that the plaintiff was not the owner of the lorry in respect of which it purported to make the hire purchase agreement. Such agreement was accordingly a nullity. Nevertheless the plaintiff contends that it is entitled to sue on foot of this agreement since the defendant is estopped from denying its validity. It has been said many times that an estoppel does not operate as a sword, but only as a shield. Accordingly, there is no agreement upon which the plaintiff is entitled to sue and its claim accordingly fails.

This rule as to the effect of an estoppel does not prevent the plaintiff from relying upon an estoppel as a defence to the defendant's counterclaim. In my view, the defendant must be taken by virtue of the fact that he signed the hire-purchase agreement and saw the invoice upon which it was based to have known that the details contained in the hire purchase agreement and in the invoice were incorrect. However, there is no suggestion on the evidence that the defendant was aware that the lorry which he was receiving was not the lorry registered number 889 OZA. Accordingly, it seems to me that while the defendant would be estopped from denying the existence of a trade-in and from denying the fact that the dealer was the third party in these proceedings he is not estopped from denying the title of the plaintiff to the lorry which he received. It may well be that the plaintiff would have a cause of action against the defendant for misrepresenting the name of the dealer and the existence of a trade-in but any such cause of action must be the subject matter of separate proceedings. Since the defendant is not estopped from denying the plaintiff's title to the lorry, it follows that his counterclaim must succeed. There has been a total failure of consideration.

Phyllis Traynor *v* Elizabeth Fegan [1985] IR 586

In October 1977 the plaintiff was injured when travelling in a car driven by a Mr Fegan, a resident of Northern Ireland. In March 1979 Mr Fegan's insurers, Eagle Star stated that they had nominated solicitors within the jurisdiction to accept service of any proceedings. Despite writing numerous letters to Eagle Star the plaintiff's solicitor heard nothing from Eagle Star until September 1980 when he contacted them by telephone. Although the plaintiff attempted to serve proceedings on the defendant, who was nominated by Eagle Star following Mr Fegan's death this proved impossible due to Eagle Star's failure to instruct the solicitors to accept these proceedings. It was December 1980 by the time Eagle Star instructed solicitors and thus the claim was time-barred under the Statute of Limitations 1957. The plaintiff pleaded that the defendant was estopped from relying on the statute.

Barrington J.:

. . .

The plaintiff's proceedings were not issued within the time limited by the Statute of Limitations and must therefore fail unless the plaintiff can show that the defendant is, in some way, estopped from setting up the statute against him. That there are circumstances in which a defendant will be estopped from setting up the statute, is clear, but what exactly these circumstances are is by no means clear. O'*Reilly v Granville* [1971] IR 90 was a motion to add the respondent as a defendant in the proceedings. The application was resisted on the grounds that it would be open to the respondent, if joined, to plead the Statute of Limitations and that the exercise was therefore pointless. The court rejected this argument and was not therefore called to decide the question of whether the case was statute barred or not. Chief Justice Ó Dálaigh, however, having reviewed the facts of the case and the possibility that the Statute of Limitations might be pleaded made the comment (at p. 98): 'A plea of the Statute of Limitations, in the circumstances, would be not only wholly unmeritorious but, I feel it my duty to add, unconscionable and plainly dishonest.' The clear implication was that the defendant would be estopped or precluded from pleading the statute in the circumstances indicated.

In *Doran v Thompson Ltd* [1978] IR 223 the plaintiff's solicitor had, in effect, convinced himself that the defendant would not plead the Statute of Limitations and had not instituted his proceedings in time. The Supreme Court held it was not a case in which the defendant could be precluded from pleading the statute. Mr Justice Henchy, however, in the course of his judgment, discussed the circumstances in which a defendant might be estopped from pleading the statute. He put the matter as follows:

Where in a claim for damages such as this a defendant has engaged in words or conduct from which it was reasonable to infer, and from which it was in fact inferred, that liability would be admitted, and on foot of that representation the plaintiff has refrained from instituting proceedings within the period prescribed by the statute, the defendant will be held estopped from escaping liability by pleading the statute. The reason is that it would be dishonest or unconscionable for the defendant, having misled the plaintiff into a feeling of security on the issue of liability and, thereby, into a justifiable belief that the statute would not be used to defeat his claim, to escape liability by pleading the statute. The representation necessary to support this kind of estoppel need not be clear and unambiguous in the sense of being susceptible of only one interpretation. It is sufficient if, despite possible ambiguity or lack of certainty, on its true construction it bears the meaning that was drawn from it. Nor is it necessary to give evidence of an express intention to deceive the plaintiff. An intention to that effect will be read into the representation if the defendant has so conducted himself that, in the opinion of the court, he ought not be heard to say that an admission of liability was not intended.

In *Smith v Ireland and Others* |1983| ILRM 300, the then President of the High Court, Mr Justice Finlay rejected an attempt to preclude the defendant from pleading the Statute of Limitations by means of equitable estoppel. But at p. 308 of his judgment he referred with approval to a dictum of Lord Denning as to the circumstances in which a plea of equitable estoppel would lie. The passage was from Lord Denning's judgment in *Crabb v Arun District Council* |1975| 3 All ER 865 and was as follows: 'Short of an actual promise, if he, by his words or conduct, so behaves as to lead another to believe that he will not insist on his strict legal rights—knowing or intending that the other will act on that belief—and he does so act, that again will raise an equity in favour of the other; and it is for a court of equity to say in what way the equity may be satisfied.'

. . .

The plaintiff's case is a more complex one and rests, in part, on the representation contained in Mr Moore's letter of 29 March 1979, that his company had in fact nominated Messrs G. D. Fottrell to accept service of proceedings. This representation, though made without ulterior motive, was false in fact and was never withdrawn. It was quite clear from subsequent negotiations and correspondence that |the plaintiff's solicitor| was acting on this representation. Had he known the true position he could have taken steps to protect his client's interest.

. . .

In the event, the insurance company took an inordinate amount of time in authorising Mr Leyden to accept service and, during this time, the statute ran out.

. . .

    . . . it appears to me that it would be unconscionable of the insurance company to plead the Statute of Limitations.

I would, therefore, hold that the company is estopped from pleading the statute.

Note

American Law Institute Restatement Contracts (2d) S. 90(1) states: 'A promise which the promisor should reasonably expect to induce action or forbearance of 'a definite and substantial character on the part of the promisee and which does induce such action or forbearance is binding if injustice can be avoided only by enforcement of the promise.' The earlier (1926) version of this section however has been criticised for failing to furnish even an approximate standard for classifying what are irrevocable gratuitous promises and what are not (Stoljar 19 MLR 237).

In the matter of J.R., a Ward of Court [1993] ILRM 657

Costello J.:

Since 1990 the ward has been living in a psychiatric hospital, unable to manage his own affairs. The ward's committee now wants to sell the dwelling house in which he formerly lived because it has fallen into a dilapidated state. The ward is unmarried but his committee has ascertained that since 1978 he had been living in the dwelling house with a lady who still resides in it and who now claims rights in relation to it. This lady has been named as the respondent to this motion, a motion seeking an order for sale. As will appear later, it is obviously in the interests of the proper management of the ward's estate that this be done, but the court is of course bound by any rights affecting the property and the court's power of sale may be restricted by rights which may have been created by the ward. The issues now for determination are the nature of the rights, if any, to which the respondent is entitled in the property, and the proper order to be made in the circumstances.

The ward is now aged seventy three years. He was admitted to a psychiatric hospital in Dublin on 19 July 1990 for investigation of a depressed mood, weight loss and inability to take care of himself. He was then depressed and disorientated, with decreased concentration and some short term and some long term loss of memory. It was established on assessment that he could not live on his own and that he required help with dressing, bathing, toileting and even with sorting out his own possessions. A diagnosis of multiple infarct dementia having been made he was transferred to a psycho-geriatric unit. Since then his mood has fluctuated and at times he is regarded as a suicide risk. In February of this year he became very agitated but a change in medication seemed to bring about an improvement for a limited time. His cognitive functions cannot improve but there is a possibility, but it is only a possibility, that his depression may improve. His life expectation is quite good, but he will need full-time institutional care for the rest of his life. I am quite satisfied that he will never be able to return to live in his former dwelling house. He made a will in 1988 and I think it is extremely unlikely that he will ever be capable of making another will.

When taken into wardship on 8 October 1990 the General Solicitor was appointed committee of his person and his estate. There is presently standing to the credit of his account the sum of £39,205.61. In addition he is the owner of a dwelling house the subject of these proceedings.

The respondent to this motion was born on 2 November 1944 so that she is now nearly forty eight years of age. She married in 1965 but her husband left her in September 1971 and she has not heard from him since. There were two children of the marriage, a son born in July 1968 and a daughter born in February 1970 but as the respondent was unable to look after them they were brought up by her mother. In 1968 she suffered a brain tumour. The operation to remove it was successful and thereafter for some years she was able to work as a tailoress. But in 1977 a second brain tumour developed and although it was successfully removed she has since been disabled; her leg is permanently weakened so that she as to use a stick, and one of her arms is almost powerless. She has been unable to work and has had only a small disability pension on which to live. She has suffered from depression. This was so severe that in 1978 she required hospitalisation in a Dublin hospital. There she met the ward. He too was undergoing psychiatric treatment. They struck up a friendship which developed into a deeper relationship and resulted in his asking her to go to live with him in the dwelling which is the subject of these proceedings. They lived together as man and wife until 1990 when the ward had to be taken into hospital because of the illnesses to which I have referred. When they lived together the ward maintained the respondent out of his resources, and in addition gave her a small allowance to augment her disability pension.

The respondent's claim to a legal interest in the ward's dwelling is based on the following facts. She says that when she went to live with him that he represented to her that he would look after her, and that she would be sure of a home for the rest of her life. She says that he continued to make these representations to her and she acted on them. Furthermore, on 2 November 1988 the ward made a will. By it he bequeathed: 'all my property of every nature and kind whatsoever both real and personal including my residence at . . . to my great friend . . . |the respondent| for her own use and benefit absolutely. . . .' and he appointed the respondent executrix of his will. The evidence establishes that the will was validly executed, and that the ward was of sound mind, memory and understanding when he executed it. 2 November was the respondent's birthday. On that day he handed her a folder which contained his will and said to her, 'it is not my house now, it's our house and eventually it will be your house'. It will be recalled that the ward was then sixty nine years of age, and that the respondent was forty four.

The ward's dwelling is now in a very dilapidated state, as appears from an architect's report of 31 July 1991. Urgent repairs are needed to the roof and the rear wall, the house timbers need to be checked and because of damp penetration their replacement may be necessary. The cost of making the house structurally sound is estimated at £34,000. The ward's only money is a sum of £39,205 and out of this liabilities will have to be discharged including (a) such sums that may be due to the hospital, (b) the cost of future maintenance, (c) costs of the committee (past and future), (d) the possibility of future specialist nursing for the ward and (e) eventually his funeral expenses. The respondent agrees that the dwelling is in need of repairs but has obtained a contractor's estimate that urgent repairs could be carried out at a cost of £3,000.

The claims advanced on behalf of the respondent are based (a) on the represent- ations made to her at the time she went to live with the ward and subsequently and (b) the representations made on 2 November 1988. She relies on the principles of the law of estoppel. For present purposes I will use the classification which is now generally accepted (see Snell's *Principles of Equity*, (28th ed.), 554 and Halsbury's *Laws of England* (4th ed.), vol. 16, 1071, 1072) and refer to (i) promissory estoppel and (ii) proprietary estoppel. A promissory estoppel will arise where by words or conduct a person makes an unambiguous representation as to his future conduct, intending that the represent- ation will be relied on, and to affect the legal relations between the parties and the representee acts on it or alters his or her position to his or her detriment the representor will not be permitted to act inconsistently with it (see Snell's *Principles of Equity*, (28th ed.), 556). If the subject matter of the representation is land, no right or interest in the land results from this estoppel—a personal right is vested in the representee which will preclude the representor from enforcing a title to the land. A proprietary estoppel is different in a number of ways. When it relates to land it may result in the creation of rights in or over the land. It has been explained as follows: 'Where one person (A) has acted to his detriment on the faith of a belief, which was known to and encouraged by another person (B), that he either has or is going to be given a right in or over B's property, B cannot insist on his strict legal rights if to do so would be inconsistent with A's belief. (See *In re Basham* |1987| 1 All ER 405 at 410).' *Maharaj v Chand* |1986| AC 898 illustrates the operation of the law relating to promis- sory estoppel. This was a case which originated in Fiji and was eventually decided by the Privy Council. The plaintiff and the defendant were living as man and wife (but unmarried) when the plaintiff applied to the housing authority for a lease to enable him to build a house. With the approval of the Native Land Trust Board he obtained a sub-lease and erected a house on the land demised to him. In reliance on a representation made by the plaintiff to her that it would be a permanent home for her and her children the defendant left her flat and went to live with the plaintiff. Their relationship later broke down. The plaintiff left the house, giving the defendant permission to remain in it. Later he revoked the permission and instituted ejectment proceedings against her. The trial judge dismissed the claim on the ground that the plaintiff was estopped from evicting her. On appeal the plaintiff succeeded on the ground that the licence he gave the defendant was an unlawful 'dealing' within the meaning of s. 12 of the Native Land Trust Act. The Privy Council allowed the defendant's appeal and restored the order of the trial judge.

In reaching its conclusions the Privy Council firstly held that s. 12 did not apply as the right on which the defendant relied was a purely personal right and no 'dealing' with the land in breach of the section had occurred. Its opinion was that it might have been possible, but for the provisions of that section, to have made out an entitlement to an equitable interest in the land but this had not been claimed. The claim advanced was a more modest one, namely that the requirements of a promissory estoppel existed. It was pointed out that the plaintiff had represented to the defendant that the house would be a permanent home for herself and her children, that in reasonable reliance on this representation she acted to her detriment by giving up her flat, that it was not possible to restore her to her former position. In these circumstances it would be 'plainly inequitable' the court concluded for the plaintiff to evict her and held that she had permission to reside permanently in the house, that this was a personal right which did not amount to a property interest diminishing the right of the plaintiff's lessor or mortgagee.

Greasley v Cooke [1980] 1 WLR 1306 is an example of proprietary estoppel. It was a case in which the owners by inheritance of a dwelling house took ejectment proceedings against an occupier whose defence was that she had reasonably believed and was encouraged by members of the family of the deceased owner so to believe that she could regard the property as her home for the rest of her life and that she was entitled to a declaration to that effect. The evidence established that in 1938 at the age of 16 she went to the house as a maid servant of the deceased, that from 1946 she had cohabited in it with one of the deceased's sons, that after the owner's death she remained in the house and looked after it and also cared for the deceased's mentally ill daughter, that she received no payment, that she had been assured by members of the family that she could regard the house as her home for the rest of her life. It was held by the Court of Appeal that once it was shown that the defendant had relied on the assurances given to her then the burden of proving that she had acted to her detriment in staying on to look after the house without payment did not rest on her and that in the absence of proof to the contrary the court could infer that her conduct was induced by the assurances given to her, that expenditure of money was not a necessary element to establish proprietary estoppel, and that it was for the courts to decide in what way the equity established by the evidence should be satisfied.

Another example of the operation of the doctrine of proprietary estoppel is to be found in *In re Basham* [1987] 1 All ER 405. The plaintiff's mother married a second time when the plaintiff was aged fifteen. The plaintiff worked for her stepfather without payment for many years, helping him to run various public houses and a service station. After she had herself married she considered moving elsewhere but she was dissuaded by her stepfather from doing so. After the death of her mother she looked after her stepfather. He owned a cottage and on many occasions he indicated to her that she would get the cottage on his death in return for what she had been doing for him and also his estate. But he died intestate and two nieces were his next of kin. The plaintiff instituted these proceedings claiming a declaration that she was entitled to the deceased's entire estate because the deceased had induced and encouraged in her the expectation or belief that she would receive the estate on his death and because she had acted to her detriment in reliance on that expectation a proprietary estoppel arose in her favour. She succeeded in her claim.

Having stated the principle of proprietary estoppel already quoted, the court pointed out that although the principle is commonly known as proprietary estoppel where the belief is that A is going to be given a right in the future it may properly be regarded as giving rise to a species of constructive trust, the concept employed by a court of equity to prevent a person from relying on his legal rights when it would be unconscionable for him to do so. The court held that a proprietary estoppel could be raised when an expectation exists that future rights would be given over a person's residuary estate. As the plaintiff's belief that she would inherit the estate had been encouraged by the deceased and as the plaintiff had acted to her detriment in subordinating her own interests to the wishes of the deceased in reliance on her belief that she would inherit, she had established a proprietary estoppel and was entitled to the estate. The court considered how effect should be given to the equity which had arisen in the plaintiff's favour. It held that the extent of the equity was to have made good, as far as could fairly be done between the parties, the expectations which the deceased had encouraged. It followed from this that the plaintiff was entitled to a declaration that the personal representatives held the whole of the net estate in trust for the plaintiff.

Conclusions

In the light of the facts and the applicable legal principles, I have come to the following conclusions:

(1) The uncontradicted evidence is that at the time that the respondent went to live with the ward and thereafter he represented to her that he would look after her and that she could be sure of a home in his dwelling house for the rest of her life. I think the respondent acted on this representation and that she did so to her detriment. The law relating to the nature of detriment suffered by a representee has been clarified by a number of recent cases. As was shown in *Maharaj v Chand* detriment may exist when a representee leaves a permanent home on the faith of a representation that another will be offered in its place. Whilst I have no evidence of where the respondent was living in 1978 I think I am entitled to assume that she had a house or a flat which she gave up to go live with the respondent and that accordingly she has made out a case of promissory estoppel as she acted on the representation made to her. It would be plainly inequitable for the ward now to deny that she has a right to live in his house and it seems to me that she has an equity which entitles her to stay in the house rent free for as long as she wishes to which the court must give effect.

(2) I do not think that any further or additional rights were conferred by the events of 2 November 1988. When on 2 November 1988 the ward handed the respondent a folder and said 'it's not my house now, it's our house and eventually will be yours' I think he was intending by those words to give a gift of an interest in the house to the respondent. But the respondent cannot claim any enforceable rights from this fact, because the gift was an imperfect one which the courts cannot enforce. I do not think that by using those words and handing her the executed will the ward thereby conferred on the respondent an immediate beneficial interest under a constructive trust—the ward intended that she would have (a) a right to reside in the house during his life and (b) ownership of it after his death, but he did not intend that she would have an

immediate beneficial interest in it—if he had so intended he would have arranged to transfer the property either to her alone or jointly with him. And the respondent cannot rely on the doctrine of estoppel because she cannot show that she acted in any way to her detriment arising from the representation which was made to her on 2 November.

In cases such as this the court must (a) ascertain the nature of the equity to which a representee is entitled and (b) decide in what way the equity may be satisfied (see Denning M.R. in *Greasley v Cooke*, op. cit., p. 1312). The equity which the respondent has been able to establish is a right to reside in the ward's dwelling house for her life and normally such a right would be satisfied by an order refusing to evict the representee or where the representor is a ward of court refusing to sell the dwelling house. But there are special circumstances in this case. The house is in a very serious state of dilapidation. Major work needs to be done on it. There has been severe damp penetration which has caused the timbers to rot. There is rising damp in the basement walls, the plumbing and electrical wiring need to be replaced. The cost of doing the work was estimated last year as being £34,000 approximately. It is quite a large three storey house and the respondent no longer uses the basement. It is not reasonable to spend the ward's limited resources in attempting to repair it and the respondent herself has no money to do so and no doubt it is declining in value all the time. The respondent's equity can be satisfied by selling the house and buying another smaller one suitable for the respondent's needs. It should be bought in the ward's name but I will declare that the respondent has a right to reside in it for as long as she wishes. This will not of course prejudice in any way the rights she will have should the ward predecease her (as would normally be expected) and should he not revoke his will (a most remote eventuality).

In order to satisfy the equity the new house should meet the respondent's reasonable needs for accommodation as a single person. It should be purchased in consultation with the respondent and should any difference arise this motion can be re-entered. The committee should take expert advice as to when to sell and when to purchase the new property.

I will therefore order that the premises be sold provided that there is made available to the respondent suitable alternative accommodation in a dwelling to be purchased in the ward's name, and I will declare that the respondent has a right to live in the newly acquired dwelling for as long as she may wish.

C. PROPRIETARY ESTOPPEL

Proprietary estoppel is a species of estoppel which operates when one party acts to his detriment on a belief that he has or will be granted an interest in or over the property of another. Unlike promissory estoppel it may give rise to a cause of action.

John Cullen v Patrick Cullen and Martin Cullen [1962] IR 268

The plaintiff owned a grocery shop, bar and 60 acres of land in Adamstown, County Waterford. The relationship between the plaintiff and his wife and children (including the defendants) was poor. The plaintiff was diagnosed as suffering from a paranoid illness. In order to avoid removal to a mental institution under an arrest order the plaintiff left his home and business in Adamstown and went to Dublin. Mr Lawton an accountant was authorised to inform Mrs Cullen that the plaintiff was prepared to make over to her the place at Adamstown. Although the plaintiff intended this transfer to be conditional upon the withdrawal of the arrest order this fact was not communicated to Mrs Cullen.

The plaintiff brought an action claiming an injunction to restrain his two sons from interfering in the family business and from trespassing on the property at Adamstown. Martin Cullen counterclaimed that he was entitled to a site on the property upon which he had constructed his house.

Kenny J.:

The plaintiff authorised Father Kavanagh to tell Mr Lawton that he was going to transfer to Mrs Cullen the place at Adamstown and every blade of grass on it and everything except the cattle on the lands and Mr Lawton told her of this. It seems to me that this was a statement of intention by the plaintiff of what he proposed to do. He offered to do this because he wanted to retain his liberty and to avoid arrest under the order made under the Mental Treatment Act, 1945. Mr Matheson has relied on the decision in *Dillwyn v Llewelyn*[1] as an authority for the proposition that the court should now compel the plaintiff to transfer the lands and premises at Adamstown to Mrs Cullen. The case is an authority for the proposition that a person claiming under a voluntary agreement will not be assisted by a court of equity but that the subsequent acts of the donor may give the donee a ground of claim which he did not acquire from the original gift. In that case a father had told his son (the plaintiff) that he should live near him and had offered him a farm in order that the plaintiff might build a house: there was a written memo in which the father confirmed that it was his wish that his widow should give the lands to his son so that he would have a house. The plaintiff expended a large sum of money in building a house on the lands. Lord Westbury held that the making of the promise to give the lands coupled with the knowledge that the plaintiff had spent a considerable sum of money in building the house on the lands gave the plaintiff an equity to call on those claiming through the father to complete the gift. In this case, however, the only act relied on by Mrs Cullen to create the equity is the putting of £403 into the business on Mr Lawton's suggestion; she has, however, been in receipt of the profits of the business since 6 June 1959, and these are considerably more than the sum which she paid in. Moreover, the balance sheet of the business as at 31 December 1960, shows a sum of £680 16s 2d to the credit of the bank account (I assume that this is the bank account in her name) and she could at any time since January 1960, have repaid out of the profits of the business the monies advanced by her. The equity referred to by Lord Westbury is a discretionary one and when I consider the circumstances in which the plaintiff made the statement that he was about to transfer the property at Adamstown to his wife and that he made it because he believed that it was the only way by which he could remain free, I have no doubt whatever that it would be grossly inequitable to regard Mrs Cullen as being entitled to a transfer of the property at Adamstown or as having acquired any proprietary interest, legal or equitable, in the property as a result of what was said. The use by Mrs Cullen of her own monies for the running of the business, particularly when she could have repaid this advance at any time, does not, in my opinion, create any claim in conscience or in equity which the court should enforce or give any ground for disregarding the general principle that equity will not aid an imperfect gift. As Mrs Cullen has no proprietary interest in the property the defendants cannot shelter behind her permission to them or her employment of them in the business. A further ground relied on was that the plaintiff made no provision for Mrs Cullen when he left, that she had to run the business to provide maintenance for herself and that she was accordingly entitled to employ the defendants and to license them to reside in the premises. In the circumstances I think that she was entitled to conduct the business when the plaintiff left, but she had no authority to employ either of the defendants in the business or to license them to reside in the premises after the letters of 14 September.

. . .

I come now to deal with the ownership of the site on which the house, won by Mrs Cullen in the competition in the *Sunday Press*, had been erected. However unfortunate the Cullens may have been in their domestic relations, they have been singularly fortunate in competitions; Seán had won a substantial prize in the Hospitals Sweepstake and in March or April, 1959, Mrs Cullen had won a fully furnished portable house. She gave this house to Martin and the plaintiff knew this in April 1959. Martin intended to erect the house on his lands at Coolnagreine and, when representatives from the *Sunday Press* visited Adamstown in April 1959, a site on his farm at Coolnagreine was selected. Shortly after this, Martin began to prepare the site for the house and did some work on the foundations. He had offered the house to his father before 6 June 1959, as he thought that his father did not approve of the position selected for it, but the offer was not accepted. When the plaintiff left Adamstown on 6 June, Mrs Cullen decided that she would like to have the house erected on the farm at Adamstown and, when she was speaking to Mr Lawton, she told him this and sought her husband's permission for it. Mr Lawton said that he did not see why the permission was necessary as the property at Adamstown would be transferred to her; she persisted and Mr Lawton undertook that he would write to Father Kavanagh and would telephone to her when he got a reply. A few days afterwards Mr Lawton wrote to Father Kavanagh who discussed the matter with the plaintiff. The plaintiff told him that it was not necessary to discuss the matter because he was making over the place at Adamstown to Mrs Cullen and that she could put the house where she liked. This discussion took place on 13 or 14 June. Father Kavanagh gave this information to Mr Lawton who then telephoned Mrs Cullen and told her that she could go ahead with 'the project as mentioned' and put the house up wherever she liked. Mrs Cullen sent a message to Martin that he was not to go on with the preparation of the site on his farm and was to put up the house on the lands at Adamstown. He then stopped the preparation of the site on his own lands and began to work on a site for the house at Adamstown. He employed a man to work with him and spent about £200 in installing a water supply and building the foundations. The house arrived at the end of July and was assembled and erected in August. Some time after it was erected Martin heard that his father objected to its being placed at Adamstown and in August 1960, Martin, who was about to get married, wrote to his father asking him to attend the wedding, and added: 'I am hoping that you will give me the site the bungalow is on and your blessing.'

I am satisfied that Martin would have erected the house on his own lands if the plaintiff had not given Mrs Cullen permission to put up the house at Adamstown and that he erected the house on the lands at Adamstown because he relied on the permission given. I am convinced that the plaintiff knew at all times that Mrs Cullen had given the house to Martin and that the house was being erected for Martin to live in. It would cost £700 at least to take it down now and to lay foundations for it elsewhere; the cost of the decoration of the house which would be made necessary by its removal would be an additional £100. It has been submitted on the authority of *Ramsden v Dyson*[2] that Martin Cullen has acquired a right to compel the plaintiff to transfer to him the site on which the house now stands. That case decides that if a stranger begins to build on land which he thinks is his and the real owner, seeing the mistake, abstains from correcting it and leaves him to continue, equity will not afterwards allow the real owner to assert his title to the land: but that if a stranger builds on land knowing it to be the property of another, equity will not prevent the real owner from claiming the lands afterwards. In this case, however, Martin knew that the land belonged to the plaintiff and his letter written in August 1960, supports this view. In my opinion the argument based on *Ramsden v Dyson* is incorrect.

I am of opinion, however, that the plaintiff is estopped by his conduct in giving consent to the erection of the house at Adamstown when he knew that the house had been given to Martin and that the plaintiff cannot now assert any title to the site on which the house has been erected. There was a representation by him that he consented to this and that representation was acted on by Martin who spent £200 at least in erecting the house and gave a considerable amount of his time to this work. It seems to me that the principle stated by Denning J. in *Central London Pty Trust Ltd v High Trees House Ltd*[3] and affirmed by the same judge when he was a Lord Justice of Appeal in *Lyle-Meller v Lewis & Co. (Westminster) Ltd*[4] applies to this aspect of the case and that the plaintiff cannot withdraw the permission which he gave for the erection of the house on the lands at Adamstown and cannot now assert a title to the site on which the house stands or to the house. While the estoppel created by the plaintiff's conduct prevents him asserting a title to the site, it does not give Martin a right to require the plaintiff to transfer the site to him: if I had jurisdiction to make such an order I would do so, but I do not think I have. However, neither the plaintiff nor any person claiming through him can now successfully assert a title to the lands on which the house is built by any proceedings and, at the end of the twelve year period from the date when the erection of the bungalow commenced, Martin will be able to bring a successful application under s. 52 of the Registration of Title Act, 1891, for his registration as owner. If this case goes further, I hope that it will be held that I was wrong in deciding that I had no power to order the plaintiff to transfer the site to Martin. There is a claim in the pleadings that Martin has acquired a lien on the lands but this was not argued. I must accordingly dismiss the counterclaim.

[1] (1862) 4 De G F & J 517.   [3] [1947] KB 130.
[2] (1866) LR 1 HL 129.   [4] [1956] 1 All ER 247.

Crabb *v* Arun District Council [1975] 3 All ER 865

Lord Denning M.R.:

. . .

. . . it is commonly supposed that estoppel is not itself a cause of action. But that is because there are estoppels and estoppels. Some do give rise to a cause of action. Some do not. In the species of estoppel called proprietary estoppel, it does give rise to a cause of action . . . The new rights and interests, so created by estoppel, in or over land, will be protected by the courts and in this way give rise to a cause of action. This was pointed out in Spencer Bower and Turner on *Estoppel by Representation*.

The basis of this proprietary estoppel—as indeed of promissory estoppel—is the interposition of equity. Equity comes in, true to form, to mitigate the rigours of strict law. The early cases did not speak of it as 'estoppel'. They spoke of it as 'raising an equity' . . . What then are the dealings which will preclude him from insisting on his strict legal rights? If he makes a binding contract that he will not insist on the strict legal position, a court of equity will hold him to his contract. Short of a binding contract, if he makes a promise that he will not insist on his strict legal rights—even though that promise may be unenforceable in point of law for want of consideration or want of writing—and if he makes the promise knowing or intending that the other will act on it, and he does act on it, then again a court of equity will not allow him to go back on that promise: see *Central London Pty Trust v High Trees House, Charles Rickards v Oppenheim*. Short of an actual promise, if he, by his words or conduct, so behaves as to lead another to believe that he will not insist on his strict legal rights—knowing or intending that the other will act on that belief—and he does so act, that again will raise an equity in favour of the other, and it is for a court of equity to say in what way the equity may be satisfied. The cases show that this equity does not depend on agreement but on words or conduct. In *Ramsden v Dyson* Lord Kingsdown spoke of a verbal agreement 'or what amounts to the same thing, an expectation, created or encouraged'. In *Birmingham Land Co. v London and North Western Rly* Cotton L.J. said that ' . . . what passed did not make a new agreement but what took place . . . raised an equity against him'. And it was the Privy Council who said that 'the court must look at the circumsta ·ces in each case to decide in what way the equity can be satisfied', giving instances: see *Plimmer v Mayor of Wellington*.

Scarman L.J.:

. . .

. . . I think the law has developed so that today it is to be considered as correctly stated by Lord Kingsdown in his dissenting speech in *Ramsen v Dyson*. . . .

. . .

> The rule of law applicable to the case appears to me to be this: If a man, under a verbal agreement with a landlord for a certain interest in land, or what amounts to the same thing, *under an expectation, created or encouraged by the landlord* [my italics], that he shall have a certain interest, takes possession of such land, with the consent of the landlord, and upon the faith of such promise or expectation, with the knowledge of the landlord, and without objection by him, lays out money upon the land, a court of equity will compel the landlord to give effect to such promise or expectation.

SECTION FOUR—DOCTRINE OF LEGITIMATE EXPECTATION

'Legitimate, or reasonable, expectation may arise either from an express promise given on behalf of a public authority or from the existence of a regular practice which the claimant can reasonably expect to continue.' Per Lord Fraser in *Council of Civil Service Unions v Minister for the Civil Service* [1985] AC 37.

Michael T. S. Webb and Michael O'Connell Webb *v* Ireland and the Attorney General [1988] IR 353

Finlay C.J.:

This is an appeal brought by the defendants against the order of the High Court made on 10 December 1986, directing the return to the plaintiffs of certain valuable antique articles constituting what has become known as 'the Derrynaflan Hoard' upon payment of £25,800 by the plaintiffs to the defendant, or in the alternative at the option of the plaintiffs an order that the plaintiffs do recover against the defendants the sum of £5,510,200.

The Derrynaflan Hoard consists of a chalice, silver paten, silver and bronze paten stand, gilt bronze strainer and a bronze basin. It has been described as one of the most significant discoveries ever made of Christian art. The chalice is believed to date from the ninth century and the entire find constitutes an immensely important contribution to knowledge.

The plaintiffs, who are father and son, on 17 February 1980, went to a place near Killenaule in County Tipperary, known as Derrynaflan, which consisted of an island of pasture land surrounded by a very large area of bog. It contains the remains of a church and other buildings which formed part of an abbey and also a tomb which is supposed to be that of the Gobán Saor. Buildings described as 'Derrynaflan Abbey' or 'Gobán's Church and Grave' were the subject matter of a preservation order made by the Minister for Finance under s. 8 of the National Monuments Act, 1930, which order was made on 8 June 1935.

The lands known as Derrynaflan were at the time of the finding of the hoard jointly owned in unequal shares by a Mr Denis O'Brien and a Mr John O'Leary.

Each of the plaintiffs had with him a metal detector and the purpose of their visit to these lands which they reached by travelling on a raised road going through the bog was to search for metal objects which might be buried in the lands. They did not seek any permission from the owners of the lands before entering on them. After a relatively short time searching with the metal detectors one of the plaintiffs got a positive reaction and upon digging into the bottom of a bank close to the abbey and buildings with a small hand trowel the plaintiffs succeeded in unearthing the objects which constitute the hoard. They brought these objects back to their house in Clonmel and having consulted an archaeologist as to their importance and also having received the advice of their solicitor, Mr Binchy, the first plaintiff delivered the articles the following day to the National Museum, bringing with him a letter written by his solicitor in the following terms:

18 February 1980

Dear Sir,

We have been consulted by Mr Michael T. S. Webb with reference to certain articles which he and his son, Mr Michael Webb, junior, found on 17 February 1980. These articles appear to be a chalice, tray and strainer and it is possible that they may constitute treasure trove. Our client is advised that these articles should, with the minimum possible delay and handling, be delivered to the care and custody of experts who have the facilities for examination and preserving same. We have accordingly advised our client that he should deliver these articles to your care for the present and pending determination of the legal ownership or status thereof; and also, of course, subject to any rights to payment or reward which our client and his son have.

Yours faithfully
O'Brien & Binchy

The articles were received by Dr Breandán Ó Riordáin, the director of the National Museum, who immediately recognised their general value and importance and it was established at the trial that Dr Ó Riordáin told Mr Webb that he thought that the articles making up the hoard were treasure trove but that with regard to that aspect of the matter he would have to be guided by the Attorney General's advice. He also told Mr Webb that he (Mr Webb) would be honourably treated.

Shortly afterwards the first plaintiff met officials of the museum and pointed out the precise place where the hoard had been found by him and his son.

Within a short time the museum, having ascertained the owners of the land and having received their permission, carried out further excavations on the site and these, which lasted for approximately six weeks, resulted in a number of missing parts and components being found, belonging either to the paten, the strainer or the bronze basin. A reconstruction was then carried out together with preservation work, partly by the National Museum and partly by the British Museum at the request of the National Museum, resulting in the restoration, to a very great extent, of the articles comprising the hoard to what must have been their original condition.

The solicitors for the plaintiffs on 9 October 1980, wrote to Dr Ó Riordáin reminding him of the undertaking that the plaintiffs would be honourably treated with regard to the finding of the hoard and asking that this promise would be implemented. To that letter a reply was sent, stating that the matter was being considered by the head of the Department of Education. No further communication was received, however, from Dr Ó Riordáin and the solicitors for the plaintiffs wrote again on 2 March 1981, asking for a firm commitment within one month. On 16 June 1981, the Chief State Solicitor wrote to the solicitors for the plaintiffs referring to the letter of 18 February 1980, addressed to Dr Ó Riordáin and stating that the government would be willing to make an award of £10,000 to the plaintiffs in respect of their interest in the finds. There does not appear to have been a direct response to that letter but on 23 November 1981, the plaintiffs' solicitors wrote seeking the return of the hoard to the plaintiffs. Reminders were sent but no response to that demand was made until 8 February 1982, when the Chief State Solicitor wrote to the solicitors for the plaintiffs pointing out that his instructions were that the hoard was the property of the State and that the government was prepared to make an award of £10,000 to the plaintiffs as had been stated in his letter of 16 June 1981. These proceedings were then instituted by plenary summons on 11 March 1982.

In March 1980, a solicitor acting on behalf of the owners of the land, Messrs O'Brien and O'Leary, had written making a claim to an award. Considerable correspondence took place between the State and these owners and eventually both agreed to accept a sum of £25,000 each, and in consideration of that payment to convey to the Minister for Education all rights, property or interest 'that they may have in the objects now known as the Derrynaflan Hoard'. Mr O'Brien and Mr O'Leary executed a document on 7 July 1981, acknowledging the payment of the sum of £25,000 and transferring to the Minister for Education all their rights and interests in accordance with the agreement.

The plaintiffs' alternative claim for the enforcement by this court of a right of reward in respect of so much of the hoard as constituted treasure trove is based on an assertion that a combination of the practices both of the British Treasury prior to 1922 and the State through the agency of the National Museum since that time and the particular conversations and conduct of the officials of the National Museum acting as agents for the State after the finding of this hoard gave to the plaintiffs a 'legitimate expectation' of the making to them of a substantial reward by the State which they are entitled to enforce in the courts.

In support of the assertion that they are entitled to rely on a 'legitimate expectation' the plaintiffs point to the evidence which was adduced, some of it undoubtedly being hearsay but apparently without objection, as to the rewards which had been paid in the past by the museum in respect of the finding of antique objects and in respect of interdepartmental or administrative minutes and decisions made with regard to the general approach to such rewards. In particular, of course, they rely on the statement already noted in this judgment and accepted by the learned trial judge, made by the director of the National Museum at the very first interview with the first plaintiff that he would be treated honourably.

It would appear that the doctrine of 'legitimate expectation' sometimes described as 'reasonable expectation', has not in those terms been the subject matter of any decision of our courts. However, the doctrine connoted by such expressions is but an aspect of the well recognised equitable concept of promissory estoppel (which has been frequently applied in our courts), whereby a promise or representation as to intention may in certain circumstances be held binding on the representor or promisor. The nature and extent of that doctrine in circumstances such as those of this case has been expressed as follows by Lord Denning M.R. in *Amalgamated Pty Co. v Texas Bank* [1982] QB 84, 122:

> When the parties to a transaction proceed on the basis of an underlying assumption—either of fact or of law—whether due to misrepresentation or mistake makes no difference—on which they have conducted the dealings between them—neither of them will be allowed to go back on that assumption when it would be unfair or unjust to allow him to do so. If one of them does seek to go back on it, the courts will give the other such remedy as the equity of the case demands.

Applying the law as there stated, which seems to me to accord with fundamental equitable principles, I am satisfied that the unqualified assurance given to the first plaintiff by the director of the National Museum that he (Mr Webb) would be honourably treated was an integral part of the transaction under which the hoard was deposited in the museum and accepted on behalf of the State, and that the State cannot now go back on the assurance. It must be given effect to in the form of a monetary award of an amount which is reasonable in the light of all the relevant circumstances.

It is not necessary to rule on the submission made on behalf of the plaintiffs that, regardless of any specific assurance given on behalf of the State, the plaintiffs are entitled as of right, as finders, to appropriate monetary payment for the treasure trove acquired by the State. As I have indicated, the right to treasure trove asserted by the State in this case is essentially the right vested in the State by reason of its sovereign nature bearing the characteristics attached to it by the common law prior to 1922. Prior to 1922 it appears to have been the practice in this country to give monetary rewards to finders of treasure trove. The defendants contend that such rewards were mere *honoraria* given as a matter of grace and not on foot of any legal liability to give them. The plaintiffs on the other hand contend that the giving of rewards to finders of treasure trove was so well established and regular that the expectation of a reward in this case was so well founded that the courts should give effect to it.

It is not necessary for the resolution of this case to choose between those two submissions. In my opinion the plaintiffs' claim for compensation rests solidly on the fact that the assurance given to Mr Webb that he would be honourably treated (which should be held to mean that he would be reasonably rewarded) was an integral part of the transaction whereby he deposited the hoard in the National Museum. It would be inequitable and unjust if the State were to be allowed to repudiate that assurance and give only a meagre and disproportionate award. For the State to avoid giving the plaintiffs a reasonable reward would not be to treat them honourably.

Evidence of the amounts paid in respect of previous finds of valuable antiques tendered in the High Court does not appear to me to assist in any particular way as to the appropriate amount which should be paid in this case for no distinction seems to have been made in those circumstances between objects of antique or historical value which were gold and silver and those which were not. In particular, the only comparable object which was found and brought into the possession of the National Museum would appear to be the Ardagh Chalice and certainly the evidence tendered with regard to the amounts paid to various people in respect of that find would indicate a total absence of relationship between its true commercial or market value and the amounts paid.

Having reached the conclusion, however, as I have done in this judgment, that treasure trove is a royalty of franchise vested in the State by virtue of its sovereign nature and having reached the further conclusion that there is associated with that a right of the plaintiffs in the particular circumstances of this case to a reasonable reward, I find that I am dealing with a situation in which a finder has got a right to a reward for which the law has not yet provided a precise method of assessment.

Whilst I have already decided that the fact that the finding of them arose from an act of trespass, namely, the digging in the land to enter which they had an implied licence would, apart from other considerations, defeat any right they had to the possession of the objects as between them and the owners of the land, I do not consider that the extent and the nature of the trespass in this case, having regard in particular to the subsequent conduct of the plaintiffs with regard to the hoard, could or should, as a matter of public policy, disentitle them to a reasonable reward. In particular, the statement upon which they rely, which was in my view properly made, by the director of the National Museum, after he had been made aware of the circumstances of the finding of this hoard, would be inconsistent with any such loss of rights.

It is not possible at this stage and in the absence of specific legislation to set out in any exhaustive detail the factors which might or should, as a matter of policy cover the assessment of what is a proper or reasonable reward for the finding of objects of treasure trove. As I have already indicated, evidence with regard to past payments made for antiquities are of little value, having particular regard to the fact that there is a great absence in most of the cases of evidence with regard to the nature of the contents of such antiquities or to any independent assessment of their value.

It would appear to me that factors which would be certainly of relevance are the general value and importance of the objects found; the circumstances of their finding; and the nature and extent of rewards granted in other instances of treasure trove. Lastly, and of very considerable importance, is the attitude and conduct of the finders of the objects after they have been found and the alacrity with which their finding is disclosed and their possession is surrendered to the appropriate authorities. Consideration must also, in my view, be given to a situation where objects are found by an act of trespass, even though that may be not of any flagrant type and even though that may not, as on the facts of this case, disentitle the finders to their reward.

It appears to me that on the evidence which is before this court and which was before the High Court, coupled with the finding by which this court is bound, with regard to the market value of the objects found, that this court is in as good a position as would be the High Court to assess a reasonable reward, having regard to the considerations which I have above outlined. In those circumstances, in litigation which has not in the courts had anything like a lengthy history but which being brought to the courts was delayed from the time of the finding of these objects, I think it is proper that this court should itself assess the appropriate reward.

Having regard to all the considerations which I have set out above, I would assess a sum of £50,000 as a reward to the finders of this hoard to be divided equally between the two plaintiffs.

Walsh J.:

With regard to the claim that the plaintiffs should be entitled to some reward for discovering and taking possession of these articles special considerations apply. I fully recognise that as a matter of prudence and indeed as a way of safeguarding similar such objects as may in the future be found that it could well be regarded as expedient on the part of the State, not merely to reward such persons but generously to reward them for the sake of ensuring, or assisting in ensuring, that the objects will be disclosed to the State and will be dealt with by the State for the benefit of the common good in accordance with the law for the time being in force. There is evidence that experience in other countries indicates that the more generous the reward the greater is the assurance of the continued availability or even survival of such objects. While it is to be hoped that the State in its legislation or in the exercise of its other powers might see matters in the same way, particularly in the case of persons as honest and as frank as the present plaintiffs that is a matter for the Oireachtas. For the reasons I have already given I take the view that the owners of the land were not entitled to assert a claim to ownership. It was their good fortune that the State saw fit to pay them. On the basis of ordinary justice it appears to me that the plaintiffs should be equally entitled, if not more entitled, legitimately to expect to be rewarded on a no less generous scale. I agree with the opinion of the Chief Justice on this topic already expressed in his judgment.

(Henchy and Griffin JJ. concurred.)

McCarthy J.:

Whilst it may be contended that the plaintiffs were merely complying with law when they brought the hoard to the attention of the National Museum, in my view, for the reasons that are set out in the judgment of the Chief Justice, they were entitled to rely on a legitimate expectation that the State would make to them a substantial reward and that they are entitled to enforce this in the courts. In this area of the case, indeed, I believe that public policy plays a significant role. Whatever criticism may be made of the plaintiffs in the use of metal detectors or for the fact that they dug below the surface in order to retrieve the hoard, their subsequent conduct and attitude had been entirely praiseworthy; I would wish that I could say the same of those responsible for the assessing of the offer of £10,000 made to the plaintiffs, when the owners of the land ignorant of the existence of the treasure until found by the plaintiffs and who had done nothing whatever save own the land, was each paid the sum of £25,000 from the same source.

I would allow the appeal accordingly and concur in the order proposed.

Note

1. One of the policy considerations that underpins the imaginative or creative features of the *Webb* case is the need to create some kind of incentive whereby persons who discover valuable items which form part of the Irish cultural heritage will come forward and declare them to the relevant authorities. A similar decision was given by Barr J. on 26 July 1994 in awarding a 'generous' reward to a group of persons who had discovered a number of Spanish Armada wrecks during 1985. S. 10 of the National Monuments (Amendment) Act 1994 now puts the payment of a reward to persons who find an archaeological object onto a statutory footing, although it remains to be seen whether the Director of the National Museum of Ireland, who is to decide several issues relating to payments, will be as generous as the courts.

2. It is interesting to note that the plaintiffs' acts in reliance (i.e. handing over the hoard to the museum) occurred before the representation. How does Finlay C.J. circumvent this?

3. Is this case consistent with the principle that promissory estoppel may be used as a 'shield but not a sword'? In *Garda Representative Association v Ireland* [1989] ILRM Murphy J. noted that the *Webb* decisions demonstrated a reluctance to recognise the doctrine as a new or separate concept within the legal system.

In **Amalgamated Investment and Pty Co. Ltd *v* Texas Commerce International Bank Ltd [1982] QB 84** referred to in the *Webb* case, the estoppel was not based on a representation by one party to the other, but on an agreed assumption. This type of estoppel is classified as 'estoppel by convention'.

In this case the plaintiff requested that the defendant would advance money to ANPP (a subsidiary of the plaintiff) in the Bahamas and covenanted to pay on demand any money owed by ANPP to the defendant. To avoid certain Bahamian trading restrictions the money was directed from the defendants to a Bahamian bank which then lent the same to ANPP. As a result of this no money was advanced directly from the defendant to ANPP. Both parties however believed that the guarantee was binding. Later the plaintiff claimed that it was under no liability to the defendants under the guarantee.

Robert Goff J.:

. . .

. . . Of all doctrines, equitable estoppel is surely one of the most flexible. . . .

. . . It is no doubt helpful to establish, in broad terms, the criteria which, in certain situations, must be fulfilled before an equitable estoppel can be established; but it cannot be right to restrict equitable estoppel to certain defined categories, and indeed some of the categories proposed are not easy to defend. Thus, in *Snell's Principles of Equity*, (27th ed. 1973), ch. 7, the editors isolate two categories of equitable estoppel, promissory estoppel and proprietary estoppel. It may be possible nowadays to identify the former with some degree of precision; but the latter is much more difficult to accept as a separate category. The cases concerned appear to derive from two distinct principles; the principle stated by Lord Cranworth L.C. in *Ramsden v Dyson*, LR 1 HL 129, and the principle stated by Lord Kingsdown in the same case—the former being concerned with an estoppel precluding a person, who stands by and allows another to incur expenditure or otherwise act on the basis of a mistaken belief as to his rights, from thereafter asserting rights inconsistent with that mistaken belief (commonly called the doctrine of acquiescence); and the other being concerned with an estoppel precluding a person who has encouraged another to improve his, the encourager's, property in the expectation that he will receive an interest in it, from denying that he is entitled to that interest. It is to be observed that the first of these principles appears to be directed towards preventing a person from fraudulently taking advantage of another's error, whereas the latter appears to derive rather from encouragement or representation. As a separate category, proprietary estoppel may perhaps be regarded as an amalgam of doubtful utility; and it is not surprising to find that the use of this term has been the subject of some criticism: see, for example, Spencer Bower and Turner, *Estoppel by Representation*, (3rd ed. 1977), para. 308. Indeed there are cases, in particular cases concerned with the acquisition of easements, and with the legal effect of contracts, which are not easy to accommodate within any of the current classifications. It is not, therefore, surprising to discover a tendency in the more recent authorities to reject any rigid classification of equitable estoppel into exclusive and defined categories. The authorities on the subject have recently been reviewed by Oliver J. in his judgment in two related actions, *Taylors Fashions Ltd v Liverpool Victoria Trustees Co. Ltd* and *Old & Campbell Ltd v Liverpool Victoria Friendly Society (Note)*, post, p. 135a; and on the basis of his analysis of the cases, which I gratefully adopt, he rejected an argument founded upon rigid categorisation. The argument was that a clear distinction must be drawn between cases of proprietary estoppel and estoppel by representation (whether express or by conduct) on the other; and that in the former class of cases it was essential that the party alleged to be estopped himself knew the true position (that is, that he knew that the other party was acting under a mistake as to his rights), the fourth of the five criteria laid down by Fry J. in *Willmott v Barber*, 15 ChD 96, as necessary to establish estoppel by acquiescence. Oliver J., however, while recognising that the strict *Willmott v Barber* criteria may be necessary requirements in cases where all that has happened is that the party alleged to be estopped has stood by without protest while his rights have been infringed, concluded that the recent authorities supported a much wider jurisdiction to interfere in cases where the assertion of strict legal rights is found by the court to be unconscionable. The cases before him were concerned with a situation where both parties had proceeded on the same mistaken assumption; and he concluded that the inquiry which he had to make was simply whether, in all the circumstances of the cases before him, it was unconscionable for the defendants to seek to take advantage of the mistake which, at the material time, all parties shared.

In my judgment, in the case before me, the inquiry which I have to make is precisely the same. But before I turn to consider the facts of the case before me, there are certain general observations which I wish to make.

First, the case advanced before me by the bank is not one of simple acquiescence by the plaintiffs in the mistaken belief of the bank; it is founded upon active encouragement by the plaintiffs or representations by the plaintiffs—encouragement and representations which I have already found were in fact given and made by the plaintiffs to the bank. Now, in my judgment, where an estoppel is alleged to be founded upon encouragement or representation, it can only be unconscionable for the encourager or representor to enforce his strict legal rights if the other party's conduct has been influenced by the encouragement or representation.

Second, it is, in my judgment, no bar to a conclusion that the other party's conduct was so influenced, that his conduct did not derive its origin only from the encouragement or representation of the first party. There may be cases where the representee has proceeded initially on the basis of a belief derived from some other source independent of the representor, but his belief has subsequently been confirmed by the encouragement or representation of the representor. ...

. . .

Third, it is in my judgment not of itself a bar to an estoppel that its effect may be to enable a party to enforce a cause of action which, without the estoppel, would not exist. It is sometimes said that an estoppel cannot create a cause of action, or that an estoppel can only act as a shield, not as a sword. In a sense this is true—in the sense that estoppel is not, as a contract is, a source of legal obligation. But, as Lord Denning M.R. pointed out in *Crabb v Arun District Council* [1976] Ch. 179, 187, an estoppel may have the effect that a party can enforce a cause of action which, without the estoppel, he would not be able to do. This is not, of course, true of all estoppels. Thus a promissory estoppel derived from *Hughes v Metropolitan Rly Co.*, 1 App Cas 439, is concerned with a representation by a party that he will not enforce his strict legal rights; of its very nature such an estoppel cannot enable a party to enforce a cause of action. But in other cases an estoppel may do so, as, for example, in cases of estoppel by acquiescence. Moreover (subject to one limitation, to which I shall shortly refer) I can see no reason, in logic or in authority, why such a cause of action should not consist of a contractual right. . . . .

Fourth, however, what I have just said has to be reconciled with the general principle that a purely gratuitous promise is unenforceable at law or in equity. In law and in equity, generally speaking a promise is only enforceable as a contractual obligation if it is supported by consideration; and neither law nor equity will perfect an imperfect gift. Furthermore, even if a purely gratuitous promise is acted upon by the promisee, generally speaking such conduct will not of itself give rise to an estoppel against the promissor; such an estoppel would be inconsistent with the general principle that purely gratuitous promises will not be enforced: see *Combe v Combe* [1951] 2 KB 215. It was suggested to me that that case provided authority that no cause of action in contract could be created by an estoppel. But that, in my judgment, is too sweeping a proposition; . . . .

. . . Indeed, there are at least three groups of cases where estoppels may be enforced despite infringement of this general principle, and I do not suggest that this list is exhaustive. The basis of all these groups of cases appears to be the same—that it would, despite the general principle, be unconscionable in all the circumstances for the encourager or representor not to give effect to his encouragement or representation. The first group concerns cases where equity would regard it as fraudulent for the party against whom the estoppel is alleged not to give effect to his encouragement or representation; an example of such a case is where, on the principle stated by Lord Kingsdown in *Ramsden v Dyson*, LR 1 HL 129, a party has encouraged another in the expectation that he shall have an interest in the encourager's land, and the other party has, on the faith of that encouragement, expended money on that land. The second group consists of cases concerned with promissory estoppel, in which one party represents to another that he will not enforce his strict legal rights under a legal relationship between the parties. The representation may be no more than a gratuitous promise; but it may nevertheless be unconscionable for the representor to go back upon it, because a representee may reasonably be expected to act in reliance upon such a forbearance, without going to the extent of requiring a contractual variation. The third group concerns cases where one party has represented to the other that a transaction between them has an effect which in law it does not have. In such a case, it may, in the circumstances, be unconscionable for the representor to go back on his representation, despite the fact that the effect is to reduce his rights or to enlarge his obligations and so give effect to what is in fact a gratuitous promise; for the effect of the representation may be to cause or contribute to the representee's error or continued error as to his true legal rights, or to deprive him of an opportunity to re-negotiate the transaction to render it legally enforceable in terms of the representation. . . .

. . .

My fifth observation is this. Where, as in cases of promissory estoppel, the estoppel is founded upon a representation by a party that he will not enforce his legal rights, it is of course a prerequisite of the estoppel that there should be an existing legal relationship between the parties. But where, for example, the estoppel relates to the legal effect of a transaction between the parties, it does not necessarily follow that the underlying transaction should constitute a binding legal relationship. In such a case the representation may well, as I have already indicated, give rise to an estoppel although the effect is to enlarge the obligations of the representor; and I can see no reason in principle why this should not be so, even if the underlying transaction would, but for the estoppel, be devoid of legal effect. Certainly the doctrine of consideration cannot of itself provide any insurmountable obstacle to this conclusion; for, whether the representation consists (as in the case of a promissory estoppel) of a forbearance, or consists of a representation as to the legal effect of a transaction, it will in any event constitute an inroad upon that doctrine.

The Court of Appeal agreed with this whilst also taking the view that as a matter of construction the guarantee did cover the loan.

Denning M.R.:

. . .

The doctrine of estoppel is one of the most flexible and useful in the armoury of the law. But it has become overloaded with cases. That is why I have not gone through them all in this judgment. It has evolved during the last 150 years in a sequence of separate developments: proprietary estoppel, estoppel by representation of fact, estoppel by acquiescence, and promissory estoppel. At the same time it has been sought to be limited by a series of maxims: estoppel is only a rule of evidence, estoppel cannot give rise to a cause of action, estoppel cannot do away with the need for consideration, and so forth. All these can now be seen to merge into one general principle shorn of limitations. When the parties to a transaction proceed on the basis of an underlying assumption—either of fact or of law—whether due to misrepresentation or mistake makes no difference—on which they have conducted the dealings between them—neither of them will be allowed to go back on that assumption when it would be unfair or unjust to allow him to do so. If one of them does seek to go back on it, the courts will give the other such remedy as the equity of the case demands.

That general principle applies to this case.

Note

In *Williams v Roffey Bros* [1990] 1 All ER 512 (see p. 160) both Glidewell and Russell L.JJ. stated that the court would have welcomed the development of an agreement based on estoppel. Russell L.J. specifically referred to the *Amalgamated Investment and Pty Co. Ltd* case as proving that 'while consideration remains a fundamental requirement before a contract not under seal can be enforced, the policy of the law in its search to do justice between the parties has developed considerably since the early nineteenth century when *Stilk v Myrick* (1809) 2 Camp. 317, 170 ER 1168 was decided.'

Isabel Kenny v James Kelly (HC) 27 July 1988, unrep.

The applicant was offered a place in Arts in UCD in September 1986. On 29 or 30 September applicant's father met an administrative officer in the Admissions Office who discussed the possibility of deferral with the Senior Administrative Officer, a Miss O'Connor. The applicant's father claims that he was told that his daughter could defer her place but that she would have to write setting out her reasons for requiring the deferral. The respondent claimed that no deferral was granted. Although the applicant wrote on 10 November, Miss O'Connor wrote to the applicant's father on 30 October stating that it was too late to consider requests for deferral. The applicant was not offered a place the following year as the entry points rose. The applicant instituted judicial review proceedings claiming to be entitled to a place in Arts in 1987. One of the grounds for UCD opposing this was that the relief being sought was not a matter of public law.

Despite this Barron J. did not rule out the possibility that the doctrine of legitimate expectation might be one of a range of possible remedies available to the applicant.

Barron J.:

. . .

The applicant's case depends upon the proper construction to be placed upon what occurred when her father called to the Admissions Office on either 29 or 30 September 1986. His evidence is that he spoke to Miss O'Connor on the telephone that morning and explained to her the reasons for the application and the need for an immediate decision. He was told that the matter could not be dealt with over the telephone and that he should come to the office. This he did in the early afternoon. He again made the same points. The official with whom he spoke went into the inner office and when she returned told him that he could have the deferral but that his daughter would have to write in to confirm the reasons which had already been given. This she did.

No one has been called to give evidence of any conversation with the applicant's father at the Admissions Office on 29 or 30 September 1986. The evidence for the respondent however accepts that he was there and made his application and I accept his evidence that he was told that his daughter could have her deferral. It is clear that the Admissions Office did not regard whatever occurred as amounting to the grant of a deferral. Otherwise the place would have been re-offered. But it is not a question of mistake or misrepresentation. Miss O'Connor to whom the request must have been put in the inner office did not intend to authorise a deferral. The official who communicated her instructions clearly misconstrued them. Nevertheless, this was not known to the applicant's father who was entitled to rely upon what she told him. As between them, there was no mistake. If she did misrepresent her instructions, this does not entitle the respondent to deny her apparent authority to bind the respondent.

The applicant seeks to rely upon the doctrine of 'legitimate expectation' as approved in *Webb v Ireland*, an unreported decision of the Supreme Court delivered on 16 December 1987. In that case, the plaintiffs, having found treasure trove, very properly handed it over to the National Museum. When doing so, they had been assured that they would be treated honourably. It was held that such assurance was an integral part of the transaction whereby the find was handed over and was enforceable. The principles of promissory estoppel upon which this decision was based apply equally in the present case. The applicant had already accepted her place and paid the deposit towards her fees. If she wanted to attend as a student in that year, she had to pay the balance of her fees and to register. If she did not do so, she would have lost her rights to attend subsequently and would also have lost her deposit. The promise of a deferral was in effect a promise not to require the applicant to register and pay the balance of her fees in 1986 but a promise to permit her to do so instead in 1987.

Such a promise to delay the enforcement of legal rights is of the essence of the doctrine of promissory estoppel as it has developed. In *Birmingham and District Land Co. v London and North Western Rly* (1888) 40 ChD 268, Bowen L.J. said at p. 286:

> It seems to me to amount to this, that if persons who have contractual rights against others induce by their conduct those against whom they have such rights to believe that such rights will either not be enforced or will be kept in suspense or abeyance for some particular time, those persons will not be allowed by a court of equity to enforce the rights until such time has elapsed, without at all events placing the parties in the same position as they were before.

In *Central London Pty Trust Co. v High Trees House Ltd* 1956, 1 All ER 256 n., the essence of promissory estoppel was said to be a promise intended to be binding, intended to be acted upon and in fact acted upon. In my view, the facts of the present case come within these principles. Each of the elements necessary to establish the estoppel is present.

Since the applicant could, if no promise had been made to her, have cancelled her acceptance and obtained a return of her deposit, then it may be argued that there was consideration for the grant of the deferral giving it contractual status. Whichever legal approach is adopted, the applicant is entitled to a declaration that she was entitled to a place in the Arts School in University College Dublin in 1987.

Duggan v An Taoiseach, Members of the Government and Fahy [1989] ILRM 710

Prior to 1 May 1985, the applicants were Land Commission Inspectors. Because of a new farm tax staff were required for a limited time span to evaluate farm holdings. The applicants applied for positions in the Office of the Farm Tax Commissioner and were promoted. The form of acceptance included a statement to the effect that the appointment would be temporary and that in the event of termination the person promoted would revert to the point on the scale of the substantive grade which that person would have reached if he had continued on their pre-promotion scale. In March 1987 it was announced that the government would not collect farm tax in 1987 and the applicants' appointments were terminated. The applicants claimed that the termination of their appointments had caused them financial difficulties; that they had altered their situations to their detriment as a result of the appointments; that they had accepted appointment on the basis that the office of Farm Tax Commissioner had been established for at least five years and that the classification work would take at least eight years to complete; that promotion was never reversed in the civil service other than on grounds of serious misconduct.

Hamilton P.:
...

Dealing with the question of legitimate expectation in the course of his opinion in the case of *Council of Civil Service Unions v Minister for the Civil Service* [1985] AC 374 Lord Fraser stated, at 400–401 of the report:

Mr Blom-Cooper submitted that the minister had a duty to consult the CCSU, on behalf of employees at GCHQ, before giving the instruction on 22 December 1983 from making an important change in their conditions of service. His main reason for so submitting was that the employees had a legitimate, or reasonable, expectation that there would be such prior consultation before any important change was made in their conditions.

It is clear that the employees did not have a legal right to prior consultation . . .

But even where a person claiming some benefit or privilege has no legal right to it, as a matter of private law, he may have a legitimate expectation of receiving the benefit or privilege, and, if so, the courts will protect his expectation by judicial review as a matter of public law . . .

Legitimate, or reasonable, expectation may arise either from an express promise given on behalf of a public authority or from the existence of a regular practice which the claimant can reasonably expect to continue . . .

Legitimate expectations such as are now under consideration will always relate to a benefit or privilege to which the claimant has no right in private law, and it may even be one which conflicts with his private rights.

[Having referred to the decision of the Chief Justice in *Webb v Ireland and Attorney General* [1988] ILRM 565 Hamilton P. continued:]

The doctrine of legitimate or reasonable expectation, being in accord with equitable principles, is recognised by the courts and if a person establishes that he had a legitimate expectation of receiving a benefit or privilege, the courts will protect his expectation by judicial review as a matter of public law.

I have in the course of this judgment set forth in detail the circumstances which led to the appointments in an acting capacity of the applicants herein to positions in the Farm Tax Office and all the relevant agreements and correspondence with regard thereto. Having carefully considered them, I can find no basis for an expectation, reasonable or otherwise, on the part of the applicants that they would be continued in the posts or positions to which they had been appointed in an acting capacity in an established or permanent capacity. The Farm Tax Office was being set up for a limited period and for a specific purpose and the work of the office was known to be of limited duration. It was specifically provided in the finalised proposals with regard to staffing that appointments would be on an acting basis and when the applicants were informed of their appointments, they were informed that they were being appointed in an acting capacity and accepted the appointments on such basis. Irrespective of what was the position prevailing in the civil service generally with regard to persons appointed to posts in an acting capacity the circumstances of the applicants' promotions were unusual and the circumstances of such appointments were known to them. Such circumstances could not, in my opinion, give rise to a reasonable expectation by them that on the termination of the work of Farm Tax Office, they would continue in the grades to which they had been appointed.

I am, however, satisfied that the applicants herein and each of them had a reasonable and legitimate expectation that they and each of them would be continued in the post to which they had been appointed in an acting capacity until the work of the Farm Tax Office as set forth in the Farm Tax Act 1985 had been completed or until the work of the Farm Tax Office upon which they were engaged was terminated in accordance with law. I am further satisfied that this legitimate expectation was frustrated by the decision of the respondents (other than the last-named respondent) and the direction of the third-named respondent given to the last-named respondent to discontinue the classification of land which was being carried out in accordance with the provisions of s.4 of the Farm Tax Act 1985. As this decision and direction adversely affected the interest of the applicants namely, their continuance in the post to which they were appointed in an acting capacity until the classification of land had been completed or the statutory requirement that agricultural land holdings be classified is repealed by the Oireachtas, I am satisfied that the applicants herein have the *locus standi* to challenge this decision by the respondents (other than the last-named respondent) as having been made contrary to law.

Note

1. However, see *Cosgrave v The Legal Aid Board* (HC) 17 October 1990, unrep., where reliance on the doctrine did not prove successful.

In *Donegal County Council v Porter, McLaughlin, McGonigal and Bredin* (HC) 23 March 1993, unrep., a number of part-time firemen who were dismissed upon reaching the age of fifty five were suing for unfair dismissal. Mr Justice Flood accepted that at the time the appellants entered the service, senior council officials considered sixty to be the age of retirement. He was thus of the view that the appellants had a legitimate expectation that they would continue to be employed until they reached the age of sixty if they were capable of performing their duties and did in fact do so.

2. For a more detailed discussion on this area see H. Delaney, 'The Doctrine of Legitimate Expectation in Irish Law' [1990] 12 DULJ 1.

Chapter Four

Intention to Create Legal Relations

INTRODUCTION

Despite the fact that consideration is supposed to filter out unenforceable promises from those that are truly contractual, there are residual lines of judicial decision which deny apparent exchanges the status of a contract. At one end of the spectrum are transactions which the judiciary do not traditionally regard as contracts because the parties are thought not to wish their promises to be 'legal' in nature, most often husband and wife agreements reached during the currency of a viable and subsisting marriage. This hostility to judicial enforcement also surfaces within the context of contracts which are contrary to public policy, but the increasing use of pre- or post-nuptial contracts will force a reconsideration of both these lines of case-law. The other end of the spectrum is presented by commercial or market-based transactions where, save in the case of ambiguity or compelling proof to the contrary, the external manifestations of the bargain will lead to enforcement *qua* contract.

'In the case of agreements regulating business arrangements it follows, almost as a matter of course, that the parties intend legal consequences to follow. In the case of arrangements requiring social arrangements it equally follows, also as a matter of course, that the parties do not intend legal consequences to follow.' Per Banks L.J. in *Rose & Frank Co. v Crompton* [1923] 2 KB 261 and [1925] AC 445

SECTION ONE—DOMESTIC AND SOCIAL AGREEMENTS

Mere social or domestic arrangements do not usually give rise to legal relations. As Atkin L.J. noted in *Balfour v Balfour* [1919] 2 KB 571 where two parties agree to take a walk together or where arrangements are made between a husband and wife 'nobody would suggest in ordinary circumstances that those agreements result in what we know as a contract'. This presumption may however be rebutted.

Jones v Padavatton [1969] 1 WLR 328

A mother suggested that if her daughter gave up her job in the United States and returned to England to study for the bar, the mother would provide her with a maintenance of $200 a month. The daughter returned in November 1962 and commenced her studies and received £42 a month (the equivalent of West Indian $200 a month). In 1964 the mother agreed to provide a house in which her daughter could reside, and let out rooms to tenants, their rents providing maintenance in place of the £42 per month. In 1967 the mother claimed possession of the house. This was refused by the court at first instance and the mother appealed.

Dankwerts L.J.:

. . .

Before us a great deal of time was spent on discussions as to what were the terms of the arrangements between the parties, . . . two questions emerged for argument: (1) Were the arrangements (such as they were) intended to produce legally binding agreements, or were they simply family arrangements depending for their fulfilment on good faith and trust, and not legally enforceable by legal proceedings? (2) Were the arrangements made so obscure and uncertain that, though intended to be legally binding, a court could not enforce them?

. . .

Of course, there is no difficulty, if they so intend, in members of families entering into legally binding contracts in regard to family affairs. A competent equity draftsman would, if properly instructed, have no difficulty in drafting such a contract. But there is possibly in family affairs a presumption against such an intention (which, of course, can be rebutted). I would refer to Atkin L.J.'s magnificent exposition of the situation in regard to such arrangements in *Balfour v Balfour* [1919] 2 KB 571, 578–580.

There is no doubt that this case is a most difficult one, but I have reached a conclusion that the present case is one of those family arrangements which depend on the good faith of the promises which are made and are not intended to be rigid, binding agreements. *Balfour v Balfour* was a case of husband and wife, but there is no doubt that the same principles apply to dealings between other relations, such as father and son and daughter and mother. This, indeed, seems to me a compelling case. Mrs Jones and her daughter seem to have been on very good terms before 1967. The mother was arranging for a career for her daughter which she hoped would lead to success. This involved a visit to England in conditions which could not be wholly foreseen. What was required was an arrangement which was to be financed by the mother, and was such as would be adaptable to circumstances, as it in fact was. The operation about the house was, in my view, not a completely fresh arrangement, but an adaptation of the mother's financial assistance to her daughter due to the situation which was found to exist in England. It was not a stiff contractual operation any more than the original arrangement.

In the result, of course, on this view, the daughter cannot resist her mother's rights as the owner of the house to the possession of which the mother is entitled.

Salmon L.J.:

I agree with the conclusion at which my Lord has arrived, but I have reached it by a different route. The first point to be decided is whether or not there was ever a legally binding agreement between the mother and daughter in relation to the daughter's reading for the bar in England. The daughter alleges that there was such an agreement, and the mother denies it. She says that there was nothing but a loose family arrangement which had no legal effect. The onus is clearly on the daughter. There is no dispute that the parties entered into some sort of arrangement. It really depends upon (a) whether the parties intended it to be legally binding, and (b) if so, whether it was sufficiently certain to be enforceable.

Did the parties intend the arrangement to be legally binding? This question has to be solved by applying what is sometimes (although perhaps unfortunately) called an objective test. The court has to consider what the parties said and wrote in the light of all the surrounding circumstances, and then decide whether the true inference is that the ordinary men and women, speaking or writing thus in such circumstances, would have intended to create a legally binding agreement.

. . . as a rule when arrangements are made between close relations, for example, between husband and wife, parent and child or uncle and nephew in relation to an allowance, there is a presumption against an intention of creating any legal relationship. This is not a presumption of law, but of fact. It derives from experience of life and human nature which shows that in such circumstances men and women usually do not intend to create legal rights and obligations, but intend to rely solely on family ties of mutual trust and affection. This has all been explained by Atkin L.J. in his celebrated judgment in *Balfour v Balfour*. There may, however, be circumstances in which this presumption, like all other presumptions of fact, can be rebutted.
. . .

On the facts as found by the County Court judge this was entirely different from the ordinary case of a mother promising her daughter an allowance whilst the daughter read for the bar, or a father promising his son an allowance at university if the son passed the necessary examinations to gain admission. The daughter here was thirty-four years of age in 1962. She had left Trinidad and settled in Washington as long ago as 1949. In Washington she had a comfortable flat and was employed as an assistant accountant in the Indian Embassy at a salary of $500 a month (over £2,000 a year). This employment carried a pension. She had a son of seven years of age who was an American citizen, and had, of course, already begun his education. There were obviously solid reasons for her staying where she was.

In the very special circumstances of this case, I consider that the true inference must be that neither the mother nor the daughter could have intended that the daughter should have no legal right to receive, and the mother no legal obligation to pay, the allowance of $200 a month.
. . .

Then again it is said that the duration of the agreement was not specified. No doubt, but I see no difficulty in implying the usual term that it was to last for a reasonable time. The parties cannot have contemplated that the daughter should go on studying for the bar and draw the allowance until she was seventy, nor on the other hand that the mother could have discontinued the allowance if the daughter did not pass her examinations within, say, eighteen months. The promise was to pay the allowance until the daughter's studies were completed, and to my mind there was a clear implication that they were to be completed within a reasonable time. Studies are completed either by the student being called to the bar or giving up the unequal struggle against the examiners.
. . .

I cannot think that a reasonable time could possibly exceed five years from November 1962, the date when she began her studies.

It follows, therefore, that on no view can she now in November 1968 be entitled to anything further under the contract . . .

Fenton Atkinson L.J.:

...

The first question in this most unhappy case is whether the arrangement made between mother and daughter in August 1962 was intended to create a legally enforceable contract between them, or was merely one of those family or domestic arrangements where the parties at the time had no thought or intention of invoking the assistance of the courts should the arrangement not be honoured.

Was the mother legally binding herself to support the daughter at the rate of £500 a year for a wholly uncertain length of time whatever changes might come about in their respective circumstances? Was the daughter assuming a contractual obligation to pursue her legal studies to successful completion whatever the difficulties she experienced, and whatever attractive alternatives might appear, such as possible marriage or well paid employment?

If the test were the giving of consideration by the daughter, the answer would be simple. She gave up well paid work and good living accommodation, and removed herself and her son to England, where she began her studies in November 1962. But the giving of consideration by the daughter cannot decide the question whether the parties intended to make a binding contract. Aktin L.J. in *Balfour v Balfour* at p. 578 of the report put it in this way:

> To my mind those agreements, or many of them, do not result in contracts at all, and they do not result in contracts even though there may be what as between other parties would constitute consideration for the agreement. The consideration, as we know, may consist either in some right, interest, profit or benefit accruing to one party, or some forbearance, detriment, loss or responsibility given, suffered or undertaken by the other. That is a well known definition, and it constantly happens, I think, that such arrangements made between husband and wife are arrangements in which there are mutual promises, or in which there is consideration in form within the definition that I have mentioned. Nevertheless they are not contracts, and they are not contracts because the parties did not intend that they should be attended by legal consequences.

On the other hand, I do not think that the lack of formality and precision in expressing the arrangement is necessarily an indication that no contract was intended having regard to what the court knows of the parties and their relationship. The problem is, in my view, a difficult one, because though one would tend to regard a promise by a parent to pay an allowance to a child during a course of study as no more than a family arrangement, on the facts of this case this particular daughter undoubtedly gave up a great deal on the strength of the mother's promise.

In my judgment it is the subsequent history which gives the best guide to the parties' intention at the material time. There are three matters which seem to me important: (1) The daughter thought that her mother was promising her US $200, or £70 a month, which she regarded as the minimum necessary for her support. The mother promised $200, but she had in mind British West Indian $200, £42 a month, and that was what she in fact paid from November 1962 to December 1964. Those payments were accepted by the daughter without any sort of suggestion at any stage that the mother had legally contracted for the larger sum. (2) When the arrangements for the purchase of No. 181, Highbury Quadrant were being discussed, and the new arrangement was made for maintenance to come out of the rents, many material matters were left open: how much accommodation was the daughter to occupy; how much money was she to have out of the rents; if the rents fell below expectation, was the mother to make up the difference below £42, or £42 less the sum saved by the daughter in rent; for how long was the arrangement to continue, and so on. The whole arrangement was, in my view, far too vague and uncertain to be itself enforceable as a contract; but at no stage did the daughter bring into the discussions her alleged legal right to £42 per month until her studies were completed, and how that right was to be affected by the new arrangement. (3) It is perhaps not without relevance to look at the daughter's evidence in cross-examination. She was asked about the occasion when her mother visited the house, and she, knowing perfectly well that her mother was there, refused for some hours to open the door. She said: 'I didn't open the door because a normal mother doesn't sue her daughter in court. Anybody with normal feelings would feel upset by what was happening.' Those answers and the daughter's conduct on that occasion provide a strong indication that she had never for a moment contemplated the possibility of her mother or herself going to court to enforce legal obligations, and that she felt it quite intolerable that a purely family arrangement should become the subject of proceedings in a court of law.

At the time when the first arrangement was made, mother and daughter were, and always had been, to use the daughter's own words, 'very close'. I am satisfied that neither party at that time intended to enter into a legally binding contract, either then or later when the house was bought. The daughter was prepared to trust her mother to honour her promise of support, just as the mother no doubt trusted her daughter to study for the bar with diligence, and to get through her examinations as early as she could.

It follows that in my view the mother's claim for possession succeeds, and her appeal should be allowed.

Rogers v Smith (SC) 16 July 1970, unrep.

The plaintiff's father carried on a money-lending business. The business was handed over to the plaintiff upon an express agreement that the plaintiff should retain £4 a week himself from the business profits and that he should also pay his mother's housekeeping expenses and the rent, rates and other sundry expenses from the business profits. Although the plaintiff paid his mother's bills he never retained the weekly sum stipulated. After the plaintiff's father died a hospital bill was furnished for £300. The plaintiff's mother suggested that the plaintiff should pay this bill himself and noted 'when I am dead and gone you will be able to claim anything you may have spent on me.' When his mother died the plaintiff claimed money owed to him against her estate.

O'Dalaigh C.J.:

. . .

Counsel for Mrs Smith has, moreover, urged on the court that in family relations, and particularly in regard to agreements entered into between son and mother, the court will readily imply that such arrangements were not intended to give rise to legal relations. Scrutton L.J. in *Rose and Frank Co. v Crompton & Bros Ltd*[1] took this point in the following language:

Now it is quite possible for parties to come to an agreement by accepting a proposal with the result that the agreement concluded does not give rise to legal relations. The reason of this is that the parties do not intend that their agreement shall give rise to legal relations. This intention may be implied from the subject matter of the agreement, but it may also be expressed by the parties. In social and family relations such an intention is readily implied, while in business matters the opposite result would ordinarily follow. But I can see no reason why, even in business matters, the parties should not intend to rely on each other's good faith and honour, and to exclude all idea of settling disputes by any outside intervention, with the accompanying necessity of expressing themselves so precisely that outsiders may have no difficulty in understanding what they mean. If they clearly express such an intention I can see no reason in public policy why effect should not be given to their intention.

Scrutton L.J. in the course of his judgment, on the same page, called attention to *Balfour v Balfour*[2] where the court declined to recognise relations of contract as flowing from an agreement between a husband and wife that he should send her £30 a month for her maintenance. There Atkin L.J. speaking of agreements and arrangements between husband and wife involving mutual promises and consideration in form, said 'They are not contracts, because the parties did not intend that they should be attended by legal consequences.'

The plaintiff's evidence, in my opinion, is much too uncertain and obscure to be acted upon. There is also the general background that the payments after John Rogers' death in 1960 were a continuation of payments which commenced six years earlier in 1954, and the post-1960 payments were treated in exactly the same way as the earlier payments. Even if the arrangement relied upon were free from the uncertainty and obscurity to which I have called attention, the court, before inferring an intention that the arrangement should have legal consequences, should have clear and unambiguous evidence. In my opinion there is in this case an absence of such evidence.

Budd J.:
...

[Counsel] stressed the necessity in law that an agreement alleged to constitute a contract in law should not leave uncertainty as to its effect or doubt as to its intention. If authority for his proposition is required it seems to me to emerge clearly from the words used by Lord O'Hagan in his judgment [sic] in *Maddison v Alderson*[3] stating his reasons for concluding that an agreement relied on in that case could not have been enforced. At p. 484 he states: 'I do not see that a bargain so obscure in its terms, so uncertain in its effect, and so doubtful in its intention, could have been properly enforced.' Counsel further submitted that there was likewise a necessity to show that a bargain had been made between mother and son as distinct from some supposition as to what would probably occur or might happen. Lord Blackburn, at p. 487 of the report of the case above referred to, clearly indicated the necessity when he stated that the evidence in the case was such from which a contract would not have been found by the jury if it had been explained to them that 'to make a contract there must be a bargain between both parties.'

It was further submitted that the matter of the intention of the parties to the alleged contract requires particular attention in this case. These parties were mother and son, and if an agreement can be spelt out of the conversations between them, it was contended that the surrounding circumstances and the words used lead to the conclusion that the parties did not intend that any agreement, which could be said to have been come to, was to have legal consequences and to be enforceable but was

rather of a purely family nature not intended to have such consequences. The learned Chief Justice in the course of his judgment has referred to passages from the judgments of Scrutton L.J. in *Rose and Frank Co. v J.R. Crompton & Bros Ltd* and Atkin L.J. in *Balfour v Balfour* which are highly relevant on this point. It clearly emerges from these passages that in social and family matters agreements may be come to which do not give rise to legal relations because such a consequence is not the intention of the parties, and in family matters, an intention *to remain free of legal obligation* will be readily implied whereas in business matters the opposite result would ordinarily follow.
. . .

Having regard to the background to the conversations between the plaintiff and his mother and the indefiniteness of the evidence both as to the making of any binding agreement and as to its terms the plaintiff has, in my view, failed to establish his case. There is also, in my view, no sufficient evidence of the intention of the parties to enter into a contract having legal consequences.

FitzGerald J.:
. . .

On the issue as to whether a contract was established or not, he contended that a family arrangement does not necessarily amount to a contract. In support of this contention he relied upon the case of *Maddison v Alderson*. This case concerned a claim by a former servant against the personal representative of her deceased master to establish a claim to a farm of land for her life, as she alleged pursuant to a contract between her and the deceased whereby he agreed to leave her the farm in consideration of her remaining on as his servant without wages. The court, on the particular facts, held that as she was not bound to remain in her master's service there was no contract but merely a promise upon which she elected to depend and that the terms of the alleged agreement were not proved with certainty and that there was no bargain. He further relied upon *Rose & Frank Co. v Crompton & Bros Ltd.*[4] This was an action for breach of a commercial contract relating to the sale of goods and the facts do not require further recital here. [Counsel], however, placed reliance on passage from the judgments in the Court of Appeal and in particular from the judgment of Lord Justice Banks, reported at p. 282, which is as follows: 'In the case of agreements regulating business arrangements it follows, almost as a matter of course, that the parties intend legal consequences to follow. In the case of arrangements requiring social engagements it equally follows, also as a matter of course, that the parties do not intend legal consequences to follow.' While I accept this as a general proposition, the question of whether an enforceable legal contract has been entered into or not must depend upon the evidence in the particular case. In the case of family arrangements it would be quite unreasonable to expect that the arrangement would be come to with all the particularity which one would expect to find in relation to a commercial contract, either formal or informal. It appears to me that the proper approach is to see whether obligations were undertaken with the mutual intention that the obligations should be carried out by one party and whether there was a consideration from the other party in return and whether, finally, those matters can be established with certainty. In the present case I am satisfied that the evidence of [the son], having been accepted by the trial judge, the true position was that [the son] had undertaken the obligation of paying the weekly amount to his mother during her lifetime and also of paying the outgoings in respect of the house which she occupied and that the consideration for his undertaking these obligations was that he should be repaid out of his mother's estate after her death. This appears to me to be a contract between them in which the terms are certain and which the parties must be taken to have intended that the agreement should be carried out which necessarily involves legal consequences.

1. [1923] 2 KB 261 at 288.							3. 8 App Cas 467.
2. [1919] 1 KB 571.							4. [1923] 2 KB 261 and [1925] AC 445.

Courtney v Courtney (1923) 57 ILTR 42

Due to the respondent's acts of cruelty the petitioner was forced to leave their home. The petitioner later returned her wedding ring and a watch and the respondent agreed to pay her £150 'in discharge of all claims of every nature and kind'. The petitioner later filed a petition for divorce *a mensa et thora* on the ground of cruelty. The respondent contended that because of the agreement the petitioner was estopped from bringing proceedings.

At first instance the jury stated that the agreement was not a good one and the trial judge opined that the agreement did not operate as a bar to the petition. The respondent appealed to the High Court.

Dodd J. (delivering the judgment of the court):

Two questions were argued before us—(1) Whether the agreement was good in law; (2) whether the evidence was sufficient to sustain the finding. Upon the first question a great many authorities were cited, but the matter is concluded so far as this court is concerned by the judgment of the Court of Appeal in Ireland in the case of *MacMahon v MacMahon; Purser v Purser* [1913] 1 IR 428 . . . The Chief Baron gives an interesting historical survey of the law, from *Wilson v Wilson* 1 H. of L. Cas 538 down, an authoritative exposition of the ecclesiastical law, and a discriminating analysis of the effect of the common law and of the procedure under the Judicature Acts upon the principle—an illuminating judgment from one who, as we know, was as devout as he was erudite. He sums up the result in the question: 'How then can it be the policy of the law that spouses cannot be free to contract that they will not co-habit?' Holmes and Cherry, L.JJ., concurred. It will, however, be of assistance to deal shortly with some of the cases in seeking to apply the principle to the facts of this case. The right is founded on contract. The judgment of the Master of the Rolls (Sir Geo. Jessel) in *Besant v Wood*, 12 ChD 605, has a paragraph that is illuminating. He says at p. 622:

> If a married woman can compromise a suit after she commences it, why not when she threatens it, or before she begins it? If, after instituting a suit for divorce, or having a suit for divorce instituted against her, and she defending it, she can compromise by agreeing to live separate on terms as regards maintenance of herself, custody of her children, and so forth, why not before? Why not after the quarrel and before the litigation commenced? The very same reasons appear to me to apply to the one case as to the other. If the wife has the right to sue for restitution of conjugal rights, for separation, or for divorce, if she has the right after beginning a suit to compromise the suit, she ought to have the right to do so before; and if she has the right afterwards in the sense of being bound by her agreement, why should she not have the same right before as regards these matters as to which she has a clear right to institute the suit, these matters being matters of personal status, and the question that of living together or not? It seems to me to follow as a necessary

corollary to the right to sue by herself, that she must have the right to contract not to sue, and I should think that there would be no difficulty at all about it. At the same time I confess there are to be found numerous dicta the other way, though there are some my way, as to what the law is. I think that the law is therefore that a woman can contract to live separate and apart from her husband. That contract, like all other contracts, if not against public policy, is one which may be upheld and enforced.

The judgment in *Clark v Clark*, 10 PD 188, is also of value. Lord Justice Bowen, alluding to the judgment of Sir Geo. Jessel in *Besant v Wood*, says: 'I think his reasoning cannot be shaken, that where a wife has power to sue her husband, she must have power to compromise any such proceeding, or to bind herself to abstain from taking it.' And again: 'It is not necessary that the contract should be in any particular form. All that is required is that there shall be evidence of a contract into which the wife entered with her eyes open, and for valuable consideration.' Baggallay L.J. gave judgment to a like effect, and Fry L.J. concurred without giving an independent judgment; but an interlocutory question by him is itself almost a judgment. He asks, at p. 191: 'The husband and wife being capable of contracting, is not the recital that they have agreed to live separate an agreement to do so?' It is to be borne in mind that there must be a contract. A contract consists of a promise and a consideration. The agreement to refrain from taking proceedings was held to be a good consideration in *Wilson v Wilson*. Mutual promises would not seem to be enough (see the judgment of Atkin L.J. in *Balfour v Balfour*, [1919] 2 KB 571). Having given a definition of what is consideration in general law, he says, at p. 578: 'It constantly happens that such arrangements made between husband and wife are arrangements in which there are mutual promises, or in which there is consideration given in form within the definition I have mentioned, nevertheless they are not contracts, and they are not contracts because the parties did not intend that they should be attended by legal consequences.' Warrington L.J. and Duke L.J. say the same, but the words of Atkin L.J. are of crystal clearness. . . . The law being as I think clear, and the cases cited giving a guide in applying it, the sole question of fact is on the plea which the learned judge at the trial allowed to be pleaded, and on which he framed question 5: 'Did the wife and the husband in May 1921, mutually agree to live separate and not to molest each other in consideration of the husband paying to his wife £150, she giving him her ring and watch?' To which the jury's answer is 'Yes.' They added a rider: 'We do not believe the agreement of May 1921, a good one,' and there being no evidence of consideration. It is not clear whether the words 'and there being no evidence of consideration' were part of the rider, or were added by the judge. That is not material, it is for the Court to say now whether there was evidence of consideration moving from the wife. It is on this that the weighty words of the judges in the cases cited become applicable. In *Wilson v Wilson*, Shadwell V.C., whose judgment was upheld in the Lords, decided that the promises of the wife not to bring proceedings in the Ecclesiastical Court, which the husband was most anxious to avoid, was a sufficient consideration. In *Besant v Wood* we have Sir Geo. Jessel's judgment that a compromise of a matrimonial quarrel before proceedings were taken was a good consideration for a contract. We also have the concluding words of the Chief Baron's judgment in *MacMahon v MacMahon*: 'Can it be the policy of the law that the spouses cannot be free to contract that they will not co-habit?' And Lord Justice Bowen's words: 'All that is required is that there shall be evidence of a contract into which the wife entered with her eyes open, and under which she has received benefits.' When this contract was entered into the wife was in a position in which she could have sued her husband. What relief could she get in a suit? A separation from bed and board, and an allowance from the court from the husband's means for alimony. The alimony would have been in the usual practice granted as an annual payment. That it was arranged for between the parties to be granted at once as a lump sum in this case throws light upon the intention of the parties. It was to be given once for all—no further dealings. The consideration from the wife was that if the husband agreed to the terms she would abstain from bringing any proceedings for separation or for alimony. She got the money—for what? It was not damages for a prior assault: it was in settlement of all claims. The handing back of the ring was a most significant matter. The husband stipulated for that. The wife at first refused. The watch, too, seems to have had some sentimental significance, if sentiment could be attributed to such a pair. But the husband's view, apparently, was to terminate, once and for all, all matrimonial relations. The wife professed she had lost the watch. Finally it was settled that pending the return of the watch £10 should be deducted from the £150 and retained by Father Courtney. The husband got the ring; the wife bought a new ring, and the priest blessed it. Was this merely an agreement between spouses, such as Atkin L.J. referred to? Or was it a bargain? Was it intended to be a bargain? Could she, next day, have brought a matrimonial suit? The priest thought the lady ought to have got more. The jury also thought so. But did she conclude the contract with her eyes open—can she keep the £150 and still sue? It is said that there is no covenant not to sue, no express contract not to sue. But if parties who are free to contract do in fact contract for the settlement of an action, or for the settlement of proceedings which might but for the settlement terminate in legal proceedings, can it be contended that the settlement having been entered into and completed by one party complying with it, the other party can keep the money and go on with an action? The contract need not be under seal, nor take the form of a covenant. Nor need it be necessarily in writing, though it is hardly conceivable that there should not be some documentary evidence forthcoming in such an issue. Nor need the bargain that no proceedings are to be taken but put in express words—though here again caution is required to ascertain the real nature of the transaction. A matrimonial tribunal must bring to the consideration of such a case great circumspection, and must not lightly sanction the severance of the marriage tie. But when all this is said, and the tribunal is satisfied that the transaction was a binding contract, the parties to it who so agree to settle a matrimonial controversy must be taken to contract that they will not go behind the settlement, and cannot be listened to saying they did not make an express bargain that they would not sue. This decision must be kept within its legitimate bounds, and is not to be taken to extend to contracts that are against public policy.

SECTION TWO—COMMERCIAL AGREEMENTS

In commercial agreements it will be presumed that the parties intended to create legally binding contracts. This presumption may however be rebutted, for example an express statement by the parties of their intention not to form a contract.

In *The Commodity Broking Co. Ltd v Fergus Meehan* [1985] IR 12 (p. 148) the presumption applied by Barron J. was that the defendant intended a promise in respect of a commercial transaction to have legal effect.

In *The Cunard Steam Ship Co. Ltd v The Revenue Commissioners* [1931] IR 297 the presumption was rebutted when a booking arrangement was held not to be a contract because it was intended that a subsequent contract be made. A similar finding was reached in *Cadbury Ireland Ltd v Kerry Co-operative Creameries Ltd* |1982| ILRM 77 (see p. 690 below).

A. LETTERS OF COMFORT

Kleinwort Benson Ltd *v* Malaysia Mining Corp. Bhd [1989] 1 All ER 785

The plaintiff bank entered into negotiations with the defendants to make a loan facility available to MMC Metals, a subsidiary of the defendants. The defendants issued a 'comfort letter' para. 3 of which stated *inter alia*: 'It is our policy to ensure that the business of MMC Metals Ltd is at all times in a position to meet its liabilities to you under the above arrangements.'

When MMC Metals went into liquidation, the plaintiffs called on the defendants to ensure payment. When they refused, the plaintiffs sued.

At first instance Hirst J. awarded the plaintiffs damages arising from breach of a warranty and/or a representation.

Gibson L.J.:

. . .

The central question in this case, in my judgment, is that considered in *Esso Petroleum Co. Ltd v Mardon* |1976| 2 All ER 5, |1976| QB 801, on which counsel for the plaintiffs relied in this court but which was not cited to Hirst J. That question is whether the words of para. 3, considered in their context, are to be treated as a warranty of contractual promise. Para. 3 contains no express words of promise. Para. 3 is in its terms a statement of present fact and not a promise as to future conduct. I agree with the submission of counsel for the defendants that, in this regard, the words of para. 3 are in sharp contrast with the words of para. 2 of the letter: 'We confirm that we will not' etc. The force of this point is not limited, as Hirst J. stated it, to the absence from para. 3 of the words 'We confirm'. The real contrast is between the words of promise, namely 'We will not' in para. 2, and the words of statement of fact, 'It is our policy' in para. 3. Hirst J. held that, by the words of para. 3, the defendants gave an undertaking that now and at all times in the future, so long as Metals should be under any liability to the plaintiffs under the facility arrangements, it is *and will be* the defendants' policy to ensure that Metals is in a position to meet their liabilities. To derive that meaning from the words it is necessary to add the words emphasised, namely 'and will be', which do not appear in para. 3. In short, the words of promise as to the future conduct of the defendants were held by Hirst J. to be part of the necessary meaning of the words used in para. 3. The question is whether that view of the words can be upheld.

The absence of express words of warranty as to present facts or the absence of express words of promise as to future conduct does not conclusively exclude a statement from the status of warranty or promise. According to the well known dictum of Holt C.J., ' . . . an affirmation can only be a warranty provided it appears on evidence to have been so intended': see Ormrod L.J. in *Esso Petroleum Co. Ltd v Mardon*, citing Viscount Haldane L.C. in *Heilbut Symons & Co. v Buckleton* |1913| AC 30 at 38, |1911–13| All ER Rep 83 at 86.

. . .

The evidence does not show that the words used in para. 3 were intended to be a promise as to the future conduct of the defendants but, in my judgment, it shows the contrary.

The concept of a comfort letter was, as counsel for the defendants acknowledged, not shown to have acquired any particular meaning at the time of the negotiations in this case with reference to the limits of any legal liability to be assumed under its terms by a parent company. A letter, which the parties might have referred to at some stage as a letter of comfort, might, after negotiation, have emerged containing in para. 3 in express terms the words used by Hirst J. to state the meaning which he gave to para. 3. The court would not, merely because the parties had referred to the document as a comfort letter, refuse to give effect to the meaning of the words used. But in this case it is clear, in my judgment, that the concept of a comfort letter, to which the parties had resort when the defendants refused to assume joint and several liability or to give a guarantee, was known by both sides at least to extend to or to include a document under which the defendants would give comfort to the plaintiffs by assuming, not a legal liability to ensure repayment of the liabilities of its subsidiary, but a moral responsibility only. Thus, when the defendants by Mr John Green in June 1984 told the plaintiffs that Mr Green would recommend that credit lines for Metals be covered by a letter of comfort rather than by guarantee, the response of Mr Irwin, before any draft of a comfort letter had been prepared, was '. . . that a letter of comfort would not be a problem, but that [he] would probably have to charge a higher rate'. The comfort letter was drafted in terms which in para. 3 do not express any contractual promise and which are consistent with being no more than a representation of fact. If they are treated as no more than a representation of fact, they are in that meaning consistent with the comfort letter containing no more than the assumption of moral responsibility by the defendants in respect of the debts of Metals. There is nothing in the evidence to show that, as a matter of commercial probability or common sense, the parties must have intended para. 3 to be a contractual promise, which is not expressly stated, rather than a mere representation of fact which is so stated.

Next, the first draft of the comfort letter was produced by the plaintiffs. Para. 1 contained confirmation that the defendants knew of and approved of the granting of the facilities in question by the plaintiffs to Metals, and para. 2 contained the express confirmation that the defendants would not reduce their current financial interest in Metals until (in effect) facilities had been paid or the plaintiffs consented. Both are relevant to the present and future moral responsibility of the defendants. If the words of para. 3 are to be treated as intended to express a contractual promise by the defendants as to their future policy, which Hirst J. held the words to contain, then the recitation of the plaintiff's approval and the promise not to reduce their current financial interest in Metals, would be of no significance. If the defendants have promised that at all times in the future it will be the defendants' policy to ensure that Metals is in a position to meet its liabilities to the plaintiffs under the facility, it would not matter whether they had approved or disapproved, or whether they had disposed of their shares in Metals. Contracts may, of course, contain statements or promises which are caused to be of no separate commercial importance by the width of a later promise in the same document. Where, however, the court is examining a statement which is by its express words no more than a representation of fact, in order to consider whether it is shown to have been intended to be of the nature of a contractual promise or warranty, it seems to me to be a fact suggesting at least the absence of such intention if, as in this case, to read the statement as a contractual promise is to reduce to no significance two paragraphs included in the plaintiffs' draft, both of which have significance if the statement is read as a representation of fact only.

That point can be made more plainly thus: if para. 3 in its original or in its final form was intended to contain a binding legal promise by the defendants to ensure the ability of Metals to pay the sums due under the facility, there was no apparent need or purpose for the plaintiffs, as bankers, to waste ink on paras 1 and 2.

As I have said, the absence of express words of promise does not by itself prevent a statement from being treated as a contractual promise. The example given in argument by counsel for the plaintiffs, namely of the shop stating by a notice that it is its policy to accept, within fourteen days of purchase, the return in good condition of any goods bought and to refund the price without question, seems to me to be a case in which a court would be likely to hold that the notice imported a promise that the policy would continue over the fourteen day period. It would be difficult on those facts to find any sensible commercial explanation for the notice other than a contractual promise not to change the policy over the fourteen day period. It would not be satisfactory or convincing to regard the notice as no more than the assumption of a moral responsibility by the shop giving such a notice to its customers. In such a case, and in the absence of any relevant factual context indicating otherwise, it seems to me that the court would probably hold that the statement was shown to have been intended to be a contractual promise.

In this case, however, the opposite seems to me to be clear.

. . .

But the evidence of the refusal by the defendants to assume legal responsibility for the liabilities of Metals to the plaintiffs in the normal form of joint and several liability or of a gaurantee, and the consequent resort by the parties to what they described as a comfort letter substantially in the terms submitted by the plaintiffs to the defendants, is, in my judgment, admissible on the question whether, for the purposes of the test applied by the court in Esso Petroleum Co. Ltd v Mardon, the defendants' affirmation in para. 3 appears on the evidence to have been intended as a warranty or contractual promise.

With that evidence before the court I find it impossible to hold that the words in para. 3 were intended to have any effect between the parties other than in accordance with the express words used. For this purpose it seems to me that the onus of demonstrating that the affirmation appears on evidence to have been intended as a contractual promise must lie on the party asserting that it does, but I do not rest my conclusion on failure by the plaintiffs to discharge any onus. I think it is clear that the words of para. 3 cannot be regarded as intended to contain a contractual promise as to the future policy of the defendants.

. . .

If my view of this case is correct, the plaintiffs have suffered grave financial loss as a result of the collapse of the tin market and the following decision by the defendant company not to honour a moral responsibility which it assumed in order to gain for its subsidiary the finance necessary for the trading operations which the defendants wished that subsidiary to pursue. The defendants have demonstrated, in my judgment, that they made no relevant contractual promise to the plaintiffs which could support the judgment in favour of the plaintiffs. The consequences of the decision of the defendants to repudiate their moral responsibility are not matters for this court.

I would allow this appeal.

Note

1. See Reynolds (1988) 104 LQR 353, and Orion Insurance Co. plc v Sphere Drake Insurance plc [1990] 1 Lloyd's Rep. 465.

2. If the letter constitutes an acceptance of a prior offer, then irrespective of its description, or cautionary language a legally binding contract will result. See *Wilson Smithett & Cape (Sugar) Ltd v Bangladesh Sugar and Food Industries Corp.* [1986] 1 Lloyd's Rep. 378.

SECTION THREE—INDUSTRIAL CONFLICT AND LEGAL INTENT

In contrast to the well known English case of *Ford v AEUW* [1969] 1 All ER 339, Irish case-law tends to favour the enforcement, via contract, of no strike clauses in industrial relations law.

Goulding Chemicals v Bolger [1977] IR 211

In anticipation of the closure of their manufacturing company, the plaintiffs reached agreement with the trade unions in regard to the manner of the closure and the amounts of the redundancy payments to be paid to the employees. All of the employees were then dismissed in accordance with the agreement. The defendants were former employees of the plaintiffs, and trade union members who refused to accept the terms of the agreement. The plaintiffs claimed an injunction to prevent the defendants picketing their premises.

O'Higgins C.J.:

The second ground of appeal put forward by the plaintiffs was based on the acceptance by all the unions concerned (including ITGWU of which the defendants are members) of the plaintiffs' proposals for the closing of their plant. These proposals were designed to ensure that the closing would be accepted by the unions as being in the circumstances unavoidable and that satisfactory monetary compensation would be paid to all employees. It was of course implicit in the proposals and in their acceptance by the unions that there would be no trade dispute and, of course, no picketing. The six-point proposal or statement from the plaintiffs which was accepted by the unions was a business-like document and had all the appearances of being intended to create legal relations between the unions which accepted and the plaintiffs who proposed. I would regard the agreement resulting from the acceptance of these proposals as being similar in effect to that dealt with in *Edwards v Skyways Ltd*[1] and, there being nothing to suggest the contrary, in my view a valid contract thereby created between these unions and the plaintiffs. However, this is not the point of this ground of appeal.

The plaintiffs' contention is that this valid enforceable agreement has the effect of binding the defendants who are all members of one of the unions involved. This submission must be considered in the light of the evidence, which was uncontradicted, that the defendants at all times opposed the conclusion of any agreement with regard to the closing of the plant and made it abundantly clear, both inside the union and to the plaintiffs, that they would not accept any agreement to this effect. I find it hard to accept that in such circumstances the defendants can be bound by an agreement which they have expressly repudiated and opposed. It seems to me that to hold them bound would be contrary to all principle. The only basis put forward for suggesting that they should be bound was that they did not resign and continued to be members of their union. The rules of the union were not put in evidence but I would find it very difficult to accept that membership of an association like a union could bind all members individually in respect of union contracts merely because such had been made by the union. I cannot accept for these reasons that this ground of appeal is well founded.

Kenny J.:

The defendants contended that the six-point statement and its acceptance by the unions did not constitute an enforceable agreement. An agreement between parties is enforceable by the law unless the agreement itself or the surrounding circumstances show that the parties did not intend to enter into legal relations (*Rose and Frank Co. v J. R. Crompton & Bros Ltd*[2]) and reliance was placed on the decision of Lane J. in *Ford Motor Co. Ltd v A.E.F.*[3] where it was held that two collective agreements did not, having regard to their background, constitute a legally enforceable agreement. In *Edwards v Skyways Ltd*[4] Megaw J. held that an agreement by the defendants to make *ex gratia* payments to their employees whom they were dismissing created an enforceable agreement. I have considerable doubts about the correctness of the decision in the *Ford Motor Co.* case particularly as Lane J. did not say anything about the decision in *Edwards v Skyways Ltd* although it was cited to him. It seems to me that the six-point agreement was intended to create legal relations and was intended to be a contract between the plaintiffs and the unions engaged in the negotiations. I think that Megaw J. was right when he said that when an apparent agreement in relation to business relations is entered into, the onus on the party who asserts that it was not intended to have legal effect is a heavy one. In my opinion the six-point statement and its acceptance created a valid enforceable contract between the plaintiffs and the unions who took part in the negotiations.

The plaintiffs then argued that if the six-point statement and its acceptance by the unions created a contract the defendants, as members of the union, were bound by it because the majority of their co-members had accepted it. No authority to support this argument was cited and the rules of the union, which would show the authority of the majority, were not referred to or proved. I think that the contention is wrong in principle and that all the reported cases on this matter are against it. Membership of a corporate body or of an association does not have the consequence that every agreement made by that corporate body or association binds every member of it. None of the defendants are parties to the agreement and as they consistently opposed it, no question of their being bound by acquiescence can arise. . . .

[1.] |1964| 1 WLR 349.   [2.] |1923| 2 KB 261.   [3.] |1969| 2 QB 303

(Henchy, Griffith and Parke JJ. agreed and the appeal was dismissed.)

Even where the agreement seems to be vague or aspirational, the courts will incline towards enforceability.

O'Rourke & Others v Talbot (Ireland) Ltd [1984] ILRM 587

Barrington J.:

. . . The defendant is a well-known firm, formerly engaged in the assembly, and now engaged in the importation and distribution, of motor cars. The plaintiffs are nine foremen formerly employed by the defendants in their motor assembly business. All were senior men with from 12 to 28 years service when they were made redundant by the defendant on 26 September 1980. A strike which attracted considerable public notoriety took place at the defendant's premises in the year 1981 so that it may be worthwhile to mention that this case has nothing to do with that strike, all of the plaintiffs having been made redundant in the previous year.

In their proceedings the plaintiffs claim a declaration that the defendant company is bound by a certain agreement dated 21 June 1979 as amended by another agreement dated 25 July 1979 whereby they allege the defendant company gave a guarantee that the plaintiffs would not be made redundant prior to 1984. The defendant, in its substantial defence to the proceedings argued before me, did not deny the existence of the said alleged agreements but pleaded that the said alleged agreements or agreement did not contemplate legal relations and do not entitle the plaintiffs to any relief in a court of law. . . .

The agreement

In 1979 the defendant company was running into difficulties. Costs were rising and sales and production were falling. Under these circumstances management were anxious to secure the agreement of the plaintiffs that foremen who had left car assembly, or were being redeployed elsewhere in the defendants' business, would not be replaced. The plaintiffs, on the other hand, were worried about their own jobs but were prepared to go along with management's proposals provided they got some security in return.

A meeting was held between management and the foremen's representatives on 20 June 1979, Mr Gould, Mr Power and Mr Oakes represented management while Mr O'Rourke, Mr Myler and Mr Coleman represented the foremen. The following extract from a memorandum from Mr Oakes, the personnel manager, to Mr Ronayne, the managing director of the defendant company, gives some insight into the problem with which management and foremen were concerned just prior to the meeting of 20 June. The memorandum is headed 'Foremen' and is dated 15 June 1979. It reads, in part, as follows:

> At the foremen's request Jim [i.e. Mr Power the production manager] and I met them on Wednesday to discuss problems which have a direct bearing on their attitudes and ultimately their behaviour.
> They expressed grave concern on the future of the plant and ultimately on employment levels. This has been brought to a head by the departure of John Ryan (foreman) and the company indicating that there will be no replacement.
> We explained in answer to their question, that for the level of production of sixteen cars a day we had surplus foremen, a fact that we had indicated some time ago.

There is very little conflict about what happened at the meeting. The foremen's representatives appeared to be of the opinion that virtually all issues were agreed, at least in principle, at the meeting of 20 June whereas the management representatives appeared to think that it took a number of meetings to reach agreement. Be that as it may I am quite satisfied that by the end of July the foremen and the management were in agreement on all outstanding points and that the foremen, in return for what they took to be a guarantee of job security, agreed that production foremen who retired or were transferred would not be replaced on the assembly line and that the remaining foremen would fill in for those who left and would work at any job to which they were assigned by management, including security work, provided they suffered no loss in pay. I am quite satisfied that the foremen, in return for agreeing to the management's plans for the redeployment of supervisory staff, asked for an assurance that their jobs would be secure and asked to have this assurance, in writing, on company notepaper.

It is not clear whether a draft of the proposed assurance was produced at the meeting of 20 June but, on the following day, the foremen received a document on company notepaper signed by Mr Gould, Mr Power and Mr Oakes and which read as follows: 'The company gives an assurance that compulsory redundancy will not be introduced among production supervisory grades should the market situation and other conditions affecting the company's performance necessitate a realignment of manning and staffing arrangements.' It will be noticed that this document contemplates changes in the 'market situation and other conditions affecting the company's performance'. Should such factors necessitate 'a realignment of manning and staffing arrangements' the company still gives an assurance that compulsory redundancy will not be introduced among production supervisory grades.

The foremen discussed this document either on the twenty first or some later date and were not satisfied with it. They wanted something that would bind the company legally. Some of the foremen—and in particular Mr Coleman—did not like the word 'assurance'. They wished to substitute the word guarantee' which they considered to be a better word from the legal point of view. They were also familiar with the term 'guarantee', in the sense of a legally binding warranty as to fitness, in the motor trade. I am quite satisfied—and indeed there is no controversy about it—that at some stage the foremen asked for a 'guarantee' instead of the 'assurance' contained in the document of 21 June. I am quite satisfied also that management created no difficulty about giving the guarantee. A meeting was held between representatives of management and representatives of the foremen on 25 July 1979. At some stage before this meeting draft minutes of the meeting were shown to the foremen's representatives and agreed to by them. These minutes contain the following paragraphs:

> The company gave a guarantee of no compulsory redundancy prior to 1984 and that surplus supervisors would be redeployed.
> On re-location a supervisor would retain all his benefits as a 'no worse off' condition.

So far as the representatives of management were concerned I am quite satisfied that they negotiated with the foremen's representatives in good faith. They were, at least, equally concerned about the future of the plant. They recognised that the foremen were senior men who had given the company loyal service They always envisaged that if a particular foreman's job became outdated that it would be possible to redeploy him in some other part of the company's business. They acknowledged that the foremen had agreed to work in any capacity and that, as senior men, they should be secure on the principle of first in last out. But things did not work out that way. The company's business deteriorated in 1980. They were five unions in the plant and it was not practicable to sack one man and replace him by a man from a different union. Neither was it practicable to have two men receiving different rates of pay for the one job. In September 1980 the company felt that it had to let all the plaintiffs go.

I think the truth of the matter is that the representatives of management did not think that they were entering into a legally binding arrangement with the foremen at all. They felt that they were entering into a productivity agreement of a kind binding in honour but not in law. Mr John Kane the secretary of the No. 2 Branch of the Irish Transport and General Workers' Union, who give evidence in the case, acknowledged that many agreements negotiated between employers and trade unions were regarded as falling into this category. Moreover, management were probably more conscious than the man of the importance of market forces and felt that no matter what was decided in negotiations, market forces would ultimately decide what would happen to the plant and to the men's jobs.

I am satisfied, however, that not only were the men looking for something which was legally binding but that management knew this. Mr Oakes admitted in cross-examination that he knew the foremen were very happy with the assurance and guarantee because they appeared to feel that their jobs were protected. They were no longer relying on the general arrangements made between the motor assemblers and the government which, while designed to maintain employment levels in the motor assembly industry, did not guarantee the particular job of any one man. They now had a further assurance which applied specifically to their jobs with the defendant company. He knew that the foremen thought they were getting more than other workers with the defendant company. The management company knew that the foremen were not getting more but did not consider it necessary to tell them.

Likewise Mr Power admitted that he knew that the plaintiffs were anxious to have a copper-fastened guarantee for the future. He knew this when they came back looking to have the word 'guarantee' substituted for the word 'assurance'. His own view was that you could not offer such things and run a viable company. He felt that the document which the men had received was not 'worth the paper it is written on' but also knew that they, having received it, were content that they had a future. They may have taken the interpretation from it that they had a secure job until 1984 but he felt that in negotiation 'you don't point out the snags in your proposal'.

Mr John Kane the branch secretary of the No. 2 Branch of the Irish Transport and General Workers' Union was not, initially, aware of the written assurance or guarantee which the foremen had received. He did not usually consider that agreements negotiated between trade unions and employers were legally binding though they might be binding in honour. He, however, regarded the document which the men had received as unique in his twenty years experience as a trade union official. He regarded it as giving cast iron and personal guarantees to each of the men concerned. He was accordingly dismayed when the guarantee was not honoured and he telephoned Mr Gould to tell him so. Mr Gould said that the document had been given in good faith and that he was sorry for what had happened. In the course of the same telephone call Mr Gould indicated that the company might be disposed to negotiate to buy back the guarantee but he could not recall if any specific sum of money was mentioned. I am satisfied that a sum of £20,000 was subsequently mentioned internally in management circles as a possible figure to redeem the assurance or guarantee, but I accept Mr Gould's evidence that he did not mention any specific sum to Mr Kane on the telephone. I also accept that what happened between Mr Gould and Mr Kane is not to be taken as any form of admission of liability but is rather to be regarded as a 'feeler' put out by Mr Gould to see if what he regarded as yet another industrial problem could be resolved by the payment of money.

The law

The agreement in the present case was a commercial agreement. It is clear from the internal memo sent by Mr Oakes to Mr Ronayne that management knew that an offer of job security would influence the men's attitude towards the scheme of redeployment in the company. It is also clear that the assurance given did influence their attitude and that the scheme of redeployment was implemented with the men's agreement and co-operation because of the assurance given. It therefore appears to me that the presumption of law is that the parties intended to create legal relations. In these circumstances as Megaw J. said in *Edwards v Skyways Ltd* [1964] 1 WLR 349, the onus is on the party who asserts that no legal effect was intended, and the onus is a heavy one.

In that case the plaintiff was an aircraft pilot employed by the defendant. At a meeting held between representatives of the defendant company and the plaintiff's trade association it had been agreed that pilots declared redundant when leaving the defendant company would be given 'an *ex gratia* payment' equivalent to the defendant's contributions to the pension fund. The plaintiff having retired, the defendant refused to make the '*ex gratia* payment'. Megaw J. held that the agreement was a binding one and that the term *ex gratia* related to the position prevailing before the plaintiff carried out his end of the agreement and not afterwards.

At p. 355 of the report the learned trial judge puts the matter as follows:

> In the present case, the subject matter of the agreement is business relations, not social or domestic matters. There was a meeting of minds—an intention to agree. There was, admittedly, consideration for the company's promise. I accept the propositions of counsel for the plaintiff that in a case of this nature the onus is on the party who asserts that no legal effect was intended, and the onus is a heavy one.
>
> Counsel for the plaintiff also submitted, with the support of the well known textbooks on the law of contract, Anson and Cheshire and Fifoot, that the test of intention to create or not to create legal relations is 'objective'. I am not sure that I know what that means in this context, I do, however, think that there are grave difficulties in trying to apply a test of the actual intention or understanding or knowledge of the parties; especially where the alleged agreement is arrived at between a limited liability company and a trade association; and especially where it is arrived at at a meeting attended by five or six representatives on each side. Whose knowledge, understanding or intention is relevant? But if it be the 'objective' test of the reasonable man, what background knowledge is to be imputed to the reasonable man, when the background knowledge of the ten or twelve persons who took part in arriving at the decision no doubt varied greatly between one and another?

The decision in *Edwards v Skyways Ltd* was cited with approval by the Chief Justice in a passage which appears at p. 231 of the report in *Gouldings Chemicals Ltd v Bolger* |1977| IR 211. But one of the matters which influenced the Chief Justice in the view he expressed in the passage quoted was that the document under discussion in that case, though negotiated between employers and a trade union, was 'a business-like document and had all the appearances of being intended to create legal relations'.

|Counsel for the defendant| says that the minute of the meeting of 25 July 1979 which contains, at para. 3, the guarantee of no compulsory redundancy prior to 1984, does not look like a business-like document or one intended to create legal relations. He points, for instance, to para. 2 which is as follows: 'The company cannot anticipate plant lay-out or supervising requirements should diversification take place but supervising ratios will be fully discussed before implementation.'

|Counsel| relies strongly on the case of *Ford Motors Co. Ltd v A.E.F.* |1969| 2 QB 303 where it was held that collective agreements negotiated between a large industrial company and various trade unions and containing many 'aspirational' clauses, were not intended to create legal relations. In the course of his judgment in that case (at p. 496) Lane J. (as he then was) put the matter as follows: 'Agreements such as these, composed largely of optimistic aspirations, presenting grave practical problems of enforcement and reached against a background of opinion adverse to enforceability, are, in my judgment, not contracts in the legal sense and are not enforceable at law.'

In *Goulding Chemicals Ltd v Bolger* Kenny J., at p. 237 of the report, expressed some reservations as to the correctness of the decision in the *Ford Motor Co. Ltd* case but I do not consider it necessary to go into these matters for three reasons. Firstly, we are not here dealing with a trade union or a group of trade unions negotiating on behalf of all the men employed in a vast concern or a particular industry but with three foremen negotiating on behalf of not more than seventeen of their peers and referring back to their peers and getting authority from time to time. Secondly, a productivity agreement which might not be legally enforceable in all its terms can still amend particular provisions in a worker's contract of employment e.g. his rate of pay. In the present case I have no doubt that the foremen made quite clear that they were looking for an alteration in their terms of employment. Finally, the plaintiffs in the present case carried out their side of the bargain and are standing over the authority of the agents who negotiated the agreement on their behalf.

As previously stated I accept the evidence of the management witnesses when they say that they did not intend to enter into legal relations with the foremen. Unfortunately, their attitude was never expressed or communicated to the foremen. The foremen's representatives, on the other hand, by demanding an assurance in writing, on company notepaper, and by insisting on the substitution of the word 'guarantee' for the word 'assurance' made clear that they were looking, not for some pious aspiration or commitment in honour, but for a guarantee, peculiar to each foreman, against being made redundant prior to 1984. I am satisfied also that when the negotiations were completed the foremen thought they had received such a guarantee and, on the basis of it, co-operated in the company's scheme of redeployment. I am satisfied also that the company, through its managers, knew that the workers thought they had received such a guarantee and did not disabuse them of the position. It therefore appears to me that the conditions of the 'objective test' referred to by Megaw J. in *Edwards v Skyways Ltd* [1964] 1 WLR 349 are met and that the company cannot rebut the presumption that the agreement was one intended to create legal relations. Under these circumstances it appears to me that the company was in breach of its agreement with the plaintiffs in making them redundant in September 1980 and that the plaintiffs are, accordingly, entitled to relief.

Chapter Five

Legal Form

INTRODUCTION

Certain contracts in order to be enforceable must be in the form prescribed by law. Some contracts must be under seal, some in writing and some evidenced in writing.

Contracts which must be under seal include contracts unsupported by consideration or conveyances of title to land.

Contracts under the Hire-Purchase Acts 1946–80 or moneylending contracts under the Moneylenders Acts 1900–1933 must be recorded in writing.

Finally the **Statute of Frauds (Ireland) 1695** lists a number of contracts which must be evidenced in writing:

2. No action shall be brought . . . . whereby to charge the defendant upon any special promise to answer for the debt, default or miscarriage of another person, or to charge any person upon any agreement made upon consideration of marriage, or upon any contract of sale of lands, tenements or hereditaments or any interest in or concerning them, or upon any agreement that is not to be formed within the space of one year from the making thereof, unless the agreement upon which such action shall be brought, or some memorandum or note thereof, shall be in writing, and signed by the party to be charged therewith, or some other person thereunto by him lawfully authorised.

SECTION ONE—FORMAL REQUIREMENTS

A. Contracts to Which the Statute Applies

Contracts to answer for the debt of another involve contracts of guarantee not contracts of indemnity. In the former case both the debtor and the promisor are liable to the creditor. In the latter case only the promisor is liable.

Fennel v Mulcahy (1845) 8 ILR 434

Brady C.B.:

. . . the case of *Walker v Taylor*[1] also shows the true view of this question, as taken by Tindal C.J.; in that case he says, 'the promise is not "I will pay if the debtor cannot," but it is "in consideration of that which is an advantage to me, I will pay you this money."'

227

There is a whole 'class of cases in which the matter is excepted from the statute, on account of a consideration arising immediately between the parties. It is a new contract; it has nothing to do with the Statute of Frauds at all.'

There is another case in which this question appears to have arisen, . . . it is the case of *Clancy v Pigott*;[2] . . . [Littledale J.] says, p. 503, 'It is clear to me, even upon the declaration in this case, that this was a promise to pay the debt of another person, notwithstanding all that is said about the lien on the goods; but upon the construction of the Statute of Frauds, it has been held that if there be a new consideration moving from the plaintiff to the defendant, though it is the promise to pay the debt of another person, it need not be in writing.'

[1.] 6 C & P 753.   [2.] 4 Nev & Man 406; SC 2 Ad & El 473.

Agreements made in consideration of marriage though common at one stage are relatively rare today.

Contracts for the sale of goods in excess of £10 are now regulated by the **Sale of Goods Act 1893 s. 4**:

4. (1) A contract for the sale of any goods of the value of ten pounds or upwards shall not be enforceable by action unless the buyer shall accept part of the goods so sold, and actually receive the same, or give something in earnest to bind the contract, or in part payment, or unless some note or memorandum in writing of the contract be made and signed by the party to be charged or his agent in that behalf.

(2) The provisions of this section apply to every such contract, notwithstanding that the goods may be intended to be delivered at some future time, or may not at the time of such contract be actually made, procured, or provided, or fit or ready for delivery, or some act may be requisite for the making or completing thereof, or rendering the same fit for delivery.

(3) There is an acceptance of goods within the meaning of this section when the buyer does any act in relation to the goods which recognises a pre-existing contract of sale whether there be an acceptance in performance of the contract or not.

To come within the category of contracts not to be performed within the year, evidence must demonstrate that at the time the contract was made the parties did not intend to perform it within one year.

Thomas Hynes *v* John Hynes (HC) 21 December 1984, unrep.

When the plaintiff's business got into financial difficulties, he entered into a verbal agreement with the defendant, his brother, whereby the latter agreed to form two new companies to complete the plaintiff's outstanding contracts and to be his successor in business. The plaintiff maintains that it was also agreed that all the profits of the new companies would, in the first instance, be used to discharge the plaintiff's debts, and thereafter to be split between the parties.

The defendant claimed *inter alia* that there was no memorandum in writing sufficient for the purposes of the Statute of Frauds.

Barrington J:

. . .

The defendant maintains that the alleged agreement between him and Tom, being a contract not to be performed within the space of one year from the making thereof, required to be evidenced by a memorandum in writing and that there is no such memorandum in existence.

. . . the plaintiff's principal submission is that the alleged agreement was not governed by the Statute of Frauds at all. In deciding whether an agreement was an agreement 'not to be performed within the spaces of one year from the making thereof' one looks at the situation which prevailed at the time when the agreement was made and at the intentions of the parties. There was no intention that the agreement should not be completed within the space of one year. It would appear that the intention was that the implementation of the agreement should commence immediately and that the completion of the agreement should take place as soon as possible.

The evidence of Mr Edmund Burke throws some light on the intention of the parties about the time of the making of the agreement. At the meeting in Jury's Hotel with John and Tom at about the time of Tom's bankruptcy Mr Burke understood that there was some scheme to pay off Tom's bankruptcy. Witness enquired how long it would take to which Tom replied that he thought it would take a year or so for him 'to come back'.

I am satisfied that there was no intention that the agreement should not be performed within the space of one year from the making thereof and I am satisfied also that it was not an agreement which, from its nature, precluded such performance. I am satisfied therefore that it was not an agreement 'not to be performed within the space of one year from the making thereof' and that the Statute of Frauds does not apply to it.

Note

In this case the defendant also claimed that the alleged agreement was not intended to constitute a binding agreement between the parties. Barrington J. held that in the circumstances the agreement was enforceable.

In a probate case, In the goods of Leslie Good, decd (HC) 14 July 1986 unrep. an agreement by a couple to leave property to their children 'on the death of either' was held to be an agreement 'that is not to be performed within the space of one year from the making thereof'. See also Naughton v Limestone Land Co. Ltd [1952] IJR 18.

Contracts for the sale of lands or interest therein form the most common category of contracts under s. 2. The remaining cases in this chapter fall under this heading.

B. CONTENTS OF A MEMORANDUM

In order to satisfy the Statute of Frauds a memorandum must include the names of the parties involved in the transaction, a description of the property to be transferred and the consideration. In addition the memorandum must include any additional terms viewed as essential by the parties.

Godley *v* Power (1961) 95 ILTR 135

The plaintiff entered into an oral agreement to sell a licensed premises to the defendant. This was confirmed by the defendant's letter which stated the purchase price, the liability of the vendor to pay half the auctioneer's fees and asked to have an enclosed inventory included in the Agreement for Sale. When the defendant attempted to withdraw from the sale, the plaintiff sued for specific performance or, in the alternative, damages for breach of contract.

The High Court dismissed the plaintiff's claim and the plaintiff appealed.

Kingsmill Moore J.:

It was next contended that the memorandum was defective, in that it did not set out correctly the terms of the contract, and did not contain all the terms of the contract.

A memorandum must contain all essential terms. The parties, the property, and the consideration must always be ascertainable from it, but it need not contain any terms which the general law would imply. The letter of 14 September contains the parties, an adequate description of the property and—apparently—the consideration. It was however objected by the defendant's counsel that it was inaccurate, in as much as it did not show the tenure of the property to be leasehold, and insufficient, in as much as it made no reference to, what was alleged to be part of the consideration for the bargain, an agreement to take over the stock in trade at cost price.

An agreement to sell land implies that the whole of the vendor's interest in the land is to be sold; *Bowen v Cooper* 2 Hare 408, and, in the absence of anything to lead to a contrary view, the interest is implied by law to be a fee simple. If, however, a purchaser has notice that the vendor is only a lessee such an implication does not arise, and the contract will have reference only to the leasehold title which the vendor possesses. . . . The question therefore arises whether the purchaser, Mr Power, had notice that the vendor could only offer a leasehold title. There is not direct evidence of this, but I think there is an irresistible inference.

. . .

The next objection was that the memorandum was incomplete, because it made no mention of an alleged agreement that the purchase should take over the balance of stock left on completion at invoice figures.

. . .

Assuming however that such an agreement had been come to would its absence from the memorandum render the memorandum invalid? A memorandum under the Statute of Frauds is only required of a contract or sale of lands. If it could be shown clearly that the agreement for the taking over of the stock was part of the consideration for the sale of the lands then the memorandum would be defective, because it did not fully set out the consideration. But it seems more likely that any such agreement was a collateral and subsidiary contract. Its execution, indeed, depended on the completion of the contract for the sale of the lands, for it was only on completion that the stock could be ascertained and its value discovered; but it appears to me to be a reversal of probability to suggest that the sale of the lands was in any way contingent on the disposal of the residue of the stock.

. . .

In argument this letter was sometimes referred to and relied on as if it was part of the formation of the contract, an acceptance of an offer, and it was urged that such acceptance was only conditional or preliminary because of the words—'Kindly let me have agreement for sale. Purchaser would like to have the enclosed inventory included in the agreement.' I do not read the letter in this way. It does not purport to be an *acceptance* of an offer. It is a formal *confirmation* of an agreement which had been already completed at an earlier period, and the terms of which it purports to set out, 'I wish to confirm that my client *has* agreed with your client to purchase from him the above premises on the following terms.' There is not the slightest suggestion that this pre-existing contract was subject to the preparation of a written agreement, or that the terms as set out were not the complete terms. The letter is evidence of what the contract was, and provides a memorandum of the contract. It is not an instrument making the contract. If the contract had already been made orally, without the incorporation of a condition requiring a written agreement, the subsequent desire or request of the purchaser to have a written agreement could not in any way affect the validity of the existing oral agreement or its enforceability, once a memorandum came into existence. This letter seems to be direct evidence that a contract containing all the necessary terms had already been concluded.

(O'Daly and Maguire JJ. agreed. Maguire C.J. dissented on the grounds that there was no sufficient memorandum as the letter did not describe the premises or the title nor did it mention a deposit, or completion times. Lavery J. also dissented.)

Note

In *Kearns v Manning* [1935] IR 869 Murnaghan J. in the Supreme Court stated that 'the date of the commencement of the term is a material part of an agreement for a lease'.

Guardian Builders Ltd *v* Patrick Kelly and Park Avenue Ltd (HC) 31 March 1981, unrep.

The defendant owned a site which he wished to sell, and for this purpose an agent, Mr O'Brien was appointed. An oral agreement was concluded with the plaintiff and the area of land to be sold was marked on a site map. The parties also agreed that the plaintiff would obtain possession within three months. Mr O'Brien stated that he would ask the defendant's solicitor to prepare a contract. Mr O'Brien then wrote a letter, which was typed by his secretary and dated 26 April. A dispute later arose as to the existence of an agreement evidenced by a sufficient memorandum.

Costello J.:

The first point that [counsel for the defendant] propounds is that Mr O'Brien had no authority to sign the memorandum. It is well established that an express authority need not be given to authorise an agent to sign a memorandum which is sufficient to satisfy the statute, and I refer to *Godley v Power*, 95 ILTR, 135. So the question arises as to whether or not Mr O'Brien had authority, either express or implied, to sign the memorandum. Now it is true that Mr Kelly did not say to Mr O'Brien: 'You're to sign a contract which is to satisfy the Statute of Frauds.' What he did was to authorise him to find a purchaser for the site. I agree with the submission of [counsel for the plaintiff] that in the circumstances of this case Mr O'Brien had an implied authority to write the letter of 26 April.

In addition to that implied authority, which arose from the relationship Mr O'Brien had with the defendant, there is the fact that Mr O'Brien stated expressly at the meeting that he was going to write a letter. It seems there is authority to be obtained from the fact that, having said this, he was not told not to write the letter; in fact, I think he obtained authority to write asking for a contract and so impliedly to write a letter to indicate that an oral agreement had been reached. I am satisfied, therefore, that Mr O'Brien had authority to sign the letter of 26 April.

What this case then turns on is whether or not this memorandum was sufficient to satisfy the statute. The first point made by |counsel for the defendant| is that the portion of the lands given in the memorandum is insufficient. The letter is headed 'The Nurseries, Park Avenue' and it states that a sale had been concluded of 'Half of the above site' and that the site area was as agreed between the plaintiff and the defendant. The parties had agreed the site area. They had marked it on a map and agreed it and in my opinion this is sufficient description to satisfy the Statute of Frauds. The test is that the property so described has to be readily identifiable. It can be identifiable on the oral evidence which produces the map agreed between the parties as being the site.

It is also suggested that the parties were not identified. I think they were. Although referred to by individual name in the case of Mr Kelly, it is nonetheless sufficient, and the error in the name of the plaintiff company does not invalidate the identity of the parties. Again the test is whether the parties can be readily identifiable, and I think they can. On this point the memorandum is adequate.

This brings me to the submission made by |counsel for the defendant| that material terms of the agreement were omitted from the memorandum and so the memorandum does not satisfy the statue. It was firstly suggested that there had been agreement in relation to possession, which is not in the memorandum, that possession would be given before six weeks of the portion of the site not claimed by Mrs Jameson. I agree that there was discussion at the meeting in relation to this part of the transaction. I do not think it was made a term of the contract that in four to six weeks the plaintiff was to be entitled to obtain possession of the site, it was merely a discussion; and even if it was a term of the contract it was not a material term because it is clear that the parties did not envisage that Mr Molloy would be able to develop the site for a year after the contract was signed.

It is said that there was agreement in relation to the building of a road by Mr Kelly. Again, I am satisfied that there was discussion about this but that it was not a material term of the contract.

It was also suggested that there was a problem in relation to rights-of-way because of the particular position of the site. There was certainly no discussion between the parties as to rights-of-way. The parties were practical businessmen and were not concerned with the legal problems which would arise, which they would leave to their solicitors to iron out. In my view there was no discussion about rights-of-way and no material term was omitted in this connection from the memorandum. I have already indicated that there was no term agreed in relation to the open spaces to be included on the site which the plaintiff was purchasing and so there was no material term omitted in this connection from the contract.

It was finally urged by |counsel| that questions of title had been discussed and that a material term in this connection was omitted from the contract in this connection, but I am quite satisfied that title was not discussed at the meeting.

I conclude, therefore, that there was an oral agreement and that there is a memorandum of this agreement sufficient to satisfy the statute. The plaintiff is entitled to the relief claimed. . . .

Note

In *Casey v Irish Intercontinental Bank Ltd* [1979] IR 364 the Supreme Court accepted that printed names on headed notepaper could constitute a sufficient signature for the purposes of the Statute of Frauds.

C. JOINDER OF DOCUMENTS

A memorandum may consist of two or more documents read together.

Michael McQuaid v Edward Lynam and James Lynam [1965] IR 564

The plaintiff inspected a house at 1 Kinvara Road belonging to the defendants. On telephoning the defendants he was told the price of the house was £2,800. On 4 September the plaintiff called to the defendants' office, informed them that he liked the house and paid a deposit of £800. He was given a receipt in these terms: 'Received from Mr Michael McQuaid the sum of £800 being deposit on no. 1 Kinvara Road.' The name 'E. & J. Lynam' was put on the receipt with a rubber stamp and, underneath this, the signature of the second defendant.

The plaintiff filled in one half of a building society loan application form at this meeting and on a later date the plaintiff completed the form. The plaintiff then signed the form and dated it 27 September. This form contained a description of the property, a statement that it was freehold, that it was vacant, and that it was being purchased for £2,800 and gave E. & J. Lynam as the name of the builder. This form was then lodged with the building society. In November the plaintiff decided to reduce the amount required from the building society and on 4 November 1963, he went to the office of the defendants, paid them an additional £500, and got a receipt which read: 'Received from Mr Michael McQuaid the sum of £500 re no. 1 Kinvara Road,' which was signed by the second-named defendant. Before the plaintiff paid this sum he was told by one of the defendants that the property would not be sold to him as freehold but would be leased to him and that the price would be reduced by £100; the plaintiff agreed to this. The defendant later refused to complete the agreement and the plaintiff sued for damages.

Kenny J.:

. . .

The first submission by the plaintiff's counsel in connection with the Statute of Frauds was that the application to the building society which was written by the second-named defendant was a sufficient memorandum or note of the oral contract. The application contains all the terms of the oral contract which was made on 4 September 1963, and the name of the defendants but it was not signed by them or either of them unless the writing in of 'E. J. Lynam' opposite the printed words, 'name of builder', was a signature. It is settled law that the memorandum or note required by the Statute of Frauds may consist of a document which was not intended to be such a note or memorandum but it must, however, be signed by the party to be charged and the signature must have been intended to authenticate the whole document of which it forms a part. This was emphasised by Lord Westbury in *Caton v Caton*[1] when he said:

> Now, what constitutes a sufficient signature has been described by different judges in different words. In the original case upon this subject, though not quite the original case, but the case most frequently referred to as of the earliest date, that of *Stokes v Moore*,[2] the language of the learned judge is, that the signature must authenticate every part of the instrument; or again, that it must give authenticity to every part of the instrument. . . . Probably the phrases 'authentic' and 'authenticity' are not quite felicitous, but their meaning is plainly this, that the signature must be so placed as to show that it was intended to relate and refer to, and that in fact it does relate and refer to, every part of the instrument. The language of Sir William Grant in *Ogilvie v Foljambe*[3] is (as his method was) much more felicitous. He says it must govern every part of the instrument. It must show that every part of the instrument emanates from the individual so signing, and that the signature was intended to have that effect. It follows, therefore, that if a signature be found in an instrument incidentally only, or having relation and reference only to a portion of the instrument, the signature cannot have that legal effect and force which it must have in order to comply with the statute, and to give authenticity to the whole of the memorandum.

The writing of 'E. J. Lynam' by the second-named defendant on the application to the building society was not a signature of that document by the defendants or by either of them as it was not intended to give authenticity to any part of it. The document was intended to be—and was—signed by the plaintiff and the writing of the name of the defendants was intended to give information to the building society. The application is not therefore a memorandum or note in writing of the contract.

The next issue is whether the receipt of 4 September 1963, and the application to the building society, dated 27 September 1963, together constitute such a memorandum or note. The receipt refers to '£800 being the deposit on no. 1 Kinvara Road.' The application to the building society has the figure £800 opposite the query, 'Amount of cash applicant is prepared to pay down?' This figure of £800 written in ink is crossed out in pencil and the figure of £1,500 was subsequently written in at this space by an official of the building society on the instructions of the plaintiff but the figure of £800 is legible. I have already stated that the application to the building society gives the address of the property to be mortgaged as 1, Kinvara Road.

. . .

The many cases on the issue whether a number of documents read together can constitute such a memorandum or note in writing show a progressively liberal approach by the courts to this question. I think that the modern cases (*Long v Millar*,[4] *Stokes v Whicher*[5] and *Timmins v Moreland Street Pty Co.*[6]) establish that a number of documents may together constitute a note or memorandum in writing if they have come into existence in connection with the same transaction or if they contain internal references which connect them with each other. But as the memorandum or note considered as a whole must be signed, it would seem to follow that the document which is signed must be the last of the documents in point of time, for it would be absurd to hold that a person who signed a document could be regarded as having signed another document which was not in existence when he signed the first. I think that the correct view on this difficult matter is that stated in the judgment of Romer L.J. in *Timmins v Moreland Street Pty Co.*, at p. 278. One of the matters discussed in that case was whether a cheque and a receipt read together constituted a valid memorandum or note and it was argued that the two documents could not unless the document signed by the party to be charged was the later one. On this matter, Romer L.J. said:

> The next point which counsel for the defendant company took was whether the cheque and receipt taken together could form a memorandum having regard to the order in which they were signed. His argument as to that was that although two separate documents can together constitute a memorandum for the purposes of s. 40, the party to be charged must have signed the second of the two; that is to say, if the defendant had signed a document, the plaintiff cannot rely on it in conjunction with a later document signed by himself. This in general must be true. A defendant cannot be bound by a document which he has not signed unless he has in effect incorporated it in the document which he had signed, in which case he would be regarded as having notionally signed both documents; but as he cannot be taken to have incorporated or signed a document which does not exist, the theory is inapplicable except where the defendant has signed the second of two documents on which the plaintiff relies as together constituting a memorandum. If, however, on the same occasion and as part of one and the same transaction—for example, as here, the payment of a deposit under an oral agreement for sale—a vendor and purchaser sit down at a table and respectively write out a receipt and a cheque, then, assuming that these documents between them sufficiently evidence the terms of the bargain, it would be going too far to say that the vendor could not rely on them as constituting a memorandum if the purchaser signed his cheque a few seconds before the vendor signed the receipt. I think it is enough to say that the documents relied on were brought into being more or less contemporaneously for the purpose of furthering a bargain which the party had made, . . .

and in the same case Jenkins L.J. said (at p. 272):

> . . . but I am, on the whole, of opinion that where two documents relied on as a memorandum are signed and exchanged at one and the same meeting as part of the same transaction, so that they may fairly be said to have been to all intents and purposes contemporaneously signed, the document signed by the party to be charged should not be treated as incapable of referring to the other document merely because the latter, on a minute investigation of the order of events at the meeting, is found to have come second in the order of preparation and signing.

The evidence is that on 4 September one half of the application to the building society was filled in by the second-named defendant immediately after the payment of the £800. The remaining half was completed at a subsequent date (probably 27 September). Thus, one half of the application to the building society and the receipt were contemporaneous: in my view, the receipt of 4 September and the whole of the application to the building society should be regarded as having come into existence in such circumstances that the signature to the receipt authenticates the building society application.

The next question is whether the receipt of 4 September and the building society application can be treated together as a memorandum or note. In my view, the reference to the deposit and 1 Kinvara Road and the close connection in time between the two documents enables me to read the documents together. The true principle on this matter was, I think, stated by Jenkins L.J. in *Timmins v Moreland Street Pty Co.*, when he said:

. . . I think it is still indispensably necessary, in order to justify the reading of documents together for this purpose [the provision of a memorandum or note in writing for the purposes of Statute of Frauds], that there should be a document signed by the party to be charged which, while not containing in itself all the necessary ingredients of the required memorandum, does contain some reference, express or implied, to some other document or transaction. Where any such reference can be spelt out of a document so signed, then parol evidence may be given to identify the other document referred to, or, as the case may be, to explain the other transaction, and to identify any document relating to it. If by this process a document is brought to light which contains in writing all the terms of the bargain so far as not contained in the document signed by the party to be charged, then the two documents can be read together so as to constitute a sufficient memorandum for the purposes of s. 40 of the Law of Property Act 1925. The laying of documents side by side may no doubt lead to the conclusion as a matter of *res ipsa loquitur* that the two are connected; but before a document signed by the party to be charged can be laid alongside another document to see if between them they constitute a sufficient memorandum, there must, I conceive, be found in the document signed by the party to be charged some reference to some other document or transaction.

If therefore the issue in the case be whether there was a sufficient memorandum or note in writing signed by the party to be charged of the agreement made on 4 September, I am of opinion that the plaintiff would succeed. But the agreement made on 4 September was varied by mutual consent on 4 November when the plaintiff and the defendants agreed that the plaintiff would purchase the house by way of lease and that the purchase money would be reduced by £100 and there is no memorandum or note in writing of this variation.

. . .

The real problem I think is whether the defendants can successfully contend that the contract of 4 September was varied by mutual agreement when there is a memorandum or note in writing of the contract of 4 September but not of the variation. In any discussion of this problem it is essential to distinguish between the case in which the parties to an agreement intend that agreement to find expression in a written contract and that in which the parties make an oral contract which is intended to be binding. If in the latter case a memorandum or note in writing is required by the Statute of Frauds, that memorandum or note does not become the contract. This distinction appears in s. 2 of the Statute of Frauds which so far as material provided: 'No action shall be brought . . . upon any contract or sale of lands, tenements or hereditaments, or any interest in or concerning them . . . unless the agreement upon which such action shall be brought, or some memorandum or note thereof, shall be in writing and signed by the party to be charged therewith or some other person thereunto by him lawfully authorised.' The same distinction was emphasised in *Thompson v The King*[7] and in *Law and Another v Robert Roberts and Co.*[8] In the first type of case, that is, where the parties intend their agreement to find expression in a written document, a subsequent oral variation of the contract is not effective unless it is evidenced by a memorandum or note in writing (see *Goss v Nugent*[9] and the speech of Lord Atkinson in *British and Beningtons Ltd v N. W. Cachar Tea Co. and Others*.[10] But in the other type of case, where the oral agreement is intended to be the contract, evidence may be given of an agreed variation even if there is a memorandum or note of the contract but not of the variation. This view is supported by the decision of the Court of Appeal in England in *Beckett v Nurse*.[11] In that case the plaintiff claimed specific performance of an alleged agreement for the sale of land and relied on a receipt as the memorandum or note in writing. The Court of Appeal held that the receipt was not the contract and that as the plaintiff was relying on an oral agreement for sale, the defendant was entitled to show that the real bargain between the parties was different from that contained in the memorandum.

In this case the evidence establishes that the oral contract made on 4 September was varied by mutual agreement on a subsequent date. The variation was that the defendants were to sell to the plaintiff not a freehold interest but a leasehold interest, but the amount of the rent to be paid and the date of the commencement of the lease were not agreed: as these were not agreed, there was never a valid contract to sell the property by lease or to grant a lease (see the judgment of the Supreme Court delivered by Mr Justice James Murnaghan in *Kerns v Manning*[12]).

Counsel for the plaintiff has also contended that the payment of £500 on 4 November was an act of part performance and that the Statute of Frauds is not therefore an answer to the plaintiff's claim. As there was not a valid contract between the parties, the question of part performance does not arise.

1. (1867) LR 2 HL 127.
2. 1 Cox 219.
3. 3 Mer. 53.
4. (1879) 4 CPD 459.
5. [1920] 1 Ch. 411.
6. [1937] 3 All ER 265.

7. [1957] 3 All ER 263, at p. 276.
8. [1920] 2 IR 365; [1921] 2 IR 438.
9. [1964] IR 292.
10. (1833) 5 B. & Ad. 58.
11. [1923] AC 48.
12. [1948] 1 All ER 81.

Note

1. In *Kelly v Ross & Ross* (HC) 29 April 1980, unrep. McWilliam J. also referred to the case of *Timmins v Moreland Street Pty Co. Ltd* [1957] 3 All ER 265 in holding that nine documents could not jointly constitute a memorandum for the purposes of the statute as the signed documents did not refer to the other documents.

2. In *Tradax (Ireland) Ltd v Irish Grain Board Ltd* [1984] IR 1 a majority of the Supreme Court held that a telex and a letter sent by the defendants with the object of cancelling the contracts constituted a sufficient note or memorandum for the purposes of s.4 of the Sale of Goods Act 1893. It was also noted in this case that even if no memorandum existed, the acceptance and receipt by the plaintiffs of part of the goods would have made the absence immaterial to the question of enforceability.

SECTION TWO—EQUITABLE MEANS OF ENFORCING THE CONTRACT

A. Part performance

The principle upon which the rule in cases of part performance was engrafted on the Statute of Frauds is, that it would be a fraud on the part of the person who had entered into an agreement by parol for a lease or sale, and had allowed expenditure to be made upon the faith of it, afterwards to turn around and say that it did not legally exist.

Per the Vice-Chancellor in *Hope v Lord Cloncurry* (1874) IR 8 Eq 555.

Lowry *v* Reid [1927] NI 142

The plaintiff's mother undertook to leave her property to the plaintiff, if he transferred his own farm together with £200 to his brother. The plaintiff did this and went to live with his mother. Although his mother made a will giving effect to their agreement, she later revoked it, leaving the plaintiff only a life interest in her property. The plaintiff sought specific performance of the agreement.

Wilson J. at first instance held that the plaintiff's action was unenforceable as there was no sufficient memorandum to evidence the agreement and that there was no part performance by the plaintiff's mother.

Moore L.C.J.:

...

Counsel for the respondents have attempted to put the case on a different ground based on certain dicta in the judgment of Lord Selborne in *Maddison v Alderson*.[1] They say that evidence of the parol contract cannot be admitted unless it is first established that the alleged acts of part performance unequivocally establish the existence of some such contract. If I have correctly stated this proposition, I can only say that I do not accept it. I think it is an inversion of the principle which should obtain. In my opinion, we must at some stage consider the contract and its effect, before we are in a position to judge, whether or not the acts relied on to take the case out of the statute are acts of part performance of the contract.

If such acts are not unequivocally referable to the performance of the contract, in whole or part, then the evidence as to them is irrelevant and the necessary proof of part performance fails. Lord Selborne's speech in *Maddison v Alderson* lays it down that 'the doctrine of part performance is applicable to any case in which a court of equity would before the statute have decreed specific performance.'

...

Now has there been such part performance of that contract as would entitle William to succeed in equity in a suit for specific performance? Would it be a fraud on the part of Mary Lowry to take advantage of the fact that there was no contract in writing pursuant to the statute?

...

In my judgment there is relief for him, because on the facts of the case, having given up his own property to his own detriment, on the faith of his mother's representation, this is a parol contract for the specific performance of which he is entitled in equity to a decree to carry those representations into execution, and if he is entitled to such a decree, he is equally entitled to rely on the doctrine of part performance to take the case out of the statute.

Andrews L.J.:

I further agree with Wilson J. that there is no sufficient note or memorandum of this parol agreement to satisfy the provisions of the Statute of Frauds; and, accordingly, the plaintiff must fail unless there has been a sufficient part performance of the contract to take the case out of the statute. Wilson J. held that the performance by William Lowry is complete. I agree. William conveyed all his estate and interest in the 48 acre Ballykeigle Farm to Andrew, who forthwith entered into and remained in possession until he sold it to his brother Hugh in 1920. William also paid Andrew the £200 agreed upon. But Wilson J. held that it was necessary that there should also be a part performance of the contract by Mary Lowry, and that the making of the will of 19 April 1916, and her allowing William to bring his wife to live at Drumhirk did not amount to such part performance.

When one considers the principle upon which the doctrine of part performance is based, it becomes, in my opinion, clear that no such performance on her part is required. In *Bond v Hopkins*[2] Lord Redesdale said: 'The Statute of Frauds says that no action or suit shall be maintained on an agreement relating to lands which is not in writing, signed by the party to be charged with it; and yet the court is in the daily habit of relieving, where the party seeking relief has been put into a situation which makes it against conscience in the other party to insist on the want of writing so signed, as a bar to his relief.' Thus the doctrine is a purely equitable one. Its underlying principle is, that the court will not allow a statute which was passed to prevent fraud to be made itself an instrument of fraud. In other words, the court disregards the absence of that formality which the statute requires when insistence upon it would render it a means of effecting, instead of a means of averting, fraud. The question in each case is, whether the plaintiff has an equity arising from part performance which is so affixed upon the conscience of the defendant that it would amount to a fraud on his part to take advantage of the fact that the contract is not in writing. The right to relief rests not so much on the contract as on what has been done in pursuance or in execution of it. Under the statute the note or memorandum of the contract must be signed by the party to be charged. Under the doctrine of part performance the equity must be possessed, not by the party to be charged, but by the plaintiff—the person who seeks relief; and this equity arises from his part performance of the contract.

. . .

I see no reason in principle, nor has any authority been cited to us to show, why a party who seeks contractual relief in regard to certain lands cannot rely as acts of part performance upon his own acts to other lands in furtherance of the same contract. . . . and, in my opinion, there could be no foundation for the suggestion that the doctrine does not apply to contracts for the exchange of lands, as in my judgment the doctrine applies to all contracts of which, before the Judicature Act, a court of equity would have granted specific performance if the alleged contract had been in writing; and these are not confined to contracts for the sale of land. . . . I would add that I can find no authority to support |counsel for the defendant's| contention that it is not permissible even to consider the terms of the parol agreement until it is clearly established that the acts of part performance refer unequivocally to the contract relied upon, and to that alone. Indeed, it would be, in my opinion, impossible to apply the proposition as so stated in practice; for how, I ask, could it be said that the acts of part performance referred unequivocally to an agreement the terms of which were *ex hypothesi* not known, unless, indeed, they were acts of such a clear, cogent, and conclusive character that they embodied and themselves proved the actual terms of the agreement, in which case it would be wholly unnecessary for the plaintiff to make any reference to or to rely in any way upon the parol agreement. In support of his contention |counsel| referred us to a passage in Lord O'Hagan's judgment in *Maddison v Alderson*, where he said:

> Next, assuming that the action must be considered maintainable, if at all, for the purpose of enforcing a parol contract, partly performed, the course of the argument appears to me to have been further erroneous in this, that, instead of seeking to establish primarily such a performance as must necessarily imply the existence of the contract, and then proceeding to ascertain its terms, it reversed the order of the

contention. The court was asked, from the findings of the jury and the testimony supporting them, to say there was a contract; and then to discover in the conduct of the parties acts of performance sufficient to validate the bargain so previously ascertained.

If these words are to be taken literally, and to be construed as deciding that the acts of performance must in themselves necessarily imply the existence of *the* contract, that is, the precise contract pleaded, I am not prepared to accept them as containing a correct statement of the law, being, as they are, at variance with the terms of the classical judgment of the Earl of Selborne C. in the same case, and, indeed, as it seems to me, with other passages of Lord O'Hagan's own judgment. Thus in the central paragraph on p. 485, he says: 'It (i.e. the act which shall amount to a part performance) must be sufficient to itself, and without any other information or evidence, to satisfy a court, from the circumstances it has created and the relations it has formed, that they are only consistent with the assumption of the existence of *a* contract, the terms of which equity requires, if possible, to be ascertained and enforced.' (The italics are my own.)

It may be said that in the next paragraph of his judgment Lord O'Hagan again reverts to the principle that the acts must, of necessity, imply the existence of *the* agreement pleaded; but this portion of his judgment follows and is inconsistent with the passage from the judgment of Sir William Grant in *Frame v Dawson*,[3] which he cited with approval on p. 484: 'The principle of the cases is, that the act must be of such a nature, that if stated, it would of itself infer the existence of *some* agreement,' (again the italics are my own); 'and then parol evidence is admitted to show what the agreement is.'

I have referred to the Earl of Selborne's judgment, from which I shall only make two extracts—the first, the passage at p. 476, to which |counsel for the plaintiff| referred us in his very forcible reply:

> It is not arbitrary or unreasonable to hold that when the statute says that no action is to be brought to charge any person upon a contract concerning land, it has in view the simple case in which he is charged upon the contract only, and not that in which there are equities resulting from *res gestae* subsequent to and arising out of the contract. So long as the connexion of those *res gestae* with the alleged contract does not depend upon mere parol testimony, but is reasonably to be inferred from the *res gestae* themselves, justice seems to require some such limitation of the scope of the statute.

The second passage is taken from p. 479, where the learned Lord Chancellor summarises the effect of the cases in the following terms: 'All the authorities show that the acts relied upon as part performance must be unequivocally and in their own nature referable to some such agreement as that alleged.' These words 'some such agreement' are also adopted as his own by Lord Fitzgerald in his judgment in the same case at p. 491.

I would like to refer to one other case of recognised authority, *Morphett v Jones*,[4] where Sir T. Plumer, referring to the equitable doctrine, says that 'Admission into possession, having unequivocal reference to the contract, has always been considered an act of part performance. The acknowledged possession of a stranger in the land of another is not explicable except on the supposition of an agreement, and has, therefore, constantly been received as evidence of an antecedent contract, and as sufficient to authorise an inquiry into the terms.' In the opinion, therefore, of this eminent authority the sole requisite preliminary to inquiry into and proof of the terms of the parol agreement is the establishment of an act which is only explicable on the basis of the existence of some contract.

I make no apology for citing, in conclusion, as a correct summary of the law a passage from *Fry on Specific Performance*, (5th ed.) 292, where the editor states that the true principle of the operation of acts of part performance seems only to require that the acts in question be such as must be referred to some contract, and may be referred to the alleged one; that they prove the existence of some contract, and are consistent with the contract alleged.

1. 8 AC 457.		3. 14 Ves. 387.	
2. 1 Sch. & L., 413 at 433.		4. 1 Swanston, 181	

(Best L.J. concurred and the appeal was allowed.)

Philip Howlin v Thomas Power (Dublin) Ltd (HC) 5 May 1978, unrep.

The defendant entered into an oral agreement to surrender a leasehold interest to the plaintiff. The plaintiff paid £200 as part of the purchase price. The defendant then refused to complete the agreement and tendered repayment of the £200. Although the agreement was not evidenced by a written memorandum, the plaintiff claimed that his actions in negotiating a new tenancy and/or paying the £200 constituted sufficient acts of part performance. The plaintiff thus sought specific performance of the oral agreement.

McWilliam J.:

. . .

The plaintiff then relies on acts of part performance as taking the case out of the statute. To take the first of these. The plaintiff has given evidence that he made an arrangement with an agent to let the premises to a building society with vacant possession of 1 February 1977, at the yearly rent of £2,500.00 and rates. It does not appear that there was any contract in writing with the building society and, in cross-examination, the plaintiff stated that he had had negotiations about letting in December, towards the end of that month, and that he wrote to the estate agent that he would have vacant possession on 31 January. On this aspect of part performance I have been referred to the following cases:

Lowry v Reid |1927| NI 142, Brough v Nettleton |1921| 2 Ch. 25, Broughton v Snook |1938| 1 Ch. 505, Daniels v Trefusis |1914| 1 Ch. 788, Estate of Earl of Longford 5 LR (Ir) 99.

I have also read the case of *Crowley v Sullivan* |1900| 2 IR 478 cited in the case of *Lowry v Reid*. In each of these cases the plaintiff had taken some conclusive or irrevocable or prejudicial step in pursuance of the contract, such as conveying land to a third party, entering into occupation of premises agreed to be let or sold to him, ejecting tenants at the request of the other party or commencing to carry on a business in partnership in pursuance of an agreement to do so. The principle established by these and other cases appears to be that, where the party seeking relief in proceedings has taken some step in pursuance of the contract which has left him in such a position that it would amount to a fraud or be inequitable on the part of the other party to rely on the fact that there was no sufficient memorandum of the contract, the case is taken out of the statute and the court will enforce the contract. With regard to negotiating a tenancy in the present case, the plaintiff does not appear to have prejudiced himself in any way by reason of the contract with the defendant or left himself in a position where he could be required to perform any act which he was not able to do. He merely appears to have consulted or instructed estate agents with regard to negotiating a letting and to have discussed terms with them and with a possible tenant but without entering into any binding contract. Accordingly, apart from causing him disappointment at the loss of his bargain, I cannot see that there is, on these facts, any special equity to take the case out of the statute.

With regard to the payment and acceptance of the sum of £200.00 as part of the purchase price, I have been referred to the cases of *Steadman v Steadman* |1976| AC 536 and *Re. Gonin decd*, |1977| 2 All ER 720. It is urged, on the authority of the former case, that, if the payment of the money is referable only to the contract alleged, it is a sufficient act of part performance. Until this case was brought to my attention, I had accepted the proposition that the mere payment of money could not constitute a sufficient act of part performance. Four of the five judges in the House of Lords and two of the three judges in the Court of Appeal refused, in Steadman's case, to accept that this proposition was well founded and, in the unusual circumstances of that case, held that the payment of £100 by a husband to his wife was a sufficient act of part performance of a contract containing four provisions for the compromise of matrimonial proceedings. I cannot disagree with the reasoning of the majority of the judges in that case but, accepting that the decision is correct on the question of the mere payment of money constituting an act of part performance sufficient to take the case out of the statute, I must keep before my mind that the statute does provide that a contract for the sale of land shall not be enforceable unless there is a sufficient note or memorandum thereof in writing and that the application of the doctrine of part performance is still confined to cases in which it would be fraudulent or inequitable for a defendant to rely on the statute because a plaintiff has prejudiced himself in some way by reason of the contract. As I have stated, this is not shown to have occurred in the present case and the following passage from the judgment of Lord Reid in *Steadman's* case at p. 541 appears to me to be relevant. It is as follows:

> Normally the consideration for the purchase of land is a sum of money and there are statements that a sum of money can never be treated as part performance. Such statements would be reasonable if the person pleading the statute tendered repayment of any part of the price which he had received and was thus able to make *restitutio in integrum*. That would remove any 'fraud' or any equity on which the purchaser could properly rely. But to make a general rule that payment of money can never be part performance would seem to me to defeat the whole purpose of the doctrine and I do not think that we are compelled to do that.

Here, not only was the sum of money paid comparatively small, but it was actually tendered in repayment to the plaintiff. Accordingly, I do not accept that this payment was sufficient to take the case out of the statute.

Note

1. In *Silver Wraith Ltd v Siuicre Eireann*, 8 June 1989 (see p. 119) Keane J. noted *obiter* that 'as a matter of probability' the plaintiff failed to establish that the expenditure incurred was unequivocally referable to the type of contract alleged. Therefore a plea of part performance was unsuccessful.
2. Even if part performance is not successful, the plaintiff may use a *quantum meruit* plea to obtain the return of wasted expenditure or the value of services rendered: *Deglman v Guarantee Trust* |1954| 3 DLR 785.

B. OTHER EQUITABLE DEVICES

A failure to satisfy the Statute of Frauds or the doctrine of part performance may not necessarily be fatal. The courts may avail of other equitable devices in oder to avoid the perpetration of fraud.

In *The McGillycuddy of the Reeks v David Joy and William Joy* [1959] IR 189 Budd J. expressly approved the dicta of Lindley L.J. in *Rochefoucauld v Boustead* [1897] 1 Ch. 196 where the latter states:

It is further established . . . that the Statute of Frauds does not prevent the proof of a fraud; and that it is a fraud on the part of a person to whom land is conveyed as a trustee, and who knows it was so conveyed, to deny the trust and claim the land himself. Consequently, notwithstanding the statute, it is competent for a person claiming land conveyed to another to prove by parol evidence that it was so conveyed upon trust for the claimant, and that the grantee, knowing the facts, is denying the trust and relying upon the form of conveyance and the statute, in order to keep the land himself.

John Doherty v John Gallagher (HC) 9 June 1975, unrep.

The plaintiff agreed to buy certain property from the defendant for £3,500 and gave him a cheque for £500 as a deposit. The property to be sold was described on the face of the cheque. The parties agreed that the defendant would be allowed keep his cattle on the property until he had a reasonable opportunity to sell them. The defendant endorsed and cashed the cheque, but later refused to complete the contract and returned the £500.When the plaintiff sued for specific performance the defendant claimed *inter alia* that the cheque was not a sufficient note or memorandum for the purposes of the Statute of Frauds because it omitted any reference to the agreement to allow the defendant graze his cattle for a time on the property.

Finlay P.:

. . .

In general I am satisfied that there must be in this context a much greater danger of permitting injustice and in that sense encouraging a fraud by a strict application of the Statute of Frauds than by a liberal application. It seems to me that where the term alleged to have been omitted from the note or memorandum relied on applies solely to the question of the date for completion of the transaction or for the giving over of vacant possession and certainly where that term was never expressed by the parties at the time of the making of the contract in a precise or definite fashion and where the party seeking to enforce the contract has before the institution of proceedings allowed an ample reasonable time for the vendor to complete his contract that it would be an injustice to refuse an order for specific performance on the grounds that what can only be considered a vague assurance of reasonable time or even of ample time was not set out in the note or memorandum.

. . .

The object of the Statute of Frauds is to prevent the mischief arising or likely to arise from proof by parol evidence of the contract or its terms.

I cannot see any logical basis for a contention that such a mischief could arise where the only alleged term of the contract not evidenced by an appropriate memorandum in writing is a vague assurance of ample time and where what can only be described as ample time is allowed to elapse before the defendant is firmly called upon to perform the contract.

In this case on the evidence before me I am satisfied that it is quite improbable that had the defendant not changed his mind for other reasons or as is expressed in the letter written on his behalf by O'Donnell & Sweeney for family reasons and refused to proceed with this sale that any term would have been written into any subsequent legal contract providing for the grazing of the cattle or the time for selling them off. I think it much more probable that the easy going dealing and general goodwill of two neighbours both of whom knew each other over a long period of time in agreement about the sale of land would have been sufficient to carry out the sort of assurance that had been given.

I am therefore satisfied that the absence of a reference to this assurance in the note or memorandum consisting of the cheque which is otherwise complete is not fatal to its compliance with the Statute of Frauds and that this defence also fails. I am therefore satisfied that the plaintiff is entitled to an order for specific performance.

Waiver

Nora Healy *v* Daniel Healy (HC) 3 December 1973, unrep.

Kenny J.:

On principle it seems to me that when a clause in a contract (whether it is a condition or a term) is inserted solely for the benefit of one party and is severable from the other clauses and when the other party on completion will get everything that he contracted for, the party for whose benefit the clause was inserted may waive performance of the clause and insist on completion despite the non-performance of the condition or term.

Anom Engineering Ltd *v* Thornton (HC) 1 February 1983, unrep.

The defendants entered into an oral agreement to sell the plaintiffs a parcel of property. The defendants' solicitors later sent the plaintiffs a draft contract and documents of title. No agreement was reached at this stage as to the power and water services and the discharge of effluent into the defendants' water course. When the defendants refused to complete the agreement the plaintiffs sued for specific performance. The defendants claimed that no memorandum existed to evidence the oral agreement.

Costello J.:
. . .

The general principle of law which I must now consider is well settled. The memorandum of the agreement which is called for by the statute must contain all the essential terms which the parties have agreed. What is or is not an essential term may be a matter of considerable debate. In *Tweddell v Henderson* [1975] 1 WLR 1496, the judgment is an indication of how a court may regard some terms of a contract as essential to the contract for sale, for example terms of the payment of the purchase price by instalments, and other terms as mainly incidental to the contract, for example, terms relating to details of the construction of the building to be built on the land. The test to be applied is a subjective one and the court is required to consider those terms as essential to the contract which were so regarded by the parties themselves. (See *Barrett v Costello* 107 ILT and SJ p. 239).

. . .

It is urged on the plaintiffs' behalf that if I were to hold that no sufficient memorandum existed relating to the terms of:

(a) the water and power supply and/or
(b) the effluent and storm water discharge

that the plaintiffs were entitled to waive the benefit of those terms and were entitled to seek the specific performance of the contract as evidenced by the memorandum of 8 May or any other memorandum contained in the correspondence. The principle of law to be applied on this aspect of the law of specific performance has been stated by Kenny J. as follows:

> My view is that when parties conclude an oral contract which contains a term wholly for the benefit of one of them and there is a written memorandum which does not contain any reference to that term the party for whose benefit the term was inserted may waive it and sue successfully on the contract of which there is a memorandum. The note in writing for the purpose of the Statute of Frauds has to be of the contract sued on not the contract made and the plaintiff may waive a term which is wholly in his favour and which is not referred to in the memorandum. (See *Barrett v Costello* quoted in Wiley *Irish Conveyancing Law* para. 9.007 and also *Tiernan Homes Ltd v Fagan and Others* (SC) 23 July 1981, unrep.).

Applying the waiver principle to this case it seems to me that the express agreement relating to the right to connect at agreed points on the defendants' land to obtain a supply of power and water was a stipulation in the agreement entirely for the benefit of the plaintiffs and that they can waive this express stipulation and obtain specific performance of the rest of the agreed terms because they were evidenced in writing. . . .

Nathaniel Black v Celine Grealy (HC) 10 November 1977, unrep.

The plaintiff entered into an agreement with Mr Finnegan, the defendant's agent to buy property from the defendant for £46,000. Mr Finnegan arranged for the plaintiff to pay the defendant £6,000 in advance and the memorandum noted a price of £40,000. When the plaintiff queried why the memorandum did not reflect the agreement, Mr Finnegan promised that matters would be organised. As a result the plaintiff signed the memorandum. When the defendant refused to complete the sale the plaintiff sued for specific performance.

Costello J.:

. . .

No action can be brought upon a contract for the sale of land unless the agreement upon which the action is brought or some note or memorandum thereof is in writing. The voluminous case law on the Statute of Frauds establishes that the memorandum to satisfy the statute must contain all the 'essential' or the 'material' terms of the agreement, and accordingly the parties, the property and the consideration must be ascertainable from the memorandum relied on (see Kingsmill Moore, J. *Godley v Power*, 95 ILTR 135 at 145). It is also clear, as pointed out by Mr Justice Kenny in *Barrett v Costello* (107 ILT and SJ p. 339) that the only terms which must appear in the written contract are those regarded by the parties as being material provisions. In that case the court granted a decree for specific performance of an oral contract, holding that the parties had not regarded a number of terms (including one relating to the deposit) as being material and that their omission from the written document relied on to satisfy the statute did not render it insufficient. It will, however, be noted that in the circumstances of the present case the document relied on does not omit the consideration—it contains a figure for the consideration for the sale which the evidence establishes is the balance of the purchase price. Nor is it a case in which an omission arose by mistake so that the jurisdiction of the court to rectify the memorandum and order specific performance of the oral agreement (see: *United States of America and Another v Motor Trucks Ltd*, |1924| AC 196 and *Nolan v Graves and Another*, |1946| IR 376) arises. This is a case in which the parties (through their agents) entered into an oral agreement for the sale of land and as part of the agreement decided that the full purchase price would not be disclosed, but that the balance after the payment of the deposit would be treated as the purchase price in the written memorandum which it was agreed should be signed by the purchaser. It is not apt to describe the resultant written document as a memorandum 'of' the parties' oral agreement (as it does not properly state the full consideration for the sale); rather it is a memorandum which is 'in accordance with' one of the stipulations of the oral agreement—which is not quite the same thing. I do not think therefore that this memorandum satisfies the statute. But the statute cannot be used as an instrument of fraud, and it would in my opinion be a fraudulent use of the statute if the court permitted the defendant to avoid liability on foot of the oral agreement on the ground that the memorandum of it, which was prepared expressly in accordance with his wishes and for his benefit, was inadequate because it treated the balance of the purchase price as the purchase price. It follows, therefore, that the plea of the statute fails and that the plaintiff is entitled to have the oral agreement specifically enforced.

I should add that the question of an estoppel arising in the circumstances of the present case was not argued before me and so I refrain from basing my decision on this ground. I should, however, point out that there may well be cases (and this could be one of them) where a party, expressly agreeing to accept the adequacy of a memorandum of an oral agreement, is in subsequent proceedings estopped from alleging its inadequacy.

The plaintiff's counsel relied on a further submission to defeat the plea of the statute. It is one which I accept and is a further reason why the order sought should in my opinion be granted. This submission was based on the principle applied in *Scott v Bradley* (|1971| 1 All ER 583) which was stated in *Williams Vendor and Purchaser* (4th ed.) vol. 1, 4, as follows:

> It is essential, however, whether the writing given in evidence is of a formal or informal nature, that the terms of the agreement sought to be proved thereby shall be sufficiently ascertained therein. The parties to the contract and the property sold must therefore be sufficiently described, and the price, or the means of ascertaining it, be stated; and any other terms of the bargain (except, of course, such as are implied by law, as that a good title should be shown) must be defined. It appears, however, that if a stipulation which is to the detriment or for the benefit of one of the parties exclusively is omitted from the memorandum, that party may submit to perform it

or waive the benefit of it (as the case may require) and may with such submission or waiver specifically enforce the contract as stated in the memorandum.

Martin v Pycroft (1852 2 De GM & G 785) is one of the cases relied on by the author to justify the principle which I have quoted. That was a case in which a tenant sought specific performance of a written agreement for a lease. The tenant had agreed to pay a premium of £200, but this term was omitted from the written agreement. In the course of the proceedings he offered to pay this sum, and as a result a decree for specific performance was made and a plea of the statute failed. Part of the judgment of Knight Bruce L.J. reads as follows:

> And our opinion is that, where persons sign a written agreement upon a subject, obnoxious or not to the statute which has been so particularly referred to, and there has been no circumvention, no fraud, nor (in the sense in which the term 'mistake' must be considered as used for this purpose) mistake, the written agreement binds at law and in equity, according to its terms, although verbally a provision was agreed to, which has not been inserted in the document; subject to this, that either of the parties sued in equity upon it may perhaps be entitled in general to ask the court to be neutral, unless the plaintiff will consent to the performance of the omitted term.

Martin v Pycroft was quoted with approval in *North v Loomes* ([1919] 1 Ch. 378) in which the plaintiff obtained an order for specific performance when he waived a term in the oral agreement which was solely to his benefit but which was omitted from the written memorandum. In *Scott v Bradley* the court was concerned with the omission from a memorandum of a term of an oral agreement which provided that the plaintiff would pay half the defendants' legal costs of the sale. Plowman J. held that this term was in fact a material term of the agreement, but notwithstanding this fact and its absence from the written memorandum of the contract a decree for specific performance was granted, on the plaintiff submitting to be bound by the missing term.

In the present case the term that is missing from the memorandum is one which is to the detriment of the plaintiff. From the memorandum of 6 October 1976 it would seem that the purchase price of the property was £40,000, but in fact the oral agreement provided that the purchase price was to be £46,000. What is missing from the memorandum are terms of the oral agreement which can be paraphrased as follows: 'the purchase price of the property is £46,000; of which £6,000 will be paid forthwith, the parties treating the balance as the purchase price in any written memorandum of the agreement which may be drawn up'. The plaintiff, through his counsel accepts that the purchase price was £46,000 has submitted to be bound by this term, accordingly the plaintiff is entitled to an order for specific performance of the oral agreement.

Note

The limits of part performance are uncertain. Contrast the US model.

American Law Institute Restatement Contracts (2d) S. 139

139. Enforcement by Virtue of Action in Reliance

    (1) A promise which the promisor should reasonably expect to induce action or forbearance on the part of the promisee or a third person and which does induce the action or forbearance is enforceable notwithstanding the Statute

of Frauds if injustice can be avoided only by enforcement of the promise. The remedy granted for breach is to be limited as justice requires.

(2) In determining whether injustice can be avoided only by enforcement of the promise, the following circumstances are significant:

(a) the availability and adequacy of other remedies, particularly cancellation and restitution;
(b) the definite and substantial character of the action of forbearance in relation to the remedy sought;
(c) the extent to which the action or forbearance corroborates evidence of the making and terms of the promise, or the making and terms are otherwise established by clear and convincing evidence;
(d) the reasonableness of the action or forbearance;
(e) the extent to which the action or forbearance was foreseeable by the promisor.

Debate on Reform

Eoin Boyle and Susan Boyle *v* Maura Lee and Eve Goyns [1992] ILRM 65
(Facts on p. 106.)

O'Flaherty J.:
. . .
. . . The Statute of Frauds was enacted to prevent perjury and subornation of perjury as well as other fraudulent practices. In due course, equity made sure that the invocation of the statute should not be used to bring about fraud and, thus, was developed the doctrine of part performance. However, it seems to me that equity has now done its work and the statute should be looked at again because what it is now necessary to prevent is the burgeoning of actions based on subtleties and niceties to get around the clear wording of the statute. For my part, I would advocate that the statute should be amended so as to provide that all contracts for the sale of land should be in writing. This is because life has not got any less complicated over the intervening centuries; nowadays, as this very case illustrates, there are often planning aspects to a sale; there is finance to be arranged; there is the tax end of matters to be sorted out (in this case there was the question of certain furnishings being part of the sale and no apportionment had been made in relation to them); family law legislation may often have some relevance, and, further, there is the fact that the boundaries of negligence in relation to people involved in the buying and selling of property have been widened over the last number of decades. In these circumstances, I would rather the occasional gazumper go unbound than that people should be involved in needless uncertainty leading often to long drawn out litigation.

I think such a law would accord with the view the average person—not versed in the mysteries of conveyancing law—would take who knows that when he buys a dwelling house or other property in the normal course of events it is necessary to have a proper contract executed to bind both parties.

Chapter Six

Express Terms

INTRODUCTION

It is an essential feature of a contract that the boundaries of the contract be capable of clear delineation. In Chapter 2 we saw that if contractual terms are ambiguous or uncertain the court may be compelled to hold the contract void for uncertainty. A number of contrasting, or indeed contradictory, statements may have been made during negotiations, and it is not unreasonable for a judge to decide that if the parties have troubled themselves to write down their agreement, they intended that document to be their agreement to the exclusion of all else. While this approach retains some vitality, the ultimate consideration is whether the contract gives effect to the intention of the parties, and it is increasingly likely that a contract may be a mixture of verbal promises, standardised clauses and custom-made documents. Indeed, the use of printed conditions is closely scrutinised by the judiciary for unfair contract practices under both the common law and under statutory fiat—see Chapter 8.

In this chapter we introduce the reader to the methods whereby contractual and non-contractual terms are identified. In Chapter 10 the reader will discover how these terms can give rise to a broad range of remedies, depending on how they are further classified.

SECTION ONE—DISTINGUISHING TERMS OF A CONTRACT FROM MERE REPRESENTATIONS

It is essential to distinguish a term of a contract, a breach of which will give rise to contractual liability and in particular liability in damages, from a mere representation which will not.

Oscar Chess Ltd *v* Williams [1957] 1 WLR 370

The defendant agreed to exchange his Morris car with the plaintiff car dealer for a new car. Both parties believed the Morris to be a 1948 model, as evidenced by its registration book. It materialised later that the car was a 1939 model. The plaintiffs sued for damages for breach of a condition or, alternatively, a warranty. At first instance damages were awarded. The defendant appealed.

Denning L.J.:

. . .

The effect of such a mistake is this: It does not make the contract a nullity from the beginning, but it does in some circumstances enable the contract to be set aside in equity. If the buyer had come promptly, he might have succeeded in getting the whole transaction set aside in equity on the ground of this mistake: see *Solle v Butcher*;[1] but he did not do so and it is now too late for him to do it; see *Leaf v International Galleries*.[2] His only remedy is in damages, and to recover these he must prove a warranty.

In saying that he must prove a warranty, I use the word 'warranty' in its ordinary English meaning to denote a binding promise. Everyone knows what a man means when he says 'I guarantee it' or 'I warrant it' or 'I give you my word on it.' He means that he binds himself to it. That is the meaning it has borne in English law for 300 years from the leading case of *Chandelor v Lopus*[3] onwards. During the last fifty years, however, some lawyers have come to use the word 'warranty' in another sense. They use it to denote a subsidiary term in a contract as distinct from a vital term which they call a 'condition'. In so doing they depart from the ordinary meaning, not only of the word 'warranty' but also of the word 'condition'. There is no harm in their doing this, so long as they confine this technical use to its proper sphere, namely to distinguish between a vital term, the breach of which gives the right to treat the contract as at an end, and a subsidiary term which does not. But the trouble comes when one person uses the word 'warranty' in its ordinary meaning and another uses it in its technical meaning. When Holt C.J., in *Crosse v Gardner*[4] and *Medina v Stoughton*,[5] made his famous ruling that an affirmation at the time of a sale is a warranty, provided it appears on evidence to be so intended, he used the word 'warranty' in its ordinary English meaning of a binding promise; and when Lord Haldane L.C. and Lord Moulton in 1913 in *Heilbut, Symons & Co. v Buckleton*,[6] adopted his ruling, they used it likewise in its ordinary meaning. These different uses of the word seem to have been the source of confusion in the present case. The judge did not ask himself, 'Was the representation (that it was a 1948 Morris) intended to be a warranty?' He asked himself, 'Was it fundamental to the contract?' He answered it by saying that it was fundamental; and therefore it was a condition and not a warranty. By concentrating on whether it was fundamental, he seems to me to have missed the crucial point in the case which is whether it was a term of the contract at all. The crucial question is: was it a binding promise or only an innocent misrepresentation? The technical distinction between a 'condition' and a 'warranty' is quite immaterial in this case, because it is far too late for the buyer to reject the car. He can at best only claim damages. The material distinction here is between a statement which is a term of the contract and a statement which is only an innocent misrepresentation. This distinction is best expressed by the ruling of Lord Holt: Was it intended as a warranty or not? using the word warranty there in its ordinary English meaning: because it gives the exact shade of meaning that is required. It is something to which a man must be taken to bind himself.

In applying Lord Holt's test, however, some misunderstanding has arisen by the use of the word 'intended'. It is sometimes supposed that the tribunal must look into the minds of the parties to see what they themselves intended. That is a mistake. Lord Moulton made it quite clear that 'The intention of the parties can only be deduced from the totality of the evidence.' The question whether a warranty was intended depends on the conduct of the parties, on their words and behaviour, rather than on their thoughts. If an intelligent bystander would reasonably infer that a warranty was intended, that will suffice. And this, when the facts are not in dispute, is a question of law.

. . .

What is the proper inference from the known facts? It must have been obvious to both that the seller had himself no personal knowledge of the year when the car was made. He only became owner after a great number of changes. He must have been relying on the registration book. It is unlikely that such a person would warrant the year of manufacture. The most he would do would be to state his belief, and then produce the registration book in verification of it. In these circumstances the intelligent bystander would, I suggest, say that the seller did not intend to bind himself so as to warrant that it was a 1948 model. If the seller was asked to pledge himself to it, he would at once have said 'I cannot do that. I have only the log book to go by, the same as you.'
. . .

One final word: It seems to me clear that the motor dealers who bought the car relied on the year stated in the log book. If they had wished to make sure of it, they could have checked it then and there, by taking the engine number and chassis number and writing to the makers. They did not do so at the time, but only eight months later. They are experts, and, not having made that check at the time, I do not think they should now be allowed to recover against the innocent seller who produced to them all the evidence he had, namely, the registration book. I agree that it is hard on the dealers to have paid more than the car is worth; but it would be equally hard on the seller to make him pay the difference. . . .

1. [1950] 1 KB 671; 66 TLR (Pt. 1) 448; [1949] 2 All ER 1107.
2. [1950] 2 KB 86; 66 TLR (Pt 1) 1031; [1950] 1 All ER 693.
3. (1603) Cro. Jac. 4.
4. (1689) Carth. 90, as glossed by Buller J. in *Pasley v Freeman* (1789) 3 Term Rep. 51, 57.
5. (1699) 1 Salk. 210.
6. [1913] AC 30, 38, 50, 51.

(Hodson L.J. concurred.)

Note

In *Dick Bentley Productions Ltd v Harold Smith (Motors) Ltd* [1965] 1 WLR the *Oscar Chess* case was distinguished. There, a dealer sold a car to a private individual and the Court of Appeal held that a statement by the dealer as to the mileage of the car constituted a warranty binding on the seller. Denning L.J. stated that the dealer was in a better position than the other party to verify the truth of the statement.

The Governor and Company of the Bank of Ireland v William Smith [1966] IR 646

An advertisement of land for sale erroneously stated that a portion of the lands was sown with barley and undersown with permanent pasture. This statement was made honestly but mistakenly by the vendor's agents. The purchaser discovered the mistake, and sued for damages for breach of a warranty.

Kenny J.:

. . .

The next argument was that the statement in the advertisement about the under-sowing of the barley was a warranty and not an innocent misrepresentation. Counsel for the defendants said that the statement was not a warranty and that the matter was concluded by the speech of Lord Moulton in *Heilbut, Symons & Co. v Buckleton*.[1] Lord Moulton, who quoted the much praised remark of Holt C.J., 'An affirmation at the time of the sale is a warranty, provided it appear on evidence to be so intended' (a statement which contains at least two ambiguities), went on to say:

> It is . . . of the greatest importance, in my opinion, that this House should maintain in its full integrity the principle that a person is not liable in damages for an innocent misrepresentation, no matter in what way or under what form the attack is made. In the present case the statement was made in answer to an inquiry for information. There is nothing which can by any possibility be taken as evidence of an intention on the part of either or both of the parties that there should be a contractual liability in respect of the accuracy of the statement. It is a representation as to a specific thing and nothing more. The judge, therefore, ought not to have left the question of warranty to the jury, and if, as a matter of prudence, he did so in order to obtain their opinion in case of an appeal, he ought then to have entered judgment for the defendants notwithstanding the verdict.

In an earlier part of his speech he had said:

> It is not contested that the only company referred to was the Filisola Rubber and Produce Estates Ltd, or that the reply of Mr Johnston to the plaintiff's question over the telephone was a representation by the defendants that the company was a 'rubber company', whatever may be the meaning of that phrase; nor is there any controversy as to the legal nature of that which the plaintiff must establish. He must show a warranty, i.e. a contract collateral to the main contract to take the shares, whereby the defendants in consideration of the plaintiff taking the shares promised that the company itself was a rubber company. The question in issue is whether there was any evidence that such a contract was made between the parties.
>
> It is evident, both on principle and on authority, that there may be a contract the consideration for which is the making of some other contract. 'If you will make such and such a contract I will give you £100,' is in every sense of the word a complete legal contract. It is collateral to the main contract, but each has an independent existence, and they do not differ in respect of their possessing to the full the character and status of a contract. But such collateral contracts must from their very nature be rare. . . . Such collateral contracts, the sole effect of which is to vary or add to the terms of the principal contract, are therefore viewed with suspicion by the law.

See also the decision in *Gilchester Properties v Gomm*,[2] in which an innocent misrepresentation made in connection with a sale was held not to be a warranty and not to entitle the purchaser to damages.

The modern cases, however, show a welcome tendency to treat a representation made in connection with a sale as being a warranty, unless the person who made it can show that he was innocent of fault in connection with it. The rule that an innocent misrepresentation causing loss does not entitle a person to recover damages for its falsity produces injustice in many cases. In *Oscar Chess Ltd v Williams*,[3] Denning L.J., having referred to the famous ruling of Holt C.J., said: 'The question whether a warranty was intended depends on the conduct of the parties, on their words and behaviour rather than on their thoughts. If an intelligent bystander would reasonably infer that a warranty was intended, that will suffice,' and in *Dick Bentley Productions Ltd v Smith (Motors) Ltd*[4] the same judge said:

> It seems to me that if a representation is made in the course of dealings for a contract for the very purpose of inducing the other party to act on it, and it actually induces him to act on it by entering into the contract, that is *prima facie* ground for inferring that the representation was intended as a warranty. It is not necessary to speak of it as being collateral. Suffice it that the representation was intended to be acted upon and was in fact acted on. But the maker of the representation can rebut this inference if he can show that it really was an innocent misrepresentation, in that he was in fact innocent of fault in making it, and that it would not be reasonable in the circumstances for him to be bound by it.

I have not had the advantage of hearing counsel on these two cases but I believe that they express the true rule.

The statement in the advertisement was a representation and was made with the intention of inducing a purchaser to act on it: the purchaser was induced to enter into the contract by it. The representation was incorrect, but was made innocently and honestly. . . . it would be against conscience that the vendor in a court sale should not be bound by a representation made by his agent in connection with that sale.

It follows, in my opinion, that the purchaser is entitled to recover damages for breach of warranty relating to the undersowing of 40 acres.

1. [1913] AC 30.
2. [1948] 1 All ER 493.
3. [1957] 1 All ER 325.
4. [1965] 2 All ER 65.

Note

1. Why does the principle of *caveat emptor* not apply to these cases?
2. In *Schawel v Reade* (1) [1913] 2 IR 64 the House of Lords held that a statement to a prospective purchaser: 'You need not look at anything; the horse is perfectly sound. If there was anything the matter with the horse I would tell you' was an express warranty made for the purposes of the sale.

SECTION TWO—CONDITIONS, WARRANTIES AND INTERMEDIATE STIPULATIONS

Sale of Goods Act 1893 (as amended by the Sale of Goods and Supply of Services Act 1980) s.11(2) states:

Whether a stipulation in a contract of sale is a condition, the breach of which may give rise to a right to treat the contract as repudiated, or a warranty, the breach of which may give rise to a claim for damages but not to a right to reject the goods and treat the contract as repudiated, depends in each case on the construction of the contract. A stipulation may be a condition though called a warranty in the contract.

S.62 of the Sale of Goods Act 1893 defines a warranty for the purposes of the Act as 'an agreement with reference to goods which are the subject of a contract of sale, but collateral to the main purpose of such contract, the breach of which gives rise to a claim for damages, but not to a right to reject the goods and treat the contract as repudiated.'

A. CONDITIONS PRECEDENT AND CONDITIONS SUBSEQUENT

Re Application of Butler [1970] IR 45

The applicant was involved in an accident on 24 June 1963. A condition of his policy required the applicant to give written notice to the company 'as soon as practicable' after any accident. As he had been informed that the insurance company was insolvent, notice of the accident was not given until a year later. Fulfilment of the conditions in the policy was stated to be 'conditions precedent to any liability'. Damages were later awarded against the applicant as a result of the accident. A special fund was set up to meet the claims of policyholders of the insurance company and the applicant sought indemnification. The Supreme Court held that no sum was due to the applicant as there had been a breach of the conditions of the policy. The applicant's belief in the futility of giving notice immediately after the accident was irrelevant.

Dorene Ltd v Suedes (Ireland) Ltd [1981] IR 312

The plaintiffs entered into negotiations to lease premises owned by the defendants. On 18 July the plaintiffs made a conditional offer to take the lease. They expressly made the offer subject to final agreement on a commencement date and a rent free period, and subject to the approval of grant aid from the IDA and to the approval of the board of its parent company. This conditional offer was conditionally accepted by the defendants who emphasised that neither party was to be bound until the lease was executed. The conditions were not fulfilled and the defendants refused to proceed with the letting. The plaintiffs sued for specific performance in the High Court.

Costello J.:

. . .

It was suggested on Dorene's behalf in counsel's closing submissions that a concluded bargain had been reached between the parties. It was urged that Dorene had not pressed for the rent-free period as required in the letter of 18 July and that agreement on the commencement date of the lease had been reached. As to the other conditions laid down by Dorene in the letter of 18 July (i.e. the approval of IDA and the approval of Doreen Holdings), it was said that these should be regarded as conditions subsequent in a concluded contract. It is, of course, important to make a distinction between a condition which must be satisfied before any legally binding contract comes into operation (a condition precedent) and a condition which is a part of a legally binding contract which, if not fulfilled, can result in the contract ceasing to be binding (a condition subsequent): see Wylie's *Irish Conveyancing Law*—para. 9.069 at pp 383–4. Dorene's counsel suggested that these conditions were conditions subsequent and were analogous to a case in which a purchaser agrees to buy a house 'subject to me getting an advance on the property'—a condition which did not prevent a binding contract for sale coming into operation in *Rooney v Byrne*.[1] He also suggested, as an alternative argument, that in any event the evidence established that these conditions had been waived by Dorene. He said that Dorene could enforce the concluded bargain which the parties had made even though the final terms of the lease had not been agreed, as the court would itself fix them in default of agreement.

I find myself unable to agree with these propositions. Dorene, as I have said, made an offer to take a lease but made the offer subject to certain conditions which had to be fulfilled before they could be legally bound. The situation was in no way similar to that of a purchaser who agrees to buy a property but safeguards himself by providing that he may avoid the bargain if, for example, he fails to obtain a loan or fails to obtain planning permissions. Even if the condition relating to the date of commencement was agreed and the condition relating to the rent-free period tacitly dropped, and even if the conditions relating to grant aid from IDA and main-board approval had been waived, there still remains an insurmountable obstacle in the way of specific performance proceedings because Suedes had made it abundantly clear that they too wished to keep their options open and because their acceptance of Dorene's offer was on the basis that Suedes would not be contractually bound to grant a lease until its terms had been finally agreed. This never happened. On 9 October 1979, the parties were still in negotiation. Therefore, it seems to me that there was no legally binding agreement to grant a lease when Dorene's proceedings were launched and, in my opinion, they were instituted without reasonable or probable cause.

[1]. [1933] IR 609.

Francis Macklin and Peter McDonald *v* Graecen and Co. Ltd [1983] IR 61

The defendants agreed to sell a licence attached to a certain public house to the plaintiffs 'provided the sale of the premises to the Northern Bank Ltd is completed'. The public house had been demolished prior to the date of this agreement. The plaintiffs sued for specific performance of this agreement.

Griffin J.:

Although the inalienability of the licence is sufficient to dispose of this appeal, one other matter deserves mention. The sale was expressed to be subject to the sale to the Northern Bank being completed. In the correspondence which took place between the solicitors for the plaintiffs and the solicitors for the defendant company and the second defendant prior to the institution of proceedings, the plaintiffs sought to make the consent of the Northern Bank, as occupier of the site in Church Square, a necessary prerequisite to the completion of the sale. Their reason was that, under s. 14 of the Intoxicating Liquor Act, 1960, the consent of the Northern Bank to the extinguishment of the licence would be necessary to enable the second plaintiff to apply for a new licence in Monaghan. The necessity of the consent of the Northern Bank was also part of the plaintiffs' case in the High Court, and it was agreed by counsel for the plaintiffs on the hearing of this appeal that the consent of the bank would be necessary. The bank was not a party to the agreement and was not bound by it. It would not therefore be permissible to read into the agreement, as the plaintiffs sought to do, a provision that the bank would give the necessary consent. Therefore, even if the plaintiffs' claim did not fail on the ground already discussed, it would have failed on this ground.

(O'Higgins C.J. and Henchy J. concurred.)

In the Matter of the Arbitration Act 1954, and of an Arbitration between Gaelcrann Teoranta and Michael Payne and others, Underwriters at Lloyds [1985] ILRM 109

Underwriters refused to indemnify a company against claims made by an employee on the grounds that the company had failed to comply with a condition in the policy which provided as follows: 'The assured shall give . . . immediate notice in writing, with full particulars of the happening of any occurrence which could give rise to a claim under this insurance, or of the receipt by the assured of notice of any claim and of the institution of any proceedings against the assured.' The policy also stated 'All conditions are precedent to liability under this assurance.' Although the company notified the underwriters of the two claims and sent them the two plenary summonses, it did not furnish written particulars of the happening of an event which could give rise to a claim. At arbitration the arbitrator stated the case for the opinion of the court on the correct interpretation of the clause.

Gannon J.:

. . . the interpretation which I advise should be applied in relation to the obligations imposed on the insured is that:

(1) In every instance in which to the knowledge of the assured an occurrence happens which he recognises could give rise to a claim under the policy he must give to the nominated agent of the underwriters immediate notice in writing of the happening of such occurrence, or alternatively give them the like immediate notice of his receipt of the claim if such be made;

(2) In the event of a claim being made or received which arises from no identifiable occurrence as a happening, or of the happening of which the assured was unaware, he must give the nominated agent of the underwriters immediate notice in writing of his receipt of notice of such claim;

(3) In every case he must give to the nominated agent of the underwriters immediate notice in writing of the institution of proceedings.

. . .

It was recognised in the course of argument that a distinction must be made between a condition expressed in a contract to be a condition precedent and one which is not so described in the contract. Counsel referred to In Re *Coleman's Depositories Ltd* [1907] 2 KB 798 and in particular to the judgment of Fletcher Moulton L.J. from which it would appear that upon non-compliance with the condition that is stated to be a condition precedent performance of the obligations of the contract cannot be enforced by the party in default. Nevertheless, Fletcher Moulton L.J. says in reference to what he calls a trifling default at p. 807 of the report: 'The courts have not always considered that they are bound to interpret provisions of this kind with unreasonable strictness, and although the word 'immediate' is no doubt a strong epithet I think that it might be fairly construed as meaning with all reasonable speed considering the circumstances of the case.' In the event of non-compliance with a condition not described as a condition precedent the party in default may be able to establish a right to the benefit of the contract subject to an assessment in damages for the consequences of the default or may be unable to enforce the contract. It was also accepted in the course of argument that compliance with a condition expressed in either form could be waived by the party to benefit by it either expressly or impliedly from conduct. But a difficulty has been created by some observations of Lord Justice Denning M.R. in his judgment in *Lickiss v Milestone Motor Policies at Lloyd's* |1966| 2 All ER 972 also reported as *Barrett Bros (Taxis) Ltd v Davies* |1966| 1 WLR 1354. In that judgment Denning M.R. stated at p. 975 of the All ER report:

> First, it was unnecessary for the motor cyclist to send the documents to the insurers. They had all the relevant facts, and that absolved the motor cyclist from doing more. The police headquarters at Blackpool by their letter of 18 January 1964 gave to the insurers all the material information. The insurers would be entitled, if they so wished, to send their own representative to the Magistrates' Court and watch the proceedings or, indeed, to take such other steps if any as they were entitled to take. Seeing that they had received the information from the police, it would be a futile thing to require the motor cyclist himself to give them the self-same information. The law never compels a person to do that which is useless and unnecessary.

In that case the motor cyclist was obliged under the terms of his policy to notify immediately the insurers of intended prosecution and had failed to do so. Towards the end of his judgment Lord Denning adds the following observation at p. 976: 'Condition 1 was inserted in the policy so as to afford a protection to the insurers so that they should know in good time about the accident and any proceedings consequent on it. If they obtain all the material knowledge from another source so that they are not prejudiced at all by the failure of the insured himself to tell them, then they cannot rely on the condition to defeat the claim.' When a similar point was taken before McKenna J. in *Farrell v Federated Employers Ltd* |1970| 1 All ER 360 those observations of Denning M.R. were cited to him. In his judgment McKenna J. says at p. 363 of the report:

> Counsel for the plaintiff in his able argument contended that there could be no breach of a condition entitling the insurers to repudiate liability unless the breach had caused actual prejudice to the insurers. For this surprising proposition he cited *Lickiss v Milestone Motor Policies at Lloyd's* |1966| 2 All ER 972. In that case the insurers relied on a failure of the insured to inform them of the receipt by the insured of a notice of intended prosecution. The insurers had received information of this matter from the police. There was also some evidence that they had waived the condition entitling them to such notice.

McKenna J., then quotes the passage which I have quoted above from the judgment of Lord Denning M.R. in the cited case, McKenna J. then went on at p. 364:

> I distinguish that case from the present. There the insurers had contemporary knowledge from another reliable source of the matter which the insured failed to notify. Here the insurers had no knowledge from any source of the issue of the writ until they received the letter of 2 March 1966. I do not regard Lord Denning M.R.'s

judgment as authority for the wider proposition that an insurer cannot rely on a breach of condition unless he has suffered actual prejudice.

An appeal from the decision of McKenna J. came before the Court of Appeal in England over which Lord Denning M.R. presided. That court in upholding unanimously the decision of McKenna J., carefully avoided expressing any approval or acceptance of the proposition advanced by Lord Denning M.R. in 1966. To the extent that any of the observations of Lord Denning M.R. as stated in the 1966 case seem to be at variance with the statements of the law as expressed by Fletcher Moulton L.J. In *Re Coleman's Depositories Ltd* I would not be prepared to adopt them.

In the policy under consideration by the arbitrator condition 5 is expressed to be a condition precedent to liability under the policy. Non-compliance with the provisions of that condition, if such there be, may be waived by the underwriters or they, the underwriters, may be found to have waived impliedly their right to rely on non-compliance. If they were found to have led the assured by their conduct to believe that their right to rely on the non-compliance was being waived by them the matter of prejudice might possibly arise for consideration. Save in the investigation of such matters of fact it seems to me there is no onus on the underwriters to show that they are prejudiced by a non-compliance with condition 5. That is to say in the absence of waiver the underwriters are entitled without the obligation of proof of prejudice to their position to rely on non-compliance with condition 5 as releasing them from liability to meet a claim under the policy.

B. Innominate Terms/Intermediate Stipulations

Hongkong Fir Shipping Co. Ltd v Kawasaki Kisen Kaisha Ltd [1962] 2 QB 26

Charterers hired a ship for a period of twenty four months ' . . . she being in every way fitted for ordinary cargo service . . . ' A clause in the charterparty provided that the ship's owners should ' . . . maintain her in a thoroughly efficient state in hull and machinery during service . . . '. The ship was delivered on 13 February 1957 and sailed on that day from Liverpool to Virginia to collect cargo and carry it to Osaka, Japan. Because the ship was twenty six years old, she required careful handling by competent and adequate staff. As the chief engineer was inefficient and the number of engine room staff insufficient, the ship broke down on numerous occasions throughout the journey. By the time the ship reached Japan on 25 May she had been off hire for about five weeks and had incurred repair expenses of £21,400. A further period of about fifteen weeks and expenses of £37,500 were then required to make her seaworthy. In June the charterers repudiated the charterparty. They sued for damages for wrongful repudiation, claiming *inter alia* that the owners had broken their obligation to deliver a seaworthy vessel. At first instance, Salmon J. held that although the owners were in breach of their duty to supply a seaworthy vessel, seaworthiness was not a condition precedent to their rights and thus the owners were entitled to damages. The charterers appealed.

Upjohn L.J.:

. . .

Why is this apparently basic and underlying condition of seaworthiness not, in fact, treated as a condition? It is for the simple reason that the seaworthiness clause is breached by the slightest failure to be fitted 'in every way' for service. Thus, to take examples from the judgments in some of the cases I have mentioned if a nail is missing from one of the timbers of a wooden vessel or if proper medical supplies or two anchors are not on board at the time of sailing, the owners are in breach of the seaworthiness stipulation. It is contrary to common sense to suppose that in such circumstances the parties contemplated that the charterer should at once be entitled to treat the contract as at an end for such trifling breaches.

. . .

It is open to the parties to a contract to make it clear either expressly or by necessary implication that a particular stipulation is to be regarded as a condition which goes to the root of the contract, so that it is clear that the parties contemplate that any breach of it entitles the other party at once to treat the contract as at an end. That matter has to be determined as a question of the proper interpretation of the contract. Bramwell B. in *Tarrabochia v Hickie*[1] has warned against the dangers of too ready an implication of such a condition. He said . . . 'No doubt it is competent for the parties, if they think fit, to declare in express terms that any matter shall be a condition precedent, but when they have not so expressed themselves, it is necessary for those who construe the instrument to see whether they intended to do it. Since, however, they could have done it, those who construe the instrument should be chary in doing for them that which they might, but have not done for themselves.' Where, however, upon the true construction of the contract, the parties have not made a particular stipulation a condition, it would in my judgment be unsound and misleading to conclude that, being a warranty, damages is necessarily a sufficient remedy.

In my judgment the remedies open to the innocent party for breach of a stipulation which is not a condition strictly so called, depend entirely upon the nature of the breach and its foreseeable consequences. Breaches of stipulation fall, naturally, into two classes. First there is the case where the owner by his conduct indicates that he considers himself no longer bound to perform his part of the contract; in that case, of course, the charterer may accept the repudiation and treat the contract as at an end. The second class of case is, of course, the more usual one and that is where, due to misfortune such as the perils of the sea, engine failures, incompetence of the crew and so on, the owner is unable to perform a particular stipulation precisely in accordance with the terms of the contract try he never so hard to remedy it. In that case the question to be answered is, does the breach of the stipulation go so much to the root of the contract that it makes further commercial performance of the contract impossible, or in other words is the whole contract frustrated? If yea, the innocent party may treat the contract as at an end. If nay, his claim sounds in damages only.

If I have correctly stated the principles, then as the stipulation as to the seaworthiness is not a condition in the strict sense the question to be answered is, did the initial unseaworthiness as found by the judge, and from which there has been no appeal, go so much to the root of the contract that the charterers were then and there entitled to treat the charterparty as at an end. The only unseaworthiness alleged, serious though it was, was the insufficiency and incompetence of the crew, but that surely cannot be treated as going to the root of the contract for the parties must have contemplated that in such an event the crew could be changed and augmented. In my judgment on this part of his case |counsel for the charterers| necessarily fails.

Diplock L.J.:

. . .

Every synallagmatic contract contains in it the seeds of the problem: in what event will a party be relieved of his undertaking to do that which he has agreed to do but has not yet done? The contract may itself expressly define some of these events, as in the cancellation clause in a charterparty; but, human prescience being limited, it seldom does so exhaustively and often fails to do so at all. In some classes of contracts such as sale of goods, marine insurance, contracts of affreightment evidenced by bills of lading and those between parties to bills of exchange, Parliament has defined by statute some of the events not provided for expressly in individual contracts of that class; but where an event occurs the occurrence of which neither the parties nor Parliament have expressly stated will discharge one of the parties from further performance of his undertakings, it is for the court to determine whether the event has this effect or not.

The test whether an event has this effect or not has been stated in a number of metaphors all of which I think amount to the same thing: does the occurrence of the event deprive the party who has further undertakings still to perform of substantially the whole benefit which it was the intention of the parties as expressed in the contract that he should obtain as the consideration for performing those undertakings?

This test is applicable whether or not the event occurs as a result of the default of one of the parties to the contract, but the consequences of the event are different in the two cases. Where the event occurs as a result of the default of one party, the party in default cannot rely upon it as relieving himself of the performance of any further undertakings on his part, and the innocent party, although entitled to, need not treat the event as relieving him of the further performance of his own undertakings. This is only a specific application of the fundamental legal and moral rule that a man should not be allowed to take advantage of his own wrong. Where the event occurs as a result of the default of neither party, each is relieved of the further performance of his own undertakings.

. . .

It was early recognised that contractual undertakings were of two different kinds: those collateral to the main purpose of the parties as expressed in the contract and those which were mutually dependent so that the non-performance by one party of an undertaking of this class was an event which excused the other party from the performance of his corresponding undertaking.

. . .

The fact that the emphasis in the earlier cases was upon the breach by one party to the contract of his contractual undertakings, for this was the commonest circumstance in which the question arose, tended to obscure the fact that it was really the event resulting from the breach which relieved the other party of further performance of his obligations, . . .

. . .

Once it is appreciated that it is the event and not the fact that the event is a result of a breach of contract which relieves the party not in default of further performance of his obligations, two consequences follow. (1) The test whether the event relied upon has this consequence is the same whether the event is the result of the other party's breach of contract or not, as Devlin J. pointed out in *Universal Cargo Carriers Corp. v Citati*.[2] (2) The question whether an event which is the result of the other party's breach of contract has this consequence cannot be answered by treating all contractual undertakings as falling into one of two separate categories: 'conditions' the breach of which gives rise to an event which relieves the party not in default of further performance of his obligations, and 'warranties' the breach of which does not give rise to such an event.

Lawyers tend to speak of this classification as if it were comprehensive, partly for the historical reasons which I have already mentioned and partly because Parliament itself adopted it in the Sale of Goods Act, 1893, as respects a number of implied terms in contracts for the sale of goods and has in that Act used the expressions 'condition' and 'warranty' in that meaning. But it is by no means true of contractual undertakings in general at common law.

No doubt there are many simple contractual undertakings, sometimes express but more often because of their very simplicity ('It goes without saying') to be implied, of which it can be predicated that every breach of such an undertaking must give rise to an event which will deprive the party not in default of substantially the whole benefit which it was intended that he should obtain from the contract. And such a stipulation, unless the parties have agreed that breach of it shall not entitle the non-defaulting party to treat the contract as repudiated, is a 'condition'. So too there may be other simple contractual undertakings of which it can be predicated that *no* breach can give rise to an event which will deprive the party not in default of substantially the whole benefit which it was intended that he should obtain from the contract; and such a stipulation, unless the parties have agreed that breach of it shall entitle the non-defaulting party to treat the contract as repudiated, is a 'warranty'.

There are, however, many contractual undertakings of a more complex character which cannot be categorised as being 'conditions' or 'warranties', if the late nineteenth century meaning adopted in the Sale of Goods Act, 1893, and used by Bowen L.J. in *Bentsen v Taylor, Sons & Co.*[3] be given to those terms. Of such undertakings all that can be predicated is that some breaches will and others will not give rise to an event which will deprive the party not in default of substantially the whole benefit which it was intended that he should obtain from the contract; and the legal consequences of a breach of such an undertaking, unless provided for expressly in the contract, depend upon the nature of the event to which the breach gives rise and do not follow automatically from a prior classification of the undertaking as a 'condition' or a 'warranty'. For instance, to take Bramwell B.'s example in *Jackson v Union Marine Insurance Co. Ltd*[4] itself, breach of an undertaking by a shipowner to sail with all possible dispatch to a named port does not necessarily relieve the charterer of further performance of his obligation under the charterparty, but if the breach is so prolonged that the contemplated voyage is frustrated it does have this effect.

. . .

As my brethren have already pointed out, the shipowners' undertaking to tender a seaworthy ship has, as a result of numerous decisions as to what can amount to 'unseaworthiness', become one of the most complex of contractual undertakings. It embraces obligations with respect to every part of the hull and machinery, stores and equipment and the crew itself. It can be broken by the presence of trivial defects easily and rapidly remediable as well as by defects which must inevitably result in a total loss of the vessel.

Consequently the problem in this case is, in my view, neither solved nor soluble by debating whether the shipowner's express or implied undertaking to tender a seaworthy ship is a 'condition' or a 'warranty'. It is like so many other contractual terms, an undertaking one breach of which may give rise to an event which relieves the charterer of further performance of his undertakings if he so elects and another breach of which may not give rise to such an event but entitle him only to monetary compensation in the form of damages.

. . .

What the judge had to do in the present case, as in any other case where one party to a contract relies upon a breach by the other party as giving him a right to elect to rescind the contract, and the contract itself makes no express provision as to this, was to look at the events which had occurred as a result of the breach at the time at which the charterers purported to rescind the charterparty and to decide whether the occurrence of those events deprived the charterers of substantially the whole benefit which it was the intention of the parties as expressed in the charterparty that the charterers should obtain from the further performance of their own contractual undertakings.

. . .

The question which the judge had to ask himself was, as he rightly decided, whether or not at the date when the charterers purported to rescind the contract, namely, 6 June 1957, or when the shipowners purported to accept such rescission, namely, 8 August 1957, the delay which had already occurred as a result of the incompetence of the engine-room staff, and the delay which was likely to occur in repairing the engines of the vessel and the conduct of the shipowners by that date in taking steps to remedy these two matters, were, when taken together, such as to deprive the charterers of substantially the whole benefit which it was the intention of the parties they should obtain from further use of the vessel under the charterparty.

In my view, in his judgment—on which I would not seek to improve—the judge took into account and gave due weight to all the relevant considerations and arrived at the right answer for the right reasons.

[1.] 1 H. & N. 183.
[2.] [1957] 2 QB 401, 434.
[3.] [1893] 2 QB 274, 280, 9 TLR 552, CA.
[4.] LR 10 CP 125, 142.

(Sellers L.J. held that the maintenance clause was merely a warranty.)

Note

In *Cehave NV v Bremer Handelsgesellschaft mbH, The Hansa Nord* [1975] 3 All ER 739 the Court of Appeal held that this flexible approach also applied to a sale of goods contract.

SECTION THREE—PAROL EVIDENCE RULE

'Parol testimony cannot be received to contradict, vary, add to or subtract from the terms of a written contract or the terms in which the parties have deliberately agreed to record any part of their contract.' Per Lord Morris in *Bank of Australasia v Palmer* [1897] AC 540.

Exceptions

1. To establish that no contract exists: parol evidence is admissible to show that what appears to be a valid contract is in fact no contract at all or that there were two distinct contracts. See *Godley v Power* (1961) 95 ILTR 135 p. 230 above.

2. To establish consideration. See *Black v Grealy* 10 November 1977 p. 245 above.

3. To explain the circumstances surrounding the agreement: parol evidence is admissible to prove the true nature of the agreement or the legal relationship of the parties.

Revenue Commissioners v Moroney [1972] IR 372

(Facts on p. 178.)

. . .

Counsel for the plaintiffs has objected to the admission of the affidavit and declaration because, he says, no evidence of extrinsic circumstances is admissible to add to, contradict, vary or alter the terms of a deed; he referred to the statement of this rule in Norton's *Treatise on Deeds* (2nd ed., 1928) 135. This rule however does not apply to the statement of the consideration in the deed (Ibid. p. 140) because 'the statement of the consideration forms no part of the terms of the deed, but is only a statement contained in the deed of an antecedent fact.' Moreover, if no evidence was admissible to contradict, vary or alter the terms of the deed, the Revenue claim would fail because there is a receipt for the consideration in the deed. It is not necessary to give authority for the proposition that evidence may be given to show that, despite the receipt, the consideration was not paid. Similarly, evidence is admissible when it is relevant to explain the circumstances in which the deed was executed and to establish that the parties did not intend that the purchase price mentioned in the deed should ever be paid.

O'Neill v Ryan (No. 3) [1992] IR 166

The plaintiff instituted contemporaneously two sets of proceedings, a petition seeking relief under s. 205 of the Companies Act 1963 and a plenary action claiming damages for *inter alia* fraudulent misrepresentation. The defendants brought a motion to consolidate the two actions and to be permitted to make a joint lodgment to all the claims in the consolidated action. Blayney J. refused to order consolidation but agreed that the two actions could be tried together. On 24 May the defendants wrote to the plaintiff's solicitors offering to settle proceedings. The plaintiff accepted this. Later the defendants claimed that the settlement related to both proceedings. The plaintiff denied this and sued for specific performance of the settlement agreement.

Costello J. in the High Court granted specific performance. After dealing with the issue of mistake Costello J. considered the admissibility of parol evidence as to the intentions of the defendants.

Costello J.:

. . .

By way of alternative it was urged that the rules of evidence relating to the construction of written documents permit the court to consider the evidence of the intention of the authors of the letter of 24 May 1990, as part of the surrounding circumstances in which the letter was written and that in the light of this evidence the offer which was made was an offer to settle the two sets of proceedings, and that as the plaintiff's solicitor intended to settle on the s. 205 proceedings the parties were not *ad idem*. In support of this submission I was referred to the passages in *Chitty on Contracts* dealing with the admissibility of extrinsic evidence to interpret and explain written agreements (26th ed.) para. 867 et seq. and *Phipson on Evidence* (12th ed.) para. 196 et seq. to *Prenn v Simmonds* [1971] 1 WLR 1381, 1383–4. The passage of *Prenn* (approved by O'Hanlon J. in *British Leyland Exports v Brittain Manufacturing Ltd* [1981] IR 335 at 346) to which I was referred is as follows:

> The time has long passed when agreements, even those under seal, were isolated from the matrix of facts in which they were set and interpreted purely on internal linguistic considerations. There is no need to appeal here to any modern, anti-literal, tendencies, for Lord Blackburn's well known judgment in *River Wear Commissioners v Adamson* (1877) 2 App Cas 743, 763 provides ample warrant for a liberal approach. We must, as he said, inquire beyond the language and see what the circumstances were with reference to which the words were used, and the object, appearing from those circumstances, which the person using them had in view.

This judgment affords justification for hearing extrinsic evidence of the general circumstances in which the offer of settlement was made and accepted, including the pleadings in the two sets of proceedings, the motion to consolidate, what transpired at its hearing and the judgment on it, as an aid to construe the written contract contained in the two letters. It is not however an authority for the proposition that the parties can adduce evidence as to their intention in entering the written agreement. In *Prenn v Simmonds* [1971] 1 WLR 1381 the court was concerned with the construction of a written contract. Counsel for the defendant, Dr Simmonds, had argued that in considering it prior negotiations could be looked at as an aid to construction. Rejecting this submission Lord Wilberforce said at p. 1385 of the report: 'In my opinion, then, evidence of negotiations, or of the parties' intentions, and *a fortiori* of Dr Simmonds' intention, ought not to be received, and evidence should be restricted to evidence of the factual background known to the parties at or before the date of the contract, including evidence of the "genesis" and objectively the "aim" of the transaction.' (emphasis added) And I do not think that the passages in *Chitty on Contracts* relating to the admissibility of extrinsic evidence to which I was referred must be taken as in some way modifying the earlier passages on the law of mistake, nor do those general principles on the same subject in *Phipson on Evidence* allow the defendant to adduce evidence which in effect contradicts the reasonable construction of the words used in the written agreement.

Finally it was submitted that the objective test as set out in *Chitty on Contracts* must be read in the light of the Supreme Court decision in *Mespil Ltd v Capaldi* [1986] ILRM 373 and that *Mespil* is authority for the proposition that in considering whether parties are *ad idem* the court is not bound by the construction of the words used in the written document but may take into account the subjective intent of the offeror when writing them.

I do not think that *Mespil Ltd v Capaldi* [1986] ILRM 373 supports this view. That was a case in which a settlement of an action had been negotiated by counsel for the plaintiff and counsel for the defendant. The result of their negotiations was reduced into writing and was headed 'Full and final settlement of all matters and acts in dispute between the parties in these proceedings.' A dispute arose as to the terms of the settlement and proceedings were instituted. Evidence was given at the trial by the plaintiff's counsel to the effect that the words did not mean that an existing dispute unrelated to the proceedings between the parties about the user of the premises was settled, whilst counsel for the defendants gave evidence that the words meant that all matters in dispute (including the user dispute) between the parties and not just those referred to in the two actions were settled. The Supreme Court held, at p. 376, that it was clear that the form of the written consent, viewed in terms of its wording and of the negotiations leading up to it, was capable of justifying the opinion of counsel for the defendant, but that it could also be said that on an objective consideration of the relevant circumstances that the plaintiff's counsel's construction was justified. There was therefore a latent ambiguity and a mutual misunderstanding which meant that in fact there was no agreement.

Mespil Ltd v Capaldi [1986] ILRM 373 is an example of a case where, looking at the words used by the parties, the court could come to the conclusion that, objectively speaking, they suffered from such ambiguity that it was impossible to conclude that the parties had reached an agreement. That is not, in my judgment, the situation which pertains in this case. In my view the words used by the defendant's solicitors could only be construed as an offer to settle the s. 205 proceedings only. This was the sense in which they were understood by the plaintiff's solicitor, and accepted by him.

(Affirmed by the Supreme Court on appeal.)

Note

See also *Re Richardson v National Trust* [1988] NI 86.

A. WHERE THE WRITTEN AGREEMENT IS NOT THE WHOLE AGREEMENT

Howden Bros v Ulster Bank Ltd [1924] IR 117

A firm of shipbuilders orally agreed to build a boat for the plaintiffs. A letter was sent by the plaintiffs confirming the order to build the boat. Instalments of the price agreed were paid by the plaintiffs, but before the boat was completed the company went into liquidation, and a receiver was appointed by the defendants, debenture holders. The defendants detained the boat and the plaintiffs sued for damages claiming the boat to be their property.

Wilson J.:

I do not doubt or impugn the settled rule of evidence, that parol evidence is not admissible to add to, vary, or contradict a written agreement or any transaction in writing: *Meres v Ansell;*[1] but in this case I have come to the conclusion that the letters are not a written agreement and do not contain or purport to contain the whole transaction, and in allowing the evidence I follow the law laid down in Roscoe's *Nisi Prius Evidence*, (18th ed.), 17; and *Allen v Pink*,[2] which decided that parol evidence of a verbal transaction is not excluded by the fact that a writing was made concerning or relating to it unless such writing was in fact the transaction itself and not merely a note or memorandum of it or portion of the transaction; and the judgment therein of Lord Abinger C.B., concurred in by Bolland and Alderson B.B.:

> The general principle is quite true that if there has been a parol agreement, which is afterwards reduced by the parties into writing, that writing alone must be looked to to ascertain the terms of the contract; but the principle does not apply here; there was no evidence of any agreement by the plaintiff that the whole contract should be reduced into writing by the defendant; the contract is first concluded by parol and afterwards the paper is drawn up, which appears to have been meant merely as a memorandum of the transaction or an informal receipt for the money, not as containing the terms of the contract itself.
> . . .

Again in *Hutton v Warren*[3] Baron Parke says that the principle on which extensive evidence is admissible to annex incidents to written contracts is a presumption that the parties did not mean to express in writing the whole of the contract by which they intended to be bound. In *Angell v Duke*[4] Blackburne J. says: 'It is a most important rule of law that people should not add to or vary a written contract, which is the record of all the terms relating to the same matter agreed upon between the parties.'

It is because it was alleged that the letters in this case on their face were not intended to be the record of all the terms agreed on between the parties that I admitted the parol evidence.

. . .

There is enough in this case, in the verbal contract, in the conduct of the parties, and in the circumstances to show that the agreement and intention of the parties was that the property in the boat should pass to the plaintiffs as she was constructed.

[1.] 3 Wilson, KB 276.
[2.] 4 M. & W. 140.
[3.] 1 M. & W. 466.
[4.] 23 WR 548.

Clayton Love & Sons (Dublin) Ltd v British and Irish Steam Packet Co. Ltd (1970) 104 ILTR 157

The defendants contracted to carry the plaintiffs' frozen food from Dublin to Liverpool. An agent of the plaintiffs telephoned the defendants prior to the shipments to explain the nature of the cargo and to request that it be shipped at a sub zero temperature. The food was damaged because the loading was conducted at atmospheric temperature and the plaintiffs sued. Evidence of the telephone conversation was admitted as the court found that the terms of the contract were to be found in the written contract and the additional terms agreed to in the telephone conversation.

Note

See Wedderburn 'Collateral Contracts' (1959) 17 CLJ 58.

B. TO IDENTIFY THE SUBJECT MATTER OF THE CONTRACT:

Ulster Bank *v* Synnott (1871) 5 IR Eq 595

The defendant, being indebted to the plaintiff, deposited debentures certificates with the plaintiff, accompanied by a letter stating that they were so deposited 'against acceptances made' on the defendant's account. The court had to determine *inter alia* whether the expression 'acceptances made' was clear or whether parol evidence was admissible to aid construction.

V.C.:

. . .

The defendant contends that the word *made*, being a past participle, grammatically excludes future acceptances, and that there is no ambiguity to warrant me in admitting parol evidence to explain it. I do not concur in this view—first, because I think that in every such case it is necessary to learn, by parol evidence, the circumstances under which the document was written, so as to enable the court to ascertain what it was with which the parties were dealing; and, also, because I think that the word *made* is capable of two different significations. That it refers to past acceptances is plain, but the question is, when past? Whether past at the time at which it was written, or past when it should afterwards come to be acted on. The expression 'against acceptances made' &c., requires to be expanded, and means, 'to be held by the bank as a security for the repayment of the sums which shall become due on foot of the acceptance made by the London and Westminster Bank on my account, and through you.' The word *made* may be read either as, which have been heretofore made, or, which shall have been made during the continuance of the security. The latter is neither a forced nor an unusual meaning, and instances of the use of the past participle with reference to future events are common.

. . .

The expression being therefore ambiguous, parol evidence of the surrounding circumstances is clearly admissible to aid the construction.

(Evidence showed that the expression meant 'acceptances which shall have been made during the continuance of the security'.)

Chambers v Kelly (1873) 7 IRCL 231

The plaintiff entered into an agreement to sell the defendant oaks growing on certain land 'together with all other trees growing through the oak plant-ation and mixed with the oak'. A dispute arose as to correct interpretation of this agreement.

Fitzgerald B.:

. . .

It appears plain, at least I think, that the term 'oak plantations', in the agreement in question does not mean plantations in which there was nothing but oak, because in the agreement itself, trees of another kind are described as being mixed up with oak, and as growing through these 'oak plantations'; and, on the other hand, that it does not mean plantations in which there was any oak at all, because otherwise there would have been no necessity whatever for the introduction of the description 'oak plantations'.

That being so, it was necessary to go outside the written agreement to ascertain the subject matter in this respect, that is to say, 'oak plantations'. I am of opinion that, for this purpose, evidence of what passed, leading, in the words of the learned judge who tried the case, 'up to' the agreement, could not be excluded.

Francis Macklin and Peter McDonald v Graecen and Co. Ltd [1983] IR 61

(Facts on p. 255.)

Griffin J.:

. . .

When (as in this case) a transaction has been reduced to writing by agreement of the parties, no evidence may be given to prove the terms of the transaction except the document itself, and extrinsic evidence is not admissible to vary the terms of the document. I agree with the learned trial judge that, in an appropriate case, an agreement made by the holder of a licence for its extinguishment is enforceable; indeed, such agreements are frequently made. Such an agreement would be more elaborate in form and would (*inter alia*) recite such matters as the agreement of the parties, that the licensee holds the licence, that the licence is subsisting and will be kept in force, the intended application to the court for a new licence, the description of the premises to which it is attached, and the agreement to consent to the extinguishment of the licence. But this is not such a case. Here, the plaintiffs' claim is, and remains, one for specific performance of an agreement to sell the licence. It is not and cannot be treated as a claim seeking rectification of the document, in which case parol evidence would be admissible in support of such a claim.

   Therefore, the plaintiffs' claim must be confined to the terms of the agreement and, unquestionably, those terms make the agreement one for the sale of the licence.
   . . .

   It follows that, as the licence is inalienable, on this ground alone the plaintiffs are not entitled to enforce the agreement of 29 August 1975, or to obtain specific performance of it.

LAC Minerals Ltd *v* Chevron Mineral Corp. of Ireland (CMCI) and Ivernia West plc (HC) 6 August 1993, unrep.

CMCI entered into an agreement with Ivernia to develop mineral deposits. A pre-emption clause provided that if either party wished to sell their interest to a third party, they were required to offer the interest first to the other party. Clause 15.3.1.4 required that the notice must state that the offer would be open for acceptance for a period of fifty five days after receipt of the offer by the offeree. Clause 15.3.2 provided that the offeree would have the 'right and option' for a period of sixty days after receipt of the offer to accept. CMCI offered their interest to Ivernia who accepted within sixty days but after forty-five days. LAC who had an agreement to buy the interest in the event of Ivernia not accepting claimed that such acceptance was not valid. LAC claimed *inter alia* that parol evidence should be admitted to explain the inconsistency between the time period allowed in the two clauses.

Keane J.:
. . .

The legal principles applicable in determining the construction of a disputed term in a contract were stated by Lord Wilberforce in *Reardon Smith Lyon v Yngvar Hansel-Tanger*, ((1976), 3 All ER 570 at pp 574–575) as follows:

> When one speaks of the intention of the parties to the contract, one is speaking objectively—the parties cannot themselves give direct evidence of what their intention was—and what must be ascertained is what is to be taken as the intention which reasonable people would have if placed in the situation of the parties. Similarly, when one is speaking of the aim, or object, or commercial purpose, one is speaking objectively of what reasonable persons would have had in mind in the situation of the parties. . . . What the court must do is to place itself in thought in the same factual matrix as that in which the parties were.

That statement of the law was expressly approved of by Griffin J. in *Rohan Construction v ICI* (1988) ILRM 373.

The extent to which a court should take into account the surrounding circumstances in construing a contract was again the subject of some observation by Lord Wilberforce in *Prenn v Simmonds* ((1971) 1 WLR 1381). He said:

> The time has long passed when agreements, even those under seal, were isolated from the matrix of facts in which they were set and interpreted purely on internal linguistic considerations. There is no need to appeal here to any modern, anti-literal, tendencies, for Lord Blackburn's well known Judgment in *River Wear Commissioners v Adamson* (1877) 2 App Cas 743, provides ample warrant for a liberal approach. We must, as he said, enquire beyond the language and see what the circumstances were with reference to which the words were used, and the object, appearing from those circumstances, which the person using them had in view.

If, however, a term of a contract is unambiguous and can only have one meaning, the court cannot go beyond that unambiguous meaning so as to seek to interpret the intention of the parties: see *Marathon Petroleum (Ireland) Ltd v Bord Gais Eireann* (SC) 31 July 1986, unrep.

The law applicable when there are inconsistent or repugnant clauses in a contract is stated as follows in *Chitty on Contract*, para. 833 as follows:

> Where the different parts of an instrument are inconsistent, effect must be given to that part which is calculated to carry into effect the real intention of the parties as gathered from the instrument as a whole, and that part which would defeat it must be rejected. The old rule was, in such a case, the earlier clause was to be received and the latter rejected, but this rule was a mere rule of thumb, totally unscientific, and out of keeping with the modern construction of documents. To be inconsistent, a term must contradict another term or be in conflict with it, such that effect cannot fairly be given to both clauses. A term may also be rejected if it is repugnant to the intention of the parties as it appears from the document. However, an effort should be made to give effect to every clause in the agreement and not to reject a clause unless it is manifestly inconsistent with or repugnant to the rest of the agreement.

It has also been said that it is not possible to look at the antecedent negotiations, where there is such an inconsistency, in order to determine the true intention of the parties: see *Prenn v Simmons*, above. Nor, it would seem, are prior drafts admissible in aid of the interpretation of the contract. As to the admissibility of evidence to explain a patent ambiguity, the law is thus stated in *Chitty*, at para. 875:

> *Patent Ambiguity.* In the case of a patent ambiguity, that is to say, a defect or ambiguity appearing on the face of the document which renders the words used unintelligible or meaningless, a rule is said to exist that any reference to matter dehors the document is forbidden. It is doubtful, however, whether such a rule applies today in respect of written contracts, except possibly in the case of total blanks in a document, although evidence will not be admitted to show what the author himself intended to say.

It is also clear that it is not legitimate to use as an aid in the construction of the contract anything which the parties said or did after it was made: see *Re Wogans Ltd*, (SC) 10 April 1992, unrep.

. . .

. . . it would seem clear that there is on the face of the document an inconsistency between the provisions of clause 15.3. 1.4, under which the notice must state that the offer is open for acceptance for a period of forty five days after receipt of the offer by the offeree, and clause 15.3.2 which provides that the offeree is to have the 'right and option' for a period of sixty days after receipt of the offer, unless enlarged in the specified circumstances, to accept.

. . .

In the light of the legal principles to which I have already referred, it is obvious that, if this action proceeds to a hearing, the court would be in a position to conduct a full investigation into the circumstances surrounding the execution of the JVA Agreement in order to ascertain whether this apparent inconsistency can be reconciled. The result of that investigation may lend support to the contentions advanced on behalf of LAC or it may not. The necessary materials for such an investigation may emerge from the process of discovery or they may not. The court may be assisted in arriving at a resolution of the difficulty by the oral evidence adduced at the hearing or it may not. It appears to me that, in these circumstances, it is not possible to say with the degree of confidence which the authorities suggest should be present in the mind of the judge when deciding an application of this nature that, no matter what may emerge on discovery or at the trial of the action, the inconsistency will be resolved only in a manner which will be fatal to the plaintiff's contentions.

In this context, I think there is a clear distinction to be drawn at this stage between the clause in *Marathon Petroleum v Bord Gais*, the subject of the decision of the Supreme Court which was much discussed during the course of the argument, and the clause in the present case. In that case, not merely was the clause in plain and unambiguous language: Finlay C.J. rejected the submission that it made no sense, saying:

> It was urged, as I have indicated, on behalf of the plaintiff that there was no meaning or sense in the parties reaching an agreement with regard to a currency exchange rate and confining it to a period of ten years with the knowledge and in the expectation that for up to four years of that period it would be inoperable and irrelevant. I do not see this as being a consideration which renders unreasonable or illogical the construction which I would put upon the clause on the basis of the actual words used in it. . . . There would be no illogicality in (the parties) deciding that they were not prepared to permit of an exchange rate fluctuation into a period beyond ten years from the time at which they were making the contract and viewing the likely movements of currency insofar as they could be prophesised.

No such reasonable or logical explanation has been put forward on behalf of the defendants of the inconsistencies in the clause in this case.

. . .

I am satisfied that, having regard to the unexplained—and it may be inexplicable— inconsistency in the wording of clauses 15.3. 1.4 and 15.3.2 of the JVA Agreement, the court of trial may well be in position where it will think it proper to admit evidence of the factual matrix, to use Lord Wilberforce's words, in which the agreement was set, and which may assist the court in arriving at a construction of the clause. In these circumstances, I am satisfied that the first issue which I have posed must be resolved in favour of LAC.

Note

Why did the plaintiff not seek to have the agreement rectified to include the correct time period in the second clause?

C. To Explain a Custom

In *Wilson and Strain v Pinkerton* (1897) 31 ILTR 86 parol evidence was admitted as an aid to construction in relation to a particular custom in contracts between bakeries and their employees.

D. To Show that the Document Should Be Rectified because the Agreed Terms which were Intended to be Reduced to Writing were Not Accurately Recorded or the Contract Document Contains a Mistake.

In *O'Neill v Ryan* (No.3) [1992] IR 166 Costello J. stated:
(Facts on p. 263.)

The court will also grant relief by way of rectification where the parties have reached an agreement but where an error is made in giving effect to the parties' common intention in a written agreement. The general rule is that where this is a common shared mistake in that the written agreement fails to record the intention of both parties the court will order its rectification. Rectification may also be ordered when a party has entered into a written agreement by mistake, if he establishes that the other party with knowledge of the mistake concluded that agreement.

Note

The Law Commission (UK), No. 154 in their study of the Parol Evidence Rule concluded that the rule does not have the effect of excluding evidence which ought to be admitted if justice is to be done between the parties. Evidence will only be excluded, the commission felt, when its reception would be inconsistent with the intention of the parties. Legislation in this area would not be helpful as it would require reference to the rule by name or a description of the rule.

Naming the rule would not be possible because, the same name is used for more than one rule of law. Describing the rule might seem to leave more scope for the production of a plausible provision. But we could not avoid the conclusion that any description consistent with our analysis of the rule would be circular, so that any purported abolition would plainly appear to be beating the air. We considered the possibility of legislation which would enact the opposite of the rule, instead of abolishing it. But this approach involved the same problem—if on a true analysis the rule cannot be said to have legal effect, nor can its opposite. [Footnotes omitted.]

Chapter Seven

Implied Terms

INTRODUCTION

Contracting parties do not generally have the time, the expertise or the opportunity, to agree or draft all the terms which they wish to include in their bargain. Few contracting parties are omniscient; fewer still are able to envisage how future developments will influence their bargain or their expectations of it. In these circumstances the express terms of the contract, whether written or verbal, will cast little or no light on how the contract should be interpreted or performed. It is at this stage that gaps in the contract will be filled, by reference to so-called implied terms. This is an important process which is intended to allow the parties to proceed towards completion of their contractual venture, often at the cost of some modification in the expectations of one or other of the parties, but in general this is viewed as preferable to a judicial declaration that the contract is void for uncertainty, invalid due to mistake, or discharged by operation of law (see Chapters 2, 9 and 18 respectively).

SECTION ONE—TERMS IMPLIED AT COMMON LAW

A. TERMS IMPLIED IN FACT

Terms will be implied into a contract where necessary to give effect to the presumed intentions of the parties. Two formulations of this test have been suggested: the 'business efficacy' test and the 'officious bystander' test:

An implied warranty, or as it is called a covenant at law, as distinguished from an express contract or express warranty, really is in every instance founded on the presumed intention of the parties and upon reason. It is the implication which the law draws from what must obviously have been the intention of the parties, an implication which the law draws with the object of giving efficacy to the transaction and preventing such a failure of consideration as cannot have been within the contemplation of either of the parties.

Per Bowen L.J. in *The Moorcock* [1886–90] All ER 530.

Prima facie that which in any contract is left to be implied and need not be expressed is something so obvious that it goes without saying; so that, if, while the parties were making their bargain, an officious bystander were to suggest some express provision for it in their agreement, they would testily suppress him with a common 'Oh, of course!'

Per MacKinnon L.J. in *Shirlaw v Southern Foundries Ltd* [1939] 2 All ER 113.

Butler v McAlpine [1904] 2 IR 445

The defendants hired a barge from the plaintiff to carry goods to a wharf which they had leased. The barge was damaged when it grounded on a block of hardened cement whose existence was unknown to the defendants. The plaintiff sued for damages for negligence. The defendants appealed against a decision of the King's Bench Division granting the plaintiff damages for breach of an implied duty to take reasonable care to ascertain that the berth was reasonably safe.

Fitzgibbon L.J.:

The defendants have contended that the *ratio decidendi* in *The Moorcock*[1] was that the defendant was a wharfinger, in the sense of a person who hires a wharf to a shipowner. With all respect, it is only necessary to read the case to see, as the Lords expressly said in *The Calliope*,[2] that the liability rested upon the fact that for good consideration the defendants had *invited* the plaintiff to moor his ship in the place where it was injured, under circumstances which, in the ordinary course of business and in reason, raised the implication that the defendants had at least undertaken to use reasonable care to *see* that the berth was safe; the wider undertaking to *make* it safe, or to *keep* it safe, was there, more than here, qualified by the evidence as to the control of the place in question. But the distinction is immaterial, because even if the lesser duty only—to see that the berth was safe—existed, the defendants here are liable for its breach.
. . .

In *The Moorcock* the defendants were held liable for injuries caused by a hardened ridge left on the natural bottom of the Thames by the weight of a previous occupant of the berth, which did not strip at low water; here the mischief was done by a bag of the defendants' cement, which either fell off their wharf, where it was in charge of their servant, or dropped overboard from a barge while unloading at their quay under the superintendence of the same servant. In addition, their general manager stated that it was the storekeeper's duty to see that the berth was clear, and he had on other occasions known bags of cement to fall into the berth, and had taken them out for the defendants.

Lord Esher said that *The Moorcock* decision went a step beyond any of the cases cited, which were not all wharfingers' cases. This case falls far short of *The Moorcock* upon the facts.

Bowen L.J. based the implied contract on the presumed intention of the parties and on reason; he held that both parties must have known that unless the ground was safe the ship would be simply 'buying an opportunity of danger' in grounding at the jetty, and although the defendants had no duty, by statute or at common law, to repair the bed of the river, and had 'no power to interfere with it unless under the license of the conservators,' he said:

> The law will not imply that the persons who have not control of the place have taken reasonable care to make it good, but it does not follow that they are relieved from all responsibility; they are on the spot; they must know that the jetty cannot be used unless reasonable care is taken, if not to make it safe, at all events to see whether it is safe. No one can tell whether reasonable safety has been secured except themselves, and if they let out their jetty for use, they at all events imply that they have taken reasonable care to see whether the berth, which is the essential part of

the use of the jetty, is safe; and if it is not safe, and if they have not taken such reasonable care, it is their duty to warn persons with whom they have dealings that they have not done so.

...

The Calliope was decided in favour of the defendants, because the Lords took a view of the facts different from that taken by the Court of Appeal. But they described the state of facts in which the defendants would have been liable in words precisely applicable to this case; and they rested the liability upon a principle not peculiar to navigation, or to wharfingers, but directly applicable to the defendants here.

Lord Halsbury said:

If the vessel had been invited to a berth at which it was unfit for a vessel under any circumstances to lie |words appropriate to a berth occupied by a bag of hardened cement|, and that by reason of the inequality and unfitness of the berth, the vessel being brought there was injured, he certainly entertained no doubt that the law, as laid down in the case of The Moorcock, would have been applicable to that state of things.

He extends the limit of the duty, where it exists, to a reasonable distance from the wharf; and refers particularly, as distinguishing the case of The Moorcock, to the fact that there was no evidence in the case of The Calliope that the alleged obstruction was not 'the normal condition of the bank.'

...

Seeing that the facts here are stronger against the defendants than were the facts in The Moorcock, and applying the decision in The Moorcock and the statements of law by the Lords in The Calliope to these facts, I am clearly of opinion that the appeal must be dismissed with costs.

[1.] 14 PD 64.   [2.] 14 PD 138; |1891| AC 11.

(Walker L.J. concurred. Holmes L.J. dissented on the ground that unlike the Moorcock case the bargemen in this case had the opportunity to examine the berth.)

Daniel Ward *v* Spivack Ltd; Noel Fagan *v* Spivack Ltd [1957] IR 40

Ward and Fagan were sales agents for the defendant company. Both operated within a defined area on a commission basis. Their contracts made no reference to the payment of commission on the termination of their agencies. Therefore when the defendant terminated their agencies they sought a declaration that there should be implied into the contracts a term that commission was to continue to be paid on all orders from customers in their respective areas who did business with the company during the period of their agencies.

Davitt P.:

Should a term then be implied with regard to it? The test is, I think, as I suggested to |counsel for the plaintiffs| during the hearing. Let us envisage the parties at the moment they have agreed on the expressed terms of their contract. Then imagine one of them saying, with regard to the term sought to be implied: 'Of course such and such is understood?' If the probability is that the other would say, 'Of course!', then the term may be implied. If the probability is that he would say, 'Certainly not, I will agree to nothing of the kind,' then clearly the term cannot be implied no matter how desirable or reasonable it may seem, as the court cannot make a contract for the parties; it can only determine what they agreed on, either expressly or impliedly. Let us apply the test here. If after the terms already mentioned had been agreed on Fagan had said: 'Of course, it is understood that in the event of my ceasing to be your agent commission will still continue to be payable to me and after my death to my executors on all business subsequently done with any customer in my territory whether introduced by me or not,' I am quite sure that Spivack would have said, 'Certainly not; I am not going to agree on commission being paid on that basis.' I must also look at it the other way round. If Spivack had said: 'Of course, it is understood that in the event of your agency coming to an end you will cease to draw any commission except on orders still to be completed; and I will continue to reap the benefit of your work and receive orders from customers introduced by you without paying you anything,' I cannot imagine Fagan entering into the contract at all.

Another way of looking at the matter is this. Consider the ordinary case of a house agent whom I employ to secure a purchaser to buy my house at a certain price. The agent produces a purchaser who is suitable and willing to pay their price, and a deal is made. I am not entitled to terminate his agency before concluding the deal so as to deprive him of his commission which he has earned.

I do therefore hold that I should imply a term to the effect that if Fagan's agency were determined he would be entitled to draw continuing commission on all orders from customers which had been introduced by him. In Ward's case I come to similar conclusions of fact and imply the same term in his contract.

The defendants appealed to the Supreme Court.

Maguire C.J.:

It is settled law that a term may be implied in a contract to repair what *Cheshire and Fifoot*, (3rd ed., 1952), 127 calls 'an intrinsic failure of expression.' Where there has been such a failure the judge may supply the further terms which will implement their (the parties') presumed intention and in a hallowed phrase give 'business efficacy' to the contract. 'In doing this he purports at least to do merely what the parties would have done themselves had they thought of the matter. The existence of this judicial power was asserted and justified in *The Moorcock*.'[1] In that case Bowen L.J. explained the nature of the implication in all the cases; he says where they were implied 'the law is raising an implication from the presumed intention of the parties, with the object of giving to the transaction such efficacy as both parties must have intended that at all events it should have.' The test to be applied by the court has been stated by several judges in much the same language: see Scrutton L.J. in *Reigate v Union Manufacturing Co. (Ramsbottom)*;[2] and MacKinnon L.J. in *Shirlaw v Southern Foundries (1926), Ltd.*[3]

It will be seen from the language used in so stating the tests that something more is required than the *probability* of which the president speaks that the parties must have agreed to the term to be implied had the matter been mentioned. There must be something approaching certainty or as put by Jenkins L.J. in *Sethia (1944) Ltd v Partabmull Rameshwar*[4] it must be 'clear beyond a peradventure that both parties intended a given term to operate, although they did not include it in so many words.'

. . .

. . . although it might have been a reasonable thing for Mr Spivack to have agreed to continue to pay commission on orders from customers introduced by the plaintiffs at least for some time after the termination of the agency I am quite unable to hold as the president does that had the matter been raised Mr Spivack must have agreed. To read such a term into the contract would in my view not be to make clear the intention of the parties unexpressed at the time but would be to make a new contract.

    I have been authorised by the other members of the court to say that they agree with the foregoing judgment.

1. (1889) 14 PD 64.   3. [1939] 3 KB 206.
2. [1918] 1 KB 592, at 605.   4. [1950] 1 All ER 51.

Murphy Buckley & Keogh v Pye (Ireland) [1971] IR 57

The defendants appointed the plaintiffs to be their sole agents for the purpose of procuring a purchaser for their factory. It was agreed that a commission would be paid to the plaintiffs if they succeeded in effecting a sale. The defendants then proceeded to negotiate a sale with a third party who had approached them directly before the plaintiff's appointment. The plaintiffs sued for commission.

Henchy J.:

The plaintiffs' case for commission, therefore, stands or falls on the submission that once they had been appointed sole selling agents commission at the agreed rate became payable when the defendants themselves sold during the currency of the sole agency. In answer to this submission, the defendants relied primarily on the decision of McCardie J. in *Bentall, Horsley and Baldry v Vicary*.[1] The headnote of that case reads as follows:

> The defendant, the owner of property, appointed the plaintiffs, who were estate agents, his sole agents for the sale of the property for a stipulated period, it being agreed that, if the plaintiffs introduced a purchaser, they should receive a commission of five per cent on the purchase price. During the period of the agency the defendant negotiated personally and quite apart from the plaintiffs with a purchaser who had never had any communication with the plaintiffs and whom the plaintiffs did not know. The result of the negotiations was that the property was sold to this purchaser. The plaintiffs thereupon claimed from the defendant damages for breach of contract on the ground that, in selling the property direct to the purchaser, he had acted in breach of his contract with them and had thereby deprived them of their commission: *Held*, that the plaintiffs were not entitled to damages, as the contract contained no express prohibition against a sale by the defendant himself, and the implication of such a prohibition was not necessary to give business efficacy to the transaction. *Held* further, on the terms of the contract, that the plaintiffs could not recover commission at the agreed rate on the purchase price received by the defendant, as they had failed to introduce the purchaser, nor could they recover on a *quantum meruit*.

. . .

Commenting on the form of the contract, McCardie J. said at p. 258 of the report:

> In the contract now before me I see nothing to prevent the business efficacy of the document by reason of the circumstance that the defendant was himself entitled to

sell. If the plaintiffs had got a purchaser within the six months and before the defendant had himself sold, then they would have gained their full commission together with their right to advertisement expenses. It is to be noted that the contract contains no express words at all indicating a prohibition against a sale by the defendant himself. If the parties intended such a prohibition nothing would have been easier than to insert the appropriate words. It is also to be noted that the defendant does not say by the contract: 'I give you the sole right to sell.' He says only: 'I appoint you sole agents for the sale', which is, in my opinion, quite a different thing.

It seems to me that these observations are fully applicable to the present case. Insofar as I have been able to ascertain the terms of the contract from the conversations that led up to it, and from the correspondence and the conduct of the parties, there was nothing in the contract which gave the plaintiffs the sole right to sell; they were merely appointed sole agents to find a purchaser who would be ready to complete at a price acceptable to the defendants, and the defendants were to have the right to revoke the agency. It is clear that the contract precluded the defendants from selling through another agent during the currency of the plaintiffs' agency; it is equally clear that the contract contained no express term which precluded the defendants themselves from selling. If I am correct in thinking that, in this respect, the contract in the present case is indistinguishable from that in the *Bentall* case, then under authority of the latter case it is not possible to read into the contract in the present case an implied term precluding the defendants from selling.

In *Luxor (Eastbourne) Ltd v Cooper*[2] it was held in the House of Lords, according to the head-note, that 'where an agent is promised a commission only if he brings about the sale which he is endeavouring to effect there is no room for an implied term that the principal will not dispose of the property himself or through other channels or otherwise act so as to prevent the agent earning his commission.' Viscount Simon L.C., having stressed the dangers of formulating general propositions as to contracts with agents for commission which depend in each case on the precise terms of the contract under consideration, said at p. 120 of the report: ' . . . in contracts made with commission agents there is no justification for introducing an implied term unless it is necessary to do so for the purpose of giving to the contract the business effect which both parties to it intended it should have.'

Viscount Simon then continued as follows:

It may be useful to point out that contracts under which an agent may be occupied in endeavouring to dispose of the property of a principal fall into several obvious classes. There is the class in which the agent is promised a commission by his principal if he succeeds in introducing to his principal a person who makes an adequate offer, usually an offer of not less than the stipulated amount. If that is all that is needed in order to earn his reward, it is obvious that he is entitled to be paid when this has been done, whether his principal accepts the offer and carries through the bargain or not. No implied term is needed to secure this result. There is another class of case in which the property is put into the hands of the agent to dispose of for the owner, and the agent accepts the employment and, it may be, expends money and time in endeavouring to carry it out. Such a form of contract may well imply the term that the principal will not withdraw the authority he has given after the agent has incurred substantial outlay, or, at any rate, after he has succeeded in finding a possible purchaser . . . But there is a third class of case (to which the present instance belongs) where, by the express language of the contract, the agent is promised his commission only upon completion of the transaction which he is endeavouring to bring about between the offeror and his principal. As I have already said, there seems to me to be no room for the suggested implied term in such a case. The agent is promised a reward in return for an event, and the event has not happened. He runs the risk of disappointment, but if he is not willing to run the risk he should introduce into the express terms of the contract the clause which protects him.

It seems to me that the contract in the present case falls into the third category of cases outlined by Viscount Simon in that passage. The contract made between the plaintiffs and the defendants was one under which the owner of the property appointed an estate agent to be the owners' sole agent for the purpose of finding a purchaser, and agreed that, if the agent through his activities was instrumental in bringing about an actual sale, the agent would be remunerated at a fixed percentage of the purchase money. In such a case it was held by McCardie J. in the *Bentall* case that there was no room for an implied term that the owner will not himself sell and thereby deprive the agent of commission; and that decision was expressly approved in the Court of Appeal in *George Trollope & Sons v Martyn Bros*[3] by Scrutton, Greer and Maugham L.JJ., and in the House of Lords in the *Luxor* case by Viscount Simon L.C. at p. 117 of the report and by Lord Wright at p. 145 of the report. . . . The result is that in my judgment, the plaintiffs are not entitled to any part of the sum claimed as being equivalent to commission.

1. |1931| 1 KB 253.   2. |1941| AC 108.   3. |1984| 2 KB 486.

Note

In *Irish Welding v Philips Electrical (Ireland) Ltd* (HC) 8 October 1976, unrep. Finlay J. implied a term into an agency agreement to the effect that reasonable notice should be given before either party terminated the agreement.

Tradax (Ireland) Ltd v Irish Grain Board Ltd [1984] IR 1

The plaintiffs agreed to acquire feed barley from the defendants for delivery during April to May 1978. The price was to be met by a letter of credit 'maturing' on 1 May 1978. Following several shipments of barley in early April the defendants repudiated the contract claiming that the plaintiffs had breached the contract by failing to supply a letter of credit. Subsequently the plaintiffs did issue a letter which would have enabled the defendants to obtain payment on 1 May. In defence to the plaintiffs action for breach of contract the defendants submitted that a term should be implied into the contract requiring the delivery of a letter of credit prior to the shipment of the barley.

O'Higgins C.J.:
. . .

It goes without question that, in any class of contract, the courts may imply a term in order to repair an intrinsic failure of expression. This is done to give business efficacy, as it is said, to a contract which would otherwise lack it. The existence of this power was asserted in the well known case of *The Moorcock*[1]. . . .
. . .

However, this power must be exercised with care. The courts have no role in acting as contract makers, or as counsellors, to advise or direct what agreement ought to have been made by two people, whether businessmen or not, who chose to enter into contractual relations with each other. The much-quoted passage, from the judgment of Bowen L.J. in *The Moorcock* was referred to by MacKinnon L.J. in *Shirlaw v Southern Foundries Ltd*[2] (at p. 227) in the following terms:

> They are sentences from an *ex tempore* judgment as sound and sensible as all the utterances of that great judge; but I fancy that he would have been rather surprised if he could have foreseen that these general remarks of his would come to be a favourite citation of a supposed principle of law, and I even think that he might sympathise with the occasional impatience of his successors when *The Moorcock* is so often flushed for them in that guise.

On the same page MacKinnon L.J. said: '*Prima facie* that which in any contract is left to be implied and need not be expressed is something so obvious that it goes without saying; so that, if, while the parties were making their bargain an officious bystander were to suggest some express provision for it in their agreement, they would testily suppress him with a common "Oh, of course!".'

Can that test be applied in this case? Is it so obvious that the parties intended, as they contracted on 23 March (Holy Thursday) that a week from then a letter of credit, providing for the payment of 1 May of £2.4m, would have been established in favour of the defendants at the plaintiffs' bank? I cannot see anything in the circumstances attendant on this contract, or in the manner in which the contract came about, to suggest that it was obviously the intention of the parties that such should be done. Nor can I see anything in what was said or done, or in the circumstances, which would suggest that such a letter should have been opened prior to the drawing of any barley. The impracticability of doing so and the subsequent actions and conduct of the parties all suggest to my mind the absence of any such intention. Further, I cannot see that the absence of any term or agreement as to when the letter of credit was to be opened in any way affected the business efficacy of the transaction: what was required was payment by a bank of the entire purchase money on the due date. This payment date was fixed and the date of the opening of the credit could not affect, alter or prejudice this payment in any way.

On reading the evidence, I am strongly of the view (a view which was shared by the learned trial judge) that the plaintiffs sought genuinely to fulfil their contract; that they never intended to repudiate it; and that they would have abided by any reasonable request made by the defendants about the date for the opening of the letter of credit. It seems to me that all that can be implied into the contract made on behalf of the two contracting parties by Mr Fitzpatrick and Mr Kyne is that Mr Fitzpatrick, on behalf of the plaintiffs, should take reasonable and proper steps to finance the opening of a letter of credit which would mature for payment of £2.4m on 1 May 1978. If he had been dilatory in securing the transfer of funds to the plaintiffs or otherwise had acted as if the contractual obligation would not be honoured, there might have been grounds for complaint by the defendants. In my view, in the circumstances, the purported cancellation of the contract on 21 April 1978, by the defendants was unjustified. Accordingly, I would hold that the plaintiffs are entitled to succeed in their action.

[1]. (1889) 14 PD 64.   [2]. [1939] 2 KB 206.

Karim Aga Khan v Firestone [1992] ILRM 31

The plaintiff entered into negotiations with the defendant with a view to purchasing a stud farm and certain company shares owned by the defendant. The plaintiff claimed that the property was offered to him for the sum of $14.2 million and he accepted. The agreement was to be confirmed in writing and was confirmed in two letters from the defendants' lawyers to the plaintiff's lawyer on 1 and 4 December 1989 setting out all the terms agreed. The defendants later claimed that there were only discussions and that no valid contract existed. The plaintiff sought specific performance of the agreement.

Morris J.:

Counsel for Mr and Mrs Firestone next argues that the circumstances of the case are such that there clearly was an implied term of the contract that the transaction would be carried through by means of a formal contract to be executed by the parties. More specifically that such a term should be implied into the contract on the basis of the principle in *The Moorcock* (1889) 14 PD 64. He is in effect saying, as Bowen L.J. said in *The Moorcock*, that I should presume that it was the intention of the parties that this provision should be in the contract 'with the object of giving the transaction such efficacy as both parties must have intended that at all events it should have'. In reply counsel for the Aga Khan has pointed out, in my view correctly, that the effect of making such an assumption or implying the existence of such a term would be to destroy the contract and far from giving efficacy to it, would in effect prevent its operation. I am satisfied that *The Moorcock* principle only applies where, through mischance, such a term as is sought to be implied has been omitted from the contract and is necessary in order to give the contract efficacy and to prevent the failure of the contract. To imply such a term into this contract would have the contrary effect. It would be to defeat it. It cannot in my view be logical to ask the court to imply into a contract a term so as to give it business efficacy when it would have the contrary effect. I do not accept this argument.

(An order for specific performance was granted.)

B. TERMS IMPLIED IN LAW

Many terms are implied in a contract as a result of rules of law. In such cases it is not necessary to refer the terms to the subjective intentions of the parties. The terms generally arise out of certain types of contracts where policy considerations are paramount.

Kevin Brown v James Norton and Bridget Norton; Roland Burgess v Same; Vincent O'Connor v Same [1954] IR 34

The plaintiffs sued the defendants claiming damages for breach of contract in selling them houses with structural defects. The plaintiffs had purchased houses which were in the course of erection.

Davitt P.:

. . .

. . . each plaintiff pleads that his purchase agreement was an agreement for the purchase of a house in the course of erection; that the defendants impliedly agreed that they would complete the erection of his house and that it would be completed of sound and suitable materials and in a proper and workmanlike manner, and when complete would be fit for human habitation. Each alleges a breach of the implied agreement as subsequently described in his evidence.

. . .

The plaintiffs rested their cases almost entirely upon the authority of the decision in *Miller v Cannon Hill Estates Ltd*[1] as accepted and applied in this country. It is sufficient at this stage to say that I consider that that case is an authority for the proposition that where a building contractor agrees to sell to a purchaser a dwelling house which is in the course of erection, and both parties understand that the purchaser is buying for the purpose of occupying it as a residence as soon as it is completed, a court may, in the absence of any circumstances negativing such an implication, hold that the vendor impliedly agrees that he will complete the house, and will do so in such a way that when complete it will be reasonably fit for immediate occupation as a residence. In this sense I believe that the decision has been readily accepted and applied during the last twenty years by the High Court and the Circuit Court in this country.

. . .

I think that the law which I have to apply in these cases may be stated thus: where there is an agreement to purchase a house in the course of erection, and it is clearly understood by the parties that what the purchaser is contracting to buy and the vendor is contracting to sell is a dwelling house in which the purchaser can live as soon as it is completed by the vendor, the court may hold, in the absence of any circumstances negativing such an implication, that the vendor impliedly agrees (1) that he will complete the building of the house; (2) that as regards what has already been done at the date of the agreement the quality of the work and materials *is* such, and as regards what then remains to be done the quality *will be* such, that the house when completed will be reasonably fit for immediate occupation as a residence; and (3) that as regards what then remains to be done the work will be carried out in a good and workmanlike manner and with sound and suitable materials. The expressions, 'completed house' and 'house in course of erection', so frequently used in cases of this kind are not, of course, to be treated as if they were expressions used in an enactment of the legislature. In no case has it been sought to define them nor would it be advisable to make an attempt at definition.

[1]. |1931| 2 KB 113.

(Davitt P. awarded damages for breach of contract to the first two defendants, but not to the third defendant as his house was found to be complete at the time of the agreement.)

Liverpool City Council *v* Irwin and Another |1976| 2 All ER 39

The tenants of a council maisonette on the ninth and tenth floors of a fifteen storey tower block refused to pay rent, and sought damages claiming that the council were in breach of their duty to repair and maintain the common parts of the building of which they retained control.

The Court of Appeal allowed an appeal from the court of first instance where the tenants were awarded damages. The tenants appealed to the House of Lords, reported at [1977] AC 239.

Lord Wilberforce:

We have then a contract which is partly, but not wholly, stated in writing. In order to complete it, in particular to give it a bilateral character, it is necessary to take account of the actions of the parties and the circumstances. As actions of the parties, we must note the granting of possession by the landlords and reservation by them of the 'common parts'—stairs, lifts, chutes, etc. As circumstances we must include the nature of the premises, *viz.*, a maisonette for family use on the ninth floor of a high block, one which is occupied by a large number of other tenants, all using the common parts and dependent upon them, none of them having any expressed obligation to maintain or repair them.

To say that the construction of a complete contract out of these elements involves a process of 'implication' may be correct; it would be so if implication means the supplying of what is not expressed. But there are varieties of implications which the courts think fit to make and they do not necessarily involve the same process. Where there is, on the face of it, a complete, bilateral contract, the courts are sometimes willing to add terms to it, as implied terms: this is very common in mercantile contracts where there is an established usage: in that case the courts are spelling out what both parties know and would, if asked, unhesitatingly agree to be part of the bargain. In other cases, where there is an apparently complete bargain, the courts are willing to add a term on the ground that without it the contract will not work—this is the case, if not of *The Moorcock* (1889) 14 PD 64 itself on its facts, at least of the doctrine of *The Moorcock* as usually applied. This is, as was pointed out by the majority in the Court of Appeal, a strict test—though the degree of strictness seems to vary with the current legal trend—and I think that they were right not to accept it as applicable here. There is a third variety of implication, that which I think Lord Denning M.R. favours, or at least did favour in this case, and that is the implication of reasonable terms. But though I agree with many of his instances, which in fact fall under one or other of the preceding heads, I cannot go so far as to endorse his principle; indeed, it seems to me, with respect, to extend a long, and undesirable, way beyond sound authority.

The present case, in my opinion, represents a fourth category, or I would rather say a fourth shade on a continuous spectrum. The court here is simply concerned to establish what the contract is, the parties not having themselves fully stated the terms. In this sense the court is searching for what must be implied.

. . .

There can be no doubt that there must be implied (i) an easement for the tenants and their licensees to use the stairs, (ii) a right in the nature of an easement to use the lifts, (iii) an easement to use the rubbish chutes.

But are these easements to be accompanied by any obligation upon the landlord, and what obligation?

. . .

In my opinion such obligation should be read into the contract as the nature of the contract itself implicitly requires, no more, no less: a test, in other words, of necessity. . . . To leave the landlord free of contractual obligation as regards these matters, and subject only to administrative or political pressure, is, in my opinion, inconsistent totally with the nature of this relationship. The subject matter of the lease (high rise blocks) and the relationship created by the tenancy demand, of their nature, some contractual obligation on the landlord.

I do not think that this approach involves any innovation as regards the law of contract. The necessity to have regard to the inherent nature of a contract and of the relationship thereby established was stated in this House in *Lister v Romford Ice and Cold Storage Co. Ltd* |1957| AC 555. That was a case between master and servant and of a search for an 'implied term'. Viscount Simonds, at p. 579, makes a clear distinction between a search for an implied term such as might be necessary to give 'business efficacy' to the particular contract and a search, based on wider considerations, for such a term as the nature of the contract might call for, or as a legal incident of this kind of contract. If the search were for the former, he says, ' . . . I should lose myself in the attempt to formulate it with the necessary precision.' (p. 576).
. . .

I accept, of course, the argument that a mere grant of an easement does not carry with it any obligation on the part of the servient owner to maintain the subject matter. The dominant owner must spend the necessary money, for example in repairing a drive leading to his house. And the same principle may apply when a landlord lets an upper floor with access by a staircase: responsibility for maintenance may well rest on the tenant. But there is a difference between that case and the case where there is an essential means of access, retained in the landlord's occupation, to units in a building of multi-occupation, for unless the obligation to maintain is, in a defined manner, placed upon the tenants, individually or collectively, the nature of the contract, and the circumstances, require that it be placed on the landlord.

It remains to define the standard. My Lords, if, as I think, the test of the existence of the term is necessity the standard must surely not exceed what is necessary having regard to the circumstances. To imply an absolute obligation to repair would go beyond what is a necessary legal incident and would indeed be unreasonable. An obligation to take reasonable care to keep in reasonable repair and usability is what fits the requirements of the case.
. . .

And in agreement, I believe, with your Lordships I would hold that it has not been shown in this case that there was any breach of that obligation. On the main point therefore I would hold that the appeal fails.

Lord Cross of Chelsea:

When it implies a term in a contract the court is sometimes laying down a general rule that in all contracts of a certain type—sale of goods, master and servant, landlord and tenant and so on—some provision is to be implied unless the parties have expressly excluded it. In deciding whether or not to lay down such a *prima facie* rule the court will naturally ask itself whether in the general run of such cases the term in question would be one which it would be reasonable to insert. Sometimes, however, there is no question of laying down any *prima facie* rule applicable to all cases of a defined type but what the court is being in effect asked to do is to rectify a particular—often a very detailed—contract by inserting in it a term which the parties have not expressed. Here it is not enough for the court to say that the suggested term is a reasonable one the presence of which would make the contract a better or fairer one; it must be able to say that the insertion of the term is necessary to give—as it is put—'business efficacy' to the contract and that if its absence had been pointed out at the time both parties— assuming them to have been reasonable men—would have agreed without hesitation to its insertion. The distinction between the two types of case was pointed out by Viscount

Simonds and Lord Tucker in their speeches in *Lister v Romford Ice and Cold Storage Co. Ltd*
|1957| AC 555, 579, 594, but I think that Lord Denning M.R. in proceeding—albeit with
some trepidation—to 'kill off' Mackinnon L.J.'s 'officious bystander' (*Shirlaw v Southern
Foundries (1926) Ltd* |1939| 2 KB 206, 227) must have overlooked it. Counsel for the
appellant did not in fact rely on this passage in the speech of Lord Denning. His main
argument was that when a landlord lets a number of flats or offices to a number of
different tenants giving all of them rights to use the staircases, corridors and lifts there is
to be implied, in the absence of any provision to the contrary, an obligation on the landlord to keep the 'common parts' in repair and the lifts in working order. But, for good
measure, he also submitted that he could succeed on the 'officious bystander' test.

I have no hesitation in rejecting this alternative submission. We are not here
dealing with an ordinary commercial contract by which a property company is letting
one of its flats for profit. The respondent council is a public body charged by law with
the duty of providing housing for members of the public selected because of their
need for it at rents which are subsidised by the general body of ratepayers. Moreover
the officials in the council's housing department would know very well that some of
the tenants in any given block might subject the chutes and lifts to rough treatment
and that there was an ever present danger of deliberate damage by young 'vandals'—
some of whom might in fact be children of the tenants in that or neighbouring blocks.
In these circumstances, if at the time when the respondents were granted their tenancy
one of them had said to the council's representative: 'I suppose that the council will
be under a legal liability to us to keep the chutes and the lifts in working order and the
staircases properly lighted,' the answer might well have been—indeed I think, as Roskill
L.J. thought |1976| QB 319, 338, in all probability would have been—'Certainly not.'

(Lord Salmon, Lord Edmund-Davies and Lord Fraser of Tullybelton concurred and the appeal was dismissed.)

Note

In relation to the third category of implication referred to by Lord Wilberforce
in this case, see *Sepes Establishment v K.S.K. Enter. Ltd* |1993| ILRM 46 where
O'Hanlon expressly approved of the following dicta of Roskill J. in *Bandar
Pty Holdings Ltd v J. S. Darwen (Successors) Ltd* |1968| 2 All ER 305:

It is axiomatic that a court will not imply a term which has not been expressed merely
because, had the parties thought of the possibility of expressing that term it would
have been reasonable for them to have done so. Before a term which has not been
expressed can be implied it has got to be shown not only that it would be reasonable
to make that implication, but that it is necessary in order to make the contract work
that such a term should be implied. It has sometimes been expressed as 'necessary for
the business efficacy of the contract'.

Patrick Siney *v* The Right Honorable the Lord Mayor, Aldermen and Burgesses of Dublin [1980] IR 400

The defendant corporation was a housing authority obliged by the Housing
Act 1966 to provide for the housing needs of the inhabitants of a
functional area. The plaintiff was let a flat in one of the defendants' blocks
of flats. Within two months water appeared under the floor covering of the
bedroom and a fungus spread over the walls. Eventually the plaintiff and

his family were forced to leave. In the Circuit Court the plaintiff claimed damages from the defendants for breach of contract, breach of statutory duty and negligence. Certain questions of law were referred by way of case stated to the Supreme Court. The first question asked if the facts constituted a breach by the defendants of their contract with the plaintiff.

O'Higgins C.J.:

The first question involves a consideration as to whether, in the particular letting of this flat to the plaintiff, a warranty can be implied as to its fitness or suitability for habitation by the plaintiff and his family. This is so because the document which was signed on 23 August 1973, contains thirty two conditions which either define the rights of the defendants or specify the obligations of the plaintiff tenant. There is no express warranty on the part of the defendants as to the suitability of the flat for any particular purpose, nor is such a warranty expressly excluded. Therefore, it becomes a question as to whether such a warranty can be implied in this particular letting in the circumstances. The law as to the circumstances under which a warranty may be implied in a contract was stated many years ago by Bowen L.J. in this well known passage from p. 68 of his judgment in *The Moorcock*[1]:

> Now, an implied warranty, or, as it is called, a covenant in law, as distinguished from an express contract or express warranty, really is in all cases founded on the presumed intention of the parties, and upon reason. The implication which the law draws from what must obviously have been the intention of the parties, the law draws with the object of giving efficacy to the transaction and preventing such a failure of consideration as cannot have been within the contemplation of either side; and I believe if one were to take all the cases, and they are many, of implied warranties or covenants in law, it will be found that in all of them the law is raising an implication from the presumed intention of the parties with the object of giving to the transaction such efficacy as both parties must have intended that at all events it should have.

At once the question arises as to whether this principle of law has any application or relevance in a case such as the present. Counsel for the defendants submit very strongly that it has not. As this was a letting of an unfurnished flat or dwelling, they assert that no such warranty can be implied. In this respect they rely on a long line of authorities as illustrated by *Sutton v Temple*;[2] *Hart v Windsor*;[3] *Brown v Norton*[4] and *Chambers v Cork Corporation*.[5] Those authorities established the proposition that the mere letting of land, with or without an unfurnished dwelling house upon it, carried no such implication of a warranty with regard to fitness for any particular purpose. Those cases applied the rule of *caveat emptor* to all lettings of land, with or without a house thereon, in the same way as it was applied to contracts for the sale of land.

An exception, which is not relevant to this case, was recognised where a furnished house was let for occupation; in such a case a covenant on the part of the landlord that the premises would be fit for such occupation at the commencement of the tenancy is implied: *Smith v Marrable*;[6] *Wilson v Finch Hatton*;[7] *Collins v Hopkins*[8] and *Brown v Norton*. A further exception was recognised where a lessor sold by way of lease a house under construction; in such circumstances terms could be implied with regard to the completion of the house, the suitability of the materials used, the quality of the workmanship and its fitness for habitation: *Norris v Staps*;[9] *Pearce v Tucker*;[10] G. H. Myers & Co. v Brent Cross Service Co.;[11] *Hall v Burke*[12] and *Brown v Norton*.

There can be no doubt that the authorities mentioned (and others which are too numerous to cite) do establish the proposition that a mere letting of land, with or without an unfurnished house thereon, carried with it no implication that either the land or the house would be fit for any particular purpose. This rule probably developed when the main subject of conveyances and leases was land, and when buildings and houses were often of secondary importance in a society that was thinly urbanised. To-day the application of such a rule in a society which is becoming more and more urbanised, and in which the building and sale of houses has become a major industry, may appear somewhat harsh and inappropriate. However, whether the rule has or has not survived changes in society is not in issue in this case. The issue is whether it can be applied, or ought to be applied, in the particular circumstances of this letting by the defendants to the plaintiff.

To answer this question, regard must be had to the Housing Act, 1966, under which this letting was made, and to the position, powers and obligations of the defendants under that Act. The Act of 1966 is a major piece of social legislation which is aimed at dealing with the distressing problem of families that are unable to provide for themselves and being either homeless or living in overcrowded, unhealthy and unfit houses. The Act sought to establish administrative machinery under which such conditions could be eliminated gradually throughout the country, and by means of which new and suitable dwellings could be provided for those in need. Under its provisions the defendant corporation became a housing authority.

. . .

Generally, it may be said that under the Act of 1966 the defendant corporation, as a housing authority, was charged with the task, in respect of its own functional area, of ending overcrowding and of eliminating substandard and unsuitable housing for poor people. The defendants were also empowered, and obliged, to let such housing accommodation as they were able to provide, on a priority basis, to people released from these conditions. In short, the aim of the Act of 1966 was to bring into existence decent housing which, in each functional area, would be introduced by the housing authority and the standards of which would be maintained by that authority. It is now necessary to consider the particular letting made to the plaintiff.

This letting was expressed to be a letting of a 'dwelling provided by the corporation under the Housing Act, 1966.' Moreover, it was a letting of one of a number of newly-built flats. Therefore, it was a letting made by the defendant corporation of a dwelling provided under its building programme and let by it in accordance with its scheme of priority for, *inter alia*, the ending of overcrowding and the elimination of houses unfit in any respect for human habitation. Under these circumstances, can it be said that such a letting carried no implication that the accommodation thereby provided for a necessitous family would be fit for habitation by them? It seems to me that to not imply such a condition or warranty would be to assume that the defendant corporation was entitled to disregard, and was disregarding, the responsibilities cast upon it by the very Act which authorised the building and letting of the accommodation in question.

. . .

Accordingly, I have come to the conclusion that the letting made to the plaintiff by the defendants did include an implied warranty that the premises let would be reasonably fit for human habitation and, therefore, I would answer affirmatively the first question in the case stated. In my view the plaintiff is entitled to damages on this account.

Henchy J.:

To determine what is implied in such a letting, it is the powers and duties of the housing authority under the Act that must be examined and, as I hope I have shown, these necessarily require the housing authority to ensure that the dwelling, when let, is fit for human habitation.

I do not find it necessary or desirable to express an opinion as to the wider question whether there should be held to be implied a condition as to habitability in the letting of every kind of dwelling house.

As I construe the law, the plaintiff is entitled to succeed in contract for the particular reason that this flat was provided under the Act of 1966. Therefore, it is academic to consider whether he would be entitled to succeed if the flat had not been provided under the Act. Whether in such circumstances he would be entitled to sue on an implied condition as to habitability is a point on which this court has never pronounced. Were it necessary to decide the point, it is not unlikely that the Chief Justice would consider it necessary to convene a full court for that purpose, for there are long-standing judicial authorities which hold that a condition as to habitability is not to be implied in the letting of an unfurnished dwelling house. If those authorities are to be set aside, it would probably be better to do so by statute, with prospective effect, rather than by judicial decision with its necessarily retrospective effect.

[1.] (1889) 14 PD 64.
[2.] (1843) 12 M. & W. 52.
[3.] (1843) 12 M. & W. 68.
[4.] [1954] IR 34.
[5.] (1958) 93 ILTR 45.
[6.] (1843) 11 M. & W. 5.
[7.] (1877) 2 ExD 336.
[8.] [1923] 2KB 617.
[9.] (1616) Hob. 210.
[10.] (1862) 3 F. & F. 136.
[11.] [1934] 1 KB 46.
[12.] (1886) 3 TLR 165.

(Kenny J. concurred.)

The court also found that in the special circumstances the defendant had owed the plaintiff a duty to take reasonable care to ensure that the flat was fit for human habitation based on the principles in *Donoghue v Stevenson* [1932] AC 562 and *Anns v Merton London Borough* [1978] AC 728. There was said however to be no cause of action for breach of a statutory duty based on an interpretation of the Act.

Note

1. Counsel for the defendants in this case argued that a term which is not expressed in a contract cannot be held to be implied merely because its implication would be reasonable. They suggested that based on the decision in *Liverpool City Council v Irwin* such a term can be inserted by implication only if its implied insertion is necessary to make the contract work. Furthermore they claimed that the liability of the landlord in *Liverpool City Council v Irwin* related to structures which were ancillary to the demised premises and which had never passed out of the landlord's control.
2. In *Ian Burke (a minor), Angela Tinkler, Celine Hickey and Lorraine Wade v The Right Honourable The Lord Mayor, Aldermen and Burgesses of Dublin* [1991] IR 341 the Supreme Court held that the implied warranty that premises were habitable acknowledged in *Siney* applied equally to the letting of a house which was not new as to a flat. The warranty was also held to apply to a

transfer under the same Act to a person entitled under the Act to be housed by the housing authority.

A. Phang 'Implied Terms Revisited' [1990] JBL 39
(Footnotes omitted.)

The distinction attacked

It would probably come as no surprise to the reader that the theoretical objections that 'attack', as it were, the distinction between the two broad categories of terms considered above are primarily radical in cast.

Before considering these theoretical critiques, it would be appropriate to recapitulate the basic difference as manifested in the precedents—although, as already demonstrated, the derivation as well as substance of this distinction is none too clear. Assuming, however, that such a distinction does indeed exist, there is, first, a narrower test based on either the 'business efficacy' criterion or 'officious bystander' criterion for 'terms implied in fact' in order to give effect to the *presumed* intention of the parties, and, secondly, a broader test based on 'reasonableness' (having regard to *public policy* considerations) for 'terms implied by law'. When terms cannot be implied on the first (and narrower) basis, the latter category offers a second string to one's legal bow, so to speak. This was indeed, the situation in the *Liverpool City Council*, *Pinios Shipping Co.*, and *Elawadi* cases, where counsel, realising that a term could not be implied on the narrower basis, opted to argue for implication on a broader and ostensibly more liberal basis. Although this approach makes sense not only from counsel's perspective but also from a logical point of view, it might, however, actually be as, if not more, difficult *in practice* for counsel to successfully argue for the implication of a 'term implied in law'. Be that as it may, the 'theoretical liberality' nevertheless remains. It would appear on the other hand, that—and there are hints to this effect in *The 'Good Luck'* where *both* categories were considered—where a party fails to obtain implication of a term under the second (and broader) category, he would almost certainly fail to obtain implication of a term under the first category as well. Again, this makes for good logic. Returning, however, to more theoretical, yet no less important, issues, let us now turn to the relevant arguments which, as just mentioned, are quite radical in nature.

A relatively less radical argument, however, would run along the following lines. The implication of terms 'in fact' (whether based upon either the 'business efficacy' test or the 'officious bystander' test, or both) must, in accordance with the present view of the modern law of contract, be effected via an *objective* test. We will not here be concerned with the exact conceptual distinctions as well as procedures by which the objective approach ought, in fact, to be applied. What, however, is important for our present purposes is the fact that this application of the objective approach does bring the category of 'terms implied in fact' much closer, in *substance* at least, to that of 'terms implied in law' than appears at first blush. This is due to the fact that the test of 'reasonableness' as applied to the second category of 'terms implied in law' itself connotes an objective ascertainment. In essence, therefore, although there is a theoretical difference between the two categories of terms, insofar as the objective approach applies to both, the outcome of each issue does rest, in many ways, in the 'hands' of the *court* itself. This (less radical) argument does not, however, go so far as to state that both tests have been merged into a broader objective test, such as that suggested by Lord Denning. It may, of course, be argued that notwithstanding the element of objectivity contained in both tests, this is merely a procedural (as opposed to a substantive) similarity, contrary to the argument just made. This reasoning is not unpersuasive, and leads us to another related (albeit more radical) argument.

The more radical argument is premised upon the rejection of the concept of 'objectivity' altogether. This approach views *every* decision as depending upon the subjective bias and convictions of the court concerned. Looked at in this light, the distinction between both categories of implied terms must perforce be a mythical one, since, *regardless* of the *ostensible* categories, everything depends, in the final analysis, on an *ad hoc* value choice by the court concerned.

Note

Treitel argues that in the *Moorcock* case itself Bowen L.J was not exclusively concerned with the actual intention of the parties but rather concentrated on objective criteria of reasonableness. (Treitel, *The Law of Contract*, (8th ed.),193–4).

C. CONTRACTS OF EMPLOYMENT

Terms may be implied into contracts of employment by operation of law.

Michael Meade Carvill v Irish Industrial Bank Ltd [1968] IR 325. The plaintiff sued for wrongful dismissal from his post as managing director of the defendant company. He had been dismissed on grounds of misconduct without any notice.

O'Keeffe J.:

I think the plaintiff must be regarded as employed under a contract from year to year as managing director, and that it must be implied also that such contract could not be determined without such notice as is appropriate to an engagement of the kind mentioned. . . . In the circumstances I see no reason for disturbing the finding of the trial judge that the appropriate period of notice was a year.

(O'Dalaigh C.J., Lavery, Haugh and Walsh JJ. concurred. Damages were thus awarded.)

Mary Grehan v The North Eastern Health Board, The Minister for Health, Ireland and the Attorney General [1989] IR 422

The plaintiff was hired by the first defendant in 1981 to provide general practitioner medical services. The schedule annexed to her contract incorporated detailed terms and conditions which had been agreed in 1972 after negotiations between the minister and the Irish Medical Organisation. These terms included provisions for the termination of the agreement in certain specified circumstances. In 1988 the minister, following further negotiations with the Irish Medical Organisation notified practitioners that the new terms and conditions would be implemented from 1 January 1989. The plaintiff instituted proceedings seeking declarations that her contract could not be terminated or altered without her consent.

Costello J.:

. . .

Should as a matter of law a further term be implied to the effect that the board could terminate the agreement at any time by giving reasonable notice? To answer that question I think I should briefly state the legal principles on the implication of terms. The legal principles applicable are not really in controversy. The debate, as so often happens, lies in their application to the facts of the case. In business transactions (and the contract between the plaintiff and the board can, for present purposes, be so regarded): 'A term can only be implied if it is necessary in the business sense to give efficacy to the contract; that is, if it is such a term that it can confidently be said that if at the time the contract was being negotiated someone had said to the parties, "What will happen in such a case", they would both have replied, "Of course, so and so will happen; we did not trouble to say that; it is too clear".'

And furthermore:

> If there is any reasonable doubt whether the parties did intend to enter into such a contract as is sought to be enforced, the document should be looked at and all the surrounding circumstances considered; and, if the document is silent and there is no bad faith on the part of the alleged promisor, the court 'ought to be extremely careful' how it implies a term. It is not enough to say that it would be reasonable to make a particular implication; nor that it would make the carrying out of the contract more convenient; nor that it is consistent with the express provisions of the contract or with the intentions of the parties as gathered from other provisions; nor will a term be implied where a contract is effective without the proposed term.
>
> Whether a term will be implied is a question of law for the court. A term will not be implied so as to contradict any express term; and, in fact, a term ought not to be implied unless on considering the whole matter in a reasonable manner it is clear that the parties must have intended that there should be the suggested stipulation. The court has no discretion to create a new contract. Where a contract contains an express obligation by a party to the contract, if is for that party to show that there is some implied term which qualifies the obligation. (see Halsbury's Laws of England, (4th ed., 1974) vol. 9 paras 355 and 356).

Only limited assistance can be obtained from previously decided cases as the facts of each case vary so much. Both parties however referred me to the speeches in the House of Lords in McClelland v Northern Ireland General Health Services Board [1957] NI 100, a case in which that court decided by a three to two majority that it would not imply a term into a term of the plaintiff's contract with the defendant health board that it could be terminated by the board on reasonable notice. I need not delay by referring to the facts as they bear little relationship to those of the instant case. What is of importance is to see what principles the court applied. It was accepted that in employment cases of general hiring for an indefinite time an employer is entitled to terminate it on reasonable notice, but the majority took the view that as the contract was not one for an indefinite period no term should be implied for its termination by such notice. The majority also considered that it should apply the 'business efficacy' test and concluded that because the parties had made express provision for the rights of the parties to determine the contract it was not necessary to imply any further right to give the transaction the efficacy that both parties must have intended it to have.

Looking at the contract which the parties entered into in this case it would, it seems to me, be an abuse of language to say that it amounted to a general hiring of the plaintiff's services by the board for an indefinite period for para. 31 quite explicitly states that the agreement was to terminate when the plaintiff reached the age of seventy (unless, of course, it had been previously terminated under one or other of the earlier provisions). Furthermore, it will be noted that the provisions relating to termination are very detailed and their comprehensive nature would strongly suggest that an implication of a further term relating to the parties' rights of termination would not be justified.

I turn, then, as I am required to do when asked to imply a term in a contract, to consider the circumstances in which this contract was negotiated and concluded. The provenance of the detailed terms and conditions in the schedule to the parties' contract is highly relevant for these were not negotiated by the parties themselves but were the result of negotiations which had previously taken place between the Minister for Health and his officials and representatives of the Irish Medical Union, negotiations which resulted in an agreement in 1972 that doctors would agree to the incorporation of these terms and conditions in their contracts with health boards. By circular 13/72 of 15 May 1972, they were circulated to health boards who were specifically instructed to enter into contracts with medical practitioners incorporating these terms and conditions. Both the plaintiff and the board in this case were, of course, aware that the terms and conditions in the schedule were in standard from and of the circumstances in which they were drafted, and I think that the intention of the parties at the time they entered into their contract was to give effect to terms and conditions agreed to by the minister and the medical unions in 1972 and that they did not intend that the terms so agreed would be altered in any way. As an implication of a term is based on the presumed intention of the parties, I cannot conclude that the parties intended that their contract would have any additional terms.

. . .

I must conclude, therefore, form the facts surrounding the making of this contract and because the suggested term is not required to give it efficacy, that as a matter of law the court cannot imply a further term into the parties' contract. It cannot therefore be terminated by the board by reasonable notice. . . .

In *Royal Trust Co. of Canada (Ireland) Ltd and the Trustee Savings Bank Dublin v Kelly and Others* (HC) 27 February 1989, unrep. Barron J. referred to *Ward v Spivack Ltd* [1957] Ir 40 before holding 'it is an implied term of every contract of employment other than for a fixed period that it can be terminated upon reasonable notice'.

Imperial Group Pension Trust Ltd and Others *v* Imperial Tobacco Ltd and Others [1991] 2 All ER 597

Browne-Wilkinson V.C.:

. . .

In every contract of employment there is an implied term: 'that the employers will not, without reasonable and proper cause, conduct themselves in a manner calculated or likely to destroy or seriously damage the relationship of confidence and trust between employer and employee . . .' (See *Woods v WM Car Services (Peterborough) Ltd* [1981] ICR 666 at 670, approved by the Court of Appeal in *Lewis v Motorworld Garages Ltd* [1986] ICR 157.) I will call this implied term 'the implied obligation of good faith'. In my judgment, that obligation of an employer applies as much to the exercise of his rights and powers under a pension scheme as they do to the other rights and powers of an employer. Say, in purported exercise of its right to give or withhold consent, the company were to say, capriciously, that it would consent to an increase in the pension benefits of members of union A but not of the members of union B. In my judgment, the members of union B would have a good claim in contract for breach of the implied obligation of good faith: see *Mihlenstedt's* case [1989] IRLR 522 at 525, 531–532 (paras 12, 64, 70).

Note

In *Scally v Southern Health and Social Services Board* [1992] 1 AC 294 the House of Lords decided that where a contract of employment negotiated between employers and a representative body contained a particular term conferring on an employer pension rights of the benefit of which he could not be expected to be aware unless the term was brought to his attention, there was an implied obligation on the employer to take reasonable steps to publicise that term. Lord Bridge of Harwich drew a clear distinction between 'the search for an implied term necessary to give business efficacy to a particular contract and the search, based on wider considerations, for a term which the law will imply as a necessary incident of a definable category of contractual relationship.'

Lord Bridge also referred to the difficulty which would arise if the implied term 'must necessarily be too wide in its ambit to be acceptable as of general application'. He suggested that 'this difficulty is surmounted if the category of contractual relationship in which the implication will arise is defined with sufficient precision'.

The *Scally* case was relied upon in *Spring v Guardian Assurances plc and Others*, [1994] 3 All ER 129. The majority of the House of Lords accepted that if a reference is given by an employer, an implied obligation arises to take reasonable care in giving the reference. Reference was also made to the sentence in Lord Edmund-Davies' judgment in *Liverpool City Council v Irwin* [1977] AC 239 to the effect that 'the touchstone is always necessity and not merely reasonableness'.

Lord Woolf:

. . .

. . . As I understand *Scally*, it recognises that, just as in the earlier authorities the courts were prepared to imply by necessary implication a term imposing a duty on an employer to exercise due care for the physical well-being of his employees, so in the appropriate circumstances would the court imply a like duty as to his economic well-being, the duty as to his economic well-being giving rise to an action for damages if it is breached.

Here, it is also possible to specify circumstances which would enable a term to be implied. The circumstances are:

(i) The existence of the contract of employment or services.

(ii) The fact that the contract relates to an engagement of a class where it is the normal practice to require a reference from a previous employer before employment is offered.

(iii) The fact that the employee cannot be expected to enter into that class of employment except on the basis that his employer will, on the request of another prospective employer made not later than a reasonable time after the termination of a former employment, provide a full and frank reference as to the employee.

This being the nature of the engagement, it is necessary to imply a term into the contract that the employer would, during the continuance of the engagement or within a reasonable time thereafter, provide a reference at the request of a prospective employer which was based on facts revealed after making those reasonably careful inquiries which, in the circumstances, a reasonable employer would make.

SECTION TWO—TERMS IMPLIED IN CUSTOM

Relevant customs of a particular market, trade, profession or region may be implied into a contract.

Patrick O'Reilly *v* The Irish Press Ltd (1937) 71 ILTR 194

The plaintiff, chief sub-editor of a paper owned by the defendants, claimed damages for wrongful dismissal on the basis that custom entitled him to six months notice.

Maguire P.:

As was said, . . . a custom or usage of any kind is a difficult thing to establish. Before a usage such as is contended for here can be held to be established it must be proved by persons whose position in the world of journalism entitles them to speak with certainty and knowledge of its existence. I have to be satisfied that it is so notorious, well known and acquiesced in that in the absence of agreement in writing it is to be taken as one of the terms of the contract between the parties.
. . .

The absence of evidence of actual instances to show the length of notice given to or by chief sub-editors does not surprise me. Having regard to the relatively small number of such posts it was natural that instances of dismissal or resignation of chief sub-editors should be exceedingly rare. A chief sub-editor generally goes higher and seldom goes down or out.
. . .

The absence of actual instances of the usage in practice would not, however, preclude me from holding that the usage existed if I were satisfied that it was well known and universally recognised.

As I have already stated, it is necessary in order to establish a custom of the kind claimed that it be shown that it was so generally known that anyone concerned should have known of it, or could easily have become aware of it.

With some hesitation and considerable regret I must hold that the evidence before me has not established such notoriety or general acquiescence for the usage as to enable me to hold it established. I say 'with considerable regret' because I would be glad to decide the case on usage. Apparently a usage with regard to dismissal of sub-editors and editors can be established. As regards chief sub-editors, notwithstanding the fact that several witnesses knew of the existence of a usage in certain circles governing the length of notice to be given I have come to the conclusion that there was not that universality of acceptance of the usage in the newspaper world in general that is required to establish it as a usage.

Note

In *O'Conaill v The Gaelic Echo* (1958) 92 ILTR 156 Hannan J. in the District Court accepted that the customary period of notice in the absence of express agreement to dismiss newspaper reporters in the Dublin City area was one month.

SECTION THREE—TERMS IMPLIED BY STATUTE

Many terms that are implied in law have been incorporated into statutes.

For example ss 12–15 of the Sale of Goods Act 1893, as amended by the Sale of Goods & Supply of Services Act 1980, in addition to s. 39 of the 1980 Act, imply terms into contracts for goods and services with the object of protecting the consumer.

12. (1) In every contract of sale, other than one to which subsection (2) applies, there is:

(*a*) an implied condition on the part of the seller that, in the case of a sale, he has a right to sell the goods and, in the case of an agreement to sell, he will have a right to sell the goods at the time when the property is to pass, and

(*b*) an implied warranty that the goods are free, and will remain free until the time when the property is to pass, from any charge or encumbrance not disclosed to the buyer before the contract is made and that the buyer will enjoy quiet possession of the goods except so far as it may be disturbed by the owner or other person entitled to the benefit of any charge or encumbrance so disclosed.

(2) In a contract of sale, in the case of which there appears from the contract or is to be inferred from the circumstances of the contract an intention that the seller should transfer only such title as he or a third person may have, there is:

(*a*) an implied warranty that all charges or encumbrances known to the seller have been disclosed to the buyer before the contract is made, and

(*b*) an implied warranty that neither:

(i) the seller, nor

(ii) in a case where the parties to the contract intend that the seller should transfer only such title as a third person may have, that person, nor

(iii) anyone claiming through or under the seller or that third person otherwise than under a charge or encumbrance disclosed to the buyer before the contract is made.

will disturb the buyer's quiet possession of the goods.

13. (1) Where there is a contract for the sale of goods by description, there is an implied condition that the goods shall correspond with the description; and if the sale be by sample as well as by description, it is not sufficient that the bulk of the goods corresponds with the sample if the goods do not also correspond with the description.

(2) A sale of goods shall not be prevented from being a sale by description by reason only that, being exposed for sale, they are selected by the buyer.

(3) A reference to goods on a label or other descriptive matter accompanying goods exposed for sale may constitute or form part of a description.

14. (1) Subject to the provisions of this Act and of any statute in that behalf, there is no implied condition or warranty as to the quality or fitness for any particular purpose of goods supplied under a contract of sale.

(2) Where the seller sells goods in the course of a business there is an implied condition that the goods supplied under the contract are of merchantable quality, except that there is no such condition:

(a) as regards defects specifically drawn to the buyer's attention before the contract is made, or

(b) if the buyer examines the goods before the contract is made, as regards defects which that examination ought to have revealed.

(3) Goods are of merchantable quality if they are as fit for the purpose or purposes for which goods of that kind are commonly bought and as durable as it is reasonable to expect having regard to any description applied to them, the price (if relevant) and all the other relevant circumstances, and any reference in this Act to unmerchantable goods shall be construed accordingly.

(4) Where the seller sells goods in the course of a business and the buyer, expressly or by implication, makes known to the seller any particular purpose for which the goods are being bought, there is an implied condition that the goods supplied under the contract are reasonably fit for that purpose, whether or not that is a purpose for which such goods are commonly supplied except where the circumstances show that the buyer does not rely, or that it is unreasonable for him to rely, on the seller's skill or judgement.

(5) An implied condition or warranty as to quality or fitness for a particular purpose may be annexed to a contract of sale by usage.

(6) The foregoing provisions of this section apply to a sale by a person who in the course of a business is acting as agent for another as they apply to a sale by a principal in the course of a business, except where that other is not selling in the course of a business and either the buyer knows that fact or reasonable steps are taken to bring it to the notice of the buyer before the contract is made.

Sale by sample

15. (1) A contract of sale is a contract for sale by sample where there is a term in the contract, express or implied, to that effect.

(2) In the case of a contract for sale by sample:

(a) There is an implied condition that the bulk shall correspond with the sample in quality;

(b) There is an implied condition that the buyer shall have a reasonable opportunity of comparing the bulk with the sample;

(c) There is an implied condition that the goods shall be free from any defect, rendering them unmerchantable, which would not be apparent on reasonable examination of the sample.

. . .

39. Subject to section 40, in every contract for the supply of a service where the supplier is acting in the course of a business, the following terms are implied:

(a) that the supplier has the necessary skill to render the service.

(b) that he will supply the service with due skill, care and diligence,

(c) that, where materials are used, they will be sound and reasonably fit for the purpose for which they are required, and

(d) that, where goods are supplied under the contract, they will be of merchantable quality within the meaning of section 14(3) of the Act of 1893 (inserted by section 10 of this Act).

Note

Many of the principal issues arising from implied terms are addressed in Chapter 8.

Chapter Eight

Risk Allocation and Consumer Protection

INTRODUCTION

The use of express contractual terms to order and regulate commercial transactions is an indispensable part of the free market system. The ability of the parties to create or transfer liability, should certain stated events occur, is an important aspect of all contract regimes and an essential feature of the principle of freedom of contract. In the Industrial Age the movement towards concluding agreements by reference to standard conditions of contract became the norm in a number of specific areas such as banking, insurance, and the carriage of goods and persons. The use of standardised contracts, in contradistinction to individualised bargaining, was explored by several distinguished American commentators, most notably perhaps Professor Karl Llewellyn:

Review of Prausnitz, O. *The Standardization of Commercial Contracts in English and Continental Law* (1937) in (1939) 52 Harv L Rev 700.

. . . when contract ceases to be a matter of dicker, bargain by bargain, and item by item, and becomes in any field or any outfit's business or any trade's practice a matter of mass production of bargains, with the background (apart from price, quantity and the like) filled in not by the general law but by standard clauses and terms, prepared often by one of the parties only—then what? One 'what' is clear: the presuppositions of our general law no longer maintain in such a situation. Those presuppositions can be stated somewhat as follows: (1) The general law is adequately specialised, and is detailed and balanced to fill in with moderate adequacy any gaps which parties leave open in their bargaining. (2) Any particular or specialised terms the parties are interested in they will bargain about. (3) Almost any particular clause included in a deal represents the parties' joint judgment as to what they want; and this alone is ground enough for letting it, for the deal in hand, displace and replace the general law. But when contracts are produced by the printing press, with the fountain pen used not for recording thought but for authentication, the adequacy of the general law for filling gaps in the conscious bargain is flatly negatived, in the view of the party preparing and ordering the form pads. And, commonly, that party is in this in good part right: specialisation of rule *is* then needed. And contracts which incorporate by reference the full 'rules' of some association stand in this on like footing. In neither case, it is to be remembered, are the individual variations from the general law bargained about. The contract is a block-contract, for one side (or both) to take or leave. If for goods, then description, quantity, delivery date, price, perhaps credit terms, may be open for actual

bargain, and these are all that at least one bargainor is in fact thinking about. Meanwhile the rest descends upon him: passage of risk, warranty, inspection requirements, exemption of seller for this or that contingency—such as strike, fire, shortage of raws or of transportation facilities—incidence of taxation, insurance, revocation of credit terms, special limitation of buyers' remedies in case of short or defective deliveries, exclusion of oral warranty or other modification, privilege of seller in the event shipping instructions are not received or goods are rejected, provision for arbitration or waiver of procedural rights—all such matters are covered *in toto* in the form or rules, to leave or to take, in block—and, commonly, to take without knowledge.
. . .

'The general law' is much too general. It needs tailoring to trades and to lines of trading. Nothing can approach in speed and sanity of readaptation the machinery of standard forms of a trade and for a line of trade, built to meet the particular needs of that trade. They save trouble in bargaining. They save time in bargaining. They infinitely simplify the task of internal administration of a business unit, of keeping tabs on transactions, of knowing where one is at, of arranging orderly expectation, orderly fulfilment, orderly planning. They ease administration by concentrating the need for discretion and decision in such personnel as can be trusted to be discreet. This reduces human wear and tear, it cheapens administration, it serves the ultimate consumer. Standardising contracts is in this a counterpart of standardising goods and production processes, as well as a device for adjustment of law to need. Prausnitz adds that such contracts, by limiting loss possibilities, can ease provision against risk (reminding us of Holmes' observation that the price paid for a contract commonly negates expectation of unusual risk). He adds, too, that it advantages a customer outfit to know that all *their* competitors are getting the same terms.

What worries Prausnitz is the combination of mass production of bargains with *one-sided* control of their detailed terms. The virtue of the 'general law', despite all inexpertness of the judges and sometimes of their formalism, has lain and does lie in a drive toward fairness, toward sane balance.
. . .

Our own concept of 'public policy' has a much more restricted field of operation. Our courts are loath indeed to throw out a contract clause under the plain justification that it is contrary to public policy, that it is such a clause as 'private' parties *cannot* make legally effective in the circumstance. Once we admit that it *is* a contract clause, and admit that it does mean what it says, we tend to regret, but to let the clause stand. And it may be that the English go even further in this than we; certainly some of the cases Prausnitz collects teach justice to shiver and shake.[1] But lacking ready recourse to *gute* Sitten or that near-equivalent in contract law, *l'ordre public* plus the *bonnes mœurs*, we have developed a whole series of semi-covert techniques for somewhat balancing these bargains. A court can 'construe' language into patently not meaning what the language is patently trying to say. It can find inconsistencies between clauses and throw out the troublesome one. It can even reject a clause as counter to the whole purpose of the transaction. It can reject enforcement by one side for want of 'mutuality', though allowing enforcement by the weaker side because 'consideration' in some other sense is present. Indeed, the law of agreeing can be subjected to divers modes of employment, to make the whole bargain or a particular clause stick or not stick according to the status of the party claiming under it: as when, in the interest of the lesser party, the whole contract is conditioned on some presupposition which is held to have failed.[2] The difficulty with these techniques of ours is threefold. First, since they all rest on the admission that the clauses in question are permissible in purpose and content, they invite the draftsman to recur to the attack. Give him time, and he will make the grade. Second, since they do not face the issue, they fail to accumulate either experience or authority in the needed direction: that of marking out for any given type of transaction what the *minimum decencies* are which a court will insist upon as essential to an enforceable bargain of a given type, or as being inherent in a bargain of that type. Third, since they purport to construe, and do not really construe, nor are intended to, but are instead tools of intentional and creative misconstruction, they seriously embarrass later efforts at true construction, later efforts to get at the true meaning of those wholly legitimate contracts and clauses which call for their meaning to be got at instead of avoided. The net effect is unnecessary confusion and unpredictability, together with inadequate remedy, and evil persisting that calls for remedy. Covert tools are never reliable tools. And the reason why Prausnitz's presentation itself rests still partly in confusion is because he does not clearly sever for separate discussion and comparison the two bodies of doctrine which run side by side in the English cases. There are, first, the doctrinal techniques of avoidance, or of misconstruction and remodelling. There are, second, the doctrinal techniques of really reading or supplementing an agreement according to its true purpose and meaning. English and American adjudication are not to be truly and fully compared with the French and German, save on the latter branch; for French and German law have the technical wherewithal for *always* trying to read accurately, and then for openly discarding objectionable clauses. Their courts have not fully grasped the opportunity, as Prausnitz's review of their decisions shows; but it is along this line that they have developed a somewhat greater clarity than have ours.[3]

[1.] *Hollis Bros & Co., Ltd v White Sea Timber Trust*, Ltd |1936| 3 All Eng 895 (KB) ('subject to seller's making necessary chartering arrangements' held to confer an option on seller to deliver or not at choice); *L'Estrange v F. Graucob, Ltd*, |1934| 2 KB 394 (small print clause: the writing includes 'All the terms and conditions under which I agree to purchase the machine specified above, and any express or implied condition, statement, or warranty, statutory or otherwise, not stated herein is hereby excluded,' stymies Scrutton himself in regard to unfitness of a slot machine for its purpose: café proprietor against manufacturer and seller; judgment on counterclaim for full unpaid price).

[2.] In such cases it is not to be expected that 'the whole contract' fails if the lesser party is claiming under it, on which Prausnitz's view of English law would be misleading if applied to American. But the further problem he raises is a fascinating one: whether, with a given clause or condition knocked out, the dominant bargainor would have entered on the deal at all. Fascinating, and hardly soluble. The practical answer lies in disregard of the problem: the type of deal was meant; the court in knocking out the clause is knocking out an inadmissible incident to that type of deal: e.g. *re* clogging an equity of redemption, or voiding usurious interest.

[3.] This is not to say that continental doctrine at large is clear. The questions surrounding the concept of contracts 'of adhesion' to which one party more affixes itself turn attention too much to the type of matter discussed by us under reality of consent; if one must take or leave in block, and needs to take, has he 'assented'? It is with a sound instinct that many writers have been impelled to answer: Yes. But that merely sets the problem. You take or leave your marriage agreement, pretty much in block; you 'adhere', you do not 'bargain'. The point is that when that is the type of choice and the only type of choice really available, it has been and still is the law's business, and in a case-law system, the judges', to see that the block to which you are indeed *assenting as a transaction* is carved into some approximation of decent balance in its detail. The 'mass' aspect properly stressed by Prausnitz goes to social importance, but it goes even more to evidencing the presence of a block of terms which is not individualised to the bargainors, and which needs re-establishment of the type of balance provided by the general 'law of sales' or 'of partnership', etc., for those who assent in block.

Note

Problems of contractual fairness and abuse of freedom of contract become particularly acute when there is a contractual imbalance as between the parties, or where one party enjoys a statutory or *de facto* monopoly. For a thoughtful analysis see H.B. Sales, Standard Form Contracts (1953) 16 MLR 318.

F. Kessler 'The Contract of Adhesion' (1943) Col L Rev 629

The development of large scale enterprise with its mass production and mass distribution made a new type of contract inevitable—the standardised mass contract.[1] A standardised contract, once its contents have been formulated by a business firm, is used in every bargain dealing with the same product or service. The individuality of the parties which so frequently gave colour to the old type contract has disappeared. The stereotyped contract of today reflects the impersonality of the market. It has reached its greatest perfection in the different types of contracts used on the various exchanges. Once the usefulness of these contracts was discovered and perfected in the transportation, insurance, and banking business, their use spread into all other fields of large scale enterprise, into international as well as national trade, and into labour relations. It is to be noted that uniformity of terms of contracts typically recurring in a business enterprise is an important factor in the exact calculation of risks. Risks which are difficult to calculate can be excluded altogether. Unforseeable contingencies affecting performance, such as strikes, fire, and transportation difficulties can be taken care of.[2] The standard clauses in insurance policies are the most striking illustrations of successful attempts on the part of business enterprises to select and control risks assumed under a contract. The insurance business probably deserves credit also for having first realised the full importance of the so-called 'juridical risk', the danger that a court or jury may be swayed by 'irrational factors' to decide against a powerful defendant. Ingenious clauses have been the result.[3] Once their practical utility was proven, they were made use of in other lines of business. It is highly probable that the desire to avoid juridical risks has been a motivating factor in the widespread use of warranty clauses in the machine industry limiting the common law remedies of the buyer to breach of an implied warranty of quality and particularly excluding his right to claim damages.[4] The same is true for arbitration clauses in international trade. Standardised contracts have thus become an important means of excluding or controlling the 'irrational factor' in litigation. In this respect they are a true reflection of the spirit of our time with its hostility to irrational factors in the judicial process, and they belong in the same category as codifications and restatements.

Insofar as the reduction of costs of production and distribution thus achieved is reflected in reduced prices, society as a whole ultimately benefits from the use of standard contracts. And there can be no doubt that this has been the case to a considerable extent. The use of standard contracts has, however, another aspect which has become increasingly important. Standard contracts are typically used by enterprises with strong bargaining power. The weaker party, in need of the goods or services, is frequently not in a position to shop around for better terms, either because the author of the standard contract has a monopoly (natural or artificial) or because all competitors use the same clauses. His contractual intention is but a subjection more or less voluntary to terms dictated by the stronger party, terms whose consequences are often understood only in a vague way, if at all. Thus, standardised contracts are frequently contracts of adhesion; they are *à prendre ou à laisser*.[5] Not infrequently the weaker party to a prospective contract even agrees in advance not to retract his offer while the offeree reserves for himself the power to accept or refuse;[6] or he submits to terms or change of terms which will be communicated to him later. To be sure, the latter type of clauses regularly provide for a power to disaffirm,[7] but as a practical matter they are acquiesced in frequently, thus becoming part of the 'living law'. Lastly, standardised contracts have also been used to control and regulate the distribution of goods from producer all the way down to the ultimate consumer. They have become one of the many devices to build up and strengthen industrial empires.

And yet the tremendous economic importance of contracts of adhesion is hardly reflected in the great texts on contracts or in the Restatement. As a matter of fact, the term 'contract of adhesion' or a similar symbol has not even found general recognition in our legal vocabulary. This will not do any harm if we remain fully aware that the use of the word 'contract' does not commit us to an indiscriminate extension of the ordinary contract rules to all contracts. But apparently the realisation of the deepgoing antinomies in the structure of our system of contracts is too painful an experience to be permitted to rise to the full level of our consciousness. Consequently, courts have made great efforts to protect the weaker contracting party and still keep 'the elementary rules' of the law of contracts intact. As a result, our common law of standardised contracts is highly contradictory and confusing, and the potentialities inherent in the common law system for coping with contracts of adhesion have not been fully developed.

1. Pausnitz, *The Standardization of Commercial Contracts in English and Continental Law* (1937) reviewed by Llewellyn (1939) 52 Harv L Rev 700; Llewellyn, 'What Price Contract—An Essay in Perspective' (1931) 40 Yale LJ 704; Issacs, 'The Standardising of Contracts' (1917) 27 Yale LJ 34; Raiser, *Das Recht der Allgemeinen Geschäftsbedingungen* (1936).
2. For a far reaching clause in a sales contract see *Hollis Bros. & Co. Ltd v White Sea Timber Trust, Ltd*, 3 All ER 895 (1936). Here the seller of timber from a port in the Arctic Circle open for navigation only about twenty one days stipulated 'this contract is subject to sellers making necessary chartering arrangements for the expedition and sold subject to shipments any goods not shipped to be cancelled.'
3. Patterson, *Essentials of Insurance Law* (1935) 282 *et seq.*
4. For an effort of the legislature to protect the interests of the buyer of agricultural machinery see North Dakota Laws (1919) c. 238, construed in *Palaniuk v Allis Chalmers Mfg Co.*, 57 ND 199, 220 NW 638 (1928).
5. The word 'contract of adhesion' has been introduced into the legal vocabulary by Patterson, 'The Delivery of a Life Insurance Policy' (1919) 33 Harv L Rev 198, 222.
6. *Cole, McIntyre, Norfleet Co. v Hollaway*, 141 Tenn. 679, 214 SW 817 (1919) discussed by Corbin in (1920) 29 Yale LJ 441.
7. See the standard form of an application for a life insurance policy, reprinted in Patterson, *Cases and Other Materials on the Law of Insurance* (1932) 819; *Robinson v US Benevolent Society*, 132 Mich. 695 (1903).

SECTION ONE—UNCONSCIONABLE BARGAIN

Schroeder Music Publishing Co. *v* Macauley [1974] 3 All ER 616

A young and inexperienced songwriter signed a music publishing contract which bound him for up to ten years while at the same time giving copyright in the songs written by him to the publisher without creating a corresponding obligation to publish all or any of these songs. The contract was standard within the music publishing industry.

The House of Lords held the contract, insofar as it was not performed, to be unenforceable.

Lord Diplock:

My Lords, the contract under consideration in this appeal is one whereby the respondent accepted restrictions on the way in which he would exploit his earning power as a song-writer for the next ten years. Because this can be classified as a contract in restraint of trade the restrictions that the respondent accepted fell within one of those limited categories of contractual promises in respect of which the courts still retain the power to relieve the promisor of his legal duty to fulfil them. In order to determine whether this case is one in which that power ought to be exercised, what your Lordships have in fact been doing has been to assess the relative bargaining power of the publisher and the song-writer at the time the contract was made and to decide whether the publisher had used his superior bargaining power to exact from the song-writer promises that were unfairly onerous to him. Your Lordships have not been concerned to enquire whether the public have in fact been deprived of the fruit of the song-writer's talents by reason of the restrictions, nor to assess the likelihood that they would be so deprived in the future if the contract were permitted to run its full course.

It is, in my view, salutary to acknowledge that in refusing to enforce provisions of a contract whereby one party agrees for the benefit of the other party to exploit or to refrain from exploiting his own earning power, the public policy which the court is implementing is not some nineteenth century economic theory about the benefit to the general public of freedom of trade, but the protection of those whose bargaining power is weak against being forced by those whose bargaining power is stronger to enter into bargains that are unconscionable. Under the influence of Bentham and of *laissez-faire* the courts in the nineteenth century abandoned the practice of applying the public policy against unconscionable bargains to contracts generally, as they had formerly done to any contract considered to be usurious; but the policy survived in its application to penalty clauses and to relief against forfeiture and also to the special category of contracts in restraint of trade. If one looks at the reasoning of nineteenth century judges in cases about contracts in restraint of trade one finds lip service paid to current economic theories but if one looks at what they said in the light of what they did, one finds that they struck down a bargain if they thought it was unconscionable as between the parties to it, and upheld it if they thought that it was not.

So I would hold that the question to be answered as respects a contract in restraint of trade of the kind with which this appeal is concerned is: was the bargain fair? The test of fairness is, no doubt, whether the restrictions are both reasonably necessary for the protection of the legitimate interest of the promisee and commensurate with the benefits secured to the promisor under the contract. For the purpose of this test all the provisions of the contract must be taken into consideration.

My Lords, the provisions of the contract have already been sufficiently stated by my noble and learned friend, Lord Reid. I agree with his analysis of them and with his conclusion that the contract is unenforceable. It does not satisfy the test of fairness as I have endeavoured to state it. I will accordingly content myself with adding some observations directed to the argument that because the contract was in a 'standard form' in common use between music publishers and song-writers, the restraints that it imposes on the song-writer's liberty to exploit his talents must be presumed to be fair and reasonable.

Standard forms of contracts are of two kinds. The first, of very ancient origin, are those which set out the terms on which mercantile transactions of common occurrence are to be carried out. Examples are bills of lading, charterparties, policies of insurance, contracts of sale in the commodity markets. The standard clauses in these contracts have been settled over the years by negotiation by representatives of the commercial interests involved and have been widely adopted because experience has shown that they facilitate the conduct of trade. Contracts of these kinds affect not only the actual parties to them but also others who may have a commercial interest in the transactions to which they relate, as buyers or sellers, charterers or shipowners, insurers or bankers. If fairness or reasonableness were relevant to their enforceability the fact that they are widely used by parties whose bargaining power is fairly matched would raise a strong presumption that their terms are fair and reasonable.

The same presumption, however, does not apply to the other kind of standard form of contract. This is of comparatively modern origin. It is the result of the concentration of particular kinds of business in relatively few hands. The ticket cases in the nineteenth century provide what are probably the first examples. The terms of this kind of standard form of contract have not been the subject of negotiation between the parties to it, or approved by any organisation representing the interests of the weaker party. They have been dictated by that party whose bargaining power, either exercised alone or in conjunction with another providing similar goods or services, enables him to say: 'If you want these goods or services at all, these are the only terms on which they are obtainable. Take it or leave it.'

To be in a position to adopt this attitude towards a party desirous of entering into a contract to obtain goods or services provides a classic instance of superior bargaining power. It is not without significance that on the evidence in the present case, music publishers in negotiating with song-writers whose success has been already established do not insist on adhering to a contract in the standard form they offered to the respondent. The fact that the appellants' bargaining power *vis-à-vis* the respondent was strong enough to enable them to adopt this take-it-or-leave it attitude raises no presumption that they used it to drive an unconscionable bargain with him, but in the field of restraint of trade it calls for vigilance on the part of the court to see that they did not.

McCord v ESB [1980] ILRM 153

O'Higgins C.J.:

The appellant is a statutory board established by s. 2 of the Electricity (Supply) Act, 1927. In accordance with the provisions of this Act it is armed with certain powers and charged with certain duties in relation to the provision of electric power throughout the country. In particular, by s. 19 it is charged with a duty to distribute, sell and promote the use of electricity and to control, co-ordinate and improve the supply of electricity generally. Over the years since its establishment the appellant has carried out these statutory functions with regard both to the supply and control of electricity to such an extent that it now exercises a virtual monopoly in relation to this essential source of energy and power. As the appellant is charged with the duty of selling electricity it is implicit, and envisaged by the Act, that it should have the power to enter into contracts with individual consumers providing for the sale of supply of electricity and for matters connected therewith. The appellant in fact does this by operating what are termed 'General Conditions relating to Supply'. These are a set of conditions, fifteen in number, which the appellant enforces throughout the country as governing the supply by it of electricity to its consumers. Every applicant for a supply of electricity is required to sign a document agreeing that such is 'to be connected, supplied and charged for in accordance with the board's general conditions relating to electrical supply.' The document contains a further acknowledgment on behalf of the applicant that he has seen and carefully read these general conditions and 'all such further or amended conditions and regulations as may be made from time to time by the board as to conditions, price or otherwise, in as full a manner as if the same were in force at the date hereof.' A postscript is added at the bottom of this document of application to the effect:

> *Important*—The board's general conditions relating to electricity supply are on display at the board's offices and showrooms, and copies are available on request. The board has the right to amend, alter or vary these conditions from time to time, and the condition of supply as so amended, altered or varied shall, while in force, be *ipso facto* binding upon the consumer.

While the ensuing relationship between the appellant and the successful applicant for a supply of electricity is termed contractual it is quite clear that it is a contract into which the person seeking a supply has no option but to enter. Not only is this so but it is one which is subject to unilateral alteration which must be accepted by the consumer if supply is to be continued. The true nature and effect of these general conditions are not in issue in this case nor has their validity been called into question. For the purpose of this case it is agreed that the relationship existing between the appellant and its consumers is based on contract and that the terms of this contract are those contained in these general conditions. I would also add, however, that these general conditions emanating as they do exclusively from the appellant must be construed strictly and must be operated fairly and reasonably.

The respondent in this appeal was and is one of the appellant's consumers. He was supplied with electricity in connection with his house at 166 Arthur Griffith Park, Lucan, in October 1973. He occupied this house with his wife and family. On 10 May 1978 one of the appellant's meter inspectors, on visiting the respondent's house, discovered that the appellant's meter therein installed had been tampered with. This meter had been opened, interfered with, and a false seal had been attached to conceal what had been done. The result was that the actual amount of electricity consumed by the household was not recorded and a considerable amount of electricity so consumed was neither charged to nor paid for by the respondent. When this was discovered the respondent and his wife disclaimed all responsibility for or knowledge of what had occurred. In ensuing interviews with representatives of the appellant the respondent was asked and required to sign a statement to the effect that while disclaiming responsibility in the manner he had indicated, he nevertheless acknowledged that the interference had taken place while the meter was in his custody and undertaking to pay for the electricity which had not been accounted for. The respondent refused to do so. Eventually and because of his attitude the appellant cut off the supply of electricity to his house. This took place on 23 May 1978. On 20 December 1978 the respondent commenced these proceedings by plenary summons claiming against the appellant damages for breach of contract and an order providing for the reconnection of supply. As a result and pending the trial of the action supply was recommenced to the respondent's house on 28 February 1979. In his statement of claim, subsequently furnished, the respondent claimed damages for the inconvenience and loss suffered by him and his family in the period in which the supply of electricity was withdrawn.

The respondent's action was tried in the High Court by the late Butler J. He came to the conclusion and so stated in his spoken judgment that the appellant was not entitled, whether for the purpose of enforcing payment of sums due or for the purpose of enforcing other terms of the contract, to cut off supply to a consumer without an order of the court. For this reason he held that the appellant had acted unreasonably and in breach of contract. However, he also held that the respondent and his wife had acted unreasonably in refusing to co-operate with the appellant's representatives and in refusing to do what was asked. He held that if the respondents had agreed to the reasonable request made of him to sign the suggested agreement and undertaking the supply of electricity would not have been cut off and none of the suffering and inconvenience which was subsequently caused would have resulted. For this reason he awarded the plaintiff only £50 damages.

The appellant brings this appeal to call into question the view expressed by Butler J. that it was not entitled to terminate or cut off supply to a consumer without first having obtained an order of the court enabling it to do so. A cross-appeal has been served by the respondent complaining that the damages awarded were inadequate.

On the hearing of the appeal, as already indicated, it was agreed that the rights of the parties depended on the contract as contained in the general conditions. The respondent did not seek to support the trial judge's view that the appellant could not act, in a situation covered by these conditions, without an order of the court. The appeal, therefore, resolved itself into a question as to whether the appellant's action, in the circumstances, was justified under the general conditions. The appellant conceded that, if not so justified, the action taken was without authority and, therefore in breach of contract. At this stage I think it proper to say that not only do these general conditions empower the appellant to cut off electricity in particular circumstances but also, that such a power is expressly given to the appellant by s. 99 of the Electricity (Supply) Act, 1927, in the circumstances to which that section applies. The question which now arises on this appeal is whether the circumstances of this particular case justified the appellant in doing what it did. In my view, these circumstances do not justify the action taken.

Counsel for the appellant rested justification for the action taken on the provisions of clause 13 of the general conditions taken in conjunction with those of clause 10. Clause 13 provides as follows:

13. Power to disconnect supply and/or terminate agreement
     The board may disconnect supply without prior notice to the consumer:

     (a) If the consumer fails to pay on demand any account issued for electricity supplied by the board, including any estimated account or any statutory charges arising in connection therewith or any other sum due to the board on foot of a contract for the supply of electricity.
     (b) If the consumer commits any breach or fails to comply with any of these terms and conditions.
     (c) To make alterations or repairs.

     The board may also disconnect from its supply mains any installation where, in the opinion of the board, such use of the energy is made as to interfere with the satisfactory distribution of electricity or where in the opinion of the board such installation interfered with the quality of supply to other consumers or where the board considers the installation to be in a dangerous condition. The board may also disconnect supply and/or terminate agreement at any time upon giving forty eight hours notice to the consumer, such notice to be left at or sent by post to the premises supplied. If the notice is sent by post it shall be deemed to have been received on the week day following the day of posting.

The particular provisions of this clause relied on was sub-clause (b). It was contended that in this case there was a breach or failure by the respondent to comply with a term or condition and that this justified the appellant in exercising its power to disconnect. The term or condition which it was contended had not been complied with or broken was that contained in clause 10. This clause reads as follows:

10. Liability of consumer for damage to board apparatus

The consumer shall be held responsible by the board for the safe keeping of all meters and other electrical apparatus, service lines and fittings belonging to the board and placed on his premises, and should any damage or injury be caused by fire, water, accident or other cause for which the board or its officers, servants or agents are not responsible, the consumer must pay to the board on demand, the cost of making good and repairing any such damage or injury.

What does this condition mean? It provides that the consumer is to be held responsible for the safe keeping of meters and other electrical apparatus placed on his premises and that this responsibility is to be discharged by paying for the cost of making good any damage caused other than damage caused by the board's servants. How can it be suggested that this clause has not been observed or will not be observed by the respondent? It was never suggested to him that he should pay for the repair of the meter nor was he required to do so. He was required to sign a statement, already indicated, which was quite a different matter. It is true, as Butler J. held, that he acted unreasonably in refusing to do so. This, however, did not constitute a breach or non-compliance with a clause which the appellant never brought to his notice or sought to enforce against him. On the contrary, at an early stage of these proceedings the appellant sought to justify the action taken by reliance on another clause, clause 7 (g). This clause is as follows:

(g) No person except an official of the board shall fix, connect or disconnect, remove or otherwise interfere with any such meter, main fuse box or other apparatus, the property of the board all of which will be sealed by the Board and such seals must on no account be broken except by Board officials. Breach of this regulation may expose the offender to prosecution. The Board reserves the right to remove any meter or meters at any time.

As, of course, there was no evidence that the respondent so interfered or caused any other person to interfere with the meter, reliance on this clause was discontinued. I am, therefore, of the opinion that there was, on the facts of this case, no evidence that the respondent has been in breach of the clause relied upon and that accordingly the appellant's action was not justified under the general conditions and was accordingly in breach of contract.

As to damages this court is bound by the finding of fact made by the learned trial judge that the appellant would not have cut off supply had the respondent co-operated in the manner already indicated. In this respect the appellant relies on the provisions of s. 34(1) of the Civil Liability Act, 1961. In the circumstances of this case, in my view, unreasonable conduct by the respondent without regard to the comfort and convenience of his family and household can fairly be regarded as contributory negligence or want of care within the meaning of the section. It cannot, however, justify an action which was unlawful and in breach of contract. The sanction which the section provides for is that the damages recoverable in respect of the wrong complained of, shall, where such damage was caused partly by the sufferer's negligence or want of care, be reduced by such amount as the court thinks just and equitable. The section authorises the reduction, not the negativing or annulment of such damage. Here the appellant was seeking to enforce its own general conditions. It cannot, in my view, seek to avoid all responsibility for an action not authorised because, through ignorance or fear or for any other reason, the threatened consumer behaved without due care and responsibility. It seems to me having regard to what was suffered by the plaintiff and his family that the award of £50 damages made by the trial judge was a reduction in damages which in the circumstances was just and equitable. I would not interfere with this award of damages.

The appellant's appeal was brought to this court because of objection to the wide nature of the ruling or decision given by the trial judge. It was not contested that the appellant was correct in this ground of appeal. The appellant, however, sought to justify the action taken on the terms of the general conditions and also relied on the respondent's contributory negligence or want of care as a ground for urging that the decree given in the High Court should not be affirmed. In the result I would dismiss the appellant's appeal and the plaintiff's cross-appeal.

Henchy J.:

The plaintiff is a builder's labourer. He is a married man with four children. He moved into his present house in Arthur Griffith Park, Lucan, Co. Dublin, in October 1973. This was a new house and he was its first occupier. He had earlier, in October 1972, entered into the normal written agreement with the Electricity Supply Board ('the board'), for the supply of electricity to the house, in accordance with the 'board's general conditions relating to electricity supply', which he acknowledged in the contract to have seen and carefully read.

From the board's point of view, the plaintiff proved to be an unsatisfactory occupier of the house. On at least two occasions the board, in exercise of the powers vested in it under the contract, had to disconnect the supply of electricity because of his failure to pay accounts due for electricity consumed. Then, in May 1978, there came to the board's notice the particular state of affairs that has led to this litigation. In that month, a routine meter inspection showed that the official seal on the meter had been removed, that it had been replaced with a bogus seal, that the voltage link inside the terminal cover of the meter was loose, as were the screws which should have been holding the terminal cover in position, so that it was possible for electrical current to be used but to be under-recorded, or not to be recorded at all. Comparison with the previous month of current used showed that approximately £166.44 worth of unrecorded current was used as a result of the wrongful tampering with the meter.

The finger of suspicion pointed to the plaintiff, but both he and his wife denied all knowledge of any interference with the meter. As they and their young children were the only persons living in the house during the relevant period, and as there was no serious suggestion that anybody else had an opportunity of interfering with the meter, the officials of the board, not unreasonably, asked the plaintiff for a written statement setting out what he knew, or did not know, about the interference with the meter, and agreeing to pay by suitable instalments an amount to be agreed for the unrecorded current used.

Both the plaintiff and his wife refused to sign such a statement. It was made clear to the plaintiff that if such a statement was not forthcoming, the supply of electricity to the house would be cut off in accordance with the rights vested in the board under the general conditions relating to supply which were incorporated into the contract. All to no avail. The plaintiff, while orally pleading ignorance of what had been done to the meter, refused to co-operate, either by recording in writing his lack of guilty knowledge or by stating in writing that he was willing to pay by agreed instalments, each to be added to his normal periodic bill, for the unrecorded electricity that had been consumed.

The board's officials dealing with the matter felt they had no option but to exercise what they believed to be the board's power to disconnect the supply of electricity. This they did in May 1978. The house remained without electricity until the end of February 1979. The discomfort and inconvenience that must have been experienced by the plaintiff, his wife and four young children during this period (which included the winter of 1979), wholly dependent as they were on electricity for light, heat, cooking, refrigeration, television, etc., must have been excruciating to bear and dangerous to their physical and psychological health. In all the circumstances and regardless of strict legal rights, the plaintiff's decision not to agree to the reasonable terms offered and to choose instead to subject his wife and family to the cruel conditions they must have suffered from living in a house without any electricity must be stigmatised as irresponsible, unconscionable and unreasonable. His intransigence was compounded by the fact that, even after the electricity had been cut off, he was told that it would be immediately restored if he would but give a statement in writing setting out the extent of his knowledge (if any) of how the meter came to be tampered with and stating his willingness to pay by reasonable and extended instalments for the unrecorded electricity that had been consumed in the house. This he adamantly refused to do. Having brought, or at least helped to bring, the misery of cold, of darkness and of the sundry unpleasant consequences of the loss of electricity to his wife and family, his unfeeling stubbornness led him to compel them to serve out their dark and chilly deprivations and discomforts for eight months.

The restoration of electricity to the plaintiff's house apparently came about as a result of proceedings taken by him in the High Court. On 20 December 1978 he issued a plenary summons, in which he sought an order directing the board to restore the supply of electricity to the house. In the statement of claim (which was delivered after the supply of electricity had been restored by the board), damages for inconvenience and suffering were claimed. The gist of the board's defence was that what it had done was done under the powers conferred on it by the contract entered into with the plaintiff, and that in any event the plaintiff had been guilty of contributory negligence within the meaning of the Civil Liability Act, 1961.

When the case came on for plenary hearing in January 1980, the only live issue was whether the plaintiff was entitled to damages, and if so, how much. At the end of the oral hearing although the trial judge held that 'if Mr and Mrs McCord had offered reasonable co-operation with the ESB on 17 May on their first visit their supply would not have been cut off', and that 'had the McCords offered reasonable co-operation with the ESB at any time after 23 May, when the supply was cut off, it would have been restored in a matter of days', he nevertheless held against the board and awarded the plaintiff damages of £50. The judge commenced his short *ex tempore* judgment as follows:

> For the reasons I have indicated |which reasons are not given in the judgment and are not referred to elsewhere in the transcript| I think the ESB are not entitled either for the purpose of enforcing the payment of sums due to them or of enforcing the terms of the contract, to cut off a supply of electricity of which they have a monopoly and which is a necessity of life. Undoubtedly, if they prove either a debt in the normal |way| in court, or if they prove a serious breach of the terms of an agreement in court, they may then on due notice abrogate the contract they have entered into, but they cannot do it arbitrarily as was done in this case.

The board has brought this appeal against the award of £50 damages, on the ground that the judge erred in law in thus limiting the board's powers. In a cross-notice the plaintiff complains that the damages awarded are inadequate and should be increased.

I should say at the outset that it has been no part of the plaintiff's case, either in the High Court or in this court, that the board is not entitled to disconnect the supply of electricity to occupiers of premises who have defaulted in the payment of their bills. In fact, as counsel for both sides have agreed in this court, the dictum of the judge that disconnection for non-payment may legally take place only after a court order has been obtained is unsupported by judicial authority and is not in accordance with the Electricity (Supply) Act, 1927. Specific powers to cut off the supply of electricity, where a debt for electricity is due, is given to the board by s. 99 of that Act. This statutory power (which is repeated in more drastic terms in condition 13(a) of the general conditions) must be deemed to be exercisable only in a reasonable manner, that is, after due notice and after giving the debtor a fair and reasonable opportunity, having regard to all the circumstances, of discharging the debt. Admittedly, any comment on this aspect of the case must be *obiter*, but because the widespread publicity given to the judge's statement that the board is not entitled to disconnect electricity to premises because of an unpaid account, until it gets a court order, it is important to clear the air by recording that it is common case that such a conclusion is unwarranted and in fact is in the teeth of the statutory powers vested in the board.

The real question in this case is whether the board has power to disconnect the supply of electricity to premises when the meter has been wrongfully interfered with (in this case without the proven knowledge of the occupier) and the occupier has refused to give a statement in writing setting out what he knows of the wrongdoing and giving an undertaking to pay by instalments for the electricity consumed but unrecorded.

Before proceeding to answer this question, it is important to point out that the contract made between the plaintiff and board (incorporating the general conditions relating to supply) is what is nowadays called a contract of adhesion: it is a standardised mass contract which must be entered into, on a take it or leave it basis, by the occupier of every premises in which electricity is to be used. The would-be consumer has no standing to ask that a single iota of the draft contract presented to him be changed before he signs it. He must lump it or leave it. But, because for reasons that are too obvious to enumerate, he cannot do without electricity, he is invariably forced by necessity into signing the contract, regardless of the fact that he may consider some of its terms arbitrary, or oppressive, or demonstrably unfair. He is compelled, from a position of weakness and necessity *vis-à-vis* a monopolist supplier of a vital commodity, to enter into what falls into the classification of a contract and which, as such, according to the theory of the common law which was evolved in the *laissez-faire* atmosphere of the nineteenth century, is to be treated by the courts as if it had emerged by choice from the forces of the market place, at the behest of parties who were at arm's length and had freedom of choice. The real facts show that such an approach is largely based on legal fictions. When a monopoly supplier of a vital public utility—which is what the board is—forces on all its consumers a common form of contract, reserving to itself sweeping powers, including the power to vary the document unilaterally as it may think fit, such an instrument has less affinity with a freely negotiated interpersonal contract than with a set of bye-laws or with any other form of autonomic legislation. As such, its terms may have to be construed not simply as contractual elements but as components of a piece of delegated legislation, the validity of which will depend on whether it has kept within the express or implied confines of the statutory delegation and, even if it has, whether the delegation granted or assumed is now consistent with the provisions of the Constitution of 1937.

However, since the present proceedings raise no issue as to question of the validity, on constitutional or other grounds, of the contract between the plaintiff and the board, the terms of reference of this case rule out a consideration of such a question; while, for similar reasons, judicial self-control requires that I withhold adverse comments on certain terms of the contract, such as that which purports to give contractual force to the idea that notices of intended disconnection may be taken as having been delivered on the weekday following the day they were posted; or on even the final term of the contract by which 'the board reserves to itself the right to add to, alter or amend any of the foregoing terms and conditions, *as it may think fit.*' However, having regard to my conclusion that the contractual powers of the board are in the nature of delegated legislation, and because a statute replacing the powers conferred on the board by the 1927 Act may result from this case, it might not be out of place to refer to what was laid down by this court in the following passage in its judgment in *Cityview Press Ltd v An Chomhairle Oiliuna* [1980] IR 381, at p. 398:

> The giving of powers to a designated minister or subordinate body to make regulations or orders under a particular statute has been a feature of legislation for many years. The practice has obvious attractions in view of the complex, intricate and ever-changing situations which confront both the legislature and the executive in a modern state. Sometimes, as in this instance, the legislature, conscious of the danger of giving too much power in the regulation or order-making process, provides that any regulation or order which is made should be subject to annulment by either House of Parliament. This retains a measure of control, if not in Parliament as such, at least in the two houses. Therefore, it is a safeguard. Nevertheless, the ultimate responsibility rests with the courts to ensure that constitutional safeguards remain, and that the exclusive authority of the national Parliament in the field of law-making is not eroded by a delegation of power which is neither contemplated nor permitted by the Constitution. In discharging that responsibility, the courts will have regard to where and by what authority the law in question purports to have been made. In the view of this court, the test is whether that which is challenged as an unauthorised delegation of parliamentary power is more than a mere giving effect to principles and policies which are contained in the statute itself. If it be, then it is not authorised; for such would constitute a purported exercise of legislative power by an authority which is not permitted to do so under the Constitution. On the other hand, if it be within the permitted limits—if the law is laid down in the statute and details only are filled in or completed by the designated minister or subordinate body—there is no unauthorised delegation of legislative power.

The precise question to be decided in this case is narrowed by the fact that counsel for the board have finally confined the board's claim (to have been entitled to disconnect the plaintiff's electricity) to the operation of the part of clause 13 of the general conditions which says:

> The board may disconnect without prior notice to the consumer . . . if the consumer commits any breach or fails to comply with any of these terms and conditions.

The particular breach or non-compliance relied on is said to be found in clause 10, which is headed 'Liability of consumer for damage to board apparatus' and which reads as follows:

> The customer will be held responsible by the board for the safe keeping of all meters and other electrical apparatus, service lines and fittings belonging to the board and placed on his premises, and should any damage or injury be caused by fire, water, accident or other cause for which the board or its officers, servants or

agents are not responsible, the consumer must pay to the board on demand the cost of making good and repairing any such damage or injury.

Apart from the fact that the power to disconnect without prior notice, contained in clause 13, does not seem to derive from any delegation of such power in the 1927 Act, I am satisfied that the plaintiff was not in breach of any obligation imposed on him by clause 10. It is true that the latter clause imposed a *responsibility* for the safe keeping of the meter and the liability set out for bearing the cost of making good any damage of it. But the plaintiff was disconnected not for failing or refusing to bear that responsibility or that cost. The clause does not bind the consumer to keep the meter safe; it merely (as its heading shows) imposes a financial liability on him if it is damaged. The cause of disconnection in this case was the refusal of the plaintiff to sign a document setting out whatever he knew of the interference with the meter and undertaking to pay for the unrecorded electricity by instalments. By no stretch of reasoning could his refusal to sign such a document be construed as a breach of clause 10, which deals exclusively with the financial liability for damage done to apparatus such as a meter. The board, therefore, was not empowered by clause 13 to disconnect. It misconstrued its powers under clauses 10 and 13. The result is that the disconnection is unlawful.

There remains the question of damages. If the plaintiff had not been guilty of contributory negligence, or had taken all reasonable steps to mitigate the damage, he would have to be awarded a substantial sum for damages. But he was plainly guilty of contributory negligence under s. 34(1) of the Civil Liability Act, 1961. By taking the reasonable step of putting his signature to a non-incriminating document which would leave him with only a liability to pay, on reasonable and extended terms, for the electricity consumed, he could have prevented the disconnection. Notwithstanding the board's misconstruction of its powers, the real source of the plaintiff's damages is to be found in his unreasonable refusal to comply with a reasonable request. He was bound to take all reasonable steps to mitigate his damage. Whether a plaintiff has done so is always a question of fact (*Payzu Ltd v Saunders* [1919] 2 KB 581), and in this case the judge found that fact against the plaintiff. Whether the matter be judged in terms of contributory negligence or failure to mitigate the damage, the plaintiff's conduct must be deemed the real and ultimate cause of both the initial disconnection and the continued disconnection for seven months. In my opinion, for the reasons adumbrated in the judgment which Griffin J. is about to read, it disentitled him to any sum for damages. I would therefore allow the defendant's appeal and dismiss the plaintiff's claim.

Finally, I would point out that this case illustrates the desirability of revising by statute the powers that were vested in the board by the 1927 Act and of giving a proper statutory foundation and realistic form to the contract that a consumer must make with the board.

(Kenny, Griffin and Parke JJ. concurred.)

Note

The Irish Times of 26 February 1985 carried the following account of a District Court case under the heading 'Bord Telecom's powers almost draconian—judge':

A District Justice yesterday said that people were 'almost dragooned' into paying telephone bills because of the near draconian powers given to Bord Telecom under the legislation.

In the Dublin District Court, District Justice McMenamin suggested that the Oireachtas, in granting monopoly powers to the telephone authorities, should have provided a 'built-in system where the customer would have some rights to protest, some very quick way of appealing to someone, some independent or quasi-independent person to examine a dispute over an account, without having his telephone cut off.

'But be that as it may I am not here to make law, I'm here to apply law,' he said.

Counsel for the board later pointed out that the Ombudsman will be empowered to deal with telephone complaints from 1 April next.

Dismissing a case brought against Bord Telecom for overcharging and abuse of personal rights under the common law of contract, the District Justice said the case had raised some interesting points of law 'but the law is clear that any constitutional issues must begin in the High Court, and only in the High Court'.

The case had been brought by Mr Garret Hooper, of Clarinda Park West, Dun Laoghaire, whose telephone was cut off in November 1980. Mr Hooper had argued that certain terms of the telephone contract were contrary to common law, and that it was therefore null and void, and that the telephone authorities had been in breach of common law duty in relation to supply of services and proper account keeping. He asked the court to state a case to the High Court as to whether common law had indeed been breached.

In particular he argued that the minister's blanket powers under the telephone regulations to determine the time and duration of calls and the amount owing in cases of dispute were such that they were prejudicial to the administration of justice and tended to promote corruption in public life.

Counsel for the board, however, replied that the state frequently limited the rights of contract such as by fixing maximum period and drink prices, and noted that the revenue commissioners and to some extent the gardai had discretionary powers to waive or amend penalties or charges.

District Justice McMenamin noted that Mr Hooper had admitted under cross-examination that during the period when the alleged overcharging had occurred, he had allowed another person to use his telephone 'to make telephone calls to exotic places like Bangkok'. Mr Hooper was not therefore on strong ground in challenging the authenticity of the telephone account.

Concluding that 'both the law and the facts are against Mr Hooper', the District Justice awarded costs to Bord Telecom.

A. Duty to Read

I. Calamari 'Duty to Read—A Changing Concept', (1974) 43 Fordham L Rev 1 341, 351–8

The Modern View—Contracts of Adhesion

There has been a tendency, particularly in recent years, to treat contracts of adhesion or standard form contracts differently from other contracts.[1] This is particularly true with respect to the duty to read.[2] There is a growing body of case law which subverts the traditional duty to read concept either upon a theory that there was not true assent to a particular term, or that, even if there was assent, the term is to be excised from the contract because it contravenes public policy or is unconscionable.[3] At times, the same decision may employ all three rationales. This modern approach to the problem and the meaning of true assent may be shown best by a brief examination of three of the leading cases on the subject.

Perhaps the most significant case is *Weaver v American Oil Co.*,[4] which considered a lease by an oil company to an individual. The lessee signed without reading the lease under which he agreed, *inter alia*, to indemnify the lessor as a result of damages caused by the lessor's negligence. The majority opinion first stated that the duty to read rule had no application to the case because '*the clause was in fine print and contained no title heading . . .*'[5] This conclusion would have ended the matter under the rules discussed above, but the court seemed anxious to break new ground for it hastened to add:

> When a party show[s] that the contract, which is . . . to be enforced, was . . . an unconscionable one, due to a prodigious amount of bargaining power on behalf of the stronger party, which is used to the stronger party's advantage and is unknown to the lesser party, the contract provision, or the contract as a whole, if the provision is not separable, should not be enforceable on the grounds that the provision is contrary to public policy. The party seeking to enforce such a contract has the burden of showing that the provisions were explained to the other party and *came to his knowledge* and there was in fact *a real and voluntary meeting of the minds and not merely an objective meeting.*[6]

Although the above quotation combines three different concepts (unconscionability, violation of public policy, and lack of true assent),[7] the court's ultimate approach appears to be that the contract is unconscionable because an objective assent which flows from a duty to read is not sufficient (despite the objective theory of contracts) to bind a party to clauses which are unusual or unfair unless the clauses are at least brought to his attention and explained.[8] The theory is that since such clauses impose a great hardship or risk on the weaker party, who is otherwise unable to protect himself, an informed and voluntary consent should be required.[9]

The same approach was employed by the court in the well known case of *Henningsen v Bloomfield Motors, Inc.*[10] which arose under the Uniform Sales Act rather than the Uniform Commercial Code.[11] In *Henningsen*, a consumer brought an action for personal injuries against both the vendor and manufacturer of his automobile. Relying upon a provision in the contract of sale that an express warranty contained therein was in lieu of all other warranties express or implied, the defendants argued that the plaintiff's action should be limited to a claim for defective parts. The heart of the *Henningsen* decision appears in a paragraph near the end of the opinion:

> True, the Sales Act authorises agreements between buyer and seller qualifying the warranty obligations. But quite obviously the legislature contemplated lawful stipulations (which are determined by the circumstances of a particular case) arrived at freely by parties of relatively equal bargaining strength. The lawmakers did not authorise the automobile manufacturer to use its grossly disproportionate bargaining power to relieve itself from liability and to impose on the ordinary buyer, who in effect has no real freedom of choice, the grave danger of injury to himself and others that attends the sale of such a dangerous instrumentality as a defectively made automobile. In the framework of this case, illuminated as it is by the facts and the many decisions noted, we are of the opinion that Chrysler's attempted disclaimer of an implied warranty of merchantability and of the obligations arising therefrom is so inimical to the public good as to compel an adjudication of its invalidity.[12]

Although there was some discussion about mutual assent, the ultimate holding was based upon the conclusion that such a clause, under the circumstances of the case (clause on reverse side, small print, disparity of bargaining power, clause on a take-it-or-leave-it basis and included by all major car manufacturers), was invalid as being contrary to public policy. This was made clear when the court further stated that it was not required to consider whether a particular charge which related to mutual assent was correct because 'the disclaimer is void as a matter of law'.[13]

Another leading case illustrating the same approach is Williams v Walker-Thomas Furniture Co.[14] There, an instalment sales agreement had a provision which resulted in 'a balance due on every item purchased until the balance due on all items, whenever purchased, was liquidated.'[15] As a result, in the event of a default on any one item, all items could be repossessed. The court in concluding that the fairness of the clause needed to be tested at trial stated:

> Ordinarily, one who signs an agreement without full knowledge of its terms might be held to assume the risk that he has entered a one-sided bargain. But when a party of little bargaining power, and hence little real choice, signs a commercially unreasonable contract with little or no knowledge of its terms, it is hardly likely that his consent, or even an objective manifestation of his consent, was ever given to all the terms. In such a case the usual rule that the terms of the agreement are not to be questioned should be abandoned and the court should consider whether the terms of the contract are so unfair that enforcement should be withheld.[16]

The three cases discussed above do not expunge the duty to read rule, but create an exception thereto if the terms (or a term) of the contract are unfair under the circumstances. In such a case, the ordinary manifestation of assent implicit in a signature or acceptance of a document is insufficient because the assent is not reasoned and knowing. Such consent involves an understanding of the clause in question[17] and a reasonable opportunity to accept or decline.[18] Even then, if the clause is sufficiently odious, it will be struck down as unconscionable or contrary to public policy.

[1.] Kessler, 'Contracts of Adhesion—Some Thoughts About Freedom of Contract', 43 Col L Rev 629 (1943). Patterson, 'The Delivery of a Life Insurance Policy', 33 Harv L Rev 198, 222 (1919) (origin of the term 'adhesion contract'). In the Kessler article, as here, the terms contract of adhesion and standardised contract are used interchangeably. But the two concepts are not always treated as coextensive. See Sheldon, 'Consumer Protection and Standard Contracts: The Swedish Experiment in Administration Control', 22 Am J Comp L 17, 18 (1974).

[2.] Ehrenzweig, 'Adhesion Contracts in the Conflict of Laws', 53 Col L Rev 1072 (1953); Note, 'Contract Clauses in Fine Print', 63 Harv L Rev 494 (1950); see Wilson, 'Freedom of Contract and Adhesion Contracts', 14 Int'l & Comp L Q 172 (1965).

[3.] The notion of condemning clauses as illegal or contrary to public policy is hardly new. However, it is being used today more often and in a wider variety of circumstances. See, e.g. von Hippel, 'The Control of Exemption Clauses—A Comparative Study', 16 Int'l & Comp L Q 591 (1967). Unconscionability is discussed in note 8 infra.

[4.] 257 Ind. 458, 276 N.E.2d 144 (1971); Annot., 49 ALR.3d 306 (1973). See also Frame v. Merrill Lynch, Pierce, Fenner & Smith, Inc., 20 Cal App 3d 668, 97 Cal Rptr 811 (1st Dist. 1971).

[5.] 257 Ind. at 462, 276 NE 2d at 147.

[6.] Ibid. at 464, 276 NE 2d at 148.

[7.] The Weaver opinion also proceeded upon a warranty analogy when it stated: 'The burden should be on the party submitting such 'a package' in printed form to show that the other party had knowledge of any unusual or unconscionable terms contained therein. The principle should be the same as that applicable to implied warranties, namely, that a package of goods sold to a purchaser is fit for the

purposes intended and contains no harmful materials other than that represented.'
Ibid., 276 NE 2d at 147–48.

8. The relationship of unconscionability to true assent and violation of public policy is
interesting. Leff, in his article, 'Unconscionability and the Code—The Emperor's
New Clause', 115 U Pa L Rev 485 (1967), distinguishes between substantive and
procedural unconscionability. Procedural unconscionability exists where there is
unfair surprise—which may be another way of saying that there was not a true,
informed and voluntary mutual assent. Substantive unconscionability exists where
a particular clause is unfair and oppressive. This is akin to a clause which is
contrary to public policy. In the latter situation (theoretically at least) questions of
true assent are unimportant. Very often, the two categories overlap. Professor Murray
prefers to restrict the notion of unconscionability to questions of mutual assent.
See Murray, 'Unconscionability: Unconscionability', 31 U Pitt L Rev 1 (1969). Although
unconscionability clearly is related to the duty to read concept, it has other aspects,
and so is treated here only incidentally. The literature on the subject is voluminous. In
addition to the articles cited above see. e.g. Braucher, 'The Unconscionable Contract
or Term', 31 U Pitt L Rev 337 (1970); Ellinghaus, 'In Defence of Unconscionability',
78 Yale LJ 757 (1969); Leff, 'Unconscionability and the Crowd—Consumers and the
Common Law Tradition', 31 U Pitt L Rev 349 (1970); Spanogle, 'Analysing Unconscionability Problems', 117 U Pa L Rev 931 (1969); Speidel, 'Unconscionability,
Assent and Consumer Protection', 31 U Pitt L Rev 359 (1970).

9. A party might be considered to be otherwise able to protect himself if he has a
bargaining power relatively equal to that of the other party, or if he were able to
obtain insurance at a reasonable rate to protect against a known risk being
imposed upon him. See, e.g. *Vitex Mfg Corp. v Caribtex Corp.*, 377 F 2d 795, 799–800
(3d Cir. 1967); Johnston, 'The Control of Exemption Clauses: A Comment', 17 Int'l &
Comp L Q 232 (1968).

10. 32 NJ 358, 161 A 2d 69 (1960), Annot., 75 ALR 2d 39 (1961).

11. If the case had arisen under the UCC, the court could have noted the provision that,
in the case of a disclaimer of the warranty of merchantability, the word merchantability must be used and the disclaimer conspicuous. UCC § 2–316(2). The term
'conspicuous' is defined in ibid. §1–201(10). What is or is not conspicuous still
appears to be a matter of controversy. A disclaimer in the smallest type preceded by
the word 'Note' printed in the largest type was held to be conspicuous in *Velez v Craine
& Clark Lumber Corp*, 41 App Div 2d 747, 341 NYS 2d 248 (2d Dep't), rev'd on other
grounds, 33 NY 2d 117, 305 NE 2d 750, 350 NYS 2d 617 (1973). But see Tennessee
Carolina Transp., Inc. v Strick Corp, 283 NC 423, 196 SE 2d 711 (1973). Even more to
the point is UCC §2–719(3) which provides: 'Consequential damages may be limited
or excluded unless the limitation or exclusion is unconscionable. Limitation of
consequential damages for injury to the person in the case of consumer goods is
prima facie unconscionable but limitation of damages where the loss is commercial
is not.' See also UCC §§2–316(1), –718, –719(1) & (2).

   Professor Murray takes the position that even if the disclaimer is conspicuous it
must, in addition, be negotiated, and comprehensible to the buyer. See Murray,
'Unconscionability: Unconscionability', 31 U Pitt L Rev 1, 48–49 (1969). Contra, Leff,
'Unconscionability and the Code—The Emperor's New Clause', 115 U Pa L Rev 485,
523–24 (1967). There are, as usual, cases which support each position. Compare
Belden-Stark Brick Corp. v Morris Rosen & Sons, Inc., 39 App Div 2d 534, 331 NYS.2d 59
(1st Dep't), aff'd, 31 NY.2d 884, 292 NE 2d 321, 340 NYS 2d 185 (1972) (mem.) with
Dobias v Western Farmers Ass'n, 6 Wash App 194, 491 P 2d 1346 (3d Div. 1971).
Professor Broude suggests that under §§2–202 and 2–316 printed form disclaimers

of warranties, even though they are contained in an integration, should not be considered to be part of the agreement because they are not truly assented to. Broude, 'The Consumer and the Parol Evidence Rule: Section 2–202 of the Uniform Commercial Code', 1970 Duke LJ 881.

12. 32 NJ at 404, 161 A 2d at 95.
13. Ibid. at 405, 161 A 2d at 95.
14. 350 F 2d 445 (DC Cir 1965), noted in 79 Harv L Rev 1299 (1966).
15. 350 F 2d at 447. See also 'Uniform Consumer Credit Code' §3.302; UCC §9–204.
16. 350 F 2d at 449–50 (footnotes omitted).
17. See, e.g. *Henningsen v Bloomfield Motors, Inc.*, 32 NJ 358, 399–400, 161 A 2d 69, 92 (1960).
18. Ibid. at 390, 161 A 2d at 87. But what is the choice being discussed? In the *Henningsen* case it was clear that a person could not buy a new car from a major manufacturer without submitting to the clause in question. But in *Weaver* there was no evidence that the lessee could not have obtained a similar lease from another oil company without the offending clause. How important should this be on the issue of true assent?

By now it should be clear that the assent discussed in Parts II and III hereof is not the same type of assent being discussed here under the label 'true assent'.

Interfoto Picture Library Ltd *v* Stiletto Visual Programmes Ltd [1988] 1 All ER 349

Dillon L.J.:

The defendants appeal against a decision of his Honour Judge Pearce QC given in the Lambeth County Court at the trial of this action on 11 March 1987 whereby the judge awarded the plaintiffs judgment against the defendants in the sum of £3,783.50 with interest and costs. The judge described the case as an interesting case, and in that I agree with him.

The plaintiffs run a library of photographic transparencies. The defendants are engaged in advertising. On 5 March 1984 Mr Beeching, a director of the defendants, wanting photographs for a presentation for a client, telephoned the plaintiffs, whom the defendants had never dealt with before. He spoke to a Miss Fraser of the plaintiffs and asked her whether the plaintiffs had any photographs of the 1950s which might be suitable for the defendants' presentation. Miss Fraser said that she would research his request, and a little later on the same day she sent round by hand to the defendants forty seven transparencies packed in a jiffy bag. Also packed in the bag, among the transparencies, was a delivery note which she had typed out, and to which I shall have to refer later.

Having received the transparencies, Mr Beeching telephoned the plaintiffs at about 3.10 on the afternoon of 5 March, and told Miss Fraser, according to a contemporary note which the judge accepted, that he was very impressed with the plaintiffs' fast service, that one or two of the transparencies could be of interest, and that he would get back to the plaintiffs.

Unfortunately he did not get back on to the plaintiffs and the transparencies seem to have been put on one side and overlooked by the defendants. The plaintiffs tried to telephone Mr Beeching on 20 March and again on 23 March, but only spoke to his secretary. In the upshot the transparencies, which the defendants did not use for their presentation, were not returned to the plaintiffs until 2 April.

The plaintiffs thereupon sent an invoice to the defendants for £3,783.50 as a holding charge for the transparencies. The invoice was rejected by the defendants, and accordingly in May 1984 the plaintiffs started this action claiming the £3,783.50, the amount of the invoice. That is the sum for which the judge awarded the plaintiffs judgment by his order now under appeal.

The plaintiffs' claim is based on conditions printed on their delivery note, which I have briefly mentioned, and must now describe in greater detail.

It is addressed to Mr Beeching of the defendants at the defendants' address and in the body of it the forty seven transparencies are listed by number. In the top right-hand corner the date of dispatch is given as 5 March 1984 and the date for return is clearly specified as 19 March. Across the bottom, under the heading 'Conditions' fairly prominently printed in capitals, there are set out nine conditions, printed in four columns. Of these the important one is no. 2 in the first column, which reads as follows: 'All transparencies must be returned to us within fourteen days from the date of posting/delivery/collection. A holding fee of £5.00 plus VAT per day will be charged for each transparency which is retained by you longer than the said period of fourteen days save where a copyright licence is granted or we agree a longer period in writing with you.' Condition 8 provides: 'When sent by post/delivered/collected the above conditions are understood to have been accepted unless the package is returned to us immediately by registered mail or by hand containing all the transparencies whole and undefaced and these conditions shall apply to all transparencies submitted to you whether or not you have completed a request form.'

The conditions purport to be merely the conditions of the bailment of transparencies to a customer. If the customer wishes to make use of transparencies so submitted to him, a fresh contract has to be agreed with the plaintiffs, but, as that did not happen so far as the defendants are concerned, it is unnecessary to consider that aspect further.

The sum of £3,783.50 is calculated by the plaintiffs in strict accordance with condition 2 as the fee for the retention of forty seven transparencies from 19 March to 2 April 1984. It is of course important to the plaintiffs to get their transparencies back reasonably quickly, if they are not wanted, since if a transparency is out with one customer it cannot be offered to another customer, should occasion arise. It has to be said, however, that the holding fee charged by the plaintiffs by condition 2 is extremely high, and in my view exorbitant. The judge held that on a *quantum meruit* a reasonable charge would have been £3.50 per transparency per week, and not £5 per day, and he had evidence before him of the terms charged by some ten other photographic libraries, most of which charged less than £3.50 per week and only one of which charged more (£4 per transparency per week). It would seem therefore that the defendants would have had a strong case for saying that condition 2 was void and unenforceable as a penalty clause; but that point was not taken in the court below or in the notice of appeal.

The primary point taken in the court below was that condition 2 was not part of the contract between the parties because the delivery note was never supplied to the defendants at all. That the judge rejected on the facts; he found that the delivery note was supplied in the same jiffy bag with the transparencies, and that finding is not challenged in this court. He made no finding however that Mr Beeching or any other representative of the defendants read condition 2 or any of the other printed conditions, and it is overwhelmingly probable that they did not.

An alternative argument for the defendants, in this court as below, was to the effect that any contract between the parties was made before the defendants knew of the existence of the delivery note, *viz.* either in the course of the preliminary telephone conversation between Mr Beeching and Miss Fraser or when the jiffy bag containing the transparencies was received in the defendants' premises but before the bag was opened. I regard these submissions as unrealistic and unarguable. The original telephone call was merely a preliminary inquiry and did not give rise to any contract. But the contract came into existence when the plaintiffs sent the transparencies to the defendants and the defendants, after opening the bag, accepted them by Mr Beeching's phone call to the plaintiffs at 3.10 on 5 March. The question is whether condition 2 was a term of that contract.

There was never any oral discussion of terms between the parties before the contract was made. In particular there was no discussion whatever of terms in the original telephone conversation when Mr Beeching made his preliminary inquiry. The question is therefore whether condition 2 was sufficiently brought to the defendants' attention to make it a term of the contract which was only concluded after the defendants had received, and must have known that they had received the transparencies *and* the delivery note.

This sort of question was posed, in relation to printed conditions, in the ticket cases, such *Parker v South Eastern Rly Co.* (1877) 2 CPD 416, |1874–80| All ER Rep 166, in the last century. At that stage the printed conditions were looked at as a whole and the question considered by the courts was whether the printed conditions as a whole had been sufficiently drawn to a customer's attention to make the whole set of conditions part of the contract; if so the customer was bound by the printed conditions even though he never read them.

More recently the question has been discussed whether it is enough to look at a set of printed conditions as a whole. When for instance one condition in a set is particularly onerous does something special need to be done to draw customers' attention to that particular condition? In an *obiter dictum* in J. *Spurling Ltd v Bradshaw* |1956| 2 All ER 121 at 125, |1956| 1 WLR 461 at 466 (cited in *Chitty on Contracts* (25th ed., 1983) vol 1, para. 742, 408) Denning L.J. stated: 'Some clauses which I have seen would need to be printed in red ink on the face of the document with a red hand pointing to it before the notice could be held to be sufficient.'

Then in *Thornton v Shoe Lane Parking Ltd* |1971| 1 All ER 686, |1971| 2 QB 163 both Lord Denning M.R. and Megaw L.J. held as one of their grounds of decision, as I read their judgments, that where a condition is particularly onerous or unusual the party seeking to enforce it must show that that condition, or an unusual condition of that particular nature, was fairly brought to the notice of the other party. Lord Denning restated and applied what he had said in the *Spurling* case, and held that the court should not hold any man bound by such a condition unless it was drawn to his attention in the most explicit way (see |1971| 1 All ER 686 at 689–90, |1971| 2 QB 163 at 169–70).

. . .

Counsel for the plaintiffs submits that *Thornton v Shoe Lane Parking Ltd* was a case of an exemption clause and that what their Lordships said must be read as limited to exemption clauses and in particular exemption clauses which would deprive the party on whom they are imposed of statutory rights. But what their Lordships said was said by way of interpretation and application of the general statement of the law by Mellish L.J. in *Parker v South Eastern Rly Co.* and the logic of it is applicable to any particularly onerous clause in a printed set of conditions of the one contracting party which would not be generally known to the other party.

Condition 2 of these plaintiffs' conditions is in my judgment a very onerous clause. The defendants could not conceivably have known, if their attention was not drawn to the clause, that the plaintiffs were proposing to charge a 'holding fee' for the retention of the transparencies at such a very high and exorbitant rate.

At the time of the ticket cases in the last century it was notorious that people hardly ever troubled to read printed conditions on a ticket or delivery note or similar document. That remains the case now. In the intervening years the printed conditions have tended to become more and more complicated and more and more one-sided in favour of the party who is imposing them, but the other parties, if they notice that there are printed conditions at all, generally still tend to assume that such conditions are only concerned with ancillary matters of form and are not of importance. In the ticket cases the courts held that the common law required that reasonable steps be taken to draw the other parties' attention to the printed conditions or they would not be part of the contract. It is in my judgment a logical development of the common law into modern conditions that it should be held, as it was in *Thornton v Shoe Lane Parking Ltd*, that, if one condition in a set of printed conditions is particularly onerous or unusual, the party seeking to enforce it must show that that particular condition was fairly brought to the attention of the other party.

In the present case, nothing whatever was done by the plaintiffs to draw the defendants' attention particularly to condition 2; it was merely one of four columns' width of conditions printed across the foot of the delivery note. Consequently condition 2 never, in my judgment, became part of the contract between the parties.

I would therefore allow this appeal and reduce the amount of the judgment which the judge awarded against the defendants to the amount which he would have awarded on a *quantum meruit* on his alternative findings, i.e. the reasonable charge of £3.50 per transparency per week for the retention of the transparencies beyond a reasonable period, which he fixed at fourteen days from the date of their receipt by the defendants.

(Bingham L.J. agreed.)

SECTION TWO—THE EXEMPTION CLAUSE

D. Yates *Exemption Clauses* (2nd ed., London: Sweet & Maxwell, 1982), 33–8

D. *Types of Exclusion Clauses*

1. *Exemption from liability for breach*

Some clauses may be in a form which purports to excuse the defendant from any liability incurred as a result of his breach; others may appear to limit or define the circumstances in which the *proferens* will be bound under the contract. . . . The flavour of the problem may, perhaps, be gleaned from the following exclusion found in an engineering company's 'back-of-order' terms:

> The company's liability under any order is limited to replacement or remedial work undertaken under these conditions of sale, to the entire exclusion of any other remedy which, but for this condition, the buyer might have. Any representation, condition, warranty or other undertaking in relation to the contract whether express or implied by statute, common law, custom or otherwise and whether made or given before or after the date of order or acceptance thereof, is hereby excluded for all purposes. Save as provided in these conditions, the company shall be under no liability of any sort (however arising) and shall not in any circumstances be liable for any damage, injury, direct consequential or other loss or loss of profits or costs, charges and expenses, howsoever arising.

2. *Limitations of liability or remedies*

These will be provisions in the contract that restrict the exercise of a right or remedy arising out of the breach of any obligation, express or implied, in the contract. So, for example, a term commonly found in building and civil engineering contracts that the contractor's liability for failure to complete on the due date shall not exceed a specified figure, is such a clause. Similar clauses are found in contracts of carriage. The following example is contained in clause 12 of the standard conditions of carriage issued by the Road Haulage Association.

> Subject to these conditions the liability of the carrier in respect of any one consignment shall in any case be limited:
>
> (1) where the loss or damage however sustained is in respect of the whole of the consignment to a sum at the rate of £800 per ton on either the gross weight of the consignment as computed for the purpose of charges under clause 9 hereof [the provisions for calculating carriage charges by weight] or where no such computation has been made, the actual gross weight;
>
> (2) where loss or damage however sustained is in respect of part of a consignment to the proportion of the sum ascertained in accordance with (1) of this condition which the actual value of that part of the consignment bears to the actual value of the whole of the consignment.

> Provided that:
>
> (a) nothing in this clause shall limit the carrier's liability below the sum of £10 in respect of any one consignment;
> (b) the carrier shall not in any case be liable for indirect or consequential damages or for loss of a particular market whether held daily or at intervals;
> (c) the carrier shall be entitled to require proof of the value of the whole of the consignment . . .
> . . .

Some clauses may go further and purport to exclude the right to damages or the right to reject altogether. It could be argued that excluding the right to damages altogether is rather different in effect from simply limiting damages. By denying the remedy of damages the promisor is depriving his promise of any contractual content. This is not the case with a clause denying the promisee the right to repudiate, since it leaves the remedy of damages intact.

3. Time limit clauses

These clauses are generally designed to limit the time within which suit must be brought. They can be of two kinds. A clause may impose a time limit shorter than that fixed by the general law for the enforcement of a right or remedy, or alternatively it may impose a time limit on action necessary (e.g. notification of claims) before any right, remedy, duty or liability arises. The purpose of a time limit clause may not always be immediately apparent. Thus, a clause whereby 'the carrier . . . shall be discharged from all liability . . . unless suit is brought within one year' was held not merely to bar the remedy but extinguished the claim. An example of a time limit clause may again be cited from the conditions of carriage of the Road Haulage Association:

> The carrier shall not be liable:
>
> (1) (a) for loss from a package or from an unpacked consignment; or,
>   (b) for damage, deviation, misdelivery, delay or detention;
> unless he is advised thereof in writing otherwise than upon a consignment note or delivery document within three days and the claim be made in writing within seven days after the termination of transit;
>
> (2) for loss or non-delivery of the whole of the consignment or of any separate package forming part of the consignment;

unless he is advised of the loss or non-delivery in writing (other than upon a consignment note or delivery document) within twenty eight days and the claim be made in writing within forty two days after the commencement of transit.

4. Controls on evidence

Some limitation clauses may attempt to affect the question of how certain items of evidence are to be treated in the event of any claim being made against the *proferens*. It may purport to alter the onus of proof of matters under the contract, or provide that one matter is to be treated as conclusive evidence of another. An old case that provides a clause combining the effect of a time limit clause and a clause affecting evidentiary matters is that of *Buchanan v Parnshaw* (1788) 2 Term Rep. 745. In that case a horse sold at auction was warranted to be six years old and sound. It was a term of the sale that, if the horse were unsound, it should be returned within two days, otherwise it should be deemed sound. The failure to return within two days was, therefore, made conclusive evidence of soundness.

5. Indemnity clauses

Any clause which requires the promisee to indemnify another as a consequence of the promisee having exercised a right or remedy under the contract can have the same effect as a straightforward exclusion clause . . .

6. Arbitration clauses

An arbitration clause would seem to be only procedural in that a provision whereby the parties agree that any disputes should be submitted to arbitration does not exclude or limit rights or remedies but simply provides a procedure under which the parties may settle their grievance. The courts have held that such a clause is not an exclusion clause proper and the parties are free, such a clause notwithstanding, to pursue their claims in the courts (see *Doleman & Sons v Ossett Corp.* [1912] 3 KB 257) subject to the right of the court to grant a stay of proceedings. However, one type of arbitration can have substantive effect in that it can make the obligation to perform contingent upon the happening of an event. This clause is the so-called *Scott v Avery* clause (see (1856) LJ Ex. 308), under which the parties agree that no action shall be brought upon the contract until the arbitrator's award has been made, or that the promisor's liability shall be to pay only such sum as an arbitrator shall award. However, notwithstanding the difference between these clauses and the more normal type of arbitration clause, the courts have still been reluctant to treat them as exclusion clauses . . .

7. Liquidated damages clauses

A liquidated damages clause, unlike a clause that simply fixes a maximum limit on the amount of damages recoverable, is a genuine attempt at a pre-estimate of damages (see *Dunlop Pneumatic Tyre Co. Ltd v New Garage & Motor Co. Ltd* [1915] AC 79).

Kenyon Son and Craven v Baxter Hoare & Co. Ltd [1971] 2 All ER 708

Donaldson J.:

The plaintiffs are the makers of K.P. salted peanuts and similar commodities. The defendants are both warehousemen. Between July 1965, and May 1966, the first defendants took delivery from ocean carriers of nine parcels of shelled groundnuts in bags.

Three of these parcels were warehoused by the second defendants and six by the first defendants. The nuts were eventually delivered to the plaintiffs in a damaged condition, the damage having occurred during the period of warehousing. Hence this action. The second defendants have admitted liability, although issues of *quantum* remain. The first defendants deny liability and agree with the plaintiffs that all issues of *quantum* shall be deferred until after the question of liability has been settled.

Liability turns upon the facts found and the true construction of two of Baxter, Hoare & Co. Ltd's conditions of business which are, I am told, not exclusive to them but are widely used by shipping and forwarding agents. The first of these conditions is: '11. The company shall not be liable for loss of or damage to goods unless such loss or damage occurs whilst the goods are in the actual custody of the company and under its actual control and unless such loss or damage is due to the wilful neglect or default of the company or its own servants.'

It is agreed that at all material times the goods were in the actual custody of the first defendants to whom I will refer hereafter as 'the defendants', and under their actual control.

The primary issue which arises is whether the damage was due to the wilful neglect or default of the company or its servants, the burden of proving that this was not the case being upon the defendants.

. . .

The second condition is: '13. In no case shall the liability of the company exceed the value of the goods or a sum at the rate of £50 per ton of 20 cwt. of goods lost or damaged, whichever shall be the smaller. . . .'

. . .

The quantity of nuts was very considerable—over 5000 bags weighing at least 250 tons. They were stored in the defendants' warehouse at Field Lane, Bootle, the first two parcels being received in September and October 1965, and the remainder in the months of February, March, April and May 1966. When received the nuts were in apparent good order and condition, but a few bags were slack or burst. When the nuts were redelivered to the plaintiffs in January 1967, they were so seriously damaged both quantitatively and qualitatively that special procedures had to be devised and operated in order to sort the nuts into categories of those which could be used after cleaning and those which were valueless. The damage alleged exceeds twenty per cent of the value of the nuts.

The effective cause of the damage was rats which ate the bags, thereby releasing the contents, ate some of the nuts and contaminated part of the remainder with urine and droppings. The plaintiffs also complained of contamination by Cellaton powder which was stored in the same warehouse, but I am quite satisfied that this powder, which is used as a filtration substance, is quite harmless and did no more damage to the nuts than would inevitably have been done by dust in the atmosphere. It, like the ordinary atmospheric dust, could easily have been removed by washing.

Before considering the history of the storage of these nuts, it may be useful to consider what was the defendants' duty in relation to them and for what breaches of that duty they would be liable on the true construction of condition 11 of their standard terms of business. The defendants were bailees for reward and as such it was their duty to redeliver the nuts in the like good order and condition as when received, subject only to such loss or damage as might arise despite the exercise of all reasonable skill and care in their preservation and custody. I put it this way rather than that simply it was the defendants' duty to exercise all reasonable skill and care in the preservation and custody of the nuts because it better reflects the burden of proof. The plaintiffs need only prove redelivery in a condition worse than when the goods were delivered to the defendants and it is then for the defendants to show that the damage arose despite the exercise of all reasonable skill and care. I doubt, however, whether it matters which way round the duty is expressed save in relation to the burden of proof.

Protective conditions are of three distinct types, namely, first, those which limit or reduce what would otherwise be the defendant's duty; second, those which exclude the defendant's liability for breach of specified aspects of that duty and third, those which limit the extent to which the defendant is bound to indemnify the plaintiff in respect of the consequences of breaches of that duty.

A condition which provided that a warehouseman should be under no obligation to take greater care of perishable goods than was appropriate to imperishable goods, would constitute a good example of the first category of protective conditions. Another example, in a different field, is provided by the well known clauses which exclude the conditions implied by the Sale of Goods Act, 1893. If, in such a case, the warehouseman takes such care of perishable goods as would be appropriate had they been imperishable and damage results, he will escape liability not because the clause exempts him from liability for breach of contract (whether fundamental or otherwise), but because there has been no breach of contract.

A. Incorporation of the Exemption Clause

The signature rule

Duff v Great Northern Rly Co. (1878) 4 LR (Ir.) 178

Palles C.B.:

It was admitted that a contract was made between the plaintiff and the defendants for the carriage by the defendants of certain cattle of the plaintiff's from Dundalk to St Ives. The terms of this contract were reduced to writing, and were signed by the plaintiff. The terms to which the plaintiff's name is attached are as follows:

> It is hereby agreed between the undersigned and Great Northern and Manchester, Sheffield, and Lincolnshire Joint Railway Companies, that the animals named on the other side are to be conveyed only *upon the conditions mentioned upon the back of the invoice*, handed to the undersigned by the company's agent, and in consideration of the reduced rate charged, at the owner's sole risk in connexion with the sea part of the transit.

> (Signed) James Duff, *Owner.*

An invoice was handed to the plaintiff by the defendants' agent, at the time of his signing these terms, having on the back certain conditions, which are therein called conditions of carriage. One of these conditions is in the following words: 'That as a drover is allowed to attend the cattle during transit, they (i.e. the defendants) will allow such drover to travel free of charge upon condition that he so travel at his own risk.'

I think it unnecessary to discuss cases which have been put during the argument, as to the effect of conditions wholly foreign to the carriage of cattle being endorsed on the invoice. It seems to me to be clear that the conditions on the invoice, including that which I have read, are the conditions referred to in the document signed by the plaintiff, and that that document must be read as if the conditions were in terms stated therein. The agreement then is to carry the cattle on the terms (*inter alia*) that the owner's drover may not only attend them during transit, but (if he elect to travel at his own risk) need not pay the ordinary fare of a passenger. The plaintiff was not bound to travel on these terms, but unless he did so he was bound to pay his fare, and an election to travel free under this contract was an election to travel at his own risk.

Now it is admitted upon the evidence that the plaintiff did elect to travel under the contract. He himself states he travelled free, and the free pass proved is identified by the figures on it with the contract for carriage of the cattle. This appears to me to conclude the case. It reduces the question from one of fact—what was the contract under which plaintiff travelled—to matter of law, what is the legal effect and validity of the particular contract under which he shows as matter of fact he did travel? This latter question admits of no doubt. Under the contract the plaintiff is without remedy against the defendants for negligence during the journey, and such a contract (being for the conveyance of a passenger, and outside the 17 & 18 Vict. c. 31, and the statutes extending the same), is valid.

I do not think it necessary to refer in detail to any of the cases relied upon for the plaintiff. In all of them the contracts were by parol, and the question was what was the contract.

In *Henderson v Stevenson*,[1] Lord Cairns distinguishes between those cases and one such as the present, in which the terms of the contract have been reduced to writing. 'There were,' he says, 'a considerable number of other cases in which, for the conveyance of animals or of goods, a ticket or paper had been *actually signed* by the owner of the animals, or by the owner of the goods. With regard again to those cases, there might indeed be a question what was the construction of the contract, or how far the contract was valid. But there could be no question whatever that the contract, such as it was, was assented to, and entered into by the person who read the ticket.'

For those reasons, I am of opinion that the defendants were entitled to have had a verdict directed for them upon the claim for personal injuries. I desire, however, to observe that my judgment is based upon the fact that the person who actually travelled as drover was the person who signed the contract. Had he been a different person, the connection of the drover with the contract might have involved a question of fact, and this might have been for the jury.

The verdict on the claim for personal injuries will be entered for the defendants, and there will be judgment accordingly.

Dowse B.:

I am of the same opinion. Suppose this was a case in which the railway company proposed in writing to carry for the plaintiff forty-two head of cattle on the following terms, namely, that the plaintiff should be at liberty to travel with the cattle free, provided he did so at his own risk. If the plaintiff had signed this and had travelled free, could he recover a verdict against the defendants for personal injuries sustained during the journey? . . .

[1] 2 Sc App 470, 474.

(Fitzgerald B. concurred.)

L'Estrange v F. Graucob Ltd [1934] 2 KB 394

Scrutton L.J.:

In this case the plaintiff commenced proceedings against the defendants in the County Court, her claim being for £9 1s as money received by the defendants to the use of the plaintiff as part of the consideration for the delivery of an automatic slot machine pursuant to a contract in writing dated 7 February 1933, which consideration was alleged to have wholly failed by reason of the fact that the machine was delivered in a condition unfit for the purpose for which it was intended. The only document which corresponds to the contract there mentioned is a long document on brown paper headed 'Sales Agreement'. By their defence the defendants denied that the machine was delivered in a condition unfit for the purpose intended, and denied that the sum claimed was payable to the plaintiff; and they counterclaimed for the balance of the price of the machine. Just before the trial the plaintiff amended her claim by adding a count for breach of an implied warranty that the machine was reasonably fit for the purpose for which it was sold; though she still claimed only £9 1s. There the pleadings stopped. At the trial, as the judge has stated in his judgment, the plaintiff's claim was put in three different ways: total failure of consideration; breach of implied conditions going to the root of the contract; and breach of warranty. The defendants pleaded: no total failure of consideration; no implied conditions; and that no action would lie for breach of implied warranty, as the agreement expressly provided for the exclusion of all implied warranties. To this last defence the plaintiff contended that she was induced to sign the contract by the misrepresentation that it was an order form, and that at the time when she signed she knew nothing of the conditions.

The County Court Judge has given judgment for the plaintiff for £70, though there is no claim by the plaintiff for that sum; and he has given judgment for the defendants on the counterclaim for £71 18s 6d, the balance of the price.

As to the defence that no action would lie for breach of implied warranty, the defendants relied upon the following clause in the contract: 'This agreement contains all the terms and conditions under which I agree to purchase the machine specified above and any express or implied condition, statement, or warranty, statutory or otherwise not stated herein is hereby excluded.' A clause of that sort has been before the courts for some time. The first reported case in which it made its appearance seems to be *Wallis, Son & Wells v Pratt & Haynes*,[1] where the exclusion clause mentioned only 'warranty' and it was held that it did not exclude conditions. In the more recent case of *Andrews Bros (Bournemouth), Ltd v Singer & Co.*,[2] where the draftsman had put into the contract of sale a clause which excluded only implied conditions, warranties and liabilities, it was held that the clause did not apply to an express term describing the article, and did not exempt the seller from liability where he delivered an article of a different description. The clause here in question would seem to have been intended to go further than any of the previous clauses and to include all terms denoting collateral stipulations, in order to avoid the result of these decisions.

The main question raised in the present case is whether that clause formed part of the contract. If it did, it clearly excluded any condition or warranty.

In the course of the argument in the County Court reference was made to the railway passenger and cloak-room ticket cases, such as *Richardson, Spence & Co. v Rowntree*.[3] In that case Lord Herschell L.C. laid down the law applicable to these cases and stated the three questions which should there be left to the jury. In the present case the learned judge asked himself the three questions appropriate to these cases, and in answering them has found as facts: (i) that the plaintiff knew that there was printed material on the document which she signed, (ii) that she did not know that the document contained conditions relating to the contract, and (iii) that the defendants did not do what was reasonably sufficient to bring these conditions to the notice of the plaintiff.

The present case is not a ticket case, and it is distinguishable from the ticket cases. In *Parker v South Eastern Rly Co.*[4] Mellish L.J. laid down in a few sentences the law which is applicable to this case. He there said: 'In an ordinary case, where an action is brought on a written agreement which is signed by the defendant, the agreement is proved by proving his signature, and, in the absence of fraud, it is wholly immaterial that he has not read the agreement and does not know its contents.' Having said that, he goes on to deal with the ticket cases, where there is no signature to the contractual document, the document being simply handed by the one party to the other: 'The parties may, however, reduce their agreement into writing, so that the writing constitutes the sole evidence of the agreement, without signing it; but in that case there must be evidence independently of the agreement itself to prove that the defendant has assented to it. In that case, also, if it is proved that the defendant has assented to the writing constituting the agreement between the parties, it is, in the absence of fraud, immaterial that the defendant had not read the agreement and did not know its contents.' In cases in which the contract is contained in a railway ticket or other unsigned document, it is necessary to prove that an alleged party was aware, or ought to have been aware, of its terms and conditions. These cases have no application when the document has been signed. When a document containing contractual terms is signed, then, in the absence of fraud, or, I will add, misrepresentation, the party signing it is bound, and it is wholly immaterial whether he has read the document or not.

The plaintiff contended at the trial that she was induced by misrepresentation to sign the contract without knowing its terms, and that on that ground they are not binding upon her. The learned judge in his judgment makes no mention of that contention of the plaintiff, and he pronounces no finding as to the alleged misrepresentation. There is a further difficulty. Fraud is not mentioned in the pleadings, and I strongly object to deal with allegations of fraud where fraud is not expressly pleaded. I have read the evidence with care, and it contains no material upon which fraud could be found. The plaintiff no doubt alleged that the defendants' agent represented to her that the document which was given her to be signed was an order form, but according to the defendants' evidence no such statement was made to her by the agent. Moreover, whether the plaintiff was or was not told that the document was an order form, it was in fact an order form, and an order form is a contractual document. It may be either an acceptance or a proposal which may be accepted, but it always contains some contractual terms. There is no evidence that the plaintiff was induced to sign the contract by misrepresentation.

In this case the plaintiff has signed a document headed 'Sales Agreement', which she admits had to do with an intended purchase, and which contained a clause excluding all conditions and warranties. That being so, the plaintiff, having put her signature to the document and not having been induced to do so by any fraud or misrepresentation, cannot be heard to say that she is not bound by the terms of the document because she has not read them.

The County Court Judge has given judgment for the defendants on the counterclaim for the balance of the price, £71 18s 6d. I do not see how he could have done that unless he found that the contract included the clause in small print providing that, if any instalment of the price should not be duly paid, all the remaining instalments should fall due for immediate payment. That judgment on the counterclaim must stand. As to the claim, judgment was given for the plaintiff for £70 for breach of an implied warranty, though only £9 1s was claimed. Such a judgment could not have been given even in the High Court without an amendment of the claim. But even if there had been an amendment, the further difficulty would have remained that the signed document contained a clause excluding any implied condition or warranty. If the view which I have expressed as to the effect of a signed document is correct, the plaintiff has no ground of claim, and the judgment in her favour cannot stand. In my opinion, the judgment for the plaintiff on the claim should be set aside and judgment entered for the defendants on the claim; and the judgment for the defendants on the counterclaim should stand.

Maugham L.J.:

I regret the decision to which I have come, but I am bound by legal rules and cannot decide the case on other considerations.
. . .

In this case it is, in my view, an irrelevant circumstance that the plaintiff did not read, or hear of, the parts of the sales document which are in small print, and that document should have effect according to its terms. I may add, however, that I could wish that the contract had been in a simpler and more usual form. It is unfortunate that the important clause excluding conditions and warranties is in such small print. I also think that the order confirmation form should have contained an express statement to the effect that it was exclusive of all conditions and warranties.

I agree that the appeal should be allowed.

[1] [1911] AC 394.
[2] [1934] 1 KB 17.
[3] [1894] AC 217.
[4] 2 CPD 416.

Slattery *v* C.I.E. (1968) 106 ILTR 71

The plaintiff's action was for breach of contract occasioned by the negligent loading of three yearlings, one of which was injured as a result. The only issue was whether the contract was concluded on the basis of the defendants' standard conditions of carriage.

Teevan J.:

In the civil bill action in the Circuit Court giving rise to this appeal the plaintiff alleged negligence in the handling of a race horse by the defendant's servant on the occasion of the carriage of the horse by the defendants from the plaintiff's residence at Milltown, near Clonmel, to Ballsbridge. The plaintiff is a breeder of bloodstock. He decided to engage the defendants to transport three unbroken yearling thoroughbred horses by road to the bloodstock sales at Ballsbridge on 8 August 1967. He made the arrangements for transport by telephone from his house to the defendants' Waterford office. The defendants accepted the business and it was agreed that one of their road horse boxes would arrive at the plaintiff's residence at 8 a.m. on 8 August 1967. No terms of contract were then arranged and nothing on either side was said about rates of charges, or conditions of carriage.

The defendants' box arrived at the plaintiff's residence as arranged. The box had been driven from Dublin that morning having left Dublin at 3 a.m. The operation of loading the horses was commenced, the loading being done by the plaintiff assisted by one of his men and the defendants' driver, Mr Peter Murphy. Mr Murphy has some twenty-two years experience of this work and it is customary for him to assist in loading the stock to be carried. Again nothing was said about rates or conditions of carriage. Mr Murphy had with him the usual combined form of consignment note and delivery sheet on which is printed in bold type: 'It is the responsibility of drivers to see that the attention of hirers or their agents . . . is drawn to the conditions on back of sheet and that their signatures are inscribed in the appropriate spaces.' There are in fact two spaces for signatures of assignor or his agent. The first of these is under the consignment note portion of the document which reads (so far as material): 'Receive and forward the undermentioned horses subject to the regulations and conditions shown on the back hereof . . .'. Then follows the space for consignor's signature. The particulars of the transaction including the charge for the carriage and the plaintiff's name and address were already inserted on this form. This should properly be signed at the commencement of carriage. This was not done nor was the plaintiff at that stage shown or informed of the terms and conditions of carriage printed on the back of the sheet. . . .

. . .

I now have to go back on the history of this contract. I have already said that the consignment note had not been signed by the plaintiff at the initiation of the carriage; neither was his attention called to the defendants' terms of carriage. If the consignment note had been signed at the commencement of the business it would of course have constituted the terms of contract and of carriage. What happened was this: on reaching the end of the journey and on off-loading the horses the driver presented the consignment note for the plaintiff's signature. The plaintiff signed both in the space acknowledging receipt of the horses (for in this case he was consignee as well as consignor) and also in the space acknowledging the regulations and conditions printed on the back of the sheet. (There was also a third signature relating to permission to him to travel personally in the box during the transit but this is of no present materiality). The plaintiff signed without demur, without reading the conditions and without making any point about holding the company liable for the horse's injury. There are two rates of carriage charges; one for owner's risk carriage and a higher rate for carriage at the carrier's risk. Even in the latter case the company's liability for loss or damage due to negligence is limited to £100 per horse unless a higher value be declared at time of delivery of the horse to the company for carriage. The charge inserted in the consignment note was at the lower rate; i.e. at the rate appropriate to 'owner's risk' carriage.

In fact the consignment note signed by the plaintiff is headed in large heavy black print '*Consignment note and delivery sheet for horses to be carried* . . . *at owner's risk.*' The plaintiff's signature stands about two inches or three inches below that heading. The plaintiff did not read the terms: he signed because, according to his evidence, he thought he was only signing a receipt or acknowledgment of completion of the carriage and did not know that he was signing a memorandum of the contract.

If the consignment note as so signed is binding on the plaintiff; that is to say if it fixes the terms of his contract, that is the end of his case. It is contended, however, that as the document was signed after completion by the defendants of the contract on their part it cannot be read as constituting terms not previously agreed upon or to bind the plaintiff by the conditions exempting liability of the defendants. The question is whether the plaintiff can be heard to deny that the conditions set out in the consignment note signed by him form part of the contract? 'The best way of proving [the terms of a contract] is by a written document signed by the party to be bound' (per Denning L.J. in *Olley v Marlborough Court Ltd* [1949] 1 KB 532 p. 549). Here we have such a document but the argument is that it must be ignored because it was signed after delivery of the horses, in other words after completion of the defendants' part of the transaction. The plaintiff could have refused to sign the document particularly as it was not shown or its terms otherwise made known to him at the inception of carriage:

the fact is that he signed it. Before signing it he was aware, needless to say, of the damage to his horse but he did not then know that the injury was likely to result in loss. In his very candid and honourable evidence in cross-examination he admitted that he was aware that the defendants had two rates of charges; that the higher rate involved the carrier's liability and that the lesser was an owner's risk rate. He said he thought the charges entered on the consignment note (£27 5s) were as he put it 'the company's rate—fully insured' but admitted that he did not look to see whether such was the case. On being asked 'Isn't it in fact at the owner's risk rate?' he replied: 'It turned out to be that but I thought it would be the 'board rate'. Had I been asked which I would prefer and if the 'board rate' had been the higher I would have taken that rate.' ('board's risk rates' is the term used to denote carriage at the defendant carrier's risk.) While the plaintiff cannot be exculpated for his own carelessness the defendants are open to criticism; in the interest of their customers they should in fairness bring the choice of rates and the consequences attending the disparity to the customer's notice at the commencement particularly where, as in this case, the conditions are lengthy complicated and set up in small type following the worst in railway tradition. If it is too much to expect that the casual as distinct from the regular customer will read and follow this complex mass of conditions, nevertheless I must repeat that the actual consignment note was headed ' . . . horses to be carried . . . at owner's risk' almost immediately above each of the spaces where the plaintiff put his signature.

If the plaintiff had declined to sign the delivery note at Ballsbridge he could not be compelled to do so nor in my opinion could he be held bound by the pleaded conditions, which could not be unilaterally imposed. He could then take the stand that he sought to take in this case: that the contract was simply on the defendants' part to carry the horses and on his part to pay for the service. It has been argued that the latter was in fact the contract agreed upon by and within the intention of the parties.

The defendants relied on *Knox v Great Northern Rly*, 29 ILTR 47; |1896| 2 IR 632. That case resembles the present case in that the terms of contract were agreed upon by the parties after the carriage had commenced, although in *Knox's* case this was done immediately after boxing and before departure of the horse on its journey: it differs in that the owner's agent consciously or with deliberation elected between the choice of rates. (This does not appear in the statement of facts but the judgments appear to proceed on that basis: see for instance Johnson J. at p. 636, '|the booking clerk| offered Creighton his choice of the two rates and Creighton with the knowledge that the horse was injured, elected to take the reduced rate with the liability incident to it.') *Knox's* case differs from the present in another respect; if Creighton, the plaintiff's agent, had refused to sign the formal contract with one effect or the other, the railway company could have refused to continue the carriage, while the defendants' driver in the case before me had effectively removed that lever by delaying to have his contract signed until journey's end had been reached. It cannot be said that Mr Slattery was in the dilemma which confronted Creighton the groom in *Knox's* case. I do not mean it to be inferred that this distinction is of any conclusive worth but at least it illustrates the present plaintiff's freedom of action. Be that as it may he signed the contract and no authority has been cited to me and no convincing argument presented to avoid the plaintiff's assent to its terms, or to support assertion that having been signed on delivery it cannot be read as the contract the parties entered into. In the words of Holmes J. in *Knox's* case in the Queen's Bench Division (p. 639): 'It is neither illegal, unreasonable, nor unusual, for the terms of a contract to be reduced to writing after the performance of the services contracted for has been begun'. To my mind the case is no different from what might have happened if in the course of the journey to Dublin, the driver had bethought himself that he had neglected to have the form of contract signed and had asked the plaintiff to sign it then. If on such an occasion the plaintiff agreed to and did sign it, I cannot see how he could escape the consequences and I fail to see any distinction between such a situation and that in which, in fact, the contract was signed at Ballsbridge. The contract was not even then wholly performed; the plaintiff had not carried out his part of it, namely to pay the carriage charge. Furthermore the signing of the contract at the lower rate put it beyond the power of the carriers to recover the higher rate for their services. [Counsel for the plaintiff] sought to distinguish the present case from Knox's case, on the submitted ground that the latter had to do with conditions laid down by statute and did not rest in contract. It is clear, on the contrary, that the judgments rest on the contract concluded between the parties.

I must hold that the plaintiff bound himself by the conditions on signing the contract note. It amounts to a declaration by the plaintiff of what the terms of the contract were. [Counsel] referred me to Anson (9th ed.) at p. 159 et seq., wherein the learned author discusses cases of standard conditions on a take-it-or-leave-it method of business, allowing of no variation. The present case materially differs from those in which the aggrieved parties were held not bound by such conditions by reason of the failure of the parties prescribing the conditions to bring the same effectively to their customers' notice. Having regard to the very prominent manner in which the defendants have called attention, almost at the very place where the plaintiff placed his signature, to the carriage being at owner's risk and subject to the condition overleaf, the plaintiff has only himself to blame for failing to notice this.

Accordingly I must regretfully find for the defendants and dismiss the claim. I say regretfully because as a matter of fair dealing these stringent conditions and the purpose or implication of the varying rates should be brought to the customer's notice at the time of engagement, unless to the knowledge of the company's officers, the customer by reason of frequency of dealing may be taken as already aware of them. The choice of rates should be left to the customer's election. Nothing could be simpler than an enquiry by the defendants' agent when the business was being placed with him, whether the customer required the service at company's, or his own risk and to make known the differential in rates and the limits of liability in the former case unless on declaration of higher value than the pre-ordained values in the standard conditions.

B. INCORPORATION BY REASONABLE NOTICE

If no condition is used or pleaded, common law or statutory liability will result.

Roche *v* Cork Blackrock and Passage Rly Co. (1889) 24 LR (Ir.) 250

Gibson J.:

The plaintiff deposited in the defendants' cloakroom a Gladstone bag, locked with an ordinary lock, and containing the sum of £10. He received a ticket in the usual way. The ticket contained no conditions in any way limiting liability. The plaintiff did not apprise the defendants that the bag contained money or valuables. On the plaintiff applying for his bag at the cloakroom he received it; but on unlocking it (which he found some difficulty in doing), he discovered the money had been abstracted. The servant in charge of the cloakroom was not examined. The plaintiff claimed the £10 against the defendants, as having been lost by their negligence.

. . .

Why this company should have omitted to protect themselves by conditions, as other railways have done for years past, I do not know. They are fortunate in having now been taught their mistake and danger at so small a cost.

Ryan v Great Southern and Western Rly Co. (1898) 12 ILTR 108

Gibson J.:

The plaintiff took from the defendants a return excursion ticket to Ennistymon, beyond the defendants' line, and the luggage was lost, not by the defendants, but by one of the other companies. On the face of the ticket there was printed in minute type a reference to the regulations and conditions of the defendants as binding the passenger, and by such conditions, if incorporated into the contract, the defendants were exonerated from liability for loss occurring beyond their own railway. The plaintiff did not read the printed matter, and could not have learned the condition, which was not disclosed on the ticket, without special inquiry. The company relied on *Zunz's* case, LR 4 QB 539. As the point seemed of some importance, I offered the company a case stated on terms which they declined to accept. The plaintiff having taken and paid the defendants for a through return ticket was *prima facie* entitled to treat them as the contracting carriers. The defendants failed to do what was reasonably sufficient to give the plaintiff notice of the restriction of liability (*Rowntree's* case, 1894, AC 217). The case is quite different from *Zunz's* case and *Burke's* case, 5 CPD 1, in each of which there was a book with express printed conditions. Where the passenger is an experienced traveller and the company have done all that is reasonably possible to bring home to him the terms on which the ticket is issued, he may not be able to better his position by the allegation of voluntary ignorance. The facts of the present case do not bring the plaintiff within any such principle. The appeal must, therefore, be allowed, and a decree given for the amount claimed, with costs.

Note

Even if the plaintiff could not, in a specific case, have seen or consented to the terms relied upon, the rule about reasonable notice will still prevail. Under earlier cases the nature of the risk run did not appear to affect the level of reasonableness.

Early v Great Southern Rly Co. [1940] IR 414

Sullivan C.J.:

I am of opinion that this appeal must be dismissed.

The material facts can be summarised in a few sentences. On the 12 April 1936, Easter Sunday, a special train was run by the defendant company from Arigna to Mohill, returning to Arigna that evening. In ordinary circumstances no train runs on this line on Sunday, and for this special train return tickets were issued at a reduced price. The plaintiff, with some companions, joined the train at a 'halt' at Fenagh and travelled to Mohill to take part in a demonstration there. Return tickets from Fenagh to Mohill had been purchased at Fenagh. Late in the evening the train with the plaintiff and his companions on board left Mohill on its return journey to Arigna, and, shortly after it had started, the tickets were taken up by the ticket collector. When the train arrived at Fenagh the plaintiff should have alighted, as his ticket was not available for any further journey, but he decided to remain in the train until it got to Cornabrone. No one except the plaintiff and his companions was aware that he should have alighted at Fenagh. When the train reached Cornabrone the accident happened in respect of which damages are claimed by the plaintiff. The question whether that accident was caused by negligence on the part of the defendants' servants was not determined at the trial and does not arise on this appeal.

The case made on behalf of the plaintiff was:

1. That he had got no reasonable notice of the conditions on which his ticket was issued, and therefore was not bound by them.

2. That if those conditions were binding upon him they were so only during the journey for which his ticket was available and were no longer operative when he travelled beyond Fenagh on the return journey.

At Fenagh, where the plaintiff purchased his ticket, there was a poster advertising the excursion to Mohill, which stated that excursion tickets and tickets issued at less than ordinary fares are issued subject to the notices and conditions shown in the company's time tables. The ticket purchased by the plaintiff bore on its face the words: 'Special train—available for day of issue only—not transferable. See back.' On the back was printed—'Issued subject to the conditions and regulations in the company's time tables, books, bills and notices.' One of those conditions was that the holder of a ticket issued at a fare less than the ordinary fare should not have any right of action against the company in respect of injury, fatal or otherwise. No copy of the time table or of any document containing those conditions was available for inspection by intending passengers at Fenagh 'halt'. The plaintiff, however, made no inquiry about them.

The learned trial judge held: (1) That the defendants had taken reasonable steps to bring to the plaintiff's notice the conditions upon which he was accepted as a passenger. (2) That the plaintiff was bound by those conditions so long as he continued to be a passenger in the train.

If the accident to the plaintiff had happened during the journey for which his ticket was available this case would be governed by the principles stated in the cases to which the learned judge referred—*Grand Trunk Rly Co. of Canada v Robinson*,[1] and *Thompson v London, Midland and Scottish Rly Co.*[2] In the former case Lord Haldane L.C. in delivering the opinion of the Privy Council said (at p. 747):

> If a passenger has entered a train on a mere invitation or permission from a railway company without more, and he receives injury in an accident caused by the negligence of its servants, the company is liable for damages for breach of a general duty to exercise care. Such a breach can be regarded as one either of an implied contract, or of a duty imposed by the general law, and in the latter case as in form a tort. But in either view this general duty may, subject to such statutory restrictions as exist in Canada and in England in different ways, be superseded by a specific contract, which may either enlarge, diminish, or exclude it. If the law authorises it, such a contract cannot be pronounced to be unreasonable by a court of justice. The specific contract, with its incidents either expressed or attached by law, becomes in such a case the only measure of the duties between the parties, and the plaintiff cannot by any device of form get more than the contract allows him.

Again, at p. 748:

> The only right to be carried will be one which arises under the terms of the contract itself, and these terms must be accepted in their entirety. The company owes the

passenger no duty which the contract is expressed on the face of it to exclude, and if he has approbated that contract by travelling under it he cannot afterwards reprobate it by claiming a right inconsistent with it. For the only footing on which he has been accepted as a passenger is simply that which the contract has defined.

In *Thompson v London, Midland and Scottish Rly Co.*, the ticket held by the plaintiff bore on its face the words: 'Excursion, for conditions see back,' and on the back: 'Issued subject to the conditions and regulations in the company's time tables and notices and excursion and other bills.' In the course of his judgment Lord Hanworth M.R. says (p. 47):

> It appears to me that the right way of considering such notices is put by Swift J. in *Nunan v Southern Rly Co.*[3] After referring to a number of cases which have been dealt with in the courts he says: 'I am of opinion that the proper method of considering such a matter is to proceed upon the assumption that where a contract is made by the delivery, by one of the contracting parties to the other, of a document in common form stating the terms upon which the person delivering it will enter into the proposed contract, such a form constitutes the offer of the party who tenders it, and if the form is accepted without objection by the person to whom it is tendered this person is as a general rule bound by its contents and his act amounts to an acceptance of the offer to him whether he reads the document or otherwise informs himself of its contents or not, and the conditions contained in the document are binding upon him.'

In a later passage Lord Hanworth says:

> It is, however, argued that it is a question of fact for the jury, whether or not sufficient notice was given of these conditions, and whether or not, therefore, the plaintiff ought to be held bound by the conditions; for it is said that the conditions are, I will not say past finding out, but difficult to ascertain. The learned commissioner who tried the case appreciated that the verdict of the jury was based probably on the fact that you have to make a considerable search before you find out the conditions. I think he is right in saying that in the line of cases, and there are many, under which this case falls, it has not ever been held that the mere circuity which has to be followed to find the actual condition prevents the passenger having notice that there was a condition.

The judgments of Lawrence L.J. and Sankey L.J. are to the same effect.

The only remaining question is whether the plaintiff, when he travelled beyond Fenagh on the return journey, was travelling subject to the special conditions or as an ordinary passenger. This was a special train on which no ordinary passengers were carried, all the passengers were carried on special terms at a reduced rate. When the plaintiff remained on the train after passing Fenagh he was, in my opinion, being carried not as an ordinary passenger but on the special conditions on which his ticket had been issued.

In my opinion the learned judge was right in holding that the defendants had taken all reasonable steps to bring to the notice of the plaintiff the conditions on which he would be carried as a passenger, and that the plaintiff was bound by those conditions at the time when he sustained the injury for which he claims damages. I do not think that the jury could properly find otherwise, and it follows that the direction given by the learned judge was right.

Murnaghan J.:

I agree, but, as this case is of some importance, I think it is right that I should give my reasons.

A contract to carry, once it is entered upon, imports a condition to carry safely; this obligation may, however, be excluded by special agreement. A passenger on a railway obtains a ticket as a receipt for payment, but the company uses that ticket to convey to the passenger that the ordinary terms of the contract have been altered.

A great number of cases have been decided on the question whether or not notice has been reasonably brought to the knowledge of the passenger. If not, the passenger is not bound by the attempted alteration. In this case the front of the ticket bears the words: 'See back', and on the back is printed: 'Issued subject to the conditions and regulations in the company's time tables, books, bills and notices.'

The point that is new in this case is that the time tables were not available at Fenagh where the ticket was issued. The plaintiff did not ask for the time tables, but he would be entitled to rely on the fact if it were the law that the absence of the time tables from the booking office amounted to a failure to give him notice of the condition. I personally sympathise with a person making a contract when the terms to which he is asked to assent are not put before him, but the law is that a document may incorporate conditions which are not expressed in it but in some other document. *Thompson's* case, was very similar to this and the court held in that case that the regulations were incorporated by the ticket.

In my opinion Hanna J., was right. I have no doubt that the principle of the law is as stated by him, and the only remedy for the present legal position would be legislation.

¹· [1915] AC 740.   ²· [1930] 1 KB 41.   ³· [1923] 2 KB 703, at p. 707.

(Geoghegan J. agreed.)

Note

The nature of the risk being displaced or excluded can now considerably influence the standard of reasonableness required before the clause will be held to have been incorporated.

Thornton v Shoe Lane Parking Ltd [1971] 2 QB 163

Lord Denning M.R.:

In 1964 Mr Thornton, the plaintiff, who was a free-lance trumpeter of the highest quality, had an engagement with the BBC at Farringdon Hall. He drove to the city in his motor car and went to park it at a multi-storey automatic car park. It had only been open a few months. He had never gone there before. There was a notice on the outside headed 'Shoe Lane Parking'. It gave the parking charges: '5s for two hours; 7s 6d for three hours', and so forth; and at the bottom: 'All Cars Parked At Owner's Risk'. Mr Thornton drove up to the entrance. There was not a man in attendance. There was a traffic light which showed red. As he drove in and got to the appropriate place, the traffic light turned green and a ticket was pushed out from the machine. Mr Thornton took it. He drove on into the garage. The motor car was taken up by mechanical means to a floor above. Mr Thornton left it there and went off to keep his appointment with the BBC. Three hours later Mr Thornton came back. He went to the office and paid the charge for the time the car was there. His car was brought down from the upper floor.

He went to put his belongings into the boot of the car. But unfortunately there was an accident. Mr Thornton was severely injured. The judge has found it was half his own fault, but half the fault of Shoe Lane Parking Ltd, the defendants. The judge awarded him £3,637 6s 11d.

On this appeal the garage company do not contest the judge's findings about the accident. They acknowledge that they were at fault, but they claim that they are protected by some exempting conditions. They rely on the ticket which was issued to Mr Thornton by the machine. They say that it was a contractual document and that it incorporated a condition which exempts them from liability to him. The ticket was headed 'Shoe Lane Parking'. Just below there was a 'box' in which was automatically recorded the time when the car went into the garage. There was a notice alongside: 'Please present this ticket to cashier to claim your car.' Just below the time, there was some small print in the left hand corner which said: 'The ticket is issued subject to the conditions of issue as displayed on the premises.' That is all.

Mr Thornton says he looked at the ticket to see the time on it, and put it in his pocket. He could see there was printing on the ticket, but he did not read it. He only read the time. He did not read the words which said that the ticket was issued subject to the conditions as displayed on the premises.

If Mr Thornton had read those words on the ticket and had looked round the premises to see where the conditions were displayed, he would have had to have driven his car on into the garage and walked round. Then he would have found, on a pillar opposite the ticket machine, a set of printed conditions in a panel. He would also have found, in the paying office (to be visited when coming back for the car) two more panels containing the printed conditions. If he had the time to read the conditions—it would take him a very considerable time—he would read:

Conditions

The following are the conditions upon which alone motor vehicles are accepted for parking:

1. The customer agrees to pay the charges of Shoe Lane Parking Developments Ltd. . . .
2. The customer is deemed to be fully insured at all times against all risks (including, without prejudice to the generality of the foregoing, fire, damage and theft, whether due to the negligence of others or not) and the company shall not be responsible or liable for any loss or misdelivery of or damage of whatever kind to the customer's motor vehicle, or any articles carried therein or thereon or of or to any accessories carried thereon or therein *or injury to the customer* or *any other person occurring when the customer's motor vehicle is in the parking building howsoever that loss, misdelivery, damage or injury shall be caused*; and it is agreed and understood that the customer's motor vehicle is parked and permitted by the company to be parked in the parking building in accordance with this licence entirely at the customer's risk. . . .

There is a lot more. I have only read about one-tenth of the conditions. The important thing to notice is that the company seek by this condition to exempt themselves from liability, not only for damage to the car, but also for injury to the customer howsoever caused. The condition talks about insurance. It is well known that the customer is usually insured against damage to the car. But he is not insured against damage to himself. If the condition is incorporated into the contract of parking, it means that Mr Thornton will be unable to recover any damages for his personal injuries which were caused by the negligence of the company.

We have been referred to the ticket cases of former times from *Parker v South Eastern Rly Co.* (1877) 2 CPD 416 to *McCutcheon v David MacBrayne Ltd* [1964] 1 WLR 125. They were concerned with railways, steamships and cloakrooms where booking clerks issued tickets to customers who took them away without reading them. In those cases the issue of the ticket was regarded as an *offer* by the company. If the customer took it and retained it without objection, his act was regarded as an acceptance of the offer: *Watkins v Rymill* (1833) 10 QBD 178, 188 and *Thompson v London, Midland and Scottish Rly Co.* [1930] 1 KB 41, 47. These cases were based on the theory that the customer, on being handed the ticket, could refuse it and decline to enter into a contract on those terms. He could ask for his money back. That theory was, of course, a fiction. No customer in a thousand ever read the conditions. If he had stopped to do so, he would have missed the train or the boat.

None of those cases has any application to a ticket which is issued by an automatic machine. The customer pays his money and gets a ticket. He cannot refuse it. He cannot get his money back. He may protest to the machine, even swear at it. But it will remain unmoved. He is committed beyond recall. He was committed at the very moment when he put his money into the machine. The contract was concluded at that time. It can be translated into offer and acceptance in this way: the offer is made when the proprietor of the machine holds it out as being ready to receive the money. The acceptance takes place when the customer puts his money into the slot. The terms of the offer are contained in the notice placed on or near the machine stating what is offered for the money. The customer is bound by those terms as long as they are sufficiently brought to his notice beforehand, but not otherwise. He is not bound by the terms printed on the ticket if they differ from the notice, because the ticket comes too late. The contract has already been made: see *Olley v Marlborough Court Ltd* [1949] 1 KB 532. The ticket is no more than a voucher or receipt for the money that has been paid (as in the deckchair case, *Chapelton v Barry Urban District Council* [1940] 1 KB 532) on terms which have been offered and accepted before the ticket is issued.

In the present case the offer was contained in the notice at the entrance giving the charges for garaging and saying 'at owner's risk', i.e. at the risk of the owner so far as damage to the car was concerned. The offer was accepted when Mr Thornton drove up to the entrance and, by the movement of his car, turned the light from red to green, and the ticket was thrust at him. The contract was then concluded, and it could not be altered by any words printed on the ticket itself. In particular, it could not be altered so as to exempt the company from liability for personal injury due to their negligence.

Assuming, however, that an automatic machine is a booking clerk in disguise—so that the old fashioned ticket cases still apply to it. We then have to go back to the three questions put by Mellish L.J. in *Parker v South Eastern Rly Co.*, subject to this qualification: Mellish L.J. used the word 'conditions' in the plural, whereas it would be more apt to use the word 'condition' in the singular, as indeed the Lord Justice himself did on the next page. After all, the only condition that matters for this purpose is the exempting condition. It is no use telling the customer that the ticket is issued subject to some 'conditions' or other, without more: for he may reasonably regard 'conditions' in general as merely regulatory, and not as taking away his rights, unless the exempting condition is drawn specifically to his attention. (Alternatively, if the plural 'conditions' is used, it would be better prefaced with the word 'exempting', because the exempting conditions are the only conditions that matter for this purpose.) Telescoping the three questions, they come to this: the customer is bound by the exempting condition if he knows that the ticket is issued subject to it; or, if the company did what was reasonably sufficient to give him notice of it.

[Counsel for the defendant] admitted here that the company did not do what was reasonably sufficient to give Mr Thornton notice of the exempting condition. That admission was properly made. I do not pause to inquire whether the exempting condition is void for unreasonableness. All I say is that it is so wide and so destructive of rights that the court should not hold any man bound by it unless it is drawn to his attention in the most explicit way. It is an instance of what I had in mind in J. *Spurling Ltd v Bradshaw* [1956] 1 WLR 461, 466. In order to give sufficient notice, it would need to be printed in red ink with a red hand pointing to it—or something equally startling.

But, although reasonable notice of it was not given, [counsel] said that this case came within the second question propounded by Mellish L.J., namely that Mr Thornton 'knew or believed that the writing contained conditions.' There was no finding to that effect. The burden was on the company to prove it, and they did not do so. Certainly there was no evidence that Mr Thornton knew of this exempting condition. He is not, therefore, bound by it.

Mr Machin relied on a case in this court last year—*Mendelssohn v Normand Ltd* [1970] 1 QB 177. Mr Mendelssohn parked his car in the Cumberland Garage at Marble Arch, and was given a ticket which contained an exempting condition. There was no discussion as to whether the condition formed part of the contract. It was conceded that it did. That is shown by the report in the Law Reports at p. 180. Yet the garage company were not entitled to rely on the exempting condition for the reasons there given.

That case does not touch the present, where the whole question is whether the exempting condition formed part of the contract. I do not think it did. Mr Thornton did not know of the condition, and the company did not do what was reasonably sufficient to give him notice of it.

I do not think the garage company can escape liability by reason of the exemption condition. I would, therefore, dismiss the appeal.

(Megaw L.J. and Wilmer J. gave judgments to the same effect.)

Western Meats Ltd *v* National Ice and Cold Storage Co. Ltd [1982] ILRM 99

Barrington J.:

The plaintiffs are a limited liability company with a registered office at Bridge Street, Longford. They operate meat factories at Dromond, County Leitrim and at Charleville, County Cork.

The defendants are two limited liability companies associated together and jointly trading under the name 'Frigoscandia'. Among their activities they maintain a cold storage freezing plant and depot at Midleton, Co. Cork.

In 1969 the plaintiffs had recently taken over a meat factory at Charleville, County Cork and had embarked on a policy which was greatly to expand the turnover and the work force in that factory. They were approached by the defendants who solicited their business, and offered them the facilities of the cold storage plant which the defendants operated at Midleton, County Cork. In September 1969 the defendants' representatives met with Mr William Lyons, who is a director of the plaintiff company, and followed up this meeting with a letter dated 22 September 1969 in which they stated:

> Our group are the largest operators of public cold stores in Europe and from their years of experience have worked out the most efficient and economical way to store customers' products. We operate a total of 7 million cubic feet of controlled temperature storage in England, with stores at Stratford, London and Kings Lynn, Norfolk. Our store at Stratford, being adjacent to the Smithfield Market, handles a high tonnage of carcass meat, boneless beef and offals. The Midleton store, which is the most modern cold store in Ireland, can offer you . . .

The letter then proceeds to describe the facilities which the Midleton store can provide.

These facilities appeared to the plaintiffs to meet their business requirements and a mutually satisfactory business relationship commenced between the parties and continued for many years. On 21 December 1973 the defendants' Mr W. S. Stephen wrote a letter to the plaintiffs which concluded in the following terms: 'Finally, I would like to take this opportunity of thanking you for your co-operation and the good business relationships that existed between our two companies in 1973. I look forward to these conditions continuing during 1974.'

Unfortunately, the difficulties which gave rise to the present action arose during the year 1974. Among the meats which the plaintiff deposited with the defendants for cold storage were various forms of pig meat including ham, bacon, pork and offals. The plaintiffs, in the course of the year, sold various forms of pig meat in the home market, and, through the Pigs and Bacon Commission, in the export market. They stored their surplus produce with the defendants in the confident expectation that they could withdraw this as and when required, and in particular for the Christmas trade. Coming up to Christmas 1974 I am satisfied that the plaintiffs had stored with the defendants very considerable quantities of gammons and other forms of pig meat and that they attempted to withdraw these to meet the Christmas demand, but were unable to do so.

I am satisfied that the reason why the plaintiffs were unable to withdraw their meat from cold storage was that the defendants, during the year 1974, had accepted into cold storage more meat than they could cope with or keep track of. I am satisfied also, that in the weeks coming up to Christmas in 1974, the plaintiffs sought to withdraw all their meat from cold storage to meet the Christmas demand but they were unable to do so simply because the defendants could not locate it and deliver it to them. The situation was so chaotic that the plaintiffs, instead of stipulating various quantities of meat which they wished to withdraw, had to resort to the device of sending their lorry to the defendants' store and giving the lorry driver a blank order book and authorising him to give a receipt for such meat as he could obtain from the defendants. I am satisfied also that the plaintiffs, being unable to withdraw their meat from cold storage, were forced in an effort to meet their customers' demands, to buy in, and slaughter, pigs in order to make available to their customers, for the Christmas trade, gammons which were in fact in cold storage and ought to have been readily available to the plaintiffs. I am quite satisfied that the reason why they were not so available, and could not be found, was that the defendants, during the year 1974, had taken into cold storage more meat than they could efficiently cope with or trace.

Under these circumstances it appears to me that, *prima facie*, the defendants, as bailees for reward, are liable for their failures to produce the plaintiffs' meat on demand and are also liable for consequential loss which befell the plaintiffs as a result of this failure.

To the plaintiffs' claim the defendants have two principal defences. The first is based on their standard conditions of trade and the second is based on the defendants' assertion that the plaintiffs were negligent in labelling, depositing, and withdrawing their goods and are consequently, at least in part, the authors of their own misfortune.

The conditions of trade, if part of the contract between the parties, appear to me to be a complete answer to the plaintiffs' claim.

Clause I of the conditions of storage provides that all goods are stored at the owner's risk. Clause II provides that the company will not be answerable for any delay, loss or damage arising (*inter alia*) from maintaining too high or too low a temperature in the stores, failure of machinery or plant, negligence, thefts, including theft by the company's servants, 'or any other cause whatsoever'.

There is no doubt that it was competent for the parties to include such clauses in their contract if they wished to do so. We are not here dealing with a monopoly providing a necessary service for an ignorant and unwary public. We are dealing with two commercial concerns one of which is providing a specialist service for the other and each of which is competent to protect its own interests. So far as this aspect of the case is concerned the relevant principles would appear to be those laid down in the House of Lords in *Photo Production Ltd v Securicor Transport Ltd* |1980| AC 827.

But the primary question is whether the plaintiffs were given reasonable notice of these conditions. Mr William Lyons says he was not aware of them an there is no evidence that they were ever expressly brought to his attention.

In later years these conditions appeared on the back of the defendants' notepaper and also on the back of many of their storage documents. We only have a photostat copy of the original letter passing between the parties dated 22 September 1969. The conditions do not appear on the back of this copy though they may have been on the back of the original.

However, in the text of the letter itself there is no reference to the conditions, though certain terms are set out in the letter. I am satisfied that the terms were never expressly brought to Mr Lyons' attention and I accept his word that he was not aware of them. I am satisfied that he is a man who carries on business by personal contact and on the telephone and that he relies greatly on his assessment of the men he is dealing with. Indeed, in the present case, even the defendants' managers do not appear to have been particularly conscious of the standard conditions. When disputes arose between the parties over the years, prior to the present dispute, these were resolved as between businessmen and, even in the present case, there was no reference to the standard conditions until the matter reached the hands of the lawyers.

It appears to me to be important that this is a case in which the defendants initially solicited the plaintiffs' business. Had they, the initial negotiators, expressly drawn to Mr Lyons' attention not only the excellence of their services but also the fact that they accepted no responsibility whatsoever for the manner in which they would handle his goods, Mr Lyons' decision of whether to retain them might well have been different. In all the circumstances of this case it appears to me that the defendants did not give the plaintiffs reasonable notice of the contents of the standard conditions. It appears to me also that a businessman, offering a specialist service, but accepting no responsibility for it, must bring home clearly to the party dealing with him that he accepts no such responsibility. In all the circumstances I think, that in the present case, the defendants were guilty of negligence and breach of contract.

With regard to the alleged negligence of the plaintiffs I am satisfied that the plaintiffs, in depositing meat for storage, clearly identified the meat as having come from their factory and also clearly distinguished, by different kinds of labels, pork from bacon.

The records of both parties, however, as to the precise amount of meat held by the defendants for the plaintiffs at various times appear to be unreliable. The fairest course to both parties is to assume that the defendants, at Christmas 1974, held for the plaintiffs only the quantity of meat which the plaintiffs received back in summer of 1975. This quantity was as follows:

(a) 131 bags 665/GR gammons 10,254 lbs @ 52p per lb. Total £5,332.08
(b) 66 bags 330/GR middle 13,240 lbs @ 40p per lb. Total £5,296.00
(c) 23 bags 113 pork loins 2,760 lbs @ 50p per lb. Total £1,380.00
(d) 31 bags 155 pork fores 2,480 lbs @ 20p per lb. Total £496.00
(e) 103 bags 515 pork backs 8,240 lbs @ 50p per lb. Total £4,120.00

Total value of meats: £16,624.08

It has been proved conclusively that all the meat was defective and unfit for human consumption in August 1975. Some of it was sold as pet food for the sum of £400 and the balance was reduced to bone meal or otherwise disposed of in a manner which scarcely paid for the cost of reduction or disposal.

Under these circumstances it appears to me that the onus of proof rests on the defendants to establish that the meat, even if delivered to the plaintiffs at Christmas 1974 would have been unfit for human consumption. It appears to me that they have succeeded in this in relation to items (c) and (d) above, i.e. the pork loins and pork fores, as they have shown that the plaintiffs left these items for so long in cold storage that they would have deteriorated even by Christmas 1974.

In these circumstances I am satisfied that the plaintiffs' loss on this score is confined to items (a), (b) and (e) which collectively total the sum of £14,748.08. In addition I am satisfied that the plaintiffs, when they could not get their meat out of cold storage at Christmas in order to satisfy their customers, purchased and slaughtered an extra 400 pigs at a premium of £2.50 per pig making a total of £1,000.

The plaintiffs did not need all of these pig carcasses for the purposes of the Christmas trade and converted the balance of the carcasses into salted bacon and it is suggested that they sustained a further loss on this. I am not satisfied however, in relation to this loss and feel I should not allow it. Portion of the meat was sold as pet food for the sum of £400 and the defendants are entitled to a credit for this. No credit is due in respect of the bone meal.

The defendants have a counterclaim for storage charges in respect of the period after Christmas 1974. As these charges would not have arisen if the defendants had returned the plaintiffs' meat on demand I dismiss the counterclaim.

C. Incorporation Through a Course of Dealing

J. Spurling Ltd v Bradshaw [1956] 1 WLR 461

The owner of barrels of orange juice left them with the plaintiff under a contract of bailment. The goods were damaged or destroyed. The plaintiff brought an action for the contracted sums. The defendant refused to pay and counterclaimed for damages. On several previous occasions the defendant had left goods with the plaintiff and had been given receipts which contained exemption clauses. At trial of the action the counterclaim was held to be defeated by these clauses. The defendant appealed.

Denning L.J.:

This brings me to the question whether this clause was part of the contract. [Counsel for the defendant] urged us to hold that the warehousemen did not do what was reasonably sufficient to give notice of the conditions within *Parker v South Eastern Rly Co.*[1] I quite agree that the more unreasonable a clause is, the greater the notice which must be given of it. Some clauses which I have seen would need to be printed in red ink on the face of the document with a red hand pointing to it before the notice could be held to be sufficient. The clause in this case, however, in my judgment, does not call for such exceptional treatment, especially when it is construed, as it should be, subject to the proviso that it only applies when the warehouseman is carrying out his contract, and not when he is deviating from it or breaking it in a radical respect. So construed, the judge was, I think, entitled to find that sufficient notice was given. It is to be noticed that the landing account on its face told Mr Bradshaw that the goods would be insured if he gave instructions; otherwise they were not insured. The invoice, on its face, told him they were warehoused 'at owner's risk'. The printed conditions, when read subject to the proviso which I have mentioned, added little or nothing to those explicit statements taken together.

Next it was said that the landing account and invoice were issued after the goods had been received and could not, therefore, be part of the contract of bailment: but Mr Bradshaw admitted that he had received many landing accounts before. True he had not troubled to read them. On receiving this landing account, he took no objection to it, left the goods there, and went on paying the warehouse rent for months afterwards. It seems to me that by the course of business and conduct of the parties, these conditions were part of the contract.

In these circumstances, the warehousemen were entitled to rely on this exempting condition. I think, therefore, that the counterclaim was properly dismissed, and this appeal also should be dismissed.

[1.] (1877) 2 CPD 416, [1874–80] All ER Rep 166.

(Morris L.J. concurred.)

D. Interpretation Contra Proferens

American Law Institute Restatement Contracts (2d) S. 206

Interpretation Against the Draftsman

In choosing among the reasonable meanings of a promise or agreement or a term thereof, that meaning is generally preferred which operates against the party who supplies the words or from whom a writing otherwise proceeds.

Comment:

a. *Rationale*. Where one party chooses the terms of a contract, he is likely to provide more carefully for the protection of his own interests than for those of the other party. He is also more likely than the other party to have reason to know of uncertainties of meaning. Indeed, he may leave meaning deliberately obscure, intending to decide at a later date what meaning to assert. In cases of doubt, therefore, so long as other factors are not decisive, there is substantial reason for preferring the meaning of the other party. The rule is often invoked in cases of standardised contracts and in cases where the drafting party has the stronger bargaining position, but it is not limited to such cases. It is in strictness a rule of legal effect, sometimes called construction, as well as interpretation: its operation depends on the positions of the parties as they appear in litigation, and sometimes the result is hard to distinguish from a denial of effect to an unconscionable clause.

Andrews Bros (Bournemouth) Ltd *v* Singer and Co. Ltd [1934] 1 KB 17

Scrutton L.J.:

This is an appeal from a judgment of Goddard J. in an action by the plaintiffs, a company carrying on business at Bournemouth, who in the agreement between them and the defendants out of which the dispute has arisen are called agents for manufac-turers, which is quite a misleading term inasmuch as they are really purchasers of motor cars which they intend to sell. They brought their action against Singer & Co. alleging that the latter delivered a car which did not comply with the terms of the contract.

The facts which are fully set out in the careful judgment of Goddard J. may be shortly summarised: the description of the kind of car the plaintiffs wanted could have been satisfied by delivery to them of a new car; but the particular car which Singer & Co. tendered to them was in this position. Another agent, who thought he had in view a purchaser for the car, had it sent to Darlington and thence it was driven some distance further to show to the prospective customer, but as that person did not like it the agent returned it to Singer & Co., the result being that it had run a very considerable mileage with the consequence no doubt that certain changes had taken place in it. When the car was tendered to the plaintiffs' representative he noticed or suspected that it had run a considerable distance, but he took it, doing nothing, however, so far as I can see, to abandon any claim for damages on the ground that it was not a new car.

At the trial two points arose: First, the plaintiffs said that the car was not a new car as that term was understood in the trade. The defendants on the other hand said it was. Goddard J. came to the conclusion that it was not a new car, and in this court his decision on that point has not been questioned and I therefore proceed on the assumption that the defendants, who were bound to supply a new car, tendered a car which was not a new one. The defendants contended secondly that they are exempted from liability by reason of clause 5 of the agreement entered into. That clause reads as follows: 'All cars sold by the company are subject to the terms of the warranty set out in schedule no. 3 of this agreement and all conditions, warranties and liabilities implied by statute, common law or otherwise are excluded.' The defendants say that their obligation to supply a car complying with the description in the contract is a condition implied by statute, and as the plaintiffs accepted the car under the agreement containing clause 5 they cannot bring an action in respect of the supplying of a car which was not a new one. Clause 5 is, I take it, a sequel to *Wallis, Son & Wells v Pratt & Haynes*.[1] In that case the subject matter of the sale was 'common English sainfoin', and the contract contained this clause: 'Sellers give no warranty express or implied as to growth, description or any other matters.' What in fact was sold under the contract was not 'common English sainfoin' but something quite different, namely, 'giant sainfoin'. On discovering this the purchasers sued for damages, to which claim the sellers replied that they gave no warranty express or implied as to description. The Court of Appeal (Moulton L.J. dissenting) took the view that the clause excluded any liability even though the seed supplied was not of the description contracted to be supplied. The House of Lords adopted Moulton L.J.'s judgment and said that the goods tendered should comply with the description in the contract, which description was not a warranty but a condition, and as the clause relied on did not include 'condition' it did not operate to protect the sellers. Those advising the present defendants in preparing this agreement appear to have thought that by the inclusion of the word 'conditions' in the relevant clause liability would be excluded, although what was supplied did not comply with the description. The question therefore is whether the defendants have succeeded in excluding liability in this case—whether they can tender under the contract goods not complying with the description in the contract and say that the plaintiffs having accepted the car cannot now sue for breach of contract.

In my opinion this was a contract for the sale of a new Singer car. The contract continually uses the phrase 'new Singer cars'. At the end of the agreement I find this: 'In the event of the dealer having purchased from the company during the period of this agreement 250 new cars of current season's models'; and in the very beginning of the agreement I find this: 'The company hereby appoint the dealer their sole dealer for the sale of new Singer cars.' The same phrase also occurs in other parts of the agreement, and the subject matter is therefore expressly stated to be 'new Singer cars'. The judge has found, and his view is not now contested, that the car tendered in this case was not a new Singer car. Does then clause 5 prevent the vendors being liable in damages for having tendered and supplied a car which is not within the express terms of the contract? Clause 5 says this: 'All conditions, warranties and liabilities implied by statute, common law or otherwise are excluded.' There are well known obligations in various classes of contracts which are not expressly mentioned but are implied. During the argument Greer L.J. mentioned an apt illustration, namely, where an agent contracts on behalf of A he warrants that he has authority to make the contract on behalf of A although no such warranty is expressed in the contract. Mr Pritt relied on s. 13 of the Sale of Goods Act, 1893, which provides that 'where there is a contract for the sale of goods by description, there is an implied condition that the goods shall correspond with the description . . . ,' and from that he says it follows that this particular condition comes within the words employed by the section. That, I think, is putting a very strained meaning on the word 'implied' in the section. Where goods are expressly described in the contract and do not comply with that description, it is quite inaccurate to say that there is an implied term; the term is expressed in the contract. Suppose the contract is for the supply of a car of 1932 manufacture, and a car is supplied which is of 1930 manufacture, there has not been a breach of an implied term; there has been a breach of an express term of the contract. It leads to a very startling result if it can be said that clause 5 allows a vendor to supply to a purchaser an article which does not comply with the express description of the article in the contract, and then, though the purchaser did not know of the matter which prevented the article supplied from complying with the express terms of the contract, to say, 'We are under no liability to you because this is a condition implied by statute and we have excluded such liability.'

In my view there has been in this case a breach of an express term of the contract. If a vendor desires to protect himself from liability in such a case he must do so by much clearer language than this, which, in my opinion, does not exempt the defendants from liability where they have failed to comply with the express term of the contract. For these reasons I think Goddard J. came to a correct conclusion, and this appeal therefore fails.

[1.] [1910] 2 KB 1003; [1911] AC 394.

(Greer L.J. and Eve J. concurred.)

Note

1. L'Estrange v F. Graucob Ltd (p. 325 above) finally closes this drafting loophole. Re-read Llewellyn (above p. 297) in order to understand how limited these techniques of 'misreading' a clause can be.
2. The two following cases illustrate graphically the pressure on the courts to construe clauses narrowly. The Ailsa Craig case (p. 346 below) however cautions against fanciful results but that case was decided after statutory controls of abusive exemption clauses were in place.

Wicklow Corn Co. Ltd *v* Edward Fitzgerald Ltd [1942] Ir Jur Rep 48

Action for damages for alleged breach of contract.

The plaintiffs purchased from the defendants in October 1939 39 barrels 11 stone of 'English Recleaned Queen Wilhelmina Winter Seed Wheat' for £71 3s 10d. The plaintiffs re-sold portions of the consignment to various customers, including one, Edmund R. Jolley, who, on the failure of his crop, sued the present plaintiffs in the Circuit Court of Justice in Wicklow and recovered £199 18s 0d damages and £47 11s 7d costs. Similar claims by other customers caused the plaintiffs the loss of a further £16 11s 8d. The damages now claimed by the plaintiffs from the defendants were comprised of the amount of the decree and costs recovered by Jolley, the costs of defending Jolley's action, amounts paid to other customers, and a sum for loss of credit.

The defence was a categorical denial together with a plea that at the time of the sale and delivery by the defendants to the plaintiffs the wheat was reasonably fit for the purpose for which it was sold.

The evidence adduced by the plaintiffs showed that the learned Circuit Judge sitting at Wicklow had held in the action by Jolley that the plaintiffs' agent had given an express warranty of fitness to Jolley which negatived the purported exclusion, set out on the invoices used by the plaintiffs, of any implied warranty.

One of the plaintiffs' witnesses in the present action deposed to the defendants' agent having given, by telephone in October 1939, about the time of the purchase by the plaintiffs from the defendants, a warranty that the purity of the seed was 99 per cent and the germination 92 per cent, while a sample of the wheat taken from Jolley's land was of only 34 per cent germination under laboratory conditions. The defendants' evidence contradicted the warranty alleged to have been expressed per telephone and it was deposed that no such warranty could then have been given and that the figures 99 per cent and 92 per cent could not have been known to the defendants until after the Department of Agriculture furnished its report on 23 November 1939. Accordingly, those figures were not communicated to the plaintiffs until March 1940, when they complained to the defendants as to the poor results of the crop.

It was further deposed in defence that, on the arrival in Dublin from Liverpool of the consignment of wheat of which the plaintiffs' purchase formed part, samples were taken and sent to the Department of Agriculture for test. No warranty was given to the plaintiffs, but a written order was given by the defendants to the plaintiffs' carter to enable him to take from the ship a consignment of seed wheat therein described as 'Queen Wilhelmina'. The next day the defendants posted to the plaintiffs an invoice which was as follows:

> Commercial Buildings, Dublin. Bought of Edward FitzGerald, Ltd, Grain Merchants. Messrs Edward FitzGerald, Ltd, give no warranty, express or implied, as to description, quality, productiveness, or any other matter, beyond the analysis required in accordance with the Seeds Act, 1920, of any seeds they send out, and will not be in any way responsible for the crop. All consignments, on being sampled and tested for germination and purity, and found up to standard requirements, it will end our liability. If the purchaser does not accept the goods on these terms, they are to be returned at once. A condition of sale is that buyers shall sell seed wheat only under the name by which it is invoiced to them.

There was evidence that invoices similarly worded had frequently been sent by the defendants in respect of consignments purchased by the plaintiffs who were aware of the terms set out. |'Queen Wilhelmina' was not a 'trade name' but was the name by which a certain species of wheat was known.|

Davitt J.:

. . . referred to the absence from the plaintiffs' correspondence of any complaint based upon the breach of an express warranty and to the fact that the evidence given on behalf of the defendants as to the warranty alleged to have been expressed over the telephone appeared to his Lordship to be more credible than that to the contrary effect offered on behalf of the plaintiffs, and continued: The plaintiffs, accordingly, cannot rely upon any express warranty while any implied warranty as to fitness is excluded by the invoice sent by the defendants to the plaintiffs. Accordingly, |counsel for the plaintiffs| is forced to rely on the allegation that a different commodity had been supplied to that which the defendants purported to supply, as in the cases he cited. There is, however, no case to show that the principle underlying those decisions can be applied where the defect complained of is one of quality only, as distinct from the supplying of a different substance. The plaintiffs are, therefore, not entitled to succeed on any of the grounds put forward, and the civil bill must be dismissed with costs.

O'Connor v McCowen and Sons Ltd (1943) 77 ILTR 64

Overend J.:

. . . The plaintiff was a farmer, and was ill at the time of the transaction. He sent his son John to Tralee to buy the seed. The son went into the shop and saw Mr Scanlan, who was in charge of the seed department. He told Mr Scanlan of his requirements, and a discussion arose as to the amount of seed that would be sufficient. There was no doubt that the nature of the purchase was clear. The amount having been arrived at, Mr Scanlan told the assistant to fill out 14 lbs. Blue Top turnip seed, and Mr Scanlan made the entry on the blue paper. This transaction was sale by description. The purchaser had no opportunity of examining the seed and if he had it would be no use for him. When he had filled up the blue docket, and before O'Connor had signed it, Mr Scanlan told John O'Connor that they had not get their seeds from their usual suppliers and could not guarantee them. These words were not sufficient to warn the buyer that the seeds might not be turnip seeds at all, and contained nothing to indicate that they would not produce turnips. If purchasers were to be precluded, when they purchased articles by description and got different goods, then the very clearest words must be used by the seller, such as: 'You may be purchasing seeds that are not turnip seeds at all.'

Mr Scanlan then asked O'Connor to sign the conditions of sale—the usual conditions which Messrs McCowen had on their dockets for a considerable time. At the time of the sale it had not entered into Mr Scanlan's head that what he was selling was not turnip seed at all. The buyer, however, got something that was not turnip seed, and, quite apart from the Sale of Goods Act, he had a cause of action. |Counsel for the defendant| had put forward the proposition that in the conditions of sale all the risk was covered. But it was not. The conditions said that they selected their seeds with the greatest care. These conditions were not applicable to the case where Messrs McCowen had not selected their goods with the greatest care, which in this case they had not, as they took what they could get.

Under the circumstances (said his Lordship) he had to decide that the defendants were liable. It was a serious case for both the plaintiff and the defendants. One of two innocent parties would suffer, but since the plaintiff did not get what he bought, the defendants, though not morally liable, were legally so, and accordingly he must affirm the decree of the Circuit Court.

Ailsa Craig Fishing Ltd *v* Malvern Fishing Ltd [1983] 1 WLR 964

Lord Fraser of Tullybelton:

My Lords, the only surviving issue in these appeals is whether the respondents ('Securicor') have succeeded in limiting their liability under a contract between themselves and the Aberdeen Fishing Vessel Owners' Association Ltd ('the association') who were acting on behalf a number of owners of fishing vessels, including the appellants. Nothing turns upon the fact that the appellants were not themselves a party to the contract and I shall proceed as if the contract had been made with them.

The appellants were the owners of the fishing vessel *Strathallan* which sank while berthed in Aberdeen Harbour on 31 December 1971, at a time when Securicor were bound, under the contract with the association, to provide security cover in the harbour. Her gallows fouled the vessel moored next to her on the starboard side, called the *George Craig*, which also sank. Both vessels became total losses. Two actions were then raised. In one the appellants claimed damages from the owners of the *George Craig* as first defenders and from Securicor as second defenders. In the other the owners of the *George Craig* claimed damages from the appellants, who brought in Securicor as a third party. The Lord Ordinary (Lord Wylie) held that the loss of both vessels had been caused by breach of contract and negligence on the part of Securicor. He found them liable to the appellants in damages for the loss of the *Strathallan*, and found them liable to relieve the appellants of their full liability to the owners of the *George Craig* for the loss of that vessel. He assessed the damages in each case at a little over £55,000. The Lord Ordinary rejected arguments on behalf of Securicor to the effect that their liability was either wholly excluded, or limited in amount, by the terms of their contract. Securicor reclaimed against the Lord Ordinary's judgment but they did not contest his findings of breach of contract and negligence. Their contention on the reclaiming motion was solely that their liability had been either excluded or limited by the terms of the contract. The First Division of the Court of Session (the Lord President, Lord Cameron and Lord Dunpark) allowed the reclaiming motion in part, holding that liability had been limited in amount but that it had not been excluded. The appellants now appeal to your Lordships' House against that decision in so far as it held that liability had been limited.

In order to appreciate the contentions of the parties, it is necessary to refer briefly to the circumstances in which the contract came to be made. Until 31 December 1971, Securicor had for some months been providing a security service for vessels of owners represented by the association. They did so under a contract dated 12 May 1971, under which the service was limited to vessels berthed at the Albert Quay in Aberdeen Harbour, and operated only during the nights and at weekends. The main object was to prevent intruders from boarding unmanned vessels and damaging them or stealing from them. Early on 31 December an official of the association realised that the service would not be adequate for the New Year period, partly because there were many more vessels than usual in the harbour and partly because they would be remaining there for several days. Owing to the unusual number of vessels they could not all be berthed at Albert Quay, where the security patrols were already provided during certain hours, and some of them would have to be berthed at the Fish Market/Commercial Quay ('the Fish Market area'). The quay in the Fish Market area was of open structure, and there was a special risk that vessels might slide under the deck of the quay and become caught or 'snubbed' by the bow. The risk arose especially on a rising tide. That was just what happened to the appellants' vessel the *Strathallan*, during the evening of 31 December 1971, and caused her to sink taking the *George Craig* with her. As Securicor accept the Lord Ordinary's findings of fault against them, it is unnecessary to refer in greater detail to the events of that evening. Securicor also accept the decision of the First Division that the liability was not wholly excluded by the contract.

The question whether Securicor's liability has been limited falls to be answered by construing the terms of the contract in accordance with the ordinary principles applicable to contracts of this kind. The argument for limitation depends upon certain special conditions attached to the contract prepared on behalf of Securicor and put forward in their interest. There is no doubt that such conditions must be construed strictly against the *proferens*, in this case Securicor, and that in order to be effective they must be 'most clearly and unambiguously expressed': see W & S *Pollock & Co. v Macrae*, 1922 SC (HL) 192, 199 per Lord Dunedin. *Pollock* was a decision on an exclusion clause but insofar as it emphasised the need for clarity in clauses to be construed *contra proferentem* it is in my opinion relevant to the present case also. It has sometimes apparently been regarded as laying down, as a proposition of law, that a clause excluding liability can never have any application where there has been a total breach of contract, but I respectfully agree with the Lord President who said in his opinion in the present case that that was a misunderstanding of *Pollock*. *Pollock* was followed by the Second Division in *Mechans Ltd v Highland Marine Charters Ltd*, 1964 SC 48 and there are passages in the judgments in that case which might seem to treat *Pollock* as having laid down some such general proposition of law, although it is not clear that they were so intended. If they were I would regard them as being erroneous. *Mechans* appears to have been relied upon by counsel for the appellants before the Second Division, but was not relied on in this house.

There are later authorities which lay down very strict principles to be applied when considering the effect of clauses of exclusion or of indemnity: see particularly the Privy Council case of *Canada Steamship Lines Ltd. v The King* |1952| AC 192, 208, where Lord Morton of Henryton, delivering the advice of the board, summarised the principles in terms which have recently been applied by this house in *Smith v U.M.B. Chrysler (Scotland) Ltd*, 1978 SC (HL) 1. In my opinion these principles are not applicable in their full rigour when considering the effect of clauses merely limiting liability. Such clauses will of course be read *contra proferentem* and must be clearly expressed, but there is no reason why they should be judged by the specially exacting standards which are applied to exclusion and indemnity clauses. The reason for imposing such standards on these clauses is the inherent improbability that the other party to a contract including such a clause intended to release the *proferens* from a liability that would otherwise fall upon him. But there is no such high degree of improbability that he would agree to a limitation of the liability of the *proferens*, especially when, as explained in condition 4 (i) of the present contract, the potential losses that might be caused by the negligence of the *proferens* or its servants are so great in proportion to the sums that can reasonably be charged for the services contracted for. It is enough in the present case that the clause must be clear and unambiguous.

The contract was arranged during the morning of 31 December 1971, in some haste. It is set out on a form partly printed and partly filled in in ink, which is headed 'Temporary Contract or Contract Change Request' and in which the association 'request Securicor Ltd to carry out the services detailed below subject to the special conditions printed overleaf.' The form requested 'continuous security cover for your |sic| vessels from 1900 hours on 31 December 1971 until 07.00 hours on 5 January 1972' and stated that the area covered was to be extended to include the Fish Market area. Nothing turns upon that part of the contract but I should mention that the appellants contended that this temporary contract, so long as it was in operation, entirely superseded the contract of 12 May 1971, and was the sole measure of parties' rights and obligations to one another. Having regard to condition 8 of the special conditions, I see no reason to question that contention.

The 'special conditions of contract' were elaborate and are applied to services of several types. So far as this appeal is concerned, the part which is most directly applicable is condition 2, and especially clause (*f*) of that condition. Condition 2 (*f*) is in the following terms: |His Lordship read clause (*f*) and continued:| On behalf of the appellants it was argued that that clause, even if apparently clear in its own terms, is not applicable when read in the context of the contract as a whole, where there has been a total failure to perform the services contracted for or what is sometimes called a total failure of contract, and that this was such a case. It was said that clause 2 (*f*) must be qualified by the opening words of condition 2 and of clause (*a*) of that condition which show that liability can only arise for some fault in the course of providing the services contracted for, and not where there has been a total failure to provide the service. I cannot accept that submission, because clause 2 (*f*) expressly states that it applies to liability arising out of 'the provision of, or purported provision of, or failure in provision of' the services contracted for. If this submission had not been so persuasively presented, I would have thought it to be unarguable in face of the provisions of clause (*f*).

The learned judge of the First Division found that this was a case of total failure or total breach of contract, in the sense of Lord Dunedin's speech in *Pollock*, 1922 SC (HL) 192. As that is the finding most favourable to the appellants on this part of the case it is not now material to consider whether this is strictly a case of total failure. If the question had been material at this stage I would have wished to give it further consideration, because there is no suggestion that the security cover was not duly maintained during the evening of 31 December 1971, in the Albert Dock area, which was part of the area covered by the temporary contract, and I think there is much to be said for the view that the contract was performed in part. But it is not necessary to come to a decision on that point.

A further argument for the appellants was that clause (*f*) of condition 2 applied only to liability which arose 'pursuant to' the provisions of the contract, and that pursuant to meant 'in accordance with the express provisions of the contract.' This meaning was said to be emphasised by the first sentence of clause 4 (iii). But that argument fails, in my opinion, if for no other reason than that clause (*f*) itself proclaims unambiguously that it applies to liability which shall arise under the 'express or implied' terms of the contract. Next, the appellants argued that there is an inconsistency between clause (*a*) of condition 2 which purports to exclude liability altogether and clause (*f*) which purports to limit the amount of liability in certain cases. The existence of that inconsistency was one of the reasons for the First Division's decision that the exclusion clause was lacking in clarity, and counsel sought to apply the same argument in reverse to the limitation clause. But the argument is in my opinion unsound. It is one thing to say, as the First Division did, that when you find a provision for limiting liability coming after a provision which is capable of being read as excluding liability altogether, the limitation provision casts doubt on the meaning of the earlier one. But it is quite a different thing to say that the inconsistency casts doubt on the meaning of the limitation clause. If the exclusion clause had succeeded in its purpose, the limitation might have been unnecessary, but its meaning as a sort of long stop is in my opinion clear and is not affected by the existence of the exclusion clause.

A separate argument was advanced to the effect that clause (*f*) was confused and uncertain in itself because the provisions of sub-paras (i) (*a*) and (*b*) did not make it clear whether the limit of liability in any particular case was £1,000 or £10,000. Perhaps the intention of subparas (*a*) and (*b*) may not be immediately clear on first reading to a person unfamiliar with provisions of this sort, but a very little consideration is enough to show, in my opinion, that the meaning is that explained by the learned judges of the First Division. Sub-para. (*a*) relates to any *claim* arising in any of the ways there mentioned and it limits the liability of Securicor to £1,000 for each claim. Sub-para. (*b*) relates to any one *incident* and limits their liability to £10,000 in respect of each incident. The two provisions overlap but they are in no way inconsistent. For example, in the present case the owner of each of the vessels has a separate claim which, if the clause is applicable, will be limited to £1,000. But both claims arise out of one incident, and if there had been more than ten claims for £1,000 each arising out of the same incident, the total liability of Securicor would have been limited to £10,000. That meaning is in my view clear and unambiguous and I reject this argument.

Having considered these particular criticisms of clause (*f*) the question remains whether in its context it is sufficiently clear and unambiguous to receive effect in limiting the liability of Securicor for its own negligence or that of its employees. in my opinion it is. It applies to any liability 'whether under the express or implied terms of this contract, or at common law, or in any other way.' Liability at common law is undoubtedly wide enough to cover liability including the negligence of the *proferens* itself, so that even without relying on the final words 'any other way', I am clearly of opinion that the negligence of Securicor is covered.

For these reasons I would refuse the appeal. The respondents must have their costs in this house.

SECTION THREE—CONSTRUCTION

A. THE MAIN PURPOSE RULE OF CONSTRUCTION

Glynn *v* Margetson & Co. [1893] AC 351

Oranges were shipped on board a vessel from Malaga to Liverpool. The bill of loading contained a 'liberty to deviate' clause which gave the master the power to proceed to Liverpool via any ports in the Mediterranean, Levant, Black Sea, Coasts of Africa, etc. The vessel left Malaga, proceeded east to another Spanish port, and then rejoined the usual route to Liverpool. The oranges were damaged when they reached Liverpool.

Lord Herschell L.C.:

. . .

My Lords, the main object and intent, as I have said, of this charterparty is the carriage of oranges from Malaga to Liverpool. That is the matter with which the shipper is concerned; and it seems to me that it would be to defeat what is the manifest object and intention of such a contract to hold that it was entered into with a power to the shipowner to proceed anywhere that he pleased, to trade in any manner that he pleased, and to arrive at the port at which the oranges were to be delivered when he pleased.

Then is there any rule of law which compels the construction contended for? I think there is not. Where general words are used in a printed form which are obviously intended to apply, so far as they are applicable, to the circumstances of a particular contract, which particular contract is to be embodied in or introduced into that printed form, I think you are justified in looking at the main object and intent of the contract and in limiting the general words used, having in view that object and intent. Therefore, it seems to me that the construction contended for would be an unreasonable one, and there is no difficulty in construing this clause to apply to a liberty in the performance of the stipulated voyage to call at a particular port or ports in the course of the voyage. That port or those ports would differ according to what the stipulated voyage was, inasmuch as at the time when this document was framed the parties who framed it did not know what the particular voyage would be, and intended it to be equally used whatever that voyage is. The ports a visit to which would be justified under this contract would, no doubt, differ according to the particular voyage stipulated for between the shipper and the shipowner; but it must, in my view, be a liberty consistent with the main object of the contract—a liberty only to proceed to and stay at the ports which are in the course of the voyage.

Lord Halsbury L.C.:

My Lords, I am entirely of the same opinion. It seems to me that in construing this document, which is a contract of carriage between the parties, one must in the first instance look at the whole of the instrument and not at one part of it only. Looking at the whole of the instrument, and seeing what one must regard, for a reason which I will give in a moment, as its main purpose, one must reject words, indeed whole provisions, if they are inconsistent with what one assumes to be the main purpose of the contract. The main purpose of the contract was to take on board at one port and to deliver at another port a perishable cargo. I do not think the learned counsel who argued this case on the part of the appellants gave sufficient effect in the argument which he addressed to your Lordships to the difference between the ordinary and formal parts of the document which are to be found in print and the written parts— indeed I gathered from him at one time that he rather contested the legitimacy of considering the difference whether the words were in print or in writing; he appeared to intimate that that doubt was justified by the terms of this particular document, because that, in the ordinary construction of a commercial document, such a principle as I have mentioned has been adopted certainly for something like a century cannot be a matter of doubt, and the reason for it appears to me to be very cogent and relevant to the case before your Lordships.

B. CONSTRUCTION OF A CONTRACT

Is liability in negligence covered?

Regan v RIAC [1990] 1 IR 278

Lynch J.:

This action arises out of an unfortunate accident which happened about 4 p.m. on Saturday 14 September 1985, in the course of a motor race being lawfully held in the Phoenix Park, Dublin. The plaintiff was officiating at the race as a flag marshal and was injured when a competing motor racing car went out of control, left the track and knocked down the plaintiff causing serious injuries to her.

The plaintiff has sued the defendants as the organisers and controllers of the race and the race-track alleging negligence against them particularly in regard to an alleged lack of protection for the flag marshals including the plaintiff at the flag marshals' post to which the plaintiff had been assigned. The plaintiff delivered her statement of claim on 30 October 1987. The defendants delivered their defence on 25 November 1988, in which they denied negligence and in general denied also the various allegations of the plaintiff in the statement of claim and furthermore in para. 9 the defendants pleaded as follows:

> And further, without prejudice to each and every matter pleaded in this defence, the defendants will say that by a contract made in writing in the year 1985 the plaintiff agreed to act in an official capacity at a Phoenix Park race-meeting to be held on 14 and 15 September 1985, and in consideration of the organising club having effected for her benefit a personal accident policy for death or benefits prescribed more specifically by RIAC requirements she agreed to absolve all persons having any connection with the promotion and/or organisation and/or conduct of the meeting including the RIAC (being the first defendant) the promoting clubs the owner of the lands entrance |sic| and drivers and owners of vehicles from liability arising out of accidents howsoever caused resulting in damage and/or personal injury to her person or property. Pursuant to the said contract, the defendants did effect for the plaintiff's benefit the said personal accident policy. In the premises, the defendant is not liable to the plaintiff for any personal injury loss or damage (which are further denied) howsoever occurring to her. Further, or in the alternative, these defendants will say that the plaintiff before the matters complained of agreed to waive her legal rights in respect thereof and the defendants have no liability to the plaintiff. And further the defendants will say that these defendants and each of them are entitled to the benefit and protection of the aforementioned agreement.

By order of this court made on 27 February 1989, it was ordered: 'That without further pleadings a preliminary issue be tried before a judge without a jury wherein the first-second- third- and fourth-named defendants shall be plaintiffs and the plaintiff defendant the question at the trial of such issue to be that raised in para. 9 of the first-second- and third-named defendants' defence herein.'

Notwithstanding the terms of the foregoing order I refer in this judgment to the plaintiff as plaintiff and to the defendants as defendants.

The plaintiff delivered her reply in the substantive action on 20 October 1989, and by para. 5, including an amendment which I allowed to be made when the matter came for trial before me on 25 October 1989, the plaintiff pleaded as follows:

> 5. By way of special reply to para. 9 of the defence herein the plaintiff denies that she entered into the alleged or any contract in writing or otherwise or agreed to waive her alleged or any rights. If the plaintiff entered into the alleged or any agreement (which is denied) the defendants negligently and in breach of contract performed their duties under the said agreement and were in fundamental breach of the same and accordingly should not be entitled to rely upon the terms of the same so as to defeat the plaintiff's claim herein.

The issue raised in para. 9 of the defendants' defence came before me for trial on 25 October 1989, and I heard evidence and submissions on that date and on 26 October 1989, relating to the said preliminary issue and also the matters relating to para. 9 of the defence as raised by para. 5 of the reply.

The evidence established to my satisfaction that the plaintiff and other officials camped in the Phoenix Park on the night of 13/14 September 1985, and reported for duty to an administration caravan between 6 a.m. and 7 a.m. on the morning of Saturday

14 September 1985. There the plaintiff and the other intending officials signed a form proffered to them by the clerical officer in charge of the administration caravan. The form contained the following passage:

> I agree to act in an official capacity at this meeting and in consideration of the organising club(s) having effected for my benefit a personal accident policy for death or benefits as prescribed more specifically by RIAC requirements, I agree to absolve all persons having any connection with the promotion and/or organisation and/or conduct of the meeting including the |RIAC| the promoting club(s) the owner of the land, entrants and drivers and owners of vehicles from liability arising out of accidents howsoever caused, resulting in damage and/or personal injury to my person and/or property.

The evidence further established that an insurance policy such as is referred to in the form had been obtained and was in existence at the time when the plaintiff signed the form although the precise amounts payable thereunder were not clearly established. This imprecision does not seem to me to be material however. The plaintiff did not know the details of the insurance policy taken out by the defendants for the benefit of officials at races but she did know that some such provision had been made and she also knew what was in the document she signed to the extent at least that it contained an exemption clause which purported to restrict her rights to compensation in the event of an accident causing injury to her.

It should be noted that at the date of the order of 27 February 1989, no reply had yet been delivered to the defence delivered on 25 November 1988. That being so a simple joinder of issue on the defence was then implied by O. 23, r. 1 of the Rules of the Superior Courts. It follows that the matter sent for trial by way of preliminary issue by the order of 27 February 1989, was the matter pleaded in para. 9 of the defence with an implied denial thereof but without the further matters specially raised by way of positive averment in the second part of para. 5 of the reply as amended before me and as quoted by me above. It is therefore appropriate that I should deal first with the matters raised in para. 9 of the defence before dealing, if at all, with the matters raised in para. 5 of the reply.

Para. 9 of the defence as impliedly denied raises the question of the construction of the terms of the form signed by the plaintiff before officiating at the motor race meeting and the really relevant portion of that form that falls for construction is the second half of the paragraph already quoted that is to say: 'I agree to absolve all persons having any connection with the promotion and/or organisation and/or conduct of the meeting including the |RIAC| the promoting club(s) the owner of the land entrants and drivers and owners of vehicles from liability arising out of accidents howsoever caused, resulting in damage and/or personal injury to my person and/or property.' Counsel for the defendants (the moving party in the issue) conceded that the form did not expressly refer to negligence but submitted that it necessarily extended to and included negligence. He cited the following authorities: *O'Hanlon v Electricity Supply Board* |1969| IR 75; *Chitty on Contract* (24th ed.) para. 818; and *Smith v South Wales Swithchgear* |1978| 1 WLR 165.

Counsel for the plaintiff submitted that in the absence of an express reference to negligence and in the light of the rule of law that the contract should be construed strictly against the person who drafted and proffered it, the document should be construed as referring only to accidents without negligence. He submitted that such accidents could readily happen at such an event as a motor race and he cited the following authorities: *Charlesworth on Negligence; Wilks v Cheltenham Cycle Club* |1971| 1 WLR 668; and *Clayton Love & Sons (Dublin) Ltd v British & Irish Steam Packet Co. Ltd* (1966) 104 ILTR 157.

I am satisfied that it is not fanciful or unreal to envisage accidents happening without negligence on the part of anyone at an event such as that at which the plaintiff was officiating. Therefore while accidents usually occur due to some carelessness or other on the part of someone and a reference to 'accidents' would usually imply and include negligent accidents the mere reference to accidents in this case would not necessarily imply negligent accidents. However I have to give effect to the words used and the word 'accidents' is not left unqualified. It is qualified by the words 'howsoever caused' and these words are obviously wide enough to embrace negligent accidents for which someone is responsible in law as well as pure accidents for which no one is responsible in law. In addition the use of the word 'liability' presupposes some form of wrong. A pure accident for which no one is responsible would create no liability in anyone and therefore the reference to liability necessarily brings within the ambit of the clause accidents resulting from the wrongful or negligent conduct of others.

It follows that my decision on the preliminary issue actually referred to me by the order of 27 February 1989, is that the plaintiff agreed for valuable consideration to absolve the defendants from liability in respect of the accident which in fact happened to her and further that the plaintiff before the accident complained of agreed to waive her legal rights as against the defendants in respect of it. Accordingly I rule that, subject to the issue as to whether there was a fundamental breach of contract by the defendants and is so the effect thereof, the plaintiff is barred from maintaining these proceedings against the defendants.

I now have to consider whether to deal at all with the matters raised by para. 5 of the reply and in particular the second part of that paragraph which, as amended before me, pleads as I have already quoted: 'If the plaintiff entered into the alleged or any agreement (which is denied) the defendants negligently and in breach of contract performed their duties under the said agreement and were in fundamental breach of the same and accordingly should not be entitled to rely upon the terms of the same so as to defeat the plaintiff's claim herein.' This issue was not referred for preliminary trial by the order of 27 February 1989. Nevertheless the plaintiff dealt extensively with the issues raised by this paragraph both in evidence and in submission before me. The defendants however adduced evidence related only to the issue actually referred for preliminary trial, their evidence being confined to proving that the defendants had provided a policy of insurance such as that referred to in the form and to proving that the plaintiff signed the form and was aware of its contents. That being so I could not possibly decide the issues raised by para. 5 of the reply against the defendants without giving them an opportunity of adducing rebutting evidence. Having heard the matter over two days however during which the greater time was taken up by the evidence and submissions on the issues raised by para. 5 of the reply I feel that I should express my views in a preliminary way because I believe that by doing so I may save the parties further litigation and expense.

The facts proved before me relevant to these issues are as follows. The plaintiff was assigned by the clerical officer in charge of the administration caravan to be a flag marshal at the end of the fastest straight on the race-track being a stretch of the main road in the Phoenix Park where the race-track makes a hairpin turn to the right onto the road leading to the Knockmaroon gate. When the plaintiff and the other flag marshals got to this post some ten minutes or so after being assigned thereto they found that the post was on the inside of the bend and did not have any solid protection particularly in the form of a skip filled with two or three tons of sand which they expected would be at the post. The plaintiff had been officiating as a flag marshal at motor races for about one and a half years before the 14 September 1985. She had however always done so at Mondello Park, County Kildare, where there was always solid protection for the marshals except on one previous occasion in 1984 when she had officiated as a flag marshal at that year's motor races in the Phoenix Park. On that occasion she was assigned to a post in the Furry Glen where there was a skip with two to three tons of sand as a form of solid protection for the marshals.

The plaintiff alleges that being posted on the inside of the bend was more dangerous than on the outside and therefore called for solid protection for the flag marshals even more than when the post was on the outside of the same bend as it was in 1984 on which occasion there was a skip at that post. The plaintiff alleges and submits that the absence of any solid protection at the post in 1985 was negligence of such a character as to constitute so fundamental a breach of agreement on the part of the defendants as to disentitle them from relying on the exemption clause in the form signed by the plaintiff.

If for the purposes of the issues raised by para. 5 of the reply I were to assume that all the allegations made by the plaintiff before me were established nevertheless my view would be that those allegations do not amount to such a fundamental breach of agreement on the part of the defendants in this case as to disentitle them from relying on the exemption clause in the form signed by the plaintiff. Moreover I am not to be taken as either accepting or rejecting the proposition that a fundamental breach of contract will necessarily have the results submitted on behalf of the plaintiff having regard to cases decided since the decision in *Clayton Love & Sons (Dublin) Ltd v British & Irish Steam Packet Co. Ltd* (1966) 104 ILTR 157.

C. THE DEVELOPMENT OF THE FUNDAMENTAL BREACH DOCTRINE

Note

There are isolated instances where the courts have developed exceptions to the general view that the application of an exemption clause depends entirely on its construction or interpretation. Most notable are the deviation cases which hold that if a contracting party seeks to rely on an exemption clause, or another defence to liability such as an act of God, it must be shown that the party invoking the defence was performing the contract in its essential respects. These cases originated in common carrier cases and eventually found their way into ordinary contracts of bailment.

Lilley v Doubleday (1881) 7 QBD 510

The facts

The action was to recover the value of certain drapery goods warehoused by the defendant for the plaintiff, which were destroyed by fire. The contract was that the goods should be deposited at the defendant's repository at Kingsland Road, but a portion of them were deposited by the defendant elsewhere, and a fire occurring they were destroyed. The plaintiff had insured the goods, giving Kingsland Road as the place where they were deposited, and in consequence lost the benefit of the insurance.

Grove J.:

I think the plaintiff is entitled to judgment. It seems to me impossible to get over this point, that by the finding of the jury there has been a breach of contract. The defendant was entrusted with the goods for a particular purpose and to keep them in a particular place. He took them to another, and must be responsible for what took place there. The only exception I see to this general rule is where the destruction of the goods must take place as inevitably at one place as at the other. If a bailee elects to deal with the property entrusted to him in a way not authorised by the bailor, he takes upon himself the risks of so doing, except where the risk is independent of his acts and inherent in the property itself. That proposition is fully supported by the case of *Davis v Garrett*,[1] which contains very little that is not applicable to this case. It was argued that that case was decided on the ground that the defendant was a common carrier, but that is not the ground of the judgment of Tindal C.J., who decided that as the loss had happened while the wrongful act of the defendant was in operation and was attributable to his wrongful act, he could not set up as an answer to the action the bare possibility of the loss if his wrongful act had never been done, and he illustrated the case by saying that a defendant who had by mistake forwarded a parcel by the wrong conveyance, if a loss had thereby ensued, would undoubtedly be liable. I do not give any opinion whether what was done here amounted to a conversion, but I base my judgment on the fact that the defendant broke his contract, by dealing with the subject matter in a manner different from that in which he contracted to deal with it.

. . .

Lindley J.:

I am of the same opinion. The plaintiff gave his goods to the defendant to be ware-housed at a particular place, the defendant warehoused them elsewhere, where, without any particular negligence on his part, they were destroyed. The consequence is that the plaintiff has a cause of action and is entitled to damages. . . .

[1] 6 Bing. 716.

(Stephen J. concurred.)

Note

These carrier cases, as extended into bailment contracts, then formed the basis of a general rule of law which found its way into sales law, the law relating to hire purchase and contracts for the provision of services. The clearest statement of principle is found in **Karsales Harrow Ltd v Wallis [1956] 1 WLR 936** per Denning L.J. In this case the defendant took a used Buick car on hire purchase, the contract containing a clause that 'no condition or warranty that the vehicle is roadworthy, or as to its age, condition or fitness for any purpose is given by the owner or implied herein.' On delivery the car was in a deplorable state and the defendant refused to make any payments under the contract.

Denning L.J.:

[Counsel] on behalf of the defendant, says that he agreed to take on hire-purchase terms a Buick motor car which he had seen a week or two before he had signed these documents. He says that it was the duty of the finance company to see that there was delivered to the defendant a motor car which corresponded to the car he had seen. He says that, owing to its condition on delivery, there was a fundamental breach by the finance company and that they cannot recover the instalments. In answer, [counsel for the plaintiff] says that there was delivered to the defendant a Buick motor car of the registration number specified in the agreement, and that they are in no way responsible for its condition on delivery. They rely on clause 3 (g) of the hire-purchase agreement: 'No condition or warranty that the vehicle is roadworthy, or as to its age, condition or fitness for any purpose is given by the owner or implied herein.' The judge held that that clause in this document meant that the hire-purchase company were not responsible in any way for the condition of this car when it was delivered, and that although it was in this deplorable condition, they could still recover the instalments due under the agreement; and that, even though the car was rejected by the defendant, they could still recover them.

In my opinion, under a hire-purchase agreement of this kind, when the hirer has himself previously seen and examined the motor car and made application for hire-purchase on the basis of his inspection of it, there is an obligation on the lender to deliver the car in substantially the same condition as when it was seen. It makes no difference that the lender is a finance company which has bought the car in the interval without seeing it. The lender must know, from the ordinary course of business, that the hirer applies on the faith of his inspection and on the understanding that the car will be delivered in substantially the same condition: and it is an implied term of the agreement that pending delivery the car will be kept in suitable order and repair for the purposes of the bailment. This is supported by *Story on Bailment*, articles 383 to 385, and *Robertson v Amazon Tug and Lighterage Co.*[1]

The plaintiffs say that there can be no such implication in this case in view of the express terms of clause 3 (g): but the law about exempting clauses has been much developed in recent years, at any rate about printed exempting clauses, which so often pass unread. Notwithstanding earlier cases which might suggest the contrary, it is now settled that exempting clauses of this kind, no matter how widely they are expressed, only avail the party when he is carrying out his contract in its essential respects. He is not allowed to use them as a cover for misconduct or indifference or to enable him to turn a blind eye to his obligations. They do not avail him when he is guilty of a breach which goes to the root of the contract. The thing to do is to look at the contract apart from the exempting clauses and see what are the terms, express or implied, which impose an obligation on the party. If he has been guilty of a breach of those obligations in a respect which goes to the very root of the contract, he cannot rely on the exempting clauses. I would refer in this regard to what was said by Roche J. in the 'copra cake' case (*Pinnock Brothers v Lewis & Peat Ltd*[2]) and the judgments of Devlin J. in *Alexander v Rly Executive*[3] and *Smeaton Hanscomb & Co. Ltd v Sassoon I. Setty, Son & Co.* (No. 1),[4] and the recent case in this court of *J. Spurling Ltd v Bradshaw*,[5] and the cases there mentioned. The principle is sometimes said to be that the party cannot rely on an exempting clause when he delivers something 'different in kind' from that contracted for, or has broken a 'fundamental term' or a 'fundamental contractual obligation', but these are, I think, all comprehended by the general principle that a breach which goes to the root of the contract disentitles the party from relying on the exempting clause. In the present case the lender was in breach of the implied obligation that I have mentioned. When the defendant inspected the car before signing the application form, the car was in excellent condition and would go: whereas the car which was subsequently delivered to him was no doubt the same car, but it was in a deplorable state and would not go. That breach went, I think, to the root of the contract and disentitles the lender from relying on the exempting clause.

The only real difficulty that I have felt in the case is whether this point is put with sufficient clarity in the pleadings. It is not put as clearly as one could wish. Nevertheless, I have always understood in modern times that it is sufficient for a pleader to plead the material facts. He need not plead the legal consequences which flow from them.

Even although he has stated the legal consequences inaccurately or incompletely, that does not shut him out from arguing points of law which arise on the facts pleaded. Looking at this defence, it is quite plain that the defence pleaded all the material facts which I have mentioned and it is, I think, sufficient.

1. (1881) 7 QBD 598.
2. [1923] 1 KB 690, 695, 39.
3. [1951] 2 KB 882.
4. [1953] 1 WLR 1468; [1953] 2 All ER 1471.
5. [1956] 1 WLR 461; [1956] 2 All ER 121.

(Birkett and Parker L.JJ. concurred.)

Clayton Love v B & I Transport (1966) 104 ILTR 157
(Facts on p. 266.)

Clark R., (op. cit) pp 149– 50 explains the case thus:

. . . The parties contracted to transport deep frozen scampi from Dublin to Liverpool. The loading was conducted at atmospheric temperature and this led to the scampi deteriorating to the extent that it was condemned when it arrived in Liverpool. The plaintiffs sued but were met by two exemption clauses, one of which was drafted widely enough to protect the defendants from liability. The second clause obliged the plaintiffs to claim within three days, otherwise the claim would be absolutely barred. Davitt P. at first instance relied on the substantive rule of law and dicta in two English cases, *Spurling Ltd v Bradshaw*[1] and *Smeaton Hanscomb & Co. Ltd v Sassoon I. Setty*[2] and refused to apply the first limiting clause. It is symptomatic of the confusion and complexity of this doctrine that Davitt P. then shifted ground and applied the second clause by holding that 'it was intended to, and does in fact cover the case of a clause arising from the breach of a fundamental term of the contract.' This reasoning seems to be unsatisfactory because Davitt P. applied a rule of law to the first clause and a rule of interpretation to the other limiting clause. The Supreme Court eliminated this inconsistency by holding that the rule of law must apply to the second limiting clause, regardless of the intention of the *proferens*. A better approach to the problem in *Clayton Love* would have been to ask if the contract had been freely negotiated; did the shipper have a choice of terms upon which he could ship his goods (as in *Slattery v CIE*). Most importantly, did the shipper know and consent to loading of such delicate frozen goods at atmospheric temperatures and did he know of the existence of this sweeping clause? It is probable that the Supreme Court would have still found in favour of the plaintiffs but they would have addressed the issues of freedom of contract and consent, factors that were not always considered by pro-fundamental breach judges.

1. [1956] 1 WLR 461.
2. [1953] 1 WLR 1468.

Note

While the Supreme Court has not had occasion to reconsider the *Clayton Love* decision, it is generally recognised that the jurisprudential basis upon which it rests is in doubt. The House of Lords, in the *Suisse Atlantique* [1967] AC 361, *obiter*, disapproved of the 'fundamental breach as a rule of law' approach. Lord Reid in particular was critical of Devlin J.'s judgment in *Smeaton Hanscomb*, the basis of *Clayton Love* itself. He continued:

. . .

If this new rule of law is to be adopted, how far does it go? In its simplest form it would be that a party is not permitted to contract out of common law liability for a fundamental breach. If that were right then a demurrage clause could not stand as limiting liability for loss resulting from a fundamental breach; and the same would apply to any clause providing for liquidated damages. I do not suppose that anyone has intended that this rule should go quite so far as that. But I would find it difficult to say just where the line would have to be drawn.

In my view no such rule of law ought to be adopted. I do not take that view merely because any such rule is new or because it goes beyond what can be done by developing or adapting existing principles. Courts have often introduced new rules when, in their view, they were required by public policy. In former times when Parliament seldom amended the common law, that could hardly have been avoided. And there are recent examples although, for reasons which I gave in *Shaw v Director of Public Prosecutions*, I think that this power ought now to be used sparingly. But my main reason is that this rule would not be a satisfactory solution of the problem which undoubtedly exists.

Exemption clauses differ greatly in many respects. Probably the most objectionable are found in the complex standard conditions which are now so common. In the ordinary way the customer has no time to read them, and if he did read them he would probably not understand them. And if he did understand and object to any of them, he would generally be told he could take it or leave it. And if he then went to another supplier the result would be the same. Freedom to contract must surely imply some choice or room for bargaining.

At the other extreme is the case where parties are bargaining on terms of equality and a stringent exemption clause is accepted by a *quid pro quo* or other good reason. But this rule appears to treat all cases alike. There is no indication in the recent cases that the courts are to consider whether the exemption is fair in all the circumstances or is harsh and unconscionable or whether it was freely agreed by the customer. And it does not seem to me to be satisfactory that the decision must always go one way if, e.g. defects in a car or other goods are just sufficient to make the breach of contract a fundamental breach, but must always go the other way if the defects fall just short of that. This is a complex problem which intimately affects millions of people and it appears to me that its solution should be left to Parliament. If your Lordships reject this new rule there will certainly be a need for urgent legislative action but that is not beyond reasonable expectation.

Note

The doctrine of fundamental breach lived on for another fourteen years, despite the admonitions of the House of Lords in *Suisse Atlantique*.

In **Photo Production Ltd v Securicor Transport Ltd [1980] 2 WLR 283** the House of Lords overruled the doctrine. Although Lord Diplock's judgment in that case gives an excellent jurisprudential analysis of the nature of an exemption clause, the judgment of Lord Wilberforce examines the policy issues with great clarity.

Lord Wilberforce:

My Lords, this appeal arises from the destruction by fire of the respondents' factory involving loss and damage agreed to amount to £615,000. The question is whether the appellant is liable to the respondents for this sum.

The appellant is a company which provides security services. In 1968 it entered into a contract with the respondents by which for a charge of £8 15s 0d (old currency) per week it agreed to 'provide their night patrol service whereby four visits per night shall be made seven nights per week and two visits shall be made during the afternoon of Saturday and four visits shall be made during the day of Sunday.' The contract incorporated printed standard conditions which, in some circumstances, might exclude or limit the appellant's liability. The questions in this appeal are (i) whether these conditions can be invoked at all in the events which happened and (ii) if so, whether either the exclusion provision, or a provision limiting liability, can be applied on the facts. The trial judge (MacKenna J.) decided these issues in favour of the appellant. The Court of Appeal decided issue (i) in the respondents' favour invoking the doctrine of fundamental breach. Waller L.J. in addition would have decided for the respondents on issue (ii).

What happened was that on a Sunday night the duty employee of the appellant was one Musgrove. It was not suggested that he was unsuitable for the job or that the appellant was negligent in employing him. He visited the factory at the correct time, but when inside he deliberately started a fire by throwing a match on to some cartons. The fire got out of control and a large part of the premises was burnt down. Though what he did was deliberate, it was not established that he intended to destroy the factory. The judge's finding was in these words: 'Whether Musgrove intended to light only a small fire (which was the very least he meant to do) or whether he intended to cause much more serious damage, and, in either case, what was the reason for his act, are mysteries I am unable to solve.' This, and it is important to bear it in mind when considering the judgments in the Court of Appeal, falls short of a finding that Musgrove deliberately burnt or intended to burn the respondents' factory.

The condition upon which the appellant relies reads, relevantly, as follows:

Under no circumstances shall the company |Securicor| be responsible for any injurious act or default by any employee of the company unless such act or default could have been foreseen and avoided by the exercise of due diligence on the part of the company as his employer; nor, in any event, shall the company be held responsible for (a) any loss suffered by the customer through burglary, theft fire or any other cause, except insofar as such loss is solely attributable to the negligence of the company's employees acting within the course of their employment. . . .

There are further provisions limiting to stated amounts the liability of the appellant upon which it relies in the alternative if held not to be totally exempt.

It is first necessary to decide upon the correct approach to a case such as this where it is sought to invoke an exception or limitation clause in the contract. The approach of Lord Denning M.R. in the Court of Appeal was to consider first whether the breach was 'fundamental'. If so, he said, the court itself deprives the party of the benefit of an exemption or limitation clause (|1978| 1 WLR 856, 863). Shaw and Waller L.JJ. substantially followed him in this argument.

Lord Denning M.R. in this was following the earlier decision of the Court of Appeal, and in particular his own judgment in *Harbutts 'Plasticine' Ltd v Wayne Tank & Pump Co. Ltd* |1970| 1 QB 447. In that case Lord Denning M.R. distinguished two cases (a) the case where as the result of a breach of contract the innocent party has, and exercises, the right to bring the contract to an end, (b) the case where the breach automatically brings the contract to an end, without the innocent party having to make an election whether to terminate the contract or to continue it. In the first case the Master of the Rolls, purportedly applying this House's decision in *Suisse Atlantique Société d'Armement*

Maritime S.A. v N.V. Rotterdamsche Kolen Centrale |1967| 1 AC 361, but in effect two citations from two of their Lordships' speeches, extracted a rule of law that the 'termination' of the contract brings it, and with it the exclusion clause, to an end. The *Suisse Atlantique* case in his view 'affirms the long line of cases in this court that when one party has been guilty of a fundamental breach of the contract . . . and the other side accepts it, so that the contract comes to an end . . . then the guilty party cannot rely on an exception or limitation clause to escape from his liability for the breach' (*Harbutt's* case |1970| 1 QB 447, 467). He then applied the same principle on the second case.

My Lords, whatever the intrinsic merit of this doctrine, as to which I shall have something to say later, it is clear to me that so far from following this House's decision in the *Suisse Atlantique* it is directly opposed to it and that the whole purpose and tenor of the *Suisse Atlantique* was to repudiate it. The lengthy, and perhaps I may say sometimes indigestible speeches of their Lordships, are correctly summarised in the headnote—holding No. 3 |1967| 1 AC 361, 362—'That the question whether an exceptions clause was applicable where there was a fundamental breach of contract was one of the true construction of the contract.' That there was any rule of law by which exceptions clauses are eliminated, or deprived of effect, regardless of their terms, was clearly not the view of Viscount Dilhorne, Lord Hodson, or of myself. The passages invoked for the contrary view of a rule of law consist only of short extracts from two of the speeches—on any view a minority. But the case for the doctrine does not even go so far as that. Lord Reid, in my respectful opinion, and I recognise that I may not be the best judge of this matter, in his speech read as a whole, cannot be claimed as a supporter of a rule of law. Indeed he expressly disagreed with the Master of the Rolls' observations in two previous cases (*Karsales (Harrow) Ltd v Wallis* |1956| 1 WLR 936 and U.G.S. *Finance Ltd v National Mortgage Bank of Greece and National Bank of Greece S.A.* |1964| 1 Lloyd's Rep. 446 in which he had put forward the 'rule of law' doctrine. In order to show how close the disapproved doctrine is to that sought to be revived in *Harbutt's* case I shall quote one passage from *Karsales* |1956| 1 WLR 936, 940:

> Notwithstanding earlier cases which might suggest the contrary, it is now settled that exempting clauses of this kind, no matter how widely they are expressed, only avail the party when he is carrying out his contract in its essential respects. He is not allowed to use them as a cover for misconduct or indifference or to enable him to turn a blind eye to his obligations. They do not avail him when he is guilty of a breach which goes to the root of the contract.

Lord Reid comments at p. 401 as to this that he could not deduce from the authorities cited in *Karsales* that the proposition stated in the judgments could be regarded as in any way 'settled law'. His conclusion is stated on p. 405: 'In my view no such rule of law ought to be adopted'—adding that there is room for legislative reform.

My Lords, in the light of this, the passage cited by Lord Denning M.R. |1970| 1 QB 447, 465 had to be considered. For convenience I restate it:

> If fundamental breach is established the next question is what effect, if any, that has on the applicability of other terms of the contract. This question has often arisen with regard to clauses excluding liability, in whole or in part, of the party in breach. I do not think that there is generally much difficulty where the innocent party has elected to treat the breach as a repudiation, bring the contract to an end and sue for damages. Then the whole contract has ceased to exist including the exclusion clause, and I do not see how that clause can then be used to exclude an action for loss which will be suffered by the innocent party after it has ceased to

exist, such as loss of the profit which would have accrued if the contract had run its full term. (*Suisse Atlantique* | 1967| 1 AC 361, 398).

It is with the utmost reluctance that, not forgetting the 'beams' that may exist elsewhere, I have to detect here a note of ambiguity or perhaps even of inconsistency. What is referred to is 'loss which will be suffered by the innocent party after |the contract| has ceased to exist' and I venture to think that all that is being said, rather elliptically, relates only to what is to happen in the future, and is not a proposition as to the immediate consequences caused by the breach: if it were that would be inconsistent with the full and reasoned discussion which follows.

It is only because of Lord Reid's great authority in the law that I have found it necessary to embark on what in the end may be superfluous analysis. For I am convinced that, with the possible exception of Lord Upjohn whose critical passage, when read in full, is somewhat ambiguous, their Lordships, fairly read, can only be taken to have rejected those suggestions for a rule of law which had appeared in the Court of Appeal and to have firmly stated that the question is one of construction not merely of course of the exclusion clause alone, but of the whole contract.

Much has been written about the *Suisse Atlantique* case. Each speech has been subjected to various degrees of analysis and criticism, much of it constructive. Speaking for myself I am conscious of imperfections of terminology, though sometimes in good company. But I do not think that I should be conducing to the clarity of the law by adding to what was already too ample a discussion a further analysis which in turn would have to be interpreted. I have no second thoughts as to the main proposition that the question whether, and to what extent, an exclusion clause is to be applied to a fundamental breach, or a breach of a fundamental term, or indeed to any breach of contract, is a matter of construction of the contract. Many difficult questions arise and will continue to arise in the infinitely varied situations in which contracts come to be breached—by repudiatory breaches, accepted or not, by anticipatory breaches, by breaches of conditions or of various terms and whether by negligent, or deliberate action or otherwise. But there are ample resources in the normal rules of contract law for dealing with these without the superimposition of a judicially invented rule of law. I am content to leave the matter there with some supplementary observations.

1. The doctrine of 'fundamental breach' in spite of its imperfections and doubtful parentage has served a useful purpose. There was a large number of problems, productive of injustice, in which it was worse than unsatisfactory to leave exception clauses to operate. Lord Reid referred to these in the *Suisse Atlantique* case | 1967| 1 AC 361, 406, pointing out at the same time that the doctrine of fundamental breach was a dubious specific. But since then Parliament has taken a hand: it has passed the Unfair Contract Terms Act 1977. This Act applies to consumer contracts and those based on standard terms and enables exception clauses to be applied with regard to what is just and reasonable. It is significant that Parliament refrained from legislating over the whole field of contract. After this Act, in commercial matters generally, when the parties are not of unequal bargaining power, and when risks are normally borne by insurance, not only is the case for judicial intervention undemonstrated, but there is everything to be said, and this seems to have been Parliament's intention, for leaving the parties free to apportion the risks as they think fit and for respecting their decisions.

At the stage of negotiation as to the consequences of a breach, there is everything to be said for allowing the parties to estimate their respective claims according to the contractual provisions they have themselves made, rather than for facing them with a legal complex so uncertain as the doctrine of fundamental breach must be. What, for example, would have been the position of the respondents' factory if instead of being destroyed it had been damaged, slightly or moderately or severely? At what point does the doctrine (with what logical justification I have not understood) decide, *ex post facto*, that the breach was (factually) fundamental before going on to ask whether legally it is to be regarded as fundamental? How is the date of 'termination' to be fixed? Is it the date of the incident causing the damage, or the date of the innocent party's election, or some other date? All these difficulties arise from the doctrine and are left unsolved by it.

At the judicial stage there is still more to be said for leaving cases to be decided straightforwardly on what the parties have bargained for rather than upon analysis, which becomes progressively more refined, of decisions in other cases leading to inevitable appeals. The learned judge was able to decide this case on normal principles of contractual law with minimal citation of authority. I am sure that most commercial judges have wished to be able to do the same: see *Trade and Transport Inc. v Iino Kaiun Kaisha Ltd* [1973] 1 WLR 210, 232 per Kerr J.). In my opinion they can and should.

2. The case of *Harbutt* [1970] 1 QB 447 must clearly be overruled. It would be enough to put that upon its radical inconsistency with the *Suisse Atlantique* case [1967] 1 AC 361. But even if the matter were *res integra* I would find the decision to be based upon unsatisfactory reasoning as to the 'termination' of the contract and the effect of 'termination' on the plaintiffs' claim for damage. I have, indeed, been unable to understand how the doctrine can be reconciled with the well accepted principle of law, stated by the highest modern authority, that when in the context of a breach of contract one speaks of 'termination', what is meant is no more than that the innocent party or, in some cases, both parties, are excused from further performance. Damages, in such cases, are then claimed under the contract, so what reason in principle can there be for disregarding what the contract itself says about damages—whether it 'liquidates' them, or limits them, or excludes them? These difficulties arise in part from uncertain or inconsistent terminology. A vast number of expressions are used to describe situations where a breach has been committed by one party of such a character as to entitle the other party to refuse further performance: discharge, rescission, termination, the contract is at an end, or dead, or displaced; clauses cannot survive, or simply go. I have come to think that some of these difficulties can be avoided; in particular the use of 'rescission', even if distinguished from rescission *ab initio*, as an equivalent for discharge, though justifiable in some contexts (see *Johnson v Agnew* [1979] 2 WLR 487) may lead to confusion in others. To plead for complete uniformity may be to cry for the moon. But what can and ought to be avoided is to make use of these confusions in order to produce a concealed and unreasoned legal innovation: to pass, for example, from saying that a party, victim of a breach of contract, is entitled to refuse further performance, to saying that he may treat the contract as at an end, or as rescinded, and to draw from this the proposition, which is not analytical but one of policy, that all or (arbitrarily) some of the clauses of the contract lose, automatically, their force, regardless of intention.

SECTION FOUR—CONSUMER SALE TRANSACTIONS

A. Statutory Control of Exemption Clauses

Note

In the area of railway transport, parliamentary regulation of the use of limiting clauses occurred in 1854 by way of the Railway and Canal Traffic Act of that year—see *Boland v Waterford, Limerick and Western Rly Co.* (1897) 31

ILTR 62. However, this legislation, which gave the courts the power to either declare contractual conditions *per se* invalid, and subject other clauses to scrutiny, by reference to whether they were unjust or unreasonable or not, was the exception that proved the rule. As Andrews J. said in *Devitt v The Glasgow, Dublin and Londonderry Steampacket Co.* (1894) 29 ILTR 30, 'Railway companies and other carriers by land are more restricted than carriers by sea; the latter may, in the absence of fraud inducing the shipper to enter the contract make almost any conceivable contract.'

In sale of goods law the Sale of Goods Act 1893 initially reinforced and improved the common law rights of the buyer by implying into every contract for the sale of goods certain statutory conditions and warranties. However, these implied terms could be displaced by a properly worded exemption clause—see *Andrews Bros (Bournemouth) Ltd v Singer and Co. Ltd* (p. 341 above).

The implied conditions and warranties found in the Sale of Goods and Supply of Services Act 1980 however (pp 294–6 above) cannot be excluded by an exemption clause as a matter of course. Consumer sale transactions, as defined in s. 3, are subject to s. 22 which provides that exemption clauses in these contracts are void. The crucial issue is whether the buyer deals as consumer.

O'Callaghan *v* Hamilton Leasing (Ireland) Ltd [1984] ILRM 146

McWilliam J.:

The plaintiff owned and operated a take away food shop known as The Magnet Take Away Foods at Main Street, Dunleer, Co. Louth. The shop sold chips, hamburgers, ice-cream, minerals and other similar types of food. There was a cigarette vending machine in the premises. In March 1982 the plaintiff purchased from the second-named defendant (Access Refrigeration) a machine known as a 'Slush Puppy Iced Drink Dispensing Machine' for use in his shop. This machine produced fruit drinks containing crushed ice. The plaintiff himself dispensed them from the machine before serving them to his customers. The purchase was financed on foot of a leasing agreement concluded between the plaintiff and the first-named defendant (Hamilton Leasing) dated 12 March 1982. The plaintiff signed this agreement 'T/A The Magnet'. On foot of the agreement, the plaintiff leased from the first-named defendant for a period of sixty months the said machine at a quarterly rent of £210.00 plus VAT. The machine proved to be defective and after the plaintiff had made the first two quarterly payments he instituted proceedings in the Circuit Court claiming a refund of the monies paid by him to the first-named defendant, as well as damages for loss of profits. The second-named defendant was later joined as a co-defendant and on 7 July 1983 Judge Roe held that the plaintiff was entitled to succeed and entered judgment against both defendants in the sum of £1,112.50. He also ordered that the first-named defendant be indemnified against the decree by the second-named defendant. The first-named defendant appealed the decision but no Appeal was filed by the second-named defendant. At the hearing of the Appeal the first-named defendant did not contest the Circuit Court finding that the machine was defective or the damages decree. It disputed the Circuit Court finding against it, solely on the basis that the plaintiff, in entering into the said leasing agreement, was not dealing as a consumer within the meaning of s. 3 of the Sale of Goods and Supply of Services Act, 1980 and that, in consequence, was not entitled to succeed against the first-named defendant, either under ss 14 or

38 of the said Act. Mr Justice McWilliam heard evidence from the plaintiff as to the nature of his business and the circumstances surrounding the conclusion of the leasing agreement. He also heard evidence from a representative of the first-named defendant, to the effect that it was its policy to only conclude leasing agreements with firms, companies or persons carrying on business.

S. 3 of the Sale of Goods and Supply of Services Act, 1980 provides as follows:

(1) In the Act of 1893 and this Act the party to a contract is said to deal as consumer in relation to another party if:

    (a) he neither makes the contract in the course of a business nor holds himself out as doing so, and

    (b) the other party does make the contract in the course of a business, and

    (c) the goods or services supplied under or in pursuance of the contract are of a type ordinarily supplied for private use or consumption.

(2) On:

    (a) a sale by competitive tender, or

    (b) a sale by auction:

        (i) of goods of a type, or

        (ii) by or on behalf of a person of a class

    defined by the Minister by Order,

the buyer is not in any circumstances to be regarded as dealing as consumer.

(3) Subject to this, it is for those claiming that a party does not deal as consumer to show that he does not.

The defendant, Hamilton Leasing (Ireland) Ltd can only be liable to the plaintiff under s. 14 of the Sale of Goods and Supply of Services Act, 1980 if the plaintiff was a buyer dealing as a consumer within the meaning of sub-s. (1) of s. 3 of the Act.

It seems to me that this contract was made in the course of the plaintiff's business. It was certainly made for the purposes of his business although I appreciate the point made on behalf of the plaintiff that this business does not in any way include a re-sale or further dealing with the goods dealt with by the contract before me.

In order to interpret the words of s. 3 otherwise I would have to amend para. (a) of sub-s. (1) by reading it as though it provided 'in the course of a business which includes a further dealing with the goods' or some words of that sort.

I cannot depart from the clear words of a statute and try to construe it in accordance with my view of an unexpressed intention of the legislature although I suspect the legislature was more concerned with the business of engaging in further dealings with the goods.

With regard to para. (c) of the subsection, I am of opinion that the expression 'ordinarily supplied for private use or consumption' should be contrasted with use for the purposes of a business rather than contrasted with use for the purpose of re-sale of or further dealings with the goods. These goods were supplied for the purpose of a business and it has not been suggested that they would ever be supplied for use other than for the purpose of a business.

Accordingly, although these goods were supplied for the personal use of the plaintiff and he is the consumer in the ordinarily accepted meaning of the word, I must hold that, in this transaction, he did not 'deal as consumer' within the meaning of the Act.

Judge McWilliam then varied the Order of the Circuit Court by allowing the first-named defendant's appeal and dismissing the plaintiff's claim against it. He allowed the first-named defendant its costs in both courts but directed that the plaintiff be indemnified against same by the second-named defendant.

Cunningham *v* Woodchester Investments Ltd (HC) 16 November 1984, unrep.

McWilliam J.:

The defendant, Woodchester Investments Ltd [trading as Hamilton Executive Services] (hereinafter called Hamilton) agreed to lease to the plaintiff a telephone system which it had been agreed would be supplied to the plaintiff by the defendant, Inter-Call Limited (hereinafter called Inter-Call). The plaintiff was then the bursar of the Salesian Agricultural College at Warrenstown, Co. Meath, which, at the time of the agreement, had a manual telephone system with fifteen extensions. Eight more were required and it was decided, on the recommendation of Inter-Call, to install a complete new electronic system as being more efficient for the purposes of the college.

The installation was not completed by Inter-Call and what was installed was most unsatisfactory. This was not contested by Hamilton.

Inter-Call did not enter an appearance or contest the claim and judgment was given in the Circuit Court against both defendants on 11 June 1984. Hamilton at all times denied liability and has appealed the judgment against it.

The plaintiff stated that the college is a non-profit-making venture but, in addition to training students in agriculture, the college sells very considerable quantities of farm produce, including cattle, pigs, vegetables, mushrooms and eggs, with a turnover appro-aching £1,000,000. The plaintiff stated that all money earned was put back into the farm.

Condition 2 of the leasing agreement provided as follows: 'The lessee's acceptance of delivery of the equipment shall be conclusive evidence that the lessee has examined the equipment and found it to be complete, in accordance with the description overleaf, in good order and condition, fit for the purpose for which it may be required, and in every way satisfactory.'

The plaintiff relies on the provisions of s. 14 of the Sale of Goods and Supply of Services Act, 1980, which provides as follows:

> Where goods are sold to a buyer dealing as consumer and in relation to the sale an agreement is entered into by the buyer with another person acting in the course of a business (in this section referred to as a finance house) for the repayment to the finance house of money paid by the finance house to the seller in respect of the price of the goods, the finance house shall be deemed to be a party to the sale and the finance house and the seller shall, jointly and severally, be answerable to the buyer for breach of the contract of sale and for any misrepresentations made by the seller with regard to the goods.

The plaintiff was the buyer within the section and, to benefit from its provisions, must have been buying as consumer within the meaning of the Act. 'Consumer' is construed at s. 3 of the Act. This section provides:

> (1) In the Act of 1893 and this Act, a party to a contract is said to deal as consumer in relation to another party if:
> (a) he neither makes the contract in the course of a business nor holds himself out as doing so, and
> (b) the other party does make the contract in the course of a business, and
> (c) the goods or services supplied under or in pursuance of the contract are of a type ordinarily supplied for private use or consumption.

Hamilton relied on the provisions of condition 2 of the leasing agreement and also on the contention that the plaintiff was not a 'consumer' within the meaning of the Act.

I was referred to my own decision in *O'Callaghan v Hamilton Leasing (Ireland) Ltd* |1984| 4 ILRM 146.

I do not accept that condition 2 can apply where only a part of the equipment was delivered. An argument advanced on behalf of the plaintiff that this condition should not be enforceable unless it was fair and reasonable seems to depend on the provisions of s. 31 which, under the provisions of s. 38, appear to apply only to lettings to a person dealing with a consumer, which is the situation arising under s. 14.

Whatever may be done with the profits accruing from the extensive agricultural activities carried on at Warrenstown, I do not see how it can be said that engaging in these activities with a turnover of the amount indicated does not constitute carrying on a business. The evidence indicated that the equipment to be supplied was mainly or largely to be used in the course of the farming activities, although I am sure it was also to be used for other purposes of the college as well. Furthermore, the equipment was quite clearly not of a type ordinarily supplied for private use or consumption.

No argument has been advanced in this case which persuades me that I should alter the view I formed in *O'Callaghan's* case.

Finally, it was suggested on behalf of the plaintiff that he was entitled to succeed at common law on the grounds that he did not get what was agreed to be supplied, that the equipment was not merchantable or fit for the purpose for which it was supplied and that what was delivered was not complete. This may be correct as against Inter-Call but, with regard to Hamilton, I was not referred to any authorities and I am not satisfied that there is any liability on a finance house in circumstances such as these.

Accordingly, I must, somewhat reluctantly, reverse the decision of the Circuit Court.

B. Is the Implied Term Broken?

If the buyer cannot be in any sense considered to purchase goods in the course of a business, the seller must seek to plead that the term has not been broken.

Two contrasting cases illustrate the tendency of Irish judges to find for the purchaser. The first is a Northern Ireland decision on the 'traditional' implied terms.

Lutton *v* Saville Tractors (Belfast) Ltd [1986] NI 327

Carswell J.:

This appeal from the County Court for the Division of Ards concerns defects found to exist in a secondhand car bought by the plaintiff and the remedies which he seeks to obtain because of their existence, but its apparent simplicity masks quite a considerable degree of complexity in the points of law involved and difficulty in determining the issues.

The car in question was a Ford Escort XR3. It was referred to in evidence as a 1981 model, but I note that in the loan document its date of 'first registration/manufacture' is given as 1 June 1980. Its exact age was not proved before me, but as no complaint was made of misdescription of its age I shall go on the assumption that at the time of sale it was approximately three years old. It had a recorded mileage of about 32,000, but, as is usual in such transactions, the correctness of the figure was not warranted by the vendors. The XR3 is a high performance version of the Ford Escort, which is designed to provide a higher top speed and faster acceleration than the standard model.

The car was bought by the plaintiff from the first defendant Saville Tractors (Belfast) Ltd, trading as Saville Motors. The date of purchase was on or shortly before 18 September 1984, but the exact date was not established in evidence.

He dealt with one of the sales staff of Saville Motors, a Mr Sinclair, who was not called to give evidence. The car was on view in Saville Motors' premises at Dunmurry, but was not then readily capable of being driven because the battery was flat. Mr Sinclair explained that numerous people inspecting the car had set the alarm off and run down the battery. He said to the plaintiff that the car was running well and all it needed was a battery charge. He assured the plaintiff that it had not sustained any accident damage and at some stage in the negotiations promised to do a full service on the car. A three month warranty was given by the dealers to the plaintiff. Under the terms of that warranty, which were not spelled out in evidence, the dealers undertook to repair defects which manifested themselves within three months of the sale. It should be said at once that Saville Motors fully carried out their obligations when called upon to do so, and nothing turns upon the terms of the warranty.

The plaintiff wished to trade in a 1980 Mazda 1400 Sp, and a transaction was agreed whereby the plaintiff would buy the Ford car for £4,250, trading in his Mazda for £1,550, the balance of £2,700 to be financed by a loan from a finance company. The plaintiff was introduced to the resident representative of Forward Trust Ltd, who had an office on Saville Motors' premises, and the necessary documents were completed for the negotiation of a loan of £2,700. The transaction was thus made up of two parts, each contained in its own written document:

(i) The sale of the Ford Escort XR3 by Saville Motors to the plaintiff for £4,250, with a credit for £1,550, the agreed price of the Mazda 1400 SP purchased by Saville Motors from him. This transaction was recorded in an undated sale document proved before me, signed by the plaintiff and by Mr Sinclair on behalf of Saville Motors. It contained a number of declarations by the purchaser and exempting clauses, to which I shall refer later.

(ii) The loan of £2,700, made by Forward Trust Ltd to the plaintiff and his father jointly. The proposal, of which a copy was furnished to me, was completed by the resident representative of Forward Trust and signed by the plaintiff and his father. It was accepted by Forward Trust on 18 September 1984. It provided for repayment of the loan, plus a credit protection insurance premium and interest charges, by thirty six monthly instalments of £119.61, the first to be paid on 18 October 1984. The plaintiff in the event paid only one such instalment.

It was agreed by all parties that the relationship between them was such as to create a debtor-creditor-supplier agreement within s. 12(b) of the Consumer Credit Act 1974, and that accordingly the provisions of s. 75 of the Act applied, making Forward Trust Ltd jointly and severally liable to the plaintiff in respect of any claim for misrepresentation or breach of contract.

The assurances given by Mr Sinclair to the plaintiff were by no means all correct. The car had been on Saville Motors' premises for some time before it was sold, and in or about July 1984 an employee had an accident with it in which the front was damaged. Both headlights and the grille were replaced and some body work repair was done to the front of the car. There was no chassis or bulkhead damage. The total repair cost charged in Saville's accounts was £401.16, of which £343.46 was for parts; the whole charge was at trade prices and rather below what the repair would have cost if charged to a customer. The occurrence of the accident and the carrying out of the repair were certainly known to the sales manager, Mr Joseph A. Ewart, who gave evidence. It was not established whether the salesman Sinclair was aware of the accident. It is difficult to suppose that he was unaware, but on the facts proved I cannot find it proved to a sufficient standard that he made the representation that the car had not been in an accident knowing it to be untrue. I bear in mind on this point, and also on the question of remedies to which I shall turn later, the evidence of Mr George Irwin, an experienced motor assessor called by the defendants, that when he saw the car in April 1985 there was no evidence visible to him of accident damage or repair and that it would not have been apparent on inspection after a few weeks. The plaintiff does not appear to have become aware of the accident damage at any time before he finally attempted to get rid of the car.

I am satisfied that Saville Motors did not carry out what can properly be regarded as a full service. The records show that what they carried out was a check designed to enable them to give a three month warranty: that is to say, their object was to trace and remedy defects which would require repair during the warranty period if not then dealt with. Mr Ewart attempted to maintain that a promise of a full service would have been met by the warranty check. I do not accept this. I consider that to the reasonable customer a full service means the carrying out of the inspection and servicing specified by the manufacturers as requisite at intervals such as 20,000 miles. It is more than a short service or inspection and would ordinarily be regarded as including a change of engine oil, replacement of plugs and points and tuning, together with all necessary greasing, oiling, checking and adjustments. This was not done before the car was delivered, although parts of it were subsequently carried out in the course of the repeated tuning to which I shall refer.

The plaintiff never found this car satisfactory and returned it constantly with lists of complaints. I did receive the impression that he was an owner who liked everything to be in as near perfect order as possible and that he had demanding standards for the performance and condition of his cars. I do not think, however, that his complaints were unfounded, and the fact that he regarded minor defects as requiring attention where less particular owners might have overlooked them does not necessarily make his complaints unreasonable. They have to be considered in the light of the type, age and cost of the car, and the fact that a three month warranty had been given with it. There was not a great deal of evidence before me about what a reasonable purchaser should expect to find when he buys a secondhand car like this one. It was established, however, that it was intended to be a car giving better than ordinary performance, and in modern conditions I think that a purchaser of a three year old car of a dependable make with a mileage of 32,000 at the price agreed could reasonably expect to find it performing well and free from minor defects, even if he is incautious enough to buy it without the opportunity of a road test or an expert's inspection.

The plaintiff complained from the very beginning that the car emitted excessive blue smoke when starting and that there was a hesitation at higher speeds. He also found when he took delivery that the radiator was losing water, the oil pressure light came on (indicating excessively low pressure or a fault in the warning light system) and the warning light also came on which indicated that the brake pads required renewal. In addition he found minor defects relating to the radio and the driver's seat belt cover winder. He took the car back to the dealers, who arranged to take it in for repair.

A new pressure cap was fitted to the radiator to cure the water loss. A new control governing the oil warning light was fitted to the dipstick, which should have solved that problem. Brake pads were ordered but not then fitted, as was a new winder. The engine was tuned on the Crypton electronic equipment, but no reason could be found for the hesitation of which the plaintiff complained. Nor could any cause be found for the emission of smoke. The engine was tuned no less than three times in all within six weeks and no fault could be found. The conclusion which the service manager, Mr Kenneth Hamilton, reached was that the smoke was not excessive for an engine at that age and that it did not indicate a need for tuning, since the readings for exhaust emission were within normal limits. He failed on road testing to detect a hesitation, and although he did not say so in so many words, he gave the impression in his evidence that he thought the plaintiff an over-fussy owner. The car was subsequently road tested by two engineers, but neither saw it in conditions in which one could judge the performance properly, since it had been lying unattended for a considerable time. Mr Dunlop thought that if the timing was fixed and the engine properly tuned it ought then to run properly, and Mr Irwin said that he obtained normal revolutions on testing the engine speed. I cannot reach any firm conclusion on this point on the evidence before me. I accept that the plaintiff did not find the engine performance satisfactory, but it cannot have been a very fundamental fault, and it remains unclear whether the hesitation was something which should not have occurred in a car of this age. Similarly, I think that the emission of smoke showed some imperfection in the engine, but that it may have been within the limits one might have to expect in a car of this age which had quite possibly been driven hard by previous owners.

The plaintiff brought the car back to Saville Motors a short time later. The brake light was still flashing and he was still dissatisfied about the emission of smoke. He also complained that a score had been caused to the roof in the course of the repairs. A suspension rattle developed, the exhaust was banging, and the oil light continued to give trouble. The car was taken in by Saville Motors on 18 October 1984, according to their records, and remedial work was done which took some 5.4 hours [sic]. The front brake pads were fitted, the rattle was checked, the warning light switches were checked and the engine tuning checked because of the smoke complaint.

A week later on 25 October the car was in again for further tuning, but no fault was found. A short time after that an electrical fault developed which left the plaintiff stranded without lights. He also said in evidence that the boot light would not go off and that he had to disconnect it to save the battery. The plaintiff took the car in to Saville Motors on 29 October, when work was done on the electrical system.

Six days later the plaintiff came back with the car and made further complaints to the service manager, who took down a list of seven items for attention, as follows (I shall set out the list, together with his own note on each item):

Lutton XR3

(1) Blue smoke from exhaust	(Acceptable level @ 36000 miles) (after idling some time)
(2) Seat belt cover winder ordered	(Ordered)
(3) Lazy starter or battery	(New battery)
(4) Oil light comes on?	(Never did with us. Checked several occasions)
(5) Rear brake squeal	(Replaced rear shoes)
(6) Hesitates	(Tuned, OK)
(7) Rear brake lights (switch ordered)	(Fitted)

Urgent

According to the servicing records new rear brake shoes and rear wheel cylinders were fitted and a new brake light switch and wires. A new battery was ordered and apparently later fitted, although Mr Hamilton averred that it was not proved really to be necessary.

On a separate day the roof was re-sprayed by a painter to cover the score mark. The reference to 36,000 miles brings out the fact that the plaintiff had done a considerable mileage, between 3,000 and 4,000 miles, since he bought the car.

On the occasion when the plaintiff took the car in and the service manager made out the list which I have quoted, which according to Saville's records was 5 November 1984, the plaintiff told him that he did not want the car back. Mr Hamilton said that he could not have his money back and suggested that he might look at other cars on show. When the plaintiff looked at a 1982 Ford Fiesta, he was told that he would lose £1,000 against his XR3, so he declined the suggestion. The plaintiff then consulted his solicitors, who wrote to Saville Motors on 9 November 1984 stating that the plaintiff wished to terminate what they referred to as his 'hire-purchase agreement' and asking for repayment of the trade-in allowance of £1,550 plus the instalment of £119.61 paid by him. No reply appears to have been received.

Meanwhile, at or about the date of their sending this letter the car broke down again, and the plaintiff had to leave it at a garage. It was examined on 14 November by Mr Dunlop, a motor assessor and engineer, who was unable to start it. His comments on the likely cause of the trouble the plaintiff had with the car were accordingly of limited assistance. It transpired eventually that the cause was a failure of the distributor. I do not think that this was something which could have been foreseen by Saville Motors when selling or servicing the car, and to judge from the other work done to the car by them they would have replaced it under the warranty without question. For the plaintiff, however, it was the last straw, and he resolved to have nothing further to do with the car. At some stage he took the keys and tax book to Mr Sinclair, but he refused to accept them. The car was eventually transported to the premises of Saville Motors, where it remained untouched for a long period. I was informed that it was recently sold, but received no details of the transaction or whether it was done by agreement between the parties.

The plaintiff's claim, as presented on the appeal before me, was based upon misrepresentation and breach of the conditions implied by statute in a sale of goods. He sought rescission of the sale and the return of the instalment paid and the value of the car which he traded in, together with damages. If he were not granted rescission, he sought damages by misrepresentation and breach of contract. I shall deal with these issues in turn.

I have already held that it has not been proved that the salesman Sinclair knew of the untruth of his representation that the car had not been in an accident. The sales manager knew of the accident, but it was not suggested the he authorised the making of the representation. The misrepresentation—for such it obviously was—was made in the course of Sinclair's employment and apparently on behalf of his employers, and therefore Saville Motors must be held to have made an innocent misrepresentation. The inference to be drawn from the plaintiff's reference to it in his evidence is that it had a material effect in inducing him to enter into the transaction, and the contrary was not suggested to him in cross-examination. The representation concerning the condition of the car might be regarded in many cases as a piece of sales talk which had no real influence on the purchaser. In the circumstances of the present case, however, the car could not be driven or tested or the engine run, and the salesman's statements about its mechanical condition assumed a greater importance. I hold that they were intended to and did constitute a material part of the inducement to the plaintiff to buy the car, although they did not become terms of the contract. Both representations therefore constituted actionable misrepresentations, for which both defendants are jointly and severally liable. It was also argued that the salesman's silence about defects constituted a misrepresentation, but I am not prepared so to hold.

A person who has been induced to enter into a contract by a misrepresentation is entitled to the equitable remedy of rescission, but that right is lost if he has affirmed the contract, in certain cases by lapse of time, or if *restitutio in integrum* is no longer possible. I do not think that the latter two defences are in point, but the question of affirmation may well be. I shall have to consider it further after deciding the issue of breach of contract, but so far as the misrepresentation about accident damage is concerned there is no evidence that the plaintiff knew its untruth at any time before the proceedings were brought, and in the absence of knowledge he cannot be held to have affirmed the contract despite the misrepresentation: see *Farnworth Finance Facilities Ltd v Attryde* [1970] 2 All ER 774, 778 per Lord Denning M.R., and cf *Peyman v Lanjani* [1984] 3 All ER 703. The fact that the plaintiff did not know of the untruth of the accident damage misrepresentation when he repudiated the contract in November 1984 is not an obstacle to his relying upon it now as a legitimate ground for the repudiation. It is a well established principle of the law of contract that a person who refuses to perform a contract on one ground may, if that is inadequate, subsequently rely upon another ground which justifies his refusal to perform, provided it in fact existed at the time of the refusal: *Benjamin's Sale of Goods*, (2nd ed.), para. 1725.

The court is, however, empowered by s. 2(2) of the Misrepresentation Act (Northern Ireland) 1967 to declare the contract subsisting and award damages in lieu of rescission, if of opinion that it would be equitable to do so, having regard to the nature of the misrepresentation and the loss that would be caused by it if the contract were upheld, as well as to the loss that rescission would cause to the other party. I shall have to consider in due course whether to exercise this power, but one can see at once that a case could be made out for doing so in respect of the accident damage misrepresentation, if it stood alone, because of the minor effect which it had upon the value of the car.

I turn then to consideration of the terms as to quality and fitness implied by the law into contracts of hire-purchase where it is appropriate on the facts to do so. The plaintiff relied first upon s. 14(2) of the Sale of Goods Act 1979, which reads as follows:

Where the seller sells goods in the course of a business, there is an implied condition that the goods supplied under the contract are of merchantable quality, except that there is no such condition:

(a) as regards defects specifically drawn to the buyer's attention before the contract is made; or
(b) if the buyer examines the goods before the contract is made, as regards defects which that examination ought to reveal.

Except for the fact that the battery was obviously flat, the provisos do not apply to this transaction. There was no evidence that any defect was drawn to the plaintiff's attention, and none of the defects of which he complains could have been revealed by any examination which he could have carried out.

'Merchantable quality' is defined by s. 14(6) in the following terms: 'Goods of any kind are of merchantable quality within the meaning of sub-s. (2) above if they are as fit for the purpose or purposes for which goods of that kind are commonly bought as it is reasonable to expect having regard to any description applied to them, the price (if relevant) and all the other relevant circumstances.' Much judicial ink has been spilled in explaining the meaning of the concept of merchantable quality, which did not have a statutory definition until the 1973 Act was passed. It is just as important not to modify a clear definition contained in a statute by incorporating inconsistent statements from previous judicial decisions as it is to avoid treating judicial observations made in the context of the facts and issues in particular cases as complete definitions. The statutory definition is generally regarded, however, as an attempt to codify the definitions advanced in the decided cases. In a case of the present nature I think that I derive most assistance from the test laid down by Dixon J. in the High Court of Australia in *Australian Knitting Mills Ltd v Grant* (1933) 50 CLR 387, 413, which was approved by several members of the House of Lords in *Henry Kendall & Sons v William Lillico & Sons Ltd* |1967| 2 AC 31: 'The condition that goods are of merchantable quality requires that they should be in such an actual state that a buyer fully acquainted with the facts and, therefore, knowing what hidden defects existed, and not being limited to their apparent condition would buy them without abatement of the price obtainable for such goods if in reasonably sound order and condition and without special terms.' This requires one qualification in particular, that the goods will only be unmerchantable where the price which would be paid by a buyer knowing of the defects is substantially lower than the contract price: see B. S. *Brown & Son Ltd v Craiks Ltd* |1970| 1 All ER 823.

Professor Atiyah points out in his book *The Sale of Goods*, (7th ed.), 133, that the tests are somewhat circular in their reliance upon reasonableness and suggests that they are somewhat vacuous in practice and give little guidance as to what kind of defects or damage will render goods unmerchantable. Lord Denning M.R. stated, however, with his customary directness in *Cehave* N. V. *v Bremer Handelsgesellschaft* mbH |1976| QB 44, 62, that it is as well to remember that one is dealing with a condition breach of which entitles the buyer to reject the goods. He went on to say: 'In these circumstances I should have thought a fair way of testing merchantability would be to ask a commercial man: was the breach such that the buyer should be able to reject the goods?' In answering that he would have regard to the matters mentioned in the statutory definition, the purpose for which the goods are bought, the description applied to them and the price.

As so often, it is easier to state the law than to apply it to a specific case or type of cases. When one is dealing with secondhand goods which have defects not known to the buyer at the time of sale, it is particularly difficult to apply it. Defects which might entitle a buyer to reject a new car may not be sufficient to make a secondhand car unmerchantable—although even in the case of a new car the existence of a manufacturer's warranty may mean that a buyer cannot reject it over a minor repairable defect: see, e.g. *Millars of Falkirk Ltd v Turpie* |1976| SLT 66. On the other hand, I would venture to express some doubt whether it is necessary in every case of a sale of a secondhand car to go so far as to find that it is unsafe to be put on the road, which might appear from the tenor of the judgments in *Lee v York Coach & Marine* |1977| RTR 35. The English Court of Appeal has regularly held that a secondhand car must not be regarded as being of unmerchantable quality merely because it has a string of defects, and before this can be found it must be shown to be unroadworthy or even unsafe: see *Porter v General Guarantee Corp. Ltd* |1982| RTR 384, 393, per Kilner Brown J. A clear statement of this approach appears in the judgment of Lord Denning M.R. in *Bartlett v Sidney Marcus Ltd* |1965| 2 All ER 753, 755: 'A buyer should realise that, when he buys a secondhand car, defects may appear sooner or later; and, in the absence of an express warranty, he has no redress. Even when he buys from a dealer the most that he can require is that it should be reasonably fit for the purpose of being driven along the road.' As always, the context is vital, and his statement has to be read in that context. I should myself respectfully suggest that it is not universally valid in sales of secondhand cars, nor would Lord Denning have intended it to be. At the end of the day a decision whether a car is of merchantable quality is a matter of fact and degree, and it is essential to take account of the factors specified in the statutory definition.

It seems to me of critical importance to preserve a proper balance between the legitimate interests of vendors and purchasers in such sales. It would not make commercial sense that a buyer of a secondhand car should be entitled to return it and claim his money back if one or more minor faults developed, and applying Lord Denning's test in the *Cehave* case one is readily brought to the conclusion that this is not intended by the concept of merchantability. By the same token, I cannot think it right that the buyer should have to endure the burden of ownership of a car with a series of defects which are commercially intolerable in a car of the type and condition which he has bought, and should have to keep getting it repaired, restricting his claim to damages. At one end of the scale is the purchase of a seven year old family car with a high mileage at a low price. A buyer of such a car would not ordinarily expect that vehicle to be free of potentially troublesome defects, and if some developed during the first weeks after his purchase he would be unlikely to be able to return the car. At the other end is a transaction concerning a luxury car, a few months old and with a small mileage, for which the price is correspondingly high. The development of defects in such a car on a scale which the buyer would have to tolerate in the case of the elderly model might well be sufficient cause for rescission of the sale, because the parties contemplated that the car would give high performance and trouble-free motoring, and these characteristics were necessary to make it of merchantable quality in the circumstances of that transaction. In between these extremes it is a matter of fact and degree on which side of the line the case falls, but it is salutary nevertheless to bear in mind the warning issued by Lord Denning M.R. in *Bartlett v Sidney Marcus Ltd.*

The car which Mr Lutton bought was three years old, and at that age and with a mileage of some 32,000 it would in my view have been reasonable for him to expect some of the mechanical and electrical parts would be worn and would need replacement or repair. It may not have been realistic to expect the performance of the engine to be up to the standard of a new one. Nevertheless, I consider that such a car, sold at such price, should still be reliable and capable of giving good service and fair performance. I think that the giving of a three month warranty, which I believe to be common in sales by reputable dealers of the better type of secondhand car, is a relevant factor. It demonstrates that the parties to the transaction regard the car as one which ought to be expected to give a period of trouble-free motoring. It is also a safeguard to both parties, in that if minor faults develop the purchaser does not have to bear the cost of repair, but the vendor can discharge his obligations by carrying out the repairs without being expected to rescind the transaction and take the car back.

In my judgment the number and seriousness of the faults which were present or developed in the car the subject of this case were such that it was not of merchantable quality. I consider that the plaintiff was entitled to expect that it would be in much better condition on the purchase of a car of this age, type and mileage at the price he agreed. I do not think that he should be required to rely solely on having these faults repaired under the warranty, faithfully though Saville Motors observed its terms.

The other implied term upon which the plaintiff relied is contained in s. 14(3) of the Sale of Goods Act 1979, the material portion of which reads as follows:

> Where the seller sells goods in the course of a business and the buyer, expressly or by implication, makes known
> (a) to the seller . . .
> any particular purpose for which the goods are being bought, there is an implied condition that the goods supplied under the contract are reasonably fit for that purpose, whether or not that is a purpose for which such goods are commonly supplied, except where the circumstances show that the buyer does not rely, or that it is unreasonable for him to rely, on the skill or judgment of the seller or credit-broker.

In view of my finding under s. 14(2) it is not strictly necessary for me to reach a decision under s. 14(3), but since the issue was argued before me, and it is likely to arise fairly regularly, I shall express my conclusions under it.

·It may be seen that this sub-section removes the need for the purchaser to prove *in limine* that he relied upon the seller's skill and judgment (see s. 14(1) of the Sale of Goods Act, 1893). It is now reduced to a matter upon which the seller may rely by way of defence, as an exception to the liability which may be imposed on him as a seller of goods in the course of a business. One may dispose of it shortly by saying that it does not arise in the present case, since the plaintiff was unusually dependent on the sales-man in the circumstances, and it was not suggested to him in cross-examination that he formed his own independent judgment and relied solely upon it.

Under the decisions given on s. 14(1) of the Sale of Goods Act 1893, it was well settled that the word 'particular' was used in the sense 'specified' rather than in contra-distinction to 'general'; *Henry Kendall & Sons v William Lillico Sons Ltd* |1969| 2 AC 31, 123, per Lord Wilberforce. The purpose may in fact be a very general purpose, for example, a car to drive on the road: Atiyah, (op. cit.), p. 141. It has also been held that the phrase 'particular purpose' would apply even if the goods could only be used for one purpose in the ordinary way. As Lord Wright said in *Grant v Australian Knitting Mills Ltd* |1936| AC 84, 99: 'There is no need to specify in terms the particular purpose for which the buyer requires the goods, which is nonetheless the particular purpose within the meaning of the section, because it is the only purpose for which anyone would ordinarily want the goods.' The change of wording from 'the particular purpose' in the 1893 Act to 'any particular purpose' in the 1979 Act seems to me to confirm the effect of those decisions.

I consider that the plaintiff impliedly made known to the dealers his purpose in taking the car, which was the only purpose for which anyone would ordinarily want it, *viz.* to have a means of transport which was reasonably suitable to drive. I would express it in these terms rather than the narrower purpose stated by Lord Denning M.R. in *Bartlett v Sidney Marcus Ltd*, as 'a motor car to drive along the road'. Even under that narrower definition, however, I think that the present car fell short of the required standard of being reasonably fit for the purpose, and *a fortiori* if one defines the purpose as I have done. It is clear from Lord Reid's speech in *Henry Kendall & Sons v William Lillico & Sons Ltd* that the statutory condition covers not only defects which the seller or dealer ought to have detected but also defects which are latent in the sense that even the utmost skill and judgment on the part of the seller would not have detected them. I therefore hold that there was in the present case a breach of both s. 14(2) and s. 14(3) of the Sale of Goods Act 1979.

I can deal shortly with the standard form parts of the sale agreement, which in my judgment were patently designed to defeat the obligations placed upon a vendor by s. 14 of the Sale of Goods Act 1979 and the law relating to misrepresentations. I consider that clause 2(b) of the terms and conditions printed on the reverse of the agreement, which provided that the vehicle was sold without any guarantee condition or warranty whatsoever other than the three month warranty, is directly contrary to s. 6(2)(a) of the Unfair Contract Terms Act 1977, and cannot stand. The final part of clause 2(b) imports an 'understanding' that the purchaser entered into the agreement relying on his own judgment and information, and the printed 'Purchaser's Declaration' on the obverse purports to contain an acknowledgment that the plaintiff had not been 'induced to make this offer by any representation as to the quality, fitness for any purpose, performance or otherwise of the goods', and a declaration that he had not relied on the 'skill, judgment or opinion of the seller, its servants or agents in relation to the goods'. I am of opinion that the portion relating to representation comes squarely within s. 3 of the Misrepresentation Act (Northern Ireland) 1967, as replaced by s. 8 of the Unfair Contract Terms Act 1977, and that the term does not satisfy the requirement of reasonableness as stated in s. 11 of the latter Act. I also consider that the 'under-standing' in clause 2(b) and the declaration concerning reliance on skill, judgment or opinion are transparent attempts to escape the operation of s. 6(2)(a) of the 1977 Act, which should not be permitted to operate successfully. I agree with the view expressed in Atiyah, (op. cit.), p. 198 that in this respect it is the facts which matter and not the printed terms of the agreement. Since the defects were not in fact drawn to the buyer's attention, and he did in fact rely, and reasonably so, on the salesman's skill and judgment, the printed disclaimer is of no contrary effect. I should make it clear in the defendants' favour, however, that they did not attempt to rely on the standard form clauses by way of defence.

Each of the implied terms which I have discussed ranks as a condition, with the concomitant right on the part of the purchaser to reject the goods for breach of condition and obtain the return of his money.

Note

The implied terms pleaded in *Lutton* are substantially identical to those found in the Sale of Goods and Supply of Services Act 1980. However, s. 13 of that Act adds a further implied condition that a motor vehicle supplied under a contract will be free from any defect that would render the vehicle a danger to members of the public, including those travelling within the vehicle.

Glorney v O'Brien (HC) 14 November 1988, unrep. decided that liability in damages will extend to even the most venerable or decrepit motor vehicle and that the court will not readily accept a plea that the vehicle was sold for spare parts rather than use on the road.

C. The Fair and Reasonable Test

If the buyer of goods, or the hirer of goods under a contract of hire-purchase does not deal as consumer, an exclusion clause may operate if the clause is fair and reasonable within the Schedule of the 1980 Act. This legislative provision was modelled upon the UK Supply of Goods (Implied Terms) Act 1973.

The leading case on that Act is **George Mitchell (Chesterhall) Ltd v Finney Lock Seeds [1983] 2 AC 805.**

Lord Bridge of Harwich:

My Lords, the appellants are seed merchants. The respondents are farmers in East Lothian. In December 1973 the respondents ordered from the appellants 30lb of Dutch winter white cabbage seeds. The seeds supplied were invoiced as 'Finney's Late Dutch Special'. The price was £201.60. 'Finney's Late Dutch Special' was the variety required by the respondents. It is a Dutch winter white cabbage which grows particularly well in the area of East Lothian where the respondents farm, and can be harvested and sold at a favourable price in the spring. The respondents planted some 63 acres of their land with seedlings grown from the seeds supplied by the appellants to produce their cabbage crop for the spring of 1975. In the event, the crop proved to be worthless and had to be ploughed in. This was for two reasons. First, the seeds supplied were not 'Finney's Late Dutch Special' or any other variety of Dutch winter white cabbage, but a variety of autumn cabbage. Secondly, even as autumn cabbage the seeds were of very inferior quality.

The issues in the appeal arise from three sentences in the conditions of sale endorsed on the appellants' invoice and admittedly embodied in the terms on which the appellants contracted. For ease of reference it will be convenient to number the sentences. Omitting immaterial words they read as follows:

1. In the event of any seeds or plants sold or agreed to be sold by us not complying with the express terms of the contract of sale . . . or any seeds or plants proving defective in varietal purity we will, at our option, replace the defective seeds or plants, free of charge to the buyer or will refund all payments made to us by the buyer in respect of the defective seeds or plants and this shall be the limit of our obligation.

2. We hereby exclude all liability for any loss or damage arising from the use of any seeds or plants supplied by us and for any consequential loss or damage arising out of such use or any failure in the performance of or any defect in any seeds or plants supplied by us or for any other loss or damage whatsoever save for, at our option, liability for any such replacement or refund as aforesaid.

3. In accordance with the established custom of the seed trade any express or implied condition, statement or warranty, statutory or otherwise, not stated in these conditions is hereby excluded.

I will refer to the whole as 'the relevant condition' and to the parts as 'clauses 1, 2 and 3' of the relevant condition.

The first issue is whether the relevant condition, on its true construction in the context of the contract as a whole, is effective to limit the appellants' liability to a refund of £201.60, the price of the seeds ('the common law issue'). The second issue is whether, if the common law issue is decided in the appellants' favour, they should nevertheless be precluded from reliance on this limitation of liability pursuant to the provisions of the modified s. 55 of the Sale of Goods Act 1979 which is set out in para. 11 of Schedule 1 to the Act and which applies to contracts made between 18 May 1973, and 1 February 1978 ('the statutory issue').

The learned trial judge, Parker J. [1981] 1 Lloyd's Rep. 476, 480, on the basis of evidence that the seeds supplied were incapable of producing a commercially saleable crop, decided the common law issue against the appellants on the ground that 'what was supplied . . . was in no commercial sense vegetable seed at all' but was 'the delivery of something wholly different in kind from that which was ordered and which the defendants had agreed to supply.' He accordingly found it unnecessary to decide the statutory issue, but helpfully made some important findings of fact, which are very relevant if that issue falls to be decided. He gave judgment in favour of the respondents for £61,513.78 damages and £30,756.00 interest. Nothing now turns on these figures, but it is perhaps significant to point out that the damages awarded do not represent merely 'loss of anticipated profit', as was erroneously suggested in the appelants' printed case. The figure includes, as [counsel] very properly accepted, all the costs incurred by the respondents in the cultivation of the worthless crop as well as the profit they would have expected to make from a successful crop if the proper seeds had been supplied.

In the Court of Appeal, the common law issue was decided in favour of the appellants by Lord Denning M.R. [1983] QB 284, 296 who said: 'On the natural interpretation, I think the condition is sufficient to limit the seed merchants to a refund of the price paid or replacement of the seeds.' Oliver L.J. |1983| QB 284, 305, 306, decided the common law issue against the appellants primarily on a ground akin to that of Parker J., albeit somewhat differently expressed. Fastening on the words 'agreed to be sold' in clause 1 of the relevant condition, he held that the clause could not be construed to mean 'in the event of the seeds sold or agreed to be sold by us not being the seeds agreed to be sold by us.' Clause 2 of the relevant condition he held to be 'merely a supplement' to clause 1. He thus arrived at the conclusion that the appellants had only succeeded in limiting their liability arising from the supply of seeds which were correctly described as 'Finney's Late Dutch Special' but were defective in quality. As the seeds supplied were not 'Finney's Late Dutch Special', the relevant condition gave them no protection. Kerr L.J. |1983| QB 284, 313, in whose reasoning Oliver L.J. also concurred, decided the common law issue against the appellants on the ground that the relevant condition was ineffective to limit the appellants' liability for a breach of contract which could not have occurred without negligence on the appellants' part, and that the supply of the wrong variety of seeds was such a breach.

The Court of Appeal, however, were unanimous in deciding the statutory issue against the appellants.

In his judgment, Lord Denning M.R. traces, in his uniquely colourful and graphic style, the history of the courts' approach to contractual clauses excluding or limiting liability, culminating in the intervention of the legislature, first by the Supply of Goods (Implied Terms) Act 1973, secondly, by the Unfair Contract Terms Act 1977. My Lords, in considering the common law issue, I will resist the temptation to follow that fascinating trail, but will content myself with references to the two recent decisions of your Lordships' House commonly called the two *Securicor* cases: *Photo Production Ltd v Securicor Transport Ltd* |1980| AC 827 ('*Securicor 1*') and *Ailsa Craig Fishing Co. Ltd v Malvern Fishing Co. Ltd* |1983| 1 WLR 964 ('*Securicor 2*').

Securicor 1 gave the final quietus to the doctrine that a 'fundamental breach' of contract deprived the party in breach of the benefit of clauses in the contract excluding or limiting his liability. *Securicor 2* drew an important distinction between exclusion and limitation clauses. This is clearly stated by Lord Fraser of Tullybelton, at p. 105:

> There are later authorities which lay down very strict principles to be applied when considering the effect of clauses of exclusion or of indemnity: see particularly the Privy Council case of *Canada Steamship Lines Ltd v The King* |1952| AC 192, 208, where Lord Morton, delivering the advice of the board, summarised the principles in terms which have recently been applied by this House in *Smith v U.M.B. Chrysler (Scotland) Ltd*, 1978 SC (HL) 1. In my opinion these principles are not applicable in their full rigour when considering the effect of conditions merely limiting liability. Such conditions will of course be read *contra proferentem* and must be clearly expressed, but there is no reason why they should be judged by the specially exacting standards which are applied to exclusion and indemnity clauses.

My Lords, it seems to me, with all due deference, that the judgments of the learned trial judge and of Oliver L.J. on the common law issue come dangerously near to re-introducing by the back door the doctrine of 'fundamental breach' which this House in *Securicor 1* |1980| AC 827, had so forcibly evicted by the front. The learned judge discusses what I may call the 'peas and beans' or 'chalk and cheese' cases, sc. those in which it has been held that exemption clauses do not apply where there has been a contract to sell one thing, e.g a motor car, and the seller has supplied quite another thing, e.g. a bicycle. I hasten to add that the judge can in no way be criticised for adopting this approach since counsel appearing for the appellants at the trial had conceded 'that if what had been delivered had been beetroot seed or carrot seed, he would not be able to rely upon the clause': |1981| 1 Lloyd's Rep. 476, 479. Different counsel appeared for the appellants in the Court of Appeal, where that concession was withdrawn.

In my opinion, this is not a 'peas and beans' case at all. The relevant condition applies to 'seeds'. Clause 1 refers to seeds 'sold' and 'seeds agreed to be sold'. Clause 2 refers to 'seeds supplied'. As I have pointed out, Oliver L.J. concentrates his attention on the phrase 'seeds agreed to be sold'. I can see no justification, with respect, for allowing this phrase alone to dictate the interpretation of the relevant condition, still less for treating clause 2 as 'merely a supplement' to clause 1. Clause 2 is perfectly clear and unambiguous. The reference to 'seeds agreed to be sold' as well as to 'seeds sold' in clause 1 reflects the same dichotomy as the definition of 'sale' in the Sale of Goods Act 1979 as including a bargain and sale as well as a sale and delivery. The defective seeds in this case were seeds sold and delivered, just as clearly as they were seeds supplied, by the appellants to the respondents. The relevant condition, read as a whole, unambiguously limits the appellants' liability to replacement of the seeds or refund of the price. It is only possible to read an ambiguity into it by the process of strained construction which was deprecated by Lord Diplock in *Securicor* 1 and by Lord Wilberforce in *Securicor* 2.

In holding that the relevant condition was ineffective to limit the appellants' liability for a breach of contract caused by their negligence, Kerr L.J. applied the principles stated by Lord Morton of Henryton giving the judgment of the Privy Council in *Canada Steamship Lines Ltd v The King* |1952| AC 192, 208. The learned Lord Justice stated correctly that this case was also referred to by Lord Fraser of Tullybelton in *Securicor* 2. He omitted, however, to notice that, as appears from the passage from Lord Fraser's speech which I have already cited the whole point of Lord Fraser's reference was to express his opinion that the very strict principles laid down in the *Canada Steamship Lines* case as applicable to exclusion and indemnity clauses cannot be applied in their full rigour to limitation clauses. Lord Wilberforce's speech contains a passage to the like effect, and Lord Elwyn-Jones, Lord Salmon and Lord Lowry agreed with both speeches. Having once reached a conclusion in the instant case that the relevant condition unambiguously limited the appellants' liability, I know of no principle of construction which can properly be applied to confine the effect of the limitation to breaches of contract arising without negligence on the part of the appellants. In agreement with Lord Denning M.R., I would decide the common law issue in the appellants' favour.

The statutory issue turns, as already indicated, on the application of the provisions of the modified s. 55 of the Sale of Goods Act 1979, as set out in paragraph 11 of Schedule 1 of the Act. The Act of 1979 is a pure consolidation. The purpose of the modified s. 55 is to preserve the law as it stood from 18 May 1973, to 1 February 1978, in relation to contracts made between those two dates. The significance of the dates is that the first was the date when the Supply of Goods (Implied Terms) Act 1973 came into force containing the provision now re-enacted by the modified s. 55, the second was the date when the Unfair Contract Terms Act 1977 came into force and super-seded the relevant provisions of the Act of 1973 by more radical and far-reaching provisions in relation to contracts made thereafter.

The relevant subsections of the modified s. 55 provide as follows:

(1) Where a right, duty or liability would arise under a contract of sale of goods by implication of law, it may be negatived or varied by express agreement . . . but the preceding provision has effect subject to the following provisions of this section. . . .

(4) In the case of a contract of sale of goods, any term of that or any other contract exempting from all or any of the provisions of ss 13, 14 or 15 above is void in the case of a consumer sale and is, in any other case, not enforceable to the extent that it is shown that it would not be fair or reasonable to allow reliance on the term. (5) In determining for the purposes of sub-s. (4) above whether or not reliance on any such term would be fair or reasonable regard shall be had to all the circumstances of the case and in particular to the following matters—(a) the strength of the bargaining positions of the seller and buyer relative to each other, taking into account, among other things, the availability of suitable alternative products and sources of supply; (b) whether the buyer received an inducement to agree to the term or in accepting it had an opportunity of buying the goods or suitable altern- atives without it from any source of supply; (c) whether the buyer knew or ought reasonably to have known of the existence and extent of the term (having regard, among other things, to any custom of the trade and any previous course of dealing between the parties); (d) where the term exempts from all or any of the provisions of ss 13, 14 or 15 above if some condition is not complied with, whether it was reason- able at the time of the contract to expect that compliance with that condition would be practicable; (e) whether the goods were manufactured, processed, or adapted to the special order of the buyer. . . . (9) Any reference in this section to a term exempt- ing from all or any of the provisions of any section of this Act is a reference to a term which purports to exclude or restrict, or has the effect of excluding or restrict- ing, the operation of all or any of the provisions of that section, or the exercise of a right conferred by any provision of that section, or any liability of the seller for breach of a condition or warranty implied by any provision of that section.

The contract between the appellants and the respondents was not a 'consumer sale', as defined for the purpose of these provisions. The effect of clause 3 of the relevant condition is to exclude, *inter alia*, the terms implied by ss 13 and 14 of the Act that the seeds sold by description should correspond to the description and be of merchantable quality and to substitute therefore the express but limited obligations undertaken by the appellants under clauses 1 and 2. The statutory issue, therefore, turns on the words in sub-s. (4) 'to the extent that it is shown that it would not be fair or reasonable to allow reliance on' this restriction of the appellants' liabilities, having regard to the matters referred to in sub-s. (5).

This is the first time your Lordships' House has had to consider a modern statutory provision giving the court power to override contractual terms excluding or restricting liability, which depends on the court's view of what is 'fair and reasonable'. The partic- ular provision of the modified s. 55 of the Act of 1979 which applies in the instant case is of limited and diminishing importance. But the several provisions of the Unfair Contract Terms Act 1977 which depend on 'the requirement of reasonableness', defined in s. 11 by reference to what is 'fair and reasonable', albeit in a different context, are likely to come before the courts with increasing frequency. It may, therefore, be appropriate to consider how an original decision as to what is 'fair and reasonable' made in the application of any of these provisions should be approached by an appellate court. It would not be accurate to describe such a decision as an exercise of discretion. But a decision under any of the provisions referred to will have this in common with the exercise of a discretion, that, in having regard to the various matters to which the modified s. 55 (5) of the Act of 1979, or s. 11 of the Act of 1977 direct attention, the court must entertain a whole range of considerations, put them in the scales on one side or the other, and decide at the end of the day on which side the balance comes down. There will sometimes be room for a legitimate difference of judicial opinion as to what the answer should be, where it will be impossible to say that one view is demonstrably wrong and the other demonstrably right. It must follow, in my view, that, when asked to review such a decision on appeal, the appellate court should treat the original decision with the utmost respect and refrain from interference with it unless satisfied that it proceeded upon some erroneous principle or was plainly and obviously wrong.

Turning back to the modified s. 55 of the Act of 1979, it is common ground that the onus was on the respondents to show that it would not be fair or reasonable to allow the appellants to rely on the relevant condition as limiting their liability. It was argued for the appellants that the court must have regard to the circumstances as at the date of the contract, not after the breach. The basis of the argument was that this was the effect of s. 11 of the Act of 1977 and that it would be wrong to construe the modified s. 55 of the Act as having a different effect. Assuming the premise is correct, the conclusion does not follow. The provisions of the Act of 1977 cannot be considered in construing the prior enactment now embodied in the modified s. 55 of the Act of 1979. But, in any event, the language of sub-ss (4) and (5) of that section is clear and unambiguous. The question whether it is fair or reasonable to allow reliance on a term excluding or limiting liability for a breach of contract can only arise after the breach. The nature of the breach and the circumstances in which it occurred cannot possibly be excluded from 'all the circumstances of the case' to which regard must be had.

The only other question of construction debated in the course of the argument was the meaning to be attached to the words 'to the extent that' in sub-s. (4) and, in particular, whether they permit the court to hold that it would be fair and reasonable to allow partial reliance on a limitation clause and, for example, to decide in the instant case that the respondents should recover, say, half their consequential damage. I incline to the view that, in their context, the words are equivalent to 'insofar as' or 'in circumstances in which' and do not permit the kind of judgment of Solomon illustrated by the example. But for the purpose of deciding this appeal I find it unnecessary to express a concluded view on this question.

My Lords, at long last I turn to the application of the statutory language to the circumstances of the case. Of the particular matters to which attention is directed by paras (a) to (e) of s. 55 (5), only those in (a) to (c) are relevant. As to para. (c), the respondents admittedly knew of the relevant condition (they had dealt with the appellants for many years) and, if they had read it, particularly clause 2, they would, I think, as laymen rather than lawyers, have had no difficulty in understanding what it said. This and the magnitude of the damages claimed in proportion to the price of the seeds sold are factors which weigh in the scales in the appellants' favour.

The question of relative bargaining strength under para. (a) and of the opportunity to buy seeds without a limitation of the seedsman's liability under para. (b) were interrelated. The evidence was that a similar limitation of liability was universally embodied in the terms of trade betwen seedsmen and farmers and had been so for very many years. The limitation had never been negotiated between representative bodies but, on the other hand, had not been the subject of any protest by the National Farmers' Union. These factors, if considered in isolation, might have been equivocal. The decisive factor, however, appears from the evidence of four witnesses called for the appellants, two independent seedsmen, the chairman of the appellant company, and a director of a sister company (both being wholly-owned subsidiaries of the same parent). They said that it had always been their practice, unsuccessfully attempted in the instant case, to negotiate settlements of farmers' claims for damages in excess of the price of the seeds, if they thought that the claims were 'genuine' and 'justified'. This evidence indicated a clear recognition by seedsmen in general, and the appellants in particular, that reliance on the limitation of liability imposed by the relevant condition would not be fair or reasonable.

Two further factors, if more were needed, weight the scales in favour of the respondents. The supply of autumn, instead of winter, cabbage seeds was due to the negligence of the appellants' sister company. Irrespective of its quality, the autumn variety supplied could not, according to the appellants' own evidence, be grown commercially in East Lothian. Finally, as the trial judge found, seedsmen could insure against the risk of crop failure caused by supplying the wrong variety of seeds without materially increasing the price of seeds.

My Lords, even if I felt doubts about the statutory issue, I should not, for the reasons explained earlier, think it right to interfere with the unanimous original decision of that issue by the Court of Appeal. As it is, I feel no such doubts. If I were making the original decision, I should conclude without hesitation that it would not be fair or reasonable to allow the appellants to rely on the contractual limitation of their liability.

I would dismiss the appeal.

(Brightman, Diplock, Scarman and Roskill L.JJ. concurred.)

The only Irish case decided on the fair and reasonable test is **McCarthy v Joe Walsh Tours [1991] ILRM 813**

Carroll J.:

The McCarthy family are the plaintiffs in this action. They booked a holiday with the defendants, Joe Walsh Tours Ltd, on 17 July 1989. The question before this court is whether their Circuit Court action claiming damages for breach of contract should be stayed under s. 5 of the Arbitration Act 1980, on the basis that there is an arbitration clause in the standard form contract signed by Mr McCarthy on behalf of the family when he booked the holiday.

Different reasons have been advanced on behalf of the plaintiffs as to why this court should refuse to stay their Circuit Court proceedings.

First, Mr McCarthy says that the contract was concluded only after he had already agreed details of the holiday with the defendants' representative in their office in Patrick Street, Cork. He considered the contract to be an oral contract. He says in his affidavit that when he was asked to sign a document he did so and paid the deposit and it was never indicated to him that the document contained any terms other than those which had been agreed and that he had no reason to suppose that the defendants were to introduce new terms into the written contract. He said that he was not offered any opportunity to read the document and that a copy of the document was not provided either before or after he signed it. The booking form which he signed contains a box for a signature which states:

The terms and conditions (see over) of this booking form have been brought to my attention and have been read, understood and fully agreed to and accepted by me, both on behalf of all persons included herein and on my own behalf. I warrant and represent that all the information herein is true and accurate and that I have been duly authorised by all persons included on this form to execute this agreement on their behalf and accordingly I sign my name on their behalf and on my own.

I consider that it was not reasonable for Mr McCarthy to suppose that the contract which he had made was an oral one and that by signing the document he had added nothing to the oral agreement. There is no suggestion that he could not have taken time to read what he had signed or that he was prevented in any way from doing so. In my opinion, this booking form constituted the written agreement between the parties.

The second argument is that the contract and the arbitration clause is affected by Part IV of the Sale of Goods and Supply of Services Act 1980. The arbitration clause reads as follows:

> 15(c)(1) If any dispute or difference should arise out of or in respect of the agreement between the parties and or in respect of any matter, or thing, directly or indirectly touching, concerning or otherwise connected with the holiday transaction between the parties, the same shall be referred to arbitration with the arbitrator being the independent arbitrator for the time being under, and with such arbitration being in accordance with the rules, provisions of the ITAA arbitration scheme. This scheme, *inter alia*, limits the liability of the company, with specific provisions about costs, and places a time limit on invoking an arbitration. Details of the scheme are available at and from the ITAA offices. Please ask for a copy. It is hereby agreed between the parties that such arbitration shall be a condition precedent to the commencement of any action of law.

S. 39 of the Sale of Goods and Supply of Services Act 1980, provides:

> Subject to s. 40, in every contract for the supply of a service where the supplier is acting in the course of a business, the following terms are implied:
>
> (a) that the supplier has the necessary skill to render the service,
> (b) that he will supply the service with due skill, care and diligence. . . .

S. 40(1) of that Act provides that any term of a contract implied by virtue of s. 39 may be 'negatived or varied', *inter alia*, by an express term of the contract 'except that where the recipient of the service deals as consumer it must be shown that the express term is fair and reasonable and has been specifically brought to his attention'. S. 40(3) explains the meaning of 'negative' and 'vary' in s. 40(1). S. 40(3) provides: 'The reference in subs. (1) to a term negativing or varying a term implied by s. 39 is a reference to a term which purports to exclude or restrict, or has the effect of excluding or restricting, the operation of any provision of that section, or the exercise of a right conferred by any provision of that section, or any liability of the supplier for breach of a term implied by any provision of that section.'

S. 40(2) adds to the definition of 'negative' by providing that 'an express term does not negative a term implied by this part unless inconsistent therewith'. The ITAA scheme itself limits liability of £5,000 for any claim. In addition, it excludes recovery in respect of personal injury although the latter exclusion is not relevant in the context of the present case as any allegation of personal injury is not substantiated by the pleadings. These limitations amount to provisions which restrict liability of the supplier for a breach of a term implied by s. 39 and are, therefore, a term 'varying' the terms implied by virtue of s. 39 into this contract. To be effective in a consumer contract such a term must be fair and reasonable and have been specifically brought to the consumer's attention. If the provisions restricting liability were contained in the general conditions of the contract then the arbitrator himself could decide whether or not the terms implied by s. 39 had been effectively negatived or varied. This would involve deciding whether the terms were fair and reasonable and had been specifically brought to the consumers' attention. However, in the present case the position is different. In this case it is the arbitration clause itself which incorporates the provisions of the ITAA scheme and an arbitrator appointed to administer that scheme could not enter into a deliberation going to his competence and enquire whether he was legally entitled to disregard the provisions of that scheme and, for example, award more than £5,000 for damages or award damages for personal injury. Therefore, since the arbitration clause is a term varying (within the meaning of s. 40 of the Act of 1980) the defendants' liability under the implied terms of s. 39 of the Act of 1980, it can only be effective in a consumer contract if it was 'fair and reasonable' and had been specifically brought to the attention of the plaintiffs.

Mr McCarthy, the first-named plaintiff, says in his affidavit, that at no time during or after negotiations was any mention made to him concerning what would happen if he was dissatisfied with the holiday or that any dispute between himself and the defendants would have to be referred to arbitration. That stands as an uncontested fact. To mention, as was done in the present case, the arbitration clause in general terms in the box for signature in the booking form is only giving general information. In order that the arbitration clause should be specifically brought to the attention of a consumer it would be necessary, in my opinion, that the consumer should be informed of the extent of the monetary limit of liability and any other limits on the defendants' liability. Accordingly, it is unnecessary for me to decide whether the arbitration term is 'fair and reasonable' as it is an uncontested fact that the arbitration clause was not specifically brought to the attention of the plaintiffs. Since this was not done, the arbitrator cannot apply the scheme.

I will therefore, make an order under s. 5 of the Arbitration Act 1980, refusing to refer the plaintiffs' action to arbitration on the ground that the arbitration clause in question is inoperative and incapable of being performed.

Note

In the US two 'statutory' solutions to problems of abuse of power have been suggested. The first, s. 2–302 of the Uniform Commercial Code, adopts a legislative position which empowers a court to rule on whether a clause is unconscionable or not. It was the product of Professor Llewellyn and critics of this approach argue that it is vague and difficult to apply consistently—see Leff (1967) 115 U.Pa L Rev. 485; contrast Ellinghaus, (1969) 78 Yale LJ 757.

The second approach is found in the **American Law Institute Restatement (2d) Contracts s. 208:**

Unconscionable Contract or Term

If a contract or term thereof is unconscionable at the time the contract is made a court may refuse to enforce the contract, or may enforce the remainder of the contract without the unconscionable term, or may so limit the application of any unconscionable term as to avoid any unconscionable result.

Comment:

a. *Scope.* Like the obligation of good faith and fair dealing (§205), the policy against unconscionable contracts or terms applies to a wide variety of types of conduct. The determination that a contract or term is or is not unconscionable is made in the light of its setting, purpose and effect. Relevant factors include weaknesses in the contracting process like those involved in more specific rules as to contractual capacity, fraud, and other invalidating causes; the policy also overlaps with rules which render particular bargains or terms unenforceable on grounds of public policy. Policing against unconscionable contracts or terms has sometimes been accomplished 'by adverse construction of language, by manipulation of the rules of offer and acceptance or by determinations that the clause is contrary to public policy or to the dominant purpose of the contract.' Uniform Commercial Code §2–302 Comment 1.

D. EUROPEAN COMMUNITY INITIATIVES

The European Communities have acted on many occasions by promoting legislation to protect consumers against improper bargaining techniques or pressurised sales techniques. Witness the so-called doorstep directive which provides cancellation rights in respect of contracts concluded away from business premises: see the European Communities (Cancellation of Contracts Negotiated away from Business Premises) Regulations 1989 (SI No. 224 of 1989). In the area of package travel, the Travel Directive 90/314/EEC also provides protection to consumers who would otherwise be subject to broad exempting provisions, but this Directive has yet to be transposed into Irish law. Further proposed legislation includes community wide protection for persons pressured into entering into holiday time-share contracts.

The Unfair Terms Directive however is the most important measure proposed to-date. For an analysis see (1993) 56 MLR 581 (Dean).

Council Directive 93/13/EEC of 5 April 1993 on Unfair Terms in Consumer Contracts

THE COUNCIL OF THE EUROPEAN COMMUNITIES,

Having regard to the Treaty establishing the European Economic Community, and in particular Article 100 A thereof,

Having regard to the proposal from the Commission,[1]

In cooperation with the European Parliament,[2]

Having regard to the opinion of the Economic and Social Committee,[3]

Whereas it is necessary to adopt measures with the aim of progressively establishing the internal market before 31 December 1992; whereas the internal market comprises an area without internal frontiers in which goods, persons, services and capital move freely;

Whereas the laws of Member States relating to the terms of contract between the seller of goods or supplier of services, on the one hand, and the consumer to them, on the other hand, show many disparities, with the result that the national markets for the sale of goods and services to consumers differ from each other and that distortions of competition may arise amongst the sellers and suppliers, notably when they sell and supply in other Member States;

Whereas, in particular, the laws of Member States relating to unfair terms in consumer contracts show marked divergences;

Whereas it is the responsibility of the Member States to ensure that contracts concluded with consumers do not contain unfair terms;

Whereas, generally speaking, consumers do not know the rules of law which, in Member States other than their own, govern contracts for the sale of goods or services; whereas this lack of awareness may deter them from direct transactions for the purchase of goods or services in another Member State;

Whereas, in order to facilitate the establishment of the internal market and to safeguard the citizen in his role as consumer when acquiring goods and services under contracts which are governed by the laws of Member States other than his own, it is essential to remove unfair terms from those contracts;

Whereas sellers of goods and suppliers of services will thereby be helped in their task of selling goods and supplying services, both at home and throughout the internal market; whereas competition will thus be stimulated, so contributing to increased choice for Community citizens as consumers;

Whereas the two Community programmes for a consumer protection and information policy [4] underlined the importance of safeguarding consumers in the matter of unfair terms of contract; whereas this protection ought to be provided by laws and regulations which are either harmonised at Community level or adopted directly at that level;

Whereas in accordance with the principle laid down under the heading 'Protection of the economic interests of the consumers', as stated in those programmes: 'acquirers of goods and services should be protected against the abuse of power by the seller or supplier, in particular against one-sided standard contracts and the unfair exclusion of essential rights in contracts';

Whereas more effective protection of the consumer can be achieved by adopting uniform rules of law in the matter of unfair terms; whereas those rules should apply to all contracts concluded between sellers or suppliers and consumers; whereas as a result *inter alia* contracts relating to employment, contracts relating to rights under family law and contracts relating to the incorporation and organisation of companies or partnership agreements must be excluded from this Directive;

Whereas the consumer must receive equal protection under contracts concluded by word of mouth and written contracts regardless, in the latter case, of whether the terms of the contract are contained in one or more documents;

Whereas, however, as they now stand, national laws allow only partial harmonisation to be envisaged; whereas, in particular, only contractual terms which have not been individually negotiated are covered by this Directive; whereas Member States should have the option, with due regard for the Treaty, to afford consumers a higher level of protection through national provisions that are more stringent than those of this Directive;

Whereas the statutory or regulatory provisions of the Member States which directly or indirectly determine the terms of consumer contracts are presumed not to contain unfair terms; whereas, therefore, it does not appear to be necessary to subject the terms which reflect mandatory statutory or regulatory provisions and the principles or provisions of international conventions to which the Member States or the Community are party; whereas in that respect the wording 'mandatory statutory or regulatory provisions' in Article 1 (2) also covers rules which, according to the law, shall apply between the contracting parties provided that no other arrangements have been established;

Whereas Member States must however ensure that unfair terms are not included, particularly because this Directive also applies to trades, business or professions of a public nature;

Whereas it is necessary to fix in a general way the criteria for assessing the unfair character of contract terms;

Whereas the assessment, according to the general criteria chosen, of the unfair character of terms, in particular in sale or supply activities of a public nature providing collective services which take account of solidarity among users, must be supplemented by a means of making an overall evaluation of the different interests involved; whereas this constitutes the requirement of good faith; whereas, in making an assessment of good faith, particular regard shall be had to the strength of the bargaining positions of the parties, whether the consumer had an inducement to agree to the term and whether the goods or services were sold or supplied to the special order of the consumer; whereas the requirement of good faith may be satisfied by the seller or supplier where he deals fairly and equitably with the other party whose legitimate interests he has to take into account;

Whereas, for the purposes of this Directive, the annexed list of terms can be of indicative value only and, because of the cause of the minimal character of the Directive, the scope of these terms may be the subject of amplification or more restrictive editing by the Member States in their national laws;

Whereas the nature of goods or services should have an influence on assessing the unfairness of contractual terms;

Whereas, for the purposes of this Directive, assessment of unfair character shall not be made of terms which describe the main subject matter of the contract nor the quality/price ratio of the goods or services supplied; whereas the main subject matter of the contract and the price/quality ratio may nevertheless be taken into account in assessing the fairness of other terms; whereas it follows, *inter alia*, that in insurance contracts, the terms which clearly define or circumscribe the insured risk and the insurer's liability shall not be subject to such assessment since these restrictions are taken into account in calculating the premium paid by the consumer;

Whereas contracts should be drafted in plain, intelligible language, the consumer should actually be given an opportunity to examine all the terms and, if in doubt, the interpretation most favourable to the consumer should prevail;

Whereas Member States should ensure that unfair terms are not used in contracts concluded with consumers by a seller or supplier and that if, nevertheless, such terms are so used, they will not bind the consumer, and the contract will continue to bind the parties upon those terms if it is capable of continuing in existence without the unfair provisions;

Whereas there is a risk that, in certain cases, the consumer may be deprived of protection under this Directive by designating the law of a non-Member country as the law applicable to the contract; whereas provisions should therefore be included in this Directive designed to avert this risk;

Whereas persons or organisations, if regarded under the law of a Member State as having a legitimate interest in the matter, must have facilities for initiating proceedings concerning terms of contract drawn up for general use in contracts concluded with consumers, and in particular unfair terms, either before a court or before an administrative authority competent to decide upon complaints or to initiate appropriate legal proceedings; whereas this possibility does not, however, entail prior verification of the general conditions obtaining in individual economic sectors;

Whereas the courts or administrative authorities of the Member States must have at their disposal adequate and effective means of preventing the continued application of unfair terms in consumer contracts,

HAS ADOPTED THIS DIRECTIVE:

Article 1

1. The purpose of this Directive is to approximate the laws, regulations and administrative provisions of the Member States relating to unfair terms in contracts concluded between a seller or supplier and a consumer.

2. The contractual terms which reflect mandatory statutory or regulatory provisions and the provisions or principles of international conventions to which the Member States or the Community are party, particularly in the transport area, shall not be subject to the provisions of this Directive.

Article 2

For the purposes of this Directive:

(a) 'unfair terms' means the contractual terms defined in Article 3;
(b) 'consumer' means any natural person who, in contracts covered by this Directive, is acting for purposes which are outside his trade, business or profession;
(c) 'seller or supplier' means any natural or legal person who, in contracts covered by this Directive, is acting for purposes relating to his trade, business or profession, whether publicly owned or privately owned.

Article 3

1. A contractual term which has not been individually negotiated shall be regarded as unfair if, contrary to the requirement of good faith, it causes a significant imbalance in the parties' rights and obligations arising under the contract, to the detriment of the consumer.

2. A term shall always be regarded as not individually negotiated where it has been drafted in advance and the consumer has therefore not been able to influence the substance of the term, particularly in the context of a pre-formulated standard contract.

The fact that certain aspects of a term or one specific term have been individually negotiated shall not exclude the application of this Article to the rest of a contract if an overall assessment of the contract indicates that it is nevertheless a pre-formulated standard contract.

Where any seller or supplier claims that a standard term has been individually negotiated, the burden of proof in this respect shall be incumbent on him.

3. The Annex shall contain an indicative and non-exhaustive list of the terms which may be regarded as unfair.

Article 4

1. Without prejudice to Article 7, the unfairness of a contractual term shall be assessed, taking into account the nature of the goods or services for which the contract was concluded and by referring, at the time of conclusion of the contract, to all the circumstances attending the conclusion of the contract and to all the other terms of the contract or of another contract on which it is dependent.

2. Assessment of the unfair nature of the terms shall relate neither to the definition of the main subject matter of the contract nor to the adequacy of the price and remuneration, on the one hand, as against the services or goods supplied in exchange, on the other, in so far as these terms are in plain intelligible language.

Article 5

In the case of contracts where all or certain terms offered to the consumer are in writing, these terms must always be drafted in plain, intelligible language. Where there is doubt about the meaning of a term, the interpretation most favourable to the consumer shall prevail. This rule on interpretation shall not apply in the context of the procedures laid down in Article 7 (2).

Article 6

1. Member States shall lay down that unfair terms used in a contract concluded with a consumer by a seller or supplier shall, as provided for under their national law, not be binding on the consumer and that the contract shall continue to bind the parties upon those terms if it is capable of continuing in existence without the unfair terms.

2. Member States shall take the necessary measures to ensure that the consumer does not lose the protection granted by this Directive by virtue of the choice of the law of a non-Member country as the law applicable to the contract if the latter has a close connection with the territory of the Member States.

Article 7

1. Member States shall ensure that, in the interests of consumers and of competitors, adequate and effective means exist to prevent the continued use of unfair terms in contracts concluded with consumers by sellers or suppliers.

2. The means referred to in paragraph 1 shall include provisions whereby persons or organisations, having a legitimate interest under national law in protecting consumers, may take action according to the national law concerned before the courts or before competent administrative bodies for a decision as to whether contractual terms drawn

up for general use are unfair, so that they can apply appropriate and effective means to prevent the continued use of such terms.

3. With due regard for national laws, the legal remedies referred to in paragraph 2 may be directed separately or jointly against a number of sellers or suppliers from the same economic sector or their associations which use or recommend the use of the same general contractual terms or similar terms.

Article 8

Member States may adopt or retain the most stringent provisions compatible with the Treaty in the area covered by this Directive, to ensure a maximum degree of protection for the consumer.

Article 9

The Commission shall present a report to the European Parliament and to the Council concerning the application of this Directive five years at the latest after the date in Article 10 (1).

Article 10

1. Member States shall bring into force the laws, regulations and administrative provisions necessary to comply with this Directive no later than 31 December 1994. They shall forthwith inform the Commission thereof.

These provisions shall be applicable to all contracts concluded after 31 December 1994.

2. When Member States adopt these measures, they shall contain a reference to this Directive or shall be accompanied by such reference on the occasion of their official publication. The methods of making such a reference shall be laid down by the Member States.

3. Member States shall communicate the main provisions of national law which they adopt in the field covered by this Directive to the Commission.

Article 11

This Directive is addressed to the Member States.

Done at Luxembourg, 5 April 1993

For the Council
The President
N. Helveg Petersen

ANNEX

TERMS REFERRED TO IN ARTICLE 3 (3)

1. *Terms which have the object or effect of*:

(a) excluding or limiting the legal liability of a seller or supplier in the event of the death of a consumer or personal injury to the latter resulting from an act or omission of that seller or supplier;

(b) inappropriately excluding or limiting the legal rights of the consumer *vis-à-vis* the seller or supplier or another party in the event of total or partial non-performance or inadequate performance by the seller or supplier of any of the contractual obligations, including the option of offsetting a debt owed to the seller or supplier against any claim which the consumer may have against him;

(c) making an agreement binding on the consumer whereas provision of services by the seller or supplier is subject to a condition whose realisation depends on his own will alone;

(d) permitting the seller or supplier to retain sums paid by the consumer where the latter decides not to conclude or perform the contract, without providing for the consumer to receive compensation of an equivalent amount from the seller or supplier where the latter is the party cancelling the contract;

(e) requiring any consumer who fails to fulfil his obligation to pay a disproportionately high sum in compensation;

(f) authorising the seller or supplier to dissolve the contract on a discretionary basis where the same facility is not granted to the consumer, or permitting the seller or supplier to retain the sums paid for services not yet supplied by him where it is the seller or supplier himself who dissolves the contract;

(g) enabling the seller or supplier to terminate a contract of indeterminate duration without reasonable notice except where there are serious grounds for doing so;

(h) automatically extending a contract of fixed duration where the consumer does not indicate otherwise, when the deadline fixed for the consumer to express this desire not to extend the contract is unreasonably early;

(i) irrevocably binding the consumer to terms with which he had no real opportunity of becoming acquainted before the conclusion of the contract;

(j) enabling the seller or supplier to alter the terms of the contract unilaterally without a valid reason which is specified in the contract;

(k) enabling the seller or supplier to alter unilaterally without a valid reason any characteristics of the product or service to be provided;

(l) providing for the price of goods to be determined at the time of delivery or allowing a seller of goods or supplier of services to increase their price without in both cases giving the consumer the corresponding right to cancel the contract if the final price is too high in relation to the price agreed when the contract was concluded;

(m) giving the seller or supplier the right to determine whether the goods or services supplied are in conformity with the contract, or giving him the exclusive right to interpret any term of the contract;

(n) limiting the seller's or supplier's obligation to respect commitments undertaken by his agents or making his commitments subject to compliance with a particular formality;

(o) obliging the consumer to fulfil all his obligations where the seller or supplier does not perform his;

(p) giving the seller or supplier the possibility of transferring his rights and obligations under the contract, where this may serve to reduce the guarantees for the consumer, without the latter's agreement;

(q) excluding or hindering the consumer's right to take legal action or exercise any other legal remedy, particularly by requiring the consumer to take disputes exclusively to arbitration not covered by legal provisions, unduly restricting the evidence available to him or imposing on him a burden of proof which, according to the applicable law, should lie with another party to the contract.

2. *Scope of subparagraphs (g), (j) and (l)*

(a) Subparagraph (g) is without hindrance to terms by which a supplier of financial services reserves the right to terminate unilaterally a contract of indeterminate duration without notice where there is a valid reason, provided that the supplier is required to inform the other contracting party or parties thereof immediately.

(b) Subparagraph (j) is without hindrance to terms under which a supplier of financial services reserves the right to alter the rate of interest payable by the consumer or due to the latter, or the amount of other charges for financial services without notice where there is a valid reason, provided that the supplier is required to inform the other contracting party or parties thereof at the earliest opportunity and that the latter are free to dissolve the contract immediately.

Subparagraph (j) is also without hindrance to terms under which a seller or supplier reserves the right to alter unilaterally the conditions of a contract of indeterminate duration, provided that he is required to inform the consumer with reasonable notice and that the consumer is free to dissolve the contract.

(c) Subparagraphs (g), (j) and (l) do not apply to:
   - transactions in transferable securities, financial instruments and other products or services where the price is linked to fluctuations in a stock exchange quotation or index or a financial market rate that the seller or supplier does not control;
   - contracts for the purchase or sale of foreign currency, traveller's cheques or international money orders denominated in foreign currency;

(d) Subparagraph (l) is without hindrance to price-indexation clauses, where lawful, provided that the method by which prices vary is explicitly described.

[1.] OJ No C 73, 24 March 1992, p. 7.
[2.] OJ No C 326, 16 December 1991, p. 108 and OJ No C 21, 25 January 1993
[3.] OJ No C 159, 17 June 1991, p. 34
[4.] OJ No C 92, 25 April 1975, p. 1 and OJ No C 133, 3 June 1981, p. 1.

Chapter Nine

Mistake

INTRODUCTION

When a contract is concluded it may later be evident that one (or both) of the parties entered into the agreement under a mistaken belief about some circumstance, fact or consequence which perhaps induced that person to enter the contract. The range and variety of such mistakes is infinite: the error may relate to the actual terms of the contract or to the results that follow (e.g. the value of the thing bought or sold). The error may be induced by the fraud of the other party or be completely self-induced. The mistake may or may not be known by the other contracting party. The financial consequences of the error will vary in their effect, and the error in question may be a 'one-off' event that could not have been envisaged or a predictable commercial risk.

The resolution of disputes where one party pleads mistake as a factor which should vitiate or modify the contract does not generally take place within any uniform conceptual framework; agreements are not *per se* void or voidable simply because a mistake is shown to have occurred. Rather, the courts tend to confine pleas of mistake within narrow boundaries in order to avoid an apparent contract from falling apart, to encourage the parties to make provision for such errors in their contract, and to avoid having to readjust the interests of the parties if the contract has in part been performed.

Nonetheless, pleas of mistake are successful in a wide variety of situations, where the contractual subject matter never existed or has perished, where the agreement is laced with latent ambiguity and the court cannot identify what has been agreed, or where the error relates to the actual terms of an executed contract and the error of one party is known to the other. Additionally, the courts do resolve disputes by reference to important matters of principle and justice such as the objective behaviour of the parties, which of the parties, if any, was responsible for the mistake, and whether either party could have avoided or mitigated the situation.

Students should pay particular attention to issues of fact, for example are both parties mistaken or is the mistake made by one party only? The jurisdictional aspect is also relevant—is the plaintiff invoking common law or equitable principles? Finally, the remedy sought is all important: the bases upon which rectification and rescission will be awarded, for example, differ substantially, as indeed does the nature of the relief itself.

SECTION ONE—MISTAKE OF LAW

It was the business of the gentlemen who settled their accounts to make themselves acquainted with that law, and to act accordingly. It is well argued, and it is not unsound in principle, that if one man gets hold of money which he ought not to get, he ought to be obliged to pay it back to the party who has paid it to him in his own wrong. But the question here is whether money paid under the circumstances of this case can be recovered back by compulsion of law, and we think it cannot. Our judgment rests on the principle that the money was paid in mistake of law.

Per Whiteside C.J. in O'*Loghlen v O'Callaghan* (1874) IR 8 Cl 116.

Elizabeth Rogers *v* Louth County Council [1981] ILRM 144

The plaintiff claimed the return of a sum of money overpaid to the defendant in redeeming an annuity in respect of a cottage under s. 99 of the Housing Act 1966. The Circuit Court Judge stated a case for the opinion of the Supreme Court as to whether payment by mistake of law was recoverable.

Griffin J.:

. . .

. . . The general rule is usually stated to be that where money is paid under the influence of a mistake, and the mistake is one of fact, an action will lie to recover it back; but that to entitle the plaintiff to recover, the mistake upon which he has acted must be one of fact, not of law. Thus in *Pollock on Contracts*, (13th ed., edited by Professor Winfield), it is stated at p. 378 that 'money paid under a mistake of law cannot in any case be recovered'. Similar statements are to be found in many textbooks. However, the Judicial Committee of the Privy Council held in *Kiriri Cotton Co. Ltd v Dewani* [1960] 2 WLR 127 that a plaintiff may recover money paid on a mistake of law provided that he is not in *pari delicto* with the defendant in mistaking the law. Delivering the advice of the Privy Council, Lord Denning said at p. 133:

> Nor is it correct to say that money paid under a mistake of law can never be recovered back. The true proposition is that money paid under a mistake of law, by itself and without more, cannot be recovered back. James L.J. pointed that out in *Rogers v Ingham*. If there is something more in addition to a mistake of law—if there is something in the defendant's conduct which shows that, of the two of them, he is the one primarily responsible for the mistake—then it may be recovered back. Thus, if as between the two of them the duty of observing the law is placed on the shoulders of the one rather than the other—it being imposed on him specially for the protection of the other—then they are not in *pari delicto* and the money can be recovered back; see *Browning v Morris*, by Lord Mansfield. Likewise, if the responsibility for the mistake lies more on the one than the other because he has misled the other when he ought to know better—then again they are not in *pari delicto* and the money can be recovered back.

This passage was cited with approval by Kenny J. in *Dolan v Neligan* [1967] IR 247, at 260. Again, even where there has been no mistake of fact, a plaintiff may still recover monies so paid in an action for money had and received upon proof that the monies were paid by him involuntarily, that is, as the result of some extortion, coercion or compulsion in the legal sense—see per Windeyer J. in *Mason v New South Wales*, 102 CLR 108, 180. He cannot recover if the payment was made voluntarily. A payment may be said to be voluntary, in this instant, when the payer makes it deliberately with a knowledge of all relevant facts, and either being indifferent to whether or not he is liable in law, or knowing, or having reason to think, himself not liable, yet intending finally to close the transaction—see per Windeyer J. ibid. at 143. Whether the payment has been voluntary in this sense may also be deduced from the relationship of the parties. As Abott C.J. said in *Morgan v Palmer*, 2 B & C 729 at 734:

> It has been well argued that the payment having been voluntary, it cannot be recovered back in an action for money had and received. I agree that such a consequence would have followed had the parties been on equal terms. But if one party has the power of saying to the other, 'That which you require shall not be done except upon the conditions I choose to impose', no person can contend that they stand upon anything like an equal footing.

In such a case, the payment is by no means to be considered to be voluntary—see per McTiernan J. in *Bell v Shire of Serpentine*, (1969) 121 CLR 137.

Applying these principles to the present case, the plaintiff is in my judgment entitled to recover the overpayment of £935.53 made by her. The payment of £1,163 made by the plaintiff was not 'voluntary' in the context aforesaid. The parties were not on equal terms; the defendants had the power, if they thought fit, to withhold permission for the redemption of the annuity; they were however prepared to allow the plaintiff to redeem it, but only on the conditions imposed by them, which included exacting a payment in excess of that permitted by the statute. The plaintiff was not in possession of all the relevant facts, and did not know, nor had she reason to think, that she was not liable to pay the sum demanded by the defendants for the redemption of the annuity. The defendants were in my view primarily responsible for the mistake and the parties were accordingly not in *pari delicto*.
...

(O'Higgins C.J. and Kenny J. concurred.)

Note

In equity a distinction may be drawn between a mistake as to public law and a mistake as to private law.

Cooper v Phibbs (1865) 17 IR Ch R 73

The plaintiff agreed to lease a fishery from the defendant. Unknown to both parties a private Act of Parliament made the plaintiff a tenant for life. The plaintiff sought to avoid their agreement.

Lord Westbury:

A private right of ownership is a matter of fact; it may be the result also of a matter of law; but if parties contract under a mutual mistake and misapprehension as to their relative and respective rights, the result is that the agreement is liable to be set aside as having proceeded upon a common mistake.

SECTION TWO—COMMON MISTAKE

A common mistake will not affect the formation of a contract since the parties are genuinely *ad idem*. However, if it later materialises that they have reached agreement on the basis of some fundamental underlying assumption which is false, consent may be nullified. It is clear that the doctrine applies to situations where the subject matter of the contract no longer exists (*res extincta*), and situations where performance of the contract is impossible because of some physical or legal impossibility (*res sua*). The doctrine may however have a wider operation than this.

Western Potato Co-operative Ltd v Peter Durnan [1985] ILRM 5

The plaintiff contracted to supply seed potatoes to the defendant in order to produce eighty tons of potatoes which were then to be resold to the plaintiff.

Clarke J. stated that since the seed potatoes were not capable of producing the crop because of physical defects in their genetic structure, both parties entered the contract on the basis of a mistaken assumption.

. . . Mistake as to the existence of a fact at the root of the contract or on the basis of an assumption which subsequently proves to be false is dealt with in *Anson's Law of Contract*, (25th ed.), in the light of the House of Lords decision in *Bell v Lever Bros. Ltd* [1932] AC 161, stated to be the leading case on the subject; and, in interpreting the decision, citing Denning L.J. in *Solle v Butcher* [1950] 1 KB 671, at p. 691: 'The correct interpretation of that case, to my mind, is that, once a contract has been made, that is to say, once the parties, whatever their inmost states of mind, have to all outward appearances agreed with sufficient certainty in the same terms on the same subject matter, then the contract is good unless and until it is set aside for failure of some condition on which the existence of the contract depends, or for fraud, or on some equitable ground . . .' And *Anson* notes at p. 287, fn.: 'Mistake can be regarded as a type of "pre-contractual frustration"'. Pursuing the implications of *Bell v Lever Bros. Ltd* in the matter of mistake as to the quality of the thing contracted for, *Anson* at p. 292 cites from Lord Atkin's speech [1932] AC 161, at p. 218 that: 'Mistake as to quality of the thing contracted for raises more difficult questions. In such a case mistake will not affect assent unless it is the mistake of both parties, and is as to the existence of some quality which makes the thing without the quality essentially different from the thing as it was believed to be.' And, under the heading of 'A False and Fundamental assumption', *Anson* at p. 296 states:

> Where the parties contract under a false and fundamental assumption, going to the root of the contract, and which both of them must be taken to have in mind at the time they entered into it as the basis of their agreement, the contract is void. This should not be regarded as a category separate and distinct from those categories of mistake already mentioned, but rather as a more compendious statement of the type of error required. . . . It is not surprising that the strictness of this test has resulted in a dearth of cases on the subject of fundamental mistake.

It seems to me that on the facts of the present case this strict test is fulfilled.

(The contract was held to be void.)

Note

See R. Clark 'Of Potatoes and Pariahs' Ir Jur (n.s.) XIX (1984) 101

Associated Japanese Bank (International) Ltd *v* Credit du Nord SA and another [1988] 3 All ER 902

Under a sale and leaseback scheme the plaintiffs bought precision engineering equipment from a Mr Bennet and leased the same back to him. This transaction was guaranteed by the defendant. Later it materialised that the equipment never existed and Mr Bennet disappeared without meeting his repayments. The plaintiff sought to enforce the guarantee.

The court held that as a matter of construction the guarantee was subject either to an express or an implied condition precedent that there was a lease in respect of existing machines. Alternatively, Steyn J. indicated that he would have been prepared to hold that the guarantee was void for common mistake.

Steyn J.:

The common law regarding mutual or common mistake

There was a lively debate about the common law rules governing a mutual or common mistake of the parties as to some essential quality of the subject matter of the contract. Counsel for CDN submitted that *Bell v Lever Bros Ltd* [1932] AC 161, [1931] All ER Rep 1 authoritatively established that a mistake by both parties as to the existence of some quality of the subject matter of the contract, which makes the subject matter of the contract without the quality essentially different from the subject matter as it was believed to be, renders the contract void *ab initio*. Counsel for AJB contested this proposition. He submitted that at common law a mistake even as to an essential quality of the subject matter of the contract will not affect the contract unless it resulted in a total failure of consideration. It was not clear to me that this formulation left any meaningful and independent scope for the application of common law rules in this area of the law. In any event, it is necessary to examine the legal position in some detail.

The landmark decision is undoubtedly *Bell v Lever Bros Ltd.* Normally a judge of first instance would simply content himself with applying the law stated by the House of Lords. There has, however, been substantial controversy about the rule established in that case. It seems right therefore to examine the effect of that decision against a somewhat wider framework. In the early history of contract law, the common law's preoccupation with consideration made the development of a doctrine of mistake impossible. Following the emergence in the nineteenth century of the theory of consensus *ad idem* it became possible to treat misrepresentation, undue influence and mistake as factors vitiating consent. Given that the will theory in English contract law was cast in objective form, judging matters by the external standard of the reasonable man, both as to contract formation and contractual interpretation, it nevertheless became possible to examine in what circumstances mistake might nullify or negative consent. But even in late Victorian times there was another powerful policy consideration militating against upsetting bargains on the ground of unexpected circumstances which occurred before or after the contract. That was the policy of *caveat emptor* which held sway outside the field of contract law subsequently codified by the Sale of Goods Act in 1893. Nevertheless, principles affecting the circumstances in which consent may be vitiated gradually emerged. The most troublesome areas proved to be two related areas, *viz.* common mistake as to an essential quality of the subject matter of the contract and post-contractual frustration. Blackburn J., an acknowledged master of the common law, who yielded to no one in his belief in the sanctity of contract, led the way in both areas.

In *Taylor v Caldwell* (1863) 3 B & S 826, |1861–73| All ER Rep 24 Blackburn J. first stated the doctrine of frustration in terms which eventually led to the adoption of the 'radical change in obligation' test of commercial frustration in modern law: see *Davis Contractors Ltd v Fareham UDC* |1956| 2 All ER 145, |1956| AC 696; *National Carriers Ltd v Panalpina (Northern) Ltd* |1981| 1 All ER 161, |1981| AC 675. In the field of mistake as to the essential quality of the subject matter Blackburn J. also gave the lead. In *Kennedy v Panama New Zealand and Australian Royal Mail Co. Ltd* (1867) LR 2 QB 580 the issue was whether a contract for the purchase of shares was vitiated by an untrue representation that the company had secured a contract to carry mail for the New Zealand government. The court upheld the contract. In passing it must be noted that the case was decided on a restrictive approach as to the circumstances in which a contract can be rescinded for innocent misrepresentation; that, of course, was remedied in due course by equity. But in the present context the importance of the case lies in the remarks of Blackburn J. about mistakes as to quality (pp 586–590). Given the fact that there was no direct authority on the point (and certainly none which could not be explained on other grounds) he turned to the civil law. He referred to the civilian doctrine of error *in substantia*. That doctrine seeks to categorise mistakes into two categories, *viz.* mistakes as to the substance of the subject matter or mistakes as to attributes (sometimes classified as mistakes in motive). Blackburn J., delivering the judgment of the court, held (p. 588): ' . . . the principle of our law is the same as that of the civil law; and the difficulty in every case is to determine whether the mistake or misapprehension is as to the substance of the whole consideration, going, as it were, to the root of the matter, or only to some point, even though a material point, an error as to which does not affect the substance of the whole consideration.' That test did not avail the plaintiff, for it was held that he got what he bought.

None of the cases between the decisions in *Kennedy v Panama New Zealand and Australian Royal Mail Co. Ltd* and *Bell v Lever Bros Ltd* significantly contributed to the development of this area of the law. But *Bell v Lever Bros Ltd* was a vitally important case. The facts of that case are so well known as to require no detailed exposition. Lever Bros had, in the modern phrase, given two employees 'golden handshakes' of £30,000 and £20,000 in consideration of the early termination of their service contracts. Subsequently, Lever Bros discovered that the contracts of service had been voidable by reason of the two employees' breach of fiduciary duties in trading for their own account. Lever Bros argued that the contracts pursuant to which the service agreements were terminated were void *ab initio* for common mistake, and sought recovery of the sums paid to the employees. The claim succeeded at first instance and in the Court of Appeal but by a three to two majority the House of Lords held that the claim failed. Lord Atkin held: ' . . . a mistake will not affect assent unless it is the mistake of both parties, and is as to the existence of some quality which makes the thing without the quality essentially different from the thing as it was believed to be.' In my view none of the other passages in Lord Atkin's speech detract from the statement of the law. Lord Thankerton came to a similar conclusion. He held that common mistake 'can only properly relate to something which both must necessarily have accepted in their minds as an essential and integral part of the subject matter'.

That seems to me exactly the same test as Lord Atkin enunciated. Clearly, Lord Atkin did not conceive of any difference between his formulation and that of Lord Thankerton, for he observed (|1932| AC 161 227, |1931| All ER Rep 1 32): 'To apply the principle to the infinite combinations of facts that arise in actual experience will continue to be difficult, but if this case results in establishing order into what has been a somewhat confused and difficult branch of the law it will have served a useful purpose.' Lord Blanesburgh's speech proceeded on different lines. It must not be forgotten that the issue of common mistake was only put forward at the eleventh hour. Lord Blanesburgh would have refused the necessary amendment, but he expressed his 'entire accord' with the substantive views of Lord Atkin and Lord Thankerton. The majority were therefore in agreement about the governing principle.

It seems to me that the better view is that the majority in *Bell v Lever Bros Ltd* had in mind only mistake at common law. That appears to be indicated by the shape of the argument, the proposed amendment placed before the House of Lords and the speeches of Lord Atkin and Lord Thankerton. But, if I am wrong on this point, it is nevertheless clear that mistake at common law was in the forefront of the analysis in the speeches of the majority.

The law has not stood still in relation to mistake in equity. Today, it is clear that mistake in equity is not circumscribed by common law definitions. A contract affected by mistake in equity is not void but may be set aside on terms: see *Solle v Butcher* |1949| 2 All ER 1107, |1950| 1 KB 671; *Magee v Pennine Insurance Co. Ltd* |1969| 2 All ER 891, |1969| 2 QB 507; *Grist v Bailey* |1966| 2 All ER 875, |1967| Ch. 532. It does not follow, however, that *Bell v Lever Bros Ltd* is no longer an authoritative statement of mistake at common law. On the contrary, in my view the principles enunciated in that case clearly still govern mistake at common law. It is true that in *Solle v Butcher* Denning L.J. interpreted *Bell v Lever Bros Ltd* differently. He said that a common mistake, even on a most fundamental matter, does not make the contract void at law. That was an individual opinion. Neither Bucknill L.J. (who agreed in the result) nor Jenkins L.J. (who dissented) even mentioned *Bell v Lever Bros Ltd*. In *Magee v Pennine Insurance Co. Ltd* Lord Denning M.R. returned to the point. About *Bell v Lever Bros Ltd* he simply said: 'I do not propose . . . to go through the speeches in that case. They have given enough trouble to commentators already.' He then repeated his conclusion in *Solle v Butcher*. Winn L.J. dissented. Fenton Atkinson L.J. agreed in the result but it is clear from his judgment that he did not agree with Lord Denning M.R.'s interpretation of *Bell v Lever Bros Ltd*. Again, Lord Denning M.R.'s observation represented only his own view. With the profoundest respect to the former Master of the Rolls, I am constrained to say that in my view his interpretation of *Bell v Lever Bros Ltd* does not do justice to the speeches of the majority.

When Lord Denning M.R. referred in *Magee v Pennine Insurance Co. Ltd* to the views of commentators he may have had in mind comments in Cheshire and Fifoot *Law of Contract* (6th ed., 1964) p. 196. In substance the argument was that the actual decision in *Bell v Lever Bros Ltd* contradicts the language of the speeches. If the test was not satisfied there, so the argument runs, it is difficult to see how it could ever be satisfied; see the latest edition of this valuable textbook for the same argument (Cheshire, Fifoot and Furmston *Law of Contract* (11th ed., 1986) pp 225–226). This is a point worth examining because at first glance it may seem persuasive. *Bell v Lever Bros Ltd* was a quite exceptional case; all their Lordships were agreed that common mistake had not been pleaded and would have required an amendment in the House of Lords if it were to succeed. The speeches do not suggest that the employees were entitled to keep both the gains secretly made and the golden handshakes. The former were clearly recoverable from them. Nevertheless, the golden handshakes were very substantial. But there are indications in the speeches that the so-called 'merits' were not all in favour of Lever Bros. The company was most anxious, because of a corporate merger, to terminate the two service agreements. There was apparently a doubt whether the voidability of the service agreements if revealed to the company *at the time of the severance contract* would have affected the company's decision. Lord Thankerton said:

'. . . I do not find sufficient material to compel the inference that the appellants, at the time of the contract, regarded the indefeasibility of the service agreements as an essential and integral element in the subject matter of the bargain.' Lord Atkin clearly regarded it as a hard case on the facts, but concluded 'on the whole' that the plea of common mistake must fail. It is noteworthy that Lord Atkin commented on the scarcity of evidence as to the subsidiaries from the boards of which the two employees resigned. Lord Blanesburgh's speech was directed to his conclusion that the amendment ought not to be allowed. He did, however, make clear that 'the mistake must go to the whole consideration', and pointed to the advantages (other than the release from the service agreements) which Lever Bros received. Lord Blanesburgh emphasised that Lever Bros secured the *future* co-operation of the two employees for the carrying through of the amalgamation. And the burden, of course, rested squarely on Lever Bros. With due deference to the distinguished authors who have argued that the actual decision in *Bell v Lever Bros Ltd* contradicts the principle enunciated in the speeches it seems to me that their analysis is altogether too simplistic, and that the actual decision was rooted in the particular facts of the case. In my judgment there is no reason to doubt the substantive reasons emerging from the speeches of the majority.

No one could fairly suggest that in this difficult area of the law there is only one correct approach or solution. But a narrow doctrine of common law mistake (as enunciated in *Bell v Lever Bros Ltd*), supplemented by the more flexible doctrine of mistake in equity (as developed in *Solle v Butcher* and later cases), seems to me to be an entirely sensible and satisfactory state of the law: see *Sheikh Bros Ltd v Ochsner* |1957| AC 136. And there ought to be no reason to struggle to avoid its application by artificial interpretation of *Bell v Lever Bros Ltd*.

It might be useful if I now summarised what appears to me to be a satisfactory way of approaching this subject. Logically, before one can turn to the rules as to mistake, whether at common law or in equity, one must first determine whether the contract itself, by express or implied condition precedent or otherwise, provides who bears the risk of the relevant mistake. It is at this hurdle that many pleas of mistake will either fail or prove to have been unnecessary. Only if the contract is silent on the point is there scope for invoking mistake. That brings me to the relationship between common law mistake and mistake in equity. Where common law mistake has been pleaded, the court must first consider this plea. If the contract is held to be void, no question of mistake in equity arises. But, if the contract is held to be valid, a plea of mistake in equity may still have to be considered: see *Grist v Bailey* |1966| 2 All ER 875, |1967| Ch. 532 and the analysis in *Anson's Law of Contract* (26th ed., 1984) pp 290–91. Turning now to the approach to common law mistake, it seems to me that the following propositions are valid although not necessarily all entitled to be dignified as propositions of law.

The first imperative must be that the law ought to uphold rather than destroy apparent contracts. Second, the common law rules as to a mistake regarding the quality of the subject matter, like the common law rules regarding commercial frustration, are designed to cope with the impact of unexpected and wholly exceptional circumstances on apparent contracts. Third, such a mistake in order to attract legal consequences must substantially be shared by both parties, and must relate to facts as they existed at the time the contract was made. Fourth, and this is the point established by *Bell v Lever Bros Ltd*, the mistake must render the subject matter of the contract essentially and radically different from the subject matter which the parties believed to exist. While the civilian distinction between the substance and attributes of the subject matter of a contract has played a role in the development of our law (and was cited in the speeches in *Bell v Lever Bros Ltd*), the principle enunciated in *Bell v Level Bros Ltd* is markedly narrower in scope than the civilian doctrine. It is therefore no longer useful to invoke the civilian distinction. The principles enunciated by Lord Atkin and Lord Thankerton represent the *ratio decidendi* of *Bell v Lever Bros Ltd*. Fifth, there is a requirement which was not specifically discussed in *Bell v Lever Bros Ltd*. What happens if the party who is seeking to rely on the mistake had no reasonable grounds for his belief? An extreme example is that of the man who makes a contract with minimal knowledge of the facts to which the mistake relates but is content that it is a good speculative risk. In my judgment a party cannot be allowed to rely on a common mistake where the mistake consists of a belief which is entertained by him without any reasonable grounds for such belief: cf *McRae v Commonwealth Disposals Commission* (1951) 84 CLR 377 at 408. That is not because principles such as estoppel or negligence require it, but simply because policy and good sense dictate that the positive rules regarding common mistake should be so qualified. Curiously enough this qualification is similar to the civilian concept where the doctrine of error *in substantia* is tempered by the principles governing *culpa in contrahendo*. More importantly, a recognition of this qualification is consistent with the approach in equity where fault on the part of the party adversely affected by the mistake will generally preclude the granting of equitable relief: see *Solle v Butcher*.

Note

It should be remembered that the subject matter of the guarantee in this case was Mr Bennet's obligation to the plaintiffs, not the machinery which was the subject matter of the original contract. Thus, this was not a case of *res extincta*. However, the subject matter of the main contract was of fundamental importance to the collateral gurantee and for this reason Steyn J. indicated the guarantee was void under the common law approach to pleas of common mistake.

Eugene P. O'Neill *v* Thomas Anthony Ryan, Declan Ryan and Kevin O'Brien [1991] ILRM 672

The plaintiff instituted proceedings under s. 205 of the Companies Act 1963 against the defendants. He then issued proceedings against a number of parties (including the first defendant) in respect of a series of alleged wrongs including misrepresentation and conspiracy. The plaintiff subsequently sought specific performance of an alleged agreement with the defendants to settle the first dispute. The defendants resisted this claim on the grounds that the agreement had been entered into by mistake. They claimed that the offer to settle was made on the basis that both sets of proceedings would be terminated.

Costello J.:
. . .

There is a category of cases in which it is accepted that there was an offer and acceptance and agreement reached between the parties but in which it is claimed that the parties shared a common mistake which has resulted in the agreement being void. For example where both parties agree on the purchase and sale of a painting believing it to be a Gainsborough and it is subsequently established that this is not so, or where both parties agree on the sale of tenanted property and both believe that the tenant is protected by the Rent Restriction Acts and subsequently ascertain that this is not so, the existence of a valid offer and acceptance is not in doubt and what is in issue is the effect on the parties' contract on what I call a shared common mistake.

. . .

There were a number of earlier cases in which a shared common mistake as to the existence of the subject matter of the contract, enabled the court to declare the contract to be void. Thus an assignment of a life assurance policy was held to be void where it was shown that at its date the person whose life was assured was wrongly assumed by both parties to have been alive, (Scott v Coulson |1903| 2 Ch. 249), and a separation deed was declared a nullity because it was made by the common and shared mistake that the parties were married to each other (Galloway v Galloway (1914) 30 TLR 531). But later cases have shown that the circumstances in which a shared common mistake will nullify a contract are extremely limited. Solle v Butcher |1950| 1 KB 671 was a case of a shared common mistake, both parties believing that a flat had been so extensively reconstructed that it was no longer controlled by the Rent Restrictions Acts as a result of which a rent was agreed that was higher than that which would have been payable had the true position been known. But the tenant failed in his claim to recover the rent he had overpaid on the ground of the common mistake. The law on the subject was stated by Denning L.J. in terms which were approved in a later case as follows at p. 691:

> . . . Once a contract has been made, that is to say, once the parties, whatever their inmost states of mind, have to all outward appearances agreed with sufficient certainty in the same terms on the same subject matter, then the contract is good unless and until it is set aside for failure of some condition on which the existence of the contract depends, or for fraud, or on some equitable ground. Neither party can rely on his own mistake to say it was a nullity from the beginning, no matter that it was a mistake which to his mind was fundamental, and no matter that the other party knew that he was under a mistake. A fortiori, if the other party did not know of the mistake, but shared it.

In most cases, then, a shared common mistake will not result in a void contract. This does not mean however that an injured party is without a remedy. As Solle v Butcher showed the court may in the exercise of equitable jurisdiction set aside an agreement even though it is not avoided by the common shared mistake. Lord Denning expressed the court's equitable jurisdiction as follows at p. 693: 'A contract is also liable in equity to be set aside if the parties were under a common misapprehension either as to facts or as to their relative and respective rights, provided that the misapprehension was fundamental and that the party seeking to set it aside was not himself at fault.'

And in that case the Court of Appeal set aside the lease on terms, the tenant being allowed to surrender the lease entirely or to remain in possession at the rent payable under the Rent Restriction Acts. The court will also grant relief by way of rectification where the parties have reached an agreement but where an error is made in giving effect to the parties' common intention in its written agreement. The general rule is that where there is a common shared mistake in that the written agreement fails to record the intention of both parties the court will order its rectification. Rectification may also be ordered when a party has entered into a written agreement by mistake if he establishes that the other party with knowledge of the mistake concluded that agreement (see Irish Life Assurance Co. Ltd v Dublin Land Securities Ltd |1989| IR 253, 260 and Monaghan County Council v Vaughan |1948| IR 306, 312). And in the exercise of its discretion the court may refuse to make an order for *specific performance* in cases of common shared mistakes. *Grist v Bailey* [1967] Ch. 532 was a case in which both the vendor and purchaser of a tenanted house contracted in the same mistaken belief that the tenancy was protected. When the mistake was ascertained the vendor tried to avoid the contract. The court held that the contract was a valid one but that in the exercise of its discretion it would refuse the purchaser's claim for specific performance and allow the defendant's counterclaim for rescission.

SECTION THREE—MUTUAL MISTAKE

A mutual mistake occurs where each party is mistaken as to the other's intention. For example, a vendor owning two cars intends to sell his 1980 model Porsche. Unknown to him the purchaser believes the vendor to be selling his 1990 model Porsche. The parties are thus bargaining at cross purposes.

Anson's Law of Contract (26th ed.), 268–9

A sells X a piece of china.

(a) X thinks that it is Dresden china. A thinks it is not. Each takes his chance. X may get a better thing than A intended to sell, or a worse thing than he himself intended to buy; in neither case is the validity of the contract affected.

(b) X thinks that it is Dresden china. A knows that X thinks so, and knows that it is not. The contract holds, A must do nothing to deceive X, but he is not bound to prevent X from deceiving himself as to the *quality* of the thing sold. X's error is one of motive alone, and although it is known to A, it is insufficient.

(c) X thinks that it is Dresden china and thinks that A intends to contract to sell it as Dresden china; and A knows that it is not Dresden china, but does not know that X thinks that he is contracting to sell it as Dresden china. A reasonably believes that X is assenting to a sale of china in general terms.

The contract holds. The misapprehension by X of the extent of A's promise, *if unknown to* A, has no effect, unless, as in *Scriven Bros & Co. v Hindley & Co.*, A has caused or contributed to X's misapprehension.

(d) X thinks it is Dresden china, and thinks that A intends to contract to sell it as Dresden china. A knows that X *thinks he is contracting to sell it as Dresden china*, but does not mean to, and in fact does not, offer more than china in general terms.

The contract is void. X's error was not one of judgment as to the quality of the china, as in (b), but was an error as to the nature of A's promise, and A, knowing that his promise was misunderstood, nevertheless allowed the mistake to continue. There can be no contract if A knows that X has accepted his offer in terms different from those in which it was in fact made.

This rule is sometimes known as the rule in *Smith v Hughes* . . .

A. ERRORS OF MOTIVE

Mistakes as to the quality of the item being sold are categorised by *Anson* as errors of motive. Such mistakes will not affect the validity of the contract, even where the mistake is known to the other party.

Smith v Hughes (1871) LR 2 QB 597

The plaintiff offered to sell oats to the defendant, a racehorse trainer. He exhibited a sample which the defendants kept for two days before accepting the offer. The defendant later refused to accept the oats on the ground that they were new and he believed he was buying old oats. The plaintiff sued for damages for breach of contract.

The trial judge left two questions to the jury: first, whether the word 'old' had been used with reference to the oats in the conversation between the plaintiff and the defendant's manager: secondly, whether the plaintiff had believed, or was under the impression, that he was contracting for old oats; in either of which cases he directed the jury to find for the defendant. The jury found for the defendant.

Cockburn C.J.:

. . .

It is to be regretted that the jury were not required to give specific answers to the questions so left to them. For, it is quite possible that their verdict may have been given for the defendant on the first ground; in which case there could, I think, be no doubt as to the propriety of the judge's direction; whereas now, as it is possible that the verdict of the jury—or at all events of some of them—may have proceeded on the second ground, we are called upon to consider and decide whether the ruling of the learned judge with reference to the second question was right.

For this purpose we must assume that nothing was said on the subject of the defendant's manager desiring to buy old oats, nor of the oats having been said to be old; while, on the other hand, we must assume that the defendant's manager believed the oats to be *old* oats, and that the plaintiff was conscious of the existence of such belief, but did nothing, directly or indirectly, to bring it about, simply offering his oats and exhibiting his sample, remaining perfectly passive as to what was passing in the mind of the other party. The question is whether, under such circumstances, the passive acquiescence of the seller in the self-deception of the buyer will entitle the latter to avoid the contract. I am of opinion that it will not.

. . .

I take the true rule to be, that where a specific article is offered for sale, without express warranty, or without circumstances from which the law will imply a warranty— as where, for instance, an article is ordered for a specific purpose—and the buyer has full opportunity of inspecting and forming his own judgment, if he chooses to act on his own judgment, the rule *caveat emptor* applies. If he gets the article he contracted to buy, and that article corresponds with what it was sold as, he gets all he is entitled to, and is bound by the contract. Here the defendant agreed to buy a specific parcel of oats. The oats were what they were sold as, namely, good oats according to the sample. The buyer persuaded himself they were old oats, when they were not so; but the seller neither said nor did anything to contribute to his deception. He has himself to blame.

. . .

If, indeed, the buyer, instead of acting on his own opinion, had asked the question whether the oats were old or new, or had said anything which intimated his understanding that the seller was selling the oats as old oats, the case would have been wholly different; or even if he had said anything which shewed that he was not acting on his own inspection and judgment, but assumed as the foundation of the contract that the oats were old, the silence of the seller, as a means of misleading him, might have amounted to a fraudulent concealment, such as would have entitled the buyer to avoid the contract. Here, however, nothing of the sort occurs. The buyer in no way refers to the seller, but acts entirely on his own judgment.

...

It only remains to deal with an argument which was pressed upon us, that the defendant in the present case intended to buy old oats, and the plaintiff to sell new, so the two minds were not *ad idem*; and that consequently there was no contract. This argument proceeds on the fallacy of confounding what was merely a motive operating on the buyer to induce him to buy with one of the essential conditions of the contract. Both parties were agreed as to the sale and purchase of this particular parcel of oats. The defendant believed the oats to be old, and was thus induced to agree to buy them, but he omitted to make their age a condition of the contract. All that can be said is, that the two minds were not *ad idem* as to the age of the oats; they certainly were *ad idem* as to the sale and purchase of them. Suppose a person to buy a horse without a warranty, believing him to be sound, and the horse turns out unsound, could it be contended that it would be open to him to say that, as he had intended to buy a sound horse, and the seller to sell an unsound one, the contract was void, because the seller must have known from the price the buyer was willing to give, or from his general habits as a buyer of horses, that he thought the horse was sound? The cases are exactly parallel.

The result is that, in my opinion, the learned judge of the County Court was wrong in leaving the second question to the jury, and that, consequently, the case must go down to a new trial.

Blackburn J.:

In this case I agree that on the sale of a specific article, unless there be a warranty making it part of the bargain that it possesses some particular quality, the purchaser must take the article he has bought though it does not possess that quality. And I agree that even if the vendor was aware that the purchaser thought that the article possessed that quality, and would not have entered into the contract unless he had so thought, still the purchaser is bound, unless the vendor was guilty of some fraud or deceit upon him, and that a mere abstinence from disabusing the purchaser of that impression is not fraud or deceit; for, whatever may be the case in a court of morals, there is no legal obligation on the vendor to inform the purchaser that he is under a mistake, not induced by the act of the vendor.

Note

It is clear from the case of *Stapleton v Prudential Assurance Co. Ltd* (1928) 62 ILTR 56 (see p. 513 below) that a self-induced mistake will not ground relief. There, a life assurance contract was valid though the plaintiff entered it under a mistake as to the nature of its terms.

Catherine Reen *v* Bank of Ireland Finance Ltd and Luceys Garage (Mallow) Ltd [1983] ILRM 507

An offer to settle action for breach of contract was made to the plaintiff. Unknown to the plaintiff the settlement did not include provision for all the legal costs involved. Although the defendant's solicitor was aware of this at the time the agreement was made, he did not notify the other party of its mistake. The plaintiff later claimed that this was a case of unilateral mistake which rendered the agreement a nullity.

McMahon J.:

. . .

The other party to the agreement |the defendant's solicitor| must have recognised that there was a possibility that |the plaintiff's solicitor| was making a mistake in overlooking the matter of his client's liability for the bank's costs but in the absence of any mistake as to the terms of the agreement |the defendant's solicitor| in my view had no duty to enquire of |the plaintiff's solicitor| whether the bank's costs had been dealt with. Blackburn J. said in *Smith v Hughes* (1871 LR 6 QB 597) the well known case as to new and old oats where a purchaser was mistaken as to the quality of goods the quality not being a term of the contract: ' . . . a mere abstinence from disabusing the purchaser of that impression is not fraud or deceit; for whatever may be the case in a court of morals there is no legal obligation on the vendor to inform the purchaser that he is under a mistake not induced by the act of the vendor.'

I therefore find that the plaintiff's claim against the motor dealers has been settled for payment by the motor dealers of a sum of £3,000 to include the plaintiff's costs.

B. ERRORS IN SUBJECT

Mistakes as to the subject matter of the contract or the nature of the offer itself may affect the validity of the contract.

If the nature of the mistake is not known to the other party the contract will stand unless the other party knew or contributed to the mistake.

Jeremiah Lucey *v* Laurel Construction Co. Ltd (HC) 18 December 1970, unrep.

The plaintiff entered into a contract to lease property from the defendants, and the defendants agreed to construct a house on this property. Although there was no discussion between the parties as to the length of the site, the site plan indicated that the plot would be 170 feet long. The site actually let was 120 feet in length, although this was later extended by the defendants to 140 feet. The defendants sought to have the lease altered to reflect their intention.

Kenny J.:

. . .

. . . Throughout, Mr Lucey believed that he was entitled to get what was shown on the site map which he signed and he asumed that the 120 feet in length which Laurel originally gave him when they built the wall was what was on the map.

. . .

The court has jurisdiction to rectify a written agreement made between parties only when either there is a mutual mistake made by the two parties in the drafting of a written agreement which is to give effect to a prior oral agreement or when one party sees a mistake in the written agreement and when he knows that the other party has not seen it and then signs the document knowing that it contains a mistake, see the unreported decision of the Supreme Court in *Lowndes v De Courcy* given on 9 April 1960 and the remarks of Lord Justice Denning in *Rove v Pim* |1953| 2 All AER 739 at p. 747:

Rectification is concerned with contracts and documents, not with intentions. In order to get rectification it is necessary to show that the parties were in complete agreement on the terms of their contract but by an error wrote them down wrongly. And in this regard, in order to ascertain the terms of their contract you do not look into the inner minds of the parties—into their intentions—any more than you do in the formation of any other contract. You look at their outward acts, i.e. at what they said or wrote to one another in coming to their agreement, and then compare it with the document which they have signed. If you can predicate with certainty what their contract was, and that it is, by a common mistake, wrongly expressed in the document, then you rectify the document. But nothing less will suffice.

There is a passage in *Crane v Hegeman Harris Co. Inc.* ([1939] 1 All AER 664) which suggests that a continuing common intention alone will suffice but I am clearly of opinion that a continuing intention is not sufficient unless it has found expression in outward agreement. There could be no certainty at all in business transactions if a party who had entered into a firm contract could afterwards turn round and claim to have it rectified on the ground that the parties intended something different. He is allowed to prove, if he can, that they agreed something different . . . but not that they intended something different. (See also *Monaghan Co. v Vaughan* [1948] IR 306).

. . .

In this case however there was not a mutual mistake. Mr Casey [a director of the defendant company] intended to give a site 120 feet in length but did not tell Mr Lucey this and did not think of the measurements shown on the site plan which Mr Lucey subsequently signed. Mr Lucey thought that he was getting what was shown on the site plan. He did not know that the agreement of 1965 or the site plan contained a mistake and he is not making a claim which he knows to be fraudulent.

(Rectification was not allowed.)

Note

This is no longer authoritative on the question of whether a common intention, or a concluded contract, is a *sine qua non* to rectification (see pp 433–6 below).

Mespil Ltd and Aramaic Ltd *v* Francis Capaldi, Philip Capaldi and Elizabeth Bowes [1986] ILRM 373

Certain actions brought by the plaintiffs against the defendants were purported to be settled by their respective counsel. The scope of the written settlement was later disputed by the parties, the defendants believing that the settlement covered all acts in dispute between the parties, and the plaintiffs believing that it covered merely the matters in issue in the proceedings in question.

Henchy J.:

. . .

Having regard to the evidence given in the High Court, I am satisfied that the finding of mutual mistake was fully justified. No blame is to be attributed to the two able and experienced counsel in question who, in the limited time available to them on the morning of the hearing, sought to achieve a binding settlement in accordance with their respective instructions. But, not having time to reduce the terms of settlement to full and unambiguous written expression, the heads of settlement which they authenticated with their signatures were not sufficiently specific to exclude ambiguity. The result was that the two counsel left court that day, each with a genuine but opposite belief as to what the settlement had achieved.

Notwithstanding the finding of mutual mistake, the judge held that the defendants were bound by the terms of the settlement to the extent of having to pay the £21,000 outstanding. This conclusion was reached on the basis of cases which have decided that when a person enters into an agreement, giving the other person the impression that he understands the nature and effect of the agreement, the general rule is that he will not be allowed to say later that he should not be bound by the agreement because he did not at the time understand its import or effect. That is undoubtedly correct law. Business relations would be thrown into undesirable uncertainty if a party to an agreement, who at the time gave no indication that he did not understand what he was doing, could later renounce the agreement on subjective considerations. If he freely and competently entered into the agreement, he will not normally escape being bound by it by saying that he misunderstood its effect.

The position is essentially different when, as is the case here, there was mutual or bilateral mistake as to the true nature of the agreement. Different and more fundamental principles of the law of contract come to be applied in such circumstances.

It is of the essence of an enforceable simple contract that there be a *consensus ad idem*, expressed in an offer and an acceptance. Such a consensus cannot be said to exist unless there is a correspondence between the offer and the acceptance. If the offer made is accepted by the other person in a fundamentally different sense from that in which it was tendered by the offeror, and the circumstances are objectively such as to justify such an acceptance, there cannot be said to be the meeting of minds which is essential for an enforceable contract. In such circumstances the alleged contract is a nullity.

Applying those basic principles to the present case, it is clear that the form of the written consent, viewed in terms of its wording and of the negotiations leading up to it, was capable of justifying the opinion of counsel for the defendants that the settlement was adequate to cover all outstanding complaints between the parties. It is also to be said, on an objective consideration of the relevant circumstances, that counsel for the plaintiffs was justified in thinking that the settlement was limited to the matters in dispute in the two actions then being settled. In those circumstances of latent ambiguity and mutual misunderstanding, it must be held that there was no real agreement between the parties. The two counsel who negotiated the settlement were understandably at cross purposes. The result was that the seeming agreement expressed in the written consent was in fact no agreement. There was a fundamental misunderstanding as to the basis of the settlement. It is clear that the defendants would not have agreed to make the payments required by the settlement if they knew that the plaintiffs could seek to oust them from the premises by means of other proceedings. It is equally clear that counsel for the plaintiffs would not have signed the settlement if he knew it would be treated by the defendants as an absolution of them from all complaints by the plaintiffs. Objectively viewed, the situation justified the misapprehension on each side. The result is that, for want of correspondence between offer and acceptance, no enforceable contract was made. The alleged settlement, whether in the interpretation of the plaintiffs or in that of the defendants, must be held to be nullity.

Note

See also *Clayton Love v B & I Transport* (1970) 104 ILTR 157 (p. 266 above).

Eugene P. O'Neill *v* Thomas Anthony Ryan, Declan Ryan and Kevin O'Brien [1991] ILRM 672.

(Facts on p. 400.)

Costello J.:

. . . I come now to the category of mistake which it is said operated in this case, that is one in which each party is mistaken as to the other's intention, although neither appreciates that he is misunderstood. This can arise, and has here arisen the defendants submit, where one party makes an offer which the other party accepts in a fundamentally different sense from that intended by the offeror. The legal principles to be applied in such cases have been long established and I adopt the following passages of *Chitty on Contracts* (1989 ed.) vol. 1 paras 351 and 352 as a correct statement of the law:

> The intention of the parties is, as a general rule, to be construed objectively. The language used by one party, whatever his real intention may be, is to be construed in the sense in which it would be reasonably understood by the other, or at least in the sense in which a reasonable person would construe it. Nevertheless cases may occur in which the terms of the offer and acceptance suffer from such latent ambiguity that it is impossible reasonably to impute any agreement between them; or it may happen that one party knowingly accepts a promise in different terms from those intended by the other. In such circumstances the mistake may render the contract void.

> In most cases the application of the objective test will preclude a party who has entered into a contract under a mistake from setting up his mistake as a defence to an action against him for breach of contract. If a reasonable man would have understood the contract in a certain sense, then despite his mistake, the court will hold that the mistaken party is bound. But where parties are genuinely at cross purposes as to the subject matter of the contract and the terms of the offer and acceptance are so ambiguous that it is not possible to point to one or other of the interpretations as the more probable, the court must necessarily hold that no contract exists.

It is the principle of law thus formulated that I applied earlier in this judgment. It required me to consider the words used by the defendants' solicitors in their letter of 24 May 1990 and to construe them objectively in the sense in which they would reasonably be understood. In doing so I concluded that they would be reasonably understood as an offer to settle the s. 205 proceedings only and not as an offer to settle those proceedings and the plenary action. It was in this sense that the offer was accepted by the letter of 30 May 1990. The defence of mistake therefore fails as I cannot take into account that the authors of the letter may have intended to make an offer of settlement different to that which a reasonable construction of the words they used disclosed.

There are a number of reasons why the court should adopt this rule. As explained by the Supreme Court:

. . . when a person enters into an agreement, giving the other person the impression that he understands the nature and effect of the agreement, the general rule is that he will not be allowed to say later that he should not be bound by the agreement because he did not at the time understand its import or effect. That is undoubtedly correct law. Business relations would be thrown into undesirable uncertainty if a party to an agreement, who at the time gave no indication that he did not understand what he was doing, could later renounce the agreement on subjective considerations. If he freely and competently entered into the agreement, he will not normally escape being bound by saying that he misunderstood its effect. (*Mespil Ltd v Capaldi* [1986] ILRM 373, 376.)

In addition to the reason there given the rule is required for the proper administration of justice. As explained, a considerable time ago, in *Fry on Specific Performance*, (5th ed.), 765: 'It seems on general principle clear that one party to a contract can never defend himself against it by setting up a misunderstanding on his part as to the real meaning and effect of the contract, or any of the terms in which it is expressed. To permit such a defence would be to open the door to perjury and to destroy the security of contracts (quoted with approval in *Eastes v Russ* [1914] 1 Ch. 468, 480.)'

Furthermore it seems to me that an estoppel arises which precludes an offeror adducing evidence of intention. If an offeror intends his offer in one sense but fails to convey that sense in the words he uses (as objectively determined) and the offeree accepts it in the sense in which the words could reasonably be construed it seems to me that the offeror is estopped from relying on his own error if detriment would thereby be suffered by the offeree. As quite clearly detriment would be suffered by the plaintiff if the defendants for the purpose of showing the parties were not *ad idem* were at liberty to adduce evidence to contradict the sense in which the words in the letter of 24 May 1990 can reasonably be construed, the law should not permit such evidence to be adduced.
. . .

There is another aspect of the principles enunciated in the quotation from *Chitty* to which I should refer. If one party knows that a mistake is made by the offeror in the offer and accepts it with this knowledge the mistaken party may give evidence of what his intention was and the fact that the parties were at cross purposes will mean that the contract was void.

This principle is illustrated by *Hartog v Colin and Shields* [1939] 3 All ER 566. That was a case dealing with the sale of hare skins by the defendant to the plaintiff. In pre-contract negotiations the parties bargained on the basis of the skins being sold at a price per piece. By mistake the defendant eventually offered them at a price based on their *weight*, an offer which the plaintiff accepted. When the defendant ascertained his mistake and refused to deliver the skins he was sued by the purchaser for damages for non-delivery. It was held that the objective test did not apply because the plaintiff must have known that the offer did not reflect the defendant's true intention and that the contract was void.

I draw attention to this principle because it was relevant to know whether the plaintiff's solicitor knew that the defendants had made an error in their letter of 24 May 1990. Had he known that they intended to make an offer to settle both sets of proceedings then the objective test would not apply and the apparent agreement would be declared void. His evidence was therefore relevant to the issues I had to consider and I do not think that by tendering it the plaintiff thereby is precluded from objecting to the relevance of the evidence of the intention of the defendant's solicitors. As he clearly did not know of their intention and could not reasonably have known it the objective test applies.

Having concluded that a valid enforceable contract came into existence I must then consider the plaintiff's remedies. Clearly the plaintiff would be entitled to damages for its breach. He has, however, claimed equitable relief—and order for specific performance. And a question arises as to whether, in the exercise of my discretion, the plaintiff should be afforded this relief. I should make clear however what the issue is. Once it is decided that an enforceable agreement exists by the application of the principles I have noted then equitable principles determine, not the validity of the contract, but the exercise of the court's discretion to grant equitable relief.

There may be circumstances in which the courts may refuse to order the specific performance of a valid contract. The manner in which the court should exercise its discretion has been stated in general terms as follows:

> It cannot be disputed that courts of equity have at all times relieved against honest mistakes in contracts, where the literal effect and the specific performance of them would be to impose a burden not contemplated, and which it would be against all reason and justice to fix, upon the person who, without the imputation of fraud, has inadvertently committed an accidental mistake, and also where not to correct the mistake would be to give an unconscionable advantage to either party. *Burrow v Scammell* (1881) 19 ChD 175, 182.

And in another case, decided at about the same time (*Tamplin v James* (1880) 15 ChD 215) James L.J. (at p. 221) pointed out that: '. . . for the most part the cases where a defendant has escaped on the ground of a mistake not contributed to by the plaintiff have been cases where a hardship amounting to injustice would have been inflicted upon him by holding him to his bargain, and it was unreasonable to hold him to it.'

In the instant case the defendants' solicitors had intended that the offer was to settle the two sets of proceedings, and so the defendants would suffer a hardship by a decision which holds them bound to a different contract. But in deciding whether the plaintiff should be left to a claim for damages rather than obtain an order that the contract be specifically enforced I have against the defendants' hardship to balance the hardship which the plaintiff would suffer if the contract was not specifically enforced. An award for damages would be based on the difference between the actual value of the shares and the price offered and the plaintiff would be left holding shares in a company engaged in business in a highly volatile industry whose value would be liable to fluctuate, and in a company from whose employment he had been dismissed (wrongly he claims) and over which he had no control. The plaintiff in no way contributed to the situation which arose. I conclude that it would not be unjust and unreasonable to require the defendants to carry out their contract and that a refusal of such an order would, on the other hand, result in considerable injustice to the plaintiff.

John O. Ferguson *v* Merchant Banking Ltd [1993] ILRM 136

The plaintiff agreed to sell the defendant lands contained in certain folios consisting of ground rental properties. Unknown to the defendant the folios also included a valuable vacant site. The plaintiff's principal was aware of this error but did not believe the vacant site to be of significant value. When the error was discovered the defendant refused to complete the contract and the plaintiff sued for specific performance. The defendant counterclaimed seeking rectification or alternatively rescission of the contract to give effect to what were claimed to be the true intentions of the parties.

Murphy J.:

...

It does seem, as the defendants contend, that a distinction may be drawn between a contract which may be rescinded by reason of the mutual mistake of the parties thereto and the avoidance of liability where it is established that there never was a *consensus ad idem*. This distinction can be made in theory but in practice it is difficult to imagine a case where there was no *consensus ad idem* to an apparent contract save in the context of some element of unilateral or mutual mistake.

The absence of the necessary meeting of minds is best exemplified by the decision of Kenny J. in *Dore v Stephenson*, (HC) (Circuit Appeal) 24 April 1980, unrep. where the parties had negotiated the sale and purchase of a cafe on the first floor premises on the High Street in Kilkenny without making any provision as to the rights of either party as to access to the premises or ownership of the foyer through which the same were entered.

In the circumstances what Kenny J. said (at p. 10 of the judgment) was as follows:

I think that the nature of the property and particularly the mutual rights in the foyer made it essential that the parties should agree on whether the plaintiff was to remain the owner of the foyer with the defendant having a right for himself and that the customers of the country shop and the occupants of the flat to pass through the foyer to go up the stairs or whether the defendant was to remain the owner of the foyer and the plaintiff and his customers to have a right to pass through it. Until agreement was reached on this point there was in my opinion no consensus between the parties. The court cannot ajudicate on what the contract should have been in relation to this. . . . I do not agree that the property to be sold had been agreed when there was no stipulation whatever about the mutual rights in the foyer which was the all important matter when the ownership of the property was being divided . . . the nature of this property made it essential that there should be agreement about the foyer and, in the absence of this, there was, in my opinion, no enforceable agreement between the plaintiff and the defendant.

In *Mespil Ltd v Capaldi* [1986] ILRM 373 the Supreme Court (per Henchy J.) accepted the proposition: ' . . . that when a person enters into an agreement, giving the other person the impression that he understands the nature and effect of the agreement, the general rule is that he will not be allowed to say later that he should not be bound by the agreement because he did not at the time understand its import or effect.'

In that case proceedings had been compromised on terms agreed between counsel. The agreement, hurriedly reached, expressed the compromise to relate to all matters in dispute between the parties 'in these proceedings' and the respective counsel by whom the agreement was reached had *bona fide* and differing views as to what they intended by the inclusion of that phrase. In the circumstances the Supreme Court held that the parties were at cross purposes and notwithstanding the seeming agreement expressed in the written consent that there was no agreement in fact. There was as, Henchy J. held, a fundamental misunderstanding as to the basis of the settlement. The concept of fundamental mistake or misunderstanding appears clearly too in the decision of the Court of Appeal in England in *Magee v Pennine Insurance Co. Ltd* [1969] 2 All ER 891. In that case an insurance company and a person claiming to be one of their insured compromised a claim on foot of a policy of insurance. After the compromise had been reached the insurance company realised that in fact there was no valid policy in existence at the time. What the court held was that a misunderstanding as to the existence of the policy on foot of which a claim was made and compromised was so fundamental as to entitle the insurance company in equity to rescind the agreement made by way of compromise.

Whether the matter is viewed as fundamental mistake or absence of consensus it seems to me that the defendants in the present case are not entitled to deprive the plaintiff of the benefit of the contract into which he entered. In my view there is no fundamental error and no absence of agreement on any fundamental term. The liquidator of the defendant company agreed to sell the property which was clearly defined in the legal documents executed by him. There was no material provision overlooked or neglected in that documentation. There was no want of consensus and no mistake as to what in substance was being sold. An error or misunderstanding may have arisen as to the extent of the undeveloped property and certainly an error on the part of the vendor as to the potential value thereof. These are not considerations which would give rise to a right of rescission in law or in equity in the absence of some abuse or sharp practice on the part of the vendor.

(Specific performance was granted to the plaintiff.)

Note

If however, the nature of the mistake is known to the other party the contract will be deemed void.

Smith v Hughes (1871) LR 2 QB 597
(Facts on p. 403.)

Blackburn J.:
. . .

But I have more difficulty about the second point raised in the case. I apprehend that if one of the parties intends to make a contract on one set of terms, and the other intends to make a contract on another set of terms, or, as it is sometimes expressed, if the parties are not *ad idem*, there is no contract, unless the circumstances are such as to preclude one of the parties from denying that he has agreed to the terms of the other. The rule of law is that stated in *Freeman v Cooke*.[1] If, whatever a man's real intention may be, he so conducts himself that a reasonable man would believe that he was assenting to the terms proposed by the other party, and that other party upon that belief enters into the contract with him, the man thus conducting himself would be equally bound as if he had intended to agree to the other party's terms.
. . .

. . . I think that, if from that direction the jury would understand that they were first to consider whether they were satisfied that the defendant intended to buy this parcel of oats on the terms that it was part of his contract with the plaintiff that they were old oats, so as to have the warranty of the plaintiff to that effect, they were properly told that, if that was so, the defendant could not be bound to a contract without any such warranty unless the plaintiff was misled. But I doubt whether the direction would bring to the minds of the jury the distinction between agreeing to take the oats under the belief that they were old, and agreeing to take the oats under the belief that the plaintiff contracted that they were old.

The difference is the same as that between buying a horse believed to be sound, and buying one believed to be warranted sound . . .

[1]. 2 Ex at p. 663; 18 LJ (Ex) at p. 119.

Note

It is often difficult to distinguish between a mistake as to identity and a mistake as to quality.

Gill v McDowell [1903] 2 IR 463

A hermaphrodite animal, as well as a bullock and a heifer, were sold together by the defendant to the plaintiff at a fair. Although no warranty was given as to the sex of the hermaphrodite animal, the plaintiff bought in the belief that it was either a bullock or a heifer.

Lord O'Brien L.C.J.:

. . .

I will now consider whether the opinion expressed in Smith v Hughes[1] applies to this case. In that case Smith sued Hughes for the price of oats. The oats were sold by sample. The jury found that the plaintiff believed that the defendant believed he was buying old oats, whereas the oats were in fact new oats. The verdict was set aside, and a new trial granted on the ground that the finding did not go far enough to warrant a verdict for the defendant; that to entitle the defendant to a verdict in the particular case the jury should have found also that the plaintiff believed that the defendant believed that the plaintiff was contracting to sell old oats.

. . .

. . . in my opinion there is evidence that the defendant believed the plaintiff believed that he (the defendant) was contracting to sell two heifers and a bullock, and if the plaintiff did so believe, the case comes, in my opinion, within the doctrine laid down in Smith v Hughes, and the defendant is responsible.

Gibson J.:

. . .

The last point is whether, on the facts found, the case comes within the principle laid down by Blackburn and Hannen, JJ., in Smith v Hughes, which is treated as clear law in the last editions of Leake, Pollock, Anson, and Benjamin. Apart from warranty or condition, a chattel must correspond with the description under which it is sold (Benjamin on Sales, p. 571). Where the seller knows that the buyer is under a mistake as to the subject matter contracted to be sold there is no enforceable contract. The plaintiff bought what he thought the defendant was professing to sell as a heifer. If the plaintiff had expressed his meaning in words, and defendant said nothing, or if the defendant had expressly sold the beast as a heifer, unquestionably there would have been no valid sale. Where nothing is said on either side, if the vendor knows that the purchaser intends a different contract from what he himself contemplates, he cannot by silence impose on the purchaser a contract which he knows the latter never intended to make. Does the principle apply here? Nothing was said as to warranty or description; the animal was there to be examined, and its defect on careful examination would have been ascertained. Does this exclude the application of the principle? I think not. The rule depends on the necessity of intelligent consent to the same contract; and it does not cease to be applicable because the buyer is guilty of some oversight or want of care. The vendor cannot force on the purchaser an article which he knows the latter never proposed to buy.

The principle does not conflict with the maxim caveat emptor, or with the legal right of the vendor to acquiesce in the silent self-deception of the purchaser, where he is under no duty to set him right. It only applies where the parties are not *ad idem* as to the contract proper. The distinction is clearly pointed out in the judgments in *Smith v Hughes* and in the text-books to which I have referred.

. . .

The determining fact in the case is that the animal did not answer the description of bullock or heifer under which description, as part of the contract, the defendant knew the plaintiff was proposing to buy. It was not a case of the animal being a bullock or a heifer with a sexual malformation or deficiency.

I hold that there was no effectual contract; that there was evidence of deceit; and that the plaintiff was at liberty to repudiate the sale.

[1.] LR 6 QB 597.

Note

In this case the majority of the court also held that there was evidence of deceit on the part of the defendant. As a result the defendant was held liable in damages to the plaintiff.

SECTION FOUR—MISTAKE IN EXECUTING A DEED

A. MISSTATED TERM

Where one party at the time of the agreement assents to a term but notices that the other party has misstated the term when executing the contract.

Annie Nolan *v* Allen Percival Graves and Willoughby Hamilton [1946] IR 376

The plaintiff's bid of £5,550 for the first defendant's property at an auction was accepted. However, due to a mistake on the part of the auctioneer, the contract stated the price to be £4,550 and the plaintiff paid a deposit and auctioneer's fees calculated as percentages of this sum. When the vendor refused to complete except at the higher price, the plaintiff sued to recover her deposit and fees. The vendor then counterclaimed to have the memorandum rectified and this new memorandum specifically enforced.

Haugh J:

. . .

. . . In my view, on the facts of this case, an innocent and very careless mistake was made by the auctioneer's servants in the conduct of this sale. The plaintiff immediately realised that a mistake had been made and attempted to take an immediate advantage of it.

. . .

The jurisdiction of the court as regards both rectification and specific performance is a delicate jurisdiction, and it is clear, from the mass of decisions cited before me, that it must be exercised with discretion and care.

. . . Mr Graves had done everything, rightly and properly, as far as he was concerned and as far as he and the plaintiff were concerned. True it is that his agent, or one of his agents, acting for these parties made a careless mistake, and, of course, if that careless mistake in any way contributed to causing her to do anything to her prejudice, I, for one moment, would not let it weigh against her. Of course I do not take that view at all. My view is that the mistake contributed nothing to her misfortunes, because it immediately lay in her power, the moment she saw it, to say to Mr Comyn, or whatever the name of the gentleman was: 'You are mistaken there. That is wrong. It is down as £4,550; it should be £5,550. That is what I bid; ask Mr Hamilton; ask any of the others.' That was the remedy of a person dealing *bona fide* and honestly. I want to make that clear. I do not think this mistake was a cause over which she had no control in respect of the subsequent controversy or the present proceedings. She (and in fact at that time she alone) had that control, because, as I have said, she, of course, knew what the price was and, in a word, could have put Mr Richardson right.

. . .

. . . I cannot see that rescission in itself will afford Mr Graves any remedy or redress for the wrong done to him. It is clear that he could have had that, on the plaintiff's submission, without ever coming into court, or without ever making a counterclaim, by simply handing back her money and having another auction on some other day by Mr Hamilton. I cannot and do not, from his point of view, regard rescission of the contract even at £4,550 without rectification, or by rectifying it to the higher figure and then rescinding it, as being a real remedy at all to the vendor, Mr Graves, though plaintiff's counsel say that that is his only right.

A great number of cases have been cited, some of which conflict. The case of *Craddock Bros v Hunt*[1] decided by the Court of Appeal in England and the case of *The United States of America v Motor Trucks, Ltd*[2] were cited by counsel for the defendants as establishing from their point of view, the principles upon which I should act. Now, these cases have been referred to over and over again; and Dr Baker points out that in *Craddock's* case the contract was an executed contract. It was a case in which the parties had gone into possession of the respective premises, portion of one of which was in dispute, and in which the persons who later became plaintiffs, actually received the rent of the yard in dispute for some years; and it was only when they sent out an architect for some building purpose who measured the yard and compared it with the parcels shown on the plaintiffs' deeds and plans and found that the plaintiffs, Craddock Bros, had never, in fact, under their conveyance got this yard, that the defendant on his part for the first time realised that it was in the conveyance to him, and immediately and for the first time sought to take advantage of what he knew he never got at the sale. He took advantage of the actual conveyance to him and refused any relief, by way of rectification or otherwise, to the plaintiffs who had paid for the yard in question. Dr Baker, with some force, pointed out that that was a case in which, if the court did not rectify the transaction the man who had bought and paid for the disputed plot could not get any other form of relief; and the defendant, who had got possession of the disputed plot, could have retained it, although he was dishonestly in possession of it, and dishonestly making claim to it, even though he knew at the auction that he never got it and only found he had got it when he examined his conveyance. The difference between that case and this case is that there is no similar conclusion between the parties. There has been no conveyance here; no parting by Mr Graves with his houses to the plaintiff, Mrs Nolan. At most there is only a contract made pursuant to the Statute of Frauds and in anticipation of the actual conveyance. For all one knows, this present contract might have broken down through some answers to the requisitions on title, as they sometimes do.

I see the difference between the altered position of the parties in *Craddock's* case against what I might call the unaltered position of the parties in this case. At p. 151 of the report, the Master of the Rolls said: 'I think I am at liberty, at any rate since the Judicature Act, 1873, to express my opinion that rectification can be granted of a written agreement on parol evidence of mutual mistake, although that agreement is complete in itself, and has been carried out by a more formal document based upon it.' Well, in this case I have a written agreement complete in itself, the parties' names are there; it recites the auction, and contains all that it should.

. . .

. . . I cannot, in equity at least, see why he should be in any weaker position by reason of the fact that her conduct is worse than that of making a mere mistake. Why should the principle stated by the Master of the Rolls in *Craddock's* case which I have just quoted, not apply here? Lord Warrington, at p. 159 of the report in *Craddock's* case says, 'The jurisdiction of courts of equity in this respect is to bring the written document executed in pursuance of an antecedent agreement into conformity with that agreement.' Now, that is the jurisdiction—to bring a written document, executed in pursuance of an antecedent agreement into conformity with that agreement. Translate that passage in reference to this case: 'The jurisdiction of courts of equity in this respect is to bring' the memorandum, 'executed in pursuance of' the bidding, 'into conformity with' the bidding. Lord Warrington goes on: 'The conditions to its exercise are that there must be an antecedent contract.' Well, the condition to the exercise of that jurisdiction in this case is that there must have been an antecedent agreement— antecedent to the memorandum. There is an offer to pay £5,500 and the acceptance of that offer. That is the antecedent agreement here. 'And the common intention of embodying or giving effect to the whole of that contract by the writing.' I am satisfied, as I have said before, that the plaintiff's bid was one of £5,550; I am satisfied that her conversation with Mr Houlihan was on the basis of such an offer. I am satisfied that it was the common intention of Mr Richardson, representing the vendor, and of the plaintiff, 'to bring the document into conformity with that agreement' (in the words of the learned Lord Justice in *Craddock's* case); they had 'the common intention of embodying or giving effect to the whole of that contract by the writing.' To put it shortly, these two parties came together with the common intention of reducing to writing a sale at £5,550, 'and', as Lord Warrington continued, 'there must be clear evidence that the document, by common mistake, failed to embody such contract and either contained provisions not agreed upon or omitted something that was agreed upon, or otherwise departed from its terms.' There is cogent, clear and preponderating evidence in this case that this document failed to embody the contract, because the price is different. It contains a provision that has a lower price which is not agreed upon and omits something agreed upon, that is the higher price, and in that respect it departs from its terms. I can only repeat that I do not see why this lady, who is in a worse position than that of making a mistake in common with the defendant, should not be at least in the same position as if common mistake and common mistake only, was the cause of this incorrect document being executed.

The case of the *United States of America v Motor Trucks Ltd*, has been referred to already. That was a case brought by the US government against Motor Trucks Ltd, who were a firm who, during the last war, agreed to make munitions for the American government, subject to hostilities ceasing, when the contract could be terminated. Some time after the armistice the US government did serve notice of termination and certain accounts had to be taken as to what amount of money the US government owed to the defen- dant company. A sum of $1.5 million was agreed upon, which included the sum of $376,000, being the amount which the company claimed in respect of certain lands and buildings which had been erected by them following their activities as munition makers. After deducting large sums from the above total, which the government had already advanced to the appellants, it was agreed that the sum of $637,812 was due.

Now, one has to bear in mind that the sum included the $376,000 for the premises, and it was agreed that a contract should be drawn up.

It was drawn up between the parties and the schedule to the contract failed to include those buildings in the conveyance although the government of the US paid for them; . . .

. . .

. . . The trial judge and the Privy Council later, in effect, ordered rectification and specific performance of the agreement. The learned judge who delivered the judgment of the Privy Council, with clarity, put his views as to the position between the parties in passages which I do not intend to read fully but some of which I shall quote. He says (at p. 200 of the report): 'And indeed the power of the court to rectify mutual mistake implies that this power may be exercised notwithstanding that the true agreement of the parties has not been expressed in writing. Nor does the rule make any inroad upon another principle, that the plaintiff must show first, that there was an actually concluded agreement antecedent to the instrument which is sought to be rectified.' (In this case the antecedent agreement is the bidding.) 'And secondly, that such agreement has been inaccurately represented in the instrument.' (I have found that it has been.) 'When this is proved either party' (be it vendor or purchaser, in the capacity of plaintiff or defendant), 'may claim, in spite of the Statute of Frauds, that the instrument on which the other insists does not represent the real agreement.'

I am satisfied from my reading of these cases that I have jurisdiction to rectify, and ought to rectify, the memorandum in such a way that it will represent the actual contract, voluntarily entered into between the plaintiff and the defendants. The mistake was one over which the plaintiff had full power to remedy, every opportunity and chance of remedying, and it in no way prejudiced her; but she knowingly sought to take advantage of it for the reasons I have stated.

. . .

I shall decree rectification and order that the first figure be changed to the higher sum of £5,550 and any consequential figures that may follow in respect of the deposit and auctioneer's fees. I shall also decree that the balance at the bottom shall be changed from £3,412 to the correct figure that follows from the purchase price being £5,550.

After rectification, there arises the question of the specific performance of the agreement. I rather think that under the circumstances I cannot give specific performance of this agreement because it is my view that the document has been rectified as against the written memorandum. It is only now that it becomes effective as an instrument required by the Statute of Frauds. From now on, at least from the time my order is made up, it remains for the plaintiff to elect whether she will, or will not, perform the sale at the price that she has contracted to buy the premises for. However, I am satisfied on the document that I rectify that the vendor will have the ordinary rights that accrue to him under what I now call the contract that correctly represents the intention of the parties, and for the same reasons I will not decree forfeiture of the deposit.

. . .

[1]. [1923] 2 Ch. 136.   [2]. [1924] AC 196.

Daniel Nolan v Maria Nolan (1954) 92 ILTR 94

A separation deed provided that the plaintiff should pay the defendant 'such sum as will after the deduction of income tax at the standard rate amount to the sum of £15 per week.' The phrase 'at the standard rate' was inserted at the defendant's request in the belief that that it would entitle her to retain refunds of income tax on the sums paid to her. The plaintiff later sought to have the deed rectified claiming that it did not reflect a prior agreement to the effect that any tax refunds would be his property.

Dixon J.:

It had been submitted on behalf of the wife that it was not a case of mutual mistake, susceptible of rectification, and that seemed to be so in a limited sense, in as much as no case of rectification could really be regarded as a case of mutual mistake; if it were there would be no contest, for the parties could rectify the instrument themselves. The whole question whether a mistake was mutual or unilateral was largely one of phrase-ology. The present position was analogous to that with which his Lordship had to deal in *Monaghan County Council v Vaughan* [1948] IR 306 and also, although expressed in a different and probably better way, in the passage quoted by counsel from Kerr on the *Law of Fraud and Mistake*. The basis of the decision in *Monaghan County Council v Vaughan* was that if there were a mistake in a document, in that it did not express the agreement between the parties and one party was not aware of that circumstance while the other party was aware of it, then that was a case of mutual mistake. The party who knew that the expression of the agreement was incorrect could not allege that there was not a mutual mistake because the other party was not aware of that mistake. What happened here came close to misrepresentation or estoppel. Mrs Nolan knew what the agreement was between herself and her husband and what was intended to be recorded in the separation deed. She knew when the alteration was made that the deed might not then correctly express the agreement, nevertheless she decided that she would have the alteration made and, if she could, take advantage of the legal consequences. In those circumstances she could not now be heard to say that there was not a mutual mistake. To hold otherwise would come close to permitting fraud.

Accordingly, his Lordship was of opinion that the plaintiff, the husband, was entitled to have the deed rectified to express what his Lordship was satisfied was the agreement between the parties, and which the husband was under the impression it did record, while the defendant, the wife, knew or suspected that it did not.

B. Error in the preparation

Where the contract is executed and one party later claims that the document does not adequately reflect the bargain struck.

In *Peter Cremer GmbH & Co. v Co-operative Molasses Traders Ltd* [1985] ILRM 564 Costello J. noted: 'Once the terms actually agreed have been established I do not think that an error in the preparation of a formal contract affects the legal consequences'

Fallon *v* Robins (1865) IR Ch R 422

The respondent agreed to let property to the petitioner for several years. Although the petitioner alleged that it was agreed that only he should have a right to determine the tenancy at the end of any third year, the memo-randum was ambiguously worded.

Smith M.R.:

. . .

So far as the petition seeks to reform the agreement, in case the court should consider that the respondent's construction of the clause authorising the determination of the tenancy by the six months' notice therein mentioned is right, I am of opinion that I can make no such decree. The case of *Fowler v Fowler*[1] is a very important case on this subject. The authorities are collected in Lord St Leonards' work on *Vendors and Purchasers*, (14th ed.), 171. A deed which agrees with the intention of one of the parties, although under a mistake as to the other, cannot be rectified.

I am also of opinion (if the petitioner's construction of the agreement be right) that the defence set up by the respondent's counsel during the argument, founded on the case of *Townsend v Stangroom*, and other cases referred to by Lord St Leonards in his work on *Vendors and Purchasers*, p. 160, is not sustainable. A respondent may no doubt insist, in a suit for specific performance, that a term of the agreement was omitted when reducing it to writing; but such a defence must be clearly established. I do not think, having regard to the evidence on both sides, that it has been established that a term in the agreement was omitted.

The affidavit of the petitioner and that of the respondent are in direct conflict. I do not see what right I have to decide, on the conflicting testimony in the case, what the agreement was. That is to be decided by reference to the agreement itself.

[1] 4 De G. & J., 273.

(According to the construction of the clause, Smith M.R. decided that the respondent had no right to determine the term.)

Young *v* Halahan (1875) 9 IR Eq 70

The plaintiff possessed a leasehold interest in certain land which he purported to sell at auction. Because of a mistake the plaintiff failed to notify the purchaser that a portion of the land had already been assigned to a railway company. However, any person viewing the land would have noticed the works constructed by the railway company. The plaintiff sought to have the deed of conveyance rectified to except the property owned by the railway company.

Chatterton V.C.:

. . .

. . . The general rule of this court in reference to the rectification of deeds is that, where it is satisfactorily proved by mutual mistake a deed as executed does not express the real contract of the parties, the court will reform it, and make it conformable to the contract. For this purpose, it is necessary that the mistake should be mutual, the principle on which the equity proceeds being that the parties are to be placed in that position in which both believed that they were placed by the deed. If one party only were under a mistake, while the other without fraud knew what the operation of the deed was, and intended that it should be so, the court cannot interfere, for otherwise it would be forcing on the latter a contract he never entered into, or depriving him of a benefit he had *bona fide* acquired by an executed deed. This rule is not confined to, though probably it originated in, cases upon marriage settlements made in pursuance of previous agreements. It is one, from its nature, of general application.

(Rectification was allowed.)

Note

Where the party pleading mistake shows that, despite the apparent assent of both parties to the written terms of the agreement, the document does not carry into effect 'the contract formula' rectification may be allowed. This is clear from the case of *Coleen Bros v The County Council of the City of Dublin* [1908] 1 IR 503.

SECTION FIVE—MISTAKE AS TO IDENTITY

Cundy v Lindsay (1978) 3 AC 459

The respondents were linen manufacturers in Belfast. A rogue, Alfred Blenkarn living at 37 Wood Street, Cheapside ordered goods from the plaintiffs signing his name to look like 'Blenkiron & Co'. The respondents believing themselves to be dealing with a highly respected firm called 'W. Blenkiron & Son' which actually operated from premises at 123, Wood Street, dispatched the goods addressed to 'Blenkiron & Co' at 37 Wood Street. The goods were later sold to the appellants who were without knowledge of the fraud. The appellants appealed against a decision of the Court of Appeal (overturning Queen's Bench) that no valid contract existed.

Lord Cairns:

. . .

. . . how is it possible to imagine that in that state of things any contract could have arisen between the respondents and Blenkarn, the dishonest man? Of him they knew nothing, and of him they never thought. With him they never intended to deal. Their minds never, even for an instant of time rested upon him, and as between him and them there was no consensus of mind which could lead to any agreement or any contract whatever. As between him and them there was merely the one side to a contract, where, in order to produce a contract, two sides would be required. With the firm of Blenkiron & Co. of course there was no contract, for as to them the matter was entirely unknown, and therefore the pretence of a contract was a failure.

   The result, therefore, my Lords, is this, that your Lordships have not here to deal with one of those cases in which there is *de facto* a contract made which may afterwards be impeached and set aside, on the ground of fraud; but you have to deal with a case which ranges itself under a completely different chapter of law, the case namely in which the contract never comes into existence. My Lords, that being so, it is idle to talk of the property passing. The property remained, as it originally had been, the property of the respondents, and the title which was attempted to be given to the appellants was a title which could not be given to them.

Note

This case was distinguished in the case of *King's Norton Metal Co. Ltd v Eldridge, Merrett & Co.* (1897) 14 TLR 98 where a contract was said to exist. In that case a rogue obtained goods by purporting to be a successful business. The court held that unlike *Cundy v Lindsay* the plaintiffs had not confused the rogue's company with any other existing company.

Phillips v Brooks Ltd [1919] 2 KB 243

A rogue entered the plaintiff's jewellery shop and offered to purchase certain items of jewellery. He wrote a cheque for the sum due saying 'You see who I am, I am Sir George Bullough', and he gave an address in St James' Square. The plaintiff knew that such a person existed and verified in a directory that the address was correct. The plaintiff allowed the rogue to take a ring with him. Later the cheque was dishonoured. In the meantime the ring was pledged to the defendants, a firm of pawnbrokers who advanced money upon it in good faith.

Horridge J.:

. . .

. . . I have carefully considered the evidence of the plaintiff, and have come to the conclusion that, although he believed the person to whom he was handing the ring was Sir George Bullough, he in fact contracted to sell and deliver it to the person who came into his shop, and who was not Sir George Bullough, but a man of the name of North, who obtained the sale and delivery by means of the false pretence that he was Sir George Bullough. It is quite true the plaintiff in re-examination said he had no intention of making any contract with any other person than Sir George Bullough; but I think I have myself to decide what is the proper inference to draw where a verbal contract is made and an article delivered to an individual describing himself as somebody else.

. . . The question, therefore, in this case is whether or not the property had so passed to the swindler as to entitle him to give a good title to any person who gave value and acted *bona fide* without notice. This question seems to have been decided in an American case of *Edmunds v Merchants' Despatch Transportation Co.*[1]

. . .

The following expressions used in the judgment of Morton C.J. seem to me to fit the facts in this case:

> The minds of the parties met and agreed upon all the terms of the sale, the thing sold, the price and time of payment, the person selling and the person buying. The fact that the seller was induced to sell by fraud of the buyer made the sale voidable, but not void. He could not have supposed that he was selling to any other person; his intention was to sell to the person present, and identified by sight and hearing; it does not defeat the sale because the buyer assumed a false name or practised any other deceit to induce the vendor to sell.

Further on, Morton C.J. says: 'In the cases before us, there was a *de facto* contract, purporting, and by which the plaintiffs intended, to pass the property and possession of the goods to the person buying them; and we are of opinion that the property did pass to the swindler who bought the goods.'

. . .

It was argued before me that the principle quoted from Pothier (Traité des Obligations, §19), in *Smith v Wheatcroft*,[2] namely, 'Whenever the consideration of the person with whom I am willing to contract enters as an element into the contract which I am willing to make, error with regard to the person destroys my consent and consequently annuls the contract' applies. I do not think, however, that that passage governs this case, because I think the seller intended to contract with the person present, and there was no error as to the person with whom he contracted, although the plaintiff would not have made the contract if there had not been a fraudulent misrepresentation. Moreover, the case of *Smith v Wheatcroft* was an action for specific performance, and was between the parties to the contract, and had no relation to rights acquired by third parties innocently under the contract, and misrepresentation would have been an answer to the enforcement of the contract. In this case, I think, there was a passing of the property and the purchaser had a good title, and there must be judgment for the defendants with costs.

[1.] 135 Mass. 283, 284.   [2.] 9 ChD 223, 230.

Ingram *v* Little [1960] 3 All ER 332

The plaintiffs advertised their car for sale and a rogue viewed it and agreed to purchase it for £717. When the plaintiffs refused to accept a cheque, the rogue claimed to be a Mr P. G. M. Hutchinson of Stanstead House, Caterham. Having checked the telephone book and ascertained that such a person did exist, the plaintiffs accepted the cheque. The cheque was dishonoured and the car was later sold to the defendant, a *bona fide* purchaser. The plaintiffs' action for conversion succeeded and the defendant appealed.

Sellers L.J.:

. . .

If Hutchinson had paid cash for the car, then it seems clear that there would have been a concluded and unimpeachable transaction in which the identity and financial stability of the buyer would have been of no moment. This is not a case where the plaintiffs wished to withhold their car from any particular person or class of persons. Their desire, made quite obvious in the negotiations, was to ensure that they received payment, and unless cash was paid the person with whom they were dealing was of major importance truly only as to his credit-worthiness and this fact was equally clear to Hutchinson from the course which the negotiations took.

It does not seem to me to matter whether the right view of the facts is, as the judge has held and as I would agree, that there was no concluded contract before the cheque book was produced and before the vital fraudulent statements were made or that there was a concluded contract which Hutchinson at once repudiated by refusing to pay cash and that this repudiation was accepted by the plaintiffs and the transaction was then and there at an end. The property would not have passed until cash had been paid and it never was paid or intended to be paid.

Was there a contract of sale subsequently made which led to the plaintiffs' taking Hutchinson's cheque and in exchange for it handing over the car and its log book? The judgment holds that there never was a concluded contract, applying, as I understand it, the elementary factors required by law to establish a contract. The learned judge, treating the plaintiffs as the offerors and the rogue Hutchinson as the offeree, finds that the plaintiffs in making their offer to sell the car not for cash but for a cheque (which in the circumstances of the Bank Holiday week-end could not be banked before the following Tuesday 6 August) were under the belief that they were dealing with, and therefore making their offer to, the honest Mr P. G. M. Hutchinson, of Caterham, who they had reason to believe was a man of substance and standing. Hutchinson, the offeree, knew precisely what was in the minds of the two ladies, for he had put it there and he knew that their offer was intended for Mr P. G. M. Hutchinson, of Caterham, and that they were making no offer to and had no intention to contract with him, as he was. There was no offer which he, Hutchinson, could accept and therefore there was no contract. The judge pointed out that the offer which the plaintiffs made was one which was capable of being accepted only by the honest Mr P. G. M. Hutchinson, of Caterham, and was incapable of acceptance by the rogue Hutchinson. In all the circumstances of this case I would accept the learned judge's findings. Indeed the conclusion so reached seems self-evident.

Is the conclusion to be held wrong in law? If it is, then, as I see it, it must be on the sole ground that as Hutchinson was present, albeit making fraudulent statements to induce the plaintiffs to part with their car to him in exchange for his worthless cheque and was successful in so doing, then a bargain must have been struck with him personally, however much he deceived the plaintiffs into thinking they were dealing with someone else.

Where two parties are negotiating together and there is no question of one or the other purporting to act as agent for another and an agreement is reached, the normal and obvious conclusion would no doubt be that they are the contracting parties. A contrary finding would not be justified unless very clear evidence demanded it. The unfortunate position of the defendant in this case illustrates how third parties who deal in good faith with the fraudulent person may be prejudiced. The mere presence of an individual cannot, however, be conclusive that an apparent bargain which he may make is made with him. If he were disguised in appearance and in dress to represent someone else and the other party, deceived by the disguise, dealt with him on the basis that he was that person and would not have contracted had he known the truth, then, it seems clear, there would be no contract established. If words are substituted for outward disguise so as to depict a different person from the one physically present, in what circumstances would the result be different?

Whether the person portrayed, by disguise or words, is known to the other party or not is important in considering whether the identity of the person is of any moment or whether it is a matter of indifference.

. . .

It would seem that there is an area of fact in cases of the type under consideration where a fraudulent person is present purporting to make a bargain with another and that the circumstances may justify a finding that, notwithstanding some fraud and deceit, the correct view may be that a bargain was struck with the person present or on the other hand they may equally justify, as here, a finding the other way.

. . .

The question in each case should be solved in my opinion by applying the test which Slade J. applied: 'How ought the promisee to have interpreted the promise?' in order to find whether a contract has been entered into. I am in agreement with the learned judge when he quotes, accepts and applies the following passage from Dr Goodhart's article (LQR 57 (1941) 231):

> It is the interpretation of the *promise* which is the essential thing. This is usually based on the interpretation which a reasonable man, in the promisee's position, would place on it, but in those cases where the promisor knows that the promisee has placed a peculiar interpretation on his words, then this is the binding one. The English law is not concerned with the motives of the parties nor with the reasons which influenced their actions. For practical reasons it has limited itself to the simple question: what did the promisor promise, and how should this be interpreted?

. . .

The legal position is, I think, well illustrated by Dr Goodhart in the article already referred to. There is a difference between the case where A makes an offer to B in the belief that B is not B but is someone else and the case where A makes an offer to B in the belief that B is X. In the first case B does in fact receive an offer, even though the offeror does not know that it is B to whom he is making it, since he believes B to be someone else. In the second case A does not in truth make any offer to B at all; he thinks that B is X, for whom alone the offer is meant. There was an offer intended for and available only to X. B cannot accept it, if he knew or ought to have known that it was not addressed to him.

Devlin L.J. (dissenting):

...

So the first thing for a judge to do is to satisfy himself that the alleged contract has been properly formed, and Dr Goodhart in the article that the learned judge has adopted has shown how easy it is to fall into error if one does not begin with that. There must be offer and acceptance. The offer must be addressed to the offeree, either as an individual or as a member of a class or of the public. The acceptance must come from one who is so addressed and must itself be addressed to the offeror.

...

Before therefore I consider mistake, I shall inquire whether there is offer and acceptance in form. There is no doubt that Hutchinson's offer was addressed to Miss Ingram and her acceptance was apparently addressed to him. But, it is argued, the acceptance was in reality addressed to P. G. M. Hutchinson, who was not the offeror, and therefore no contract was made. There can be no doubt on the authorities that this argument must be settled by inquiring with whom Miss Ingram intended to contract: Was it with the person to whom she was speaking or was it with the person whom he represented himself to be? It has been pressed on us that this is a question of fact and that we ought to give great weight to the answer to it provided by the trial judge. It is, I think, a mixed question.

...

In my judgment the court cannot arrive at a satisfactory solution in this case except by formulating a presumption and taking it at least as a starting point. The presumption that a person is intending to contract with the person to whom he is actually addressing the words of contract seems to me to be a simple and sensible one and supported by some good authority. It is adopted in *Benjamin on Sale* (8th ed.), 102, where two decisions in the US are referred to, *Edmunds v Merchants' Despatch Transportation Co.*,[1] and *Phelps v McQuade*.[2] The reasoning in the former case was adopted by Horridge J., in *Phillips v Brooks Ltd*[3] and the latter case is a decision of the New York Court of Appeals. All these three cases still stand as the law in their respective jurisdictions. *Corbin on Contracts* Vol. 3, s. 602 cites them and a number of others and states the general principles in the US as follows: 'The courts hold that if A appeared in person before B, impersonating C, an innocent purchaser from A gets property in the goods as against B.'

I do not think that it can be said that the presumption is conclusive, since there is at least one class of case in which it can be rebutted. If the person addressed is posing only as an agent, it is plain that the party deceived has no thought of contracting with him but only with his supposed principal; if then there is no actual or ostensible authority, there can be no contract; *Hardman v Booth*[4] is, I think, an example of this. Are there any other circumstances in which the presumption can be rebutted? It is not necessary to strain to find them, for we are here dealing only with offer and acceptance; contracts in which identity really matters may still be avoided on the ground of mistake. I am content to leave the question open and do not propose to speculate on what other exceptions there may be to the general rule. What seems plain to me is that the presumption cannot in the present case be rebutted by piling up the evidence to show that Miss Ingram would never have contracted with Hutchinson unless she had thought him to be Mr P. G. M. Hutchinson. That fact is conceded and, whether it is proved *simpliciter* or proved to the hilt, it does not go any further than to show that she was the victim of fraud. With great respect to the learned judge, the question that he propounded as the test is not calculated to show any more than that. He said: 'Is it to be seriously suggested that they were willing to accept the cheque of the rogue other than in the belief, created by the rogue himself, that he, the rogue, was in fact the honest Mr P. G. M. Hutchinson of the address in Caterham with the telephone number which they had verified?' In my judgment there is everything to show that Miss Ingram would never have accepted Hutchinson's offer if she had known the truth, but nothing to rebut the ordinary presumption that she was addressing her acceptance, in law as well as in fact, to the person to whom she was speaking. I think therefore that there was offer and acceptance in form.

On my view of the law, it therefore becomes necessary to consider next whether there has been a mistake that vitiates the contract.

. . .

In my judgment there has been no such mistake. I shall assume without argument what I take to be the widest view of mistake that is to be found in the authorities; and that is that a mistake avoids the contract if at the time when it is made there exists some state of fact which, as assumed, is the basis of the contract and, as it is in truth, frustrates its object.

. . .

The fact that Miss Ingram refused to contract with Hutchinson until his supposed name and address had been 'verified' goes to show that she regarded his identity as fundamental. In this she was misguided. She should have concerned herself with credit-worthiness rather than with identity. The fact that Hutchinson gave Mr P. G. M. Hutchinson's address in the directory was no proof that he was Mr P. G. M. Hutchinson; and, if he had been, that fact alone was no proof that his cheque would be met. Identity therefore did not really matter. Nevertheless, it may truly be said that to Miss Ingram, as she looked at it, it did. In my judgment Miss Ingram's state of mind is immaterial to this question. When the law avoids a contract *ab initio*, it does so irrespective of the intentions or opinions or wishes of the parties themselves. That is the rule in the case of frustration; see *Hirji Mulji v Cheong Yue S.S. Co.*[5] It is the rule also in a case such as G. *Scammell & Nephew Ltd v Ouston*,[6] where the parties believed themselves to have contracted but had failed to reach agreement on essentials with sufficient particularity. This rule applies in the case of mistake because the reason for the avoidance is the same, viz., that the consent is vitiated by non-agreement about essentials. It is for the court to determine what in the light of all the circumstances is to be deemed essential. In my judgment, in this case Hutchinson's identity was immaterial. The credit-worthiness was not, but credit-worthiness in relation to contract is not a basic fact; it is only a way of expressing the belief that each party normally holds that the other will honour his promise.

[1.] (1883), 135 Mass. Rep. 283.
[2.] (1917), 220 N.Y. 232.
[3.] [1919] 2 KB 243.
[4.] (1863), 1 H & C 803.
[5.] [1926] All ER Rep. 51; [1926] AC 497.
[6.] [1941] 1 All ER 14; [1941] AC 251.

Lewis v Averay [1971] 3 All ER 907

A rogue arranged to view a car advertised for sale by the plaintiff in a newspaper. The rogue tested the car that evening, introducing himself as 'Richard Green' a well known actor. He then offered to buy the car and a price was agreed. The rogue then wrote a cheque intending to take the car immediately. When the plaintiff asked for proof of identity, he was shown a special stamped admission pass to Pinewood Studios bearing a photograph of the rogue and the name 'Richard A. Green'. Satisfied, the plaintiff allowed the rogue take the car away. Later the cheque was proved to be worthless. In the meantime the defendant had purchased the car in good faith from the rogue. The plaintiff brought an action against the defendant for conversion.

Lord Denning M.R.:

. . .

What is the effect of this mistake? There are two cases in our books which cannot to my mind, be reconciled the one with the other. One of them is *Philips v Brooks*[1] where a jeweller had a ring for sale. The other is *Ingram v Little*,[2] where two ladies had a car for sale.

. . .

It seems to me that the material facts in each case are quite indistinguishable the one from the other. In each case there was, to all outward appearance, a contract but there was a mistake by the seller as to the identity of the buyer. This mistake was fundamental. In each case it led to the handing over of the goods. Without it the seller would not have parted with them.

. . .

. . . in *Ingram v Little* the majority of the court suggested that the difference between *Phillips v Brooks* and *Ingram v Little* was that in *Phillips v Brooks* the contract of sale was concluded (so as to pass the property to the rogue) before the rogue made the fraudulent misrepresentation, whereas in *Ingram v Little* the rogue made the fraudulent misrepresentation before the contract was concluded. My own view is that in each case the property in the goods did not pass until the seller let the rogue have the goods.

Again it has been suggested that a mistake as to the identity of a person is one thing; and a mistake as to his attributes is another. A mistake as to identity, it is said, avoids a contract; whereas a mistake as to attributes does not. But this is a distinction without a difference. A man's very name is one of his attributes. It is also a key to his identity. If then, he gives a false name, is it a mistake as to his identity? or a mistake as to his attributes? These fine distinctions do no good to the law.

As I listened to the argument in this case, I felt it wrong that an innocent purchaser (who knew nothing of what passed between the seller and the rogue) should have his title depend on such refinements. After all, he has acted with complete circumspection and in entire good faith; whereas it was the seller who let the rogue have the goods and thus enabled him to commit the fraud. I do not, therefore, accept the theory that a mistake as to identity renders a contract void.

I think the true principle is that which underlies the decision of this court in *King's Norton Metal Co. Ltd v Eldridge, Merrett & Co. Ltd*[3] and of Horridge J. in *Phillips v Brooks Ltd* which has stood for these last fifty years. It is this: when two parties have come to a contract—or rather what appears, on the face of it, to be a contract—the fact that one party is mistaken as to the identity of the other does not mean that there is no contract, or that the contract is a nullity and void from the beginning. It only means that the contract is voidable, that is, liable to be set aside at the instance of the mistaken person, so long as he does so before third parties have in good faith acquired rights under it.

Applied to the cases such as the present, this principle is in full accord with the presumption stated by Pearce L.J. and also by Devlin L.J. in *Ingram v Little*. When dealing is had between a seller like Mr Lewis and a person who is actually there present before him, then the presumption in law is that there is a contract, even though there is a fraudulent impersonation by the buyer representing himself as a different man than he is. There is a contract made with the very person there, who is present in person. It is liable no doubt to be avoided for fraud but it is still a good contract under which title will pass unless and until it is avoided. In support of that presumption, Devlin L.J. quoted, not only the English case of *Phillips v Brooks*, but other cases in the US where:[4] 'The courts hold that if A appeared in person before B, impersonating C, an innocent purchaser from A gets the property in the goods against B.' It seems to me to be right in principle in this country also.

In this case Mr Lewis made a contract of sale with the very man, the rogue, who came to the flat. I say that he 'made a contract' because in this regard we do not look into his intentions, or into his mind to know what he was thinking or into the mind of the rogue. We look to the outward appearances. On the face of the dealing Mr Lewis made a contract under which he sold the car to the rogue, delivered the car and the log book to him, and took a cheque in return. The contract is evidenced by the receipts which were signed. It was, of course, induced by fraud. The rogue made false represent-ations as to his identity. But it was still a contract though voidable for fraud. It was a contract under which this property passed to the rogue, and in due course passed from the rogue to Mr Averay, before the contract was avoided.

Although I very much regret that either of these good and reliable gentleman should suffer, in my judgment it is Mr Lewis who should do so. I think the appeal should be allowed and judgment entered for the defendant.

[1.] [1919] 2 KB 243, [1918–19] All ER Rep 246
[2.] [1960] 3 All ER 332, [1961] 1 QB 31
[3.] (1897) 14 TLR 98
[4.] This quotation is from *Corbin on Contracts*, vol. 3, s. 602

SECTION SIX—REMEDIES

A. RESCISSION

Irish Life Assurance Co. Ltd v Dublin Land Securities Ltd [1989] IR 253
The defendants offered to buy a large portfolio of ground rents owned by the plaintiffs. Due to a mistake by the plaintiff's legal department, certain property in Palmerstown also owned by the plaintiffs was included in the portfolio. Although the auctioneer was aware that the land in Palmerstown was not included, the defendant was not informed of this. The defendants refused to alter the contract when the mistake was discovered. The plaintiff sought rectification of the contract claiming that the contract was signed under a mutual mistake of fact. The defendant counterclaimed for an order of specific performance. The High Court dismissed the plaintiff's claim on the grounds that there was no common intention between the parties to exclude the property in Palmerstown. The plaintiff appealed to the Supreme Court.

Griffin J. noted *obiter* that a claim for rescission of the contract might have been appropriate

In *Monaghan County Council v Vaughan* |1948| IR 306 Dixon J., in contrasting rescission and rectification, stated that where the parties contract under a mutual mistake of fact the agreement is liable to be rescinded at the instance of either party, since in such a case no contract comes into being; likewise, where there is a unilateral mistake, and one of two or more parties is not *ad idem* with the other party or parties, there is no real agreement between them and rescission may also be appropriate.

The plaintiff, however did not desire to rescind the agreement.

John O. Ferguson *v* Merchant Banking Ltd [1993] ILRM 136
(Facts on p. 410.)

Murphy J.:

...

As no claim for rescission was made in *Irish Life Assurance Co. Ltd v Dublin Land Securities* Ltd the Supreme Court judgment provides no guidance as to the circumstances in which that remedy may be available. However, in the High Court Keane J., whilst recognising that it was unnecessary for him to consider in detail a claim of that nature, described as 'apposite' the observations of Russell L.J. in *Riverlate Properties Ltd v Paul* |1975| Ch. 133 at pp 140–41 as follows:

> Is the lessor entitled to rescission of the lease on the mere ground that it made a serious mistake in the drafting of the lease which it put forward and subsequently executed, when:
>
> (a) the lessee did not share the mistake,
> (b) the lessee did not know that the document did not give effect to the lessor's intention, and
> (c) the mistake of the lessor was in no way attributable to anything said or done by the lessee?

> What is there in principle, or in authority binding upon this court, which requires a person who has acquired a leasehold interest on terms upon which he intended to obtain it, and who thought when he obtained it that the lessor intended him to obtain it on those terms, either to lose the leasehold interest, or, if he wised to keep it, to submit to keep it only on the terms which the lessor meant to impose but did not? In point of principle, we cannot find that this should be so. If reference be made to principles of equity, it operates on conscience. If conscience is clear at the time of the transaction, why should equity disrupt the transaction?

> If a man may be said to have been fortunate in obtaining a property at a bargain price, or on terms that make it a good bargain, because the other party unknown to him has made a miscalculation or other mistake, some high-minded men might consider it appropriate that he should agree to a fresh bargain to cure the miscalculation or mistake, abandoning his good fortune. But if equity were to enforce the views of those high-minded men, we have no doubt that it would run counter to the attitudes of much the greater part of ordinary mankind (not least the world of commerce), and would be venturing upon the field of moral philosophy in which it would soon be in difficulties.

Accepting as I do that the foregoing is a correct statement of the law and accepting as I have done that the purchaser believed that 'the development lands' were included in the contract; that he did not appreciate that they were of significant value and was not aware that an error had occurred on the part of the vendor, the claim for rescission too must fail.

B. RECTIFICATION

Rooney & McParland Ltd v Carlin [1981] NI 138

In order to settle an earlier action for nuisance caused by the plaintiffs' quarrying operations, the plaintiffs agreed to buy all the defendant's land in the vicinity of the quarry. The written agreement, however, only provided for the transfer of a portion of the property. The plaintiffs sued for rectification of the agreement claiming that the written agreement did not conform with the prior oral agreement and common intention of the parties. The trial judge granted rectification and ordered specific performance and the defendant appealed.

Lord Lowry:

. . .

. . . it is clear that this is not the straightforward case of a simple written error being made in the reduction of an antecedent concluded verbal agreement to writing in the sense that counsel having knowledge of the existence of the field and having directed their minds to it during negotiations, verbally agreed to include it or exclude it from the settlement. The antecedent concluded verbal agreement did not include the field *as such* for the simple reason that neither counsel knew of the field.

. . .

Have the plaintiffs positively shown that there was an antecedent common intention to include in the settlement what was not recorded in the written settlement and what was not referred to in terms during negotiations? I have used the phrase 'antecedent common intention' because the authorities make it clear it is the *intention* of the parties in the antecedent agreement which must be looked for. In *Joscelyne v Nissen* [1970] 2 WLR 509 there was not a complete antecedent concluded oral contract between the parties but the Court of Appeal held that it was sufficient to find a common continuing intention in regard to a particular provision or aspect of the agreement (confirming the view of Simonds J. in *Crane v Hegeman-Harris Co. Inc.* [1939] 1 All ER 662, 664 and Clausen J. in *Shipley Urban District Council v Bradford Corporation* [1936] 1 Ch. 375) together with some outward expression of accord. The Court of Appeal also noted what Harman L.J. said at p. 470 in *Earl v Hector Whaling Ltd* [1961] 1 Lloyd's Rep. 459:

'As to the facts it does not appear to me that there ever was an oral agreement. There was a common intention and that is enough . . . .' Buckley L.J. said in *Lovell & Christmas Ltd v Wall* (1911)104 LT 85 at p. 93: 'What you have got to find out is what intention was communicated by one side to the other and with what common intention and common agreement they made their bargain.' To find this out, it seems to me that you must look at all the circumstances of the negotiations, at everything touching their course including what was said and done and understood by counsel during them and also at what the respective parties to the action were seeking to resolve and achieve by these negotiations. Then you must ask what would a reasonable third party objectively conclude from all this? Was there a common continuing intention to include the field as part of the settlement, or on the other hand, were the parties so genuinely at cross purposes that it is not possible to impute a common intention or infer the existence of an agreement?

The learned trial judge contemplated only two alternative answers here, the one leading to rectification and the other to rescission, but he did not mention the possibility of a common intention to transfer only the house and garden.

. . .

With respect I consider that the learned trial judge's statement of conclusions wrongly equated motive, object and belief with intention (which in a contract case must crystallise as a *common intention*) . . . I do not see how it could have been the common intention of counsel to transfer a field which neither gave any thought to or knew to be part of the defendant's property.

. . .

. . . What is clear, however, is that both counsel intended the triangle to pass and that they communicated that fact to each other and agreed upon it.

. . .

To describe counsel's misapprehension concerning the extent of the defendant's lands as a 'mutual mistake as to quality', which causes all the defendant's lands to be included in the transaction, is not correct. Cases such as *Bell v Lever Bros Ltd* |1932| AC 161 and *Harris & Jones Ltd v Bunten & Lancaster Ltd* |1953| 1 QB 646 have little to contribute to the solution of the present problem, because their facts are unrelated to the point at issue. They can be pressed into the service of the plaintiffs only by assuming facts in this case which were not found, or open to be found, by the learned trial judge. Likewise, if *Frederick E. Rose (London) Ltd v Wm. H. Pim Jnr & Co. Ltd* |1953| 2 QB 450 were closer to this case, it could only help the defendant. Indeed what is said at pp 461–2 is directly opposed to the plaintiffs' agreement:

> In order to get rectification it is necessary to show that the parties were in complete agreement on the terms of their contract, but by an error wrote them down wrongly; and in this regard, in order to ascertain the terms of their contract, you do not look into the inner minds of the parties—into their intentions—any more than you do in the formation of any other contract. You look at their outward acts, that is, at what they said or wrote to one another in coming to their agreement, and then compare it with the document which they have signed. If you can predicate with certainty what their contract was, and that it is, by a common mistake, wrongly expressed in the document, then you rectify the document; but nothing less will suffice. It is not necessary that all the formalities of the contract should have been executed so as to make it enforceable at law (see *Shipley Urban District Council v Bradford Corporation* |1936| Ch. 375) but, formalities apart, there must have been a concluded contract. There is a passage in *Crane v Hegeman-Harris Co. Inc.* |1939| 1 All ER 662, 664 which suggests that a continuing common intention alone will suffice; but I am clearly of opinion that a continuing common intention is not sufficient unless it has found expression in outward agreement. There could be no certainty at all in business transactions if a party who had entered into a firm contract could afterwards turn round and claim to have it rectified on the ground that the parties intended something different. He is allowed to prove, if he can, that they *agreed something different*: see *Lovell & Christmas v Wall* per Lord Cozens-Hardy M.R., and per Buckley L.J., 104 L.T. 85, 88, 93 but not that they *intended* something different. Per Denning L.J.

The fallacy of the plaintiffs' argument, both in this court and in the court below, lay in the misuse of the phrases 'common intention', 'objective approach' and 'the sense of the promise'. This can readily be appreciated by a study of *Joscelyne v Nissen* |1970| 2 QB 86, in which Russell L.J. (who delivered the judgment of the court) sets out and lucidly explains the guiding principles on which claims for rectification should be decided. The entire judgment is worthy of close attention. I shall simply highlight the points which appear to be decisive of this case.

The plaintiff in *Joscelyne v Nissen* and his wife shared a house with their daughter (the defendant). The plaintiff arranged to transfer his business to the defendant in return for which she was to pay certain household expenses. The written agreement which was to implement this arrangement failed to provide clearly for the payment of household expenses by the defendant. She paid some of these for a while and then gave up. The County Court, which was affirmed by the Court of Appeal, ordered rectification of the written agreement so as specifically to include an obligation by the defendant to pay household expenses.

This was done on the ground that it was not necessary to have a concluded contract antecedent to the written agreement: it was enough if there was a common continuing intention in regard to a particular provision of the agreement (namely, the undertaking of the defendant to pay the household expenses); but an outward expression of accord, as well as convincing proof that the concluded instrument did not represent the parties' common intention, was required.

Russell L.J. clarified certain principles with the aid of *Lovell & Christmas Ltd v Wall*, *USA v Motor Trucks Ltd* |1924| AC 196, *Shipley Urban District Council v Bradford Corporation*, *Crane v Hegeman-Harris Co. Inc.*, *Frederick E. Rose (London) Ltd v William H. Pim Jnr & Co. Ltd* and a number of other authorities:

1. There must be a concluded agreement antecedent to the instrument which is sought to be rectified; but
2. The antecedent agreement need not be binding in law (for example, it need not be under seal if made by a public authority or in writing and signed by the party if relating to a sale of land) nor need it be in writing: such incidents merely help to discharge the heavy burden of proof; and
3. A complete antecedent concluded contract is not required, so long as there was prior accord on a term of a proposed agreement, outwardly expressed and communicated between the parties, as in *Joscelyne v Nissen*.

The statement of principles, while dispensing with the straitjacket of complete antecedent formal contract, continues to insist on the need for communication and outwardly expressed accord between the parties, and in that respect differs from the plaintiffs' argument and from the judgment appealed from. It is in the light of this requirement that one must understand the phrase 'common continuing intention', which means that the parties not only *have* the same intention but *are agreed* upon it. As Denning L.J. said in *Rose v Pim* at p. 461: 'There is a passage in *Crane v Hegeman-Harris Co. Inc.* which suggests that a continuing common intention alone will suffice; but I am clearly of opinion that a continuing common intention is not sufficient unless it has found expression in outward agreement.' On referring to the judgment of Simonds J. in the case cited one sees that he, too, after mentioning continuing common intention, speaks of the parties being 'in agreement' (p. 664E). In *Earl v Hector Whaling Ltd* (noticed by Russell L.J. at p. 97G) Harman L.J. said (at p. 470):

As to the facts it does not appear to me that there ever was an oral agreement. There was a common intention and that is enough. In spite of Denning L.J.'s observations in *Frederick E. Rose (London) Ltd v William H. Pim Jnr. & Co. Ltd*, I think that Clauson J.'s original decision in *Shipley Urban District Council v Bradford Corporation* (as followed by Simonds J. in *Crane v. Hegeman-Harris Company Inc.*) that you do not need a prior contract, but a prior common intention, is right: and here, as it seems to me, both parties always intended that there should be a written agreement, and they came to a common intention as to what that written agreement was to be, or thought they did: and if the evidence satisfied one that that common intention did not appear in the written document, then you would have a case for rectification.'

But the plaintiffs cannot profit from this statement (which itself relies on *Crane v Hegeman-Harris*) in face of Russell L.J.'s further observation at p. 98C: 'In our judgment the law is as expounded by Simonds J. in *Crane's* case with the qualification that some outward expression of accord is required.'

The plaintiffs' argument disregards the following facts:

1. Both counsel intended to transfer a house and garden delineated by the red triangle and comprised in Folio 24184;
2. Neither counsel was even aware of the existence of the field as a part of the defendant's lands;
3. The plaintiffs' counsel did not stipulate to the defendant's counsel that he was contracting to buy the defendant's entire lands in the vicinity;
4. The defendant's counsel did not warrant expressly or by implication that the lands contracted to be sold comprised the defendant's entire lands in the vicinity;
5. The price of £17,000 left out of account the value of the field;
6. The property described in the agreement is precisely that which the parties, through their counsel, agreed to transfer for the price specified in the agreement.

In other words, the plaintiffs' counsel knew exactly what he was buying and the defendant's counsel exactly what he was selling, and the written instrument correctly recorded their agreement, including the price. But the plaintiffs' argument is that because both counsel believed that their agreement accounted for all the defendant's lands in the vicinity and because neither counsel knew that the defendant owned in addition a field worth £800, the written instrument ought to be rectified (although 'altered' would be a better word) so as to include the field with no alteration in the price. Even before one considers the law on the subject, this contention seems scarcely reasonable unless the defendant was guilty of fraud, which is not proved or even alleged.

. . .

. . . there is no justification for saying that the omission of Folios 24369 and 25329 from the agreement was a common mistake in expressing *the terms which had been agreed*. Nor is there evidence to show that Mr Comerton told Mr Cahill that all the defendant's lands adjoining the quarrying business were contained in Folio 24184, or that the defendant mistakenly thought that all his lands (and not merely the house and garden) were comprised in Folio 24184. The question as to what the defendant owned simply never came up between counsel. To say that Folios 24369 and 25329 were omitted by mistake would be correct only if the parties had agreed that the land comprised in those folios was to be sold.

. . .

. . . the mistaken *belief* by Mr Cahill that the house and garden comprised all the defendant's relevant lands and the common intention that the house and garden should pass do not add up to a belief and intention on the part of the plaintiffs that the defendant intended to sell and the plaintiffs intended to buy something *more* than the house and garden.

. . .

Even if both counsel intended all the defendant's property to pass and believed that this was the effect of their agreement, this does not mean that clear terms of agreement ought to be altered so as to make property pass (for the same price) which neither side contemplated as forming part of the subject matter of the sale and of the value and extent of which neither side had any idea.

Accordingly I would allow the appeal, refuse rectification and dismiss the plaintiffs' action.

Irish Life Assurance Co. Ltd *v* Dublin Land Securities Ltd [1989] IR 253
(Facts on p. 427.)

Griffin J.:

. . .

It should be emphasised that the claim of the appellant in this case is solely for rectification of the contract for sale. There is no claim for rescission although it is quite clear, and the learned judge so held, that it was at all times the intention of the appellant to exclude the lands in question. In *Monaghan County Council v Vaughan* [1948] IR 306 at p. 312, Dixon J., in contrasting rescission and rectification, stated that where the parties contract under a mutual mistake of fact the agreement is liable to be rescinded at the instance of either party, since in such a case no contract came into being; likewise, where there is a unilateral mistake, and one of two or more parties is not *ad idem* with the other party or parties, there is no real agreement between them and rescission may also be appropriate. During the course of the hearing of this appeal the court indicated to counsel for the appellant that, even at this late stage, it would consider an application to amend the pleadings to include a claim for rescission of the agreement if the appellant wished to apply for such amendment, in case it should transpire that this was a more appropriate remedy when all the matters in issue were being considered. The appellant however steadfastly refused to apply for any such amendment, as it did not seek nor did it want rescission of the agreement. The appellant's attitude is readily understandable having regard to its reasons for selling the rent roll in the first instance. The appellant was supported in this attitude by the respondent, so that neither party wished to contemplate rescission of the agreement. In these circumstances, this court is solely concerned with the issue of rectification, upon which the claim of the appellant must stand or fall, and I would express no view on the question as to whether the remedy of rescission is appropriate or otherwise.

Rectification is concerned with defects in the recording, not in the making, of an agreement. 'Courts of equity do not rectify contracts; they may and do rectify instruments purporting to have been made in pursuance of terms of contracts', per James V.C. in *Mackenzie v Coulson* (1869) LR 8 Eq. 368 at p. 375.

As a general rule, the courts only rectify an agreement in writing where there has been mutual mistake—i.e. where it fails to record the intention of *both* parties. Although that was the original conception of reformation of an instrument by rectification, nowadays a party who has entered into a written agreement by mistake will also be entitled to rectification if he establishes by convincing evidence that the other party, with knowledge of such intention and mistake, nevertheless concluded the agreement— see Kenny J. in *Lucey v Laurel Construction Co. Ltd* (HC), 18 December 1970, unrep.; *Roberts and Co. Ltd v Leicestershire County Council* [1961] Ch. 555; *Riverlate Properties Ltd v Paul* [1975] 1 Ch. 133. In the last case it was considered by the Court of Appeal that the knowledge of such other party must be such as to involve him in a degree of sharp practice.

. . .

It was formerly considered that the court could not rectify a document in writing unless it was preceded by a concluded oral contract. In taking this view, Kenny J. in *Lucey v Laurel Construction Co. Ltd* cited with approval what was said by Denning L.J. (as he then was) in *Rose v Pim* [1953] 2 QB 450 at p. 461:

> Rectification is concerned with contracts and documents, not with intentions. In order to get rectification it is necessary to show that the parties were in complete agreement on the terms of their contract, but by an error wrote them down wrongly; and in this regard, in order to ascertain the terms of their contract, you do not look into the inner minds of the parties—into their intentions—any more than you do in the formation of any other contract. You look at their outward acts, that is, at what they said or wrote to one another in coming to their agreement, and then compare it with the document which they have signed. If you can predicate with certainty what their contract was, and that it is, by a common mistake, wrongly expressed in the document, then you rectify the document; but nothing less will suffice. [It is not necessary that all the formalities of the contract should have been executed so as to make it enforceable at law (see *Shipley Urban District Council v Bradford Corporation* [1936] Ch. 375) but, formalities apart, there must have been a concluded contract]. There is a passage in *Crane v Hegeman-Harris Co. Inc.* [1939] 1 All ER 662, 664 which suggests that a continuing common intention alone will suffice; but I am clearly of opinion that a continuing common intention is not sufficient unless it has found expression in outward agreement. There could be no certainty at all in business transactions if a party who had entered into a firm contract could afterwards turn around and claim to have it rectified on the ground that the parties intended something different. He is allowed to prove, if he can, that *they agreed something different*: see *Lovell & Christmas v Wall*, per Lord Cozens-Hardy M.R., and per Buckley L.J. (1911) 104 LT 85, 88, 93, but not that they *intended* something different.

Two things need to be noted—the emphasis was Denning L.J.'s; and the sentence inside square brackets was inadvertently omitted from the quotation by Kenny J., presumably in transcription.

Kenny J. does not appear to have been referred to *Joscelyne v Nissen* [1970] 2 QB 86, a decision of the Court of Appeal reported some months before *Lucey v Laurel Construction Ltd*. In *Joscelyne v Nissen* the judgment was delivered by Russell L.J. and was the judgment of the court. In giving judgment he reviewed what he himself described as 'the train of this undoubtedly formidable array of judicial opinion' from the decision of *MacKenzie v Coulson* (one hundred years earlier) onwards. Amongst the cases considered was *Crane v Hegeman-Harris Co. Inc.* [1939] 1 All ER 662 decided by Simonds J. Buckley L.J. at p. 95 (*inter alia*) cited the following passage from the judgment of Simonds J. at p. 664:

> I am clear that I must follow the decision of Clauson J., as he then was, in *Shipley Urban District Council v Bradford Corporation* [1936] 1 Ch. 375, the point of which is that, in order that this court may exercise its jurisdiction to rectify a written instrument, it is not necessary to find a concluded and binding contract between the parties antecedent to the agreement which it is sought to rectify. The judge held, and I respectfully concur with his reasoning and his conclusion, that it is sufficient to find a common continuing intention in regard to a particular provision or aspect of the agreement. If one finds that, in regard to a particular point, the parties were in agreement up to the moment when they executed their formal instrument, and the formal instrument does not conform with the common agreement, then this court has jurisdiction to rectify, although it may be that there was, until the formal instrument was executed, no concluded and binding contract between the parties . . .

Secondly, I want to say this upon the principle of the jurisdiction. It is a jurisdiction which is to be exercised only upon convincing proof that the concluded instrument does not represent the common intention of the parties. That is particularly the case where one finds prolonged negotiations between the parties eventually assuming the shape of a formal instrument in which they have been advised by their respective skilled legal advisers. The assumption is very strong in such a case that the instrument does represent their real intention, and it must be only upon proof which Lord Eldon, I think, in a somewhat picturesque phrase described as 'irrefragable' that the court can act, I would rather, I think say that the court can only act if it is satisfied beyond all reasonable doubt that the instrument does not represent their common intention, and is further satisfied as to what their common intention was. For let it be clear that it is not sufficient to show that the written instrument does not represent their common intention unless positively also one can show what their common intention was.

In *Joscelyne v Nissen* Russell L.J. in considering what was said in *Rose v Pim* said at p. 97: 'The decision in our judgment does not assert or reinstate the view that an antecedent complete concluded contract is required for rectification: it only shows that prior accord on a term or the meaning of a phrase to be used must have been outwardly expressed or communicated between the parties.'

He then referred to the passage from the judgment of Denning L.J. already cited, and said: 'Insofar as this passage might be taken to suggest that an antecedent complete concluded contract is necessary it would be in conflict with the views of both courts in *Crane v Hegeman-Harris* and is not supported by the other judgments' (those of Singleton L.J. and Morris L.J. who were the other members of the court in *Rose v Pim*). And at p. 98 he said:

> In our judgment the law is as expounded by Simonds J. in *Crane's* case with the qualification that some outward expression of accord is required. We do not wish to attempt to state in any different phrase that with which we entirely agree, except to say that it is our view better to use only the phrase 'convincing proof' without echoing an old fashioned word such as 'irrefragable' and without importing from the criminal law the phrase 'beyond all reasonable doubt'.

In *Rooney and McParland Ltd v Carlin* [1981] NI 138 at p. 146 Lord Lowry L.C.J. summarised the principles clarified by Russell L.J. in the following terms:

1. There must be a concluded agreement antecedent to the instrument which is sought to be rectified; but
2. The antecedent agreement need not be binding in law (for example, it need not be under seal if made by a public authority or in writing and signed by the party if relating to a sale of land) nor need it be in writing: such incidents merely help to discharge the heavy burden of proof; and
3. A complete antecedent concluded contract is not required, so long as there was prior accord on a term of a proposed agreement, outwardly expressed and communicated between the parties, as in *Joscelyne v Nissen*.

Like the learned trial judge, I would adopt what was said by Russell L.J. and Lord Lowry L.C.J. as representing the law on the subject in question in this jurisdiction.

Applying those principles to the facts of this case, and bearing in mind the heavy burden of proof that lies on those seeking rectification, the question to be addressed is whether there was convincing proof, reflected in some outward expression of accord, that the contract in writing did not represent the common continuing intention of the parties on which the court can act, and whether the plaintiff can positively show what that common intention was in relation to the provisions which the appellant says were intended to exclude the vacant lands at Palmerstown.

. . .

. . . Like the learned trial judge, I am quite satisfied that the instant case is one of unilateral mistake and not of common or mutual mistake.

Note

This decision was affirmed in *John O. Ferguson v Merchant Banking Ltd* |1993| ILRM 136 and in *R. McD v V. McD* |1993| ILRM 717.

SECTION SEVEN—NON EST FACTUM

The Governors and Company of the Bank of Ireland *v* Patrick McManamy and Others |1916| 2 IR 161

Cherry L.C.J.:

. . .

The action was brought on foot of a guarantee by the defendant to the Bank of Ireland of the debts and liabilities to the bank of the Boyle Co-operative Society, Ltd. The guarantee is in the ordinary form. It is dated 7 April 1911, and signed by all the defendants. Although the document is dated on that day, it was not, as a matter of fact, signed by many of the defendants until long afterwards. Some of the signatures were obtained as late as the year 1913. The whole transaction was, indeed, a very strange one. It appears that there was an earlier guarantee to the bank for £500; that a man named Ahern, who was manager of the Co-operative Society, asked the local bank manager to increase the amount to £1000, which he agreed to do, provided additional names were put to a new contract. The guarantee for £1000 now sued upon was then prepared by the bank's solicitor, and given to Ahern, who took the document away with him, and kept it at the office of the society, where nearly all the defendants signed it, their signatures being witnessed by Ahern.

At the trial Ahern swore that he explained the nature of the document to all the defendants whose signatures he witnessed, and that they all knew the purport of what they were signing. These defendants, on the other hand, positively denied this, and swore that they signed the document without being aware of its nature, and believing it to be of an entirely different character. Most of them swore that they were under the impression, when signing the guarantee, that it was a receipt for manure supplied to them. Others said that they thought that it was a receipt for a dividend, while others said that they thought that it was for milk supplied.

Madden J., at the trial, submitted to the jury a series of questions as to the knowledge and belief of each of the defendants, according to the evidence given by each of them as to his state of mind when signing the guarantee. The jury found in answer to these questions that in the case of all the defendants, save one, the document was signed by them in the honest belief that it was one of an entirely different character from what it really was, and that it was signed by them without negligence on their part. The jury also found that none of the defendants, except

Healy, knew that the document was a guarantee of any debt which the society owed to other persons. But upon one question (No. 7)—'Were the signatures of the defendants obtained by the fraudulent representation of Ahern that the document in question was one which did not involve them in any liability to the plaintiffs in respect of any money due or to become due by the creamery to the plaintiffs?' they disagreed. Upon the findings in answer to the other questions I have mentioned, however, the judge gave judgment for all the defendants (except Healy) as against the plaintiffs; and the question now is, was he right in so doing?

The principle of law which the learned judge evidently had in his mind when framing the questions for the jury, was that laid down by Byles J., in delivering the judgment of the court in the well known case of *Foster v McKinnon*,[1] namely this: That where a party signs a document under a fundamental mistake as to its nature and character, and that mistake is not due to negligence on his part, he is not bound by his signature, upon the ground that there is, in reality, no contact at all binding him on his part. It is true that in *Foster v McKinnon*, and I think also in nearly all the cases which have followed it, the cause of the error has been fraud on the part of some person, but this is due to the fact that such error as to the nature of the document can scarcely ever exist without fraud on somebody's part. The principle of the cases is not, however, that fraud vitiates consent, but rather that there is an entire absence of consent. That the mind of the party who signs under a fundamental error does not go with the act of signing, and that there is consequently no contract at all in fact. The defendant, if he succeeds, does so upon the issue *non est factum*, not upon the issue of fraud, though fraud, as I have said, is usually present, and is generally found by the jury to have existed.

The following passage, frequently quoted with approval from the judgment of Byles J. in *Foster v McKinnon*, at p. 711, clearly lays down the principle in that way:

It seems plain, on principle and on authority, that if a blind man, or a man who cannot read, or who for some reason (not implying negligence) forbears to read, has a written contract falsely read over to him the reader misreading to such a degree that the written contract is of a nature altogether different from the contract pretended to be read from the paper which the blind or illiterate man afterwards signs; then, at least if there be no negligence, the signature so obtained is of no force. And it is invalid not merely on the ground of fraud, where fraud exists, but on the ground that the mind of the signer did not accompany the signature; in other words, that he never intended to sign, and, therefore, in contemplation of law never did sign, the contract to which his name is appended.

This passage plainly indicates that the fundamental error as to the nature of the document which vitiates the contract need not necessarily have been induced by fraud, though in the great majority of such cases fraud is present, and is the cause of the error.

In the recent case of *Carlisle and Cumberland Co. v Bragg*,[2] where the defendant was induced by the fraud of a third party to sign a guarantee to the plaintiff company in entire ignorance of the nature of the document, the decision of the Court of Appeal in England was based upon the same principle. This most clearly appears from the judgment of Kennedy L.J.: 'I entirely assent,' he says, 'to the exposition which has been given of the law with regard to *non est factum* as a defence. The principle involved, as I understand it, is that a consenting mind is essential to the making of a contract, and that in such a case as this there was really no consensus, because there was no intention to make a contract of the kind in question.'

In *Lewis v Clay*,[3] a case tried by Lord Russell of Killowen, where the defendant was induced by a fraudulent misrepresentation to sign a promissory note, judgment was given in his favour upon this ground, though the question of fraud was not left to the jury at all.

1. LR 4 CP 704.   2. [1911] 1 KB 489.   3. 67 LJ (QB) 224.

Saunders v Anglia Building Society [1971] AC 1004
[On appeal from *Gallie v Lee*]

Lord Reid:
. . .

The plea of *non est factum* obviously applies when the person sought to be held liable did not in fact sign the document. But at least since the sixteenth century it has also been held to apply in certain cases so as to enable a person who in fact signed a document to say that it is not his deed. Obviously any such extension must be kept within narrow limits if it is not to shake the confidence of those who habitually and rightly rely on signatures when there is no obvious reason to doubt their validity. Originally this extension appears to have been made in favour of those who were unable to read owing to blindness or illiteracy and who therefore had to trust someone to tell them what they were signing. I think it must also apply in favour of those who are permanently or temporarily unable through no fault of their own to have without explanation any real understanding of the purport of a particular document, whether that be from defective education, illness or innate incapacity.

But that does not excuse them from taking such precautions as they reasonably can. The matter generally arises where an innocent third party has relied on a signed document in ignorance of the circumstances in which it was signed, and where he will suffer loss if the maker of the document is allowed to have it declared a nullity. So there must be a heavy burden of proof on the person who seeks to invoke this remedy. He must prove all the circumstances necessary to justify its being granted to him, and that necessarily involves his proving that he took all reasonable precautions in the circumstances. I do not say that the remedy can never be available to a man of full capacity. But that could only be in very exceptional circumstances: certainly not where his reason for not scrutinising the document before signing it was that he was too busy or too lazy. In general I do not think he can be heard to say that he signed in reliance on someone he trusted. But, particularly when he was led to believe that the document which he signed was not one which affected his legal rights, there may be cases where this plea can properly be applied in favour of a man of full capacity.

The plea cannot be available to anyone who was content to sign without taking the trouble to try to find out at least the general effect of the document. Many people do frequently sign documents put before them for signature by their solicitor or other trusted advisers without making any inquiry as to their purpose or effect. But the essence of the plea *non est factum* is that the person signing believed that the document he signed had one character or one effect whereas in fact its character or effect was quite different. He could not have such a belief unless he had taken steps or been given information which gave him some grounds for his belief. The amount of information he must have and the sufficiency of the particularity of his belief must depend on the circumstances of each case.

Further, the plea cannot be available to a person whose mistake was really a mistake as to the legal effect of the document, whether that was his own mistake or that of his adviser.
. . .

Finally, there is the question as to what extent or in what way must there be a difference between that which in fact he signed and that which he believed he was signing.

. . .

There must, I think, be a radical difference between what he signed and what he thought he was signing—or one could use the words 'fundamental' or 'serious' or 'very substantial'. But what amounts to a radical difference will depend on all the circumstances.

Lord Hodson:

. . .

The plea of *non est factum* requires clear and positive evidence before it can be established. As Donovan L.J. said, delivering the judgment of the Court of Appeal in *Muskham Finance Ltd v Howard* [1963] 1 QB 904, 912: 'The plea of *non est factum* is a plea which must necessarily be kept within narrow limits.' To take an example, the man who in the course of his business signs a pile of documents without checking them takes the responsibility for them by appending his signature. It would be surprising if he was allowed to repudiate one of those documents on the ground of *non est factum*.

. . .

Want of care on the part of the person who signs a document which he afterwards seeks to disown is relevant. The burden of proving *non est factum* is on the party disowning his signature; this includes proof that he or she took care. There is no burden on the opposite party to prove want of care. The word 'negligence' in this connection does not involve the proposition that want of care is irrelevant unless there can be found a specific duty to the opposite party to take care.

Lord Wilberforce:

. . .

How, then, ought the principle, on which a plea of *non est factum* is admissible, to be stated? In my opinion, a document should be held to be void (as opposed to voidable) only when the element of consent to it is totally lacking, that is, more concretely, when the transaction which the document purports to effect is essentially different in substance or in kind from the transaction intended.

. . .

To this general test it is necessary to add certain amplifications. First, there is the case of fraud. The law as to this is best stated in the words of the judgment in *Foster v Mackinnon* (1869) LR 4 CP 704, 711 where it is said that a signature obtained by fraud 'is invalid not merely on the ground of fraud, where fraud exists, but on the ground that the mind of the signer did not accompany the signature; in other words, that he never intended to sign, and therefore in contemplation of law never did sign, the contract to which his name is appended.' In other words, it is the lack of consent that matters, not the means by which this result was brought about. Fraud by itself may do no more than make the contract voidable.

Secondly, a man cannot escape from the consequences, as regards innocent third parties, of signing a document if, being a man of ordinary education and competence, he chooses to sign it without informing himself of its purport and effect. This principle is sometimes found expressed in the language that he is 'doing something with his estate' (*Hunter v Walters* (1871) LR 7 Ch App 75, 88, *Howatson v Webb* [1907] 1 Ch. 537, 547) but it really reflects a rule of common sense on the exigency of busy lives.

Thirdly, there is the case where the signer has been careless in not taking ordinary precautions against being deceived.

. . .

In my opinion, the correct rule is that, leaving aside negotiable instruments to which special rules may apply, a person who signs a document, and parts with it so that it may come into other hands, has a responsibility, that of the normal man of prudence, to take care what he signs, which, if neglected, prevents him from denying his liability under the document according to its tenor. I would add that the onus of proof in this matter rests upon him, i.e. to prove that he acted carefully, and not upon the third party to prove the contrary. I consider therefore that *Carlisle and Cumberland Banking Co. v Bragg* [1911] 1 KB 489, was wrong, both in the principle it states and in its decision, and that it should no longer be cited as an authority for any purpose.

The preceding paragraphs contemplate persons who are adult and literate: the conclusion as to such persons is that, while there are cases in which they may successfully plead *non est factum* these cases will, in modern times, be rare.

As to persons who are illiterate, or blind, or lacking in understanding, the law is in a dilemma. On the one hand, the law is traditionally, and rightly, ready to relieve them against hardship and imposition. On the other hand, regard has to be paid to the position of innocent third parties who cannot be expected, and often would have no means, to know the condition or status of the signer. I do not think that a defined solution can be provided for all cases. The law ought, in my opinion, to give relief if satisfied that consent was truly lacking but will require of signers even in this class that they act responsibly and carefully according to their circumstances in putting their signature to legal documents.

United Dominions Trust Ltd *v* Western B.S. Romanay [1976] 1 QB 513

The defendant agreed to acquire a car on hire-purchase from a firm of car dealers. He signed the plaintiff finance company's standard form in blank, leaving the dealers to fill in the form. The dealers later inserted false figures.

Megaw L.J.:

. . .

For the defendant appellant in this case [counsel], to whose argument I would like to pay tribute, has submitted—and this really is the essence of his submission—that there is a material distinction, for the purpose of the doctrine of *non est factum*, between, on the one hand, the careless signing of a document which is complete when it is signed, as in *Gallie v Lee* [1971] AC 1004 and, on the other hand, the sort of situation that arose in this case, the careless signature of a document in blank; where it is left to somebody (not being an agent of the other party) who is trusted to fill it in in a particular way but who, perhaps from fraud (as it would seem to have been in this case), or perhaps from mistake, in fact fills it in in some different way. [Counsel] argues that the principles which apply to the former type of case do not apply to the latter. With great respect to [counsel's] argument, I am unable to see either that that is right on authority or that it would be acceptable to common sense. Why should a careless act which results in the opposite party being misled as to one's contractual intentions be of less legal significance and effect than a careless act of not reading, or failing to understand, an existing completed document which is put before one to sign?

. . .

. . . On the principle of *Gallie v Lee* [1971] AC 1004 the onus was on the defendant to show that in permitting the intended contractual document to be filled in by the dealer he acted carefully. He wholly failed to do so.

Lloyds Bank plc v Waterhouse [1991] Fam Law 23

The defendant guaranteed his son's loan in the belief that he was doing no more than guaranteeing enough money to enable his son to buy a farm and that his position would be protected by the sale of the land if necessary. In fact the guarantee was in respect of all monies advanced to his son. The defendant was illiterate although the plaintiff was not aware of this. The plaintiff later sued the defendant on foot of the guarantee.

Purchas L.J.:

For the defence of *non est factum* to succeed the father must establish three things: (a) that he was under a disability, in the present case, illiteracy. There was no challenge to that as an existing fact and for that purpose it was irrelevant that the bank was not aware of the disability; (b) that the document which the father signed was 'fundamentally different' or 'totally different' or 'radically different' from the document which he thought he was signing; and (c) that he was not careless or that he did not fail to take proper precautions to ascertain the contents or significance of the document he was signing (see *Saunders (Execution of the will of Rose Maude Gallie, decd) v Anglia Building Society* [1971] AC 1004).

The first requirement above was not in dispute. As regards (b) it was submitted for the father that an 'all monies' guarantee was a fundamentally different document from a guarantee restricted to the money borrowed for the purpose of purchasing the land and that the court ought to accept the father's evidence that he would never guarantee an overdraft, unlimited apart from the overall limit of the guarantee, whether for his son or any other person. In considering that requirement of the defence one must look at the respective liabilities which each type of document would have imposed on the person seeking to take advantage of the defence, rather than what in fact happened subsequently. In his Lordship's judgment the father had established his incapacity and the document which he had signed was different within the concept of *non est factum* from the document which he thought he was signing.

The third aspect of the defence had given his Lordship the greatest difficulty, but after a careful review of the position he had formed the conclusion that there was ample evidence before the judge which would discharge the onus of proof, strict as it was in those particular circumstances, imposed upon the father in order to establish his defence of *non est factum*. Having made exhaustive inquiries of the bank's representatives, and having received answers which gave no hint of any liability beyond guaranteeing the son's indebtedness arising out of the purchase of the farmland and farmhouse, the father was excused from making any specific inquiry about the contents of the guarantee which had been the sole object of his earlier inquiries.

The defence of negligence or breach of duty relied essentially on the answer given by the bank's representative in the context of the father's inquiries about the extent of his guarantee, to the effect that the reason why the bank required a guarantee over and above the value of the land was that it was a matter of the bank's standard practice to obtain security greater than the value of the land being purchased. Even if the defence of *non est factum* were to fail his Lordship would consider that in the conduct of the bank's negotiations with the father, the father was misled by that answer. The father had established, *vis-à-vis* the bank, a defence of negligent misrepresentation and a defence of *non est factum* and, therefore, the appeal should be allowed.

Woolf L.J. (concurring):

said that he had some difficulty in relation to the plea of *non est factum*. He was not satisfied that the consequences to the father of signing the guarantees which he in fact signed when compared with the guarantees he thought he was signing were sufficiently fundamental to fulfil the requirements in *Gallie v Lee* [1971] AC 1004. As regards the third requirement of the defence, he was concerned as to whether the questions asked by the father were sufficient to comply with the obligation he was under if he wished to raise a plea of *non est factum*. For those reasons his Lordship preferred not to determine the appeal on that plea. He preferred to allow the appeal on the basis of misrepresentation—the second ground relied upon by Purchas L.J.— while making no distinction between misrepresentation and breach of duty.

Sir Edward Eveleigh (concurring):

suggested another approach. In all the circumstances, the bank's representative ought to have known that the defendant was not aware of the extent of the obligation in the guarantee; that the defendant would only be willing to undertake a liability which would be largely covered by a sale of the farm, and that the guarantee as printed would lead to the defendant suffering a loss far greater than he was prepared to accept. Consequently, the guarantee was signed under a mistake which was negligently induced by the bank's representative and, therefore, the mistake prevented the signature from having a binding effect *inter partes* (see *Scriven Bros v Hindley & Co.* [1913] 3 KB 564).

Chapter Ten

Misrepresentation

INTRODUCTION

The law relating to pre-contractual misrepresentation, that is, the law which controls the range of reliefs available to a person who has entered into a contract following upon a misstatement made to that person, involves a complex network of common law and contract rules, tortious causes of action and equitable and statutory rules and principles. In this chapter it is hoped to introduce the student to this area of the law. It is essential for the student to grasp that the range of options available to the misrepresentee traverses the broad expanse of civil liability and is not purely contract related.

In general, there have been a significant number of developments within the law of misrepresentation. New tortious (*Hedley Byrne*) and statutory (s. 45 (1) of the 1980 Act) causes of action have become available to the misrepresentee. Several obstacles to the granting of certain remedies such as rescission have been removed either by way of practical decision or under the 1980 legislation. The courts, both in England and Ireland have made considerable efforts to reinterpret the boundary between actionable misrepresentation and non-actionable bare representation (*Dick Bentley*, and the *Bank of Ireland* cases respectively) and the judicial trend is towards creating overlapping or concurrent liability in contract and tort. These trends make good contract drafting more (not less) important, than ever.

SECTION ONE—REPRESENTATION

In order to claim relief, the general rule is that a representation of existing fact must have been made by one party to induce the other party to enter into a contract.

Esso Petroleum Co. Ltd v Mardon [1976] 1 QB 801

The defendant entered into a tenancy agreement with the plaintiffs in respect of a filling station on the basis of a representation made by one of the plaintiffs' agents. This agent, a man with forty years' experience of the trade, calculated that the potential throughput was likely to reach 200,000 gallons by the third year of operation. This figure proved to be over-optimistic because planning restrictions had been overlooked by the agent and the defendant lost his business. He claimed damages for breach of the warranty as to the potential throughput, or alternatively for negligent misrepresentation.

Lord Denning M.R.:

. . .

Now I would quite agree with [counsel for the plaintiff] that it was not a warranty—in this sense—that it did not *guarantee* that the throughput *would be* 200,000 gallons. But, nevertheless, it was a forecast made by a party—Esso—who had special knowledge and skill. It was the yardstick (the e.a.c.) by which they measured the worth of a filling station. They knew the facts. They knew the traffic in the town. They knew the throughput of comparable stations. They had much experience and expertise at their disposal. They were in a much better position than Mr Mardon to make a forecast. It seems to me that if such a person makes a forecast, intending that the other should act upon it—and he does act upon it, it can well be interpreted as a warranty that the forecast is sound and reliable in the sense that they made it with reasonable care and skill. It is just as if Esso said to Mr Mardon: 'Our forecast of throughput is 200,000 gallons. You can rely upon it as being a sound forecast of what the service station should do. The rent is calculated on that footing.' If the forecast turned out to be an unsound forecast such as no person of skill or experience should have made, there is a breach of warranty. Just as there is a breach of warranty when a forecast is made—'expected to load' by a certain date—if the maker has no reasonable grounds for it: see *Samuel Sanday and Co. v Keighley, Maxted and Co.* (1922) 27 Com Cas 296; or bunkers 'expected 600/700 tons': see *Efploia Shipping Corp. Ltd v Canadian Transport Co. Ltd (The Pantanassa)* [1958] 2 Lloyd's Rep. 449, 455–7 by Diplock J. It is very different from the New Zealand case where the land had never been used as a sheep farm and both parties were equally able to form an opinion as to its carrying capacity: see particularly *Bisset v Wilkinson* [1927] AC 177, 183–4.

In the present case it seems to me that there was a warranty that the forecast was sound, that is, Esso made it with reasonable care and skill. That warranty was broken. Most negligently Esso made a 'fatal error' in the forecast they stated to Mr Mardon, and on which he took the tenancy. For this they are liable in damages.

. . .

. . . It seems to me that *Hedley Byrne & Co. Ltd v Heller & Partners Ltd* [1964] AC 465, properly understood, covers this particular proposition: if a man, who has or professes to have special knowledge or skill, makes a representation by virtue thereof to another—be it advice, information or opinion—with the intention of inducing him to enter into a contract with him, he is under a duty to use reasonable care to see that the representation is correct, and that the advice, information or opinion is reliable. If he negligently gives unsound advice or misleading information or expresses an erroneous opinion, and thereby induces the other side to enter into a contract with him, he is liable in damages.

Note

This case was distinguished in the Canadian case of 447927 *Ontario Inc. v Pizza Pizza Ltd* (1987) 44 DLR (4th) 366 affd. (1990) 64 DLR (4th) 160. The plaintiff claimed to have entered a franchise agreement with the defendant franchisor, on the basis of representations made by the defendant's agent to the effect that, properly managed, the franchise could enjoy possibly average sales. When sales fell below average the plaintiff sought damages for *inter alia* misrepresentation and breach of warranty.

Anderson J.:

. . .

Based on *Esso* and *Hedley Byrne*, I am prepared to conclude that, the defendant having held itself out as having special expertise in the operation of such franchise business as those with which the action is concerned, the relationship between the defendant and the plaintiff in the pre-contractual negotiations was such as to give rise to a duty of care. I am also prepared to conclude that the representation made by Davis as to the potential of the site was an inducement to the plaintiff in entering into the franchise agreement. I think what was said by Davis bears a reasonable analogy to what was said by the plaintiff's representative in *Esso*. In *Esso* the phrases 'negligent representation' and 'negligent misrepresentation' are used as though they were interchangeable. With great deference to the learned judges of the Court of Appeal, I think that speaking precisely the appropriate phrase is 'negligent misrepresentation', in other words, the proper connotation is that the words spoken were not true. There then remains the further question of whether they were spoken negligently. In my view, the plaintiff in the case at bar has difficulty in both aspects.

. . .

. . . I could not find on the evidence that, when Davis said what he did say in May and June of 1980, that what he said was untrue.

In view of that conclusion, it may not be essential, but I consider it appropriate to consider whether there was negligence. It is in this area that there is a conspicuous variance between the facts in *Esso* and the facts in the case at bar.

To return to *Esso* for the moment, and to consider the facts in that case, the potential throughput for the station had been estimated by its representatives predicated upon a certain anticipated design. As events developed, the planning authorities would not permit construction according to that design, and the final layout was such that the potential of the station was materially reduced. No new calculation was made by *Esso* based on the altered design. This was described by the trial judge, Lawson J. ([1975] QB 819), as a 'fatal error'. On this point a paragraph from the judgment of Lord Denning M.R., at pp 814–5, is appropriate:

> Now at this point Esso made an error which the judge described as a 'fatal error'. They did not revise their original estimate which they had made in 1961. They still assessed the e.a.c. (estimated annual consumption) of petrol at 200,000 gallons. Whereas they should have made a re-appraisal in the light of the building being now 'back to front'. This adversely affected the site's potential: because passing traffic could not see the station. It would reduce the throughput greatly. The judge found that this 'fatal error' was due to want of care on the part of Esso. There can be no doubt about it.

There is simply no such error demonstrated on the evidence in the case at bar.

. . .

In my view, the plaintiff has failed to establish misrepresentation and has failed to establish negligence.

. . .

The agreement contains an exclusionary clause in the following terms:

22. No Warranty
The franchisor makes and has made no warranties, inducements, promises or representations to the franchisee respecting the subject matter of this agreement, except as may be expressly stated in this agreement, or is otherwise stated in writing in a document executed by the franchisor and the franchisee and has made

no representations to the franchisee in respect of income or profit to be derived by the franchisee pursuant to this agreement.

This clause must be considered in deciding whether a warranty should be found (quite apart from any result the clause might have upon the right to enforce a warranty, if one were found). It seems to me more difficult to conclude that a collateral oral warranty was intended, when, after it was alleged to have been made, a formal written agreement was submitted for consideration by the plaintiff, was negotiated and amended, and ultimately executed, containing a clause flatly asserting that no warranty had been made. It is significant that in _Esso_ the agreement contained no such clause.

Smyth v Lynn (1954) 85 ILTR 57

A property which was advertised as being 'in excellent structural and decorative repair' was auctioned. The plaintiff was successful in the auction outbidding the defendant. Six weeks later the plaintiff advertised the property for sale by auction again, using the same advertisement. This time the property was knocked down to the defendant. Upon inspecting the house the defendant discovered extensive woodworm infestation, and refused to complete. The plaintiff sued for specific performance.

Curran J.:

The principles underlying the contentions of counsel and what are the relevant inquiries in a case such as the present are discussed in the judgment of the Privy Council in the case of _Bisset v Wilkinson & Anor_, |1927| AC 177, in which a vendor of land in New Zealand brought an action to recover under the contract. The purchaser claimed to rescind the contract on the ground of the falseness of a statement as to the carrying capacity of the land for sheep. The headnote of this case contains the following proposition: ' . . . When it is sought to rescind a contract on the ground of the falseness of a statement of opinion by which it was induced, it must be enquired what was the meaning of the statement made, and whether it was true. Relevant to those inquiries are, the material facts of the transaction, the knowledge of the parties, the words used, and the actual condition of the subject matter.'

It was held, on the evidence, applying the above considerations, that the statement was merely of an opinion which the vendor honestly held; and accordingly that the defence failed, and the judgment of the Court of Appeal was reversed.

The learned judge who tried the action, (Sim J.) based his judgment in favour of the appellant upon the conclusions at which he arrived upon his examination of the evidence, firstly, that the representation made by the plaintiff was a representation only of his opinion of the capacity of the farm, not a representation of what that capacity in fact was; and secondly, that this representation of opinion was honestly made by the appellant. By these conclusions the whole case of misrepresentation was disposed of and the charge of fraud was specifically negatived. At p. 181 Lord Merivale says:

In an action for rescission, as in an action for specific performance of an executory contract, when misrepresentation repudiates the contract, it is, of course, essential to ascertain whether that which is relied upon is representation of fact, or a statement of opinion, since an erroneous opinion stated by the party affirming the contract, though it may have been relied upon and induced the contract on the part of the party who seeks rescission, gives no title to relief unless fraud is established.

The learned judge then cited _Karberg's_ case |1892| 3 Ch. 1. and _Smith v Land and House Property Corp._ (1884) 28 ChD 7. In _Karberg's_ case the test used to ascertain whether a representation was one of opinion or belief, was: 'Was the statement of expectation a statement of things not really expected?' In *Smith v Land and House Property Corp.* a tenant was described as 'a most desirable tenant'. This description was held by the Court of Appeal to be a misrepresentation of fact, which, without proof of fraud, disentitled the vendor to specific performance of the contract. In *Smith v Chadwick* (1884) 9 App Cas 187; (1882) 20 ChD 27, the words under consideration involved an inquiry in relation to the sale of an industrial concern. The question was, was a statement of 'the present value of the turnover or output' a statement of fact that the produce of the works was of the amount mentioned or a statement that the productive power of the works was estimated at so much. The words were held to be capable of the second of these meanings. The decisive enquiries came to be: what meaning was actually conveyed to the party complaining; was he deceived, and, as the action was based on a charge of fraud, was the statement in question made fraudulently?

I now proceed to consider the application of the foregoing principles to the present case. The advertisement contains statements which are undoubtedly statements of fact such as 'the property is brick-built, pebble-dashed and slated.' No question of standard or degree enters into these statements. When the advertisement goes on, however, to state that the property is 'in excellent structural and decorative repair and ready for immediate owner occupation' one is forced with the question 'What standard has the person making these statements applied?'

It is my view that the statements referred to are expressions of opinion, and that the opinions expressed are erroneous. Was the position of the parties such that, nevertheless, those expressions of opinion constituted statements of fact? Both parties inspected the premises prior to the auction on 11 March 1949, when the plaintiff purchased the property. It is clear that neither of them had discovered the woodworm infestation before that date. It is suggested that the plaintiff either personally or by her agents had discovered the woodworm infestation after the first and before the second sale. On the evidence before me I find it difficult to believe that the plaintiff had discovered the woodworm prior to the execution of the assignment of 2 April, or prior to the payment of the purchase money on 11 or 12 April.

It is not my view that the words used in the advertisement were apt to describe the actual condition of the premises. The law gives no special sanctity to statements contained in an advertisement for the sale of property. They may, for example, be made the subject of proceedings based upon misrepresentation or may be relied upon as grounds for rescission of a contract or in answer to a claim for specific performance— provided the necessary elements are present. Such advertisements, however, must be looked at in their true perspective. They do not purport to be detailed reports by experts as to the condition of the property to be sold. It is common knowledge that the purpose of such advertisements is to draw attention to the good points of the property, and that one usually finds in such advertisements rather flourishing statements.

In my opinion the defendant is not the type of person to rely on 'Auctioneers' encomiums.' There is something to be said for the contention that the defendant placed more reliance upon the description of the property in the second advertisement by reason of the fact that the plaintiff was reselling the property so soon after she had purchased it. I am inclined to the view that the statement in the advertisement assumed a more positive importance in the defendant's mind after his discovery of the woodworm and when he came to consider with his advisers what grounds he had for getting out of his contract.

On the evidence I am satisfied that the statements complained of did not in any positive sense induce the defendant to purchase or contribute to the inducement of the defendant. If I were satisfied that the defendant was so induced or if I had a reasonable doubt as to whether he was so induced or not I would find it necessary to give further consideration to the question as to whether specific performance of the contract should be granted. In all the circumstances of the case the plaintiff is entitled to specific performance of the contract. This may be a hardship to the defendant, but that, by itself, is not a ground for refusing the enforcement of the contract.

Note

In *Doolan v Murray, Murray, Murray Cheevers, Aziz and Dun Laoghaire Corporation* (HC), 21 December 1993, unrep., considered in detail at p. 465 below, Keane J. further expanded on the scope of a permissible plea of misrepresentation.

. . .

It is also to be borne in mind—and this is of obvious relevance in the present case—that the representation, to give rise to legal consequences, must normally be a representation of fact and not of law. While the leading cases on this aspect of the law, such as *Cooper v Phibbs* (1867) LR 2 HL 149 concern cases of mistake, I think Dr Robert Clark, in *Contract Law in Ireland*, (3rd ed.), 229, is correct in stating that that principle also applies to misrepresentation cases. (A similar view seems to be taken by the learned editors of *Chitty on Contracts*, (26th ed.) vol I, 274. That law, as demonstrated by the decision in *Cooper v Phibbs*, draws a distinction between mistakes as to the law in general as distinct from mistakes as to private rights. Thus, a misrepresentation as to private rights may still afford a cause of action.

A. RELIANCE

Reliance on the representation is essential. Thus a representation will not be actionable if it did not come to the attention of the other party, or if the other party already knew the truth, or took a deliberate risk as to the truth, or if the other party relied on their own information.

Phelps v White (1881) 5 LR (Ir.) 318

The plaintiff agreed to purchase property from the defendant. The agreement of sale represented in substance that the timber on the estate was reserved to the vendor and formed part of the property to be sold. However, an examination of the contents of the abstract of title which was delivered to the plaintiff would have indicated that the vendor had no title to the timber. Upon discovering the error the plaintiff sought compensation.

The Vice Chancellor held that the plaintiff entered the contract on the basis of a material misrepresentation. He then continued:

. . . The real question here has throughout appeared to me to be, what is the effect which the possession of those means of knowledge should have upon the plaintiff's right to compensation? If the defendant had brought home actual knowledge of the fact that the timber was not the defendant's to convey, the case would wear a different aspect; for if the plaintiff, knowing that this was the case, had proceeded to complete his purchase without objection, he could scarcely be entitled afterwards to claim rescission or compensation. But as I believe, from the evidence, that the defendant had not by himself or his agent such actual knowledge till after completion, and that he went on with his purchase believing the timber was to be his, the question is, whether his neglect to avail himself of the information afforded him debars him from relief? I find negligence on the one hand, but legal fraud on the other. Assuming that the defendant had not discovered the error in his rental, which is far the more favourable view for him, I cannot see how he can rely on the plaintiff's failure to discover the mistake. It was the defendant's duty to have discovered it, and at once called the plaintiff's attention expressly to it. The plaintiff has the excuse of relying on the defendant's express and unequivocal representation of that which it was his duty to the plaintiff to know and to remember, and to represent truly. The plaintiff had no duty towards the defendant to discover the defendant's mistake. He cannot, as has more than once been well observed, complain of the plaintiff's having relied too implicitly on the truth of what he has himself stated. The critical time, too, at which this misrepresentation operated on the plaintiff's mind was that when he estimated the price he should offer, and made his offer. That offer was accepted, and upon this basis the whole of the subsequent dealings took place. During all those dealings the error was never pointed out to him, and I believe he never discovered it. His neglect was, therefore, innocent as compared with the fraudulent negligence of the defendant.

In the case of Horner v Williams,[1] the purchaser had accepted his conveyance, which stated correctly the term of the lease, which had been misrepresented in the rental under which he had purchased; and though his acceptance of the conveyance with this statement was relied on as a waiver of his claim to compensation, Pennefather B. held he was entitled to it. In Stewart v Alliston,[2] the nature of the rent, which had been misrepresented as a ground rent in the printed particulars of sale, was truly stated as in fact a rack-rent in the abstract of title furnished to the defendant, and which was submitted by him to counsel: but there, as here, the error remained undiscovered by the purchaser, notwithstanding the information thus afforded. The title was approved of, subject to certain queries, which had no reference to the subject of the misrepresentation. The conduct of the purchaser was relied on by the plaintiff as a waiver of the objection, but this was decided against him. This case, so far as it goes, is in accordance with the opinion I have expressed; but it cannot be considered as a decision upon the question, as the transaction did not proceed to a conveyance. On these grounds I am of opinion that the plaintiff has not waived his right to compensation.

[1] Jo. & Car. 274.   [2] 1 Mer. 26.

Donal Gahan v Maurice Boland and Wendy Boland (SC) 20 January 1984, unrep.

Henchy J.:

The defendants Maurice and Wendy Boland are husband and wife. In February 1981 they had on offer for sale the property known as Glencarrig, situate at Bride's Glen, Loughlinstown, Co. Dublin. That property consists of a dwelling house and some 3 ¼ acres of land.

The plaintiff, who is a solicitor, entered into a written contract on Monday 16 February 1981 for the purchase of the property for £135,000. In the present proceedings he has sought an order for the rescission of that contract. When his case came for hearing before Murphy J. in the High Court he succeeded in getting that order. The defendants now appeal.

The order for rescission was made as a result of certain events which are said to have taken place on Friday 13 February 1981. On that day the plaintiff visited the defendants at Glencarrig. The purpose of the visit was to inspect the property and to make certain inquiries about it. The plaintiff says that amongst the inquiries he made was one as to whether a projected motorway connecting Dublin and Wicklow would affect the Glencarrig property. His evidence was that Mr Boland assured him that the property would not be affected by the proposed motorway and that this assurance led him to enter into a written contract on the following Monday for the purchase of the property. It seems to be common case that the proposed motorway is in fact routed to pass through the Glencarrig property. That is something the plaintiff did not discover until after he had signed the contract.

There was a conflict of evidence as to what representation, if any, was made as to the motorway. The judge, however, having reviewed the evidence was of the clear opinion that an innocent but false representation was made by Mr Boland to the effect that the property would not be affected by the motorway, if and when it came to be constructed; that this representation was a material one made with the intention of inducing the plaintiff to act on it; and that it was one of the factors that induced the plaintiff to enter into the written contract on the following Monday to purchase the property.

Having perused the transcript of the evidence, I am satisfied that there was ample evidence to support those findings as to the misrepresentation relied on by the plaintiff for rescission of the contract. Once there was evidence to support the judge's findings in that respect, the defendants' main ground of appeal, namely that the findings as to misrepresentation are unsustainable, must be held to fail. This court cannot set aside primary facts of that nature found by the judge and supported by evidence.

The alternative or secondary ground of appeal argued was that, even if the defendants' argument as to the misrepresentation fails, the claim for rescission should have been rejected because the plaintiff should be held to have had constructive notice of the true position as to the route of the proposed motorway. It was suggested that the plaintiff, a solicitor and an intending purchaser, having made inquiries of the vendors as to whether the property would be affected by the motorway, was required, by the application of the doctrine of constructive notice, to pursue those inquiries in quarters where he would have been reliably informed as to the true position. For that reason, it is submitted, he should be held disentitled, for the purposes of rescission, to rely on the misrepresentation made and should be deemed to have constructive notice of the true position as to the route of the motorway.

I was unable to accept this argument. I consider it to be well settled law that the only knowledge that will debar a purchaser from repudiating a contract he has been induced into by the vendor's misrepresentation is actual and complete knowledge of the true situation. It does not lie with a vendor, who has by his misrepresentation induced the purchaser to enter into a contract to purchase, to have his misrepresentation excused or overlooked and to have the purchaser deprived of a right to rescind because he did not ignore the misrepresentation and pursue matters further so as to establish the truth of what was misrepresented. That would be unconscionable and unfair. The doctrine of constructive notice, as it arises under s. 3 of the Conveyancing Act, 1882 and as it was applied by this court in *Somers v W* 1979 IR 94, has no application to the facts of this case.

I would dismiss this appeal.

Note

The situation will be different if the representee can be proven to be actually aware of the truth. For example in *Grafton Court Ltd v Wadson Sales Ltd* (HC) 17 February 1975, unrep., the defendant claimed to have leased a unit in a shopping complex on the basis of representations by the lessor that the other tenants would be 'of high quality retail type'. The court stated that since the majority of the other units were occupied at the time of the lease, the defendant knew the quality and nature of those tenants and was not thus relying on any representations made.

S. Pearson & Son Ltd *v* Lord Mayor &c. of Dublin [1907] AC 351

Agents for Dublin Corporation furnished the appellants with plans, drawings and specifications as a result of which the appellants contracted to execute certain work. In the plans representations were made as to the position of a certain wall:

... In the contract (clauses 43, 46, 47, 48) it was stipulated that the contractor should satisfy himself as to the dimensions, levels and nature of all existing works and other things connected with the contract works; that the corporation did not hold itself responsible for the accuracy of the information as to the sections or foundations of existing walls and works; and that no charges for extra work or otherwise would be allowed in consequence of incorrect information or inaccuracies in the drawings or specifications. The appellants performed the contract, and brought an action of deceit against the corporation, claiming damages for false representations as to the position, dimensions and foundations of the wall, whereby the appellants were compelled to execute more costly works than would otherwise have been required.

Palles C.B. refused to leave any question to the jury, and entered judgment for the respondents on the ground that the contractors were bound by their contracts to verify for themselves all the information contained in the plans.

Lord Loreburn L.C.:

...

... Inasmuch as I am about to propose that the case be remitted for a new trial, it is desirable that I should say no more than is necessary to explain my view.

The plaintiffs' case is that they were induced to enter into a contract for the construction of certain sewage works by statements made by and on behalf of the defendants as to the existence to a depth of nine feet below ordnance datum of an old wall. Undoubtedly evidence was adduced at the trial from which the jury might, if they thought right, conclude that the plaintiffs were so induced by statements made on behalf of the defendants. Also, there was evidence for the jury that those statements were made either with a knowledge of their falsity, or (which is the same thing) with a reckless indifference whether they were true or false, on the part of the engineers employed by the defendants to make the plans which were submitted to plaintiffs as the basis of the tender. And had the case rested there I gather that the Chief Baron would have left the case to the jury, and that the learned judges who subsequently had this litigation before them would have approved this course.

But another feature of the case was considered fatal to the plaintiffs' claim. The contract contained clauses, which I need not cite at length, to the effect that the contractors must not rely on any representation made in plans or elsewhere, but must ascertain and judge of the facts for themselves. And, therefore, the Chief Baron withdrew the case from the jury. As I understand it, the view he held, in substance confirmed by the Court of Appeal, was that the plaintiffs, so forewarned, had no right to rely on any representation, and could not be heard to say they were induced by statements on which by contract they were not to rely. Or, at all events, it was said that the defendants, being themselves innocent, are protected by such clauses against the consequence of contractors acting on false statements made by defendants' agents, however fraudulent those agents might be.

Now it seems clear that no one can escape liability for his own fraudulent statements by inserting in a contract a clause that the other party shall not rely upon them. I will not say that a man himself innocent may not under any circumstances, however peculiar, guard himself by apt and express clauses from liability for the fraud of his own agents. It suffices to say that in my opinion the clauses before us do not admit of such a construction. They contemplate honesty on both sides and protect only against honest mistakes. The principal and the agent are one, and it does not signify which of them made the incriminated statement or which of them possessed the guilty knowledge.

Lord Ashbourne:

. . . I cannot think that in face of the evidence in the case this clause 43 could be regarded as establishing a defence. Such a clause might in some cases be part of a fraud, and might advance and disguise a fraud, and I cannot think that on the facts and circumstances of this case it can have such a wide and perilous application as was contended for. Such a clause may be appropriate and fairly apply to errors, inaccuracies, and mistakes, but not to cases like the present.

(The Earl of Halsbury and Lord James of Hereford delivered concurring judgments. Lord Macnaghten and Lord Collins agreed.)

Note

1. In *Dublin Port and Docks Board v Brittania Dredging Co. Ltd* |1968| IR 136 Lord Loreburn's observations were noted but as the misrepresentations in that case were innocent a clause avoiding liability for misrepresentation or lack of information was deemed effective.
2. It is clear from the case of *Sargent v Irish Multiwheel Ltd* (1955) 21–22 IJR 42 that it is not necessary for a representee to inform the representor that he or she is relying on the representation.
3. S. 46 of the Sale of Goods and Supply of Services Act 1980 regulates the extent to which an express clause can exclude or limit the right of a misrepresentee to bring an action in respect of an otherwise actionable, non-fraudulent misrepresentation. Such clauses are permissible if they pass the 'fair and reasonable' test. For English cases on the same statutory provision in English law see *Walker v Boyle* |1982| 1 WLR 495 and *South Western General Pty Co. v Marton* (1982) 263 EG 1090

SECTION TWO—MISREPRESENTATION AND TORT

A. Fraudulent Misrepresentation

Delany *v* Keogh |1905| 2 IR 267

The facts

The defendant, an auctioneer, was employed by Bradley, a solicitor, to sell the latter's interest in leasehold property. The conditions of sale stated that although the annual rent was £25, a rent of £18 had been accepted for several years. Prior to the auction, the defendant was informed that the landlord was insisting on a rent of £25 *per annum*. Bradley opined however that the landlord would be estopped from such an action. The conditions of sale were read out at the auction, and the plaintiff purchased the leasehold interest. He was later obliged to pay full rent, and sued the defendant for deceit. The majority of the King's Bench Division entered judgment for the defendant.

Johnson J.:

To succeed in this action, the plaintiff must prove fraud by the defendant, and damage to the plaintiff thereby induced to act on fraud—nothing short of that will be sufficient to maintain the action. Proof of damage without proof of fraud will not suffice. The plaintiff's case is that he sustained damage by having been induced by the defendant's false and fraudulent misrepresentations and false and fraudulent concealment of facts known to the defendant to purchase a leasehold public house and 3 acres of land at a public auction for a price larger than he would otherwise have given.

For the purpose of the present action, I dismiss from consideration the class of authorities in which equity relieves from contracts on the ground of misrepresentation—to which some of the cases cited in argument apply. There is a distinct cleavage between that class of authorities and those by which the case in hand is now to be determined, and in which, as I understand the law, the authorities establish that the alleged fraud must be such as would sustain an action for deceit, viz. *mala fides*—intentional deceit to deceive the plaintiff, which is a question of fact on the evidence, and is of the very essence of the alleged cause of action. A statement untrue in fact, but made without *mala fides*, and in the honest belief that it is true, is not evidence of fraud, although made through want of care or even through negligent carelessness or without reasonable grounds for belief in its truth, provided always it is made without *mala fides* and in honest belief of its truth. Of course it is not sufficient for a person making a representation to induce another to act on it, and who does act on it, to say I honestly believed what I said was true. The grounds on which the honest belief is really entertained and *mala fides* is absent necessarily depend on the facts of the particular case; and it is obviously of the last importance to investigate and ascertain whether on the evidence the person making the representation has really such honest belief. The authorities supply some tests.

For instance, if a person states what he knows to be false to induce another to act on that statement, it is plain that he has no honest belief in his statement; if he wilfully shuts his eyes to the facts, or purposely abstains from inquiry into them, no reasonable person would in such circumstances infer he had any honest belief in the matter. For the present purpose it is not necessary to multiply illustrations. False and fraudulent misrepresentation to induce another to act on it may be effectuated by *mala fide* active concealment (so to speak) with intent to deceive as by actual *mala fide* false statement. The same principles are equally applicable to such cases, whether the concealment is of a fact, or part of a fact, or by apparent disclosure of a fact, while there is *mala fide* concealment of that which, if disclosed, would put a wholly different complexion on the disclosure, and show what only is disclosed is false, and fraudulent, and dishonest, because it was not the whole truth.

A lie which is all a lie may be met and fought with outright;
But a lie which is part a truth is a harder matter to fight.

In all such cases the question is whether the representation is effected by actual statement or actual concealment; whether it was made dishonestly and intentionally to deceive another, and with intent that the other shall act on it, and so to induce him to act on it; or whether it was made *bona fide* in the honest belief of its truth; and the solution of this question depends on the evidence in the particular case in which it lies on the plaintiff to prove the alleged fraud and damage.

. . .

. . . The defendant, who was not a lawyer, *bona fide* inquired from Bradley, the solicitor who employed him, and who was the best source of information accessible to him, what he ought to do in the circumstances. This was the defendant's reasonable and proper course to pursue. Bradley was a solicitor, and personally acquainted with all the facts. Bradley, as a lawyer, gave the defendant his opinion that no more than £18 a year could be recovered, and directed him to proceed with the auction under the published advertisements and particulars and conditions of sale. The defendant states: 'I believed Bradley's statement, and acted on his opinion. I thought the rent was £18 a year and no more, outgoings 11s weekly, on the basis that the rent was only £18.' The defendant also says that no authority was given him to alter the particulars, and he sold the premises by Bradley's orders under the published particulars and conditions of sale, which he read then at the auction, without comment or alteration. He believed they truly represented the state and condition of the subject matter of the sale, and Mr Justice Wright, who saw and heard all the witnesses, with his experience at the bar and on the bench, believed the defendant. I think the decision of the House of Lords in *Derry v Peek*,[1] both on the facts of the case and in law, practically covers the present case.

The defendant knew nothing of the correspondence between Tench and Bradley, and it is not evidence against him.

I fail, on the facts, to discover any intention on the part of the defendant to deceive any person, either before or at the auction; he appears to me to have been honest and straightforward in the matter.

[1] 14 AC 337.

Holmes L.J. in the Court of Appeal:

. . . There is no doubt that to sustain an action for misrepresentation, there must be proof of fraud on the part of the defendant. It is, I think, equally certain that fraud is proved when it is shown that the defendant made the misrepresentation, knowing it to be false. To use the words of Lord Herschell, in *Derry v Peek*: 'To prevent a false statement being fraudulent, there must always be an honest belief in its truth.' To these propositions I add another, suggested by the peculiar facts of the present case. It is not necessary that the misrepresentation which will sustain an action of deceit should be made in actual terms. Words may be used in such circumstances, and in such a connection, as to convey to the person to whom they are addressed a meaning or inference beyond what is expressed; and if it appears that the person employing them knew this, and also knew that such meaning or inference was false, there is sufficient proof of fraud.

Of course whether the misstatement be express or implied, the plaintiff must show that he has suffered loss by acting on it; . . .

. . .

. . . The statement was not made for the purpose of informing a would-be purchaser of a past incident with which he was not concerned. It was intended that he should draw the inference that the reduction hitherto made would probably be continued, and, in my opinion, it clearly implied a representation that the vendor had no reason to believe that it would be discontinued. . . .

The question is whether, in the foregoing circumstances, the particulars of sale, taken in connection with the suppression of the contents of the landlord's letter, showed fraud of the kind that entitles the plaintiff to recover in an action of deceit such damages, if any, as he sustained therefrom?

Let me present the case in a way suggested by |counsel for the respondent|. Let me assume that the defendant, after he received the particulars from Mr Bradley, but before he made them public, had ascertained from the landlord that he would insist on the full rent for the future, would it not have been manifestly dishonest to frame the advertisement as he did? His doing so would be an example of the trick described by Lord Blackburn in *Smith v Chadwick*:[2]

> If, with intent to lead the plaintiff to act upon it, they |i.e. the defendants| put forth a statement which they know may bear two meanings, one of which is false to their knowledge, and thereby the plaintiff, putting that meaning on it, is misled, I do not think they can escape by saying he ought to have put the other. If they palter with him in a double sense, it may be that they lie *like* truth; but I think they lie, and it is a fraud. Indeed, as a question of casuistry, I am inclined to think the fraud is aggravated by a shabby attempt to get the benefit of a fraud without incurring the responsibility.

But the information, which would have made the statement fraudulent if it had been obtained before the advertisement was issued, reached the defendant in time to enable him to prevent persons attending the auction from being misled; and the fact that the landlord communicated with him as auctioneer ought to have impressed, and I am sure did impress, him with the importance of correcting the false inference which his language was calculated and intended to convey. All that was necessary for Mr Keogh to do was, after reading the particulars at the auction, to have added, that since they had been prepared the landlord had expressed his intention to insist on the rent of £25, but that the vendor's solicitor was of opinion that he was legally estopped from obtaining more than £18. He did not do this. He allowed the sale to proceed on the basis that the reduced rent might be voluntarily received in the future as in the past, or, at least, that he knew nothing to the contrary.

How does the defendant himself account for this? His evidence on this point is clear: 'The conditions were Bradley's. I did not get authority to make any change. I was selling under Bradley's orders. I acted on Bradley's directions to me to go on with the sale.' In other words, an intelligent auctioneer, who admits that 'it would have been material to have let those at the auction know of Tench's determination to enforce the higher rent', kept back this information, because the solicitor under whose orders he was acting did not authorise him to disclose it or make any change in the particulars. In matters of truth and falsehood, of honesty and dishonesty, our law requires a man to judge for himself, and will not allow him to escape responsibility by pleading that he was carrying out the directions of another. Knowing that he could not thus free himself from liability, his counsel relied on his belief in the soundness of Mr Bradley's legal opinion. I accept Mr Keogh's statement that he believed what he was told by the solicitor, although this was not his reason for suppressing Tench's letter, and although the solicitor himself had not ventured to state it in the particulars of sale; but the defendant must have understood the difference between a landlord accepting voluntarily an abated rent, and a tenant being forced to fight for the abatement in a doubtful lawsuit. I do not understand either the legal or ethical aspect of |counsel's| argument on this point.

I have observed, not for the first time, in the discussion of this case the prevalence of an idea that *Derry v Peek* has laid down a new rule in actions of deceit, and has given a latitude to falsehood that did not previously exist. This seems to me to be a great mistake. The directors of a Tramway Co. that had authority to use steam power with the consent of the Board of Trade, believing that this consent would be given as a matter of course, issued a prospectus in which it was stated that they had the right to use steam power without reference to any condition. It was held that this was not actionable, inasmuch as the statement was made in the honest belief that it was true. This is, I think, old law; but if the directors had known, before they issued the prospectus, that the Board of Trade had refused to consent, or had announced its intention to refuse, the case would have been like this, and the directors would have had no defence; nor in such case would their position have been improved if their solicitor had assured them that there would be no difficulty in obtaining from Parliament an amending Act removing the condition.

I am satisfied that when the defendant read in his auction mart to the assembled bidders the particulars of sale, unaccompanied with a statement that there would be no longer a voluntary abatement of the rent, he was knowingly deceiving them, and that the natural effect of the deception was to obtain a higher price for the public house than it was worth.

I believe that the plaintiff's bid of £430 was considerably higher than what he would have offered if he had the knowledge which the auctioneer possessed; and than the real value of the premises.

The measure of damages is the difference between such real value and £430 . . .

1. 14 AC 374.   2. 9 AC 201.

Mary Carbin *v* Patrick Sommerville [1933] IR 276

The plaintiff claimed to have entered into a contract to purchase a house from the defendant on the basis of a false misrepresentation that the house was free from damp and that the roof was in good condition. She then claimed rescission of the contract, return of the purchase money and damages for misrepresentation. Alternatively, she claimed damages for breach of warranty of the condition of the house.

The trial judge found that the defendant was asked if the house was dry and if the roof was adequate, and replied to each question that it was. He also found that neither statement was justified and that the plaintiff had entered the contract upon the truth of these statements. However he refused the relief claimed on the ground that fraud had not been proven.

FitzGibbon J.:

. . .

Now, that the house was neither dry nor free from damp, and that the roof was not perfect, as stated by the defendant, has been abundantly proved, but the question which we have to decide is whether it is so clear that the defendant knew his statement to be untrue (as the judge has found it was), or that he made it so recklessly without regard to its truth or falsehood, that the judge's findings that he was no more than 'unduly optimistic', that he was 'inclined to believe what he wanted to believe', and that 'his reticence on the question' which he was not asked, 'will not convict him of fraud', cannot stand.

. . .

'Early in 1928' he noticed cracks in the compo which he had put on in March, and late in June 1929, he treated them with waterex. In June 1929, he again repapered the house. More damp patches appeared in February or March 1930, in the dining-room and the kitchen, and the defendant then found several fresh cracks in the walls, which he 'supposed would be admitting damp into the house'. He then 'completely repapered' the dining-room and the kitchen. This occurred only five or six weeks before he described the house to the plaintiff as 'dry and free from damp'. His own case is that he did not so describe the house, and that he could not have so described it, because it would not have been honest to do so. . . .

. . . 'Was this house free from damp and dry?' The judge has found that this question was put; the defendant agrees that if the question had been put, honesty must have compelled him to point out, or tell the plaintiff of, the damp patches, and the judge has found that he answered the question with an unconditional and unqualified affirmative. To my mind this alone, having regard to the defendant's knowledge of the facts, suffices to establish the plaintiff's case that the misrepresentation was fraudulent, but the Chief Justice, in the course of the argument, has directed attention to an equally convincing proof of the defendant's lack of belief in the truth of the assertion that the house was 'free from damp'. He had repapered the house, in whole or in part, in consequence of patches of damp and discoloration appearing upon the walls, on no less than three occasions between June 1927, and March 1930. In February or March 1930 he applied black pitch paint on the *interior* walls of the house. This he admits was done to prevent 'the damp that was still in the walls' from discolouring the new paper. That damp was there, in spite of the cementing and waterexing of 1929, and the second application of waterex in 1930. Now, if the defendant applied pitch to the *interior* surface of a wall to prevent the new paper from destruction by damp, it is clear that he must have believed that the damp had penetrated, or would penetrate, from the outside through the wall, for it could not by any other means attack the paper on the inside surface, and if the defendant had believed that the outside surface of the wall was waterproof, there could be no necessity for coating the inside face with pitch to protect the paper from damp. To my mind his action, and his own explanation of his action, in applying pitch to the interior surface of the walls, demonstrates his knowledge that the walls were not free from the damp, which, indeed, he admits in his replies to many questions, was in the walls, and it was because of this knowledge that he said he could not honestly have described the house as dry and free from damp.
. . .

. . . It is perfectly clear that when the defendant answered the question in the affirmative, as the judge has found he did, he intended his answer to be taken in the sense in which the question was asked, and in the sense in which the judge has found the plaintiff did take it and act upon it, and so given, the misrepresentation was false and fraudulent.

If there be no other ground for denying the plaintiff's claim to the relief by way of rescission, the conclusions I have stated establish it, in accordance with the statement of the law by Blackburn J. in *Kennedy v Panama, etc., Mail Co.*:[1]

> It is enough to show that there was a *fraudulent* representation as to any part of that which induced the party to enter into the contract which he seeks to rescind; but where there has been an *innocent* misrepresentation or misapprehension, it does not authorise a rescission unless it is such as to show that there is a complete difference in substance between what was supposed to be, and what was, taken, so as to constitute a failure of consideration.

The plaintiff has contended that there was such 'a complete difference' in the present case, and that even if the defendant's representation that the house was dry and free from damp was innocent or inadvertent, she is still entitled to rescind her bargain upon the ground of 'a failure of consideration'. I do not agree with this contention. To sell a leaky house or a leaky ship on a fraudulent misrepresentation that it is sound entitles the party defrauded to rescind the contract, but if the misrepresentation be innocent there is not that difference in the subject matter of the sale which would entitle the party to be relieved of his bargain on the ground of defect of substance when there is really only an inferiority of quality. Any remedy the purchaser may have in such a case would sound in damages only.

...

We have not been referred to any decision of any court, or to any opinion of any reputable text-writer, to the effect that when a party to a contract has been induced to enter into it by fraudulent misrepresentation he loses his right to repudiate it on discovery of the fraud because the subject matter cannot be restored to the defendant in the identical condition in which it was at the date of the contract, where the alteration is due to the nature of the subject matter itself and cannot be attributed to any act of the plaintiff. In *Adam v Newbigging*[2] the House of Lords, Lords Halsbury, Watson, FitzGerald and Herschell, considered that the circumstance that the business, in which the plaintiff had been induced to become a partner by the misrepresentation of the defendants made without any fraud on their part, had become totally insolvent and worthless between 1 February 1883, the date of the contract, and November 1884, the date of the commencement of proceedings for rescission, did not disentitle the plaintiff to rescission and repayment of his capital although the defendants could not recover against him for money lent and goods sold by them to the partnership during the interval. It was held unanimously that the mere deterioration of the business, though it might have been anticipated if the plaintiff had known the actual state of affairs in the beginning of 1883, could not stand in the way of the plaintiff's claim for mutual restitution, and that was a case of innocent misrepresentation only. The present defendant sold the plaintiff a defective house, by fraudulent misrepresentation as to its condition. He will get back his own defective house, which has deteriorated since he sold it through its own inherent vice, and has not been depreciated by any act of the plaintiff, who has simply refrained from spending any more of her own money upon the defendant's house in a vain endeavour to make it what he contracted to sell her.

Having arrived at a clear determination that the plaintiff is entitled to rescission of her contract and the return of her purchase money upon the ground that the contract was induced by the fraudulent misrepresentation of the defendant, it is unnecessary to consider the question, to which the greater portion of the time occupied by the appeal was devoted, whether the plaintiff could recover damages for breach of warranty. The question was not dealt with specifically by the learned judge in his decision, but we have been asked to infer from his dismissal of the action that he held that no warranty had been given. Having held, as he did, that the plaintiff asked, before any discussion as to the price of the house, whether it was dry and free from damp, and that she received an affirmative answer and acted upon it, I find it difficult to understand a decision that no warranty was given except upon the assumption that he was persuaded by the arguments on behalf of the defendant to hold that there can be no warranty unless the word 'warrant' or some equivalent expression is used.

Whether the parties understood an affirmation made at the time of a sale to be a warranty, that is a contract connected with, but collateral to, the contract of sale itself, must depend not only upon the actual words used but upon the context, and all the surrounding circumstances. In my opinion an affirmation, in circumstances such as those deposed to in the present case, that the house was dry and free from damp, might well amount to a warranty, breach of which would give rise to a claim for damages, although the statement was made with an honest belief in its truth, but I base my decision in the plaintiff's favour upon the ground of fraudulent misrepresentation, and not upon any alleged breach of warranty.

[1.] LR 2 QB 580, p. 587.　　　　　　　　[2.] 13 AC 308.

Consumer Information Act 1978 ss 6 (1) & (2) & 17 (3)

6. (1) If a person, in the course or for the purposes of a trade, business or profession:

(a) makes a statement which he knows to be false, or

(b) recklessly makes a statement which is false

as to any of the following matters, that is to say

(i) the provision in the course of the trade, business or profession of any services, accommodation or facilities,

(ii) the nature, effect or fitness for purpose of any services, accommodation or facilities provided in the course of the trade, business or profession,

(iii) the time at which, manner in which or persons by whom any services, accommodation or facilities are so provided,

(iv) the examination, approval, use or evaluation by any person of any services, accommodation or facilities so provided,

(v) the place where any service, facility or accommodation is so provided or the amenities of any such accommodation,

he shall be guilty of an offence.

(2) For the purposes of this section

(a) anything (whether or not a statement as to any of the matters specified in the preceding subsection) likely to be taken for such a statement as to any of those matters as would be false shall be deemed to be a false statement as to that matter; and

(b) a statement made regardless of whether it is true or false shall be deemed to be made recklessly, unless the person making it had adequate reasons for believing that it was true.

. . .

17. (3) (a) Where a court imposes a fine or affirms or varies a fine imposed by another court for an offence referred to in subsection (1) of this section of which a person was convicted summarily, it may, at its discretion, on the application (made before the time of such imposition or affirmation) of any person who was summoned as a witness on behalf of the prosecution in the proceedings in which the fine was imposed and who suffered personal injury, loss or damage resulting, wholly or partly, from the offence provide by order for the payment of the amount of the fine or of a specified part of it as compensation in respect of the injury, loss or damage to the person making the application.

(b) An application shall not lie under paragraph (a) of this subsection in respect of any personal injury, loss or damage if proceedings claiming damages for the injury, loss or damage have been instituted in any court.

(c) Where the whole or part of a fine imposed under this section is paid to a person pursuant to this subsection and the person is awarded damages by a court in respect of the personal injury, loss or damage to which the payment relates, the payment shall be deemed to be in satisfaction of so much of the damages as is equal to the amount of the payment.

B. NEGLIGENT MISREPRESENTATION

The Governor and Company of the Bank of Ireland v William Smith and Others [1966] IR 646
(Facts on p. 251.)

Kenny J.:

. . .

The next contention was that the decision of the House of Lords in *Hedley Byrne & Co. Ltd v Heller*[1] had established that a person who relies on an innocent misrepresentation and suffers loss as a result is entitled to damages. The speeches in that case establish that, in some cases, a negligent misrepresentation made to anyone who, to the knowledge of the speaker or writer will rely on it and will be damaged if it is incorrect, gives a right to damages: they do not establish that every innocent misrepresentation gives such a right. . . .

. . . It was said that an auctioneer acting for a vendor should anticipate that any statements made by him about the property will be relied on by the purchaser and that he, therefore, owes a duty of care to the purchaser and is liable in damages to him if the statement was incorrect and was made carelessly. In my opinion, the decision in *Hedley Byrne & Co. Ltd v Heller* does not give any support to this startling proposition. It decides that, if a person seeks information from another in circumstances in which a reasonable man would know that his judgment is being relied on, the person giving the information must use reasonable care to ensure that his answer is correct, and if he does not do so, he is liable in damages: but the relationship between the person seeking the information and the person giving it, if not fiduciary or arising out of a contract for consideration, must be, to use the words of Lord Devlin, 'equivalent to contract', before any liability can arise. The basis of the decision in *Hedley Byrne & Co. Ltd v Heller* is, I think, contained in the speech of Lord Devlin when he said (at p. 528):

> I think, therefore, that there is ample authority to justify your Lordships in saying now that the categories of special relationships which may give rise to a duty to take care in word as well as in deed are not limited to contractual relationships or to relationships of fiduciary duty, but include also relationships which in the words of Lord Shaw in *Nocton v Lord Ashburton*[2] are 'equivalent to contract', that is, where there is an assumption of responsibility in circumstances in which, but for the absence of consideration, there would be a contract . . .

Even if an auctioneer's fees are paid by the purchaser (and in this case the vendors are liable for them), a contractual relationship between the vendors' auctioneers and the purchaser does not exist. The decision of Davitt P. in *Securities Trust Ltd v Hugh Moore & Alexander Ltd*[3] supports this conclusion. Moreover, the purchaser has not proved that Mr Mulcahy was negligent. He was told by an employee of Mr Smith that the lands had been undersown, he visited them on many occasions and the error which he made is one which could be made by the most careful of auctioneers. The claim in negligence against the vendors fails.

[1.] [1964] AC 465.   [2.] [1914] AC 932, 972.   [3.] [1964] IR 417.

Patrick Stafford v Denis Mahony & Others [1980] ILRM 53

The plaintiff claimed to have entered into a contract on the basis of a misrepresentation by the defendants, a firm of auctioneers as to the potential resale value of certain property purchased. The defendants denied making any representation to the plaintiff and stated that they had been acting exclusively for the plaintiff's brother Mr James Stafford prior to the signing of the contract.

Doyle J. in the High Court found that the evidence indicated that no representations had been made. However Doyle J. considered the legal situation which would have arisen had these representations actually been made:

. . .

Based upon the assumption that Mr Patrick Stafford did have discussions with Mr Mahony and Mr Palmer in the course of which he obtained some information amounting to representations, innocent but mistaken, which induced him to purchase the premises, |counsel for the plaintiff| directs a legal argument founded in the first instance upon the doctrine of innocent misrepresentation and its consequences. |Counsel| relied chiefly upon the doctrine as expounded by the Court of Appeal in England in *Esso Petroleum Co. Ltd v Mardon* |1976| QB 801. In this case the Court of Appeal purported to found their judgment upon the decision of the House of Lords in *Hedley Byrne & Co. Ltd v Heller*, the well known authority which expounded for the first time in a full way the question as to how far the duty to exercise care was imposed upon a person giving information or advice to another. It would, I think, be generally considered that the Court of Appeal in *Esso v Mardon* considerably extended the application of the principle which had been laid down in *Hedley Byrne*. The principle upon which this decision was based was summarised by Lord Denning M.R. at p. 820 as follows:

> It seems to me that *Hedley Byrne* . . . . , properly understood, covers this particular proposition: if a man, who has or professes to have special knowledge or skill, makes a representation by virtue thereof to another—be it advice, information or opinion—with the intention of inducing him to enter into a contract with him, he is under a duty to use reasonable care to see that the representation is correct, and that the advice, information or opinion is reliable. If he negligently gives unsound advice or misleading information or expresses an erroneous opinion, and thereby induces the other side to enter into a contract with him, he is liable in damages.

Omrod L.J. at p. 287, after analysing the principles which he said underlay the decision in *Hedley Byrne*, stated:

> The parties were in the kind of relationship which is sufficient to give rise to a duty on the part of the plaintiffs. There is no magic in the phrase 'special relationship'; it means no more than a relationship the nature of which is such that one party, for a variety of possible reasons, would be regarded by the law as under a duty of care to the other. In this case the plaintiff had all the expertise, experience and authority of a large and efficient organisation carrying on the business of developing service stations to sell their petroleum through dealers who were expected to invest a substantial amount of capital in the business. . . . On the evidence they clearly assumed responsibility for the reliability of their own |estimated annual consumption|.

Similar views were expressed by Shaw L.J. and it is difficult to avoid the suspicion that the views of these learned judges were to some extent coloured by the provisions of the English Misrepresentation Act of 1967 which was already law for some years at the date of the judgment but which had not been effective in 1963 at the date of the matters complained of by Mr Mardon the applicant.

Hedley Byrne is reported at |1964| AC 465. It is difficult to state compendiously the effect of this very important decision, but I think it may perhaps be summarised by adopting the words of Lord Devlin at p. 530. He is reported as saying:

> I shall therefore content myself with the proposition that wherever there is a relationship equivalent to contract, there is a duty of care. Such a relationship may be either general or particular. Examples of a general relationship are those of solicitor and client and of banker and customer. . . . There may well be others yet to be established. Where there is a general relationship of this sort, it is unnecessary to do more than prove its existence and the duty follows. Where, as in the present case, what is relied on is a particular relationship created *ad hoc*, it will be necessary to examine the particular facts to see whether there is an express or implied undertaking of responsibility.

He goes on in the next sentence to state an aspect of the doctrine which appears important in considering the present case, namely: 'I regard this proposition as an application of the general conception of proximity'.

In the speech of Lord Morris there is to be found an analysis of *Derry v Peek* (1889) 14 App Cas 337, in the course of which he also referred to the speech of Lord Shaw in *Nocton v Lord Ashburton* |1914| AC 932, at p. 972:

> . . . Once the relations of parties have been ascertained to be those in which a duty is laid upon one person of giving information or advice to another upon which that other is entitled to rely as the basis of a transaction, responsibility for error amounting to misrepresentation in any statement made will attach to the adviser or informer, although the information and advice have been given not fraudulently but in good faith.

Having discussed other speeches in *Derry v Peek*, Lord Morris went on to comment |1964| AC 465, at p. 502:

> The enquiry in the present case, and in similar cases, becomes, therefore, an enquiry as to whether there was a relationship between the parties which created a duty and, if so, whether such duty included a duty of care.

Lord Morris continued:

> I consider that it follows that it should not be regarded as settled that if someone possessed of a special skill undertakes, quite irrespective of contract, to apply that skill for the assistance of another person who relies upon such skill, a duty of care will arise.

He follows this with an observation which might be thought to be of assistance to the plaintiff in the present case:

> Furthermore, if in a sphere in which a person is so placed that others could reasonably rely upon his judgment or his skill or upon his ability to make careful

enquiry, a person takes upon himself to give information or advice to, or allow his information or advice to be passed on to, another person who, as he knows or should know, will place reliance upon it, then a duty of care will arise.

The force of this last observation, as I understand it, is that if advice had been given to Mr James Stafford which might reasonably have been expected to be passed on to or have come to the knowledge of his brother Mr Patrick Stafford and if Mr Patrick Stafford had placed reliance upon it, then the duty of care would have extended to him. The observation however clearly contemplates that there must be a person making the representation and another person to whom the representation is made or to whom it is likely to be conveyed.

In my view the application and extent of the doctrine of negligent although innocent misrepresentations giving rise to an action for damages have been correctly stated by Davitt P. in *Securities Trust Ltd v Hugh Moore and Alexander Ltd* |1964| IR 417. Having at p. 421 stated his view that, contrary to the narrow interpretation formerly given to *Derry v Peek*, the law now provided that an action for damages might be based on innocent, that is non-fraudulent, but negligent misrepresentation, the learned judge went on to consider the then recent decision of *Hedley Byrne*. He stated:

> The proposition that circumstances may create a relationship between two parties in which, if one seeks information from the other and is given it, that other is under a duty to take reasonable care to ensure that the information given is correct, has been accepted and applied in the case of *Hedley Byrne & Co. Ltd v Heller*, recently decided by the House of Lords.

Having considered the circumstances in the case which he was then deciding, under which Mr Kevin Anderson, the chairman and managing director of the plaintiff company, had sought information from the defendant company, the learned judge pointed out that Mr Anderson, who had made the request, was a shareholder but that the plaintiff company had not then been registered as owner of any shares in the defendant company. Davitt J. stated the plaintiff was entitled to the information and entitled to receive it personally *qua member*; he was not entitled to receive it *qua agent* of the plaintiff company, and he later went on to say:

> It seems to me that there was no relationship between the parties in this case |that is to say the plaintiff company and the defendant company| other than such as would exist between the defendant company and any person (other than Mr Anderson) who might chance to read the copy supplied to him; or, indeed, between that company and any members of the community at large, individual or corporate, who chanced to become aware of the last sentence in Article 155 of the defective reprint of the Memorandum of Articles.

This was the document which had given rise to the misrepresentation. The learned judge went on to say:

> It can hardly be seriously contended that the defendant company owed a duty to the world at large to take care to avoid mistakes and printers' errors in the reprint of their articles. In my opinion, counsel is correct in his submission that in this case the defendant company owed no duty to the plaintiff company to take care to ensure that the copy of the article supplied to Mr Anderson was a correct copy.

Adopting the principles thus laid down by Davitt P., I have come to the conclusion that in order to establish the liability for negligent or non-fraudulent misrepresentation giving rise to an action there must first of all be a person conveying the information or the representation relied upon; secondly, that there must be a person to whom that information is intended to be conveyed or to whom it might reasonably be expected that the information would be conveyed; thirdly, that the person must act upon such information or representation to his detriment so as to show that he is entitled to damages. It follows, I think, that if Mr James Stafford had been the plaintiff in the present case and had made out to the satisfaction of the court that misrepresentations had been made to him by the defendants or any member of the firm upon which he acted to his detriment relying upon their skill and experience, then he would have made out such a case. I do not think that this liability would extend to his brother Patrick, even if he had learned in the course of his various visits to the offices of the defendant firm the nature of the transaction which his brother James was conducting up to the date upon which the contract of sale was executed. . . .

C. INNOCENT MISREPRESENTATION

Connor *v* Potts [1897] 1 IR 534 (ch.)

The plaintiff agreed to purchase land from the defendant for £5,500 calculated on the basis of 442 acres at £12 10s per acre. The plaintiff accepted the defendant's representation as to the total acreage involved. Later the area proved to be 67 acres less. The plaintiff sought specific performance to the extent of the real acreage.

V.C.:

. . . Fraudulent misrepresentation is not necessary for the plaintiff to establish, for a mistaken representation by the defendant of a matter that it was his duty to state correctly, and on the faith of which he knew the plaintiff acted, is sufficient, though he may himself have believed it to be true.

. . .

The general principle applicable to this case is well established that where a misrepresentation is made by a vendor as to a matter within his knowledge even though it may be founded upon an honest belief in the truth of what he states, and the purchaser has been misled by such misrepresentation, the purchaser is entitled to have the contract specifically performed so far as the vendor is able to do so, and to have compensation for the deficiency.

. . .

On the whole case I am of opinion that the plaintiff is entitled to judgment for the specific performance of the contract as to the portion of Knockcairn to which the defendant can show title, being 249 acres and the entire of Fourscore 126a. 2r. 10p., and that he is entitled to compensation for the 67 acres' deficiency of the acreage of Knockcairn . . .

Note

This case was referred to in *Keating & Others v Bank of Ireland & Others* [1983] ILRM 295 where it was held that if the purchasers of property were entitled to compensation for a misdescription, they were entitled to it out of the purchase money, and thus they could not be forced to close the sale until such time as the amount of compensation, if any, and therefore the amount of the balance of the purchase price, had been ascertained.

Doolan *v* Murray, Murray, Murray, Cheever, Aziz and Dun Laoghaire Corporation (HC) 21 December 1993, unrep.

The plaintiff purchased a mews house from the first and second defendants, aware that there was a right of way in favour of the third and fourth defendants. Prior to completion the vendors executed a deed which affirmed that the right of way was a pedestrian way only. Following completion the plaintiff discovered that the right of way was more extensive and that planning restrictions, of which the first and second defendants, as well as the plaintiff, had not known, prevented the plaintiff from carrying out improvements to her property. The third defendant however was aware of these restrictions. The plaintiff sought damages against the various defendants for misrepresentation.

Keane J.:
. . .
As to the liability that arises in law from a misrepresentation, whether innocent, negligent or fraudulent, and whether made by parties to a contract or made in other circumstances, the law in Ireland appears to be as follows. A fraudulent misrepresentation will unquestionably give rise to an action for damages for deceit. An innocent misrepresentation will not *in general* give rise to any action for damages, although it may afford grounds for rescission of a contract or a defence to an action for specific performance. There are, however, two broad categories of cases in which a person may be entitled to recover damages for an innocent misrepresentation. They are:

(a) Where a representation is made for the purpose of inducing a person to enter into a contract, and it actually induces him or her to act on it by entering into the contract;

(b) Where the representation is made negligently by a person owing a duty of care in relation to the making of such a statement to the person to whom the representation is made.

The representation in the first category of cases has been described in some of the English authorities as a 'collateral warranty' and that is the way in which it has been pleaded and relied on in the present case. The suggestion also appears to have been made that the 'warranty' is enforceable because it is a 'promise', presumably supported by consideration in the form of a corresponding promise by the person to whom the representation is made to enter into the contract. (See, for example, the observations of Denning L.J. as he then was, in *Oscar Chess Ltd v Williams* |1957| 1 All ER 325 at p. 328). . . .

With those qualifications in mind, one can safely adopt the following statement of the law by Denning L.J., as he then was, in *Bentley (Dick) Productions Ltd v Harold Smith (Motors) Ltd* |1965| 1 WLR 623:

Looking at the cases once more, as we have done so often, it seems to me that if a representation is made in the course of dealings for a contract for the very purpose of inducing the other party to act on it, and it actually induces him to act upon it by entering into the contract, that is *prima facie* ground for inferring that the representation was intended as a warranty. It is not necessary to speak of it as being collateral. Suffice it that the representation was intended to be acted on and was in fact acted on.

It is also clear that the 'collateral warranty' principle may apply where the main contract is not between the plaintiff and the defendant, but between the plaintiff and a third party: see *Shanklin Pier Ltd v Detel Products Ltd* |1951| 2 KB 854.

As to the second category of cases, the cause of action, if any, here derives from the legal principle enunciated by the House of Lords in *Hedley Byrne and Co. Ltd v Heller* |1964| AC 465 and adopted by the High Court in *Securities Trust Ltd v Hugh Moore and Alexander Ltd,* |1964| IR 417 and *Bank of Ireland v Smith* |1966| IR 646. In the first of the Irish decisions, Davitt P. succinctly defined the context in which liability may arise as follows: 'Circumstances may create a relationship between two parties in which, if one seeks information from the other, and is given it, that other is under a duty to take reasonable care to ensure that the information is correct.'

The decision in *Hedley Byrne* had reversed in England the view of the majority of the Court of Appeal in *Candler v Crane Christmas and Co.* |1951| 2 KB 164 that no liability arose for purely economic loss (as contrasted with physical injury) caused by a negligent misstatement. Before *Hedley Byrne,* the generally accepted view was that such negligent misstatements causing economic loss did not come within the ambit of Lord Atkin's often quoted 'neighbour' principle in *Donoghue v Stevenson* |1932| AC 562, *viz.*:

> The rule that you are to love your neighbour becomes in law you must not injure your neighbour; and the lawyer's question, who is my neighbour? receives a restrictive reply. You must take reasonable care to avoid acts or omissions which you can reasonably foresee would be liable to injure your neighbour. Who, then, in law is my neighbour? The answer seems to be—persons who are so closely and directly affected by my act that I ought reasonably to have them in contemplation as being so affected when I am directing my mind to the acts or omissions which are called in question.

Some passages in the speeches in *Hedley Byrne* are important as specifying in more detail the circumstances which will create a duty in law to take care in relation to the making of statements. Lord Reid, having cited an extract from the speech of Lord Haldane in *Robinson v National Bank of Scotland* |1916| SC 154, says:

> This passage makes it clear that Lord Haldane did not think that a duty to take care must be limited to cases of fiduciary relationship in the narrow sense of relationships which had been recognised by the Court of Chancery as being of a fiduciary character. He speaks of other special relationships, and I can see no logical stopping place short of all those relationships where it is plain that the party seeking information or advice was trusting the other to exercise such a degree of care as the circumstances required, where it was reasonable for him to do that, and where the other gave the information or advice when he knew or ought to have known that the inquirer was relying on him. I say 'ought to have known' because in questions of negligence we now apply the objective standard of what the reasonable man would have done.

Lord Devlin puts the matter thus:

I think, therefore, that there is ample authority to justify Your Lordships in saying now that the categories of special relationships, which may give rise to a duty to take care in word as well as in deed, are not limited to contractual relationships or to relationships of fiduciary duty, but include also relationships which in the words of Lord Shaw in *Nocton v Lord Ashburton* are 'equivalent to contract' that is, where there is an assumption of responsibility in circumstances in which, but for the absence of consideration, there would be a contract. Where there is an express undertaking, an express warranty as distinct from a mere representation, there can be little difficulty. The difficulty arises in discerning those cases in which the undertaking is to be implied. In this respect the absence of consideration is not irrelevant. Payment for information or advice is very good evidence that it is being relied on and that the informer and adviser knows that it is. Where there is no consideration, it will be necessary to exercise greater care in distinguishing between social and professional relationships and between those which are of a contractual character and those which are not. It may often be material to consider whether the adviser is acting purely out of good nature or whether he is getting his reward in some indirect form.

It was urged in *Esso Petroleum Co. Ltd v Mardon* |1976| 2 All ER 5 that, where negotiations between two parties resulted in a contract between them, their rights and duties were governed by the law of contract and not by the law of tort and there was therefore no place in their relationship for *Hedley Byrne* which related solely to liability in tort. That view was rejected by the Court of Appeal. Lord Denning M.R., in the course of his judgment, said that: 'If a man, who has or professes to have special knowledge or skill, makes a representation by virtue thereof to another—be it advice, information or opinion—with the intention of inducing him to enter into a contract with him, he is under a duty to use reasonable care to see that the representation is correct, and that the advice, information or opinion is reliable.'

That statement of the law was cited, without apparent disapproval, by Doyle J. in *Stafford v Mahony Smith and Palmer* |1980| IRLM 53.

There remains the question as to whether, in considering either of these categories, mere silence can ever amount to an actionable misrepresentation or a negligent misstatement. In the case of parties to a contract, the authorities suggest that there are three categories of cases in which silence can amount to a misrepresentation giving rise to a cause of action. One of them, where a contract requires *uberrima fides*, does not arise in the present case. The others are where the silence distorts a positive representation and where a fiduciary relation exists between the contracting parties. I would adopt as a correct statement of the law in this jurisdiction the following statement in Cheshire, Fifoot and Furmston's *Law of Contract*, (12th ed.), 273:

> Silence upon some of the relevant factors may obviously distort a positive assertion. A party to a contract may be legally justified in remaining silent about some material fact, but if he ventures to make a representation upon the matter it must be a full and frank statement, and not a partial and fragmentary account that what is withheld makes that which is said absolutely false. A half truth may be in fact false because of what it leaves unsaid and although what a man actually says may be true in every detail, he is guilty of misrepresentation unless he tells the whole truth.

And at p. 308, dealing with the nature of the confidential relationship, the learned authors have this to say:

Such a confidential relationship is deemed to exist between persons connected by certain recognised ties, such as parent and child, principal and agent, solicitor and client, religious superior and inferior, and trustee and beneficiary. But the courts have always refused to confine this equitable jurisdiction to such familiar relations. They are prepared to interfere in a contract wherever one party deliberately and voluntarily places himself in such a position that it become his duty to act fairly and to have due regard to the interest of the other party.

These passages are concerned with the position of parties to a contract. It should not be assumed that they are applicable without qualification when one is considering liability for an alleged negligent misstatement. In the first place, while Lord Atkin's statement of the 'neighbour' principle expressly extends to omissions, the authorities both in England and other common law jurisdictions have reflected a reluctance to extend liability to cases of 'pure omissions'. Giving the judgment of the Court of Appeal in *Banque Financiere v Westgate Insurance Co.* |1989| 2 All ER 952, Slade L.J. said at p. 1009:

The same reluctance on the part of the courts to give a remedy in tort for pure omission applies, perhaps even more so, when the omission is a failure to prevent economic harm . . . a corresponding distinction is drawn by the law of contract which in general imposes no liability by virtue of a failure to speak as opposed to a misrepresentation.

In the second place, as this citation suggests, the general principle of *caveat emptor*, based on it is on the recognition by the law that parties should be left free to determine their obligations to each other, is not to be eroded by the inappropriate invocation of tortious liability.

Where, however, a person elects to make a representation on a matter which is capable of being misleading because of its partial nature, there seems no reason why liability in tort for negligent misstatement should not arise, provided there was a duty to take care in relation to the making of the representation. Whether such a duty of care arose in the circumstances of the present case must be determined having regard to the legal principles laid down in *Hedley Byrne* and subsequently adopted in our courts.

Note

Keane J., in applying these principles to the facts before him, found the first two defendants and the fourth defendant had not made a fraudulent misrepresentation nor had the first two defendants made any pre-contractual warranties, negligent misstatements or breached covenants of quiet enjoyment. The third defendant was held liable under *Hedley Byrne*.

SECTION THREE—REMEDIES

A. DAMAGES

As we have seen in the *Delany* case (p. 452 above) an entitlement to damages depends on establishing that the representation was made either fraudulently or negligently.

Sale of Goods and Supply of Services Act 1980 s. 45 (1)

45. (1) Where a person has entered into a contract after a misrepresentation has been made to him by another party thereto and as a result thereof he has suffered loss, then, if the person making the misrepresentation would be liable to damages in respect thereof had the misrepresentation been made fraudulently, that person shall be so liable notwithstanding that the misrepresentation was not made fraudulently, unless he proves that he had reasonable ground to believe and did believe up to the time the contract was made that the facts represented were true.

(2) Where a person has entered into a contract after a misrepresentation has been made to him otherwise than fraudulently, and he would be entitled, by reason of the misrepresentation, to rescind the contract, then, if it is claimed in any proceedings arising out of the contract that the contract ought to be or has been rescinded, the court may declare the contract subsisting and award damages in lieu of rescission, if of opinion that it would be equitable to do so, having regard to the nature of the misrepresentation and the loss that would be caused by it if the contract were upheld, as well as to the loss that rescission would cause to the other party.

(3) Damages may be awarded against a person under subsection (2) whether or not he is liable to damages under subsection (1), but where he is so liable any award under subsection (2) shall be taken into account in assessing his liability under subsection (1).

In the *Phelps v White* case (p. 448 above) the Vice Chancellor noted that the case of fraudulent misrepresentation is an exception to the rule that relief is unavailable after completion of purchase:

. . . In every case where relief was refused on the ground that it was sought after the completion of the purchase, I find that the case of a fraudulent misrepresentation is stated to be an exception to the rule on which those decisions were founded. Malins V.C., in *Manson v Thacker*,[1] says, 'No doubt, if there has been a fraudulent misrepresentation on the part of the vendor, there may be compensation even after completion.' The fraudulent misrepresentation spoken of in those cases means a misrepresentation fraudulent in a legal sense, within the principles I have already stated, and does not necessarily involve moral fraud. The recent case of *Hart v Swaine*,[2] before Fry J., is a very clear authority for this proposition, and bears a close resemblance to the present case in every respect save one, which I shall afterwards consider. That was an action to set aside a sale after conveyance, on the ground of misrepresentation. Fry J. said, during the argument, that he saw no evidence of actual fraud on the part of the defendant, and that he had only made a mistake; but that, as the defendant had taken on himself to assert that the land was freehold, he was not at liberty to look into the state of his mind. The land there proved to be copyhold. In his judgment he said that the defendant took upon himself to assert that to be true which had turned out to be false, and made this assertion for the purpose of benefiting himself; and, that though he might have done this believing it to be true, he had, in the view of a court of law, committed a fraud. He quoted from the judgment of Maule J., in *Evans v Edmonds*,[3] a passage which it is unnecessary to repeat, and from that of Turner L.J., in *Rawlins v Wickham*,[4] the passage which I have already mentioned, and held that there had been a legal fraud committed by the defendant, which had resulted in a sale to the plaintiffs, and that he was bound by the authorities to give the plaintiffs the relief which they asked; and accordingly set aside the sale. If this misrepresentation authorised the setting aside the sale, it would at least equally entitle the purchaser to compensation, if he elected to hold his purchase. . . .

1. 7 ChD 620.   3. 13 CB 777, 786.
2. 7 ChD 42.   4. 3 De G. & J. 316, 317.

B. RESCISSION

Where the contract is executed

There are certain situations in which the remedy of rescission may not be available to the injured party.

In *Seddon v North Eastern Salt* [1905] 1 Ch. 326 the court determined that an executed contract may only be set aside in equity where there has been equitable fraud.

This rule however is not confined to cases where land formed the subject matter of the contract.

Lecky *v* Walter [1914] 1 IR 378 (Ch.)

The plaintiff entered into a contract to purchase bonds of a Dutch oil company on the basis of the defendant's representation that they were secured by company property in the US. When this proved to be untrue the plaintiff sought to have the contract set aside.

O'Connor M.R.:

. . . I am satisfied from the plaintiff's evidence that the statement that the bonds were charged on the oil-fields was, if not the only inducement, a material inducement to purchase them.

I need not pause to establish the proposition that it is not necessary to prove that a particular representation was the sole cause of the transaction, and that it is enough that it constituted a material inducement. I have now come to the point when I consider it established that the plaintiff purchased the bonds from the defendant, and that he was induced to make the purchase by misrepresentation by the defendant's agent, which is equivalent to misrepresentation by the defendant himself. The purely legal question then arises, does this state of affairs give the plaintiff the right to set aside a transaction which has been in fact completed, and is not merely in the process of completion? It must be borne in mind that there is no allegation of fraudulent misrepresentation, and therefore the case is to be treated as one in which a *bona fide* mistake was made by the defendant.

. . . counsel for the defendant, contended that in such circumstances the plaintiff had no cause of action, and he relied upon the judgment of Lord Campbell in the House of Lords in *Wilde v Gibson*,[1] where he says:

My Lords, after the very attentive and anxious consideration which this case has received, I have come to the clear conclusion that the decree appealed against ought to be reversed; and I must say that in the court below the distinction between a bill for carrying into execution an executory contract, and a bill to set aside a conveyance that has been executed, has not been very distinctly borne in mind. With regard to the first: if there be, in any way whatever, misrepresentation or concealment, which is material to the purchaser, a court of equity will not compel him to complete the purchase; but where the conveyance has been executed, I apprehend, my Lords, that a court of equity will set aside the conveyance only on the ground of actual fraud. And there would be no safety for the transactions of mankind, if, upon a discovery being made at any distance of time of a material fact not disclosed to the purchaser, of which the vendor had merely constructive notice, a conveyance which had been executed could be set aside.

In *Brownlie v Campbell*,[2] Lord Selborne affirms the same principle. He says there:

Passing from the stage of correspondence and negotiation to the stage of written agreement, the purchaser takes upon himself the risk of errors. I assume them to be errors unconnected with fraud in the particulars, and when the conveyance takes place it is not, so far as I know, in either country the principle of equity that relief should afterwards be given against that conveyance, unless there be a case of fraud, or a case of misrepresentation amounting to fraud, by which the purchaser may have been deceived.

There appears to be no doubt that the law established by these cases is just as applicable to the sale of a chattel or a chose in action as to the sale of real property which is carried out by conveyance: *Seddon v The North Eastern Salt Co. Ltd.*[3]

How are these authorities met by the plaintiff's counsel? |Counsel| in reply admitted, as of course he was obliged to admit, that the authorities referred to were binding on this court, but argued that they only apply to cases in which the purchaser has got in substance what he contracted to buy, and have no application when he has got something substantially different; and he relies upon the judgment of Blackburn J. in *Kennedy v Panama, New Zealand, and Australian Mail Co.*,[4] and particularly on the passage quoted by Joyce J., in *Seddon v The North Eastern Salt Co. Ltd.*[3] Lord Blackburn, then Blackburn J., says at p. 587:

There is, however, a very important difference between cases where a contract may be rescinded on account of fraud, and those in which it may be rescinded on the ground that there is a difference in substance between the thing bargained for and that obtained. It is enough to show that there was fraudulent representation as to *any part* of that which induced the party to enter into the contract which he seeks to rescind; but where there has been an innocent misrepresentation or misapprehension, it does not authorise a rescission unless it is such as to show that there is a complete difference in substance between what was supposed to be and what was taken, so as to constitute a failure of consideration. For example, where a horse is bought under the belief that it is sound, if the purchaser was induced to buy by a fraudulent representation as to the horse's soundness, the contract may be rescinded. If he was induced by an honest misrepresentation as to its soundness, though it may be clear that both vendor and purchaser thought they were dealing about a sound horse and were in error, yet the purchaser must pay the whole price, unless there was a warranty; even if there was a warranty, he cannot return the horse and claim back the whole price, unless there was a condition to that effect in the contract.

Now, if I may so speak of such an eminent judge as Lord Blackburn, the proposition which he there lays down must commend itself, not only to all lawyers, but to all persons of sound judgment. If there is a complete difference in substance between the thing contracted for and the thing delivered, there is a complete failure of consideration, and the price may be recovered. But if the thing delivered is in substance what was contracted for, and the price is paid, the transaction stands, and the purchaser has no remedy unless there has been a warranty. I am speaking of course of cases in which there has been no fraud, and where any misrepresentation which has induced the contract was a wholly innocent misrepresentation. Lord Blackburn gives as an example the common case of a horse bought on the representation that it was sound. The purchaser has no remedy unless he has got a warranty; and why? Because he has got in substance what he contracted for, *viz.* a horse. The horse may be in fact unsound, but still it is a horse, even though a very inferior one; and there is not a complete failure of consideration.

There would, of course, be a complete difference in substance if some animal other than a horse had been delivered, if such a thing can be imagined. I will try to give an example nearer akin to the present case. If a man contracts to purchase mortgage debentures of a public company, and takes delivery of what he believes to be such, but what he afterwards discovers to be ordinary shares, he has not got in substance what he bargained for, but something quite different, one being a specifically secured liability of the company, the other being a share in the company's undertaking on which the liability is imposed. Here again there is a complete failure of consideration. In *Kennedy v Panama, New Zealand, and Australian Mail Co.*, the plaintiff sought to set aside the contract for taking shares in the company on the ground that it was induced by an untrue statement in the company's prospectus that the company had a contract with the government of New Zealand for an important monthly mail service. The statement was made quite innocently, and as the result of mistake. It was held that the plaintiff was not entitled to any relief, there having been no fraud, and he having got what he contracted for, *viz.* shares, although not so valuable as they would have been if the company had had the mail contract mentioned. Lord Blackburn, in his judgment, referred to two reported cases: *Gompertz v Barlett*[5] and *Gurney v Wormersley*,[6] in which the plaintiffs got relief on the ground that they did not get what they bargained for. In each case there was a sale of a bill of exchange: in one case the bill was a forgery; in the other the bill was void under the stamp laws. In neither case did the plaintiff get what he contracted for—a valid bill of exchange.

I think that these decisions make it easy to determine whether in the present case the plaintiff got in substance what he agreed to buy.

. . . He agreed to buy bonds and he has got bonds. They may be of little or no value, but they are bonds. It is not alleged that they are forgeries. Their validity is not in any way impeached. In substance, then, the plaintiff has got what he bargained for. . . .

. . .

. . . if the representation was part of the contract, there might have been a warranty which would give the plaintiff the right to relief. But a representation is not necessarily a warranty. It may be only an inducement, and such it appears to me to have been in the present case. I am, therefore, bound to hold that inasmuch as the contract was completed, and there was no fraud, the sale cannot be set aside, and the action must be dismissed.

[1] 1 HLC 605, 632–3.	[4] LR 2 QB 580.
[2] 5 AC 925, 937.	[5] 2 E & B 849.
[3] [1905] 1 Ch. 326.	[6] 4 E & B 133.

Note

S. 44(b) of the Sale of Goods and Supply of Services Act 1980 removes the rule in *Seddon v* N.E. *Salt* as an objection to the grant of rescission. However, because s. 43 makes s. 44 (b) applicable only to contracts of sale of goods, hire-purchase, and supply of services the rule is not abrogated in sale of real property transactions.

Where the contract is affirmed

Lutton v Saville Tractors (Belfast) Ltd [1986] NI 327. (See this case in Chapter 18 especially at 888).

Note

Compare the *Lutton* decision to the case of *Thomas Dillon-Leetch v Maxwell Motors Ltd* [1984] ILRM 624. There the plaintiff bought a car from the defendant in May of 1981 following representations that the car was free from any defect and suitable for substantive journeys. Two months later the car manifested a significant defect in the braking system, which despite several attempts at repair recurred a second time during the following month. The plaintiff notified the defendant of the recurrence of the defect but did not return the car for further repair until November, having used the car in the interim period with a disconnected handbrake. Later the plaintiff wrote to the defendant stating that if the car failed again he would seek compensation. The car failed again the same month and the car was returned. Although the car was repaired the defendant failed to meet the plaintiff's proposals for compensation. Murphy J. held that as it would not be possible to restore parties to their pre-contractual positions rescission was not possible. He noted however that the defendants' unequivocal acceptance of the return of the car in November implied in the absence of any counter proposals by the defendant, that he had accepted the proposal of the plaintiff for the return of the car and payment of compensation.

Where there has been a delay in seeking relief

Delay in seeking rescission may prevent equitable relief. However, where fraud or oppression exists as a fact the courts are more lenient. In *O'Kelly and Wife v Glenny* (1846) 9 Ir Eq R 25 a delay of twelve years was held not to be fatal. There the plaintiff had been the victim of fraudulent misrepresentation.

In cases of innocent misrepresentation the courts may be less indulgent. See for example *Leaf v International Galleries* [1950] 2 KB 86.

Where third party rights are affected

John Anderson v Matthew Ryan [1967] IR 34

Henchy J.:

In January 1965, an advertisement appeared in a Dublin evening paper for the sale of an Austin-Healey (Sprite) motor car. A Mr Edwin Davis saw it and, being interested in cars, he telephoned a number indicated in the advertisement. As a result, two men called to his house with the Sprite. It happened that Mr Davis had an Austin (Mini) motor car. The two men seemed to take a fancy to the Mini, as Mr Davis did to the

Sprite, and the upshot of the negotiations was that it was agreed to exchange the Mini for the Sprite. The two men left with the Mini and Mr Davis found himself with the Sprite. No money had passed; it was a straight swop. The unfortunate part of the transaction was that, unknown to Mr Davis, the Sprite was a car that had been stolen in Northern Ireland. Within a week detectives descended upon him and took it away. Later a man pleaded guilty in the Dublin Circuit Court to fraudulently obtaining the Mini from Mr Davis by falsely pretending that he was the owner of the Sprite. Mr Davis eventually recovered the Mini and has since sold it.

In the meantime, someone approached the defendant in this action, who carries on business as a panel beater in Cork Street, Dublin, and indicated that he was prepared to sell the defendant a Mini for £200. It was, in fact, the Mini belonging to Mr Davis. The defendant was interested in the purchase but was not prepared to go through with it until he had obtained a purchaser to whom he could sell the car at a profit. The plaintiff, who is a garage owner in Bray, turned out to be such a person. He visited the defendant's premises, where the Mini happened to be, inspected the car, and agreed to buy it for £225 plus £22 for panel repairs to it, which the defendant agreed to do. The plaintiff, having made enquiries which showed that the car was not subject to a hire-purchase agreement, there and then, on 15 January 1965, made out a cheque in favour of the defendant for the sum of £244 10s 0d to cover the £225 for the Mini and also to cover an account that the plaintiff owed to the defendant for panel beating which had been previously done for the plaintiff by the defendant. The defendant lodged the cheque to his account on the following day. My impression from the evidence is that the defendant had no title to the Mini when that deal was made. But, later, on the same evening as he got the cheque from the plaintiff, the defendant gave a cheque for £200 for the car to someone who purported to be, but was not Mr Davis. The defendant proceeded to do the panel beating which he had arranged with the plaintiff to do.

A few days later the plaintiff called to the defendant's premises, paid the defendant the sum of £22 for the further panel beating, collected the registration book (which showed Mr Davis to be the owner) and took the Mini away. He then placed it on display in the forecourt of his garage in Bray as a second-hand car for sale. Once again the arm of the law reached out. Two detectives called and said that the Mini was the subject matter of criminal proceedings. They told the plaintiff that he would have to allow them to take it away and that if he did not give it to them they would return with a warrant. He let them take it away. That is the last he saw of the car or his £247. The plaintiff recovered judgment in the Circuit Court against the defendant for the sum of £247, and the defendant has appealed against that judgment.

. . .

In the present case, it is clear that, if the defendant was not the owner of the Mini at the time he sold it to the plaintiff, the plaintiff got nothing for his money and he would be entitled to recover the £247 as money paid upon a consideration that had wholly failed. Counsel for the plaintiff says that the car was sold on 15 January 1965, when the plaintiff inspected it, agreed on the price and gave a cheque for £244 10s 0d; and that the defendant then had no title.

. . .

The transaction between the plaintiff and the defendant on 15 January 1965, was no more than an agreement to sell. The property in the car did not pass. It was plainly the intention of the parties that the property would not pass until the panel beating had been done by the defendant and the balance of £22 had been paid; until that had happened the agreement to sell would not have merged into a sale.

. . .

. . . the central question is: 'Did the defendant have a good title to the car when he sold and delivered it to the plaintiff?' To decide this question one must go back to the circumstances under which the original owner, Mr Davis, parted with possession of the car. As I have said, he exchanged it for the Sprite. The inducement for him to do so was not alone the desirability to him of the exchange but also the representation by the other party that the Sprite was his property. That was a false and fraudulent representation as to an existing fact. The contract of exchange was, therefore, a voidable contract. Since Mr Davis intended to pass the ownership of the Mini, the person who got the car in exchange acquired a title to it, but it was a voidable title, that is, voidable at the option of Mr Davis. It would have been different if Mr Davis had parted with the Mini as a result of larceny by a trick, for then no title would have passed. Authority for the conclusion that what passed on the exchange was a voidable title is to be found in *Cundy v Lindsay*;[1] *Robin & Rambler Coaches, Ltd v Turner*;[2] *Central Newbury Car Auctions Ltd v Unity Finance Ltd*[3] and *Archbold on Criminal Pleading* (36th ed.) para. 1497.

There is no evidence that there was any intermediate sale of the Mini between the fraudulent exchange and the sale to the defendant. In fact, all the likelihood is that the car was sold to the defendant by or on behalf of the person who effected the fraudulent exchange. One looks then to see what title, if any, such person conveyed to the defendant. The answer is to be found in s. 23 of the Act, which is as follows: 'When the seller of goods has a voidable title thereto, but his title has not been avoided at the time of the sale, the buyer acquires a good title to the goods, provided he buys them in good faith and without notice of the seller's defect of title.' It is clear from the evidence that Mr Davis had not avoided the title of the person who sold the car to the defendant at the time to that sale, and it has not been suggested that the defendant bought otherwise than in good faith and without notice of the seller's defect of title. I am satisfied, therefore, that the defendant acquired a good title to the car and that he in turn passed a good title to the plaintiff. It is unfortunate that the plaintiff has been deprived of a car of which he was the rightful owner, but the fault for that does not lie with the defendant.

. . .

. . . I go no further than saying that no liability attaches to the defendant for the plaintiff's loss and that the plaintiff's claim must be dismissed.

[1] 3 App Cas 459, 464   [2] [1947] 2 All ER 284.   [3] [1957] 1 QB 371, 382.

Abatement of Price

If property is purchased for a given price and the quantity delivered is less than that promised, there can be an abatement or reduction in price, *pro rata*. (See p. 464 above and p. 1046 below.)

Equitable Indemnity

Costs contractually incurred under a contract can be recovered in equity, even if damages are not available. See *Whittington v Seale Hayne* (1890) 82 LT 49.

Chapter Eleven

Disclosure

INTRODUCTION

In the previous chapter we considered how verbal or written misstatements could be actionable. Liability in those cases depended on proof of a misstatement being made in breach of a contractual or tortious duty, the duty being either strict or based on some other standard such as reasonable care. There is no general duty to provide a full and frank explanation of all surrounding circumstances (e.g. that the car being offered for sale has been involved in an accident) that may influence a decision whether to contract or not. In an arms' length transaction, the seller and buyer, for example, are regarded as being of equal competence and if the buyer wants an assurance that the thing being offered meets the buyer's requirements the buyer should inspect the subject matter, seek to extract an express promise by way of warranty, or invoke whatever consumer protection or general statute law remedies there are at the buyer's disposal. Additional relief is possible through the law of mistake (see Chapter 9) but contractual mistake is difficult to invoke in this context.

However, fraudulent concealment or misrepresentation in a pre-contractual context, have always been actionable, but the boundary between fraudulent concealment and non-disclosure is a difficult one to draw at times. The law relating to non-marine insurance contracts establishes a general duty of disclosure of all material circumstances: this duty is often explained away on the basis of the applicant being in the best position to know the material circumstances surrounding the liability being covered by the policy, and, because of this imbalance as between the parties, the duty is defended on the grounds of economic efficiency; the insured can more cheaply disclose material circumstances as against the insurer seeking to establish these circumstances.

However, in *Banque Keyser Ullman S.A. v Skandia (UK) Insurance Co.* [1990] 1 KB 665, the right to avoid a contract for non-disclosure was stated by the Court of Appeal to depend not on contract but upon underlying principles of equity. This is an important observation because it helps to explain a number of recent Irish cases which have readjusted the scope of the duty so as to require the insurer to show greater clarity and uniformity in relation to business activities.

As a general rule there is no liability for non-disclosure of material facts.

Smith *v* Hughes (1871) LR 6 QB 597
(Facts on p. 403.)

Cockburn C.J.:
. . .

I take the true rule to be, that where a specific article is offered for sale, without express warranty, or without circumstances from which the law will imply a warranty— as where, for instance, an article is ordered for a specific purpose—and the buyer has full opportunity of inspecting and forming his own judgment, if he chooses to act on his own judgment, the rule *caveat emptor* applies. If he gets the article he contracted to buy, and that article corresponds with what it was sold as, he gets all he is entitled to, and is bound by the contract. Here the defendant agreed to buy a specific parcel of oats. The oats were what they were sold as, namely, good oats according to the sample. The buyer persuaded himself they were old oats, when they were not so; but the seller neither said nor did anything to contribute to his deception. He has himself to blame. The question is not what a man of scrupulous morality or nice honour would do under such circumstances. The case put of the purchase of an estate, in which there is a mine under the surface, but the fact is unknown to the seller, is one in which a man of tender conscience or high honour would be unwilling to take advantage of the ignorance of the seller; but there can be no doubt that the contract for the sale of the estate would be binding.

SECTION ONE—EXCEPTIONS TO THE GENERAL RULE

A. RESTRICTIVE COVENANTS IN THE SALE OF LEASEHOLD PREMISES

Power *v* Barrett (1887) 19 LR (Ir) 450
The plaintiff held a leasehold interest in certain premises which he agreed to sell to the defendant, a chandler and oil merchant. The lease contained a covenant not to use the premises to carry on *inter alia* any 'dangerous, noxious, or offensive trade, business, or profession whatsoever'. The plaintiff did not disclose the existence of this covenant to the defendant. When the defendant discovered it he refused to complete and the plaintiff sued for specific performance.

V.C.:
. . .

The plaintiff was aware at the time of the negotiations, of the object and purpose of the defendant in agreeing to take the premises. He was perfectly aware of the nature of the business intended to be carried on there, namely, that of chandler and oil merchant, which implies the sale of all goods ordinarily sold and stored by a person engaged in such a trade. The defendant, accompanied by two friends, visited the premises in question, when a conversation arose involving knowledge by the plaintiff of the purpose of the defendant; and the parties then discussed the quantity of oil with which the vaults and stores could be filled. It is idle to contend that the sale and storing of petroleum or paraffin is not within the business of the defendant as an oil merchant. It was, therefore, well known to the plaintiff that the defendant required the premises for the purpose of storing quantities of this substance—whether 1000 barrels or 100 barrels is unimportant—and it is clear that on the occasion of the defendant's visit there was mention of the quantity of oil the premises could contain.

This being so, it was the duty of the plaintiff to inform the defendant of the existence of the restrictive clause in the lease—to inform him of the existence of every covenant which could reasonably be a prohibition against carrying on the trade for which the defendant desired to take the premises.

It is immaterial whether the plaintiff was himself actually aware of the extent, or even of the existence, of this covenant. It was his duty to be aware and to know of it. Lord St Leonards, in his work on *Vendors and Purchasers* (14th ed.), 214, quoting the case of *Flight v Barton*,[1] states the law on the subject. I take the law to be as there laid down, and that there is now no question that it is so—that if the purchaser state the object which he has in purchasing, and the seller is silent as to a covenant in the lease prohibiting or interfering with that object, his silence would be equivalent to a representation that there was no such prohibitory covenant, although he was not aware of the extent or operation of the covenant. I am of opinion that a vendor in the position of the plaintiff here is bound to know what covenants are in his lease, and that he is bound, moreover, to communicate such knowledge to an intending purchaser—provided such covenant can be reasonably interpreted as affecting the object which he is aware the purchaser has in view in purchasing the premises, and I think that the plaintiff has not fulfilled that obligation.

The plaintiff states he was not aware of the existence of this covenant. On this point, however, I entertain great doubt. I cannot understand why he should have paid a visit to the defendant, and inquired whether he was a manufacturer, unless he was aware of some restriction. The defendant says the plaintiff added a statement that the lease under which he held the premises contained a clause prohibiting the manufacture of certain articles. This is denied by the plaintiff, but I rather incline to believe the defendant's testimony on this point. Why should the plaintiff ask the defendant if he was a manufacturer, unless to avoid the consequences of not informing him of something which would interfere with his manufacture? I must assume the plaintiff to have been aware that the restriction in the lease was not confined to manufacture. It would be an extraordinary conclusion of law that the defendant is affected with constructive notice solely because he was informed that there was a lease, while the plaintiff should not be deemed to know the contents of that lease, under which he held, and which he was about to sell.

The plaintiff went farther than this; for the very fact that he made the inquiry as to whether the defendant was a manufacturer—even if there was no mention on that occasion by the plaintiff of a prohibition in the lease—was sufficient to induce the defendant to suppose that any such prohibition did not prevent anything but manufacturing. The plaintiff goes beyond mere silence, because his observations constituted an implied misrepresentation that there was no restriction except as to manufacturing.

. . .

. . . I must dismiss this action, with costs.

[1] 3 My. & K. 282. 2M 2.

Note

Equity requires the vendor of property to disclose unusual defects in the title of the property.

B. Error in Advertisement

Sargent v Irish Multiwheel Ltd (1955) 21–22 Ir Jur Rep 42

The defendants advertised in the following terms: 'Among our large selection of new and secondhand cars, vans, and trucks, we have to offer: . . . Vans—1947 Austin 10 cwt. English assembled van for sale, taxed for year £55.' The one van only was priced at £55 in the advertisement. The plaintiff saw the advertisement and approached the defendants. He asked to see 'some vans' for sale. The defendants showed him various vans, including one and only one, priced at £55. The plaintiff believed this was the van advertised, but did not verify this fact with the defendants. The defendants admitted in evidence that in fact this was the same van. They knew it was Irish-assembled. They also knew that by an error it had been described in the advertisement as English-assembled. When negotiating with the plaintiff they did not mention that it was Irish-assembled, nor did the plaintiff say that he required an English-assembled van. The plaintiff purchased the van in the belief that it was English-assembled. He subsequently sold it and warranted it to the purchaser as English-assembled. In due course its country of assembly was discovered and the plaintiff was sued for breach of warranty. He suffered, as a result, loss and expense. The plaintiff failed to recover this loss and expense from the defendants in the District Court and appealed to the Circuit Court.

MacCarthy J.:

I have no hesitation in finding for the plaintiff in this case. The plaintiff came to the defendants and purchased from them a van in full reliance on a representation as to that van given in the defendants' advertisement. That representation was false, to the knowledge of the defendants. The defendants have said that the representation was made in error. It may be so. But once the plaintiff came to the defendants in consequence of their advertisement and was shown the subject of it, there was a duty on the defendants to warn the plaintiff of the error. They failed in this duty, and are liable to the plaintiff for the loss he suffered.

C. Animal Sales

Gill v McDowell [1903] IR 463
(Facts on p. 413.)

O'Brien L.C.J.:

. . .

I think also there is evidence of misrepresentation sufficient to sustain the action. It is perfectly notorious that a bad animal is often placed among good, so that the defects of the bad animal may, by association with the general lot, escape detection. In the case before us the animal of itself was calculated to give occasion to mistake; from one point of view it might be regarded as a heifer, and from another point of view it might be regarded as a bullock. It would, indeed, be hard to find anything more calculated of itself to deceive, and the defendant, well knowing that it was not a bullock or heifer, drove it into a fair where bullocks and heifers are sold, and deliberately put it into a category to which it did not belong, and to which he knew it did not belong. He associates it with a heifer and a bullock, makes it as one of a lot, and thereby the purchaser was, as a matter of fact, deceived, there being, I think, a tacit representation that this animal, standing in this cattle fair with a heifer and bullock, and offered for sale with them, was either a heifer and bullock. The plaintiff was, as a matter of fact, deceived; the defendant knew he was deceived. In my opinion there is some evidence that he was thrown off his guard by the action of the defendant.

Note

See also *Kennedy v Hennessy* (1906) 40 ILTR 84.

SECTION TWO—CONTRACTS UBERRIMAE FIDEI—INSURANCE CONTRACTS

A duty to disclose material facts exists in certain types of contract in which one of the parties is in a stronger position to know the truth of the statements made. Examples of these type of contracts include family settlements and insurance contracts.

A. DISCLOSURE OF A MATERIAL FACT

Chariot Inns Ltd *v* Assicurazioni Generali SPA and Coyle Hamilton Hamilton Phillips Ltd [1981] ILRM 173

Kenny J.:

. . .

. . . A contract of insurance requires the highest standard of accuracy, good faith, candour and disclosure by the insured when making a proposal for insurance to an insurance company. It has become usual for an insurance company to whom a proposal for insurance is made, to ask the proposed insured to answer a number of questions. Any misstatement in the answers given, when they relate to a material matter affecting the insurance, entitles the insurance company to avoid the policy and to repudiate liability if the event insured against happens. But the correct answering of any questions asked is not the entire obligation of the person seeking insurance; he is bound, in addition, to disclose to the insurance company every matter which is material to the risk against which he is seeking indemnity.

What then is to be regarded as material to the risk against which the insurance is sought? It is not what the person seeking insurance regards as material nor is it what the insurance company regards as material. It is a matter or circumstance which would reasonably influence the judgment of a prudent insurer in deciding whether he would take the risk and, if so, in determining the premium which he would demand. The standard by which materiality is to be determined is objective, not subjective. The matter has, in the last resort, to be determined by the court: the parties to the litigation may call experts in insurance matters as witnesses to give evidence of what they would have regarded as material but the question of materiality is not to be determined by such witnesses.

The generally accepted test of materiality in all forms of insurance against risks when property of any kind is involved is stated in s.18(2) of the Marine Insurance Act, 1906: 'Every circumstance is material which would influence the judgment of a prudent insurer in fixing the premium or determining whether he will take the risk'. Although this test is stated in an Act dealing with marine insurance, it has been accepted as a correct guide to the law in insurance against damage to property or goods of all types.

The rule to determine the materiality of a fact not disclosed to the insurers was expressed by Lord Justice MacKinnon with his customary pungency in *Zurich General Accident and Liability Insurance Co. Ltd v Morrison* [1942] 1 All ER 529 at 539:

> Under the general law of insurance an insurer can avoid a policy if he proves that there has been misrepresentation or concealment of a material fact by the insured. What is material is that which would influence the mind of a prudent insurer in deciding whether to accept the risk or fix the premium. If this be proved, it is not necessary further to prove that the mind of that actual insurer was so affected. In other words the insurer could not rebut the claim to avoid the policy because of a material misrepresentation by a plea that the particular insurer concerned was so stupid, ignorant or reckless that he could not exercise the judgment of a prudent insurer and was in fact unaffected by anything the insured had represented or concealed.

The statement of Samuels J. of the rules relating to the law about materiality of facts not disclosed in insurance law in *Mayne Nickless Ltd v Pegler* (1974) 1 NSWLR 228 has the authority of having been approved and followed by the Judicial Committee of the Privy Council in *Marene Knitting Mills Pty Ltd v Greater Pacific General Insurances Ltd* [1976] 2 L1. LR 631:

> Accordingly I do not think that it is generally open to examine what the insurer would in fact have done had he had the information not disclosed. The question is whether that information would have been relevant to the exercise of the insurers' option to accept or reject the insurance proposed. It seems to me that the test of materiality is this: a fact is material if it would have reasonably affected the mind of a prudent insurer in determining whether he will accept the insurance, and if so, at what premium and on what conditions.

In January 1976, the plaintiffs ('Chariot')—whose directors and shareholders were Mr and Mrs Wootton—bought licensed premises at Ranelagh, Dublin. The directors decided to run the premises as a public house and also to have a cabaret entertainment. This made it necessary to build a larger room at the back. There were furnishings in the existing room at the back and as the extension could not be built without removing them, the directors decided to store them in 82 Lower Leeson Street. This latter premises was owned by Consolidated Investment Holdings Limited ('Consolidated') whose shares had been purchased by Mr Wootton and his business partner, Mr Mockler, but had been registered in the maiden names of their wives. Mr Wootton and Mr Mockler intended to use the premises as a hotel and discotheque and as Mr Wootton had been associated with a number of night clubs which had been prosecuted for breaches of the licensing laws, the directors expected considerable local opposition when their application for permission for a change of user was made if it became known that his wife or he were associated with Consolidated.

The insurance brokers acting for Mr Wootton were Coyle Hamilton Hamilton Phillips Ltd ('the brokers'), the second-named defendants. Mr Wootton had almost all his dealings with the brokers through Mr John Hart, an employee of theirs. The brokers placed the insurance on 82 Lower Leeson Street with the Sun Alliance and London Insurance Group and, in the policy, the premises were described and it was stated that the property was 'at present unoccupied'. When the directors of Chariot decided to store their furnishings in 82 Lower Leeson Street, Mr Hart advised them that further insurance cover on the furnishings was necessary. An endorsement on the policy in connection with the furnishings valuing them at £15,000, was made. As the premises at Lower Leeson Street were unoccupied, they were broken into by squatters almost nightly between November 1975 and the happening of the fire on 19 April 1976. These squatters lit fires and cooked there but left each morning before Mr Wootton arrived. The premises and Chariot's furnishings, which Consolidated held as bailees, were badly damaged. A claim for malicious damage was lodged with the local authority and was compromised by an agreed award of £55,000. Chariot was paid £8,000 by Consolidated who forwarded them a Sun Alliance cheque for this sum made out in favour of Chariot in respect of the furnishings. The claim by Consolidated against their insurance company was handled by Corcoran Insurances Ltd. Mr Mockler and Mr Wootton were so dissatisfied with the type of cover which the brokers had negotiated in connection with the Lower Leeson Street premises that they had changed their brokers and had given their business to Corcoran Insurances Ltd in December 1975.

When the plaintiffs bought the Chariot Inn, it was insured with the General Accident Insurance Co. Ltd ('the General Accident') and this policy was renewed subsequently. The principal in Corcoran Insurances Ltd advised Mr Wootton that a different and wider insurance cover was advisable in respect of the Chariot Inn, but when the General Accident were asked to quote for this, they increased the premium which they would require by 50 per cent. Mr Wootton was most reluctant to pay such a large increase and decided to get his brokers to ask for tenders for the insurance. The first-named defendants, who are an Italian insurance company, are represented and carry on business in the Republic of Ireland through their agents, International Underwriters Ltd and they sent in the lowest tender. Mr Hart had remained on friendly terms with Mr Wootton and frequently called to his premises. Chariot wanted cover against fire risk, employer's liability, liability to the public and loss of profits. Separate proposal forms for each type of insurance were sent out by the first-named defendants and Mr Hart got these. On 22 February 1978 Mr Hart called to Chariot's premises in Ranelagh with these proposal forms. They were issued by International Underwriters Ltd. One related to material damage. Mr Hart asked the questions necessary to fill in the answers to the questions and gave any other information required. It was not disputed by anyone during the trial that the handwriting in which the answers appeared was Mr Hart's. There was a discussion about the fire at Leeson Street and Mr Hart said that it was totally unnecessary to disclose this on the proposal forms because (as Mr Wootton said) 'we were dealing with a separate company and only had to show what was relevant to the Chariot Inn' (Question 167 first day). It is of importance that there is a question in this case as to who were the brokers who negotiated the policy with the first-named defendants and Mr Hart wrote in 'Coyle Hamilton'. In the form dealing with material damage this appeared:

MATERIAL DAMAGE
Give claims experience for loss over the last 5 years (i.e. date, nature of loss, amount paid or outstanding. Brief details of how loss occurred).
If none in any class say so.

The answer written in by Mr Hart was 'None'.

The first-named defendants subsequently issued policies to the plaintiffs in respect of the various forms of liability for which the plaintiffs sought insurance cover and in respect of indemnity against material loss. On 14 May 1978 a serious fire occurred at the plaintiffs premises which caused extensive damage. In June 1978, the first-named defendants repudiated liability because of the non-disclosure of the fire in Leeson Street. From the time of the fire, the first-named defendants suspected that Mr Wootton had set fire to the premises and stated during the hearing of the case that they would not have raised the issue of non-disclosure if they had not suspected that this was a case of arson.

When the first-named defendants repudiated liability, the plaintiffs brought this action against them claiming a declaration that the policy issued by them giving indemnity against material losses was valid and as against the brokers, damages for breach of contract and negligence.

. . .

Three experts on insurance business gave evidence. Their unanimous view was that the fire at Leeson Street and the damage to the plaintiffs' goods were matters that were material to the risk which the first-named defendants were asked to insure. Their opinions were not conclusive on this matter. The question whether any of these matters were material is essentially an inference from facts established by evidence. The circumstance that Mr Wootton was a director of Chariot and of Consolidated would not of itself make a fire on the premises owned by Consolidated a fact material to the risk undertaken by the first-named defendants when they insured Chariot against fire in the latters' premises.

I think, however, that it was material to the insurance effected by Chariot with the first-named defendants that goods belonging to Chariot were damaged by fire in premises owned by Consolidated. The answer to the query about claims made by Chariot for loss over the last five years was literally correct, but though Chariot had no claim against the insurance company which had issued a policy in respect of the Leeson Street premises, they were paid by Sun Alliance the sum negotiated in respect of the furnishings stored.

The circumstances in which the goods of Chariot were stored in the Leeson Street premises and the fact that Chariot ultimately got payment in respect of them were, in my view, matters which would reasonably have affected the judgment of a prudent insurer in deciding whether to take the risk or in fixing the premium, particularly as Mr Wootton was a director of and managed and controlled Chariot and Consolidated.

It was strenuously contended by counsel for the brokers that the onus of establishing that the matter not disclosed was material to the risk undertaken lay on the first-named defendants and that to discharge this onus, they had to establish that the matter not disclosed did affect, and not might have affected the judgment of the first-named defendants. I accept the first part of this proposition but not the second. It is necessary to establish that the fact not disclosed would have reasonably affected the judgment of a prudent insurer . . .

(Henchy and Griffin JJ. concurred.)

Note

This standard of disclosure has been substantially revised by the Supreme Court in the following two cases.

B. LIMITS

Aro Road and Land Vehicles Ltd v The Insurance Corporation of Ireland Ltd [1986] IR 403

The plaintiff agreed to sell and deliver goods to a company in Northern Ireland. The carriers organised insurance cover for the consignment. The only information sought by the underwriters was the names and addresses of the consignor and consignee and the nature and value of the goods. When the consignment was hijacked and lost, the defendants sought to repudiate liability on the basis that the plaintiff had failed to disclose the fact that Mr Mansfield, its managing director and principal shareholder had been convicted of a number of offences involving dishonesty twenty years previously.

Carroll J. in the High Court applied the test for the duty of disclosure laid down in the Chariot Inns case, and accepted that a reasonable underwriter may have regarded the conviction as relevant to the risk.

Henchy J.:

. . .

I accept without question that it is a general principle of the law of insurance that a person seeking insurance, whether acting personally or through a limited company, is bound to disclose every circumstance within his knowledge which would have influenced the judgment of a reasonable and prudent insurer in fixing the premium or in deciding whether to take on the risk. Carroll J., while personally of opinion that Mr Mansfield's non-disclosure of his convictions and imprisonment was not material, deferred to the expert opinion given in the High Court (which she accepted and considered to transcend her personal opinion) that a reasonable and prudent underwriter would regard that matter as material and would have regarded its non-disclosure as a good reason for refusing to underwrite the risk. Accordingly, she held that the insurers were entitled to avoid the policies in question and to repudiate liability. On the assumption that full disclosure of all known material facts was obligatory, I consider that the judge's conclusion could not be interfered with by this court: see *Northern Bank Finance v Charlton* |1979| IR 149.

It emerged, however, in the course of the hearing of this appeal, that a particular aspect of the case was not adverted to, either in the pleadings or in the argument in the High Court. This was whether the circumstances of the case showed it to be an exception to the usual requirement of full disclosure.

. . .

Generally speaking, contracts of insurance are contracts *uberrimae fidei*, which means that utmost good faith must be shown by the person seeking the insurance. Not alone must that person answer to the best of his knowledge any question put to him in a proposal form, but, even when there is no proposal form, he is bound to divulge all matters within his knowledge which a reasonable and prudent insurer would consider material in deciding whether to underwrite the risk or to underwrite it on special terms.

That is the general rule. Like most general legal rules, however, it is subject to exceptions. For instance, the contract itself may expressly or by necessary implication exclude the requirement of full disclosure. It is for the parties to make their own bargain— subject to any relevant statutory requirements—and if the insurer shows himself to be prepared to underwrite the risk without requiring full disclosure, he cannot later avoid the contract and repudiate liability on the ground of non-disclosure.

An example of a contract of insurance which excludes full disclosure is where the circumstances are such as to preclude the possibility of full disclosure; or where the requirement of full disclosure would be so difficult, or so impractical, or so unreasonable, that the insurer must be held by his conduct to have ruled it out as a requirement. This is exemplified by many forms of what I may call 'over-the-counter insurance'. Because this case is concerned only with fire and theft cover, I am addressing myself only to property insurance. Many concerns, such as airlines, shipping companies and travel agents—acting as agents for an insurance company and usually under the umbrella of a master policy—are prepared to insure travellers or consignors of goods in respect of luggage or of goods consigned, in circumstances in which full disclosure is neither asked for nor could reasonably be given effect to. The time factor, if nothing else, would rule out the requirement of full disclosure in many instances: an air traveller who buys insurance of his luggage in an airport just before boarding an aeroplane could not be expected to have time to make disclosure of *all* material circumstances. Insurance sold in that way obviously implies a willingness on the part of the insurer to provide the cover asked for without requiring disclosure of all material circumstances. The question in this case is whether this insurance, which the judge has held was entered into by Mr Mansfield's company in good faith and without any intention to defraud, was attended by circumstances which show that the insurers are precluded from claiming that full disclosure was a prerequisite of a valid contract of insurance.

Consider the relevant circumstances. Mr Mansfield, through his company, was sold this insurance. He did not look for it. It was suggested by CIE. He was reluctant to take it out; he considered it a waste of money. CIE as agents for the insurers arranged the rates and filled in the relevant certificates of insurance. Once that was done, CIE were ready to transport the goods. They sought no further information from Mr Mansfield and apparently deemed none necessary. Before collecting and transporting the goods, they did not furnish the certificates of insurance to Mr Mansfield or his company. They did not even inform Mr Mansfield or his company of the identity of the insurers. It is conceded by counsel for the insurers that if Mr Mansfield was to make full disclosure he would have to make such inquiries as would bring the identity of the insurers to his knowledge—or alternatively to pass the relevant information to CIE as their agents. CIE as well as being the insurers' agents, were to be the carriers of the goods insured. Everything points to the conclusion that when, as carriers of the goods, they got the information necessary for their purposes as carriers, and then arranged insurance of the goods during transit, the insurance was for all practical purposes concluded, so that no further information could have thereafter been asked for.

The circumstances of this case seem to me to show that CIE, acting as agents for the insurers, accepted this insurance without expecting or requiring disclosure of *all* relevant circumstances. The informal, almost perfunctory, way in which CIE effected this insurance, their readiness to collect the premium and proceed to carry the goods to their destination as soon as they had ascertained the premium, showed a failure or unwillingness to give the insured company an opportunity to make full disclosure before the contract of insurance was concluded. The relevant circumstances indicate an indifference on the part of CIE as agents for the insurers as to matters such as the personal circumstances of the managing director of the insured company.

It may well be the law that even in a case such as this certain types of information may not be knowingly withheld by the insured, but this case calls only for an answer to the question whether in the circumstances of the case an innocent non-disclosure of an incident in the past life of the managing director of the insured company entitled the insurers to avoid the policy. In my opinion it did not. Insurers who allow agents such as shippers, carriers, airlines, travel agents and the like to insure on their behalf goods being carried, and to sell that insurance to virtually all and sundry who ask for it, with minimal formality or inquiry, and with no indication that full disclosure is to be made of any matter which the insurers may *ex post facto* deem to be material, cannot be held to contract subject to a condition that the insured must furnish *all* material information.

I would allow the plaintiff's appeal and remit the case to the High Court for the assessment of damages.

(Griffin J. concurred.)

McCarthy J.:

...

In my view, if the judgment of an insurer is such as to require disclosure of what he thinks is relevant but which a reasonable insured, if he thought of it at all, would not think relevant, then, in the absence of a question directed towards the disclosure of such a fact, the insurer, albeit prudent, cannot properly be held to be acting reasonably. A contract of insurance is a contract of the utmost good faith on both sides; the insured is bound to disclose every matter which might reasonably be thought to be material to the risk against which he is seeking indemnity; that test of reasonableness is an objective one not to be determined by the opinion of underwriter, broker or insurance agent, but by, and only by, the tribunal determining the issue. Whilst accepted standards of conduct and practice are of significance in determining issues of alleged professional negligence, they are not to be elevated into being an absolute shield against allegations of malpractice—see O'Donovan v Cork County Council |1967| IR 173 and Roche v Peilow |1985| IR 232. In disputes concerning professional competence, a profession is not to be permitted to be the final arbiter of standards of competence. In the instant case, the insurance profession is not to be permitted to dictate a binding definition of what is reasonable. The learned trial judge depended part of her judgment upon the decision of this court in Chariot Inns v Assicurazioni Generali |1981| IR 199. In his judgment, with which Henchy and Griffin JJ. agreed, Kenny J. stated at p. 225:

> A contract of insurance requires the highest standard of accuracy, good faith, candour and disclosure by the insured when making a proposal for insurance to an insurance company. It has become usual for an insurance company to whom a proposal for insurance is made to ask the proposed insured to answer a number of questions. Any misstatement in the answers given, when they relate to a material matter affecting the insurance, entitles the insurance company to avoid the policy and to repudiate liability if the event insured against happens. But the correct answering of any questions asked is not the entire obligation of the person seeking insurance: he is bound, in addition, to disclose to the insurance company every matter which is material to the risk against which he is seeking indemnity.

> What is to be regarded as material to the risk against which the insurance is sought? It is not what the person seeking insurance regards as material, nor is it what the insurance company regards as material. It is a matter of circumstance which would reasonably influence the judgment of a prudent insurer in deciding whether he would take the risk, and, if so, in determining the premium which he would demand. The standard by which materiality is to be determined is objective and not subjective. In the last resort the matter has to be determined by the court: the parties to the litigation may call experts in insurance matters as witnesses to give evidence of what they would have regarded as material, but the question of materiality is not to be determined by such witnesses.

These observations were made in a case in which there was a proposal form, there were questions asked by the insurer and, as this court held, there was a non-disclosure of a matter material to the risk. In the High Court (in Chariot Inns) Keane J., at p. 209, said:

> The most widely accepted test of materiality in all forms of insurance on property and goods appears to be that set out in s. 18, sub-s. 2, of the Marine Insurance Act, 1906, which is in the following terms:
>> 'Every circumstance is material which would influence the judgment of a prudent insurer in fixing the premium, or determining whether he will take the risk.'

That test has been frequently stated to be applicable to non-marine insurance as well: see *Joel v Law Union & Crown Insurance Co.* and *March Cabaret v London Assurance*. Another test has sometimes been proposed, i.e. the test of whether a reasonable man in the position of the assured and with knowledge of the facts in dispute ought to have realised that they were material to the risk. But this test has been confined normally in its application to cases of life see *MacGillivray & Parkington on Insurance Law* (6th ed.) paras 749, 750. It was not suggested by any of the parties as the appropriate test in the present case and, accordingly, I propose to apply the test set out in s. 18, sub-s. 2 of the Act of 1906.

Kenny J. did not expressly advert to this proposition but it reflects the argument advanced by the plaintiff here touching on what the insured might consider relevant or material. Keane J., at p. 207, referred to the judgment of Fletcher Moulton L.J. in *Joel v Law Union & Crown Insurance Co.* |1908| 2 KB 863 at p. 892. There it was said: 'Over and above the two documents signed by the applicant, and in my opinion unaffected by them, there remained the common law obligation of disclosure of all knowledge possessed by the applicant material to the risk about to be undertaken by the company, such materiality being a matter to be judged of by the jury and not by the court.'

The same Lord Justice, at p. 885, had some critical comments to make on the practices on the part of insurance offices of requiring that the accuracy of the answers to the proposal form should be the basis of the contract. I point to this so as to emphasise that *Joel v Law Union & Crown Insurance Co.* |1908| 2 KB 863 was a case concerned with a proposal form and insurance effected on foot of it as was *Chariot Inns* |1981| IR 199. This is not such a case, but the test remains one of the utmost good faith. Yet, how does one depart from such a standard if reasonably and genuinely one does not consider some fact material; how much the less does one depart from such a standard when the failure to disclose is entirely due to a failure of recollection? Where there is no spur to the memory, where there is no proposal form with its presumably relevant questions, how can a failure of recollection lessen the quality of good faith? Good faith is not raised in its standard by being described as the utmost good faith; good faith requires candour and disclosure, not, I think, accuracy in itself, but a genuine effort to achieve the same using all reasonably available sources, a factor well illustrated by Fletcher Moulton L.J. at p. 885 of *Joel*. If the duty is one that requires disclosure by the insured of all material facts which are known to him, then it may well require an impossible level of performance. Is it reasonable of an underwriter to say: 'I expect disclosure of what I think is relevant or what I may think is relevant but which a reasonable proposer may not think of at all or, if he does, may not think is relevant'? The classic authority is the judgment of Lord Mansfield in *Carter v Boehm* (1766) 3 Burr. 1905 where, in terms free from exaggeration, he stated at p. 1911:

> The *reason* of the rule which obliges parties to disclose, is to prevent fraud and to encourage good faith. It is adapted to *such* facts as vary the nature of the contract; which one privately knows, and the other is ignorant of, and has no reason to suspect.
> The question therefore must always be 'Whether there was, under all the circumstances at the time the policy was underwritten, a *fair representation*; or a *concealment*; fraudulent, if *designed*; or, though not designed, *varying materially the object* of the policy, and *changing the risque* understood to be run.

If the determination of what is material were to lie with the insurer alone I do not know how the average citizen is to know what goes on in the insurer's mind, unless the insurer asks him by way of the questions in a proposal form or otherwise. I do not accept that he must seek out the proposed insurer and question him as to his reason-ableness, his prudence, and what he considers material. The proposal form will ordinarily contain a wide ranging series of questions followed by an omnibus question as to any other matters that are material. In the instant case, if Mr Mansfield had ever had the opportunity of completing a proposal form, which, due to the convenient arrangement made between the insurers and CIE, he did not, there is no reason to think that he would have recounted petty convictions of about twenty years before the time. For the reasons I have sought to illustrate, in my view, the learned trial judge failed correctly to apply the very stringent test; in my judgment, the insurers failed to discharge the onus of proof that lay on them.

There is a second ground upon which, also, in my view the plaintiff is entitled to succeed. Without detracting from what I have said in respect of the general law of insurance, in my judgment, that law is materially affected by over-the-counter insurance such as found in cases of the present kind, in other forms of transit and in personal travel, including holiday insurance. If no questions are asked of the insured, then, in the absence of fraud, the insurer is not entitled to repudiate on grounds of non-disclosure. Fraud might arise in such an instance as where an intending traveller has been told of imminent risk of death and then takes out life insurance in a slot machine at an airport. Otherwise, the insured need but answer correctly the questions asked; these questions must be limited in kind and number; if the insurer were to have the opportunity of denying or loading the insurance one purpose of the transaction would be defeated. Expedition is the hallmark of this form of insurance. [Counsel for the defendant] suggested that the whole basis of insurance could be seriously damaged if there was any weakening in the rigidity and, I must add, the severity, of the principle he sought to support. The force of such an argument as a proposition of law is matched by the improbability of the event.

(Walsh and Hederman JJ. agreed.)

Note

1. Is McCarthy J.'s reference to the reasonable insured compatible with Kenny J.'s test in the *Chariot Inns* case of the prudent underwriter?
2. See 'Contract Property Insurance—A Return to Utmost Good Faith by Both Sides' by R. Clark in (1987) 9 DULJ 117.

Elizabeth Ann Keating v New Ireland Assurance Co. plc [1990] ILRM 110

The plaintiff and her husband entered a life assurance policy in June 1985. At a medical examination prior to entering the insurance policy, Mr Keating disclosed that he had undergone examination for what appeared to be a digestive ailment and he made available the names of the doctors who had treated him. Unknown to Mr Keating he had been diagnosed as suffering from angina at that time and the drugs he had been subse-quently prescribed were to treat this condition. Later Mr Keating died as a result of the angina and the defendants sought to repudiate the plaintiff's claim on the basis *inter alia* of non-disclosure of a material fact.

McCarthy J.:

. . .

The insurer might well contend that the deceased *ought* to have known that there was some problem arising with his heart; the onus, however, of proving that he *did* know lies upon the insurer; it is not sufficient to prove that he *ought* to have known. The fact that the three doctors concerned *did* know does not impute knowledge to the deceased, to whom the medical examiner for the insurer (Dr Duffy), was enjoined by the examination form to give no information as to the result of the examination.

The insurers were not informed of these material facts; was it a non-disclosure? One cannot disclose what one does not know, albeit that this puts a premium on ignorance. It may well be that wilful ignorance would raise significant other issues; such is not the case here. If the proposer for life insurance has answered all the questions asked to the best of his ability and truthfully, his next-of-kin are not to be damnified because of his ignorance or obtuseness which may be sometimes due to a mental block on matters affecting one's health.

Support for this view is to be found in my judgment, with which Walsh and Hederman JJ. agreed, in *Aro Road and Land Vehicles Ltd v Insurance Corporation of Ireland Ltd* |1986| IR 403. In that case, as in this, reliance was placed on the observations of Kenny J. in *Chariot Inns v Assicurazioni Generali* |1981| IR 199. *Chariot Inns* was, like this, a proposal form case; the decision turned upon the determination of what is material; such is not the issue here. The *Aro Road and Land Vehicles Ltd* case was decided upon a preliminary point as to materiality and, accordingly, the expressed challenge to the reasonably prudent test as outlined in *Chariot Inns* did not arise.

Note

It should be noted that limits to the duty to disclose relate to other areas apart from situations where no proposal form exists. For example if specific questions are asked in proposal forms this may waive the insurer's right to further disclosure.

Hilda Kelleher *v* Irish Life Assurance Co. Ltd (SC) 8 February 1993, unrep.

A 'special promotional offer' was made available, and accepted by the plaintiff who assured her husband's life in 1985. This offer consisted of two documents, one being a general application form containing general questions concerning the health and history of the life assured such as 'Has the life suffered at any time from any illness, injury requiring medical or psychiatric attention?' Through these questions was drawn a line of cancellation indicating that these questions need not be answered in the special promotion. The second document titled a 'special proposal' form merely declared that the assured has not undergone medical treatment in the previous six months.

When Mr Kelleher died the defendant rejected the plaintiff's claim due to the non-disclosure of the fact that Mr Kelleher had received treatment for cancer in 1981. The High Court dismissed the plaintiff's claim against the defendant, and the plaintiff appealed.

Finlay C.J.:

. . .

. . . The learned trial judge in the course of his judgment held that the special promotional offer was obviating the necessity for producing medical evidence but that it did not obviate the obligation to make full disclosure, and that that was in fact underlined on the other document which was sent to persons availing of the special scheme. The ratio of his decision is to be found in a paragraph contained at p. 9 of the judgment which is as follows: 'In these circumstances it seems to me that there was no waiver by the defendants of the obligation which was on the plaintiff and on the person whose life was insured. There was no variation of the common law duty. There was a contractual duty to disclose which was stated in clear terms. In my view, the breach of that contractual duty entitles the defendants to repudiate liability.'

No challenge was made on the hearing of this appeal to the general proposition of the implied obligation on persons proposing insurance to disclose, first stated by Lord Mansfield in *Carter v Boehm* (1766) 3 Burr 1905, and subsequently confirmed and repeated in many decisions both in England and in Ireland.

The sole issue raised by the appellant on the hearing of this appeal is a submission that upon the true construction of the two forms of proposal and, in particular, upon the true construction of the special form of proposal that the policy which is based on the two forms of proposal must be read as excluding a requirement of full disclosure with regard to the medical history of the life assured from the years 1981 to 1985 and that in addition the terms of those documents exclude any implied obligation arising under the doctrine laid down in the case of *Carter v Boehm*.

This doctrine was recently dealt with by this court in the case of *Aro Road and Land Vehicles Ltd v ICI* [1986] IR 403. In that case, Henchy J. in the course of his judgment at p. 408 stated as follows:

Generally speaking contracts of insurance are contracts *uberrimae fidei*, which means that utmost good faith must be shown by the person seeking the insurance. Not alone must that person answer to the best of his knowledge any question put to him in a proposal form, but, even when there is no proposal form, he is bound to divulge all matters within his knowledge which a reasonable and prudent insurer would consider material in deciding whether to underwrite the risk or to underwrite it on special terms.

That is the general rule. Like most general legal rules, however, it is subject to exceptions. For instance, the contract itself may expressly or by necessary implication exclude the requirement of full disclosure. It is for the parties to make their own bargain—subject to any relevant statutory requirements—and if the insurer shows himself to be prepared to underwrite the risk without requiring full disclosure, he cannot later avoid the contract and repudiate liability on the ground of non-disclosure.

The appellant in this case says it comes precisely within the exception referred to in that portion of the judgment as being an instance where the contract itself formed on the two proposals, by necessary implication, excludes the requirement of full disclosure.

Special emphasis is placed upon the unambiguous statement contained under the heading 'Special Promotional Offer on Life Assurance and Disability Benefit' in the special proposal form, whereby the insurance company, in effect, guarantees that 'for any member who is under sixty years old and who *satisfactorily completed the declaration of health below* we can offer life cover of £80,000 *free of medical evidence* and annual disability benefit cover of £10,000 *per annum.*' (Emphasis added). This it is submitted is the clearest possible assertion that completion of 'the declaration of health below' is the sufficient entry for a person who also is a member of the organisation, namely, the IMO, and who is under sixty years of age. The 'declaration of health below', there referred to, I have set out in this judgment and it is one expressly confined to the work experience and the negativing of excessive absence through illness for a period of three months prior to the date of the signing of the form and the absence of taking or seeking medical treatment during six months prior to the signing of the form. Such an unequivocal statement, it is submitted, not only clearly excludes the ordinary doctrine of *uberrima fides* or the implied obligation to make full disclosure with regard to the risk, but also must be read as confining clause 6 of the provisions, privileges and conditions in the policy of assurance to misrepresentation or non-disclosure confined to the precise questions and periods raised in the declaration of health. This topic is dealt with as a matter of general principle in *MacGillivray and Parkington* (8th ed., 1988). There, having set out the possibility that the form of questions asked in a proposal form may make the applicant's duty to disclose more strict than the general duty arising under the doctrine laid down in *Carter v Boehm*, at para. 646 it is stated as follows:

It is more likely, however, that the questions asked will limit the duty of disclosure, in that, if questions are asked on particular subjects and the answers to them are warranted, it may be inferred that the insurer has waived his right to information, either on the same matters but outside the scope of the questions, or on matters kindred to the subject matter of the questions. Thus, if an insurer asks 'How many accidents have you had in the last three years?', it may well be implied that he does not want to know of accidents before that time, though these would still be material. If it were asked whether any of the proposer's parents, brothers or sisters had died of consumption or been afflicted with insanity, it might well be inferred that the insurer had waived similar information concerning more remote relatives, so that he could not avoid the policy for non-disclosure of an aunt's death of consumption or an uncle's insanity. Whether or not such waiver is present depends on a true construction of the proposal form, the test being would a reasonable man reading the proposal form be justified in thinking that the insurer had restricted his right to receive all material information, and consented to the omission of the particular information in issue?

This identical paragraph which was contained in an earlier edition of the text-book involved, is cited with full approval by Woolf J. (as he then was) in *Hair v The Prudential Assurance Co. Ltd* | 1983| 2 Lloyd's Rep., 667, at p. 673 of his judgment. In applying that principle to the facts of that particular case, Woolf J. laid particular emphasis on the last sentence of the paragraph.

I too would accept this as an accurate statement of the principle of limitation of the obligation for disclosure arising from the particular form of questions. I would also be satisfied that the true and acid test must be as to whether a reasonable man reading the proposal form would conclude that the information over and above it which is in issue was not required.

Applying that test to the form of the special proposal form in this case, I have no doubt that a reasonable man reading that would assume that, provided he could truthfully answer the two questions, namely, his absence from work due to illness being confined to not more than two weeks in the previous three months, and the second question, as to his not having undergone, taken or sought medical treatment within six months, he would be entitled, having fulfilled the other necessary qualifications of being a member of the IMO under the age of sixty years, to the insurance.

In essence, the grounds on which the defendants now seek to avoid payment on this policy consist precisely of a non-disclosure by the life assured, Dr Kelleher, of his having sought and obtained medical treatment in the year 1981 and in succeeding years, but outside of the time of six months provided for in the declaration of health contained in the special proposal form.

Whilst it is not necessary to go outside the forms of the proposal themselves, it is not without importance that what was described as the 'special promotional offer' being offered by the assurance company after negotiation through the brokers to all the members of the Irish Medical Organisation constitutes a very sound and probable commercial manner in which to attract a very substantial quantity of new business by one single project. That fact constitutes a probable reason why the defendant should significantly limit the disclosure required from proposers for that insurance.

I would, therefore, allow this appeal, vary the order made in the High Court and enter judgment for the plaintiff for the sum of £80,000.

C. Basis of the Contract Clauses

Often insurance contracts contain a clause stating that the answers given in a proposal form and the making of full and honest disclosure are the basis of the contract and the policy is thus conditional upon full disclosure.

The Insurance Act 1936 ss 61–64

61. (1) Every proposal for an industrial assurance policy shall, unless

   (a) such policy is proposed to be effected on the life and on behalf of a child under the age of sixteen years, or
   (b) the person whose life is proposed to be assured under such policy is a person in whom the proposer has an insurable interest,

contain a declaration by the person whose life is proposed to be assured under such policy that such policy is proposed to be taken out by him and that the premiums thereon will be paid by him.

(2) Where the person whose life is proposed to be assured under an industrial assurance policy is a person in whom the proposer has an insurable interest, the proposal for such policy shall contain a statement of the nature of such interest.

(3) Every industrial assurance company which fails to comply with or to observe the foregoing provisions of this section shall be deemed to have failed to comply with the provisions of this Act and every collector or agent of such company who takes part or is concerned in such failure shall be guilty of an offence under this sub-section and shall be liable on summary conviction thereof to a fine not exceeding five pounds.

(4) Whenever a proposal for an industrial assurance policy contains a statement, which is not true in fact, that the person in respect of whose life such proposal has been made is not at the time of making such proposal a person on whose life any other policy has been issued by the industrial assurance company to which such proposal is made, and a policy of assurance on the life of such person is issued by such company in pursuance of such proposal, such company shall, notwithstanding that such statement is not true and that the truth of such statement is made a condition of such policy, not be relieved because such statement is not true from liability on foot of such policy.

(5) Whenever a proposal for an industrial assurance policy consists of a form or proposal filled in, wholly or partly, by a person employed by the industrial assurance company to which such proposal is made and a misstatement which is not fraudulent has been made in some material particular by the proposer and embodied in such proposal, the following provisions shall have effect, that is to say:

(a) where such proposal has been filled in wholly by any person so employed, such company shall not be entitled to question the validity of the policy founded on such proposal on the ground of such misstatement so made by the proposer and embodied in such proposal, and

(b) where such proposal has been filled in partly by any person so employed, such company shall not be entitled to question the validity of the policy founded on such proposal on the ground of such misstatement so made by the proposer and embodied in such proposal unless such statement occurs in some part of such proposal which has not been filled in by any person so employed.

(6) Where, but for the provisions of the next preceding sub-section of this section, the validity of a policy issued by an industrial assurance company could have been questioned on the grounds of a misstatement in the proposal for such policy relating to the state of health at the date of such proposal of the person upon whose life such policy is proposed to be taken out, nothing in the said next preceding sub-section shall prevent such question being raised by such company within two years from the date of issue of such policy.

(7) Notwithstanding the provisions of this section, whenever a proposal for a policy of industrial assurance which was effected before the commencement of this Part of this Act contains an incorrect statement of the age of the person whose life is assured under such policy, the industrial assurance company which issued such policy may so adjust the terms of the policy, or of any policy which may be issued in lieu thereof, that such terms shall conform to the terms which would have been applicable if the true age of such person had been inserted in such proposal, and accordingly no industrial assurance policy issued before the commencement of this Part of this Act shall be invalidated on the ground that the age of the person in respect of whose life such policy was issued was incorrectly stated in such policy or in the proposal for such policy.

62. (1) Every policy of industrial assurance issued after the commencement of this Part of this Act shall, subject to the provisions of this section, contain a copy of such of the provisions of this Act as shall from time to time be prescribed by orders made by the Minister under this sub-section.

(2) The Minister may, if he thinks fit, grant permission to an industrial assurance company to insert and every such company shall thereupon insert in every policy of industrial assurance effected by such company after the commencement of this Part of this Act a statement setting forth the effect of the provisions of this Act for the time being prescribed by order made under the next preceding sub-section of this section, and such insertion shall be in lieu of and be deemed to be a compliance with the obligation imposed on every such company by the said next preceding sub-section.

(3) Every industrial assurance company which, after the commencement of this Part of this Act, issues a policy of industrial assurance which does not comply with whichever of the foregoing sub-sections of this section is applicable to such company shall be deemed to have failed to comply with the provisions of this Act, and shall, without prejudice to the liability incurred in respect of such failure, either (at the election of the person who has paid the premiums due on foot of such policy) rectify

such policy or pay to such person a sum equal to the amount of the premiums so paid, but such company shall not be liable further or otherwise to such person, and such premiums may be recovered by such person from such company in any court of competent jurisdiction.

63. (1) The Minister may, if and whenever he so thinks proper, by notice in writing left in the case of an industrial assurance company which is registered in Saorstát Eireann, at the registered office of such company in Saorstát Eireann, and in the case of an industrial assurance company which is not registered in Saorstát Eireann, at the principal office of such company in Saorstát Eireann, require such company to delete or amend any term, condition, question, or provision contained in any form of proposal for a policy of industrial assurance issued by such company on or after the date specified in that behalf in such notice.

(2) The Minister may, if and whenever he so thinks proper, by notice in writing left in the case of an industrial assurance company which is registered in Saorstát Eireann, at the registered office of such company in Saorstát Eireann, and in the case of an industrial assurance company which is not registered in Saorstát Eireann, at the principal office of such company in Saorstát Eireann, require such company to delete or amend any term, condition, or provision contained in any form of policy of industrial assurance proposed to be issued by such company on or after the date specified in that behalf in such notice.

(3) Every industrial assurance company to which a notice is given by the Minister under this section shall forthwith comply with such notice and, for that purpose, do all such things as such company is required by such notice to do.

(4) Nothing in this section shall authorise or empower the Minister to require an industrial assurance company to alter either the premium payable under or the sum assured by or the date of maturity of a policy of industrial assurance.

64. (1) Every policy of industrial assurance issued after the commencement of this Part of this Act shall be deemed to be made on the terms that the age, at the date of the issue of such policy, of the person in respect of whose life such policy is issued is admitted by the company issuing such policy to be the age stated in that behalf in such policy or, where such age is not dated in such policy, to be the age stated in that behalf in the proposal for such policy, and accordingly no industrial assurance policy shall be invalidated or questioned on the ground that the age of the person in respect of whose life such policy is issued is incorrectly stated in such policy or in the proposal for such policy.

(2) Whenever an industrial assurance company receives a proposal for a policy of industrial assurance and such proposal contains an incorrect statement of the age of the person whose life is thereby proposed to be assured, such company may, within twelve months after the date on which it receives such proposal, to adjust the terms of the policy issued or about to be issued in pursuance of such proposal as to make such terms conform to the terms applicable to the true age of such person.

(3) Where an industrial assurance company requires, as a condition precedent to the issue of an industrial assurance policy, for the age of the person in respect of whose life such policy is to be issued shall be verified by production of a certified copy of the entry of the birth of such person or other evidence, and such company defrays the cost of obtaining such certified copy or other evidence, such company may adjust the amount of the money payable by such company under such policy by deducting

from such money the amount of the said cost so defrayed by such company, if, but only if, the proposal form contained a clause to the effect that the production of such certified copy or other evidence would be required as aforesaid and that the cost thereof, if defrayed by such company, would be deducted from the money payable by such company under such policy.

(4) Every registrar of births, every assistant registrar of births and every other person having the custody of a register of births shall, on an application being made to him by an industrial assurance company in such form and manner as may be approved by the Registrar-General of Births, Deaths and Marriages and on being paid by such company a fee not exceeding six pence for each certified copy, furnish to such company a certified copy of the entry of the birth of any person whose birth is registered in such register of births and in respect of whom a proposal for a policy of industrial assurance has been received or a policy of industrial assurance has been issued by such company.

(5) Every registrar of marriages, every deputy registrar of marriages and every other person having the custody of a register of marriages shall, on an application being made to him by an industrial assurance company in such form and manner as may be approved by the Registrar-General of Births, Deaths and Marriages used on being paid by such company a fee not exceeding one shilling for each certified copy, furnish to such company a certified copy of the entry of the marriage of any married woman or widow whose marriage is entered into such register and in respect of whom a proposal for a policy of industrial assurance has been approved or a policy of industrial assurance has been issued by such company.

In *Patrick Keenan v Shield Insurance Co.* [1987] IR 113 Blayney J. in the High Court noted that while at common law only a misstatement of a material fact would entitle an insurer to repudiate, the situation is different where the insured has expressly warranted the accuracy of his or her answers and agreed that they would be made the basis of the insurance contract. In such cases he said the following passage from *MacGillivray & Parkington* (7th ed.) para. 725 must be applied:

Blayney J.:

. . .

It has always been the law since Lord Mansfield's day that there must be strict and exact compliance with the obligation or statement which is warranted, so that, as he himself said in *Pawson v Watson* (1778) 2 Cowp. 785, 787, 'Nothing tantamount will do or answer the purpose.' It is, therefore, not open to the assured to say that the obligation has been substantially complied with, or that the answer he made to a question was more or less accurate. This rule is presumably related to the general doctrine that a warranty is independent of any question of materiality, since an assured who gave an answer which was false only in trifling detail, and contended that it was accurate, might in a sense be contending that the difference was not material or important to the insurers' calculations.

Note

See also *John B. Farrell v South East Lancashire Insurance Co. Ltd* [1933] IR 36.

Patrick Brady v Irish National Insurance Co. Ltd [1986] IR 698

The plaintiff insured his boat under a policy which incorporated *inter alia* a warranty as to the purpose and intended use of the boat and a warranty that the vessel would be 'laid up' over the winter in a place of safety, dismantled, not fitted out or used for any purpose whatsoever other than dismantling, fitting out or customary overhauling. The plaintiff did not disclose his intention to use the boat to cook meals during the maintenance works. When the boat was damaged the defendants resisted the claim on the basis *inter alia* of non-disclosure of a material fact. The plaintiff's action seeking indemnification was dismissed in the High Court and he appealed to the Supreme Court.

Finlay C.J.:

. . .

The principle applicable to this interpretation is, I am satisfied, similar to the principle which would be applicable to the interpretation of a contract proffered by one person to another. District Judge Walter E. Hoffman in *The Cristie* [1975] 2 Lloyd's Rep. 100, dealing with an express warranty in a marine insurance policy, states at p. 106: 'As far as the vagueness claim is concerned, plaintiffs are quite correct in stating that if the warranty was vague it should be construed against the insurer.'

In this case the phrase contained in special warranty number (ii), 'customary overhauling' is not expanded or amplified by any further definition in the policy, nor is it a phrase which has any special legal meaning. It must, in my view, therefore, be interpreted against the insurer in the light of evidence as to what is customary in this context. In the course of his judgment the learned trial judge dealing admittedly with the provisions of s. 18, but on the same topic, stated as follows:

A good deal of evidence was tendered for the purpose of establishing that owners of boats of the type damaged in the explosions, commonly lay them up for the winter, either on the hard or afloat, and spend much of their spare time getting the boats ready for the new season; that it is common practice in such circumstances for the galley to be used while works of overhaul and refurbishing are in progress, and that this was well known to the boat-owning fraternity and to their insurers—a 'matter of common notoriety' to use the words of the Act. I am prepared to accept that there is and always has been a common practice of the type referred to.

This finding was, as I have already indicated, not only well founded, on the evidence, but inevitable from it, and indeed in examining the only witness called on behalf of the defendant in the High Court, counsel on behalf of the defendant, at Question 490, summarised what the effect of the plaintiff's evidence so far had been, in the following question: 'We have had evidence which I think is uncontrovertible that it is within the contemplation of people overhauling boats during the laying up period that the cooker will be used. Is the boat fit for such use if the geyser has been disconnected in the circumstances described?'

I can not see any conceivable distinction between what has been described by the learned trial judge as a common practice which is and always has been, in this context, and a custom. I, therefore, conclude that on the true construction of special warranty number (ii), having regard to the findings of the learned trial judge, the use of the galley was part of the customary overhaul and ancillary to it and not a failure exactly to comply with this special warranty. The ground, therefore, on which the learned trial judge found against the plaintiff must, in my view, fail.

Elizabeth Ann Keating v New Ireland Assurance Co. plc [1990] ILRM 110
(Facts on p. 488.)

Walsh J.:

. . .

Insurers may stipulate for any warranty they please and if an assured undertakes that warranty, although it may be something not within his or her knowledge, he or she must abide the consequences. But when insurers intend that there is to be a warranty of that sort they must make it perfectly plain that such is their intention and they must use unequivocal language, such as persons with ordinary intelligence may without any difficulty understand. No such language is to be found in the proposal form in the present case. What has been sought to be established in the present case is that there was a warranty which amounted to a pure and absolute condition that the proposer was a good life irrespective of his knowledge of the subject. Therefore it would follow that because it subsequently transpired that the proposer had, although unknown to himself, such an impairment of his health as not to be a good life the contract would be void upon that fact being established. In a case where there is such a warranty or condition then nothing need be told but it must in subsequent litigation, if that question is raised, be proved that the life in fact was a good one. Even in such circumstances the life may be a good one even though it may be suffering from some particular infirmity. The question would be whether it was in a reasonably good state of health and was such that it could be insured on ordinary common terms.

A life insurance contract is in essence a wagering contract. In a life policy obviously it is not a wager that the assured would never die.

It is appropriate to recall the words of Lord Mansfield in *Ross v Bradshaw* (1761) 1 Wm Bl 312 that: ' . . . such a warranty could never mean that a man has not in him the seeds of some disorder. We are all born with the seed of mortality in us. A man, subject to the gout, is a life capable of being insured, if he has no sickness at the time to make it an unequal contract.'

If the present case had been one of warranty or pure condition then the insured would have taken it upon themselves to prove in the case of death that at the time the insurance was effected the parties were in such a good state of health as not to suffer from anything which was dangerous to life at the time of the insurance. If it was proved that he simply had some ailment which was troublesome or inconvenient but not a danger to his life then there would have been no breach of the warranty. In the present case the condition of angina was a danger to life but the policy was not written on the basis of a warranty. Therefore the insurers took the risk upon themselves and cannot avoid the policy unless they can prove that there was a misrepresentation fraudulent or innocent in some material circumstance.

In my view, that has not been established from the evidence and the policy therefore cannot be avoided.

McCarthy J.:

. . .

The legal basis
S. 2 of the policy reads:

  1. Legal basis
  (a) The policy is conditional upon full and true disclosure having been made in the proposal and medical statement, if any, of all material facts of which the company ought to have been informed for the purposes of the contract of assurance.

(b) The allocation of units to the policy shall not constitute the company or any other person a trustee of such units on behalf of the owner of the policy.

Accepting, as he does for the purpose of this part of the argument, that neither the deceased nor the plaintiff were aware of the heart condition, counsel for the insurer contends that on the true construction of the policy, combined with the proposal form, there was an absolute warranty by the deceased as to the state of his health; that his health was not as warranted and, accordingly, the insurer was entitled to repudiate liability under the policy. In short, he says, the deceased warranted the answer to be correct—it was not correct. It is argued that it is immaterial that the insured believed his health to be satisfactory save as to the stomach upset, if the fact was that he had a heart condition. He points to the declaration contained in the proposal form:

We, the proposer/s and the life/lives proposed, have read the statements and answers written in this proposal and we declare that they are true and complete.

I/we, the proposer/s, agree that they, together with the written statements and answers, if any, made or to be made by the life/lives proposed to the company's medical examiner in connection with the proposal and together also with this declaration, shall form the basis of the proposed contract between me/us and the company.

I/we, the proposer/s, hereby apply for a policy subject to such privileges, terms and conditions as are contained in the policy ordinarily used by the company for a contract of the kind proposed.

I, the life proposed and I, the second life proposed, hereby respectively consent to the company seeking information from any doctor who at any time has attended me and from any insurance office to which at any time a proposal of insurance of any kind on my life has been made and I authorise the giving of such information.

Such declarations and provisions are known as 'basis of the contract' clauses. The contention is that their effect in law is that all answers in the proposal form are incorporated into the contract as warranties and that, if any one of them is inaccurate, the insurer may repudiate the contract for breach of warranty without regard to the materiality of the particular answer to the risk (see *Thomson v Weems* (1884) 9 App Cas 671, 689). The corollary is that the fact that the insured may have answered the questions in good faith and to the best of his knowledge and belief is irrelevant if the answers are in fact inaccurate. It is not difficult to think of instances where a serious symptomless condition exists affecting the life expectancy of a proposer for insurance and is unknown and unknowable; yet if he were to die and it be discovered that such condition had existed at the time of the creation of the contract of insurance, the contract, it is said, is vitiated. In support of this argument, counsel for the insurer relied upon a wealth of authority as cited in *MacGillivray and Parkington* (8th ed.) at paras 732 and 737 and cited some of the authorities (*Duckett v Williams* (1834) 2 Cr & M 348, *McDonald v Law Union* (1874) LR 9 QB 328, *Thomson v Weems* (1884) 9 App Cas 671, *Reid & Co. v Employers Accident* [1898] SC (1031). In *Duckett v Williams* (1834) 2 Cr & M 348 an insurance company in proposing a re-insurance of its risk on a life policy stated in the proposal that it agreed that if any untrue answers were contained in the proposal or if the facts required to be set forth therein were not truly stated the insurance would become void. It was held that 'untrue' did not mean untrue to the knowledge of the party but simply 'inaccurate' without reference to his knowledge. But in *Joel v Law Union and Crown* [1908] 2 KB 863 at 886, Fletcher Moulton L.J. appeared to question this when he said:

To make the accuracy of these answers a condition of the contract is a contractual act, and if there is the slightest doubt that the insurers have failed to make clear to the man on whom they have exercised their right of requiring full information that he is consenting thus to contract, we ought to refuse to regard the correctness of the answers given as being a condition of the validity of the policy. In other words, the insurers must prove by clear and express language the *animus contrahendi* on the part of the applicant; it will not be inferred from the fact that questions were answered, and that the party interrogated declared that his answers were true.

It was in the course of that judgment that Fletcher Moulton L.J. said at 885: 'Unfortunately the desire to make themselves (insurance companies) doubly secure has made them depart widely from this position by requiring the assured to agree that the accuracy, as well as the *bona fides*, of his answers to various questions put to him by them or on their behalf shall be a condition of the validity of the policy. . . . I wish I could adequately warn the public against such practices on the part of the insurance offices.'

In *Zurich General Insurance Co. v Morrison* [1942] 1 All ER 529 Lord Greene M.R. at 537 described such clauses as being traps for the insured. In *Anderson v Fitzgerald* (1853) 4 HL Cas 484 Lord St Leonards (the dual Lord Chancellor) was of opinion that to give effect to such a clause would render the policy not worth the paper upon which it was written and liable to produce a result whereby (at 514):

No prudent man (would) effect a policy of insurance with any company without having an attorney at his elbow to tell him what the true construction of the document is.

A policy ought to be so framed that he who runs can read. It ought to be framed with such deliberate care that no form of expression by which, on the one hand, the party assured can be cut, or by which, on the other, the company can be cheated shall be found upon the face of it. Nothing ought to be wanting in it, the absence of which may lead to such results.

Whilst acknowledging that parties are free, subject to legislative interference; to make such lawful contracts as they may wish, in my view there are certain clear principles that must be applied in construing a contract of insurance of the kind with which the court is presently concerned. Some of these may be stated as follows:

1. Parties of full age and competence are, subject to any statutory impediment, entitled to contract as they wish.

2. Whilst acknowledging the right of parties to express the pre-contract representations as being the basis of the contract, same must be read in the light of the actual terms of the contract subsequently executed. The contract, so to speak, takes over from the proposal.

3. If insurers desire to found the contract upon any particular warranty, it must be expressed in clear terms without any ambiguity.

4. If there is any ambiguity, it must be read against the persons who prepared it (see *Anderson v Fitzgerald* at 503, 507, 514 and *Thomson v Weems* at 682, 687).

5. Like any commercial contract, such a policy must be given a reasonable interpretation.

'The policy is conditional upon full and true disclosure' means that it is a condition of the policy that there has been full and true disclosure. Disclosure can, plainly, be only of matters within the knowledge of the person making the disclosure. What are to be disclosed are 'all material facts of which the company ought to have been informed for the purposes of the contract of assurance.' This must be construed as related to the questions asked in the proposal form and in the answers to the examining doctor. As the learned trial judge said in his observation of enviable brevity when dealing with this matter—'How can it be said that a person ought to disclose some fact which he does not know about?'

How is the proposer for life insurance to comply with the requirement of full and true disclosure in answer to questions in a proposal form and from the medical examiner of all material facts of which the company ought to have been informed, if he does not know of some fact of which the company might well say it ought to have been informed? To read s. 2 (the legal basis) as conveying a warranty that the proposer is accepting a contract on the basis that he has disclosed something of whose existence he was wholly ignorant is demonstrably an irrational interpretation. It is neither irrational nor inappropriate in seeking to find a reasonable interpretation of a commercial contract to pose the question as to how the casual onlooker or, indeed, the officious bystander, would react if told of the construction favoured by one party or another. I would think such an individual would react in more forceful terms than those used by Fletcher Moulton L.J. as I have quoted. An alternative test of reasonable interpretation may be to extend Lord St Leonards' observation thus. If the proposal form were to contain a statement by the proposer that the statements and answers written in the proposal together with the written statements and answers made to the company's medical examiner shall form the basis of the proposed contract 'even if they are untrue and incomplete for reasons of which I am wholly unaware', would there be any takers for such a policy?

In my judgment, upon a reasonable interpretation of what is called the legal basis of the policy, the insurer has failed to establish either material non-disclosure or a breach of warranty as alleged. . . .

SECTION THREE—FRAUD

Since the policy holder is under a duty to observe the utmost good faith in dealings with the insurers, a fraudulent claim will result in the invalidation of the contract, whether there is a condition to that effect or not.

The definition of 'fraud' for the purposes of an insurance contract differs slightly from the common law definition.

Michael Fagan *v* General Accident Fire and Life Assurance (HC) 19 February 1993, unrep.

The defendants issued a policy insuring the contents of the plaintiff's house. Following a fire the plaintiff put in a large claim in respect of his loss. The defendants attempted to repudiate the policy stating that the plaintiff's claim was grossly exaggerated and that the values set out in the claim, in respect of the individual items were in many cases grossly inflated. Furthermore they noted that the explanations given by the plaintiff in respect of the existence and the value of many of the items were unsatisfactory and often contradictory. Certain claims were submitted for items which were subsequently withdrawn and were later admitted not to have been damaged or to have already been claimed under a different heading.

Murphy J.:

...

There was no dispute between counsel on behalf of the parties as to the nature of the duty of an insured in putting forward a claim on foot of a policy of insurance. Obviously the insured must refrain from making any statement which is fraudulent in any material respect and in that context 'a claim is false not only if it is deliberately invented but also if it is made recklessly, not caring whether it is true or false but only seeking to succeed in the claim' see *Lek and Mathews* 1927 29 LL LR 141 at 145. In addition, the duty to exercise the utmost good faith (upon which attention is more frequently focused at the stage when the assurance company is considering whether or not to accept the risk offered) continues throughout the relationship up to and including the making of a claim on foot of a policy. Mr Justice Hirst dealt with that aspect of the matter in *Black King Shipping Corp. and Massie* 1985 1 LL LR 437 at 512 in the following terms:

> Moreover, in the leading and now authoritative textbook, the law relating to fire insurance, by Baker Wellford and Otter-Barry (4th ed., 1948) the paragraph under the heading 'fraudulent claims' on p. 289 starts: 'Since it the duty of the assured to observe the utmost good faith in his dealings with the insurers throughout, the claim which he puts forward must be honestly made . . . ' However, in contrast to the pre-contract situation, the precise ambit of the duty in the claims context has not been developed by the authorities; indeed no case has been cited to me where it has been considered outside the fraud context in relation to claims. It must be right, I think, by comparison with the *Style* and *Liberain* cases to go so far as to hold that the duty in the claims sphere extends to culpable misrepresentation or non-disclosure.

The consequence of making a fraudulent claim is summarised in *MacGillivray and Parkington* (8th ed.) at para. 1926 in the following terms:

> The law is, that a person who has made such a fraudulent claim could not be permitted to recover at all. The contract of insurance is one of perfect good faith on both sides, and it is most important that such good faith should be maintained. It is common practice to insert in fire policies conditions that they should be void in the event of a fraudulent claim; and there was such a condition in the present case. Such a condition is only in accordance with legal principle and sound policy. It would be dangerous to permit parties to practice such frauds, and then, notwithstanding their falsehood and fraud, to recover the real value of the goods consumed. And if there is wilful falsehood and fraud in claim, the insured forfeits all claim whatever upon the policy.

The author having quoted the foregoing passage from *Britton and Royal Insurance Co.* 1866 4F and F905 went on to say as follows: 'The clause is most frequently invoked where the assured includes a claim for goods which he either never had or disposed of before the fire. It may also be invoked where the assured makes a deliberate over-valuation of the stock . . . '

Attention was also directed to the decision of the Supreme Court in *Banco Ambrosiano and Ansbacher* [1987] ILRM 669. Counsel on behalf of the company referred to that judgment as authority for the proposition that the onus of proof in a case of fraud is no more and no less than the ordinary burden of proof in a civil action. Counsel on behalf of Mr Fagan drew attention to the remarks of Mr Justice Henchy in the same judgment to the effect that the inference of fraud must not be drawn lightly or without due regard to all the relevant circumstances (p. 702). Counsel on behalf of the company referred to the observations of the Official Referee in *Albian Mills and Hill* 1922 Lloyd's Rep. where (at p. 98) the Official Referee said in relation to a claim under a policy of insurance as follows:

> What was the motive for making this claim in this way? Whether there was a motive or not is immaterial. It was made by the man who was trusted by the plaintiffs, and one cannot suppose that he did not know perfectly well what he was doing. I believe there was ample motive having regard to Mr Harry Simmons' position. I have come to the conclusion that the plea of fraud has been made out and therefore I have not gone into the question as to whether there was fraud in the prices charged.
>
> . . .
>
> The company has contended originally and proved in the course of the hearing that the insured has ascribed values or prices to a small but significant number of goods which were grossly excessive. Counsel for the insured emphasised the problems with which the insured was faced in compiling the various lists discussed in evidence. It was not surprising—counsel argued—that errors, even substantial errors, should arise with regard to the value or cost of a relatively small number of the goods in the circumstances. If such errors occurred or if, in the absence of specific information or appropriate documentation, the insured had claimed for figures which were excessive in the sense that they represented an extremely optimistic view of the value of the items in question, that would not, in my view, justify the company in repudiating liability on foot of the policy.
>
> This was not a case in which an insured sought to correct or explain errors or to revise claims proved to be unsupportable. So far from it the insured and his family sought to justify as correct facts and figures which, in my view, were untrue.
>
> . . .
>
> In the circumstances it seems to me to have been established on the evidence as a whole that the insured, in breach of both his general and contractual obligations to the company, claimed a loss under the policy based on figures which were deliberately over-stated in the original claims and persisted in on the hearing of the action. In those circumstances it seems to me that the company is entitled to repudiate liability on foot of the policy issued by it and to have such declaration as may be necessary to give effect to that decision.

Orakpo v Barclays Insurance Services, Court of Appeal 29 March 1994, unrep.

The plaintiff claimed for damages for loss of rent from thirteen bedsitter flats caused by flooding, storms and vandalism. The insurance company defended as to liability claiming that the claim was fraudulent as only three of the flats had been occupied when the storm and flood damage occurred and only one when the vandalism occurred.

The first judge held that the claim was fraudulent with the result that all the benefit under the insurance policy was forfeited. Mr Orakpo appealed.

Hoffmann L.J.:

. . .

. . . In principle insurance is a contract of good faith. I do not see why the duty of good faith on the part of the assured should expire when the contract has been made. The reasons for requiring good faith continue to exist. Just as the nature of the risk will usually be within the peculiar knowledge of the insured, so will the circumstances of the casualty; it will rarely be within the knowledge of the insurance company. I think that the insurance company should be able to trust the assured to put forward a claim in good faith. Any fraud in making the claim goes to the root of the contract and entitles the insurer to be discharged. One should naturally not readily infer fraud from the fact that the insured has made a doubtful or even exaggerated claim. In cases where nothing is misrepresented or concealed, and the loss adjuster is in as good a position to form a view of the validity or value of the claim as the insured, it will be a legitimate reason that the assured was merely putting forward a starting figure for negotiation. But in cases in which fraud in the making of the claim has been averred and proved, I think it should discharge the insurer from all liability. It is true that an express term to this effect is commonly inserted into insurance policies and that there is no such term in this one. But in my view the direction to the jury by Willes J. in *Britton v The Royal Insurance Co.* |1866| F & F, is sufficient authority for holding that such a term is implied by law as one which, in the absence of contrary agreement, it would be reasonable to regard as forming part of a contract of insurance: see Lord Cross of Chelsea in *Liverpool City Council v Irwin* |1877| AC 239, 257 H to 258 A, 13 HLR 38; see also Hirst J. in The 'Litsian Pride', (*Black King Shipping Corp. and Wayang (Panama) SA v Massie)* |1985| 1 Lloyd's Rep. 437, 518.

Sir Roger Parker:
. . .
On what basis can an assured who asserts, for example, that he has been robbed of five fur coats and some valuable silver, when he has only been robbed of one fur and no silver, be allowed, when found out, to say, 'You must still pay me for the one of which I was truly robbed'? I can see none and every reason why he should not recover at all. Just as on inception the insurer has to a large extent to rely on what the assured tells him, so also is it so when a claim is made. In both cases there is therefore an incentive to honesty, if the assured knows that, if he is fraudulent, at least to a substantial extent, he will recover nothing, even if his claim is in part good. In my view, the law so provides. . . .

(The appeal was dismissed.)

SECTION FOUR—MATERIAL CIRCUMSTANCES IN MARINE INSURANCE CONTRACTS

Pan Atlantic Insurance Co. Ltd and Another *v* Pine Top Insurance Co. Ltd TLR 27 July 1994

A 'material circumstance' in s. 18 of the Marine Insurance Act 1906 was one that would have an effect, not necessarily a decisive influence, on the mind of the prudent underwriter in deciding whether to accept the risk or as to the premium to be charged.

To avoid a contract for non-disclosure of a material circumstance he had to show that he had been induced by the non-disclosure to enter into the policy on the relevant terms.

The House of Lords (Lord Templeman and Lord Lloyd dissenting on the first point) dismissed an appeal by the plaintiffs, Pan Atlantic and Republic Insurance Co. acting on their own behalf and on behalf of all members of the Pan Atlantic Group Reinsurance

Syndicate and/or the Pan Atlantic Reinsurance Group in 1982, from the Court of Appeal (Sir Donald Nicholls, Vice-Chancellor, Lord Justice Farquharson and Lord Justice Steyn) (*The Times* 8 March 1993; [1993] 1 Lloyd's Rep. 496), who had dismissed the plaintiffs' appeal from Mr Justice Waller ([1992] 1 Lloyd's Rep. 101) who had dismissed their claims in their action against the defendants, Pine Top.

S. 17 of the 1906 Act provides: 'A contract of insurance is a contract based on the utmost good faith, and, if the utmost good faith be not observed by either party, the contract may be avoided by the other party.'

S. 18 provides: '(1) . . . the assured must disclose to the insurer, before the contract is concluded, every material circumstance which is known to the assured. . . . If the assured fails to make such disclosure, the insurer may avoid the contract.

(2) Every circumstance is material which would influence the judgment of a prudent insurer in fixing the premium, or determining whether he will take the risk . . .'

Lord Mustill:

said that although the issues arose under a policy of non-marine insurance, it was convenient to state them by reference to the 1906 Act since it had been accepted in argument, and was laid down in several authorities, that in relevant respects the common law relating to the two types of insurance was the same and that the Act embodied a partial codification of the common law.

Between 1977 and 1982 Pan Atlantic had written a quantity of direct American liability insurance. Much of that was 'long-tail' business, in which a long time might elapse before claims matured. Such business could involve the insurer in disastrous losses. The present case was no exception.

For 1977 to 1979 Pan Atlantic's casualty account had been reinsured with other insurers for excess of loss above a certain figure. For 1980, 1981 and 1982 Pine Top had been the reinsurer.

Disputes had subsequently arisen in relation to all three years. Judgment had been given in favour of Pan Atlantic in an action under 1980 and 1981 contracts. The present appeal was concerned only with its claim under the 1982 contract.

The basis on which Pine Top sought to avoid the 1982 contract on the ground of non-disclosure was the presentation that had been made by Pan Atlantic's broker to Pine Top's underwriter of the loss record for the previous years.

As against the disclosed losses of US$235,768 for the underwriting year 1981 it was common ground that the true losses had been US$468,168, that Pan Atlantic had had information about those additional losses available before the slip had been signed on 13 January 1982 and that those losses had not been disclosed.

The judge had upheld Pine Top's defence based on the understatement of the losses for 1981.

Two questions of law arose:

First, in considering the materiality of a circumstance under ss 18(2) and 20(2) of the 1906 Act, did it have to be shown that full and accurate disclosure would have led the prudent underwriter to a different decision on accepting or rating the risk or was a lesser standard of impact on his mind sufficient, and, if so, what was that lesser standard?

Second, was the establishment of a material misrepresentation or non-disclosure sufficient to enable the underwriter to avoid the policy, or was it also necessary that the misrepresentation or non-disclosure had induced the making of the policy, either at all or on the terms on which it had been made? If the latter, where did the burden of proof lie?

Both the judge and the Court of Appeal had been bound by the previous decision of the Court of Appeal in *Container Transport International Inc. v Oceanus Mutual Underwriting Association (Bermuda) Ltd* [1984] 1 Lloyd's Rep 476, (the CTI case).

The judge had directed himself (at p. 103) that the law laid down in the CTI case was that:

> any circumstance is material . . . if it . . .'would have had an impact on the formation of his opinion and on his decision-making process'.
>
> That is to say, 'judgment' was equal to 'formation of opinion' rather than the 'final decision.'
>
> The case also made clear that the test in relation to non-disclosure or misrepresentation was influence on the judgment of a 'prudent insurer' and that thus the right to avoid did not depend on whether the particular insurer was influenced as a fact in relation to determining the premium he charged or in his decision whether or not to take the risk.

In the Court of Appeal, the Vice-Chancellor (at p. 508), with the concurrence of his brethren, had expressed his unease at the consequence to which inadvertent non-disclosure had led, for the result was that the reinsurer had avoided all liability for his own bad bargain and, moreover, had done so even though full disclosure would have resulted not in his declining to take the risk but only in an increased premium.

Justice and fairness would suggest that, when the inadvertent non-disclosure had come to light, what had been required was an adjustment in the premium or, perhaps, in the amount of cover, but those were not options available under English law.

In substance, the present was an appeal against the decision in the CTI case. Lord Justice Steyn had said that it had proved to be a remarkably unpopular decision not only in the legal profession but also in the insurance markets.

The books and articles produced in argument all adopted a critical stance. Nevertheless, although the unanimous disapprobation of the CTI case was striking, equally striking was the lack of unanimity about what exactly was wrong with it.

As to materiality, the main thrust of Pan Atlantic's argument was that the expression in ss 18(2) and 20(2) of the 1906 Act called for the disclosure only of such circumstances as would, if disclosed to the hypothetical prudent underwriter, have caused him to decline the risk or charge an increased premium.

His Lordship could not accept that argument. In the first place, he could not find the suggested meaning in the Act. The legislature had not said 'decisively influence' or 'conclusively influence'. It had left 'influence' unadorned. It therefore bore its ordinary meaning.

'Influence the mind' was not the same as 'change the mind'. The expression in ss 18(2) and 20(2) clearly denoted an effect on the thought processes of the insurer in weighing up the risk, quite different from words that might have been used but had not been, such as 'influencing the insurer to take the risk'.

Treating the matter simply as one of statutory interpretation, his Lordship would feel little hesitation in rejecting the test of decisive influence.

Having considered decisions and writings before and after 1906, he considered that the House was free to interpret ss 18(2) and 20(2) as proposed.

As to inducement, the question was as to the need, or otherwise, for a causal connection between the misrepresentation or non-disclosure and the making of the insurance contract.

Ss 17, 18(1) and 20(1) said that the other party or the insurer 'may avoid the contract'. There was no mention of a connection between the wrongful dealing and the writing of the risk.

But for that, his Lordship doubted whether it would nowadays occur to anyone that it would be possible for the underwriter to escape liability even if the matter complained of had had no effect on his processes of thought.

How did it happen that the Act seemed to contemplate that once a material misrepresentation or non-disclosure was established the underwriter had an invariable right to avoid?

His Lordship could not accept the proposition that the omission of an express requirement of inducement had been due to an oversight by the draftsman unless he was forced to do so by want of any other explanations. The draftsman, Sir Mackenzie Chalmers, had been a most learned and careful scholar.

There appeared to be three reasons why the Act might have taken the form that it had:

First, the common law had not required inducement and had been correctly reproduced by the Act. Second, the common law had required inducement but the promoters of the Act had wished the law to be changed and Parliament had changed it. Third, the common law had required inducement and the Act, properly understood, was to the same effect.

To make a choice one had to look behind the Act to the developing history of marine insurance law, and for that, again, particular regard had to be paid to the scholarly writings, the older cases having practically nothing useful to say on the matter.

Having done so, his Lordship concluded that there was to be implied into the Act a requirement that neither a material misrepresentation nor a wrongful non-disclosure would entitle the underwriter to avoid the policy unless it had induced the making of the contract, using 'induced' in the sense in which it was used in the general law of contract. The contrary view expressed in the CTI case should not be upheld. His Lordship's conclusion held good also for non-marine insurance.

As to the facts, his Lordship agreed with Lord Lloyd that the misrepresentation by Pan Atlantic had been material and that the position regarding causation was so clear that the appeal could be decided in favour of Pine Top without the need for remittal to the judge.

Lord Lloyd (dissenting in part):

said that, taken as a whole, the phrase 'would influence the judgment of a prudent insurer' pointed to something more than what the prudent insurer would want to know, or take into account. At the very least it pointed to what the prudent insurer would perceive as increasing, or tending to increase, the risk.

If one analysed the phrase word for word, the ordinary meaning of 'influence' was to affect or alter.

'Judgment' in a legal or quasi-legal context was often used in the sense of a decision or determination. Lord Justice Kerr in the CTI case had considered (at p. 492) that it meant not the decision itself but the decision-making process, but his Lordship saw no reason to give it that meaning in the present context.

In a commercial context, 'judgment' was often used in the sense of 'assessment'.

A market assessment meant a judgment as to what the market was going to do, not the process by which a stockbroker arrived at that judgment. That was the sense in which 'judgment' was used in s. 18(2) of the 1906 Act.

His Lordship's provisional conclusion, before going to the authorities, was that to avoid a contract for non-disclosure it had to be shown that a prudent insurer, if he had known of the undisclosed fact, would either have declined the risk altogether or charged an increased premium.

Having considered the authorities, his Lordship's view was that they did not help greatly one way or the other but on balance were in favour of Pan Atlantic's argument.

As to inducement, there were two separate but closely related questions to ask: had the misrepresentation or non-disclosure induced the actual insurer to enter into the contract on the terms in question, and would the prudent insurer have entered into the contract on the same terms if he had known of the misrepresentation or non-disclosure immediately before the contract had been concluded?

If both questions were answered in favour of the insurer he would be entitled to avoid the contract, but not otherwise. On the facts, the judge's conclusions had to be accepted.

(Lord Templeman agreed with Lord Lloyd; Lord Goff agreed with Lord Mustill and Lord Slynn agreed with Lord Mustill.)

Chapter Twelve

Capacity to Contract

Certain categories of person are deemed to lack the legal capacity to enter into binding contracts.

SECTION ONE—INFANTS

The Age of Majority Act 1985 s. 2 (1) and (2)

2. (1) Where a person has not attained the age of twenty-one years prior to the commencement of this Act, he shall, subject to *section* 4, attain full age:

(a) on such commencement if he has attained the age of eighteen years or is or has been married, or

(b) after such commencement when he attains the age of eighteen years or, in case he married before attaining that age, upon his marriage.

(2) *Subsection* (1) applies for the purposes of any rule of law and, in the absence of a definition or of any indication of a contrary intention, for the construction of 'age of majority', 'full age', 'infancy', 'infant', 'minor', 'minority' and of other cognate words and expressions in

(a) any statutory provision passed or made before, on or after the commencement of this Act, and

(b) any deed, will, court order or other instrument (not being a statutory provision) made on or after such commencement.

Irish Current Law Statutes Annotated at 85/2-11 (Binchy)

. . .

It is arguably a policy of debatable merit that where, for example, an immature minor aged between sixteen and eighteen contracts a marriage voidable on the ground of incapacity to form a caring or considerate relationship, he or she should on that account lose minority status.

The practical implications of this general question are reasonably significant. One of the main purposes of the legislation is to encourage banks, building societies and other businesses to enter into contracts with young people without fear of having the contracts later set aside because the young people were not of full age. If, in order to attain full age, a marriage must be neither void or voidable—a fact very difficult, if not impossible, for outsiders to determine—then the commercial institutions may be cautious about entering into contracts with persons under the age of eighteen who have married.

This issue provokes consideration of a wider question, which has application even where the marriage is valid. To what extent will the statutory conferment of full age on

508

a person of eighteen or younger guarantee that third parties may contract with that person with confidence that the contract may not be vitiated on the ground of undue influence, inequality of bargaining power or lack of mental capacity?

Note

The purpose of the law of infants is to protect infants against their own lack of experience.

The general rule is that a contract entered into by an infant is voidable.

Exceptions to this rule exist where valid contracts for necessaries or for beneficial contracts of service are binding on minors.

A. CONTRACTS THAT ARE BINDING ON THE MINOR

Contracts for Necessaries

Sale of Goods Act 1893 s. 2

2. Capacity to buy and sell is regulated by the general law concerning capacity to contract, and to transfer and acquire property:

Provided that where necessaries are sold and delivered to an infant, or minor, or to a person who by reason of mental incapacity or drunkenness is incompetent to contract, he must pay a reasonable price therefor.

Necessaries in this section mean goods suitable to the condition in life of such infant or minor or other person, and to his actual requirements at the time of the sale and delivery.

Nash *v* Inman [1908] 2 KB 1

Cozens-Hardy M.R.:

. . . The plaintiff sues for goods sold and delivered. The defendant pleads infancy. The plaintiff must then reply, 'The goods sold were necessaries within the meaning of the definition in s. 2 of the Sale of Goods Act, 1893.' It is not sufficient, in my view, for him to say, 'I have discharged the onus which rests upon me if I simply shew that the goods supplied were suitable to the condition in life of the infant at the time.' There is another branch of the definition which cannot be disregarded. Having shewn that the goods were suitable to the condition in life of the infant, he must then go on to shew that they were suitable to his actual requirements at the time of the sale and delivery. Unless he establishes that fact either by evidence adduced by himself or by cross-examination of the defendant's witnesses, as the case may be, in my opinion he has not discharged the burden which the law imposes upon him.

Skrine *v* Gordon (1875) 9 IR CL 479

Lawson J.:

. . .

. . . The question argued before us was whether the learned baron was right in leaving the question to the jury; i.e. whether there was any evidence fit to be submitted to a jury that the hunter was a necessary article for an infant in the defendant's position.

The subject matter of the action, as I have said, was the price of a hunter sold and delivered. It appeared that the plaintiff sold this horse to the defendant, who was a young English gentleman on a visit with a country gentleman in the North of Ireland. At the time of the bargain, which took place at a ball, the defendant stated he would pay for the horse by his bill at six months, and that it should be endorsed by his friend, and he stated that in six months he would be of age. The price agreed on was £150. The evidence before the court as to the property and station of the defendant is very scanty. The plaintiff says that the defendant talked of having an allowance of £600 a year from his father, and that he would be of age in June 1875, and said he belonged to the Surrey Hunt, and rode his step-father's hunters. Are we to hold that this is any evidence, having regard to the social position of the defendant, such as would justify a question being left to a jury, whether a hunter was a necessary for him? We think not; and we consider that there was no evidence proper to be submitted to a jury to find that a hunter was a necessary for the defendant. *Ryder v Wombell*[1] correctly lays down the principles applicable to this case. And we think that, as shown by that case, the question of 'necessaries', or 'not necessaries', is one of fact for the jury; but, like all other questions of fact, it should not be left to the jury by the judge unless there is evidence on which they can reasonably find in the affirmative. In my opinion that rule, within proper limits, is very much calculated to keep the law in a certain and steady condition, and prevent juries rendering it uncertain by finding upon insufficient evidence in favour of a plaintiff, on the ground, as Mr Justice Willes says, that it is a shabby thing to plead infancy. Of course we all know that hunting is a good sport and a manly exercise, but still that only shows it is a sport, and luxuries or amusement are quite distinct from necessaries. We are, therefore, of opinion that the rule should be made absolute for entering up a verdict for the defendant.

[1.] LR 4 Ex. 32.

Beneficial Contracts of Service

De Francesco *v* Barnum [1890] 45 ChD 430

Fry L.J.:

I approach this subject with the observation that it appears to me that the question is this, Is the contract for the benefit of the infant? Not, Is any one particular stipulation for the benefit of the infant? Because it is obvious that the contract of apprenticeship or the contract of labour must, like any other contract, contain some stipulations for the benefit of the one contracting party, and some for the benefit of the other. It is not because you can lay your hand on a particular stipulation which you may say is against the infant's benefit, that therefore the whole contract is not for the benefit of the infant. The court must look at the whole contract, having regard to the circumstances of the case, and determine, subject to any principles of law which may be ascertained by the cases, whether the contract is or is not beneficial. That appears to me to be in substance a question of fact.

Margaret Keays *v* The Great Southern Rly Co. [1941] IR 534

The plaintiff, a twelve year old girl, sued the defendant for injuries sustained as a result of the defendant's negligence. The defendant claimed that as the plaintiff was a holder of a 'school season ticket' issued at a reduced price, she was bound by the conditions applying to such tickets, one of which absolved the defendant from all liability for injuries caused by their negligence. Counsel for the plaintiff argued that as an infant she should not be bound by a contract which was not for her benefit. Counsel for the defendant argued that the contract considered as a whole was for her benefit as it allowed her get a better education than was available locally by travelling to the city at a cheap rate.

Hanna J.:

An important point is raised in this case, namely, that by reason of the contract that was made by the railway company with the plaintiff, she is disentitled to maintain any action for injuries received through the negligence of the company's servants. This matter has been decided forty-six years ago in *Flower's* case,[1] and that decision has been accepted as the law, both in this country and in England, for that long period. It is a clear enunciation by eminent judges that, in considering a contract of this kind made with an infant, the court has to peruse and consider the entire contract to decide whether it is for the benefit of the infant.

An infant *prima facie* cannot make a contract, but an infant has certain rights in law, and a contract made by an infant is not in itself a void contract; it is only a voidable contract. That means that it is open to the infant at any time to repudiate the contract. In determining whether the contract is for the benefit of the infant, the court must consider the contract as a whole. It is not sufficient that the infant gets some benefit from the contract. The court has to take into consideration the obligations or limitations imposed by the company on the natural or legal rights of the infant.

In this case, the benefit to the infant is to be carried for 6s 3d per month, but her common law rights are entirely wrested from her by the clauses in the contract, which prevent her from making a claim against the railway company for any injury she may sustain through any negligence on the part of the company, or the servants of the company. It goes even further: that, in the case of her death, her parents or representatives are prohibited by the terms of the contract from making a claim that might otherwise be sustainable. These conditions are contained in a large notice which is properly put up, both in Irish and English, somewhere in the booking office.

It is, to my mind, manifestly absurd to think that a school child, even of twelve years of age, and even of the intelligence of this young girl, should be expected to be aware of the limitation on her rights. This contract is not a contract made with her father or mother; it is a contract made with the child, and while it is a valid contract, and capable of being acted upon while in operation, it is the law that the child is entitled to repudiate it and to have determined by the court whether a contract of this kind is for her benefit or not.

At first I thought this might be a serious matter for the railway company, but, apparently, all the railway companies have been quite satisfied for the past forty-six years to have the case of *Flower v London and North Western Rly Co.* stand as law, and it is probably for this reason that the railway companies and their servants undoubtedly take very great care of children going to school; it may be that the railway companies are quite satisfied to allow the law to stand as it is, and in view of the rare cases in which children may be injured through the negligence of their servants, not to have the matter tested.

I am of opinion that the contract in this case is very unfair to the infant because it deprives her of practically every common law right that she has against the railway company in respect of the negligence of themselves or their servants. For that reason, I think it is not for her benefit, and accordingly, her case must go to the jury on ordinary principles of law, namely, whether the servants of the company were guilty of negligence, and whether there was any negligence on the part of the plaintiff.

1. [1894] 2 QB 65.

Philly Harnedy v The National Greyhound Racing Co. Ltd IR [1944] 160

The plaintiff sued the defendant for damages for negligence or alternatively for breach of contract as a result of injuries sustained by her dog. The dog was injured during a race organised by the defendant as part of a greyhound auction.

Geoghegan J.:

The plaintiff was nine years of age at the time of the accident to her dog. Some time previously her father, Patrick Harnedy, had, according to himself, given the animal to her as a gift, and had registered it in her name. This piece of evidence is of substantial importance. There has been skilful cross-examination to elicit an admission that the dog remained the property of the plaintiff's father, Patrick Harnedy, and that the plaintiff was a mere nominee on his behalf, but the plaintiff's father was not shaken in his testimony that the dog was actually the property of the plaintiff. Therefore I find myself compelled to hold on the evidence presented here that at the time of the accident the infant plaintiff was the legal and beneficial owner of the dog, notwithstanding any instinctive feelings of my own as to the realities of the transaction between father and daughter.

I now have to consider the terms and implications of the contract made between the infant plaintiff and the defendants.

The terms of the contract are to be found on the face of the entry form, in the 'Conditions of Sale' printed on the back, and on the front cover of the catalogue prepared by the defendants for the purpose of the sale.

The entry form declares that the defendants 'accept no responsibility for accidents or disease during trials or sales', and the catalogue contains a similar provision together with a notice stating that 'the National Greyhound Racing Co., Ltd, or the auctioneer accept no responsibility for loss or damage suffered or incurred whether from death, disease, accident or any other cause whatsoever to owners, trainers, or their charges during trials or sales.'

The entry form and the catalogue constitute the contract. The effect of the contract, if binding on the infant plaintiff, is to relieve the company of all liability for negligence by its servants in connection with trials or sales of dogs held in pursuance of the contract. The comprehensiveness of the stipulation in the catalogue need not be stressed.

It follows that a person contracting with the defendants on this basis is deprived of certain rights which otherwise would be afforded to him by common law. Some of these rights might be of such a nature as to arise only in rare and unusual circumstances, but others might arise frequently. No doubt, an owner of a dog who sells the animal through the medium of the sales held by the defendants may obtain an enhanced price as compared with a sale by private negotiation or otherwise, but, in my opinion, the possible disadvantages from a legal standpoint flowing from the express terms of the contract to which I have adverted oblige me to disregard them as against this plaintiff, and to treat the special contract (taken as a whole) as one substantially to the detriment of the plaintiff. I must regard the sale as having been held on an open contract of employment affording no protection to the defendants against their common law liability for negligence.

In arriving at this conclusion I have followed the decisions in *Keays v Great Southern Rly Co.*[1] and *Flower v London and North Western Rly Co.*[2] I have dealt with the law point relied upon by the defendants. No point was taken as to the authority of the plaintiff's father to offer for sale the plaintiff's dog.

Turning to the evidence before me I have come to the conclusion that, while in the conduct of their business generally the defendants and their servants did their work with skill, knowledge, and consideration for those with whom they were dealing, there was negligence in the present instance. It has been established that on the occasion in question the dogs were prematurely released by reason of a defect in the mechanism of the traps, thereby creating the danger that some of the dogs might be attacked and bitten by others. The premature opening of the door of the trap was the effective cause of the accident. This constitutes negligence on the part of the defendants, for which they are answerable to the plaintiff.

[1] [1941] IR 534.   [2] [1894] 2 QB 65.

B. Contracts that are Binding unless and until Repudiated by a Minor, generally described as Voidable Contracts

Certain transactions which involve recuring obligations will be binding unless disaffirmed by the infant during or within a reasonable time after infancy. Examples include family settlements, insurance contracts, liability for share calls and leases. In *Paget v Paget* (1882) 11 LR (Ir.) 26, Law C. accepted the principle that 'if an infant, having executed a deed, repudiates it on attaining his majority, or within a reasonable time afterwards, the instrument thereupon becomes null and void *ab initio*, so far as he is concerned.' Thus in that case an infant who repudiated a re-settlement immediately upon learning that he had been an infant at the date of the re-settlement rendered the agreement void *ab initio*.

Stapleton *v* Prudential Assurance Co. Ltd (1928) 62 ILTR 56

A nineteen year old girl entered into a life assurance contract under a mistake as to the nature of its terms. She paid premiums until she was thirty, at which stage she sued the company for the return of her premiums. The Circuit Judge ordered that the premiums be returned.

Sullivan P.:

. . . adopted the facts as found by the Circuit Judge, that there was no misrepresentation by the defendant, but *bona fide* mistake on the part of the plaintiff. This was a continuing contract, and the plaintiff if she wished to repudiate it on attaining full age was bound to do so within a reasonable time. Even if she could now repudiate, it did not follow that the premiums should be returned to her. If she had died between 1916 and 1927, the company would have been bound to pay, so it could not be held that no consideration had passed during those years. Accordingly the Circuit Judge's decision should be reversed, but his Lordship hoped that the company might deal with the young lady in a way that the court could not order.

(O'Byrne J. agreed. The appeal was allowed with costs.)

Note

In *Griffiths v Delaney* (1938) 4 Ir Jur Rep 1 the plaintiff sued three partners, for money due for goods sold and delivered. The goods were not necessaries. One of the partners John Delaney was an infant. The action against the infant was dismissed, O'Byrne J. in the High Court noting however, that he would have considered an argument that the plaintiff was misled, had it been raised.

Walter Blake *v* Charles Concannon (1870) 4 IR CL 323

Pigot C.B.:

In this case I decided, in point of fact, at the hearing at the Assizes, that the defendant, under a letting made to him of the lands in question, in May 1866, possessed and enjoyed the lands until 20 April 1867; that he was under the age of twenty-one years when the letting was made; and that he still continued an infant on 20 April 1867; that he, on that day, left the possession of the lands; and that, in due time after he had attained his majority (which event occurred shortly after he had left the possession), he repudiated the contract of tenancy, and the tenancy under it; but that in the interval, before he had repudiated, and while he continued in possession and enjoyment of the lands, a gale of the rent sued for became due on 1 November 1866.

Upon these facts I reserved the point, whether, by the repudiation, the defendant not only became exonerated from liability for the rent, which, if he was liable for it at all, became due on 1 May 1867, but also for that which became due on 1 November 1866, while he continued in possession and enjoyment of the lands.

. . .

That an infant is liable to an action of debt for rent reserved on a lease for years made to him for land which he has occupied and used until after the rent became due, appears from very ancient authority. A case in the Year Book, 21 Hen. 6, 31 b., is referred to by Baron Parke in his judgments in the case in 5 Ex, and is also referred to twice in *Ketley's* case,[1] in which the following is stated as law by Newton J.: 'If one lease for a term of years, rendering rent, *in fait*' (that is, not by matter of record, see Co. Litt., 380) 'to an infant within age, if he manures the land, a writ of debt is maintainable against him; the cause is, he has a *quid pro quo.*'

Four cases were decided in the Court of Exchequer in England, in which actions were brought for calls on railway shares, and in each of which actions the defendant relied upon his having been an infant when he became the holder of the shares. In each of these cases the court considered the liability of the defendant with reference to the law affecting infant lessees, and infant purchasers of land. The first was *The Newry and Enniskillen Rly Co. v Coombe.*[2] There the court treated the defendant as having become the holder of the shares only by reason of his having contracted with the company, and subscribed for the shares; and having been an infant when he did so, and having disaffirmed and repudiated the contract and subscription before the action was brought, he was held exonerated from liability. The next case was *The Leeds and Thirsk Rly Co. v Fearnly.*[3] There the defendant pleaded that, at the time of his becoming and being the holder of the shares, and of the contracting of the debt in respect of the calls, the defendant was an infant. The plea did not state either that he had become the owner of the shares by reason of a contract with the company, or that he had repudiated the shares. On demurrer, the court held him liable. The two next cases were *The North-Western Rly Co. v McMichael*, and *The Birkenhead, Lancashire, and Cheshire Rly*

Co. v Pilcher; both reported together in 5 Ex, 114. In each, the defence was, that the defendant became the holder of the shares while he was an infant. In neither did it appear that he became the holder only by contract with the company, in neither was there any repudiation. And, although in one of the cases (*The North-Western Rly Co. v McMichael*), it was alleged in the plea, that the defendant had derived no profits from the shares, it did not appear that the defendant was still an infant. The court, on demurrer to the plea in each case, held the defendant liable, following their former decision in *The Leeds and Thirsk Rly Co. v Fearnly*, and a case previously decided in the Court of Queen's Bench—*The Cork and Bandon Rly Co. v Cazenove*.[4] In 5 Ex, 123, Baron Parke stated the views which the courts took of persons becoming shareholders when infants. After stating that, if the effect of the infant becoming a shareholder by an original agreement with the company, ought to be treated as a contract for a future partnership, and to contribute to the capital for carrying on the undertaking, such a contract could not be presumably beneficial to the infant, and would be not binding on the infant at all; he proceeded to explain the grounds on which infants had, in cases already decided, been held liable. He said:

> they have been treated as persons in a different situation from mere contractors, for they then would have been exempt; but, in truth, they were purchasers, who have acquired an interest, not in a mere chattel, but in a subject of a permanent nature, either by contract with the company, or purchase, or devolution from those who have contracted, and with obligations attached to it, which they were bound to discharge; and have been thereby placed in a situation analogous to an infant purchaser of real estate, who has taken possession, and thereby become liable to all the obligations attached to the estate; for instance, to pay rent in the case of a lease rendering rent, and to pay a fine due on admission to a copyhold to which an infant has been admitted: *Evelyn v Chichester*;[5] unless they have elected to waive or disagree with the purchase altogether, either during infancy or after full age, at either of which times it is competent for an infant to do so: Bac. Abridgment, *Infancy and Age* (I.); Co. Litt. 380. This court accordingly held, in *The Newry and Enniskillen Rly Co. v Coombe*, that an infant who did avoid the contract of purchase during minority was not liable for calls. In the subsequent case of *The Leeds and Thirsk Rly Co. v Fearnly*, where there had been no waiver or repudiation of the purchase, we held, in conformity with the previous decision of the Queen's Bench, that the plaintiff continued liable.

Baron Parke then proceeded to state the dissent of the court from one of the reasons of the Court of Queen's Bench in *The Cork and Bandon Rly Co. v Cazenove*; and to state, at length, the reasons of the Court of Exchequer for holding, in each case, that the defendant, by analogy to the liability of infant lessees, was liable for the calls.

Long before those decisions the Court of Exchequer in Ireland (in the year 1829) made a similar decision in *Billing v Osbrey*, in an action brought for rent upon a lease by the assignee of the reversion against an infant, sued as assignee of the lessee. The defendant, by his guardian, pleaded, that at the time the rent became due he was, and at the time of the bringing of the action he still continued, an infant. On demurrer to this plea, the court held that the infant was answerable for the rent during his enjoyment of the premises. The decision is to be found stated in 1 Furl. Landl. and Ten. 912. It is there stated from a manuscript note of the learned author, whose well known care and accuracy may be fully relied on.

Two cases have been more recently decided in this country: *Mahon v O'Ferrall*,[6] and *Kelly v Coote*.[7] In each of these cases (as in that cited by Mr Furlong), the defendant was sued, as assignee of a lease, for rent reserved in it; and pleaded, as his defence, that he was an infant when the rent accrued. In each, the liability of the infant was affirmed. But there was not in any of them a repudiation of the estate or tenancy in respect of which the defendant was sued, and which, upon the record, was treated as having vested in him.

Upon a review of all the authorities, and I am not aware of any others materially affecting the question arising on this Civil Bill, I am satisfied that I was wrong in forming the opinion, which I did reluctantly, that, upon the view which I at first took of the passages in Bacon's Abridgment and in Rolle's Abridgment of the case referred to, and of the judgments of Baron Parke, in 5 Ex, the respondent, the defendant in the Civil Bill, was discharged from liability to the first gale of rent.

It appears to me now, upon a consideration of the grounds on which an infant is held to be liable where, by the authorities to which I have referred, his liability is established, if he does not waive or repudiate the tenancy and the land, that he ought to be held bound by that liability when it has been once attached to the payment of the rent which accrued while he has occupied, and before he has repudiated. He is not, in an action of debt for the rent, held liable upon the contract of tenancy alone. His liability arises from his occupation and enjoyment of the land, under the tenancy so created. If his liability arose from the contract alone, the repudiation of the contract, by annulling it, would annul its obligations, which would then exist only by reason of the contract. But the infant, though he can repudiate the contract of demise, and the tenancy under it, and can so revest the land in the landlord, cannot repudiate an occupation and enjoyment which are past, or restore to the landlord what he has lost by that occupation and enjoyment of the infant. The reason given by Justice Newton, in 21 Hen. 6, 31, b., lies at the root of the infant's liability: 'he has had a *quid pro quo*'. Though quaintly expressed, it is a reason sanctioned by common sense, and in accordance with plain justice. The infant owed the rent because he has an equivalent in the occupation and enjoyment of the lands. The authorities to which I have referred appear to me sufficiently to indicate that, if the infant does not avoid the tenancy under which he occupies before the rent becomes due, the mere fact of infancy constitutes no defence. If, therefore, he continues so to occupy without repudiation, the landlord, on the accruing of the rent, has a vested right of suit against the infant for the rent which has so accrued. I cannot, on consideration, hold that such vested right can be divested by the mere repudiation of the infant, without a direct decision, or some unequivocal and acknowledged authority, sustained by general acquiescence or clear analogy of law. I have found none. The dictum of Baron Parke in 5 Ex, 125, must be regarded with all the respect due to everything that fell from that eminent judge. But it was not necessary for the decision of the case before him; and it was manifestly founded on the passage in Bac. Abr. *Infancy and Age*, (I.) 8, or was influenced by that passage. And I have shown that the proposition in Bacon's Abridgment, which is there contained, and which appears to have been thus adopted by Baron Parke, was not warranted by the authorities cited in support of it.

On the whole, I am of opinion that the respondent, the defendant in the Civil Bill, was, and is, liable for the first gale of rent, but is not liable for the second. . . .

1. Brownlow, 120.
2. 3 Ex 565.
3. 4 Ex 26.
4. 11 Jur. 802; 10 QB 935.

5. 3 Bur. 1717.
6. 10 ILR 527.
7. 5 IR CL 469; 2 Ir Jur. NS 195.

C. CONTRACTS DEEMED VOID BY THE INFANTS RELIEF ACT 1874

The Infants Relief Act 1874 ss 1 & 2

1.

All contracts, whether by specialty or by simple contract, henceforth entered into by infants for the repayment of money lent or to be lent, or for goods supplied or to be supplied (other than contracts for necessaries), and all accounts stated with infants, shall be absolutely void: provided always that this enactment shall not invalidate any contract into which the infant may, by existing or future statute, or by the rule of common law or equity, enter, except such as now by law are voidable.

2.

No action shall be brought whereby to charge any person upon any promise made after full age to pay any debt contracted during infancy, or upon any ratification made after full age of any promise or contract made during infancy, whether there shall or shall not be any new consideration for such promise or ratification after full age.

G. H. Treitel 'The Infants Relief Act 1874' 73 LQR 194
(Footnotes abridged.)

The Infants Relief Act 1874, is a somewhat mysterious statute. No convincing reason has ever been advanced to explain exactly why it was passed. Its object may be gathered, in general terms, from the preamble: it is 'to amend the law as to the contracts of infants, and as to the ratification made by persons of full age of contracts made by them during infancy, and as to necessaries.' As regards the first section, this object has been largely, if not entirely, frustrated by the orthodox interpretation placed upon it. As regards the second section, the object has indeed been achieved, but the language of the section is such as to give rise to some unexpected and curious results.

. . .

II. S. 1

. . .

1. *'All contracts . . . henceforth entered into by infants.'* It is submitted that this phrase refers to cases where money is lent, or goods are supplied to the infant, and does not cover cases where money is lent, or goods are supplied, by the infant. This is made clear by the exception as to necessaries. A contract by which an infant is to supply goods to a person of full capacity cannot properly be termed a contract for necessaries since the law recognises no special category of contracts for necessaries supplied or to be supplied to a person of full capacity. The exception can therefore only make sense if, in the contracts to which it refers, goods are supplied or to be supplied to an infant. The same applies, *mutatis mutandis*, to contracts for money lent. Thus an infant's overdraft at a bank is within s. 1, but his credit account is not.

2. *'For goods supplied.'* It has been held that this phrase covers contracts of sale and contracts of exchange. Although the point has never been decided, it seems that the phrase is wide enough also to cover contracts of hire and hire-purchase.

3. *The Exception: 'other than contracts for necessaries.'* The first problem is to determine to what contracts the exception refers.

It is submitted in the first place that the exception refers to contracts for the repayment of money lent or to be lent for buying, or otherwise acquiring, necessaries. The section deals with:

'All contracts, . . . for the repayment of money lent or to be lent, or for goods supplied . . . (other than *contracts* for necessaries). . . .'

When the word 'contracts' occurs in the exception, it must refer back to the word 'contracts' in the only other place where it previously occurs in the section, that is, in the opening two words. These refer to contracts of loan as well as to contracts for the supply of goods, and the exception likewise refers to both types of contract. . . .

. . .

It is submitted, secondly, that the exception refers to executory contracts for the supply of necessary goods. This submission is based on the position of the exception. S. 1 deals with:

'All contracts, . . . for goods supplied or to be supplied (other than contracts for necessaries). . . .'

Contracts for necessary goods 'to be supplied' are thus within the exception.

. . .

The next problem is to determine the effect of the exception on these contracts. It is, of course, arguable that the exception merely saves them from being made absolutely void and that it has no validating effect whatsoever. But it must be borne in mind that one of the declared objects of the Act is 'to amend the law . . . as to necessaries' and that the exception is the only part of the Act which can possibly achieve this object. It is submitted that the exception does achieve this object, and that this becomes clear when one considers the exception in relation to the law as it stood before the Act. Contracts of loan and contracts for the supply of goods must be dealt with separately.

We have seen that, before the Act, the lender for necessaries had certain equitable remedies, but that he could not sue on the contract of loan. If he took legal advice the day before the Act came into force, he would be told 'all contracts for the repayment of money lent to infants are void.' If he took legal advice again the next day he would be given a different statement of the law: 'all contracts for the repayment of money lent to infants, *other than* contracts for the repayment of money lent for necessaries, are void.' The contrast between these two statements is sufficiently strong to justify the inference that the law as to contracts for the repayment of money lent to infants for necessaries had been changed, and that such contracts are no longer void but valid. Contrary to this view, the Court of Appeal held in *Lewis v Alleyne*[1] that the lender's cause of action was still based on the expenditure of the loan on necessaries, and not on the contract to repay it. But since the Act was not even cited, it is submitted that the case was decided *per incuriam*. Again, in *Martin v Gale*[2] Sir George Jessel M.R. applied the pre-1874 principles, but this is hardly surprising since the lender did not claim repayment of the loan but merely asked for an account of money expended on necessaries and for the repayment of such sum. On the other hand, in *Gardner v Wainfur*,[3] where the Act was at any rate cited by counsel, Eve J. spoke of a 'debt owing . . . in respect of . . . *advances for necessaries*' thus implying that the lender's cause of action is now based on the loan rather than on the expenditure. It must, however, be admitted that that case is not direct authority for the view here put forward, since the whole loan was spent on necessaries.

It is submitted that the present view is in full accord with the general attitude of the law towards contracts with infants for necessaries. As we have seen, an infant is liable for necessaries 'not for the benefit of the tradesman who may trust the infant, but for the benefit of the infant himself.' On the same principle, a person who paid money directly to the tradesman to induce him to deliver necessaries to the infant could recover that money from the infant. It is submitted that the same principle still applies if the lender does not pay the money directly to the tradesman but into the hands of the infant. The distinction between these two cases is largely technical, and it is submitted that it was one of the objects of the Infants Relief Act to abolish it. It is true that, by paying the money into the hands of the infant, the lender puts it into the infant's power to misapply the money. But an infant does not cease to be liable for a shirt merely because he may gamble it away. It would, moreover, be perfectly consistent with the Act to impose on the lender the burden of proving that the loan was made to enable the infant to buy necessaries, and that the lender believed in good faith and on reasonable grounds that the money would be used for this purpose.

The effect of the exception on executory contracts for necessary goods is less clear for two reasons. First, the phrase 'contracts, . . . for goods to be supplied . . . ' differs from the phrase 'contracts, . . . for the *repayment* of money lent . . . ' in that it is wide enough to refer to the obligations of the adult as well as to those of the infant. Secondly, the legal effect of executory contracts for the supply of necessary goods before 1874 is uncertain. If such contracts were fully valid, the Act has clearly not invalidated them. If they were binding on the other party, but not on the infant, the exception probably has no effect on them whatsoever. If a man took legal advice on this point the day before the Act came into force, he would be told that 'all contracts for goods to be supplied to infants do not bind the infant but bind the other party.' If he took further legal advice the next day, he would be told that 'all contracts for goods to be supplied to infants, other than contracts for necessaries, are void.' A comparison of these two statements does not justify any inference that the law as to contracts for necessary goods to be supplied has been changed: if anything, it favours the opposite view. The question whether an infant is liable on an executory contract for necessary goods therefore cannot be solved with reference to the Act.

4. '*Absolutely void.*' When a contract is void, two legal consequences normally follow. First, neither party can enforce the contract by legal proceeding. Secondly, either party can, subject to certain conditions, recover back any money paid or thing transferred in purported performance of the contract. If a contract is in some way impeachable but these consequences do not follow, the contract is at most voidable. One would have thought that the effect of s. 1 is to make the contracts with which it deals void in the full legal sense of the term. 'It is hopeless,' Lord Halsbury has said, 'to try to get rid of the express language of the statute which renders the loan . . . absolutely and entirely void.' Nonetheless, the orthodox view is that s. 1 does not render the contracts with which it deals void, but only voidable at the infant's option. Of course it is true that the use of the word 'void' in a statute does not always produce all the legal consequences of voidness. But it is hardly credible that 'void' should mean 'voidable' in a section which draws a sharp distinction between those contracts which 'now by law are voidable' and those which 'shall be absolutely void'. A number of specific problems call for discussion in this connection.

(a) *Can the infant sue?* We have seen that before 1874 the general rule was that an infant's contracts were not binding on him but were binding on the other party. Equity had long recognised that this rule might cause unnecessary injustice to the other party. Hence it was laid down that an infant could not obtain specific performance of a contract which was not binding on him. It is submitted that in 1874 the legislature, too, recognised the injustice of the common law and therefore repealed it. That this was the effect of s. 1 appears from the judgment of Buckley L.J. in *Nash v Inman*[4] where the learned Lord Justice, having expounded the old law, continued: 'The obligation was in contract, but contract of such a kind that as against the infant at any rate it could not be enforced. It was a voidable contract. In that state of things the Act of 1874 was passed. The Act relates to certain contracts and renders them form the first time void.' Nonetheless, the statement that an infant can sue on an absolutely void contract is still commonly found in the books. But it is submitted that none of the arguments which have been advanced in favour of this view are sufficiently cogent to stand up against the clear words and apparent object of the Act.

. . .

(b) *Can the infant recover back money paid?* It is clear that before 1874 an infant could not recover back money which he had paid under a contract which was not binding upon him. This rule might well defeat the policy of the law, which was to protect infants against their own lack of experience: an infant who paid ready money for trash, or for useless luxuries, was not protected at all. The object of s. 1 of the Act seems to have been to remedy this defect in the law by making certain contracts absolutely void so as to allow the infant to recover back money paid under such contracts in accordance with the usual common law rules. Unfortunately this provision was first considered in a somewhat hard case, and the result was very nearly bad law.

In *Valentini v Canali*[5] the infant plaintiff agreed with the defendant to take the lease of a house and to pay £102 for the furniture in it. Having paid £68 on account, and used the furniture for some months, he repudiated the contract and sued to recover back the £68. The court rejected this claim. The crucial part of Lord Coleridge's brief judgment reads as follows: 'When an infant has paid for something and has consumed or used it, it is contrary to natural justice that he should recover back the money which he has paid. Here the infant plaintiff . . . had had the use of a quantity of furniture for some months. He could not give back this benefit or replace the defendant in the position in which he was before the contract.'

It must be noted, in the first place, that this passage does not lay down the sweeping principle that an infant can only recover back money paid under an absolutely void contract if there has been a total failure of consideration. An infant who had paid for unnecessary goods which he had neither consumed nor used would, according to this passage, be entitled to have his money back.

On the other hand, the passage is wider than necessary for the decision of the case in that it states that an infant cannot recover back money paid under an absolutely void contract in two circumstances, namely (i) if he has taken a benefit under the contracts; or (ii) if *restitutio in integrum* has become impossible. But the first circumstance, standing alone, is indecisive. The mere fact that a person has taken a benefit under a void contract does not destroy his right to recover money paid under it. The justification of *Valentini v Canali* lies in the second circumstance. A person who claims rescission of a void or voidable contract will only succeed if he is both able and willing to give back what he received under the contract. This rule is relaxed in equity to the extent that a person who can make substantial, though not precise, restitution is allowed to rescind if he accounts for the profits, and makes allowance for the deterioration, of what he has received in addition to returning the thing in its altered state. This equitable relaxation, however, could hardly be applied in favour of an infant who has bought unnecessary goods: to apply it would amount, in effect, to making him pay for the hire of such goods. In *Valentini v Canali*, then, the infant was not allowed to recover back the money he had paid because he could not make precise restitution. He had used the furniture for some months, and it was presumably the worse for wear.

Thus explained, the decision becomes perfectly consistent with the Act. An infant who has consumed unnecessary goods cannot recover back the money he has paid for them. But it is submitted that an infant who has used such goods but has not consumed them is entitled to recover back the price.

In *Pearce v Brain*[6] the infant plaintiff exchanged his motor cycle for the defendant's motor car. Four days later the car broke down because of a defect which was already in existence at the time of the contract. The plaintiff's claim to recover the motor cycle in return for the damaged car failed. The reason given was that *Valentini v Canali* was 'direct authority that money paid under a void contract cannot be recovered unless there has been a total failure of consideration,' and that a chattel given in exchange stood in the same position as money paid. It has already been suggested that Lord Coleridge did not, in *Valentini v Canali*, lay down the wide proposition that an infant can only recover back money paid under a void contract if there has been a total failure of consideration. *Pearce v Brain* can, however, be justified on the explanation of *Valentini v Canali* which has been given above. The infant could not recover the motor cycle because he was unable to restore the car in the same condition in which he had received it. It must be noted, in this connection, that the defendant had given no warranty as to the car and that it was admitted that he had acted in good faith. Had the defendant been guilty of breach of warranty, or of fraud, the plaintiff could have recovered the motor-cycle in spite of his inability to make restitution. To the principle that rescission is conditional on restitution there is an exception, namely that inability to make restitution is no bar to rescission if that inability is imputable to the fault of the party against whom rescission is sought. For instance, a person who has sold a thing which does not belong to him can be compelled to repay the price although the buyer has in the meantime had to give the thing up to the true owner since in such a case the buyer's inability to restore the thing is imputable to the seller's breach of condition.

In the present submission, then, the phrase 'absolutely void' has changed the law in two respects: it has deprived the infant of his former right to sue, and it has given him a new right to recover back money paid. On the orthodox interpretation of the phrase, s. 1 does not change the law in these, or in any other, respects. Yet the Act was passed 'to amend the law as to the contracts of infants.' It is respectfully submitted that a view which ignores not only the plain meaning but also the declared object of the Act cannot be right.

(c) *Does property pass?* The question whether the property in goods which are the subject matter of an absolutely void contract may pass as a result of the transaction cannot be answered with any degree of assurance. In *Stocks v Wilson*[7] Lush J. in an *obiter dictum* expressed the view that the property in the goods did pass. This view certainly has the attraction that it enables the law to protect a person who in good faith buys such goods from the infant. Nor is it necessarily in violent conflict with the Act since it is by no means uncommon for property to pass under a contract which is declared to be void or illegal by statute. Thus in *Elder v Kelly*[8] a person was charged with 'having sold' adulterated milk contrary to s. 6 of the Food and Drugs Act 1875. His defence was that the purported sale was void as it had taken place on a Sunday, in breach of the Sunday Observance Act 1677. The court, rejecting this defence, said: 'The transaction clearly operated to pass the property in the milk . . . and it was to that extent an effective sale.' The court might easily have reached the same conclusion had the milk been 'sold' to an infant who was already plentifully supplied with milk. In any event, it does not appear that the legislature in 1874 intended to make any particular provision on this point.

5. *The proviso.* The object of the proviso is to save certain contracts from the invalidating effect of the enacting words of s. 1.

. . .

(a) *Contracts valid by statute.* In the first place, the proviso saves contracts into which an infant may 'by any existing or future statute' enter.

. . .

(b) *Contracts valid at common law or in equity.* The proviso secondly saves contracts into which an infant may 'by the rules of common law or equity enter.' This phrase seems to refer to contracts for necessaries and to beneficial contracts of service. Contracts for necessary goods are already exempted from the invalidating provisions of s. 1 by the exception as to necessaries. Contracts for other necessaries, such as education, and beneficial contracts of service are not within the enacting words of s. 1 at all. It is therefore difficult to see the need for this part of the proviso.

(c) *'Except such as now by law are voidable.'* The proviso concludes with the puzzling phrase 'except such as now by law are voidable.' One possible meaning of this phrase is: this section shall not invalidate contracts which are valid by statute, common law or equity, but *shall* invalidate such contracts as are now voidable. But this interpretation has been rejected: the proviso does not in this way enlarge the effect of the enacting words of s. 1. The true meaning of the phrase therefore appears to be: this section shall not invalidate contracts which are valid by statute, common law or equity, but *may* invalidate such contracts as are now voidable. If 'voidable' is here used in its correct sense the phrase permits the enacting words to invalidate contracts for the acquisition of a permanent interest in property; but in fact there is nothing in the enacting part to invalidate such contracts. If 'voidable' means 'not binding on the infant unless he ratifies on reaching full age, but binding on the other party' all that the phrase does is to permit the enacting words to invalidate a number of contracts, two of which are in fact invalidated. Why the legislature chose to invalidate these two, and no others, is a mystery.

II. Section 2

. . .

1. *'No action shall be brought.'* In 1828 it was still thought that these words had an invalidating effect. But this view was exploded in 1852 when it was decided in *Leroux v Brown*[9] that their effect was only procedural. The promises and ratifications dealt with in s. 2 are therefore only unenforceable and not void.

. . .

2. *'To charge any person.'* This must mean 'to charge the infant' since it is he, and not the other party, who is charged 'upon' the promise or ratification made after full age. If the action is brought by the former infant, it is brought 'upon' the original transaction. As we have seen, the infant can no longer sue where the transaction is made void by s. 1. But since that section only avoids certain specified contracts it is still possible in a number of cases for an infant to sue on a contract which is not binding on him. If he ratifies such a contract on reaching full age, he cannot now be sued 'upon' the ratification. But he himself can still sue on the original transaction.

3. *'Debt'* and *'promise or contract.'* The distinction drawn in s. 2 between 'debt' and 'promise or contract' in no way corresponds with that drawn in s. 1 between contracts of loan and contracts for the supply of goods. 'Debt' here means any sum certain due under contract and may arise from a contract of loan, or from a contract for the supply of goods, or from a contract which is not within s. 1 at all, for instance from a contract

under which some service has been rendered to an infant for a fixed reward. Although the word 'debt' may frequently include a sum certain due otherwise than under contract, it does not have this meaning in s. 2, which deals only with 'debt *contracted*'. Thus in *Re Seager*[10] an infant failed to account to his employer for money received on his behalf. After reaching full age he acknowledged the debt and charged it on a legacy to which he had become entitled. It was held that the master could recover the money. S. 2 did not apply since there was no 'debt contracted'. On the other hand, the section refers to '*any* debt contracted' and thus covers debts for necessaries. If a person of full age promises to pay a debt contracted during infancy for necessaries, he can be sued on the original transaction but not on the subsequent promise to pay. A 'contract' means an agreement by the infant to do something other than to pay a definite sum of money, for instance an agreement under which some service is to be rendered by the infant. Beneficial contracts of service are included in the same way as debts for necessaries.

4. '*Promise*' and '*ratification*.' In determining the effect of these words, it is important to bear in mind that they were copied from a statute passed in 1828.
. . .

It has been suggested that the retention of the old terminology has the following effect: that a ratification after full age of a contract made during infancy is not actionable; that a fresh promise after full age to pay a debt contracted during infancy is not actionable; but that a fresh promise after full age to perform a contract made during infancy is actionable. It is submitted, with respect, that this view is untenable for a number of reasons. In the first place, it is difficult to see why the legislature should have wanted to distinguish between, for instance, a fresh promise to pay for services rendered to a person during infancy and a fresh promise to perform a contract made by a person during infancy whereby he was to render services. Secondly, the concluding words of s. 2—'whether there shall or shall not be any new consideration for such promise or ratification after full age'—suggest that no such distinction was intended. Thirdly, there is authority not only for the proposition that a fresh promise to perform a contract made during infancy is actionable but also for the proposition that a fresh promise to pay a debt contracted during infancy is actionable. It is submitted that the true effect of s. 2 is as follows. There is no longer any distinction between promises to pay debts and ratifications of contracts. Both are unenforceable. There is, however, a distinction between promises to pay debts and ratifications of contracts on the one hand, and *fresh* promises to pay debts and to perform contracts on the other. Fresh promises are perfectly valid. To this rule there is an exception, which is not due to the Infants Relief Act at all, but to s. 5 of the Betting and Loans (Infants) Act 1892: a fresh promise to pay a debt due under a void contract of loan made during infancy is itself void.

No satisfactory test has yet been formulated to distinguish between promises to pay debts and ratifications of contracts on the one hand, and fresh promises on the other hand. In one case a man who, after reaching full age, continued to treat himself as engaged was held merely to have ratified his promise to marry; but in another a man who, after reaching full age, continued to serve his former employer at an increased wage was held to have entered into a new contract of service. The question whether a fresh promise has been made is, according to the authorities, one of fact depending on the intention of the parties. Of course, where the alleged fresh promise merely amounts to a colourable device to secure performance of the old obligation, it will not be enforced.

1. (1888) 4 TLR 560	6. [1929] 2 KB 310.
2. (1876) 4 ChD 428.	7. [1913] 2 KB 235, 246–247.
3. (1920) 89 LJ Ch 98.	8. [1919] 2 KB 179.
4. [1908] 2 KB 1, 12.	9. (1852) 12 CB 501.
5. (1889) 24 QBD 166.	10. (1869) 60 LT 665.

D. Reform

The **Law Reform Commission Report on Minors' Contracts (1985) LRC 15** recommended adopting a restitutionary approach:

The restitutionary approach has been perceived by some lawyers as having several advantages. First, it will provide some degree of encouragement for adults to provide goods or services for minors. Although the adult will lose the chance of a profit in a case where the minor repudiates the contract, he will have a reasonable prospect of being restored (in part or in full) to the position he would have been in had he not made the contract.[1] It may be argued that, for responsible adults contemplating a contract with a minor, the prospect of a fair system of restitution will be a sufficient incentive to them to enter the contract, provided, of course, the independent commercial incentives are sufficient.

As against this it can be argued that it would be too narrow to regard contracts between adults and minors as necessarily isolated events. Commercial realities dictate otherwise. In many cases the adult (or business company) will not be contemplating making *a* contract with a minor, but will instead have to make a decision as to whether to contract with minors *as a class*. Whereas an adult contemplating a single contract with a minor might well be satisfied with the prospect of a restitutionary principle being applied if the minor seeks to resile from the contract, a large scale business concern might well be less enthusiastic where the risks are multiplied by the large number of possible contracts involved.

The second advantage to the restitutionary approach is that it goes a good way to ensuring that a minor may not, as he may under the present law, use the defence of minority as a means of wrongfully profiting at the expense of the adult.[2]

The third advantage of the restitutionary approach is that to some degree it resolves the problem where (under present law) a minor who repudiates a contract may be unable to recover money he has paid or the value of services he has rendered.

Of course, support for the introduction of the restitutionary principle as a general rule does not exclude the possibility of exceptions being made in the proposed legislation for specific categories of contract, where different rules may apply.

The restitutionary approach has not attracted universal support. The English Law Commission in its Working Paper No. 81, *Minors' Contracts*, published in 1982, criticised[3] the recommendations of the Latey Committee that had favoured the restitutionary approach.

One objection was that the Latey Committee had not put forward any detailed proposals or guidelines to be followed by the courts in determining the question of restitution. This of course is not, in itself, a fundamental objection to the restitutionary principle since it is possible for the legislation to include specific guidelines for the court—indeed the English Law Commission itself envisages and spells out possible detailed guidelines.

Another objection to the restitutionary principle is its uncertainty of application. The English Law Commission, in its examination of the Latey Committee's proposals, expressed this objection in the following terms:

The need for a relative degree of certainty in the law is, in our view, of very great importance. The law serves not only to solve disputes when they arise but also regulate conduct so as to avoid them. In order to avoid disputes the law must be reasonably certain in its application. If contracts are unenforceable against minors, that is, in most cases, the end of it. While such a rule may in some cases lead to unjust enrichment it also avoids much fruitless litigation. Those who know the law can take precautions against its abuse by unscrupulous minors. Potential abuse of the law or its procedures is not limited to minors; many adults avoid paying their just debts by refusing to pay and leaving the creditors to the expense of trying to trace them and of getting and enforcing a judgment. The best protection, as is widely known, is not to give credit to the untrustworthy.

Under the Latey Committee's proposals of a general duty to account, coupled with a relieving power in the court, the outcome of any case would be uncertain and this uncertainty would exist on several levels: on the valuation of the benefit conferred; on the question of whether the minor should be relieved of his liability to account; and, if so, on the extent to which such relief should go. These uncertainties would make out of court settlement less likely. The scheme might well cause some increase in litigation: and, in a large number of cases, there would be a need for legal aid on one or both sides.[4]

We appreciate the force of this argument but we consider that it overstates the problem. Obviously a rule of absolute enforceability 'avoids much fruitless litigation' but if the rule is not itself an entirely fair one[5] it seems to us that this factor should not be given much weight. So far as the likely volume of litigation is concerned, we do not consider that the existence of a judicial discretion would necessarily increase the incidence of litigation. It is of course, quite possible that, under the restitutionary principle, litigation would be threatened or commenced; we do not see this as necessarily a bad thing, and we do not consider that what the English Law Commission stigmatise as the 'uncertainties' of the restitutionary principle would make an out-of-court settlement significantly less likely than in the normal run of litigation.

Whether the restitutionary approach would leave the law in a more or less 'uncertain' condition is a matter of prediction on which there may be differing views[6] but we do not consider that a discretionary principle is to be dismissed on account of its very flexibility.

On balance we consider that the restitutionary principle affords the most satisfactory general approach for the proposed legislation to take. We consider that it best resolves the divergent policies of protecting minors against unscrupulous adults and the risks that their youthfulness and lack of experience involve, on the one hand, and of protecting the interests of adults who contract with minors in good faith, on the other.

. . .

Summary of Recommendations

1. The legislation should introduce a general principle of restitution whereby a contract made by a minor with an adult party would be enforceable by the minor against the adult but unenforceable by the adult against him; the adult would, however, be entitled to apply to the court for compensation from the minor based on restitutionary rather than contractual principles.

2. The legislation should be drafted so as to enable the court in proceedings for restitution to grant to any party such relief by way of compensation or restitution

of property or both as is proper, and, upon doing so, to discharge the parties from further obligations specified by the contract if it considers it proper to do so.

3. In making any order under these powers the court should have regard to:

    (a) the subject matter and nature of the contract;

    (b) where the contract relates (in part or entirely) to property, the nature and value of the property;

    (c) the age, mental capacity and general experience of the minor at the time of making the contract, and at the time of the hearing, respectively;

    (d) the specific experience and knowledge of the minor relative to the particular circumstances of the contract;

    (e) the respective economic circumstances of the parties, at the time of the making of the contract and at the time of the hearing, respectively;

    (f) the circumstances surrounding the making of the contract and, in particular, the reasonableness and fairness, or otherwise, of the conduct of each party relative thereto;

    (g) the extent and value of any actual benefit obtained by each party as a result of making the contract;

    (h) the amount, if any, of any benefit still retained by each party at the time of the hearing;

    (i) the expenses or losses sustained and likely to be sustained by each party in the making and discharge of the contract;

    (j) all other circumstances that appear to the court to be relevant.

4. The legislation should not give any one of these factors greater weight than the others.

5. The restitutionary principle should apply to both concluded transactions and to those that have not yet been concluded.

6. The legislation should include a provision that, in exercising its discretion when applying the restitutionary principle in cases where the contract has been concluded, the court should have regard to the extent of the difficulties likely to result for the party who contracted with the minor from re-opening the contract.

7. The legislation should provide that property passes in an unenforceable contract; a person who receives any property should not have to concern himself or herself as to whether the donor, grantor, vendor or lessor, as the case may be, derived the article from a minor; this should apply whether or not *bona fide* purchasers for value are involved. However, so far as the parties to the contract—the minor and adult (or other minor, as the case may be)—are concerned, the court should be free to make any order affecting title to the property (to the extent that either of them retains title) as it may consider proper, in its application of the restitutionary principle.

8. The legislation should include specific provisions enabling the court, in applying the restitutionary principle, to have regard to whether the goods or services which were the subject matter of the contract were suitable to the condition in life of the minor and to his actual requirements at the time of the making of the contract, so far as the other party was, or could reasonably be, aware, having regard to the circumstances, including any information given by the minor on this question.

9. Subject to recommendation 10, a contract of employment or for personal services should bind a minor if, taken as a whole, it is for his or her benefit.

10. Where the court finds that a contract, taken as a whole, is not for the minor's benefit, because it contains a particular term or terms, then, rather than being obliged to declare the contract unenforceable against the minor, the court should have power to strike out the term or terms in question, if severable from the rest of the contract. In exercising this power, the court should not be entitled to re-draft the contract, and the contract as enforced should be substantially the same as the original contract. The court should, moreover, take into account the interests of the employer before deciding to enforce the contract without the unduly onerous term or terms.

11. For the avoidance of doubt, the legislation should specifically provide that minority may be relevant in determining whether a covenant in restraint of trade is reasonable.

12. Minors' trading contracts should be governed by the restitutionary principle rather than treated in the same manner as employment contracts and contracts for personal services.

13. Contracts of loans to minors should continue to be void.

14. No action should be capable of being brought on a promise made after full age to pay any debt contracted during infancy.

15. A fresh promise after majority to pay a loan that is void in law, and any negotiable instrument given in respect of such a loan should be void and incapable of enforcement against a former minor.

16. Recommendations 13 to 15 should apply to all contracts of loans, including loans for necessaries.

17. Minors, once they come of age, should be free, if they wish, to ratify undertakings made during minority as well as to make new contracts with a fresh consideration with respect to such undertakings.

18. After a minor comes of age, a contract involving continuing obligations should become fully enforceable, with respect to obligations contracted and to be dis-charged by the parties whether before or after the minor comes of age.

19. The legislation should include a validation procedure, whereby approval may be obtained for a contract to which a minor is a party, and for the granting of contractual capacity (general or subject of limitations) to a minor.

20. Parents should not be given powers in respect of the validation procedure prop-osed in recommendation 19.

21. The courts should have jurisdiction to make an order validating contracts or granting contractual capacity. The District Court should have jurisdiction where the consideration of the contract or value of the property concerned does not exceed £2,500. The Circuit Court should have jurisdiction up to a value of £15,000; the High Court would have jurisdiction without monetary limit.

22. Any party to the contract should be permitted to apply to the court for an order for validation; but such application should be made only before the contract has been made or, if it has already been made, only when the contract contains a condition precedent that application for validation will be obtained.

23. As regards the considerations to be taken into account by the court in deciding whether or not to validate a proposed contract or confer contractual capacity (whether general or subject to limitations) the court should have regard to all the circumstances, but, without prejudice to the generality of this discretion, the court may take into account:

    (a) the age of the minor;

    (b) the nature, subject matter and terms of the contract;

    (c) the reasonable likelihood of performance of the contract by each of the parties to it;

    (d) the requirements of the minor, having regard to his particular circumstances;

    (e) the financial resources of the minor;

    (f) the wishes, where they can reasonably be ascertained, of the guardian or guardians of the minor.

24. Where a contract is made between minors, the law should not treat the minors as adults: the restitutionary principle should apply.

25. The legislation should retain the rule that a minor should not be exposed to an action in tort where this would amount to an indirect enforcement of an unenforceable contract.

26. The restitutionary principle should apply to cases of misrepresentation as to age.

27. A guarantor should not be relieved of liability in respect of a guarantee by reason only of the fact that the person in respect of whom the guarantee is given is a minor.

28. So far as the minor's relationship with the guarantor is concerned, the restitutionary principle should apply, whether or not the minor has entered into a binding contract.

[1.] Law Reform Commission of British Columbia, *Report on Minors' Contracts*, p. 49 (LRC 26–1976).

[2.] Ibid.

[3.] W.P. No. 81, paras 4.6–4.15.

[4.] Ibid., paras 4.12–4.13.

[5.] As the English Law Commission (para. 4.12) appeared willing to concede.

[6.] It is worthy of note that one commentator has commended the *Latey Report* as follows: 'The principal virtue of the recommendations is their simplicity and *the relative certainty which they would provide in the law*': Evans, 'The Need for Reform in the Law of Infants' Contracts—Some Comments on the Latey Report,' Auckland UL Rev 65 at 75 (1970) (emphasis added).

SECTION TWO—LUNATICS—MENTAL INCAPACITY

Hassard *v* Smith (1872) 6 IR Eq 429

V.C.:

This suit has been instituted to set aside a lease, made by the plaintiff Richard John Hassard to the defendant, on the ground that the defendant procured the signature

thereto of the lessor at a time when he was, from the state of his mental health, incompetent to bind himself by any deed or contract, and that the reserved rent was much less than the value of the demised premises.
. . .

The plaintiff R.J. Hassard was found a lunatic, by inquisition, on 23 January 1872; and by a special direction under s. 19 of the 34 Vict. c. 22, added at the instance of the co-plaintiff Mrs Hassard, as the petitioner of the lunacy matter, the jury found the time at which the lunacy commenced, which they fixed at the date of 29 October 1870, being anterior to the execution of the lease in question. It was contended by the plaintiffs that, consequently, R. J. Hassard must be, *prima facie*, taken to have been insane when he executed the lease, and that it lies upon the defendant to make out clearly and satisfactorily that he was of capacity to do so.

The presumption of sanity and capacity which ordinarily exists is, no doubt, removed by such a finding, and the onus of proof shifted; but such a finding, usually *ex parte*, is not conclusive, and the contrary may be averred and proved. No instance could show more clearly than the present the necessity of this latter principle, for the co-plaintiff, Mrs Hassard, who has been the promovent in all these proceedings, was obliged to admit, which she did with great reluctance, upon her cross-examination, that the purpose for which the lunacy proceedings were instituted was that of breaking the defendant's lease. To aid in this object, the special direction to inquire as to the commencement of the lunacy was obtained, and there was, of course, but little difficulty in such a proceeding (which was entirely in the hands of the petitioner, and behind the back of the party interested in resisting it) in obtaining a finding, that Richard J. Hassard was a lunatic from a time anterior to the making of the lease. It seems to me not improbable, that if the case had come before the jury in the same way in which it came before the court here, they might have seen reason to modify that opinion. The plaintiffs are, however, entitled to the benefit of it; but beyond the legal principle which, in consequence of it, throws the onus of proof on the defendant, I am not disposed to attribute to it any special importance. It was urged by the plaintiffs that, after such a finding, this court ought not to arrive at a contrary conclusion on its own unaided judgment. The authorities, however, show that I have full jurisdiction to do so; but still, except in a clear case, which this may or may not be, I should hesitate in deciding against a finding, even on an *ex parte* inquisition, without submitting the question to another jury. In the view I take of the present case, it will not be necessary for me to do so. I do not, for the same reason, enter upon the consideration, whether, assuming Mr Hassard to have been a lunatic from an antecedent period, the lease was executed by him in a lucid interval—a proposition which there is much evidence to sustain. The rule which now prevails, both at law and in equity, in reference to contracts entered into by a person apparently of sound mind, and not known by the other contracting party to be insane, is, that such contracts, if executed and completed, and if fair and *bona fide*, will not be held void or set aside. The principal case at law upon this subject is that of *Molton v Camroux*,[1] in the Court of Exchequer, and affirmed by the Court of Exchequer Chamber.[2] That was followed by the case of *Bearan v McDonnell*,[3] where the contract was one for the purchase of land, entered into by the plaintiff, who paid a deposit on account of the purchase money. He afterwards brought an action to recover back the money so paid, and, although it was proved that he was a lunatic at the time of the contract, and incapable of understanding its meaning, yet, as the defendant had entered into the contract and received the money fairly and in good faith, and without knowledge of the lunacy, it was held that the plaintiff could not recover back the money. But in courts of equity this principle is carried farther, for, even in cases where the contract may possibly be void at law, they will not interfere to set it aside, except in the case of fraud. In Storey's Eq Jur, s. 227, the rule is laid down thus: 'The ground upon which courts of equity now interfere to set aside the contracts and other acts, however solemn, of persons who are idiots, lunatics, and otherwise *non compotes mentis*, is fraud.' The learned commentator, in the following section, says: 'And so, if a purchase is made in good faith, without any knowledge of the incapacity, and no advantage has been taken, courts of equity will not interfere to set aside the contract, if injustice will be thereby done to the other side, and the parties cannot be placed *in statu quo*, or in the state in which they were before the purchase.' This principle is fully borne out by the case of *Niell v Morley*,[4] where Sir William Grant refused to interfere, and left the party seeking to invalidate an executed contract, entered into *bona fide*, and without knowledge of the plaintiff's insanity, to his remedy, if any, at law. In *Price v Berrington*,[5] Lord Truro acted upon the same principle, and dismissed a bill to set aside a conveyance, although the jury, on an issue directed by Lord Langdale, had found that the grantor was not of sound mind when he executed it, he having been already found a lunatic, by inquisition, from a date anterior to the conveyance, and without lucid intervals. In the case of *Elliot v Ince*,[6] Lord Cranworth considered the law upon this subject, and referred with approbation to the case of *Molton v Camroux*,[7] stating the principle of that case to be very sound—namely, that an executed contract, where parties have been dealing fairly, and in ignorance of the lunacy, shall not afterwards be set aside. He adds, 'that was a doctrine of necessity, and a contrary doctrine would render all ordinary dealings between man and man unsafe.' He states that the result of the authorities seems to be, that dealings of sale of purchase by a person apparently sane, though subsequently found to be insane, will not be set aside against those who have dealt with him on the faith of his being a person of competent understanding. He showed that that principle did not affect the case before him, on grounds which do not touch the present case. The same principle was applied to a mortgage by a lunatic, in *Campbell v Hooper*.[8]

The knowledge of the lunacy or incapacity above mentioned must be understood to mean not merely actual knowledge, but that which must be presumed, from circumstances known to the other contracting party, sufficient to lead any reasonable person to conclude that, at the time the contract was made, the person with whom he was dealing was of unsound mind. The plaintiffs here contended that the transaction itself could not be relied on by the defendant as affording any evidence of sanity. In this proposition I cannot agree, and I think the circumstances attending the contract, though not conclusive, are, perhaps, of the greatest importance on the one side or the other. I have not to investigate the different theories put forward in the cases on this subject as to the effect of delusions not actually leading to the doing of the act in question, or as to partial unsoundness of mind, though, if I had, I should feel more disposed to concur in the views expressed by Lord Chief Justice Cockburn, in *Banks v Goodfellow*,[9] than in those of an opposite tendency. But here, on the hypothesis on which I am proceeding, it is unnecessary for me to enter upon these difficult matters, for I assume the finding to be correct.

On the evidence in the case, it cannot be contended that the mind of R. J. Hassard, when he made this lease, was wholly unsound. His insanity was, at the most, partial; and he was proved beyond doubt to have acted in other transactions, at or after the date of the lease, as a sane man, and as quite capable of managing his affairs, and to have been so treated by his family. This consideration is of great importance upon the question whether knowledge of the plaintiff's insanity is to be imputed to the defendant. There is not a particle of evidence to show that the defendant had any actual knowledge of this insanity, and the contrary has been positively deposed to by him. Were, then, the circumstances of which the defendant is shown to have been aware, such as might lead him, as a reasonable man, to conclude that Mr Hassard was of unsound mind? So far from their being so, it appears to me that every act of the plaintiff in this transaction, laying aside for the present the nature of the lease itself, had a directly opposite tendency. The only witnesses produced to prove facts leading to the conclusion that he was insane depose to matters of which, the defendant could not have had any knowledge. They speak of changes in habit and manner, which probably were sufficient to attract the attention of members of his family and persons in daily intercourse with Mr Hassard, but not of a nature to be known to, or observed by, others. . . .

. . .

The case of *Greenslade v Dare*[10] is an important authority in the present case, in more points than one; and it was there held by Lord Romilly, that even a general reputation of insanity in the neighbourhood where the party resided was not evidence of notice of insanity. This is all the evidence of the plaintiffs, and it has, in my opinion, wholly failed to show that the defendant had knowledge or notice of Mr Hassard being of unsound mind. But there is a great deal more in the case than this—namely, a number of circumstances admitted, or sufficiently proved, which show that any ordinary person would have been justified in believing Mr Hassard to have been perfectly sane in his conduct in reference to this lease. . . .

. . .

. . . In my opinion the plaintiffs have failed to prove that the lease was at an undervalue. . . .

. . .

I have now gone through this case in detail, and have examined the facts proved, in reference to the rules of law by which it is governed. I have shown that, in my opinion, assuming Mr Hassard to have been of unsound mind at the time of the treaty for an execution of the lease, this was not known to the defendant; that to him he appeared to be of sound mind; that the contract was complete and executed; that it was an honest and *bona fide* transaction, and that the rent reserved was the fair value of the place. Under these circumstances, I am of opinion that the plaintiffs have failed to sustain their case.

A good deal was said at the one side and at the other as to the way in which the defendant proceeded to treat the land, but with that I have nothing to do. He has undertaken obligations respecting the premises which he must honestly and faithfully observe. If he violate or neglect them, he should remember that he can be prevented from commissive injury, and held liable in damages for breaches of his contract.

I must dismiss the bill with costs.

[1] 2 Ex 487.		[6] 7 De G. M. & N. 475.
[2] 4 Ex 17.		[7] 2 Ex 592; 4 Ex 17.
[3] 9 Ex 309.		[8] 3 Sm. & G. 153.
[4] 9 Ves. 482.		[9] LR 5 QB 560 2F2.
[5] 3 McN. & G. 496.		[10] 20 Beav. 284.

Note

Compare this decision to the decision of the Privy Council in *Hart v O'Connor* [1985] 3 WLR 214 where Lord Brightman stated:

If a contract is stigmatised as 'unfair', it may be unfair in one of two ways. It may be unfair by reason of the unfair manner in which it was brought into existence; a contract induced by undue influence is unfair in this sense. It will be convenient to call

this 'procedural unfairness'. It may also, in some contexts, be described (accurately or inaccurately) as 'unfair' by reason of the fact that the terms of the contract are more favourable to one party than to the other. In order to distinguish this 'unfairness' from procedural unfairness, it will be convenient to call it 'contractual imbalance'. The two concepts may overlap. Contractual imbalance may be so extreme as to raise a presumption of procedural unfairness, such as undue influence or some other form of victimisation. Equity will relieve a party from a contract which he has been induced to make as a result of victimisation. Equity will not relieve a party from a contract on the ground only that there is contractual imbalance not amounting to unconscionable dealing.
. . .

. . . in the opinion of their Lordships, the validity of a contract entered into by a lunatic who is ostensibly sane is to be judged by the same standards as a contract by a person of sound mind, and is not voidable by the lunatic or his representative by reason of 'unfairness' unless such unfairness amounts to equitable fraud which would have enabled the complaining party to avoid the contract even if he had been sane.

SECTION THREE—DRUNKARDS

In *Leslie White v Kevin McCooey* (HC) 26 April 1976, unrep. the defendant sought to avoid a contract for the sale of a licensed premises on the grounds that at the time it was made he was so drunk that he was incapable of contracting. Also, he argued that whatever agreement was made was unfair because he was in an unequal bargaining position of which the other party took advantage.

Gannon J. stated that 'two issues of fact fall to be determined namely whether and to what extent the defendant was so intoxicated as to be incapable as he alleged, and whether this was known to the plaintiff at the time, and on these issues the onus of proof lies on the defendant.' He also stated that the onus of proof lies on the defendant to prove that the transaction was unfair and unconscionable.

On the evidence before the court Gannon J. felt that the defendant had not discharged the onus of proof in respect of the three issues.

Note

Even if infancy, lunacy or drunkenness is not made out as a defence, the relative disparity in age as between the parties, the mental condition of the parties *vis-à-vis* each other, or proof of intoxication or a history of alcoholism, are pertinent factors in establishing the equitable defences of undue influence, unconscionable bargain or improvident transaction. These matters are considered in Chapter 14.

SECTION FOUR—COMPANIES

The Directors &c. of the Ashbury Rly Carriage and Iron Co. (Ltd) *v* Hector Riche (1875) LR 7 HL 653

Lord Cairns:

. . . Your Lordships are well aware that this is the Act which put upon its present permanent footing the regulation of joint stock companies, and more especially of those joint stock companies which were to be authorised to trade with a limit to their liability.

The provisions under which that system of limiting liability was inaugurated, were provisions not merely, perhaps I might say not mainly, for the benefit of the shareholders for the time being in the company, but were enactments intended also to provide for the interests of two other very important bodies; in the first place, those who might become shareholders in succession to the persons who were shareholders for the time being; and secondly, the outside public, and more particularly those who might be creditors of companies of this kind. And I will ask your Lordships to observe, as I refer to some of the clauses, the marked and entire difference there is between the two documents which form the title deeds of companies of this description—I mean the memorandum of association on the one hand, and the articles of association on the other hand. With regard to the memorandum of association, your Lordships will find, as has often already been pointed out, although it appears somewhat to have been overlooked in the present case, that that is, as it were, the charter, and defines the limitation of the powers of a company to be established under the Act. With regard to the articles of association, those articles play a part subsidiary to the memorandum of association. They accept the memorandum of association as the charter of incoporation of the company, and so accepting it, the articles proceed to define the duties, the rights and the powers of the governing body as between themselves and the company at large, and the mode and form in which the business of the company is to be carried on, and the mode and form in which changes in the internal regulations of the company may from time to time be made. With regard, therefore, to the memorandum of associations, if you find anything which goes beyond that memorandum, or is not warranted by it, the question will arise whether that which is so done is *ultra vires*, not only of the directors of the company, but of the company itself. With regard to the articles of association, if you find anything which, still keeping within the memorandum of association, is a violation of the articles of associations, or in excess of them, the question will arise whether that is anything more than an act *extra vires* the directors, but *intra vires* the company.

. . .

. . . It appears to me that it would be perfectly fatal to the whole scheme of legislation to which I have referred, if you were to hold that, in the first place, directors might do that which even the whole company could not do, and that then, the shareholders finding out what had been done, could sanction, subsequently, what they could not antecedently have authorised.

Companies Act 1963 s. 8 (1) and (2)

8.

(1) Any act or thing done by a company which if the company had been empowered to do the same would have been lawfully and effectively done, shall, notwithstanding

that the company had no power to do such act or thing, be effective in favour of any person relying on such act or thing who is not shown to have been actually aware, at the time when he so relied thereon, that such act or thing was not within the powers of the company, but any director or officer of the company who was responsible for the doing by the company of such act or thing shall be liable to the company for any loss or damage suffered by the company in consequence thereof.

(2) The court may, on the application of any member or holder of debentures of a company, restrain such company from doing any act or thing which the company has no power to do.

Northern Bank Finance Corp. Ltd v Bernard Quinn & Achates Investment Co. [1979] ILRM 221

A company guaranteed a bank loan made to the first defendant. When he defaulted on his payments, the bank called in the guarantee at which stage the company pleaded *ultra vires*. The bank sought to rely on s. 8 (1) to validate the guarantee. The bank's solicitor possessed copies of the memorandum and articles and Keane J. decided that he probably read the memorandum but believed the guarantee to be *intra vires*.

Keane J.:

. . . The question accordingly arises as to whether, in these circumstances, the bank were 'actually aware', within the meaning of s. 8 (1) of the lack of *vires*. [Counsel for the plaintiff] submitted that the language of s. 8 (1) clearly demonstrated that the onus of establishing actual knowledge within the meaning of the section is on the person who asserts that such knowledge existed and that, accordingly, the onus was on the company, to establish that the bank were 'actually aware' of the lack of *vires*. This may very well be so, but I do not think it is material to the issue which has to be resolved in the present case. . . . The only question that arises is as to whether, having regard to that evidence and the inferences, which, in my view, necessarily follow from it, the bank can be said to have been 'actually aware' of the lack of *vires*.

[Counsel for the plaintiff] submitted that actual, as distinguished from constructive, notice of the lack of *vires* was essential if a third party was to lose the protection of s. 8 (1). I accept that this is so: altogether apart from authority, the language used would suggest that what the legislature had in mind was actual and not constructive notice. Moreover, to interpret the section in any other way would be to frustrate its manifest object. While there is no authority of which counsel were aware or which I have been able to discover on the section, the mischief which it was designed to avoid is clear. Prior to the enactment of the section, all persons dealing with a company were deemed to have notice of the contents of the company's public documents, including its memorandum and articles. If a transaction was *ultra vires*, the other party to it, speaking generally, had no rights at all. The manifest injustice and inconvenience which followed from this rule is amply illustrated by the decision in re: *John Beauforte Ltd* (1953) Ch. 131, which was referred to in the argument.

But if constructive notice can still be relied on in answer to a party claiming the protection of this action, the protection in question would be, to a significant extent, eroded. It is clear, moreover, that the doctrine of constructive notice should not normally be applied to purely commercial transactions, such as the advancing of money. (See the observations of Mr Justice Kenny delivering the judgment of the Supreme Court in *Bank of Ireland Finance Ltd v Rockfield Ltd* 1976 No. 46 Sp: 28 July 1978, unrep.)

But while I am satisfied that the doctrine of constructive notice does not apply to the sub-section under consideration, this does not dispose of the matter. The bank, because of the knowledge of their agent, Mr O'Connell, which must be imputed to them, were aware of the objects of the company. There were no further *facts* of which they could be put on notice. But they failed to draw the appropriate inference from those facts, i.e. that the transaction was *ultra vires*.

[Counsel for the plaintiff] submits that, even accepting this to be so, this is not the actual knowledge which the section contemplates.

A great number of transactions are entered into every day by companies, public and private, without any of the parties looking at the memorandum in order to see whether the transaction in question is in fact authorised by the memorandum. I think it probable that, on the occasions when the memorandum is looked at before a transaction is entered into, it is normally because the company's solicitor or a solicitor for a third party wishes to satisfy himself that the proposed transaction is *intra vires* the memorandum. I think it is clear that the section was designed to ensure that, in the first category of cases, persons who had entered into transactions in good faith with the company without ever reading the memorandum and accordingly with no actual knowledge that the transaction was *ultra vires* were not to suffer. I can see no reason in logic or justice why the legislature should have intended to afford the same protection to persons who had actually read the memorandum and simply failed to appreciate the lack of *vires*. The maxim *ignorantia juris haud neminem excusat* may not be of universal application, but this is certainly one situation where it seems fair that it should apply.

This is best illustrated by an example. The directors of a public company decide to invest the bulk of the company's resources in a disastrous property speculation as a result of which the company suffers enormous losses. The company in fact had no power to enter into any such transaction, but the vendors' solicitors, although furnished with the memorandum and articles, failed to appreciate this. If the submission advance on behalf of the bank in this case is well founded, it would mean that, in such circumstances, the innocent shareholders would be the victims rather than the vendors. There seems no reason why the consequences of the vendors' failure to appreciate the lack of *vires* should be visited on the heads of the blameless shareholders. I do not overlook the fact that the sub-section gives the company a remedy against any director or officer of the company who is responsible for the *ultra vires* act; but such a remedy may not necessarily enable the innocent shareholder to recoup all his losses.

It is interesting in this context to note that in the UK the Jenkins Committee recommended that even actual knowledge of the contents of the memorandum should not deprive a third party of his right to enforce a contract if he honestly and reasonably failed to appreciate that they precluded the company or its officers from entering into the contract. (See Cmnd. 1749, paras 35–42). Writing in the early days of the operation of our Act, Mr Alexis Fitzgerald said of s. 8. 'The draughtsmen wisely reject the advice of the Jenkins Committee, which would have given contractual rights even to third parties with actual knowledge, where such a third party could prove he honestly and reasonably failed to appreciate the effect of the lack of power. Acceptance of this recommendation would have created uncertain and therefore bad law'.

(See 'A Consideration of the Companies Act, 1948, the Companies Act (Northern Ireland) 1960, and Companies' Act, 1965; I', Ir Jur Vol. One (New Series) Part One at p. 16).

In England, the *ultra vires* rule was modified by 9(1) of the European Communities Act, 1972, and while the language of the section is different from that of s. 8 of our 1963 Act, the requirement being that the third party should have acted in good faith, it is interesting to note that the editors of *Palmer's Company Law* (22nd ed.) take the view that it would not protect the third party in circumstances such as the present. (See vol. 1, p. 97).

I am satisfied that, where a party is shown to have been actually aware of the contents of the memorandum but failed to appreciate that the company were not empowered thereby to enter into the transaction in issue, s. 8 (1) has no application. It follows that, in the present case, the bank cannot successfully rely on s. 8 (1).

European Communities (Companies) Regulations 1973 S.I. No. 163

6. (1) In favour of a person dealing with a company in good faith, any transaction entered into by any organ of the company, being its board of directors or any person registered under these regulations as a person authorised to bind the company, shall be deemed to be within the capacity of the company and any limitation of the powers of that board or person, whether imposed by the memorandum or articles of association or otherwise, may not be relied upon as against any person so dealing with the company.

(2) Any such person shall be presumed to have acted in good faith unless the contrary is proved.

(3) For the purpose of this regulation, the registration of a person authorised to bind the company shall be effected by delivering to the registrar of companies a notice giving the name and description of the person concerned.

Note

In *Re Frederick Inns Ltd (In Liquidation)* (SC) 5 November 1993, unrep. Regulation 6 was discussed but found not to apply. In this case the payment by a company, while insolvent, of revenue debts owing by a sister company was found to be *ultra vires*. Regulation 6 could not be relied upon to validate the payment as it was not a transaction entered into by the board of directors of the company as required. The payment in question was agreed to in informal meetings between accountants acting for the company and a representative of the Revenue Commissioners.

Chapter Thirteen

Duress

INTRODUCTION

The existence of equitable concepts such as undue influence and unconscionable bargain have been useful ways of counteracting improper bargaining practices and coercion. Similarly, the doctrine of consideration and in particular the rule about the adequacy of consideration being ultimately a matter for the judiciary has been an important, if covert, method of frustrating persons who exert their superior bargaining position to coerce a further advantage after the contract has been concluded.

However, the concept of duress being a distinct vitiating factor has, in historical terms, only a limited scope. Initially, duress was confined to cases of physical restraint in the form of coercion or personal restraint.

Lessee of Blackwood v Gregg (1831) Hayes 277

This was an action for ejectment brought on the equity side. A man of ninety two, having executed a will leaving property to the plaintiff, was abducted by the defendant who prevailed upon the old man to both execute a new will and sell lands to the plaintiff's confederate. One plea set up was duress or coercion by imprisonment. The Court of Exchequer held that a plea of coercion had been properly left before the jury by the trial judge.

Smith B.:

But if the old man's sudden abandonment of his own house, and his subsequent absence from it, are not open to the observations which I have been making; if they were acts, not voluntary, but the result of compulsion; then they become a part of the evidence of duress. Without them, there is evidence of this. Persons are refused access to him. This is without his knowledge; and consequently not *with*, probably, on the evidence, *against* his consent. Is this no *direct* evidence of the coercion of personal restraint. Does it involve no *presumptive* evidence of still further coercion and control? Would he too, who had not scrupled to spoliate, hesitate to intimidate or to coerce?

Barton v Armstrong [1975] 2 All ER 465

Armstrong, the chairman of a company, became involved with Barton, the managing director of Landmark, in a struggle for control of the company. Ultimately, a deed was executed under which Armstrong's interest in Landmark would be purchased for a total consideration of A$320,000. Barton executed the deed on behalf of Landmark. Barton later sought a declaration that as against him the deed was void because his signature had been obtained following threats made by Armstrong against Barton's life and members of his family. Lord Cross gave judgment for the majority of the Privy Council.

Lord Cross:

. . .

. . . It is hardly surprising that there is no direct authority on the point, for if A threatens B with death if he does not execute some document and B, who takes A's threats seriously, executes the document it can be only in the most unusual circumstances that there can be any doubt whether the threats operated to induce him to execute the document. But this is a most unusual case and the findings of fact made below do undoubtedly raise the question whether it was necessary for Barton in order to obtain relief to establish that he would not have executed the deed in question but for the threats. In answering this question in favour of Barton Jacobs J.A. relied both on a number of old common law authorities on the subject of 'duress' and also—by way of analogy—on later decisions in equity with regard to the avoidance of deeds on the ground of fraud. Their Lordships do not think that the common law authorities are of any real assistance for it seems most unlikely that the authors of the statements relied on had the sort of problem which has arisen here in mind at all. On the other hand they think that the conclusion to which Jacobs J.A. came was right and that it is supported by the equity decisions. The scope of common law duress was very limited and at a comparatively early date equity began to grant relief in cases where the disposition in question had been procured by the exercise of pressure which the Chancellor considered to be illegitimate—although it did not amount to common law duress. There was a parallel development in the field of dispositions induced by fraud. At common law the only remedy available to the man defrauded was an action for deceit but equity in the same period in which it was building up the doctrine of 'undue influence' came to entertain proceedings to set aside dispositions which had been obtained by fraud: see *Holdsworth's History of English Law*.[1] There is an obvious analogy between setting aside a disposition for duress or undue influence and setting it aside for fraud. In each case—to quote the words of Holmes J. in *Fairbanks v Snow*[2]—'the party has been subjected to an improper motive for action'. Again the similarity of the effect in law of *metus* and *dolus* in connection with dispositions of property is noted by Stair in his *Institutions of the Law of Scotland*.[3] Had Armstrong made a fraudulent misrepresentation to Barton for the purpose of inducing him to execute the deed of 17 January 1967 the answer to the problem which has arisen would have been clear. If it were established that Barton did not allow the representation to affect his judgment then he could not make it a ground for relief even though the representation was designed and known by Barton to be designed to affect his judgment. If on the other hand Barton relied on the misrepresentation Armstrong could not have defeated his claim to relief by showing that there were other more weighty causes which contributed to his decision to execute the deed, for in this field the court does not allow an examination into the relative importance of contributory causes. 'Once make out that there has been anything like deception, and no contract resting in any degree on that foundation can stand' (per Lord Cranworth L.J. in *Reynell v Sprye*;[4] see also the other cases referred to in Cheshire and Fifoot's *Law of Contract*[5]). Their Lordships think that the same rule should apply in cases of duress and that if Armstrong's threats were 'a' reason for Barton's executing the deed he is entitled to relief even though he might well have entered into the contract if Armstrong had uttered no threats to induce him to do so.

[1]. Vol. 38, p. 51.	[4]. (1852) 1 De G. M. & G. 660 at 708.
[2]. (1887) 13 NE at 598.	[5]. (8th ed., 1972) 250, 251.
[3]. Book IV, tit 40, 25.	

(Lords Wilberforce and Simon of Glaisdale dissented on the facts.)

SECTION ONE—DURESS OF GOODS

Related to the law governing coercion by physical restraint or harm are the rules found in quasi-contract, or restitution. Where a person pays money, or an excess charge, in order to gain access to property, or perhaps a business opportunity, that should have been available as of right, or on other terms, then the money improperly extracted will be returnable.

These demands, often made under colour of office, are seen as improper, even if made *bona fide*, and made following a mistake, such as an incorrect interpretation of the law.

Great Southern & Western Rly *v* Robertson (1878) 2 LR (Ir) 548

Ball C.:

The appellant is a carrier who, under and in pursuance of a contract with the military authorities, conveyed upon the Great Southern and Western Railway (Ireland) public baggage stores and ammunition; and having been by the company charged in excess of the rate prescribed by the Act 7 & 8 Vict. c. 85, for the carriage of such goods, sues to recover back this excess. The Court of Exchequer determined that he could not succeed.

The statutable provisions relating to the charges for the carriage of goods of the character of those forwarded by the defendant will be found in the Acts 5 & 6 Vict. c. 55, and 7 & 8 Vict. c. 85. Both oblige soldiers, with their baggage, stores, ammunition, and other necessaries and things, to be carried by railways; but the first left the payment to be settled between the Secretary-at-War and the company; and the second substituted for this a fixed rate of 2d per ton per mile.

The case of *The Attorney General v Great Southern and Western Rly Co.*[1] decided that, in order to take advantage of the provisions of s. 12 of the second Act (that which regulates the charges by the company), it was not necessary that the public baggage, stores, &c., should be accompanied by the whole regiment or battalion to whom they appertained, as passengers at the same time upon the railway. This section, in its recitals from the previous statute, quotes the words, 'whenever it shall be necessary to move any of Her Majesty's officers or soldiers, with their baggage, stores &c.' and these words were held to be satisfied by any officers or soldiers accompanying the baggage, stores &c., the public baggage, stores &c., being theirs in the only sense in which what is public can be theirs, as having the present custody of it, whether designed for their use or not. I am by no means satisfied that the true construction of this section is not that the provision as to the rate of charge for carriage of public baggage, stores &c., is quite independent of the circumstance whether or not such baggage, stores &c., are accompanied by soldiers; but as the view taken in the case I have cited is that suggested in the pleadings and argument of the appeal before us, I also shall for my judgment adopt it.

The question before us is raised upon a demurrer and the pleadings preceding it. The carrier alleges that a necessity had arisen for moving upon the railway military forces, with their public baggage, stores &c.—a contract by him with the proper authorities for moving such baggage &c., at the rates provided by the Act; that officers and soldiers accompanied such baggage &c.; that the military forces were always ready and willing to give their assistance in loading and unloading such goods—that is, he avers in pleading all the various matters which, if the baggage, stores &c., were transmitted and accompanied only by military persons, can be suggested as conditions to the assertion of their rights to have the goods carried at the statutable rate—and then complains that, notwithstanding, the railway company exacted charges exceeding 2d per ton per mile. Upon the assumption of all the matters thus stated having occurred, which in the argument of a demurrer we must make—it seems uncontroverted that if there had been no contract between the military authorities and the carriers, and if the baggage, stores &c., had been solely in charge of officers and soldiers, the rate of charge for carriage would have been 2d per ton per mile.

Then did the fact of the interposition of a contract with the carrier alter the rate of charge, and if so can the carrier sue to recover for overcharge? The Court of Exchequer seem to me to have answered the first question in the affirmative, and the second in the negative. We have arrived at conclusions differing from theirs; but it must be observed that cases have been cited before us, and principles deduced from those cases, which do not seem to have been submitted for their consideration.

With respect to the first question, namely, whether the rate of charge was different because of the contract with the carrier—it is to be observed that a route or order from the proper military authorities was produced to the officer of the railway company; that no doubt or controversy, either at the time of transmission or since, has arisen as to the baggage &c., being public baggage &c.; and that it was accompanied by soldiers. Then why should the addition of a civilian to the soldiers, whether he were contractor or overseer, or attendant, make the baggage &c., less public baggage, or alter the rate for which as such public baggage &c., when accompanied by soldiers, it ought to be carried? The object was to diminish the cost to the nation of transmitting military stores &c., and this object may be attained alike whether they are in charge of soldiers and a contractor, or of soldiers only. We cannot doubt that the payment under a contract, upon the basis of the carrier having to pay railway companies only the statutable fares, would be less expensive to the War Department than it otherwise would be; indeed in the present instance it is pleaded that on the railway the carrier was to convey at these rates. In the case of *Read v Willan*[2] cited in argument, a contractor supplying horses for the artillery was held entitled to the benefit of the Billeting Act, which obliged dragoon horses to be fed without charge. I fail to see the distinction in principle between that and the present case.

Then, if the true rate was 2d per ton per mile, is not the appellant, who paid more, entitled to have the excess refunded? The very learned judge, who delivered the judgment of the Court of Exchequer now appealed from, adopts and approves of the *dictum* of Mr Justice Willes in *The Great Western Rly Co. v Sutton*,[3] as I do also, that when a man pays more than he is bound to do for the performance of a duty which the law says is owed to him for nothing, or for less than he has paid, there is a compulsion in respect of which he is entitled to recover the excess by action for money had and received. Mr Robertson, in order to have the goods conveyed to their destination, was obliged to pay the fares required by the officers of the railway company, and he is entitled to demand back the amount by which he overpaid them.

May C.J.:

The first Act, 5 & 6 Vict. c. 55, s. 20, provided that railway companies should carry troops and stores at the usual hours of railway trains, at such prices as should from time to time be agreed upon between the Secretary-at-War and such companies; and this Act is still in force as to all companies in existence at its date, and who have not since acquired fresh powers from parliament. This Act was followed by the Act 7 & 8 Vict. c. 85, which recited that 'it is expedient that the concession of powers for the establishment of new lines of railway should be subjected to such conditions as were thereinafter contained for the benefit of the public.' The s. 12 then is as follows: [His Lordship here read the section]. It appears, therefore, that with respect to all railways which obtained powers from Parliament after the passing of this Act, a bargain was, as it were, made between the company and the legislature, that troops and stores should be conveyed at certain fixed prices—and this was provided for the public benefit of the state; and the policy of the provision is obvious. Under the various Mutiny Acts it was provided that the owners of private vehicles should be obliged to carry military baggage, the moving of which was necessary, at certain fixed rates; and it was very reasonable that when railway companies became so numerous, and obtained as it were a monopoly of the carriage of passengers and goods on the principal public roads, similar obligations should be imposed on them.

Now it is clear, I think, upon the pleadings, that every circumstance in the present case had concurred, necessary in order to impose on the railway company the obligation of conveying the baggage in question at the fixed parliamentary rates. It was necessary to move the troops and baggage by the railway; a route was properly presented; troops accompanied the baggage; and these troops were ready and willing to assist in loading and unloading the stores. This point in fact is not disputed; it is admitted, I think, that the railway company, if required by the military authorities to convey at the parliamentary rates, must have complied with that requisition.

But the argument is that, inasmuch as the defendant had contracted for the carriage of this baggage from its point of departure to its ultimate destination—including the middle space occupied by the railway line, and, as the baggage was delivered to him for that purpose—he, the defendant, could not legally require the company to convey at the fixed parliamentary rate.

No privity, it is argued, existed between the military authorities and the company in the present case; they were not conveying the baggage by the railway: that was done by the contractor, the defendant; and the enactment was one of which a private individual could not claim the benefit.

I think the obligation imposed on the company was an obligation arising out of the act of the legislature, and for the benefit of the state; and I see no reason why this obligation in this particular case should be held to be discharged because the military authorities thought proper to enter into a contract with the defendant, covering the entire route, and including the portion of the line of railway to be traversed by the troops. Notwithstanding the contract with the defendant, it continued to be for the public benefit that the troops should be conveyed by the railway, and at the reduced fares; for it must, I think, be assumed that the contractor agreed with the authorities, having regard to the fact that for a considerable portion of the route the railway would be not only available, but the proper and peculiar mode of transit; it being admitted on the pleadings that it was necessary that the troops and baggage should be conveyed by the railway.

It appears to me, therefore, that the public obligation on the railway company continuing, they were not justified in refusing to carry the baggage at the parliamentary rates, and, as they refused to carry except on the payment by the defendant of the increased charges, and, as the exigency of the case obliged him to pay the demand illegally made, he is entitled to recover back the overcharge. The case of *Read v Willan* I think entirely supports this view of the case. Though the facts are not accurately stated, the principle of decision seems in favour of the defendant in this case.

542   *Duress*

14 Ir CLR 447, 2 U2.   ^{2.} 2 Doug. 422.   ^{3.} LR 4 HL 226, 249.

(Morris C.J. concurred.)

Smelter Corp. of Ireland *v* O'Driscoll (SC) 27 July 1977, unrep.

O'Higgins C.J.:

This is an appeal brought by the plaintiffs from the decision and judgment of Butler J. refusing their claim for specific performance of an agreement entered into by the defendant for the sale to them of 55 acres 0 roods 36 perches of land situate at Carrigrenan, Co. Cork. The plaintiff is a limited liability company formed for the purpose of establishing in Ireland a smelter or base metal reduction plant and in pursuance of this aim was at the time of the agreement sought to be enforced engaged in the acquisition of land as a suitable site for such a plant in the Little Island area of Cork. The defendant is the owner of the land the subject of the agreement but the negotiations in relation to the agreement were conducted on her behalf by her husband Michael O'Driscoll and later by her solicitor who has since died, also named Michael O'Driscoll. The agreement necessarily took the form of an option to purchase dated 25 November 1969 under which for the sum of £7,000 the plaintiffs were given for twelve months an option to purchase at a price to be determined by Mr Owen MacCarthy, the well known arbitrator to the Land Values Reference Committee, on an arbitration specially held for that purpose.

Provision was made for the extension of the option for a further period of six months on the payment of a further sum of £3,250 and there were other clauses not relevant to the issues raised in this appeal. It was provided that the option payments should in the event of the option being exercised be credited against the purchase money and if the option was not exercised for any of the three grounds set out in clause 9 then one half of such sums should be returned to the plaintiffs and in the meantime such one half should be secured on deposit. On 10 January 1970 Mr Owen MacCarthy determined in his arbitration award that the purchase price of the land should be at the rate of £1,500 per acre, making a purchase price of £82,857.50. By letter dated 23 November 1970 the plaintiffs took a second option for six months for the sum of £3,250 thereupon paid to the defendant's solicitors. A second option for six months was then purchased by the plaintiffs as a result of negotiations between the auctioneer acting for the plaintiffs, Mr Ahern, and the defendant's solicitor. The consideration for this option was also £3,250 but this sum was not to be credited against the purchase money should the plaintiffs exercise the option. At the expiration of this third option a fourth was negotiated as evidenced by a letter dated 24 November 1971 from the defendant's solicitor to the plaintiffs. This option was for a further six months for a nominal consideration but on the terms that the option monies paid under the original option should now be freed to the defendant and should not be credited against the purchase money in the event of the option being exercised. In effect this arrangement constituted the ground of a fresh option to purchase for a fixed price of £93,087.50 being £82,837.50 as fixed by Mr MacCarthy, plus the £10,250 paid in respect of the options under the agreement of 25 November 1967. By letter dated 15 May 1972 the plaintiffs purported to exercise this final option. The defendant being unwilling and refusing to complete, these proceedings were commenced by the plaintiffs seeking specific performance of the agreement to sell and associated relief.

The defendants' defence to the plaintiffs' claim is based on two main grounds. In the first place it is contended that the option or options to purchase were given by her,

I quote from para. 3 of the defence: 'Subject to a condition precedent that a smelter plant, otherwise a base metal reduction plant, would be built on the said lands and that the said lands would be used for no other purpose, but the defendants do not propose to build or utilise a smelter plant or base metal reduction plant on the said lands and the said option has not been fulfilled and will not be fulfilled and the plaintiff is thereby debarred from exercising the said or any option.' It was further contended with regard to the option and I quote from para. 4 of the defence:

> The same was obtained from the plaintiff under duress and coercion whereby the plaintiff caused or permitted a local authority to clearly give her to understand that if she did not sell the said lands or give an option under the same to the plaintiff for the purpose of a smelter plant or base metal reduction plant, then the said lands would be acquired by compulsory acquisition by the said local authority and given to the plaintiffs for the stated purpose, and the defendant believed that this threat would be carried out to her damage and it was further represented to the defendant that she had a national and patriotic duty to permit employment on a large scale to be afforded by the plaintiffs at the said smelter plant or base metal reduction plant and it was in those circumstances and only on the understanding and pre-condition, express or implied, as hereinbefore indicated, that the defendant afforded such option to the plaintiffs.

To assess the validity of these two grounds of defence or of either of them, regard must of course be had to the evidence adduced at the trial before the learned High Court Judge. Apart from the documents already referred to which relate to evidence of the option arrangements entered into between the parties it appears that much happened before these arrangements became possible. The plaintiffs had engaged a Mr Ahern, the principal of the firm of March & Co., Auctioneers, to conduct negotiations on their behalf with local land owners including the defendant.

On behalf of the plaintiffs Mr Ahern interviewed Mr Michael O'Driscoll, the defendant's husband, and offered £800 per acre for the land which was subsequently the subject of the options. Believing that the Cork County Council as the Planning Authority had power under s. 77 of the Planning Act, 1963, to acquire these lands compulsorily for the development which the plaintiffs aimed at and further believing that this power would as a matter of probability be exercised, Mr Ahern so informed Mr O'Driscoll. He did this in good faith, as the learned trial judge has found, believing his statement to represent the reality of the situation facing the defendant. Mr Ahern followed up this verbal statement with a letter dated 11 August 1969 which was written to Mr Michael O'Driscoll, the solicitor acting for the defendant. In this letter he again made an offer of £800 per acre but added: 'We are suggesting that since the probability of a compulsory purchase order being made is admitted that the necessity of having the order made be dispensed with and that the value of the land be submitted to an independent arbitrator acceptable to both parties and that both parties be bound by his decision.' This letter was a clear indication of Mr Ahern's view as the negotiator on behalf of the plaintiffs that if the £800 was not acceptable the defendant to avoid a compulsory purchase order ought to agree to the price being determined by an independent arbitrator. It seems clear that Mr Michael O'Driscoll's solicitor did not for a moment doubt the soundness of the view expressed by Mr Ahern and that subsequent negotiations were carried on on the basis that if agreement was not possible compulsory purchase would be the next step. It appears that Mr Filer, the managing director of the plaintiffs, was made aware of the manner in which Mr Ahern was negotiating with the defendant and of the arguments and representations he used and made. This appears from the fact that Mr Filer was given Mr Ahern's complete file of correspondence at the end of August 1969, which file of course included the letter already mentioned of 11 August. Despite the efforts of Mr Ahern the defendant through her husband could not be persuaded to sell although the offer made on behalf of the plaintiffs was substantially increased.

By 9 October 1969 all negotiations had come to an end and the possibility of the plaintiffs securing the defendant's lands by agreement seemed remote in the extreme. On that date a number of people representing the plaintiffs called to the County Hall in Cork, the headquarters of the Cork County Council. These included Mr Filer, the managing director, and Mr Ahern, the auctioneer. They there met the County Manger, Mr Conlon,· the Chairman of the county council, Mr Michael Pat Murphy, the Vice-Chairman, Mr Denis O'Sullivan, and the Development Officer, Mr David Murphy. There appears to have been some slight conflict in the evidence at the trial as to the immediate purpose of this meeting. It is, however, clear that following this meeting the County Manager, the Chairman, the Vice-Chairman, Mr Ahern and Mr David Murphy went in a body to see Mr O'Driscoll for the purpose of urging him to resume negotiations with the plaintiffs for the sale of his land. As to what was said at this interview with Mr O'Driscoll, there was again a conflict in the evidence at the trial. Mr O'Driscoll maintained that it was made clear to him by the gentlemen who called to see him that if he was not willing to sell, his lands would be acquired compulsorily by the county council. This was disputed by the county council witnesses. The learned trial judge was, however satisfied that at this interview there had been a reference to the compulsory purchase of the lands and that this, coupled with what had previously been said and written by Mr Ahern, operated on Mr O'Driscoll's mind. This, of course, is a finding of fact by the learned trial judge which is binding on this court. The following day Mr O'Driscoll telephoned Mr David Murphy, the Development Officer, to say that he was prepared to negotiate with the plaintiffs and on 25 November 1969 the agreement the subject of these proceedings was entered into.

It was made clear at the trial by the County Manager, Mr Conlon, when he gave evidence, that the belief held and expressed by Mr Ahern was incorrect. Mr Conlon made it perfectly clear in his evidence that there was no question of the county council acquiring these lands for the plaintiffs. Whatever views he may have had as to the Council's powers in this respect he said that such an exercise of compulsory acquisition had never been attempted and certainly was neither planned nor contemplated in this case. From this it follows that all suggestions made to Mr O'Driscoll to the effect that if the lands were not sold voluntarily they would be acquired compulsorily were ill-founded.

I now turn to the grounds relied on by the defendant for resisting the order for specific performance claimed in this case. I wish to say at once that I find no substance in the first ground of objection. In my view the purpose for which the plaintiffs sought to purchase lands or the use to which they intended to put them in no way affected the transaction entered into. I can see no basis for suggesting that the proposed acquisition of the defendant's lands depended on the smelter project proceeding.

The second objection must, however, be viewed in a different light. Specific performance is a discretionary remedy. The discretion to grant or refuse the relief must be exercised in a manner which is neither arbitrary nor capricious but which has regard to the essential fairness of the transaction involved. Here it is, in effect, suggested that the defendant was coerced or forced into granting the option or options to the plaintiffs by the threat of compulsory purchase. It does not seem to me on the evidence that a threat as such was ever used. At the same time it seems perfectly clear that the defendant was at a serious disadvantage. Mr O'Driscoll, the defendant's husband, who acted for her throughout the negotiations, believed that if there was not a voluntary sale there would be a compulsory acquisition of the lands. He so believed because he was told this by the plaintiffs' agent, Mr Ahern. It is quite clear that this view was repeated to him by his own solicitor, Mr Michael O'Driscoll, and on 9 October 1969 further corroboration was provided by those who came to see him representing the Cork County Council. Believing this to be the situation there was no real purpose in refusing to sell or to give an option once, as was suggested, the price was to be determined by an agreed arbitrator. To refuse in these circumstances meant acquisition anyway and the determination of the price by an arbitrator in whose appointment the defendant might have no say. It now transpires that the situation was not as was intimated to the defendant's husband, Michael O'Driscoll. It is now clear that at the time that these negotiations were proceeding the county council had no plans whatsoever to interfere by way of the compulsory acquisition of the defendant's lands. It is well established that the discretion to grant specific performance should not be exercised if the contract is not equal and fair. In this instance the defendant was under a fundamental misapprehension as to the true facts. This misapprehension was brought about by the plaintiffs' agent, Mr Ahern. While Mr Ahern acted *bona fide* this does not alter the situation which he created. He led the defendant's husband, Mr O'Driscoll, and his solicitor to believe that if the defendant did not agree to sell the lands would be acquired. It appears clear also that Mr Filer, the plaintiffs' managing director was aware of the true position so far as compulsory acquisition was concerned. It is to be noted that he had Mr Ahern's file of correspondence and should from this file have been aware of the incorrect picture which Mr Ahern had painted. Nevertheless Mr Filer allowed the negotiations to proceed. In these circumstances it appears to me that there was a fundamental unfairness in the transaction. The defendant agreed to sell believing she had no real option and the plaintiffs accepted her agreement to sell knowing that this was not so. In my view it would create a hardship and would be unjust to decree specific performance in this case. I agree with the decision of the learned trial judge. I would refuse specific performance but would order that all monies paid to the defendant by the plaintiffs be returned to the plaintiffs by the defendant.

SECTION TWO—SETTLEMENT OF DISPUTES AND CLAIMS

A. ABUSE OF PROCESS

Rourke v Mealy (1879) 13 ILTR 52
The defendant accepted a bill of exchange in favour of the plaintiff. The bill was dishonoured and the defendant pleaded that the bill had been given by the defendant in order to discontinue proceedings brought by the plaintiff alleging a forgery by a relative of the defendant, such proceedings being a matter of some shame to the family. The defence, as set out, was one of public policy rather than coercion.

Palles C.B.:

...

The second argument which pressed me was that, the plaintiff having threatened to resort to criminal proceedings, and thereby obtained the bill now sued on, he ought to be estopped from denying that without which his threat would have been unjustifiable and idle—*viz.* that the bill was a forgery. I fully appreciate the weight of this argument, and the pressure which may be exercised by unscrupulous holders of instruments alleged to be forged, who, by threats of prosecution, extort from the fears of criminals or others, contracts which otherwise would not be entered into. I see too the danger of permitting the validity of the contract to depend upon its being possible to prove guilt at a time after the contract has been performed, and the evidence of that guilt probably destroyed. But, upon full consideration, I think that this threat constituted part of a different line of defence—*viz.* that to which I adverted in the commencement of my judgment. If we had here a defence of duress or extortion relying upon the threat, and the circumstances under which it was made, as amounting to such pressure as rendered the contract unjust or inequitable, a different question would arise. We should then have to deal, not as we have here, with a matter of illegality alone. We should have to determine to what extent, if at all, the threat prevented the defendant from acting as a free agent; and I confess that in determining the effect which might reasonably be produced upon his mind by a statement of forgery, I should be slow to listen to a statement by the utterer of the threat that it was one for which there was no solid or reasonable foundation. If the defence here clearly showed that the plaintiff ground-lessly had alleged or represented that the former bill was in fact forged, that the representation was made to the defendant, and that the defendant believed that allegation, and in consequence accepted the bill sued upon, it would take much more argument than I have yet heard to convince me that such a defence was bad. These allegations, however, are not in the defence here. It does not rely either upon estoppel or upon pressure. Its sole ground is that the contract was against public policy, and, for the reasons I have already stated, I have been coerced to arrive at the conclusion that it cannot be sustained.

Rogers *v* Louth County Council [1981] ILRM 144

Griffin J.:

In proceedings brought against the defendants in the Circuit Court for the County of Louth the plaintiff, who is the personal representative of James Murphy deceased, claims the return to her of the sum of £935.53 which it is alleged had been overpaid by her to the defendants in redeeming an annuity in respect of a cottage the property of the deceased at Rathnure, Co. Louth. The annuity was redeemed under and in pursuance of the provisions of s. 99 of the Housing Act, 1966.

James Murphy was, at the time of his death, the owner of the said cottage, which by a vesting order made under the Labourers Act, 1936, was vested in him in fee simple free from encumbrances but subject to an annuity of £19 10s *per annum* for the period of forty nine years from 2 April 1958, and to the statutory conditions, being those set out in s. 17 of the 1936 Act. In 1968, he was anxious to redeem the said annuity, and on 25 November 1968 his solicitors wrote to the defendants stating that their client 'wished to purchase the fee simple of his property. We would be obliged if you would let us have a note of the amount due'. The letter erroneously referred to the purchase of the fee simple; it was the purchase of the annuity which was intended. James Murphy died on 17 October 1968, and after some further correspondence the defendants wrote to the solicitors for the personal representatives of the deceased on 22 September 1969 stating that the amount required to redeem the outstanding annuity on the vested cottage would be £1,163. The personal representatives had some difficulty in raising that sum and the redemption was not concluded until 12 October 1972 when £1,163 was paid to the defendants. On 18 October 1972, the county council certified that the annuity had been redeemed in full.

As already stated, the redemption took place under s. 99 of the Housing Act, 1966. That section provides:

An annuity at any time outstanding may, if the housing authority entitled to receive the annuity think fit, be redeemed by the person liable to pay the annuity by payment to the authority of such amount as may be approved by the Minister, and the premises, which but for this section would be subject to and charged with the payment of the annuity or the part, shall, on receipt by the authority of the amount so approved, stand freed and discharged from the payment of the annuity.

The minister therein referred to was the Minister for Local Government, now the Minister for the Environment. Under s. 100 where an annuity is redeemed under s. 99, all the provisions of the Act of 1936, including the statutory conditions, shall cease to apply in respect of the cottage.

The sum of £1,163, as being the redemption value of the annuity, was arrived at by the defendants in accordance with directions included at para. 147D of a circular No.H.5/67 issued by the Department for Local Government (as it then was) in 1967, requiring the redemption value of the annuity to be based not on the capitalised value of the annuity, but on the current market value of the cottage, due allowance being made for the number of years for which the annuity had been paid on the cottage. In *Meade v Cork County Council* (SC) 31 July 1974, unrep., this court decided that the method of assessment of the redemption value of an annuity assessed in accordance with para. 147D of the said circular was incorrect, the correct amount being the capitalised value of the annuity outstanding at the time when redemption took place. In the instant case, it is agreed that the redemption value of the annuity under s. 99 of the 1966 Act, in accordance with the principles laid down by this court in *Meade v Cork County Council*, is the sum of £227.47.

There was therefore an overpayment by the plaintiff of the sum of £935.53. After *Meade's* case had been decided, the plaintiff claimed the return of the sums so overpaid by her in respect of the redemption of the annuity, but the defendants refused to refund such overpayment.

The defendants having failed to repay the overpayments made by the plaintiff, these proceedings were instituted, and the defendants pleaded that the sum of £1,163 was paid by the plaintiff voluntarily and with full knowledge of the facts, and that if any sum had been overpaid by the plaintiff, it was paid under a mistake of law and is irrecoverable. When the matter came for hearing before the Circuit Court Judge, he referred to this court for determination the following questions:

1. Whether the defendants were entitled to require payment by the plaintiff of the sum actually paid in respect of redemption of the said annuity?.
2. If the defendants were not entitled to require the said sum to be paid, whether the sum was paid by a mistake either of law or of fact?
3. If the said sum was paid by the plaintiff by mistake, whether the said sum or any part thereof is now recoverable?

As to the first question, having regard to the decision of this court in *Meade v Cork County Council*, counsel for the defendants very properly conceded that the county council were not entitled to require payment by the plaintiff of the sum of £1,163 and that, as stated earlier in this judgment, it was agreed that the sum of £227.47 was the correct redemption value of the annuity.

Likewise, in respect of the second question, the argument in this court proceeded on the basis that the mistake was not one of fact but of law. Both parties were agreed that the mistake was one of law; the defendants submitted that, as it was a voluntary payment, no sum was recoverable by the plaintiff, whilst the plaintiff submitted that whilst the mistake was one of law, it was one made by the defendants when they were in a privileged position with the right to withhold that privilege and that therefore the payment was not voluntary.

The real question therefore for determination is whether a payment made, in circumstances such as the present, in mistake of law is recoverable. The general rule is usually stated to be that where money is paid under the influence of a mistake, and the mistake is one of fact, an action will lie to recover it back; but that to entitle the plaintiff to recover, the mistake upon which he has acted must be one of fact, not of law. Thus in *Pollock on Contracts*, (13th ed.), edited by Professor Winfield, it is stated at p. 378 that 'money paid under a mistake of law cannot in any case be recovered'. Similar statements are to be found in many textbooks. However, the Judicial Committee of the Privy Council held in *Kiriri Cotton Co. Ltd v Dewani* [1960] 2 WLR 127 that a plaintiff may recover money paid on a mistake of law provided that he is not in *pari delicto* with the defendant in mistaking the law. Delivering the advice of the Privy Council, Lord Denning said at p. 133:

> Nor is it correct to say that money paid under a mistake of law can never be recovered back. The true proposition is that money paid under a mistake of law, by itself and without more, cannot be recovered back. James L.J. pointed that out in *Rogers v Ingham*. If there is something more in addition to a mistake of law—if there is something in the defendant's conduct which shows that, of the two of them, he is the one primarily responsible for the mistake—then it may be recovered back. Thus, if as between the two of them the duty of observing the law is placed on the shoulders of the one rather than the other—it being imposed on him specially for the protection of the other—then they are not in *pari delicto* and the money can be recovered back; see *Browning v Morris*, by Lord Mansfield. Likewise, if the responsibility for the mistake lies more on the one than the other because he has misled the other when he ought to know better—then again they are not in *pari delicto* and the money can be recovered back.

This passage was cited with approval by Kenny J. in *Dolan v Neligan* [1967] IR 247, at 260. Again, even where there has been no mistake of fact, a plaintiff may still recover monies so paid in an action for money had and received upon proof that the monies were paid by him involuntarily, that is, as the result of some extortion, coercion or compulsion in the legal sense—see per Windeyer J. in *Mason v New South Wales*, 102 CLR 108, 139. He cannot recover if the payment was made voluntarily. A payment may be said to be voluntary, in this context, when the payer makes it deliberately with a knowledge of all relevant facts, and either being indifferent to whether or not he is liable in law, or knowing, or having reason to think, himself not liable, yet intending finally to close the transaction—see per Windeyer J. at p. 143. Whether the payment has been voluntary in this sense may also be deduced from the relationship of the parties. As Abott C.J. said in *Morgan v Palmer*, 2 B & C 729 at p. 734:

> It has been well argued that the payment having been voluntary, it cannot be recovered back in an action for money had and received. I agree that such a consequence would have followed had the parties been on equal terms. But if one party has the power of saying to the other, 'That which you require shall not be done except upon the conditions I choose to impose', no person can contend that they stand upon anything like an equal footing.

In such a case, the payment is by no means to be considered to be voluntary—see per McTiernan J. in *Bell v Shire of Serpentine*, (1969) 121 CLR 137.

Applying these principles to the present case, the plaintiff is in my judgment entitled to recover the overpayment of £935.43 made by her. The payment of £1,163 made by the plaintiff was not 'voluntary' in the context aforesaid. The parties were not on equal terms; the defendants had the power, if they thought fit, to withhold permission for the redemption of the annuity; they were however prepared to allow the plaintiff to redeem it, but only on the conditions imposed by them, which included exacting a payment in excess of that permitted by the statute. The plaintiff was not in possession of all the relevant facts, and did not know, nor had she reason to think, that she was not liable to pay the sum demanded by the defendants for the redemption of the annuity. The defendants were in my view primarily responsible for the mistake and the parties were accordingly not in *pari delicto*.

I would accordingly answer the questions submitted by the learned Circuit Court Judge as follows: Question 1 No. Question 2 The sum paid was paid by a mistake of law. Question 3 Yes.

Kenny J.:

. . . The aphorism 'money paid under a mistake of fact may be recovered but money paid under a mistake of law cannot' is grossly inaccurate. It has the advantage of simplicity but the matter is much more complex than it suggests. I have no doubt that the excessive sum fixed by the county council for the redemption was caused by the circular sent by the Department of Local Government which was based on an entirely wrong interpretation of s. 99 and which was, therefore, a mistake of law. The recovery of a sum so paid is well dealt with in *Law of Restitution* by Goff J. and Professor Jones (2nd ed., 1978) ch. 4. It has also been dealt with in the case law; my judgment when I was a judge of the High Court in *Dolan v Neligan* [1967] IR 245 and the decision of the Privy Council in *Kiriri Cotton Co. Ltd v Ranchoddas* [1960] AC 192.

In the latter Lord Denning said:

It is not correct to say that everyone is presumed to know the law. The true proposition is that no man can excuse himself from doing his duty by saying that he did not know the law on the matter. *Ignorantia juris neminem excusat.* Nor is it correct to say that money paid under a mistake of law can never be recovered back. The true proposition is that money paid under a mistake of law by itself and without more cannot be recovered back . . . If there is something more in addition to a mistake of law—if there is something in the defendant's conduct which shows that of the two of them, he is the one primarily responsible for the mistake,—then it may be recovered back . . . if the responsibility for the mistake lies more on the one than the other—because he has misled the other when he ought to know better—then again they are not in *pari delicto* and the money can be recovered back.

In the instant case the plaintiff's solicitor wrote to the defendants asking what was the redemption price of the annuity. The plaintiff's solicitor could not be expected to know the redemption price. He relied on the defendants to give him the correct figure. Nor could he be expected to anticipate the decision of the Supreme Court in *Meade's* case. It is important to bear in mind that the decision of the Supreme Court reversed that of a High Court Judge who thought that the excessive amount of the redemption price of an annuity could not be recovered back from the defendants in that case.

I have no doubt that the plaintiff is entitled to recover the £935.53 from the defendants.

The answers to the questions posed by the Circuit Court Judge should, in my opinion be: (i) The defendants were not entitled to require payment by the plaintiff of the sum actually paid in respect of the redemption of the annuity. (ii) The amount of the redemption price of the annuity was paid under a mistake of law. (iii) £935.53, part of the redemption price paid, is recoverable by the plaintiff as personal representative from the defendants.

(O'Higgins C.J. concurred.)

B. Duress by Threatened Breach of Contract.

In Re Hooper and Grass Contract [1949] VLR 269

Fullagar J.:

Vendor and purchaser summons issued under s. 49 of the Property Law Act 1928 at the instance of the purchaser. The contract was made on 27 January 1948, and the date provided for payment of balance of purchase money was, in the events which happened, 24 February 1948.

The question in issue relates to an irrigation charge imposed by a by-law made by the State Rivers and Water Supply Commission under s. 66 of the Water Act 1928. The total amount of the charge is £26 2s. The by-law was published in the Gazette of 29 October 1947, and it provided, in compliance with s. 66, that the charge was made and should be levied for the period beginning 1 September 1947, and ending 30 April 1948, and that it should be payable at specified places on 31 October 1947. By virtue of ss. 324 and 326 of the Water Act the irrigation charge in question became a charge on the land on the day when it became payable, i.e. 31 October 1947. Apart, therefore, from special provision in the contract, the vendor would be bound either to pay the amount himself, or to allow it in account on completion. See *Re Sneesby and Ades and Bowes' Contract*, [1919] VLR 497, at p. 504: the question which actually arose for decision in that case does not arise here. The contract, however, incorporates Table A of the Transfer of Land Act 1928, and clause 10 of Table A provides that all rates, taxes, assessments, fire insurance premiums and other outgoings in respect of the land shall be borne and paid by the purchaser as from the date on which he becomes entitled to possession and the same shall, if necessary, be apportioned between the vendor and purchaser. On the argument before me it was common ground that this clause applies to the irrigation charge in question, and I should think that it was clearly an outgoing in respect of the land. The purchaser, however, contended that the apportionment should be on the basis of time, while the vendor contended that it should be on the basis of water consumed. If the first contention were correct, then, the period for which the charge was imposed being from 1 September 1947, to 30 April 1948, the vendor would be responsible for £17 1s 10d. If the second contention were correct, then, since the vendor had used no water before the date of possession, the whole of the amount in question would fall on the purchaser.

I am clearly of opinion that the contention of the purchaser is correct. The first part of clause 10 of Table A makes it plain, I think, that the apportionment contemplated is to be made by reference to the time after the purchaser becomes entitled to possession. Nor is there, in my opinion, anything in the nature of a charge under the Water Act to take it outside the provision for apportionment in clause 10 or to support the view that it is apportionable on some other basis than a time basis. I need not refer in detail to the relevant provisions of the Act. It is true that under s. 66 the amount of the irrigation charge in respect of any land is arrived at by reference to the quantity of water apportioned to that land as a right in pursuance of ss. 56 and 61. But it has no relation to water used. It is payable in full if no water is used or more or less water than the quantity apportioned to the land as a right. More may be used under the last two paragraphs of s. 61, and, if more is used, it must be paid for at a rate per unit of volume fixed by by-law. The irrigation charge had nothing to do with water actually used, and I do not think that the vendor's contention can be supported.

The summons asks for a declaration and an order for payment by the vendor to the purchaser. The vendor, however, argues that I cannot make an order for payment, and that I should not therefore make a declaration of a right which cannot be enforced. This argument arises in this way. At the time of settlement the amount of the charges had not been paid, and the purchaser's solicitor sought to debit the vendor with this amount in making the various adjustments of rates etc., to arrive at the net amount payable by him. The vendor's solicitor refused to allow this to be done, and in a letter written on 1 March stated that the amount payable was £1,456 17s 4d, an amount which did not allow for a deduction of £17 1s 10d. He added that he was ready to settle if that amount was paid at once, and he added: 'Otherwise, as your client is now in default, he must suffer the penalties provided for in the contract and any other loss he may sustain.' Thereupon the sum of £1,456 17s 4d was paid under protest with an intimation that a vendor and purchaser summons would be issued. The summons was issued a few days later. The argument now is that the payment made was a voluntary payment and the amount thereof cannot be recovered as money had and received. Reliance was placed on *Donaldson v Gray*, |1920| VLR 379.

If no action would lie for the recovery of the sum in question, I do not think that I ought to make a declaration. Nothing more, however, appears from the report of *Donaldson v Gray* than that 'for the purposes of not delaying the settlement the purchaser's solicitors agreed under protest' to the vendor's demand. Cussen J. said, at p. 382: 'They agreed at the time, and they are not in a position to recover the money back.' He held that the mere fact of protest could not alter the position. I think that a good deal more appears in this case than appeared in *Donaldson v Gray*. There is a certain ambiguity—perhaps a studied ambiguity—about the letter of the vendor's solicitor, but the time for completion had passed, and the purchaser's solicitor certainly could not be blamed if he read that letter as a threat to cancel the contract if a sum in excess of what was really due were not paid. At least it purported to treat the purchaser as in default, and, in effect, while offering to waive the default if the purchaser paid the whole of the charge in question, threatened to exercise any remedy available for default if the purchaser did not pay the whole of that charge.

Now, time is expressly made of the essence of the contract in this case, and, if the purchaser were really in default, and the vendor demanded a price for refraining from taking any step which he was entitled to take on default, and the purchaser, rather than have any such step taken, paid the price, it would seem clear that he could not recover the price so paid as money had and received. The position would not be affected by his paying expressly 'under protest'. This was really, I think, in substance the position in *Smith v William Charlick Ltd*, (1924) 34 CLR 38. A says to B: 'I am not bound to do a certain thing. I will, however, do it if, but not unless, you pay me £10.' B says: 'I pay you the £10. The consequences of not paying it would be disastrous. But, though I pay it, I pay it under protest.' That is plainly, in my opinion, not this case. The due date for completion under the contract was 24 February 1948. A letter written by the vendor's solicitor on that date shows that the vendor was not insisting on completion on that precise date. He had waived the condition that time was of the essence, and he could not thereafter insist on completion by any definite date unless and until he had given a notice requiring the purchaser to pay on or before some reasonable date in the future. What the vendor was doing was not threatening to exercise a legal right unless he were paid a price for not exercising it: he was threatening to withhold that to which the other party was legally entitled unless he were paid a price which he had no right to receive. In such a case I think the true rule of law is that a payment under protest is not a voluntary payment, whatever the position may be where the payment is not made under protest. It makes no difference that the vendor honestly believed that he was legally entitled in any case to the price which he asked. In these cases there is very reasonably said to be a practical compulsion to pay a demand not justified by law. The following authorities, to which Mr Adam referred me are all, I think, relevant: *Fraser v Pendlebury*, |1861| 31 LJ CP 1, *Close v Phipps*, |1844| 7 M & G 586, *Atkinson v Denby*, |1862| 31 LJ Ex 362, *Ashmole v Wainwright*, |1842| 2 QB 837, *Green v Duckett*, |1883| 11 QBD 275, and *Knutson v The Bourkes Syndicate*, |1941| SCR (Can.) 419. The Canadian case is criticised in a note in Can B Rev, 19, p. 694, but I am much more impressed by the decision than by the criticism. Kerwin J., who delivered the judgment of himself and four other judges, cited, at p. 423, two very pertinent passages from the judgments of Bayley J. and Holroyd J. in *Shaw v Woodcock*, |1827| 7 B & C 73. Holroyd J. put it very shortly. He said, at p. 85: 'Upon the question whether a payment be voluntary or not, the law is quite clear. If a party making the payment is obliged to pay, in order to obtain possession of things to which he is entitled, the money so paid is not a voluntary, but a compulsory payment, and may be recovered back.'

Bayley J. also rejected the argument, which had been put, that the owner must be shown to be under an immediate pressing necessity of receiving his property.

In cases of this type the withholding of another's legal right is, I think, itself treated as a 'practical compulsion'. Cases like *Criterion Theatres Ltd v Melbourne & Metropolitan Board of Works*, |1945| VLR 267 seem to differ only in that the 'practical compulsion' takes a different form. In the *Criterion Theatres* case, the plaintiff, if the water had been cut off, would in all probability have suffered very serious damage through the deterioration or practical destruction of its racing track. Such cases may be described in the words of Lord Ellenborough C.J. in *Smith v Cuff*, |1817| 6 M & S 160, at p. 165, as cases where 'one holds the rod, and the other bows to it', or in the words of Cockburn C.J. in *Atkinson v Denby*, |1862| 31 LJ Ex 362, as cases 'where one person can dictate and the other has hardly any other alternative but to submit'.

Possibly in both classes of case the underlying basis on which the money paid, but not legally payable, is recoverable is that it was paid without consideration. This basis would not support the action if the payment was made voluntarily and with full knowledge of the facts. But payments made in certain circumstances are not treated by the law as being made voluntarily for the purposes of this principle. The manner in which the question whether the payment was 'voluntary' is discussed in the cases seems to suggest that the voluntary character of the payment will take it outside a general rule which would make it recoverable. The other possible analysis is that the money is paid under duress, a widely extended meaning being attached to the word 'duress'. But I think that there is really more to be said in favour of the former suggested analysis.

In *Donaldson v Gray*, |1920| VLR 379, the purchaser, although he paid or allowed in account sums for which the vendor was in law responsible, was held, I think, not to have proved enough to entitle him to maintain money had and received. I would regard it as a decision on particular facts: the 'practical compulsion', which was established in the cases cited above, was not established in *Donaldson v Gray* to the satisfaction of Cussen J. Those cases afford, to my mind, ample justification for holding here that the 'practical compulsion' is established.

The question asked by the summons is answered: Yes. It is apportionable in respect of time. Order that vendor pay to purchaser the sum of £17 1s 10d. Order that costs of summons be paid by vendor to purchaser.

Maskell v Horner [1915] 3 KB 106

Lord Reading C.J.:

From the year 1900 till 1912 the plaintiff carried on business at Spitalfields Market as a dealer in produce and the defendant throughout this period demanded and received payment by the plaintiff of market tolls on goods sold by the plaintiff in the market. It was decided by the Court of Appeal in *Attorney General v Horner* (No. 2)[1] that the defendant Horner was not entitled to demand tolls from the sellers, and it follows from this decision, which has not been and could not be challenged in this court, that the plaintiff was never under legal obligation to pay tolls to the defendant. The plaintiff having, during this period of years, paid a number of small sums of money as market tolls to the defendant, now sues to recover these sums as money had and received by the defendant to the use of the plaintiff. The action came for trial before Rowlatt J., who decided in favour of the defendant, and the plaintiff appeals to this court for a reversal of this judgment.

The question is whether the plaintiff made these payments in such circumstances as entitle him to recover them from the defendant in an action at law for money had and received.

. . .

Upon the second head of claim the plaintiff asserts that he paid the money not voluntarily but under the pressure of actual or threatened seizure of his goods, and that he is therefore entitled to recover it as money had and received. If the facts proved support this assertion the plaintiff would, in my opinion, be entitled to succeed in this action.

If a person with knowledge of the facts pays money, which he is not in law bound to pay, and in circumstances implying that he is paying it voluntarily to close the transaction, he cannot recover it. Such a payment is in law like a gift, and the transaction cannot be reopened. If a person pays money, which he is not bound to pay, under the compulsion of urgent and pressing necessity or of seizure, actual or threatened, of his goods he can recover it as money had and received. The money is paid not under duress in the strict sense of the term, as that implies duress of person, but under the pressure of seizure or detention of goods which is analogous to that of duress. Payment under such pressure establishes that the payment is not made voluntarily to close the transaction (per Lord Abinger C.B. and per Parke B. in *Atlee v Backhouse*[2]). The payment is made for the purpose of averting a threatened evil and is made not with the intention of giving up a right but under immediate necessity and with the intention of preserving the right to dispute the legality of the demand (per Tindal C.J. in *Valpy v Manley*[3]). There are numerous instances in the books of successful claims in this form of action to recover money paid to relieve goods from seizure. Other familiar instances are cases such as *Parker v Great Western Rly. Co.*,[4] where the money was paid to the railway company under protest in order to induce them to carry goods which they were refusing to carry except at rates in excess of those they were legally entitled to demand. These payments were made throughout a period of twelve months, always accompanied by the assertion that they were made under protest, and it was held that the plaintiffs were entitled to recover the excess payments as money had and received, on the ground that the payments were made under the compulsion of urgent and pressing necessity. That case was approved in *Great Western Rly. Co. v Sutton*,[5] when the judges were summoned to the House of Lords to give their opinion. Willes J., in stating his view of the law, said: 'When a man pays more than he is bound to do by law for the performance of a duty which the law says is owed to him for nothing, or for less than he had paid, there is a compulsion or concussion in respect of which he is entitled to recover the excess by *condictio indebiti*, or action for money had and received. This is every day's practice as to excess freight.' That is a clear and accurate statement in accordance with the views expressed by Blackburn J. in the same case and adopted by the House of Lords. It treats such claims made in this form of action as matters of ordinary practice and beyond discussion. (See also per Lord Chelmsford in *Lancashire and Yorkshire Rly. Co. v Gidlow*[6]).

[1.] |1913| 2 Ch. 140. [3.] 1 CB 594, 602, 603. [5.] LR 4 HL 226, 249.
[2.] 3 M & W 633, 646, 650. [4.] 7 Man. & G. 253. [6.] LR 7 HL 517, 527.

(Buckley L.J. concurred with Lord Reading. Pickford L.J. dissented.)

Note

In *Maskell v Horner*, Pickford L.J., while not doubting the principle, found that the plaintiff had not on the facts 'established' quasi-duress of goods. As we shall see, the inferences to be drawn from facts are highly problematical in this area.

The Australian and Canadian courts have developed a doctrine of practical compulsion by building on decisions such as *Maskell v Horner*: see Sutton, (1974) 20 McGill LJ 555. In England, Beatson's observations on the limited role afforded to duress ((1974) CLJ 97) in that jurisdiction provided an interesting contrast. However, judicial pronouncements on economic duress were not universally negative.

Ogilvie, 'Economic Duress, Inequality of Bargaining Power and Threatened Breach of Contract' (1981) 27 McGill LJ 289 at 296–9

. . .

Relying on *Rookes v Barnard*, Lord Denning M.R., in *D. & C. Builders v Rees* made some comments which until recently have been overlooked in the discussion of economic duress. In that well known case the plaintiffs were owed about £480 by the defendants and, to the knowledge of the defendants, were in desperate financial straits. Exploiting this knowledge, the defendants said that they could pay only £300, which the plaintiffs accepted, signing a receipt 'in completion of the account' at the insistence of Mrs Rees. The Court of Appeal held that the plaintiffs were entitled to recover the remaining £180 on two grounds: first, because there was no consideration for the settlement and, second, that there was no true accord because, as Lord Denning said, '|n|o person can insist on a settlement procured by intimidation'. This could be viewed as economic duress; moreover, *D. & C. Builders* could also be viewed as a case of two-party intimidation.

II. *Recent developments in England*

The significance of Lord Denning's remark was not lost on Kerr J. in *The Siboen and the Sibotre*, which is the fresh starting point for recent cases which recognise economic duress by threatened breach of contract. Two oil tankers were chartered in 1970 to Concord Petroleum Ltd, at the rate of £4.40 per ton per month on standard charterparties, for use in transporting oil from the Persian Gulf in the event that Concord was shut out from its Libyan supplies. The market slumped and Concord's parent company, Occidental Petroleum Inc., sought to renegotiate the rate, and they devised a scheme to give the owners the false impression that they had not substantial assets and had suffered great losses. Occidental threatened to repudiate the charter and allow Concord to go into liquidation if the rates were not lowered. The pressure on the owners was exacerbated by the fact that if the charterparties were repudiated the ships would have to be laid up because of the depressed market. The ships were mortgaged and the owners relied on the charterparties' income to repay the mortgages, as the charterers well knew. In such a squeeze the owners seemed to have no alternative but to concede the rate reduction. By mid-1973 the market was rising steeply again and the charterers were making huge profits. The owners asked them to revert to the original rate or the charterparties would be cancelled on the ground of coercion. The charterers declined to reinstate the original rate, the owners withdrew the ships and the charterers sued. The owners alleged that the renegotiated terms were void for misrepresentation or for duress, and Kerr J. held that the charterers were liable for fraudulent and innocent misrepresentation, but that the action in duress could not succeed.

The learned judge conceded that there was room for the development of the law in regard to contracts concluded under some form of compulsion not amounting to duress to the person, and stipulated the appropriate test:

> . . . the court must in every case at least be satisfied that the consent of the other party was overborne by compulsion so as to deprive him of any *animus contrahendi*. This would depend on the facts of each case. One relevant factor would be whether the party relying on the duress made any protest at the time or shortly thereafter. Another would be to consider whether or not he treated the settlement as closing the transaction in question and as binding upon him, or whether he made it clear that he regarded the position as still open.

In the instant case Kerr, J. decided that there was neither sufficient coercion of the will nor protest, and that the owners had admitted that they regarded the agreement as binding, thus 'acting under great pressure, but only commercial pressure, and not under anything which could in law be regarded as a coercion of his will so as to vitiate his consent.'

This approach is unsatisfactory. Undoubtedly, it was convenient for the court that the threatened breach of contract took the form of fraudulent and innocent misrepresentations. But if there had been no misrepresentations would the charterers have escaped liability? Or would the judge have made an extra effort to find an alternative ground of liability? One would hope so. Here was a situation in which the owners were apparently under the greatest type of commercial pressure possible, submitting to the charterer's demands or risking insolvency, in the event that they proved unable to renegotiate the mortgages or find some other adequate solution. On the presumption that insolvency was the only alternative to submission (and the court's failure to probe the existence of alternatives should be noted), the owners could hardly be said not to have entered the agreement voluntarily. In this Kerr J. was quite right; there had indeed been a voluntary submission. But there always will be when the only alternatives available are worse. Thus it is questionable whether coercion of the will is a satisfactory criterion for distinguishing real economic duress from acceptable 'commercial pressure'. Indeed, there is coercion in *all* contracts: if I wish to purchase a loaf of bread I must pay its price, although I would much rather have the bread and the money in my pocket. The coercion here is a vital matter, yet in the absence of other factors it is most unlikely that courts would allow avoidance of the contract for economic duress.

But even if coercion of the will is accepted as the key to the presence of economic duress, how is it to be distinguished from mere commercial pressure?

Kerr J. suggested several other relevant factors in the determination of the presence of economic duress, notably whether the victim protested or regarded the agreement as forever binding. The relevance of these factors is minimal. At the very least the victim might not be the 'protesting sort' or might consider protest superfluous. Moreover, a victim at the time of submission to duress is likely to consider himself fully bound and will only question the transaction later. The learned judge might have considered other factors, such as an initial inequality of bargaining power, or a subsequent inequality of bargaining power, the 'wrongfulness' of the coercive act, the adequacy of the consideration, the actual availability of other alternatives and the seriousness of the consequences to the victim of not submitting. These will be considered later.

Issues similar to those in *The Siboen and the Sibotre* were raised in *The Atlantic Baron*. A contract was agreed to between the plaintiffs and a South Korean shipbuilding company to build an oil tanker, 'The Atlantic Baron', for £30, 950,000. Article XI stated that the price was to be paid in five instalments and that the builders were to open a letter of credit to provide security for the repayment of the instalments in the event of their default. Ten months later the American dollar was devalued by ten per cent and the builders demanded a ten per cent increase in the purchase price in respect of the four instalments payable after the devaluation. The plaintiffs took legal advice and were told that the claim lacked foundation. Correspondence ensued with the plaintiffs noting that they too were adversely affected by the devaluation, yet had not increased freight rates under existing contracts; but to no avail. On 26 June 1973 the builders sent a telex requesting a final and decisive reply by 30 June; otherwise the contract would be terminated. The plaintiffs were caught because on 22 May they had concluded a three-year charterparty with Shell and could not get a substitute tanker. The builders were ignorant of this fact as well as of the fact that the plaintiffs would still be left with a handsome profit from the Shell contract after paying the ten per cent. They replied to the telex on 28 June 1973 that they would pay, 'in order to maintain an amicable relationship and without prejudice to our rights'. They asked that the letter of credit be increased accordingly and this was done. In an action to recover the ten per cent, the plaintiffs argued, first, that there was no additional consideration for the payments and, second, that the agreement was voidable because made involuntarily under economic duress. Mocatta J. held, though with some doubt, that there was consideration in the detriment to the builders in increasing the letter of credit, thus showing yet again that the courts can find consideration whenever it suits them. With respect to the second question, the learned judge opined that even when there was good consideration, where a threatened breach of contract had led to a further contract, that contract could be voidable for economic duress. Just what economic duress is, he did not decide. He did not have to because the plaintiff's subsequent failure to protest or litigate the transaction for almost two years was an affirmation of it; thus they were not entitled to claim a refund.

SECTION THREE—ECONOMIC DURESS AND INDUSTRIAL CONFLICT

The first decision of the House of Lords to establish economic duress was *Universe Tankships Inc. of Monrovia v International Transport Workers Federation* (1982) 2 WLR 803.

The decision was not universally welcomed.

Atiyah, 'Economic Duress and "The Overborne Will"' (1982) 98 LQR 197

Since 1976 there have been four English and one Privy Council decision recognising the existence in principle of the concept of 'economic duress' as furnishing a defence to an action on a contract, or as providing a ground for the recovery of money paid: *The Siboen and the Sibotre* |1976| 1 Lloyd's Rep. 293; *North Ocean Shipping Co. Ltd v Hyundai Construction (The Atlantic Baron)* |1979| QB 705; *Pao On v Lau Yiu* |1980| AC 614; *Universe Tankships of Monrovia Inc. v International Transport Workers' Federation* |1981| ICR 129; *Syros Shipping Co. S.A. v Elaghill Trading Co.* |1981| 3 All ER 189. It is true that in only two of these cases (*The Atlantic Baron* and the *Universe Tankships* case) was the court satisfied that economic duress had been made out on the facts, and that even in these two cases relief for economic duress was ultimately denied, in the first because the contract was held to have been affirmed by the innocent party, and in the other because the guilty party was a trade union entitled to rely on the 'trade dispute' statutory immunities. Nevertheless, it is clear that here is a growth area of the law of contract of considerable potential importance.

It is, therefore, particularly desirable that this new doctrine should start life on a sound conceptual basis and not be shunted into a blind alley for lack of adequate analysis. Yet, as a result of an oversight of monumental proportions, this latter fate appears at present to be a serious danger, because all five of these cases have attempted to justify, to a greater or lesser degree, the concept of economic duress by invoking the traditional theory that duress 'overbears the will' of the party subject to it. The purpose of this note is to draw the attention of the practising profession to the fact that all these five cases have overlooked a crucially important case decided by the House of Lords as recently as 1975, namely *Lynch v DPP of Northern Ireland* |1975| AC 653, which totally demolishes the theory that duress operates by 'overbearing the will' of the party subject to it.

The 'overborne will' theory has, of course, a long history in cases of common law duress as well as in many equitable cases of undue influence, so it is hardly surprising that it should be used by the courts to justify the new concept of economic duress, and (as stated above) it was so used, to some extent, in all five of the cases listed above. It will suffice here to refer to the discussion in the *Pao On* case as this contains the fullest analysis of the basis of the new doctrine of economic duress. It is unnecessary to refer to the facts except to mention that the context was a complex commercial transaction in which the defendant alleged that he had been induced to make the promise sued on as a result of threats to break other contractual obligations. Delivering the opinion of the Privy Council, Lord Scarman several times reiterated that economic (or indeed, any other form of) duress operated by overbearing the will of the person subject to it. 'Duress, whatever form it takes, is a coercion of the will so as to vitiate consent' (p. 635). Again, where commercial pressures were alleged to constitute economic coercion, the duress 'must be such that the victim must have entered the contract against his will, must have had no alternative course open to him . . .' (p. 636). Further, it must even be shown that the victim's act 'was not a voluntary act on his part' (p. 636).

This analysis, it is submitted, is totally inconsistent with the speeches in the House of Lords in *Lynch's* case, which does not appear to have been cited in any of the five cases mentioned above. *Lynch's* case was, of course, a decision on the criminal law, concerning the applicability of the defence of duress to a charge of murder, where the accused was charged as an accessory and not a principal. The defence was upheld by a majority of three to two; but all five members of the House discussed the theoretical basis of the defence of duress, some of them at considerable length, and all five of them agreed in rejection of the 'overborne will' theory. Thus Lord Morris of Borth-y-

Gest accepts that a person subjected to duress has a moment of time to decide whether he will submit or not. If he submits, 'what is done will be done most unwillingly but intentionally' (p. 670). Lord Wilberforce says that the best opinion is that duress does not negative intention, but is superimposed on the other ingredients of the offence. *Coactus volui* sums up the combination: the victim completes the act and knows that he is doing so; but the addition of the element of duress prevents the law from treating what he has done as a crime' (p. 680). Lord Simon of Glaisdale, dissenting in the result, concurred on this point in the fullest analysis to be found in the speeches (or, indeed, anywhere else in English law) on the nature of the concept of duress. He stresses that 'an *intention* to bring about a consequence of an act can co-exist with a *desire* that such consequence should not ensue' (p. 690). He distinguishes a case of 'true necessity' from a case of duress. In the former, there is no choice of action and the act is not a product of the will at all, and is not even an 'act' of the person constrained. But this is not the case with other (not 'true') cases of necessity, nor with cases of duress. 'In both |such| sets of circumstances there is power of choice between two alternatives, but one of the alternatives is so disagreeable that even serious infraction of the criminal law seems preferable. In both, the consequence of the act is intended, within any permissible definition of intention' (p. 692). At the end of his analysis, Lord Simon concludes by saying, 'I hope, indeed, to have demonstrated that duress is not inconsistent with act and will, the will being deflected, not destroyed . . . ' (p. 695). Similar passages are to be found in the speeches of Lord Kilbrandon (p. 703) and Lord Edmund-Davies (p. 709). It appears from the latter's speech that the 'overborne will' theory was actually adopted by the trial judge and fully canvassed in argument before the House of Lords.

Thus what we have here is an unanimous and authoritative rejection of the 'overborne will' theory, doubtless overlooked in the contract cases mentioned above because this was a criminal case. But any suggestion that these remarks are, for that reason, inapplicable in the law of contract is surely unacceptable. First, it is clear that in the passages referred to above, the Law Lords were not discussing a doctrine of peculiar application to the criminal law, but the very nature and meaning of the concept of duress. They were addressing themselves to fundamentally juristic questions involved in the meaning of concepts like intention, act, will and voluntary conduct—all concepts which are just as relevant in contract law as in the criminal law. Secondly, two of their lordships, Lord Wilberforce and Lord Simon, actually referred, if only *en passant*, to the analogy of contract law (see pp 680 and 695) to justify the views they were upholding in relation to the criminal law. In doing this, Lord Wilberforce and Lord Simon may well have been guilty of a certain disingenuousness having regard to the fact that the 'overborne will' theory has undoubtedly held the field in contract law for many years, but that does not alter the fact that these two, at least, showed clearly enough that they regarded the new analysis as applicable to the law of contract.

But even if the speeches in *Lynch's* case are not finally authoritative in the law of contract, it is nevertheless submitted that they ought to be followed, both because they are far more rationally persuasive than the 'overborne will' theory, and also because they are more consistent with the developing rules of the doctrine of economic duress. As to the first point it is difficult to disagree with the various speeches in *Lynch's* case which demonstrate the difficulties of the 'overborne will' theory. A victim of duress *does* normally know what he is doing, does choose to submit, and *does* intend to do so. Indeed, as has often been pointed out by American writers (see, e.g. Dawson, 'Economic Duress—An Essay in Perspective' (1947) 45 Michigan LR 253, 267) the more extreme the pressure, the more real is the consent of the victim. The victim of the modern mugger who surrenders his wallet with a knife at his throat certainly knows what he is doing, and intends to do it. (This analysis may cause difficulty for other aspects of the criminal law—e.g. the victim's voluntary surrender of his wallet is clearly not such a consent as to negative a charge of theft—but that need not be pursued here.)

In the second place, the 'overborne will' theory is internally inconsistent and contradictory, even as enounced in the *Pao On* case. I have already cited a passage from Lord Scarman's speech (on p. 636 of the report) in which the defence of duress is confined to those cases in which the victim 'had no alternative course open to him'. Yet it is clear that this cannot be taken literally because on the very same page Lord Scarman indicates that one of the factors to be considered in deciding whether economic duress has been established, is the *effectiveness* of the alternative remedies open to the victim. So it is clear that the defence may be available even where the victim does have alternative courses of action open to him; indeed, on the analysis in *Lynch's* case, the victim *always* has such alternatives open to him. Even the victim of the mugger may resist at the price of his own life, if he has the courage to do so (as the late Professor W. Friedmann had).

Thirdly, as pointed out by Lord Simon in *Lynch's* case, the 'overborne will' theory is difficult to reconcile with the now established rule that duress renders a contract voidable and not void. As Lord Simon also points out, the contrast is with the defence of *non est factum*. That is a case where there is a total lack of consent. No doubt it is possible to envisage rare cases of duress or even undue influence where the victim is reduced to such a stage of submission that he acts as though in a trance without knowing what he is doing, in which case a different analysis may be appropriate. But that is certainly not the ordinary case of duress, still less is such an analysis likely to be relevant in the commercial contexts in which economic duress is pleaded.

It may, of course, be argued that all this is a highly theoretical debate, or perhaps even that it is merely a terminological or conceptual debate without practical import- ance. Provided that the courts evolve, as they seem to be doing, subsidiary rules which are to be applied to determine if and when the victim's will is to be 'taken' to have been 'overborne', it may not matter what formula is used to describe the process. For myself, I would reject this argument, if only because it is desirable that rules should be formulated in a way which commands rational assent. A rule which declares that it only operates when a person has no choice, but then requires examination of the choices open to him, does not inspire confidence among rational beings. But there are also practical reasons for desiring that the 'overborne will' theory should now be consigned to the historical scrapheap. So long as the law is stated in terms of this theory, there is a real danger that the formula may be taken too literally by those whose business it is to apply the law—and it must be remembered that this includes arbitrators as well as solicitors and counsel advising their clients. In the *Syros Shipping* case, for instance, Lloyd J., in remitting the case to the arbitrator to reconsider (among other issues) a plea of economic duress, simply said that the decisions cited above appeared to establish 'that the question of duress turns on whether the commercial pressure exercised by one party on the other was such as to vitiate the other party's consent by coercion of his will' (p. 192). This seems a clear invitation to the arbitrator to treat the issue as one of fact, but if the issue is so treated, it is surely bound to divert attention into quite irrelevant inquiries into the psychological motivations of the party pleading duress.

Careful study of the cases referred to above will show that this is the wrong approach. Duress is clearly only partly a question of fact. Once it is appreciated that the victim of duress has chosen between evils, it becomes necessary to examine the nature and acceptability of the choice he was presented with. That clearly involves important questions of law, and cannot be treated as a pure question of fact. To treat the issue as one of fact diverts inquiry from the really vital issues in a case of economic duress, namely what sort of threats is it permissible to make, and when is it permissible for a victim of duress to reopen a question which has apparently been closed by his submission to the coercion.

It is much to be hoped that the next case to involve a plea of economic duress will see *Lynch's* case drawn to the attention of the court, and the law placed on a sounder theoretical footing.

Lord Wedderburn (1982) 45 MLR 556 was also critical of this new line of authority:

In 1976, there began a line of judgments in commercial cases which swept this old learning aside. They were attempts to introduce a new element of 'fairness' into some commercial bargains by judges insufficiently reckless (or courageous, according to taste) to go the whole hog and limit private enterprise by judicial reference to 'inequality of bargaining power'.[1] Instead, the Privy Council and Kerr J. introduced the more limited concept that has come to be known as 'economic duress'. This operates whenever 'the consent of the other party was overborne by compulsion so as to deprive him of any *animus contrahendi*'.[2] Mere 'commercial pressure' by itself is not enough (how could it be?). But any 'coercion of the will which vitiates consent' suffices.[3] While English judges have not stretched the doctrine to the length of their American counterparts,[4] and most of the cases in which the doctrine has been applied have involved duress by way of acts wrongful in themselves,[5] judges have now stated the doctrine in wider terms.[6] Economic duress turns upon whether 'the commercial pressure exercised by one party on the other was such as to vitiate the other party's consent by coercion of his will.'[7]

Although approved by today's modish liberalism, this fashionable new doctrine suffers, even in commercial law, from a number of profoundly unsatisfactory features. First, as Professor Atiyah has amply demonstrated, its conceptual apparatus of the 'overborne will' is wrongheaded, 'internally inconsistent and contradictory.'[8] A victim of this sort of duress does choose to submit. His remedy stems from the fact not that he has no choice but that the alternatives left open to him were in the court's eyes inadequate. And a contract induced by such duress is voidable (not void).[9]

Secondly, is there not something absurd in asking whether, for the purposes of our commercial law, one large corporate trading entity has 'overborne the will' of another? Indeed, lawyers should now no doubt be eagerly seeking out the *alter ego* in each such corporation, the men whose (real) will must be 'coerced' before the corporate (fictional) consent is vitiated.[10]

Thirdly, consent is vitiated where the court decides that the pressure is not 'legitimate'.[11] And illegitimate pressure may not involve (though it usually will involve) an act unlawful in itself. 'Duress can of course exist even if the threat is one of lawful action; whether it does so depends upon the nature of the demand.'[12] At this critical point, 'economic duress' becomes a formidable and uncertain liability. It is not in itself a tort. But if it is threatened or employed deliberately to injure, would the judges, if it suited them, not treat it as such? Would a combination to impose 'economic duress' not be treated (if need be) as a conspiracy to damage 'by unlawful means thereby giving rise to liability in damages and an injunction? Is the liability for economic duress (even if limited to restitution of benefits and rescission of contracts) not broadly equivalent to a civil liability for intentional injury without combination—the so-called wrong of '*Quinn v Leathem* without the conspiracy'?[13] Such a liability outflanks, in part at least, the liberal decision in *Allen v Flood*,[14] long disliked by many judges for having 'damned a stream of thought that . . . would have had a beneficial effect on the law of tort.'[15] Paradoxically, though, these strands of judicial interventionism are being woven into society at the very time when orthodox economic and political thinking is moving in the opposite direction, towards the hegemony of 'market forces'. In claiming more control over the fairness of commercial bargains through such instruments as 'economic duress', perhaps some judges have seen themselves as seeking to introduce a countervailing factor to that trend in the interest of social or economic 'stability', always the 'supreme law' for the judiciary.[16]

But whatever the general merits of the new 'economic duress' doctrine, its application to labour relations gives it a quite novel social function. Not that it is being applied to employment in what might be considered the most obvious way. The *individual* employment relationship is indeed based upon 'coercion'. The contract of employment is a 'command in the guise of an agreement'; the employer 'fills in the blank' constituted by the legal institution of 'contract'.[17] The individual worker who accepts engagement rather than starve or who obeys an employer's orders rather than be dismissed into unemployment[18] is not normally understood by lawyers to have suffered from 'economic duress' (though his will may surely have been 'overborne'). Few judges are likely to understand their new doctrine to apply to such cases.

1. As would Lord Denning M.R., *Lloyds Bank v Bundy* |1975| QB 326, 339.
2. Per Kerr J. *The Siboen*, p. 336; *Barton v Armstrong* |1976| AC 104 (PC).
3. Per Lord Scarman *Pao On v Lau Yiu Long* |1980| AC 614, 635. On burden of proof see *Barton v Armstrong* |1976| AC 104.
4. See J. P. Dawson 'Economic Duress' (1947) 45 Michigan LR 253.
5. E.g. torts or threats to break contracts: *North Ocean Shipping Co. Ltd v Hyundai Construction Co. Ltd* |1979| QB 705; the *Universe Tankships* case |1982| 2 WLR 803 (inducing breach of contract).
6. See Lord Scarman, *Burmah Oil Ltd v Bank of England* |1980| AC 1090, 1140; *Pao On v Lau Yiu Long* |1980| AC 614, 635–636. 'As yet the cases do not answer the question whether a threatened breach of contract marks the boundaries of economic duress,' A. Evans |1981| JBL 188, 192; G. Treitel, op. cit. p. 307 states that 'legally wrongful conduct . . . is necessary to constitute duress'. See too P. Baker (1979) 95 LQR 475; J. Adams (1979) 42 MLR 557; J. Beatson |1974| CLJ 97 and (1976) 92 LQR 496.
7. Per Lloyd J. *Syros Shipping S.A. v Elaghill Trading Co.* |1981| 3 All ER 189, 192.
8. 'Economic Duress and the Overborne Will' (1982) 98 LQR 197, 201 (also pointing out the 'monumental oversight' of the reasoning in *Lynch v DPP Northern Ireland* |1975| AC 653, in the recent civil cases). Atiyah's criticism is especially applicable to the judgment of Parker J. who found as a *'question of fact'* that the loss to the shipowners was 'so potentially disastrous that they had no practical option but to submit' |1981| ICR 141.
9. Confirmed by Lord Diplock, *Universe Tankships* |1982| 2 WLR 812.
10. See: *The Lady Gwendolen* |1965| p. 294; *The Garden City, Financial Times*, 12 March 1982; *Bolton (Engineering) Ltd v Graham* |1957| 1 QB 159; *Lennard's Carrying Co. v Asiatic Petroleum* |1915| AC 705, 713; *Tesco Supermarkerts Ltd v Nattrass* |1972| AC 153; *Thomson & Son v Deakin* |1952| Ch. 646; *Belmont Finance Corp. v Williams Furniture* |1979| Ch. 250; (No.2) |1980| 1 All ER 393.
11. Per Lord Diplock, *Universe Tankships* |1982| 2 WLR 813–814; per Lord Wilberforce, *Barton v Armstrong* |1976| AC 104, 121: 'the pressure must be one of a kind that the law does not regard as legitimate.'
12. Per Lord Scarman, ibid. at p. 829, citing *Thorne v M.T.A.* |1937| AC 797, 806; see too Goff and Jones, *The Law of Restitution*, p. 182.

13. Per Lord Devlin, *Rookes v Barnard* |1964| AC 1215–1216. But this is the same House of Lords which has recently restricted the ambit of the tort of conspiracy to use unlawful means; see *Lonrho Ltd v Shell Ltd* |1982| AC 173; and Clerk and Lindsell, *Torts* (15th ed., 1982) paras 15–06, 15–15, 15–20 and 15–23 (Wedderburn).

14. |1898| AC 1 (HL). Lord Brandon in *Universe Tankships* actually states that duress is 'actionable as a tort if it causes damage or loss' |1982| 2 WLR 828. But the orthodox view is that it is not a tort as such; see, e.g. Lord Diplock, ibid. at p. 814. Compare the progress of 'breach of confidence' towards the character of a liability in tort; Law Commission, *Breach of Confidence* (Cmnd. 8388 (1981)).

15. Lord Devlin, 'Samples of Lawmaking' 1962, p. 11.

16. J. A. G. Griffith, *The Politics of the Judiciary* (2nd ed., 1981) p. 235: see too, J. Clark and Wedderburn, Chap. 6, *Labour Law and Industrial Relations—Building on Kahn-Freund* (Wedderburn, R. Lewis and J. Clark, eds forthcoming, O.U.P.).

17. O. Kahn-Freund, Introduction to K. Renner *The Institutions of Private Law and their Social Functions* (1949), p. 28; cf. his *Labour and the Law* (2nd ed., 1977) p. 6: the employee's 'submission' and 'subordination' is 'concealed by that indispensable figment of the legal mind known as the "contract of employment".'

18. Cf. *Latter v Braddell* (1881) 50 LJQB 448; (1880) 50 LJCP 166 (order to submit to medical examination obeyed under protest; no threat of force, therefore no duress; it seems unlikely that judges today would reverse the finding on duress).

B. & S. Contracts and Design Ltd *v* Victor Green Publications Ltd [1984] ICR 419

Eveleigh L.J.:

In September 1978 the plaintiffs agreed to erect stands for the defendants at Olympia for an international fire, security and safety exhibition, which was to be open to the public from 23 April 1979 until 27 April 1979. The contract price was £11,731.50. The contract contained a *force majeure* clause in these terms: 'Every effort will be made to carry out any contract based on an estimate, but the due performance of it is subject to variation or cancellation owing to an act of God, war, strikes, civil commotions, work to rule or go-slow or overtime bans, lock-out, fire, flood, drought or any other cause beyond our control, or owing to our inability to procure materials or articles except at increased prices due to any of the foregoing causes.'

The plaintiffs had a subsidiary company in Wales. That company was in some financial difficulty and indeed at the end of 1978 had become insolvent. In February 1979 that company gave notice to its employees that there was a danger that they would have to close down the works and it was later indicated that the directors were contemplating closing down the works on 27 April 1979. In the event sixty days' notice was given to that work force, terminating on 27 April 1979.

The contract provided for the dismantling of the stands and that would take place perhaps on 27 but probably on 28 and perhaps 29 April. The plaintiffs decided to use the men who were threatened with redundancy in the subsidiary company and some eighteen of them were brought to Olympia to do the work, and they arrived on 12 April. In the meantime there had been some negotiations between the subsidiary and trade union officials, and of course the plaintiffs were concerned in controlling that situation. The workmen were demanding severance pay. They asked for sixty days' wages. They were not entitled to any severance pay, and at some stage the plaintiffs did indicate that they would be prepared to pay two weeks' wages *ex gratia*. When the men arrived on 12 April at Olympia they stopped work: they wanted their sixty days' severance pay. They were also annoyed at the fact that the plaintiffs intended to use other labour to dismantle the equipment.

News of the stoppage reached Mr Barnes, who was the director responsible for the exhibition on behalf of the defendants, and he discussed the matter with the plaintiffs' financial director, Mr Fenech, on 17 April. The men had for a short while resumed work in the interval, but on that day, 17, they stopped working again. On 13, 14, 15 and 16 there was no work because Olympia was closed for the Bank Holiday period. Mr Fenech told Mr Barnes that the workforce had stated that they would settle for twenty eight days' severance pay and Mr Barnes said that he would have to refer that to his board.

There came the moment when Mr Barnes, realising that the plaintiffs were short of money, in the sense that their cash flow was not good, offered Mr Fenech £4,500. He intended that offer to be an advance payment on the contract price. Mr Fenech apparently understood it as an offer over and above the contract price, and when Mr Fenech subsequently, on 18 April, spoke with Mr Barnes and said that the plaintiffs were prepared to pay £4,500 towards the severance pay and to accept Mr Barnes' offer of £4,500—which figures together would have amounted to a sum acceptable to the men, namely £9,000—it then became clear to Mr Fenech that Mr Barnes' offer had been an advance payment and not one over and above the contract price. Mr Fenech then said that it would be necessary for him to consult the managing director as to whether or not the plaintiffs would be prepared to pay £4,500 and accept the £4,500 from the defendants as an advance payment only. Later Mr Fenech told Mr Barnes that that offer was not acceptable and it was made clear during these discussions to Mr Barnes that the plaintiffs would not be able to carry out their obligations under the contract unless the men could be persuaded to stay at work. When Mr Fenech told Mr Barnes that his proposition was not acceptable Mr Barnes said, 'Well, you have me over a barrel' and he paid £4,500 to the plaintiffs.

The men were paid and the work was done. The plaintiffs sent in their bill and the defendants deducted £4,500 from the price and sent a cheque for the balance. The plaintiffs sued for £4,500, the remainder, as they regarded it, of the contract price. The defence was that the money had been paid under duress and consequently the defendants were entitled to claim back the sum of £4,500.

The matter came before Sir Douglas Frank QC, sitting as a deputy judge of the High Court, and he said [1982] ICR 654, 658:

The realities of the situation were this: leaving aside the *force majeure* clause, the plaintiffs were under a contractual obligation to carry out this work for the contract sum. The plaintiffs were saying 'We are not going to carry out that work; we are going to repudiate that contract because we are not prepared to pay the additional £4,500 demanded by the men.' It is necessarily implicit in that attitude adopted by the plaintiffs that unless somebody—and who else but the defendants—paid off the men, they would not carry out the contract. If the work was not done, then the exhibition would go with what would have been disastrous consequences to the defendants and I would think to the exhibitors. As I see it, Mr Barnes really had no alternative but to agree to pay that money. That seems to me to be a clear case of duress and it does not need any authorities to support it. It speaks for itself.

He then considered the *force majeure* clause and concluded that it could not come to the rescue of the plaintiffs, and consequently he held that their intimation that they would not carry on with the work amounted to a breach of contract and therefore they had caused the defendants to pay the £4,500 unlawfully under duress.

The matters that have to be established in order to substantiate a claim for the return of money on the ground that it was paid under duress have been stated in a number of different ways. We have been referred to a number of cases and indeed we have been taken through the history of the common law on duress, so thoroughly set out in the judgment of Mocatta J. in *North Ocean Shipping Co. Ltd v Hyundai Construction Co. Ltd* |1979| QB 705. It is not necessary to consider these cases: for the purpose of my judgment all I require to read is a passage from the speech of Lord Diplock in *Universe Tankships Inc. of Monrovia v International Transport Workers Federation* |1982| ICR 262. He said, referring to the law on duress, at pp 272–273:

> The rationale is that his apparent consent was induced by pressure exercised upon him by that other party which the law does not regard as legitimate, with the consequence that the consent is treated in law as revocable unless approbated either expressly or by implication after the illegitimate pressure has ceased to operate on his mind. It is a rationale similar to that which underlies the avoidability of contracts entered into and the recovery of money exacted under colour of office, or under undue influence or in consequence of threats of physical duress.

It is not necessary to consider precisely the meaning of the word 'legitimate' in that context. For the purpose of this case it is sufficient to say that if the claimant has been influenced against his will to pay money under the threat of unlawful damage to his economic interest he will be entitled to claim that money back, and as I understand it that proposition was not dissented from.

In this case the plaintiffs say that there was no threat; that Mr Fenech was really stating the obvious, stating the factual situation, namely, that unless they could retain the workforce they would be unable to perform their contract. I have had some difficulty in deciding whether or not the evidence in this case did disclose a threat, but on a full reading of the evidence of Mr Fenech and Mr Barnes and the cross-examination of Mr Fenech I have come to the conclusion that the judge was right in the way in which he put it. There was here, as I understand the evidence, a veiled threat although there was no specific demand, and this conclusion is very much supported, as I see it, by Mr Barnes' reaction, which must have been apparent to Mr Fenech when Mr Barnes said, 'You have got me over a barrel.' On 18 April what was happening was this. Mr Fenech was in effect saying, 'We are not going on unless you are prepared to pay another £4,500 in addition to the contract price,' and it was clear at that stage that there was no other way for Mr Barnes to avoid the consequences that would ensue if the exhibition could not be held from his stands than by paying the £4,500 to secure the workforce. But, the plaintiffs now say, 'Even so, this was not an unlawful threat or a threat of unlawful action because seeing that there was a strike the strike clause— the *force majeure* clause—applied and the plaintiffs were entitled to take advantage of that clause and to cancel the contract, and so there was here no threat of unlawful action.' They also drew the court's attention to authorities on the obligations of a contracting party when a strike arose. They did so in the context of a contention that they were under an obligation to take steps to avoid the consequence of the strike, which they had not done. Mr Hodgson for the plaintiffs referred the court to *Bulman & Dickson v Fenwick & Co.* |1894| 1 QB 179, in which it was held that there was no obligation upon the charterers to change the order to the vessel to proceed to another port when the port that they had originally ordered was strike-bound. In the context of the present case I do not find it necessary to consider the effect of such a case as *Bulman & Dickson v Fenwick & Co.* on the law generally because we are concerned with the words of a specific clause. I would say in passing, however, that the *Bulman v Fenwick* case is to my mind to be regarded as one where it was shown to be impossible to carry out the contract as finally crystallised once the port had been ordered by the charterers. Be that as it may, as I have said, it is not necessary to go into that matter because we are concerned with the words of the particular clause, and that clause begins, 'Every effort will be made to carry out any contract,' and the question, to my mind, in this case is whether or not every effort was made to carry out that contract in the face of the strike. I will of course have regard to the argument that the contracting party is only required to make efforts that will be reasonable in the circumstances.

Well, what are the circumstances in this case? To pay what for the plaintiffs would have been an extra £4,500, or indeed to pay the whole of the £9,000, would in the circumstances of this case have been reasonable. It was a simple solution to the problem. Mr Hodgson has argued that if an employer is required to give in to the demands of the workmen in these cases where a strike clause is inserted in the contract, the clause would have no meaning; it would be valueless. But I do not say that an employer must in every case give in: I simply say that on the facts of this case the evidence shows that it would have been reasonable for the plaintiff to have done so. It might have been distasteful to some employers to pay the workforce in this situation, but I do not think that the plaintiffs can claim that it would have been obnoxious to them to do so. They were prepared to do so provided the defendants paid half the price. Furthermore, they would not be creating a rod for their own backs because the workmen were not in their immediate employment and the workmen were not workmen with whom they were intending to have any further dealings after 27 April, so they could not, by giving in, have fed an appetite that in the future was likely to make even greater demands upon them. That being so, it seems to me that the only objection which the plaintiffs had to this easy solution of the problem was the sum of £4,500. It does not appear from the evidence in this case that it was impossible for them to find £4,500 for indeed £4,500 was offered to them as an advance payment.

In those circumstances I have come to the conclusion that every effort was not made to perform this contract, and consequently reliance cannot be placed upon that *force majeure* clause. Having come to that conclusion there is no need for me to deal with other arguments that have been put forward by the defendants in this case, for example to the effect that the plaintiffs, by their conduct in employing workmen who were on the brink of dismissal, were bringing strike troubles upon themselves. In my judgment that does not arise.

I would dismiss the appeal.

Griffiths L.J.:

I agree. The law on economic pressure creating a situation which will be recognised as duress is in the course of development, and it is clear that many difficult decisions lie ahead of the courts. Many commercial contracts are varied during their currency because the parties are faced with changing circumstances during the performance of the contract, and it is certainly not on every occasion when one of the parties unwillingly agrees to a variation that the law would consider that he had acted by reason of duress. The cases will have to be examined in the light of their particular circumstances. But two recent decisions of the highest authority—the decision of the Privy Council in *Pao On v Lau Yiu Long* [1980] AC 614 and *Universe Tankships Inc. of Monrovia v International Transport Workers Federation* [1982] ICR 262—establish that a threatened breach of contract may impose such economic pressure that the law will recognise that a payment made as a result of the threatened breach is recoverable on the grounds of duress.

The facts of this case appear to me to be as follows. The plaintiffs intended to break their contract, subject to the effect of the *force majeure* clause, by allowing their workforce to walk off the job in circumstances in which they could not possibly replace it with another workforce. The defendants offered to advance the sum of £4,500 on the contract price, which would have enabled the plaintiffs to pay the men a sufficient extra sum of money to induce them to remain on the job. The plaintiffs refused this sum of money. There is no question that they refused to pay as a matter of principle. They refused to pay because they did not want to reduce the sum they would receive for the contract. They said to the defendants, 'If you will give us £4,500 we will complete the contract.' The defendants, faced with this demand, were in an impossible position. If they refused to hand over the sum of £4,500 they would not be able to erect the stands in this part of the exhibition, which would have clearly caused grave damage to their reputation and I would have thought might have exposed them to very heavy claims from the exhibitors who had leased space from them and hoped to use those stands in the ensuing exhibition. They seem to me to have been placed in the position envisaged by Lord Scarman in the Privy Council decision, *Pao On v Lau Yiu Long* |1980| AC 614, in which they were faced with no alternative course of action but to pay the sum demanded of them. It was submitted to us that there was no overt demand, but it was implicit in negotiations between the parties that the plaintiffs were putting the defendants into a corner and it was quite apparent to the defendants, by reason of the plaintiffs' conduct, that unless they handed over £4,500 the plaintiffs would walk off the job. This is, in my view, a situation in which the judge was fully entitled to find in the circumstances of this case that there was duress. As the defendants' director said, he was over a barrel, he had no alternative but to pay; he had no chance of going to any other source of labour to erect the stands. That being so, the only fall-back position for the plaintiffs was the *force majeure* clause. Clauses of this kind have to be construed upon the basis that those relying on them will have taken all reasonable efforts to avoid the effect of the various matters set out in the clause which entitle them to vary or cancel the contract: see *Bulman & Dickson v Fenwick & Co.* |1894| 1 QB 179, in the speech of Lord Esher M.R. at p. 185. Quite apart from that general principle this particular clause starts with the following wording: 'Every effort will be made to carry out any contract based on an estimate,' which is saying in express terms that which the law will imply when construing such a clause.

There is no doubt that the plaintiffs were faced with a strike situation and the question is, did they behave reasonably when faced with this situation? I, like Eveleigh L.J., am far from saying that whenever a contracting party with such a clause is faced with a strike situation he must give in to it in order to perform his contract. If that were the situation the clause would be absolutely worthless. But the special circumstances of this case, as I see it, are as follows. The plaintiffs were going to close down their subsidiary company; they had already dismissed the workforce and the men were working out their time. There is no question here of any ongoing industrial situation between the plaintiffs' subsidiary company and the workforce. There was no question of principle at stake; the plaintiffs were perfectly prepared to pay what the men were demanding save for the fact, they said, they did not have the money available. Well, then there came the offer of the defendants to make the money available by giving them an advance. In those circumstances I can see no reason why they should not have accepted the money and paid the workforce save their own immediate economic interests, and they chose not to do that but to put pressure on the defendants by refusing the offer and indicating that the only way out was for the defendants to hand over the £4,500 as a gift rather than as an advance.

I think that was thoroughly unreasonable behaviour, and that being so they are not entitled to rely upon the *force majeure* clause, and for these reasons I agree this appeal fails.

Kerr L.J.:

I agree that this appeal must be dismissed for the reasons which have been given, and there is little that I wish to add. I think it convenient to begin by considering what the terms of the contract were, *viz.* whether or not the plaintiffs were entitled to rely on the *force majeure* clause and on the exception of strikes on the facts of this case. To rely upon a strike of one's own workforce is difficult for a party seeking to rely on an exception of strikes, but I entirely agree that it is perfectly possible if the circumstances justify such reliance. The cases cited in the books have generally been concerned with situations where a place of performance was strike-bound, particularly in the shipping cases referred to in *Carver, Carriage by Sea*, (13th ed., 1982) vol. 2 paras 1053 et seq. But in either case it is clear that where an exception of strikes is invoked, then like all other exceptions it is subject to the principle that the party seeking to rely on it must show that the strike and its consequences could not have been avoided by taking steps which were reasonable in the particular circumstances: see, in relation to the shipping cases, the authorities cited in *Carver* in para. 1056, and in particular the judgment of Lord Esher M.R. in *Bulman & Dickson v Fenwick & Co.* [1894] 1 QB 179, 185 to which Griffiths L.J. has already referred.

Generally speaking, also, a mere difficulty of additional expense is not a sufficient ground to enable a party to invoke an exception clause, and *Brauer & Co. (Great Britain) Ltd v James Clark (Brush Materials) Ltd* [1952] 2 All ER 497, to which the judge referred, is an illustration of this principle. However, I entirely agree with what has been said: that in strike situations where a party's own employees are concerned, the question of the amount which is payable is liable to be far from conclusive, because all sorts of other considerations may play a part as to what was reasonable in the circumstances.

All these matters are really implicit in the words '*force majeure*', the heading of this clause. The situation and its consequences must be beyond the reasonable control of the party seeking to rely on the exceptions clause. In the present case the situation is still simpler, because what I have been referring to as being implied by law generally, is expressed in the opening words of the clause: 'Every effort will be made to carry out any contract.'

On the facts of the present case it is unnecessary to decide whether the plaintiffs could have avoided the effect of this strike, either because it was foreseeable due to the difficulty which had been existing for some two months between their subsidiary and the subsidiary's workforce, or because no alternative steps were taken at a late stage to use labour from their London office. It is sufficient, as has been pointed out, that the sum of £4,500 needed to overcome the effect of the strike was put on the table and available to the plaintiffs. But they decided not to accept it on the terms offered; they wanted it as an extra, and that in itself is wholly fatal to the plaintiffs' attempt to rely on the strike clause in this case, quite apart from the fact that it has not been established that they could not have raised this additional sum of £4,500 themselves. As Griffiths L.J. pointed out, no question of principle is at stake in this case: the plaintiffs were perfectly willing to pay the men in order to have this contract performed, provided that they could extort—which I think is really the right word in the circumstances—one half of the total cost of £9,000 from the defendants.

Turning to the other half of the case, what is the position if the *force majeure* clause is left out of the account? On that basis the plaintiffs were clearly saying in effect, 'This contract will not be performed by us unless you pay an additional sum of £4,500.' This faced the defendants with a disastrous situation in which there was no way out for them, and in the face of this threat—which is what it was—they paid the £4,500. In the light of the authorities it is perhaps important to emphasise that there is no question in this case of the defendants having subsequently approbated this payment or failed to seek to avoid it, which in some cases (such as the *North Ocean Shipping Co. Ltd v Hyundai Construction Co. Ltd* [1979] QB 705, a decision of Mocatta J., to which Eveleigh L.J. has referred) would be fatal. In the present case the defendants took immediate action by deducting that £4,500 from the invoice price.

I also bear in mind that a threat to break a contract unless money is paid by the other party can, but by no means always will, constitute duress. It appears from the authorities that it will only constitute duress if the consequences of a refusal would be serious and immediate so that there is no reasonable alternative open, such as by legal redress, obtaining an injunction, etc. I think that this is implicit in the authorities to which we have been referred, of which the most recent one is *Universe Tankships Inc. of Monrovia v International Transport Workers Federation* [1982] ICR 262. I would only refer to one passage from the speech of Lord Scarman, not because he states anything that differs from what was stated elsewhere, but because I wonder whether this passage may not contain a typographical error. Lord Scarman is reported at pp 288–289 as having said—and it applies to the facts of this case: 'The classic case of duress is, however, not the lack of will to submit but the victim's intentional submission arising from the realisation that there is no other practical choice open to him.'

I wonder whether 'the lack of will to submit' should not have been 'the lack of will to resist' or 'the lack of will in submitting.' However that may be, there was no other practical choice open to the defendants in the present case, and accordingly I agree that this is a case where money has been paid under duress, which was accordingly recoverable by the defendants provided they acted promptly as they did, and which they have recovered by deducting it from the contract price. In these circumstances the plaintiffs' claim for this additional sum must fail.

Appeal dismissed with costs.

Atlas Express Ltd *v* Kafco (Importers and Distributors) Ltd [1989] NLJR 111

The facts:

In June 1986 the plaintiffs, a national road carrier, entered into a contract with the defendants, a small company which imported and distributed basketware to the retail trade, to deliver cartons of basketware to branches of Woolworths for the defendants. The plaintiffs' depot manager inspected the cartons, which were of different sizes, before the contract was entered into and estimated that each load would contain a minimum of 400 and possibly as many as 600 cartons and on that basis he agreed a rate of carriage of £1.10 per carton. In fact the first load contained only 200 cartons and the plaintiffs' depot manager told the defendants that the plaintiffs would not carry any more cartons unless the defendants agreed to pay a minimum of £440 per load. The defendants were heavily dependent on the Woolworths' contract and were unable at that time of the year to find an alternative carrier. The defendants accordingly agreed to the new terms on 18 November 1986 but later refused to pay the new rate. The plaintiffs brought an action to recover the amount owing under the new rate.

Tucker J.:

I find that when Mr Armiger [a director of the defendants] signed [the amended] agreement he did so unwillingly and under compulsion. He believed on reasonable grounds that it would be very difficult if not impossible to negotiate with another contractor. He did not regard the fact that he had signed the new agreement as binding the defendants to its terms. He had no bargaining power. He did not regard it as a genuine arms length renegotiation in which he had a free and equal say and, in my judgment, that view was fully justified.

In the words of his co-director, Mr Fox, he felt that he was 'over a barrel'. He tried in vain to contact Mr Hope [the plaintiffs' depot manager] but, as he said to Mr Armiger, they really had no option but to sign. I accept the evidence of Woolworths' manager, Mr Graham, that if the defendants had told them that they could not supply the goods, Woolworths would have sued them for loss of profit and would have ceased trading with them. I find that this was well known to the defendants' directors . . . The defendants made their position quite clear through their solicitors, who wrote to the plaintiffs on 2 March 1987, saying that the revised contract was signed under duress. This was three months before the plaintiffs commenced proceedings.

The issue which I have to determine is whether the defendants are bound by the agreement signed on their behalf on 18 November 1986. The defendants contend that they are not bound, for two reasons: first because the agreement was signed under duress; second because there was no consideration for it.

The first question raises a particularly interesting point of law: whether economic duress is a concept known to English law.

Economic duress must be distinguished from commercial pressure, which on any view is not sufficient to vitiate consent. The borderline between the two may in some cases be indistinct. But the authors of *Chitty on Contracts* and of *Goff and Jones on the Law of Restitution* appear to recognise that in appropriate cases economic duress may afford a defence, and in my judgment it does. It is clear to me that in a number of English cases judges have acknowledged the existence of this concept. Thus, in *D & C Builders Ltd v Rees* |1965| 3 All ER 837 at 841 Lord Denning M.R. said: 'No person can insist on a settlement procured by intimidation.' And in *Occidental Worldwide Investment Corp. v Skibs A/S Avanti (The 'Siboen' v The 'Sibotre')* |1976| Lloyd's Rep. 293 at 336 Kerr J. appeared to accept that economic duress could operate in appropriate circumstances. A similar conclusion was reached by Mocatta J. in *North Ocean Shipping Co. Ltd v Hyundai Construction Co. Ltd* |1978| 3 All ER 1170. In particular, there are passages in the judgment of Lord Scarman in *Pao On v Lau Yiu Long* |1979| 3 All ER 65 at 78–79 which clearly indicate the recognition of the concept . . .

A further case, which was not cited to me, was *B & S Contracts v V. G. Publications* (1984) ICR 419 at 423 where Eveleigh L.J. referred to the speech of Lord Diplock in another uncited case. *Universe Tankship Inc. of Monrovia v International Transport Workers Federation* |1982| 2 All ER 67 at 75–76: 'The rationale is that this apparent consent was induced by pressure exercised upon him by that other party which the law does not regard as legitimate with the consequence that the consent is treated in law as revocable unless approbated either expressly or by implication after the illegitimate pressure has ceased to operate on his mind.'

In commenting on this, Eveleigh L.J. said of the word 'legitimate': 'For the purpose of this case, it is sufficient to say that if the claimant has been influenced against his will to pay money under the threat of unlawful damage to his economic interest, he will be entitled to claim that money back . . . '

Reverting to the case before me, I find that the defendants' apparent consent to the agreement was induced by pressure which was illegitimate and I find that it was not approbated. In my judgment that pressure can properly be described as economic duress, which is a concept recognised by English law, and which in the circumstances of the present case vitiates the defendants' apparent consent to the agreement.

In any event, I find that there was no consideration for the new agreement. The plaintiffs were already obliged to deliver the defendants' goods at the rates agreed under the terms of the original agreement.

There was no consideration for the increased minimum charge of £440 per trailer.

Accordingly, I find that the plaintiffs' claim fails and there will be judgment for the defendants with costs.

Chapter Fourteen

Equitable Intervention

SECTION ONE—UNDUE INFLUENCE

The equitable doctrine of undue influence is intended to provide relief to persons who enter into transactions in circumstances where there are potential or actual grounds for suspecting that an abuse of position has taken place, or that improper pressure has been brought to bear upon one of the contracting parties.

A. THE PRESUMPTION

Kirwan v Cullen (1854) 2 Ir Ch R 322

A Catholic lady transferred property to the Archbishop of Dublin, under a trust instrument, the trustees including a priest who had previously been the lady's spiritual confessor. On her death her brother sought to have the transfer set aside.

Lord St Leonards L.C.:

I feel no doubt in this case that this petition cannot be sustained. In substance this petition is to recall, for the purpose of administration, a sum of £3000 stock, which now stands in the names of Archbishop Cullen and Dr Curtis, to whom it was transferred by Miss Kirwan in the year 1851, when she was still living. I said that the object of this suit is to recall this sum from these two gentlemen, for the purpose of administration, as part of the assets of Miss Clare Kirwan; and it is insisted that these respondents cannot retain it, on the ground that the donation to them was made in consequence of undue influence over the mind of the lady, the exercise of which was the probable cause of their obtaining the gift; and further, that even if no undue influence had caused the gift, it was made for purposes which the law does not recognise, and that being thus given to the respondents upon trusts which were void in their inception, Miss Kirwan had a resulting interest in it which passed to her administrator. As to the first point, I do not think it necessary to go through a detailed examination of the authorities to which the counsel referred; this case seems perfectly distinct from all of them. Here was a lady of full age and competent understanding, moving in the world, living with her family, who possessed a sum of money; this she transferred through the medium of a duly authorised agent, to the names of these gentlemen of high position in the church to which she belonged. We find the respondents not claiming any personal interest, admitting that they are mere trustees for the objects of Miss Kirwan's bounty, and that they are bound to carry out purposes not connected with themselves individually. We find the donation effected by Miss Kirwan through the intervention of a third person, whose name has been mentioned here, who was

570

admittedly without interest in the subject of the gift, and who never has received the smallest portion of it. I do not think it possible to contend that this can be classed with the cases in which donations and gifts have been held by this court to have been tainted by the fact that they were made to a person who was placed in a situation giving him power to exercise undue influence over the donor, with which other cases certainly conflict as to the extent to which they have gone. . . . none of them seem to me to interfere with the decision of this case, which is, I think, to be resolved into this question, whether, in fact, there is evidence to show that when this lady made this gift, any influence was exercised to induce her to do so? On that subject the petitioner's case is wholly without evidence. I do not say that we can at all wonder at this, for it is conceded by the respondents that the knowledge of the transaction was wholly confined to this lady herself, and the gentleman to whom she confided the arrange-ment of the business; but unquestionably there is no evidence to impeach the gift, beyond the broad circumstances of the case. Then, as I said, here is a lady of mature age and undoubted understanding, living with her sisters, making this gift more than a year before her death. She never complained of it to any one, not even to her sisters with whom she resided. It appears that some dividends on the sum were received by the trustees, and that she made no objection to the fact of their receiving them, but that some discussion arose as to the application: all these circumstances showing that she perfectly well knew of and approved of the transaction; and I must therefore say that I consider the case made by the petition entirely destitute of foundation. No doubt, the court would not have been satisfied unless some explanation had been given of this transfer, which in itself seems a little remarkable; but that has been fully given. We have here affidavits of Dr Curtis and Archbishop Cullen, which show that so far as they are concerned they were wholly without influence. Dr Cullen swears 'that he never saw the said Clare Kirwan, or had the slightest intimacy or acquaintance with her, or with any of her family, and did not know there was such a person until he was asked to become a trustee of the fund.'

Dr Curtis seems to have had a more intimate acquaintance with this lady, he had filled the position of her spiritual adviser; but the relation between them had ceased two years before the transaction occurred, and she had been before this perfectly inde-pendent of him. Dr Curtis and Dr Cullen both swear that they had no knowledge of the transaction; Dr Curtis until he was informed by another person; Dr Cullen until he was told by Dr Curtis. Dr Curtis says that he declined to accept the burden of this trust alone, and that he suggested that Dr Cullen, the spiritual superior of himself and of all other members of his church in Ireland, should be associated with him in the trust. He also states that they had an interview with this lady after the transfer, in which it did not appear that she had any wish to retract from the arrangement. There is then the affidavit of a gentleman who intervened in the transaction, at least so far as procuring the assent of the trustees. He also was in the position of a person not taking any personal benefit from the transaction, and seems to have declined to be in any way concerned in it, beyond procuring these persons to act as trustees. His statement is not in any way controverted, and his evidence is so full, clear and creditable to him, that though on the whole it may not be absolutely necessary, I shall read some portion of it. . . . This is, I may say, the whole evidence in the case, and it is not contro-verted. There was not any other person to whom the facts were communicated, and therefore no other evidence could exist. I will not say that the case might not assume a very different aspect if this claim were made by Miss Kirwan in her lifetime, and if she were to make affidavits contradicting these; but here we have the uncontroverted evidence of persons who appear only to have intervened between this lady and the objects of her bounty, without taking any personal benefit. To apply to this case of doctrine of *Huguenin v Basely*,[1] and the other similar cases, would be to strain it much beyond its legitimate bounds. It is said that such a gift is most extraordinary in its amount as well as in its circumstances; but this lady appears to have been of an unusually charitable and pious disposition. She does seem to have denuded herself of much property, but she still retained a considerable amount, which may have been enough for her desires. She frequently visited this institution which she benefited, and she seems to have esteemed it highly. She saw the purposes to which her bounty was to be devoted, and being of a charitable and religious disposition, she may have come to the conclusion that those were purposes which she ought to sustain, and to which her property ought to be devoted. I do not mean in saying this to call in aid of this gift the opinion that the object was charitable in a legal point of view; I do not mean to decide that these were what are legally denominated charitable purposes; I merely mean to show the motive, acting as it did seem to act on the mind of a person who was perhaps, if that be possible, religious and charitable even to excess—who approved of the purposes of this community, and who in consequence devoted a large portion of her property to its support. It may be that, in the opinion of some persons, she pursued her purposes not wisely, but too well; but, sitting in this court, I cannot venture to set a limit to her bounty.

[1]. 14 Ves 273.

The Queen (Proctor) *v* Hutton [1978] NI 139

Jones L.J.:

This is an appeal by Thomas David Rainey (hereinafter called 'the appellant') the lawfully appointed attorney of Richard Quinn and Tony Schneider both of New Jersey, USA, who are the executors appointed by the will of Mrs Mary Founds, deceased, dated 17 February 1968. The appeal arises in the following circumstances. Mrs Founds was an old lady who was born in Portadown eighty five years ago. She emigrated to the USA about the year 1905 when she was about twenty years old and there she married Mr Founds. There were no children of the marriage. Mr Founds died in May 1967 and thereafter Mrs Founds continued to live in Philadelphia where on 17 February 1968, she made her last will whereby she bequeathed her entire estate in equal shares to (1) Richard Harold Quinn (2) Richard Quinn (3) William Robert Rainey (4) Thomas David Rainey (5) James Cecil Rainey (6) Sarah Ann Proctor (7) Margaret Jane Jackson (8) Minnie McAteer (9) Anna May Schneider and (10) Minnie Todd. Of those legatees Nos (3), (4), (5), (7) and (8) were nephews and nieces of Mrs Founds and brothers and sisters of Mrs Proctor the person named as prosecutrix in the title hereof and hereinafter so referred to. Thomas David Rainey was also the administrator with will annexed of Mrs Founds, Richard Quinn I think was one of the executors named in the will and the three remaining legatees were relatives or acquaintances of Mrs Founds in America. On 4 July 1969, the prosecutrix flew out to visit Mrs Founds in Philadelphia and on 28 July 1969 (in circumstances which are fully set out in the judgment of the Lord Chief Justice) Mrs Founds and the prosecutrix arrived back in Northern Ireland but prior to leaving Philadelphia it was arranged that all Mrs Founds' funds, which amounted to $33,052 71c or £13,816 1s 10d, should with certain small exceptions for personal expenses be transferred from a bank in Philadelphia to the Portadown branch of the Belfast Savings Bank where on 29 July 1969, Mrs Founds and the prosecutrix opened two accounts payable to either of them or the survivor—or actually opened a joint ordinary account and applied to open a joint special investment account when the bulk of the monies should arrive from USA. The pass books in respect of these accounts were subsequently handed by Mrs Founds to the prosecutrix with a request to keep them safe. As stated the two accounts into which this money was paid were a joint ordinary account and a joint special investment account from the former of which no withdrawals were made and from the latter of which two withdrawals were made, namely £50.00 on 5 August 1969, and £300.00 on 15 August 1969, on the afternoon of which latter day Mrs Founds died. Thereafter by letter dated 21 May 1970, Messrs T. D. Gibson & Co., the solicitors for the administrator (Mr T. D. Rainey) applied to the bank for payment of the monies in the accounts which application was refused by the bank by letter of 1 June and at the suggestion of the bank the matter was referred to a deputy appointed by the Chief Registrar of Friendly Societies under Article 23 of the Government of Ireland (Companies, Societies, etc.) Order 1922 (S.R. & O. 1922 No. 184) for determination under s. 27 of the Trustee Savings Banks Act 1969. I should say that at the date of the hearing before the learned deputy the amounts standing to the credit of the two accounts were:

Account No. 08–038744–1–0 (Ordinary Department)	£ 51 0s 7d
Account No. 08–038744–7–4 (Special Investment Department)	£14,014 9s 2d
Total	£14,065 9s 9d

The learned deputy, having heard the evidence and submissions held that the payments into the two joint accounts should be set aside on the ground that there was a presumption that the payments were made when Mrs Founds was subject to the undue influence of the prosecutrix which presumption the prosecutrix had failed to rebut. He accordingly held that the monies in the two accounts, together with the interest accrued thereon, formed part of the estate of Mrs Founds and he thereupon made certain consequential orders for costs and incidental matters.

Thereafter an application was made to the Queen's Bench Division by way of *certiorari* to bring up the order of the learned deputy and to have the same quashed. This application was made in two stages. The first stage consisted of an argument as to the jurisdiction of the learned deputy on the ground that there was no dispute within s. 27 of the Trustee Savings Banks Act 1969 to which the trustees and managers of the savings bank were party. The Lord Chief Justice, before whom the matter came on *certiorari*, held that there was such a dispute and so jurisdiction in him to entertain the matter and though that ruling was made the subject of a cross appeal to this court that cross appeal was abandoned at the outset of the hearing before us. But the second stage was fully argued before the Lord Chief Justice who held—and here I quote the last two paragraphs of his judgment:

Accordingly, I hold that there was no evidence to justify the finding that a relationship of trust and confidence existed from which the exercise of undue influence by the applicant (that is the prosecutrix) on the deceased could be presumed and that there is no room for the presumption in this case, because the exercise of undue influence has been conclusively negatived.

I therefore hold that the applicant is entitled to an order of *certiorari* to quash the learned deputy's decision.

From that decision of the learned Lord Chief Justice the appellant appealed to this court. And when the matter came before us the area of debate was still further reduced by the prosecutrix's abandonment of the rebuttal contention. It may well be that this was a prudent attitude to be adopted by the prosecutrix because as Mr Sheil (for the appellant) accepted that in considering whether the presumption existed or not one had to look at all the facts of the matter the real question centred on the existence of the presumption the evidence relevant to which was really the same as that which would have been relevant to its rebuttal. This indeed is very much the same result as that at which the learned Lord Chief Justice arrived at p. 16 of his judgment when he said: 'When this proof is forthcoming (as in this case) *pari passu* with the evidence which is said to prove the relationship of trust and confidence, it is more accurate to say that the presumption never arises rather than to say that it has been rebutted.'

The legal principles applicable to cases of this type are to be found in Hanbury and Maudsley's *Modern Equity* (10th ed.) 628 where it is stated:

> It is possible to divide the cases up into those, first, in which equity readily perceives the possibility of such influence, such as parent and child, guardian and ward, doctor and patient, religious adviser and pupil, and other situations where it is shown that a similar relationship of confidence existed, cases in which equity requires positive evidence that no undue influence was in fact exerted; and, secondly, those in which equity requires positive proof of influence having actually been exerted. But in all cases the question is whether a defendant has taken advantage of his position, or, *per contra*, has been assiduous not to do so. The question can only be answered in each case by a meticulous consideration of the facts.

The present case is said by the appellant to fall into the first of the above categories, because of the finding that there was a relationship of confidence and trust between Mrs Founds and the prosecutrix. It is of course dangerous to seek to compare the facts of one case with those of another but it is not dangerous to observe that the facts of *Tate v Williamson* (1866) 1 Eq 528, to which the learned deputy referred at this stage of his judgment, were very markedly different from those of the present case—I need refer to no more than that the purchaser of the estate in that case had obtained a valuation from a mining engineer which was very material but which was not communicated to the vendor who died in Plymouth, aged twenty three, of *delerium tremens*. No doubt the prosecutrix did say in evidence before the learned deputy that Mrs Founds put great confidence in her. I am sure she did. After all the prosecutrix was the one person who had come half way across the world to assist, I might say rescue, her but I am satisfied that if the learned deputy was thereby inferring the existence of any trust and confidence placed by Mrs Founds in the prosecutrix in relation to the disposal of her property which could give any foundation to a suggestion of undue influence in relation thereto there was no evidence to support such an inference. Indeed, so far as Mrs Founds' property was concerned, the prosecutrix's suggestion that all the family should share or that the monies should not be put into a joint account was rejected by Mrs Founds. I feel that the finding of a relationship of trust and confidence in the learned deputy's decision is one that can be reviewed. It is not a finding of a primary fact but is more like a deduction from other facts or an expression of opinion, and in either case it is reviewable on the ground that there is no support for it, and that it is therefore erroneous in point of law, having regard to the decision read as a whole.

Now the presumption of undue influence may arise in two sorts of cases. The evidence may show a particular relationship, for example that of solicitor and client, trustee and *cestui que trust*, doctor and patient or religious adviser and pupil. Those cases or some of them, depending on the facts, may of themselves raise the presumption. Such examples, as regards undue influence, have much in common with the doctrine of *res ipsa loquitur* in relation to negligence. But then there is the other sort of case, the precise range of which is indeterminate, in which the whole evidence, when meticulously considered, may disclose facts from which it should be inferred that a relationship is disclosed which justifies a finding that there is a presumption of undue influence. In other words the presumption enables a party to achieve justice by bridging a gap in the evidence, where there is a gap, because the evidence is difficult or impossible to come by.

Is the present that other sort of case? Here it is necessary to look at the facts properly found. The facts are conveniently summarised at pp 64–8 of the judgment of the learned Lord Chief Justice. This summary was accepted by Mr Sheil, though he did refer to certain omissions such as (1) failure to mention the dates of the prosecutrix's arrival in the USA, of the flight back and of Mrs Founds' death (2) failure to mention the possibility of Mrs Founds having to go into an old people's home if she remained in the USA (3) Mrs Founds' worry about her apartment being broken into and (4) that Mrs Founds was excited when the prosecutrix arrived in Philadelphia. However, I take the learned Lord Chief Justice's summary of the facts, with Mr Sheil's reservations to the extent I have indicated, as full and accurate and, like the learned Lord Chief Justice, I place great importance on his seventeenth finding or observation which was as follows:

(17) The learned deputy concluded his review of the facts with the following observations:

From her (that is the prosecutrix's) demeanour and from the way in which she gave her evidence I formed the view that Mrs Proctor was a truthful and reliable witness, and, on the basis of her own evidence, I formed the view that when she went out to bring her aunt home from Philadelphia and when she gave her a home in Portadown, she was not concerned about what money her aunt might have or about what money she might receive from her aunt. I also formed the view that Mr [sic but I think the quotation should read 'Mrs'] Proctor is a kind, warm-hearted person, who went out to America and brought her aunt home out of feelings of kindness and sympathy for a lonely old lady, and not by reason of hope or desire of receiving or extracting a financial reward or benefit from her aunt. I think that this view of Mrs Proctor's feeling and motives is supported by the terms of the letters which she wrote home from Philadelphia and which are set out above. I further consider that this view is supported by the evidence of Mr Dennison that in the discussion in the bank between him and Mrs Founds as to whose name or names the money should be lodged in, Mrs Proctor did not intervene and adopted the attitude that it was for her aunt to decide what to do with the money.

Indeed, like the learned Lord Chief Justice, I regard that as a salient point and the key to the whole situation.

I do not overlook the observation of Lindley L.J. in *Allcard v Skinner*, 36 ChD 145 at p. 183, about setting aside gifts even when there is no proof of undue influence. But of course in *Allcard's* case there was a relationship—indeed one of the recognised relationships—and the facts of the case were quite unlike those of the present. And when one follows the guidance of the learned editor of *Hanbury* and considers the facts meticulously (including not only what I might call the negative facts that the prosecutrix had done nothing whatsoever improper or 'sharp' but also the positive facts that, as accepted by the learned deputy, she had actually discouraged the giving of benefits to herself), I just cannot find any relationship of trust and confidence in the present case such as would give rise to a presumption of undue influence. Indeed the case is one in

which the following observations of Lawton L.J. and Bridge L.J. in *re Brocklehurst* |1978|
1 AER 767 might well have been made, namely that at p. 777 where Lawton L.J.,
referring of course to the decision at first instance in that case, said: 'Many common
lawyers would expect that finding to result in judgment for the defendant. Yet the court
ordered the lease to be set aside for the reason alleged in the writ. I found this an
unexpected result.' and where Bridge L.J. on p. 782 in reference to the same decision
said: 'I find the result a very surprising one.' and like those learned judges I would find
it unfortunate and unfair that the law should require the prosecutrix to justify the gift
in this case and, if she failed to do so, to adjudge that she should suffer the smear of
having exerted or of being presumed to have exerted undue influence on the donor—
see p. 779 h of 1978 1 AER 767. Should such be the result I would feel that an equitable
doctrine was being used to work inequity, which as Black J. said in *Provincial Bank of
Ireland v McKeever* |1941| IR 471 at 491, should not be allowed. Having read the case
many times and listened, I hope carefully, to the contentions of counsel, I have arrived
at the conclusion that, on the proper findings of the learned deputy, the judgment of
the learned Lord Chief Justice is correct and I would therefore dismiss this appeal.

(McGonigal L.J. and O'Donnell J. concurred.)

McGonigle *v* Black (HC) 14 November 1988, unrep.

Barr J.:

The relevant facts in this case are as follows: Edward McGonigle, deceased, (Mr
McGonigle) formerly of Flemingstown, Convoy, Co. Donegal, died intestate on 1 October
1983. He lived for over twenty years with his uncle and aunt, Mr and Mrs James
McClure, on a farm at Convoy then owned by Mr McClure which is the subject matter
of these proceedings. The McClures had no children. Mr McGonigle helped in running
the farm and seems to have been regarded by them as a son. Mr McClure died in 1978
and left the farm by will to Mr McGonigle subject to Mrs McClure's life interest. After
the death of his uncle, Mr McGonigle ran the farm and continued to reside with his
aunt. At that time the property comprised three holdings; the home farm of 36 acres,
which also included an old dwelling house, and two separate holdings not far away of
9½ acres and 6 acres respectively. The entire comprised good quality land which at all
material times had a value in excess of £1,000 per acre. Some time after Mr McClure's
death the dwelling house on the home farm became derelict and thereafter Mr
McGonigle and his aunt vacated the premises and lived in a mobile home on the land.
However, it appears that Mrs McClure was in poor health and was transferred to hospital
in or about 1979 where she remained until she died in 1981. After his aunt entered
hospital there was no one to keep house for Mr McGonigle and he was obliged to fend
for himself. It is evident that he was unable to do so satisfactorily and the effective
loss of his aunt caused him to develop a serious drink problem which became more
acute as time went on.

I accept the evidence of Mr Thomas Morrow, senior partner in David Wilson and
Co., solicitors. He had a long-standing connection with Mr and Mrs McClure for whom
he had acted as solicitor. He had also acted for Mr McGonigle whom he had known for
many years. He first noticed that the latter was addicted to alcohol in 1980. Thereafter
he often saw him in town and he personally observed that Mr McGonigle's drink
problem was becoming progressively worse in the following years. He was barred from
local pubs. The primary reason was that when intoxicated he insisted on buying drinks
for everyone because, it seems, the was lonely and was anxious to make friends.

The defendant is a married man aged thirty nine years who owns a farm of 26 acres where he resides with his wife and three young children. That property is about half a mile from the McGonigle farm. The defendant knew the latter for about fourteen or fifteen years and for most of that time he rented 20 acres of the McClure lands on conacre. It appears that a friendship developed between them and in the latter years of Mr McGonigle's life, after the departure of his aunt to hospital, they spent much time together. Mr McGonigle often had breakfast in the Black household and sometimes other meals also.

Dr Brian Lavelle of Convoy gave evidence that he had been the McClure family doctor and had also known Mr McGonigle for many years. In April and May 1983, he treated him for a urinary tract infection. He did not return for further treatment as intended. Dr Lavelle was aware that Mr McGonigle had a drink problem but he was not consulted in that regard. Mr McGonigle died on 1 October 1983.

The plaintiff is thirty years of age and was a nephew of Mr McGonigle. He is married and lives about 2½ miles from his uncle's mobile home. I accept his evidence that each Sunday evening he brought Mr McGonigle to see Mrs McClure in hospital until she died in July 1981. He described that his uncle came to his home occasionally for meals and that quite often he had drink taken on those occasions. He also confirmed that his uncle's alcoholism became more acute after Mrs McClure's death. At that time he used to visit his nephew two or three times a week with occasional gaps of a fortnight or so. He described that for some years Mr McGonigle had a urinary problem which caused him to wet himself involuntarily when he had drink taken and this happened more frequently from 1981 when his health seemed to deteriorate. The mobile home was very well kept in Mrs McClure's time. Mr McGonigle continued to maintain it reasonably well during her life but after her death it became, as the plaintiff described, 'rougher and rougher'. On his death it was found to be in an appalling condition and it was evident that no one had attempted to clean the place for a long time.

Mr McGonigle was not entitled to social welfare benefits because of the amount of land owned by him. It appears that from time to time he bought and sold a few cattle (though probably not in the last year of his life). He was dependent on that activity and on conacre lettings for his livelihood. In his latter years his income from those sources was not sufficient to support his drinking habits, including his insistence on buying drink for others. He had an overdraft in the Bank of Ireland, Ballybofey, which amounted to £2,786.17 on 26 October 1982 when the account was closed. The defendant also had an account in the same branch.

The first land transaction between Mr McGonigle and the defendant was in or about December 1980. Mr Morrow gave evidence that in that month Mr McGonigle called to his office and told him that he had agreed to sell his 9½ acre holding to the defendant for £3,500. Mr Morrow informed his client that in his view the price was very cheap, but the vendor insisted that he wished to go on with the sale. A contract dated 9 December 1980 was duly drawn up and executed by the parties. £500 was paid to the vendor on signing the contract; £250 on completion and the balance of £2,750 was to be paid by three annual instalments, the last one being due in December, 1983.

Three months later, in March 1981 Mr Morrow received a message from V. P. McMullin and Son, solicitors for the defendant, to the effect that Mr McGonigle had agreed to sell his 6 acre holding to the defendant for £3,000. Shortly afterwards the vendor came to see Mr Morrow and he told him that the sale was for far less than the true value of the land. He (Mr Morrow) formed the opinion at that time that Mr McGonigle was under the influence of the defendant. It was evident that he was not looking after himself properly and that his drink problem was getting worse. He did not accept Mr Morrow's advice and insisted on proceeding with the sale of the 6 acres for £500 an acre—the going rate at that time being in the region of three times that amount.

On 24 June 1982 Mr McGonigle and the defendant came to see Mr Morrow in his office. The former was quite unsteady and incoherent. The defendant spoke for him and said that Mr McGonigle wished to give him the home farm of 36 acres (i.e. all of his remaining lands) as a gift. Mr McGonigle signified his consent but at the time was clearly unfit to transact business. Mr Morrow told him to come back when he was sober. He did not do so.

The defendant's account of his business dealings with Mr McGonigle was as follows: He said that the plaintiff asked him to buy the 9$\frac{1}{2}$ acre plot because he was short of money. He had said that he wanted £3,000 and would give the defendant three years to pay for it. In the following year he again approached the defendant and asked him to buy the 6 acre plot and said that he wanted £3,000 in his hand to buy cattle. This contract was duly completed and the entire purchase price was paid in one sum. The explanation given by the defendant as to the background to his purchase of the home farm from Mr McGonigle in July 1982 was that about two months earlier the latter had received a letter from the bank regarding repayment of his overdraft which was then in the region of £2,500. The defendant alleged that Mr McGonigle asked him would he buy the home farm on terms that he would pay off the bank and give the vendor £1,000 over and above the bank debt. The defendant stated that Mr McGonigle was aware that the farm was worth about £40,000 but stated that he wished to give him the lands. At that point both men went to Mr Morrow but it was not possible to transact business as Mr McGonigle had too much drink taken at the time. I do not accept the defendant's evidence as to how Mr McGonigle came to transfer the home farm to him and I also doubt his explanation of the other transactions. First of all, his version of the deal relating to the home farm does not accord with Mr Morrow's account of the meeting which he had with Mr McGonigle and the defendant on 24 June 1982. Mr Morrow was not told anything about the debt due by Mr McGonigle to the bank; that he was being pressed for payment or that the plaintiff had initiated the transaction by offering to sell the home farm to the defendant in return for clearance of the bank debt and a further payment of £1,000. On the contrary, the defendant's explanation at that time was simply that Mr McGonigle wished to make a gift to him of the home farm. Secondly, the defendant went on to state in evidence that he was told by Mr McGonigle that he would not go back to Mr Morrow but instead had decided to consult James Boyle and Co., solicitors, in the matter of the home farm deal. He denied specifically that Messrs McMullin and Son, his own solicitors, had advised him to bring Mr McGonigle to Boyle and Co.. This also is patently untrue. It is specifically pleaded in para. 11 of the defence that acting upon the advice of his solicitors the defendant had brought Mr McGonigle to the firm of James Boyle and Co. for independent legal advice. It also emerged from the evidence of Mr John Heverin, manager of the Bank of Ireland, Ballybofey, that Mr McGonigle had obtained an overdraft of £2,500 on 8 March 1982 for the purpose of buying stock and providing for living expenses. This loan was to be repaid out of the sale of stock in November 1982. In fact the account was closed in the previous month when the outstanding balance at that time was discharged by the defendant. Mr Heverin had no note of any letter having been sent to Mr McGonigle earlier that year regarding the overdraft, nor was there any need for the bank to write to him because the loan was not due for repayment until the following November. I am satisfied that Mr McGonigle did not receive any demand from the bank about repayment of his overdraft and that in the period May, June and July, 1982 he was unlikely to have been concerned about it.

Miss McCrory, solicitor, of James Boyle and Co., gave evidence which I also accept. She said that in or about the last week of June 1982 Mr McGonigle accompanied by the defendant came to her office. The former was obviously under the influence of drink and she sent them away without enquiring into their business. About three weeks later on 16 July they both returned to her office again. Mr McGonigle was sober on this occasion. He explained that he wanted to transfer his home farm to the defendant. The latter was asked to leave the room and the remainder of Miss McCrory's interview with Mr McGonigle took place in private. She ascertained that the title deeds of the property were being held in the Bank of Ireland, Ballybofey as security against an overdraft. She telephoned the bank and ascertained the acreage of the farm as Mr McGonigle was not sure of the precise acreage. He told her that the purchase price of the land was to be £1,000 in cash and the purchaser was to clear the vendor's overdraft which Miss McCrory had ascertained from the bank then amounted to the sum of £2,623. She advised Mr McGonigle that the purchase price was not a realistic value and that it should be in the region of £30,000 to £35,000. She went on to advise that if he sold the farm on the open market he could expect to obtain about £1,000 per acre for it. Despite that advice Mr McGonigle insisted that he wanted to transfer the farm to the defendant. He also told her that he had already received £500 from the purchaser as a deposit. Miss McCrory made a written attendance immediately after the interview. A transfer deed was made out. No consideration was shown because the debt to the bank was rising daily as interest mounted. She asked Mr McGonigle to sign the transfer document and he did so. She then held it in trust until the consideration was paid in full. The transaction was completed on 19 November 1982. She handed over the title . deeds to Mr Brian O'Mahony of V. P. McMullin and Son and in exchange received the sum of £300 which was purported to be the balance of the purchase price over and above the clearance of the overdraft and sums already paid by the purchaser to the vendor. She was not informed by Mr McGonigle or anyone else that at the time of the transfer the defendant already owed £1,000 to the vendor on an earlier transaction; nor was she given any family history by her client or told that Mr Morrow had acted for him and for the McClures for many years. The only observation Mr McGonigle made to her by way of explanation for wishing to transfer his farm to the defendant was that the latter and his wife were the only people who had bothered about him. In fact this was not true as I am satisfied that the plaintiff and his wife had also taken an interest in Mr McGonigle and had endeavoured to help him from the time when his aunt had gone into hospital.

It is well settled that equity will set aside a contract where one party thereto has exercised undue influence over the other party as a result of which the latter has been induced to enter into an improvident transaction against his own interest. Certain relationships give rise to a presumption of undue influence and the onus is on the benefiting party to prove that none was exercised in fact. The catalogue of relationships which may give rise to that presumption is unlimited and in that regard I adopt with respect the following passage from the judgment of Lowry L.C.J. in R. (*Proctor*) *v Hutton* (No. 2) [1978] NI 139 at 147–8:

> The relationships which raise the presumption are left unlimited by definition, wide open for identification on the facts and in all the circumstances of each particular case as it arises . . . it is a common but not necessary feature of the relationship that the person on whose part undue influence is alleged assumed a responsibility for advising the donor or even managing his property. There are certain relationships which are recognised as giving rise to the presumption, but there are also those which, upon a consideration of the particular facts, may raise the same presumption.

I am satisfied that for several years prior to his death Mr McGonigle had a serious drink problem which became progressively worse as time went on and caused a deterioration in his health and general well-being. He was a bachelor and it is evident that he was particularly dependent on his aunt, Mrs McClure, to provide a home for him and generally to look after him. It seems that, essentially, his problems date from the time when she went into hospital some two years before her death and he was obliged for the first time to fend for himself. It is clear that this was too much for him and that he took refuge in alcohol. It is evident that he was a lonely man who was anxious to please and to be liked by his associates.

The defendant lived nearby Mr McGonigle and had been taking land from him on conacre for many years. I am satisfied that after Mrs McClure's departure to hospital he built up a dominant relationship with Mr McGonigle, who was then vulnerable to exploitation, through frequent contact and by providing him with some home comforts, though it seems that his help did not extend to giving any assistance to Mr McGonigle in maintaining his dwelling in habitable condition. I am also satisfied that the nature of that relationship was such as to raise a presumption of undue influence exercised by the defendant over Mr McGonigle in the matter of the transfer of the home farm thus casting an onus on the former to establish that that transaction was not brought about by any such improper influence. I have taken into account also that, although frequent drunkenness does not constitute absolute incapacity, it does lead a court to examine with particular care any transaction which may have been influenced by over-indulgence in alcohol even though the person so affected may have been sober at the time when the particular contract was made. I have no doubt that the defendant has failed to satisfy the onus upon him of establishing that his acquisition of Mr McGonigle's family farm for a small fraction of its true value was not brought about by his undue influence over the vendor. The evidence of Miss McCrory falls far short of discharging that onus. It is also eminently likely that the defendant was instrumental in persuading Mr McGonigle to leave his long-standing solicitor, Mr Morrow, because he (the defendant) was well aware that the former would be very loath indeed to allow his client to sell his last remaining asset for hardly more than a pittance.

Mr McGonigle was not sober on the first occasion when brought to Miss McCrory by the defendant. I appreciate that he was sober at the time of the crucial second visit to James Boyle and Co., but, for whatever reason, he failed to instruct Miss McCrory sufficiently about his relationship with the defendant and other relevant matters to enable her to assess the situation adequately and fully advise him. In particular, she was not informed that the defendant already owed Mr McGonigle £1,000 on an earlier transaction; that he was in the final stage of acquiring all of the defendant's lands at a gross undervalue and that before bringing him to Miss McCrory for so called independent advice, Mr McGonigle had been encouraged to leave the solicitor who had been advising him and his family for forty years. I have no doubt that Miss McCrory behaved with complete propriety in this matter, but if she had been appraised of all the salient information, including the fact that the lands comprised in the proposed transfer constituted Mr McGonigle's last remaining asset, she might well have advised him differently and probably would have refused to accept his instructions.

I am satisfied that the purported acquisition by the defendant of Mr McGonigle's home farm was for the vendor a grossly improvident transaction which was brought about by undue influence persistently exercised by the defendant over Mr McGonigle who, because of a combination of bereavement, inability to cope, loneliness, alcoholism and ill-health, was vulnerable to manipulation and was so manipulated by the dependant to the vendor's obvious disadvantage. It follows, therefore, that the plaintiff, as personal representative of Edward McGonigle, deceased, is entitled to the following relief:

(a) A declaration that the defendant holds the property which is the subject matter of this action in trust for the plaintiff; and

(b) an order that the defendant shall vacate the said property and shall take all such steps as are necessary to enable the plaintiff to be registered as owner of the same in his capacity as administrator of the estate of the said deceased.

(c) There shall be an enquiry in the Circuit Court as to damages limited to £15,000.

(d) The plaintiff shall have liberty to make further application to the High Court in these proceedings, if necessary.

Scope of the Presumption

Gregg v Kidd [1956] IR 183

Budd J.:

In these proceedings the plaintiff seeks to set aside a deed of 28 September 1953, whereby George Gregg, since deceased, in consideration of his affection for his nephew, John George Kidd, transferred his farm, situate at Tinryland in County Carlow, to William Gregg Kidd to hold in trust for the settlor for his life and in remainder in trust for John George Kidd (usually known as Jack Kidd) in fee simple.

Some months prior to the execution of the deed the settlor had made his will, dated 20 March 1953, whereby he devised all his property to his brother, Richard, for life and after his death to his nephew, Mark Gregg, the plaintiff. He appointed Richard Gregg and Mark Gregg his executors. He died on 29 December 1953, being then about fifty nine years of age. Richard Gregg pre-deceased him, but Mark Gregg, as sole surviving executor, proved the will on 2 April 1954, and thereafter launched these proceedings.

The defendants are the trustee and beneficiary under the deed, respectively, and are both sons of Mrs Hannah Kidd, a sister of the settlor. She and her family reside at Bohermore, near Bagenalstown, where they have a farm. John George Kidd is a young man of about thirty years of age.

It is alleged by the plaintiff that at the time of the making of the deed the settlor was reduced by mental ill-health or physical and mental debility to a state of help-lessness and was at the time residing in the house of the defendants and their mother, Mrs Hannah Kidd, and under their care; that the deed was improvident and was thus executed when the parties were not on equal terms. The deceased, it is alleged, was not competent by reason of mental illness to comprehend the nature and effect of the settlement. It is also alleged that the deed was obtained by the undue influence brought to bear upon the deceased by the defendants or on their behalf by Mrs Hannah Kidd, Mr Dawson Miller or one or other of them. These allegations the defendants deny and claim that the deed constitutes a valid settlement.

George Gregg acquired the farm by a transfer from his brother, Richard, on 13 January 1928, subject to a charge in favour of Richard for £500. He occupied the lands there-after up to about a year before his death. In January 1953, he was living at Tinryland, but being in bad health he went to reside with his brother, Richard, in his house at Kilmeany and was also for a time with his sister, Mrs Miller, at Shamrock Lodge, Carlow. He returned later to Kilmeany, Richard's place, and while there he had a stroke on 26 February 1953, which paralysed his left side. From 26 February to 13 March 1953, he was in Carlow Infirmary. From then until 1 May 1953, he was in the Meath Hospital in Dublin under the care of Dr Mayne. While in the Meath Hospital George Gregg made the will I have already referred to. From the Meath Hospital he returned to Carlow and went to reside again with his sister Mrs Miller. She went to London on holidays at the end of May 1953, and on 27 May George Gregg was taken to Mrs Hannah Kidd's house at Bohermore. While he was there he had two further serious relapses, (probably strokes, but that is uncertain) one in the beginning, and another at the end, of June. He remained in his sister's, Mrs Kidd's, house until he died on 29 December 1953.

During the early part of his illness George Gregg was attended by Dr Seale who had known him for about thirty years. Dr Seale, in the course of his evidence, stated that when he had the stroke George Gregg's left side became paralysed and for a time he could not speak. He had improved somewhat in May. Dr Seale saw the patient for the last time on 11 August 1953, and I shall refer later to his evidence as to his condition then. As he did not see him after that date he could not say what his condition was at the date of the execution of the deed.

Dr Mayne found George Gregg suffering from the result of the stroke and widespread arteriosclerotic disease; his mental capacity was impaired and his reasoning capacities to some extent affected. Dr Mayne said that the progress of the disease from which he was suffering would as a rule be one of deterioration but there might be improvement. Another stroke would, as one would expect, make deterioration probable.

During the period from June to September certain events took place which throw considerable light on the circumstances leading up to the execution of the deed of 28 September 1953, and I wish to refer to certain portions of the evidence which I regard as relevant to the issues which I have to decide. It is apparent that some discussions with regard to the recompense of the Kidd family for looking after George Gregg went on early in June 1953, between the Kidd family and Mr Dawson Miller, George Gregg's brother-in-law. These culminated in a visit by Dawson Miller and Jack Kidd to Mr Jeffers, who had up to then acted as George Gregg's solicitor, on 15 June. The burden of what they had to say was that George Gregg was living with the Kidds and that some arrangement should be made for the transfer of George Gregg's farm to Mrs Kidd or one of her sons subject to the payment of £500 to Mark Gregg. It transpired, however, that George Gregg was then very ill and had not himself sent for Mr Jeffers. In fact George Gregg had not, it appeared, mentioned settling his affairs and the whole idea of the purported transfer had apparently originated with Mr Miller and the Kidd family. The suggestion was no doubt made because the Kidds had taken on themselves the onerous duty of looking after George Gregg and there is no doubt Mr Miller supported the idea. Mr Jeffers very properly said that unless George Gregg himself wished to see him he could not do anything. Since George Gregg was very ill Mr Jeffers added that Dr Seale would have to certify him fit for business before he would take his instructions. They left, saying that they would see Dr Seale and get him to go out to see George Gregg.

On 22 June Mrs Hannah Kidd herself called at Mr Jeffers' office. She told him that Dr Seale had seen George and said he was incapable of doing business. She pointed out the work and cost involved in looking after her brother and asked what could be done about the matter. Mr Jeffers' view was that the moneys coming from the lettings of George's farm should be utilised to meet the expenses. He offered to ask Chancellor Nelson, George Gregg's rector, to approach George to see if he would be satisfied with the suggestion. Mr Jeffers did not know the precise income of the farm, but considered it would be ample to recompense the Kidds.

Towards the end of June 1953, Dr Seale formed the view that George Gregg should be sent to Dublin for further treatment by Dr Mayne. He engaged a room for him at a nursing home. Mrs Miller called out to Bohermore on 28 June to take him in her car to Dublin, but he was not removed on that occasion, and I am satisfied that this was mainly owing to Mrs Kidd's attitude.

On 25 July Jack Kidd called on Mr Jeffers and informed him that George Gregg wanted to see Mr Dawson Miller and himself the following Monday 27 July, for the purpose of making a will. Jack Kidd said that George Gregg was now recovered and was perfect. That was, to say the least of it, an overstatement as to George Gregg's condition. It transpired during the interview that Mrs Kidd had a short time before been to see the Reverend Mr Willis, the rector of the parish in which she resided, to get him to approach George Gregg to make a will, but he had declined to interfere. Jack Kidd further said that Mrs Kidd had also been to see Chancellor Nelson with the same object, that the Chancellor had called to see George, but that George Gregg would not discuss matters with him. He added that Dawson Miller had a week before told George Gregg that he should give the place to the Kidds. George Gregg was, he said, unwilling to adopt a suggestion that he should go to live with Edie Gregg, the plaintiff's sister, and, when told that the plaintiff had been tidying up at Tinryland, said that he would have him thrown out on the road. George Gregg, he said, had told his mother that he wanted to make a will giving her and Mark Gregg some money.

As a result of the interview with Jack Kidd Mr Jeffers repaired to Bohermore on 27 July with Mr Dawson Miller. What transpired at the interview is of importance and I should say that I accept what Mr Jeffers said in this evidence as a correct account of what occurred on that occasion. From what George Gregg said to Mr Jeffers it was obvious that Mrs Kidd was anxious that George Gregg would make a will and that at that stage he was unwilling to do so. In fact he said that he was being rushed by his sister. Mr Jeffers was anxious that George Gregg should state his attitude in the presence of Mr Miller and Mrs Kidd. George Gregg did not wish to see Mr Miller but consented to see Mrs Kidd. He told her that he could make no arrangements because he could not think clearly. An argument ensued in the course of which Mrs Kidd stated that she could not keep him unless he made a will. She was insistent that he would have to make a will or get out. He stated that he wished to have his existing will destroyed but appeared at some stages not to recollect what was in it. He directed Mr Jeffers to state what was in it in Mrs Kidd's presence, which he did. He was distressed and worried by this interview, fearing he would have to leave the house, which he did not wish to do. Mr Jeffers explained to him that entirely apart from making a will he should make provision for his maintenance and for paying Mrs Kidd for looking after him. He agreed to give her £50 out of the money in the auctioneers' hands in respect of the grazing rents of his lands. Mr Jeffers informed Mrs Kidd of this but she refused the offer and insisted that a will should be made. On this being reported to George Gregg, he was again worried and felt he would have to leave. Before Mr Jeffers left he saw Mrs Kidd again, along with Mr Miller, and both insisted to him that George Gregg would have to make a will or be put out. Mr Miller added that he would not be able to stand being moved if he was put out. Mr Miller and Mrs Kidd then returned to George Gregg's room, and, when they came out, Mr Miller said that George had refused to make a will, and, from what they said to Mr Jeffers, it was clear to him that they had made it clear to George Gregg that he must take a will or get out. Mr Jeffers told them that a will made under undue influence would be invalid, but he says that no attention was paid to what he said, and he then left having pointed out that while Mrs Kidd was quite justified in seeking some arrangement to be made for George's maintenance, no one had the right to insist upon his making a will if he did not wish to do so. I have dealt in some detail with this interview because it indicates what the attitude and aims of Mrs Kidd were at that early stage. Strong pressure was being put on George Gregg to make a will at a time when he was in poor condition to resist, and that pressure was backed by a threat which was bound to have a strong affect on George Gregg's mind. I have no doubt that the will which Mrs Kidd wished him to make was one in favour of some one or other of the members of the Kidd family.

Mrs Kidd was not satisfied to allow things to remain as they were. Dr Gavin, who had not attended George Gregg before, was summoned to visit him. He saw him on 31 July and again on 3 and 11 August. On 31 July he found George suffering from residual haemo-plegia. His blood pressure was raised; his left arm was not as strong as his right; his hearing was affected but that was put right. He explained his condition, but things would have to be dragged out of him, as the doctor put it. On 3 August he was satisfied that he was capable of looking after his affairs; but he had not known George Gregg when he was in good health and admitted that his opinion would have been affected if he had known of George Gregg's previously cheerful and voluble disposition. He was then quiet and difficult to get answers from and required to have things explained slowly to him.

Having again received information, this time from the Reverend Mr Willis, to the effect that George Gregg wished to make a will, Mr Jeffers again went to Bohermore on 11 August. Mr Willis had informed him that it was Jack Kidd who had asked him to phone and that he had said that Dr Gavin had certified George Gregg fit to make a will. Mr Jeffers brought Dr Seale with him so that he could have the benefit of Dr Seale's views, as George Gregg's medical attendant, as to his capacity to make a will. Dr Seale formed the view that George Gregg was not competent to make a will. The doctor found that certain answers George Gregg gave to his questions were not correct and that his mental condition had deteriorated since June. He just answered, 'yes' or 'no', to questions and made no effort to chat, which was quite different from his normal habits. He was clear intermittently, but not for long enough to know what he was doing. His view was that George Gregg could not understand or appreciate affairs of business and that he could not evaluate or resist suggestions made to him. The doctor thought he could be persuaded to do anything. He never saw George Gregg again nor was his assistance with regard to George Gregg's medical history sought after that date by any other doctor. He did not on that occasion put any question to George Gregg about the extent of his property or about his family or generally about his making a will as he thought there was no use in doing so.

To Mr Jeffers George Gregg also seemed to have deteriorated. Although normally cheerful and chatty, he had little to say. His answers were short, his speech was not very clear and he was inclined to ramble a little at times. He informed George Gregg that having regard to Dr Seale's view he could not make a will for him, but later asked him what he would do if he was able to make a will. He replied that he would give the place to his sister, Hannah, and her son, Jack Kidd. When he was asked whether he meant to give them the place jointly or one after the other he seemed incapable of understanding what Mr Jeffers meant and mumbled something that Mr Jeffers could not hear. He also said he would like to benefit Dick's little girl. He said her name was Edie, but later said the name was Markey, the name he usually used to refer to the plaintiff. According to Mr Jeffers he seemed very confused but made some remark about paying Mrs Kidd for looking after him.

Mrs Kidd asked Mr Jeffers why he could not make a will having regard to the views of Dr Mansfield, who had also seen George Gregg prior to that date. Mr Jeffers replied that Dr Seale had better knowledge of the case than Dr Mansfield. Mrs Kidd was again not satisfied. She went that same evening to see Dr Gavin, and, as a result, he went out to see George Gregg. He was satisfied that George Gregg wanted to make some change in his affairs and was capable of making that change and of determining what he wanted to do. He admitted that he was slow in his answers and that he took no steps to test their accuracy. He might have lingered on for two or three years, he thought.

On 12 August Mrs Kidd again came to Mr Jeffers' office and asked him whether George's will had been destroyed, a question Mr Jeffers declined to answer. She stated that Dr Gavin had been called in to see George Gregg on the previous night, after Dr Seale and Mr Jeffers had left, and had certified George Gregg fit to make a will and that George Gregg had said that Mr Jeffers had let him down in not making a will for him. Mr

Jeffers pointed out that George Gregg could get another solicitor if he was not satisfied. He had no more dealings with the parties up to the time of George Gregg's death.

On 15 August Mrs Kidd wrote a letter to her sister, Mrs Miller. She states that she wrote that letter at the dictation of Chancellor Nelson, a suggestion that I do not believe. The letter reads:

> Dear Susan. I want you to get a bed ready for your brother George in Tinryland, or the only alternative a bed in the county hospital. I have done all in my capacity for him. I cannot continue any longer. Please let me have a reply immediately.
>
> Yours
>
> H. M. Kidd.

Ken Miller, Mrs Miller's son, was given this letter to take to Bohermore to read to his uncle. He did so. While Mrs Miller's action in sending the letter to her brother may be open to criticism, it is hardly to be suggested that Mrs Kidd did not intend her attitude to be made known to him. The letter was, of course, a great shock to George Gregg.

Early in September Mrs Kidd betook herself to consult Mr Cody, a solicitor practising in Bagenalstown. She had several interviews with him. Her object, Mr Cody understood, was to get something done about George's affairs and to have her position as regards his maintenance secured. She gave him certain information about George Gregg, told him she was looking after him, that he had had a stroke and was possessed of the farm. She was Mr Cody's source of information as to the background. Mr Cody did not keep a note of his attendances on Mrs Kidd and does not remember what exactly passed between them, but he recalled that Mrs Kidd had said that Mr Jeffers had refused to make a will for George Gregg on the advice of Dr Seale. Mr Cody gave Mrs Kidd certain advice. He anticipated litigation and suggested the advisability of having George Gregg examined by two doctors. Mr Cody had not up to this time been sent for or consulted by George Gregg himself.

In accordance with Mr Cody's advice Dr Mansfield and Dr Humphries examined George Gregg on 25 September. Dr Humphries did not know him before and was about ten minutes with him. He asked him some questions about simple every day affairs, which he answered apparently to the doctor's satisfaction. Dr Humphries came to the conclusion that he was capable of doing business and altering the settlement of his affairs by a procedure of question and answer. While his mental processes were somewhat impaired he thought he could make a simple will if matters were explained slowly to him. The doctor expressed the view that he did not think that George Gregg would be influenced by the views of others but it would seem to me that the doctor's lack of knowledge of the background put him in a poor position to form any such view after so short an interview. He thought from what he saw that George Gregg might have lingered on for three or four years.

Dr Mansfield had previously seen George Gregg on 4 June. He was uncertain then whether he had had a second stroke or not, but he had just previously become worse and had little use of his arm and leg on the left side. When he saw him again on 6 June he answered simple questions and was clear to that extent. He saw him later on 6 July and on 26 and 27 August but there was not much change in his condition. Mrs Kidd it was who asked Dr Mansfield to see George Gregg on 25 September, the object being to see if he was fit to make a will. He asked him about his farm and whom he wished to leave it to; he said he wished to leave it to one of the Kidd family. His answers were satisfactory and the doctor came to the conclusion he could make a simple will but that he was not capable of making a complicated disposition of a lot of property; he was incapable of continuing a long process of thought or of concentration. As to his general observations of the patient, he agreed that any change would be towards deterioration. The disorder of haemoplegia, he agreed, affects the brain processes and there may be periods of clarity followed by periods of confusion. He also thought that he might have lingered on a few years.

William Kidd having informed Mr Cody that George Gregg wished to settle his affairs and wanted him to go out, Mr Cody went to Bohermore on 26 September and saw the deceased. He spent from half an hour to three quarters of an hour with him. He said that George Gregg looked all right to him and that he could see nothing wrong with him. He was able to talk to Mr Cody who said that he understood he wished to settle his affairs. Mr Cody spoke to him of his previous will and its contents and about his farm. George Gregg answered such questions as he was asked satisfactorily but was slow to answer and generally confined his answer to the one word, 'yes'. George Gregg said that he wanted to leave the farm at Tinryland to Jack Kidd by deed. Mr Cody explained to George Gregg the two ways in which he could dispose of his property, by will or by deed. He pointed out the salient differences between a deed and a will and in particular that a will can be changed but that a deed cannot be altered. Mr Cody was satisfied that George Gregg understood what he was told. Before leaving the house Mr Cody told the Kidds of the instructions he had received and asked William Kidd if he would act as trustee, which he agreed to do.

On 28 September Mr Cody returned with the engrossment of a deed which he had prepared in the meantime. By it the farm was transferred to William Gregg Kidd upon trust for George Gregg for life and in remainder to the use of John George Kidd in fee simple. The deed was read over to George Gregg. Mr Cody explained its effect and asked George Gregg if he understood it. George Gregg said that he did and executed it, after which Mr Cody departed.

Mr Cody says that George Gregg was on that occasion as clear as on the previous day he saw him and as far as he could judge understood what he was saying to him and knew what he was doing. He had not had the benefit of the views of the doctors who had examined George Gregg just before. He relied on what he saw himself. He did not realise that George Gregg was permanently paralysed, nor did he consider how long he might possibly live. He said that he did not consider what position George Gregg would be in if he changed his mind. He did not at the time of taking instructions or drawing the deed know that pressure was being brought to bear on George Gregg; he only discovered that when the affidavit of discovery was filed by the plaintiffs, when presumably he had the advantage of reading Mr Jeffers' notes of his attendances on the parties. He was in no way on guard against the possibility that the Kidds might be influencing George Gregg nor did he apparently appreciate that George Gregg was in a position in which he would require protection. He did not give George Gregg any advice as to the possibility or desirability of inserting in the deed a clause of revocation or any provision that would provide for him being permitted to reside at Bohermore or binding the Kidds to care for him for the rest of his life, nor did he consider the desirability of making any provision compelling Jack Kidd to work the lands during his life. In short, he did not give any serious consideration to the possibility that the Kidds might fall out with George Gregg after the deed was executed nor what would happen to George Gregg if they did. He got a payment on account of the costs relative to drawing the deed from Jack Kidd and intended to furnish the bill of costs to Jack Kidd later on.

Voluntary gifts, made *inter vivos*, obtained by persons standing in a confidential, fiduciary, or other relation to the donor in which dominion may be exercised over him may, upon principles of general public policy, be set aside where there has been some improper conduct, overreaching or coercion exercised against the donor. The general principles are well stated in White and Tudor's *Leading Cases in Equity* in the notes appended to the case of *Huguenin v Basely*.[1] As Lord Cottenham states in *Dent v Bennett*:[2] 'The relief . . . stands upon a general principle, applying to all variety of relations in which dominion may be exercised by one person over another.' It applies of course where the gift is the result of influence expressly used by the donee and also 'where the relations between the donor and donee have at or shortly before the execution of the gift been such as to raise a presumption that the donee had influence over the donor. In such a case the court sets aside a voluntary gift, unless it is proved that in fact the gift was the spontaneous act of the donor acting under circumstances which enabled him to exercise an independent will and which justifies the court in holding that the gift was the result of a free exercise of the donor's will', per Cotton L.J. in *Allcard v Skinner*.[3]

The courts have never confined the application of the principle to any stated forms of relationship. To do so would fetter that wide jurisdiction to relieve against all manner of constructive fraud which courts administering equitable principles have always exercised. The principle has been exercised in the case of an improvident voluntary settlement by a younger sister in favour of an elder sister, who had obtained great ascendancy and influence over the younger sister, the younger sister not having the benefit of independent advice: *Harvey v Mount*.[4] In *Sharp v Leach*[5] a voluntary deed, under which a brother obtained an advantage from a sister who lived with him and consulted him about her affairs, was set aside. The improvidence of the transaction was held to cast the onus on the defendant to show that the deed emanated from the free will of the sister after it had been explained to her. Similarly in *Griffiths v Robins*,[6] an old lady, nearly blind, who reserving only a life estate to herself, made a deed of gift of all her property to her niece and her husband, on whose kindness and assistance she depended, was held entitled to have the deed set aside. The onus was held to be upon the recipients to establish that the deed was made of her own free will and effected through the intervention of some indifferent person.

The authorities cited leave no doubt that the principle can be extended to the relationship of brother and sister, where a sister has for one reason or another acquired an influence or dominion over a brother and uses that influence improperly for her own ends. Likewise it can be extended in similar circumstances to the relationship between uncle and nephew. The influence may arise or be acquired in many ways, such as through disparity of age or the mental or physical incapacity of the donor or, indeed, out of a mere dependence upon the kindness and assistance of another. To bring the principle into play it must be shown that the opportunity for the exercise of the influence or ascendancy on the donor existed, as where the parties reside together or meet frequently. While close family relationship creates a situation where influence is readily acquired, mere blood relationship is not sufficient of itself to call the principle into play; it must be shown that the actual relations between the parties give rise to a presumption of influence.

Although the exercise of undue influence is pleaded against the donee of the deed impugned, as well as against others, it is true to say that the evidence was mainly directed to establishing that influence had been obtained and exercised over the donor by Mrs Hannah Kidd, mother of the donee. There is in my mind no doubt that if it be shown that his deed was obtained by the undue influence of Mrs Hannah Kidd or as a result of her dominion of mind over her brother, improperly exercised to benefit a member of her family, this deed cannot stand. Indeed, it is only right to say that a contention to the contrary was never made by the advisers of the defendants. Although authority is scarcely required on the point, I recall the words of Lord Eldon in the first paragraph of his judgment in *Huguenin v Basely* where he says: 'I should regret that any doubt could be entertained, whether it is not competent to a court of equity to take away from third persons the benefits which they have derived from the fraud, imposition, or undue influence of others.' If the proper deductions from the evidence adduced are that Jack Kidd knew perfectly well that his mother had acquired influence over the donor and that they acted together in order to obtain some advantage from the donor, the grounds for interfering are all the stronger.

Some debate took place during the hearing as to where the onus of proof lay. In the case of a voluntary gift where the relations between the donor and donee are such as to raise a presumption that the donee had influence over the donor, the onus lies, in my view, on the donee to establish that the gift was the spontaneous act of the donor acting in circumstances which enabled him to exercise an independent will and that the gift was the result of a free exercise of the donor's will. This proposition I believe to be one well established. Authority will be found for it in the cases of *Allcard v Skinner*, *Sharp v Leach*, and *Griffiths v Robins*, already referred to, and also in the observations of Lord Romilly in *Cooke v Lamotte*.[7] If more modern authority is required it will be found in the judgment of Lord Hailsham in the comparatively recent case of *Inche Noriah v Shaik Allie Bin Omar*.[8] Where the relations between the donor and another person raise a presumption that that other person had influence over the donor and the evidence shows that that third party is both closely related to the donee and was closely associated in action and interest with the donee at the time of the events leading to the transaction, it would seem to me on principle that the onus in such circumstances must be likewise thrown on the donee to establish that the gift resulted from the free exercise of the donor's will.

The presumption may, of course, be rebutted either by showing that the donor has had competent independent advice and acted of his own free will or in some other way. As Lord Hailsham says, in *Inche Noriah v Shaik Allie Bin Omar*: 'The most obvious way to prove |that the gift was the result of the free exercise of independent will is to establish| that the gift was made after the nature and effect of the transaction had been fully explained to the donor by some independent and qualified person so completely as to satisfy the court that the donor was acting independently of any influence from the donee and with full appreciation of what he was doing.' If that method of rebutting the presumption is adopted, and it is not the only method open, the advice relied on must, in the words of Lord Hailsham, 'be given with a knowledge of all relevant circumstances and must be such as a competent and honest adviser would give if acting solely in the interests of the donor.' The nature of that advice naturally must vary with the circumstances of each particular case.

Although there is considerable difference of medical opinion as to George Gregg's mental and physical condition at the time when the deed was executed and during the period immediately preceding that event, I have formed these conclusions as to his health during the relevant period: he had had at least one stroke and two serious relapses; he was partially paralysed and virtually bedridden; he suffered from a condition the usual progress of which is one of deterioration; during the summer and autumn his reasoning faculties became impaired; at times his memory was intermittent and faulty and I believe that he could not concentrate for any appreciable length of time; he had periods of confusion of mind. In character he had formerly been voluble and cheerful but had changed to saying little and had become difficult to get answers from. I believe that his capacity to make rational decisions was, by the autumn, definitely impaired and that his capacity to resist influence and suggestions was very slight and easily overcome. At times, I think, he might have been fit to make a simple officious will or simple disposition of his property if uninfluenced and properly advised, but it would, in my view, have been difficult to discover just when he was in that condition and equally difficult to bring him to a full understanding of the transaction. Someone well acquainted with him would obviously be the best person to make the attempt, but even such a person would require to exercise care and patience in examining him before coming to a conclusion as to his capacity. Even if he could be shown to have had the capacity to bring a reasoning mind to bear on such a disposition there would still remain the formidable difficulty of ascertaining and ensuring that his mind was emancipated from the influence and dominion of others alleged to have existed.

The last above-mentioned matter brings me to a consideration of the relations between the donor, on the one hand, and the donee and his mother, Mrs Hannah Kidd, on the other hand, at and immediately before the execution of the deed. As far back as the end of May 1953, George Gregg had been moved to the Kidds' house and he had remained with them until his death. During most of that time he was a very sick man, only a wreck of his former self. He was during that period entirely dependent on the Kidd family for all the attention his helpless condition required. If and when he was fit for company and conversation it would naturally be members of that family whom he would generally see and he does not seem to have seen much of other members of his family from June onwards. I believe that he knew with more or less clarity, according to the varying state of his health, that he was then dependent on the Kidd family and that he was at times at least most apprehensive as to what would become of him were they to refuse to look after him any longer. In short, his circumstances and condition laid him open in a high degree to the influence of that family, more particularly to that of Mrs Hannah Kidd, having regard to her relationship to him and her position in the household. Mrs Kidd's character as revealed by her evidence and demeanour is not, in this connection, by any means irrelevant to what I am dealing with, and I should say that she struck me as a woman of forceful and determined character, who believed in having her own way without much regard to the views or advice of others.

Apart from these circumstances which I have mentioned, there is a considerable body of evidence as to the actual relations existing between George Gregg and his relatives, the Kidds, and of their attitude to him, to which I must briefly refer. Before doing so I should say that it must, in all fairness, be recognised that the Kidds acted with kindness in taking George Gregg into their house, having regard to his condition, and I see no reason to doubt that they treated him kindly and looked after him to the best of their ability. No one would suggest that it would have been unreasonable for Mrs Kidd to seek reasonable recompense for the onerous services she performed. Unfortunately, I regret to say that the evidence does not lead me to believe that the Kidds' motives were by any means solely altruistic and moreover I was forced to take an unfavourable view of the veracity of such members of the family as gave evidence before me in respect of a good deal of what they told me.

The evidence leads me to believe that from an early stage Mrs Kidd formed the view, shared by her son, Jack Kidd, that George Gregg's farm at Tinryland should go to the Kidds in return for looking after him. It does not matter, to my mind, whether the idea originated with Dawson Miller or Mrs Kidd herself or her son. The attempts to get George Gregg to make some further settlement of his affairs, other than that provided for in his existing will, indicated by the approaches of Mrs Kidd and Jack Kidd to Mr Jeffers and of Mrs Kidd to Mr Cody, all indicate their frame of mind. Likewise, the fact that they kept stressing that doctors other than Dr Seale thought George Gregg fit to transact business betrayed their anxiety to have something done and I am satisfied that what was aimed at was the making of some disposition of George Gregg's property in favour of Mrs Kidd or some of her family and not merely obtaining some reasonable recompense for her services.

That Mrs Kidd realised that she was in a position to influence her brother and was prepared to put pressure upon him is revealed strikingly on several occasions. Dr Seale's view was that George Gregg should go to Dublin for further examination and treatment by Dr Mayne towards the end of June. He did not go and the real reason is to be found in Mrs Kidd's attitude. Having regard to all the circumstances, especially the burden he must have been to her, it is difficult to avoid drawing the inference that she wished to keep him in her house for purposes of her own not difficult to seek. She showed her hand clearly on 27 July when she insisted that George Gregg should make a will, although he was unwilling to do so, and brought what must be regarded as strong pressure to bear on him to do so, having regard to his condition, by threatening to put him out if he did not do so. At the same time she rejected the suggestion that a money payment might be arranged for and insisted on a will being made, and there can be little doubt that it was one benefiting the Kidds that she had in view. That she was of the same mind in August and still prepared to exercise pressure is shown by the terms of her letter of 15 August indicating that George would have to go to Tinryland or the county hospital. She must have known that her attitude as revealed in this letter would be made known to George Gregg and would profoundly affect him. In September she made several visits to Mr Cody, who was not George Gregg's solicitor, and I believe that her object again was to see if she could get something done, through the intervention of Mr Cody, which would achieve her objects. Mr Miller in the beginning, I believe, supported her, but he only plays a secondary role.

Although he plays a lesser part than his mother the evidence establishes also that the defendant, John George Kidd, was a party to his mother's activities and took an active part in the endeavours made to get George Gregg to make a fresh disposition of his property in a fashion favourable to the Kidd family. He was party, along with Mr Dawson Miller, to the original suggestion made in Mr Jeffers' office on 15 June that arrangements should be made to have the farm at Tinryland transferred to Mrs Kidd or one of the family, an idea that originated with them and not with George Gregg, who had at that stage not even mentioned settling his affairs. It was Jack Kidd again who went to Mr Jeffers on 25 July to get him to go out to make a will for George Gregg. He did not scruple on that occasion to make what I regard as an untrue statement as to George Gregg's health with the object, I am satisfied, of allaying Mr Jeffers' anxieties as to George Gregg's capacity. Indeed, that was not the only occasion on which he saw fit to suggest that George Gregg's health was better than it was so as to induce Mr Jeffers to go out and make a will for him. He knew all about his mother's efforts to get the clergy to intervene to get George Gregg to make a will, but saw fit to deny that he had told Mr Jeffers of these approaches by his mother. His testimony was so uncandid as to lead me to the belief that he was involved even more than the direct evidence indicates. The evidence satisfies me that Jack Kidd was of one mind with his mother. He was, I believe, perfectly aware of his mother's influence over his uncle and perfectly willing to accept the benefit of its exercise on his behalf.

The facts as proved are such as to lead me to the conclusion not only that the relations between George Gregg and his sister were such as to raise a presumption that she had influence over him, but that she was exercising that influence towards securing his farm for some one or other of her family. She was certainly using active pressure on 27 July 1953, and her subsequent activities lead me to believe that that pressure was not relaxed to the date on which the deed was executed; that influence was such, having regard to George Gregg's incapacity and circumstances, as to preclude the exercise by him of a free and independent judgment. The facts are sufficient to support a finding of the actual exercise of undue influence, but it is sufficient to say that the relations between the donor, on the one hand, and his sister and nephew, on the other, were such as to raise a presumption that the donee's mother had influence over the donor. I am satisfied that the donee was aware of this influence and acted in combination with his mother; the onus consequently lies on the defendants to establish that the gift resulted from the free exercise of the donor's will acting in circumstances which enabled him to exercise an independent will.

Before passing to a consideration of the evidence of Mr Cody, relied upon by the defendants to show that the deed was the free act of the settlor acting in circumstances which enabled him to exercise an independent will, I wish to say something about the deed itself, since its form and contents may, apart from the other circumstances of the case, afford some evidence that the donor did not understand the transaction and so of undue influence. After reserving a life estate to the donor, the effect of the deed is to transfer an estate in remainder to the donee of practically all the donor's property, since apart from the farm he only possessed chattel property of small value. It contains no covenants or other safeguards to ensure that George Gregg would be looked after for the rest of his life by the Kidds or to secure that his farm would be worked during his lifetime. The medical evidence satisfies me that George Gregg might well have lingered on for a matter of years and, while I do not suggest that they would have done so, there was nothing to prevent the Kidds from putting him out of their house after he had executed the deed, in which event he would only have the value of his life estate as a bargaining factor to secure his future comfort. This deed was therefore on the face of it improvident, a fact affording at least some indication militating against the contention that it was the spontaneous product of an independent mind.

Another factor of weight in connection with the form of the deed is that it contains no power of revocation, a fact not brought to the attention of the donor. I accept the view contended for by the defendants that the absence of a power of revocation in a voluntary deed is not of itself a sufficient ground for the cancelling of the deed. It is, as Turner L.J. states in *Toher v Toher*,[9] approved by James L.J. in *Hall v Hall*,[10] a circumstance to be taken into consideration and it is a circumstance of more or less weight according to the facts of each particular case. It is, I apprehend, a material factor where the deed is improvident unless the donor is protected by such a power. FitzGibbon L.J. in *Horan v MacMahon*[11] stated at p. 654 his view, frequently quoted, that to get over the absence of the clause in a voluntary deed the 'other circumstances must show . . . that it is the free act of a settlor who knows what he is doing; and, 2, either that it is a deed provident and just in itself, or that any apparent improvidence and injustice is in accordance with the actual intention of the settlor.' I shall have to revert to these considerations after considering the effect of Mr Cody's evidence.

The duty of a solicitor advising a donor suffering from a degree of mental or physical infirmity about to make a voluntary settlement of the greater portion of his property is not an easy one. The judgment of Farwell J. in *Powell v Powell*[12] has been relied on as stating the duty. Having stated that in his view a solicitor who acts for both parties cannot be independent of the donee in fact and that it is not sufficient that the donor should have an independent adviser unless he acts on the advice, Farwell J. points out that it is the duty of the solicitor to protect the donor against himself and not merely against the personal influence of the donee. He was dealing with a case of child and step-parent but the same considerations apply, in my view, to a case such as the present. He goes on to say that the solicitor does not discharge his duty by satisfying himself simply that the donor understands and wished to carry out the particular transaction, and adds (at p. 247): 'He must also satisfy himself that the gift is one that it is right and proper for the donor to make under all the circumstances; and if he is not so satisfied, his duty is to advise his client not to go on with the transaction, and to refuse to act further for him if he persists.' He found that the solicitor in question had not, *inter alia*, advised the donor in that case of the proper course to adopt or recommended the insertion in the settlement of a power of revocation. The Privy Council in *Inche Noriah v Shaik Allie Bin Omar* were not prepared to affirm that independent legal advice, when given, does not rebut the presumption unless it be shown that the advice was taken. What is necessary, Lord Hailsham said, is that the donee should prove that the gift was the result of the free exercise of independent will. He adds that the most obvious way to prove this is by establishing that the gift was made after the nature and effect of the transaction had been fully explained to the donor by some independent and qualified person so completely as to satisfy the court that the donor was acting independently of any influence from the donee and with the full appreciation of what he was doing. Finally, he says, the advice must be given with a knowledge of all relevant circumstances and must be such as a competent adviser would give if acting solely in the interests of the donor. With great respect to that learned judge there are two statements in his judgment on which I venture to differ from the views of Farwell J. In accordance with the view of the Privy Council it seems to me that independent legal advice may in certain circumstances rebut the presumption even though that advice is not taken. Moreover, I do not think that a solicitor is bound to refuse to act further for his client in all cases of the nature I am dealing with where his advice to his client not to proceed with the transaction is not taken, though in some extreme cases that may be the proper course. Apart from these two matters I adopt the views of Farwell J. and Lord Hailsham as to the duties of a solicitor in similar cases, observing, however, that they are not necessarily exhaustive. The nature of the advice to be given must in all instances depend upon the facts and circumstances of each case.

These views of a general nature as to the duties of a solicitor in cases of this kind have now to be applied in a practical fashion to the particular circumstances of this case and, without purporting to deal with every detail, I conceive that a solicitor advising one in the circumstances of George Gregg is at least under the following obligations to his client. To begin with, he should apprise himself of the surrounding circumstances in so far as he reasonably can; if he does not do this he can never put himself in a position to advise his client fully and effectively. He would need to discover the nature of the donor's illness so as to be able to estimate in some reasonable degree the nature of his incapacity. He would need to know how far his reasoning capacity was affected and how far he was capable of comprehending the manner in which the proposed transaction would affect his own interests and his future and to what extent he was competent to come to a rational decision. Without knowing all that, he could not be said to have sufficient knowledge of his client to enable him to judge the nature of the advice he should give him and the degree of protection he would require. With the knowledge that he would have gained upon inquiry that the donor was incapacitated to some degree both mentally and physically and had been living for some time with the family of the proposed transferee, by one of whom the solicitor in this case had originally been consulted with a view to having something done about the donor's affairs, he ought then to have been put on his guard and he should, in my view, then endeavour to discover whether his client was subject to the influence of the donee or any member of his family and, if so, the extent of that influence. Having discovered the extent of the donor's incapacity he should make sure that he was capable of fully understanding the nature and results of a transaction such as that proposed. Without that capacity the transaction could not be proceeded with, but, assuming that the solicitor satisfies himself that it exists, he should then make sure that his client did thoroughly understand what he was doing and how it would affect him. He would need in this connection to consider very carefully whether the transaction was one for his benefit and, as I see it, this was a case that called for positive and definite advice, not mere explanation. The suggested transfer was, on the face of it, an improvident transaction. The plight of the donor demanded that he should be protected against himself. He should have been told clearly that the transaction was improvident, that it secured nothing for him in return for what he was giving, and that he was not only depriving himself of most of what he possessed, but also the means of securing his future comfort. He should have been advised against entering into the proposed transaction unless he was adequately and properly safeguarded. In particular, he should have been told that he might safeguard himself to a great degree by having a power of revocation inserted in the instrument. Before he could conscientiously advise his client to proceed with the transaction the solicitor would also need to satisfy himself that his intervention and advice had emancipated the donor from any adverse influence he lay under and that he was acting of his own free will.

Mr Cody was faced with an unenviable task of difficulty and delicacy when he was called upon to attend George Gregg in September 1953. It is easy to be wise after the event and I feel sure that Mr Cody would have acted differently had he appreciated what the real circumstances were. It may well be that he was to some extent misled and it is right to say the he was quite candid about the advice he gave. I must, however, consider whether such advice as he did give could have the results contended for by the defendants. While I am alive to the fact that it was Mrs Kidd, and not the donee, who had previously consulted him I have the gravest doubts whether Mr Cody could be properly described as an independent solicitor; but even assuming for the moment that he was, Mr Cody did not, I fear, appreciate the full extent of George Gregg's physical and mental incapacity. He had not known his client previously and was not in a position to judge how much he had deteriorated and I believe he did not appreciate the extent to which his reasoning power and ability to make rational decisions was affected. He did not sufficiently consider what effect the transaction would have on George Gregg's future nor what would happen should he fall out with the Kidds, nor did he consider in what way George Gregg might be safeguarded, nor did he, I believe, appreciate the entire improvidence of the transaction. It follows that he did not feel called upon to give, nor did he give, George Gregg any positive advice in the way of dissuading him from entering into the transaction as proposed nor did he advise George Gregg as to the various ways in which he might be safeguarded from the improvidence he contemplated nor urge him to adopt any suggestions calculated to safeguard him. In particular, he never brought to his notice the possibility of inserting a power of revocation in the deed nor did he urge on him the desirability of such a course, which I believe the circumstances called for. Furthermore, Mr Cody did not appreciate the true nature of the relations existing between the donor and Mrs Kidd and the donor and the donee, to a lesser degree. Deprived of that knowledge, he was never in a position to consider what advice and warning he should properly give to the donor and what steps he should take to make sure that the settlor was acting with a free and independent mind and was emancipated from the influence of his sister. As a result, no steps were taken to ensure that George Gregg acted independently and freed from the effects of his sister's influence. The advice received by the donor was not therefore sufficient to enable the donor to understand fully and properly the nature of the entire transaction nor such as to protect the donor against himself; nor was it sufficient to rebut the presumption, nor does it satisfy me that the gift was the spontaneous act of a donor who knew what he was doing.

The findings I have so far made are sufficient to determine the action, but the plaintiff does not rest his case solely on the contentions I have dealt with. He also relies on the decision in *Grealish v Murphy*,[13] a decision of Gavan Duffy J., as he then was, and says that the circumstances of this case cause it to fall within the principle of that decision.

The plaintiff in that proceeding, who was mentally deficient, executed a deed transferring his farm to a much younger man. The deed reserved a life estate to the plaintiff but the lands were charged with the defendant's right of residence and maintenance during the plaintiff's life. The defendant covenanted to reside on, and to work and manage, the farm without reward during the plaintiff's lifetime, to account for money received and expended and to pay the plaintiff £1 for every week in which he failed to reside on the farm and to indemnify the plaintiff for any loss or expense incurred or the maintenance or wages of any person employed to do work which the defendant failed to do. I have only taken the salient factors of the deed. They show that the plaintiff was more adequately protected than was George Gregg. Gavan Duffy J. took the view that the circumstances of the case brought into operation the principle stated by Lord Hatherley, in *O'Rourke v Bolingbroke*[14] (in which he dissented on facts), that equity comes to the rescue whenever the parties to a contract have not met upon equal terms, the corollary being, he said, that the court must inquire whether a grantor, shown to be unequal to protecting himself, has had the protection which was his due by reason of his infirmity. Having stated that the principle applies to improvident grants and that in several instances the inadequacy of the explanations given to the grantor has been a decisive factor in the court's action against an improvident deed, the learned judge set aside the improvident deed by reason of the plaintiff's weakness of mind coupled with the deficiencies of the legal advice under which he acted and his unawareness.

The late president expressly stated that the deed could not be avoided by reason of any undue influence and that the case was not one where any presumption of undue influence arose from the relationship of the parties. The degree of the plaintiff's incapacity coupled with deficiencies of advice and the improvidence of the transaction was held sufficient in the circumstances of that case to entitle the donor to relief. That degree of incapacity was that the donor had not attained the normal power of an adult. I have already expressed the view that the deed made by George Gregg was improvident. He was suffering from such incapacity as would prevent him from understanding anything but the simplest transaction. His solicitor had not got the facts as to the nature of his illness or his incapacity. Apart from any question of the donor being subject to influence, he did not consider what safeguards might be necessary to protect George Gregg for the future nor warn him as to the improvidence of what he contemplated and against entering into the transaction as proposed. He did not advise him as to what steps he ought to take to protect himself, such as the insertion of a power of revocation. Since he was not warned of the improvidence of the transaction nor told what steps could be taken to safeguard himself, George Gregg was never fully aware of what he was doing or its consequences and could not, in my view, be said to have fully understood the transaction. The case therefore in some of its essential features falls within the principle of the decision of Gavan Duffy J. in *Grealish v Murphy*, but as, in my view, the case falls more properly within the principles laid down in the other cases I have dealt with, I prefer to rest my judgment on the basis that the relations existing between the donor, on the one hand, and the donee and his mother, on the other, were such as to raise a presumption that the donee's mother and the donee acting through and with her had influence over the donor and that that presumption has not been rebutted by showing that in fact the gift was the spontaneous act of the donor acting under circumstances which enabled him to exercise an independent will and that the gift resulted from a free exercise of the donor's will.

The indenture of 28 September 1953, must, therefore, be set aside and the deed must be delivered up to be cancelled.

1. 14 Ves 273.
2. 4 My & C 277.
3. 36 ChD 145, at p. 171.
4. 8 Beav 439.
5. 31 Beav 491.
6. 3 Madd 181.
7. 15 Beav 234.

8. [1929] AC 127.
9. 3 D J & S 487 at p. 491.
10. 8 Ch App 430.
11. 17 LRI 641.
12. [1900] 1 Ch. 243.
13. [1946] IR 35.
14. 2 App Cas 814, at p. 823.

B. COHABITING PARTIES—THE OLD LAW

Hargreave v Everard (1856) 6 Ir Ch R 678

In this case a woman living in adultery with a married man assigned some of her property to secure a debt contracted by him. She later sought to have the transaction set aside.

In giving his judgment Lord St Leonards could not disguise his distaste at the conduct of the parties but he went on to consider the plea of undue influence:

. . . The question which I am obliged to consider is merely whether the petitioner is entitled to claim the interposition of this court to set aside the deed?

That interposition has been sought upon grounds which have been acted on in many cases in this court; but, from the first opening of this petition, I have felt great difficulty in applying the doctrine established in such cases to the present one. Those cases will be found, on examination, wholly distinct from the case now before the court. In the case of parties between whom certain recognised and lawful relations exist, calculated to give a strong influence to the one over the mind of the other, the court interferes on high grounds of public policy; not so much in many cases, for the sake of remedying injustice in the particular case, as for the sake of the relation itself, and to secure that those relations may stand free from risk, so that no one need fear to enter upon them, and that trustees, parents and guardians, may be relieved from any temptation to seek their own advantage in the discharge of their duties. Protected by this principle, the parent intrusts his child to a guardian, with the firm conviction that that guardian will not be allowed to make his office the means of working on the fears or affections of the child, in his own favour. So likewise, property may be given to a child, whom the law intrusts to the guardianship of the parent, and the giver may be sure that the parent will not be allowed, by any abuse of power or influence, to obtain any portion of the gift. Nor is the protection confined to the case of infancy. In legal relations between adult persons, in those, for example, of physician and patient, clergyman and penitent, and so on from one lawful relation to another, the law recognises the relation, and guards it in a similar manner. But all these are lawful relations, and necessary to the community; and this court therefore endeavours to keep them in a pure atmosphere, and to make it certain that the influence which arises out of them shall not be used for any purpose connected with the acquisition of property. But when we come to consider the relation which is put forward as the ground of relief in the present case, I know of no law, no public policy, which seeks to encourage it, or intervenes to protect one of the parties to such a relation from the other. In the eye of the law, they stand isolated from one another: there is no legal or recognised relation between them from which influence will be presumed. That, of course, does not exclude the consideration of any facts which may be proved to have occurred, and which may in themselves be strong enough to induce the court to set aside a transaction which has taken place between the parties. But the case made must be apart from the consideration of any connection between the parties, and facts must be shown strong enough to demonstrate the necessity of the court interfering to protect the weaker against the stronger. I do not see how these cases of parent and child, and the like, can be applied, considering the reasons upon which the decisions in these cases were grounded. The rule they establish was introduced for the purpose of protecting and encouraging certain relations recognised by the law, and has no bearing upon such a connection as is disclosed in this case. Here there is no legal presumption of influence at one side or the other, and conjecture is not sufficient ground to rely upon; nor could we with any certainty conjecture at which side the influence exists. It is much more frequently the woman who influences the man, than the man who influences the woman; and the cases in our books as to wills are much more frequently of the former class than the latter. No doubt, the influence may be brought to bear on the woman; but that is a question of fact to be made out from all the circumstances of the case, and not to be reasoned out by inferences from the existence of the connection. It is said, however, that the court would at all events interpose as against Mr Thomas himself, the great delinquent in this case, if this suit was instituted against him alone, on behalf of this unhappy woman, to refuse a restitution of the gifts which she has made to him. I am not sure of that. True it may be, that this court would not assist him to enforce any claim arising out of such a transaction, but it does not necessarily follow that it would set aside a deed which she had executed for his benefit, or give her relief even as against him. As I said before, it is difficult to say what influence there is, apart from the intensity of affection, which must exist in these cases. The cases which we have every day upon the separate property of married women are expressly in point. We have constantly suits by creditors of the husband, to enforce securities which they have got from the wife upon her separate estate; but who ever heard of a petition by a wife, to be relieved from such an engagement, on the ground of its having been procured through her affection for her husband? It is plain therefore there is a distinction recognised, and which we ought to bear in mind, though it may be sometimes difficult to make, between the effects of intense affection, such as a person in the position of the petitioner here may perhaps be presumed to feel, and what the law calls undue influence.

But let us examine the particular circumstances of the case itself. Here is a lady, not in her very early youth, but of mature intelligence, evidently not devoid of knowledge of business, possessed of and managing considerable property, who, making a case in her petition of delusion and weakness, in her affidavit avows, almost with exultation, the part which she has borne in the abandonment by this gentleman of the objects of his legitimate affection. Certainly, comparing her petition with her affidavit, and bearing in mind the case made by that petition, one is struck by the nervous language she uses, and the strong and business-like manner in which she speaks. It turns out also that this deed, instead of being procured, as alleged, by a sudden demand pressed unduly upon her, was the result of long deliberation and discussion. It forms part of the means adopted by this lady to relieve Mr Thomas from the consequences of the legal proceedings against him. It follows up a security, which is not impeached, given by her for the purpose of freeing him from imprisonment; for she gave her bond with warrant of attorney to the Sheriff, on Mr Thomas' arrest, not a month before the present matter took place. The suit against Mr Thomas went on, and there can be no doubt that the public hearing of the cause would have been an undesirable event both for her and him. It is pretty clear that, under these circumstances, the means of compromising the matter were suggested by him, or his sister, or his friends. It is to be lamented that this lady did not find some professional adviser to manage her affairs; but I do not wonder that no one would wish to take them up, seeing them involved with such a person. But she did find one gentleman, who, on her application to him, did caution and warn her not to give this security; and it is quite plain, from what she states, that she had a strong inclination and will in the other direction, that she determined to carry out the compromise, and that she acted on that determination.

C. Married Persons and Cohabitees—The New Law

Barclays Bank plc v O'Brien [1993] 4 All ER 417

Browne-Wilkinson L.J.:

My Lords, in this appeal your Lordships for the first time have to consider a problem which has given rise to reported decisions of the Court of Appeal on no less than eleven occasions in the last eight years and which has led to a difference of judicial view. Shortly stated the question is whether a bank is entitled to enforce against a wife an obligation to secure a debt owed by her husband to the bank where the wife has been induced to stand as surety for her husband's debt by the undue influence or misrepresentation of the husband.

The facts

The facts of the present case are very fully set out in the judgment of Scott L.J. in the Court of Appeal ([1992] 4 All ER 983, [1993] QB 109). I will only state them in summary form. Mr and Mrs O'Brien were husband and wife. The matrimonial home, 151 Farnham Lane, Slough, was in their joint names subject to a mortgage of approximately £25,000 to a building society. Mr O'Brien was a chartered accountant and had an interest in a company, Heathrow Fabrications Ltd. The company's bank account was at the Woolwich branch of Barclays Bank. In the first three months of 1987 the company frequently exceeded its overdraft facility of £40,000 and a number of its cheques were dishonoured on presentation. In discussions in April 1981 between Mr O'Brien and the manager of the Woolwich branch, Mr Tucker, Mr O'Brien told Mr Tucker that he was remortgaging the matrimonial home; Mr Tucker made a note that Mrs O'Brien might be a problem. The overdraft limit was raised at that stage to £60,000 for one month. Even though no additional security was provided, by 15 June 1987 the company's overdraft had risen to £98,000 and its cheques were again being dishonoured.

On 22 June 1987 Mr O'Brien and Mr Tucker agreed (1) that the company's overdraft limit would be raised to £135,000 reducing to £120,000 after three weeks, (2) that Mr O'Brien would guarantee the company's indebtedness and (3) that Mr O'Brien's liability would be secured by a second charge on the matrimonial home.

The necessary security documents were prepared by the bank. They consisted of an unlimited guarantee by Mr O'Brien of the company's liability and a legal charge by both Mr and Mrs O'Brien of the matrimonial home to secure any liability of Mr O'Brien to the bank. Mr Tucker arranged for the documents, together with a side letter, to be sent to the Burnham branch of the bank for execution by Mr and Mrs O'Brien. In a covering memorandum Mr Tucker requested the Burnham branch to advise the O'Briens as to the current level of the facilities afforded to the bank (£107,000) and the projected increase to £135,000. The Burnham branch was also asked to ensure that the O'Briens were 'fully aware of the nature of the documentation to be signed and advised that if they are in any doubt they should contact their solicitors before signing'.

Unfortunately the Burnham branch did not follow Mr Tucker's instructions. On 1 July Mr O'Brien alone signed the guarantee and legal charge at the Burnham branch, the document simply being produced for signature and witnessed by a clerk. On the following day Mrs O'Brien went to the branch with her husband. There were produced for signature by Mrs O'Brien the legal charge on the matrimonial home together with a side letter, which reads:

> We hereby agree acknowledge and confirm as follows: (1) That we have each received from you a copy of the guarantee dated 3 July 1987 (a copy of which is attached hereto) under which Nicholas Edward O'Brien guarantees the payment and discharge of all moneys and liabilities now or hereafter due owing or incurred by Heathrow Fabrications Ltd to you. (2) That the liability of the said Nicholas Edward O'Brien to you pursuant to the said guarantee is and will be secured by the legal charge dated 3 July 1987 over the property described above made between (1) Nicholas Edward O'Brien (2) Nicholas Edward O'Brien and Bridget Mary O'Brien and (3) Barclays Bank Plc. (3) That you recommended that we should obtain independent legal advice before signing this letter.

In fact the Burnham branch gave Mrs O'Brien no explanation of the effect of the documents. No one suggested that she should take independent legal advice. She did not read the documents or the side letter. She simply signed the legal charge and side letter and her signature was witnessed by the clerk. She was not given a copy of the guarantee.

The company did not prosper and by October 1987 its indebtedness to the bank was over £154,000. In November 1987 demand was made against Mr O'Brien under his guarantee. When the demand was not met possession proceedings under the legal charge were brought by the bank against Mr and Mrs O'Brien. Mrs O'Brien seeks to defend these proceedings by alleging that she was induced to execute the legal charge on the matrimonial home by the undue influence of Mr O'Brien and by his misrepresentation. The trial judge, Judge Marder Q.C., and the Court of Appeal rejected the claim based on undue influence: on the appeal to this House the claim based on undue influence is not pursued. However, the judge did find that Mr O'Brien had falsely represented to Mrs O'Brien that the charge was to secure only £60,000 and that even this liability would be released in a short time when the house was remortgaged. On those findings of fact the trial judge granted an order for possession against Mrs O'Brien holding that the bank could not be held responsible for the misrepresentation made by Mr O'Brien.

The decision of the Court of Appeal

The Court of Appeal (Purchas, Butler-Sloss and Scott L.JJ.) reversed his decision. The leading judgment in the Court of Appeal was given by Scott L.J., who found that there were two lines of authority. One line would afford no special protection to married women: the rights of the creditor bank could only be adversely affected by the wrongful acts of the principal debtor, the husband, in procuring the surety's liability if the principal debtor was acting as the agent of the creditor in procuring the surety to join or the creditor had knowledge of the relevant facts. I will call this theory 'the agency theory'. The other line of authority (which I will call 'the special equity theory') detected by Scott L.J. considers that equity affords special protection to a protected class of surety, *viz.* those where the relationship between the debtor and the surety is such that influence by the debtor over the surety and reliance by the surety on the debtor are natural features of the relationship. In cases where a surety is one of this protected class, the surety obligation is unenforceable by the creditor bank if (1) the relationship between the debtor and the surety was known to the creditor, (2) the surety's consent was obtained by undue influence or by misrepresentation or without 'an adequate understanding of the nature and effect of the transaction' and (3) the creditor had failed to take reasonable steps to ensure that the surety had given a true and informed consent to the transaction. The Court of Appeal preferred the special equity principle. They held that the legal charge on the O'Briens' matrimonial home was not enforceable by the bank against Mrs O'Brien save to the extent of the £60,000 which she had thought she was agreeing to secure.

Policy considerations

The large number of cases of this type coming before the courts in recent years reflects the rapid changes in social attitudes and the distribution of wealth which have recently occurred. Wealth is now more widely spread. Moreover a high proportion of privately owned wealth is invested in the matrimonial home. Because of the recognition by society of the equality of the sexes, the majority of matrimonial homes are now in the joint names of both spouses. Therefore in order to raise finance for the business enterprises of one or other of the spouses, the jointly owned home has become a main source of security. The provision of such security requires the consent of both spouses.

In parallel with these financial developments, society's recognition of the equality of the sexes has led to a rejection of the concept that the wife is subservient to the husband in the management of the family's finances. A number of the authorities reflect an unwillingness in the court to perpetuate law based on this outmoded concept. Yet, as Scott L.J. in the Court of Appeal rightly points out, although the concept of the ignorant wife leaving all financial decisions to the husband is outmoded, the practice does not yet coincide with the ideal (see [1992] 4 All ER 983 at 1008, [1993] QB 109 at 139). In a substantial proportion of marriages it is still the husband who has the business experience and the wife is willing to follow his advice without bringing a truly independent mind and will to bear on financial decisions. The number of recent cases in this field shows that in practice many wives are still subjected to, and yield to, undue influence by their husbands. Such wives can reasonably look to the law for some protection when their husbands have abused the trust and confidence reposed in them.

On the other hand, it is important to keep a sense of balance in approaching these cases. It is easy to allow sympathy for the wife who is threatened with the loss of her home at the suit of a rich bank to obscure an important public interest, viz. the need to ensure that the wealth currently tied up in the matrimonial home does not become economically sterile. If the rights secured to wives by the law renders vulnerable loans granted on the security of matrimonial homes, institutions will be unwilling to accept such security, thereby reducing the flow of loan capital to business enterprises. It is therefore essential that a law designed to protect the vulnerable does not render the matrimonial home unacceptable as security to financial institutions.

With these policy considerations in mind I turn to consider the existing state of the law. The whole of the modern law is derived from the decision of the Privy Council in *Turnbull & Co. v Duval* [1902] AC 429 which, as I will seek to demonstrate, provides an uncertain foundation. Before considering that case however, I must consider the law of undue influence which (though not directly applicable in the present case) underlies both *Turnbull v Duval* and most of the later authorities.

Undue influence

A person who has been induced to enter into a transaction by the undue influence of another (the wrongdoer) is entitled to set that transaction aside as against the wrongdoer. Such undue influence is either actual or presumed. In *Bank of Credit and*

Commerce International SA v Aboody (1988) |1992| 4 All ER 955 at 964, |1990| 1 QB 923 at 953 the Court of Appeal helpfully adopted the following classification.

Class 1: actual undue influence. In these cases it is necessary for the claimant to prove affirmatively that the wrongdoer exerted undue influence on the complainant to enter into the particular transaction which is impugned.

Class 2: presumed undue influence. In these cases the complainant only has to show, in the first instance, that there was a relationship of trust and confidence between the complainant and the wrongdoer of such a nature that it is fair to presume that the wrongdoer abused that relationship in procuring the complainant to enter into the impugned transaction. In class 2 cases therefore there is no need to produce evidence that actual undue influence was exerted in relation to the particular transaction impugned: once a confidential relationship has been proved, the burden then shifts to the wrongdoer to prove that the complainant entered into the impugned transaction freely, for example by showing that the complainant had independent advice. Such a confidential relationship can be established in two ways, *viz.*:

Class 2A. Certain relationships (for example solicitor and client, medical advisor and patient) as a matter of law raise the presumption that undue influence has been exercised.

Class 2B. Even if there is no relationship falling within class 2A, if the complainant proves the *de facto* existence of a relationship under which the complainant generally reposed trust and confidence in the wrongdoer, the existence of such relationship raises the presumption of undue influence. In a class 2B case therefore, in the absence of evidence disproving undue influence, the complainant will succeed in setting aside the impugned transaction merely by proof that the complainant reposed trust and confidence in the wrongdoer without having to prove that the wrongdoer exerted actual undue influence or otherwise abused such trust and confidence in relation to the particular transaction impugned.

As to dispositions by a wife in favour of her husband, the law for long remained in an unsettled state. In the nineteenth century some judges took the view that the relationship was such that it fell into class 2A, i.e. as a matter of law undue influence by the husband over the wife was presumed. It was not until the decisions in *Howes v Bishop* |1909| 2 KB 390 and *Bank of Montreal v Stuart* |1911| AC 120 that it was finally determined that the relationship of husband and wife did not as a matter of law raise a presumption of undue influence within class 2A. It is to be noted therefore that when *Turnbull v Duval* was decided in 1902 the question whether there was a class 2A presumption of undue influence as between husband and wife was still unresolved.

An invalidating tendency?

Although there is no class 2A presumption of undue influence as between husband and wife, it should be emphasised that in any particular case a wife may well be able to demonstrate that *de facto* she did leave decisions on financial affairs to her husband thereby bringing herself within class 2B, i.e. that the relationship between husband and wife in the particular case was such that the wife reposed confidence and trust in her husband in relation to their financial affairs and therefore undue influence is to be presumed. Thus, in those cases which still occur where the wife relies in all financial matters on her husband and simply does what he suggests, a presumption of undue influence within class 2B can be established solely from the proof of such trust and confidence without proof of actual undue influence.

In the appeal in CIBC *Mortgages plc v Pitt* [1993] 4 All ER 433 (judgment in which is to be given immediately after that in the present appeal) Mr Price Q.C. for the wife argued that in the case of transactions between husband and wife there was an 'invalidating tendency', i.e. although there was no class 2A presumption of undue influence, the courts were more ready to find that a husband had exercised undue influence over his wife than in other cases. Scott L.J. in the present case also referred to the law treating married women 'more tenderly' than others. This approach is based on dicta in early authorities. In *Grigby v Cox* (1750) 1 Ves Sen 517, 27 ER 1178 Lord Hardwicke L.C., whilst rejecting any presumption of undue influence, said that a court of equity 'will have more jealousy' over dispositions by a wife to a husband. In *Yerkey v Jones* (1939) 63 CLR 649 at 675 Dixon J. refers to this 'invalidating tendency'. He also refers (at 677) to the court recognising 'the opportunities which a wife's confidence in her husband gives him of unfairly or improperly procuring her to become surety'.

In my judgment this special tenderness of treatment afforded to wives by the courts is properly attributable to two factors. First, many cases may well fall into the class 2B category of undue influence because the wife demonstrates that she placed trust and confidence in her husband in relation to her financial affairs and therefore raises a presumption of undue influence. Second, the sexual and emotional ties between the parties provide a ready weapon for undue influence: a wife's true wishes can easily be overborne because of her fear of destroying or damaging the wider relationship between her and her husband if she opposes his wishes.

For myself, I accept that the risk of undue influence affecting a voluntary disposition by a wife in favour of a husband is greater than in the ordinary run of cases where no sexual or emotional ties affect the free exercise of the individual's will.

Undue influence, misrepresentation and third parties

Up to this point I have been considering the right of a claimant wife to set aside a transaction as against the wrongdoing husband when the transaction has been procured by his undue influence. But in surety cases the decisive question is whether the claimant wife can set aside the transaction, not against the wrongdoing husband, but against the creditor bank. Of course, if the wrongdoing husband is acting as agent for the creditor bank in obtaining the surety from the wife, the creditor will be fixed with the wrongdoing of its own agent and the surety contract can be set aside as against the creditor. Apart from this, if the creditor bank has notice, actual or constructive, of the undue influence exercised by the husband (and consequentially of the wife's equity to set aside the transaction) the creditor will take subject to that equity and the wife can set aside the transaction against the creditor (albeit a purchaser for value) as well as against the husband: see *Bainbrigge v Browne* (1881) 18 ChD 188 and BCCI *v Aboody* [1992] 4 All ER 955 at 980, [1990] 1 QB 923 at 973. Similarly, in cases such as the present where the wife has been induced to enter into the transaction by the husband's misrepresentation, her equity to set aside the transaction will be enforceable against the creditor if either the husband was acting as the creditor's agent or the creditor had actual or constructive notice.

Turnbull v Duval

This case provides the foundation of the modern law: the basis on which it was decided is, to say the least, obscure. Mr Duval owed three separate sums to a firm, Turnbull & Co., including £1,000 owed to the Jamaican branch for beer. Turnbulls' manager and agent in Jamaica was a Mr Campbell. Mr Campbell was also an executor and trustee of a will under which Mrs Duval had a beneficial interest. Mr Campbell threatened to stop supplying beer to Mr Duval unless security was given for the debts owed and, with Mr Campbell's knowledge, a document was prepared under which Mrs Duval charged her beneficial interest under the will to secure the payment of all debts owed by Mr Duval to Turnbull, i.e. not only the money owed for beer but all the debts. Mr Duval put pressure on Mrs Duval to sign the document. She was under the impression that the document was to secure the beer debt only.

The trial judge and the Court of Appeal in Jamaica held that the security document should be set aside as against Turnbulls on the sole ground that Mr Campbell, as executor of the will, was in a fiduciary capacity *vis-à-vis* his beneficiary, Mrs Duval, and his employers could not uphold the security document unless they could show that Mrs Duval was fully aware of what she was doing when she entered into it and did it freely. The Privy Council dismissed Turnbulls' appeal, Lord Lindley expressing the ratio in these terms ([1902] AC 429 at 434–5):

> In the face of such evidence, their Lordships are of opinion that it is quite impossible to uphold the security given by Mrs Duval. It is open to the double objection of having been obtained by a trustee from his *cestui que trust* by pressure through her husband and without independent advice, and of having been obtained by a husband from his wife by pressure and concealment of material facts. Whether the security could be upheld if the only ground for impeaching it was that Mrs Duval had no independent advice has not really to be determined. Their Lordships are not prepared to say it could not. But there is an additional and even stronger ground for impeaching it. It is, in their Lordships' opinion, quite clear that Mrs Duval was pressed by her husband to sign, and did sign, the document, which was very different from what she supposed it to be, and a document of the true nature of which she had no conception. It is impossible to hold that Campbell or Turnbull & Co. are unaffected by such pressure and ignorance. They left everything to Duval, and must abide the consequences.

The first ground mentioned by Lord Lindley (i.e. Campbell's breach of fiduciary duties) raises no problems. It is the second ground which has spawned the whole line of cases with which your Lordships are concerned. It raises two problems. The passage appears to suggest that Mr Duval had acted in some way wrongfully *vis-à-vis* his wife, and that Turnbulls who 'had left everything to Duval' were held liable for Duval's wrong. What was the wrongful act of Duval *vis-à-vis* his wife? Second, why did the fact that Turnbulls 'left everything to Duval' render them unable to enforce their security?

Turnbull v Duval: was the husband in breach of duty to his wife?

Thanks to the industry of counsel, we have seen the case lodged on the appeal to the Privy Council. The pleadings contain no allegation of undue influence or misrepresentation by Mr Duval. Mrs Duval did not in evidence allege actual or presumptive undue influence. The sole ground of decision in the courts below was Campbell's fiduciary position. There is no finding of undue influence against Mr Duval. No one appeared for Mrs Duval before the Privy Council. Therefore the second ground of decision sprang wholly from the board and Lord Lindley's speech gives little insight into their reasoning.

For myself I can only assume that, if the board considered that Mr Duval had committed a wrongful act *vis-à-vis* his wife, it proceeded on a mistaken basis. It will be remembered that in 1902 it had not been finally established that a presumption of undue influence within class 2A did not apply as between husband and wife. The board may therefore have been proceeding on the basis that the presumption of undue influence applied as between Mr and Mrs Duval. This was certainly one contemporary understanding of the *ratio decidendi*: see *Bishoff's Trustee v Frank* (1903) 89 LT 188. Alternatively, the board may have been mistakenly applying the heresy propounded by Lord Romilly to the effect that when a person has made a large voluntary disposition the burden is thrown on the party benefiting to show that a disposition was made fairly and honestly and in full understanding of the nature and consequences of the transaction: see *Hoghton v Hoghton* (1852) 15 Beav 278, 51 ER 545. Although this heresy has never been formally overruled, it has rightly been regarded as bad law for a very long time: see the account given by Dixon J. in *Yerkey v Jones* (1939) 63 CLR 649 at 678 et seq. It is impossible to find a sound basis for holding that Mrs Duval was entitled to set aside the transaction as against her husband. How then could she set it aside as against Turnbulls?

Turnbull v Duval: was the creditor under a direct duty to the wife?

It is the lack of any sound basis for holding that Mr Duval was guilty of a legal wrong for which Turnbulls were indirectly held liable which has led to the theory that the creditor, Turnbulls, were themselves in breach of some duty owed by them as creditors directly to the surety, Mrs Duval. No one has ever suggested that in the ordinary case of principal and surety the creditor owes any duty of case to the surety: in the normal case it is for the surety to satisfy himself as to the nature and extent of the obligations he is assuming. Therefore, it is said, there must be some special feature of the case where a wife stands surety for her husband's debt which gives rise to some special duty. This is the explanation of the decision of *Turnbull v Duval* given by Dixon J. in *Yerkey v Jones* (1939) 63 CLR 649 at 675, which, in turn, is the basis on which the Court of Appeal in the present case adopted the view that the law imposed on the creditor itself a duty to take steps to ensure not only that the husband had not used undue influence or made a misrepresentation but also that the wife had 'an adequate understanding of the nature and effect' of what she was doing. If this interpretation of *Turnbull v Duval* is correct, the law not only imposes on the creditor a duty *vis-à-vis* a particular class of surety (where ordinarily there would be none) but the extent of that duty is greater than that which, under the ordinary law, a husband would owe to his wife: a transaction between husband and wife cannot, in the absence of undue influence or misrepresentation, be set aside simply on the ground that the wife did not fully understand the transaction.

Turnbull v Duval: 'They left everything to Duval and must abide the consequences'

These words provide the only guidance as to the circumstances which led the board to set aside the surety agreement as against Turnbulls. In later cases the words have often been treated as indicating that Mr Duval (but not Turnbulls themselves) acted in breach of duty to Mrs Duval, that Mr Duval was Turnbulls' agent and that Turnbulls could not be in a better position than its agent. Quite apart from the difficulty of identifying what was the breach of duty committed by Mr Duval, the concept of Mr Duval having acted as agent for Turnbulls to procure his wife to become surety for the debt was artificial in *Turnbull v Duval* itself and in some of the later cases becomes even more artificial. As the Court of Appeal in this case point out, in the majority of cases the reality of the relationship is that, the creditor having required of the principal debtor that there must be a surety, the principal debtor on his own account in order to raise the necessary finance seeks to procure the support of the surety. In so doing he is acting for himself not for the creditor.

The subsequent authorities

The authorities in which the principle derived from *Turnbull v Duval* has been applied are fully analysed in the judgment of Scott L.J. and it is unnecessary to review them fully again.

Scott L.J. analyses the cases as indicating that down to 1985 there was no decision which indicated that the agency theory, rather than the special equity theory, was the basis of the decision in *Turnbull v Duval*. I agree. But that is attributable more to the application of the *Turnbull v Duval* principle than to any analysis of its jurisprudential basis. The only attempts to analyse the basis of the decision in *Turnbull v Duval* were the Australian decisions in *Bank of Victoria Ltd v Mueller* (1914) |1925| VLR 642 and the judgment of Dixon J. in *Yerkey v Jones* (1939) 63 CLR 649. The former decision was reached by applying the Romilly heresy which, as I have already said, is bad law. The judgment of Dixon J. undoubtedly supports the special equity theory.

From 1985 down to the decision of the Court of Appeal in the present case the decisions have all been based on the agency theory, i.e. that the principal debtor has acted in breach of duty to his wife, the surety, and that, if the principal debtor was acting as the creditor's agent but not otherwise, the creditor cannot be in any better position than its agent, the husband. In all the cases since 1985 the principal debtor has procured the agreement of the surety by a legal wrong (undue influence or misrepresentation). In all the cases emphasis was placed on the question whether the creditor was infected by the debtor's wrongdoing because the debtor was acting as the agent of the creditor in procuring the wife's agreement to stand as surety. I am unable to agree with Scott L.J. that the decision in *Kingsnorth Trust Ltd v Bell* |1986| 1 All ER 423, |1986| 1 WLR 119 was not based on the agency theory: Dillon L.J. expressly makes it a necessary condition that the creditor has entrusted to the husband the task of obtaining his wife's signature (see |1986| 1 All ER 423 at 427, |1986| 1 WLR 119 at 123).

However, in four of the cases since 1985 attention has been drawn to the fact that, even in the absence of agency, if the debtor has been guilty of undue influence or misrepresentation the creditor may not be able to enforce the surety contract if the creditor had notice, actual or constructive, of the debtor's conduct: see *Avon Finance Co. Ltd v Bridger* (1979) |1985| 2 All ER 281 at 287 per Brandon L.J., *Coldunell Ltd v Gallon* |1986| 1 All ER 429 at 439, |1986| QB 1184 at 1199, *Midland Bank plc v Shephard* |1988| 3 All ER 17 at 23 and *BCCI v Aboody* |1992| 4 All ER 955 at 980, |1990| 1 QB 923 at 973. As will appear, in my view it is the proper application of the doctrine of notice which provides the key to finding a principled basis for the law.

Accordingly, the present law is built on the unsure foundations of *Turnbull v Duval*. Like most law founded on obscure and possibly mistaken foundations it has developed in an artificial way, giving rise to artificial distinctions and conflicting decisions. In my judgment your Lordships should seek to restate the law in a form which is principled, reflects the current requirements of society and provides as much certainty as possible.

Conclusions

(a) *Wives*
My starting point is to clarify the basis of the law. Should wives (and perhaps others) be accorded special rights in relation to surety transactions by the recognition of a special equity applicable only to such persons engaged in such transactions? Or should they enjoy only the same protection as they would enjoy in relation to their other dealings? In my judgment, the special equity theory should be rejected. First, I can find no basis in principle for affording special protection to a limited class in relation to one type of transaction only. Second, to require the creditor to prove knowledge and understanding by the wife in all cases is to reintroduce by the back door either a presumption of undue influence of class 2A (which has been decisively rejected) or the Romilly heresy (which has long been treated as bad law). Third, although Scott L.J. found that there were two lines of cases one of which supported the special equity theory, on analysis although many decisions are not inconsistent

with that theory the only two cases which support it are *Yerkey v Jones* and the decision of the Court of Appeal in the present case. Finally, it is not necessary to have recourse to a special equity theory for the proper protection of the legitimate interests of wives as I will seek to show.

In my judgment, if the doctrine of notice is properly applied, there is no need for the introduction of a special equity in these types of cases. A wife who has been induced to stand as a surety for her husband's debts by his undue influence, misrepresentation or some other legal wrong has an equity as against him to set aside that transaction. Under the ordinary principles of equity, her right to set aside that transaction will be enforceable against third parties (e.g. against a creditor) if either the husband was acting as the third party's agent or the third party had actual or constructive notice of the facts giving rise to her equity. Although there may be cases where, without artificiality, it can properly be held that the husband was acting as the agent of the creditor in procuring the wife to stand as surety, such cases will be of very rare occurrence. The key to the problem is to identify the circumstances in which the creditor will be taken to have had notice of the wife's equity to set aside the transaction.

The doctrine of notice lies at the heart of equity. Given that there are two innocent parties, each enjoying rights, the earlier right prevails against the later right if the acquirer of the later right knows of the earlier rights (actual notice) or would have discovered it had he taken proper steps (constructive notice). In particular, if the party asserting that he takes free of the earlier rights of another knows of certain facts which put him on inquiry as to the possible existence of the rights of that other and he fails to make such inquiry or take such other steps as are reasonable to verify whether such earlier right does or does not exist, he will have constructive notice of the earlier right and take subject to it. Therefore where a wife has agreed to stand surety for her husband's debts as a result of undue influence or misrepresentation, the creditor will take subject to the wife's equity to set aside the transaction if the circumstances are such as to put the creditor on inquiry as to the circumstances in which she agreed to stand surety.

It is at this stage that, in my view, the 'invalidating tendency' or the law's 'tender treatment' of married women, becomes relevant. As I have said above in dealing with undue influence, this tenderness of the law towards married women is due to the fact that, even today, many wives repose confidence and trust in their husbands in relation to their financial affairs. This tenderness of the law is reflected by the fact that voluntary dispositions by the wife in favour of her husband are more likely to be set aside than other dispositions by her: a wife is more likely to establish presumed undue influence of class 2B by her husband than by others because, in practice, many wives do repose in their husbands trust and confidence in relation to their financial affairs. Moreover the informality of business dealings between spouses raises a substantial risk that the husband has not accurately stated to the wife the nature of the liability she is undertaking, i.e. he has misrepresented the position, albeit negligently.

Therefore, in my judgment a creditor is put on inquiry when a wife offers to stand surety for her husband's debts by the combination of two factors: (a) the transaction is on its face not to the financial advantage of the wife; and (b) there is a substantial risk in transactions of that kind that, in procuring the wife to act as surety, the husband has committed a legal or equitable wrong that entitles the wife to set aside the transaction.

It follows that, unless the creditor who is put on inquiry takes reasonable steps to satisfy himself that the wife's agreement to stand surety has been properly obtained, the creditor will have constructive notice of the wife's rights.

What, then are the reasonable steps which the creditor should take to ensure that it does not have constructive notice of the wife's rights, if any? Normally the reasonable steps necessary to avoid being fixed with constructive notice consist of making inquiry of the person who may have the earlier right (i.e. the wife) to see whether such right is asserted. It is plainly impossible to require of banks and other financial institutions that they should inquire of one spouse whether he or she has been unduly influenced or misled by the other. But in my judgment the creditor, in order to avoid being fixed with constructive notice, can reasonably be expected to take steps to bring home to the wife the risk she is running by standing as surety and to advise her to take independent advice. As to past transactions, it will depend on the facts of each case whether the steps taken by the creditor satisfy this test. However for the future in my judgment a creditor will have satisfied these requirements if it insists that the wife attend a private meeting (in the absence of the husband) with a representative of the creditor at which she is told of the extent of her liability as surety, warned of the risk she is running and urged to take independent legal advice. If these steps are taken in my judgment the creditor will have taken such reasonable steps as are necessary to preclude a subsequent claim that it had constructive notice of the wife's rights. I should make it clear that I have been considering the ordinary case where the creditor knows only that the wife is to stand surety for her husband's debts. I would not exclude exceptional cases where a creditor has knowledge of further facts which render the presence of undue influence not only possible but probable. In such cases, the creditor to be safe will have to insist that the wife is separately advised.

I am conscious that in treating the creditor as having constructive notice because of the risk of class 2B undue influence or misrepresentation by the husband I may be extending the law as stated by Fry J. in *Bainbrigge v Browne* (1881) 18 ChD 188 at 197 and the Court of Appeal in BCCI *v Aboody* |1992| 4 All ER 955 at 980, |1990| 1 QB 923 at 973. Those cases suggest that for a third party to be affected by constructive notice of presumed undue influence the third party must actually know of the circumstances which give rise to a presumption of undue influence. In contrast, my view is that the risk of class 2B undue influence or misrepresentation is sufficient to put the creditor on inquiry. But my statement accords with the principles of notice: if the known facts are such as to indicate the possibility of an adverse claim that is sufficient to put a third party on inquiry.

If the law is established as I have suggested, it will hold the balance fairly between on the one hand the vulnerability of the wife who relies implicitly on her husband and, on the other hand, the practical problems of financial institutions asked to accept a secured or unsecured surety obligation from the wife for her husband's debts. In the context of suretyship, the wife will not have any right to disown her obligations just because subsequently she proves that she did not fully understand the transaction: she will, as in all other areas of her affairs, be bound by her obligations unless her husband has, by misrepresentation, undue influence or other wrong, committed an actionable wrong against her. In the normal case, a financial institution will be able to lend with confidence in reliance on the wife's surety obligation provided that it warns her (in the absence of the husband) of the amount of her potential liability and of the risk of standing surety and advises her to take independent advice.

|Counsel| for the bank urged that this is to impose too heavy a burden on financial institutions. I am not impressed by this submission. The report by Professor Jack's Review Committee on *Banking Services: Law and Practice* (1989), (Cmnd. 622) recommended that prospective guarantors should be adequately warned of the legal effects and possible consequences of their guarantee and of the importance of receiving independent advice. Pursuant to this recommendation, the Code of Banking Practice (adopted by banks and building societies in March 1992) provides in para. 12.1 as follows:

Banks and building societies will advise private individuals proposing to give them a guarantee or other security for another person's liabilities that: (i) by giving the guarantee or third party security he or she might become liable instead of or as well as that other person; (ii) he or she should seek independent legal advice before entering into the guarantee or third party security. Guarantees and other third party security forms will contain a clear and prominent notice to the above effect.

Thus good banking practice (which applies to all guarantees, not only those given by a wife) largely accords with what I consider the law should require when a wife is offered as surety. The only further substantial step required by law beyond that good practice is that the position should be explained by the bank to the wife in a personal interview. I regard this as being essential because a number of the decided cases show that written warnings are often not read and are sometimes intercepted by the husband. It does not seem to me that the requirement of a personal interview imposes such an additional administrative burden as to render the bank's position unworkable.

(b) *Other persons*

I have hitherto dealt only with the position where a wife stands surety for her husband's debts. But in my judgment the same principles are applicable to all other cases where there is an emotional relationship between cohabitees. The 'tenderness' shown by the law to married women is not based on the marriage ceremony but reflects the underlying risk of one cohabitee exploiting the emotional involvement and trust of the other. Now that unmarried cohabitation, whether heterosexual or homosexual, is widespread in our society, the law should recognise this. Legal wives are not the only group which are now exposed to the emotional pressure of cohabitation. Therefore if, but only if, the creditor is aware that the surety is cohabiting with the principal debtor, in my judgment the same principles should apply to them as apply to husband and wife.

In addition to the cases of cohabitees, the decision of the Court of Appeal in *Avon Finance Co. Ltd v Bridger* [1985] 2 All ER 281 shows (rightly in my view) that other relationships can give rise to a similar result. In that case a son, by means of misrepresentation, persuaded his elderly parents to stand surety for his debts. The surety obligation was held to be unenforceable by the creditor *inter alia* because to the bank's knowledge the parents trusted the son in their financial dealings. In my judgment that case was rightly decided: in a case where the creditor is aware that the surety reposes trust and confidence in the principal debtor in relation to his financial affairs, the creditor is put on inquiry in just the same way as it is in relation to husband and wife.

Summary

I can therefore summarise my views as follows. Where one cohabitee has entered into an obligation to stand as surety for the debts of the other cohabitee and the creditor is aware that they are cohabitees: (1) the surety obligation will be valid and enforceable by the creditor unless the suretyship was procured by the undue influence, misrepresentation or other legal wrong of the principal debtor; (2) if there has been undue influence, misrepresentation or other legal wrong by the principal debtor, unless the creditor has taken reasonable steps to satisfy himself that the surety entered into the obligation freely and in knowledge of the true facts, the creditor will be unable to enforce the surety obligation because he will be fixed with constructive notice of the surety's right to set aside the transaction; (3) unless there are special exceptional circumstances, a creditor will have taken such reasonable steps to avoid being fixed with constructive notice if the creditor warns the surety (at a meeting not attended by the principal debtor) of the amount of her potential liability and of the risks involved and advises the surety to take independent legal advice.

I should make it clear that in referring to the husband's debts I include the debts of a company in which the husband (but not the wife) has a direct financial interest.

The decision of this case

Applying those principles to this case, to the knowledge of the bank Mr and Mrs O'Brien were man and wife. The bank took a surety obligation from Mrs O'Brien, secured on the matrimonial home, to secure the debts of a company in which Mr O'Brien was interested but in which Mrs O'Brien had no direct pecuniary interest. The bank should therefore have been put on inquiry as to the circumstances in which Mrs O'Brien had agreed to stand as surety for the debt of her husband. If the Burnham branch had properly carried out the instructions from Mr Tucker of the Woolwich branch, Mrs O'Brien would have been informed that she and the matrimonial home were potentially liable for the debts of a company which had an existing liability of £107,000 and which was to be afforded an overdraft facility of £135,000. If she had been told this, it would have counteracted Mr O'Brien's misrepresentation that the liability was limited to £60,000 and would last for only three weeks. In addition according to the side letter she would have been recommended to take independent legal advice.

Unfortunately Mr Tucker's instructions were not followed and to the knowledge of the bank (through the clerk at the Burnham branch) Mrs O'Brien signed the documents without any warning of the risks or any recommendation to take legal advice. In the circumstances the bank (having failed to take reasonable steps) is fixed with constructive notice of the wrongful misrepresentation made by Mr O'Brien to Mrs O'Brien. Mrs O'Brien is therefore entitled as against the bank to set aside the legal charge on the matrimonial home securing her husband's liability to the bank.

For these reasons I would dismiss the appeal with costs.

(Templeman, Lowry, Slynn of Hedley and Woolf L.JJ. agreed.)

Note

1. In CIBC *Mortgages plc v Pitt* [1993] 4 All ER 433, (mentioned by Lord Browne-Wilkinson in his judgment in *Barclays Bank plc v O'Brien* at p. 601 above) their Lordships found on the facts that a wife who had consented to remortgaging the family home under pressure from her husband, was the victim of undue influence. In such a case the wife is not required to prove that the transaction was manifestly disadvantageous to her, their Lordships reasoning that the victim of fraud may still plead the fraud even if the transaction is beneficial to that person. However, the House of Lords did not set the transaction aside *vis-à-vis* the bank because the person exercising undue influence was in no sense acting as the agent of the bank and the transaction itself was a normal banking transaction.

2. Irish case-law on this matter is both indirect and somewhat in need of review, viz. *Northern Banking Co. v Carpenter* [1931] IR 268. The Scottish court of session in *Mumford v Bank of Scotland* TLR 4 August 1994, has recently had occasion to consider *Barclays Bank plc v O'Brien*. Lord Johnston observed that *O'Brien* seemed to create a presumption in favour of the wife of a wrong having been committed against her in appropriate circumstances,

particularly when the transaction did not benefit her *vis-à-vis* debts being guaranteed and, as a whole, the transaction was to her disadvantage. Lord Johnston declined to impose any duty on a bank in circumstances where the bank was in ignorance of the circumstances surrounding the transaction, observing that O'*Brien* was based on English equitable principles and did not represent the law in Scotland.

D. Undue Influence as of Fact

McCrystal v O'Kane [1986] NI 123

Murray J.:

This is a purchaser's action for specific performance of a written contract dated 22 October 1984 ('the contract') for the sale of about 25 acres of farm land in the townland of Shriff in the Omagh area of Co. Tyrone: The contract is in the Law Society's printed 'Particulars and Conditions of Sale' form. The plaintiff purchaser is a nephew of the defendant and farms some 170 acres of land (some of it leased) in the Omagh area: he is thirty eight, unmarried and lives with his mother. The defendant vendor, who is his uncle (on his mother's side) is also a bachelor and has just passed his sixty first birthday: before the present dispute between the parties he had a room in the house where the plaintiff and his mother live and the two men were on good terms with each other.

The land the subject of the contract ('the contract land') had not been farmed by the defendant for about ten years before the contract, his practice having been to let it each year in conacre to his brother Peter. The defendant himself does casual labouring work both on farms and farm buildings and before the present dispute often worked for the plaintiff. The contract land is about two hundred yards from land which the plaintiff has on lease and his object in acquiring the contract land is to work it in conjunction with that leased land.

The late Mr T. T. Montague solicitor (who died in July last) acted for both parties and witnessed their signatures to the contract which was executed in the evening of Monday 22 October 1984 at an office which Mr Montague maintained in his own home at Fintona. Because of his illness the evidence of Mr Montague was taken on commission in May last and later in this judgment I shall be referring to a transcript of it.

The contract fixed a price of £20,000 for the contract land but it was unusual in that it provided for payment by instalments over ten years in the following words: ' . . . payable interest free by equal annual payments of £2,000, the first said payments to be made on 30 November 1984 and each subsequent payment on the anniversary of the said date in each succeeding year. The purchaser shall be entitled to possession as from 30 November 1984.' The completion date is stated to be 30 November 1984 and the endorsed memorandum provided for a deposit of £2,000 to be paid by the plaintiff to Mr Montague.

The original defence delivered on 18 March 1986, in addition to denying any contract, pleaded the Statute of Frauds, and also pleaded the supercession of the contract by an oral agreement of 29 October 1984 under which (it was alleged) the plaintiff was to pay the £20,000 purchase price in one lump sum. At the beginning of the trial, however, |counsel| for the defendant, sought leave to amend the defence by adding two additional paragraphs pleading duress and undue influence and incapacity to contract because of drink, the texts of the two paragraphs being as follows:

5. If any agreement existed as alleged in para. 2 of the Statement of Claim, which is denied, the defendant says that it was made under duress and as a result of undue influence by the plaintiff.

Particulars of Duress and Undue Influence

(i) Since in or around the death of the defendant's friend Mr Frank O'Hagan, who died on 11 September 1984 the defendant commenced drinking heavily and persistently throughout the rest of that year and into 1985.

(ii) The plaintiff was fully aware of the defendant's spate of heavy drinking at that time and the effect it was having on him.

(iii) In or around 22 October 1984, whilst the defendant was drinking as aforesaid, the plaintiff, after having previously failed to purchase the property which is the subject of this action, induced the defendant to accompany him to meet their mutual solicitor to draw up terms of a sale of the said property.

(iv) The defendant says that at that time he was not fully in control of his mental faculties and that this was known to the plaintiff who wrongfully and fraudulently took advantage of this situation.

6. The defendant says that any agreement entered into on 22 October 1984 was null and void by reason of the incapacity of the defendant arising from his drinking at that time.

|Counsel| for the plaintiff, did not object to these amendments and I allowed them to be made.

I must say, however, that the explanation given in the witness box by the defendant himself for these late amendments—an explanation based on his alleged heavy drinking—struck me as quite unbelievable. Since the dispute started the defendant has (it appears) at all material times lived in the house of a very elderly widow, a Mrs Mary O'Hagan, who apparently does not hold with strong drink and who (he said) expressed objection to the publication in court of the fact that a heavy consumer of alcohol, in the person of the defendant himself, was lodging in her house. However, subsequent to the delivery of the original defence (said the defendant) he discovered and explained to the widow that details of cases in the courts here are not published in the press and this explanation (he alleged) cleared the way for his putting forward the defences based on his drinking. I feel that comment on this explanation would be superfluous. I do not doubt that on occasions—mainly weekends and at wakes and weddings—the defendant drinks excessively but I reject as without merit his late defences based on his alleged excessive drinking. The onus is on him to establish such defences, no expert evidence of any kind was called, and his own evidence did not, in my view, come anywhere near to proving either (a) that because of drink he did not know what he was doing when he signed the contract or (b) that the plaintiff took any advantage whatever of his alleged lack of control of his mental faculties due to drink. The cross-examination of the plaintiff by |counsel| suggested that the defendant is a man who is slow in the uptake but the plaintiff rejected the suggestion and I saw no sign of it at all. I must add that I had the opportunity of observing the defendant over two days in court—including a substantial period in the witness box—and at all times he appeared to me to be as sober as the judge who tried the case.

The plaintiff's account of the formation of the contract was this; about the end of September 1984 he had discussed with the defendant the possibility of leasing the contract land for ten years at a rent which was agreed at £800 *per annum*, the defendant having originally asked for £1,000 *per annum*, but the long standing conacre letting arrangements for the land between the defendant and his brother Peter was an obstacle which in fact prevented the lease being made. However, about two weeks before the date of the contract, i.e. in the first week of October, the plaintiff called at Mrs O'Hagan's house to see the defendant and my note of the plaintiff's evidence from this point on is as follows: 'I said "Would you ever sell it [i.e. the contract land] to me? I can't pay for it now but could pay a reasonable price over a number of years" and I asked him to put it over a number of years. He said "I'd need £20,000 at that rate; would five years be enough?" I said "ten years would help me." I agreed £20,000. It was in Mrs O'Hagan's house: she was there, and probably heard the discussion . . . I left to go home at 11.30 p.m.' The plaintiff explained that subsequently he telephoned his solicitor, Mr Montague, told him about the purchase, and asked him to act in the matter, the first step required being a meeting between the plaintiff, the defendant and Mr Montague. Mr Montague agreed to this and proposed the evening of Monday 22 October for the meeting, the place being the office he maintained in his home at Fintona. The plaintiff said that in the afternoon of that day he went over to O'Hagan's where he saw the defendant who showed him over a nearby house in which he (the defendant) was working for a contractor (also called Montague) who was renovating the house for Frank O'Hagan, the son of the widow Mary O'Hagan. The plaintiff told the defendant of the arrangement with Mr Montague, the solicitor, and the defendant agreed to the plaintiff's collecting him by car that evening and going with him to Mr Montague's office. The plaintiff's further evidence was that he did in fact collect the defendant that evening and go with him to Mr Montague's office in Fintona. The plaintiff also gave evidence of Mr Montague asking the defendant if he had a solicitor and of the defendant saying 'The one solicitor will do the two of us.' The plaintiff also said that Mr Montague asked about interest and he (the plaintiff) told him that interest was included in the price of £20,000. According to the plaintiff, Mr Montague then prepared the contract, read out its terms, and had it signed by the plaintiff and defendant whose signatures were witnessed by Mr Montague. The plaintiff went on to describe a discussion with the defendant at O'Hagan's about a week later when the defendant spoke of a conversation which he (the defendant) had had over a drink with the 'dole man' [i.e. a supplement-ary benefit office official] to the effect that the dole man had told him that he would qualify for benefit if he got rid of the contract land but that the deal he had done of £20,000 over ten years was a bad one. If he had received the £20,000 into his hand he (the defendant) would have been able to buy a house and even with it he would qualify for benefit. The plaintiff said that he suggested to the defendant that he (the defendant) should build himself a house and that he (the plaintiff) would give him a site for it on the contract land. The plaintiff also gave evidence of telling the defendant that he (the plaintiff) did not have £20,000 to give to the defendant for the contract land but that out of the £2,000 *per annum* the defendant would get under the contract he could pay for a house. The plaintiff explained that he saw the defendant three or four times in the period following this conversation but on Monday 17 December 1984—two days before the plaintiff left for a holiday in America—he had his final discussion with the defendant when the latter told him that he was not selling because 'he [the defendant] never got the £20,000.' The plaintiff replied that the defendant was only to get £2,000 and how could he in any event expect to get money until the title deeds were available. The reference to the title deeds arose in this way: the defendant's deeds for the contract land had earlier been given by the defendant to another firm of solicitors, Messrs Orr and Rountree of Omagh, in connection with a transaction under which the defendant had bought a caravan, and although at the time of the contract the defendant had signed an authorisation to Mr Montague to collect his deeds, they could not in fact be found in Messrs Orr and Rountree's office and were not found until the following March. Despite the fact that the plaintiff had paid Mr Montague the deposit of £2,000 required by the contract and had paid it on the signing of the contract Mr Montague did not pass it on to the defendant on 30 November, the completion date, because the deeds had not been found at that date and not surprisingly the solicitor was not willing to part with his purchaser-client's money otherwise than in return for the vendor's deeds of the property sold.

Under cross-examination the plaintiff admitted that he knew the defendant did drink and did use any money he had on drink but he said that weekends were his drinking periods and that 22 October 1984, the day on which the contract was signed, was a Monday (a working day), and that the defendant at the time had no drink on him and was fully aware of what was happening. He rejected counsel's suggestions that the defendant 'was slow in his understanding' and he denied 'pulling the wool over the defendant's eyes' or taking any advantage of him. He said that in a down payment transaction for the contract land he would not have agreed to pay £20,000, but probably would have been willing to pay £12,000–£14,000. He also said that there were 14 or 15 acres of good land in the 25 acres and that £1,000 per acre for good land in the area was a possible price at the time. He also agreed that at auction the defendant might have done better than under the contract. He firmly rejected counsel's suggestion that subsequent to the contract a new deal had been made under which he (the plaintiff) was to pay the £20,000 in one lump sum.

In the witness box the defendant said that he had been a drinker for seventeen or eighteen years and that on occasions he drank spirits and stout from morning till night. His account of the suggested leasing of the land to the plaintiff substantially agreed with that of the plaintiff but his account of the oral part of the sale was as follows:

> One night he [the plaintiff] called in [at O'Hagan's] and said 'I will give you £20,000 for your land.' I was boozing and I didn't know what to do . . . I said that was all right i.e. it was sold: the next thing he said was 'I have no money can you give it to me for ten years at £2,000 a year.' I said OK that's all right. We had an agreement that he would come some night and take me to a solicitor: he took me to a solicitor in Fintona Mr Montague about 8.30 or 9 p.m. one night. It was a Monday. I was in not very good shape, just hard to describe, my stomach was rumbling and I didn't want to sit: I wanted to keep walking. I was drinking vodka and white. I knew I was going to settle a farm of land. As regards my state of mind I really didn't care—that was the way it was—what I done. I signed for the farm of land to sell it to my nephew, £20,000 over ten years.

The defendant went on to explain that he was glad to get out through the door of Mr Montague's house and that his stomach was 'revving' as he put it. He said he felt anything but good and went out and lay across the bonnet of the plaintiff's car and vomited a little. He said he stayed there until the plaintiff came out but he did not pass any remarks on the contract and he then added 'I wasn't in a way annoyed about it'. [I interpose the comment that the plaintiff was not cross-examined about the alleged incident on the bonnet of his car and therefore did not have an opportunity of saying whether he agreed that that took place or not.] The defendant's evidence continued as follows:

> The plaintiff arrived back one night at O'Hagan's about a week later and he came in and got tea: the old woman asked him when was this man [i.e. the defendant himself] getting his big lump of money to borrow to drink and maybe leave her. The plaintiff said that he was going to get it [i.e. the big lump of money] on 30 November.

She said that he would start his drinking. I talked about buying a house; the next thing he said was that I had no stamps on and I was going to get no dole money. I was not then getting dole money—no stamps. He asked me then to sign him the place and I would get dole: 'Sign you me the place and you'll get dole' that's what he said. I didn't see no other signing or talked about at all—then he came to another agreement that he didn't bother signing. That he'd put up the £20,000 on 30 November and collect me at Mrs O'Hagan's the same as he had done before and take me up to the solicitor at Fintona to get the £20,000. The agreement of £20,000 over the years was going to be cut out. He was going to give me £20,000 and I could buy a house (he said) and this would still get me the dole. I am telling the truth, the absolute truth. I had a conversation with the dole man in Omagh. He (i.e. the dole man) said for me to buy a house—this was before the new agreement to pay £20,000 the Saturday before that . . .

The defendant, after describing his conversation with the dole man continued:

The plaintiff never came on 30 but on 17 December which was a Monday the plaintiff landed in [i.e. into O'Hagan's] and asked me to go up to work for him . . . I asked him about not getting the money on the thirtieth and he seemed to fool 'A man like you wouldn't be looking for money'. He gave no explanation of why he did not come on the thirtieth. I told him the deal was off with me, that is to say the selling of the land was off . . . I have a couple of reasons why I am not going through with the deal. (1) I don't want the money. (2) I don't want to have no deal with McCrystal any more. Even I got the £20,000 it just could be the end of me. I would start taking too much booze. I think the plaintiff was too cheeky coming down—he knew that I was drinking down there [i.e. at O'Hagan's] and I still thought why did he not buy the land of me that night we went to my brother's—buy the land of me at £20,000 that night. He didn't talk about buying the land till he got me drinking down at O'Hagans . . .

Under cross-examination the defendant said that the plaintiff promised to give him the £20,000 on 30 November and he was then asked if he did not know of the problem about the deeds; his answer was: 'No problem about the deeds. The plaintiff phoned Montague who told him there was no problem about the deeds.' In answer to a question as to whether he had told anyone about the alleged change in the contract he said he had told no one. His answer about the deeds does not square with the letter he wrote to Mr Montague on 4 March 1985 in which, inter alia, he wrote: 'I am now advising you to take action against Orr and Rountree for loss of deeds and set back of sale of farm on 30 November.'

I must now refer to some passages in Mr Montague's evidence on commission since certain important points clearly emerge from them. First, as one would expect, Mr Montague advised the defendant to be separately represented but the defendant refused to adopt this course: 'When I ascertained the nature of the transaction I advised Owen O'Kane that Peter McCrystal was my client and it would be in his own interest that though I could represent him he should have separate representation.' Then there was this question to Mr Montague:

'What was his attitude?' and the answer was: 'He did not require separate represent-ation. He and his nephew were very close and friendly and there was no need for another solicitor: subsequently when I learned of the nature of the purchase money I again advised Owen O'Kane relative to separate representation and advices consider-ing his age, method of payment and the question of interest.'

Mr Montague was told by the defendant himself that he (the defendant) had a drink problem:

> Mr Owen O'Kane did not want any interest stating that his nephew had always been very good to him and he did not expect any change if he was short of a pound or two.
>   It was made clear to me at this stage by Owen O'Kane that he had a drink problem and he did not want nor could he handle the purchase monies *in toto*.
> . . .
> Q. Did they ask you your advice in relation to the adequacy of the purchase price?
> A. Obviously [due to] the fact that the payment was over such a long period I indicated to both parties that Mr Peter McCrystal was getting a substantial advantage.

On the issue of whether the parties agreed to substitute a lump-sum contract for the contract (i.e. for the instalment contract) I come down in favour of the plaintiff, that is to say, that they did not do so. In general I much preferred his evidence to that of the defendant. Some of the defendant's evidence was obviously untruthful: for example para. 5(1) of the amended defence referred to the defendant's heavy and persistent drinking from 11 September 1984 (the date of the death of the defendant's friend O'Hagan, Mary O'Hagan's husband) for the rest of the year and beyond, and in direct evidence the defendant actually said that he did not work from September to Christmas of that year. This plainly was an untruthful answer as indeed emerged from his own witness, Frank O'Hagan (the son of the deceased O'Hagan) who told the court that the defendant had worked on his (Frank O'Hagan's) house for four months from August to Christmas of that year, and indeed the defendant, shortly after his original statement, contradicted himself. Again he quite seriously suggested that the plaintiff asked him to convey the contract land to the plaintiff for nothing, as part of a plan to enable the defendant to obtain the dole. To be more specific on this central issue, I must say that the defendant's evidence of the substitution of a lump-sum contract, did not at all have the ring of truth in my ears. he said that the plaintiff did not bother about signing anything for the alleged new contract and that the plaintiff simply said that he would pay him (the defendant) the £20,000 on 30 November. I cannot believe that the plaintiff, who was careful to have the original bargain put into legal form and witnessed by his solicitor, was going to part with £20,000 to the defendant without a properly drawn fresh contract to protect himself and, moreover, a fresh contract which varied or in some appropriate way dealt with the then existing contract which had been signed by the two parties on 22 October. There is no evidence whatever that either the defendant or the plaintiff ever told Mr Montague about the substitution of a lump-sum contract. Again it is clear that the defendant's deeds were not found until March 1985 and if, in the absence of the deeds, Mr Montague would not let his client, the plaintiff, part with the £2,000 deposit, it is highly unlikely that in the absence of those deeds and any proper contract the plaintiff, without any advice, was going to part with £20,000.

Despite the fact that undervalue was not pleaded even in the amended defence [counsel for the defendant] led evidence of this through a valuer, one McLernon. [Counsel for the plaintiff] despite being put at a disadvantage by this move, did not ask me to rule out the valuer's evidence. I gave [counsel] the opportunity overnight to take instructions upon the value matter and I also indicated that I would allow him to call rebutting evidence if necessary; but in the result he was unable to have a valuer present in court the second day of the trial to give evidence for the plaintiff, and had to confine himself to cross-examining the defendant's valuer. Mr McLernon said that in his opinion £20,000 was light for the contract land and he was of the opinion that

£28,000 was a possible price in the market in October 1984. I need not pursue the question of whether a lump-sum of £20,000 in October 1984 would have been an undervalue because I have no doubt whatever that at that time £20,000 payable at £2,000 a year over ten years was a substantial undervalue and a distinct advantage to the plaintiff. I do not however hold that it was so gross an undervalue as to be evidence itself of fraud and [counsel for the defendant] did not attempt to say it was. I shall return later in this judgment to the undervalue point.

I now list the following further conclusions as relevant to my ultimate decision:

(1) There was no acceptable evidence (a) that drink played any part either in the defendant's oral agreement to sell the contract land to the plaintiff for £20,000 over ten years, or in his signing the contract itself, or (b) that the plaintiff at any material time found the defendant affected by drink and used undue influence to induce him to make the oral agreement, to sign the contract, or to take advantage of the defendant in any way whatever.

(2) When the oral agreement was made there was no question of the plaintiff's rushing the defendant to a solicitor to have the contract signed. In fact a considerable time elapsed before the parties went to Mr Montague and the defendant had ample time to reflect on the proposed transaction and therefore an ample *locus poenitentiae* in relation to it.

(3) When the parties did get to the solicitor, Mr Montague, he advised the defendant not once but twice to be separately represented and drew attention to the distinct advantage conferred on the plaintiff by the proposed transaction. As Megarry J. (as he then was) remarked in one case 'Nobody, of course, can be compelled to seek independent advice . . . '. *Cresswell v Potter* [1978] 1 WLR 255 at 259B. In view of Mr Montague's careful approach to the matter it is to me quite inconceivable that he would have taken part in a transaction if there had been any question of the defendant's being affected either intellectually or emotionally by drink.

My general conclusion is that the contract is an enforceable contract between the plaintiff and the defendant for the sale of the contract land to the plaintiff.

Having reached this general conclusion I now have to consider whether I should in the exercise of my discretion withhold from the plaintiff the normal equitable remedy granted in this type of case, *viz.* specific performance of the contract. The matter is succinctly and in my view correctly stated in the recent work intituled *Specific Performance* by Jones and Goodhart p. 1: 'The remedy of specific performance is an equitable remedy which the court will grant if the plaintiff requires it and it is just to do so. No plaintiff therefore is entitled to specific performance as of right . . . but the discretion to grant or refuse specific performance is not exercised capriciously but with regard to principles established by previous authorities.' There is no doubt, however, that the normal rule is for the court to grant specific performance of a contract for the sale of land and in such a case the onus is on the defendant of establishing a ground or grounds upon which the remedy should be refused: *Broughton v Snook* [1938] Ch. 505 at p. 513. The grounds relied upon by [counsel] for the defendant in this case were as follows: (1) The defendant is not 'an astute commercial person: he is impecunious and socially inadequate': by contrast the plaintiff is a man of acumen and substance. (2) The defendant was not separately advised and this was particularly unfortunate since he is a man who, because of his fondness for drink, cannot be trusted with money, as he himself confessed to Mr Montague. (3) The sale was at an undervalue. (4) The contract was vague and uncertain in respect of certain matters, for example whether £2,000 or £4,000 (i.e. two instalments) were to be paid in the first year of the contract, *viz.* 1984.

(5) The plaintiff lacked candour in the witness box about his knowledge of the defendant's weakness for drink, vulnerability and certain other matters.

In support of his arguments |counsel| cited the two Northern Ireland cases *Conlon v Murray* |1958| NI 6 (CA) and *Buckley v Irwin* |1960| NI 98. In the former case the Court of Appeal confirmed the decision of the Chancery Judge who not only refused the vendor specific performance of a contract for the sale of farm land but dismissed the action, i.e. did not even award damages. In the second case McVeigh J. (as he then was) did likewise: he refused both specific performance and damages. I have to say straight-away that in my view this case is a very far cry from either *Conlon* or *Buckley*. In *Conlon* an elderly widow, the owner of a farm who was seriously ill with a malignant disease, was wandering the countryside at night in a distressed condition after a serious row with her brother with whom she lived. She met a man called Collins who advised her to sell the farm for £2,000—an undervalue but not a gross undervalue—and to go and live with her sister. The sale was arranged with indecent haste at 11 p.m. the following night when Collins (who was to benefit from the sale) brought the plaintiff Conlon along as the purchaser and the widow, impulsively and without proper advice, agreed to sell the farm to him.

In *Buckley* the defendant was not of unsound mind but was described by the learned judge as a person who 'requires protection and guidance in carrying out business affairs, even of a comparatively simple nature': she was induced to sell her farm at a substantial undervalue in a deal which arose out of a casual conversation she had with the plaintiff and another man, the judge describing the pair as 'two sharp-eyed and experienced dealers'. The defendant had no advice of any kind before she signed the contract. The learned judge said in the course of his judgment: ' . . . it is my view that this was a snap bargain at a considerable undervalue even if it was not a gross under-value: and that, above all, the plaintiff with the ready assistance of W. J. Irwin took advantage of the defendant's incompetence. I am satisfied that this was an unethical bargain and infringed the principles of fairness.'

The cases including *Buckley* draw a distinction between two categories of undervalue cases, *viz.* those in which there is a substantial undervalue and those in which the undervalue is so gross as to be evidence in itself of fraud. I have already said that in my view the £20,000 over ten years was a substantial undervalue but I repeat that I do not regard the undervalue as falling in the second category, and (as I have said) Mr Kennedy did not attempt to argue the contrary. How then stands a case in the first category? I now wish to refer to a recent and important Privy Council case which I found myself and have considered in this general area of the law. Counsel did not cite it and if it had altered, as distinct from confirming, my view of this case, I would have re-listed the action for further argument by counsel on it. I refer to *Hart v O'Connor* |1985| AC 1000 (PC). It was a complicated contract case which, *inter alia*, involved as a contracting party a person who was in fact of unsound mind but was ostensibly sane and was believed by the other contracting party to be sane; the case also involved the effect of unfairness in a contract and it is this aspect of it which is relevant here. In giving the opinion of the Privy Council Lord Brightman summarised the law in this way at p. 1027: 'To sum the matter up, in the opinion of their Lordships, the validity of a contract entered into by a lunatic who is ostensibly sane is to be judged by the same standards as a contract by a person of sound mind, and is not voidable by the lunatic or his representatives by reason of 'unfairness' unless such unfairness amounts to equitable fraud which would have enabled the complaining party to avoid the contract even if he had been sane.'

Another very recent case which was not cited by counsel but to which I wish to refer is *Morgan v National Westminster Bank* |1985| AC 686. It was a case involving an allegation of undue influence against a bank mortgagee and in the course of his speech Lord

Scarman expressed disapproval of the notion of inequality of bargaining power as in itself a vitiating element in a contract: he said this:

> The question which the House does have to answer is: did the court in *Lloyds Bank Ltd v Bundy* accurately state the law?
>
> Lord Denning M.R. believed that the doctrine of undue influence could be subsumed under a general principle that English courts will grant relief where there has been 'inequality of bargaining power' (p. 9). He deliberately avoided reference to the will of one party being dominated or overcome by another. The majority of the court did not follow him; they based their decision on the orthodox view of the doctrine as expounded in *Allcard v Skinner*, 36 ChD 145. The opinion of the Master of the Rolls, therefore, was not the ground of the court's decision, which was to be found in the view of the majority, for whom Sir Eric Sachs delivered the leading judgment.
>
> Nor has counsel for the respondent sought to rely on Lord Denning M.R.'s general principle: and, in my view, he was right not to do so. The doctrine of undue influence has been sufficiently developed not to need the support of a principle which by its formulation in the language of the law of contract is not appropriate to cover transactions of gift where there is no bargain. The fact of an unequal bargain will, of course, be a relevant feature in some cases of undue influence. But it can never become an appropriate basis of principle of an equitable doctrine which is concerned with transactions 'not to be reasonably accounted for on the ground of friendship, relationship, charity, or other ordinary motives on which ordinary men act' (Lindley L.J. in *Allcard v Skinner*, at p. 185). And even in the field of contract I question whether there is any need in the modern law to erect a general principle of relief against inequality of bargaining power. Parliament has undertaken the task—and it is essentially a legislative task—of enacting such restrictions upon freedom of contract as are in its judgment necessary to relieve against the mischief: for example, the hire-purchase and consumer protection legislation, of which the Supply of Goods (Implied Terms) Act 1973, Consumer Credit Act 1974, Consumer Safety Act 1978, Supply of Goods and Services Act 1982 and Insurance Companies Act 1982 are examples. I doubt whether the courts should assume the burden of formulating further restrictions.
>
> I shall refer to one other matter. A defence which can be raised to a specific performance claim is that such an order would inflict great hardship on the defendant, but according to *Snell's Principles of Equity* (28th ed.), 596 and authorities there cited: 'the fact that one party has made a poor bargain . . . is not hardship . . . nor is inadequacy of price a ground for refusing specific performance, unless the purchaser stands in a fiduciary position to the vendor, or fraud enters into the contract.' Neither of these last two conditions is present in this case. If, as I think, the price represents an undervalue, though not a gross one, it must be pointed out that the normal rule under which the vendor is entitled to hold the deeds until he is fully paid will make the plaintiff's position somewhat unenviable over the next eight years since he will be at the serious disadvantage of having to pay out substantial sums of money and yet not be in control of the title deeds.
>
> In the result I hold that specific performance should be ordered: there is a well-established jurisdiction to attach conditions to the order and one which I shall attach to this order arises out of the slight doubt which exists over the true construction of the contract, *viz.* whether £4,000 was to be paid in the period October–November 1984 (i.e. the deposit of £2,000 and a further £2,000 on 30 November 1984) or only one amount of £2,000, the deposit, which was to double duty as deposit with the first instalment of the price. Whatever the true construction of the contract in this respect I

shall insert a condition in the order to the effect that the plaintiff must pay £8,000 down, i.e. £4,000 and the two instalments of £2,000 each for 1985 and 1986. He will, of course, remain liable to pay the balance of £12,000 over the next six years. Since the contract is an instalment one a special form of order will probably be required: see *Halsbury's Laws* (4th ed.) vol. 42 para. 134. It is a curious result of the whole matter that if the defendant's own evidence is accurate, this method of receiving the £20,000 will be much better for his health and welfare than if he received the whole £20,000 'into his hands' in one lump sum which he said 'could be the end of him'.

O'Flanagan v Ray-ger and Others (HC) 28 April 1983, unrep.

In this action the plaintiff sought to set aside a transaction entered into by his late father in relation to a company in which the late Mr O'Flanagan held shares, the plaintiff alleging that one of the defendants, a Mr Pope had exercised undue influence over the plaintiff's late father.

Costello J.:

. . .

. . . The equitable principles which the plaintiffs call in aid are well established. The cases where a plaintiff seeks to set aside a gift or other transaction on the ground that it was procured by undue influence have been divided into two classes; firstly, those in which it can be expressly proved that undue influence was exercised, in which circumstances the court intervenes on the principle that no one should be allowed to retain any benefit arising from his own fraud or wrongful act; secondly, those in which the relations between the donor and donee have at or shortly before the execution of a gift been such as to raise a presumption that the donor had influence over the donee. Then, the court intervenes, not on the ground that any wrongful act has in fact been committed by the donee but on the ground of public policy and to prevent the relations which existed between the parties and the influence arising therefrom being abused. The court will set aside the gift unless it is proved (and the onus is on the donee in such cases) that in fact the gift was the result of a free exercise of the donor's will (see *Allcard v Skinner* 36 ChD 145 at 171). The courts have not defined the degree of confidence and trust which must exist in a relationship before it can be said that a donee is in a position to exert undue influence. It has been long established that the relationship of parent and child, guardian and ward, doctor and patient, religious adviser and pupil are relationships which give rise to the presumption to which I have referred. But the categories are not closed and in *Gregg v Kidd* [1956] IR 183 Budd J. held that the relationship raised the presumption to which I have referred in a case in which an uncle settled property on his nephew. Recently in England a majority of the Court of Appeal (in *Re Brocklehurst's Estate* [1978] 1 Ch. 21) took the view that the presumption did not arise from the relationship of friendship between an elderly man and a companion from a different class in the social structure, whilst in in *Re Craig* [1971] 1 Ch. 95 it was held that the relationship between an elderly man and his secretary gave rise to the presumption. The presumption does not arise in the case of Mills (see, *In the goods of Kavanagh, decd* 24 October 1978, unrep. in which I held that express undue influence was proved).

Just as the courts have declined to define the exact categories of relationship which will give rise to the presumption of undue influence so too they have declined to define exactly what undue influence is. The approach which courts of equity should adopt was suggested by Sir Samuel Romilly (a distinguished chancery lawyer and former Solicitor General) in one of the early leading cases on the matter (*Huguenin v*

Basely (1807) 14 Ves 273), an approach which subsequently obtained judicial approval from Lord Cottendham in *Dent v Bennett* (4 My Cr 277) and from Byrne J., in *Cavendish v Strutt* (19 TLR 483). The passage to which I refer reads as follows:

> Where a gift is immoderate, bears no proportion to the circumstances of the giver, where no reason appears, or the reason given is falsified, and the giver is a weak man, liable to be imposed upon, this court will look upon such a gift with a very jealous eye, and very strictly examine the conduct of the person in whose favour it is made; and if it sees that any arts or stratagems, or any undue influence have been used— if it sees the least speck of imposition at the bottom, or that the donor is in such a situation with respect to the donee as may naturally give an influence over him—if there be the least scintilla of fraud, this court will and ought to interpose . . . (quoted in White and Tudor *Leading Cases in Equity* vol. I p. 216).

The plaintiffs do not reply solely on the equitable principles relating to undue influence. They claim in the alternative that the agreement of 15 March 1976 should be set aside on the ground that it is an unconscionable bargain. The principle relied on was stated by Lord Hatherley in a dissenting judgment in *O'Rourke v Bolingbroke* 2 App Cas 814, 823, a case dealing with a sale at undervalue by an expectant heir but which enunciated a principle of wider application. The passage reads as follows:

> It . . . appears that the principle on which equity originally proceeded to set aside such transactions was for the protection of family property; but this principle being once established, the court extended its aid to all cases in which the parties to a contract have not met upon equal terms. In ordinary cases each party to a bargain must take care of his own interest, and it will not be presumed that undue advantage or contrivance has been resorted to on either side; but in the case of expectant heirs or of persons under pressure without adequate protection and in the case of dealings with uneducated ignorant persons, the burden of showing the fairness of the transaction is thrown on the person who seeks to obtain the benefit of the contract.

This passage was quoted with approval by Gavan Duffy J. in *Grealish v Murphy* [1946] IR 35, a case in which the plaintiff was a mentally retarded adult but in which no undue influence was shown to have been exercised. The transaction which he entered into, however, was set aside on the ground that equity comes to the rescue in cases where the parties to a contract have not met on equal terms, the court holding that the deed was an improvident one and that the plaintiff's weakness of mind coupled with the inadequacy of the advice he obtained justified the intervention of the court in that case (see also *Fry v Lane* 10 ChD 312, at 322)

As the evidence relating to the relationship between the deceased and the defendant and the evidence relating to the allegation of undue influence are inextricably mixed I propose to examine the facts surrounding the making of the agreement of 15 March 1976 and then give my opinion as to whether or not the plaintiff has made out a case for the intervention of the court on the ground that undue influence was exercised by the defendant in relation to it.

Costello J. reviewed the evidence and summarised the material facts and continued:

I have the following observations to make on the agreement and the defendant's evidence in relation to it:

(a) I found the defendant's evidence unconvincing and must record my view that he was not telling the truth as to how the agreement came to be made. He failed to give any or any acceptable explanation as to why (a) he insisted on a 'private meeting' with the deceased or (b) why he and Mr O'Flanagan should agree that the surviving partner should be entitled to the entire of the company's assets. I am also quite satisfied that the defendant, contrary to what he stated in the course of his testimony, knew full well that Mr O'Flanagan had had two major operations for cancer.

(b) I do not accept (as pleaded in para. 8 of the defence) that the defendant in March 1976 wished to wind up the company and that he was prevailed upon by the deceased not to do so. I think it is much more probable that the defendant used the threat to wind up the company as a means for procuring the deceased's signature to the agreement and that he used the IOUs which the deceased had signed for the same purpose.

(c) The written agreement refers to the fact that each of the partners should receive a copy of it. No copy was ever found amongst the deceased's effects after his death and Mrs O'Flanagan knew nothing about the agreement until the reply to the notice for particulars in this action. I think it is reasonable to assume that the defendant did not give Mr O'Flanagan a copy of it.

(d) In March 1976 the deceased was a very sick man. He had undergone a very serious operation the previous November and a letter written by him on 10 March a couple of days before he met the defendant shows that he had been ill in bed and had been unable to attend a business appointment.

(e) The deceased was aware that he was terminally ill with cancer and must have realised that his chances of surviving Mr Pope were slight. He was not well off and notwithstanding this he was apparently agreeing that on his death the defendant and not his wife or any of his eight children would obtain the benefit of two valuable commercial properties. There is nothing to suggest that Mr O'Flanagan had not the normal love and affection which a husband and father has for his wife and children and no explanation has been forthcoming as to why he should fail to give expression to that love and affection and instead give what was virtually a gift of these properties to Mr Pope.

(f) After Mr O'Flanagan's death, as we will see, the defendant sought advice from his accountant as to his right to appoint a new director and issue the balance of the share capital to himself and a nominee. In doing so he did not show him the secret agreement of 15 March 1976. His failure to do so demonstrates a lack of confidence in its validity, which could only have arisen if it was tainted by some wrongdoing on his part.

Taking into account all the evidence in the case I think there is only one conclusion to be reached in relation to this agreement namely that the defendant must have used undue influence to procure it. The defendant has a strong and forceful personality and had obviously exercised considerable influence amounting to domination of the deceased on previous occasions. The deceased was infirm and ill when he signed it. The agreement was egregiously unfair to the deceased's wife and family. The mutual promises it contained were largely illusory in that both parties knew that it was highly probable that the deceased would predecease the defendant. Furthermore the lack of candour of the defendant raises very serious suspicions about the circumstances in which it came to be executed. It is unnecessary for me to decide whether the relationship which existed raises any presumption as to what happened. The evidence satisfies me that I should set the agreement aside.

Elton John and Others v James and Others [1991] FSR 397

The facts

The action concerned a series of publishing, recording and management agreements entered into by Elton John and his lyricist, Bernie Taupin, beginning in 1967, when they were unknown and still minors.

By the first agreement, they assigned to the second defendant, for a renewable period of three years, the full copyright throughout the world in every musical composition of theirs for the full period of such copyrights. The plaintiffs agreed to supply in each three year period at least eighteen compositions approved by the second defendant, each period to be extended until the minimum number had been supplied. The defendant was to pay them (a) 10 per cent of the market retail price of each copy of the composition, (b) 50 per cent of the mechanical royalties in the UK and Ireland, less the costs of collection, (c) 50 per cent of royalties received from the rest of the world, and (d) 50 per cent of performing and broadcasting fees. The agreement was exclusive, except in respect of compositions rejected by the second defendants. Also in 1967, Elton John entered into an agreement with the third defendant in which he was to perform his songs for recording purposes as and when required for a royalty of 20 per cent of net monies received. This agreement was for five years.

In 1968, the plaintiffs entered into five-year management agreements whereby it [sic] was to be their sole manager in return for 30 per cent of all money received by them in respect of any branch of the entertainment industry during the currency of the agreements.

The agreements were extended and varied from time to time. In 1970 new management agreements were signed, *inter alia* specifically excluding Mr John's activities as a composer and reducing the commission payable to 20 per cent, but separating from the commission sums due under certain agency agreements. By a later rider, recording activities were also excluded. In March 1971, the royalty rates under heads (b) and (c) of the copyright agreement were increased to 60 per cent, while in March 1970 the recording agreement was extended for a further five years, with an increased minimum number of recordings and an increase in royalties to 40 per cent in respect of recordings made before February 1972 and 60 per cent thereafter. Other amendments, mainly to royalty rates, followed.

In March 1971, Mr John entered into a tax mitigation scheme whereby all three agreements were to be terminated. In their place came two employment contracts, one relating to all his activities in the entertainment industry in the UK and Ireland, and the other covering the rest of the world. Each was for five years. Under the first he was to receive a salary, and under the other £1,000 plus a royalty of $92^1/_2$ per cent of his employer's gross earnings up to £200,000 and 95 per cent above that sum. The defendants then began to set up a network of wholly-owned subsidiaries in the most lucrative world markets in order to sub-publish the plaintiffs' works there, they to receive substantial rates of commission which, together with the expense of maintaining offices and employing staff, substantially reduced the net earnings of the second defendant, and thus the plaintiffs' share of the gross revenues from their work.

In October 1972, following the judgment in *Instone v A. Schroeder Music Publishing Co. Ltd*, the plaintiffs, defendants and their respective legal advisers sought counsel's opinion on the implications of that case for their own agreements. Counsel concluded that the publishing agreement was unobjectionable, but that the publisher was under a duty not unfairly to deplete the source of income of which part was payable to the writers. He advised that the accounts of the subsidiaries and other documents should be obtained.

There began a long correspondence between the parties in an attempt to ascertain the true facts, and Mr John was given separate advice that the device of using wholly-owned sub-publishers, at least in the USA, was probably improper.

In November 1973, the 1971 publishing agreements expired, and in February 1975, the two recording agreements ended. Following unsuccessful attempts to obtain proper information about the sub-publishing agreements, the writ was issued in October 1982.

The plaintiffs' primary claims were for the setting aside, on the ground of undue influence, of the publishing and recording agreements, the return of the copyrights in all compositions and recordings covered by the agreements and delivery up of all master recordings. The copyrights involved were of 144 compositions and 169 song recordings, the retail sales value of which probably exceeded £200 million. The plaintiffs conceded that the defendants should retain all sums received by them so far, save that they should account for (a) all sums wrongly retained by them by way of the sub-publishing agreements, (b) the difference between the royalty rates in the agreements being set aside and the best possible rates obtainable in the market, and (c) compound interest on the above. Alternatively, they claimed payment of substantial additional sums which they alleged ought to have been paid under the publishing agreements as mechanical royalties on original recordings, or the sums retained by the second defendant's subsidiaries in excess of the normal commercial sub-publishing rates.

Nichols J.:

I turn to the plaintiffs' primary claim, to have the various recording and publishing agreements set aside on the basis that they were procured by undue influence. On the law I have the advantage of the recent authoritative exposition given by the House of Lords in the case of *National Westminster Bank Ltd v Morgan* [1985] 2 WLR 588,1 which concerned a claim by a wife that her signature to a mortgage of the matrimonial home in favour of a bank had been procured by the bank manager exercising undue influence over her. In the leading speech Lord Scarman (at pp 597–8) observed that the principle justifying the court in setting aside a transaction for undue influence was the need to protect one party from being victimised by the other. He quoted approvingly a passage from the judgment of Lord Shaw of Dunfermline in the Privy Council case of *Poosathurai v Kannappa Chettiar* LR 47 IA 1 on the subject of undue influence, which commenced with the sentence: 'It must be established that the person in a position of domination has used that position to obtain unfair advantage for himself, and so to cause injury to the person relying upon his authority or aid.' Lord Scarman then said (at p. 599):

> The wrongfulness of the transaction must, therefore, be shown: it must be one in which an unfair advantage has been taken of another. The doctrine is not limited to transactions of gift. A commercial relationship can become a relationship in which one party assumes a role of dominating influence over the other. In *Poosathurai's* case, LR 47 IA 1 the board recognised that a sale at an undervalue could be a transaction which a court could set aside as unconscionable if it was shown or could be presumed to have been procured by the exercise of undue influence. Similarly a relationship of banker and customer may become one in which the banker acquires a dominating influence. If he does and a manifestly disadvantageous transaction is proved, there would then be room for the court to presume that it resulted from the exercise of undue influence.

So, in short, and whatever be the precise form of words used, the substance of the two ingredients required before the court will set aside a transaction is, first, a relationship in which one person has a dominating influence over the other and, secondly, a manifestly disadvantageous transaction resulting from the exercise of that influence. In appropriate circumstances presumptions may be employed regarding either of the two ingredients: in appropriate circumstances the existence of a dominating influence may be presumed; the court may also, again in appropriate circumstances, presume that where a dominating influence exists, a manifestly disadvantageous transaction was the result of the exercise of undue influence.

This is all subject to the warning given by Lord Scarman at the conclusion of his speech (at p. 602):

> There is no precisely defined law setting limits to the equitable jurisdiction of a court to relieve against undue influence. This is the world of doctrine, not of neat and tidy rules. The courts of equity have developed a body of learning enabling relief to be granted where the law has to treat the transaction as unimpeachable unless it can be held to have been procured by undue influence. It is the unimpeachability at law of a disadvantageous transaction which is the starting point from which the court advances to consider whether the transaction is the product merely of one's own folly or of the undue influence exercised by another. A court in the exercise of this equitable jurisdiction is a court of conscience. Definition is a poor instrument when used to determine whether a transaction is or is not unconscionable: this is a question which depends upon the particular facts of the case.

The defendants' case was that neither of the necessary ingredients existed in this case regarding any of the agreements. Thus, for example, as to the 1967 publishing agreement, DJM never acquired a dominating influence over Mr John or Mr Taupin, nor was the transaction manifestly disadvantageous either at its inception or as it was subsequently implemented. On whether Mr James (because he alone was the person concerned for DJM) assumed a role of dominating influence, the gist of the defendants' submission was that although DJM, like the banker in the *Morgan* case, was in a much stronger bargaining position, the relationship of music publisher and would-be writers did not *per se* give rise to a presumption of undue influence, and Mr James never crossed the line which divides a normal business relationship from one of undue influence. Mr James never sought to persuade or encourage the two individual plaintiffs to enter the publishing agreement.

I shall consider the various agreements in turn, starting with the 1967 publishing agreement. Under this the writers tied themselves exclusively to DJM for what would be a period of six years if DJM exercised its option. DJM was entitled to obtain and retain for all time the full copyright in all their works produced in that period (unless, as was unlikely, DJM rejected any work as unsuitable) and to do so even if DJM never published the work or works in question. In return for this, viewed in strict terms of legal obligations of DJM, the writers obtained precious little. They obtained a right to royalties. The defendants claimed that the writers also obtained the benefit of an implied obligation that DJM would use reasonable diligence to publish, promote and exploit the compositions accepted, but even if this was so such an obligation was necessarily so loose and imprecise that it would have afforded the writers little protection.

The defendants further claimed that under an oral contract made at the same time as the written agreement DJM was obliged to pay Mr John and Mr Taupin £20 per week between them during the currency of the 1967 publishing agreement as an advance on royalties. Mr James' evidence was that he intended to commit himself to pay this sum for the whole life of the agreement come what may. He explained that he suggested to Mr John that the weekly payments should not be mentioned in the agreement, even though they were to endure for its full term, because the sum might be increased from time to time, in which event letters would have to be exchanged if the payments were included in the written agreement. I am unable to accept Mr James' evidence on this. I have no doubt that if, for example, the two writers had failed miserably to produce any work of any potential and there was no realistic prospect of them earning any royalties other than of a minimal amount and Mr James had wished not to continue with the 1967 publishing agreement, he would have considered himself free, after a reasonable time and on giving reasonable notice, to discontinue the weekly payments long before the end of the six year period (the renewal option was exercisable by the writers as well as by the publisher). I am not satisfied that there was a binding contract beyond this.

It may be inherent in the nature of this type of publishing agreement that the publisher's strictly legal obligations will be very limited. What Mr John and Mr Taupin wanted was a foot in the door, the *entrée* to the popular music publishing world, and in practice they obtained this by the 1967 publishing agreement. They were put on the 'books' of a leading publisher; they obtained the use of a studio; and they also obtained the financial means enabling them to pursue their ambitions. The value of this to the two young would-be writers is not to be underestimated. They were fortunate to have found in Mr James a leading music publisher who was willing to encourage and support them. But the agreement contained no provision for early termination or return of copyrights if, for example, successful publication was not achieved and the writers became aware of another publisher who had more confidence in their songs. Conversely, and more importantly, if, as was no doubt the hope in every case, the writers succeeded enormously, their entire output for six years was bound to DJM effectively for ever, whether published or not, and there was no provision for any increase in royalty rates.

Obviously it takes time for a new writer to succeed. Mr James' estimate was that on average between one and two years is needed before there is any success, if there is to be any. The publisher is entitled to a reasonable period to obtain a proper reward for taking on the new writers, paying the (comparatively modest) costs of making demonstration records, providing studio facilities, seeking to promote the works and, in this case, paying the writers their weekly retainer. But six years is an appreciable time in anyone's professional career, particularly at the threshold of so uncertain a career as that of pop music writer. I consider that to have tied these two young men to DJM in 1967 for six years on the terms in question represented an unacceptably hard bargain.

Did Mr Dick James assume a role of dominating influence? I consider that, brief though their acquaintance had been at this stage, he did. Once he had decided that the two young men, who like so many others were anxious to be signed by him, were worth pursuing and encouraging, he really took charge of the arrangements. At his request they assigned the copyright in the seventeen songs to Gralto Music Ltd, even though they were under no obligation to do so. And although, understandably after so many years, some obscurity now surrounds precisely what was said at the relevant meetings, and, indeed, it is uncertain how many meetings there were, what does emerge clearly is that Mr James did not regard himself as obliged to give Mr John or Mr Taupin, nor did he give them, a thorough explanation of the terms of the proposed agreement. In particular, he did not explain to them that, whatever might happen in practice, under the agreement all the songs they wrote over the next three years, or six years if DJM exercised its option, would belong to DJM for ever, regardless of how successful those songs might be and whether published or not, and that for those songs, again regardless of how successful they might be, they would be entitled to receive only the one fixed rate of royalties. When the typed form of agreement was produced, no one went through the four and a half pages, explaining the practical implications of the eighteen clauses. Mr John and Mr Taupin were young and inexperienced minors. They were very apprehensive at meeting such a giant in the music publishing industry, and they were very anxious to be taken on by him. No negotiation took place. They would have been disinclined to question the terms of any agreement Mr James put before them, the more so when he told them that the terms were the standard terms within the industry. They were, as must have been obvious to him, trusting and relying on him that the contractual terms were fair and reasonable. The formality of requiring parental signature in the circumstances of these two young men and their parents was not an adequate counterbalance to this. In my view it is clear that the reason why Mr John and Mr Taupin signed the agreement for such an onerously long period lies not only in their keenness to be signed by Mr James but also, and importantly, and this is partly why they were so keen, in the trust they reposed in him as a man of stature in the industry that he would treat them fairly.

My conclusion is that, in respect of the period for which the artists were bound and because of the circumstances in which the agreement was entered into, at its inception the 1967 publishing agreement was an unfair transaction (I prefer to use this expression rather than 'unconscionable transaction', but without intending any different meaning).

In stating this conclusion I wish to emphasise that there is no question of Mr James having sought consciously to obtain an unfair advantage. At the time he thought his normal terms for a publishing agreement were standard in the trade and therefore fair. And if, contrary to what normally happened in the popular music business, these two young writers succeeded spectacularly, it would have been his intention to increase their royalty rates, as indeed in the event happened. But finding, as I do unhesitatingly, that in this transaction Mr James was acting in good faith does not in my view provide a complete answer to the undue influence claim. One can obtain an unfair advantage by the exercise of a dominating influence without intending to act unfairly.

I come next to the 1967 recording agreement, regarding which I make the same finding on Mr James' good faith. Under this agreement Mr John bound himself exclusively to TRC in respect of all his recording activities, with some immaterial exceptions, for a period which, when the agreement was signed in January 1968, had some $4^3/4$ years to run. TRC became the owner of the master recordings for all time and, under the annexed 'standard artists condition' no. 6, TRC was expressed to have the right in its discretion to decide whether and when to start, stop or re-start production of records. Mr John was precluded from making recordings of any work performed by him under the agreement for five years from the date when it was recorded for TRC. In return TRC was, as the plaintiffs accepted, under an obligation to make master recordings sufficient to produce the agreed minimum of four sides of single records. TRC was also obliged to pay a royalty of one fifth of all 'net monies' received by TRC in respect of the master recordings. The defendants alleged that in addition TRC was under an implied obligation to use reasonable diligence to procure the distribution, sale, promotion and exploitation of records embodying the minimum number of master recordings. Such an implication is far from easy to make having regard to condition 6, but I do not pursue this further for the same reason as mentioned earlier when dealing with the comparable allegation regarding the 1967 publishing agreement.

I am in no doubt that at its inception this agreement was significantly disadvantageous to the artist Mr John, in one important respect. At the time he was unknown as a writer or artist and the royalty rate specified was not unreasonable for such an artist. TRC was entitled to protection in the form of exclusivity for a reasonable period, so that it would have a fair opportunity to recoup and benefit from the expenses incurred by it on unsuccessful master recordings. The success rate in this field is low. As a rough guide, a recording company will recoup its recording costs with not more than one artist in ten, and it will make a significant profit with not more than one artist in thirty. Bearing this in mind, and that on average a new artist will take three years to become established, a five year tie in this instance may not have been unreasonable. But whether this was so or not, where the agreement fell short of striking a reasonable balance was that it made no provision for any improvement in the royalty rate if, as happened here, the artist became a major success. The experts called by the parties were in agreement that clause 5 was a most unusual provision, the defendants' expert (Mr David Betteridge) saying that he had not seen a royalty clause like this before. In 1967 the royalty rate was normally a percentage of retail sale prices, there being one percentage for UK sales, and another smaller percentage (of the order of one half or two thirds of the UK rate) for overseas sales. The UK market represented about $6\frac{1}{2}$ per cent of the worldwide record market at all times material in this action, although obviously the sales in different countries will vary greatly from one artist to another. In January 1968 20 per cent of 'net monies' received by TRC under the Philips agreement equalled approximately 2 per cent of the retail selling price in the UK. This was somewhat less than the average going rate for the UK for an untried artist at the beginning of his career, but since under clause 5 the same rate applied worldwide, the overall result probably was to leave Mr John in a not significantly better or worse position than other untried, unknown artists. But for Mr John to have remained tied to TRC for five years at this beginners' rate, however successful he might be, would have been obviously unfair.

As with the 1967 publishing agreement, so with this agreement, I think it is clear that at the time it was entered into, some two or three months after Mr John had become linked to Mr James and his organisation, Mr James was exercising a dominating influence over Mr John regarding his career. Again, no proper explanation was given on the substantial implications of the agreement. Mr John, to whom to be given any recording agreement was 'heaven sent', could not recall being furnished with any explanation of its terms before signing it. Although Mr James' evidence was that he gave some explanation, I am satisfied from the general tenor of his evidence that in this case also he did not feel obliged to give and he did not give a proper explanation of the way in which the basic provisions of this agreement concerning its length and one fixed royalty rate would, under the agreement as it stood, work unfairly to Mr John if he were to become a major success. Mr John, for his part, as he stated in evidence, 'just trusted Mr James and the contract.' In my view it was because of this trust, which Mr James must have known Mr John was placing in him, that Mr John entered into this agreement. I consider that in these circumstances this agreement also, with the single fixed low royalty rate, if for no other reason, constituted an unfair transaction.

I must come now to the 1970 recording agreement, prefacing what I have to say on this by reference to an issue which arose on whether or not, having regard to the terms of the 1968 management agreement, DJM was acting as Mr John's manager in March 1970 in respect of his recording activities. The management agreement proposal arose some weeks after the 1967 publishing agreement had been entered into, at a time when, although the 1967 recording agreement had probably not yet been signed by the parties, Mr John had accepted that he should enter into a recording agreement with the DJM group. The defendants' case was that in respect of his composing and recording activities Mr John did not need a manager, and they pointed out that DJM never took a management commission from Mr John on his publishing and recording royalties. Mr Dick James' evidence was that he never intended to assume managerial responsibility for recording and publishing, and that Mr John clearly understood from what Mr James said to him at the time that recording and publishing were not included in the management arrangements. Mr Stephen James' evidence was to the like effect. Mr John's recollection was far less certain, but he accepted frankly that when the 1970 recording agreement was made in March 1970 he did not expect Mr James to advise him on its terms.

There is force in the consideration that, publishing and recording arrangements with the DJM group having already been seen to, there would have been no point in DJM assuming a managerial responsibility for Mr John in February 1968 in those fields. Moreover, I think Mr John was told that there would be no further deductions, by way of a management commission, from the publishing and recording royalties. But the opening words on the management agreement are unambiguous: 'the artist hereby appoints the managers to be his sole managers to manage on behalf of the artist all the affairs of the artist relating to his professional career in any medium of professional entertainment,' and phonographic recording was one of the six branches of the entertainment industry then specified. If the width of these clear terms is to be cut down in reliance on an oral agreement or the common intention of the parties, convincing proof is required. I would have to be satisfied that both parties understood and accepted that, despite the terms of the agreement, none of those terms was to apply at all to any of Mr John's activities as a composer or in the recording field. Having heard the evidence I am not satisfied on this. In particular, whatever was said to Mr John at the time, I do not think that he clearly understood that regarding his composing and recording activities DJM was to have no functions whatever as his manager. Rather he thought that, although the management would be primarily in the field of live performances, DJM as manager would generally guide his career.

With that preface I turn to consider whether the 1970 recording agreement was an unfair transaction. On this, in the first place, I am in no doubt that in March 1970 Mr James with his genial, ebullient personality was exercising a dominating influence over the young artist, all of whose professional activities were, under one agreement or another, bound so closely to the DJM group. This was so in practice, whether or not as a matter of strict law DJM was Mr John's manager in respect of his recording activities. As Mr John said in his evidence regarding entering into this new recording agreement, 'everything was built on trust anyway.' He always regarded Mr James as a 'benevolent father-figure'. I add that at the time, when the 'Elton John' album had not yet been released and tested in the market place, Mr John thought that the new contract was a very generous one.

In considering whether indeed any unfair advantage was taken of Mr John, several points must be borne in mind. The genesis of the new agreement was that by March 1970 Mr John had not had a hit record, but he was well considered as an up and coming artist. The suggestion of a new agreement came from Mr James. He was concerned to extend the period for which Mr John would remain tied to him (the expiry date was deferred from 9 November 1972 to 28 February 1975) and to improve the royalty rates. By March 1970 Mr John had been with DJM for over two years. Although still a young man, not quite twenty three years of age, he was no longer without personal experience of long-term publishing and recording contracts (and in passing I refer to the events of 1969 involving Mr Gee and Island Records). Mr John knew Mr James and his organisation, and he knew whether he wanted to remain signed with them. In fact he was very pleased with the efforts DJM had been making on his behalf regarding the 'Elton John' album. Mr John also understood that the new contract involved a commitment for five years, and he was happy to accept that. The royalty rates were increased to 40 per cent in respect of master recordings produced in the first two years of the five year term of the new agreement, and 60 per cent in respect of master recordings produced in the remaining three years. Under the licensing agreement then in force in the USA and the arrangement being implemented between TRC and DJM Records, the 40 per cent rate equalled about 4 per cent of the retail sale prices in the USA and the UK. On the expert evidence this 4 per cent rate at the time, even on a worldwide basis, for an artist placed as was Mr John in 1970, was not generous.

Weighing all these matters, my conclusion is that, given the significant increase in Mr John's experience and his awareness of what the new agreement involved, and given also the improved and escalating royalty rates, this agreement taken as a whole and having regard to the circumstances in which it was entered into was not an unfair transaction.

I add that this was so, although, as I have found, DJM's management agreement at the time extended to Mr John's recording activities. This is an important circumstance to be taken into account. But even if an arm's length negotiation by DJM as Mr John's manager with another record company at the time would have resulted in better terms for Mr John, as it might well have done, I do not think it necessarily follows, and I do not think that it was the case here, that the transaction entered into between DJM and Mr John was unfair. All the circumstances have to be taken into account.

I move on to 1971. The defendants placed considerable reliance on the termination of the existing publishing and recording agreements effected by the new agreements entered into in March and April 1971 as part of Mr John's and Mr Taupin's double employment schemes. For the defendants it was emphasised that in relation to the 1971 agreements the individual plaintiffs were advised by independent solicitors experienced in the field of entertainment agreements (and it is right to recognise that it was at Mr James' suggestion that Mr John first consulted solicitors). The 1971 agreements could not have been, and indeed were not alleged to have been, procured by undue influence.

I am unable to accept the defendants' argument on this. Berger Oliver were not instructed to consider whether the existing agreements were unfair or impeachable on any ground. Mr Oliver (who did not give evidence) seems, not surprisingly, to have proceeded on the footing that there were in existence valid contracts and that one of the parties had offered to vary the terms of one of those contracts. Mr Oliver took part in negotiations with Mr James concerning the proposed variations, and advised Mr John and Mr Taupin thereon, and his firm prepared the documents required for the tax mitigation scheme, reflecting therein the agreed variation. No one suggested that the defendants' rights under the existing contracts might be impeachable, and with the one exception of the improvement in the publishing royalty rates, the defendants stood on their rights under the existing agreements and the terms of those agreements were carried over into the new agreements. Thus the negotiations took place, and the independent advice was given, not against a background of Mr John and Mr Taupin being free or possibly being free from any existing obligations to the defendants, but against a background of the existing agreements upon which, with one exception, the defendants were standing firm. I do not see how such negotiations and advice, followed by the 1971 agreements, by themselves can have been operated to cure the taint attaching to the 1967 agreements. On the contrary, any existing taint was carried over and, subject to any complications arising from the difference in the parties to the 1971 agreements, insofar as the existing publishing and recording agreements were then still capable of being set aside on the ground that they were procured by undue influence, so also at their inception were the corresponding 1971 agreements.

E. PROBLEMS OF PROOF—UPHOLDING THE TRANSACTION

McCormack v Bennett (HC) 2 July 1973, unrep.

Finlay J.:

The plaintiff Philomena McCormack brings this action as legal personal representative of her father James Seery to set aside and cancel an indenture of transfer dated 4 October 1967 executed by James Seery and for other relief. By that transfer James Seery transferred the lands of which he was then registered as full owner on folio no. 7790 of the County of Westmeath to the defendant Teresa Bennett subject to his life estate. The defendant is a sister of the plaintiff being another daughter of James Seery.

The grounds on which this deed is challenged as stated in the original pleadings were that it was improvident; that at the time of its execution the transferor had no independent advice and that he did not know or appreciate the consequences of the deed.

The proceedings were commenced by the late James Seery in his lifetime by a plenary summons dated 27 February 1970. A statement of claim purports to have been filed on his behalf on 9 March 1971 although he had in fact died on 22 May 1970. By order of 5 November 1971 the proceedings were continued in the name of the present plaintiff and an amended statement of claim was filed on 27 January 1972 which did not enlarge or amend the grounds already alleged for setting aside the deed.

By notice dated 15 June 1973 the plaintiff gave notice to the defendant of her intention to apply at the hearing of the action to amend the statement of claim by additional allegations of 1) undue influence by the defendant 2) the absence of a revocation clause in the deed 3) the absence of covenants on the part of the defendant to look after James Seery and to work the lands for his benefit and 4) the absence of covenants on the part of the defendant to look after James Seery's wife.

The case came on for hearing before me on 20 June and I allowed this amendment notwithstanding its extreme lateness upon the grounds that it was desirable that all issues between the parties should be tried and because I concluded that the defendant did not require any adjournment of the case to put herself in a position to meet these additional allegations.

Some of the facts of the case were agreed or admitted and some were in dispute. The facts as I find them to be are as follows:

James Seery was on 4 October 1967 when he executed this deed aged seventy nine years and his wife Mary who lived with him at that time was eighty. She died in November 1968.

James Seery was the registered owner of approximately 22 statute acres of land and a small house on it which I am satisfied was situated in an inaccessible place and probably had in the year 1967 a market value of approximately £1,500.

The lands were let by James Seery at that time at £80 per year and the only other income which he and his wife had were their social welfare benefits probably amounting though the figure was not clearly established to about £5,00.

Much of the disputed evidence concerned the mental and physical condition of James Seery and to some extent the condition of his wife. I am satisfied that Mary Seery was in October 1967 in extremely bad physical condition and that she was commencing to be affected by senility and as far as her condition is relevant to the issues in this case I am satisfied that she needed some sort of relatively constant attention from a person able in effect to give her unskilled nursing and that she also required from time to time skilled medical attention.

James Seery was I am satisfied at the time of this deed in 1967 suffering from no form of mental abnormality. He was suffering from the loss of the sight of one eye.

Some evidence was given that he was hard of hearing but I am satisfied that this was not so and certainly was not to an extent which affected his capacity to hear people nor did he ever complain of it to Doctor Kelly. He had had a bowel complaint in 1963 and a perforated ulcer when he had been obliged to go to hospital and undergo an operation but I am satisfied that operation was a success and that he was not suffering from any particular form of physical disability which would impair his capacity to transact business. Doctor Kelly who was his constant medical attendant during the relevant period gave evidence that James Seery was of a nervous and fretful condition and that he was more anxious about his future and that of his wife than could be expected to be normal. Doctor Kelly expressed the view that it was not desirable for him to have to transact worrying business but I am satisfied that this view was expressed more in the light of the effect it might have on the health of James Seery than in the light of an expression of opinion by the doctor that he was unfit to carry out serious business. I am satisfied that he was very anxious about both his own future and that of his wife but I am not completely satisfied that this anxiety having regard to his wife's general condition which was extremely bad and to his own age and hers was necessarily abnormal or exaggerated.

James and Mary Seery had nine children consisting of one son and eight daughters. With the exception of the plaintiff Mrs McCormack who was though not constantly for long periods living at home all these children had departed for a considerable time from their home, one of them Hannah was a nun known in religion as Sister Xavier and the others were married. The son Patrick was married and settled in England. Two sisters the defendant Mrs Bennett and a Mrs Ann Seery were married and living close to where the deceased and his wife lived. Prior to the transactions of October 1967 James Seery had made two dispositions of his property by two successive wills. In the year 1956 he made a will leaving his property substantially to Mrs Seery and making minor provisions for some other members of the family after the lifetime of his wife. In the year 1963 he changed this will and made his substantial beneficiary his son Patrick. Some evidence was given that a dispute had arisen between the late James Seery and his daughter Mrs Ann Seery which led to the change of will. Mrs Ann Seery in evidence denied that such a dispute occurred and I am satisfied that it was not necessary or relevant for the purpose of the issues in this case to enquire further into that matter.

Two conflicting accounts are given by the plaintiff and defendant respectively with regard to the circumstances preceding the transactions of October 1967. The plaintiff in evidence said that the defendant was constantly urging the deceased James Seery to benefit her with the lands upon promises of looking after him and his wife. The defendant on the other hand stated in evidence that Patrick Seery the son of James having returned home on a holiday in the summer of 1967 pointed out to his father that he was not going to return to Ireland and could not look after his father and mother and suggested to him that he should instead give the lands to his daughter the defendant Mrs Bennett who was the logical and most likely person to look after himself and his wife. The defendant said in evidence that her brother Patrick told her about this conversation with her father and that subsequently her father came to her and asked her if he gave her over the place would she be prepared to take care of himself and his wife as long as they lived. She said that she would but that she would prefer to buy the place as after his death there might be arguments from the other members of the family. The defendant's account of this conversation then went on to say that they agreed a price of £300 that she knew that that was below the value of the place and that her father who also knew it was below the value of the place thought it was sufficient. The defendant admitted that it was she who suggested a sale rather than a transfer or voluntary gift of the lands.

I accept as being substantially accurate the account of the origin of this transaction given by the defendant and I reject the account given by the plaintiff, I am therefore satisfied as a matter of fact that the idea of a giving of the land to the defendant in some form originated with James Seery on the suggestion of his son Patrick and I am satisfied that Mrs Bennett did not exercise any influence over James Seery her father to induce him to enter into this transaction. I am satisfied that after this conversation James Seery brought the defendant Mrs Bennett into Mullingar on 26 September to visit Mr Kevin Wallace of the firm of N. J. Downes and Co.. I am quite satisfied on the evidence that it was James Seery who chose Mr Wallace as solicitor to transact this business and that he did so because he had previously done all his business including making his two wills with the firm of N. J. Downes and Co. and had made the will of 1963 specifically with Mr Kevin Wallace.

I have had evidence from Mr Kevin Wallace of the interview which then took place with James Seery and with Mrs Teresa Bennett present the whole time. I accept as being accurate and correct that account of that interview. Mr Wallace's recollection of what occurred is fortified by a full note which he took in the form of an attendance and which has been produced before me. In general it was Mr Seery who gave all the instructions and did all the discussion with Mr Wallace and Mrs Bennett made practically no intervention in the proceedings.

James Seery then instructed Mr Wallace that his daughter Mrs McCormack the plaintiff and his other daughter Mrs Ann Seery were kicking up a row and having given a full outline of the members of his family where they were and how they were situated he informed Mr Wallace that he wished to sell the farm outright to the defendant Mrs Bennett for the sum of £300,00. Mr Wallace advised Mr Seery strongly against this course, and urged him instead to make a will. I am satisfied that a considerable part of the time occupied in the attendance of Mr Wallace on Mr Seery which was approximately an hour and a half was taken up with a discussion in which Mr Wallace was urging upon Mr Seery the desirability of simply making a new will. Mr Seery was not content to make a new will only and was then informed by Mr Wallace of the alternative of making a deed retaining to himself a life interest in the lands and transferring them in remainder to the defendant Mrs Bennett. This alternative he James Seery I am satisfied specifically chose. Although there is no note of it in the attendance Mr Wallace told me in evidence and I accept it as being accurate that he informed Mr Seery of the possibility of inserting a revocation clause in this deed. He said however that he did not emphasise the desirability of a revocation clause largely as I understand his evidence because he had urged upon Mr Seery the even more easily revocable method of giving these lands by will to Mrs Bennett and that Mr Seery had definitely refused to adopt that course. Mr Wallace also I am satisfied made specific enquiry as to the position of James Seery's wife particularly if he were to die before her. Mr James Seery in reply indicated that his wife would not want for anything and in fact indicated that he placed a total reliance upon Mrs Bennett to look after her mother. At the conclusion of this interview Mr Wallace arranged that he would send out to Mr Seery addressed to him care of Mrs Bennett at his request a draft of the proposed deed. This was done and a deed in the simple form of a transfer of the remainder interest reserving a life interest to James Seery was sent in draft form to him. He returned to Mr Wallace's Office on 30 September 1967 accompanied again by Mrs Bennett. On this occasion James Seery demanded that he should in addition make a new will asserting that it was undesirable that he would have a will leaving the place to one member of the family and a deed transferring it to another. Mr Wallace took some care again to enquire from James Seery as to whether he was totally satisfied with the arrangement which he proposed to make and in particular to the position of his wife and having done so and

James Seery appearing totally satisfied with it the deed was then executed and was subsequently dated 4 October 1967.

At no time during any of the discussions between James Seery and Mr Kevin Wallace did James Seery ever mention to Mr Wallace the fact that his proposal to transfer an interest in the lands to his daughter Mrs Bennett had originated in association with a promise requested by him and given by her that she would look after him and his wife to the end of their lives. Mr Wallace in evidence properly conceded that had he been aware of the existence of that sort of arrangement he would have had to take cognisance of it. The possibility in these circumstances of inserting into the deed covenants on the part of Mrs Bennett for the support and maintenance and care of James Seery and or his wife was never considered at any of the discussions in the solicitor's office.

Much of the evidence was concerned with events which occurred after the execution of this deed. Except in relation to a claim by the plaintiff against the defendant that she unlawfully trespassed on her father's land during his lifetime, the issues arising from this part of the evidence seem to me to be irrelevant to the question of the validity of the deed. If as is alleged by the plaintiff the defendant Mrs Bennett subsequent to the execution of this deed failed to fulfil the promise which she had given to look after her mother and father this would not of itself affect the validity of the deed. If on the other hand the deed is in fact invalid then no matter how much care Mrs Bennett bestowed on her mother and father after its execution it would not render it valid. Since the issues have been raised however and the allegations have been made I should say that in general I accept and prefer the account of these contentious issues given by Mrs Bennett than the account given by Mrs McCormack or by Sister Xavier. In particular I find it a fact that Mrs Bennett was in occupation of her father's land during his lifetime by his permission and under an arrangement to pay him for that occupation which she fulfilled.

It is necessary to summarise the above rather lengthy findings of fact in order to clarify the legal position as between the parties. The summary is as follows:

I find that this deed was not executed as a result of any undue influence on the part of Mrs Bennett. I find that James Seery had no mental or physical infirmity which prevented him from fully understanding the nature and consequences of this deed. I find that James Seery had the benefit of independent advice from the solicitor of his choice and that that was fully and carefully available to him. I find that the possibility of a clause of revocation was explained to James Seery and that the desirability of making a revocable disposition of his property was urged upon him. I find that the deed is on the face of it improvident in that James Seery disposed of the remainder interest in his only piece of property without any valuable consideration moving to him in respect of that disposition. I find that by reason of the failure of James Seery and or Mrs Bennett to inform Mr Wallace of the promises made by Mrs Bennett in respect of the care and maintenance of her father and mother that he was not aware of all the circumstances of the case when he was advising James Seery.

On these findings of fact I am satisfied that the legal position is as follows:

I accept and adopt as applicable to this case the reasoning of Mr Justice Budd in the case of *Gregg v Kidd* [1956] IR 183. In particular I would adopt and repeat the portion of his judgment at p. 196 [see above p. 588] where he says:

> Where the relations between the donor and another person raise a presumption that that other person had influence over the donor and the evidence shows that the third party is both closely related to the donee and was closely associated in action and interest with the donee at the time of events leading to the transaction it would seem to be on principle that the onus in such circumstances must be

likewise thrown on the donee to establish that the gift resulted from the free exercise of the donor's will. The presumption may of course be rebutted either by showing that the donor has had competent independent advice and acted of his own free will or in some other way.

As Lord Hailsham says in *Inche Noriah v Shaik Allie Bin Omar*:

The most obvious way to prove that the gift was the result of the free exercise of independent will is to establish that the gift was made after the nature and effect of the transaction had been fully explained to the donor by some independent and qualified person so completely as to satisfy the court that the donor was acting independently of any influence from the donee and with full appreciation of what he was doing.

If that method of rebutting the presumption is adopted and it is not the only method open the advice relied on must in the words of Lord Hailsham be given 'with a knowledge of all relevant circumstances and must be such as a competent and honest adviser would give if acting solely in the interests of the donor.'

The ignorance by Mr Wallace at the time when he was advising the late James Seery of the promises made by Mrs Bennett in respect of a transfer of the land meant that he was not a person with knowledge of all relevant circumstances. If to defend this deed and to discharge the onus which is in my view upon her the defendant must rely only on the independent advice of Mr Wallace she must therefore fail. However from the passage which I have quoted Mr Justice Budd was of this view and in this I am in full agreement with his judgment that the presence of full and satisfactory independent advice is not the only way of proving that a voluntary deed even though it may be on the face of it improvident resulted from the free exercise of the donor's will. I am satisfied that James Seery in October 1967 himself was particularly concerned to make an out and out transfer of these lands by deed to his daughter Mrs Bennett. I am satisfied that that idea for practical purposes originated with him and certainly did not originate with the defendant Mrs Bennett. His reason for making such a transfer instead of a will which would have been revocable was I am satisfied that he wanted a permanency and finality with regard to the disposition of his affairs. I think it is a reasonable inference from the evidence which I have heard that he was a sufficiently astute man to know that no form of bargain or commercial transaction concerned with his land was likely to secure for himself and his wife what they really needed and that was personal care and attention granted largely through affection and kindness by a member of their family. I believe therefore that James Seery when he executed this deed did so as an act entirely of his own free will and did so in the expectation and belief which was his own and not induced to them that by so doing he would secure or reinforce what he believed to be the affectionate attendance of his daughter for both himself and his wife. In these circumstances I conclude that there is evidence before me which I accept other than and in addition to the evidence of the independent advice which James Seery received before executing the deed which satisfies me that the deed was his own act and resulted from an exercise of his own free will. In these circumstances as I understand the legal principles applicable I must uphold this deed even though it may on the face of it appear improvident and even though events which occurred after its execution may have made James Seery in his lifetime dissatisfied with it. Having already concluded that there was no trespass on the life interest of James Seery in these lands I therefore dismiss this action.

SECTION TWO—UNCONSCIONABLE BARGAIN

A. SALES OF REVERSIONS

A general equitable jurisdiction to protect persons from their own weakness or vulnerability developed from early case-law which gave relief to the sons of the aristocracy who had dealt in their future property rights— e.g. by mortgaging or charging landed estates—in order to satisfy present needs or requirements. The jurisdiction expanded in order to protect the more feckless or underprivileged members of society.

Fry v Lane (1888) 90 ChD 312

Property was left to five 'poor persons in a humble position' in society. The defendant Lane induced them to sell the property to him, on less than favourable terms. Various actions were brought to set these transactions aside, *inter alia*, under 31 Vict. c.4. (The Sale of Reversions Act 1867).

Kay J.:

. . .

. . . Long before the passing of that Act it was settled that the court of chancery would relieve against a sale of or other dealing with a remainder or revision at an undervalue on that ground alone, and this even where the remainderman was of mature age and accustomed to business: *Wiseman v Beake*;[1] *Berkley-Freeman v Bishop*;[2] *Davis v Duke of Marlborough*;[3] *Earl of Portmore v Taylor*;[4] *Boothby v Boothby*;[5] *Foster v Roberts*;[6] *Beynon v Cook*.[7] In such cases it was held that the onus lay upon the purchaser to shew that he had given the 'fair' value as it was called in *Earl of Aldborough v Trye*,[8] or 'the market value': *Talbot v Staniforth*.[9]

By the 31 Vict. c. 4, reciting that it was expedient to amend the law as administered in courts of equity with respect to sales of reversions, it was enacted (by s. 1) that 'no purchase, made *bona fide* and without fraud or unfair dealing, of any reversionary interest in real or personal estate shall hereafter be opened or set aside merely on the ground of undervalue,' and by s. 2 the word 'purchase' in the Act is to include 'every kind of contract, conveyance, or assignment, under or by which any beneficial interest in any kind of property may be acquired.' This Act came into operation on 1 January 1868.

It is obvious that the words 'merely on the ground of undervalue' do not include the case of an undervalue so gross as to amount of itself to evidence of fraud, and in *Earl of Aylesford v Morris*[10] Lord Selborne said that this Act:

> leaves undervalue still a material element in cases in which it is not the sole equitable ground for relief. These changes of the law have in no degree whatever altered the *onus probandi* in those cases, which, according to the language of Lord Hardwicke, raise 'from the circumstances or conditions of the parties contracting— weakness on one side, usury on the other, or extortion, or advantage taken of that weakness'—a presumption of fraud. Fraud, does not here mean deceit or circumvention; it means an unconscientious use of the power arising out of these circumstances and conditions; and when the relative position of the parties is such as *prima facie* to raise this presumption, the transaction cannot stand unless the person claiming the benefit of it is able to repel the presumption by contrary evidence, proving it to have been in point of fact fair, just, and reasonable.

The most common case for the interference of a court of equity is that of an expect-ant heir, reversioner, or remainderman who is just of age, his youth being treated as an important circumstance. Another analogous case is where the vendor is a poor man with imperfect education, as in Evans v Llewellin;[11] Haygarth v Wearing.[12]

In the case of a poor man, in distress for money, a sale, even of property in posses-sion, at an undervalue has been set aside in many cases, as in Wood v Abrey,[13] where the only professional person employed was the purchaser's attorney, and the price was one fourth of the value, Sir John Leach saying: 'A court of equity will inquire whether the parties really did meet on equal terms; and if it be found that the vendor was in dis-tressed circumstances, and that advantage was taken of that distress, it will avoid the contract.' So in Longmate v Ledger[14] (which it seems, was affirmed on appeal),[15] where property in possession was sold for a price greatly below the value, and one solicitor acted for vendor and purchaser, and the vendor was a man advanced in years, and known to have been of a weak and eccentric disposition.

In Clark v Malpas,[16] an improvident sale of property in possession by a poor and illiterate man, the same solicitor being employed by both parties, was set aside. Again, the same thing was done in Baker v Monk,[17] where the vendor was an elderly woman in humble life, and the purchaser a substantial tradesman, whose solicitor carried out the transaction for both parties, the consideration being an annuity of 9s a week for the life of the vendor. In that case Turner L.J. distinguishes Harrison v Guest[18]—a case in which the transaction was allowed to stand—on the ground that there the offer came first from the vendor, and the purchaser advised him to take time to consider and to consult some one else about it, no such advice having been given by the vendor in Baker v Monk.

The result of the decisions is that where a purchase is made from a poor and ignorant man at a considerable undervalue, the vendor having no independent advice, a court of equity will set aside the transaction.

This will be done even in the case of property in possession, and a fortiori if the interest be reversionary.

The circumstances of poverty and ignorance of the vendor, and absence of independ-ent advice, throw upon the purchaser, when the transaction is impeached, the onus of proving, in Lord Selborne's words, that the purchase was 'fair, just, and reasonable'.

Upon the evidence before me I cannot hesitate to conclude that the price of £170 in J. B. Fry's case and £270 in George Fry's case were both considerably below the real value. The property has been subjected to the costs of appointing new trustees, and also to part of the costs of an administration suit, and yet the net produce of one fifth share is £730. Managed in a more careful manner it might have produced more.

Both J. B. Fry and his brother George were poor, ignorant men, to whom the temptation of the immediate possession of £100 would be very great. Neither of them in the transaction of the sale of his share, was, in the word of Sir J. Leach, 'on equal terms' with the purchaser. Neither had independent advice. The solicitor who acted for both parties in each transaction seems from the Law List, to have been admitted in March 1877. In October 1878, at the time of completing the sale of J. B. Fry's share he had not been more than a year and a half on the roll. His inexperience probably in some degree accounts for his allowing himself to be put in the position of solicitor for both parties in such a case. I think in each transaction he must have been considering the purchaser's interest too much properly to guard that of the vendors. Nothing could be more obvious than to test the value by obtaining an offer from one or more of the leading offices in London, which deal in purchases of this kind. But, although when borrowing money for one of the beneficiaries, he did make some application to the Law Reversionary Society, he says it never occurred to him to do so when he had to effect a sale. He found it was easy to borrow £200 upon an interest of this kind before he completed the sale of J. B. Fry's share for £170. He does not seem even to have informed either of the vendors that one of the £250 legacies had been satisfied, and he allowed the sale by auction of William's share to proceed without correcting the inaccurate statement in the particulars that this legacy was still due, though he says that he informed the intending purchaser of William's share, that the legacy had been discharged. I regret that I must come to the conclusion that, though there was a semblance of bargaining by the solicitor in each case, he did not properly protect the vendors, but gave a great advantage to the purchasers, who had been former clients, and for whom he was then acting. The circumstances illustrate the wisdom and necessity of the rule that a poor, ignorant man, selling an interest of this kind, should have independent advice, and that a purchase from him at an undervalue should be set aside, if he has not.

1. 2 Vern 121.
2. 2 Atk 39.
3. 2 Sw 108, 143.
4. 4 Sim 182.
5. 1 Mac. & G. 604; SC 15 Beav 212.
6. 29 Beav 467.
7. Law Rep 10 Ch. 389.
8. 7 Cl. & F. 436, 456.
9. 1 J. & H. 484, 503.
10. Law Rep 8 Ch. 484, 490.
11. 1 Cox, 333.
12. Law Rep 12 Eq. 320.
13. 3 Madd. 417, 423.
14. 2 Giff. 157.
15. See 3 D. F. & J. 402.
16. 4 D. F. & J. 401.
17. 4 D. J. & S. 388.
18. 8 HLC 481.

Note

In *Slator v Nolan* (1877) 11 Ir Eq R 367, at 407–8 the jurisdiction was stated very broadly by Sullivan M.R.:

It is an idle thing to suppose that the relation of trustee *cestui que trust*, or guardian and ward, or attorney and client, or some other confidential relation, must exist to entitle a man to get aid in this court in setting aside an unconscionable transaction. I take the law of the court to be that if two persons—no matter whether a confidential relation exists between them or not—stand in such a relation to each other that one can take an undue advantage of the other, whether by reason of distress or recklessness or wildness or want of care and where the facts show that one party has taken undue advantage of the other, by reason of the circumstances I have mentioned—a transaction resting upon such unconscionable dealing will not be allowed to stand: and there are several cases which show, even where no confidential relation exist; that, where parties are not on equal terms, the party who gets a benefit cannot hold it without proving that everything has been right and fair and reasonable on his part.

Sometimes the position of weakness involves the combination of a number of circumstances. These could include illiteracy, old age, physical or mental illness, to name just a few. In *Rae v Joyce* (1892) 29 LR (Ir.) 500, the plaintiff entered into an unfavourable property mortgage while in severe financial need and in poor health as a result of a complicated pregnancy. Disparate socio-economic status is also a factor.

Kelly *v* Morrisroe (1919) 53 ILTR 145

Pim J.:

Two cases came before me on appeal from the decisions of the County Court Judge of Mayo. In the first case the plaintiff, Andrew J. Kelly, issued a civil bill for ejectment on the title against the defendants, Michael Morrisroe and Honoria Morrisroe, in respect of a plot of ground in Chapel Street, in the town of Swinford. The plaintiff claimed the premises by virtue of a deed of 23 May 1918, under which a woman called Mary Gaven, the owner-in-fee, granted and conveyed to him the estate in the premises for the sum of £25, subject to her right to the use during her lifetime, rent free, of a cottage on the said plot. Mary Gaven died on 14 June 1918. The County Court Judge gave a decree in ejectment for possession of the premises. In the second case (the matter of the case stated) the plaintiff, Michael Morrisroe, and the sole executor and universal legatee and devisee under the will of Mary Gaven (dated 12 June 1918, and proved on 16 August 1918), claimed to have the deed of 23 May 1918, rescinded and delivered up to be cancelled. The County Court Judge dismissed the equity civil bill with costs. The premises in respect of which the two civil bills were issued consist of a plot of ground upon which two cottages formerly stood, but one has for some years past been in ruins, and the other, in which Mary Gaven resided, is in a state of considerable dilapidation. The valuation of the whole plot is 10s. The engineers called on each side agreed in stating, and I find as a fact, that the substantial value of the plot is its site value, and that apart from the site it is not worth much. The plot is situated between the business premises of the plaintiff, Andrew J. Kelly, and of one, Martin Campbell, both of whom stated in their evidence before me that it would be of substantial value to them as a site. I am satisfied from the evidence, and I so find, that either Andrew J. Kelly or Martin Campbell would have been willing to give Mary Gaven a very much larger sum for the premises than £25 (Martin Campbell stated that he was ready to give £100). Apart from its value to either of these parties as a means of improving their business premises, it would not have been worth to a third person more than £25, if, indeed, so much. It was stated by Andrew J. Kelly that the first suggestion of a sale of the premises was made to him by Mary Gaven, that she asked £30 and a life interest in the cottage, and that he offered her £20. Evidence was given by Mr E. H. Dolphin, a baker and merchant in Swinford, a magistrate, and a former employer of Mary Gaven, that she came to him for advice as to the offer made to her, and that he suggested the sum of £25. Mr Dolphin's account of the negotiations before the sale was not seriously disputed, and I find it to be substantially correct, but I am not satisfied that the first suggestion of a sale came from Mary Gaven. On 22 May 1918, Andrew J. Kelly instructed Mr P. O'Connor, solicitor, of Swinford, to prepare a conveyance, and on 23 May the parties, with Mr Dolphin, called at Mr O'Connor's office. Mr O'Connor stated that he read over the conveyance to Mary Gaven and explained it to her, and that in his opinion she understood its nature and effect. He said she stated that she was expecting to get £30, but that Mr Kelly was only willing to give her £25. She then executed the conveyance and memorial, Mr O'Connor holding her hand to assist her in signing. The £25 was then paid by Mr Kelly, who also paid Mr O'Connor's costs and the stamp duty. I accept Mr O'Connor's evidence so far as it goes. Mr Kelly has almost completed an entrance to his premises on the portion of the premises sold to him, which was not covered by Mary Gaven's cottage. Mary Gaven never appears to have made any objection, and there was no evidence offered showing that she was at any time dissatisfied with her bargain. I am satisfied that Mary Gaven was not in the strict sense of the word insane, but she was between seventy and eighty years of age, evidently senile, very eccentric in her habits, and altogether mentally abnormal. I find as a fact that she understood that she was selling the premises for £25, subject to her life interest therein; but I also find as a fact that owing to age and mental weakness she was not capable of duly and properly judging the fairness of the offer made to her; that she was unaware that a larger—possibly a much larger—price might have been obtained owing to the value of the site to Messrs Campbell and Kelly, and to the competition between these two gentlemen; and that neither the plaintiff nor his solicitor gave her any information as to matters which she ought to have known. It was admitted that she had not any independent advice in the transaction, and I have no doubt that an independent solicitor would have succeeded in making a much better bargain on her behalf. I do not impute any intention of fraud either to Mr Kelly or to Mr O'Connor. They thought they were making a good bargain for Mr Kelly, that they had a right to do what they did, and I dare say they also thought the bargain was not a bad one for Mary Gaven. I reversed the decision of the County Court Judge on the grounds: (1) That Mary Gaven had no independent legal advice; (2) that she was very old, and evidently infirm of mind; (3) that the premises had a competitive site value, of which she was unaware, and concerning which the purchaser's solicitor would hardly be expected to inform her; (4) that no information as to the site value was given to her either by the plaintiff or by his solicitor, and that the premises were in consequence sold at a figure much below their real value. The question of law arising for the determination of the court is as follows: Are the above facts sufficient in law to justify the court in setting aside the deed of purchase at the suit of the executor and legatee of Mary Gaven?

Sir James Campbell L.C.:

In this case the learned judge has asked us the following question: 'Are the facts as set out in the case stated sufficient in law to justify the court in setting aside the deed of purchase at the suit of the executor and legatee of Mary Gaven?' Speaking for myself, the only conceivable difficulty that I would have is the suggestion made by Mr McCormack, that there was some evidence on which the judge might come to the determination he did, and therefore that we ought not to interfere. But that argument would really evade the object which Pim J. had in view in stating the case, otherwise he never would have stated it in the way in which he did. What he really meant in stating a case was, that he wished us to decide the question whether, in our view, the evidence was reasonably sufficient for setting aside the deed that has been impeached—in other words, did the evidence justify the conclusion that the deed must be set aside? The facts in the case are few, and are not disputed. An old lady was living alone in humble circumstances in this dilapidated cottage. She had no near relatives or dependants. She had two neighbours, Mr Kelly and Mr Campbell, but the latter had never had any negotiations with her up to the date of the impeached transaction: the only offer that was made to her came from Mr Kelly, and he offered her £20. The valuation of the place is 10s. It is a remarkable fact that there is no evidence that any individual whatever would give even a shilling for it except Mr Kelly or Mr Campbell. Be that as it may, she got this offer from Mr Kelly, and she went to her former employer, Mr Dolphin, in whom she trusted, and who lives in the same town—a man of position and respectability, and a justice of the peace. Here is what Pim J. says of him: 'Evidence was given by Mr E. H. Dolphin, a baker and merchant in Swinford, a magistrate, and a former employer of Mary Gaven, that she came to him for advice as to the offer made to her, and that he suggested the sum of £25. Mr Dolphin's account of the negotiations before the sale was not seriously disputed, and I find it to be substantially correct.' How is it possible, then, to say that this old lady was without advice, or the best possible advice? The learned judge does not say that this old lady was not capable of transacting business, but that she was eccentric in habits and mentally abnormal. It would have been a dangerous contention for the plaintiff to have put forward—that the old lady was not capable of transacting business, seeing that he claims as executor under a subsequent will. The judge merely says that she was eccentric and not normal, but we have all had experience of eccentric old ladies—eccentric in habits and eccentric in dress, but as cute as possible in money matters, and quite well able to understand the value of money and transact business, yet not mentally normal. Mr Kelly's offer having been accepted, he went to Mr O'Connor, solicitor, Swinford, and instructed him to prepare a conveyance, and on the next day the old lady, accompanied by Mr Dolphin, called at Mr O'Connor's office, and Mr O'Connor—whose evidence the judge accepts—read out and explained the deed to her, and swears she understood it. The judge finds that she understood that she was getting £25, but he says the place had a sort of fancy value owing to the competition for it between the two merchants, Mr Kelly and Mr Campbell. But, apart from Mr Campbell's offer of £100 in court, its fancy value up to that time was something between £20 or £30, and there is no evidence that it was of any value except to these two gentlemen, and even for its adventitious value at that date neither went above £25. It is said that because Mr Campbell stated in court that he would have given £100, that there was something in Mr Kelly's mind about Mr Campbell's anxiety to get the place, which should have been communicated to this old lady, but the price of £100 was apparently never suggested until after her death. There is no evidence upon which the judge could reasonably find that this deed could be set aside. This old lady had all the protection necessary: her former employer, whom she trusted, advised her in the matter, and was present when the deed was completed. It was a fair and honest transaction, and although the age of the old lady threw the onus on Mr Kelly of showing that he took no advantage, that onus has been discharged by him. There is no ground whatever for any imputation either against him or Mr O'Connor, and the validity of the deed cannot be impeached. Accordingly, the question put to us by the learned judge must be answered in the negative.

(Ronan and O'Connor L.JJ. concurred.)

The leading case is **Grealish v Murphy [1946] IR 35**

Gavan Duffy J.:

The plaintiff sues (1) to have an indenture of settlement of October 1942, set aside, either (a) as improvident, or (b) for his own mental infirmity and incapacity to understand the deed, coupled with undue influence by the defendant; (2) to assert his sole title to a sum of £2,000 standing at the National Bank, Galway, in the joint names of plaintiff and defendant; (3) to recover two sums of £500 and £645, as money improperly obtained or retained by the defendant from the plaintiff; and (4) to have an account taken. The defendant justifies his action under each head.

Peter Grealish, the plaintiff, is by way of being a farmer; he is a bachelor in the sixties; he is a man of a generous turn, but obstinate; he can hardly read and he signs as a marksman; he is afflicted with a worse than Boeotian headpiece and a very poor memory; a long life has not taught him sense. At the opening of the year 1942 this poor old victim of his circumstances was living under rather dismal conditions; Peter, for as Peter he is known, had a couple of labouring men sleeping under his roof, but otherwise lived alone on a remote farm and ranch of some 180 acres at Carnmore in the Oranmore district of the County of Galway, neglected by his relatives and almost bereft of friends; he was loaded with possessions, far above his modest wants and far beyond his modest capacity for management; moneys exceeding £5,500 lay to his credit on deposit at a bank in Galway, though considerable portions of this fortune were destined to be dissipated in the course of the year 1942; he had some cattle and his land had for many years brought him into frequent conflict with certain of his smaller neighbours, who were in the habit of taking conacre from him; he felt, as I surmise, that he could not by himself hope to hold his own in any considerable purchases or sales of cattle; he also owned a little farm a few miles away from Carnmore; and he needed, and realised that he needed, a reliable factotum as manager and as protector.

Peter had tried hard, and failed, to solve his problem; he had sought to marry first a cousin of his, then a niece, and finally another niece, to one, Thomas Fox, who had promised to bring in a marriage portion, payable to the plaintiff, first of £400, then of £1,000 and lastly of £500, and to look after Peter and his affairs, in exchange for a settlement of the big farm, as from Peter's death, on Fox and his bride, and their maintenance on the farm during Peter's life: Fox had eventually refused the first two ladies; the third deed had been executed on 3 December 1941; but a few weeks later the third lady had positively said 'No.'

Peter was bitterly disappointed, but he was not defeated. His family had known a family of Murphys, who lived as far away as Headford, and he resolved to invite one of the sons to step into the breach. Accordingly Thomas Murphy, the defendant, whom Peter had never seen, presented himself at Carnmore on 26 January 1942; Peter liked his looks and at once came to business; he admits that he promised to give Murphy the farm after his own (Peter's) death, if Murphy would in the meantime work the land for him. In view of that admission, borne out by Peter's later instructions to his own solicitor, I need not determine precisely how much further Peter's promises may have gone, though Murphy is much more explicit; his evidence is that Peter explained that he was boycotted and that his land had been forcibly seized and that he wished to put an end to the conacre holdings on his land and to have a man to manage and work the farm and live with him; he says that Peter went on to promise that, if Murphy would come, Peter would leave him the farm, buy him a new lorry and also, if he wished, a new car, settle on Murphy any sum of money he required and let him marry any girl he liked; Murphy says that Peter wanted to go to a solicitor the very next day to 'sign me over the farm.'

Murphy's reply, he says, was that he must see his own solicitor, Mr McDonagh, at Tuam, and he saw him on 27 January, and discovered the Fox settlement of the previous month; he returned at once to Carnmore, when Peter assured him that he had already given instructions for a suit to set that deed aside; they agreed, Murphy continues, to call on Mr Concannon, Peter's solicitor, at Galway on the following day; they did so, according to Murphy, and during that visit he and Peter agreed, in the presence of the solicitor and his clerk, Costello, that pending the setting aside of the Fox settlement, Murphy should manage for Peter Grealish, take him into town to buy and sell generally and do any business that Peter might ask him to do. This agreement of 28 January 1942, is decisive upon the onus of proof for any transaction prior to the impugned indenture of October 1942. This agreement is not corroborated; Peter is incapable of affirming or disputing it; Concannon denies it; Costello, called as a witness by Murphy, was asked nothing about it, and his answer, were it available, would have carried little weight; but, as against Murphy, I must accept his own evidence as proving at least that on some day at the outset of his dealings with Peter he undertook in consideration of Peter's promises, to act for him in business matters generally, pending the action against Fox. And during the time that elapsed before October 1942, when that action was heard, Murphy must have discovered beyond doubt, if he did not know from the first day, that Peter needed decidedly more protection than the ordinary western farmer and cattle dealer.

|Counsel for the defendant| pressed on me vigorously the view that Peter is merely a simple-minded and not a feeble-minded old man, but that is not the impression made on me by his performance as a witness; I must go with the medical evidence to the extent of classifying him among the mentally deficient, though I should not myself assimilate him to a child of twelve. I cannot measure his deficiency in scientific terms and I need say no more than this, that, as I appraise him, the brain, while it must have developed with time, has never since childhood attained the normal powers of an adult; and he is liable to be erratic, especially outside the daily routine of his life at home. The trial threw occasional side-lights on Peter's faculties; for instance, he can read the clock, but cannot tell the time; Murphy virtually admitted that Peter was unable to count £2,000 in £50, £10 and £5 notes; and, having made to Murphy in October 1942, an astounding present of, as Murphy says, £700, Peter was unable, as I must necessarily infer from the pleadings, to give his advisers in this action any instructions whatever on the matter, which came to light only through a question in Murphy's cross-examination by |counsel for the plaintiff| at the trial; I gather, moreover, that Peter had completely lost all trace of a further large sum of money, which he drew from the bank at the same time.

Murphy, who comes of farming stock, had been a road worker and he was a haulier in a small way, with a car and a lorry of his own, when Peter's proposal burst upon him and a bright vista suddenly opened out before his eyes. True, he was being asked to give up his freedom, he had no idea what sort of principal Peter would prove to be and he could not tell what stings he would have to endure from waspish neighbours. But he was only thirty two years of age and the possible difficulties may well have loomed dim in the dazzle of the glittering reward proffered by his glowing benefactor; the golden prospect was that he would be a rich man after a few years of not too arduous labour and surely he could well bear any little passing troubles that the venture might entail. Murphy accepted Peter's proposal, but did nothing at this time to rush the old man; I do not think he called on him again until the following March. Then he began to see him, as he says himself, about twice a week until June, and I see no reason to believe that his attentions slackened during the summer; he used to take Peter for shopping or business purposes to Galway by car; he drove him at different dates as far as Dublin and Limerick and to several fairs; he says he bought cattle for him to the value of £480 at Gort Fair in May, and early in October sold cattle for him at Tuam Fair, taking £530 net, and immediately afterwards bought cattle for him at Westport Fair. He was kind to Peter and that solicitude did not go unrewarded; Peter gave Murphy £450 towards a motor lorry in May 1942, and (at about the same time, I think, or earlier) £250 for a Chrysler car. In June Peter actually placed a sum of £2,000 in the joint names of himself and Murphy at the National Bank, in Galway, though not necessarily out of munificence towards Murphy and primarily, I think, as a strategic diversion to defeat the apprehended machinations of a rapacious Estate Duty Office.

In June 1942, the court adjourned the Fox action, and Peter, blaming Mr Concannon and chafing at the delay, entrusted his case to another solicitor, Dr Comyn of Loughrea. On 10 October 1942, the Circuit Court in Galway annulled the Fox deed on Peter's evidence, Fox not appearing, and on 13 October Peter gave the instructions upon which Dr Comyn drew the settlement that is the chief bone of contention in this action. The deed was executed on 20 October, and bears date 24 October 1942, and Peter, there-tofore full owner of the Carnmore land, was registered as limited owner by reference to this document. The stamp duty puts the net value of the farm at some £1,000. The deed, in pursuance of the January agreement, gave Murphy a position at Carnmore equivalent to, but really better than, that of an adopted son.

On 30 October 1942, Peter drew out £1,900, standing on deposit in his own name at the Bank of Ireland in Galway, thus closing the account, which was distinct from the still subsisting joint account for £2,000 with the National Bank. There is some evidence that Peter, when taking the money out, alleged that he was buying a farm. Murphy avowed in cross-examination that Peter had given him £700 of this money and had lodged £1,000 out of the £1,900 in the National Bank (presumably at Galway). I understand that, until this admission by Murphy as to his £700, the whole sum drawn had vanished, and, unless the money has been discovered during the long vacation, the sum of £1,000 still has to be found. Murphy may be mistaken as to the precise bank, but his evidence of a bank lodgment is specific, and the mystery cannot be brushed aside as if a mere bagatelle were involved. I am not to be understood as throwing blame on Murphy for the loss of the money; I do not know who is to blame. This extraordinary disappearance of the money of an irresponsible old man calls, in my view, for close and persistent investigation, with the aid, if necessary, of the Gárda Síochána; but that matter is outside the purview of this action on the pleadings and the evidence.

Murphy says that he did not go to live at Carnmore in pursuance of the settlement until early in December 1942, when he lodged, hard by Peter's own house, with a Mrs Fahy; a young Fahy lived with Peter and worked for him. Local hostility had declared itself against Murphy as early as October, but, after his arrival, a quite unforeseen and particularly unpleasant series of attacks came from one of Peter's sisters, a bedlam, living some three miles away, who would descend in wrath upon Carnmore at intervals, giving tongue to loud maledictions upon the grabber of her brother's land. Murphy, I think actually went in fear of his life from some of the local roughs, a number of whom had stoned his car; and he found the onslaughts of the termagant almost equally hard to endure.

Early in January 1943, I find (in a conflict of evidence) that Murphy, as Peter says, told Peter that he must have money or he would leave; I find that Peter offered him £500 and that Murphy refused this sum and went off to Galway; and that Peter at once sent him an urgent message with an offer, if he would come back. Murphy's evidence, for which there is some corroboration, is that the messenger brought him an offer of £500 and of all Peter's cattle, and that Peter also promised to keep his sister away; so he returned and accepted the offer. I find that Murphy did return and come to terms with Peter, but, as his witness, the messenger, says 'I suppose he really meant to stay anyway'; my reading of the position is that Murphy knew that Peter was afraid of being beaten or killed, if deprived of Murphy's protection, and knew that Peter was sure to succumb to the demand for money, to prevent his desertion by Murphy. Murphy now says that he had not decided to abandon the undertaking, but he could not live there nor work the farm 'on account of the trouble', he did not like the place 'inside or outside', he was under police protection (in fact the Gárdaí had not yet come) and he wanted to go home to see his own people and to consult his solicitor. He admits having gone away, but denies having demanded money before he left. Peter (whose evidence here I do not accept) says that Murphy got the £500 before leaving and he denies having sent a messenger with an offer to bring him back. The fact that Murphy got the money is not in dispute. But I do not know where Peter got the £500; he says that he drew it from the Bank of Ireland, Murphy having driven him to Galway for the purpose; Murphy, as I follow him, says that Peter drew the money from the National Bank and paid him on 15 January 1943. But neither bank account shows any such drawing and no witness has suggested that the justly timorous owner kept any large sum of money at home.

On the night of 12 January 1943, a day or two after Murphy's return, shots were fired into Mrs Fahy's house; the incident was described by the police as 'an attempted murder on the house of Fahy'; young Fahy was afraid to work for Peter or live with him any more, though the other labourer stayed; Peter's house and Fahy's were kept under police protection for eighteen months thereafter, as was also Murphy's person on dark nights, while he remained at Carnmore.

On 10 March, Murphy sold on the land thirty nine head of cattle (Peter's alleged present to him), realising £643, for his own account. The deal was not carried out as openly as the circumstances required. I see no need to determine whether Peter had given Murphy the cattle or not; Peter vehemently denies the gift; but I think the probabilities are that Peter had regretted and repudiated his excessive liberality in a crisis and that Murphy felt uneasy about the whole discreditable affair. On 3 May Murphy fell ill and went home; he and Peter parted on good terms. But Murphy's amazing statement that, when leaving, he was 'under the impression' (sic!) that Peter knew that the cattle were gone, throws a nasty light on the rape of the cattle. On 28 May Murphy returned; Peter was angry and at once taxed him with having sold Peter's cattle surreptitiously. By this time Peter had another man, a relative, living in the house. Early in June Peter consulted Mr Conway, his present solicitor, with a view to taking action against Murphy. By 22 June Peter and Murphy were not on speaking terms and on that night Murphy was locked out by Peter and went five miles away for a bed, under police protection. At the end of June, Murphy, feeling that he was in effect supplanted by the new arrival, left Carnmore.

That is the story in outline. But the difficulty of ascertaining the facts has been prodigious. I could not depend much on Peter's memory, nor on the accuracy of either contestant; the other local witnesses did not impress me; and several witnesses who might have been called did not appear.

Let me now examine the making of the settlement which the plaintiff seeks to set aside. We have Peter's promise to Murphy at the very outset of their connection; that was a promise, according to Murphy, to 'leave me the farm' and 'settle any sum of money I wanted on me', and Peter had wished to go to a solicitor at once to 'sign me over the farm'. Then, according to Murphy, 'he used to say every time I would meet him that he had decided to leave the place to me and that the marriage settlement would be set aside.' And there is ample evidence (whatever the terms actually were in which Peter expressed himself to Murphy) that Peter was fuming with impatience to rid himself of his commitments to Fox, obviously in order to be free to conclude his arrangements with Murphy. There is evidence that Costello, Mr Concannon's clerk, who claims to have been an old friend of Peter's and was called as a witness for Murphy, in March 1942, definitely ascertained that Mr Concannon would have nothing to do with any settlement of the land by Grealish upon Murphy, and I cannot doubt that Costello made this fact known to Murphy, if not to Peter, who changed his solicitor in June 1942, as I have said. Costello lost his place in the Concannon office early in July. Peter paid several visits to Dr Comyn during the summer, always accompanied, I think by Murphy and by Costello; Costello's presence on these occasions is unexplained, but Peter clearly trusted him and afterwards rewarded him liberally for his miscellaneous services. According to Dr Comyn's recollection, Costello occasionally made some remarks on these occasions, but Peter did the talking, while Murphy 'never uttered a word', a singularly modest attitude for the heir-presumptive during the long wait from June to October; if this persistent silence is an example of western caution, it suggests tactical caution carried rather too far.

On 13 October 1942, three days after the court had set aside the Fox deed, Peter, duly accompanied by Murphy and Costello, called on Dr Comyn. In the outer office Peter intimated to the solicitor that he intended to 'take in' a man and Dr Comyn understood the man to be Murphy, whereupon Dr Comyn took Peter by himself upstairs and wrote down his instructions; he had no conversation at all with Murphy. If Murphy is to be believed (and there are limits to my credulity), Peter (who may fairly be said to have been living for this day) did not tell Murphy when he came down, that he had actually given the instructions; but Murphy did admit in cross-examination that Peter had said he was going in (that is, to Dr Comyn) in order to transfer the land to Murphy.

The effect of the detailed instructions, as taken down, was that, being old, delicate and unable to work his land without loss, Peter wished to take Murphy, who was not a relative, into his house as factotum and general worker and, while keeping a life interest, to transfer the big farm after his death to Murphy, who was to be supported and to live at Carnmore in the meantime; Peter meant to deal with the other farm and with his stock and moneys later. The instructions were read to Peter, who approved of them, and upon them Dr Comyn instructed counsel, verbally, as I understand, to settle the deed.

On 20 October the engrossment was read to Peter, who executed the deed as a marksman. The solicitor was acting for Peter alone; he was not told that Murphy had a solicitor of his own; Murphy had no adviser at all and had not been consulted in any way during the preparation of the settlement. Dr Comyn himself 'knew about the boycotting thoroughly well'; 'boycott' was counsel's term and it is right to say that the evidence, so far as it goes, suggests that the facts do not warrant so strong an expression to describe Peter's annoyances from his neighbours up to this time. Dr Comyn says that he explained Murphy's covenants to him and that Murphy also then executed the deed. Finally he 'told Peter, in the presence of Murphy, that, if Murphy did not comply with the covenants, he, Peter, knew where to find me.' He did not give Murphy any copy or duplicate of the deed. It is not suggested that Murphy made any claim to a money settlement.

The settlement purports to make Peter Grealish, as beneficial owner, assign the farm absolutely as from Peter's death to Thomas Murphy, his heirs and assigns, subject to a life interest in Peter; the land is expressly charged with a right for Murphy to reside in Peter's house and to be supported and maintained out of the land during Peter's life; Murphy for his part covenants with Peter, during Peter's life, without reward to reside in the house and work and manage the land and sow and harvest the crops and attend to and take proper care of all farm stock and implements and the buying and selling of stock and generally to perform all the farm work and the duties of a labourer as required by Peter and (a very important covenant) duly and properly to account for all moneys expended or received by him on behalf of Peter; and Murphy covenants to pay Peter £1 a week for every week in which he fails to reside with Peter and to indemnify Peter for any loss and expense incurred on the maintenance or wages of any person employed by Peter to perform any work that Murphy may fail to do.

Thus Peter executed an improvident settlement, surrendering irrevocably his own absolute title for a life interest in consideration of personal covenants, backed by no adequate sanction; the farm itself was hypothecated to secure the newcomer, beside whom Peter was a Croesus; and Peter was to be left for the remainder of his life very much at the mercy of a rather impecunious young man, who had no ties of blood and was still unproved as a friend. I think effective safeguards for Peter could have been devised, if there was to be a settlement, or alternatively Peter might have contracted to settle the property on Murphy by will, upon the lines suggested by *Coverdale v Eastwood*;[1] whatever plan was adopted, I think that suitable conditions could and should have been determined in negotiation between the solicitors for the parties, each of whom ought to have been separately represented. But these reflections are otiose, if the conclusive answer to Peter's present claim is that he was separately advised by an independent solicitor.

That contention deserves careful examination and I have examined it with great care. I am satisfied that Peter received from an experienced solicitor advice that was absolutely independent and I am satisfied that the draft deed was settled by very able counsel, upon instructions reflecting, of course, the state of mind and knowledge of the solicitor. Nevertheless, the question of Peter's actual understanding of the solemn document that he executed on 20 October 1942, is a question of first importance. Dr Comyn, who avows that he looked upon the settlement as a transaction similar to the three attempts which, as Peter told him, had broken down, says that he was absolutely satisfied that Peter understood the instructions he gave for the deed. I have no doubt that Peter did know that the deed would secure the land to Murphy at Peter's death and that he knew generally the undertakings that Murphy was giving in return; Peter showed his own understanding of the young man's obligations, when he formulated his grievance in his own words: 'He (Murphy) did not do anything about the agreement; he failed. . . . He was bound to look after me and buy and sell and give up the money—what he did not do.' But the trouble is that the solicitor, whose advice was essential to Peter, did not advise *en connaissance de cause* and that Peter's actual knowledge of what he was doing fell very short of the knowledge that the settlor ought to have had. That is the result in my mind of candid evidence from Dr Comyn himself and of inferences therefrom. Consequently the principle of *Harrison v Guest*[2] and *Coomber v Coomber*;[3] that a competent assignor, who knows what he is doing, must be held to his deed, does not apply here.

The evidence proves that the solicitor did not know all the material facts, that he did not give Peter a complete explanation of the nature and effect of the deed, and that the duty of illuminating Peter's benighted mind was more imperative and more formidable, if the task was possible, than the solicitor supposed.

First. Dr Comyn did not get the facts. He did not ascertain the total of Peter's property, nor the proportion between that total and the value of the farm at Carnmore; yet that was relevant and material information for an adviser. Still more important to be known was the fact that Peter had already placed £2,000 on deposit in the joint names of himself and Murphy, with Murphy's ready acquiescence, under the illusion, known to Murphy, that this device would ward off the imaginary terrors of Dublin Castle. Murphy, knowing Peter for what he was, could not assume that Peter had mentioned the episode, still less that he had given an accurate account of it; Murphy ought to have told the solicitor all about it, but he persisted in his curious policy of silence. Perhaps Murphy did not know positively how silly Peter's ruse was as a measure of defence, but he is intelligent enough, in my estimate of him, to have felt the transaction to be one of questionable virtue and of very dubious value, and, both for this reason and because he stood to gain a large sum of money from his pitiable patron, he ought to have spoken out at this juncture. Here was cogent evidence, had the solicitor and counsel known it, that Peter was and would be incapable of taking care of his own interests and that Peter and Murphy combined were and would be unequal to the burden of taking care of his property. Instead of favouring the projected settlement, as he did, Dr Comyn must have gone into the whole affair very much more warily, had he known. He did not know, because, by agreement or coincidence, each of the two men vitally concerned said nothing.

Secondly. Peter was not told and did not realise how gravely he was committing himself and jeopardising his own interest; he probably understood neither the immediate pledging of his favour to Murphy nor the effect of that charge; certainly the difference between the deed and a will was not explained to him, nor the fact that the settlement was to be irrevocable and his alienation irretrievable, no matter how badly Murphy might behave, no matter what untoward development might supervene; and he was certainly not a man to apprehend the risks, at least without the clearest and most insistent exposition of them. What precautions were taken in the deed against the vicissitudes of life? Murphy might have mismanaged the farm hopelessly, for all the solicitor could tell; or, for all he could tell, Murphy might have taken to drink or gone to the devil or married a shrew who would make Peter's life a torture; he might have become a bankrupt; he might have been sent to hospital for years, or been committed for some time to an asylum; he might even have been sentenced to imprisonment. Unlikely events, very unlikely? Perhaps, but why do I insure my house against fire, and how was the solicitor, a stranger to Murphy, to gauge the probabilities of an ensuing incapacity or incompetence? An act of God is always unlikely (before it happens) and the devil's action may often seem unlikely too. And if some such calamity had smitten Peter, the law might or might not have given him some costly redress. It was unlikely, perhaps very unlikely, that the young man would predecease the old; but how deplorable would Peter's position have been, if Murphy had died after a few months' work under the deed and perhaps twenty years before Peter himself! However, Peter's advisers had no more dark forebodings than their client. Clearly there were some important aspects of the deed far outside poor Peter's ken, when he scratched his rude mark upon the paper.

Thirdly. The solicitor quite erroneously considered and treated Peter as a normal member of the farming community; in fact I think he treated him as a man of high intelligence. Taking his client to be a competent judge of his own man, the solicitor, who just knew Murphy to be a farmer's son and no relative and Peter's dumb attendant, made no inquiries at all as to Murphy's antecedents, character, capacity or financial position; he assumed both the fitness of Murphy and the value of his covenants; he did not suspect how easily the young man might become master of the situation, nor how much he would be tempted to abuse his trust; and the deed reflects that kindly confidence; whether Dr Comyn seriously expected Murphy to keep accounts, I do not know. No need was felt to appoint trustees; perhaps they would have been hard to find, but, had the solicitor realised the settlor's weakness, he would have seen that Peter required and must have the protection for which trusts were invented. Unless there be a legal presumption of undue influence against Murphy, making other questions quite subordinate, I regard it as a matter of high importance that Peter's advisers in this particular transaction should have been equipped to advise him with a just appreciation of his mental debility and his special need of protection. They were not so equipped and Peter did not get the circumspect advice and protection so necessary to him.

Now, how is Murphy affected by any criticism reflecting upon the advice under which Peter acted? I have shown that Murphy's own conduct in the matter was not beyond reproach, but any impartial person will see that it is quite impossible to say that the deed was procured through Murphy's undue influence, even if he did his part during nearly nine months, as he naturally would, to keep the old man's ardour alive. Nor is this the familiar case in which the court, from the relation of the parties, must presume undue influence until disproved positively by the recipient of the bounty; Murphy had constituted himself Peter's interim confidential agent in January 1942, and had thus placed himself in a very delicate position, an exceptionally delicate position in view of Peter's mentality; but the undoubted fact is that some such transaction as that eventuating in the actual settlement had been expressly envisaged by the parties from the outset, before Murphy can have acquired any influence whatsoever; therefore I cannot fairly impute to him Peter's decision to put the business on a legal basis as soon as the way was made clear by the final elimination of the Fox interest, the only obstacle. And Murphy in no way interfered with the drafting of the deed in the particular form which it took.

Peter had intended all through to leave the property to Murphy and to bind himself to that effect, in return for the precious services to be rendered by the vigorous young man to the rather helpless old one. As from January 1942, Murphy had only to be kind to Peter, as he was, and to retain his goodwill, as he certainly did, in order to secure his reward from that eager benefactor.

Besides, the plan was not originated by Murphy, but by Peter, and by Peter alone. Murphy on his side had faced appreciable risks in accepting Peter's advances; and any picture of him as an adventurer, inveigling his witless victim into a trap in the October settlement, would be a caricature. Much as I blame Murphy for his reticence (partly perhaps through ignorance) as to the existence of his own solicitor and for his want of candour in suppressing the eccentric and disquieting £2,000 deposit in the joint names, I could not in common sense treat these faults as any evidence of undue influence in relation to the settlement on the facts; and, if Murphy throws doubt on the veracity of his own evidence concerning Peter's alleged original offer to settle money on him, by his failure to mention that important promise to Dr Comyn and his failure to call upon the solicitor to make good that promise in the deed, here again my criticism of Murphy as a witness is foreign to the issue of undue influence in fact and remote from any evidence that would raise a legal presumption of undue influence against Murphy, so far as the settlement is concerned.

The result is that the plaintiff's attempt to set aside the deed on the ground of undue influence, whether actual or presumptive, by Murphy cannot succeed, and, if the deed had to stand or fall upon that issue, there would be nothing more to say. But the position in law as I see it, upon the pleadings, is not so simple as that; there is another crucial matter to be determined.

Peter cannot avoid the deed for undue influence; but his claim is further based on the improvidence of the transaction and also he directly alleges (though in connection with the charge of undue influence) his own mental incapacity; I think I can reasonably read these averments together without calling for an amendment of his pleadings.

The issue thus raised brings into play Lord Hatherley's cardinal principle (from which the exceptions are rare) that equity comes to the rescue whenever the parties to a contract have not met upon equal terms, see Lord Hatherley's judgment (dissenting on facts) in O'Rourke v Bolingbroke;[4] the corollary is that the court must inquire whether a grantor, shown to be unequal to protecting himself, has had the protection which was his due by reason of his infirmity, and the infirmity may take various forms. The deed here was in law a transaction for value: Colreavy v Colreavy;[5] however tenuous the value may have proved to be in fact, and, of course, a court must be very much slower to undo a transaction for value; but the fundamental principle to justify radical interference by the court is the identical principle, whether value be shown or not, and the recorded examples run from gifts and voluntary settlements (including an abortive marriage settlement) to assignments for a money consideration. The principle has been applied to improvident grants, whether the particular disadvantage entailing the need for protection to the grantor were merely low station and surprise (though the grantor's rights were fully explained): Evans v Llewellin,[6] or youth and inexperience: Prideaux v Londsdale;[7] Everitt v Everitt,[8] or age and weak intellect, short of total incapacity, with no fiduciary relation and no 'arts of inducement' to condemn the grantee: Longmate v Ledger;[9] Anderson v Elsworth.[10] Even the exuberant or ill-considered dispositions of feckless middle-aged women have had to yield to the same principle: Phillipson v Kerry;[11] Wollaston v Tribe.[12]

The principle prevailed, when the deed was 'the most honest thing in the world' so far as the settlor and her solicitor were concerned: Everitt v Everitt, and though the evidence of the solicitor acting for the grantor was fully accepted: Phillipson v Kerry, and again where the deed had been prepared by the grantor's own solicitor, a man of honour, but the grantor, while fully understanding the benefit to accrue to the grantee, had not fully understood the effect of her deed as it affected her own interests: *Anderson v Elsworth*; in several other instances the inadequacy of the explanations given to the grantor has been a conspicuous, indeed a decisive, factor in the court's action against an improvident deed, the court either assuming: *Prideaux v Lonsdale*, or having direct evidence: *Phillipson v Kerry*; *Wollaston v Tribe*, to prove a serious lack of understanding. The least the court can demand is that an infirm grantor shall have known what he was doing. In the much more frequent, but analogous, instances of deeds attacked for undue influence the Judicial Committee has insisted that the donor must have had a complete explanation of the nature and effect of the transaction, from an adviser who himself knew all the relevant circumstances: *Inche Noriah v Shaik Allie Bin Omar*,[13] even where the adviser was selected by the donor: *Williams v Williams*,[14] and the same imperative requirement was stressed in a transaction for value by Isaacs J. upon a deed closely resembling the deed in this action in some aspects, but obtained by undue influence: *Watkins v Combes*.[15]

In my judgment, without any regard to any question of undue influence, upon Lord Hatherley's principle and the concurrent authorities the plaintiff by reason of his own weakness of mind, coupled with the deficiencies in the legal advice under which he acted and his unawareness, is entitled to have the improvident indenture of settlement, dated 24 October 1942, set aside and the Register of Freeholders rectified.

I may add that the balancing of equities is not complicated here by any plea of estoppel, nor have I on the evidence any reason to suppose that the defendant has suffered any prejudice worth mentioning through executing the settlement.

I pass to the other heads of complaint and first to the £2,000 deposit. On 19 June 1942, Peter, with Murphy at his elbow, first called at the Bank of Ireland in Galway, and removed in notes a sum of £2,000 standing on deposit there in this own sole name, and then went to the National Bank in Galway, and put the money on deposit there in a new account made out in the joint names of himself and Murphy. He had had some difficulty concerning another deposit account in the Bank of Ireland, standing in his own name and that of a deceased brother, because the bank had demurred to paying Peter from that deposit without being satisfied that the duty payable to the state on his brother's death had been discharged; the brother had died some years before, and, as the beneficial owner of the money, fiercely resenting the suggestion of its depletion by fiscal claims and the delay, Peter was angry at the bank's attitude. I cannot, on the evidence of a single witness, a partisan, hold as a fact that Murphy pressed Peter to make the change to another bank by frightening him with the Revenue bogey, even though Peter in part supports the story. But the following answers by Murphy himself show that the money was withdrawn under a delusion, in fear of the Revenue Commissioners, and discover Murphy with varying explanations for the insertion of his own name in the second bank's account:

Q. 1570. (In chief) 'Was he (Peter) going to assail the Bank of Ireland again?' (The reference is to a visit to the bank on the previous day.)

'Yes. He said, when leaving the office (that is the bank) the day before that he noticed a Customs and Excise man leaving the office. He said "If I don't take my money out of the Bank, they will rob me completely."'

'Was the £2,000 eventually paid over on to the counter to him?' 'Yes.'

'Before he got to the National did he say anything about what he was going to do with the money?'

'I asked him first what he was going to do and he said "I'm going to put it into the National."'

'After that, did he tell you what he was going to do with the money?'

'He said, "I will put your name in with it."'

'Was that the first time he ever said anything to you about putting your name on the deposit?' 'Yes.'

'What did you say?'

'I said nothing at all for the time being (sic!). Then a bit further down he said, "I don't want my relatives to get any of the money."'

(In cross-examination.) 'And, according to your case, you had got a gift of £2,000?'

'I don't know about the £2,000. I left it at that.'

'You are claiming it here in this action as a gift?'

'I am. Grealish told me he intended leaving it to me after his death.'

'You are claiming that £2,000 as a gift; did I hear you say that Grealish told you he intended leaving that after his death?' 'Yes.'

'When did he say that?'

'He said, "I intend leaving all my money to you"; he did not mention £2,000 or £3,000.'

'When did he make that interesting announcement to you?'

'On the day down to the bank.'

'What day was that?'

'19 June.'

'The day you went down to the bank?' 'Yes.'

'He made that interesting announcement, which you forgot in your direct evidence, that he was going to leave you all his money, not mentioning this particular sum?'

'Yes'

'He intended leaving you everything he had after his death?' 'Yes'

Mr Thunder, the manager of the National Bank, who knew that the money belonged to Grealish, says that he saw the plaintiff privately, because he was a marksman; he told him that both signatures would be required to draw any money, and explained to him, and was satisfied that Grealish understood, that a lodgment in joint names meant that the survivor would be entitled to the money, if one of them died; Peter just replied that. 'Murphy was managing his business and looking after him in general'; he said nothing about wanting to make a present to Murphy.

> 'Were you able to form any impression of his intention about the money, whether he intended making a present of it to Murphy?'
> 'No, I could not tell you that.'

Mr Thunder says that Peter was quite clear with him. The deposit receipt was given to Peter.

The unsatisfactory features of this episode are patent. The transaction was shocking and the two men did not stand on equal terms, so that I think I might, following Lord Hatherley's principle, or perhaps the even more emphatic language of Sullivan M.R. in *Slator v Nolan*,[16] against any party taking undue advantage of another, uphold the plaintiff's claim, without any regard to the peculiar relations of the parties. But Murphy, on his own evidence had become Peter's interim manager and business agent, his confidential man, as early as January 1942; their relations were such that the court must on long settled principles assume undue influence, if not rebutted, and for this issue the burden of proof is definitely upon Murphy, who has wholly failed to discharge it. Murphy had put himself into such a position towards this old man as to be bound to protect his patron in money matters, even against the patron himself; and Murphy was bound to refuse any gross prodigality in his own favour, made in secret or without competent advice. Moreover, quite apart from any confidential relations, the presumption of a resulting trust stands unrebutted, for I must discount Murphy's own evidence here. I need not labour this matter. I disregard the fact that interest on the deposit was paid to the joint holders and shared between them. Peter's vagary in the matter of the £2,000 must be redressed. The transaction cannot stand.

I come to the present of Peter's cattle to Murphy after the deed of settlement and Murphy's realisation of the cattle for his own use. I need say nothing more of Murphy's method of acquisition, for his position under the deed puts him out of court. Here was a flagrant abuse by Murphy and he must make good Peter's loss, which I measure, on Murphy's evidence, at the sum of £643.

Finally, the plaintiff is entitled to an account. He is entitled to an account of all dealings by the defendant with, or in relation to, cattle for, or on behalf of, the plaintiff during the calendar year 1942, and a further account of all moneys, the property of the plaintiff, come to the hand of the defendant.

The first account (which I hope the plaintiff will be advised to waive) relates in particular to the sale of cattle for some £530 by Murphy at the Tuam Fair in October 1942; Murphy says that he bought cattle at Westport Fair immediately afterwards for the plaintiff to the value of £500, and he was at pains to give some account of the balance. But Murphy has in his power or procurement one or more banking documents in this connection, which he omitted from his affidavit of documents. That is why I have to order the first account, if it is sought, but I do not think that Peter has anything to gain from it. Murphy's purchase of cattle for Peter at Gort in May 1942, to the value of £480 is not disputed and must be allowed in the account.

The second account is necessitated by Murphy's admission in cross-examination that he received on 30 October 1942, from Peter a sum of £700, whereof (though he may be able to justify more) he has so far accounted to my satisfaction for only £115 paid by Peter's direction to Costello; for the moment I shall extend the charity of silence to the remainder of his evidence on this subject, including the reappearance of the fiscal vampire. This account will deal also with the £500 paid by Peter to Murphy in January 1943. Murphy may object that the statement of claim does not complain of this particular payment, and it does not; that is why I deal with the matter by way of an account instead of giving judgment for the amount; but I think the answer to the objection is that Peter's advisers probably did their best upon incoherent instructions; they did complain of a gift of £500 by Peter to Murphy and properly attributed it to undue influence upon Murphy's threat to abandon Peter, but they placed the gift in October 1942, confusing it with the price (£530 on Murphy's evidence) realised at that time by the aforesaid sale of Peter's cattle at Tuam Fair. I think the mistake was understandable in lawyers who had Peter for a client, and Peter did in fact depose to this payment in his evidence. I see no need for the statement of claim to be amended, because the prayer for an account seems to me sufficiently to cover this claim and Murphy has not been misled.

I have said nothing about the two cars for Murphy, bought with Peter's moneys; I do not regard these gifts as tainted; I am satisfied that the private car was promised by

Peter at his first interview with Murphy; probably he promised the lorry too, though here Murphy's evidence is not corroborated. The statement of claim makes no specific claim under this head and the moneys paid by Peter for the two cars may reasonably be treated as having been properly expended by Murphy. In all the circumstances the accounts will be directed without interest.

1. 15 Eq. 121.
2. 6 De G. M. & G. 424; 8 HLC 481.
3. |1911| 1 Ch. 723.
4. 2 AC 814, at p. 823.
5. |1940| IR 71.
6. 1 Cox, Eq Cas 333.
7. 1 de G. J. & S. 433.
8. 10 Eq. 405.
9. 2 Giff. 157.
10. 3 Giff. 154.
11. 32 Beav. 628.
12. 9 Eq. 44.
13. |1929| AC 127, 135.
14. |1937| 4 All ER 34, 83.
15. 30 CLR 180, 196–7.
16. IR 11 Eq. 367, at p. 386.

Note

See *Gregg v Kidd* (pp 593–4 above) where the same plea was raised.

Lydon *v* Coyne (1946) 12 Ir Jur Rep 64

O'Byrne J.:

This is an action to set aside a deed dated 25 January 1943, and made between Martin Lydon of the one part and Martin Coyne of the other part. Martin Lydon, the transferor, died within a few months, namely, on 10 April 1943, and the present proceedings have been brought by his widow, Bridget Lydon, who sues personally and as his personal representative.

Martin Lydon owned a very small farm of land in the neighbourhood of Tourmakeady. Early on the morning of 25 January 1943, Martin Coyne came to the offices of Messrs Michael Moran & Co., in Castlebar, and asked Mr Michael Moran to come out to Tourmakeady. Mr Moran arrived at Tourmakeady between 11 and 12 o'clock that morning. He had been told beforehand that the old man was making over his land; but when he got to the house it appeared that the matter was not so simple, and a very long discussion took place between the parties. I can appreciate the very great difficulty in which Mr Moran was placed, wishing to draw up the deed and finding that the parties had not come to any firm agreement. But solicitors must often protect parties against themselves.

The deed is technically not a voluntary deed by reason of two provisions therein. Firstly, there is the covenant to support the old couple, which is in the following terms: 'That he will support, clothe and maintain the said assignor and his said wife Bridget Lydon during their lives out of the rents and profits of the said lands.' It is to be noted that Bridget Lydon, who takes a benefit under the deed, is not a party to it. Secondly, there is a covenant by the assignee for payment of £100 in the following terms: 'The assignee hereby covenants with the assignor for the payment of the sum of £100 to the assignor by instalments on demand in writing by the assignor such instalments not to exceed the sum of £10 in any year.' That covenant, while technically sufficient, is in all the circumstances of this case quite illusory. I do not deal with the deed as a voluntary deed, but as one of a highly improvident character. In one respect it is quite unique; the *habendum* is worded as follows: 'To hold the same unto the assignee to the use of the assignor for his life and should Bridget Lydon wife of the assignor survive the assignor then and in such event to the use of said Bridget Lydon for her life and from and after the death of the assignor or the said Bridget Lydon or the death of the survivor of them then unto and to the use of the assignee his heirs executors administrators and assigns for all the estate right title term and interest of the assignor therein.'

It is clear to me that Lydon never intended parting with the dominion over his property during his lifetime, for he kept insisting that his name should be in the rent receipt, showing in this way his intention that he should remain the owner while he lived. The limitation in the *habendum* purports to be controlled and governed by a subsequent covenant by the assignee in the following terms: 'And the assignee hereby covenants with the assignor that he will reside in the dwelling house on the said lands and that he will manage and work the said lands in a good and husbandlike manner during the lifetime of the assignor and his said wife Bridget Lydon or the survivor of them . . . and the assignor hereby covenants with the assignee that he will allow the assignee to manage and to work the said lands during the lifetime of the assignor and during the lifetime of the said Bridget Lydon and the survivor of them and to retain the rents and profits of the said lands for his own use and benefit.' If (as I think is the fact) it was intended to reserve a life estate to the assignor, the terms of the deed with reference to the application of the rents and profits during the lifetime of the assignor are extremely peculiar. Apart from the peculiarity of form, it throws some light upon the value of the covenant to support, for this is enforceable only out of the rents and profits.

There is one question—the main question to which I must address myself—and it is whether the assignor understood the transaction into which he was entering. If this were a voluntary deed there would be an absolute onus upon the assignee to show that the transaction was the free and voluntary act of the assignor and that he understood the transaction. Owing to the circumstances of this case, the onus here is not so great. It seems to me that Mr Moran, though undoubtedly doing his best for all parties, must be looked upon as Coyne's solicitor. He had acted for him before; Coyne brought him out and paid his fees for drawing the deed. But, approaching the transaction in that way and having regard to the improvidence of the transaction and the difficulty of interpreting some of the clauses in the deed, can I be satisfied that the settlor understood the transaction? I am quite satisfied he did not understand it. I do not understand it myself nor can I see how effect can be given to some of its provisions. That being so, and having regard to the fact that the deed contained no power of revocation and that no independent advice was given, this assignment cannot be allowed to stand.

I see the difficulty of inserting a power of revocation in the circumstances of this case since it would probably have resulted in the transaction falling through, but, in my opinion, that would have been the lesser of two evils. I see the difficulty of getting independent advice having regard to the remoteness of the place where the settlor lived and the cost of getting a second solicitor out. I realise that Mr Moran did the best he could, but, making full allowance for these facts, I am of opinion that the deed cannot be allowed to stand and, accordingly, I shall declare that the defendant is a trustee of the lands for the plaintiff as personal representative of the settlor. I shall order a reconveyance of the lands and I shall direct the defendant to pay the plaintiff's costs.

SECTION THREE—UNCONSCIONABLE BARGAINS IN COMMERCIAL CONTRACTS

INTRODUCTION

One celebrated attempt to compel the English courts to recognise the general application of inequality of bargaining power as a general invalidating factor was made by Denning M.R., in the Court of Appeal in *Lloyds*

Bank v Bundy [1974] 3 All ER 757. While the *ratio decidendi* of the case is a narrow one, turning upon the peculiar circumstances in which the bank was placed by its customer in this particular instance, Denning M.R. examined a diverse range of cases (e.g. *Fry v Lane*, *D. & C. Builders v Rees*, *Maskell v Horner*) and sought to extract the following general principle:

Gathering all together, I would suggest that through all these instances there runs a single thread. They rest on 'inequality of bargaining power'. By virtue of it, the English law gives relief to one who, without independent advice, enters into a contract on terms which are very unfair or transfers property for a consideration which is grossly inadequate, when his bargaining power is grievously impaired by reason of his own needs or desires, or by his own ignorance or infirmity, coupled with undue influences or pressures brought to bear on him by or for the benefit of the other. When I use the word 'undue' I do not mean to suggest that the principle depends on proof of any wrongdoing. The one who stipulates for an unfair advantage may be moved solely by his own self-interest, unconscious of the distress he is bringing to the other. I have also avoided any reference to the will of the one being 'dominated' or 'overcome' by the other. One who is in extreme need may knowingly consent to a most improvident bargain, solely to relieve the straits in which he finds himself. Again, I do not mean to suggest that every transaction is saved by independent advice. But the absence of it may be fatal.

Note

The breadth of this principle is such that it has not found favour with other members of the English judiciary, particularly the House of Lords: see Lord Scarman in *National Westminster Bank v Morgan* [1985] 1 All ER 821 at 829–30. Nor has it been supported in Northern Ireland (see p. 617 above).

The case has been more enthusiastically received in Canada and Australia. Indeed, these courts have utilised this general principle in a great number of cases. Three examples of the application of equitable principles in commercial cases are taken from non-English case-law.

A. BANK GUARANTEES

Commercial Bank of Australia v Amadio (1983) 151 CLR 447

Two elderly people of Italian origin who had emigrated to Australia gave a guarantee by way of mortgage to secure their son's business debts. The mortgage was not explained to them—their grasp of English was poor—and the bank was aware that they had been misinformed about the document. Gibbs C.J., Mason, Wilson and Deane JJ., set the transaction aside, the latter three judges on the grounds of unconscionability.

Mason J.:

I agree with Deane J.'s comprehensive statement of the facts and with his conclusion that the respondents are entitled to relief on the ground that the bank was guilty of unconscionable conduct in procuring the execution of the mortgage guarantee by the respondents.

Historically, courts have exercised jurisdiction to set aside contracts and other dealings on a variety of equitable grounds. They include fraud, misrepresentation, breach of fiduciary duty, undue influence and unconscionable conduct. In one sense they all constitute species of unconscionable conduct on the part of a party who stands to receive a benefit under a transaction which, in the eye of equity, cannot be enforced because to do so would be inconsistent with equity and good conscience. But relief on the ground of 'unconscionable conduct' is usually taken to refer to the class of case in which a party makes unconscientious use of his superior position or bargaining power to the detriment of a party who suffers from some special disability or is placed in some special situation of disadvantage, e.g. a catching bargain with an expectant heir or an unfair contract made by taking advantage of a person who is seriously affected by intoxicating drink. Although unconscionable conduct in this narrow sense bears some resemblance to the doctrine of undue influence, there is a difference between the two. In the latter the will of the innocent party is not independent and voluntary because it is overborne. In the former the will of the innocent party, even if independent and voluntary, is the result of the disadvantageous position in which he is placed and of the other party unconscientiously taking advantage of that position.

There is no reason for thinking that the two remedies are mutually exclusive in the sense that only one of them is available in a particular situation of the exclusion of the other. Relief on the ground of unconscionable conduct will be granted when unconscientious advantage is taken of an innocent party whose will is overborne so that it is not independent and voluntary, just as it will be granted when such advantage is taken of an innocent party who, though not deprived of an independent and voluntary will, is unable to make a worthwhile judgment as to what is in his best interest.

It goes almost without saying that it is impossible to describe definitively all the situations in which relief will be granted on the ground of unconscionable conduct. As Fullagar J. said in *Blomley v Ryan*:[1]

> The circumstances adversely affecting a party, which may induce a court of equity either to refuse its aid or to set a transaction aside, are of great variety and can hardly be satisfactorily classified. Among them are poverty or need of any kind, sickness, age, sex, infirmity of body or mind, drunkenness, illiteracy or lack of education, lack of assistance or explanation where assistance or explanation is necessary. The common characteristic seems to be that they have the effect of placing one party at a serious disadvantage *vis-à-vis* the other.

Likewise Kitto J.[2] spoke of it as 'a well known head of equity' which '. . . . applies whenever one party to a transaction is at a special disadvantage in dealing with the other party because illness, ignorance, inexperience, impaired faculties, financial need or other circumstances affect his ability to conserve his own interests, and the other party unconscientiously takes advantage of the opportunity thus placed in his hands.'

It is not to be thought that relief will be granted only in the particular situations mentioned by their Honours. It is made plain enough, especially by Fullagar J., that the situations mentioned are no more than particular exemplifications of an underlying general principle which may be invoked whenever one party by reason of some condition of circumstance is placed at a special disadvantage *vis-à-vis* another and unfair or unconscientious advantage is then taken of the opportunity thereby created. I qualify the word 'disadvantage' by the adjective 'special' in order to disavow any suggestion that the principle applies whenever there is some difference in the bargaining power of the parties and in order to emphasise that the disabling condition or circumstance is one which seriously affects the ability of the innocent party to make a judgment as to his own best interests, when the other party knows or ought to know of the existence of that condition or circumstance and of its effect on the innocent party.

Because times have changed new situations have arisen in which it may be appropriate to invoke the underlying principle. Take, for example, entry into a standard form of contract dictated by a party whose bargaining power is greatly superior, a relationship which was discussed by Lord Reid and Lord Diplock in A. *Schroeder Music Publishing Co. Ltd v Macaulay.*[3] See also *Clifford Davis Management Ltd v W.E.A Records Ltd.*[4] In situations of this kind it is necessary for the plaintiff who seeks relief to establish unconscionable conduct, namely that unconscientious advantage has been taken of his disabling condition or circumstances.

Of course the relationship between the present parties and the transaction into which they entered were by no means novel, viewed as a situation to which the general principle can apply. That the principle might justify the setting aside of a guarantee is established by decisions such as *Owen and Gutch v Homan*[5] and *Bank of Victoria Ltd v Mueller.*[6]

To say this involves no contradiction of the well entrenched proposition that a guarantee is not a contract *uberrimae fidei*, that is, a contract which of itself calls for full disclosure. However, it is accepted that the principal creditor is under a duty:

> . . . to disclose to the intending surety anything which has taken place between the bank and the principal debtor 'which was not naturally to be expected', or as it was put by Pollock M.R., in *Lloyds Bank Ltd. v Harrison*[7] cited in *Paget's Law of Banking*, (7th ed., 1966), 583 'the necessity for disclosure only goes to the extent of requiring it where there are some unusual features in the particular case relating to the particular account which is to be guaranteed.
>
> (*Goodwin v National Bank of Australasia Ltd*,[8] per Barwick C.J.).

It has been said that this duty to disclose does not require a bank to give information as to matters affecting the credit of the debtor or of any circumstances connected with the transaction in which he is about to engage which will render his position more hazardous (*Wythes v Labouchere*,[9] per Lord Chelmsford L.C.). No surety is entitled to assume that the debtor has not been overdrawing, the proper presumption being in most instances that he has been doing so and wishes to do so again (*London General Omnibus Co. Ltd v Holloway*[10]).

But the fact that a bank's duty to make disclosure to its intending surety, arising from the mere relationship between principal creditor and surety, is so limited has no bearing on the availability of equitable relief on the ground of unconscionable conduct. A bank, though not guilty of any breach of its limited duty to make disclosure to the intending surety, may nonetheless be considered to have engaged in unconscionable conduct in procuring the surety's entry into the contract of guarantee.

It is to be hoped that the respondents' amended statement of claim does not find its way into the precedent books. It leaves much to be desired. It alleges unconscionable conduct and alternatively undue influence on the part of the bank. It does not, as it might have done, allege undue influence on the part of the respondents' son Vincenzo, with notice on the part of the bank. The findings, and indeed the evidence, contradict or fail to support the alleged case of undue influence on the part of the bank. The critical issue then is whether, in accordance with the principle already explained, the respondents are entitled to relief on the ground of unconscionable conduct.

There are a number of factors which go to establish that there was a gross inequality of bargaining power between the bank and the respondents, so much so that the respondents stood in a position of special disadvantage *vis-à-vis* the bank in relation to the proposed mortgage guarantee. By way of contrast to the bank, the respondents' ability to judge whether entry into the transaction was in their own best interests, having due regard to their desire to assist their son, was sadly lacking. The situation of special disadvantage in which the respondents were placed was the outcome of their reliance on and their confidence in their son who, in order to serve his own interests, urged them to provide the mortgage guarantee which the bank required as a condition of increasing the approved overdraft limit of his company, V. Amadio Builders Pty. Ltd ('the company'), from $80,000 to $270,000 and misled them as to the financial position of the company. Their reliance on their son was due in no small degree to their infirmities—they were Italians of advanced years, aged seventy six and seventy one respectively, having a limited command of written English and no experience of business in the field or at the level in which their son and the company engaged. They believed that the company's business was a flourishing and prosperous enterprise, though temporarily in need of funds. In reality, as the bank well knew, the company was in a perilous financial condition.

In the weeks immediately preceding the execution of the mortgage guarantee the company was unable to pay its debts as they fell due. In this situation the bank had selectively paid cheques drawn by the company in favour of suppliers in order to ensure continuity in the supply of building materials, the company being a building contractor. In this period the bank had regularly and continuously dishonoured other cheques, the payment of which was not essential to the maintenance of the supply of building materials. In pursuing this course and in agreeing to an increase in the company's overdraft limit, the bank was substantially influenced by a special consideration. The company was a major customer of the bank, indeed the largest customer at the Glynde branch of the bank, and the company's continuation in business was advantageous to General Credits Ltd, a finance company and subsidiary of the bank. In fact the company built houses for a joint venture comprising General Credits Ltd and another company of Vincenzo's at cost plus ten per cent, this figure being designed to cover building costs and administration charges. It was not intended to yield a profit to the company. General Credits Ltd's share of the joint venture profits was sixty per cent. In addition it provided the bulk of the finance required for the joint venture's operations. The respondents, needless to say, were quite unaware of these circumstances.

The effect of the respondents' execution of the mortgage guarantee was disastrous for them though advantageous to the bank. The bank agreed to increase Vincenzo's overdraft limit in the light of his statement that the property comprising four shops which was the subject of the mortgage guarantee was valued in the vicinity of $200,000.
. . .

No doubt the respondents' age and lack of business experience played a part in their reliance on their son's judgment and in their failure to make any inquiries as to the financial position of the company and their failure to seek advice as to the probable or possible consequences of the transaction into which they entered. Their lack of command of English, especially written English, apart from contributing to their reliance on their son, had an additional importance. Vincenzo had informed them that the bank would present for signature a guarantee and very probably a security of some sort, though the precise nature of that security, i.e. mortgage or charge, was not specified. He had incorrectly said that the liability would be limited to a period of six months and to an amount of $50,000. Mr Virgo, the bank manager, in the conversation which took place immediately before execution, informed them that their liability under the instrument was unlimited in time, the question having been raised by Mr Amadio senior. Mr Virgo said nothing on the topic of unlimited liability because the respondents did not mention it.

The primary judge found that if Vincenzo 'had disabused his parents' minds of their confidence in him, his parents would not have helped him.' The correctness of this finding has not been challenged. Nor could it be for the simple reason that any rational person knowing the circumstances of the company at the time would not have executed the instrument which they signed.

In deciding whether the bank took unconscientious advantage of the position of disadvantage in which the respondents were placed, we must ask, first, what knowledge did the bank have of the respondents' situation?

Mr Virgo was aware that the respondents were Italians, that they were of advanced years and that they did not have a good command of English. He knew that Vincenzo had procured their agreement to sign the mortgage guarantee. He had no reason to think that they had received advice and guidance from anyone but their son. In cross-examination he conceded that he believed that Vincenzo had acted in the 'role of adviser/explainer' in relation to the transaction and referred to him as acting 'in his capacity as dominant member of the family'. Mr Virgo also knew that, in the light of the then financial condition of the company, it was vital to Vincenzo to secure his parents' signature to the mortgage guarantee so that the company could continue in business. It must have been obvious to Mr Virgo, as to anyone else having knowledge of the facts, that the transaction was improvident from the viewpoint of the respondents. In these circumstances it is inconceivable that the possibility did not occur to Mr Virgo that the respondents' entry into the transaction was due to their inability to make a judgment as to what was in their best interests, owing to their reliance on their son, whose interests would inevitably incline him to urge them to sign the instrument put forward by the bank.

Indeed, the inquiry by Mr Amadio senior as to the duration of the arrangement should have alerted Mr Virgo to the likelihood that Vincenzo had not adequately or accurately explained the intended transaction to them, let alone the possible or probable consequences which attended it.

Whether it be correct or incorrect to attribute to Mr Virgo knowledge of this possibility, the facts as known to him were such as to raise in the mind of any reasonable person a very real question as to the respondents' ability to make a judgment as to what was in their own best interests. In *Owen and Gutch v Homan*, Lord Cranworth L.C. said: '. . . it may safely be stated that if the dealings are such as fairly to lead a reasonable man to believe that fraud must have been used in order to obtain [the concurrence of the survey], he is bound to make inquiry, and cannot shelter himself under the plea that he was not called on to ask, and did not ask, any questions on the subject. In some cases wilful ignorance is not to be distinguished in its equitable consequences from knowledge.' The principle there stated applies with equal force to this case. The concept of fraud in equity is not limited to common law deceit; it extends to conduct of the kind engaged in by the respondents' son when he took advantage of the confidence and reliance reposed in him to induce his parents to enter into a transaction in order to serve his ends, thereby depriving them of the ability to make a judgment as to what is in their interests.

As we have seen, if A having actual knowledge that B occupies a situation of special disadvantage in relation to an intended transaction, so that B cannot make a judgment as to what is in his own interests, takes unfair advantage of his (A's) superior bargaining power or position by entering into that transaction, his conduct in so doing is unconscionable. And if, instead of having actual knowledge of that situation, A is aware of the possibility that that situation may exist or is aware of facts that would raise that possibility in the mind of any reasonable person, the result will be the same.

The knowledge of Mr Virgo was the knowledge of the bank.

1. (1956) 99 CLR 362, at p. 405.
2. (1956) 99 CLR, at p. 415.
3. [1974] 1 WLR 1308, at pp 1314–5, 1316; [1974] 3 All ER 616, at pp 622–3, 624.
4. [1975] 1 WLR 61, at pp 64–5; [1975] 1 All ER 237, at p. 240.
5. (1853) 14 HLC 997, at pp 1034–5 [10 ER 752, at p. 767].
6. [1925] VLR 642, at p. 649.
7. (1925) Unrep.
8. (1968) 117 CLR 173, at p. 175.

9. (1859) 3 De G. & J. 593, at p. 609.   10. |1912| 2 KB 72, at pp 83–4, 87.
|44 ER 1397, at p. 1404|.

B. Insurance Settlements

Doan *v* Insurance Corporation of British Columbia (1987) 18 BCLR 286

Paris J.:

The plaintiff, Mr Doan, suffered a brain injury when struck down in a crosswalk by the defendant Bassey on 24 September 1982. The defendants' negligence is admitted.

The Insurance Corporation of British Columbia (ICBC) appointed Mr David Slessor to adjust the claim and he dealt directly with Mr and Mrs Doan.

On 12 August 1983 they signed a release settling their claim for a total of $60,000 including Pt. 7 benefits, loss of income, non-pecuniary damages and all other claims.

The brain damage suffered by Mr Doan left him incapacitated and the incapacitation has become progressively worse since the accident. Mrs Doan has had to quit her job to look after him.

[After finding that Doan was not independently represented, relied on Slessor's advice and that Slessor was in a position of conflict of interest, Paris J. continued:]

The result was predictable. The bargain arrived at was clearly improvident and seriously so. At first Slessor offered the Doans $40,000 in full settlement. They declined. He then came back with an offer of $60,000 which they accepted. He told them that this was $20,000 more than they should be receiving. In fact, ICBC's own reserve estimate for the file at that time, as set out in Ex. 119, was in the neighbourhood of $110,000. The breakdown by ICBC of the settlement proceeds given by Slessor to the Doans allocated $30,000 for non-pecuniary damages. However, it is agreed by the parties that non-pecuniary damages should be fixed by the court at $140,000, assuming that there is no apportionment of those damages to some cause other than the motor vehicle accident.

Incidentally, I say parenthetically, in my view this is a fair assessment of those non-pecuniary damages.

I will deal in due course with the other aspects of the plaintiffs' claim to which they are entitled. Suffice it to say for the moment that they are very greatly out of proportion to what the settlement represented, particularly bearing in mind the pay-back which had to be made by the plaintiffs to the long term disability plan. And further, that the settlement included the Pt. 7 no fault benefits to which they were entitled as insured persons under the universal coverage aspect of the public motor vehicle insurance scheme in place in this province.

Finally, Slessor told Mrs Doan that she personally had no claim although, of course, he got her to sign the release.

In sum, by any of the three tests set out in the *Towers v Affleck*[1] and *Harry v Kreutziger*[2] cases, the test of unconscionable bargain is met and the release must be set aside.

1. |1974| 1 WWR 714.   2. (1978) 95 DLR (30) 231.

C. Sale of Real Property to a Commercial Developer

Fusty *v* McLean Construction Ltd (1978) 6 Alberta LR (2d) 216

Rowbotham D.C.J.:

The plaintiff asks for rescission of a certain contract made between himself and the defendant and dated 30 May 1975, respecting the sale by the plaintiff to the defendant of a certain parcel of land described as lot 11, block 2, plan Drumheller 561JK.

The plaintiff came to Canada from Hungary in 1927 and despite the fact that he has been in Canada for fifty years has very great difficulty in understanding the English language let alone the details of a real estate transaction. He is now an old man and has recently suffered some illness and undergone several operations. Insofar as I could understand his testimony he said that he had a discussion with the agent of the defendant company in which he stated that if he returned to his native Hungary to live he would sell the land in question, on which his house is situated, to the defendant for the sum of $3,300. He delivered his duplicate certificate of title to the agent for the defendant, subsequently attended at the office of the solicitor for the defendant and signed several documents without receiving any independent advice and subsequently received the sum of $3,300. After the completion of the transaction he attempted to pay the taxes on his house as he described it and was informed that he would not be permitted to do so because it was no longer his house.

The value of the house and lot according to the witness Raymond Page of Page Agencies Drumheller Limited is between $11,000 and $13,000.

According to the testimony of Mr D. E. Harrison, the real estate agent involved, the defendant McLean Construction Ltd is, to use his words, 'the mother company of McLean Agencies', the real estate firm involved.

The plaintiff argues that this is a case where the doctrine of Fry v Lane; Re Fry, Whittet and Bush (1888), 40 ChD 312, should be applied. The doctrine is found in the judgment of Kay J. at p. 322 in these words:

> The result of the decisions is that where a purchase is made from a poor and ignorant man at a considerable undervalue, the vendor having no independent advice, a court of equity will set aside the transaction.
>
> This will be done even in the case of property in possession, and a fortiori if the interest be reversionary.
>
> The circumstances of poverty and ignorance of the vendor, and absence of independent advice, throw upon the purchase, when the transaction is impeached, the onus of proving, in Lord Selborne's words, that the purchase was fair, just and reasonable.

The plaintiff argues that the defendant has tendered no evidence to show that the purchase was fair, just and reasonable and I agree with him.

The plaintiff also cited Earl of Aylesford v Morris (1873) 8 Ch App 484, and Butler v Miller (1867) 1 IR Eq 195.

Fry v Lane was first followed in Canada in Hrynyk v Hrynyk 40 Man R 173, [1932] 1 WWR 82, [1932] 1 DLR 672 (CA). A seventy seven year old ignorant and apparently worn out man transferred his land to his son in consideration for a lease back to the father on the house and garden found on the same parcel of land for $1 consideration. The Manitoba Court of Appeal held (p. 84): 'I look on this as an improvident transaction, made practically without consideration and without advice, in favour of a person who had a duty at least to see that the transaction went no farther than was actually necessary. I think that on this ground and following the principles of equity jurisprudence in such a case the transaction cannot be allowed to stand.'

The Supreme Court of British Columbia in Hnatuk v Chretian (1960) 31 WWR 130 refused specific performance of an agreement for sale where the plaintiff had taken advantage of illiterate defendants who were in difficult financial circumstances.

The British Columbia Court of Appeal in *Morrison v Coast Finance Ltd* (1965) 54 WWR 257, 55 DLR (2d) 710, set aside a mortgage as an unconscionable transaction in circumstances where a seventy nine year old widow of meagre means granted a mortgage on her house and lot under unfavourable circumstances without any independent advice.

Davey J.A. set out the distinction between undue influence and unconscionable bargains at p. 259:

> The equitable principles relating to undue influence and relief against unconscionable bargains are closely related, but the doctrines are separate and distinct. The finding here against undue influence does not conclude the question whether the appellant is entitled to relief against an unconscionable transaction. A plea of undue influence attacks the sufficiency of consent; a plea that a bargain is unconscionable invokes relief against an unfair advantage gained by an unconscientious use of power by a stronger party against a weaker. On such a claim the material ingredients are proof of inequality in the position of the parties arising out of the ignorance, need or distress of the weaker, which left him in the power of the stronger, and proof of substantial unfairness of the bargain obtained by the stronger. On proof of those circumstances, it creates a presumption of fraud which the stronger must repeal by proving that the bargain was fair, just and reasonable: *Earl of Aylesford v Morris*, per Lord Selborne at p. 491, or perhaps by showing that no advantage was taken: See *Harrison v Guest* (1855), 6 De G. M. & G. 424 at 438, affirmed 8 HL Cas 481 at 492, 493, 11 ER 517. In *Fry v Lane; Re Fry, Whittet and Bush* Kay J. accurately stated the modern scope and application of the principle, and discussed the earlier authorities upon which it rests.

The Saskatchewan Court of Appeal in *Knupp v Bell* (1968), 67 DLR (2d) 256, refused to uphold an agreement for sale of land by an eighty five year old senile woman without any business experience at a value of approximately half of its market value.

Beck J. in *Anderson v Morgan* 11 Alta LR 526, |1917| 2 WWR 969, 34 DLR 728 (CA), concerning alleged misrepresentations made in negotiations resulting in an exchange of lands said at pp 971–72:

> It is not necessary that that relationship should arise by reason of a previous contractual or quasi-contractual relationship (per Lord Shaw |in *Nocton v Lord Ashburton*, |1914 AC 932| p. 971, but applies to such a case as *Waters v Donnelly* (1884), 9 OR 391, cited by my brother Walsh which holds that if two persons, no matter whether a confidential relationship exists between them or not, stand in such a relation to each other that one can take an undue advantage of the other, and advantage is taken, the transaction will not be allowed to stand.
>
> Boyd C. in *Waters v Donnelly*, at p. 401 says that the method of investigation is to determine first whether the parties were on equal terms; if not, and the transaction is one of purchase, and any matters requiring explanation arise, *then it lies on the purchaser* to show affirmatively that the price given was the value.

In view of the foregoing the contract between the plaintiff and the defendant is rescinded and the plaintiff shall have an order directing the Registrar of the South Alberta Land Registration District to cancel certificate of title 751060460 in the name of McLean Construction Ltd and issue a new certificate of title in the name of the plaintiff.

Because the plaintiff has remained in possession of the property he shall be responsible for the payment of property taxes during the period of time in question.

The plaintiff shall have costs of the action.

Chapter Fifteen

Privity of Contract

INTRODUCTION

The doctrine of privity of contract states that only a party to a contract may sue on or be bound by that contract.

Murphy and Others v Bower (1868) IR 2 CL 506

The defendant was an engineer employed by a railway company. A contract was made between the railway company and contractors obliging the latter to build a railway to the defendant's specifications. Remuneration under the contract was contingent upon obtaining a certificate from the defendant to the effect that the work was completed. Although the railway was finished the defendant refused to furnish such a certificate. The plaintiffs in this case were the assignees of the contractors' estate.

Monahan C.J.:

It therefore appears that the engineer was not a party to the original agreement between the Messrs Moore and the company; and that the alleged duty of the defendant to give a certificate, so far as it exists, arises from the simple fact that he was employed by the company as their engineer to superintend their works. The question then arises, whether the defendant has rendered himself liable to plaintiffs' action by merely refusing to give his certificate, though aware that the plaintiffs, or those under whom they derive, had done everything to entitle themselves to it, and how far the matter would be affected by the fact of his being actuated by a fraudulent motive in withholding such certificate, or having done so in collusion with the company.

The argument for the defendant is, that since the duty of the engineer to give a certificate arises, if at all, out of a contract, the Messrs Moore or their assignees, not being parties to it, cannot maintain an action for its breach, and this argument is equally applicable, whether the contract out of which the duty arises is a contract between the engineer and the company, or, as has been suggested, between the railway company and the Messrs Moore—assuming them to have contracted on the part of their engineer, that he, as their employee, should do his duty, and give such certificate.

It was also contended on the part of the plaintiff that, inasmuch as the defendant has taken upon himself the duty of engineer, it might be inferred that he has expressly contracted with the Messrs Moore to perform his duty as such engineer; but the answer to this suggestion is, that, if any such contract was intended to be relied on, it should have been stated that such a contract was in fact entered into; the consideration for that contract should have been also stated, and it would have been then competent for the defendant to traverse the alleged consideration. If the contract stated in the summons and plaint was an express contract between the railway company and the Messrs Moore, by which the railway company contracted that their engineer should do his duty properly, there is no doubt but that a right to maintain an action against the

661

railway company would have accrued to them upon the engineer's default; but some cases have been referred to in which it has been decided that, where the foundation of the right of action is rested upon contract, no one can maintain an action who is not a party to the contract. In *Alton v The Midland Rly Co.*,[1] an action was brought by the employer of a commercial traveller for the loss of the services of his servant, who, it was alleged, had taken his railway ticket in the usual way, and, while proceeding upon his journey thereunder, sustained injuries through the negligence of the company. There was no doubt but that if no contract had existed between the injured man and the company—if, for instance, he had been walking upon the line, and had been injured through the default of the company—his employer would have been enabled to recover damages for the loss of his services; nevertheless the court held that the action having been in fact founded upon the contract between the traveller and the company to carry him to the place for which he had obtained a ticket, the action could not be maintained by one who was not a party to that contract. The cases of *Tollit v Sherstone*,[2] and *Winterbottom v Wright*,[3] were decided upon the same principle. The only case in which this principle has been apparently overlooked was that of *Langridge v Levy*,[4] in which it was held that an action for false representation could be maintained by a plaintiff whose father had purchased a gun for his use from the defendant, a gunsmith, and the defendant, though knowing it to be unsafe, guaranteed it safe, and the gun subsequently exploded, and injured the plaintiff. I do not now mean to question the decision in that case—although it has been questioned, and the principle of it is one of difficult application.

The question then arises, are the plaintiffs remediless? There is authority to show that, if collusion did exist between the engineer and the company, he has a remedy against the railway company. The case of *Clarke v Watson*[5] decides that, in the absence of fraud or collusion, he has not. But here fraud and collusion with the company have been alleged; and if fraud exists—most certainly if collusion—there *must* be a remedy. In *Milner v Field*[6] the court expressed an opinion that an action at law would lie against parties who fraudulently prevented such a certificate from being given, and thus attempted to shelter themselves from liability on their contract. In *Batherboy v Vyne*,[7] a declaration upon a contract by an employer who stood in the position of the present railway company, charging as a breach thereof that the architect had improperly refused to give his certificate and had neglected to do so, in collusion with the defendant and by his procurement, was supported upon demurrer.

The proper course, therefore, for the plaintiff to adopt is, to proceed, not against the engineer alone, but against both the engineer and railway company: if he go into a court of equity, or if he elect to sue at law, he must proceed against the company who contracted with him.

[1]. 19 CBNS 213.
[2]. 5 M & W 283.
[3]. 10 M & W 109.
[4]. 2 M & W 519; and in error, 4 M & W 337.
[5]. 18 CBNS 278.
[6]. 5 Ex 829.
[7]. 2 H & C 12.

SECTION ONE—CONSIDERATION—JOINT PROMISEES

The doctrine of privity is very similar to the rule (noted in Chapter 3 at p. 150) that consideration must move from the promisee.

Dunlop Pneumatic Tyre Co. Ltd *v* Selfridge & Co. Ltd [1915] AC 847

Viscount Haldane L.C.:

My Lords, in the law of England certain principles are fundamental. One is that only a person who is a party to a contract can sue on it. Our law knows nothing of a *jus quaesitum tertio* arising by way of contract. Such a right may be conferred by property, as, for example, under a trust, but it cannot be conferred on a stranger to a contract as a right to enforce the contract *in personam*. A second principle is that if a person with whom a contract not under seal has been made is to be able to enforce it consideration must have been given by him to the promisor or to some other person at the promisor's request. . . . A third proposition is that a principal not named in the contract may sue upon it if the promisee really contracted as his agent. But again, in order to entitle him so to sue, he must have given consideration either personally or through the promisee, acting as his agent in giving it.

It is clear from Viscount Haldane's argument that the requirements of privity and consideration are seen as cumulative. It would seem difficult to reconcile this with the concept of joint promisees as expressed in the cases of *McEvoy v The Belfast Banking Co. Ltd* [1935] AC 24 or *Coulls v Bagot's Executor and Trustee Co. Ltd* (1967) 119 CLR 460.

McEvoy v The Belfast Banking Co. Ltd [1935] AC 24

The appellant's father deposited £10,000 in the respondents' bank and received a deposit receipt in the following form: '£10,000 . . . Received from John McEvoy Esq. and Mr Joseph McEvoy (a minor), Newry, the sum of ten thousand pounds sterling for credit in Deposit Account. Not transferable . . . Payable to either or the survivor. . . . This receipt must be produced when payment of either principal or interest is desired.'

When the appellant's father died the executors were empowered under his will to hold the rest of his property in trust for the appellant until he was twenty five years old and to carry on the business. The £10,000 deposit was transferred to an account in the name of the executors. This money was gradually exhausted in meeting the expenses of the business. Soon after becoming of age the appellant sued the bank to recover the sum as having been wrongfully and without his authority paid by the bank to the executors.

Lord Atkin:

. . .

I am compelled to notice an elaborate argument addressed to this House on behalf of the bank to the effect that the legal title never was in the son. It is said that the effect of the contract created by the deposit of £10,000 by the father in the names of himself and his son, the opening of the joint deposit account and the giving and acceptance of the deposit receipt was the formation of a contract between the father alone and the bank. Neither the father nor the bank, it is said, purported to contract for or with the son; the son was a third party who could acquire no rights against the bank. It was as though the father had opened an account in his own name making the sums payable to himself or his son, in which case it was said the son would clearly have to prove an independent contract between himself and the bank before he could sue the bank. My Lords, this contention seems to me to raise the one question of general importance in the case. It involves the whole question of the legal relations created by a bank deposit in this form. The argument, if correct, appears to me inconsistent with well established banking practice and likely to impair the confidence in deposits made in joint names. I consider it to be quite unfounded. It is, I think, significant that there appears no trace of such an argument having been put forward in the courts below. It would not have been attractive hearing for customers or potential customers of the bank in Belfast. It seems to have been reserved for the rarer atmosphere of your Lordships' House.

The suggestion is that where A deposits a sum of money with his bank in the names of A and B, payable to A or B, if B comes to the bank with the deposit receipt he has no right to demand the money from the bank or to sue them if his demand is refused. The bank is entitled to demand proof that the money was in fact partly B's, or possibly that A had acted with B's actual authority. For the contract, it is said is between the bank and A alone. My Lords, to say this is to ignore the vital difference between a contract purporting to be made by A with the bank to pay A or B and a contract purporting to be made by A and B with the bank to pay A or B. In both cases of course payment to B would discharge the bank whether the bank contracted with A alone or with A and B. But the question is whether in the case put B has any rights against the bank if payment to him is refused. I have myself no doubt that in such a case B can sue the bank. The contract on the face of it purports to be made with A and B, and I think with them jointly and severally. A purports to make the contract on behalf of B as well as himself and the consideration supports such a contract. If A has actual authority from B to make such a contract, B is a party to the contract *ab initio*. If he has no actual authority then subject to the ordinary principles of ratification B can ratify the contract purporting to have been made on his behalf and his ratification relates back to the original formation of the contract. If no events had happened to preclude B from ratifying, then on compliance with the contract conditions, including notice and production of the deposit receipt, B would have the right to demand from the bank so much of the money as was due on the deposit account.

In my view, therefore, if nothing had happened to prevent the son from ratifying the contract, he could sue the bank on the original deposit account. It would be no answer to say that the bank had paid the executors, for the contract was not to pay to the executors of either of the two names, but to the survivor. I think the case is rightly put on ratification, for I can find no sufficient evidence that the father had the actual authority of the son to enter into this contract on the son's behalf.

. . .

It remains then to consider whether the son still had the right to ratify, as I think he first sought to do, in October 1930, ten years after the original contract and four years after he had attained his majority. It is, I think, clear that he had from the beginning known: (1) That the contract purported to be made on his behalf; (2) that the money had been claimed and paid to his father's executors. I ignore any dealings with the money while the son was a minor, but in the period between November 1926, and October 1930, there was a series of transactions to the knowledge of the son, in which he played an active part and which were only consistent with the money having formed part of the father's estate and being paid to the executors as part of the estate. It has been said that ratification must take place, if at all, within a reasonable time. I would prefer in this case to say that ratification cannot take place after the purported principal has by words or conduct intimated to the other party that he does not intend to ratify. I have come to the conclusion that the only reasonable inference that the bank would draw from the son's conduct was that he was content that the money should be applied as part of his father's estate and that he did not propose to make a claim on his own behalf. I do not think for this purpose that it is necessary that he should have known the full extent of his rights. The facts are that ratification, or no ratification, was in suspense, and that the son by his conduct gave the bank reasonably to believe that the decision was no ratification.

I come to the conclusion therefore that the son never acquired the right to sue the bank on the contract. It becomes unnecessary on this view to consider whether if the son had acquired the right to sue, the bank could have relied on their plea of payment. I am much impressed by the view taken by Best L.J. on this question, but I express no final opinion. I agree that the appeal should be dismissed.

Lord Warrington:

. . .

Did the father purport to act as agent for his infant son so as to make the latter a party to the contract, or was the contract made with the father alone for the benefit of the son as a third party? In my opinion it is unnecessary to answer this question, for I think the real question is not whether the appellant would, as the effect in law of the contract, have been held entitled to be paid the money by the respondents, but what in the view of a court of equity would be the position between him and the executors; would he be held entitled to retain the moneys, if so paid, for his own benefit, or must he hand them over to the executors to be dealt with as part of the testator's estate? The material circumstances are these: the money deposited was that of the father alone, the son was a mere volunteer. The intention of the father as to the disposition of his estate was clearly expressed at the interview of 19 July 1921. The form of the deposit receipt in no way operated to alter this intention; it was adopted for another purpose. The money was entirely at the father's disposal during his life. The will as actually made gives effect to the expressed intention of the father and there is no evidence of any *animus donandi* except subject to the testamentary directions. The residuary personal estate including the deposit of £2,000, but excluding the £10,000, in question was so small that it is impossible to suppose that the testator deliberately intended to withdraw so important an item as the £10,000 from the fund to be administered by the executors and trustees until the son should attain twenty five. Finally the illegal proceedings of the executors, so much relied on by the trial judge, were entirely irrelevant, inasmuch as the testator was not in any way implicated in them. On the whole then I am satisfied that if the matter had been brought before a court of equity the decision would have been in favour of the executors, namely, that they alone were entitled to receive the money and to apply it in due course of administration as directed by the testator's will.

(Lord Macmillan concurred. Lord Thankerton agreed that in the circumstances the father alone contracted with the bank. He stated, however that if the father had purported to make the son a contracting party he would have agreed with Lord Atkin.)

Coulls v Bagot's Executor and Trustee Co. Ltd (1967) 119 CLR 460

The respondent's late husband contracted to grant a licence to a quarrying company to quarry and remove stone from a quarry which he owned. The last paragraph of the contract stated: 'I authorise the above company to pay all moneys connected with this agreement to my wife, Doris Sophia Coulls and myself, Arthur Leopold Coulls as joint tenants (or tenants in common?) (the one which goes to living partner).'

The contract was signed by both husband and wife.

Barwick C.J.:

. . .

It must be accepted that, according to our law, a person not a party to a contract may not himself sue upon it so as directly to enforce its obligations. For my part, I find no difficulty or embarrassment in this conclusion. Indeed, I would find it odd that a person to whom no promise was made could himself in his own right force a promise made to another. But that does not mean that it is not possible for that person to obtain the benefit of a promise made with another for his benefit by steps other than enforcement by himself in his own right: see the recent case of *Beswick v Beswick*.[1] I would myself, with great respect agree with the conclusion that where A promises B for a consideration supplied by B to pay C then B may obtain specific performance of A's promise, at least where the nature of the consideration given would have allowed the debtor to have obtained specific performance. I can see no reason whatever why A in those circumstances should not be bound to perform his promise. That C provided no part of the consideration seems to me irrelevant. Questions of consideration and of privity are not always kept distinct. Indeed, on some occasions when lack of privity is the real reason for not allowing a plaintiff to succeed on a promise not made with him, an unnecessary and irrelevant reason is given that the plaintiff was a stranger to the consideration; that is to say, that he was not merely not a party to the agreement but was not a party to the bargain. In *Dunlop Pneumatic Tyre Co. Ltd v Selfridge & Co. Ltd*[2] privity was not lacking because it was assumed, but the promise made by the defendant to the plaintiff was as between them gratuitous. But in this case whether the promise was made by the company to the deceased alone or to the deceased and the respondent, it was not as between promisor and promisee a gratuitous promise.

But as I construe this writing, we have here not a promise by A with B for consideration supplied by B to pay C. It was, in my opinion, a promise by A made to B and C for consideration to pay B and C. In such a case it cannot lie in the mouth of A, in my opinion, to question whether the consideration which he received for his promise moved from both B and C or, as between themselves, only from one of them. His promise is not a gratuitous promise as between himself and the promisees as on the view I take of the agreement it was a promise in respect of which there was privity between A on the one hand and B and C on the other. Such a promise, in my opinion, is clearly enforceable in the joint lifetime of B and C: But it is only enforceable if both B and C are parties to the action to enforce it. B, though he only supplied the consideration, could not sue alone. If C were unwilling to join in the action as plaintiff, B no doubt, after suitable tender of costs, could join C as a defendant. And A's promise could be enforced. But the judgment would be for payment to B and C. If B would not join in an action to enforce A's promise, I see no reason why C should not sue joining B as a defendant. Again, in my opinion, A's promise would be enforced and a judgment in favour of B and C would result. In neither of these cases could A successfully deny either privity or consideration. . . .

[1] [1966] Ch. 538.   [2] [1915] AC 847.

Taylor and Owen JJ.:

. . .

. . . If, however, the correct conclusion is that the widow was a party to the contract it is, to our minds, clear that she is entitled to receive the royalties payable after her husband's death notwithstanding that she, personally, gave no consideration for the company's promise. We do not accept the contention advanced on behalf of the appellant that if one, only, of two joint promisees provides the consideration for a promisor's promise the other promisee cannot, in any circumstances, sue to recover moneys payable according to the promise.

. . .

But the mere fact that her signature appears does not make her a party; this is a question to be resolved upon a consideration of the written instrument itself. It seems to us that the terms of the last paragraph do not prescribe the persons who are to be *entitled* to demand and receive the royalties payable under the agreement and, therefore, do not negative the certain implication which would otherwise arise that it was the testator who was to be so entitled. On what other basis could the husband, alone, 'authorise' the survivor to receive them after the death of either himself or his wife? It is, of course, obvious that in the preparation of this informal agreement the persons concerned contemplated, and provided for, the contingency of the death of the testator or his wife during its currency and it is not without significance that, whereas the testator authorised his wife to receive the royalties payable after his death, there is no corresponding authorisation by the wife in the event of her husband surviving her. We think it is clear that the only person entitled to demand royalties under the contract was the testator and that his wife was not a party to it. . . .

(McTiernan J. agreed that the wife was not a party to the contract.)

Windeyer J.:

. . .

Still, it was said, no consideration moved from her. But that, I consider, mistakes the nature of a contract made with two or more persons jointly. The promise is made to them collectively. It must, of course, be supported by consideration, but that does not mean by considerations furnished by them separately. It means a consideration given on behalf of them all, and therefore moving from all of them. In such a case the promise of the promisor is not gratuitous; and, as between him and the joint promisees, it matters not how they were able to provide the price of his promise to them. . . .

Note

In 'Consideration and the Joint Promisee' [1978] CLJ 301, Brian Coote argues that the joint promisee doctrine enunciated in *Coulls* was based on a misapprehension of what constitutes 'consideration' and of what constitutes a 'party' to a contract. He states that as a contract is a species of bargain, an essential condition of a contract is the reciprocal exchange of consideration between the parties. Thus only those who provide consideration can be parties. In the case of bilateral contracts, however, the consideration is not the payment by the promisee, but his initial acceptance of an obligation to pay. If this is accepted, Coote argues, it is easy to see how there can exist a series of cases where a person was held able to enforce a contract even though the contract price had been paid by someone else. He thus explains how, while a majority of their Lordships in *McEvoy v Belfast Banking Co.* rejected the son's claim because he was not a party to any contract with the bank it was quite possible in law for Lord Thankerton, while concurring with the majority, to agree with Lord Atkin that had the son been a party it would have been immaterial that the father had provided all the funds for the deposit. What could have made the son a party, Coote suggests, would have been an acceptance by him of an obligation to make or join in making the deposit, or even a mere acceptance by him, through his father, of the ordinary duties of a customer to the bank.

M.P. Furmston, 'Return to Dunlop v Selfridge?' (1960) 23 MLR 373. (Footnotes abridged.)

[Having discussed the rule that only a party to a contract may sue upon it, and the rule that consideration must move from the promisee, Furmston continued]

. . . The prevailing view is that the two rules are separate, although in many circumstances they overlap. This seems to be one of the more unfortunate legacies of comparative law. When English lawyers discovered that continental systems of law which knew nothing of consideration nevertheless had the rule that a contract could only benefit and bind the parties, they assumed that this must be a fundamental characteristic of a contract and promptly transferred it to English law although the situation was already provided for. It has been felt necessary to justify this dichotomy by giving illustrations of cases where the two rules do not overlap. Thus it is said that if 'by the terms of a joint agreement, A promises B and C to pay C £100 if B will carry out work desired by A, C is a contracting party, but he cannot sue A, because B alone has given consideration for A's promise.' With respect, this view is not completely convincing. In English law a contract is not a mere promise but a promise supported by consideration, or, in modern rationalisation, a bargain. If A were to promise C to pay him £100 *simpliciter*, we should not say that there is a contract but that C cannot enforce it because he has not given consideration. We should simply say that there is no contract. To do otherwise is to deprive the word contract of any legal meaning. Similarly a promise to C to pay him £100 if B carries out work is not a contract but a mere gratuitous promise. It is not easy to see why when we do not describe a gratuitous promise to C as a contract, we should suddenly describe it as a contract, albeit one C cannot enforce, because B has bargained for and bought the same promise. If C is not a party to the bargain he is not a party to the contract.

A converse case is sometimes put. A promises B to pay C £100 if C does work. It is said that if C does the work he cannot recover because, although he has furnished consideration, he was not a party to the contract. This analysis again is not completely convincing. If C does the work in ignorance of the offer he would seem not to provide consideration, because although he has no doubt suffered a detriment, the detriment is not causally connected with the offer. This is clearly the case where there are only two parties. Thus, for example, in *Wigan v English and Scottish Law Life Assurance Assn*[1] one Hackblock had a life assurance policy for £5,000 which was to be void if the assured died by his own hand 'but without prejudice to the *bona fide* interests of third parties based on valuable consideration.' He owed Wigan, who was pressing for payment, over £5,000 and executed an assignment to him of the policy, which was to be revealed in negotiations if necessary. In fact Wigan forebore without the assignment being revealed, and Parker J. held that there was no consideration because, although the assignment had been executed with the object of obtaining further time and further time had in fact been obtained, it had not been obtained in exchange for the assignment. The presence of a third party may obscure but should not confuse the issue. Even if C knew of the promise when he acted there would not strictly be consideration unless the offer was addressed to him. It might well be, however, that the court would infer from the express promise to B an implied offer to C of £100 for his doing the work—a unilateral contract.

There does not seem to be any binding authority against this view. *Corney and Curtis v Colidon*[2] is too poorly reported to be of much assistance. No doubt *obiter dicta* can be found which treat the principles as separate, notably those of Lord Haldane in *Dunlop v Selfridge*,[3] but it does not appear that these remarks have ever had any practical effect. Indeed, if the above conditions are correct, the question is one which never can arise in practice.

It is submitted, therefore, that there is no difference in the English law of simple contracts between the doctrine of privity of contract and the rule that consideration must move from the promisee.

[1.] [1909] 1 Ch. 291.   [2.] (1674) 1 Freem KB 284.   [3.] [1915] AC 847.

In considering the available remedies, it should be noted that the parties to a contract who are entitled to sue for breach may not have occasioned any loss. Often the loss will be sustained by the third party.

For example, A promises to pay B £10 if B gives C a book. If A pays B but B refuses to complete this contract, C will suffer a loss, yet only A can sue. In an action for breach A's damages will be measured by reference to his loss which in this case is minimal. An argument that A should be allowed to sue for C's loss was rejected by the House of Lords in *Woodar Investment Development Ltd v Wimpey Construction (UK) Ltd* [1980] 1 All ER 571.

An action by A for specific performance would however provide C with a remedy.

Beswick *v* Beswick [1968] AC 58

Lord Reid:

My Lords, before 1962 the respondent's deceased husband carried on business as a coal merchant. By agreement of 14 March 1962, he assigned to his nephew, the appellant, the assets of the business and the appellant undertook first to pay to him £6 10s per week for the remainder of his life and then to pay to the respondent an annuity of £5 per week in the event of her husband's death. The husband died in November 1963. Thereupon, the appellant made one payment of £5 to the respondent but he refused to make any further payment to her. The respondent now sues for £175 arrears of the annuity and for an order for specific performance of the continuing obligation to pay the annuity.

. . .

It so happens that the respondent is administratrix of the estate of her deceased husband and she sues both in that capacity and in her personal capacity. So it is necessary to consider her rights in each capacity.

For clarity I think it best to begin by considering a simple case where, in consideration of a sale by A to B, B agrees to pay the price of £1,000 to a third party X. Then the first question appears to me to be whether the parties intended that X should receive the money simply as A's nominee so that he would hold the money for behoof of A and be accountable to him for it, or whether the parties intended that X should receive the money for his own behoof and be entitled to keep it. That appears to me to be a question of construction of the agreement read in light of all the circumstances which were known to the parties.

. . .

In the present case I think it clear that parties to the agreement intended that the respondent should receive the weekly sums of £5 in her own behoof and should not be accountable to her deceased husband's estate for them. Indeed the contrary was not argued.

Reverting to my simple example the next question appears to me to be: Where the intention was that X should keep the £1,000 as his own, what is the nature of B's obligation and who is entitled to enforce it? It was not argued that the law of England regards B's obligation as a nullity, and I have not observed in any of the authorities any suggestion that it would be a nullity.

. . .

Lord Denning's view, expressed in this case not for the first time, is that X could enforce this obligation. But the view more commonly held in recent times has been that such a contract confers no right on X and that X could not sue for the £1,000.

. . .

What then is A's position? I assume that A has not made himself a trustee for X, because it was not argued in this appeal that any trust had been created. So, if X has no right, A can at any time grant a discharge to B or make some new contract with B. If there were a trust the position would be different. X would have an equitable right and A would be entitled and, indeed, bound to recover the money and account for it to X. And A would have no right to grant a discharge to B. If there is no trust and A wishes to enforce the obligation, how does he set about it? He cannot sue B for the £1,000 because under the contract the money is not payable to him, and, if the contract were performed according to its terms, he would never have any right to get the money. So he must seek to make B pay X.

The argument for the appellant is that A's only remedy is to sue B for damages for B's breach of contract in failing to pay the £1,000 to X. Then the appellant says that A can only recover nominal damages of 40s because the fact that X has not received the money will generally cause no loss to A. He admits that there may be cases where A would suffer damage if X did not receive the money but says that the present is not such a case.

Applying what I have said to the circumstances of the present case, the respondent in her personal capacity has no right to sue, but she has a right as administratrix of her husband's estate to require the appellant to perform his obligation under the agreement. He has refused to do so and he maintains that the respondent's only right is to sue him for damages for breach of his contract. If that were so, I shall assume that he is right in maintaining that the administratrix could then only recover nominal damages because his breach of contract has caused no loss to the estate of her deceased husband.

If that were the only remedy available the result would be grossly unjust. It would mean that the appellant keeps the business which he bought and for which he has only paid a small part of the price which he agreed to pay. He would avoid paying the rest of the price, the annuity to the respondent, by paying a mere 40s damages.

. . .

The respondent's second argument is that she is entitled in her capacity of administratrix of her deceased husband's estate to enforce the provision of the agreement for the benefit of herself in her personal capacity, and that a proper way of enforcing that provision is to order specific performance. That would produce a just result, and, unless there is some technical objection, I am of opinion that specific performance ought to be ordered.

Lord Pearce:

My Lords, if the annuity had been payable to a third party in the lifetime of Beswick senior and there had been default, he could have sued in respect of the breach. His administratrix is now entitled to stand in his shoes and to sue in respect of the breach which has occurred since his death.

It is argued that the estate can only recover nominal damages and that no other remedy is open, either to the estate or to the personal plaintiff. Such a result would be wholly repugnant to justice and commonsense. And if the argument were right it would show a very serious defect in the law.

In the first place, I do not accept the view that damages must be nominal. Lush L.J. in *Lloyd's v Harper*[1] said:

> Then the next question which, no doubt, is a very important and substantial one, is, that Lloyd's, having sustained no damage themselves, could not recover for the losses sustained by third parties by reason of the default of Robert Henry Harper as an underwriter. That, to my mind, is a startling and alarming doctrine, and a novelty, because I consider it to be an established rule of law that where a contract is made with A for the benefit of B, A can sue on the contract for the benefit of B, and recover all that B could have recovered if the contract had been made with B himself.

(See also *Drimmie v Davies*.[2]) I agree with the comment of Windeyer J. in the case of *Coulls v Bagot's Executor and Trustee Co. Ltd*[3] in the High Court of Australia that the words of Lush L.J. cannot be accepted without qualification and regardless of context and also with his statement: 'I can see no reason why in such cases the damages which A would suffer upon B's breach of his contract to pay C $500 would be merely nominal: I think that in accordance with the ordinary rules for the assessment of damages for breach of contract they could be substantial. They would not necessarily be $500; they could I think be less or more.' In the present case I think that the damages, if assessed, must be substantial. It is not necessary, however, to consider the amount of damages more closely since this is a case in which, as the Court of Appeal rightly decided, the more appropriate remedy is that of specific performance.

The administratrix is entitled, if she so prefers, to enforce the agreement rather than accept its repudiation, and specific performance is more convenient than an action for arrears of payment followed by separate actions as each sum falls due. Moreover, damages for breach would be a less appropriate remedy since the parties to the agreement were intending an annuity for a widow; and a lump sum of damages does not accord with this. And if (contrary to my view) the argument that a derisory sum of damages is all that can be obtained be right, the remedy of damages in this case is manifestly useless.

The present case presents all the features which led the equity courts to apply their remedy of specific performance. The contract was for the sale of a business. The defendant could on his part clearly have obtained specific performance of it if Beswick senior or his administratrix had defaulted. Mutuality is a ground in favour of specific performance.

Moreover, the defendant on his side has received the whole benefit of the contract and it is a matter of conscience for the court to see that he now performs his part of it. Kay J. said in *Hart v Hart*[4]: ' . . . when an agreement for valuable consideration . . . has been partially performed, the court ought to do its utmost to carry out that agreement by a decree for specific performance.'

What, then, is the obstacle to granting specific performance?

It is argued that since the widow personally had no rights which she personally could enforce the court will not make an order which will have the effect of enforcing those rights. I can find no principle to this effect. The condition as to payment of an annuity to the widow personally was valid. The estate (though not the widow personally) can enforce it. Why should the estate be barred from exercising its full contractual rights merely because in doing so it secures justice for the widow who, by a mechanical defect of our law, is unable to assert her own rights? Such a principle would be repugnant to justice and fulfil no other object than that of aiding the wrongdoer. I can find no ground on which such a principle should exist.

In *Hohler v Aston*[5] Sargant J. enforced a contract relating to the purchase of a house for the benefit of third parties. The third parties were joined as plaintiffs, but the relief was given to the plaintiff who had made the contract for their benefit: 'The third parties, of course, cannot themselves enforce a contract made for their benefit, but the person with whom the contract is made is entitled to enforce the contract.' In *Keenan v Handley*[6] the court enforced an agreement providing the benefit of an annuity in favour of a mother who was a party to the agreement and, after her death, to her child, who was not a party to it.

And in *Drimmie v Davies* the Court of Appeal in Ireland ordered specific performance of an agreement whereby annuities were provided for third parties. Holmes L.J. there said:

> In this case Davies, junior, covenanted for valuable consideration with Davies, senior, that in certain events he would pay certain annuities to the children of the latter. If such annuities had become payable in the life of the covenantee, and they were not paid, what legal obstacle would there be to his suing the covenantor? Indeed, I believe that it is admitted that such an action would lie, but that it would only result in nominal damages. A result more repugnant to justice, as well as to legal principle, I can hardly imagine. The defendant would thereby escape from paying what he had undertaken to pay by making an illusory payment never contemplated by either party. Well, if Davies, senior, would have been entitled to sue in his lifetime if the annuities were then payable, his executors would have the same right of action after his death. As I have already said, the question is elementary.

Recently in *Coulls v Bagot's Executor and Trustee Co. Ltd* the learned Chief Justice of Australia, Sir Garfield Barwick, in commenting on the report of the Court of Appeal's decision in the present case, said:

> I would myself, with great respect, agree with the conclusion that where A promises B for a consideration supplied by B to pay C that B may obtain specific performance of A's promise, at least where the nature of the consideration given would have allowed the debtor to have obtained specific performance. I can see no reason whatever why A in those circumstances should not be bound to perform his promise. That C provided no part of the consideration seems to me irrelevant.

Windeyer J. in that case said:

> It seems to me that contracts to pay money or transfer property to a third person are always, or at all events very often, contracts for breach of which damages would be an inadequate remedy—all the more so if it be right (I do not think it is) that damages recoverable by the promisee are only nominal. Nominal or substantial, the question seems to be the same, for when specific relief is given in lieu of damages it is is because the remedy, damages, cannot satisfy the demands of justice. 'The court,' said Lord Selbourne, 'gives specific performance instead of damages, only when it can by that means do more perfect and complete justice': *Wilson v Northampton and Banbury Junction Rly Co.*[7] Lord Erskine in *Alley v Deschamps*[8] said of the doctrine of specific performance: 'This court assumed the jurisdiction upon this simple principle; that the party had a legal right to the performance of the contract; to which right the courts of law, whose jurisdiction did not extend beyond damages, had not the means of giving effect.' Complete and perfect justice to a promisee may

well require that a promisor perform his promise to pay money or transfer property to a third party. I see no reason why specific performance should not be had in such cases—but of course not where the promise was to render some personal service. There is no reason to-day for limiting by particular categories, rather than by general principle, the cases in which orders for specific performance will be made. The days are long past when the common law courts looked with jealousy upon what they thought was a usurpation by the Chancery court of their jurisdiction.

He continued later:

It is, I think, a faulty analysis of legal obligations to say that the law treats the promisor as having a right to elect either to perform his promise or to pay damages. Rather, using one sentence from the passage from Lord Erskine's judgment which I have quoted above, the promisee has 'a legal right to the performance of the contract.' Moreover we are concerned with what Fullagar J. once called 'a system which has never regarded strict logic as its sole inspiration.' *Tatham v Huxtable.*[9]

I respectfully agree with these observations.

[1.] (1880) 16 ChD 290, 321, CA.	[6.] 2 De G. J. & Sm. 283.
[2.] [1899] 1 IR 176.	[7.] (1874) 9 Ch App 279, 284.
[3.] (1967) 40 ALJR 471, 486.	[8.] (1806) 13 Ves 225, 227–8.
[4.] 18 ChD 670, 685.	[9.] (1950) 81 CLR 639, 649.
[5.] [1920] 2 Ch. 420.	

(Lords Hodson, Guest and Upjohn agreed that the respondent was entitled to a decree of specific performance.)

Note

For a critical comment on this case see Treitel, 'Specific Performance and Third Parties' (1967) 30 MLR 687.

Ian Burke (a minor) *v* Dublin Corporation [1991] IR 340

The plaintiff lived in a house built by the defendant, a housing authority. The plaintiff sued the defendant, *inter alia* for damages for breach of contract in providing defective heaters rendering the house unfit for habitation. (See p. 287 above.)

The plaintiff claimed to be a party to the tenancy contract between his parents and the defendant as it was a contract made for his benefit. Blayney J. in the High Court dismissed the plaintiff's claim.

Finlay C.J.:

. . .

With regard to the broader submission on the alternative ground, particular reliance was placed on the decision of the Court of Appeal in England in the case of *Jackson v Horizon Holidays Ltd* [1975] 1 WLR 1468. In that case it was held that a man who entered into a contract for the provision of a holiday for himself, his wife and two children, making specific requirements as to what was to be contracted for in relation not only to himself but also to his wife and children, was entitled to sue upon breach of that contract, for damages in respect of his own discomfort, vexation and disappointment and the diminution of the value of the holiday, but also, although he was not held to be a trustee, in respect of the same damages suffered by his wife and two children. It seems to me, first, that the facts of that case and above all else the fact that the other contracting party was expressly aware of the persons for whose benefit the contract was being made and whose position was at risk if the contract was broken, make it entirely distinguishable from the present contract of tenancy entered into at a time when this plaintiff had not been born. I am also impressed by the submission made on behalf of the defendant in this case that the decision of the Court of Appeal in *Jackson v Horizon Holidays Ltd* has already been the subject matter of persuasive adverse comment in a judgment of Lord Wilberforce in *Woodar Investment v Wimpey Construction* [1980] 1 WLR 277 at p. 283 suggesting that it should be confined in effect to a decision on the measure of damages or possibly as an example of a type of contract, examples of which are persons contracting for family holidays, ordering meals in restaurants and hiring a taxi for a group, calling for special treatment.

It is attractive to view as a disturbing disparity and unnecessary discrimination a significant difference between the parties entering into a tenancy agreement of a house provided by a housing authority and other members of the family enjoying the same *de facto* rights and privileges who are not parties to that agreement. An argument based on this wider problem of equality before the law was not made in this case and I express no view about it.

I would therefore conclude, as did the learned trial judge, though apparently based on his belief that a concession to that effect had been made, that the issue of liability in the case of the first plaintiff depends upon his successfully establishing negligence on the part of the defendant.

Darlington Borough Council *v* Wiltshier Northern Ltd (CA) TLR 28 June 1994

The defendant a building contractor, entered into a contract with Morgan Grenfell (Local Authority Services) Ltd to construct a recreational centre. The latter assigned to the plaintiff all rights it had against the defendant. The plaintiff then sued for damages for defects in the performance of the contract.

Dillon L.J.:

. . .

Thus, in the first place, the general principle for the assessment of damages for breach of contract was compensatory: to compensate the plaintiff for damage, loss or injury he had suffered through the breach: see, for example, *Johnson v Agnew* [1980] AC 367, 400.

In the second place, it remained the law that a third party could not sue for damages on a contract to which he was not a party: see, for example, *Dunlop Pneumatic Tyre Co. Ltd v Selfridge & Co. Ltd* [1915] AC 847.

In the third place, the general position was that if a plaintiff contracted with a defendant for the defendant to make a payment or confer some other benefit on a third party who was not a party to the contract, the plaintiff could not recover substantial damages from the defendant for breach of that obligation on the part of the defendant: see *Woodar Investment Development v Wimpey Construction UK Ltd* [1980] 1 WLR 277. The plaintiff could, *prima facie*, only recover for his own loss.

Thus the case of the defendant which the judge accepted was simply that Morgan Grenfell, the employer under the building contracts, having no proprietary interest in the Dolphin Centre and no obligation to the plaintiff for the quality of the defendant's workmanship or for the defendant's due performance of the building contracts, had suffered no damages or loss from whatever defects there might have been in the construction of the centre, and could not recover by way of damages from the defendant whatever loss the plaintiff might have suffered from the defects.

It had been recognised in the House of Lords, however, that there were certain exceptions to the general principles to which his Lordship had referred.

One exception recognised in the *Woodar Investment* case was where the plaintiff made the contract as agent or trustee for the third party, and was enforcing the rights of a beneficiary.

A further exception was to be found, in the law as to carriage of goods by sea, in the recognition in *The Albazero* [1977] AC 774 of the continuing validity, in such a context, of the earlier decision in *Dunlop v Lambert* (1839) 6 Cl & F 600. The rule laid down in *Dunlop v Lambert* was applied by the House of Lords in a building contract context in *Linden Gardens Trust Ltd v Lenesta Sludge Disposals Ltd* [1994] AC 85, 114–5.

The present case was *a fortiori* since, so far from there being a prohibition on the assignment of Morgan Grenfell's rights against the defendant under the building contracts, the covenant agreement, of which the defendant was aware, gave the plaintiff the right to call for an assignment of such rights.

Accordingly, his Lordship would allow the appeal by direct application of the rule in *Dunlop v Lambert* as recognised in a building contract context.

His Lordship reached the same result by a slightly different route. In the light of the covenant agreement, if Morgan Grenfell had, before any assignment, sued in its own name for damages for the alleged breaches of the building contracts, it would have held any damages recovered as a constructive trustee for the plaintiff and would have been accountable accordingly in equity. Morgan Grenfell could have recovered from the defendant the losses of the plaintiff to whom it stood, in that respect, in a fiduciary relationship.

(Steyn and Waite L.JJ. concurred.)

Privity of Contract: Contracts for the Benefit of Third Parties. The Law Commission (UK) Consultation Paper No. 121. (Footnotes omitted.)

2. Test of enforceable benefit

5. 8 This is the central issue involved in reform of the third party rule. It is an issue on which there is no consensus among the various jurisdictions which we have examined. There are several options, including the following:

  (i) A third party may enforce a contract which expressly in its terms purports to confer a benefit directly on him.

 (ii) A third party may enforce a contract in which the parties intend that he should receive the benefit of the promised performance, regardless of whether they intend him to have an enforceable right of action.

(iii) A third party may enforce a contract in which the parties intend that he should receive the benefit of the promised performance and also intend to create a legal obligation enforceable by him.

(iv) A third party may enforce a contract where to do so would effectuate the intentions of the parties and either the performance of the promise satisfies a monetary obligation of the promisee to him or it is the intention of the promisee to confer a gift on him.

 (v) A third party may enforce a contract on which he justifiably and reasonably relies, regardless of the intentions of the parties.

5.9 We think that the options of allowing a third party to sue on any contract which happens to confer a benefit on him or on which he justifiably and reasonably relied would be unacceptably wide. They raise the possibility of an unacceptable volume of litigation and leave promisors open to liability to a potentially indeterminate class of third parties. The option of allowing a third party to sue on a contract which expressly in its terms purports to benefit him would not cater for those contracts under which the parties intend to confer an enforceable benefit on him but have not spelled this out expressly. Likewise, we do not think it sufficient that the contracting parties intend that the third party should receive the benefit of the promised performance: again, for the reasons that the parties' intentions could be defeated and an unacceptably large number of potential plaintiffs created. For instance, in the example discussed earlier of a building company contracting with a highway authority for the construction of a new road, the road may be intended for the benefit of all road-users, or even for an identified number of users (such as the residents of a private estate). However, it is a different issue whether individual road-users should have a right of action on the agreement in the event of delay in construction.

5.10 We provisionally recommend that a third party should be able to enforce a contract in which the parties intend that he should receive the benefit of the promised performance and also intend to create a legal obligation enforceable by him. From this it follows that the creation of a right in a third party should not be inferred from the mere fact that he will derive benefit from performance of the contract. Equally, a third party should not be allowed to sue on any contract which is simply made for his benefit or which merely happens to benefit him or on which he has happened to rely.

5.11 The basic principle on which our proposal rests is to allow a remedy to the third party when to do so would give effect to the intentions of the contracting parties. Intention should not necessarily be associated with motive. If A, in buying property from B, promises to pay the purchase price to C, A's motive or purpose in making the promise may be simply to comply with the proposed bargain. Likewise, the reason why B extracted the promise may have been to make a gift to a close friend or to fulfil a duty to a sworn enemy. Whether or not a contract is intended to create a legal obligation enforceable by the third party is to be derived from the terms of the contract and the surrounding circumstances.

5.12 Furthermore, it is the objectively determined intentions of the parties which matter rather than their private thoughts. Parties to the contract may frequently omit provisions from their contract, whilst relying on prior dealing, trade customs or other shared beliefs. We provisionally recommend that reform should enable consideration of the circumstances surrounding the making of the contract when deducing the parties' intentions.

5.13 Although we provisionally recommend the dual intention test, we are aware of the criticisms of it.

(i) Where the contract is silent or ambiguous on the question of enforcement by a third party, the ascertainment of a contractual intention may be difficult.

(ii) Concentration on the intention of the parties has been argued to be a substitute for the real enquiry, which should be on the third party's actual reliance and the needs of the market in which the parties operate. Where a third party becomes involved, generally by reliance on the contract, a court may be unduly restricted if it only has regard to the intent of the contracting parties.

5.14 However, we do not regard these circumstances as convincing. First, the problem of detecting an unexpressed intention is a familiar one for courts as is the idea of giving effect to the intentions of the parties. We do not think that ascertainment of the parties' intentions in a three-party situation poses any more difficulties than in a two-party situation. Indeed, even if such ascertainment is difficult, this does not of itself point in favour of a laxer rule which may not reflect the intentions of the contracting parties. Secondly, we have already stated why we think that it would be unacceptable if a third could sue on any contract on which he justifiably and reasonably relied.

5.15 A reform of the third party rule would allow, in principle, contractual actions by consumers against manufacturers if the contract between manufacturer and wholesaler/retailer were to be construed as a contract for the benefit of a third party within the terms discussed earlier. Whether or not this would occur frequently in practice is debatable, since under our provisional recommendations, if the parties to the contract do not make it clear that they intend to create a legal obligation enforceable by the third party, the third party will have no remedy. In a context in which such intent may be inferred by the court it is open for the contracting parties to make the position clear by inserting a contractual term in effect excluding any action by a third party. In the context of s. 4 of the New Zealand Contracts (Privity) Act 1982, one commentator has noted that if the parties wish to escape the application of the Act, they need only to declare in their contract, in a manner clear enough to be proof against interpretation *contra proferentum*, their intention that the third party beneficiary be not entitled to sue.[1] We are of the provisional view that the ability of parties to do this is an important component of any reform which is to be compatible with a consensual view of contractual relations.

[1.] Coote, (1984) NZ Recent Law 107, 112.

Note

See also Beatson [1992] CLP 1.

SECTION TWO—EXCEPTIONS

A. RESTRICTIVE COVENANTS

The rule in *Tulk v Moxhay* (1848) 2 Ph. 774 states that the burden of a restrictive covenant will run with the land to which it relates, and thus may be enforced against successors in title, with the exception of a *bona fide* purchaser for value without notice of the covenant. This rule is based on the premise that the restrictive covenant concerns the preservation of the value of the land. (See Wylie, *Irish Land Law*, (2nd ed.) ch. 19 'Restrictive Covenants').

In *James Whelan and Deirdre Whelan v Cork Corporation* [1991] ILRM 19, Murphy J. accepted that when a lessee contemplates acquiring the interest of his immediate lessor with a view to relieving himself of the burden of covenants in the lease, he or she is put upon enquiry as to the existence and identity of third parties who might have the right to enforce covenants of a like effect as those contained in the lease.

Law Debenture Trust Corp. plc *v* Ural Caspian Oil Corp. Ltd and others
[1993] 2 All ER 355

Hoffman J.:

The first four defendants (the Russian companies) are English registered companies which carried on business in Russia before the Bolshevik revolution. The Soviets confiscated all their assets and for many years rejected their claims for compensation.

In April 1986 a company called Leisure Investments (Overseas) Ltd (Leisure Overseas) made an offer for the entire issued share capitals of the Russian companies. By then, an improvement in our relations with the Soviet Union had made payment of compensation a practical possibility. The controlling shareholder in each of the Russian companies was the Shell Petroleum Co. Ltd (Shell) but there were a fair number of small shareholders as well. Shell agreed to accept the offer on condition that Leisure Overseas and the Russian companies entered into covenants to apply any compensations which might be paid for the benefit of the existing shareholders. Accordingly by four separate agreements dated 2 May 1986 (the agreements), each of the Russian companies and Leisure Overseas entered into covenants with the plaintiff, Law Debenture Trust Corp. plc as trustee for the shareholders. Each Russian company covenanted to take whatever steps were necessary to pursue its compensation claim and to pay the net amount of any compensation it received (after deduction of expenses and costs) to the plaintiff as trustee. In each agreement, Leisure Overseas covenanted, first, to procure that the Russian company would perform its covenants and, secondly, not to part with control of the Russian company except on terms that the transferee entered into covenants in similar form. After the execution of the agreements, Shell and certain other shareholders who had accepted the offer transferred their shares to Leisure Overseas, which thereby acquired control.

On 15 December 1989 the Russian companies were paid about £7.2m. compensation through the Foreign Compensation Commission. Very shortly before the payment was received, Leisure Overseas agreed to sell its entire shareholdings to the fifth defendant, Hilldon Ltd (Hilldon), an Isle of Man company. In breach of its covenant, Leisure Overseas imposed no requirement that Hilldon should covenant with the plaintiff and Hilldon did not do so. On 5 March 1990 the shares were transferred to Hilldon. A further tranche of about £6m. compensation was paid on 4 June 1990. On 20 June 1990 the sixth defendant, Caspian Resources Ltd (Caspian) made an offer for the entire issued share capitals of the Russian companies. Hilldon accepted the offer and in October 1990 transferred its shares to Caspian.

The Russian companies refused to pay any part of the compensation to the plaintiff and on 15 November 1990 the plaintiff commenced proceedings against the Russian companies, Hilldon and Caspian.

Hilldon and Caspian apply to have these claims struck out. Hilldon says that, whatever may be its liability in tort, there are no grounds for implying any contract between itself and the plaintiff. Caspian says that, as against it, the statement of claim discloses no arguable case because it is all predicated upon the allegation that Hilldon was under a contractual liability which Caspian induced it to break.

These submissions are in my judgment correct. Neither Hilldon nor Caspian was party to a contract with the plaintiff. Nor are there any grounds for implying a collateral contract. One would have to imply a promise by Hilldon to the plaintiff, made for consideration and with intention to contract: *Wells (Merstham) Ltd v Buckland Sand and Silica Ltd* [1964] 1 All ER 41 at 45–6, [1965] 2 QB 170 at 180. The acts alleged against

Hilldon and Caspian do not suggest any such intention. As for the plaintiff, there is no allegation that it had even heard of Hilldon or Caspian at the time when it is alleged to have impliedly contracted with them. It follows that para. 9(b) of the statement of claim is liable to be struck out as against Hilldon and the whole as against Caspian.

At the commencement of the hearing, |counsel| for the plaintiff applied for leave to amend the statement of claim so as to formulate the claim in alternative ways and to seek additional relief.

. . .

A proposed new para. 9A says that, because Hilldon took the shares with knowledge of the agreements and their breach by Leisure Overseas, it also took the burden of those covenants and thereby came under a legal or equitable obligation to perform them. A new para. 11A makes similar allegations against Caspian. In argument, |counsel| submitted that the obligation to perform the covenants arose either in equity under the principle of De Mattos v Gibson (1858) 4 De G. & J. 276 at 282, |1843–60| All ER Rep 803 at 805 or at law or in equity under a developing principle relating to benefits and burdens.

The De Mattos principle was formulated by Knight-Bruce L.J. in a well known passage:

> Reason and justice seem to prescribe that, at least as a general rule, where a man, by gift or purchase, acquires property from another, with knowledge of a previous contract, lawfully and for valuable consideration made by him with a third person, to use and employ the property for a particular purpose in a specified manner, the acquirer shall not, to the material change of the third person, in opposition to the contract and inconsistently with it, use and employ the property in a manner not allowable to the giver or seller. This rule, applicable alike in general as I conceive to moveable and immoveable property, and recognised and adopted, as I apprehend, by the English law, may, like other general rules, be liable to exceptions arising from special circumstances; but I see at present no room for any exception in the instance before us.

This generalisation has had its ups and downs over the past 130 years. The enforceability of a restrictive covenant against a purchaser of land was first taken to be its paradigm example. But restrictive covenants turned out to be equitable interests in land whose enforceability owed nothing to the De Mattos principle. The actual knowledge of the purchaser was neither necessary nor sufficient. Like other equitable interests, they bound any purchaser who could not show that he had acquired a legal estate in good faith and for value without actual or constructive notice of the covenant: see Re Nisbet and Potts' Contract |1906| 1 Ch. 386, |1904–7| All ER Rep 865. But the right of enforcement, even against purchasers with actual knowledge, was confined to owners of neighbouring land for whose benefit it had been imposed: see London CC v Allen |1914| 3 KB 642, |1914–15| All ER Rep 1008.

The defection of restrictive covenants was not the only setback. The De Mattos principle also failed to secure the enforceability of resale price maintenance agreements against retailers who acquired stock with full knowledge of the covenants into which their wholesalers had entered: see Taddy & Co. v Sterious & Co. |1904| 1 Ch. 354 and McGruther v Pitcher |1904| 2 Ch. 306. (See the comment on the inconsistency between these cases and De Mattos by Buckley L.J. in London CC v Allen |1914| 3 KB 642 at 658–9, |1914–15| All ER Rep 1008 at 1014.) These cases, Scrutton L.J. later said in Barker v Stickney |1919| 1 KB 121 at 132, showed that 'the general rule of Knight-Bruce L.J. was quite impracticable'. It was however, applied by the Privy Council in Lord Strathcona Steamship Co. Ltd v Dominion Coal Co. Ltd |1926| AC 108, |1925| All ER Rep 87 to restrain the owner of a ship from using it inconsistently with a charter granted by a predecessor in title.

Diplock J. thought that the *Strathcona* case had been wrongly decided: see *Port Line Ltd v Ben Line Steamer Ltd* [1958] 1 All ER 787, [1958] 2 QB 146. But *Swiss Bank Corp. v Lloyds Bank Ltd* [1979] 2 All ER 853, [1979] Ch. 548 declared the principle to have continuing validity. I am bound to say that neither *Strathcona* nor *Swiss Bank* make it entirely clear when the principle applies and when it does not. Why, for example, does it apply to a time charter but not to a resale price maintenance agreement? But I need not explore this question in a motion to strike out. I shall assume that the principle applies in this case.

The plaintiff's difficulty, as it seems to me, is not whether the principle applies but the extent of the remedy which it provides. One thing is beyond doubt: it does not provide a panacea for outflanking the doctrine of privity of contract. In the *Strathcona* case [1926] AC 108 at 119, [1925] All ER Rep at 92 Lord Shaw said:

> It has sometimes been considered that *Tulk v Moxhay* (1848) 2 Ph. 774 at 777, 41 ER 1143 at 1144 and *De Mattos v Gibson* carried forward to and laid upon the shoulders of an alienee with notice the obligations of the alienor, and, therefore, that the former is liable to the covenantee in specific performance as by the law of contract, and under a species of implied privity. This is not so; the remedy is a remedy in equity by way of injunction against acts inconsistent with the covenant, with notice of which the land was acquired.

Thus the *De Mattos* principle permits no more than the grant of a negative injunction, to restrain the third party from doing acts which would be inconsistent with performance of the contract by the original contracting party. The terms of the injunction must be such that refraining altogether from action would constitute compliance. A time charter, as Diplock J. pointed out in *Port Line Ltd v Ben Line Steamer Ltd*, is a contract under which the owner is under a positive obligation to provide the vessel. It is clear that Lord Shaw did not intend to order the purchase to fulfil this obligation. The injunction only prohibited him from doing an inconsistent act, namely chartering the vessel to someone else. In practice, the board thought that this would provide the owner with an economic incentive to perform the charter: as Lord Shaw said ([1926] AC 108 at 125, [1925] All ER Rep 87 at 95): 'it is incredible that the owners will lay up the vessel rather than permit its use under the contract' but such dog-in-the-manager behaviour would not have been a breach of the injunction.

In the *Swiss Bank* case Browne-Wilkinson J. analysed the other cases in which it appeared that the *De Mattos* principle had been applied and showed that in each case the remedy was a purely negative restraint. In *Lumley v Wagner* (1852) 1 De G. M. & G. 604 at 618, [1843–60] All ER Rep 368 at 373 Lord St Leonards L.C. restrained Johanna Wagner from singing at Covent Garden and also injuncted Mr Gye from employing her there. But he did not order her to sing at Her Majesty's Theatre or require Mr Gye to procure that she did so. In *De Mattos v Gibson* itself, the plaintiff had chartered a ship to carry his coals from the Tyne to Suez. In the Channel it suffered damage and put into Penzance for expensive repairs. The owner had no money to pay for them and Gibson, who held a mortgage over the ship, proposed himself to discharge the repairer's lien and order the ship back to Newcastle so that he could exercise his power of sale. Knight Bruce and Turner L.JJ. granted an interlocutory injunction to restrain him from doing so on the ground that this would be inconsistent with the performance of the charter, of which he had knowledge. But there was never any question of ordering Gibson to sail the ship to Suez and Lord Chelmsford L.C. later discharged the injunction on the grounds that it was useless to De Mattos because the owner did not have the resources to sail to Suez either. In *Manchester Ship Canal Co. v Chester Racecourse Co.* [1901] 2 Ch. 37 the defendant, which had given the plaintiff a right of pre-emption over its land, was proposing to sell it to a third party. The Court of Appeal, following Lumley v Wagner, granted an injunction to restrain the defendant from selling without first offering the land to the plaintiff and also injuncted the third party from purchasing until such an offer had been made and rejected. Similarly in Earl of Sefton v Tophams Ltd |1965| 3 All ER 1, |1965| Ch. 1140 the Court of Appeal, having decided by a majority that the sale of Aintree Racecourse by Tophams Ltd to a third party for building houses would infringe a covenant with Lord Sefton not to 'cause or permit the land to be used other- wise than for the purpose of horse racing and for agricultural purposes', granted an injunction in the Manchester Ship Canal form, restraining Tophams Ltd and the third party from completing the sale (the House of Lords disagreed on construction and held that the sale would not infringe the covenant: see Tophams Ltd v Earl of Sefton |1966| 1 All ER 1039, |1967| 1 AC 50).

These cases of negative injunctions may be contrasted with Barker v Stickney |1919| 1 KB 121, in which the plaintiff wanted an order that the purchaser positively perform the covenants in the agreement of which he had notice. Barker had assigned the copyright in his book to a publisher on terms which provided for a royalty as well as a lump sum payment and the publisher expressly covenanted not to assign the copyright except subject to the terms of the agreement. The publisher went into receivership and by its receiver assigned the copyright to Stickney without any stipulation as to payment of royalties. Barker claimed that Stickney should have to pay the royalties because he had acquired the copyright with full knowledge of the agreement with the publisher. This claim was emphatically rejected by the Court of Appeal. Although Diplock J. regarded this decision as writing finis to the entire De Mattos principle (see Port Line Ltd v Ben Line Steamers Ltd |1958| 1 All ER 787 at 797, |1958| 2 QB 146 at 168), Browne-Wilkinson J. has more recently explained it as a case in which the plaintiff was trying to push the principle too far by securing positive performance of the contract (see Swiss Bank Corp. v Lloyds Bank Ltd |1979| 2 All ER 853 at 874, |1979| Ch. 548 at 575). He agreed however with Diplock J.'s statement of the limits of Strathcona in Port Line Ltd v Ben Line Steamers Ltd |1958| 1 All ER 787 at 797–8, |1958| 2 QB 146 at 168: ' . . . I do not think that it purported to decide . . . (2) that the charterer has any remedy against the subsequent purchaser with notice except a right to restrain the use of the vessel by such purchaser in a manner inconsistent with the terms of the charter; (3) that the charterer has any positive right against the subsequent purchaser to have the vessel in accordance with the terms of his charter.'

Thus there is not a single case in which the De Mattos principle has been used to impose upon a purchaser a positive duty to perform the covenants of his predecessor. It cannot therefore save the claim to performance of the covenants by Hilldon and Caspian from being struck out. The negative injunction granted in De Mattos and the Strathcona is of no use to the plaintiff. Hilldon and Caspian are not proposing to do any particular acts inconsistent with the covenant given by Leisure Overseas. They are proposing in fact to do nothing whatever. Under the De Mattos principle, this cannot give rise to any liability.

. . .

In the alternative, the plaintiff relies upon the principle that he who takes the benefit of a transaction must also take the burden. In Tito v Waddell (No 2) |1977| 3 All ER 129 at 280, |1977| Ch. 106 at 289 Megarry V.C. examined all the cases which could be said to exemplify the principle. Many were cases in which, upon the true construction of the instrument, enjoyment of the benefit is conditional upon assumption of the burden. There is little difficulty about such cases and this is plainly not one of them. But Megarry V.C. found a handful of cases which he said embodied the 'pure principle' of benefit and burden (|1977| 3 All ER 129 at 281, |1977| Ch. 106 at 290): ' . . . the right and burden, although arising under the same instrument, are independent of each other: X grants a right to Y, and by the same instrument Y independently covenants with Y to do some act'.

The leading example of the 'pure principle' is *Halsall v Brizell* |1957| 1 All ER 371, |1957| Ch. 169. Upjohn J. said, *obiter*, that successors in title to the original purchasers of houses on an estate laid out in 1851 could not take the benefit of rights to use the estate roads and sewers which had been granted by a deed between the owners and the original purchasers unless they also accepted obligations in the deed to contribute to the upkeep of the estate (see |1957| 1 All ER 371 at 377, |1957| Ch. 169 at 183). The two other cases mentioned by the judge also concerned rights of property conferred by an instrument or transaction which created reciprocal obligations.

The present case differs from any case which might embody the 'pure principle'. The right and burden do not arise under the same instrument. The shares were transferred to Leisure Overseas by transfers from some of the registered shareholders, while the covenant was made by Leisure Overseas with the plaintiff as trustee for all shareholders. Nor are the obligations clearly reciprocal. There is nothing in any transfer of the shares to which Hilldon and Caspian become successors in title which links them to the agreements. The connection between the shares and the obligations of Leisure Overseas is that use of the voting rights attached to the shares is the most obvious way in which Leisure Overseas can give effect to its covenant to procure that the Russian companies observe their obligations. It is not however the only way.

More important, Megarry V.C. in *Tito v Waddell* (No. 2) |1977| 3 All ER 129, |1977| Ch. 106 recognised that, without some limits, the 'pure principle' could completely subvert the doctrine of privity of contract and the principle that a purchaser of goods or the assignee of a contract or other *chose* in action is not bound to perform the obligations undertaken by the seller or assignor. So, for example, it is hard to believe that *Barker v Stickney* would have been decided differently if counsel (who was already scraping the barrel for arguments) had put forward the pure principle of benefit and burden. Some explanation is required for why the application of the principle would have been rejected. Megarry V.C. proposed various limits, including the following (|1977| 3 All ER 129 at 291–2, |1977| 1 Ch. 106 at 302):

> If the initial transaction has created benefits and burdens which, on its true con-
> struction, are distinct, the question whether a person who is not an original party
> can take one without the other will *prima facie* depend on the circumstances in which
> he comes into the transaction. If, for instance, all that is assigned to him is the
> benefit of a contract, and the assignor, who is a party to the contract, undertakes to
> continue to discharge the burdens of it, it would be remarkable if it were held that
> the assignee could not take the benefit without assuming the burden. The circum-
> stances show that the assignee was intended to take only the benefit, and that the
> burden was intended to be borne in the same way as it had been borne previously.

The right of the covenantee to enforce his covenant against an assignee therefore depends, perhaps rather curiously, upon the circumstances of a transaction to which he is not a party. One must be able to infer from that transaction that the assignee was intended to assume the burden. If correct, this would explain *Barker v Stickney*, where the assignments by the receiver contained no provision that the purchaser should pay royalties. Equally, no such inference can be drawn here. On the contrary, the plaintiff asserts that the whole object of the transaction was to ensure that Hilldon and Caspian would not be subject to the burden of the agreements. In my judgment, therefore, the benefit and burden doctrine does not assist the plaintiff.

B. Statutory Exceptions to the Privity Doctrine

In certain cases it has been enacted that a contract may be enforceable by a person who is not a party to the contract.

Married Women's Status Act 1957 s. 7 (1)–(3), s. 8 (1)–(2)

7. (1) This section applies to a policy of life assurance or endowment expressed to be for the benefit of, or by its express terms purporting to confer a benefit upon, the wife, husband or child of the insured.

(2) The policy shall create a trust in favour of the objects therein named.

(3) The moneys payable under the policy shall not, so long as any part of the trust remains unperformed, form part of the estate of the insured or be subject to his or her debts.

. . .

8. (1) Where a contract (other than a contract to which s. 7 applies) is expressed to be for the benefit of, or by its express terms, purports to confer a benefit upon, a third person being the wife, husband or child of one of the contracting parties, it shall be enforceable by the third person in his or her own name as if he or she were a party to it.

(2) The right conferred on a third person by this section shall be subject to any defence that would have been valid between the parties to the contract.

Note

In *Ian Burke (a minor) v Dublin Corporation* [1991] IR 340 (see p. 673 above) the Supreme Court rejected a submission that a minor had an interest in a tenancy agreement by virtue of s. 8 (1), Finlay C.J. stated that:

Such a submission would place upon s. 8 sub-s 1 of the Act of 1957, which is clearly restricted to contracts which are expressed to be for, or whose express terms confer benefits upon third persons, a much wider implied effect than the terms of the section would warrant. In the terms of the written letting agreement there is nothing which confines it to a case in which a family has children or which deals with any particular category or child or children in regard to the rights vested in the occupiers of the house by the letting agreement.

Road Traffic Act 1961 s. 76 (1)

76. (1) Where a person (in this section referred to as the claimant) claims to be entitled to recover from the owner of a mechanically propelled vehicle or from a person (other than the owner) using a mechanically propelled vehicle (in this section referred to as the user), or has in any court of justice (in proceedings of which the vehicle insurer or vehicle guarantor hereinafter mentioned had prior notification) recovered judgment against the owner or user for, a sum (whether liquidated or unliquidated) against the liability for which the owner or user is insured by an approved policy of insurance or by the payment of which, by the owner or user is guaranteed by an approved guarantee, the claimant may serve by registered post, on the vehicle insurer by whom the policy was issued, or on the vehicle insurer or the vehicle guarantor by whom the guarantee was issued, a notice in writing of the claim or judgment for the sum, and upon the service of the notice such of the following provisions as are applicable shall, subject to sub-s. (2) of this section, have effect:

- (a) the insurer shall not after service of the notice pay to the owner or user in respect of the sum any greater amount than the amount (if any) which the owner or user has actually paid to the claimant in respect of the sum;
- (b) where the claimant has so recovered judgment for the sum, or after service of the notice so recovers judgment for the sum or any part thereof, the insurer or guarantor shall pay to the claimant so much of the moneys (whether damages or costs) for which judgment was or is so recovered as the insurer or guarantor has insured or guaranteed and is not otherwise paid to the claimant, and the payment shall, as against the insured or principal debtor, be a valid payment under the policy or guarantee;
- (c) where the claimant has so recovered judgment for the sum, or after service of the notice so recovers judgment for the sum or any part thereof, and has not recovered from the owner or user or such insurer or guarantor the whole amount of the judgment, the claimant may apply to the court in which he recovered against the insurer or guarantor, grant the application either in respect of the whole amount of the judgment or in respect of any specified part of that amount;
- (d) where the claimant has not so recovered judgment for the sum, the claimant may apply to any court of competent jurisdiction in which he might institute proceedings for the recovery of the sum from the owner or user for leave to institute and prosecute those proceedings against the insurer or guarantor (as the case may be) in lieu of the owner or user, and the court, if satisfied that the owner or user is not in the State, or cannot be found or cannot be served with the process of the court, or that it is for any other reason just and equitable that the application and thereupon the claimant shall be entitled to institute and prosecute those proceedings against the insurer or guarantor any sum which he would be entitled to recover from the owner or user and the payment of which the insurer or guarantor has insured or guaranteed;
- (e) the insurer or guarantor shall not, as a ground for refusing payment of moneys to the claimant or as a defence to proceedings by the claimant, rely on or plead any invalidity of the policy or guarantee arising from any fraud or any misrepresentation or false statement (whether fraudulent or innocent) to which the claimant was not a party or privy and which, if constituting a misdemeanour under this Part of this Act, was not the subject of a prosecution and conviction under the relevant section of this Act.

Sale of Goods and Supply of Services Act 1980

S. 13 of the Act gives a cause of action in respect of persons who are injured whilst travelling in an unroadworthy vehicle which has been sold to a purchaser within the terms of the section. See *Glorney v O'Brien* (HC) 14 November 1988, unrep. (Chapter 8, p. 375 above).

C. TRUSTS

If A promises B to give C £50, C may be able to avoid the privity rule and enforce the contract, if equity will treat B as the trustee for C for the benefit of the contract. C will thus be entitled 'by way of property' to the benefit of the contract. C may thus sue on foot of the contract, although as the legal right vests in B, B would have to be joined as a party to the action.

Drimmie v Davies [1899] 1 IR 176

A father and son entered into a partnership agreement which included a clause obliging the son to pay his brothers and sisters certain annuities in the event of the father dying during the continuance of the partnership. When the father died, the executors of the will, and the brothers and sisters sued to enforce payment of the annuities.

Chatterton V.C.:

. . .

The case therefore comes to this, whether any action can be brought by any one against the defendant for his breach of his contract. I say 'by any one', because both the daughters and sons of F. Davies, senior, as the beneficiaries, and his acting executors are joined as co-plaintiffs, the latter of course suing only for the benefit of the former.

The defendant's contention is based on the common law rule that in the case of contracts under seal no one can sue who is not a party to the deed. That rule is fully stated in the case of *Tweddle v Atkinson*,[1] namely, that a stranger to the contract, that is to say, a person who is not a party to the contract and from whom no consideration moved, cannot sue upon it. The test seems to be whether such a person could be sued upon the contract. Now here the daughters and sons were not parties to the contract, nor did any consideration move from them, nor could they be sued upon the contract. But this rule did not prevail in equity, and since the Judicature Act the rules in equity are to prevail in cases where such a conflict exists. The equitable rule was that the party to whose use or for whose benefit the contract had been entered into has a remedy in equity against the person with whom it was expressed to be made. The court deems the latter a trustee for the former, and would compel him to execute his trust according to the apparent intention of the contracting parties. In the case of *Page v Cox*,[2] which has much resemblance to the present case, an agreement was held to amount to a trust which, as stated by Wood V.C., may well be created, though there may be an absence of any expression in terms importing confidence, and a trust cannot be the less capable of being enforced, because it is founded on contract. It was sought to distinguish that case on the ground that there a trust was imposed to pay out of specific property, which, as I have stated, did not exist here, but it seems to me that as the contract here was such that, if the executors of the deceased partner had a right to sue on it, any money recovered by them must have been held by them in trust for the daughters and sons, there is sufficient to create an equity in favour of the beneficiaries. The case chiefly relied on by the defendant was that of the *Empress Engineering Co.*[3] where it was held that a contract made by the promoters of the company with third parties for payment of a sum of money, and which was in itself null and void, could not be made the subject of a claim against the company when formed by reason of its having been mentioned in the purchase deed as a charge subject to which the business was purchased by the company. The case was decided principally on the ground that the agreement with the third parties being in itself null and void was not capable of ratification, but certainly the learned judges who decided the appeal drew a distinction between cases where there was intended to be a charge in favour of the third party on specific property, and cases where there was a mere agreement to

pay a sum of money to a third party. Jessel M.R., guards his decision by the observation that he was far from saying that there might not be agreements which may
make the third party a *cestui que trust*.

In the case of *Lloyd's v Harper*[4] a question bearing on the principle applicable to
such transactions was considered first by Fry J., and afterwards by the Court of Appeal,
namely, whether a guarantee given by a father to Lloyd's Assocation on the admission
of his son as an underwriter could be sued on by persons who had been underwritten
by the son. Lloyd's were co-plaintiffs in the action with outside persons, not members
of Lloyd's, who had been underwritten by the son. One of the questions raised was
that Lloyd's not having sustained any damage, could only recover nominal damages
for themselves, and could not recover for the losses sustained by third parties by reason
of the default of the son as an underwriter. This contention was disallowed. As to it,
Lush L.J. (p. 321), says 'To my mind it is a startling and an alarming doctrine, and a
novelty, because I consider it to be an established rule of law that where a contract is
made with A for the benefit of B, A can sue on the contract for the benefit of B, and
recover all that B could have recovered if the contract had been made with B himself.'
This principle shows that if the executors of F. Davies the elder, who are co-plaintiffs in
this action, had sued alone, they could recover all that the defendant agreed with his
father to pay, and of any sums so recovered they would of course be trustees for the
daughters and sons.

In the case of *Murray v Flavell*[5] before North J., and afterwards on appeal, in which
the decision in *Lloyd's v Harper* was referred to, the question arose as to the effect of
partnership articles, in which it was provided that from the determination of the partnership the retiring partner or his widow should be entitled to receive out of the profits
for a stated period an annuity; and it was contended that this was a mere bargain
between the partners, and that no trust was created for the widow, and that she could
not enforce an agreement to which she was not a party, and which was not communicated to her. The cases of *Gregory v Williams*;[6] *In re Empress Engineering Co.*; and *Lloyd's v
Harper* were considered, and it was held both by North J. and the Court of Appeal that
a valid trust for the widow was created by the articles.

The last case referred to, *Gandy v Gandy*,[7] is probably the most important. The
action there was brought upon a deed of separation containing a covenant by the
husband with trustees to maintain the children. The husband afterwards refused to
maintain one of the children, and she sued the husband and the trustees to carry out
the trusts of the deed. The husband raised an objection that the plaintiff was not
competent to sue upon the deed, and that the only proper parties to sue were the
trustees; and it was contended that the children were not parties to the deed, and that
the consideration did not move from them. Bacon V.C. held that there was a relation
of trustee and *cestui que trust* existing, and that as the trustees refused to sue, the *cestui
que trust* could sue. From this the husband appealed, and the judgement of the Vice-
Chancellor was reversed. Cotton L.J. stated the rule of law to be as follows:

> As a general rule, a contract cannot be enforced except by a party to the contract;
> and either of two persons contracting together can sue the other, if the other is
> guilty of a breach of or does not perform the obligations of that contract. But a
> third person—a person who is not a party to the contract—cannot do so. That rule,
> however, is subject to this exception: if the contract, although in form it is with A, is
> intended to secure a benefit to B, so that B is entitled to say he has a beneficial
> right as *cestui que trust* under that contract; then B would, in a court of equity, be
> allowed to insist upon and enforce the contract.

He considered the objection to the plaintiff suing as fatal to the action in its present form, but he allowed the case to stand over to see whether the plaintiff could induce the trustees to sue. Bowen L.J. concurred, and said that whatever may have been the common law doctrine, if the true intent and effect of the deed were to give to the children a beneficial right under it, that is to say, to give them a right to have the covenants performed, and to call upon the trustees to protect their rights and interests under it, then the children would be outside the common law doctrine, and would in a court of equity be allowed to enforce their rights under the deed, but the whole application of that doctrine depends upon its being made out that upon the true construction of the deed, it was a deed which gave the children such a beneficial right.

The case was allowed to stand over. The trustees refused to become plaintiffs. The statement of claim was amended by making the wife and her two eldest daughters co-plaintiffs, and the case came on again for hearing; and it was held that the wife was entitled to sue, for that the agreement was really one between the husband and wife, and the trustees were introduced merely to obviate the objection to the wife suing her husband, and that the case came within the authorities referred to, that where a covenant is entered into with one person for the benefit of another, then if the covenantee will not sue, the person beneficially interested may sue in equity. The case was accordingly heard on the merits and disposed of.

The difficulties raised in these cases do not arise here. In *Gandy v Gandy* it was not disputed that the trustees could sue, and again that the wife could sue, these being parties to the contract. Here we have the personal representatives of F. Davies, senior, who was a party to the contract, and the persons beneficially interested joined as co-plaintiffs suing the defendant. He it was who expressly bound himself to pay these annual sums, and his obligation was to his father, who is now represented by his executors. The defendant having got the full benefit of that contract, now inequitably declines to perform his part of it. Consequently it is not necessary to decide the question whether a fiduciary relation exists between the executors and the beneficiaries for the purpose of enabling the suit to be maintained by the latter. The executors of course admit that any moneys recovered by them from the defendant will be held by them for the benefit of the daughters and sons as provided by the deed.

There must be judgment for payment by the defendant to the executors of the sums due on foot of the arrears of the annuities, and for payment of the accruing gales to be applied by them in accordance with the terms of the 15th clause of the deed.

(The decision was upheld by the Court of Appeal.)

Holmes L.J.:

. . .

I decide this case on very simple—even elementary—grounds. The proposition affirmed in *Tweddle v Atkinson* is excellent law; but it has no application to the present case. In that case it was held that a contract by which a benefit was provided for a person not a party to it cannot be sued on by such person: but it contains no suggestion that the contract could not have been enforced by the person with whom it was made. In this case Davies, junior, covenanted for valuable consideration with Davies, senior, that in certain events he would pay certain annuities to the children of the latter. If such annuities had become payable in the life of the covenantee, and they were not paid, what legal obstacle would there be to his suing the covenantor? Indeed, I believe that it is admitted that such an action would lie, but that it would only result in nominal damages. A result more repugnant to justice, as well as to legal principle, I can hardly imagine. The defendant would thereby escape from paying what he had undertaken to pay by making an illusory payment never contemplated by either party. Well, if Davies, senior, would have been entitled to sue in his lifetime if the annuities were then payable, his executors would have the same right of action after his death. As I have already said, the question is elementary.

I desire to add that I am not to be understood as holding that in the circumstances of this case the children could not have maintained the action without the personal representatives. I see grounds resting on both authority and legal principle for thinking that *Tweddle v Atkinson* is distinguishable; but it is unnecessary to consider this.

1. 1 B & S 393.	4. 16 ChD 290.	7. 30 ChD 57.
2. 10 Ha. 163.	5. 25 ChD 89.	
3. 16 ChD 125.	6. 3 Mer 582.	

Kenney v Employers' Liability Assurance Corp. [1901] 1 IR 301

Holmes L.J.:

...

All the material facts are admitted. Charles Kenney mortgaged his lands of Rocksavage to the National Bank to secure the sum of £4,738 or such further or other sums as might thereafter become due. The interest on the mortgage debt having been allowed to fall into arrear and the mortgagee being entitled to appoint a receiver pursuant to the provisions of the Conveyancing and Law of Property Act, 1881, appointed Plunkett Kenney receiver. Although Plunkett Kenney was the son of the mortgagor, he was not nominated by the latter, who it must be assumed had nothing to do with the appointment. The mortgagee, as security for the faithful discharge by Plunkett Kenney of his duties as receiver, took from him and the defendant company a joint bond. . . . Plunkett Kenney subsequently made default in the sum of £667, but before any effective steps were taken to enforce payment from either of the obligors, the entire amount due under the mortgage was discharged partly out of subsequent rents and partly out of the proceeds of a sale of portion of the mortgaged premises.

Under these circumstances this action has been brought to recover the sum in default from the defendant company, it being admitted that, although both the mortgagor and mortgagee are joined as plaintiffs, the suit is for the sole benefit of the former. The foregoing statement will serve to show the novelty and difficulty of the case. The plaintiff with whom the defendant entered into the contract sustained no damage; the loss fell entirely on the other plaintiff, who was no party to it. . . .

There are cases in which one of two contracting parties constitutes himself a trustee for others, and the contract is entered into on this basis. In such circumstances the trustee is bound to act in the interest of the beneficiaries; and if he is slack or careless, may be compelled to do so. But such is not the relationship of mortgagee and mortgagor; and although the bank may be at liberty to use the bond given by the defendant company so as to benefit the mortgagor, it must, I think be assumed that in requiring its execution the mortgagee was looking to his own interest and convenience. The question, however, still remains, what is the measure of the obligation imposed by it? It appears that on 14 October 1896, Plunkett Kenney was a defaulter to the extent of £667. If this sum had been properly applied by him, £339 of it would have gone to the payment of head rents, tithe rent charge, and income tax that had become due up to that date, and the remainder would have been applicable to the payment of interest on the bank's mortgage, of which £443 was then in arrear. Now, I suppose it cannot be denied that if the bank had then put the bond in suit, it would have been entitled to judgment for the full sum of £667. But the whole of this when recovered would have inured for the benefit not of the mortgagee but of the mortgagor. The mortgaged estate was solvent; the bank has received thereout the amount due without being obliged to enforce payment of the £667; and the only result of recovering on the bond would have been to relieve the mortgagor's property to the extent of what would have been thus realised.

Let me now assume, by way of illustration, that the receiver had paid out of the rents collected by him all the outgoings of the property, and discharged in full the interest due to the bank, but had applied to his own use a considerable surplus that would have been payable under the condition of the bond to the mortgagor. Could this sum have been recovered by the mortgagee? There is no doubt that the contract embodied in the bond was that the receiver should so apply the money; and it seems to me that if the obligee would not be entitled to sue for the amount, it would follow that our law does not recognise a contract by which one of the contracting parties agrees with the other to pay a sum of money to or perform services for a third person. But there is nothing illegal or contrary to public policy in such a contract. Why, therefore, will not an action lie for its breach?

[Holmes L.J. then referred to the cases of *Lloyd's v Harper* and *Drimmie v Davies.*]

I am of opinion that the bond in the present case comes within the same principle, nor do I think that this would be doubted, were it not for the relation of mortgagor and mortgagee that exists between the two plaintiffs. . . . but it is said that a difficulty is created by s. 24 (2), of the Act of 1881, which provides that a receiver appointed by a mortgagee 'shall be deemed to be the agent of the mortgagor, and the mortgagor shall be solely responsible for the receiver's acts or defaults, unless the mortgage deed otherwise provides.' It is argued that as the mortgagor is himself primarily responsible for the defaults of the receiver, he cannot be indemnified at the expense of a surety. There is, I think, some confusion of ideas at the root of this argument. The defendant company was not surety for the mortgagor but for the receiver, and by the terms of the contract undertook that the receiver would do his duty to both mortgagee and mortgagor. No doubt as between the two last-named, the latter was to be responsible for the receiver's act and defaults; but the surety must be assumed to have been aware of this when he entered into the bond, and yet he accepted the obligation in the form in which it stands. I understand the defendants' case, if it can be shown that the condition of the bond was to save the bank from the consequences of any default by the receiver. The bank has not been damnified, and a condition in that form has not been broken. I cannot, however, conceive any mortgagee taking such a security for the faithful discharge of a receiver's duties, as the right to recover in such a case would depend not upon proof of default, but upon, whether by reason of the default, the mortgage debt was put in peril. The bank in this case has been too well advised to allow itself to be thus embarrassed. The terms of the contract made with it by the defendant company are free from all ambiguity, and I am of opinion that it is entitled to recover the full amount sued for.

. . . For these reasons I am of opinion that the appeal ought to be allowed.

Walker L.J. (dissenting):

. . .

I am of opinion that the Master of the Rolls was right, and that the mortgagor has no equity to obtain the relief he seeks. If the bond had not been executed, I do not think it could be contended successfully that the mortgagor had any right to compel the mortgagees to sue Plunkett Kenney for his defaults. The mortgagor was responsible for such as between him and the mortgagees, and the bank owed him no duty in respect of them, or of the debt created by reason of them, no more than I think he owed a duty to the other members of the class I have mentioned. Then take the case of the bond. It was obtained by the mortgagees at their sole option, and solely for their own security. They might have cancelled it any time. The statute says the mortgagee may remove the receiver and appoint another, and the mortgagees were at liberty to pursue all their remedies against the mortgagor, independently of it, as they in fact did.

[Having referred to the cases of *Lloyd's v Harper*, *Drimmie v Davies*, *Gandy v Gandy*, *Tomlinson v Gill* and *re Empress Engineering Co.*, Walker L.J. continued:]

Let us apply the tests furnished by the authorities to the case before the court— was it the object of intent or effect of the deed and bond, according to their true construction, to confer a beneficial right upon the mortgagor, or to make the mortgagees in any sense trustees for the mortgagor? . . . There is nothing from which it can be inferred that the benefit of the mortgagor was in any way in contemplation. The object of the mortgagee was solely to protect his own interest, and guard against the loss which, directly or indirectly, might fall upon him by putting a receiver in receipt of the rents, and this is natural, though the mortgagor and the mortgagor's estate were still between him and ultimate loss. The mortgagor indirectly gets a benefit from the due application of the rents, but it is not from his being a *cestui que trust*, or object of the bond or deed. If he was not a *cestui que trust*, the mortgagee cannot be a trustee for him, and therefore when the mortgagee was paid off, as he was before action, the mortgagor could recover nothing on that which was solely the security obtained by and held for the benefit of the mortgagee.

I am of opinion that neither the mortgagor, or, on the facts, the mortgagee who was paid off, could separately maintain this action, and if that be so, they could not maintain it together.

Cadbury Ireland Ltd *v* Kerry Co-operative Creameries Ltd and Dairy Disposal Co. Ltd [1982] ILRM 77

The second defendant owned a number of creameries which supplied milk to the plaintiff. To encourage the plaintiff to expand its operations the second defendant, with the endorsement of the Minister for Agriculture, agreed to adequately supply the plaintiff in the event of their expansion. The plaintiff proceeded with expansion. When the second defendant was negotiating the sale of certain of its creameries to the first defendant, it emphasised that adequate milk supplies to the plaintiff would have to be ensured. In a subsequent agreement between the first and second defendants for the transfer, a clause was inserted ('clause 19') containing an undertaking by the first defendant to continue supplying the plaintiff, subject to price and total supply stipulations. The plaintiff was not however a party to this agreement. Later, when milk supplies were threatened, the plaintiff attempted to rely on this undertaking.

Barrington J.:

. . .

. . . In my view clause 19 was inserted in the agreement by the second-named defendant for the benefit of the plaintiffs.

The plaintiffs accordingly maintain that, though not a party to the contract, they are entitled to sue upon clause 19 of it because the Dairy Disposal Co. Ltd is, in the circumstances of this case, a trustee of the benefit of that clause for the plaintiff company. They rely upon the principle laid down in *Lloyd's v Harper* (1880–1) 16 ChD 290 and in particular on the law as stated by Fry J., at 309: 'It appears to me from the cases which were cited in the course of the argument, especially *Tomlinson v Gill* Amb 330 and *Lamb v Vice* 6 M & W 467 that where a contract is made for the benefit and on behalf of a third person, there is an equity in that third person to sue on the contract, and the person who has entered into the contract may be treated as a trustee for the person for whose benefit it has been entered into.'

The principle that the parties to a contract can create a trust of contractual rights for the benefit of a third party and that that third party can himself enforce those rights, if his trustee does not enforce them for him, by suing the person placed under a duty to him by the contract and by joining his trustee as a co-defendant, is well established. It is discussed in *Anson on Contract* (1975 ed.), 408 and on which the plaintiffs rely. It is also discussed in *Cheshire and Fifoot on Contract* (1976 ed.), 440 and on which the defendants rely. The latter authors (at 442) quote Lord Wright as referring to the doctrine of a trust of contractual rights as 'a cumbrous fiction' and suggest that the courts are reluctant to extend it. A similar view is expressed in the *Halsbury* (4th ed.) vol. 9 para. 341 and, in *Chitty on Contracts* (24th ed.) vol. 1, 528 para. 1122, it is stated that the trust device has so far only been applied to promises to pay money or to transfer property. The passage continues: 'It is sometimes suggested that it might be applied to other kinds of promises, e.g. that an employer might hold the benefit of an exemption clause on trust for his employee. In view of the present judicial tendency to confine the trust device within narrow limits, it seems unlikely that such extensions will be made; though other techniques may be used for making the benefit of exemption clauses available to third parties.'

As previously stated, it seems clear to me, that in the present case the minister and the Dairy Disposal Co. Ltd intended to benefit Cadburys, not indeed because they wished to confer any favours on Cadburys, but because they wished, through the Cadbury factory at Rathmore, to advance their view of what the public interest required. One factor which makes the courts more ready to infer that the promisee in a contract is a trustee for the third party is that the promisee should have some contractual or fiduciary duty to the third party. In the present case there was certainly no fiduciary relationship between the Dairy Disposal Co. Ltd and the plaintiffs. It seems improbable that there was a contractual relationship between them. What there was was an undertaking given by the Dairy Disposal Co. Ltd to the plaintiffs with the knowledge and approval of the minister. The value of such an undertaking to the plaintiffs lay not so much in any legal sanction as in the fact that it committed the good faith of the public authority. This undoubtedly provided the motive for the Dairy Disposal Co. Ltd to attempt to protect the interest of the plaintiffs when they were selling creameries the produce of which was covered by the undertaking, but it does not necessarily follow that the Dairy Disposal Co. Ltd intended to, or did in fact, constitute itself a trustee of its rights under clause 19 for the benefit of the plaintiffs. The answer to this question depends, at least in part, on whether clause 19 in fact created legal rights which either the Dairy Disposal Co. Ltd or the plaintiffs can now enforce.

. . .

It appears to me that the imprecision of the language in clause 19 is explained by the fact that the clause was concerned with policy considerations and that the draughtsman assumed that clause 19 would be supplemented by a bilateral agreement between the plaintiffs and the first-named defendants in which the precise rights and duties of

both parties would be set out. Put another way one could say that clause 19 contemplated a further agreement between the plaintiffs and the first-named defendants to
give it business efficacy.

. . .

If the first-named defendants had any legal commitments to the plaintiffs under
the provisions of clause 19 it appears to me that this was, at most, a commitment to
enter into honest negotiations for a legal trading agreement to govern future relations
between the parties. In the past the plaintiffs had the benefit of an undertaking which
they had received from the Dairy Disposal Co. Ltd with the approval of the minister. The
chief value of that undertaking appears to me to have been that, despite the fact that the
Dairy Disposal Co. Ltd was in form a company incorporated under the Companies Acts,
the undertaking committed the good faith of the public authorities. When, therefore,
the Dairy Disposal Co. Ltd was selling its creameries and placing itself in a position
where it could no longer fulfil its undertaking, it would have been appropriate for the
plaintiffs to have entered into a properly binding legal agreement with the private
body which was acquiring the creameries in order to protect the plaintiff's interests in
the future.

They did not do so at the time and it appears to me that it is now too late for them
to do so pursuant to the provisions of clause 19. Seven years have elapsed and, in the
interval, conditions in the dairying industry have totally changed from those which
prevailed at the end of 1973 and early 1974.

. . .

Moreover I do not believe that the concept of a trust of contractual rights for the
benefit of a third party can be extended to cover a case as complex and unusual as the
present one.

Note

1. This case was referred to in **Inspector of Taxes' Association v The
Minister for Public Service, Ireland and the Attorney General [1986]
ILRM 296** where Murphy J. had to decide whether the plaintiff staff
association or its members could take advantage of a conciliation and
arbitration contract to which they were not parties. The *Cadbury* case was
cited as support for the right of the plaintiffs to maintain an action.

Murphy J.:

. . .

. . . It does not seem to me that that decision supports the plaintiffs' claim. In fact
Barrington J. accepted that the principle for which the plaintiffs contended in that case
was the well established proposition that parties to a contract can create a trust of
contractual rights for the benefit of a third party and indeed went on to hold that no
such trust had been created therein. Similarly in the present case I would find it very
difficult to infer that the various staff associations who were parties to the original C.
& A. agreement purported to contract by implication as trustees on behalf of other
associations which might be formed thereafter.

In my view the only basis on which the plaintiffs could rely upon the C. & A. scheme
and the contract which constitutes it is on the basis that the members of the plaintiff
association are officers or employees of the State whose terms of employment include
by implication a provision that each of them shall have the benefit of the contract and
scheme in accordance with its terms and provisions.

(The Supreme Court confirmed this decision on appeal see [1986] ILRM 296.)

2. The trust concept has been used in recent years to try to enable an employee to recover as against an insurance policy taken out by an employer when the employee has been injured in a work-related accident. These applications have generally been unsuccessful: see *Green v Russell* [1959] 2 QB 226, *Bradley v Eagle Star Insurance Co.* [1989] 1 All ER 961, and the decision of Morris J. in *McManus v Cable Management (Ireland) Ltd and Others* (HC) 8 July 1994, unrep.

SECTION THREE—AGENCY

'It is certainly true, that when a contract is made by an agent, ostensibly acting as principal himself, or as agent for an undisclosed principal, the principal may assume the place of his agent, disclose himself, and sue upon the contract. But this assumes that there were both a principal and an agent when the contract was made.' per Vice-Chancellor Chatterton in *Sheppard v Murphy* (1867) 1 IR Eq 490.

Scruttons Ltd v Midland Silicones Ltd [1962] AC 446

A drum of chemicals was consigned to the respondents from America by ship under a bill of lading signed on behalf of the shipowners. The bill included a clause limiting the liability of the carrier for damage to $500. The appellants, a stevedoring company, were employed by the shipowners to discharge the ship at London port and deliver goods to the consignees. The contract between the appellants and the shipowners stated that the appellants should have 'such protection as is afforded by the terms . . . of the bills of lading'. The respondents were not aware of this contract. When the chemicals were damaged as a result of the appellants' negligence, the respondents sued the stevedores who attempted to rely on the bill of lading. The court of first instance and the Court of Appeal held that the appellants were not protected by the bill of lading.

Lord Reid:

. . .

. . . Although I may regret it I find it impossible to deny the existence of the general rule that a stranger to a contract cannot in a question with either of the contracting parties take advantage of provisions of the contract even where it is clear from the contract that some provision in it was intended to benefit him. That rule appears to have been crystallised a century ago in *Tweddle v Atkinson*[1] and finally established in this House in *Dunlop Pneumatic Tyre Co. Ltd v Selfridge & Co. Ltd.*[2] There are it is true certain well established exceptions to that rule—though I am not sure that they are really exceptions and do not arise from other principles. But none of these in any way touches the present case.

The actual words used by Viscount Haldane L.C., in the *Dunlop* case were made the basis of an agreement that, although a stranger to a contract may not be able to sue

for any benefit under it, he can rely on the contract as a defence if one of the parties to
it sues him in breach of his contractual obligation—that he can use the contract as a
shield though not as a sword. I can find no justification for that. If the other contracting
party can prevent the breach of contract well and good, but if he cannot I do not see how
the stranger can. As was said in *Tweddle v Atkinson* the stranger cannot 'take advantage'
from the contract.

It may be that in a roundabout way the stranger could be protected. If A, wishing to
protect X, gives to X an enforceable indemnity, and contracts with B that B will not sue
X, informing B of the indemnity, and then B does sue X in breach of his contract with A,
it may be that A can recover from B as damages the sum which he has to pay X under
the indemnity, X having had to pay it to B. But there is nothing remotely resembling
that in the present case.

The appellants in this case seek to get round this rule in three different ways. In the
first place they say that the decision in *Elder, Dempster & Co. v Paterson Zochonis & Co.*[3]
establishes an exception to the rule sufficiently wide to cover the present case. I shall
later return to consider this case. Secondly, they say that through the agency of the
carrier they were brought into contractual relation with the shipper and that they can
now found on that against the consignees, the respondents. And thirdly, they say that
there should be inferred from the facts an implied contract, independent of the bill of
lading, between them and the respondents. It was not argued that they had not committed a tort in damaging the respondents' goods.

I can see a possibility of success of the agency argument if (first) the bill of lading
makes it clear that the stevedore is intended to be protected by the provisions in it
which limit liability, (secondly) the bill of lading makes it clear that the carrier, in
addition to contracting for these provisions on his own behalf, is also contracting as
agent for the stevedore that these provisions should apply to the stevedore, (thirdly)
the carrier has authority from the stevedore to do that, or perhaps later ratification by
the stevedore would suffice, and (fourthly) that any difficulties about consideration
moving from the stevedore were overcome. And then to affect the consignee it would
be necessary to show that the provisions of the Bills of Lading Act, 1855, apply.

But again there is nothing of that kind in the present case. I agree with your
Lordships that 'carrier' in the bill of lading does not include stevedore, and if that is so
I can find nothing in the bill of lading which states or even implies that the parties to
it intended the limitation of liability to extend to stevedores. Even if it could be said that
reasonable men in the shoes of these parties would have agreed that the stevedores
should have this benefit that would not be enough to make this an implied term of the
contract. And even if one could spell out of the bill of lading an intention to benefit
the stevedores there is certainly nothing to indicate that the carrier was contracting as
agent for the stevedores in addition to contracting on his own behalf. So it appears to
me that the agency argument must fail.

And the implied contract argument seems to me to be equally unsound. From the
stevedores' angle, they are employed by the carrier to deal with the goods in the ship.
They can assume that the carrier is acting properly in employing them and they need
not know to whom the goods belong. There was in their contract with the carrier a
provision that they should be protected, but that could not by itself bind the consignee.
They might assume that the carrier would obtain protection for them against the
consignee and feel aggrieved when they found that the carrier did not or could not do
that. But a provision in the contract between them and the carrier is irrelevant in a
question between them and the consignee. Then from the consignees' angle they would
know that stevedores would be employed to handle their goods but if they read the
bill of lading they would find nothing to show that the shippers had agreed to limit the

liability of the stevedores. There is nothing to show that they ever thought about this or that if they had they would have agreed or ought as reasonable men to have agreed to this benefit to the stevedores. I can find no basis in this for implying a contract between them and the stevedores. It cannot be said that such a contract was in any way necessary for business efficiency.

So this case depends on the proper interpretation of the *Elder, Dempster* case. What was there decided is clear enough. The ship was under time charter, the bill of lading made by the shippers and the charterers provided for exemption from liability in the event which happened and this exemption was held to inure to the benefit of the shipowners who were not parties to the bill of lading, but whose servant the master caused damage to the shippers' goods by his negligence. The decision is binding on us but I agree that the decision by itself will not avail the present appellants because the facts of this case are very different from those in the *Elder, Dempster* case. For the appellants to succeed it would be necessary to find from the speeches in this House a *ratio decidendi* which would cover this case and then to follow that *ratio decidendi*.

. . .

I would certainly not lightly disregard or depart from any *ratio decidendi* of this House. But there are at least three classes of case where I think we are entitled to question or limit it: first, where it is obscure, secondly, where the decision itself is out of line with other authorities or established principles, and thirdly, where it is much wider than was necessary for the decision so that it becomes a question of how far it is proper to distinguish the earlier decision. The first two of these grounds appear to me to apply to the present case.

It can hardly be denied that the *ratio decidendi* of the *Elder, Dempster* decision is very obscure. A number of eminent judges have tried to discover it, hardly any two have reached the same result, and none of the explanations hitherto given seems to me very convincing. If I had to try, the result might depend on whether or not I was striving to obtain a narrow ratio. So I turn to the decision itself. Two quite separate points were involved in the case. The first was whether the damage to the cargo was caused by bad stowage or by the ship being unseaworthy. This was very fully considered and the decision was bad stowage. On the conditions in the bill of lading this clearly freed the charterer of liability. The other question was whether those conditions were also available as a defence to the shipowner. From the report of the case it would seem that this was not very fully argued, and none of the three noble Lords who spoke devoted more than a page of print to it. They cannot have thought that any important question of law or any novel principle was involved. Viscount Finlay said that a decision against the shipowner would be absurd and the other noble Lords probably thought the same. They must all have thought that they were merely applying an established principle to the facts of the particular case.

But when I look for such a principle I cannot find it, and the existence and able arguments of counsel in this case have failed to discover it.

. . .

In such circumstances I do not think that it is my duty to pursue the unrewarding task of seeking to extract a *ratio decidendi* from what was said in this House in *Elder, Dempster*. Nor is it my duty to seek to rationalise the decision by determining in any other way just how far the scope of the decision should extend. I must treat the decision as an anomalous and unexplained exception to the general principle that a stranger cannot rely for his protection on provisions in a contract to which he is not a party. The decision of this House is authoritative in cases of which the circumstances are not reasonably distinguishable from those which gave rise to the decision. The circumstances in the present case are clearly distinguishable in several respects. Therefore I must decide this case on the established principles of the law of England apart from that decision, and on that basis I have no doubt that this appeal must be dismissed.

[1.] (1861), 1 B & S 393.   [2.] |1915| AC 847.   [3.] |1924| All ER Rep 135; |1924| AC 522.

(Viscount Simonds, Lord Keith and Lord Morris agreed. Lord Denning dissented.)

Note

It should be noted that the stevedores were not bailees of the drum.

New Zealand Shipping Co. Ltd *v* A.M. Satterthwaite & Co. Ltd (The Eurymedon) [1975] AC 154

Lord Wilberforce gave the leading judgment for the majority:

. . .

The question in the appeal is whether the stevedore can take the benefit of the time limitation provision. The starting point, in discussion of this question, is provided by the House of Lords decision in *Midland Silicones Ltd v Scruttons Ltd* |1962| AC 446. There is no need to question or even to qualify that case in so far as it affirms the general proposition that a contract between two parties cannot be sued on by a third person even though the contract is expressed to be for his benefit. Nor is it necessary to disagree with anything which was said to the same effect in the Australian case of *Wilson v Darling Island Stevedoring and Lighterage Co. Ltd* (1956) 95 CLR 43. Each of these cases was dealing with a simple case of a contract the benefit of which was sought to be taken by a third party to it, and the emphatic pronouncements in the speeches and judgments were directed to this situation. But *Midland Silicones* left open the case where one of the parties contracts as agent for the third person: in particular Lord Reid's speech spelt out, in four propositions, the prerequisites for the validity of such an agency contract. There is of course nothing unique to this case in the conception of agency contracts: well known and common instances exist in the field of hire purchase, of bankers' commercial credits and other transactions.

. . .

The question in this appeal is whether the contract satisfies these propositions.

Clause 1 of the bill of lading, whatever the defects in its drafting, is clear in its relevant terms. The carrier, on his own account, stipulates for certain exemptions and immunities: among these is that conferred by article III, rule 6, of the Hague Rules which discharges the carrier from all liability for loss or damage unless suit is brought within one year after delivery. In addition, to these stipulations on his own account, the carrier as agent for, *inter alios*, independent contractors stipulates for the same exemptions.

Much was made of the fact that the carrier also contracts as agent for numerous other persons; the relevance of this argument is not apparent. It cannot be disputed that among such independent contractors, for whom, as agent, the carrier contracted, is the appellant company which habitually acts as stevedore in New Zealand by arrangement with the carrier and which is, moreover, the parent company of the carrier. The carrier was, indisputably, authorised by the appellant to contract as its agent for the purposes of clause 1. All of this is quite straightforward and was accepted by all the judges in New Zealand. The only question was, and is, the fourth question presented by Lord Reid, namely that of consideration.

. . .

It [the present contract] is one of carriage from Liverpool to Wellington. The carrier assumes an obligation to transport the goods and to discharge at the port of arrival. The goods are to be carried and discharged, so the transaction is inherently contractual. It is contemplated that a part of this contract, *viz.* discharge, may be performed by independent contractors—*viz.* the appellant. By clause 1 of the bill of lading the shipper agrees to exempt from liability the carrier, his servants and independent contractors in respect of the performance of this contract of carriage. Thus, if the carriage, including the discharge, is wholly carried out by the carrier, he is exempt. If part is carried out by him, and part by his servants, he and they are exempt. If part is carried out by him and part by an independent contractor, he and the independent contractor are exempt. The exemption is designed to cover the whole carriage from loading to discharge, by whomsoever it is performed: the performance attracts the exemption or immunity in favour of whoever the performer turns out to be. There is possibly more than one way of analysing this business transaction into the necessary components, that which their Lordships would accept is to say that the bill of lading brought into existence a bargain initially unilateral but capable of becoming mutual, between the shipper and the appellant, made through the carrier as agent. This became a full contract when the appellant performed services by discharging the goods. The performance of these services for the benefit of the shipper was the consideration for the agreement by the shipper that the appellant should have the benefit of the exemptions and limitations contained in the bill of lading. The conception of a 'unilateral' contract of this kind was recognised in *Great Northern Rly Co. v Witham* (1873) LR 9 CP 16 and is well established. This way of regarding the matter is very close to if not identical to that accepted by Beattie J. in the Supreme Court: he analysed the transaction as one of an offer open to acceptance by action such as was found in *Carlill v Carbolic Smoke Ball Co.* [1893] 1 QB 256. But whether one describes the shipper's promise to exempt as an offer to be accepted by performance or as a promise in exchange for an act seems in the present context to be a matter of semantics. The words of Bowen L.J. in *Carlill v Carbolic Smoke Ball Co.* at p. 268: 'why should not an offer be made to all the world which is to ripen into a contract with anybody who comes forward and performs the condition?' seem to bridge both conceptions: he certainly seems to draw no distinction between an offer which matures into a contract when accepted and a promise which matures into a contract after performance, and, though in some special contexts (such as in connection with the right to withdraw) some further refinements may be needed, either analysis may be equally valid.

. . .

In their Lordship's opinion, consideration may quite well be provided by the appellant, as suggested, even though (or if) it was already under an obligation to discharge to the carrier. (There is no direct evidence of the existence or nature of this obligation, but their Lordships are prepared to assume it.) An agreement to do an act which the promisor is under an existing obligation to a third party to do, may quite well amount to valid consideration and does so in the present case: the promisee obtains the benefit of a direct obligation which he can enforce. This proposition is illustrated and supported by *Scotson v Pegg* (1861) 6 H & N 295 which their Lordships consider to be good law.

. . .

In the opinion of their Lordships, to give the appellant the benefit of the exemptions and limitations contained in the bill of lading is to give effect to the clear intentions of a commercial document, and can be given within existing principles. They see no reason to strain the law or the facts in order to defeat these intentions. It should not be overlooked that the effect of denying validity to the clause would be to encourage actions against servants, agents and independent contractors in order to get round exemptions (which are almost invariable and often compulsory) accepted by shippers against carriers, the existence, and presumed efficacy, of which is reflected in the rates of freight. They see no attraction in this consequence.

Their Lordships will humbly advise Her Majesty that the appeal be allowed.

(Viscount Dilhorne and Lord Simon dissented.)

Note

1. Was it relevant that the consignees had possession of the bill of lading in the *Eurymedon* case but not in the *Midland Silicones* case?
2. This decision was applied in *Port Jackson Stevedoring Pty Ltd v Salmond & Spraggon Pty (Australia) Ltd (The New York Star)* [1980] 3 All ER 257 but was distinguished in *Southern Water Authority v Carey* [1985] 2 All ER 1077. In the latter case a building subcontractor was held not to be entitled to benefit from an exemption clause in the main contract as he was selected only after the main contract had been signed. He was not thus entitled to ratify the contract.

See also *Norwich City Council v Harvey* [1989] 1 All ER 1180.

P. J. Davies & N. E. Palmer, 'The Eurymedon, Five Years On' 1979 JBL 334. (Footnotes abridged.)

The Eurymedon explained: bilateral unilateral or nudum pactum?

[In *The Eurymedon*] the stevedore had three contentions which are relevant here. The first was the simple agency argument, where what was spelled out was an immediate bilateral contract between shipper and stevedore concluded at the time of the contract between shipper and carrier. The other two contentions involved a unilateral contract argument, where at the time of the main contract the consignor makes an offer at large accepted by the stevedore only when he undertakes the work, and alternatively, a solution involving the creation of a *nudum pactum* with a condition that it should become binding when the work is commenced.[1]

There are at least three reasons why Lord Wilberforce's judgement must be closely examined to see just which contentions he accepted. First, on the simple unilateral analysis the acceptance is the undertaking of the work: this will generally be the unloading of the goods. If the goods are damaged before unloading has commenced the damage will have occurred before the contract is complete, and the stevedore will be unable to rely on the protective clauses. According to the bilateral contract explanation the contract is completed at the time the main contract is concluded. This is true also of the *nudum pactum* analysis.

Secondly, it might be argued that if the unilateral contract analysis is accepted there is no need for compliance with Lord Reid's propositions; he almost certainly had in mind the bilateral contract argument when he formulated them. When a 'unilateral offer' is conveyed from the shipper to the stevedore by the intermediary, the carrier, it might be argued that the carrier is not acting as an agent in the proper sense of the term: he is transmitting an offer rather than acting as negotiator or participant in the conclusion of the contract which results. It is arguable, then, that he need not describe himself as agent or have authority, though it will still be necessary that the offeror knows that the offer will be transmitted. No such argument however appears to have been put in any of the reported cases. This seems surprising (if the argument is sound), since Lord Wilberforce did express a preference for the unilateral contract analysis.

The third distinction concerns what is necessary to satisfy the fourth condition set down by Lord Reid. The discussion by Lord Wilberforce of the consideration problem indicates either that he had missed the distinctions between the contentions or (and this is more likely) that he was not fully committed to the unilateral contract analysis despite his expressed preference for it.

The Eurymedon undermined: the problem of consideration

The fourth condition presents great difficulty on the bilateral contract analysis. Lord Wilberforce was clearly concerned with the question of consideration. He 'solved' the difficulty arising from the apparent lack of consideration by finding it in 'the commercial character' of the relationship between all the parties involved; and he made it clear that technical points must give way to a 'practical approach'. But if his Lordship was accepting the unilateral contract analysis, what exactly is the problem? The minority did not point to any consideration problem in the unilateral contract analysis; the act of performance was at once acceptance and consideration. The problem with the unilateral contract explanation was to discover an offer. Viscount Dilhorne said that to discover an offer would 'not mean just straining the language of the clause but rewriting it.' This problem was at least one which it is possible to overcome by revised drafting, and it is surprising to find that little effort has been expended to this end. Lord Simon of Glaisdale said: ' . . . there seems no reason to question that . . . a bill of lading could, if appropriately drafted, contain an offer giving rise to a unilateral contract with a stevedore.' Thus even the minority saw a possibility of the successful exploitation of this argument. For Viscount Dilhorne and Lord Simon, there was a consideration problem, and they thought it insuperable; but it arose only on the bilateral contract analysis. As Turner P. had pointed out when The Eurymedon was before the New Zealand Court of Appeal, it is impossible to see what consideration moved from the stevedore at the time of the signing and delivery of the bill of lading.[2] The argument advanced at first instance and on appeal (that there was an implied obligation on the stevedore under the bill of lading to discharge the consigned goods, which obligation provided sufficient consideration) was rejected as not tenable on the facts. Before the Privy Council the stevedore argued that the consideration moving from the carrier (as agent of the stevedore) would suffice. Lord Simon thought this 'wrong in law';[3] and moreover the agency arrangement here existed only as regards the immunity arrangements, while the consideration was given in respect of the (allegedly separate) contract of carriage. The alternative contention (that the carrier's consideration was sufficient, the carrier and stevedore being joint promisees) Lord Simon felt to be correct in law[4] but untenable on the facts because the joint promise too extended only to cover the clause purporting to grant immunity.

It would seem then that the unilateral contract analysis marks the way forward because of the lack of consideration problems. Yet in the New York Star,[5] before the New South Wales Court of Appeal, this very point proved fatal to the stevedores. The plaintiffs, consignees of a cargo of razor blades, sued the defendant stevedores from whose custody the cargo was stolen. The latter sought to rely on exception clauses in the bill of lading. The first two of Lord Reid's conditions were clearly satisfied. The New South Wales Court of Appeal held the third condition satisfied by implying authorisation[6] and the point was not contested before the High Court. In the Court of Appeal, however, for the first time, the plaintiffs had contested the fourth prerequisite, submitting that there fell to be considered a rule which had not been considered in *The Eurymedon*—'the rule that where conduct is relied on as the acceptance of and consideration for an offer the acceptor must be shown to have acted on the offer.' They cited as authority for this requirement R v *Clarke*.[7] It was not enough that the stevedore know of the shippers' offer to exempt; there needed to be evidence of his 'reliance' on that offer. Quite what needs to be proved is uncertain. English law at least seems, as far as the authorities go, firmly set against a search for evidence of motivation by the offer;[8] but there are English cases which mention some requirement of 'acting on' or 'acting in reliance on' the offer.[9] *Some* mental element is clearly necessary. In the High Court of Australia four of the judges (Barwick C.J., Mason, Jacobs and Murphy JJ.) indicated that the reliance requirement, though a valid one was usually easily satisfied. Mason and Jacobs JJ. for instance said: 'Common sense and knowledge of human affairs indicate the evident probability of the appellant acting in reliance on the shipper's promise or offer when he discharges the goods so long as he has knowledge of the existence of that promise or offer.' Thus it seems that this requirement will usually be assumed to be satisfied.[10] There does, of course, remain a problem. What if evidence suggesting that the work is done without reliance on the offer is brought forward? It is submitted that this requirement ought rarely to be fatal (as the Court of Appeal had held it to be) in this sort of case. Courts should show the sort of attitude that was shown in cases like *The Satanita*[11] (where a contract was spelled out in the absence of compliance with the details of the rule relating to the formation of contracts) provided that the notions of offer, acceptance and consideration are not too greatly attenuated. It is submitted that while the bilateral contract analysis may involve too great a departure from the traditional requirements the unilateral contract analysis involves only a pragmatic approach which can be accommodated within the common law framework.

The unilateral contract analysis is not then without difficulties. As well as this consideration point there is also the point that it often requires a rather strained construction to spell out from a bill of lading a unilateral offer. Indeed, it was this fact which drove Barwick C.J. in the *New York Star* to reject the simple unilateral contract analysis. He said: ' . . . I do not think the bill can be interpreted as containing an offer at large by the consignor.' Rather he felt there was an offer by the consignor to grant immunity to the stevedore on his doing the work. The stevedore accepted this offer when the bill of lading was agreed to. There then existed an 'arrangement' which became an enforceable contract only when the stevedore actually did the work and thereby provided the consideration. This is something like the *nudum pactum* argument put in *The Eurymedon* itself. Barwick C.J. felt that this was in fact the argument that had been accepted in *The Eurymedon*. In his opinion it was because their Lordships accepted this rationalisation that they failed to take the 'reliance' point and found the consideration requirement satisfied: ' . . . there is a fundamental difference between providing consideration to support a consensual arrangement otherwise made and the acceptance by performance of an act of an offer not otherwise accepted.' But what *is* the difference? Surely the 'consideration' must be made in reliance on the arrangement: might this not sometimes be equally problematical? Moreover, how exactly is the juridical nature of the 'arrangement' to be analysed? Barwick C.J. agreed that it is unenforceable; can it, also, like an offer, be revoked? If so, for how long? What if the work is begun but never completed?[12] Moreover, like the bilateral contract analysis, this rationalisation of *The Eurymedon* gives rise to all the problems consequent upon holding that no contract is created until the work is done. It is clear that Barwick C.J.'s analysis of *The Eurymedon* decision is not without problems: it is also submitted that it is not consonant with what was actually decided by the majority in that case.

The solution to the whole question would seem to lie in the adoption of the simple unilateral contract analysis. It is true it might often be difficult to spell out an offer from the bill of lading and that there could be problems in finding 'reliance'. One would however expect it to be pursued in most cases in which it might be of assistance to a party.

1. This version of the argument was introduced to defeat the view that the unilateral contract theory could not be right because the bill of lading clearly contemplated an immediate contract.
2. |1973| 1 NZLR at p. 178.
3. He felt that in so far as *Fleming v Bank of New Zealand* |1900| AC 577, could be read as supporting this contention it was inconsistent with *Dunlop v Selfridge* |1915| AC 847.
4. This proposition derived from dicta in *McEvoy v Belfast Banking Co. Ltd* |1935| AC 24 and *Coulls v Bagot's Executor and Trustee Co. Ltd* |1967| ALR 471. See Coote |1978| CLJ 301 for a critique.
5. |1977| 1 Lloyd's Rep. 445.
6. The trial judge had held there to have been ratification when the point had been argued before him. It is submitted that the Court of Appeal were right to imply authorisation if that was possible. Glass J. held that such implication could be made if reasonable: after *Liverpool CC v Irwin*, |1977| AC 239. The test must surely be necessity for business efficacy.
7. (1927) 40 CLR 227.
8. See especially *William v Carwardine* (1835) 5 C & P 566.
9. e.g. *Carlill v Carbolic Smoke Ball Co.* |1893| 1 QB 256, at pp 264, 268–9; *Taylor v Allon* |1966| 1 QB 304.
10. There have been dicta suggesting that knowledge plus action will not raise a presumption that the requirement is satisfied: see *Dalgety Australia Ltd v Harris* |1977| NSWLR 34.
11. *Clarke v Dunraven* |1897| AC 59. In *Manchester City Council v Gibson* |1979| 1 All ER 972, the House of Lords consented to this attitude in certain 'exceptional' circumstances.
12. In *Daulia Ltd v Four Millbank Nominees Ltd* |1987| 2 All ER 557 (CA), it was stated that in a unilateral contract the offeror is not entitled to revoke the offer once performance is *commenced*. Will such reasoning apply here?

Fox *v* Higgins (1912) 46 ILTR 22

The plaintiff was appointed as a national school teacher by the current school manager. After a period of absence due to ill health, the plaintiff attempted to recommence work. When the new manager refused to allow him do so, the plaintiff sued for damages for breach of an implied contract.

This contract was implied, *inter alia*, by the defendant having undertaken to observe the rules of the National Board of Education.

Gibson J.:

. . .

. . . I think the question whether the manager has entered into an implied contract with the teacher is one which is full of difficulty. There is no authority on these rules or on analogous legislation, and the matter is one on which different judges might come to different conclusions. On this somewhat confused legislation the fair inference is that the national board, the manager, and the teacher are put together in a kind of triangular pact, and if the manager accepts the terms of the national board for the school, and undertakes for the teacher that he shall have the benefit of the national board rules, and if the teacher has signed a contact which would bind him, then the manager is bound, in my opinion, in the same way and to the same extent as if he had signed the contract. If he is bound that way, what is the plaintiff's measure of damages? He cannot be in a better position than if the defendant had signed the contract, and that would entitle him only to damages measured at the amount of his salary for three months. I shall, therefore, give him that amount, and nothing over and above it.

Note

1. Tripartite contracts such as these are, however, exceptional as may be seen in the case of *Michael Halpin v Samuel Rothwell and United Dominions Trust (Ireland) Ltd* [1984] ILRM 613. There, the plaintiff purchased a lorry from the first defendant, who held the lorry under a hire-purchase contract with the second defendant. The plaintiff later sued both defendants for alleged breach of warranties as to the age of the lorry and as to the existence of certain liabilities and charges in respect of the lorry. The court dismissed the action against the second defendant. O'Hanlon J. in the High Court noted that at the time of the sale only the first defendant had title to the lorry, as he had paid all moneys due to the second defendant from funds provided by the plaintiff. Accordingly no privity existed between the plaintiff and the second defendant.
2. In *Owners of cargo lately laden on board* K.H. *Enterprise v Owners of Pioneer Container* [1994] 2 All ER 250 the Privy Council held that a person who voluntarily took another person's goods into his custody held them as bailee of the owner and that he could only invoke terms of a sub-bailment under which he received the goods from an intermediate bailee as qualifying or otherwise affecting his responsibility to the owner if the owner consented.

R. Flannigan, 'Privity—The End of an Era' (1987) 103 LQR 565
(Footnotes abridged.)

Privity Pro and Con

Arguments offered to justify the doctrine of privity only rarely get beyond the level of axiomatic assertion. Indeed, the infamous Professor Langdell thought the mere recitation of the privity phrase was sufficient. In his view, 'this latter proposition [i.e. privity] is so plain upon its face that it is difficult to make it plainer by argument.' Argument, as it turns out, is not something to which the doctrine stands up well.

Another American commentator, writing at a time when the US was in the middle of a process of ridding itself of the privity bar, argued for the doctrine in this way:

A perfect, well rounded contract requires not only a promise and a consideration, but a participation by each party in both of these elements. Possibly a privity as to only one might not always be fatal, though even this is doubtful; but a want of privity as to both the promise and the consideration certainly seems to be an insuperable obstacle to an action, upon the strict principles of the common law. If no other reason existed, the fact that the person who furnished the consideration, and to whom the promise was made, could always maintain an action upon it, seems to be a sufficient reason why another person could not, even though interested in the performance. To allow two actions by two disconnected persons, having opposite interests, upon the same promise, would indeed be anomalous.

That a plaintiff cannot maintain an action when the whole consideration moves from a third person to the defendant, and the defendant's promise is made wholly to such third person, has been the law of England for over two centuries.[1]

Once beyond the question-begging appeal to 'the strict principles of the common law', we find in these lines two arguments for privity. The first argument, presumably, is that otherwise the promisor would be subject to double performance liability.[2] This, of course, is preposterous. There is only one promise and once it is enforced by the promisee *or* the third party the promisor has fulfilled the promise and is subject to no further liability. The second argument offered by this American writer (in 1895) was that the doctrine had been the law of England for the previous two centuries. We have already examined how accurate that historical argument is.

A modern summary of the arguments advanced to justify the privity rule is given by Professor Treitel. As is apparent, he is reluctant to confirm or endorse any one of these arguments:

> One possible reason for it [i.e. the doctrine] is that a contract is a personal affair affecting only the parties to it; but this is rather a restatement of the doctrine than a reason for its existence. Another possible reason is that it would be unjust to allow a person to sue on a contract on which he could not be sued; but the law enforces unilateral contracts, to which the same argument applies. A third possible reason is that, if third parties could enforce contracts made for their benefit, the rights of contracting parties to rescind or vary such contracts would be unduly hampered; this reasoning has certainly been influential in limiting the development of one of the exceptions to the doctrine. Yet a fourth possible reason is that the third party is often a mere donee. A system of law which does not give a gratuitous promisee a right to enforce the promise is not likely to give this right to a gratuitous beneficiary who is not even a promisee.[3]

Professor Treitel himself dismisses the first argument and the second has been addressed in our earlier discussion of *Tweddle v Atkinson*.[4] The third reason or argument is one occasionally brought forward as a supposed disadvantage in the use of the trust device to circumvent the doctrine of privity.[5] But the reason is quite irrelevant as a concern with respect to third party actions if the original parties can always rescind or vary their contract or even if they can only do so prior to a certain event such as third party acceptance or reliance. It is worth noting, in any event, that no case involving a third party complaint that the original parties rescinded or varied the contract ever came before a court when third party actions were maintainable. Usually it is because of the death or disappearance of the original promisee, or because the promisee (while still intending the benefit) does not wish to incur the litigation or other costs of enforcing the contract, that the third party is or would be forced to bring an action to compel the promisor merely to do what he or she had promised to do and was paid to do. The substance of this argument, in the end, is illusory. The fourth reason or argument is no more significant. It is in fact quite misleading to point out that the law does not give a 'gratuitous promisee' a right to enforce a promise. Consider, rather that what the law *does do* is enforce promises which are paid for. As Professor Furmston points out: 'It is one thing to say that a gratuitous promise will not be enforced; it is quite another to say that a promise seriously made and bargained for may be repudiated because the person who bought the promise is not the person who seeks to enforce it.' In the third party beneficiary situation, the promise was paid for and there is both a promisee and a third party who expect and have an interest in its performance. This is quite different from the 'gratuitous promisee' situation.

A sustainable legal argument for the doctrine of privity has yet to surface. Perhaps because of that fact a variety of sociological explanations for the creation, continuation or utility of the doctrine have been advanced. Professor Atiyah's guess is economic:

> There is a sense in which the new doctrine of privity was an important development in the law at a time of increasing complexity in multilateral commercial relationships. The appearance of middlemen in all sorts of commercial situations served to separate the parties at either end of the transaction, and it was generally accepted that no privity existed between them. Economically, this may have served a useful purpose, in that it encouraged the development of a more market-based concept of enterprise liability. But on some occasions the results were not only economically dubious but socially disastrous.[6]

Another writer describes the theory that it was actually the *Vandepitte* case[7] which established the privity rule and that it did so in order to close what were wide-open floodgates:

> Perhaps *Vandepitte v Preferred Accident Insurance Corp. of New York*, |1933| AC 70 (PC (Can.)); aff'g., |1932| SCR 22; rev'g., |1930| 4 DLR 654 (BCCA), aff'g., |1930| 2 DLR 562 (BCSC), established the rule, not *Dunlop Tyre*. *Vandepitte* cited *Dunlop Tyre* simply to tie into precedent, but *Dunlop Tyre* came to be perceived as the authority itself. Thus the views about the law effected in *Vandepitte* became seen as current when *Dunlop Tyre* was decided.
>
> A speculative explanation for this theory goes like this. Sometimes as the law gives, the law ensures that not too much is taken. The seminal case is *Donoghue v Stevenson*, |1932| AC 562 (HL (Sc)). In those days, eliminating privity as a requisite, particularly according to Lord Atkin's formula, would have been seen as leading to a horrifying flood of litigation. *Vandepitte* ensured that *Donoghue v Stevenson's* uncertain impact was limited to tort. The Privy Council cited precedent for this position, as any competent court would; its precedent was *Dunlop Tyre*.[8]

Yet another explanation sometimes advanced is that judges have consciously retained the privity doctrine as a device to combat the scope and operation of third party exculpation clauses, for example, clauses in retail sales contracts that seek to exclude the liability of third party manufacturers. But if this were true, we would be paying a very high third party price for what amounts to modest consumer protection. Moreover, for other clauses of the same variety there is a different view of the utility of the privity doctrine.[9] Thus, it is complained that it is wrong for a third party exculpation clause which attempts to exclude the liability of the servants, agents and independent contractors of one of the contracting parties to be rendered ineffective by the doctrine. Such a result is said to be inefficient and commercially unexpected.[10]

These sociological explanations are, for the most part, pure conjecture. As such, they provide no real basis for excusing the continuation of the doctrine's application. Moreover, and more significantly, nothing in any of them provides a compelling justification for the doctrine. In the end, there just doesn't seem to be a satisfactory historical, legal or other argument to support the doctrine. Perhaps the most that can be argued is that to change the rule would upset the *status quo*. But this is hardly an acceptable basis for continuing to allow the pernicious consequences of the application of the doctrine. If we are concerned with retaining the *status quo* in order to protect the planning interest, it is well to point out that those who plan on the basis of the rule are those who contract with the knowledge that they will not have to perform the contract, a very odd position for the common law to support.

In addition to historical criticism the case *against* the doctrine of privity has been made in a variety of ways. Firstly, it is commonly argued that there are a number of other legal concepts that are inconsistent with or have the effect of displacing or subverting the doctrine. Thus, it is noted that finding a trust relationship is a simple and, for a while, an often-used procedure for overcoming a privity bar. It is also pointed out that agency principles can be used to create a direct relationship between the third party and the promisor so as to thereby avoid the doctrine. These are the major concepts proffered but others enlisted for this argument include assignment, collateral contract, attornment and tortious liability.

A second line of attack involves listing the various statutory exceptions to the application of the rule. The point of doing so as to show just how unfair or inconvenient the doctrine has appeared to the legislature. It is a useful exercise, in this respect, because many would not otherwise appreciate the iniquitous consequences of the common law rule. Indeed, but for the statutory exceptions, the doctrine of privity would undoubtedly have been abolished long ago upon it having become widely appreciated that, for example, third parties had no right to the proceeds of life insurance policies taken out for their benefit.

Another argument involves pointing out that here is clearly no objection to the third party actually getting the benefit promised since the original promisee is allowed to obtain specific performance of the promise. The third party will get the benefit notwithstanding that he or she gave no consideration.

Added to this are the 'joint promisee' cases where persons were allowed to enforce contracts even though they gave no consideration. Creditor compensation agreements and the payment of the debts of third parties are other instances where the third party, without having provided any consideration, is still able to insist on the benefit of the contract. It is sometimes said that these latter cases were decided on the basis that it would otherwise be a fraud on the promisee but, of course, there is not 'fraud' here that would be any different than the 'fraud' on the promisee in the ordinary third party beneficiary situation. So, if 'privity' is really only another name for consideration, the foregoing cases appear to show that it is only necessary that consideration be provided by somebody. It is not necessary that the beneficiary of the promise should have given further consideration to be able to enforce the promise directly or indirectly. There are yet other cases that are equally inconsistent with a supposed fundamental and inviolable rule that third parties cannot take advantage of contracts made for their benefit. The mere existence of all of these cases is highly problematic for the doctrine of privity.

It has also been noted that the doctrine is not found in many jurisdictions. The English rule was actually in place in the US well into the last century but was then widely rejected. This point is lost on those who remain confident that English common law is singularly fastidious and not prone, as might be the case in other jurisdictions, to allowing concessions from theoretical rigour. But raising this fact does lead one to the conclusion that our legal system is unlikely to come crashing down around our ears if we were to allow third parties to pursue performance of the promise made for their benefit.

There are other arguments, but what is perhaps the most compelling reason for jettisoning the doctrine of privity is the continuous parade of judges, law reformers and commentators in this century who are of the opinion that the doctrine generates hardship and injustice and ought to be either abolished or at least reconsidered. It is undoubtedly because of this unrelenting effort on the part of these authorities that the issue continues to remain, essentially, an open one.

1. Langdell, C. C., A *Summary of the Law of Contracts* (2nd ed.), Boston: Little, Brown and Co., 1880, s. 62

2. Bennett, E. H, *Considerations Moving from Third Persons* (1895) 9 Harv L Rev 31, at 31–32.

3. The authorities cited were *Bourne v Mason* (1669) 1 Vent. 6, 86 ERS, *Crow v Rogers* (1724) 1 Str. 591, 93 ER 719 and *Price v Easton* (1883) 4 B. & Ad. 433, 110 ER 518.

4. Treitel, G. H., *The Law of Contract* (6th ed.) London: Stevens & Sons, 1983, 458.

5. (1861) 1 B. & S. 393.

6. Furmston M. P., 'Return to *Dunlop v Selfridge*' (1960) 23 MLR 373.

7. Atiyah, P. S., *The Rise and Fall of Freedom of Contract*, Oxford: Clarendon Press, 1979, 413–44.

8. [1933] AC 70.

9. Arymowicz, C. M. (1982) 60 Can Bar Rev 467. The theory is attributed to Professor Gilmore.

10. E.g. *New Zealand Shipping Co. Ltd v A. M. Satterthwaite & Co. Ltd* [1975] AC 154 at 469 (per Lord Wilberforce).

Chapter Sixteen

Illegality

INTRODUCTION

We have already seen instances where the courts will deny a contract the right to enforcement on a number of grounds. In Chapter 3 the doctrine of consideration, through the notion that consideration, 'must be something of value in the eyes of the law' (i.e. the judge) was shown to have denied enforceability to some exchanges which were not devoid of substance, while allowing enforceability to others when the content was less easy to identify: compare O'*Donnell v O'Sullivan* (p. 160 above), with *Williams v Roffey Bros & Nicholls (Contractors) Ltd* (p. 145 above). In both cases the judges alluded to principles of public policy as crucial elements in shaping consideration. Similarly, in Chapter 4, the policy issues presented by contracts as between husband and wife proved dispositive for Atkin L.J. in *Balfour v Balfour* (see p. 207 above). The entire development of pleas of economic duress (Chapter 13) points up how universal issues such as 'improper' pressure or unfair bargaining practices can be addressed by the judiciary, often covertly.

In this chapter we consider a substantial body of case-law in which the courts have denied the enforceability of certain contracts on overt grounds of public policy. The policy values that the courts strive to defend are both various and shifting. Certainly, in relation to so-called common law illegality, many of the social institutions and policy considerations of the eighteenth and nineteenth centuries that shaped the law are increasingly under review. While contracts should not encourage the commission of crimes, if the thing done is no longer criminal (e.g. suicide under the Criminal Law (Suicide) Act 1993) should the courts strike down related contracts or review the law in the light of legislative developments? The movement towards greater competition in the provision of legal and other professional services (e.g. the Solicitors (Amendment) Bill 1994) and the fact that many key litigations have been conducted on a 'no foal, no fee' basis make many of the cases on maintenance and champerty look curious indeed. In the area of human relationships, the desire to uphold the institution of marriage is laudable, but in other legal jurisdictions there has been substantial acceptance of property-related agreements between cohabitees and resort to pre-cohabitation contracts is an increasingly common phenomenon. The *a priori* application of precedents from a different era or another social or moral culture is undesirable, and some judges are sensitive to these issues.

Where the source of the illegality is statutory—often a technical, regulatory or fiscal rule that lacks any moral imperative other than the fact that it is parliamentary in origin—the judges are more sensitive to the extreme result that follows from a declaration that any related contract is illegal. Public policy may be better served by enforcement of such a contract, rather than by denying the agreement legal force, and the judges are edging their way towards a more rational, if *ad hoc*, set of solutions, based upon a more generous use of the *in pari delicto* exceptions, the severance of clauses, and a balancing of equities. While this is more evident in statutory illegality cases, decisions like *Saunders v Edwards* (see p. 754 below), show that certain perceptible shifts in approach are possible across the board, thus causing us to recall Borrough J.'s dictum that public policy is 'a very unruly horse, and when once you get astride it you never know where it will carry you. It may lead you from the sound law', *Richardson v Mellish* (1824) 2 Bing. 229 at 252. However, other judges with a more pronounced taste for judicial activism have stressed the utility of public policy considerations e.g. Denning M.R. in *Enderby Town F.C. Ltd v The F.A. Ltd* [1971] Ch. 591 at 606.

SECTION ONE—ILLEGAL CONTRACTS AT COMMON LAW

A. CONTRACTS TO COMMIT A CRIME OR A TORT

Una Gray *v* Hibernian Insurance Co. Ltd (HC) 27 May 1993, unrep.

Barron J.:

The Bolton Horse public house was destroyed by fire on 30 November 1982. The premises were owned by the plaintiff's husband ('the deceased') and were insured with the defendant company. Following the fire the deceased made a claim against the defendant under his policy. At the same time he commenced proceedings to recover damages for malicious injury. These proceedings came on for hearing on 25 June 1984. On that date the deceased was arrested and charged with being implicated in the fire. The malicious injury proceedings were accordingly adjourned.

The deceased was charged with arson. His trial took place on 19 June 1985. The nature of the evidence against him was that of two persons ('the accomplices') who maintained that they had been instructed by the deceased to set fire to the premises. The deceased himself gave evidence on his own behalf. In the event the jury acquitted him of the charge.

On 8 July 1985 the deceased called upon the defendant to admit liability under the policy. The defendant refused to admit liability until such time as the malicious injury application was concluded. It claimed to be so entitled pursuant to a term of the policy.

On 25 February 1986 the deceased commenced proceedings to enforce the policy. These proceedings were referred to arbitration by an order of this court on 13 June 1986. The arbitration was held on 24 July 1987 and the arbitrator gave his award on 9 September 1987. The arbitrator held against the defendant, and found that the deceased was not obliged to proceed with the malicious injury application in the absence of the determination by the defendant as to whether or not to accept liability under the policy.

On 11 November 1987 the defendant accepted liability under the policy and on 15 March 1988 made a payment of £100,000 on account. The parties could not agree upon the amount to be paid on foot of the policy, nor could they agree upon the appointment of an arbitrator. Accordingly further proceedings were commenced on 28 March 1988 to obtain an order for the appointment of an arbitrator. This arbitrator was appointed by the court on 20 June 1988 and proceedings took place before him, including a preliminary hearing which took place on 12 June 1989.

Meanwhile, the plaintiff's husband had died on 17 September 1988. Prior to his death some correspondence had taken place between the solicitors for the parties as to evidence to be given in relation to *quantum* at the application. Following the deceased's death the solicitors for the defendant wrote on 27 September 1988 indicating that they were being prejudiced by the lengthy delay in bringing forward the malicious injury application for hearing. By a further letter dated 27 February 1989 they indicated that their client was no longer prepared to continue with the arbitration as to *quantum* and regarded themselves as no longer bound under the terms of the arbitration agreement.

On 7 July 1989 they commenced proceedings to stay the arbitration until the plaintiff had disposed of the malicious injury application. These proceedings were compromised on 12 February 1991 in the following terms:

> This action is hereby settled and all further proceedings herein stayed upon the terms following:
>
> (1) The defendant will pursue a malicious injury application against Dublin Corporation in accordance with the request already made herein pursuant to condition 6 of the policy of insurance and with the benefit of the indemnity as to costs already given, with all reasonable expedition up to the conclusion of the same in the Circuit Court.
>
> (2) Upon the delivery of judgment by the Circuit Court on the said application, the defendant shall be at liberty to proceed with the arbitration of her claim under the said policy.
>
> (3) The plaintiff undertakes unconditionally that it will not withdraw its agreement to indemnify the defendant in respect of her claim under the said policy.
>
> (4) Each party will bear his own costs of this action.

The malicious injury application came on for hearing on 7 May 1991. At that hearing evidence was given by the accomplices on behalf of Dublin Corporation. The Circuit Court Judge found that the accomplices were probably telling the truth and dismissed the application. On the following day the defendant repudiated liability under the policy and on the day following such repudiation the present proceedings were commenced.

The defendant submits that the plaintiff is disentitled to succeed because the loss upon which she relies was caused by the deliberate act of her husband. Two bases are put forward for this submission. First, as a matter of public policy that a man may not recover for loss sustained by his own deliberate act. Secondly, that it is a rule of insurance law that an insured cannot recover when he has deliberately caused the event upon which policy specifies that indemnity should be payable. The defendant relies upon the decision of the Circuit Court Judge in dismissing the malicious injury application. The plaintiff contends that that decision does not create any estoppel as between the plaintiff and the defendant in these proceedings, and that the onus of establishing the wrongdoing on the part of the deceased lies upon the defendant.

The two propositions for which the defendant contends are fully dealt with by the House of Lords in England in *Beresford v Royal Insurance Co. Ltd* [1938] 2 All ER 602. In that case there was a policy of life assurance. It provided that if the life assured should die by his own hand whether sane or insane within one year from the commencement of the insurance the policy should be void as against any person claiming the amount thereby assured or any part thereof. In June 1934 he became insolvent. He had no means of repaying his creditors save with the insurance moneys. Just before the policy expired he shot himself. It was held in those circumstances that it would be contrary to public policy to allow the personal representative of the assured to recover under the policy. In the judgment of Lord Atkin he considered that there were two questions to be answered: '(1) What was the contract made by the parties? (2) How was that contract affected by public policy?' In dealing with the first of those questions he said at 604:

> On ordinary principles of insurance law, an assured cannot by his own deliberate act cause the event upon which the insurance money is payable. The insurers have not agreed to pay on that happening. The fire assured cannot recover if he intentionally burns down his house, nor the marine assured if he scuttles his ship, nor the life assured if he deliberately ends his own life. This is not the result of public policy, but of the correct construction of the contract.

Then at 605 he said:

> . . . I entertain no doubt that, on the true construction of this contract, the insurance company have agreed with the assured to pay to his executors or assignees on his death the sum assured, if he dies by his own hand whether sane or insane, after the expiration of one year from the commencement of the assurance. . . . the meaning is clear, and one may assume from what one knows of tariff conditions that it is a usual clause. There is no doubt, therefore, that, on the proper construction of this contract, the insurance company promised (its insured) that, if he, in full possession of his senses, intentionally killed himself, they would pay his executors or assignees the sum assured.

Dealing with the second question, he said at 607:

> I think that the principle is that a man is not to be allowed to have recourse to a court of justice to claim a benefit from his crime, whether under a contract or under a gift. No doubt the rule pays regard to the fact that to hold otherwise would in some cases offer an inducement to crime, or remove a restraint to crime, and that its effect is to act as a deterrent to crime, but, apart from these considerations, the absolute rule is that the courts will not recognise the benefit accruing to a criminal on his crime.

In the event, the claim failed.

The reason for the first rule is that an insurer must be presumed as a matter of construction of the contract when it is silent as to suicide not to have intended to be on cover in such circumstances. Where, on the proper construction of the contract, he did so intend, then he cannot rely upon the criminal act as a pure matter of contract to repudiate liability. In my view, that is how the acceptance of liability by the defendant should be viewed. It agreed knowing the full allegations being made against the deceased that it would honour the policy. . . .

. . .

The issue of public policy was considered in R v National Insurance Commissioner Ex-parte Connor 1981 1 All ER 769. An application by a widow for a widow's allowances pursuant to the Social Security Acts was refused upon the basis that she had become a widow through her own intentional criminal act. She had been convicted of manslaughter of her husband and the court accepted that the verdict of the jury must have been based upon a belief that she had deliberately caused the act which caused his death. In the judgment of Lord Lane C.J. at p. 773 he quotes a passage from the charge by the trial judge to the jury in which the trial judge put the evidence of the wife to the jury. In that passage he ended by saying: 'The only issue is whether what happened was done deliberately in order to hurt, or whether it happened accidently, and from the start to the finish, from the very first moment she opened her mouth to the police, she has maintained it was an accident.' In that case the court decided that as a matter of public policy that the widow was not entitled to the allowance she claimed.

The two submissions made on behalf of the defendant assumed an onus of proof upon the balance of probabilities. In my view, this is not so. The defence of illegality in relation to insurance law is a question of contract. Here, if the defendant had not admitted liability, it would have had to prove the deceased's involvement in the malicious damage as a matter of probability. Once that defence fails, the defendant is asking the court to deny to the plaintiff upon grounds of public policy the benefit of the cause of action which she has established. To succeed on this defence it must therefore establish that the deceased committed a crime. The issue arises in civil proceedings, but the defence is permitted only because to refuse it would be to allow an unconscionable result. In my view, that requires a heavier standard of proof than the balance of probabilities.

There are only two pieces of evidence which have been adduced upon this issue:

(1) the acquittal of the deceased upon the charge of arson; and
(2) the finding by the Circuit Court that the evidence of the accomplices was probably correct.

The admissibility of the latter finding has been challenged on the ground that it does not found an estoppel against the plaintiff. I do not accept that submission. The issue being raised is not strictly an issue *in personam*. It is in reality an issue *in rem*.

There is a considerable difference in interpretation between a verdict of guilty and a verdict of not guilty. The meaning of the former is clear. The jury is satisfied beyond reasonable doubt that the accused has committed the crime with which he is charged. In the present case, no such certainty can be inferred from the verdict that the deceased was not guilty. The jury may have had a reasonable doubt, they may have believed the deceased totally, or they might have taken a view somewhere between the two. It is not appropriate in my view, as the defendant submits, to ignore this verdict upon the basis that it is not of any value where the onus of proof is not beyond reasonable doubt, but on the balance of probabilities. That submission is based as I have already indicated upon a false premise as to the onus of proof upon the present issue.

The deceased was acquitted by a jury in a criminal trial. In the course of that trial he gave evidence on his own behalf and evidence was given against him by the accomplices. Before the Circuit Court the accomplices gave the same evidence. At this date the deceased was dead and was unable to give evidence on his own behalf. In those circumstances, can the court be satisfied even on the balance of probabilities that if the deceased had given evidence before the Circuit Court that the Circuit Court decision would have been the same? Obviously, it cannot.

The position accordingly is as follows. The accused was acquitted at his own trial when he was there to defend himself. The evidence of the accomplices was accepted on the probabilities when he was not there to defend himself. In my view, public policy could not require the court on such evidence to deny to his estate the benefits to which it is entitled by contract. To do so would neither be fair nor be seen to be fair. Whatever the onus of proof upon the defendant upon this issue, it could not be so low as to be satisfied by the evidence adduced. It is accordingly unnecessary to indicate the proper standard of proof nor the evidence by which it should be established.

Namlooze Venootschap De Faam v The Dorset Manufacturing Co. Ltd [1949] IR 203

The plaintiff, a Dutch company, sued the defendant, an Irish company, for the price of goods sold and delivered. The defendant claimed that such payment either in Dutch guilders or in sterling would constitute a breach of the currency regulations of Ireland which prohibited the export of foreign exchange and the making of payments to persons outside the State without ministerial permission. The permission obtained by the defendant was in respect of a lower figure than required and had in any case expired.

Dixon J.:

The goods in this case were sold and delivered while the Emergency Powers (Finance) (No. 7) Order 1941, was in force. I do not find that the contract, or several contracts, under which the goods were ordered was or were thereby made either void or illegal. One reason is that the prohibitions in article 3 of the order, although void, related rather to what might be a contemplated or possible sequel to the contract rather than its essential nature. Another, and perhaps stronger, reason is that I think the qualification in that article enabling any of the prohibited acts to be done with the permission of the Minister for Finance places the contract in the category dealt with in J. W. *Taylor & Co. v Landauer & Co.*,[1] viz. as being a legal contract with an implied representation that, so far as permission of the minister might be necessary, such permission existed or would be applied for.

. . .

Whatever the terms of the court's order, the legal effect of it would be to put the plaintiffs in a position to secure payment of the amount in question and it would thus, even if indirectly, compel the defendants to do an act prohibited by the law for the time being in force. Put thus, I feel that on general principles it would be improper and contrary to public policy for the court to give judgment for the plaintiffs on their claim as now framed. There is persuasive authority for this view in a recent decision of the Court of Appeal in England in *Stockholms Enskilda Bank Aktiebolag v Schering Ltd.*[2] There, the claim was for an instalment provided for in a contract entered into before the Trading with the Enemy Act, 1939, but falling due after the coming into operation of that Act, and it was held that such payment would, in the circumstances of the case, be for the benefit of an enemy and would also be a payment of money to or for the benefit of an enemy. The court accordingly dismissed the action, thereby implying that they considered that an order enabling the recovery of the instalment by the plaintiffs would amount to the same thing as a payment of it by the defendants.

As a statement of principles applicable to the present case, and allowing for the different circumstances of the two cases, I adopt the following passage from the judgment of Lord (then Sir Wilfred) Greene M.R., at 440–441:

> He is claiming payment of a sum of money, and he is claiming it at a time when the law of this country declares that the thing which he is asking for, namely, payment, is illegal, and the fact that illegality has struck what in its origin was a perfectly innocent and proper transaction is, it seems to me, an answer to the claim. It is

true that, so far as anything in this Act of Parliament is concerned, the prohibition of payment is a temporary one. It only exists so long as the payee, or the person to receive the benefit, is an enemy. If and when he ceases to be an enemy, and in the absence of further legislation affecting his rights, he will, according to ordinary principles, be entitled to receive the benefit which was to flow to him under the machinery of these agreements. At the moment that benefit is prohibited, and it seems to me that that circumstance in this case is a defence to the action.

He later added: 'The true analogy seems to me to be the case of an action prematurely brought.'

This passage was primarily directed to an argument that the plaintiffs were at least entitled to a judgment which would declare and settle their rights, but with some sort of stay to prevent payment from being made during the continuance of the war or until a licence was obtained; and I think similar reasoning would preclude the adoption of any such course in this case.

. . .

The present claim is for the price of goods sold and delivered. Cases such as In re *Anglo-Russian Merchant Traders and John Ball & Co. (London)*;[3] *Mertens v Home Freeholds Co.*[4] and J. W. *Taylor & Co. v Landauer & Co.* suggest that the existence or terms of the relevant orders would not prevent the plaintiffs maintaining an action for damages for failure to use reasonable diligence to obtain the necessary permission or possibly for allowing the permission obtained to expire before it was fully exhausted, if the plaintiffs are in a position to adduce the necessary proofs. No such claim is before me, and I have not the necessary materials, even if I were so inclined, to express any view on that aspect of the matter. I have, however, considered the question whether I could enable justice to be done between the parties by adjourning the matter for plenary hearing so that a claim on the lines indicated could be formulated; but I feel I am precluded from this course by the consideration that such a claim would be one for unliquidated damages and, thus, unappropriate to proceedings commenced by summary summons and within the decision, now of long standing, in *Meares v Connolly*.[5]

For these reasons, the action must be dismissed.

1. |1940| 4 All ER 335.
2. |1941| 1 KB 424.
3. |1917| 2 KB 679.
4. |1921| 2 KB 526.
5. |1930| IR 333.

Note

This decision was affirmed by the Supreme Court in *Fibretex (Société Personnes à Responsabilité Limitée) v Beleir Ltd* (1958) 89 ILTR 141, a case involving an action for goods sold and delivered. The court also noted in that case that when the controlling legislation lapsed or was revoked the plaintiff would be in a position to take action, and if successful, to have an order for payment.

In *Westpac Banking Corp. v Anthony Matthew Dempsey* (HC) 19 November 1992, unrep., the defendant appealed against an order of the Master to enforce a judgment against him, awarded in the English High Court, in respect of money owed to the plaintiffs. The plaintiffs were a London-based banking company. The money was owed on foot of a loan agreement which the defendant claimed was void due to non-compliance with the Exchange Control Act 1954. Having referred to both the *Fibretex* and the *Namlooze* cases Morris J. noted that the exchange control restrictions had been relaxed on a gradual basis and from 1 January 1992 all restrictions on residents in respect of guarantees had been removed. As a result he stated 'The payments necessary under such guarantees may now be effected. It appears to me that precisely the circumstances envisaged for the removal of such restrictions by the Supreme Court in *Fibretex* have in fact occurred.'

B. CONTRACTS PREJUDICIAL TO THE ADMINISTRATION OF JUSTICE

In Re Adam Boyd (1885) 15 LR (Ir.) 521

On the eve of bankruptcy, a grocer who was both a customer and a commission agent of Leathem and Howard, a wholesale grocery firm, provided security to the firm for moneys due to them. Evidence suggested that the firm had threatened to prosecute the grocer for embezzlement if security was not provided.

Sullivan C.:

The question arose whether what occurred between these gentlemen and the bankrupt amounted to an agreement to stifle a prosecution. Lord Justice FitzGibbon thinks that there was an agreement to stifle a prosecution; and that this being the consideration for the equitable mortgage, that mortgage fails as being founded on an illegal consideration. I cannot agree in this view. *Ward v Lloyd*[1] is a most distinct authority that a threat of prosecution will not invalidate a security thereupon given, if there was no agreement to abandon the prosecution ultimately. I see no agreement here not to prosecute. The result is that this mortgage security stands according to the opinion of the majority of the court.

[1]. 7 Sc. NR 499.

Nolan v Shiels (1926) 60 ILTR 143

The defendant gave the plaintiff a cheque for £50 in consideration of the plaintiff's abandonment of an intended prosecution against a third party for an indecent assault. When the cheque was dishonoured, the plaintiff sued.

Pigot K.C.:

Indecent assault is a statutory offence punishable with two years' imprisonment. Common assault is punishable with one year's imprisonment and was indictable at common law. There is a clear distinction between compromising an indictable misdemeanour and 'stifling' a prosecution in respect of such an offence. By the latter phrase is to be understood an agreement not to take or refusing to take any part in a prosecution of a criminal nature. Before the time of Blackstone it had become a common practice, in the course of a criminal trial for a misdemeanour, for the defendant after conviction 'to speak with the prosecutor', and as a result, in consideration of compensation agreed to be given to the latter, the penalty was frequently made a nominal one. In one case reported the imprisonment was reduced from six to three months. Notwithstanding the adverse comments of that learned writer against such a custom, I have no doubt that it had become (and still is) a recognised part of the procedure in criminal trials for misdemeanour if rarely practised. And it is in that sense that the compromising of prosecutions is to be read as being allowable in criminal cases. From the earliest times we read that to agree not to prosecute in a criminal case was illegal; that a promise to pay money for such a promise is an illegal consideration, and that such a contract is void. To constitute such illegality there must be reasonable grounds for believing that the offence had been actually committed and that each party must have entered on the agreement on that assumption: *Rourke v Mealy* 4 LR Ir 166. Is there any exception to this general rule? The words used by Wilmot C.J., in *Collins v Blantern* 2nd Wils. 341, giving the grounds and reason for this rule, are of general application, and would appear to cover the 'stifling' of any indictable prosecution. But as was admitted in argument in the Exchequer Chamber in the hearing on writ of error in *Keir v Leeman* 9 QB 371, exceptions to this general rule are to be found. And in the course of his judgment at p. 375, Tyndall C.J., says: 'It is said, indeed, that in the case of an assault he (that is, the injured party) may also undertake not to prosecute on behalf of the public. It may be so. But we are not disposed to extend this any further.' That was a case of riot, a crime of a more public nature than assault. The ground upon which it was supposed that an agreement might be made not to prosecute in such a case was that compensation to the prosecutor might be commensurate with the possible penalty. And no doubt the elements of common assault regarded as an offence at common law were essentially the same as those giving rise to the right for assault in a civil action. If such an exception to a well known and general principle is to be recognised as still in existence (and I doubt whether it is), I am of opinion that any distinction should be laid hold of to prevent an interference with the right of the public to have protection through the criminal law. Inasmuch as no civil action could be brought for an indecent assault as distinguished from an ordinary assault, as the penalty to be possibly awarded by the court is a higher one for one offence than for the other, therein differing again from actionable assault; as I consider that the exception (if any) is probably founded on an historical development of our law rather than on principle; and finally because I am of opinion that the old and sound rule of the law should be restricted in the interests of the public welfare, I decide that this agreement was founded on an illegal consideration, that the contract was void and that the action fails.

David McElroy (t/a Irish Genealogical Services) *v* Catherine Josephine Flynn and Daniel O'Flynn [1991] ILRM 294

An advertisement was inserted in various papers by the British Treasury Secretary seeking next-of-kin for one Mary Creedon who had died intestate. The plaintiff, a professional next-of-kin agent, traced the defendants who were relations of Mary Creedon. He informed them that they might be entitled to a share in the estate of a deceased person but claimed not to know the name of the deceased. He offered to represent them and lodge a claim on their behalf and they signed deeds of assignment stating that in consideration of the plaintiff informing them that they might be entitled to a share in the estate of the deceased, they would assign to him twenty five per cent of their respective shares in the estate. Later they notified him of their intention to repudiate their agreement.

Blayney J.:

The leading case on what amounts to an agreement savouring of champerty, and how it is viewed in equity, is *Rees v De Bernardy* [1896] 2 Ch. 437, a decision of Romer J. The facts were as follows. In 1863 W. Howells died intestate in New Zealand possessed of real estate of considerable value. In 1884 the defendant, a next-of-kin agent, became aware of the intestacy and set to work to discover the heir at law. Having first found a relative who was thought erroneously to be the heir, he ultimately discovered that two widows both over seventy years of age, uneducated, illiterate and living in humble circumstances in England, were entitled as co-heiresses. He got them to sign a document by which they agreed, in consideration of being given particulars of the estate, to pay the defendant one half of what they would receive from the estate. The two widows died before receiving the entire of the property and their personal representatives sued to set aside the agreement. Romer J. said in his judgment at 446:

> But I think the plaintiffs are also entitled to relief on another ground—namely, that the agreement induced by the defendant is one in the nature of champerty and void as being contrary to the policy of the law. It is not necessary in cases of this kind, in order that the agreement should be held void, that it should amount strictly in point of law to champerty or maintenance so as to constitute a punishable offence: see, amongst other cases, *Reynell v Sprye* 1 DM & G 660. In that case Knight Bruce L.J., with reference to the agreement there impeached, said: 'Such an understanding, such an agreement . . . may or may not have amounted strictly in point of law to champerty or maintenance so as to constitute a punishable offence, but must in my judgment be considered clearly against the policy of the law, clearly mischievous, clearly such as a court of equity ought to discourage and relieve against.'

Now in the case before me I think the true agreement made by the defendants was one contrary to the policy of the law. I agree that a contract by a person to communicate information on terms of getting a share of any property that may thereby be recovered by the person to whom the information is to be given, and nothing more, is not champerty or void: see *Sprye v Porter* (1856) 7 E & B 58. But if the arrangement come to is not merely that information shall be given, but also that the person who gives it and who is to share in what may be recovered shall himself recover the property or actively assist in the recovery of it by procuring evidence or similar means, then I think the arrangement is contrary to the policy of the law and void: see *Sprye v Porter* and also *Stanley v Jones* (1831) 7 Bing. 369, where the agreement held void was one by Stanley to communicate information to enable the defendant to recover a sum of money and to use and exert his utmost influence and means for procuring such evidence as should be requisite to substantiate the claims of the defendant. And in *Hutley v Hutley* (1872) LR 8 QB 112 Blackburn J. says, with reference to the contract there held void: 'If that stood without more, it is clear that it is champerty by the English law, which says that a bargain, whereby the one party is to assist the other in recovering property, and is to share in the proceeds of the action, is illegal.'

. . .

Having considered the evidence of the plaintiff and of the defendants, the conclusion I have come to is that the real agreement here was that the plaintiff should do more than merely inform the defendants of the name of the deceased. I consider that the plaintiff agreed in addition to assist actively in the recovery of the defendants' shares in the estate and that the agreement accordingly is void.

Simon Fraser and Another v Denis Buckle and Others [1994] 1 ILRM 276
The two plaintiffs, professional next-of-kin agents, informed the three defendants that they could be heirs to an estate in New Jersey. The name of the deceased though known to the plaintiffs was not mentioned at this stage. The defendants entered into contracts agreeing to give the plaintiffs a one third share of any sums they might subsequently inherit from the estate in return for which the plaintiffs agreed to disclose the identity of the deceased and to assist in the presentation of the defendants' claim. The contracts stipulated that the proper law of the contract was to be the law of England and Wales. The plaintiffs performed their part of the agreement but the defendants refused to pay the agreed sum claiming that the agreements were unenforceable because they were champertous.

Costello J.:

If *Rees v De Bernardy* and *McElroy v Flynn* are still good law then if the agreements entered into between the parties in this case had related to an Irish estate and to the maintenance of a claim to an estate in an Irish court it would clearly be unenforceable. This is because the plaintiff in this case had not only supplied information to the defendants in return for a share in the estate arising from the court proceedings but had agreed actively to assist in collecting evidence and presenting the evidence collected to support the claim to the court and did in fact do so.

The plaintiffs advance three main arguments as to why these cases should not be followed and why the enforcement of those agreements is not contrary to Irish public policy.

Firstly, they submit that the law has been developed by decisions of the English courts (which our courts should follow) which mean that heir-locator agreements should no longer be regarded as champertous.

Secondly, and in the alternative, they submit that if the law of champerty still applies to heir-locator agreements then modern developments in the law would lead to the conclusion that the plaintiffs in this case had a legitimate business interest in the New Jersey proceedings and accordingly they were not unlawfully 'maintaining' the New Jersey proceedings, and the agreements are therefore not champertous.

Thirdly, and in the further alternative, they submit that agreements which relate to proceedings outside Ireland cannot be said to be contrary to Irish public policy and as the principles of private international law relied on by the defendants do not apply the court should apply the principles of the proper law of the contract (i.e. the law of England and Wales) to those agreements.

Before referring in more detail to the principal cases cited in argument there are two general observations to be made. Firstly, none of the modern cases were concerned with heir-locator agreements—they all dealt with the assignment of rights of action. Secondly, all of the cases (with the exception of one) turned on the question whether the interest which the maintainer had in the action in suit was sufficient to disprove the claim that the action was being unlawfully 'maintained' by him.

Martell v Consett Iron Co. [1955] 1 Ch. 363 was a case in which a riparian owner and the trustees of an angling club claimed injunctive relief against the defendant company who were said to be polluting a river by effluent from iron works. An association for the protection of the rights of riparian owners and for the prevention of pollution supported the plaintiffs (who were members of the association) in the form of an indemnity in respect of costs. The defendants moved to strike out the claim on the ground that it was tainted with illegality and an abuse of the process of the court because it was being maintained by a third party who had not got a sufficient common interest in the subject matter of the action. The court held on the facts of the case that the association had a sufficient common interest in the subject matter of the plaintiffs' action in maintaining the action and was not therefore acting illegally.

Laurent v Sale & Co. |1963| 1 WLR 829 was a case of an assignment of a debt owed by the defendant company to two businessmen, one carrying on business in Belgium, the other in Germany. The assignees sued the defendant company in England and the defence raised was that the assignment amounted to a champertous agreement and was therefore unenforceable. The plaintiff assignee unsuccessfully argued that no champerty was involved in the transaction, Megaw J. holding that the assignment was effected so that the plaintiff could conduct litigation at his own risk and expense for the agreed benefit he would obtain if the case was successful.

In re Trepca Mines Ltd (No. 2) was a case concerning the winding-up in England of an insolvent company. A person claiming to be a creditor had applied to the liquidator for payment of a considerable sum he claimed the company owed him. The proof of his debt was rejected. He had no funds with which to appeal. He was contacted by a Frenchman, M. Teyssou, who entered into agreements by which M. Teyssou paid £4,000 to a solicitor to finance an appeal in return for one fourth of the proceeds which might result from it. The court held that this was a champertous agreement and unenforceable and that the solicitor being aware of the champertous nature of the agreement was unable to recover costs in relation to it.

Trendtex Trading Corp. v Credit Suisse was a case in which the judgments of the Court of Appeal were reported in |1980| QB 629 and the judgments of the House of Lords in |1982| AC 679. It concerned the assignment of a cause of action by a plaintiff in an English action against the well known bank, Credit Suisse. The parties had entered into an agreement which provided that it was to be governed by Swiss law and that any dispute arising under it was to be 'judged by the Court of Geneva, exclusive of any other jurisdiction'. Credit Suisse moved to stay the English proceedings and one of the issues raised was whether the assignment of the cause of action was champertous. The Court of Appeal held (1) that the assignment was valid because the assignee had a legitimate and genuine interest in the suit, and (2) that the English proceedings should be stayed because of the exclusive jurisdiction clause in the contract. The House of Lords took a different view of the assignment holding that it was champertous, but agreed nonetheless that the action should be stayed because of the parties' agreement that the Swiss courts were to have exclusive jurisdiction.

I was also referred to recent decisions in the Court of Appeal and the House of Lords in proceedings entitled Sanders v Templar, Giles v Thompson and Devlin v Baslington. The judgments in the Court of Appeal were delivered on 11 January 1993 (and have not yet been reported (see The Times, 13 January 1993) but a transcript has been obtained) whilst the judgments in the House of Lords are reported in |1993| 2 WLR 908. These proceedings concerned the hiring of cars to persons injured in road accidents who claimed damages for the hiring charges as well as for their personal injuries. Although the agreements in the three cases were different it will suffice if I indicate in a general way their subject matter. Each of the injured plaintiffs entered into agreements with rental companies which provided that the companies should have the right to pursue the defendants in the plaintiffs' names, the companies having hired a car to the plaintiffs on terms that no hiring charges would be immediately payable but would be paid when damages were recovered. It was claimed that these agreements were champertous, a claim dismissed in both the Court of Appeal and the House of Lords. In his judgment in the Court of Appeal Bingham M.R. pointed out (p. 5 of the transcript) that the essence of both maintenance and champerty was the wanton intermeddling in the litigation of another without justification or excuse and that what had to be considered was the sort of interest which a maintainer has to show to justify his intervention. He pointed out that when an outsider has no legitimate business interest beyond the agreement which is alleged to be unlawful then he is trafficking in litigation. But he held (as did his colleagues in the Court of Appeal) that the rental companies were not trafficking in litigation, that they were not wantonly and officiously meddling in the disputes of others because they had a legitimate business interest in recovering a reasonable award for services which they had actually performed. This approach to the case was also adopted by Lord Muskill in the House of Lords.

None of these cases either expressly or impliedly overruled the decision of *Rees v De Bernardy*; none dealt with heir-locator agreements or the enforceability of such agreements. It is true that Lord Muskill in *Giles v Thompson* at 911 of his judgment stated that in recent decades maintenance and champerty had in practice only maintained a living presence in two respects, first as a source of the rule which forbids a solicitor from accepting payment calculated as a proportion of a sum recovered and secondly, as the ground for denying recognition to the assignment of a bare right of action. But he was referring to a factual position and his comments cannot be taken as meaning that the class of agreements condemned in *Rees v De Bernardy* should not now be regarded as champertous. I must reject therefore the plaintiffs' general submission that modern developments in the law mean that their heir-locator agreements no longer infringe the law of champerty.

The second submission based on these cases is that the courts in England have expanded the situations in which it can be said that persons have a legitimate interest in the litigation which they are maintaining so that no wrongdoing occurs. I cannot however agree that any of the decisions in the cases to which I have been referred or any part of the judgments in those cases oblige me to hold that the plaintiffs in this action had a legitimate and genuine interest in the proceedings in the New Jersey court such as would entitle them lawfully to maintain the defendants' claim in them. They had no interest in the estate of Evelyn Herbert, apart from the interest they acquired in the November 1988 agreements. As it is well established that the interest which the maintainer enjoys in a suit which he is maintaining must exist independently of the agreement which gives him a share in the proceeds of the suit, and as the plaintiffs have no such interest in this case, I cannot agree that the agreements in this case are not champertous because of some interest which the plaintiffs had in Evelyn Herbert's estate prior to their November 1988 agreements.

I come now to the third, and what I conceive to be the principal, submission advanced on the plaintiffs' behalf. It is urged that the law of champerty only renders unenforceable heir-locator agreements relating to an estate or fund which is situated in Ireland and does not apply where the agreement relates to an estate or fund outside Ireland.

It will be observed that if this submission is correct then *Rees v De Bernardy* was incorrectly decided because the agreement in that case was made in England and related to the share of an estate in New Zealand. Furthermore it would follow that *McElroy v Flynn* was wrongly decided as the agreements in the case were made in Ireland and related to an estate in England. The plaintiffs submit that the point now urged was not raised in either of these cases and accordingly the courts are not bound to follow those decisions as they were incorrectly reached.

For the purpose of this submission the plaintiffs accept that some heir-locator agreements may be champertous but argue that only those that relate to litigation in Ireland are champertous because Irish public policy is only concerned with proceedings in this country and cannot be concerned with proceedings in a foreign country, for example, New Jersey.

The term 'public policy' needs to be understood. It is used in different senses and there are different and distinct heads of public policy which the courts will seek to enforce. Steyn L.J. in *Sanders v Templar*, recently identified them under three separate headings:

> The criterion of public policy or public interest in the restraint of trade field is based on an economic view of the needs of society. Other contracts may be held illegal on the ground that they endanger fundamental moral values of our society, such as certain agreements in restraint of marriage. A third head of public policy serves to protect the integrity of the institutions of government in the broad sense of the word. And the public policy which render champertous agreements illegal clearly falls in this third category. It will be seen that this head of public policy rests on the perceived need to protect the integrity of public justice.

Relying on this concept of public policy it is claimed that Irish public policy is not and should not be concerned with the integrity of the administration of justice in New Jersey. It follows that the agreements in suit are not offensive to Irish public policy and, accordingly, the defendants cannot rely on the principle of private international law they have quoted.

To consider the validity of these submissions it is necessary to recall firstly that the agreements which the law of champerty condemns are agreements by which one party agrees to maintain litigation in which he has no genuine interest in consideration of a promise to receive a share of the proceeds of the litigation. Secondly, the reason why the law condemns champertous agreements, is because of the dangers associated with such agreements, namely the temptation that the maintainer might inflame the damages, suppress evidence or suborn witnesses. It is necessary also to appreciate that the reason why such agreements are contrary to public policy is that these associated dangers, if realised, could compromise the proper administration of justice because of the unjust adjudications likely to result. I can see no reason for restricting the law of champerty in relation to heir-locator agreements as suggested by the plaintiffs because it seems to me that the dangers with which such agreements are associated exist whether the estate to be shared with the maintainer (and the litigation associated with it) is situated in Ireland or is situated abroad. I cannot agree that the law should provide that heir-locator agreements are contrary to Irish public policy when they relate to claims to estates in Ireland but are not contrary to Irish public policy when they relate to claims to estates situated abroad. When such agreements relate to estates situated abroad litigation in relation to them may come before the Irish courts when a question of the enforceability of the agreement arises. The recognised dangers associated with such agreements could lead to unjust adjudications in such litigation and it seems to me to be reasonable that in heir-locator cases Irish public policy should seek to protect the integrity of public justice in this country both in litigation relating to the enforceability of the agreements and in litigation determining the persons entitled to share in an Irish estate. It follows that Irish public policy should condemn heir-locator agreements whether they relate to estates abroad or not.

I think, with respect, that the novel point raised by the plaintiffs has been based on a misconstruction of some observations of Lord Denning in the *Trepca Mines* case and of Steyn L.J. in the *Sanders v Templar* case. *Trepca Mines* was, as I have said, a case dealing with the winding-up of a company in England. The enforceability of agreements by which M. Teyssou paid £4,000 to a solicitor to finance an appeal in consideration of one fourth of the proceeds of the appeal was one of the issues in the case. In the course of his judgment, having commented that the agreements were clearly champertous, Lord Denning went on to remark that had the agreements concerned French litigation they might have been lawful 'because I understand champerty is lawful in France' (at 218). But he pointed out that this was not the case as they concerned English litigation against an English company to recover sums in England. He clearly was not making any reference to the point of law I am now considering as his remarks related to the legal position in France had proceedings taken place in that country.

It is necessary to stress that *Sanders v Templar* was a case relating to assignments of rights of action. In the course of his judgment Steyn L.J. having considered various aspects of the law of maintenance and champerty, went on to point out that the doctrine he was considering 'only applies to agreements governing English litigation' and that 'an agreement of a champertous nature made in England is valid if it relates to litigation in a country where champerty is lawful' (pp 17 and 18 of the transcript). It seems to me that the observations on which the plaintiffs rely are to be read in the context in which they appear, namely in a case dealing with the assignment of rights of actions in England. The judgment expressed no views or comments on the law relating to heir-locator agreements, or on the legal issues which arise when the court is required to enforce such an agreement as has happened in this case.

I must conclude therefore (a) that the agreements sued on in these proceedings are unenforceable under Irish law because they are champertous, (b) that such agreements are opposed to Irish public policy, (c) that I should therefore apply Irish law to these contracts whether or not they are enforceable under their proper law, and (d) that in doing so I should dismiss the plaintiffs' claim.

Note

The boundary between champertous contracts and everyday agreements that are beneficial to both parties, indeed agreements that have been sanctioned in legislation, is a difficult one to draw. In *Grovewood Holding plc v James Capel & Co. Ltd* TLR 15 August 1994 Lightman J. held that a company liquidator who sought to pursue a claim in negligence against a firm of stockbrokers that had allegedly provided negligent advice to the company could not do so by entering into an agreement with some anonymous backers who would fund the litigation in return for one half of the recoveries in the action. Lightman J. drew an admittedly fine line between an acceptable course of action, assignment of the cause of action, and an illegal one, namely sale of the fruits of a cause of action. The fact that the liquidator may have been acting meritoriously and in the interest of creditors could not, in Lightman J.'s view, outweigh the fact that Parliament had not created a broad exception to champerty in passing s. 436 and para. 6 of schedule 4 to the UK Insolvency Act 1986.

C. AGREEMENTS WHICH SERVE TO DEFRAUD THE REVENUE

Starling Securities Ltd *v* Francis Woods, Thomas Woods and Investment Holdings International Ltd (HC) 24 May 1977, unrep.
The plaintiff agreed to sell a hotel to the defendants for £215,000. The contract, however only stated a price of £190,000. The desired effect of this

was to reduce the defendant's stamp duty liability. Later, when the plaintiff sought specific performance of this contract, the defendant claimed *inter alia* that there was no sufficient memorandum to satisfy the Statute of Frauds and that the contract was illegal.

The court found that there was a sufficient act of part performance to take the case out of the statute and then it proceeded to deal with the issue of illegality.

McWilliam J.:

. . .

. . . With regard to the defence of illegality it is argued that, *prima facie*, there is nothing to show any illegality and that full duty could have been paid on a transaction completed in this manner and that, in any event, the defendants cannot rely on illegality without pleading it. . . . The only interpretation I can put on the very peculiar method adopted to conduct these transactions is that both parties were trying to conceal from the Revenue authorities the true nature of the transactions. Certainly no other possible explanation has been suggested to me. Accordingly, on these two authorities, it appears to me that I am not entitled to countenance such attempted frauds on the Revenue by enforcing the performance of the contracts at the instance of either party. The issue of illegality should certainly have been pleaded but, once the evidence of it has been properly introduced in respect to one issue in the case, namely, with regard to the sufficiency of the memorandum, I am not entitled to ignore it. . . .

Stanley R. Lewis *v* Squash Ireland Ltd [1983] ILRM 363

The claimant was employed as managing director of the respondent company. His salary was £16,000 *per annum*, £2,000 of which was described as 'expenses' in the respondent's accounts. This figure actually represented a salary increase and was misdescribed in order to reduce the respondent's tax liability. When the claimant was dismissed he sued for unfair dismissal and the Employment Appeals Tribunal had to consider whether the contract of employment was tainted with illegality.

Determination

1.37 Applying the test of probability (*Whitecross Potatoes International Ltd v R. Coyle*) [see p. 750 below] we find that the scheme adopted in relation to the £2,000 *per annum* increase was illegal.

2. *We consider the possibility of severence*

2.01 [Counsel for the claimant] submitted that if the tribunal were to find that the agreement regarding the £2,000 was illegal and not enforceable that it could and should, in that event, be severed from the remainder of the claimant's contract of employment which was a normal contract of its type, legal as to its object and its performance.

2.02 The tribunal accepts that it is mathematically possible to sever the illegal agreement from the remainder of the claimant's salary but we feel that the parties knowingly incorporated the illegal agreement into the contract through a vital term *viz.* the claimant's consideration (his salary/remuneration) and the illegality infected the whole of the claimant's consideration and through it the whole of the contract.

2.03 The illegal term entered the contract by consent and became part of it.

2.04 In *Miller v Karlinski* (1945) 62 TLR 85, CA, du Parcq L.J. said:

> The argument for the plaintiff has been attractively presented to the court and in some ways appeals to my sympathy. If, but for the fact that the contract is illegal, the defendant ought to pay, it is not altogether satisfactory that the plaintiff should go without reward and that the defendant should escape liability. I do not, however, think that it is possible to hold that this part of the agreement is a separate part to be treated as an independent covenant, and to say that the plaintiff is entitled to sue for any salary alleged to be owing to him. Authorities have been cited one of which decides that, where an agreement is capable of two constructions, one of which will make the agreement legal and the other of which will make it illegal, that construction is to be preferred which will make it lawful. That is a well settled principle which does not help us here. The other lays down that the question whether a covenant is independent is one of construction. I need not refer further to those authorities. I find it impossible to say that, where a man agrees to work and to be paid according to a scheme devised, as was that in the present case, so as to defraud the revenue, the whole agreement is not an illegal agreement which the courts will not enforce. It is as well that people who enter into this kind of agreement should know that if either party fails to observe any of its terms the courts will not entertain an action to enforce them.

2.05 We find that the contract as existing at the time of the dismissal and from the time of the agreement regarding the £2,000 increase was a contract which was wholly tainted with the illegality as stated, and that the illegal arrangement could not be severed from the contract of employment as a whole, leaving, as [counsel] submitted, the other parts of the contract enforceable and thus, *pro tanto*, the claimant's claim before this tribunal.

3.01 We *considered the consequences of the illegality.*

3.02 Did *it render the contract void?*

We do not hold the view that the illegality rendered the contract void, i.e. at law deemed to have no effect.

3.03 In this case the contract as originally made was, as far as we are concerned, perfectly legal and continued as such until tainted by the later agreement.

3.04 If we are wrong in this then the claimant's claim must fail as there would be no contract of employment to support his entitlement to claim under the Unfair Dismissals Act 1977.

3.05 Did *it render the contract unenforceable?*

3.06/3.07 In *Tomlinson v Dick Evans 'U' Drive Ltd* [1978] ICR 639–643 the employee received a £15.00 per week pay rise paid to the knowledge of employer and employee out of petty cash against 'bogus vouchers' for collection and delivery charges. On a claim for compensation for unfair dismissal and a redundancy payment, the industrial tribunal held that the payment was a fraud on the Revenue and, therefore, as the contract of employment was unenforceable, they dismissed the claim.

3.08/3.09 She appealed and her appeal was dismissed by the Employment Appeal Tribunal (EAT). In its judgment the EAT said:

> The reason why rights and obligations which arise from a contract which is illegal will not be enforced in the courts was expressed by Lord Mansfield as long ago as 1775 in *Holman v Johnson* (1775) 1 Cowp. 341, 343 to be founded on general principles of public

policy. 'The principle of public policy is this: *ex dolo malo non oritur actio'*. A distinguished judge using the idiom of 1977 and borrowing from A. P. Herbert has expressed it in language more apt to be used amongst those concerned with this branch of the law as 'the dirty dog gets no dinner here'. We take it to be clear law that someone who tries to assert in the courts a right contained in an illegal contract will not succeed.

It is not suggested on this appeal that the industrial tribunal was wrong in finding that it had to do with a deliberate fraud on the Revenue. It is clear that both Mr Evans and the employee knew exactly what they were doing and that both were in it up to the neck. Both in their evidence were what it is kinder to call candid than shameless about it. No doubt there are cases in which a junior employee goes along with an employer's tax fraud knowing it to be dishonest in circumstances where more blame attaches to the employer than to him. But even in such cases the evil lies in the dishonesty in which the employee knowingly participated and the law leaves the balancing of the respective degrees of blame to the discretion of the Revenue in deciding who is to be subjected to penalties or prosecuted, and the criminal court which has to decide upon what sentence to inflict. There is, for good reason, no relaxation in the rule that the dishonest party to the swindle cannot recover upon the contract.

3.10 In *Newland v Simons and Willer (Hairdressers) Ltd* |1981| ICR 521 the EAT, in a fraud on the Revenue case, stated (May J. delivering the majority decision):

> In the view of the majority of this appeal tribunal, however, where both employer and employee knowingly commit an illegality by way of a fraud on the Revenue in the payment and receipt of the employee's remuneration under the contract of employment, which is an essential part of such a contract, then we think that there can be no doubt that this does turn it into a contract that is prohibited by statute or common law, and consequently the employee is precluded from enforcing any employment rights she might otherwise have against her employer. The incidence of income tax frauds both large and small is so rife that they cannot be brushed on one side and the blame for them laid only at the feet of the employers (at p. 530).

3.11 In *Newland's* case at 531, May J. stated that in the view of the majority the essential question is 'Has the employee knowingly been a party to a deception on the Revenue?'

3.12 Adopting this question, the tribunal has decided that on a subjective test the answer is yes.

3.13 It is public policy that the courts and this tribunal, should not lend themselves to the enforcement of contracts either illegal on their face or in which the intended performance of obligations thereunder was illegal to the knowledge of the party seeking to enforce the contract.

3.14 In *Newland v Simons and Willer Ltd* it was argued that public policy in relation to illegal contracts should be set against the public policy that employees be entitled to the rights under the protective legislation as in the Unfair Dismissals Act 1977.

3.15 *Shaw v Groom* |1970| 2 QB 504 was referred to in *Newland's* case and particularly a dictum of Sachs L.J.:

> This conclusion is reached on the footing that there has been no change in recent years in the relevant public policy. If, however, it be on the contrary said that the conclusion postulates a less rigid public policy today than obtained in 1924, so be it. Public policy has been often spoken of as an unruly horse: all the more reason

then why its riders should not themselves in these changing times wear blinkers, be oblivious to the scene around, and thus ride for a fall. Sound policy must be flexible enough to take into account the circumstances of its own generation. Today's generation is dominated by that ever-mounting mass of legislative control to which reference has already been made: in support of that control numberless offences have been created each with its appropriate penalty, and it is for the courts to see that this does not result in additional forfeitures and injustices which the legislature cannot have intended (at 523).

3.16 The dictum was elaborated upon by Miss Mogridge, honorary employment adviser to Fulham Citizen's Advice Bureau, for the employee and her submission and the majority view of the EAT with which we agree is stated in the *Newland* judgment at 533 as follows:

> Miss Mogridge contended that if one applies the principles contained in that dictum to the circumstances of the present case, Parliament cannot have intended that an employee should be deprived of his rights under his contract of employment, once that has been accurately ascertained, namely because it on its face or its performance to his knowledge involves a fraud on the revenue. In the climate of 1981 those rights of employees should not be so summarily disregarded merely because of the illegality involved. There are ways and means of redressing the illegality: the Revenue has full powers to recover, either from the employer or the employee or from both, any tax which has been lost; the employee has in the circumstances no similar right to recover his or her *prima facie* entitlement under the employment legislation if this is denied on the ground of public policy because of illegality.
>
> This is indeed a bold submission and one to which the majority of us can in no way accede. If an employee wishes to be entitled to the statutory rights given him by the relevant legislation, then the contract of employment in respect of which he seeks those rights and its performance both by himself and by his employer to his knowledge must each be legal. That is to say, that they conform to the law. We have no doubt that Parliament never intended to give the statutory rights provided for by the relevant employment legislation to those who were knowingly breaking the law by committing or participating in a fraud on the Revenue (at 533).

3.17 The tribunal considers that the contract herein is not enforceable at the suit of the claimant by virtue of public policy being set against such enforcement.

4. *Can statutory rights be based on an illegal contract?*

4.01 Although the contract in this case is unenforceable it is not, as stated, void and [counsel] submitted that the mere existence of the contract of employment is sufficient to establish that the claimant was an employee of the respondent and he, having the requisite qualifying service, had met the requirement of the Unfair Dismissals Act 1977, to the extent that the tribunal should and could review the dismissal in accordance with the Act, the onus being on the respondent to justify the dismissal.

4.02 The tribunal notes that the respondent had not throughout this lengthy hearing sought to raise any issue of illegality but sought to discharge the onus as it was seen to exist.

4.03 In *Tomlinson v Dick Evans 'U' Drive* the judgment, referring to the British Act, of course, dealt with this question as follows:

> Does it make any difference that the right which it is sought to enforce, the right to redress if you are unfairly dismissed and to redundancy money, is not a right

contained in the contract itself but a right given to the dismissed employee by the Trade Union and Labour Relations Act, 1974 and the Redundancy Payments Act, 1965?

In our judgment it does not. It is true that the rights with which we are concerned are creatures of statute, superimposed upon the contractual rights of employees and employers which they enjoy under the common law. But the prerequisite to the existence of these rights is that the person who seeks to enforce them has been employed under a contract. The rights, though creatures of statute, in our judgment depend on, or arise from the contract just as do the common law rights which arise from the contract itself.

It is said that the statutory rights can be asserted irrespective of the illegality of the contract from which they arise or upon which they depend because the result of the employment legislation is to give the employee a protected status. While it may be a convenient shorthand to say that the effect of the employment legislation is that the law is moving away from contract in this field and towards status, it is misleading if such shorthand tends to disguise the fact that it is the employee's situation as a party to a contract of employment which is the subject of protection by the legislation which it did not enjoy under the common law. Unless he was a party to a contract of employment, the statute cannot and does not give him a right not to be unfairly dismissed, or a right to receive a redundancy payment (at 642).

4.04 In *Newland v Simons and Willer Ltd*, the EAT considered the matter and stated:

In the view of the majority of this appeal tribunal, the question whether the employee is in her turn in such circumstances also affected by the illegal performance of the contract by the employers depends upon whether she was a party to or knew of her employer's illegality. If she did take part in or continued working knowing of the illegal mode of performance by her employers of her contract of employment then she too was affected by that illegality and cannot now rely upon the statutory rights to which she would otherwise be entitled under the relevant employment legislation (at 528). (See also 3.10 above.)

4.05 The tribunal considers that in order that an employee be able to have his claim dealt with under the Unfair Dismissals Act 1977, he must be an 'employee' at law.

4.06 An employee is defined as a person who has entered into or works under a contract of employment.

4.07 The existence of the contract, therefore, establishes the status of employee which status is essential to the existence of his rights under the Act.

4.08 In the case of an illegal contract as in this case public policy renders it unenforceable.

4.09 In our view an employee's statutory rights under the Unfair Dismissals Act 1977, are dependant on his holding his employment under a legal and enforceable contract of employment, which the claimant did not.

Tony Haden *v* Sean Quinn Properties Ltd (HC) 6 December 1993, unrep.

The plaintiff was appointed general manager of a hotel in Cavan owned by the defendant. A basic salary of £22,000 was agreed and added to this was a sum of £6,000 non-taxable allowance to cover expenses. Eight months later the plaintiff was dismissed and sued for damages for breach of contract. On the evidence Barron J. found that the grounds for dismissal given by the defendant were spurious and that there was no legal justification for the plaintiff's dismissal. However, he then considered the legal status of the contract.

Barron J.:

...

... In the course of his evidence the plaintiff said that this was never intended to cover expenses of which there were none but was to enable him to have an after-tax salary equal to that being received by him in England. ...

... I am satisfied that the plaintiff would not have come to the hotel for less than he was getting and that the device of expenses was for the benefit of the defendant. ...

...

The defendant is clearly in breach of contract in that the plaintiff's dismissal was wrongful. However, the contract itself was an illegal one. It contained a term designed to lessen the defendant's liability at the expense of the Revenue, something with which the plaintiff concurred. In *Napier v National Business Agency Ltd*, 1951 2 All ER 264 the facts were almost identical. Part of the plaintiff's salary purported to be in respect of expenses, which at best were only minimal. The plaintiff had claimed to have been dismissed wrongfully. He sued for damages. His claim was dismissed upon the ground that the contract was unlawful and so unenforceable. Sir Raymond Evershed said at 266:

> ... it must surely be that, by making an agreement in that form the parties to it were doing that which they must be taken to know would be liable to defeat the proper claims of the Inland Revenue and to avoid altogether, or at least to post-pone, the proper payment of income tax. If that is the right conclusion, it seems to me equally clear ... that the agreement must be regarded as contrary to public policy. There is a strong legal obligation placed on all citizens to make true and faith-ful returns for tax purposes, and, if parties make an agreement which is designed to do the contrary, i.e. to mislead and to delay, it seems to me impossible for this court to enforce that contract at the suit of one party to it.

The learned judge then went on to consider whether or not the fraudulent part of the agreement could be severed and held that it could not.

In my view that case would have been decided in the same way and upon the same grounds in this jurisdiction at that date. Notwithstanding the very great changes that have occurred in society in this country since then I do not believe that public policy on this issue would have changed in any way. The plaintiff allowed himself to agree to something which would benefit the defendant at the expense of the Revenue. Such an agreement is unenforceable and the plaintiff's claim must therefore fail.

D. Agreements which Serve to Corrupt Public Officials

The Lord Mayor, Aldermen, and Burgesses of Dublin *v* Michael Angelo Hayes (1876) 10 IRCL 226

Morris C.J.:

The defendant was City Marshal, and as such was Marshal of the Borough Court, and also Marshal of the Court of Conscience, and by the provisions of the Irish Statutes 26 Geo. 43, c. 3, and 28 Geo. 3, c. 49, as Marshal, he became Registrar of pawnbrokers, and received considerable fees much exceeding the salary he was appointed at by the plaintiffs. The arrangement the plaintiffs entered into with the defendant on his appointment and the bond entered into by him in compliance with the arrangement provides that he is to pay over all the fees and emoluments of his office to the treasurer of the plaintiffs. Such an arrangement, it has been admitted on the part of the plaintiffs during the argument, would be clearly illegal prior to the passing of the Municipal Corporations Act, 3 & 4 Vict. c. 108. It would be illegal as a bargain of an office of trust by which the plaintiffs who were appointing the defendant were to obtain a large benefit by the receipt of the fees of the office. . . .

E. Contracts Tending to Promote Immorality

Pearce and Another *v* Brooks (1866) 1 Ex 213

The plaintiffs hired a carriage to the defendant knowing the latter to be a prostitute. When the carriage was returned damaged they attempted to sue her for unpaid fees and for the damage.

Pollock C.B.:

. . . I have always considered it as settled law, that any person who contributes to the performance of an illegal act by supplying a thing with the knowledge that it is going to be used for that purpose, cannot recover the price of the thing so supplied. If, to create that incapacity, it was ever considered necessary that the price should be bargained or expected to be paid out of the fruits of the illegal act (which I do not stop to examine), that proposition has been overruled by the cases I have referred to, and has now ceased to be law. Nor can any distinction be made between an illegal and an immoral purpose; the rule which is applicable to the matter is, Ex *turpi causa non oritur actio*, and whether it is an immoral or an illegal purpose in which the plaintiff has participated, it comes equally within the terms of that maxim, and the effect is the same; no cause of action can arise out of either the one or the other. The rule of law was well settled in *Cannan v Bryce*;[1] . . .

. . . If, therefore, this article was furnished to the defendant for the purpose of enabling her to make a display favourable to her immoral purposes, the plaintiffs can derive no cause of action from the bargain. . . .

. . . If evidence is given which is sufficient to satisfy the jury of the fact of the immoral purpose, and of the plaintiffs' knowledge of it, and that the article was required and furnished to facilitate that object, it is sufficient . . .

Martin B.:

I am of the same opinion. The real question is, whether sufficient has been found by the jury to make a legal defence to the action under the third plea. The plea states first the fact that the defendant was to the plaintiffs' knowledge a prostitute; second, that the brougham was furnished to enable her to exercise her immoral calling; third, that the plaintiffs expected to be paid out of the earnings of her prostitution. In my opinion the plea is good if the third averment be struck out; and if, therefore, there is evidence that the brougham was, to the knowledge of the plaintiffs, hired for the purpose of such display as would assist the defendant in her immoral occupation, the substance of the plea is proved, and the contract was illegal. When the rule was moved I did not clearly apprehend that the evidence went to that point; had I done so, I should not have concurred in granting it. It is now plain that enough was proved to support the verdict.

As to the case of *Cannan v Bryce*, I have a strong impression that it has been questioned to this extent, that if money is lent, the lender merely handing it over into the absolute control of the borrower, although he may have reason to suppose that it will be employed illegally, he will not be disentitled from recovering. But, no doubt, if it were part of the contract that the money should be so applied, the contract would be illegal.

Pollock C.B.:

I wish to add that I entirely agree with what has fallen from my brother Martin, as to the case of *Cannan v Bryce*. If a person lends money, but with a doubt in his mind whether it is to be actually applied to an illegal purpose, it will be a question for the jury whether he meant it to be so applied; but if it were advanced in such a way that it could not possibly be a bribe to an illegal purpose, and afterwards it was turned to that use, neither *Cannan v Bryce*, nor any other case, decides that his act would be illegal. The case cited rests on the fact that the money was borrowed with the very object of satisfying an illegal purpose.

[1.] 3 B & A 179.

Devine *v* Scott and Johnston (1931) 66 ILTR 107

The plaintiff let premises to the second defendant, the first defendant acting as a guarantor. The contract did not refer to the purposes for which the premises were to be used. At the date of this contract, the premises had been sub-let by a former tenant to the second defendant who was already carrying on therein an illegal bookmaking business. The plaintiff then sued the defendants to recover rent due.

Thompson J.:

Since the letting was to the knowledge of the plaintiff's agent for the purpose of carrying on the business of a ready-money bookmaker, such purpose being illegal, the rent payable under the agreement cannot be recovered. I am also of opinion that the letting must be treated as a whole, and that no rent can be recovered in respect of a portion of the premises which was not being used for illegal purposes. The civil bill must be dismissed with costs.

F. CONTRACTS TO TRADE WITH ENEMIES OF THE STATE

Ross Bros Ltd *v* Edward Shaw & Co. [1917] 2 IR 367

In October 1915 the plaintiff sued the defendant for failure to deliver Belgian yarn pursuant to two contracts made in March 1914. Due to the German invasion of Ghent the yarn was unavailable to the defendant.

Gibson J.:

The problem before us, ... relates to illegality or impossibility created by our own law in consequence of war. Taking the contract embodying the custom as meaning that the yarn was to be drafted from Belgium (where meanwhile the contract assumes it might be legitimately kept), in pursuance of notifications delivered by the buyers to the sellers, the price of each lot when delivered constituting a debt referable-to the primary contract, what was the effect of the war and the occupation of Belgium on the contract and its fulfilment? The situation is not one where the inability to carry out the contract results from enemy blockade, or stoppage of trade routes, or destruction of a mail steamer carrying the order or of the cargo vessel returning. Suppose Belfast as well as Belgium was held by the enemy, could the plaintiffs serve a specification and insist that reasonable time was to be deemed to run at once? The delivery of each lot ordered would make a debt from plaintiffs to defendants, and from defendants to the Belgian companies. The constitution of these companies was not proved, nor is there any evidence of what is the Belgian law regulating them, whether they are local or created by the general law of the country, as is likely. The contracts to be performed as contemplated by the custom assumed as a tacit condition that delivery could, as regards our own law, be legally carried out from Belgium. Once Belgium became an enemy territory by reason of German occupation this was impossible.

. . . *Daimler Co. v Continental Tyre Co.*[1] shows that the companies, being under enemy control, could not have lawful business relations with Belfast. *Horlock v Beal*,[2] *Moss v Donohoe*,[3] and *Jager v Tolme & Runge*[4] also illustrate the effect of war on contracts. If import of goods from Belgium had been expressly prohibited by statute, would not such prohibition have made performance in the manner contemplated by the custom unlawful? Taking the custom as part of the contract terms, I am of opinion that when the writ was issued, on 31 January 1915, there was no enforceable cause of action. . . .

[1.] [1916] 1 AC 307.   [3.] 32 TLR 343.
[2.] [1916] 1 AC 496.   [4.] [1916] 1 KB 939.

Note

Gibson J. stated also that a contract for the sale and delivery 'as required' of particular goods of which the vendor is not producer must incorporate a trade custom that delivery need not be made until a reasonable time to enable the vendor to obtain the goods from the particular source from the receipt of the purchaser's specification.

G. Contracts that Breach Foreign Law

Stanhope v Hospitals Trust Ltd (No. 2) [1936] Ir J Rep 25

The plaintiff sold Irish sweepstakes tickets in Natal notwithstanding the fact that sweepstakes were illegal in Natal. He then posted the counter-foils to the defendant's Dublin office where the draw was to take place. When the tickets were not included in the draw, the plaintiff sued for damages for alleged breach of contract, negligence and consequent loss of reputation. The trial judge withdrew the case from the jury and dismissed the action on the ground that a court of law in this country will not lend its aid in enforcing a contract entered into expressly for an unlawful purpose.

Fitzgibbon J.:

In my opinion, the judgment for the defendants cannot stand. The learned trial judge based his direction upon the view taken by him that the whole cause of action was so tainted with illegality that the plaintiff cannot apply to the courts in this country to enforce any claim he may have for damages for breach of contract, or for negligence in the performance by the defendants of their contract with him. In the first place, one must see what the contract was before considering the question as to its illegality. In my opinion, the contract between the plaintiff and the defendants was contained in the offer by the latter, made upon the tickets issued by them and accepted by the plaintiff when he returned the counterfoils and the appropriate money, that they would put into the draw the counterfoils transmitted to them by him with the appropriate fee, and that such counterfoils would have their chance in a draw that was to take place on the result of the 'Grand National'. The contract seems to be created by the offer held out on the tickets, to be accepted by anyone who returns a counterfoil with the sum of 10s.

The plaintiff gave evidence from which the jury might have come to the conclusion—if that evidence should not be displaced by evidence to the contrary presented on the part of the defendants—that he returned a number of counterfoils with the appropriate sum of money, and that, through the negligence of the defendants, these counterfoils did not find their way into the drum, but of course the case was not heard to the end. It is quite possible that there might have been evidence produced by the defendants which would have negatived the receipt of the counterfoils by them, but all I can say is that on the plaintiff's evidence there was a case upon which it was open to the jury to find that the defendants received a number of counterfoils, and that, through their negligence, they did not find their way into the drum.

The contract was one which, to my mind, was to be performed in Dublin, and to be governed by the law of the place of performance, that is, the law of the Irish Free State, and I can find no evidence that the contract was illegal either by the law of this country or by the law of Natal. It was a contract entirely to be performed in Dublin—completed, possibly, by the posting, by the plaintiff in Natal, of the counterfoils and the appropriate money—but to be carried out in the Irish Free State where it was perfectly legal. In my opinion, therefore, the learned judge was not entitled to withdraw from the jury the issue whether there had been a breach of that contract, and to what damages, if any, the plaintiff had established his right in respect of that breach.

But the plaintiff has also claimed damages for a totally different thing, that is to say, damages occasioned to him by the loss of his trade as a professional seller of sweepstake tickets in Durban, a trade which the learned judge has decided was illegal by the law of the country in which it was carried on. I agree with the learned judge that the courts in this country will not allow themselves to be used for the purpose of establishing a claim for damages for the loss of an illegal business, and I think also that the judge has a duty, where the illegality appears either on the face of the pleadings or from the evidence, to take notice of it himself: Gedge's case; North Western Salt Co. Ltd v Electrolytic Alkali Co. Ltd. I do not think that the parties, even by agreement, could call upon the court, on an apparent illegality, to assist them to carry out an illegal transaction between themselves.

I confess I am unable to follow the contention that because no South African lawyer was called to prove that the trade carried on by the plaintiff in the town of Durban was illegal there, the court was entitled to disregard the express evidence of the plaintiff himself on the point. I agree that if foreign law is in dispute the proper evidence to establish what the foreign law is is that of a person who is an expert on that law, but if no issue is raised as to what the foreign law is, then I confess that it seems to me that the admissions of the parties themselves are as good legal evidence of foreign law as they are of any other question of fact on which the court has to come to a conclusion, and that where the plaintiff himself admits three times over that the trade he is carrying on is illegal there is no need to call any further evidence of its illegality. I do not know who should call evidence to contradict it, but at any rate the onus was on the defendants. That being so, it seems to me that the court had specific evidence that the plaintiff was claiming damages for the loss of an illegal trade, and that the court was not only justified in taking, but was bound to take, notice of that specific evidence, and was bound to see that the courts in this country were not made the means of enforcing that illegality.

As to the question of breach of contract, I do not think that the trial judge was justified in withdrawing it from the jury. There was not, in my opinion, a claim for damages for breach of an illegal contract. The contract in question was with the Hospitals Trust to put the plaintiff's tickets into the drum, and his claim is for whatever damages he can get, if he succeeds. Therefore, I think the judgment ought to be set aside, and the case sent back for trial on the question whether the plaintiff is entitled to damages, and, if so, how much, for breach of contract to put his tickets into the drum, provided that he can prove to the satisfaction of the jury that he did in fact send the money and the tickets, and that the defendants received them and failed to put the counterfoils into the drum.

(Murnaghan J. agreed and Kennedy C.J., while agreeing with the main issues, felt that non-expert evidence as to foreign law should not be sufficient evidence of legality or illegality.)

SECTION TWO—STATUTORY ILLEGALITY

Contracts may be invalidated by express or implied prohibitions in Acts of the Oireachtas or statutory instruments.

Gavin Low Ltd v William Field [1942] IR 86

Sullivan C.J.:

The plaintiffs are livestock salesmen and auctioneers, and on 12 December 1940, they exposed for sale in their sale yard a cow intended for human consumption which they had received for sale in the ordinary course of their business. It was bought by the defendant, a licensed victualler, for the sum of £16 10s, of which £4 was paid in cash and the balance £12 10s by cheque drawn by him in the plaintiffs' favour. On the same day the cow was slaughtered on the defendant's premises at Dun Laoghaire in the presence of the Veterinary Inspector of the Public Health Department of the Dun Laoghaire Borough Corporation, and he found that the carcase was infected with tuberculosis. On the following day 13 December, the carcase was destroyed in the corporation destructor as being unfit for human consumption, and the defendant stopped payment of his cheque. The plaintiff subsequently brought this action in the District Court to recover £12 10s, being the amount of the defendant's cheque, and recovered a decree for that amount. The defendant appealed to the Circuit Court, and on the hearing of that appeal this case was stated.

The learned judge of the Circuit Court found as a fact that the cow was unsound and unfit for human consumption at the time of its exposure for sale, but that this fact was unknown to the plaintiffs and could not have been ascertained prior to its slaughter without a veterinary test, the results of which would not be known for at least twenty four hours. The question submitted for the opinion of this court is whether upon the true construction of s. 133 of the Public Health (Ir.) Act 1878, as amended by ss 12 and 28 of the Public Health Acts Amendment Act 1890, the decree of the District Court should be reversed and the plaintiffs' claim dismissed on the ground that the said cheque was given for an illegal consideration.

S. 132 of the Act of 1878 empowers any sanitary officer of the sanitary authority to inspect and examine—*inter alia*—any animal exposed for sale or deposited in any place for the purpose of sale or of preparation for sale . . . and intended for the food of man, and, if such animal appears to be diseased, or unsound, or unwholesome, or unfit for the food of man, to seize and carry it away in order to have the same dealt with by a justice. S. 133 provides that if it appear to the justice that any animal so seized is diseased, or unsound, or unwholesome, or unfit for the food of man, he shall condemn the same and order it to be destroyed so as to prevent it being exposed for sale or used for the food of man; and that the person to whom the same belongs or did belong at the time of exposure for sale, or in whose possession or on whose premises the same was found, shall be liable to a penalty not exceeding £20 for every animal . . . so condemned, or at the discretion of the justice, without the infliction of a fine, to imprisonment for a term of not more than three months.

The English Public Health Act, 1875, contains in ss 116 and 117 similar provisions to those contained in ss 132 and 133 of the Irish Act.

The Public Health Acts Amendment Act 1890, s. 28, provides:

> (1) Ss 116 to 119 of the Public Health Act, 1875, ... shall extend and apply to all articles intended for the food of man, sold or exposed for sale, or deposited in any place for the purpose of sale, or of preparation for sale within the district of any local authority.
>
> (2) A Justice may condemn any such article, and order it to be destroyed or disposed of, as mentioned in s. 117 of the Public Health Act, 1875, if satisfied on complaint being made to him that such article is diseased, unsound, unwholesome, or unfit for the food of man, although the same has not been seized as mentioned in s. 116 of the said Act.

S. 12 provides that in the application of the Act to Ireland references to ss 116–119 of the Public Health Act 1875, shall be taken to be references to ss 132–135 of the Public Health (Ireland) Act 1878.

The question raised in this case is whether the effect of these sections is to render illegal the contract entered into by the plaintiffs and defendant on 12 December 1940. If that be the effect of the sections, then unquestionably the cheque given to the plaintiffs by the defendant as security for his liability under that contract is, as between the plaintiffs and the defendant, void. The contract is illegal if it is prohibited either expressly by those sections or by implication arising from the imposition of a penalty on the parties with the intention of prohibiting the contract. No question of express prohibition of the contract arises in this case—admittedly there is none; but it is conceded by counsel for the plaintiffs that, if the effect of the sections be to impose a penalty on the plaintiffs for entering into the contract, then the object of the legislature in this case was to prohibit such a contract, and it is prohibited by implication, and is therefore illegal.

It was contended on behalf of the plaintiffs: (1) that the effect of these sections was to impose a penalty, not on the *sale* of animals or articles intended for human consumption and unfit for that purpose, but on the exposure for sale, or deposit for the purposes of sale or of preparation for sale, of such animals or articles; and (2) that condemnation by a Justice of the Peace—now a Peace Commissioner (Courts of Justice Act 1924, s. 88, sub-s. 3)—is a condition precedent to a conviction for such offence.

In support of the first branch of this argument we were referred to the case of *Bothamley v Jolly*[1] in which the Court of King's Bench in England—Reading C.J., Ridley,

Darling, Avory and Rowlatt JJ.—held that the appellant, who had sold diseased meat but had not exposed it for sale, was not liable to conviction under the provisions of s. 117 of the Public Health Act 1875, as amended by s. 28 of the Public Health Acts Amendment Act 1890.

. . .

The authority of *Bothamley v Jolly* was not challenged by counsel for the defendant, in fact [counsel] said that it was an authority in their favour. They did not contend that the sections in question expressly penalised the contract for sale of a diseased animal or of unsound articles of food, what they did contend was that, if a contract be made for the sale of such animal or article when it is exposed for sale, then the exposure for sale and the sale together form one transaction, the entire of which is vitiated by the illegal exposure. In support of their argument they relied on the object that the legislature had in view in enacting the sections in question, as stated by Lord Coleridge C.J. in *Blaker v Tillstone*[2]: 'The object of the Act is that people shall not be exposed to the danger of eating and drinking poison, that anything that is likely to injure life shall not be sold,' and restated, in terms practically identical, by the judges of the Court of Appeal in *Hobbs v Winchester Corporation*.[3] That object would, they submitted, be defeated if the vendor could recover the price of the 'poison' which the purchaser had been induced to buy by seeing it exposed for sale.

The argument based on the policy of the Act loses in my mind much of its force when it is admitted that the Act does not penalise the sale of diseased or unsound articles of food. In my opinion the defendant's counsel, in order to succeed, must satisfy the court that the contract for sale and the exposure for sale should be regarded as together constituting one unlawful transaction. Sir Frederick Pollock in his *Principles of Contract* (6th ed.), 354–5 expresses the opinion that an agreement may be made void by its connection with an unlawful purpose, though subsequent to the execution of it. 'To have that effect, however,' he says, 'the connection must be something more than a mere conjunction of circumstances into which the unlawful transaction enters so that without it there would have been no occasion for the agreement. It must amount to a unity of design and purpose such that the agreement is really part and parcel of one entire unlawful scheme.'

I accept that as a correct statement of a legal principle which is, I think, applicable in the present case. In the view that I take of the facts in this case the connection between the unlawful exposure and the sale does not amount to a unity of design and purpose such that the sale is part of one entire unlawful scheme.

I am, therefore, of opinion that the contract for sale between the plaintiff and the defendant was not an illegal contract, and that the cheque, upon which the plaintiff sues, was not given for an illegal consideration.

Having come to that conclusion it is unnecessary that I should express any opinion on the question whether condemnation by a Peace Commissioner of the diseased animal is a condition precedent to conviction for unlawfully exposing it for sale. . . .

Murnaghan J.:

. . .

In the present case there was no seizure and condemnation, which, as I think, is by this statute made essential before a penalty can be imposed. In these circumstances no illegality has been shown to have existed, and in my opinion there is no defence to the action. . . .

(Geoghegan J. concurred.)

Meredith J.:

Counsel for the plaintiffs did not dispute the proposition established in *Cope v Rowlands*[4] that where a penalty is imposed by statute the penalty implies a prohibition; but he contended, in effect, that what is impliedly prohibited and that in respect of which the penalty is imposed must be identical, in other words, that the implied prohibition and the offence as punishable must be co-extensive. This contention puts too narrow a construction on the well established principle.

First of all, it is clear that wherever a penalty is imposed something is impliedly prohibited, and the only question is what that something is. That for which alone the penalty is imposed may contain elements or ingredients, such as conditions subsequent, that from the nature of the case could not form a subject matter of prohibition, so that if the prohibition and the punishable offence had to be co-extensive, nothing would be impliedly prohibited at all, which is absurd.

Secondly, the question is from first to last simply one of implication, and implication depends on considerations of logic and common sense. On these considerations elements or ingredients of the offence as punishable may be rejected in the statement of what is impliedly prohibited, or something may be prohibited by implication that is not part of the punishable offence at all. . . .

. . . That disposes of the two points relied on by the defendant. |Counsel for the plaintiffs'| submission that a sale *per se* is not an offence under the Act is perfectly sound; but the inference, that a sale for the very purpose of which there was an impliedly prohibited exposure for sale is not impliedly prohibited, just as much as the exposure for that sale, is a *non sequitur*.

The legislature may choose to intervene *in limine* and cut short action that may in the natural course of events lead to what is the real mischief aimed at—it may, in other words, seek to nip the mischief in the bud. Prohibition of the bud is then prohibition of the blossom. If exposure for sale is impliedly prohibited, then the sale on such exposure is also impliedly prohibited.

But—and this was the defendant's second point—the exposure for sale is not an offence under the statute, unless there is subsequent condemnation. But that is not the point. The question is whether the exposure for sale of the cow, when it was, as the learned Circuit Court Judge has held, in fact unfit for human consumption, was *impliedly* prohibited. From the nature of the case a prohibited act must be prohibited and the offence be complete, at the time it is committed, and the prohibition cannot be conditional on a subsequent condemnation. A commandment against stealing provided the theft is discovered would be an absurdity.

It is clear, therefore, that the exposure for sale in this case was unlawful, and that so also was the sale on that exposure, and that the consideration for the cheque was an illegal consideration, and that the contract was void *ab initio*, and that the plaintiffs' claim must be dismissed and the question asked by the learned Circuit Court Judge answered in the affirmative.

O'Byrne J.:

For the purpose of attaining its object, the legislature penalises the various preliminary steps which normally precede and lead up to a contract of sale. Exposure of such food for sale for human consumption is an offence, so also is conveying it for sale or depositing it any place for the purpose of sale or of preparation for sale. Did the legislature by these penalties seek to prevent the sale of such food, and was that the intention, or part of the intention, of Parliament, as gathered from a reasonable construction of the Act? I have come to the conclusion that the answer to that question must be in the affirmative. When one considers the general scope and nature of the Acts, it seems difficult to justify such a construction as would recognise the validity of a contract arising out of an exposure for sale, though the exposure itself is made a criminal offence and, as it seems to me, is made such offence for the very purpose of preventing the sale.

For these reasons I am of opinion that the question submitted to us by the Circuit Court Judge should be answered in the affirmative.

1. [1915] 3 KB 415.
2. [1894] 1 QB 335, at p. 347.
3. [1910] 2 KB 471.
4. 2 M & W 149.

St John Shipping Corp. v Joseph Rank Ltd [1957] 1 QB 267

The plaintiffs, ship owners, contracted to transport grain to the defendants in England. On arrival the ship was found to be overloaded contrary to the Merchant Shipping (Safety and Load Line Conventions) Act, 1932 and the master was prosecuted and fined. The defendants withheld a sum equivalent to the freight on overall additional cargo carried by which the ship was found to be overloaded. The plaintiffs sued for the unpaid portion. The defendants claimed that since the contract of carriage was performed in such a way as to infringe the Act, the plaintiffs permitted an illegality which prevented them from enforcing the contract at all.

Devlin J.:

. . . It is a misfortune for the defendants that the legal weapon which they are wielding is so much more potent than it need be to achieve their purpose. Believing, rightly or wrongly, that the plaintiffs have deliberately committed a serious infraction of the Act and one which has placed their property in jeopardy, the defendants wish to do no more than to take the profit out of the plaintiffs' dealing. But the principle which they invoke for this purpose cares not at all for the element of deliberation or for the gravity of the infraction, and does not adjust the penalty to the profits unjustifiably earned. The defendants cannot succeed unless they claim the right to retain the whole freight and to keep it whether the offence was accidental or deliberate, serious or trivial. The application of this principle to a case such as this is bound to lead to startling results. . . . A shipowner who accidentally overloads by a fraction of an inch will not be able to recover from any of the shippers or consignees a penny of the freight. There are numerous other illegalities which a ship might commit in the course of the voyage which would have the same effect. . . . Carriers by land are in no better position; again [counsel for the defendants] does not shrink from saying that the owner of a lorry could not recover against the consignees the cost of goods transported in it if in the course of the journey it was driven a mile an hour over its permitted speed. If this is really the law, it is very unenterprising of cargo owners and consignees to wait until a criminal conviction has been secured before denying their liabilities. A service of trained observers on all our main roads would soon pay for itself. An effective patrol of the high seas would probably prove too expensive, but the maintenance of a corps of vigilantes in all principal ports would be well worthwhile when one considers that the smallest infringement of the statute or a regulation made thereunder would relieve all the cargo owners on the ship from all liability for freight.

Of course, as [counsel] says, one must not be deterred from enunciating the correct principle of law because it may have startling or even calamitous results. But I confess I approach the investigation of a legal proposition which has results of this character with a prejudice in favour of the idea that there may be a flaw in the argument somewhere.

. . . There are two general principles. The first is that a contract which is entered into with the object of committing an illegal act is unenforceable. The application of this principle depends upon proof of the intent, at the time the contract was made, to break the law; if the intent is mutual the contract is not enforceable at all, and, if unilateral, it is unenforceable at the suit of the party who is proved to have it. This principle is not involved here. Whether or not the overloading was deliberate when it was done, there is no proof that it was contemplated when the contract of carriage was made. The second principle is that the court will not enforce a contract which is expressly or impliedly prohibited by statute. If the contract is of this class it does not matter what the intent of the parties is; if the statute prohibits the contract, it is unenforceable whether the parties meant to break the law or not. A significant distinction between the two classes is this. In the former class you have only to look and see what acts the statute prohibits; it does not matter whether or not it prohibits a contract; if a contract is deliberately made to do a prohibited act, that contract will be unenforceable. In the latter class, you have to consider not what acts the statute prohibits, but what contracts it prohibits; but you are not concerned at all with the intent of the parties; if the parties enter into a prohibited contract, that contract is unenforceable.
. . .

. . . the question always is whether the statute meant to prohibit the contract which is sued upon. One of the tests commonly used, and frequently mentioned in the later cases, in order to ascertain the true meaning of the statute is to inquire whether or not the object of the statute was to protect the public or a class of persons, . . . If in considering the effect of the statute the only inquiry that you have to make is whether an act is illegal, it cannot matter for whose benefit the statute was passed; the fact that the statute makes the act illegal is of itself enough. But if you are considering whether a contract not expressly prohibited by the Act is impliedly prohibited, such considerations are relevant in order to determine the scope of the statute. . . .

. . . The fundamental question is whether the statute means to prohibit the contract. The statute is to be construed in the ordinary way; one must have regard to all relevant considerations and no single consideration, however important, is conclusive.

Two questions are involved. The first—and the one which hitherto has usually settled the matter—is: does the statute mean to prohibit contracts at all? But if this be answered in the affirmative, then one must ask: does this contract belong to the class which the statute intends to prohibit? For example, a person is forbidden by statute from using an unlicensed vehicle on the highway. If one asks oneself whether there is in such an enactment an implied prohibition of all contracts for the use of unlicensed vehicles, the answer may well be that there is, and that contracts of hire would be unenforceable. But if one asks oneself whether there is an implied prohibition of contracts for the carriage of goods by unlicensed vehicles or for the repairing of unlicensed vehicles or for the garaging of unlicensed vehicles, the answer may well be different. The answer might be that collateral contracts of this sort are not within the ambit of the statute.

. . .

In my judgment, contracts for the carriage of goods are not within the ambit of this statute at all. A court should not hold that any contract or class of contracts is prohibited by statute unless there is a clear implication, or 'necessary inference', as Parke B. put it, that the statute so intended.[1] If a contract has as its whole object the doing of the very act which the statute prohibits, it can be argued that you can hardly make sense of a statute which forbids an act and yet permits to be made a contract to do it; that is a clear implication. But unless you get a clear implication of that sort, I think that a court ought to be very slow to hold that a statute intends to interfere with the rights and remedies given by the ordinary law of contract. Caution in this respect is, I think, especially necessary in these times when so much of commercial life is governed by regulations of one sort or another, which may easily be broken without wicked intent. Persons who deliberately set out to break the law cannot expect to be aided in a court of justice, but it is a different matter when the law is unwittingly broken. To nullify a bargain in such circumstances frequently means that in a case— perhaps of such triviality that no authority would have felt it worthwhile to prosecute—a seller, because he cannot enforce his civil rights, may forfeit a sum vastly in excess of any penalty that a criminal court would impose; and the sum forfeited will not go into the public purse but into the pockets of someone who is lucky enough to pick up the windfall or astute enough to have contrived to get it. It is questionable how far this contributes to public morality. . . .

. . .

On [counsel for the defendants'] third point I take the law from the dictum in *Beresford v Royal Insurance Co. Ltd*[2] that was adopted and applied by Lord Atkin: 'no system of jurisprudence can with reason include amongst the rights which it enforces rights directly resulting to the person asserting them from the crime of that person.' I observe in the first place that in the Court of Appeal in the same case Lord Wright[3] doubted whether this principle applied to all statutory offences. His doubt was referred to by Denning L.J. in *Marles v Philip Trant & Sons*,[4] which I have already cited. The distinction is much to the point here. The Act of 1932 imposes a penalty which is itself designed to deprive the offender of the benefits of his crime. It would be a curious thing if the operation could be performed twice—once by the criminal law and then again by the civil. It would be curious, too, if in a case in which the magistrates had thought fit to impose only a nominal fine, their decision could, in effect, be overridden in a civil action. But the question whether the rule applies to statutory offences is an important one which I do not wish to decide in the present case. The dicta of Lord Wright and Denning L.J. suggest that there are cases where its application would be morally unjustifiable; but it is not clear that they go as far as saying that the application would not be justified in law. I prefer, therefore, to deal with [counsel's] submission in another way.

The rights which cannot be enforced must be those 'directly resulting' from the crime. That means, I think, that for a right to money or to property to be unenforceable the property or money must be identifiable as something to which, but for the crime, the plaintiff would have had no right or title. That cannot be said in this case. The amount of the profit which the plaintiffs made from the crime, that is to say, the amount of freight which, but for the overloading, they could not have earned on this voyage, was, as I have said, £2,295. The quantity of cargo consigned to the defendants was approximately thirty five per cent of the whole and, therefore, even if it were permissible to treat the benefit as being divisible *pro rata* over the whole of the cargo, the amount embodied in the claim against the defendants would not be more than thirty five per cent of £2,300. That would not justify the withholding of £2,000. The fact is that the defendants and another cargo owner have between them withheld money, not on a basis that is proportionate to the claim against them, but so as to wipe out the improper profit on the whole of the cargo. . . .

. . .

The result is that there must be judgment for the plaintiffs for £2,000. . . .

[1] 2 M & W 159.
[2] [1938] AC 586; 54 TLR 789; [1938] 2 All ER 602.
[3] [1937] 2 KB 197, 220; 53 TLR 583; [1937] 2 All ER 243.
[4] [1954] 1 QB 29, 37.

Archbolds (Freightage) Ltd v S. Spanglett Ltd [1961] 1 QB 375
The defendant questioned the validity of a contract to transport goods
when the carrier was not properly licensed. Under the Road Traffic Act
1933 the use of goods vehicles for carriage of goods without a licence was
prohibited.

Pearce L.J.:

[Having referred to Devlin J.'s judgment in St John Shipping Corp. v Rank
[1957] 1 QB 267 he continued:]

The object of the Road and Rail Traffic Act 1933 was not (in this connection) to
interfere with the owner of goods or his facilities for transport, but to control those
who provided the transport, with a view to promoting its efficiency. Transport of goods
was not made illegal but the various licence holders were prohibited from encroaching
on one another's territory, the intention of the Act being to provide an orderly and
comprehensive service. Penalties were provided for those licence holders who went
outside the bounds of their allotted spheres. These penalties apply to those using the
vehicle but not to the goods owner. Though the latter could be convicted of aiding and
abetting any breach, the restrictions were not aimed at him. Thus a contract of
carriage was, in the sense used by Devlin J., 'collateral', and it was not impliedly
forbidden by the statute.

This view is supported by common sense and convenience. If the other view were
held it would have far-reaching effects. For instance, if a carrier induces me (who am in
fact ignorant of any illegality) to entrust goods to him and negligently destroys them,
he would only have to show that (though unknown to me) his licence had expired, or
did not properly cover the transportation, or that he was uninsured, and I should then
be without a remedy against him. Or, again, if I ride in a taxicab and the driver leaves
me stranded in some deserted spot, he would only have to show that he was (though
unknown to me) unlicensed or uninsured, and I should be without remedy. This
appears to me an undesirable extension of the implications of a statute.

Lord Wright said in Vita Food Products Inc. v Unus Shipping Co. Ltd[1]: 'Each case has to
be considered on its merits. Nor must it be forgotten that the rule by which contracts
not expressly forbidden by statute or declared to be void are in proper cases nullified
for disobedience to a statute is a rule of public policy only, and public policy understood
in a wider sense may at times be better served by refusing to nullify a bargain save on
serious and sufficient grounds.' If the court too readily implies that a contract is forbidden by statute, it takes it out of its own power (so far as that contract is concerned)
to discriminate between guilt and innocence. But if the court makes no such implication, it still leaves itself with the general power, based on public policy, to hold those
contracts unenforceable which are ex facie unlawful, and also to refuse its aid to guilty
parties in respect of contracts which to the knowledge of both can only be performed
by a contravention of the statute: see Nash v Stevenson Transport Ltd,[2] or which though
apparently lawful are intended to be performed illegally or for an illegal purpose, for
example, Pearce v Brooks.[3]

It is for the defendants to show that contracts by the owner for the carriage of
goods are within the ambit of the implied prohibition of the Road and Rail Traffic Act
1933. In my judgment they have not done so.

[1] [1939] AC 277, 293; 55 TLR 402;   [2] [1936] 2 KB 128; 52 TLR 331.
    [1939] 1 All ER 513.   [3] (1866) LR 1 Ex 213.

Hortensius Ltd and John Durack *v* Kenneth L. Bishop and Others, Trustees of the Trustee Savings Bank, Dublin [1989] ILRM 294

The defendants purchased all the loans and the securities given thereon of the Royal Trust Bank when the latter ceased to carry on banking business. The consent of the Minister for Finance was obtained for this purchase. The portfolio included a loan secured by a mortgage on premises owned by the first plaintiff and a personal guarantee from the second plaintiff. The first plaintiff failed to meet its obligations under the loan agreement and proceedings were instituted seeking *inter alia* declarations that the sale of the debt and the assignment of the mortgage to the defendants was void and unlawful. They claimed that since s. 3 of the Trustee Savings Bank Act 1965 did not authorise the use of depositors' funds for the purchase of funds any consent given by the minister was *ultra vires* and void. The transaction thus fell to be considered under s. 15 of the Trustee Savings Bank Act 1863 which did not give the defendants power to purchase the Royal Trust Bank's portfolio.

Costello J.:

(1) The doctrine of *ultra vires* contracts is one which relates to the acts and contracts of public authorities and companies. As applied to companies it means that any contract made otherwise than in the exercise of powers conferred by the company's memorandum of association is void. But the bank in this case is not a company and s. 15 is a section which imposes a statutory duty on trustees and prohibits the use of funds otherwise than in accordance with that duty. The *ultra vires* doctrine does not apply in such circumstances. What was involved here was a contract entered into in breach of duty imposed by statute, not an *ultra vires* contract. The plaintiffs cannot therefore successfully claim that the contracts are unenforceable because they were *ultra vires* the trustees' powers.

(2) At common law the enforcement of certain contracts was regarded as being against public policy and such contracts were termed 'illegal'. Illegal contracts included those which tend to injure the public service, or pervert the course of justice, or abuse the legal process, or are contrary to good morals, or restrain trade. Also included are those whose objects are clearly illegal, so that a contract which cannot be performed without a breach of the criminal law is unenforceable at common law. But in this case we are concerned with a statutory provision which prohibits the trustees from entering into the contracts of 19 December 1983, not a provision which made illegal the objects of the contracts they entered into. It seems to me therefore that the plaintiffs cannot rely on the common law rules relating to the unenforceability of illegal contracts to justify the claims for relief made in this action.

(3) It remains then to consider whether on a true construction of the 1863 Act the contracts in suit are void and therefore unenforceable. Some statutes may expressly declare certain types of contract to be void and unenforceable (without declaring them to be illegal) as does s. 18 of the Gaming Act 1845 which provides that all agreements by way of wagering shall be null and void and which prohibits any action brought to recover a sum alleged to have been won on a wager. Others may prohibit the making of certain contracts and impose penalties for doing so but remain silent as to the civil rights of the parties to them; it is then a question of the construction of the statute as to whether the contract entered into between the parties is to be regarded as an illegal one. But in this case the 1863 Act did not make illegal *contracts* for the purchase of

loans—it prohibited the trustees *from entering into* such contracts, which is not the same thing. There is, it seems to me, an important distinction between a statutory provision which makes it illegal for a trustee to enter into certain types of contracts and a statutory provision which makes certain types of contract illegal. In the former case (which is what happened on 19 December 1983) what the courts have to consider is what are the legal consequences which flow from a contract entered into by trustees contrary to the statutory provisions by which their trust is governed, in the latter case (which is not this case) what the court would have to consider are the consequences of entering into a contract declared by statute to be an illegal one.

(4) I have no doubt that had the Royal Trust Bank attempted to resile from their agreement with the trustees and had the trustees claimed that it be specifically performed their claim would have failed because the courts of equity will not give relief to a trustee acting in breach of trust. But here we have a completed transaction. It is well established that if a trustee has, in breach of trust, converted trust property into some other form, the property into which it has been converted becomes subject to the trust (see Underhill *Law of Trusts and Trustees*, (1987 ed.), 751). And so if a trustee actually acquires any property in breach of trust his wrongful act does not render the transaction void. That seems to me the position in this case. The statute can properly be regarded as one regulating the manner in which the trustees of savings banks to which the Act applies are to manage the funds which come into their possession. Should they act contrary to its provisions then the law relating to breach of trust by trustees should apply. This means that the property in the choses in action assigned to the trustees and in the freehold and leasehold conveyed and assigned to them by the agreements of 19 December 1983 vested in the trustees notwithstanding their breach of trust. And it follows that they can enforce the rights they thus obtained against the plaintiffs. In reaching this conclusion I have not overlooked the argument advanced by |counsel| on their behalf based on the long established principles most recently illustrated in *Euro-Diam Ltd v Bathurst* |1988| 2 WLR 517. That was a case involving a consignment of diamonds to Germany which were there stolen and which resulted in proceedings to enforce a policy of insurance relating to them. A false value had been inserted in the invoice sent to the German consignee for the purpose of avoiding German import tax and the claim on foot of the policy of insurance was resisted on the ground *inter alia* that the contract of insurance was tainted by the illegality relating to the consignment contract and was therefore unenforceable. The law relating to a defence based on the maxim *ex turpi causa non oritur actio* was helpfully summarised by Kerr L.J. at 526–7. But for reasons already explained I do not think that this maxim is of any avail to the plaintiffs in the present case. In my view the plaintiffs could not resist a claim brought against them by the trustees on the ground that the illegality of the contracts of 19 December 1983 has so tainted the original contracts between the plaintiffs and Royal Trust Bank (Ireland) Ltd that the court would not allow the trustees to enforce them. For reasons already pointed out the contracts of 19 December 1983 were not themselves 'illegal' contracts, so that the doctrine of tainting does not arise. Furthermore public policy has never required that trustees should be deprived of the right to enforce propriety claims over property acquired in breach of trust. In my judgment therefore the contravention of s. 15 which occurred does not invalidate the transaction of 19 December 1983 and the trustees are entitled to enforce the rights they acquired in the agreement and mortgage of 6 July 1982.

I turn now to deal with the alternative final submission made on the trustees' behalf by |counsel|. He argues, and I think argues correctly, that even if the transaction of 19 December 1983 can be regarded as an illegal one, once property has been delivered under it the fact that by reason of the illegality the trustees could not originally have enforced the agreement does not mean that the property in the interests they acquired has not passed to them. I think the statement to this effect in *Chitty on Contracts*, (25th ed.) para. 1169 is correct and is borne out by the authorities. *Singh v Ali* |1960| AC 167 was a case dealing with the unlawful sale of a motor lorry. In the course of his judgment Lord Denning made some observations of a general nature (subsequently approved of in *Belvoir Finance Co. v Stapleton* |1971| 1 QB 210 at 219). 'Although the transaction between the plaintiff and the defendant was illegal', he said:

> nevertheless it was fully executed and carried out; and on that account it was effective to pass the property in the lorry to the plaintiff. . . . The reason is because the transferor, having fully achieved his unworthy end, cannot be allowed to turn around and repudiate the means by which he did it—he cannot throw over the transfer. And the transferee, having obtained the property, can assert this title to it against all the world, not because he has any merit of his own, but because there is no one who can assert a better title to it. The court does not confiscate the property because of the illegality. . . .

And as Chitty points out (in para. 1169) this principle also applies in the case of real property so that where a person takes a lease intending to use it for an immoral purpose he acquires an interest in the executed lease despite the intention to use it for the immoral purpose. I think it follows that even if the agreements of 19 December 1983 can be regarded as illegal contracts which the trustees could not have enforced against the Royal Trust Bank (Ireland) Ltd once the consideration provided in them has been paid, and the property referred to in them transferred to the trustees they are not void contracts. I think therefore the trustees now have a good title to the choses in action (including the debt due by the plaintiff company and the right to enforce the guarantee of the second-named plaintiff under the agreements of 6 July 1982) as well as to the properties transferred to them by the agreements (including the fee simple of No. 62 Clontarf Road, Dublin). This means that the trustees are entitled to enforce the rights they have acquired by virtue of these agreements against both plaintiffs.

The claims the plaintiffs have made in this action must fail. To avoid doubts I would propose to dismiss the claims having recited that the court is satisfied that the defendants have acquired a good title to the property real and personal referred to in the agreements of 19 December 1983 and that they are entitled to enforce the rights obtained by them against the plaintiffs. The order should also declare the trustees' entitlement to the moneys on deposit in the joint names of the parties' solicitors.

Note

The High Court of Australia has adopted a more logical approach to this area.

Yango Pastoral Co. Pty Ltd and Others *v* First Chicago Australia Ltd and Others [1978] 139 CLR 410

S. 8 of The Banking Act 1959 (Cth) prohibited a corporate body from carrying on banking business in Australia without authority. Despite the fact that First Chicago Australia Ltd did not possess the relevant authority, it made a loan to the first appellant which was secured by a mortgage incorporating a guarantee given by the other appellants. When the respondent sued for default in repayment, the appellants pleaded illegality.

Gibbs A.C.J.:

There are four main ways in which the enforceability of a contract may be affected by a statutory provision which renders particular conduct unlawful: (1) The contract may be to do something which the statute forbids; (2) The contract may be one which the statute expressly or impliedly prohibits; (3) The contract, although lawful on its face, may be made in order to effect a purpose which the statute renders unlawful; or (4) The contract, although lawful according to its own terms, may be performed in a manner which the statute prohibits.

In the present case we are not concerned with the first of these possible situations. Clearly s. 8 does not render it unlawful to borrow or lend money or to give and take a mortgage, supported by guarantees, to secure its repayment. The contract sued upon was therefore not to do anything which s. 8 forbids. The principal question in the case is whether s. 8, on its proper construction, prohibited the making or performance of the contract. As will be seen if that question is answered in the negative, it will not be possible to say that the contract cannot be enforced on the ground that it was made in order to effect an unlawful purpose or was performed in an unlawful manner.

It is often said that a contract expressly or impliedly prohibited by statute is void and unenforceable. That statement is true as a general rule, but for complete accuracy it needs qualification, because it is possible for a statute in terms to prohibit a contract and yet to provide, expressly or impliedly, that the contract will be valid and enforceable. However, cases are likely to be rare in which a statute prohibits a contract but nevertheless reveals an intention that it shall be valid and enforceable, and in most cases it is sufficient to say, as has been said in many cases of authority, that the test is whether the contract is prohibited by the statute. Where a statute imposes a penalty upon the making or performance of a contract, it is a question of construction whether the statute intends to prohibit the contract in this sense, that is, to render it void and unenforceable, or whether it intends only that the penalty for which it provides shall be inflicted if the contract is made or performed.

The question whether a statute, on its proper construction, intends to vitiate a contract made in breach of its provisions, is one which must be determined in accordance with the ordinary principles that govern the construction of statutes. 'The determining factor is the true effect and meaning of the statute' (St John Shipping Corp. v Joseph Rank Ltd[1]). 'One must have regard to the language used and to the scope and purpose of the statute.' (Archbolds Freightage Ltd. v S. Spanglett Ltd[2]). One consideration that has been regarded as important in a great many cases, . . . is whether the object of the statute— or one of its objects—is the protection of the public. An antithesis is commonly suggested between an intention to protect the public and an intention simply to secure the revenue, and it is said that when the former intention appears the contract must be taken to be prohibited, whereas if the intention is only to protect the revenue the statute will not be construed as imposing a prohibition on contracts. The question whether the statute was passed for the protection of the public is one test of whether it was intended to vitiate a contract made in breach of its provisions, but I am with respect in full agreement with the views expressed in St John Shipping Corp. v Joseph Rank Ltd and Shaw v Groom[3] that it is not the only test. It would be contrary to reason and principle to allow one circumstance to override all other considerations in the interpretation of a statute. As Devlin J. said in St John Shipping Corp. v Joseph Rank Ltd: 'The fundamental question is whether the statute means to prohibit the contract. The statute is to be construed in the ordinary way: one must have regard to all relevant considerations and no single consideration, however important is conclusive.'

Mason J.:

. . .

The principle that a contract the making of which is expressly or impliedly prohibited by statute is illegal and void is one of long standing but it has always been recognised that the principle is necessarily subject to any contrary intention manifested by the statute. It is perhaps more accurate to say that the question whether a contract prohibited by statute is void is, like the associated question whether the statute prohibits the contract, a question of statutory construction and that the principle to which I have referred does no more than enunciate the ordinary rule which will be applied when the statute itself is silent upon the question. Primarily, then, it is a matter of construing the statute and in construing the statute the court will have regard not only to its language, which may or may not touch upon the question, but also to the scope and purpose of the statute for which inferences may be drawn as to the legislative intention regarding the extent and the effect of the prohibition which the statute contains.

The first question is: Does s. 8 expressly prohibit the making of a contract of loan? The question must, I think, be answered in the negative. . . .

. . .

The next question is whether by implication, that is by way of necessary inference, such a prohibition can be discovered in the section. . . .

. . .

Where, as here, a statute imposes a penalty for contravention of an express prohibition against carrying on a business without a licence or an authority and the business is carried on by entry into contracts, the question is whether the statute intends merely to penalise the person who contravenes the prohibition or whether it intends to go further and prohibit contracts the making of which constitute the carrying on of the business. In deciding this question the court will take into account the scope and purpose of the statute and the consequences of the suggested implication with a view to ascertaining whether it would conduce to, or frustrate, the object of the statute.

. . .

In this context there is little to be said for the view that the statute intends to prohibit contracts made by unauthorised banks in the course of carrying on banking business. To do so would be to prejudice depositors, not to protect them. The implication of such a prohibition would deny to innocent depositors the right to recover moneys deposited unlawfully with persons carrying on banking business because *ex hypothesi* the prohibited contract would be illegal and void. To place the defendants' interpretation upon the statute would confer an extraordinary advantage on the wrongdoer in enabling it to resist repayment of moneys deposited with it. In this respect the advantage given to the wrongdoer might conceivably go some distance towards outweighing the punishment imposed upon it by way of penalty under s. 8.

It is not rational to suppose that the Parliament intended to inflict such dire consequences on innocent depositors. Nor is it rational to suppose that the Parliament intended to advantage innocent borrowers whilst penalising innocent depositors. Even less is it to be supposed that the Parliament intended to invalidate the wide range of commercial and other securities which are brought into existence in the course of carrying on a banking business and thereby to inflict loss on the many persons acquiring such securities. I therefore conclude that the purpose of the Act is adequately served by the imposition of the very heavy penalty which is prescribed for a contravention of s. 8 and that it does not prohibit and thereby invalidate contracts and transactions entered into in the course of carrying on banking business in breach of the section.

. . .

In my opinion the plaintiff is able to enforce the mortgage against the defendants in this case as the contract is not rendered void, either expressly or impliedly, by the Act and considerations of public policy operate, in the circumstances, so as to make inapplicable the maxim *ex turpi causa non oritur actio*.

1. [1957] 1 QB 267, at 286.
2. [1961] 1 QB 374, at 390.
3. [1970] 2 QB 504, at 518.

Note

The *Yango Pastoral Co.* decision was relied upon by Leggatt J. in *Stewart v Oriental Fire and Marine Insurance Co. Ltd* [1984] 3 All ER 777. This latter case was, however, overruled in the case of *Phoenix General Insurance Co. of Greece SA v Administratia Asigurarilor de Stat* [1987] 2 All ER 125.

Phoenix General Insurance Co. of Greece SA *v* Administratia Asigurarilor de Stat [1987] 2 All ER 125

The plaintiffs were insurers authorised under the Insurance Companies Act 1974. In 1978 new regulations were introduced reclassifying the various categories of insurance. The plaintiffs entered into reinsurance contracts with the defendants, but when they submitted their claims, the defendants refused to pay claiming that the contracts were illegal due to the plaintiff's lack of authorisation. The Court of Appeal held that transitional provisions in the regulations provided the necessary authorisation. However it went on to consider what the position would have been if no authorisation existed.

Kerr L.J.:

(i) Where a statute prohibits both parties from concluding or performing a contract when both or either of them have no authority to do so, the contract is impliedly prohibited: see *Mahmoud and Ispahani's* case [1921] 2 KB 716, [1921] All ER Rep 217 and its analysis by Pearce L.J. in the *Archbolds* case [1961] 1 All ER 417, [1961] 1 QB 374 with which Devlin L.J. agreed.

(ii) But where a statute merely prohibits one party from entering into a contract without authority and/or imposes a penalty on him if he does so (i.e. a unilateral prohibition) it does not follow that the contract itself is impliedly prohibited so as to render it illegal and void. Whether or not the statute has this effect depends on considerations of public policy in the light of the mischief which the statute is designed to prevent, its language, scope and purpose, the consequences for the innocent party, and any other relevant considerations. . . .

(iii) The Insurance Companies Act 1974 only imposes a unilateral prohibition on unauthorised insurers. If this were merely to prohibit them from carrying on 'the business of effecting contracts of insurance' of a class for which they have no authority, then it would clearly be open to the court to hold that considerations of public policy preclude the implication that such contracts are prohibited and void. But unfortunately the unilateral prohibition is not limited to the business of 'effecting contracts of insurance' but extends to the business of 'carrying out contracts of insurance'. This is a form of statutory prohibition, albeit only unilateral, which is not covered by any authority. However, . . . I can see no convincing escape from the conclusion that this extension of the prohibition has the unfortunate effect that contracts made without authorisation are prohibited by necessary implication and therefore void. Since the statute prohibits the insurer from carrying out the contract (of which the most obvious example is paying claims), how can the insured require the insurer to do an act which is expressly forbidden by statute? And how can a court enforce a contract against an unauthorised insurer when Parliament has expressly prohibited him from carrying it out? In that situation there is simply no room for the introduction of considerations of public policy. As Parker J. said in the *Bedford* case [1984] 3 All ER 766 at 775, [1985] QB 966 at 986: ' . . . once it is concluded that on its true construction the Act prohibited both contract and performance, that is the public policy'.

(iv) It follows that, however reluctantly, I feel bound to agree with the analysis of Parker J. in the *Bedford* case and his conclusion that contracts of insurance made by unauthorised insurers are prohibited by the 1974 Act in the sense that they are illegal and void, and therefore unenforceable.

. . .

. . . But, with all due respect, the reliance which Leggatt J. placed on the decision of the High Court of Australia in the *Yango* case appears to me to be untenable. The statutory prohibition in that case (s. 8 of the Banking Act 1959) merely prohibited a body corporate from carrying on any banking business without authority, and imposed a daily penalty for contravention. It made no reference whatever to any contracts concluded by persons carrying on banking business without authority. This was the main basis for the conclusion of the High Court, but it cannot have any direct application here. Furthermore, it was held that the contracts in question, a loan, mortgage and guarantee, were not central to the business of banking. But this would be an obviously impossible argument in relation to contracts of insurance in the context of insurance business.

Note

It was observed in this case that this decision was based very much on its own facts, most statutes leaving room for a more purposive approach.

SECTION THREE—THE CONSEQUENCES OF ILLEGALITY

A. WHERE THE CONTRACT IS UNLAWFUL ON ITS FACE

Gray v Cathcart (1899) 33 ILTR 35

Under the Belfast Corporation Acts it was a penal offence to occupy a house not provided with proper yard accommodation. Despite being ordered to leave his house for this reason by the local authority the plaintiff let the house to the defendant. The latter was informed of the local authority's orders. Later the plaintiff sued for the balance of rent due under the letting agreement.

Johnson J.:

Everyone commits a misdemeanour who does any act forbidden by a statute; accordingly when these parties entered into the agreement to occupy a house which had been condemned it was a contract to do that which the statute says that you could not do. It was a contract to do an illegal thing, and, though the parties might go through the form, yet such a contract is not binding, and cannot be sued upon.

James L. Murphy & Co. Ltd v Crean [1915] 1 IR 111

The facts:

The defendant was married in 1890 to Mr Eugene Crean, who had a leasehold interest in the premises No. 3 Douglas Street. They had been married for about two years, when it appears to have been arranged between the defendant and her husband that she should commence to trade as a publican in her own name in these premises. She had not, however, a publican's licence, nor, so far as the evidence goes, was there ever a publican's licence attached to No. 3 Douglas Street. As the law then stood, it was legally possible to obtain a licence for a house which was previously unlicensed, but an applicant for a new licence was almost invariably confronted by the objection that the number of houses already licensed in the locality were ample for the wants of the community. To meet this objection a certain practice, of which the court has judicial notice, sprung up; and this was, that the applicant for a licence for a house previously unlicensed should acquire an existing licence attached to another house, and, in order to remove the objection that the new licence would increase the number of public-houses, should give an undertaking to the court to extinguish the existing licence which he had acquired. In substance this was the course adopted by the defendant when she applied for a licence for the house 3 Douglas Street. She did not indeed herself acquire a licence which had been attached to other premises, but one was acquired for her, and placed at her disposal, so that she might remove any objection on the ground of an increase in the number of licensed houses. The matter was carried out in the following way: One Joseph Healy was licensed for the sale of beer, wine, and spirits in a house known as 32 Blarney Street, in the City of Cork. The plaintiffs, by arrangement with the defendant, purchased this licence from Healy at the price of £160, which the plaintiffs paid out of their own moneys. Having so acquired it, they concurred with the defendant in her application for a licence for No. 3 Douglas Street by giving her authority to agree for a surrender of the existing licence, so as to obviate an objection that the new licence would increase the number of public houses. In these circumstances the defendant was granted the licence for No. 3 Douglas Street.

This is the strictly legal account of the transaction, but it will be seen that contemporaneous documents describe it as a transfer of the licence from 32 Blarney Street to 3 Douglas Street. There was really no such thing known to the law, but the practice I have referred to became so usual that, in common parlance, the suppression of a licence for one public house and the consequential grant of a licence for another was described as a transfer, as in substance it was. Indeed, so much had the idea of transfer dominated not merely the lay, but the legal, mind, that the use of the term 'transfer' actually found its way into legal documents, and even into court records. In the present case we find that the defendant on 26 May 1892, served a notice on the clerk of the peace that she would apply at the next general quarter sessions of the peace to be held at Cork on 17 June 1892, for a certificate to obtain a transfer of a licence lately held by Joseph Healy at 32 Blarney Street to 3 Douglas Street; that on 17 June the application for a transfer was granted, and that on 6 October 1892, the transfer was confirmed at the Cork annual licensing quarter sessions.

The acquisition by the plaintiffs of the licence attached to 32 Blarney Street, at a cost to them of £160, and the use allowed by them to be made of it by the defendant, were of course not mere acts of benevolence. In return, the plaintiffs were to have the exclusive right of supplying the defendant with porter and stout. . . . As ancillary to this agreement, the defendant gave certain powers to the plaintiffs, and further agreed not, under any circumstances, to transfer or attempt to transfer the licence to any person or to any other house without the plaintiffs' consent, . . .

(The plaintiffs later sought damages for breach of contract caused by the defendant selling porter and stout manufactured by another brewery.)

Palles C.B.:

Applications to licensing authorities for certificates authorising the grant of licenses for the sale of beer, wine, and spirits . . . in respect of . . . houses which at the time of the application are licensed, . . . are divisible into those where (a) the application is for a certificate to the then licensed person to enable him to trade for another year—in other words, for a renewal; and (b) where it is for a transfer of the licence from the licensed person to another to enable that other to trade on the then licensed premises. As the licence is an authority to a named person to carry on trade in a described house, it is not only essentially personal to the named licensee, but is also attached to the described premises; and, if by reason either of the licensee's death, or of his ceasing to occupy the described house during the period covered by the licence, trade cannot be lawfully carried on in the house without further authority, and if that authority be conferred by transfer, it is confined to trade in the specified house. . . .
. . .

   I refer to this elementary matter to emphasise this, that the sale of excisable liquors authorised by such a transfer—the only transfer known to the Licensing Acts—is sale *in the premises licensed* by the existing licence. The transfer affects the licensed person only—not the licensed premises. There is not in the whole licensing code any provision for the transfer of a licence from one house to another house. If the house in which it is desired to carry on a publican's business be not licensed in the then current year, the application must be for an original licence, and upon hearing such an application the licensing authority is bound to consider the number of previously licensed houses in the neighbourhood—a matter which *Clitheroe's* case[1] decides cannot be entered upon on applications by licensed persons for renewals of their licences authorising them to continue to trade in the same licensed premises, or upon a transfer authorising a person other than the original licensee to continue to trade in the same licensed premises.
. . .

   . . . In my judgment it is wholly inconsistent with the licensing code that anyone should hold, either legally or equitably, such a licence as it were *in gross*, that is, so that there should be a right enforceable either at law or in equity to have it transferred at his request to any house he should direct.
. . .

   I have no doubt that at a previous time the plaintiffs must have given the renewal licence to Mrs Crean, with a view to her procuring an order transferring it to her, to enable her to trade in Douglas Street; but I must express my surprise that the licensing authority in Cork allowed such a transfer to be made. Their doing so was wholly beyond their jurisdiction. The order of transfer was void; the subsequent confirmation by the licensing justices was without jurisdiction and void; and, as far as I can see, the carrying on of the publican's business in the defendant's house in Douglas Street, up to the present time, was unauthorised and illegal. . . .
. . .

   In my judgment it is clear that the effect of this agreement is to provide for the carrying on of the publican's trade under a document purporting to be a licence, but which in truth is waste paper—that is, to carry it on without a licence, with an obligation on the defendant, at the plaintiffs' request, to transfer the licence to any house directed by them. Such an agreement is, in my opinion, illegal and incapable of enforcement. If there had been any valuable consideration for it, it consists in assistance in procuring a void licence by producing a document to the licensing authority, and thereby persuading it to purport to transfer it without authority from one house to another house, and thus to procure a licence for such other house without an inquiry as to the number of public houses in the neighbourhood.

Thus I am of opinion that the illegality pervades the entire agreement, both consideration and promises. It appears on the face of the document, and consequently need not have been pleaded.

The answer to |counsel for the plaintiff's| argument that the clause of the agreement sought to be enforced is legal, and that, where the consideration is not illegal, if there be two promises, one legal and the other illegal, the former can be enforced (which, of course, assumes the consideration to be legal, and therefore, in my opinion, is inapplicable), is that the two promises are not independent. The promise sought to be enforced here is that the porter and stout *which are to be illegally sold in the house* are, with a view to their being so sold, to be purchased from the plaintiffs, and a decree which would enforce that term would necessarily involve a direction that the illegal trade should be carried on.

Ritchie v Smith[2] is one of several authorities which demonstrate the illegality of the agreement as a whole. That was an action on an agreement whereby the plaintiffs agreed to let to one Newman, *inter alia*, a spirit shop or tap, part of Fendall's Hotel and Coffee House, at the weekly payment of £4, and whereby Newman agreed with the plaintiff to carry on the business of the tap, and to purchase all the porter, ale, and other malt liquors he might sell therein, from Messrs Kempson of the Mortlake Brewery, and the defendant agreed with the plaintiff that if Newman made default in the performance of the agreement he (the defendant) would pay the plaintiff £200 as liquidated damages. The declaration averred several breaches. The third plea alleged that the agreement was entered into for the express purpose of enabling Newman to sell for his own use excisable liquors by retail to be consumed on the premises without being duly licensed. It appeared at the trial that Newman carried on the business under the supposed protection of the hotel licence, the whole premises being contained in the one licence. A verdict for the defendant was obtained on the third plea, and the case came before the court upon an application for a new trial or for judgment *non obstante veredicto*. Chief Justice Wilde, in giving judgment, says: 'It seems to me that the jury could not possibly have come to any other conclusion,' and then proceeded to consider the second part of the rule, which had been argued upon the ground that the plea did not disclose any matter which rendered the agreement illegal. 'It is said,' says the Chief Justice 'that, though the agreement was entered into for the purpose of *enabling* Newman to do this, it did not of necessity follow that he *would* be guilty of any infraction of the law. But I think it is impossible to look at this agreement without seeing that the parties contemplated the doing of an illegal thing, in the infraction of a law enacted, not simply for revenue purposes, but for the safety and protection of the public morals.' All the court—Coltman, Maule, and Williams JJ.—agreed. Maule J. said:

> Although, in terms, the agreement is *enabling* only, and the act contemplated to be done is not, expressly and in terms, prohibited by the statute, I think there can be no doubt that it was an illegal act, and that the agreement is void. It is said that there is no authority that goes precisely that length. But it appears to me that the cases as to matters contrary to public policy do directly apply. If two parties enter into an agreement whereby it is stipulated that one of them shall be enabled to commit an act that is contrary to public policy, and contrary to the provisions of an Act of Parliament, though not expressly prohibited thereby except by the imposition

of a penalty, I apprehend the agreement is clearly illegal and void. But I do not think it necessary to enter into that question here; for I am clearly of opinion that an agreement having for its object the contravention of the excise laws is illegal.

It will be observed that there was no inquiry in that case whether the parties believed that the business could be lawfully carried on under the old hotel licence. So, too, here the belief of the parties in the legality of the transaction is immaterial.

1. IR 11 CL 412.   2. 6 CB 462.

Note

This approach was reaffirmed in *Francis Macklin and Peter McDonald v Graecen and Co. Ltd* [1983] IR 61 (see p. 255 above).

B. WHERE THE CONTRACT IS LAWFUL ON ITS FACE BUT ONE PERSON INTENDS
   TO PERFORM UNLAWFULLY

Whitecross Potatoes (International) Ltd *v* Raymond Coyle [1978] ILRM 31

Finlay P.:

. . . The sole issue arising on the question of liability in this case is as to whether the contract admittedly made between the plaintiff company and the defendant and dated 16 July 1976 is an illegal contract or not. This contract has undoubtedly been broken by the defendant without any justification and unless it is, as he asserts, an illegal contract there must be damages for its breach. I am satisfied as a matter of law that the onus is on the defendant to establish to my satisfaction as a matter of probability that the contract was, at the time of its formation, an illegal contract.

The plaintiff company is a company incorporated in England and carrying on business in Yorkshire whose business is the purchasing of potatoes and the reselling of them to processors of potatoes in England such as fish and chip merchants. It is jointly owned by a Mr Gilchrist and a Mr David Kemp. The defendant is a grower of potatoes in an extensive fashion carrying on business at Kilbrew, Ashbourne in the County of Meath but he is not and has not, I am satisfied on the evidence, ever been a dealer in potatoes purchasing them and reselling them, but purchases only such seed potatoes as are necessary for the purposes of growing on acreage which, at material times was as much as 900 acres of potatoes. After preliminary negotiations and discussions by telephone and letter Mr Gilchrist on behalf of the plaintiff company and the defendant on his own behalf signed a contract in writing on 16 July 1976 for the purchase by the plaintiff company from the defendant of a total amount of 700 tonnes of ware potatoes to be supplied at various dates scheduled to the agreement in various quantities over a period between August of 1976 and 7 January 1977. The price of the potatoes was fixed at £58 per tonne. The contract provides, *inter alia*, that the potatoes were to be collected by the plaintiff company from the defendant at the defendant's premises at Ashbourne. At clause 11 of the contract however it was provided as follows: 'In the event of import, export controls by either government the potatoes will be supplied from Northern Ireland and a supplement of £5.50 (five pounds fifty pence) will be paid by Whitecross Potatoes Ltd in this event to Mr Coyle.'

Whilst the matter is not expressly provided for in the contract it was the agreed evidence of the parties before me that this was, undoubtedly, a contract for the export of potatoes by the defendant to the UK for use by the plaintiff company in the UK. . . .

Again on the agreed evidence of the parties at the time of the making of this contract it was the belief or estimate of Mr Gilchrist who negotiated the contract on behalf of the plaintiff company that potatoes would be in short supply both in the UK and in Ireland and that the price of potatoes would rise and he therefore feared that the government of Ireland might introduce at some future date a restriction or total ban on the export of potatoes from Ireland. It was the belief and expectation of the defendant on the other hand that there would be a glut of potatoes, that the price would fall and that there was a possibility that the UK government would introduce to protect producers in their area a control or prohibition of import of potatoes into the UK.

Both these estimates or beliefs were discussed by Mr Gilchrist and Mr Coyle prior to the signing of the contract. The contract was created by a typed or printed form of contract in general use by the plaintiff company in England which left space for the provision of two additional paragraphs and after discussion into one of those additional paragraphs was introduced the clause which I have just quoted in full. This clause was actually introduced after the signing of the contract and was then initialled by both the parties and I am satisfied in law became part of the contractual relationship.

The case on behalf of the plaintiff is that the defendant assured him that he had associations and contacts in Northern Ireland with whom he had dealt on previous occasions and that in the event of there being a restriction of the export or import of potatoes it would be possible for him, the defendant, to sell the potatoes originally intended for the purpose of completing this contract in the Republic of Ireland and to purchase from these contacts or connections in Northern Ireland potatoes to fulfil his obligations under the contract.

The contention of the defendant on the other hand is that he, when the question of import and export control came up, expressly stated to Mr Gilchrist on behalf of the plaintiff company that he, the defendant, would be able to get men to run the potatoes which he, the defendant, was growing and had available for the completion of this contract, across the border and so make them available to be collected in Northern Ireland by Mr Gilchrist. . . . I am satisfied that the legal principles applicable to this conflict of evidence are relatively straightforward. If this was a contract which, on the apparent intention of the parties at the time of its formation, could be and would be carried out in a legal fashion then even though one of the parties, namely the defendant, in reality intended to carry it out in an illegal fashion it is enforceable. If, on the other hand, the acknowledged and accepted intention of both the parties at the time of the formation of the contract was that in the event of this export or import control being imposed the contract would be carried out by a smuggling operation, it is unenforceable and is contrary to public policy and cannot be upheld by the court.

I have had the greatest possible difficulty in reaching a conclusion as to which of the two accounts of this transaction I should accept. I have ultimately come to the conclusion that the onus being on the defendant he has failed to discharge it and to establish to my satisfaction as a matter of probability that the agreed understanding between him and the plaintiff was that this contract should, in the event of a restriction on export, be carried out by a smuggling operation.

Patrick Martin v Messrs Galbraith Ltd [1942] IR 37

The plaintiff, a bread server, sold goods supplied by the defendants from a horse and van. Despite the fact that the plaintiff was working for longer periods of time than allowed by s. 20 sub-s. 2 of the Shops (Conditions of Employment) Act 1938, rendering the defendant guilty of an offence under s. 20 sub-s. 11 the plaintiff claimed to be entitled to overtime payments under s. 20 sub-s. 6 of the Act.

Murnaghan J.:

The object of s. 20, sub-s. 6, was to give the employee overtime pay for the excess hours worked. This sub-section does not say expressly that overtime is only to be paid in respect of excess hours permitted by the Act, but, in my opinion, this result follows from the general rules of law. Parties to a contract, which produces illegality under a statute passed for the benefit of the public, cannot sue upon the contract unless the legislature has clearly given a right to sue. Overtime can only be legally worked by a person who is aged sixteen or upwards, and a young person who worked overtime illegally cannot, in my opinion, sue for it under s. 20, sub-s. 6. Similarly, where overtime is permitted, the employee can recover the statutory remuneration for the amount of the permitted overtime. In s. 20, sub-s. 6, the legislature enacts that the employer shall be *deemed to have agreed to pay*, and he cannot, in my opinion, be deemed to have made a contract which the statute declares to be illegal.

(Sullivan C.J. and Geoghegan J. agreed.)

Meredith J.:

With regard to the contention that, where a proprietor permits a member of the staff to work for a number of hours that makes him guilty of an offence punishable under s. 5, he is not liable to pay the member of the staff for the prohibited excess, I agree with the conclusion and reasons stated in the judgment of O'Byrne J. which I have had the advantage of reading. I would, however, be inclined to go a step further. The question seems to me to be one of the avoidance of a contract simply on the ground that the party called upon to perform the contract has at some stage been guilty of an illegal act, which act has made him liable to perform an obligation under the contract. The contract implied under s. 20, sub-s. 6, cannot, in my opinion, be regarded as *per se* a void or illegal contract. Also, it was not suggested that Martin himself was guilty of an offence under the Act for working hours in excess of the permitted excess over sixty hours per week. He was not *in delicto*. The suggestion is that, because the proprietors were guilty of an offence in doing what made them liable to perform the legal contract by an act in itself legal, they are excused from performance of their contract. No authority for that proposition was cited and I know of none. In *Wetherell v Jones*[1] Lord Tenterden said:

> Where a contract which a plaintiff seeks to enforce is expressly, or by implication, forbidden by the statute or common law, no court will lend its assistance to give it effect; and there are numerous cases in the books where an action on the contract has failed, because either the consideration for the promise or the act to be done was illegal, as being against the express provisions of the law, or contrary to justice, morality, and sound policy.
>
> But where the consideration and the matter to be performed are both legal, we are not aware that a plaintiff has ever been precluded from recovering by an infringement of the law, not contemplated by the contract, in the performance of something to be done on his part.

The last qualification was approved in *Forster v Taylor*.[2]

O'Byrne J.:

It was contended, on behalf of the defendants, that where a member of the staff is allowed to work for any hours in excess of those permitted by the section, the statutory contract to pay for overtime is unenforceable as regards such excessive hours. If this contention be well founded, the plaintiff could not, in any circumstances, recover overtime pay, under the section, for periods in excess of (1) sixty hours in any week, or (2) 216 hours in any four consecutive weeks, or (3) 2,600 hours in any year.

The basis of this contention, as I understand it, is that where a member of the staff is permitted to work beyond the limits aforesaid, the proprietor is guilty of an offence, in respect of which he may be convicted and penalised under s. 5, and it is alleged that he cannot, in addition, be compelled to pay as for overtime under s. 20. I must say that I can find, in the Act, no foundation for this contention. Sub-s. 6 seems to me to be quite clear, and I do not think it is in any way dependent upon a question as to whether or not an offence has been committed.

The contention seems to me to be quite inconsistent with the sub-section as enacted. . . .

. . .

Further, I am of opinion that construing the section in the manner contended for, so far from giving effect to the intentions of the legislature, would tend to defeat such intentions. To allow a member of the staff to do shop work during periods in excess of those permitted by s. 20 is undoubtedly an offence, but it is an offence on the part of the proprietor and not on the part of the servant. Why, in such circumstances, should the latter be penalised by being prevented from recovering overtime pay in respect of such excessive work—particularly in view of the fact that one of the expressed intentions of the legislature was to make provision for ensuring the payment of wages at fair rates to employees?

I consider that the sub-section is free from all ambiguity and that it should be so construed as to effectuate the object of the legislature and to give the fullest effect to the beneficial provisions of the Act.

[1] 3 B & Ad 221.   [2] 5 B & Ad 887, at 900.

Exceptions to ex turpi causa and in pari delicto

Sumner v Sumner (1935) 69 ILTR 101

In contemplation of divorce the plaintiff and defendant entered an agreement by which the plaintiff agreed to settle certain securities on the defendant and their infant child. Later a settlement setting out the trust conditions was made by the plaintiff on the defendant. The plaintiff then attempted to have the settlement set aside on the grounds of illegality.

Megaw J.:

. . .

The plaintiff had said that he had instituted this action at the instance of his legal advisers to upset an illegal bargain. If his Lordship might speculate as to the framework adopted in putting forward the plaintiff's case he should trace the ground work of the claim to a short statement in *The Laws of England*, vol. 7 p. 408 (old edition), *viz*. 'The illegality of a contract may be set up by way of defence to an action on the contract, even if it does not appear on the face of the contract; but in order to obtain relief in equity by getting the contract set aside, the applicant must prove, not only that the contract was illegal, but that he was *induced to enter into it by pressure or undue influence.*' He accepted that statement of the law. It was clearly stated by Lindley L.J., in *Jones v Merionethshire Permanent Building Society*, |1892| 1 Ch. 173 at p. 182: 'A plaintiff is not entitled to relief in a court of equity on the ground of the illegality of his own conduct. In order to obtain relief in equity he must prove not only that the transaction is illegal but something more; he must prove either pressure or undue influence.'

At common law the same principle was recognised. Lord Mansfield in *Holman v Johnston* 1 Cowp. 343 put it in this way:

> The principle of public policy is this: *ex dolo malo non oritur actio* . . . . No court will lend its aid to a man who founds his cause of action on an immoral or an illegal act.
>
> If from the plaintiff's own statement or otherwise the cause of action appear to arise '*ex turpi causa*', or the transgression of a positive law of the country, then the court says he had no right to be assisted. It had been on that ground that the court went; not for the sake of the defendant but because they will not lend their aid to such a plaintiff. So, if the plaintiff and defendant were to change sides, and the defendant were to bring his action against the plaintiff, the latter would have the advantage of it; for when both are equally in fault *potior est conditio defendentis*.

That had been recognised in such cases as *Scott v Brown* |1892| 2 QB 724, and *Gedge v Royal Exchange Assurance Corp.* |1900| 2 QB 214.

There were two old maxims of equity which should not be left out of sight entirely. 'He who seeks equity must do equity' and 'He who comes into equity must come with clean hands.' The plaintiff did not comply with either of these maxims, but it was not necessary to investigate how much or little weight was to be attached to them.

. . .

The principle that, where property had been transferred by an instrument that was tainted with illegality, the estate should lie where it fell, had been recognised from the time of Lord Eldon. The doctrine was accepted in a case of *Gascoigne v Gascoigne* |1918| 1 KB 223, and in his opinion the principle there recognised was applicable to the present case. The plaintiff sought an equitable remedy, and his Lordship was of opinion that in the circumstances he had pointed out he was not entitled to succeed.

. . .

The action was dismissed with costs.

Note

See Meredith J.'s dissenting judgment in *Martin v Galbraith* |1942| IR 37 (see p. 752 above).

Saunders and Another *v* Edwards and Another [1987] 2 All ER 651

The defendant sold a leasehold interest in a flat to the plaintiff on the basis of a fraudulent misrepresentation that the flat included a roof terrace. The agreed price was £45,000 but in order to minimise the plaintiff's stamp duty liability the parties agreed to apportion the price in the contract of sale on the basis of £40,000 for the flat and £5,000 for the chattels. The chattels were only worth between £500 and £1,000. The plaintiffs were subsequently awarded damages for fraudulent misrepresentation and the defendant appealed.

Kerr L.J.:

. . .

. . . Counsel for the defendant submitted that, if the plaintiffs sought to open up the apportionment and rely on the true value of the chattels, they were in the same breath admitting that they had been parties to a fraud, or an attempted fraud, on the Revenue by seeking to avoid stamp duty by understating the true value of the flat. He relied on two maxims, *ex turpi causa* (or *ex dolo malo*) *non oritur actio*, and the related maxim, in *pari delicto potior est conditio defendentis*. These apply in different circumstances, which it is necessary to analyse for present purposes: I will refer to this line of defence for short as the '*ex turpi causa* defence'.

This submission requires serious consideration. What happened in this case may well be common practice. But it cannot be condoned. If a solicitor is involved in an apportionment of this kind, which he knows not to be in accordance with the facts, then he must be guilty of professional misconduct. Furthermore, apart from this and possible criminal offences, the consequence for buyers may well be that their contract becomes unenforceable.

In that connection counsel for the plaintiffs rightly reminded us of the important decision of this court in *Alexander v Rayson* |1936| 1 KB 169, |1935| All ER Rep 185. In that case a landlord persuaded his tenant to agree that the true rent should be expressed in two documents, one as a figure for rent and the other for fictitious services to be rendered by the tenant. The landlord's object was to present only the first document to the local authority in order to secure a low rateable value. He claimed for arrears of rent under both documents and the tenant relied on the true facts. In the result the landlord's action for rent was dismissed on the basis of the *ex turpi causa* defence. Solicitors should bear this case in mind when considering an unreal apportionment between the purchase price of a real property and fixtures and fittings.

However, the present action, unlike *Alexander v Rayson*, is not brought on the contract, but on the tort of deceit based on the defendant's fraudulent misrepresentation. I therefore do not propose to consider what would have been the position if, for instance, the defendant had declined to complete in this case and the plaintiffs had sought to sue on the contract, either for specific performance or for damages. Nor do I express any view on the relevance of two other points made by counsel for the plaintiffs in that connection. First, while I find it impossible to escape from the conclusion that there was an intention to avoid payment of the full amount of stamp duty, counsel for the plaintiffs pointed out that in the event there was no underpayment, because the flat did not include the roof terrace and was therefore substantially less valuable than had been supposed. She also drew attention to evidence from the first plaintiff that he personally, as he said, had not been aware of anything wrong and that he had had no intention of defrauding the Revenue.

I put all those matters on one side. This is not an action based on the contract but on the defendant's fraudulent misrepresentation. The plaintiffs are not seeking to enforce the contract by relying on it or seeking any relief in connection with it. They have to prove, firstly, the fraudulent misrepresentation, which they have done, and, secondly, the resulting loss, the transfer of £45,000. Thirdly, they must then give credit for the value received, the value of the flat and chattels without the roof terrace. That process does not involve any reliance on the contract, let alone the apportionment. The figures in the contract and the fact of the apportionment, as counsel for the plaintiffs concedes, may of course be relevant evidence in relation to the dispute about the value received. But they are not the foundation of the plaintiffs' claim in any way.

That approach is supported by a number of authorities which show that the relevance of the *ex turpi causa* defence lies mainly in the field of contractual claims and only rarely in tort.

An illuminating passage for this proposition appears in the speech of Lord Asquith in *National Coal Board v England* |1954| 1 All ER 546, |1954| AC 403. The plaintiff had been injured in an explosion. He sued his employers for damages for breach of statutory duty although he himself, and the shot-firer with whom he was working, had acted in concert in breach of the relevant regulations. One of the defences raised by the employers was the *ex turpi causa* defence. That was unanimously rejected, but I need only read from the speech of Lord Asquith (|1954| 1 All ER 546 at 558, |1954| AC 403 at 428–9):

> The point which exercised some of your Lordships, and certainly myself, was the argument that the respondent and the appellants' shot-firer were parties to an agreement in breach of the regulations whereby they agreed that the respondent should couple the electric leads with the detonators, a function committed by the regulations to the sole province of the shot-firer; and that the damage which followed resulted from that illegal agreement. The appellants relied on the maxim *ex turpi causa non oritur actio* as absolving them of liability. The short answer to this contention has, no doubt, been found by those of your Lordships who pointed out the definition of 'fault' in the Law Reform (Contributory Negligence) Act 1945. But, for myself, I should have decided in the same sense in the absence of any such definition. The vast majority of cases in which the maxim has been applied have been cases where, there being an illegal agreement between A and B, either seeks to sue the other for its enforcement or for damages for its breach. That, of course, is not this case. Cases where an action in tort has been defeated by the maxim are exceedingly rare. Possibly a party to an illegal prize fight who is damaged in the conflict cannot sue for assault: *Boulter v Clark* (1747) Bull NP 16. But it seems to me in principle that the plaintiff cannot be precluded from suing simply because the wrongful act is committed after the illegal agreement is made and during the period involved in its execution. The act must, I should have supposed, at least be a step in the execution of the common illegal purpose. If two burglars, A and B, agree to open a safe by means of explosives, and A so negligently handles the explosive charge as to injure B, B might find some difficulty in maintaining an action for negligence against A. But if A and B are proceeding to the premises which they intend burglariously to enter, and before they enter them B picks A's pocket and steals his watch, I cannot prevail on myself to believe that A could not sue in tort . . . The theft is totally unconnected with the burglary. There is, however, a surprising dearth of authority on this point. Certain cases were cited to us decided under the Factory Acts, but none of them was, to my mind, really in point.

A number of other cases illustrate the approach on which counsel for the plaintiffs relies. There had been the earlier well known decision of this court in *Bowmakers Ltd v Barnet Instruments Ltd* |1944| 2 All ER 579, |1945| KB 65. As in *Alexander v Rayson* |1936| 1 KB 169 at 188, |1935| All ER Rep 185 at 194, the court referred to a succinct statement by Lindley L.J. in *Scott v Brown Doering McNab & Co.* |1892| 2 QB 724 at 729, |1891–4| All ER Rep 654 at 657, as follows (see |1944| 2 All ER 579 at 582, |1945| KB 65 at 71): 'Any rights which he |a plaintiff| may have irrespective of his illegal contract will, of course, be recognised and enforced.'

One illustration of this principle, and a strong case on its facts, was the decision of the Privy Council in *Sajan Singh v Sardara Ali* |1960| 1 All ER 269, |1960| AC 167. The plaintiff and the defendant concluded an illegal contract for the sale of a lorry and jointly engaged in its unlawful and fraudulent operation contrary to certain Malaysian regulations. The defendant then removed the lorry from the plaintiff and he refused to return it. The plaintiff sued in detinue. He recovered the lorry and damages for its wrongful detention, despite his own participation in the illegal contract and in the unlawful scheme involved. It was held that the property in the lorry had passed to the plaintiff under the contract, notwithstanding its illegality and that he was therefore entitled to enforce his cause of action in detinue despite the *ex turpi causa* defence.

That case was distinguished in *Chettiar v Chettiar* [1962] 1 All ER 494, [1962] AC 294 (also in the Privy Council) because the plaintiff had to rely on the illegal transaction itself. But the full picture is more complex, as shown by two more recent cases to which we were also referred. I will not analyse them in detail, but they show that there are no rigid rules for or against the application of the *ex turpi causa* defence. This is not surprising, since it involves issues of public policy. To some extent these must depend on the circumstances of each case.

The first was *Shelley v Paddock* [1978] 3 All ER 129, [1979] QB 120, a decision of Bristow J. affirmed by this court (see [1980] 1 All ER 1009, [1980] QB 348). The second was a recent decision of Hutchison J. in *Thackwell v Barclays Bank plc* [1986] 1 All ER 676, which contains a valuable discussion of the jurisprudence in this field.

These cases show that the conduct and relative moral culpability of the parties may be relevant in determining whether or not the *ex turpi causa* defence falls to be applied as a matter of public policy. Thus, in the former case the plaintiff recovered money paid by her under a contract which was illegal under the exchange control legislation. She did not know of the illegality, whereas the defendants were swindlers who had induced the contract by fraudulent misrepresentations and had then made off with her money. In the latter case on the other hand, the *ex turpi causa* defence succeeded although the plaintiff's cause of action lay in tort. His claim was for negligence or the wrongful conversion of a cheque. This was rejected because the cheque formed part of the proceeds of a crime in which he had been involved and in whose perpetration the cheque had played an essential part.

What these cases show is that the earlier authorities to which I have referred, including in particular the statement of Lindley L.J., cannot be applied literally in every situation. However, I have no doubt on which side of the line the present case falls. The plaintiffs have an unanswerable claim for damages for fraudulent misrepresentation. The possible illegality involved in the apportionment of the price in the contract is wholly unconnected with their cause of action. The plaintiffs' loss caused by the defendant's fraudulent misrepresentation would have been the same even if the contract had not contained this illegal element. Their claim for damages is in no way seeking to enforce the contract or any relief in connection with it. The moral culpability of the defendant greatly outweighs any on the part of the plaintiffs. He cannot be allowed to keep the fruits of his fraud. I therefore hold that the *ex turpi causa* defence fails.

(Bingham L.J. agreed.)

Euro-Diam Ltd *v* Bathurst [1988] 2 All ER 23

The plaintiffs, diamond merchants, supplied a quantity of diamonds worth over $223,000 to Verena GmbH, a client in Germany. In order to enable the client to avoid payment of German customs duty, the invoice stated the value of the diamonds to be $131,411. Later, when some of the diamonds were stolen the plaintiffs valued the missing diamonds at $142,174 and claimed under their insurance policy. The insurers argued that the plaintiffs' claims were tainted by illegality.

Kerr L.J.:
. . .

. . . [The trial judge] concluded that the *ex turpi causa* defence fails in this case. I entirely agree with his conclusion and can summarise my reasons as follows:

(a) Mr Laub's issue of the understated invoice was undoubtedly reprehensible. He realised that it would probably be used to deceive the German customs, and his action was criminal under the laws of West Germany. But he did not issue the invoice for his own or Euro-Diam's purposes, but at the request of Mr Bonim. Subject to the argument on subrogation to which I come in a moment, the understated invoice had no bearing on the loss of the diamonds, which is now admitted to have been covered by Euro-Diam's policy. The understated invoice also involved no deception of the insurers, since the true value of the diamonds was recorded in Euro-Diam's register and the correct premium was paid. In these circumstances there could in my view be no question of any affront to the public conscience, if Euro-Diam's claim were to be upheld. On the contrary, it might be considered surprising if in these circumstances the insurers were entitled to refuse payment. But, even if that is putting it too high, I have no doubt that public policy does not require the court to hold that Euro-Diam's claim must be rejected *in limine* on the basis of the *ex turpi causa* defence.

(b) . . . Counsel for the insurers strenuously argued that Euro-Diam could not prove consignment of the diamonds to Verena without relying on the invoice showing the number of carats dispatched. He also said that, in order to show that the title in the diamonds remained in Euro-Diam, Mr Laub would have to give evidence that the contract was sale or return, and that in these circumstances Mr Laub would have to rely on, or at any rate to disclose, all the terms of the contract without picking and choosing, including his agreement to understate the value of the goods. But I do not accept any of these submissions. In particular, Euro-Diam did not have to rely on the invoice to establish their claim, since the policy provided that the basis of valuation should be 'as per Register', and since Euro-Diam's register contained a correct record of the value.

(c) . . . [Euro-Diam] derived no tangible benefit from the understated invoice. In *St John Shipping Corp. v Joseph Rank Ltd* [1956] 3 All ER 683 at 693–4, [1957] 1 QB 267 at 292–3 Devlin J. appears to have considered that the *ex turpi causa* defence cannot be asserted unless the defendant is able to show to what extent the plaintiff derived a benefit from his illegality. It may be that this goes too far. But in the present case the possible goodwill advantage to Euro-Diam of having acceded to Mr Bonim's request is so shadowy that it is not surprising that the judge made no mention of it at all. Although I felt bound to accept for the submission of counsel for the insurers that the potential benefit of the understated invoice was not exclusively on the side of Verena, the impact of this aspect is virtually negligible.

(d) I then turn to the position as between Euro-Diam and Verena in so far as this may be relevant. I have great difficulty in seeing how Verena could successfully rely on the *ex turpi causa* defence in relation to almost any claim by Euro-Diam against Verena that one can imagine, assuming that English law would apply or that German law is the same. Mr Bonim would clearly have to be treated as having acted on behalf of Verena in asking for the understated invoice, and in any event Verena must be treated as having ratified his conduct when they used it to deceive the German customs, as the judge held they did. It follows that on the question of public policy and the relative culpability of the parties the scales would be heavily weighted against Verena. They alone made a tangible profit out of the transaction. An action against Verena for conversion or for the negligent loss of the diamonds would in my view succeed. . . .

The only situation in which I could envisage that Euro-Diam would be in the difficulty of having to rely on the understated invoice is an ingenious scenario suggested by counsel for the insurers. He said that if Verena failed to return the diamonds and failed to pay the price, and if Euro-Diam thereupon sued them for the price, Verena might merely pay the amount stated in the invoice, and that it would then not be open to Mr Laub to contradict the invoice by relying on the true agreed price. But whether or not this is correct, and it is unnecessary to express any view about it, is irrelevant to Euro-Diam's claim in this action. Since any failure on the part of Verena to return the diamonds or to pay the agreed price was not a risk insured under Euro-Diam's policy, there could be no question of Euro-Diam's insurers claiming payment of their price by subrogation.

(e) These matters also deal with the new point of counsel for the insurers on the alleged prejudice to the insurers' rights to subrogation. But in any event it seems to me that this line of argumentation goes too far. The successful exercise by underwriters of their full rights of subrogation is often impossible, in many cases due to acts or omissions by their assured. Admittedly, in this case there was no question of Mr Laub having merely acted negligently. His conduct was unlawful by German law and in effect dishonest. But if underwriters wish to exclude their liability in such circumstances, and if they cannot succeed on the grounds of public policy already discussed, then their remedy must be to include some appropriate term in the policy. The mere fact that the understated invoice might prove an embarrassment to them in any subrogation proceedings concerning the diamonds, as counsel for Euro-Diam frankly conceded it might, cannot in itself be sufficient to tip the scales of public policy in their favour.

. . .

For all these reasons I am in full agreement with the judge that the *ex turpi causa* defence fails.

Note

This case was referred to in *Hortensius Ltd and John Durack v Kenneth L. Bishop and Others, Trustees of the Trustee Savings Bank Dublin* [1989] ILRM 294 (see p. 740 above).

Howard *v* Shirlstar Container Transport Ltd and Another [1990] 3 All ER 366

The plaintiff, a pilot, contracted to remove an aeroplane from Nigeria pursuant to a contract with the defendants. He travelled to Nigeria with a wireless operator. Then, believing their lives to be in danger, he took off in the aeroplane and flew to Lagos. Contrary to Nigerian law he did not obtain permission from air traffic control to depart. He later sued the defendants for non-payment of the agreed fee. The defendants claimed that the contract was unenforceable as it had been performed illegally in Nigeria.

Staughton L.J.:

. . .

I turn then to the second point, the effect of illegality under a contract of English domestic law. This was dealt with in three propositions by Kerr L.J. in the *Euro-Diam* case [1988] 2 All ER 23 at 28–29, [1990] 1 QB 1 at 35. I can abbreviate them for present purposes. (1) The *ex turpi causa* defence rests on a principle of public policy. It applies where the plaintiff has been guilty of illegal (or immoral) conduct, if in all the circumstances it would be an affront to the public conscience to grant the plaintiff relief, because the court would thereby appear to assist or encourage the plaintiff in his illegal conduct or to encourage others in similar acts. (2) The main situations where the defence will *prima facie* succeed are (i) where the plaintiff seeks, or is forced, to found his claim on an illegal contract or to plead illegality in order to support his claim, either in the statement of claim or in a reply; (ii) where the grant of relief to the plaintiff would enable him to benefit from his criminal conduct; (iii) where the situation is residually covered by the general principle in (i) above. (3) However, the *ex turpi causa* defence must be approached pragmatically and with caution, depending on the circumstances.

We were referred to *Pitts v Hunt* [1990] 3 All ER 344, [1990] 3 WLR 542 decided on 13 April. There Dillon L.J. said that he did not find the 'public conscience' test satisfactory. One reason was that appeal to the public conscience would be likely to lead to a graph of illegalities according to moral turpitude. The difficulty of formulating a criterion for separating cases of serious illegality from ones which were not so serious was insoluble. However, Beldam L.J. in that case recorded that, in *Saunders v Edwards* [1987] 2 All ER 651, [1987] 1 WLR 1116, the 'public conscience' test, first clearly set out by Hutchinson J. in *Thackwell v Barclays Bank plc* [1986] 1 All ER 676, was approved. . . .

. . .

. . . To take off from a Nigerian airport in breach of regulations was central to his performance of the contract, as it was in fact performed. It was in no sense incidental illegality. . . .

. . .

. . . it is to be noted that proposition 2 (ii) of Kerr L.J. in the *Euro-Diam* case, dealing with the recovery of a benefit from the plaintiff's criminal conduct, is expressed to be an example of the main principle in proposition (1), that the court will not assist a plaintiff if to do so would be an affront to the public conscience. Can there then be circumstances where the public conscience is not affronted, even though a plaintiff does not recover a benefit from his criminal conduct? In my judgment, there can be. . . .

. . .

. . . this case is in my judgment plainly one where the plaintiff's claim should not fail, because the conscience of the court is not affronted. The offence, or offences, which Captain Howard committed were, on the judge's findings which are not now challenged, designed to free himself and Miss Spalding from pressing danger.

Tinsley v Milligan [1993] 3 All ER 65
The parties jointly purchased a house. The house was registered in the sole name of the appellant in order to allow the respondent make false claims for social welfare benefits. Two years later the parties quarrelled and the appellant left the house. She subsequently brought an action seeking possession of the house and asserting ownership. The respondent counterclaimed for an order for an order for sale and a declaration that the house was held by the appellant on trust for the parties in equal share.

Lord Goff:
. . .

The appeal, which is brought by leave of the Court of Appeal, raises the question whether the claim of the respondent to an interest in the property in question is defeated by reason of frauds practised on the Department of Social Security.

. . . the principle invoked by the appellant in the present case, [is] that, if A puts property in the name of B intending to conceal his (A's) interest in the property for a fraudulent or illegal purpose, neither law nor equity will allow A to recover the property, and equity will not assist him in asserting an equitable interest in it. This principle applies whether the transaction takes the form of a transfer of property by A to B, or the purchase by A of property in the name of B.

. . . the case which has for nearly 200 years been regarded as the authoritative source of the principle is *Muckleston v Brown* (1801) 6 Ves. 52 at 68–9, [1775–1802] All ER Rep 501 at 506, in which Lord Eldon L.C. said in a much-quoted passage: ' . . . the plaintiff stating, he had been guilty of a fraud upon the law, to evade, to disappoint, the provision of the legislature, to which he is bound to submit, and coming to equity to be relieved against his own act, and the defence being dishonest, between the two species of dishonesty the court would not act; but would say "Let the estate lie, where it falls."'
. . .

It is against the background of these established principles that I turn to consider the judgments of the majority of the Court of Appeal. As I have recorded, Nicholls L.J. in particular invoked a line of recent cases, largely developed in the Court of Appeal, from which he deduced the proposition that, in cases of illegality, the underlying principle is the so-called public conscience test, under which the court must weigh, or balance, the adverse consequences of respectively granting or refusing relief. This is little different, if at all, from stating that the court has a discretion whether to grant or refuse relief. . . . It is necessary to examine with some care the authorities relied upon by Nicholls L.J. in support of his statement of the applicable law.

The first case is *Thackwell v Barclays Bank plc* [1986] 1 All ER 676. In that case the plaintiff claimed damages from the defendant bank for negligence and conversion of a cheque by the bank. The point was taken that the cheque formed part of a fraudulent financing scheme, to which the plaintiff was a party; and the bank (whose defence under s. 4 of the Cheques Act 1957 failed, because the judge, Hutchison J., held that the bank ought to have been put on inquiry) pleaded that the plaintiff's claim must fail by reason of the maxim *ex turpi causa non oritur actio*. It was conceded on behalf of the plaintiff that, if he knew at the time that there was such a scheme, his claim must fail. Hutchison J. held that the plaintiff knew from the outset that the scheme was fraudulent and willingly participated in it. Accordingly the plaintiff's claim failed. However, the defendant had advanced an alternative argument on the basis of which he submitted that, even if the plaintiff was innocent, his claim should fail. The judge accepted this alternative argument, and indicated that, even if he had held the plaintiff to be innocent, he would have denied him recovery. In this argument, we find the origin of the so-called public conscience test, which involved:

> the court looking at the quality of the illegality relied on by the defendant and all the surrounding circumstances, without fine distinctions, and seeking to answer two questions: first, whether there had been illegality of which the court should take notice and, second, whether in all the circumstances it would be an affront to the public conscience if by affording him the relief sought the court was seen to be indirectly assisting or encouraging the plaintiff in his criminal act. (See [1986] 1 All ER 676 at 687.)

It is to be observed that the test is not stated as a general principle, but as a limited principle under which the court may deny relief in certain specific circumstances, even though the claimant is not implicated in the illegality. Furthermore, the test does not as stated involve any balancing exercise of the kind described by Nicholls L.J. in the present case. It is unnecessary for your Lordships' House to consider for present purposes whether the test accepted by Hutchison J. is good law or not. I wish only to refer to the fact that of the four cases relied upon as providing support for it, the first

(*Burns v Edman* |1970| 1 All ER 886, |1970| 2 QB 541) was concerned with a claim under the Fatal Accidents Acts founded upon the income from the deceased as a burglar, the second (*Murphy v Culhane* |1976| 3 All ER 533, |1977| QB 94) was concerned with a claim for damages by the deceased's widow, the deceased having been killed by the defendant during a criminal affray initiated by the deceased), the third (*Shelley v Paddock* |1980| 1 All ER 1009, |1980| QB 348) was concerned with a claim for damages for fraud, where the defendant had swindled the plaintiff out of the price paid by her for property in Spain, the plaintiff having innocently paid the money in breach of the Exchange Control Act 1947, and the fourth (*Geismar v Sun Alliance and London Insurance Ltd* |1977| 3 All ER 570, |1978| QB 383) was a case in which the plaintiff's claim to an indemnity under a contract of insurance, in respect of the loss of jewellery deliberately imported in breach of the Customs and Excise Act 1952, failed because recovery of such an indemnity would indirectly enable the plaintiff to profit from his deliberate breach of the law. It is by no means easy to see how any broadly applicable public conscience test could be derived from these authorities.

However, in three subsequent cases the principle so accepted by Hutchison J. was adopted and expanded by the Court of Appeal. The first was *Saunders v Edwards* |1987| 2 All ER 651, |1987| 1 WLR 1116. The case was concerned with a claim by the purchasers of the lease of a flat against the vendor for damages for fraudulently misrepresenting that the flat included a roof terrace. In answer, the defendant pleaded illegality, on the ground that the respective values of the flat and certain chattels in it had been distorted in the contract at the suggestion of the plaintiffs by exaggerating the value of the chattels and so diminishing the value of the flat, in order to reduce the stamp duty payable on the transaction. The plaintiffs succeeded in their claim, having an unassailable claim for damages for fraud which did not involve any reliance on the contract of sale itself; but reference was made to Hutchison J.'s judgment in *Thackwell v Barclays Bank plc* |1986| 1 All ER 676, and Nicholls L.J. in particular adopted and applied the public conscience test as being applicable in a case concerned with a claim in tort arising out of fraudulent activities.

A further step was taken by the Court of Appeal in *Euro-Diam Ltd v Bathurst* |1988| 2 All ER 23, |1990| 1 QB 1, a case concerned with a claim under an insurance policy in respect of a consignment of precious stones exported to West Germany which was stolen from a German company's warehouse. The defendant raised an issue of illegality, which was rejected both at first instance and by the Court of Appeal. It is enough for present purposes to record that Kerr L.J., citing *Saunders v Edwards*, stated the principles relating to illegality in a series of numbered paragraphs, in the first of which he stated that: 'the *ex turpi causa* defence . . . applies if in all the circumstances it would be an affront to the public conscience to grant the plaintiff the relief which he seeks because the court would thereby appear to assist or encourage the plaintiff in his illegal conduct or to encourage others in similar acts . . . ' (See |1988| 2 All ER 23 at 28–29 1 QB 1 at 35.)

This broad general statement appears to have been qualified in a later paragraph in Kerr L.J.'s statement of the law; even so, we can here see the limited principle accepted by Hutchison J. being given a new and wider role, apparently with the purpose of softening the rigour of the principle of policy established in the older authorities.

A more decisive step was taken in the third case, *Howard v Shirlstar Container Transport Ltd* |1990| 3 All ER 366, |1990| 1 WLR 1292. The case was concerned with a contract for the recovery from Nigeria of an aircraft owned by the defendants which was being detained by the Nigerian authorities at Lagos. Under the contract, the plaintiff was entitled to recover a fee of £25,000 if he 'successfully' removed the aircraft from Nigerian airspace. He succeeded in so doing, insofar as he, at some risk to his life, flew the aircraft out of Lagos as far as the Ivory Coast, where however the aircraft was impounded by the authorities and returned by them to Nigeria. The plaintiff's claim for the balance of his fee was met by the defence of illegality, on the ground that he took off without obtaining the necessary clearance in breach of air traffic control regulations at Lagos; in fact he had left in a hurry, without obtaining clearance, because he had been warned that his and his wireless operator's lives were in danger and that he would not be given permission to take off. The Court of Appeal, deciding that the defence of illegality failed, relied explicitly on the public conscience test, holding that the conscience of the court would not be affronted by enforcing the plaintiff's claim under the contract for the balance of his fee. This appears to have been a case concerned not so much with an illegal contract as such, but with illegality committed in the performance of the contract. In normal circumstances, one would have expected it to be decided on the principle stated by Devlin J. in *St John Shipping Corp. v Joseph Rank Ltd* [1956] 3 All ER 683, [1957] 1 QB 267. In any event, there was evidence that the plaintiff's and his companion's lives were in danger, and that this might well have provided a defence to the alleged breach of Nigerian law—a point left open by the Court of Appeal.

Finally there came the explicit reliance on the public conscience test by Nicholls L.J. in the present case.

I feel driven to say that what appears to have happened is that a principle, developed by counsel for the defendant bank in *Thackwell v Barclays Bank plc* [1986] 1 All ER 676 for a limited purpose in the context of a claim in tort, has been allowed to expand, both in its terms and in its range of application, so that it is now suggested that it operates as a broad qualifying principle, modifying and indeed transforming the long-established principles applicable in cases of illegality, and in particular in relation to the principle established as applicable in cases such as the present. Furthermore, this development has been allowed to occur without addressing the questions (1) whether the test is consistent with earlier authority, (2) if it was not so consistent, whether such a development could take place consistently with the doctrine of precedent as applied in the Court of Appeal, or (3) whether the resulting change in the law, if permissible, was desirable. It is unnecessary for your Lordships to decide whether any such test is applicable in the limited context in which it originally emerged before Hutchison J. It is sufficient for present purposes to say, with the greatest respect, that to apply the public conscience test as qualifying the principle established for nearly 200 years as applicable in cases such as the present is, for reasons I have already stated, inconsistent with numerous authorities binding on the Court of Appeal.

. . . I have been unable to discover any development in the law. As I read the authorities, they reveal a consistent application of the principle, subject only to the recognition of a *locus poenitentiae* for the claimant where the illegal purpose has not been carried into effect.

I would allow this Appeal.

(Keith L.J. agreed.)

Lord Lowry:

My Lords, I have had the advantage of reading in draft the speeches prepared by your Lordships and find myself in agreement with the conclusions reached by my noble and learned friends Lord Jauncey of Tullichettle and Lord Browne-Wilkinson.

. . .

The rule of policy which is said to justify the wide principle should be closely examined. A and B buy property in equal shares and by agreement B acquires the legal title. A, either by himself or in conspiracy with B (who may or may not stand to benefit from the fraud), plans to obtain a financial advantage by falsely pretending that he owns no property: if A goes through with the scheme, the wide principle applies, although, in order to assert his rights against B, A does not need to rely on his own fraud. Indeed, where the presumption of advancement does not apply, it is B who will have to rely on the fraud (to which in some cases he had been privy) as a defence. If, on the other hand, the property has been innocently acquired and A later takes advantage of his lack of legal title to make the same false pretence, his claim against B on foot of a resulting trust cannot be defeated. The criminal sanction against A is the same in either case.

I am not impressed by the argument that the wide principle acts as a deterrent to persons in A's position. In the first place, they may not be aware of the principle and are unlikely to consult a reputable solicitor. Secondly, if they commit a fraud, they will not have been deterred by the possibility of being found out and prosecuted. Furthermore, the wide principle could be a positive encouragement to B, if he is aware of the principle, because by means of his complicity he may become not only the legal owner but the beneficial owner.

For A to take proceedings in order to vindicate his equitable rights as sole or joint beneficial owner is not an example of the maxim *ex turpi causa non oritur actio* because his equitable title and his cause of action do not arise out of his illegal or immoral act. It is B who must rely on the *turpis causa* as a defence.

The foregoing considerations render me all the more convinced that the right view is that a party cannot rely on his own illegality in order to prove his equitable right, and not that a party cannot recover if his illegality is proved as a defence to his claim. I consider that the wide principle is not well founded and, since it is not binding on your Lordships, that your Lordships should not follow it.

Lord Browne-Wilkinson:

My Lords, I agree with the speech of my noble and learned friend Lord Goff of Chieveley that the consequences of being a party to an illegal transaction cannot depend, as the majority in the Court of Appeal held, on such an imponderable factor as the extent to which the public conscience would be affronted by recognising rights created by illegal transactions. However, I have the misfortune to disagree with him as to the correct principle to be applied in a case where equitable property rights are acquired as a result of an illegal transaction.

Neither at law nor in equity will the court enforce an illegal contract which has been partially, but not fully, performed. However, it does not follow that all acts done under a partially performed contract are of no effect. In particular it is now clearly established that at law (as opposed to in equity) property in goods or land can pass under, or pursuant to, such a contract. If so, the rights of the owner of the legal title thereby acquired will be enforced, provided that the plaintiff can establish such title without pleading or leading evidence of the illegality. It is said that the property lies where it falls, even though legal title to the property was acquired as a result of the property passing under the illegal contract itself. I will first consider the modern authorities laying down the circumstances under which a legal proprietary interest acquired under an illegal transaction will be enforced by the courts. I will then consider whether the courts adopt a different attitude to equitable proprietary interests so acquired.

The position at law is well illustrated by the decision in *Bowmakers Ltd v Barnet Instruments Ltd* [1944] 2 All ER 579, [1945] KB 65. In that case Barnet acquired three parcels of machine tools which had previously belonged to Smith. The transaction was carried through by three hire-purchase agreements under which Smith sold the goods to Bowmakers, who then hired them to Barnet. All three agreements were unlawful as being in breach of defence regulations: it is important to note that in the case of at least two of the parcels the illegality lay in the contract under which Bowmakers acquired the machine tools from Smith (see [1944] 2 All ER 579 at 581, [1945] KB 65 at 69). Bowmakers succeeded in an action for conversion against Barnet. Even though it appeared from the pleadings and the evidence that the contract under which Bowmakers acquired the goods was illegal, such contract was effective to pass the property in the goods to Bowmakers, who could therefore found their claim on the property right so acquired.

The position at law is further illustrated by Feret v Hill (1854) 15 CB 207, [1843–60] All ER Rep 924, where A, with intent to use premises as a brothel, took a lease from B. B, having discovered that the premises were being used as a brothel, ejected A. A was held entitled to maintain ejectment against B notwithstanding that A entered into the lease for an illegal purpose.

In Taylor v Chester (1869) LR 4 QB 309, [1861–73] All ER Rep 154 the plaintiff had deposited with the defendant half a £50 note as security for payment due under an illegal contract with the defendant. The plaintiff was held unable to recover the half note as a special property in it (i.e. the security interest) had passed to the defendant.

In Alexander v Rayson [1936] 1 KB 169, [1935] All ER Rep 185 the plaintiff had leased a property to the defendant. For the purpose of defrauding the rating authorities, the plaintiff had carried through the transaction by two documents, one a lease which expressed a low rent the other a service agreement providing for additional payments sufficient to bring up the annual payment to the actual rent agreed. The plaintiff failed in an action to recover rent due under the agreements but the Court of Appeal said that, if the plaintiff had let the flat to be used for an illegal purpose, the leasehold interest in the flat would have vested in the defendant, who would have been entitled to remain in possession of the flat until and unless the plaintiff could eject her without relying on the unlawful agreement (see [1936] 1 KB 169 at 186, [1935] All ER Rep 185 at 193).

From these authorities the following propositions emerge.

(1) Property in chattels and land can pass under a contract which is illegal and therefore would have been unenforceable as a contract.

(2) A plaintiff can at law enforce property rights so acquired provided that he does not need to rely on the illegal contract for any purpose other than providing the basis of his claim to a property right.

(3) It is irrelevant that the illegality of the underlying agreement was either pleaded or emerged in evidence: if the plaintiff has acquired legal title under the illegal contract that is enough.

I have stressed the common law rules as to the impact of illegality on the acquisition and enforcement of property rights because it is the appellant's contention that different principles apply in equity. In particular it is said that equity will not aid the respondent to assert, establish or enforce an equitable, as opposed to a legal, proprietary interest since she was a party to the fraud on the Department of Social Security. The house was put in the name of the appellant alone (instead of joint names) to facilitate the fraud. Therefore, it is said, the respondent does not come to equity with clean hands: consequently, equity will not aid her.

. . .

In my judgment to draw such distinctions between property rights enforceable at law and those which require the intervention of equity would be surprising. More than 100 years has elapsed since the fusion of the administration of law and equity. The reality of the matter is that, in 1993, English law has one single law of property made up of legal and equitable interests. Although for historical reasons legal estates and equitable estates have differing incidents, the person owning either type of estate has a right of property, a right *in rem* not merely a right *in personam*. If the law is that a party is entitled to enforce a property right acquired under an illegal transaction, in my judgment the same rule ought to apply to any property right so acquired, whether such right is legal or equitable.

In the present case, the respondent claims under a resulting or implied trust. The courts below have found, and it is now disputed, that apart from the question of illegality the respondent would have been entitled in equity to a half share in the house in accordance with the principles exemplified in *Gissing v Gissing* [1970] 2 All ER 780, [1971] AC 886, *Grant v Edwards* [1986] 2 All ER 426, [1986] Ch. 638 and *Lloyds Bank plc v Rosset* [1990] 1 All ER 1111, [1991] 1 AC 107. The creation of such an equitable interest does not depend upon a contractual obligation but on a common intention acted upon by the parties to their detriment. It is a development of the old law of resulting trust under which, where two parties have provided the purchase money to buy a property which is conveyed into the name of one of them alone, the latter is presumed to hold the property on a resulting trust for both parties in shares proportionate to their contributions to the purchase price. In argument, no distinction was drawn between strict resulting trusts and a *Gissing v Gissing* type of trust.

A presumption of resulting trust also arises in equity when A transfers personalty or money to B: see *Snell's Equity* (29th ed., 1990), 183–184, *Standing v Bowring* (1885) 31 ChD 282 at 287, [1881–85] All ER Rep 702 at 704 per Cotton L.J. and *Dewar v Dewar* [1975] 2 All ER 728 at 732, [1975] 1 WLR 1532 at 1537. Before 1925 there was also a presumption of resulting trust when land was voluntarily transferred by A to B; it is arguable, however, that the position has been altered by the 1925 property legislation: see *Snell* (op. cit.), 182. The presumption of a resulting trust is, in my view, crucial in considering the authorities. On that presumption (and on the contrary presumption of advancement) hinges the answer to the crucial question: does a plaintiff claiming under a resulting trust have to rely on the underlying illegality? Where the presumption of resulting trust applies, the plaintiff does not have to rely on the illegality. If he proves that the property is vested in the defendant alone but that the plaintiff provided part of the purchase money, or voluntarily transferred the property to the defendant, the plaintiff establishes his claim under a resulting trust unless either the contrary presumption of advancement displaces the presumption of resulting trust or the defendant leads evidence to rebut the presumption of resulting trust. Therefore, in cases where the presumption of advancement does not apply, a plaintiff can establish his equitable interest in the property without relying in any way on the underlying illegal transaction. In this case the respondent as defendant simply pleaded the common intention that the property should belong to both of them and that she contributed to the purchase price: she claimed that in consequence the property belonged to them equally. To the same effect was her evidence-in-chief. Therefore the respondent was not forced to rely on the illegality to prove her equitable interest. Only in the reply and the course of the respondent's cross-examination did such illegality emerge: it was the appellant who had to rely on that illegality.

. . .

Against this background, I turn to consider the authorities dealing with the position in equity where A transferred property to B for an illegal purpose. The earlier authorities, primarily Lord Eldon, support the appellant's proposition that equity will not aid a plaintiff who has transferred property to another for an illegal purpose.

. . . in *Curtis v Perry* (1802) 6 Ves 739, 31 ER 1285 Nantes and Chiswell (who was a Member of Parliament) were partners. Ships had been purchased by Nantes out of partnership assets but registered in the sole name of Nantes. When Chiswell discovered the position, the ships were shown in the partnership books as being partnership property. However, with Chiswell's connivance the ships remained registered in the sole name of Nantes so as to evade a statutory prohibition against the ships being used for government contracts if owned by a Member of Parliament. In a dispute between the partnership creditors and Nantes's separate creditors, Lord Eldon L.C. held in favour of the latter. He said (6 Ves 739 at 747, 31 ER 1285 at 1288–9):

> The moment the purpose to defeat the policy of the law by fraudulently concealing, that this was his property, is admitted, it is very clear, he ought not to be heard in this court to say, that is his property. In the case of a bill filed to have a reconveyance of a qualification given by the plaintiff to his son to enable him to sit in Parliament, the purpose being answered, the bill was very properly dismissed by Lord Kenyon with costs.

See also Ex p Yallop (1808) 15 Ves. 60, 33 ER 677.

The same broad principle was applied by the Exchequer Chamber in equity in *Groves v Groves* (1828) 3 Y & J 163, 148 ER 1136. In that case the plaintiff had purchased land in the name of his brother so as to give the brother a necessary qualification to vote. The plaintiff claimed to recover the land under a resulting trust. His claim was dismissed on the grounds, *inter alia*, ' . . . that the illegal purpose for which this conveyance was made bars that equity' (see 3 Y & J 163 at 172, 148 ER 1136 at 1141). There are many other cases in the first half of the nineteenth century where the same principle was applied.

However, in my view, the law was not so firmly established as at first sight it appears to have been.
. . .

The law was developing in another direction during the nineteenth century. There was originally a difference of view as to whether a transaction entered into for an illegal purpose would be enforced at law or in equity if the party had repented of his illegal purpose before it had been put into operation, i.e. the doctrine of *locus poenitentiae*. It was eventually recognised both at law and in equity that, if the plaintiff had repented before the illegal purpose was carried through, he could recover his property: see *Taylor v Bowers* (1876) 1 QBD 291, [1874–80] All ER Rep 405, *Symes v Hughes* (1870) LR 9 Eq 475. The principle of *locus poenitentiae* is in my judgment irreconcilable with any rule that where property is transferred for an illegal purpose no equitable proprietary right exists. The equitable right, if any, must arise at the time at which the property was voluntarily transferred for an illegal purpose no equitable proprietary right exists. The equitable right, if any, must arise at the time at which the property was voluntarily transferred to the third party or purchased in the name of the third party. The existence of the equitable interest cannot depend upon events occurring after that date. Therefore if, under the principle of *locus poenitentiae*, the courts recognise that an equitable interest did arise out of the underlying transaction, the same must be true where the illegal purpose was carried through. The carrying out of the illegal purpose cannot, by itself, destroy the pre-existing equitable interest. The doctrine of *locus poenitentiae* therefore demonstrates that the effect of illegality is not to prevent a proprietary interest in equity from arising or to produce a forfeiture of such right: the effect is to render the equitable interest unenforceable in certain circumstances. The effect of illegality is not substantive but procedural. The question therefore is: in what circumstances will equity refuse to enforce equitable rights which undoubtedly exist?

It is against this background that one has to assess the more recent law. Although in the cases decided during the last 100 years there are frequent references to Lord

Eldon L.C.'s wide principle, with one exception (*Cantor v Cox* (1975) 239 EG 121) none of the English decisions are decided by simply applying that principle.
. . .

In my judgment, the explanation for this departure from Lord Eldon L.C.'s absolute rule is that the fusion of the administration of law and equity has led the courts to adopt a single rule (applicable both at law and in equity) as to the circumstances in which the court will enforce property interests acquired in pursuance of an illegal transaction, *viz* the *Bowmaker* rule (see *Bowmakers Ltd v Barnet Instruments Ltd* |1944| 2 All ER 579, |1945| KB 65). A party to an illegality can recover by virtue of a legal or equitable property interest if, but only if, he can establish his title without relying on his own illegality. In cases where the presumption of advancement applies, the plaintiff is faced with the presumption of gift and therefore cannot claim under a resulting trust unless and until he has rebutted that presumption of gift: for those purposes the plaintiff does have to rely on the underlying illegality and therefore fails.

The position is well illustrated by two decisions in the Privy Council. In the first, *Sajan Singh v Sardara Ali* |1960| 1 All ER 269, |1960| AC 167 a plaintiff who had acquired legal title to a lorry under an illegal transaction was held entitled to succeed against the other party to the illegality in detinue and trespass. The board approved the *Bowmaker* test. Two years later in *Chettiar v Chettiar* |1962| 1 All ER 494, |1962| AC 294 the board had to consider the case where a father, who had transferred land to his son for an illegal purpose, sought to recover it under a resulting trust. It was held that he could not, since he had to rely on his illegal purpose in order to rebut the presumption of advancement. The board distinguished the decision in *Haigh v Kaye* (1872) LR 7 Ch. 469 on the following ground (|1962| 1 All ER 494 at 497, |1962| AC 294 at 301):

> It appears to their Lordships, however, that there is a clear distinction between *Haigh v Kaye* and the present case. In *Haigh v Kaye* the plaintiff conveyed a freehold estate to the defendant. In the conveyance it was stated that a sum of £850 had been paid by the defendant for it. The plaintiff proved that no such sum was paid and claimed that the defendant was a trustee for him. Now in that case the plaintiff had no reason to disclose any illegality and did not do so. It was the defendant who suggested that the transaction was entered into for a fraudulent purpose. He sought to drag it in without pleading it distinctly and he was not allowed to do so. In the present case, however, the father had of necessity to disclose his own illegality to the court and for this reason: He had not only to get over the fact that the transfer stated that the son paid $7,000 for the land. He had also to get over the presumption of advancement for whenever a father transfers property to his son, there is a presumption that he intended it as a gift to his son: and if he wishes to rebut that presumption and to say that his son took as trustee for him, he must prove the trust clearly and distinctly, by evidence properly admissible for the purpose, and not leave it to be inferred from slight circumstances; see *Shephard v Cartwright* (|1954| 3 All ER 649 at 652, |1955| AC 431 at 445).

Further, the board distinguished *Sajan Singh v Sardara Ali*. It was pointed out that in *Sajan Singh v Sardara Ali* the plaintiff founded his claim on a right of property in the lorry and his possession of it. The board continued (|1962| 1 All ER 494 at 498, |1962| AC 294 at 303):

> |The plaintiff| did not have to found his cause of action on an immoral or illegal act. He was held entitled to recover. In the present case the father has of necessity to put forward, and indeed, assert, his own fraudulent purpose, which he has fully

achieved. He is met therefore by the principle stated long ago by Lord Mansfield: "No court will lend its aid to a man who founds his cause of action upon an immoral or illegal act" (see *Holman v Johnson* ((1775) 1 Cowp 341 at 343, [1775–1802] All ER Rep 98 at 99).

In my judgment these two cases show that the Privy Council was applying exactly the same principle in both cases although in one case the plaintiff's claim rested on a legal title and in the other on an equitable title. The claim based on the equitable title did not fail simply because the plaintiff was a party to the illegal transaction; it only failed because the plaintiff was bound to disclose and rely upon his own illegal purpose in order to rebut the presumption of advancement. The Privy Council was plainly treating the principle applicable both at law and in equity as being that a man can recover property provided that he is not forced to rely on his own illegality.

I therefore reach the conclusion that, although there is no case overruling the wide principle stated by Lord Eldon L.C., as the law has developed the equitable principle has become elided into the common law rule. In my judgment the time has come to decide clearly that the rule is the same whether a plaintiff founds himself on a legal or equitable title: he is entitled to recover if he is not forced to plead or rely on the illegality, even if it emerges that the title on which he relied was acquired in the course of carrying through an illegal transaction.

As applied in the present case, that principle would operate as follows. The respondent established a resulting trust by showing that she had contributed to the purchase price of the house and that there was a common understanding between her and the appellant that they owned the house equally. She had no need to allege or prove *why* the house was conveyed into the name of the appellant alone, since that fact was irrelevant to her claim: it was enough to show that the house was in fact vested in the appellant alone. The illegality only emerged at all because the appellant sought to raise it. Having proved these facts, the respondent had raised a presumption of resulting trust. There was no evidence to rebut that presumption. Therefore the respondent should succeed. This is exactly the process of reasoning adopted by the Ontario Court of Appeal in *Gorog v Kiss* (1977) 78 DLR (3d) 690, which in my judgment was rightly decided.

Finally, I should mention a further point which was relied on by the appellant. It is said that, once the illegality of the transaction emerges, the court must refuse to enforce the transaction and all claims under it whether pleaded or not: see *Scott v Brown Doering McNab & Co.* [1892] 2 QB 724, [1891–4] All ER Rep 654. Therefore, it is said, it does not matter whether a plaintiff relies on or gives evidence of the illegality: the court will not enforce the plaintiff's rights. In my judgment, this submission is plainly ill-founded. There are many cases where a plaintiff has succeeded, notwithstanding that the illegality of the transaction under which she acquired the property has emerged: see, for example, *Bowmakers Ltd v Barnet Instruments Ltd* and *Sajan Singh v Sardara Ali*. In my judgment the court is only entitled and bound to dismiss a claim on the basis that it is founded on an illegality in those cases where the illegality is of a kind which would have provided a good defence if raised by the defendant. In a case where the plaintiff is not seeking to enforce an unlawful contract but founds his case on collateral rights acquired under the contract (such as a right of property) the court is neither bound nor entitled to reject the claim unless the illegality of necessity forms part of the plaintiff's case.

I would therefore dismiss the appeal.

(Jauncey L.J. agreed.)

SECTION FOUR—SEVERANCE

Sheehy v Sheehy [1901] 1 IR 239

An equity civil bill was brought to foreclose a £56 mortgage. Consideration for the mortgage included alcohol sold upon credit in violation of the Tippling Acts. The amount did not exceed £1. It was contended that this figure invalidated the entire transaction. The trial judge dismissed the suit but stated a case for the decision of the Court of Appeal. There were two questions—(1) Was the mortgage in whole or in part enforceable? (2) Was the order dismissing the suit right?

Fitzgibbon L.J.:

. . . Here we have to deal with legislation which does not expressly avoid anything, but which is in effect prohibitive. What is prohibited? Plainly not the sale of spirits: the sale is not illegal, either in itself, or where the price is paid—sale of small quantities on credit is what is aimed at, and where this has been done, the recovery of the price is prohibited. With all deference for expressions to be found in some of the cases, I am not prepared to hold that there is any such prohibition of selling drink on credit as would make the act indictable; if anything is prohibited, or is made illegal, by a statute, doing it must be a misdemeanour. I am not prepared to say that a publican who supplies drink without being paid for it, commits a misdemeanour, even though the statute imposes a penalty, and enacts a disability, for so doing. I think that the statute with which we are dealing is analogous, in its effect, and for our present purpose, rather to the Statute of Frauds and the Statutes of Limitations, than to a prohibitory Act, disobedience to which is a crime. It bars and takes away the remedy, but the transaction or contract is not made void. If a man orders drink and gets it, the publican thinking that he is going to get cash across the counter, the publican gives it at the risk of being unable to recover the price, but I cannot believe that he commits a misdemeanour. The sale is legal, but recovering the price is illegal; this construction of the law makes the punishment fit the crime, because it limits the illegality to the amount of the credit; and I think that it will reconcile most of the authorities, and will lead to a just result in this case.

If giving credit is illegal, it follows that any security given for the amount of the illegal credit is equally illegal. But the question remains whether such illegality necessarily vitiates the entire security, where part only of the consideration is affected by it. If the prohibition be what I think it is, namely, only a prohibition to recover the amount of the credit, this indiscriminate result will not follow. The part of the consideration which is good is severable, and full effect is given to the prohibition by preventing the recovery of so much as consists of credit illegally given. . . .

. . . In my opinion, the plaintiff's claim, to the extent of the credit given for drink within the Tippling Acts, cannot be recovered; but those Acts vitiate or affect nothing more. In *Burnyeat v Hutchinson*[1] the verdict was sustained for the amount of the tavern bill, omitting the charge for spiritous liquors. In my own experience, on County Court appeals, in actions for the price of goods, and upon promissory notes, including the price of drink, the practice has been to deduct the irrecoverable items and to give decrees for the rest, and I think that this case should be decided in the same way.

[1] 5 B & Ald. 241.

Furnival & Co. *v* O'Neill [1902] 2 IR 422

In 1879, following a creditor's composition, the defendant's husband and the plaintiff, one of his creditors, entered into a contract under which the latter was to receive a secret benefit. In 1890 the defendant's husband mortgaged certain property to the plaintiff to secure the repayment of his debt. The defendant later provided promissory notes to the plaintiff to secure the outstanding debt. The plaintiff then sued the defendant on foot of those notes.

Andrews J.:

. . .

I think it clear that the main and leading consideration for the agreement of 14 October 1879, without which it would not have been entered into, was the undertaking that the plaintiffs' debt of £215 8s should be paid in full, and that the main and loading object of the deed of 1880, without which it would not have been entered into, was to secure the carrying out of that agreement, which was plainly illegal as being contrary to the settled principle and policy of the law, applicable to composition arrangements with creditors as well as to bankruptcy, that no creditor shall be allowed to obtain for himself, without the assent of the other creditors, a preference and exclusive advantage over the others.

. . .

Now I do not think that it can be disputed that where there are several considerations, some illegal and bad, and some good, and several agreements are entered into in the same instrument, founded on all the considerations, all the agreements are void, because it is impossible to say that the illegal consideration did not enter into each agreement and was not the main consideration which induced it. It is, in my opinion, beyond doubt that the illegal agreement to pay the plaintiffs' debt in full was the main and operative foundation for the entire of the deed of 1880, without which that deed would not have been entered into at all, and it follows that the entire deed was and is void and incapable of enforcement by reason of the illegality to which it sought to give effect.

In the recent case of *Sheehy v Sheehy*,[1] decided on the Tippling Acts, the ground of the decision was that what was prohibited was not the sale of liquors in small or any quantities, but the recovery of the price of certain small quantities sold on credit; and so the security in that case was vitiated only to the extent of the irrecoverable part of the consideration. That decision does not affect this case, in which the main consideration was illegal as being against the principle and policy of the law.

[1]. [1901] 1 IR 239.

John McIlvenna and David McIlvenna *v* Owen Ferris and Arthur Green [1955] IR 318

In September 1951 the plaintiffs contracted to build a factory for the defendants. This contract was in contravention of the Emergency Powers Order of 1945 which prohibited building work without a ministerial licence. In February 1952, during the building of the factory the plaintiffs orally agreed to perform additional work. When all the work was completed the defendants refused to pay the agreed price and the plaintiffs sued. The defence of illegality was not pleaded by the defendants.

O'Daly J.:

. . .

. . . It is, in my opinion, clearly established that the contract of September 1951, was made in contravention of art. 5 (1) of the Emergency Powers (No. 358) Order 1945.

. . .

The contracts for extras on the evidence before me were made after 15 February 1952, and at a time when building operations were not subject to statutory restriction. I think [counsel for the defendant's] submission on this head would have much force if the Emergency Powers Order had not been revoked. But the order having been revoked, contracts entered into subsequently (as the contracts for the extras were) clearly cannot be affected.

. . .

In my opinion it is well settled that the court will not assist a plaintiff in the circumstances of this case—I refer only to the contract of September 1951. The law is stated by Lindley L.J. with characteristic forthrightness in *Scott v Brown, Doering, McNab & Co.*[1]:

> *Ex turpi causa non oritur actio.* This old and well known legal maxim is founded in good sense, and expresses a clear and well recognised legal principle, which is not confined to indictable offences. No court ought to enforce an illegal contract or allow itself to be made the instrument of enforcing obligations alleged to arise out of a contract or transaction which is illegal, if the illegality is duly brought to the notice of the court, and if the person invoking the aid of the court is himself implicated in the illegality. It matters not whether the defendant has pleaded the illegality or whether he has not. If the evidence adduced by the plaintiff proves the illegality the court ought not to assist him.

. . .

. . . I might also refer to *Harry Parker Ltd v Mason*[2] where McKinnon L.J. (at 601) says: 'The rule *ex turpi causa non oritur actio* is, of course, not a matter by way of defence,' and Luxmoore L.J. (at 610) says that 'this court will not assist either party once the illegality of the transaction has been brought to its notice.'

[1] [1892] 2 QB 724 at p. 728.   [2] [1940] 2 KB 590.

Ailion *v* Spiekermann and Others [1976] 1 Ch. 158

Templeman J.:

. . . The question in this case is whether a vendor who contracts to sell a lease for an illegal premium can be compelled to assign the lease to the purchaser without the premium.

By a contract dated 8 April 1974, the vendor, Mr Ailion, agreed to assign to the purchasers, Mr and Mrs Spiekermann, the flat 59, Oakwood Court, London, held under a lease for a term expiring on 24 December 1976, at a yearly rent of £850. The contract provided for the lease to be assigned in consideration of the usual covenants by the purchasers to indemnify the vendor. The contract also provided for the purchasers to pay £3,750 for certain specified chattels. The chattels were subsequently valued at £604.75. Although this valuation has not been proved or accepted, it is common ground that at all material times the chattels were worth much less than £3,750. It is also common ground that at the date of the contract the vendor and the purchasers were aware that the chattels were not worth £3,750 and that it was not lawful for the vendor to require or receive more than the value of the chattels. The vendor wanted the money and the purchasers needed the flat.

The illegality arises from the admitted fact that possession under the lease of the flat 59, Oakwood Court constituted a protected tenancy within the Rent Act 1968. S. 86 (1) provides that any person who as a condition of the assignment of a protected tenancy requires the payment of any premium shall be guilty of an offence. By s. 86 (2) any person who, in connection with the assignment of a protected tenancy, receives any premium shall be guilty of an offence. By s. 88 where the purchase of any furniture has been required as a condition of the assignment of a protected tenancy, then, if the price exceeds the reasonable price of the furniture, the excess shall be treated as if it were a premium required to be paid as a condition of the assignment of the protected tenancy. S. 92 (1) defines furniture in a way which includes the chattels the subject of the contract dated 8 April 1974. By s. 89 any person who, in connection with the proposed assignment, on terms which require the purchase of furniture, of a protected tenancy offers the furniture at a price which he knows or ought to know is unreasonably high, or otherwise seeks to obtain such a price for the furniture is guilty of an offence.

The vendor in the present case infringed s. 89 when he offered the chattels to the purchasers for £3,750 and committed an offence under s. 86 (1) when he required the purchasers to contract to take the chattels for £3,750. If the contract had been completed according to its terms the vendor would have infringed s. 86 (2) by receiving a premium in the form of an excessive price for the chattels.

After the date of the contract the purchasers were allowed into possession of the flat as licensees on the terms of a letter dated 26 April 1974, namely that they 'should be licensees only and that they will vacate the premises on demand in the event of them failing to complete the purchase in accordance with the contract.'

The date for completion fixed by the contract was 6 May. The purchasers had trouble in raising the money and on 16 May, the vendor served a notice to complete and thereby committed another offence under s. 86 (1). The vendor also revoked the purchasers' licence to occupy the flat and demanded possession by the following day. Litigation followed. The vendor claims possession and rescission. The purchasers claim specific performance of the contract on payment of the reasonable value of the chattels.

For present purposes it does not matter whether the vendor committed all the offences which are alleged. It is admitted, and it is sufficient, that the contract originated in an illegal offer by the vendor under s. 89, and cannot be completed without an illegal receipt by the vendor under s. 86 (2). The vendor has fallen foul of the statutory control of rented residential accommodation. I am not concerned with the merits or demerits of the statutory control of residential accommodation which includes control of rent and security of tenure. But one of the objects of the Rent Act 1968 is plainly to protect a purchaser requiring accommodation from a vendor seeking to exploit the financial value of the controlled rent and security of tenure established by Parliament.

A purchaser negotiating with a vendor is protected by ss 86, 88 and 89 of the Act. But Parliament thought it necessary to give further protection to a purchaser against a vendor who is undeterred by the possibility of punishment for an offence, and who pursues a purchaser, desperate for residential accommodation, who dares not invoke the law until he obtains the accommodation. Thus, s. 90 of the Act provides that where under any agreement any premium is paid which could not lawfully be required or received, the premium shall be recoverable by the person by whom it is paid. In the present case it is common ground that if the purchasers had kept quiet and had paid £3,750 they could have sprung the trap after taking an assignment and sued successfully for the recovery of the amount by which £3,750 exceeds the reasonable value of the chattels.

It is submitted for the purchasers that they are only seeking in these proceedings, without any further breach of the law, the result which s. 90 was designed to achieve, namely, an assignment without the loss of the premium. It defeats the purpose of the Act and brings the law into disrepute if a purchaser who is offered and contracts to purchase furniture at an unreasonable price as a condition of acquiring a protected tenancy obtains the tenancy and recovers the premium if he enables the vendor to commit the further offence of receiving an illegal premium, but fails to obtain the tenancy if he declines to pay the premium which can only be illegally received. The argument is that the Rent Act 1968 on its true construction requires an illegal premium to be deleted or deducted from a contract for the assignment of a protected tenancy. Such is the logical result of all the provisions and the purpose of the Act.

The argument for the vendor counters logic with logic; the contract is illegal and cannot be performed in accordance with its express terms. Therefore both parties are released from the contract. The parties bargained for the assignment of the lease and for the delivery of the chattels on payment of £3,750. The court has no power to inflict on the parties a different bargain for the assignment of the lease and for the delivery of the chattels on payment of the reasonable value of the chattels.

In my judgment the answer to this conundrum is that Parliament has not made illegal the contract or the assignment which the vendor agreed to execute. Parliament only requires the vendor to decline with thanks any sum of money which constitutes a premium. The court is now asked to compel the vendor to assign the lease which he contracted to assign without the money which Parliament forbids him to accept.

On behalf of the vendor it was argued that severance between the good and bad parts of the contract was not possible, or alternatively, was unprecedented. In my judgment the effect of the Rent Act 1968 and in particular the effect of s. 88 is to divide the contract into three separate elements. The vendor is contractually and legally bound to assign the lease in return for a covenant of indemnity. The vendor is contractually and legally bound to transfer the chattels in return for the reasonable value of the chattels. The vendor is contractually but illegally entitled to receive a premium which consists of the amount by which £3,750 exceeds the reasonable value of the chattels. Parliament having effected this clear and distinct division between the legal and illegal elements of the contracts, the court is not powerless to remove the gilt and leave the gingerbread. The absence of precedent does not worry me so long as there is no lack of principle.

Where there are legal and illegal elements in a contract which are capable of severance, the jurisdiction to enforce the legal elements will only be exercised in a proper case and if the severance is in accordance with the enforcement of the principles which induced Parliament to outlaw the elements which are illegal. The fact that the purchasers knew of the illegality at the outset is a powerful reason why they should not obtain any relief. But the Rent Act is designed to protect persons in the position of the purchasers. They could not insist on the elimination from the draft contract of the illegal premium without losing the flat. They had no choice if they needed somewhere to live. They committed no offence.

If the purchasers by obtaining specific performance without payment of the illegal premium were able to put themselves in a better position than if they had completed the contract according to its terms, that would be a good reason for the court to decline to assist the purchasers. But in this case s. 90 makes all the difference. By that section whether a purchaser knows of the illegality or not, he can enjoy the fruits of his bargain and recover the illegal payment which he has made, even if he hands over a cheque and a writ in exchange for an assignment.

It does not follow that every purchaser for a protected tenancy at a premium is entitled to specific performance. The remedy of specific performance is discretionary.

If the vendor is ignorant of the facts or the law, or if the purchaser tempts the vendor with a cheque book, or if the vendor changes his mind before the purchaser alters his position in reliance on the contract, the court may decline to make a specific performance order. It all depends on the circumstances. In the present case the initiative came wholly from the vendor and he now wants to recoil from the contract because he cannot obtain the illegal payment on which he insisted until the illegality became public. Moreover the purchasers have been allowed to go into occupation of the flat. If they are now evicted by the court, as the vendor requires, it will appear that the purchasers have been turned out because they failed to raise and pay an illegal premium and to keep quiet about the illegality until after the contract had been completed by an assignment. This appearance is not consistent with the purpose of the Act or the administration of justice. If I make no order for possession in favour of the vendor and no order for specific performance in favour of the purchasers, thus following the historical precedent of washing my hands of a contract which contains an illegal element, the vendor will remain liable for the rent and covenants under the lease and the position of both the vendor and the purchasers will be unsatisfactory. In these circumstances I propose to order specific performance of the contract to assign the lease and transfer the chattels in return for the consideration to which the vendor has been confined by Parliament.

Philip Carney v John Herbert and Others [1985] 1 AC 301

The plaintiffs agreed to sell shares in a company 'Airfoil' to the defendant. The purchase price was to be paid in instalments secured by a personal guarantee by the defendant and mortgages by a subsidiary of Airfoil. These mortgages were illegal under s. 67 of the Companies Act 1961 which prohibited the provision of security by a subsidiary in connection with the purchase of shares in its holding company. When the plaintiff sued the defendant under his guarantees the defendant claimed that the illegality of the mortgages tainted the whole contract rendering it unenforceable.

Lord Brightman:

. . .

Questions of severability are often difficult. There are not set rules which will decide all cases. As was said by Kitto J. in Brooks v Burns Philp Trustee Co. Ltd (1969) 121 CLR 432, 438, tests for deciding questions of severability that have been formulated as useful in particular cases are not always satisfactory for cases of other kinds.

To some extent each case must depend on its own circumstances, and in particular on the nature of the illegality. Two colliery cases, Netherseal Colliery Co. Ltd v Bourne (1889) 14 App Cas 228 and Kearney v Whitehaven Colliery Co. |1893| 1 QB 700, provide a useful starting point for a consideration of this branch of the law.

In the Netherseal case two miners were suing for the balance of their wages. In the Kearney case the colliery was suing a miner for damages for his failure to give the contractual period of notice before leaving his employment. In the latter case the miner sought to defeat the claim by relying on the illegality of a term in the contract which, it was said, rendered the entire contract of employment void. The same illegal term was present in both cases. It was a term, illegal by statute, which purported to authorise the colliery owner to make a deduction from a miner's wages in respect of coal brought to the surface of the mine which was so small as to pass through a screening device known as 'Billy Fairplay'. Neither the House of Lords nor the Court of Appeal had difficulty in upholding the claims of the respective plaintiffs despite the presence of this illegal term. It was not argued in the *Netherseal* case that the illegal term vitiated the whole contract, so severability was not an issue. It was nevertheless raised and disposed of by Lord Halsbury L.C. in his concluding observations, at 236: 'as the whole contract is not illegal but the deductions are not enforceable, the plaintiffs had a right to sue for the wages due to them without any such deduction.'

Severability was directly in issue in the second case, and it may be helpful to quote from the judgment of Lopes L.J. at 713:

> The law is clear that where the consideration for a promise or promises contained in the contract is unlawful, the whole agreement is void. The reason is that it is impossible to discriminate between the weight to be given to different parts of the consideration, and therefore you cannot sever the legal from the illegal part. But where there is no illegality in the consideration, and some of the provisions are legal and others illegal, the illegality of those which are bad does not communicate itself to, or contaminate, those which are good, unless they are inseparable from and dependent upon one another. Here the consideration moving from the master to the men is the employment and the payment of wages. The consideration moving from the men to the master is the services rendered by them. Both are good and lawful considerations. Then we come to the stipulation with respect to deductions. I am of opinion that that stipulation is altogether separable from and independent of the consideration.

This approach was echoed by Jordan C.J. in *McFarlane v Daniell* (1938) 38 SR (NSW) 337. This was a case in which an actor sued for his remuneration under a contract of employment which contained a restrictive covenant which was void as being in unreasonable restraint of trade. The employer boldly contended that the actor could not recover his remuneration because the contract was wholly void. Jordan C.J. said, at 345:

> When valid promises supported by legal consideration are associated with, but separate in form from, invalid promises, the test of whether they are severable is whether they are in substance so connected with the others as to form an indivisible whole which cannot be taken to pieces without altering its nature . . . If the elimination of the invalid promises changes the extent only but not the kind of the contract, the valid promises are severable . . . If the substantial promises were all illegal or void, merely ancillary promises would be inseverable.

He added later, at 346:

> The exact scope and limits of the doctrine that a legal promise associated with, but severable from, an illegal promise is capable of enforcement, are not clear. It can hardly be imagined that a court would enforce a promise, however inherently valid and however severable, if contained in a contract one of the terms of which provided for assassination.

Their Lordships agree with both observations. There are therefore two matters to be considered where a contract contains an illegal term, first, whether as a matter of construction the lawful part of the contract can be severed from the unlawful part, thus enabling the plaintiff to sue on a promise unaffected by any illegality; secondly, whether, despite severability, there is a bar to enforceability arising out of the nature of the illegality.

. . .

The classic case where a contract containing an illegal provision was severed into its lawful and unlawful parts, and the lawful part enforced, was decided in 1962 by the High Court of Australia, *Thomas Brown & Sons Ltd v Fazal Deen* (1962) 108 CLR 391. In that case the plaintiff Fazal Deen had lodged with the defendant in 1943 a safe containing gold and gems under a contract of bailment. The bailment was illegal as regards the gold, which ought to have been delivered to the Commonwealth Bank under exchange control regulations. The contents of the safe disappeared in unexplained circumstances at some time during the ensuing sixteen years, whereupon the plaintiff sued the company in detinue. The company resisted the claim on the ground, *inter alia*, that the entire contract of bailment was tainted by the illegality of the bailment of the gold. The High Court, at 411, approved the observation of Jordan C.J. in *McFarlane's* case, 38 SR (NSW) 337, 345: 'If the elimination of the invalid promises changes the extent only but not the kind of the contract, the valid promises are severable.' That test was clearly passed, because under the contract of bailment the plaintiff was entitled at any time to demand the return of part only of the property bailed without thereby affecting the bailment of the residue. Accordingly the plaintiff could sue in detinue on the contract of bailment in respect of the safe and the gems. The High Court rejected the submission of the company's counsel, at 393, that: 'If any part of the contract is illegal, public policy will not allow any part of the contract to be enforced.'

These principles were applied by the Supreme Court of Victoria in *Niemann v Smedley* [1973] VR 769. In that case employees were given the right to an allotment to shares on terms that the company would if desired finance their acquisition over a five year period. The company became insolvent three years later, and the question arose whether the allottees, whose names had been entered on the register, were personally liable for the amounts unpaid on their shares, or whether they could claim that the allotments were illegal and void. One question which arose was whether the illegal provision for company finance was severable from the remainder of the contract constituted by the employee's application of shares (the offer) and notice to him of the allotment (the acceptance). It was held that the promise of the company to finance the acquisition of the shares was not the whole or the main consideration to support the promises of the applicants to pay for the shares, but was subsidiary to the main purpose of the contract—a contract to acquire fully paid shares in the company. Accordingly, the term by which the company agreed to provide finance was severable from the rest of the agreement, which remained valid, and accordingly the liquidator could recover capital unpaid on the shares. In the course of their decision, the Full Court said, at 778:

> An illegal term, as distinct from one merely void [for uncertainty], may raise different considerations for if it is of a kind involving a serious element of moral turpitude or is obviously inimical to the interest of the community so as to offend almost any concept of public policy it will so infect the rest of the contract that the courts will refuse to give any recognition at all to the contract, e.g. a promise to commit a burglary or to defraud the revenue or one *contra bonos mores*. But such class of cases apart, where the illegality has no such taint, the other terms will stand if the illegal portion can be severed.

It is necessary to refer briefly to a recent decision of the Court of Appeal of New South Wales, *DJE Constructions Pty Ltd v Maddocks* [1982] 1 NSWLR 5, in which the *Niemann* case was distinguished. The company, which had in issue only two one-dollar shares, needed to increase its issued capital by $5,998 in order to qualify for a licence from the Builder's Licensing Board. In order to achieve this result Reilly, who did not however possess the requisite funds, drew a cheque on her bank account in favour of the company for $5,990 to pay for an allotment of shares in favour of Maddocks. In order to cover Reilly's cheque, the company then drew a cheque on its own banking account in favour of Logan for the same amount, which Logan deposited in Reilly's bank account. This sum was shown in the company's account as a loan to Logan. The 5,998 shares intended to be issued appeared in the company's statutory returns as allotted to Maddocks, but only an unsealed share certificate in his name existed and his name was not entered on the register of members. Maddocks took proceedings against the company for rectification of the register by the entry of his name as the holder of 5,998 shares. His claim failed. In the course of his judgment Street C.J. said, at 10:

> Whilst the doctrine of severance can be applied in proceedings brought in the context of a contract illegal and void by reason of an infringement of a statutory provision (*Thomas Brown & Sons Ltd v Fazal Deen*), I know of no case in which it has been applied in a claim for the actual enforcement of such a contract. The principles relating to severability were developed in connection with contractual clauses void for uncertainty and for restraint of trade, and not in cases involving contracts *illegal* and void.

He then considered the *Niemann* case [1973] VR 769 and added, at 11–12:

> With the greatest of respect I do not consider that the doctrine of severability is available to save an integral term of an agreement such as the method of paying for shares that are being agreed to be issued in contravention of a section such as is presently under consideration. The distinction to be observed in the operation of the doctrine of severability as between contracts that are merely void and those that are *illegal* and void is adequately noted in *Halsbury* [certain references being given]. In the light of the long standing distinctions between a clause which is purely void and a clause which is illegal and void, I have some difficulty in accepting the correctness of applying the doctrine of severability in a situation such as existed in *Niemann v Smedley*.

The approach of Samuels J.A. was somewhat different. He said, at 21:

> It is arguable that a contractual term cannot be severed if it involves the doing of an act which is *contra bonos mores* or illegal at common law . . . or by statute . . . and the company's loan to Mr Logan amounted to a criminal offence under s. 67 (3) punishable by imprisonment. It appears, however, that this limitation cannot stand with the decision of the High Court in *Thomas Brown & Sons Ltd v Fazal Deen*, where one term of a contract was severed from the rest, although its performance necessarily contravened a provision of the National Security (Exchange Control) Regulations and was thus subject to any penalty prescribed by the regulations, or constituted an indictable misdemeanour at common law.

He came however to the same conclusion as Street C.J. on the ground that:

> the allotment was dependent upon the loan, and the illegality of the loan infected the whole of the contract. This was not an ordinary contract to take shares. Its fundamental objective was to enable the company to satisfy the requirements of the Builders' Licensing Board. It was a device to achieve that purpose; and an unsuccessful one as it turned out because the shares never were paid up in cash.

Glass J.A., who was the third member of the court, at p. 13, agreed with the result, but did not express a preference between the two approaches.

With great respect to Street C.J., their Lordships consider that the approach of Samuels J.A. was correct. Furthermore, so far as the Court of Appeal was concerned, the *Fazal Deen* case was a decision of the High Court and concluded the matter; in that case the plaintiff sued to enforce a contract of bailment a part of which contract was illegal, but he was allowed to succeed in relation to the lawful part of the contract.

In the light of the law as it has been developed in Australia and England, and also in Scotland though their Lordships have not been referred to the Scottish case law, their Lordships feel no doubt in the instant case that the illegal provision of the debentures can be severed from the composite transaction, leaving the plaintiffs free to enforce the sale agreements against Ilerain and the guarantee against the defendant; and that the nature of the illegality is not such as to preclude the plaintiffs on the ground of public policy from enforcing their rights under those documents.

. . .

The contract in the present case was basically one for the sale by the plaintiffs to the defendant or his nominated company of shares in Airfoil. The mortgages, like the guarantee, were ancillary to that contract for the sole purpose of ensuring the due performance of the contract by the purchaser. The defendant wanted only the shares in Airfoil. The plaintiffs wanted only the purchase money. It made no difference to the plaintiffs, or to the nature of the transaction, what security was provided so long as it was satisfactory security. The mortgage did not go to the heart of the transaction, and its elimination would leave unchanged the subject matter of the contract and the primary obligations of the vendors and the purchaser. The debenture is therefore capable of being severed from the remainder of the transaction, and its illegality does not taint the whole contract. There is no public policy objection to the enforcement of the contract from which the debenture has been divorced. The *Mineral Water* case |1967| 1 WLR 1110 is an authority that there is no public policy objection to such a course so far as the law of England and Wales is concerned. The *Firmin* case, 2 ACLC 338 is a like authority so far as the State of Queensland is concerned. There is no reason to suppose that the public policy of the State of new South Wales is any different.

. . .

Subject to a caveat that it is undesirable, if not impossible, to lay down any principles which will cover all problems in this field, their Lordships venture to suggest that, as a general rule, where parties enter into a lawful contract of, for example, sale and purchase, and there is an ancillary provision which is illegal but exists for the exclusive benefit of the plaintiff, the court may and probably will, if the justice of the case so requires, and there is no public policy objection, permit the plaintiff if he so wishes to enforce the contract without the illegal provision.

SECTION FIVE—CONTRACTS VOID AT COMMON LAW

A. AGREEMENTS WHICH OUST THE JURISDICTION OF THE COURT

Gregg & Co. v Fraser & Sons [1906] 2 KB 545

Lord O'Brien L.C.J.:

The defendants, by instrument in writing, contracted with the plaintiffs to supply them with certain timber, and by that instrument in writing warranted that the timber should be of a certain specified description and quality. There was also contained in the instrument the following provision, upon which the principal controversy arises:

> Should any difference arise under this contract, the buyers shall not reject the goods, if shipped, nor refuse payment for same as above stipulated, but such difference shall be referred to two arbitrators in the trade, one to be chosen by each party, said arbitrators having power to appoint an umpire, who shall decide whether any, or what, allowance shall be made; the decision of such arbitrators or their umpire shall be final and binding upon buyers and sellers, and this submission shall, and may, be made a rule of His Majesty's High Court of Justice. The cost of the arbitration to be borne as directed by arbitrators or umpire. In case of the non-compliance by the buyers with any of the terms of this contract, sellers to have immediate power of resale.

This is the provision upon which, as I said, the principal controversy arises. An action was brought by the plaintiffs on an award, and for breach of warranty, and the defendants allege, as the fact was, that the award was bad as not having been made within the prescribed time, and, relying upon the provision I have read, contended that it was a condition precedent to the plaintiffs' right to sue that there should have been an arbitration and award legally effectual under the clause in question. There was an award in point of fact, but it was not, as I have said, made within the prescribed time, and was, therefore, bad. I will at least assume for this part of my judgment that the defendants are not precluded from contending that it was invalid. I shall assume the award to have been ineffectual whilst discussing the question on the count for breach of warranty, namely, what was the true character of the so called arbitration clause, whether it was a merely collateral agreement or whether compliance with it was a condition precedent to a right of action: *Scott v Avery*[1] is the leading authority on this subject. The true limits of that decision have been the subject of much controversy. Did it sanction an agreement wholly ousting the jurisdiction of the courts, or did it stop short of such a result? Notwithstanding the opinion of Baron Martin, it has been held that it did not sanction any such agreement. Lord Cranworth, in giving judgment in that case in the House of Lords (see p. 847), is reported to have said:

> There is no doubt that where a right of action has accrued, parties cannot by contract say that there shall not be jurisdiction to enforce damages in respect of that right of action. Now this doctrine depends upon the general policy of the law, that parties cannot enter into a contract which gives rise to a right of an action for the breach of it, and then withdraw such a case from the jurisdiction of the ordinary tribunals. But surely there can be no principle or policy of the law which prevents parties from entering into such a contract as that no breach shall occur until after a reference has been made to arbitration. It appears to me that in such cases as that, the policy of the law is left untouched.

I find in the same case (see pp 853 and 854 of the report) that Lord Campbell said:

> But I am glad to think that there is no case that I am aware of that will be overturned by your Lordships affirming the judgment now in dispute. Because all that has been hitherto decided in *Thompson v Charnock*,[2] and the other cases referred to, is this, that if the contract between the parties simply contains a clause or covenant to refer to arbitration, and goes no further, then an action may be brought in spite of the clause, although there has been no arbitration. But there is no case that goes

the length of saying that where the contract is, as it is here, that no right of action shall accrue until there has been an arbitration, then an action may be brought, although there has been no arbitration. Now, in this contract of insurance it is stipulated, in the most express terms, that until the arbitrators have determined, no action shall lie in any court whatsoever. That is not ousting the courts of their jurisdiction, because they have no jurisdiction whatsoever, and no cause of action accrues until the arbitrators have determined.

True, that in the case before us there is no express provision that until the arbitrator or umpire has made an award no action shall lie; but if an intention to this effect is plainly inferable from the language used, the result is the same.

Before I apply myself to the language of the arbitration clause in this case I desire to refer to what Lord Esher (then Mr Justice Brett) said in the case of *Edwards v The Aberayron Mutual Ship Insurance Society*.[3] He is reported, at 596 of the report, to have said:

> The true limitation of *Scott v Avery* seems to me to be that which was expressed in it, and which, as I have pointed out, has so often been expressed about it, that if parties to a contract agree to a stipulation in it, which imposes, as a condition precedent to the maintenance of a suit or action for a breach of it, the settling by arbitration the amount of damage, or the time of paying it, or any matters of that kind, which do not go to the root of the action, i.e. which do not prevent any action at all from being maintained, such stipulation prevents any action being maintained until the particular facts have been settled by arbitration; but a stipulation in a contract which in terms would submit every dispute arising on the contract to arbitration, and so prevent the suffering or complaining party from maintaining any suit or action at all in respect of any breach of the contract, does not prevent an action from being maintained; it gives, at most, a right of action for not submitting to arbitration, and for damages, probably nominal. And the rule is founded on public policy. It in no way prevents parties from referring disputes, which have arisen, to arbitration; but it does prevent them from establishing as it were, before they dispute, a private tribunal, which may from ignorance do what the invented tribunal here did, namely, act in contravention, and insist on acting in contravention, of the most elementary principles of the administration of justice.

This is what Lord Esher said after an exhaustive view of the authorities. There is a succinct statement of the law on this subject by the Lord Chief Baron in the case of *Gorman v Hand-in-Hand Insurance Co.*[4] He said:

> The law upon the matter has been, at least since *Scott v Avery*, and, as I believe, from a far earlier period, settled beyond controversy. That law, as I understand, is that if two or more persons, whether in the instrument which creates the liability, or in any other way, agree to refer the matter on which that liability arises to arbitration, that agreement does not take away the right of action. But if the original agreement be, not simply to pay a sum of money, or to do an act, but to pay such sum of money, or do such an act, as a third person shall ascertain or direct, or to pay a sum of money or do an act in a certain event, such, for instance, as an arbitrator arriving at a certain conclusion, in any of these cases no cause of action arises unless, in the one case, that third person has so ascertained or directed, or, in the other, the stipulated event has happened. The question is, in every case, one of construction of the instrument— What is the meaning of the parties as evidenced by the language they have used?

Then, bearing in mind what Lords Cranworth and Campbell said in *Scott v Avery*, and what Lord Esher said in *Edwards v The Aberayron Mutual Insurance Society*, and what the Lord Chief Baron said in *Gorman v Hand-in-Hand Insurance Co.*, I turn to the clause before us, premising, as Lord Cranworth said in *Scott v Avery*, that we have to deduce the intention of the parties from the language used by them in the instrument of contract. What, then, is that language? I have already set it forth at length. It is, in my opinion, in its essence, a provision to maintain the existence of the contract by providing that in case of damage, shortage, or defect of quality, an 'allowance' shall be made. It is not a mere collateral agreement, but is a provision which creates a condition precedent to the right to sue, that the arbitrators or an umpire shall, as an exclusive authority, determine the amount of the allowance to be sued for. The function of the arbitrators was to determine what amount (if any) was to be 'allowed'. The words 'who shall decided what allowance is to be made' are all-important. The clause prescribes a function for the arbitrators or umpire to discharge, and constitutes the arbitrators or umpire the sole tribunal to discharge that function. In case of default of the character I have mentioned an 'allowance' was to be determined by the arbitrators or umpire, and when that was done the jurisdiction of the court of law attached to enforce payment of the 'allowance'. This was no ouster of the jurisdiction of the courts; it was merely the creation of a condition precedent to their jurisdiction attaching. I refer again to what Lord Campbell said in *Scott v Avery*, that is to say, the proceedings in arbitration and award 'is not ousting the courts of their jurisdiction, because they have no jurisdiction whatsoever, and no cause of action accrues until the arbitrators have determined' (see p. 854).

It appears to me that this case falls within the proposition laid down by the Lord Chief Baron in *Gorman v Hand-in-Hand Insurance Co.* Looking at the instrument of contract as a whole, I think the agreement is to pay a sum of money in a certain event, that is to say, to pay an allowance if made by the arbitrators or umpire as the case may be.

The provision that the award shall be final and binding on all parties means that so far as relates to its true function, that is to say, the determination as to whether an allowance is to be made or not, it shall be final and binding on all parties. It had not in any way the effect of preventing access to the courts to enforce payment once an award was made. I am of opinion that this case falls within the principle laid down in *Scott v Avery*, that the agreement as to arbitration does not oust the jurisdiction of the courts, but merely creates a condition precedent to the right to sue. . . .

[1.] 5 HL Cas 811.	[3.] 1 QBD 563.
[2.] 8 TR 139.	[4.] IR 11 CL 224, at 233.

Note

See also *Winterthur Swiss Insurance Co. v ICI* [1990] ILRM 159.

B. Contracts which Subvert the Sanctity of Marriage

Dalton v Dalton [1982] ILRM 418

An application was made to have a separation agreement made a rule of court under s. 8 of the Family Law (Maintenance of Spouses and Children) Act 1976. The agreement contained a clause whereby the parties, both domiciled in Ireland agreed to obtain a divorce *a vinculo* outside the jurisdiction.

O'Hanlon J.:

Considerations of public policy require that the court should not lend its support to an agreement provided for the obtaining of a divorce *vinculo* by a husband and wife and this may well be the position even if the parties are domiciled elsewhere than in Ireland when the application is made or proposed to take up such foreign domicile in the future . . . I am of the opinion that to ask the court to make the agreement which has been concluded between the parties in the present case a rule of court is to ask the court to lend its support to a course of conduct which is contrary to public policy within its jurisdiction.

Note

Contracts in restraint of trade will be considered in Chapter 17.

Chapter Seventeen

Restraint of Trade

INTRODUCTION

In the age of Queen Elizabeth all restraints of trade, whatever they were, general or partial, were thought to be contrary to public policy, and therefore void (*Colgate v Bacheler*[1]). In time, however, it was found that a rule so rigid and far reaching must seriously interfere with transactions of every day occurrence. Traders could hardly venture to let their shops out of their own hands; the purchaser of a business was at the mercy of the seller; every apprentice was a possible rival. So the rule was relaxed. . . .
. . .

The true view at the present time I think, is this: The public have an interest in every person's carrying on his trade freely: so has the individual. All interference with individual liberty of action in trading, and all restraints of trade of themselves, if there is nothing more, are contrary to public policy, and therefore void. That is the general rule. But there are exceptions: restraints of trade and interference with individual liberty of action may be justified by the special circumstances of a particular case. It is a sufficient justification, and indeed it is the only justification, if the restriction is reasonable—reasonable, that is, in reference to the interests of the parties concerned and reasonable in reference to the interests of the public, so framed and so guarded as to afford adequate protection to the party in whose favour it is imposed, while at the same time it is in no way injurious to the public. That, I think, is the fair result of all the authorities.

[1] Cro Eliz 872.

Per Lord Macnaghten in *Nordenfelt v Maxim Nordenfelt Guns and Ammunition Co.* [1894] AC 535.

John Orr Ltd and Vescom B.V. *v* John Orr [1987] ILRM 702

Costello J.:
. . .

The principles of law to be applied in the issue are not in controversy and can be briefly stated. All restraints of trade in the absence of special justifying circumstances are contrary to public policy and are therefore void. A restraint may be justified if it is reasonable in the interests of the contracting parties and in the interests of the public. The onus of showing that a restraint is reasonable between the parties rests on the person alleging that it is so. Greater freedom of contract is allowable in a covenant entered into between the seller and the buyer of a business than in the case of one entered into between an employer and employee. A covenant against competition entered into by the seller of a business which is reasonably necessary to protect the business sold is valid and enforceable. A covenant by an employee not to compete

784

may also be valid and enforceable if it is reasonably necessary to protect some proprietary interest of the covenantee such as may exist in a trade connection or trade secrets. The courts may in certain circumstances enforce a covenant in restraint of trade even though taken as a whole the covenant exceeds what is reasonable, by the severance of the void parts from the valid parts.

The facts established at the hearing are as follows. John Orr Ltd was established by the defendant in 1971 and carried on a business in Navan, County Meath, manufacturing and selling upholstery fabrics and garment fabrics. It had two members, the defendant and a Mr Jerry Linscheid. In the early part of 1977 it was failing badly—indeed it was insolvent. In an endeavour to revitalise the company (an attempt which in the event proved eminently successful) an agreement was entered into on 11 March of that year (the 'share-transfer agreement') by which Vescom B.V. (a company registered in Holland) would purchase the business of John Orr Ltd and invest £50,000 in it. It did this by purchasing the shares in the company owned by the defendant and Mr Linscheid for a nominal sum. As part of the financial package then negotiated the Industrial Development Authority agreed to make grants to the company, Foir Teoranta agreed to make available certain financial facilities, and certain major creditors agreed to write off their debts. As a result of this agreement John Orr Ltd became a wholly owned subsidiary of Vescom B.V. The share transfer agreement also contained provisions for the future role of the defendant and Mr Linscheid in John Orr Ltd, requiring both to enter into service agreements with the company by which the defendant would be appointed as its commercial director and Mr Linscheid its technical director. The share transfer agreement also contained a clause, clause 6(c) which falls for consideration in these proceedings. It provided that until the expiry of one year from the determination of his service agreements the defendant should:

(i) not have any interest in any other firm or company nor be employed by, or act as representative or agent for any other person firm or company which manufactures or trades or markets similar or competing goods to those manufactured or traded or marketed by the company or by Vescom;
or
(ii) not solicit nor seek to obtain orders from nor interfere with nor endeavour to entice away any person firm or company which at any time within the period of twelve months ending with the termination of employment of Mr Orr or Mr Linscheid (as the case may require) were customers of or in the habit of dealing with the company or Vescom or any associated or subsidiary company.

The following points are to be noticed about the restraints on competition; (a) they are for a twelve month period; (b) they are world wide; (c) they apply to goods similar to and competing with goods manufactured by (i) John Orr Ltd and (ii) its parent company, Vescom B.V. As to the restraints on soliciting customers it is to be noted (a) that they, too, are to operate for a twelve month period; (b) they apply worldwide; and (c) they apply not only to customers of John Orr Ltd, but also to customers of Vescom B.V. and to customers of any subsidiary or associated companies of Vescom B.V.

The defendant also on 11 March 1977 entered into a service agreement with John Orr Ltd. This took the form of a letter sent to him by the company which he signed. This confirmed that the defendant was to be employed as commercial director of the company as from 11 March 1977 and that the appointment should continue until terminated by a six months notice given by either side. It contained a clause restricting the defendants' trading activities for a period of one year after termination in exactly the same terms as those of the share transfer agreement and a non-solicitation obligation in exactly similar terms.

The defendant took up his duties under the service agreement. The company prospered (sales expanding to £1.7m in 1984). But the defendant decided to resign in 1985 and his resignation, having been accepted, became effective from 31 October of that year, from which date the restraints began to run. Unknown to the plaintiffs the defendant had established in England a company called Rossbrae Ltd which began trading on 1 November 1985 in upholstery fabrics. Early this year the plaintiffs ascertained that Rossbrae Ltd was doing business with one of John Orr Ltd's most important customers in England and furthermore that the defendant had been visiting some of its most valuable customers in the US soliciting business for his new company. These proceedings followed shortly thereafter.

The reasonableness of the restraints imposed on the defendant is to be tested by reference to the commercial realities of the situation which existed when they were imposed, that is in the year 1977. So the question for determination is whether in that year it was reasonably necessary for the protection of Vescom's investment in John Orr Ltd to impose the restraints contained in the share-purchase agreement and whether it was reasonably necessary for the protection of John Orr Ltd's trade connections that it should impose the restraints contained in the service agreement. The business actually carried on by John Orr Ltd in that year is obviously of crucial importance. But what was in the reasonable contemplation of the parties for its future development is also relevant and some limited assistance on this aspect of the case can be obtained from evidence of what happened to the business in subsequent years.

The evidences show that:

(a) In 1977 John Orr Ltd manufactured and sold upholstery fabrics and garment fabrics, both of high quality and design. It did not then trade in wall coverings nor did the parties contemplate that it would ever do so. This was the product manufactured by Vescom B.V.

(b) In 1977, 36.7 per cent of the sales of John Orr Ltd were sales of garment fabrics and these were almost exclusively on the home market. Virtually all its production of upholstery fabrics was exported. But its export markets were limited in area. Of its total turnover 39.8 per cent was sold to five customers in the US. Outside North America it only traded in Europe, having three customers in the UK, three in Germany, and one in Holland, Switzerland, Belgium, Denmark, France and Italy. The one customer in Holland was Vescom B.V. and it was an important customer. The quantities sold in other European countries was insignificant. Its business was obviously heavily dependent on its trade connection with a small number of customers. In that year nearly eighty per cent of its total turnover was sold to ten customers (five of which, as I have already pointed out being in the US).

(c) Its export trade was carried out (apart from its sales to its parent company) by means of orders obtained from wholesale distributors. To obtain a distributor in a foreign country required a considerable amount of persuasion and active promotion of the company's products. When referring to 'customers' of John Orr Ltd the parties had particularly in mind these distributors rather than the ultimate purchasers of their products. Having agreed to act as a distributor the foreign wholesaler purchased a small quantity of the company's fabrics and endeavoured to obtain orders for them. In a given year the 'customers' of John Orr Ltd included those distributors who had agreed to distribute the company's fabrics even though no sale in fact took place. The ultimate purchasers of these fabrics were mainly institutions or large commercial undertakings rather than domestic users, and the market for them was a highly specialised one. But the company faced competition from manufacturers of upholstery fabrics of a different quality to theirs, such as producers of damask, and from manufacturers using different looms to those employed by John Orr Ltd.

(d) At the time of their agreements the parties contemplated that one of the benefits from them would be the trade connection established between John Orr Ltd and its new parent company. This benefit in fact materialised. In 1978 export total sales were £445,077 (compared to £302,895 in the previous year) but thirty five per cent of its total turnover was with the parent company. In 1978 it obtained one new customer in Norway, one in Sweden and one in Australia but the pattern of its trade remained the same as it had been in 1977. 42.3 per cent of the volume of goods sold were sold in North America (principally the US), 20.7 per cent on the home market, and thirty five per cent in Holland. Twelve customers took 84.2 per cent of the total volume of sales.
(e) In later years the trade in garment fabrics fell off so that by 1985 the company's business was exclusively in upholstery fabrics. It had in 1985 extended its trading and had one customer in Japan, Hong Kong and the Middle East, but in each case the quantity sold was very small. Nearly ninety per cent of its turnover comprised sales to eight customers and nearly fifty per cent of its business was to the US.

I have no doubt that in 1977 the parties hoped that the company's business would expand and that new markets would be entered. But there is no evidence to suggest that the parties had at that time any plans to develop it on a worldwide basis. North America and Europe were then the only areas in which the company's products were sold, sales in those areas being confined in the main to a small number of customers.

These findings lead me to the following conclusions on the enforceability of the restraint of trade clauses in the two contracts on 11 March 1977.

(1) *The non-solicitation clauses*
(a) I am quite satisfied that it was reasonably necessary for the protection of Vescom's investment in John Orr Ltd that it should require the defendant not to solicit the customers of John Orr Ltd for a period of twelve months after the termination of his service agreement with that company. But the protection of that investment did not require the defendant to agree not to solicit the customers of Vescom Ltd or its subsidiaries or associated companies because John Orr Ltd was not manufacturing or trading in wall coverings and had no intention of doing so. The plaintiffs' counsel submitted, a submission with which the defendant's counsel agreed, that the severance rule could be applied to this clause. I will therefore hold that in respect of the share-purchase agreement of 11 March 1977 clause 6(c)(ii) is valid and enforceable with the deletion of the words 'or Vescom or any associated or subsidiary company' at the end of the paragraph.
(b) I am also quite satisfied that it was reasonably necessary for the protection of the proprietary interest of John Orr Ltd in its trade connection with its customers that it should require the defendant not to solicit its customers for twelve months after the termination of his service agreement with the company. But the protection of that interest did not require that he would not solicit the customers of Vescom or its associates and subsidiaries. As in the case of the share-purchase agreement counsel agree that the severance rule can be applied to the service agreement. Accordingly I will declare that para. 7(II) of that agreement is enforceable with the deletion of the words 'or the parent company or any associated or subsidiary company' at the end of the paragraph. In neither case will there be any adverse effect on the public interest.

(2) *The non-competition clauses*
(a) it will be recalled that the share-purchase agreement restrained the defendant for one year after the termination of his service agreement from manufacturing or selling (either personally or through a company) goods manufactured or sold by the parent Dutch firm Vescom as well as goods manufactured or sold by John Orr Ltd. In 1977 John Orr Ltd manufactured and sold upholstery and garment fabrics and did not manufacture or trade in wall coverings, which were the goods manufactured by Vescom

B.V. It had no intention of entering the market in these goods. The range of goods subjected to the restraints in clause 6(c)(i) of the share-purchase agreement was therefore unreasonably wide as it was not necessary for the protection of Vescom's investment in John Orr Ltd that the defendant should be restrained from manufacturing or trading in wall coverings. The clause therefore imposes an excessive restraint.

It is also excessively restrictive for another reason. It prohibited the defendant from manufacturing or trading in upholstery fabrics in any part of the world during the limitation period. In 1977 the vast bulk of the business of John Orr Ltd was done with a limited number of customers in a limited number of countries. A restriction on the defendant which would prohibit him for one year after termination of his service contract from manufacturing or selling in the countries in which John Orr Ltd had customers could well have been justified as necessary to protect Vescom's investment in this case. Indeed, it might even have been possible to justify a wider restriction if it could have been shown that in 1977 John Orr Ltd had definite proposals for expanding into markets outside North America and Europe. But a blanket worldwide restraint based merely on the possibility that markets in other parts of the world might be entered by the company is to my mind an unreasonable one as it was not reasonably required for the protection of Vescom's investment in the company.

(b) Exactly the same considerations apply to the restrictions contained in clause 7(1) of the service agreement. The protection of the trade connection of John Orr Ltd did not require that the defendant should be restrained from manufacturing or trading in goods manufactured or sold by Vescom B.V. And the protection of its trade connections could be assured without prohibiting the defendant from manufacturing or selling upholstery fabrics in any part of the world.

The defendant's counsel had urged that if I found that the restraints imposed by clause 6(c)(i) of the share-purchase agreement and clause 7(1) of the service agreement were excessive and therefore unreasonable that the clauses were unenforceable because I could not apply the severance rule to them as to do so would amount to re-writing the parties' contracts. The plaintiffs' counsel forcibly submitted that the worldwide restraints in the two agreements were reasonable ones, but did not suggest that if I were to hold otherwise that the infirmities could be cured by severing the unenforceable parts. In these circumstances I must hold that these two clauses are unenforceable.

That brings me to the plaintiff's motion for an interlocutory injunction. In the light of my decision on the preliminary issue it follows that if the trial of this action takes place before 31 October 1986 the trial judge would grant an injunction, (damages being an inadequate remedy) limited in the way I have described, and would in addition decide whether any breaches of the enforceable part of the non-solicitation clauses had occurred and if so what damages resulted. This means that I do not consider the plaintiffs' claim to interlocutory relief by the principles established in *American Cyanamid Co. v Ethicon Ltd* [1975] AC 396 but rather on the basis that the plaintiffs' right to an injunction has in fact been established. Although the defendant through his counsel has offered to give an undertaking not to solicit I think that to avoid any doubts as to the parties' rights I should formally make an order. This will restrain until 31 October 1986 the defendant either personally or by means of Rossbrae Ltd or any other company or firm with which he may be associated either directly or indirectly from soliciting or seeking orders from or interfering with or endeavouring to entice away any person firm or company which were customers of John Orr Ltd or were in the habit of dealing with John Orr Ltd at any time within the period of twelve months ending 31 October 1986.

Eddie Macken *v* Frank O'Reilly and Others [1979] ILRM 79

O'Higgins C.J.:

This is an appeal brought by the defendants against the judgment and order of Hamilton J. in the High Court in which he declared that a certain resolution adopted by them was void, as being, contrary to public policy, an unreasonable restraint of trade. The plaintiff is a professional show jumper and horseman and is resident and domiciled within the country. The defendants are members of and constitute the Equestrian Federation of Ireland (hereinafter referred to as the federation) which is the body responsible for both national and international aspects of all equestrian sports in Ireland. The resolution which led to the initiation of these proceedings was passed at a meeting of the federation on 21 January 1978.

. . .

The effect of this resolution was to reiterate and repeat the consistent policy of the federation which was not to permit Irish competitors at international events to be mounted on other than Irish horses, but to make a special exception in favour of the plaintiff, who was then resident in Germany, in respect of those international events (C.A.s and C.I.s) at which competitors from the different countries could compete as individuals. The plaintiff, who is now again resident in Ireland and whose standing and reputation as a showjumper and horseman is among the highest in the world, complains that the decision incorporated in this resolution interferes with his freedom to earn his living and is a restraint of trade which cannot be justified as being reasonable. . . .

. . .

All interference with an individual's freedom of action in trading is *per se* contrary to public policy and, therefore, void. This general prohibition is subject to the exception that certain restraints may be justified. Restraints, restrictions or interferences are permitted if they are, in the circumstances obtaining, fair and reasonable. Whether what is complained of can be justified on this basis involves a careful examination of all the circumstances—the need for the restraint, the object sought to be attained, the interests sought to be protected and the general interest of the public. What is done or sought to be done must be established as being reasonable and necessary and on balance to serve the public interest. The fact that the body or group imposing the restraint has the power to do so does not of itself justify its imposition. Any arbitrary or unreasonable use of power by those who have control or authority over a particular trade or profession would come within the prohibition. In this case the fact that its constitution and the FEI regulations appear to authorise the federation to act as it did, does not of itself authorise what was done. The question is whether in all the circumstances the action taken by the federation can be said to be fair and reasonable and in the public interest.

The learned trial judge in holding that the federation acted within its powers in passing the resolution in question said as follows:

The federation is, under its constitution, the body responsible for both the national and international aspects of all equestrian sports in Ireland which are recognised by the federation and has sole jurisdiction in respect of international and ultimate authority in respect of national equestrian affairs. As such a body, it has, in my opinion, an interest in ensuring that the Irish half-bred breeding industry is in a healthy and thriving condition so as to ensure a reasonable supply of suitable horses available for all equestrian sports and is entitled to endeavour to take steps to protect that industry. Being so satisfied, I consider that the policy of the federation and the resolutions giving effect thereto are *intra vires* the power of the federation. . . .

This view is amply supported by the evidence and as already indicated it is a view with which I entirely agree. The learned judge went on to say:

> There is nothing unreasonable and the interest of all parties including the public, probably require that the federation do everything possible to encourage Irish riders to ride Irish-bred horses in international competitions. . . .

Having expressed this view he rather surprisingly went on to hold that by reason of the policy being inflexible he regarded it as an unreasonable restraint of trade in relation to the plaintiff. He gave his reasons as follows:

> None of the other national federations affiliated to the FIE have such a policy or rule. I accept Mr Macken's evidence that there are not available to him at this point of time sufficient Irish-bred horses of the necessary quality to enable him to maintain his position as one of the world's leading showjumpers. I consider that a policy which has the effect of inhibiting his efforts to maintain such a position to be unjust and unfair and that if he fails to maintain that position the public will be deprived of a great deal of pleasure. Having regard to the worldwide reputation of Irish half-bred horses I do not consider that the interests of the industry require that such a policy be maintained by the federation with regard to individual riders participating in international showjumping competitions as individuals and not representing their country officially.

It seems to me that in this part of his judgment the learned trial judge was in error. Having already held that the federation's policy was reasonable in the interest of all parties including the public, he nevertheless concluded that in its application to the plaintiff it was unjust and unfair. A policy of restraint which is held to be reasonable, having regard to all interests affected, including the public, cannot, in my view, properly be described as being unjust and unfair simply because in its particular application to one individual an inconvenience or loss is experienced. The trial judge was also influenced by the rule or policy being regarded as inflexible. This, it seems to me, is of the essence of any rule or policy until it is altered or changed. Any policy or ruling of this kind must be regarded in the light of all the circumstances to test whether it is reasonable or not. The mere fact that those who advocate it to enforce it are insistent as to their views cannot make what is otherwise reasonable suddenly unreasonable. In addition, it seems to me that the trial judge disregarded entirely the undisputed evidence as to the effect a change of policy would have on the horse breeding industry and on equestrian sport in Ireland. This ought to have been considered as a balance to the harm or inconvenience caused to the plaintiff by adhering to the rule. Finally, in my view the trial judge misinterpreted the FEI regulations when he referred to individual riders in international showjumping competitions competing as individuals and not as representatives of their country. As I have already indicated, in my view, this is just not possible under the regulations which apply.

I take a different view on the evidence and facts established before the learned trial judge. I accept that the plaintiff has been, as the trial judge put it, 'inhibited in his efforts to maintain his position as one of the world's leading show jumpers' by reason of the federation's rule. He is engaged on the international showjumping circuit from March to December each year. He has not the time to school or bring on young horses. As he said in his evidence he is faced by the fact that 'the majority of quality young horses in

Ireland are sold at a very early stage'. It would be easier for him while on the circuit to look around for what he described as 'a talented young horse with a lesser rider'. This would be a horse already trained for jumping that he could include in his string without too excessive a loss of time or undue effort being involved. If he were free to buy such a horse, irrespective of its breeding, his interests would be well served and he could continue on the international circuit without any cessation. This is quite understandable if only the plaintiff's position were to be considered. This, however, is not the case. Also to be considered are the interests of the public as represented by those concerned with the horsebreeding industry in Ireland and also the interests of those already engaged in showjumping in this country who are looking for recognition and advancement in international events. The evidence established beyond question that if the plaintiff were permitted to ride foreign-bred horses as an accredited Irish competitor at international events then all others who wished to do so would have to get the same permission. This process once started would, through sponsorship and money, affect the standing of the Irish horse breeding industry. It would also have the effect of depriving young riders at home, particularly those of limited means, of any reasonable opportunity of advancement. It seems to me that on balance the policy and ruling of the federation can be justified as being reasonable, necessary and fair, having regard to all the tests which should be applied. The need for the rule in the first instance and the object of maintaining it was and is to build up the Irish half-bred horse industry in the interests of equestrian sport generally in the country. It is the view of the federation fairly and reasonably held, that in doing so it is serving the interests of the generality of young riders of limited means and thereby serving the general interests of the public. It is not a new rule. It is as old as the federation itself. It has been accepted and complied with by all Irish riders over the years and was of course so accepted by the plaintiff himself until recently. It can be said fairly that the plaintiff is where he is today because this policy was in operation over the years. The fact that his very success as a showjumper on the world circuit makes the application of the rule to him, now, inconvenient and expensive is no basis for condemning it as being unreasonable and unfair.

In my view, therefore, the resolution and ruling of the federation although in restraint of trade is, in the circumstances, reasonable and fair.

(Griffin and Parke JJ. agreed.)

Note

The restraint of trade doctrine was the judicial response to contractual or market practices which sterilised or constrained the power of individuals, groups, or companies to trade in a free or open market. The desire to maintain the supply of essential commodities such as foodstuffs, allow skilled artisans to carry on their trade to the benefit of themselves and the public, and avoid the creation of monopolies and artificial markets, are all evident in the voluminous body of case-law that restraint of trade produced. The restraint of trade doctrine was readily applied to employment and sale of business restraints and to exclusive selling and buying agreements; in recent years the courts have tested trade and professional association restraints, showing that the boundaries of restraint of trade are never closed.

The existing state of the authorities suggests that Lord Macnaghten's observations in *Nordenfelt* are only approximate guides to the methodology to be used in testing the agreement in question. In *Esso v Harpers* (see p. 827

below) the House of Lords suggested that certain contractual arrangements (conveyancing ties, ordinary supply agreements) are outside the
doctrine altogether so that most but not all agreements that are manifestly a restraint upon a person's freedom to trade are *prima facie* void.
Once this is established the question turns to whether the tie can be
justified as being in the public interest; is it reasonable as between the
parties and is it reasonable *vis-à-vis* the public generally?

In fact, reasonableness *inter partes* tended to be the main issue by which
enforceability was determined. Very few cases dealt with the public interest
in an abstract or realistically economic sense, and the judges tended to
adopt negative positions when arguments about the inflationary or market
distorting effects of an agreement were presented e.g. Ungoed-Thomas J.
in *Texaco Ltd v Mulberry Filling Station* [1972] 1 All ER 513, at 525–6. While it is
doubtless understandable to expect judges to admit that the balancing of
several conflicting economic or business decisions is best left to Parliament,
such observations help to point up the fact that the common law doctrine
could not adequately deal with more complex economic or distributive
issues, and the Oireachtas has intervened, firstly, through legislative control
of certain kinds of agreement, such as motor fuel solus agreements in
1972, and secondly, through the Competition Act 1991.

Restraint of trade will remain a relevant ground for invalidity and some
agreements, particularly employment restraints, will tend to fall outside
the legislation, thus making these restraints enforceable only if they pass
through the common law doctrine.

The objectives of the **Competition Act 1991**, as set out in the explana-
tory memorandum, are to prohibit, by analogy with Articles 85 and 86 of
the EEC Treaty, the prevention, restriction or distortion of competition and
the abuse of dominant positions:

S. 4. (1)–(4)

4. (1) Subject to the provisions of this section, all agreements between undertakings,
decisions by associations of undertakings and concerted practices which have as their
object or effect the prevention, restriction or distortion of competition in trade in any
goods or services in the State or in any part of the State are prohibited and void, including in particular, without prejudice to the generality of this subsection, those which:

- (a) directly or indirectly fix purchase or selling prices or any other trading conditions;
- (b) limit or control production, markets, technical development or investment;
- (c) share markets or sources of supply;
- (d) apply dissimilar conditions to equivalent transactions with other trading parties
  thereby placing them at a competitive disadvantage;
- (e) make the conclusion of contracts subject to acceptance by the other parties of
  supplementary obligations which by their nature or according to commercial
  usage have no connection with the subject of such contracts.

(2) The Competition Authority established by this Act ('the Authority') may in
accordance with s. 8 grant a licence for the purposes of this section in the case of:

- (a) any agreement or category of agreements,
- (b) any decision or category of decisions,
- (c) any concerted practice or category of concerted practices,

which in the opinion of the Authority, having regard to all relevant market conditions, contributes to improving the production or distribution of goods or provision of services or to promoting technical or economic progress, while allowing consumers a fair share of the resulting benefit and which does not:

      (i) impose on the undertakings concerned terms which are not indispensable to the attainment of those objectives;

      (ii) afford undertakings the possibility of eliminating competition in respect of a substantial part of the products or services in question.

(3)(a) A licence under sub-s. (2) shall, while it is in force, and in accordance with its terms, permit the doing of acts which would otherwise be prohibited and void under sub-s. (1).

  (b) Where a licence under sub-s. (2) covers a category of agreements, decisions or concerted practices, any agreements, decisions or concerted practices (as the case may be) within that category which comply with the terms of the licence *need not be notified* under s. 7 to benefit from the licence while it is in force.

(4) The Authority may certify that in its opinion, on the basis of the facts in its possession, an agreement, decision or concerted practice notified under s. 7 does not offend against sub-s. (1).

Note

If the Competition Act does not apply to a transaction, the common law position must be considered.

SECTION ONE—COMMON LAW POSITION

A. SALE OF A BUSINESS

Competition Authority Decision No. 1, Nallen/O'Toole (Belmullet) 2 April 1992

Notification was made with a request for a certificate under s. 4(4) of the Competition Act, 1991 or, in the event of a refusal by the Competition Authority to issue a certificate, a licence under s. 4(2), by Mr Nallen and Mr O'Toole, Belmullet, on 21 November 1991 in respect of an agreement to transfer a business interest.

. . .

This notification concerns an agreement between the vendor and the purchaser of an interest in a business in which they had previously been partners. In the agreement the vendor agrees, as part of the arrangements in selling his share of the business to his partner, to refrain from engaging in the business concerned for a specific period in a defined geographical area.

The Authority decided that Mr Nallen and Mr O'Toole were 'undertakings' within the meaning of s. 3 of the Competition Act and that the arrangements in question constituted an agreement which applied within a part of the State. However, the Authority found that the agreement did not prevent, restrict or distort competition as it involved no reduction in the actual number of competitors in the market in question and did not reduce the threat of potential competition within the defined market. The Authority then proceeded to consider the non-competition clause:

35. The Authority now turns to the specific issue of the non-competition clause which is a key element of the present agreement. There are a series of EC cases dealing with similar agreements under Article 85(1). The Commission view, which has been confirmed by the European Court of Justice, is that arrangements of this type are essential to secure the transfer of the goodwill of a business to a new owner. They are regarded as not involving any restriction on competition but as essential to allow the full transfer of ownership, provided their duration and extent is only that which is necessary to secure the full transfer of the goodwill. If an agreement satisfies these criteria it has been found not to be in breach of Article 85(1).

36. In the *Nutricia* and *Reuter*/BASF cases the Commission ruled that the agreements were in breach of Article 85(1) of the Treaty of Rome. The Commission decision was, however, based on the view that the duration of the non-competition clause was longer than was necessary for the proper transfer of the goodwill of the business to the new owner. It is clear from both decisions that a shorter non-competition clause would have been acceptable. Indeed in the *Nutricia* case, although the agreements had operated since 1979, the Commission ruled that the infringement only dated from 1983, four years after the agreement came into effect. The Commission decision in this case was upheld by the Court of Justice. In the *Mecaniver*-PPG case the Commission granted a negative clearance to the agreement for a specified period of time.[1]

37. It is clear from the Commission's decisions that the length of time necessary for the full transfer of the goodwill of a business will vary from industry to industry.

In general, the assessment under Article 85(1) of non-competition obligations imposed on sellers of businesses will depend on the particular circumstances of each individual case and no universal rule can therefore be established as to the permissible duration of such clauses.[2]

38. Thus what may be regarded as a reasonable length of time for a non-competition clause in one case may be regarded as excessive in another. In the former case such a clause would not be regarded as a breach of Article 85(1) whereas in the latter it would.

In the absence of circumstances which deviate greatly from those in the *Reuter/* BASF or *Nutricia* cases, these decisions, however, indicate as [a] general guide that where the transfer of a business also involves the transfer of goodwill and know-how, a period of approximately five years will normally be acceptable, whereas a period of approximately two years will normally apply if the sale involves only the transfer of goodwill.[3]

39. In the *Nutricia* case the Commission indicated that among the factors to be taken into account in evaluating the duration of such clauses were:

(i) how frequently consumers in the relevant market change brands and type (in relation to the degree of brand loyalty shown by them),
(ii) for how long, after the sale of the business, the seller, without a restrictive clause, would be able to make a successful comeback to the market and regain his old customers.

40. The European Commission also decided in the *Nutricia* case that: 'The geographical scope of a non-competition clause also has to be limited to the extent which is objectively necessary to achieve the aforementioned goal. As a rule, it should there-

fore only cover the markets where the products concerned were manufactured or sold at the time of the agreements.'

41. The view that such arrangements are essential in order to secure the transfer of the goodwill of a business and that they do not, therefore, involve a restriction of competition, appears to be well established under both US competition law and common law in the UK and Ireland. Such a view has prevailed in the US for almost 100 years, following the decision of Judge Taft in the *Addyston Pipe*[3] case which stated that:

It was equally for the good of the public and trade, when partners dissolved, and one took the business, or they divided the business, that each partner might bind himself not to do anything in trade thereafter which would derogate from his grant of the interest conveyed to his former partner. Again, when two men became partners in a business, although their union might reduce competition, this effect was only an incident to the main purpose of a union of their capital, enterprise, and energy to carry on a successful business, and one useful to the community. For the reasons given, then, covenants in partial restraint of trade are generally upheld as valid.

42. The EC competition rules are themselves based on US antitrust legislation.

43. The courts in Ireland and the UK have tended to take a favourable view of restraint clauses of this nature in the past. Such views were based on common law rather than competition legislation.

The purchaser of a business can restrict the seller from engaging in similar enterprises in the future. The need to impose such a restriction is accepted by the courts because the proprietary interest in the goodwill of the business may be worthy of protection. But such restrictions will not be upheld should they be deemed to be wider than are reasonably necessary for that protection.[4]

44. In deciding whether the restraint imposed is reasonable, the courts have regarded two factors as particularly relevant. Firstly the buyer must establish a proprietary interest which the clause is seeking to protect. Secondly the clause must be reasonable in the light of all the circumstances of the case. In this respect the restraint must not go further than reasonably necessary for the protection of the purchaser's interest in point of space, time or subject matter.[5]

45. It is therefore widely recognised in competition law in other countries and in our own common law that some restraint on a party disposing of all or part of his interest in a business is essential for the proper transfer of the goodwill of the business to take place, and that without the transfer of such goodwill, the transfer of ownership would be incomplete. Without such a restraint proper transfer of goodwill could take place. The Authority agrees with this view. This restraint must, however, be limited in terms of its duration, geographical coverage and subject matter to that which is necessary to secure the adequate transfer of the goodwill. Provided this is the case, then clearly the intention of such a restraint is not to restrict competition in the market in question.

46. The restraint on Mr O'Toole in this agreement is for a period of three years, although the agreement involves a transfer of goodwill only. While the Authority would tend to agree at this stage with the EC view that a period of two years would

generally be sufficient for the complete transfer of the goodwill of a business, it believes that a longer period is justified in this case. Consumers tend to purchase the products in question infrequently. In addition, in this case, close personal contact with customers was a major factor in the business. This is a small rural community where most consumers would know, or at least know of, Mr O'Toole as someone engaged in the particular business. In addition, Mr O'Toole is still active in business within the area. For these reasons it would appear that the period specified in the agreement is no more than is required to secure the complete transfer of the goodwill.

47. In this case the restraint applies to an area within a radius of 20 miles from the town of Belmullet and appears to correspond to the area within which Mr Nallen and Mr O'Toole previously carried on their business. Finally the restriction applies only to the lines of business in which Mr O'Toole was previously engaged in partnership with Mr Nallen. The restrictions involved are no more than are necessary to ensure the adequate transfer of the goodwill of the business to Mr Nallen and on those grounds are not in breach of s. 4(1) of the Competition Act.

1. *Reuter/BASF, Nutricia/deRooij* and *Nutricia/Zuid Hollandse Conservenfabriek*, and *Mecaniver-PPG* (85/78/EEC) (OJ L35, 7 February 1985, p. 54). The European Court of Justice dealt with an appeal in the *Nutricia* case, see *Remia B.V. and Others v European Commission*, Case 42/84 |1985| ECR 2545.
2. European Commission (1983); 'Thirteenth Report on Competition Policy', para. 88.
3. *United States v Addyston Pipe & Steel Co. et al.*, 1898. See W. Breit and K. Elinzga; *The Antitrust Casebook: Milestones in Economic Regulation*, (2nd ed.), New York: Dryden Press 1989, 17–23.
4. B Doolan A *Casebook of Irish Contract Law*, (1989), 254. See also the decision of Costello J. in the case of *John Orr Ltd v Orr* (HC) 1987.
5. See E. McKendrick *Contract Law*, London: Macmillan 1990.

B. Employment Agreements

Faccenda Chicken Ltd *v* Fowler and Others [1986] 1 All ER 617

Fowler was employed by the plaintiff, a poultry breeding and marketing company as its sales manager. Fresh chickens were sold from refrigerated vans which operated on certain routes within a defined area. Fowler left the plaintiff and set up his own business in the same area selling fresh chickens from refrigerated vans. Eight of the plaintiff's employees resigned and joined him in his business. Fowler's vans operated on the same routes and serviced similar customers to the plaintiff's. The plaintiff sued the defendants alleging breach of their employment contracts. The trial judge dismissed this action and the plaintiff appealed to the Court of Appeal.

Neill L.J.:

In these two appeals it will be necessary to consider the interaction of three separate legal concepts. (1) The duty of an employee during the period of his employment to act with good faith towards his employer; this duty is sometimes called the duty of fidelity. (2) The duty of an employee not to use or disclose after his employment has ceased any confidential information which he has obtained during his employment about his employer's affairs. (3) The *prima facie* right of any person to use and to exploit for the purpose of earning his living all the skill, experience and knowledge which he has at his disposal, including skill, experience and knowledge which he has acquired in the course of previous periods of employment.

. . .

Having considered the cases to which we were referred, we would venture to state these principles as follows.

(1) Where the parties are, or have been, linked by a contract of employment, the obligations of the employee are to be determined by the contract between him and his employer: cf *Vokes Ltd v Heather* (1945) 62 RPC 135 at 141.

(2) In the absence of any express term, the obligations of the employee in respect of the use and disclosure of information are the subject of implied terms.

(3) While the employee remains in the employment of the employer the obligations are included in the implied term which imposes a duty of good faith or fidelity on the employee. For the purpose of the present appeal it is not necessary to consider the precise limits of this implied term, but it may be noted: (a) that the extent of the duty of good faith will vary according to the nature of the contract (see *Vokes Ltd v Heather*); (b) that the duty of good faith will be broken if an employee makes or copies a list of the customers of the employer for use after his employment ends or deliberately memorises such a list, even though, except in special circumstances, there is no general restriction on an ex-employee canvassing or doing business with customers of his former employer (see *Robb v Green* |1895| 2 QB 315, |1895–9| All ER Rep 1053 and *Wessex Dairies Ltd v Smith* |1935| 2 KB 80, |1935| All ER Rep 75).

(4) The implied term which imposes an obligation on the employee as to his conduct after the determination of the employment is more restricted in its scope than that which imposes a general duty of good faith. It is clear that the obligation not to use or disclose information may cover secret processes of manufacture such as chemical formulae (see *Amber Size and Chemical Co. Ltd v Menzel* |1913| 2 Ch. 239), or designs or special methods of construction (see *Reid Sigrist Ltd v Moss Mechanism Ltd* (1932) 49 RPC 461), and other information which is of a sufficiently high degree of confidentiality as to amount to a trade secret.

The obligation does not extend, however, to cover all information which is given to or acquired by the employee while in his employment, and in particular may not cover information which is only 'confidential' in the sense that an unauthorised disclosure of such information to a third party while the employment subsisted would be a clear breach of the duty of good faith.

This distinction is clearly set out in the judgment of Cross J. in *Printers and Finishers Ltd v Holloway* |1964| 3 All ER 731, |1965| 1 WLR 1, where he had to consider whether an ex-employee should be restrained by injunction from making use of his recollection of the contents of certain written printing instructions which had been made available to him when he was working in his former employers' flock printing factory. In his judgment, delivered on 29 April 1964 (not reported on this point in the WLR), Cross J. said (|1964| 3 All ER 731 at 738n):

> In this connection one must bear in mind that not all information which is given to a servant in confidence and which it would be a breach of his duty for him to disclose to another person during his employment is a trade secret which he can be prevented from using for his own advantage after the employment is over, even though he has entered into no express covenant with regard to the matter in hand. For example, the printing instructions were handed to |the first defendant| to be used by him during his employment exclusively for the plaintiffs' benefit. It would have been a breach of duty on his part to divulge any of the contents to a stranger while he was employed, but many of these instructions are not really 'trade secrets'

at all. [The first defendant] was not, indeed, entitled to take a copy of the instructions away with him; but insofar as the instructions cannot be called 'trade secrets' and he carried them in his head, he is entitled to use them for his own benefit or the benefit of any future employer.

The same distinction is to be found in E. *Worsley & Co. Ltd v Cooper* [1939] 1 All ER 290, where it was held that the defendant was entitled, after he had ceased to be employed, to make use of his knowledge of the source of the paper supplied to his previous employer. In our view it is quite plain that this knowledge was nevertheless 'confidential' in the sense that it would have been a breach of the duty of good faith for the employee, while the employment subsisted, to have used it for his own purposes or to have disclosed it to a competitor of his employer.

(5) In order to determine whether any particular item of information falls within the implied term so as to prevent its use or disclosure by an employee after his employment has ceased, it is necessary to consider all the circumstances of the case. We are satisfied that the following matters are among those to which attention must be paid. (a) The nature of the employment. Thus employment in a capacity where 'confidential' material is habitually handled may impose a high obligation of confidentiality because the employee can be expected to realise its sensitive nature to a greater extent than if he were employed in a capacity where such material reaches him only occasionally or incidentally. (b) The nature of the information itself. In our judgment the information will only be protected if it can properly be classed as a trade secret or as material which, while not properly to be described as a trade secret, is in all the circumstances of such a highly confidential nature as to require the same protection as a trade secret *eo nomine*. The restrictive covenant cases demonstrate that a covenant will not be upheld on the basis of the status of the information which might be disclosed by the former employee if he is not restrained unless it can be regarded as a trade secret or the equivalent of a trade secret: see for example *Herbert Morris Ltd v Saxelby* [1916] 1 AC 688 at 710, [1916–17] All ER Rep 305 at 317 per Lord Parker and *Littlewoods Organisation Ltd v Harris* [1978] 1 All ER 1026 at 1037, [1977] 1 WLR 1472 at 1484 per Megaw L.J.

We must therefore express our respectful disagreement with the passage in Goulding J.'s judgment where he suggested that an employer can protect the use of information in his second category, even though it does not include either a trade secret or its equivalent by means of a restrictive covenant (see [1985] 1 All ER 724 at 731). As Lord Parker made clear in *Herbert Morris Ltd v Saxelby* [1916] 1 AC 688 at 709, [1916–17] All ER Rep 305 at 317, in a passage to which counsel for Faccenda Chicken Ltd drew our attention, a restrictive covenant will not be enforced unless the protection sought is reasonably necessary to protect a trade secret or to prevent some personal influence over customers being abused in order to entice them away.

In our view the circumstances in which a restrictive covenant would be appropriate and could be successfully invoked emerge very clearly from the words used by Cross J. in *Printers and Finishers Ltd v Holloway* [1964] 3 All ER 731 at 736, [1965] 1 WLR 1 at 6 (in a passage quoted later in his judgment by Goulding J. (see [1985] 1 All ER 724 at 732–3):

If [the managing director] is right in thinking that there are features in his process which can fairly be regarded as trade secrets and which his employees will inevitably carry away with them in their heads, then the proper way for the plaintiffs to protect themselves would be by exacting covenants from their employees restricting their field of activity after they have left their employment, not by asking the court to extend the general equitable doctrine to prevent breaking confidence beyond all reasonable bounds.

It is clearly impossible to provide a list of matters which will qualify as trade secrets or their equivalent. Secret processes of manufacture provide obvious examples, but innumerable other pieces of information are *capable* of being trade secrets, though the secrecy of some information may be only short-lived. In addition, the fact that the circulation of certain information is restricted to a limited number of individuals may throw light on the status of the information and its degree of confidentiality. (c) Whether the employer impressed on the employee the confidentiality of the information. Thus, though an employer cannot prevent the use or disclosure *merely* by telling the employee that certain information is confidential, the attitude of the employer towards the information provides evidence which may assist in determining whether or not the information can properly be regarded as a trade secret. It is to be observed that in *E. Worsley & Co. Ltd v Cooper* [1939] 1 All ER 290 at 307 Morton J. attached significance to the fact that no warning had been given to the defendant that 'the source from which the paper came was to be treated as confidential'. (d) Whether the relevant information can be easily isolated from other information which the employee is free to use or disclose. In *Printers and Finishers Ltd v Holloway* [1964] 3 All ER 731 at 736, [1965] 1 WLR 1 at 6 Cross J. considered the protection which might be afforded the information which had been memorised by an ex-employee. He put on one side the memorising of a formula or a list of customers or what had been said (obviously in confidence) at a particular meeting, and continued:

> The employee might well not realise that the feature or expedient in question was in fact peculiar to his late employer's process and factory; but even if he did such knowledge is not readily separable from his general knowledge of the flock printing process and his acquired skill in manipulating a flock printing plant, and I do not think that any man of average intelligence and honesty would think that there was anything improper in his putting his memory of particular features of his late employer's plant at the disposal of his new employer.

For our part we would not regard the separability of the information in question as being conclusive, but the fact that the alleged 'confidential' information is part of a package and that the remainder of the package is not confidential is likely to throw light on whether the information in question is really a trade secret.

These then are the principles of law which we consider to be applicable to a case such as the present one. We would wish to leave open, however, for further examination on some other occasion the question whether additional protection should be afforded to an employer where the former employee is not seeking to earn his living by making use of the body of skill, knowledge and experience which he has acquired in the course of his career, but is merely selling to a third party information which he acquired in confidence in the course of his former employment.

We turn now to the facts of the instant case. It will be remembered that the case of Faccenda Chicken Ltd was that Mr Fowler and the other defendants were in breach of an implied term of their contracts of employment in using or disclosing the sales information that they had acquired while in the employment of Faccenda Chicken Ltd or, alternatively, that they were in breach of this implied term by using or disclosing their knowledge of the prices charged by Faccenda Chicken Ltd to individual customers. It will also be remembered that the sales information contained five elements: the names and addresses of customers; the most convenient routes to be taken to reach the individual customers; the usual requirements of individual customers; the days of the week and the times of day when deliveries were made to individual customers; and the prices charged to individual customers.

Counsel for Faccenda Chicken Ltd was prepared to concede that, if these pieces of information were looked at separately, some of them did not constitute confidential information at all. Thus he accepted that Mr Fowler and the other defendants were entitled to make use of any recollection they might have of the names and addresses of Faccenda Chicken Ltd customers as well as of the most convenient routes by which the premises of such customers could be reached. Moreover, we did not understand him to argue otherwise than rather faintly that Mr Fowler and the other defendants would have been in breach of contract if they had merely made use of their knowledge of the usual requirements of Faccenda Chicken Ltd customers or of the times when deliveries were made to them.

The central plank of the argument of counsel for Faccenda Chicken Ltd was that any information about the prices charged to individual Faccenda Chicken Ltd customers was confidential, and that, as this information about prices formed part of the package of sales information, the package taken as a whole was confidential too. It is therefore necessary to consider the information about prices more closely. It seems clear that, apart from the fact that the three main groups of customers, butchers, chains of shops and catering establishments, were charged slightly different prices, there were a number of individual variations inside these groups to take account, no doubt, of such matters as the size of the orders placed and the length of time that the traders concerned had been customers. It was this information, submitted counsel for Faccenda Chicken Ltd, which was confidential.

Counsel relied in particular on the following passage in the judgment of Goulding J. ([1985] 1 All ER 724 at 727): 'I find that an experienced salesman quickly acquires a good idea of the prices obtained by his employer's competitors, but usually such knowledge is only approximate; and in this field accurate information is valuable, because a difference of even a penny a pound may be important.' He also relied on the references to the confidentiality of prices in the three authorities which we have already mentioned.

We find ourselves unable to accept the submissions of counsel for Faccenda Chicken Ltd either as to the information about prices or as to the sales information as a whole. We can well appreciate that in certain circumstances information about prices can be invested with a sufficient degree of confidentiality to render that information a trade secret or its equivalent. The price put forward in a tender document is an obvious example. But there may be many other cases where the circumstances show that a price or prices are matters of great importance and highly confidential.

Information about the price to be charged for a new model of a car or some other product or about the prices negotiated, for example, for various grades of oil in a highly competitive market in which it is known that prices are to be kept secret from competitors occur to us as providing possible further instances of information which is entitled to protection as having the requisite degree of confidentiality.

But in the present case the following factors appear to us to lead to the clear conclusion that neither the information about prices nor the sales information as a whole had the degree of confidentiality necessary to support Faccenda Chicken Ltd's case. We would list these factors as follows: (1) the sales information contained some material which Faccenda Chicken Ltd conceded was not confidential if looked at in isolation; (2) the information about the prices was not clearly severable from the rest of the sales information; (3) neither the sales information in general, nor the information about the prices in particular, though of some value to a competitor, could reasonably be regarded as plainly secret or sensitive; (4) the sales information, including the information about prices, was necessarily acquired by the defendants in order that they could do their work. Moreover, as the judge observed in the course of his judgment, each salesman could quickly commit the whole of the sales information relating to his own area to memory; (5) the sales information was generally known among the van drivers who were employees, as were the secretaries, at quite junior level. This was not a case where the relevant information was restricted to senior management or to confidential staff; (6) there was no evidence that Faccenda Chicken Ltd had ever given any express instructions that the sales information or the information about prices was to be treated as confidential.

We are satisfied that, in the light of all the matters set out by the judge in his judgment, neither the sales information as a whole nor the information about prices looked at by itself fell within the class of confidential information which an employee is bound by an implied term of his contract of employment or otherwise not to use or disclose after his employment has come to an end.

Accordingly these appeals must be dismissed.

Panayiotou and Others v Sony Music Entertainment (UK) Ltd TLR, 30 June 1994

Parker J.:

said that George Michael was claiming against the Sony Group that the agreement in 1988 for the delivery of eight albums of records over a period of time was void and unenforceable because it was an unreasonable restraint of trade and was in any event rendered void by article 85(2) of the EEC Treaty, directed at maintaining freedom of competition within the common market.

Restraint of trade

On the restraint of trade issue it had to be borne in mind that the 1988 agreement was a renegotiation of an agreement made in 1984; that by 1988 George Michael was already an established artist and that the essence of the renegotiation was a substantial improvement in the financial terms in exchange for additional albums.

In any event, his Lordship concluded that it was not open to the plaintiff to challenge the 1988 agreement on the ground of restraint of trade because:

1 There was a public interest in enforcing agreements reached by way of compromise of disputes. The 1984 agreement was such a compromise and as the 1988 agreement was a renegotiation of the 1984 agreement, the same applied.

2 It would be unjust to Sony if the 1988 agreement were treated as unenforceable or void because: (i) George Michael at all times had expert legal advice from Russels and was well aware of the doctrine of restraint of trade; (ii) Sony had agreed to bring forward dates of various payments for tax reasons; (iii) There was a further renegotiation in 1990 improving the plaintiff's terms; (iv) George Michael made a request for payment in advance in 1992 for a third album.

3 By requesting the advance for the third album when he knew it was open to him to challenge the 1988 agreement on the ground of restraint of trade, George Michael affirmed the 1988 agreement and he could not now resile from that affirmation.

Article 85

On the article 85 issue, it was necessary to consider the general European approach to the rules on competition. The need was for a broad and flexible approach, paying attention to substance rather than form (*Nungesser v Commission* (Case 2588/78) ([1982] ECR 2015)) and considering an agreement in its legal, economic and commercial context rather than applying a set of *a priori* principles.

That broad approach generally meant the need for a detailed investigation and analysis of the surrounding facts as the basis for a consideration of whether the agreement in question contravened the competition rules.

It should be said, however, that certain factors, the so-called rule of reason, the *de minimis* rule, and intellectual property rights, limited to some degree the scope for the application of article 85.

A further point was that where an agreement was said to contravene the competition rules, the particular aspect of competition said to be affected had to be identified: *Italian Flat Glass* (Cases T–68/69 and T–77/78/89) (1992) 5 CMLR 302, 342).

Also, the effect of an agreement for the purposes of article 85 had to be judged by reference to the competition which would occur in its absence: *Petrofina SA v Commission* (Case T–2/89)([1991] 2 ECR 1087).

As to the application to those rules to the 1988 agreement, it was said for George Michael, *inter alia*:

1 The effect of the agreement on trade between member states was that it prevented him from producing recordings in the field of pop music for other record companies in other member states;

2 It had the requisite effect on the end-product market in that it affected the flow of trade in records of his work since trade in his records was undertaken by Sony and not by some other record company;

3 Those actual or potential effects were appreciable, not *de minimis*, given the status and size of Sony and the fact that George Michael was a highly successful recording artist whose records had achieved substantial sales;

4 It was a fact that the 1988 agreement formed part of a network of similar agreements, that is, agreements between other recording artists and other artists.

It was an essential feature of George Michael's case that the market should be a Community wide market and not merely a national or domestic market since a national or domestic market would not attract article 85: *Hugin Kassaregister AB v Commission* (Case 22/78) ([1979] ECR 1869); yet, on the restraint of trade issue, it was said that there was a lack of evidence to indicate that UK recording artists signed with non-UK record companies, let alone with record companies from member states.

Indeed, the evidence before his Lordship was to the effect that the market for the services of UK recording artists in the pop field was a purely national and domestic market limited territorially to the UK.

It was unfortunate that the article 85 issue was not specifically addressed in evidence.

On the evidence before his Lordship however, he could only conclude that there was no Community wide market for the services of UK recording artists in the field of popular music since it was only in exceptional cases that UK recording artists signed to a non-UK record company.

Thus, so far as George Michael was concerned, in 1982 and again in 1984, the relevant market for his services was the UK market, consisting of UK record companies.

It followed that for the purposes of article 85(1), the 1988 agreement did not affect trade between member states at the raw material end of the chain of supply, that is, the market for George Michael's recording services.

The result therefore was that both George Michael's claims would be dismissed.

(An appeal has been lodged against this decision.)

Competition Authority; Employment Agreements and The Competition Act, Iris Oifigiuil 18 September 1992, 632–3

The Competition Authority has received numerous requests regarding the position of employment contracts or agreements between employers and employees under the Competition Act. Since this indicates that many employment contracts may include non-competition clauses, the Authority considers that it would be useful to give some indication of its views regarding such agreements. The Authority points out that the interpretation of the provisions of the Competition Act is ultimately a matter for the courts.

The prohibition in s. 4 (1) of the Competition Act relates to agreements between undertakings, decisions of associations of undertakings and concerted practices. Clearly most employers are undertakings. The Authority does not consider, however, that employees as such are undertakings within the meaning of the Act. Employees normally act on behalf of an undertaking and do not, therefore, constitute an undertaking themselves. This view is in accord with that expressed by the European Court of Justice in the *Suiker Unie* case, which involved article 85 (1) of the Treaty of Rome, upon which s. 4 (1) is based. The court indicated that employees should be regarded as an integral part of the undertaking which empowered them and were not therefore undertakings themselves. The view that employees are not undertakings was endorsed in a written answer to the European Parliament by the European Commission in relation to professional soccer players which stated that: 'individuals participating in professional sports normally do so as employees of a club on the basis of an employment contract and as such are not undertakings.'[1]

Although there is a difference between Irish and EC legislation, in that the Irish Act defines an undertaking as being engaged for gain, the Authority believes that employees as such should not be regarded as undertakings under s. 4 on the basis of the reasoning advanced by the Court of Justice in the *Suiker Unie* case.

As it does not consider that employees are undertakings, the Authority believes that an agreement between an employer and an employee is not an agreement between undertakings and is not therefore within the scope of s. 4 (1). It follows also that an employment agreement as such is not notifiable to the Authority, as ss 7 (1) and (2) of the Act only provide for the notification of agreements of a kind described in s. 4 (1).

The position changes, however, once an employee leaves an employer and seeks to set up his or her own business. They would then be regarded as an undertaking. This view is in accord with EC treatment of such cases. As Van Bael and Bellis point out: 'Employees are normally acting on behalf of an undertaking and therefore do not constitute an undertaking themselves. However, from the moment an employee pursues his own economic interests, and where they are different from his employer's interests, he might well become an undertaking within the sense of article 85.'[2]

At this stage the Authority would regard the agreement as an agreement between undertakings which could then be notified. If the former employer were to seek to enforce a non-competition clause in an employment contract in respect of an employee who had left and was seeking to establish his or her own business, the Authority believes that this would represent a restriction of competition within the meaning of s. 4 (1). While such an agreement between one individual and an employer may not have a substantial impact on competition, the existence of such agreements in many sectors of the economy means that their combined effect would be to greatly restrict competition. The Authority therefore believes that it would be difficult for such an agreement to satisfy the requirements specified for the grant of a licence in s. 4 (2) of the Act.

Should an employee in addition own or control the undertaking, the view of the Authority, expressed in several decisions, is that the individual can then be regarded as an undertaking.[3]

[1.] Written question no. 2391/83, OJ 1984 C222/21, 23 August 1984.
[2.] I. Van Bael and J. F. Bellis, *Competition Law of the EEC*, (2nd ed.), CCH Editions Ltd, 1990, point 206.
[3.] Notification nos CA/9/91 *Nallen/O'Toole (Belmullet)*, decision of 2 April 1992, CA/9/91 *ACT/Kindle*, decision of 4 September 1992 and CA/1/92 *Budget Travel/Phil Fortune*, decision of 14 September 1992.

Note

It must be remembered that it is the function of the courts to interpret the provisions of the Competition Act, and thus, the notices and decisions of the authority are subject to review by the courts.

C. Employee or Undertaking

Competition Authority Decision No. 9 Budget Travel/Phil Fortune (CA/1/92) 14 September 1992

An agreement for the sale by Budget Travel Ltd of their shares in Budget Travel Schools Abroad Ltd (hereinafter referred to as BTSA) to Phil Fortune, a former employee of BTSA, was notified to the Competition Authority on 17 January 1992 for the purposes of obtaining a licence under s. 4 (2) of the Competition Act 1991.

. . .

The agreement for the sale and purchase of BTSA was made on 7 November 1991. Under the agreement, Budget Travel Ltd agreed to sell BTSA to Phil Fortune and to accept a number of restrictions on their future activity in the market for group tours. Specifically, Budget Travel Ltd gave undertakings in clause 13(b) of the agreement not to:

(i) For a period of two years from completion be directly or indirectly interested or concerned in or assist in carrying on any business, undertaking, company or firm actively marketing, promoting, or selling, tours or holidays catering for school or academic institutions, *provided always* that nothing in this clause shall prevent the vendor from accepting group bookings from school and other academic institutions for holidays the nature of which the vendor presently promotes, or

(ii) For a period of *four years* from completion either on their own or each of their own account or on behalf of any person, firm or company solicit the employment of or enter into partnership with or appoint as consultant any person who is at completion or who has within the six months prior to completion [been] an officer or employee of the company or,

(iii) At *any time* hereafter make use of or disclose or divulge to any third party any *information* of a secret or *confidential* nature relating to the business of the company.

. . .

Assessment

(b) *The undertakings and the agreement*

19. The Authority is concerned with an agreement between Phil Fortune and Budget Travel Ltd. S. 3(1) of the Competition Act defines an undertaking as 'a person being an

individual, a body corporate or an unincorporated body of persons engaged for gain in the production, supply or distribution of goods or the provision of a service'.

20. Budget Travel Ltd is a subsidiary of the UK publicly quoted Granada group. It acts as a tour operator on the Irish market and is clearly an undertaking within the meaning of s. 3 of the Act. Prior to this agreement Budget Travel Ltd was the owner of BTSA.

21. Phil Fortune, a former employee of BTSA, has bought the company from Budget Travel Ltd. S. 3 of the Act explicitly states that individuals may come within the definition of undertakings if they are 'engaged for gain in the production, supply or distribution of goods or the provision of a service'.

22. The Competition Authority has decided in previous cases that individuals who either own or control a business are undertakings for the purposes of the Act[1] provided they are engaged for gain in the production, supply and distribution of goods and services through the firms which they control.

23. In this respect the Authority has followed the approach taken by the European Commission which has ruled in a number of cases under article 85(1) of the Treaty of Rome, on which s. 4(1) of the Act is based, that individuals can be undertakings in certain circumstances. In the *Nutricia* case the Commission decided, and the European Court of Justice agreed, that individuals were undertakings by virtue of their being the future proprietors of a business.[2] This ruling is of particular relevance to the present agreement as Phil Fortune became the owner of BTSA under the agreement.

24. For the reasons detailed above, Budget Travel Ltd and Phil Fortune are considered to be undertakings within the meaning of s. 4(1) of the Act. The present arrangements constitute an agreement between undertakings which applies within the State as both parties to the agreement operate within the State.

. . .

The Authority has given its views on non-competition clauses in *Nallen/O'Toole* and a number of other decisions. In these cases the Authority took the view that some restraint on the business activities of the vendors may be necessary to ensure the adequate transfer of the goodwill of the business concerned. The Authority decided that the restraint must be limited in terms of its scope, duration and geographical coverage to that which is necessary to fully secure that transfer of the goodwill. Provided this is the case, then such a restraint does not restrict competition in the market in question. In this respect the Authority has followed the views of the EC Commission in respect of similar agreements under article 85(1) which have been endorsed by the European Court of Justice.

29. The Authority accepts that in the present case some restriction on Budget Travel competing in the relevant market is necessary to secure the complete transfer of the goodwill of BTSA. The issue therefore is whether the restrictions in the notified agreement are limited to what is necessary to secure the transfer of the goodwill.

Clause 13(b)(i)

30. In clause 13(b)(i), Budget Travel Ltd have undertaken not to become involved in the relevant market for a period of two years. The Authority has indicated in previous decisions that it would normally regard a time limit of two years as being adequate for

the transfer of goodwill. This clause, does not, therefore, offend against s. 4(1) of the Act by virtue of its duration.

31. On the question of the geographical scope of the non-competition clause in 13 (b)(i), no specific geographical area to which it applies is specified.

32. The European Commission ruled in the *Nutricia* case that: 'The geographical scope of a non-competition clause also has to be limited to the extent which is objectively necessary to achieve the aforementioned goal. As a rule, it should therefore only cover the markets where the products concerned were manufactured or sold at the time of the agreements.'

33: The Authority took a similar view in the *Nallen/O'Toole* and *ACT/Kindle* cases. In the latter case, no specific geographical area was mentioned in the restrictive clauses. This was found to be acceptable by the Authority given that, prior to the agreement, Kindle was operating on a worldwide basis.

34. It has been argued that Budget could compete directly with BTSA by establishing a company either in Northern Ireland or England and retaining sales persons on a commission or other basis. Accordingly, the application of the non-competition clause in 13(b)(i) was not limited to the Irish market. The Authority accepts the validity of this argument and does not consider that this restriction offends against s. 4(1) of the Act.

35. In relation to the scope of the clause, Budget Travel Ltd are required not to compete in the market for group tours which is the market in which BTSA was involved at the time of the agreement. Therefore, the scope of the restriction does not restrain the vendors from being active in any market outside of the one served by BTSA. It is evident that the scope of the restriction does not go beyond what is necessary for the transfer of the goodwill and does not offend against s. 4(1) of the Act.

Clause 13(b)(ii)

36. This clause prevents Budget Travel Ltd from soliciting into employment, entering into partnership with or appointing as consultants employees of BTSA for a period of four years.

37. The justification advanced for the restriction was that it was essential for BTSA to 'retain its qualified and trained staff, who constituted one of its principal assets', and that it was 'essential to the preservation of the transferred worth of the undertaking'.

38. There is little doubt that BTSA employees who have worked in this area over a number of years have become familiar with the various facets of the business and will be efficient in dealing with them. However, this knowledge does not constitute technical know-how as defined by the Authority in *ACT/Kindle*. Accordingly, it is the Authority's view that the expertise of the employees of BTSA represents primarily part of the goodwill of the company.

39. In principle, there is nothing wrong with preventing the vendors from soliciting the services of BTSA employees for a period of time. Such a restriction ensures that the goodwill of the company being purchased is transferred.[3] In this case, however, the original clause may have gone beyond what was required to secure the transfer of the

goodwill of BTSA because of its duration. Phil Fortune has agreed to accept a lesser period of three years. The Authority believes that, given the fact that personal contacts are quite important in this business, Ms Fortune, despite her background in the business, will need some time to establish a reputation for the newly managed entity, and that the restriction on Budget Travel competing in the group tour market is for only two years, the three years duration now proposed for this clause is acceptable and does not offend against s. 4(1).

Clause 13(b)(iii)

40. This clause prevents Budget Travel Ltd from using, disclosing or divulging information of a secret or confidential nature about BTSA. The restriction is not limited in terms of its duration.

41. In advancing a case to support this clause a distinction was made by Phil Fortune between business information in the public domain and other business information such as profits, margins, turnover, overheads and other financial matters not in the public domain. The intention is to prevent the disclosure and use of the latter type of information. Phil Fortune's main argument in relation to this clause was that it was essential to 'transfer the entire worth of the company'.

42. Confidential business information may constitute an important part of the value of the transferred undertaking. The use of such information may confer a competitive advantage on the vendor. Nonetheless, the value of the type of confidential business information referred to in this case will be eroded over time. Eventually, it will be worthless and restrictions on its disclosure or use will become meaningless.

43. The Authority is concerned, however, that such a clause should not be used to impede any possible re-entry into the market by Budget once the two year non-competition clause in 13(b)(i) has expired. In particular, the Authority would be concerned that the effect of this could be to prevent Budget using its knowledge of the market for group tours if they decided to engage in that market in the future. The Authority accepts Phil Fortune's undertaking not to 'use or attempt to use this clause in any manner which would prevent the vendor re-entering the market after the period provided by clause (b)(i) has expired'. In the light of this undertaking the Authority considers that this clause does not offend against s. 4(1) of the Act.

1. Notification Nos CA/8/91—*Nallen/O'Toole* (Belmullet), decision of 2 April 1992 and CA/9/91—ACT/*Kindle*, decision of 4 September 1992.
2. *Nutricia/De Rooij* and *Nutricia/Zuid Hollandse Conservenfabriek* (83/670/EEC, OJ L 376, 31 December 1983, p. 22), on appeal *Remia BV and Others v European Commission*, Case 42/84, [1985] ECR 2545.
3. The Authority took a similar view in *Woodchester Bank/UDT Bank*.

Competition Authority Decision No. 12 Scully Tyrrell/Edberg (CA/57/92) 29 January 1993

Arrangements for the purchase of Scully Tyrrell & Co. (STC) by Edberg Ltd were notified to the Competition Authority on 31 July 1992. The notification requested a certificate, or in the event of a refusal by the Authority to grant a certificate, a licence.
. . .

Assessment

. . . because the vendors have a substantial share in Edberg, exercise extensive control over its operations and could pursue interests which differ from those of the company, they can continue to be regarded as undertakings following completion of the notified arrangements.

. . .

Collectively the vendors have retained a significant shareholding (thirty eight per cent) in Edberg Ltd as part of the agreement for the sale of STC. RHL have acquired the option to buy this shareholding from the vendors in 1995. In the interim, it is proposed that the vendors be employed in Edberg for an initial period of three years under clause 2.2 of the service agreement. Their employment may be terminated thereafter by either party giving not less than six months written notice to the other.

68. If any of the vendors terminated their employment contract before the initial three years has expired, they would have been deemed to have breached that contract and RHL could have exercised the right to acquire their shares in Edberg within three months. The consideration payable to the vendor in these circumstances would have been £1.

69. Clause 12 of the STC Agreement set out restrictions on the future activities of the vendors. 12.1 contained a non-competition clause which applied to the vendors for a period of the longer of (i) three years from completion and (ii) a second period. The second period was two years from termination of the vendor's employment with the purchaser if such termination occurred within three years of completion. This non-competition provision was also included in clause 14.1 of the service agreement. After the initial three year period had elapsed there would be no second period if the vendor's employment was terminated by the purchaser in breach of the terms thereof. The second period would be six months if the vendor's employment was terminated by notice in accordance with clause 2.2 of the service agreement.

70. It is evident that termination by the vendors of their employment within the first three years was not a feasible option in the light of the return on their shareholding provided for under the option agreement. The vendors were therefore tied to Edberg for an initial period of three years. In these circumstances the additional six months provided for under clause 12.1(b) of the STC agreement (the second period) meant that the duration of the non-competition clause was effectively a minimum of three and a half years.

71. In relation to the duration of the non-competition clause, the purchasers had stressed the importance of customer/client loyalty built up over the year by the vendors. They argued that the duration of the clause was the minimum that was objectively necessary for Edberg to assume, by active competitive behaviour, the place in the market previously occupied by the vendors through STC. They added that 'the duration of the covenants in clause 12 may potentially, in certain circumstances, exceed three years since the second period' of protection afforded by clause 12 was equally objectively necessary to protect and preserve the value of the investment by SGS and Edberg in the STC business in view of the nature of the business as a service business where customer/client loyalty was invaluable and persisted for a period which might well exceed three years.'

72. The Authority's view on the duration of non-competition clauses in the case of the sale of a business has been stated in several previous decisions. Its view is that some

restriction on the seller is generally necessary in order to ensure the complete transfer of the goodwill of the business. It stated that provided the restriction was limited in terms of its duration, geographical coverage and subject matter to that which was necessary for the complete transfer of the goodwill, then the restriction did not offend against s. 4(1) of the Act. Most recently in *General Semiconductor*, the Authority indicated that, having had an opportunity to consider a number of such agreements, it would generally consider a non-competition clause exceeding two years in a sale of business agreement to offend against s. 4(1).[1]

73. Given its previous decisions, the Authority regarded the non-competition clauses in the notified arrangements, which were effectively for a minimum of three and half years, as being more than was necessary to secure the complete transfer of goodwill. It is relevant that insurers would be dealing with the firm frequently and in such circumstances a period of two years was considered sufficient for the new owners to acquire the complete goodwill. It must also be considered that figures for commission paid to the vendors in respect of fee income earned by them in 1991, indicated that a lot of the company's business was attributable to its other employees.

74. In this case it was not clear that the arrangements could be viewed as a simple sale of business, since the vendors are to remain on as shareholders and employees following the sale. This raised the question of the date from which the non-compete clause should have effect. The arrangements could be viewed as akin to the creation of a partnership involving RHL and the vendors. An agreement between parties to engage in business together could not operate if the parties were free to compete with the business or with each other. The Authority believes that individuals could not jointly engage in business together if they were free to compete with each other. It is clear, even if it is not explicitly stated, that an agreement between parties to carry on business together implies that they will not compete against the business or against each other so long as they remain in the business together.

75. Where individuals agree to engage in business together as part of a single economic entity and not to compete with one another, the Authority believes there is a case for not regarding such arrangements, of themselves, as offending against s. 4(1). Indeed such arrangements may be pro-competitive in that the combined entity may be in a better position to compete with other undertakings in the relevant market. The position changes, however, if the parties are prevented from withdrawing from such arrangements. If a party wishes to withdraw from such arrangements then measures designed to prevent him doing so may restrict competition. In the event that one of the parties to such an arrangement decides to withdraw then, given the Authority's view in *Nallen/O'Toole*, where one partner bought out the other partner's share in the business, a provision which restricts the vendor from competing with the business for a time may be justified in order to allow the purchaser obtain the goodwill of the business for which he had paid.

76. In the present case Edberg has purchased the business of STC from the vendors, who are to become shareholders in, and employees of Edberg. The Authority believes that in such circumstances the vendors could not be expected to compete with Edberg for so long as they continue to be significant shareholders and enjoy a degree of control over the running of the business and that in such circumstances any agreement not to compete does not offend against s. 4(1). The Authority does not believe that such a restriction would be acceptable if the shareholding was held for purely

investment purposes or if it was part of an artificial arrangement which had the object or effect of evading the prohibition contained in s. 4(1).

77. The original restrictions went beyond what was necessary to secure the complete transfer of the goodwill of the business to the extent that they did not just prevent the vendors competing with the business while they remained involved in it, but sought to tie them to the business for a minimum period of time. The vendors were effectively tied to Edberg for at least three years by virtue of the service and option agreements. In addition they would have been prevented from competing with Edberg for a further six months if they then left. The combined effect of the non-compete clauses, the option agreement and related provisions therefore was to exclude potential competitors—the vendors—from the market for at least three and a half years. This period exceeded what the Authority generally regards as necessary to secure the transfer of the goodwill of a business and the Authority therefore considered that the effect of the arrangements was to prevent competition. The restrictions, therefore, offended against s. 4(1).

78. Clause 12.2 (a) of the STC agreement prevented the vendors canvassing orders from clients of Edberg. This restriction applied for the 'longer of a period of three years from completion or a period of two years from termination of the relevant vendor's employment with the purchaser . . . ' As already explained, it was not in the vendors' interests to break their three year service contracts. Therefore, the duration of this clause was effectively a minimum of five years. Given the nature of the business, in particular the relatively small number of users of loss adjusters' services, the Authority believes that a restriction on canvassing former clients would make it extremely difficult if not impossible to compete in this market. In the Authority's opinion, this clause would have served to reinforce the duration of the other non-competition provisions in the arrangements and would have had the effect of preventing the vendors from competing with Edberg for an excessive period of time. Clause 14.2 of the service agreements also included this restriction. The Authority concluded that both of these clauses offended against s. 4(1) of the act for the reasons outlined in the previous paragraph.

79. On balance the Authority believes that in a case such as this a restriction on competition should be limited to the period during which the vendors remain as shareholders, employees and enjoy a degree of control over the business. Should they sell their shareholding at some stage then a restriction on their competing with the business may be justified to enable the purchaser to acquire the remaining goodwill of the business. Such a restriction generally ought not to exceed two years from the time of such sale.

80. In a supplemental agreement dated 18 December 1992, the parties amended the offending provisions of the agreement. Under the amended agreement the vendors agree not to compete with Edberg for so long as they remain shareholders and/or employees of Edberg and for a period of two years after they dispose of their shareholding in accord with the terms of the option agreement. In addition the option agreement has been amended to provide that, in the event that the vendors leave Edberg before 31 December 1994, the buy out price pursuant to clause 3.2 (a) of that agreement would be 'such sum as equals the price determined by the auditors of Edberg to be the market value on the basis of a willing seller and a willing buyer and on the basis that the relevant shares constitute a minority shareholding less an agreed discount of five per cent.'

81. The Authority believes that while the option agreement as amended means that there may still be some disincentive for the vendors to leave the business before 31 December 1994, this is not now so great as to effectively exclude such a possibility. The Authority considers that a restriction on the vendors competing with the business for so long as they remain employees and shareholders and for a further two years after they dispose of their shareholding is acceptable in such circumstances as being no more than is necessary to secure the transfer of the goodwill of the business to the purchaser. For these reasons the Authority considers that the amended provisions do not offend against s. 4(1).

82. The Authority wishes to make clear that the restrictions contained in the arrangements as amended were acceptable in the context of the parties having agreed to engage in business together as part of a single economic entity. As stated above, in its view a restriction on individuals competing with a business in which they were shareholders would offend against s. 4(1) where such shareholding was purely for investment purposes or was an artificial arrangement whose object or effect was to evade the prohibition contained in that section. It would take a similar view of an employment contract that was an artificial arrangement whose object or effect was to evade the prohibition contained in that section.

83. The scope of clause 12.1 is limited to the business of loss adjusting. Accordingly, the scope of the restriction does not offend against s. 4(1) of the Competition Act 1991. It applies to Ireland, Northern Ireland, England, Wales, Scotland, the Channel Islands and the Isle of Man. In view of the fact that insurance loss adjusting services can be easily provided across international borders, the Authority is satisfied that the geographical impact of the clause is limited to that which is necessary for the transfer of the goodwill of STC.

84. Clause 12.2(b) of the STC agreement prevents the vendors using the words 'Scully' or 'Tyrrell' or 'Scully Tyrrell' as a trade name or mark in the relevant market. It is necessary to prevent the possibility of the vendors passing themselves off to their customers or suppliers as representing STC in the event that they should decide to compete against the purchasers. This restraint does not involve any restriction on competition within the State or any part of the State and does not offend against s. 4(1).

85. Clause 15 of the STC agreement, clause 14.1 of the shareholders' agreement and clause 11.1 of the service agreements involve undertakings by the vendors concerning the disclosure or use of confidential information and related matters. These clauses prevent the vendors from disclosing or making use of trade secrets. There is no time limit on these clauses. The Authority has considered the question of preventing the use of non-technical know-how in Budget Travel. As in that case, the Authority was concerned that such a clause should not be used to impede any possible re-entry into the market by the vendors once the non-competition clauses had expired. The parties indicated by letter dated 23 November 1992 that the confidentiality provisions in clause 15 of the STC agreement, clause 14.1 of the shareholders' agreement and clause 11.1 of the service agreements 'are not intended or designed to prevent the vendors from competing with the business carried on by Edberg but rather are intended and designed simply to prohibit a vendor from using or abusing information that is confidential to Edberg or any of the Edberg shareholders.' In these circumstances, the Authority finds that these clauses do not offend against s. 4(1) of the Act.

The decision

86. Edberg, RHL and the vendors are undertakings within the meaning of s. 3(1) of the Competition Act and the notified arrangements for the sale of the business of STC to Edberg constitute an agreement between undertakings which applies within the State.

87. The Authority believes that the agreement for the purchase and sale of STC does not offend against s. 4(1) of the Competition Act.

88. The Authority has previously stated that, in the case of a sale of business, some restriction on the seller competing with the purchaser is normally justified in order for the purchaser to acquire the complete goodwill of the business. A non-competition clause which is limited in terms of duration, geographic coverage and subject matter to what is necessary to secure the complete transfer of the goodwill of the business does not prevent, restrict or distort competition within the meaning of s. 4(1) of the Competition Act. In this instance the vendors have decided to remain on and effectively agreed to engage in business with the purchaser as part of a single economic entity. The Authority believes that, in such circumstances, an agreement by the vendors not to compete with Edberg for so long as they remain shareholders and employees of that company does not offend against s. 4(1) of the Competition Act, provided the shareholding is not held for purely investment purposes and provided that the arrangements are not an artificial construction whose object or effect is to evade the prohibition contained in that section.

89. The Authority believes that the restriction on the vendors competing with Edberg for two years after they sell their shares is limited in terms of duration, geographic coverage and subject matter to what is necessary to secure the complete transfer of the goodwill of the business following such a sale. In the Authority's view the restrictions contained in the various agreements, as amended by the supplemental agreement of 18 December 1992, together with the undertaking in respect of the confidentiality clauses in the letter of 23 November 1991, do not prevent, restrict or distort competition in the State or any part of the State.

90. The present agreement for the transfer of ownership of Scully Tyrrell & Co. between Robins Holdings Ltd, Edberg Ltd and Messrs Scully, Tyrrell, Crawford, Herbert, Sleater, Conroy, O'Donoghue and Putnam does not, in the Authority's opinion offend against s. 4(1) of the Competition Act, 1991.

[1.] Competition Authority decision no. 10, notification nos CA/51/92 and CA/52/92—GI/ *General Semiconductor Industries*, 23 October 1992.

Note

In Competition Authority decision No. 24, *Cambridge/Imari* (CA/8/92E), 21 June 1993 an individual was regarded as an 'undertaking' by virtue of the fact that he was a part owner and managing director of a company, exercising 'considerable *de facto* control over the business'. The Authority noted that he was thus 'engaged for gain in the provision of services'.

Competition Authority Decision No. 13 Peter Mark/Majella Stapleton (CA/1011/92E) 18 February 1993

This decision concerns a contract of employment between Peter Mark and Ms Majella Stapleton, who is now a former employee of Peter Mark. The arrangements were notified to the Competition Authority on 30 September 1992 under s. 7 of Competition Act 1991 for the purpose of obtaining a certificate under s. 4(4) or, in the event of a refusal by the Authority to issue a certificate, a licence under s. 4(2).

. . .

Assessment
The agreement
    The contract of employment between Peter Mark and their former employee, Majella Stapleton, was made on 16 July 1990 on commencement of her employment with Peter Mark. The relevant clauses in the notified agreement in these proceedings are clauses 4, 5 and 6 which provide as follows:

Clause 4: The employee upon ceasing employment with the employer shall not take up employment with any competitor of the employer nor commence business in competition with the employer within a radius of one mile of Peter Mark, Wine Street, Sligo for the term of six months from the date that such employment ceases.

Clause 5: As and from the termination of the employment the employee shall not canvas, circularise or solicit business from the employer's customers using the name Peter Mark.

Clause 6: In the event that the restraint provisions in this contract are modified by any court, then such provisions as are considered reasonable by such court shall apply in lieu of the foregoing provisions.

. . .

Peter Mark
16. Peter Mark, an unlimited company and subsidiary of Glenberg, is a body corporate engaged in the provision of hairdressing and hairstyling services for gain and is therefore an undertaking within the meaning of the Act.

Majella Stapleton
17. The Competition Authority in its Notice on Employee Agreements and the Competition Act outlined its views on the employee as an undertaking and on agreements between employers and employees.

18. In its decision in the *Aga Khan* case[2] the Authority indicated that it: 'had also taken the view that the provisions of ss 4(1), 4(4), 7(1) and 7(2) taken together, imply that an agreement may be notified, and a certificate requested, where the parties are in some doubt as to whether that agreement would offend against s. 4(1), but not otherwise. In the Authority's view, there must be reasonable grounds for such doubts.'

19. In the Notice on Employee Agreements it was further indicated by the Authority that once an employee leaves an employer and seeks to set up his or her own business they would then be regarded as an undertaking. The Authority, however, did not deal directly with the question of an employee taking up employment with another

employer in the notice. It was also noted that Van Bael & Bellis, had, in the context of Article 85, stated: 'However, from the moment an employee pursues his own economic interests, and where they are different from his employer's interests, he might well become an undertaking within the sense of Article 85.'[3]

20. Ms Stapleton's solicitors have claimed that she is an undertaking within the meaning of the Competition Act because she profits from an increase in the business of her employer through the payment of a commission. For these reasons the Authority believes that there was reasonable doubt in this instance, and it has considered the notified agreement in the context of the Competition Act 1991.

21. Majella Stapleton was employed by Peter Mark from July 1990 to September 1992 as a stylist. She left Peter Mark to take up employment in a competing hairdressing salon. Her position with Peter Mark was solely that of an employee. Her position with her new employer is also solely that of an employee. She had or has no ownership or control in her previous or present employment. The fact that Ms Stapleton is paid partly on a commission basis and, as a result, benefits directly from any increase in business, is not sufficient to establish, in the Authority's view, that she is an undertaking by virtue of pursuing her own economic interests. Accordingly, in the Authority's view she was not and is not an undertaking under s. 3(1) of the Competition Act 1991.

22. The position would of course be wholly different if Ms Stapleton were seeking to set up her own business. As the notified agreement is, therefore, not an agreement between undertakings the arguments submitted by Ms Stapleton's solicitor in support of a certificate or a licence in relation to clauses 4, 5 and 6 need not be considered by the Authority.

The decision

23. This decision applies solely to the contract of employment between Peter Mark and Ms Majella Stapleton, dated 16 July 1990. In the opinion of the Authority, that contract does not constitute an 'agreement between undertakings' for the purposes of the Competition Act 1991 because one of the contracting parties, Ms Stapleton, was not at any material time an 'undertaking' within the meaning of the Act. Accordingly, the agreement, not being 'of a kind described in s. 4(1)', falls outside the scope of s. 7 of the Act and the Authority refuses to grant a certificate or a licence under the Act.

[1.] Written question No. 2391/83, OJ 1984 C222/21, 23 August 1984.
[2.] Notification Nos CA/673/92E—*Thoroughbred Promotion and Development Co. Ltd/Grenfell Ltd* and CA/674/92E—*Bertram and Diana Firestone/His Highness Karim Aga Khan.*
[3.] I. Van Bael and J. F. Bellis, *Competition Law of the EEC,* (2nd ed.), CCH Editions Ltd, 1990, point 206.

Competition Authority Decision No. 20 APEX Fire Protection Ltd/Noel Murtagh (CA/1130/92) 10 June 1993

1. This decision concerns a contract of employment between Apex Fire Protection Ltd and Mr Noel Murtagh. The arrangements were notified on 11 November 1992 under s. 7(1) of the Competition Act 1991 for the purpose of obtaining a certificate under s. 4(4) or, in the event of a refusal by the Authority to issue a certificate, a licence under s. 4(2).

. . .

The decision concerns an employment contract between Apex Fire Protection Ltd and Mr Noel Murtagh a former employee of Apex, who has now set up his own business dealing in fire protection products and related services. The employment contract includes certain restrictions on the employee in the event of termination of employment.

. . .

The relevant clause in the notified agreement in these proceedings is clause 15 which provides as follows:

Clause 15: On the termination of this agreement howsoever occasioned, the representative shall not for the period of two years next after such termination within the district of which he has operated during the course of this agreement solicit any of the persons who were customers of the employer within two years immediately preceding the date of such termination and shall not divulge or disclose to any other party any information gained as a result of employment with the employer.

. . .

Assessment

(b) The undertakings

. . .

Apex Fire Protection Ltd

28. Apex Fire Protection Ltd is a limited company involved in the provision of fire protection and detection goods and services for various premises for gain and is therefore an undertaking within the meaning of the Act.

Mr Noel Murtagh

29. Mr Noel Murtagh, a former employee of Apex Fire Protection Ltd, set up his own business in October 1992 called A & A Fire Prevention Ltd. The Authority in its Notice on Employee agreements and the Competition Act[1] stated that it did not consider an employee to be an undertaking within the meaning of the Act and, as such, agreements between employers and employees did not come within the scope of the Act. It was further indicated that when an employee left an employer and set up his or her own business they would then be regarded as an undertaking. The Authority in its decision on *Phil Fortune/Budget Travel*[2] considered an ex-employee who acquired and became the proprietor of her former employer's business to be an undertaking. In this respect, the Authority has followed the approach taken under European Competition Law. For example, in the *Nutricia* case the Commission decided, and the Court of Justice agreed, that an individual who owns or controls a business is an undertaking. As Mr Murtagh now owns and controls his own business—A & A Fire Prevention Ltd which provides goods and services for gain—he is an undertaking within the meaning of s. 3(1) of the Act.

(c) The agreement

30. Apex Fire Protection Ltd and Mr Noel Murtagh, carrying on business under the name A & A Fire Prevention Ltd, are both undertakings within the meaning of the Act and consequently the agreement between Apex and Mr Murtagh is now an agreement between undertakings as defined in s. 4(1) of the Competition Act, 1991. The relevant product market is the market for the sale and servicing of portable fire equipment and the relevant geographical market is the city and county of Dublin.

(d) Restriction of competition

31. The provisions of the notified agreement, other than clause 15, concerned matters appropriate to contracts of employment such as the duties of the employee,

remuneration, working conditions etc. They are no longer operative since the employment has ceased.

32. In clause 15, two restrictions are imposed on the employee in the event of termination of the employment. These restrictions are to apply for a period of two years after termination. During that period, the employee may not, within the district in which he operated,

(a) solicit any of the persons who were customers of the employer within two years preceding the date of termination.
(b) divulge or disclose to any other party any information gained as a result of the employment.

33. In its Notice on Employee Agreements and the Competition Act the Authority has already given general guidance on the subject of non-competition clauses in contracts of employment.

34. The Authority therefore believes that a restriction which seeks to prevent a former employee entering the market as a competitor offends against s. 4(1). The restrictions in this instance are confined to soliciting the former employer's customers and to disclosing information confidential to the employer's business. The Authority considers that there is a difference between a restriction which seeks to prevent a former employee from entering the business and one which seeks only to protect the proprietary interests of the employer in his own business. The Authority believes that it is essential to employer/employee relationships that an individual should not be able to take up employment solely for the purpose of gaining an introduction to the employer's customers in order to solicit such customers. A restriction on soliciting the former employer's customers may therefore be regarded as essential both to protect the employer's proprietary interest in the goodwill of his business and to normal employer/employee relationships. Such a restriction must not, however, exceed what is absolutely necessary to protect the employer's interests or it would be regarded as an attempt to prevent competition by the ex-employee.

35. The Authority has considered carefully the arguments submitted by Apex in support of the proposition that the agreement does not restrict competition. Insofar as the company are arguing that the non-solicit clause is necessary to protect the public from the provision of unsatisfactory goods or services, the Authority would say that this function is not one for private firms and that it cannot afford any justification for the imposition of clauses of the kind under consideration. It is clear that the main purpose of the clause is to protect the interests of the company itself from what it may consider to be unfair competition. The company is seeking by this clause to protect the goodwill of its customer base for a certain period and in relation to a particular area. The company considers that the restrictions involved do not exceed reasonable limits.

Restriction on soliciting

36. The Authority recognises that the restriction on soliciting in the present case is by no means a total prohibition of all forms of competition. The Authority understands, on the basis of the facts in its possession, that the restriction does not cover more than a small proportion of all customers in the relevant market. Mr Murtagh remains free to transact unsolicited business with Apex customers within the designated area, all business with Apex customers elsewhere, and all business with non-Apex customers

everywhere. He may engage in normal forms of advertising to attract customers. After the expiry of the restriction, he will be completely free to carry on business everywhere without any restriction. It must be recognised that the clause places some restrictions on Mr Murtagh's commercial freedom. Mr Murtagh is seeking to earn a livelihood and build up a new business using the sources he has, including his knowledge and expertise of the business and his relationships with various customers, all acquired, admittedly while in the employment of Apex. He considers that he should be free to offer his services to any customer; it should be for the customer alone to decide whether to do business with him or Apex or any other firm.

37. Apex has provided important training to Mr Murtagh. He has had personal access to some of the customers of the company as well as access to information about the company's manner of operation. Besides having knowledge of the identity of Apex's customers, he also possesses confidential information concerning their requirements, the service dates and prices charged to them. His employment with the company has put him in possession of information which would place him at a competitive advantage *vis-à-vis* the company were he to commence business himself (as he has done). The company is, in the Authority's view, entitled to some protection against its former employee in these circumstances.

Scope of restricted activities

38. The restriction applies to 'soliciting' certain customers. Two issues arise here (i) whether this could extend to general advertising e.g an advertisement in the Yellow Pages and (ii) whether it could extend to 'passive' sales i.e. a sale resulting from an approach by the customer to the employee. The Authority understands the clause not to apply in either of these situations and Apex have confirmed that that is their interpretation also. On that basis, the Authority would raise no objection to this aspect of the clause.

Scope by reference to customers and area

39. The persons who may not be solicited by Mr Murtagh are those persons who were customers of Apex within two years of the termination of Mr Murtagh's employment. The reference to the area ('within the district of which he has operated') is somewhat ambiguous but it is understood (and Apex confirm) that the customers concerned are those who are based within the area of Dublin City and County only (and not the whole country) and this is unobjectionable as far as geographic scope is concerned. Of more significance is the determination of the class of customers affected. No distinction is drawn between customers with whom Mr Murtagh had dealings and other customers. It is mainly in relation to the former category that the arguments in favour of the restriction generally derive their force. The Authority accepts, however, that due account must be taken of the particular post occupied by Mr Murtagh in the Apex organisation. As a 'Field Training Supervisor', Mr Murtagh had access directly and indirectly to a wider range of customers than those dealt with previously by himself. Accordingly, the scope of the restriction in this respect does not appear to be excessive. A second difficulty which the Authority sees under this heading is that the class of customers, as defined, includes persons who have ceased to be 'customers' of Apex before Mr Murtagh established his business as well as persons who chose to leave Apex during the period of the restriction. In the Authority's view, the company is not entitled to protection from soliciting of these persons. This conclusion does not apply, of course to persons who ceased to be customers as a result of soliciting by Mr Murtagh in breach of the clause. The Authority therefore concludes that the agreement offends against s. 4(1) of

the Act in that it applies to persons who are no longer customers of Apex other than as a result of soliciting by Mr Murtagh and this exceeds what is required for the legitimate commercial interests of Apex.

40. Apex offered to amend this clause, by letter of 28 May 1993, so as to apply only to those persons who were customers at the date of termination of employment. Since this would now permit Mr Murtagh to solicit those persons who ceased to be customers of Apex in the two years prior to the date when his employment ceased, the Authority considers that this aspect of the agreement no longer offends against s. 4(1) of the Act. While this would still prevent Mr Murtagh from soliciting those persons who ceased to be customers during a period after his employment ceased, the Authority considers that this would have no real effect on competition, and that its removal would not lead to any practical difference in the situation since Mr Murtagh would not be aware, of his own knowledge, that such persons had ceased to be customers. In the circumstances, the Authority considers that the scope of the agreement by reference to customers, as amended, does not offend against s. 4(1) of the Act.

Scope by reference to duration

41. In the view of the Authority, the company has shown that a two year period after termination is necessary for the protection of its legitimate commercial interests. In coming to this view, the Authority has taken into account the fact that the period of time during which items of fire protection equipment normally require servicing is one year. A one year period of protection, in the view of the Authority, would provide the company with ample opportunity to confirm its business connection and goodwill with its existing customers prior to facing competition for those customers from Mr Murtagh subsequently. In reaching this conclusion the Authority has also taken account of the following factors:

(i) Insofar as the purpose of the restriction is to protect the company's goodwill, it must be admitted that only some of the goodwill in question is exclusively attributable to Mr Murtagh. Most of the goodwill must be attributable to the company itself and to the business reputation of its services, products and the back-up support provided by the company to its representatives.

(ii) In the case of sale of business agreements, the Authority accepted that a two year period of protection was normally necessary to protect the goodwill of the business being acquired. In such a case however, the starting position for the purchaser is one in which he normally possesses none of the goodwill. He has to secure all of that goodwill unlike the employer who already holds most of it. This consideration would suggest that a period of less than two years should normally be necessary in the case of employment contracts.

(iii) Notwithstanding his previous employment with Apex, Mr Murtagh is in a position somewhat akin to a new entrant into the market. He has to convince customers that the products and services he is offering are as good as or better than those of others, including Apex, and that he is in a position to ensure adequate back-up service.

(iv) Apex is one of the leading firms in that market.

(v) While there is obviously some degree of technical expertise involved in the provision of the services concerned, that degree is not such as to justify a lengthy period of protection. The Authority does not consider that the suggested period of eighteen months, as proposed in the letter of 28 May 1993, is necessary to protect the legitimate interests of Apex.

42. The Authority therefore concludes that the agreement offends against s. 4(1) of the Act in that it applies for a period of two years after the termination of the employment and exceeds what is required for the legitimate commercial interests of Apex.

Restriction on divulging information

43. In some previous cases concerning sale of business or shareholder agreements the Authority considered obligations not to disclose information. For example in the *Budget Travel* case the Authority accepted a clause preventing one party from using, disclosing or divulging information of a secret or confidential nature, following the sale of a business after the second party had given an undertaking not to use this clause to prevent the first party from re-entering the market. In another case, *Scully/Tyrrell*[4] the Authority decided that a clause preventing the use and disclosure of confidential information did not offend against s. 4(1) of the Act, after the parties involved had stated that the restriction would not be used to prevent the second party from competing in business. In those cases, the Authority was concerned to ensure that obligations of this kind were not used as a means of preventing or impeding a party from re-entering the market after the expiry of a non-competition clause. The restriction in the present case only involves disclosure. Apex have indicated that the clause under consideration will not be used in this way and will only be used to protect information covered by normal business confidentiality.

44. Unless confidentiality can be ensured, employer/employee relationships, and many others, just could not occur. This is relevant during the term of an agreement, and afterwards. It is akin to the goodwill being transferred as part of the sale of a business, but is probably even more important. It is hard to see how an employer would be prepared to give confidential information to employees if they were allowed to use this or disclose it to competitors when employment ceased. At the same time, it often has to be disclosed to employees for them to be able to do their job. Confidentiality may therefore be seen as ancillary in the sense of being fundamentally necessary for such relationships.

45. In the view of the Authority the restriction on disclosure does not offend against s. 4(1) of the Act.

Applicability of S. 4(2)

. . .

47. As the restriction on soliciting exceeds what is required for the legitimate commercial interests of Apex, it cannot be considered to be 'indispensable' within the meaning of s. 4(2) of the Act. Since all of the four tests of the subsection must be met in order to qualify for a licence, it follows that the agreement in its present form cannot be granted a licence. It is not necessary to consider the position in relation to the other three requirements of s. 4(2).

The decision

48. Apex Fire Protection Ltd, and Mr Noel Murtagh are undertakings within the meaning of the Competition Act and the contract of employment between them, dated 29 October 1991 (CA/1130/92), is an agreement between undertakings. The agreement, as amended in the letter of 28 May 1993, offends against s. 4(1) of the Act insofar as it contains a restriction on soliciting certain customers which exceeds what is required for the legitimate commercial interests of Apex in that it still applies for a period of eighteen months after termination of employment. The agreement may not benefit

from the provisions of s. 4(2) of the Act because it contains terms which are not indispensable to the attainment of any benefits achieved by the agreement. The Authority therefore refuses to grant a licence to the agreement between Apex Fire Protection Ltd and Mr Noel Murtagh.

1. Competition Authority Notice on Employee Agreements and the Competition Act, *Iris Oifigiuil*, No. 75, 18 September 1992, pp 632–3.
2. Notification No. CA/1/92—*Budget Travel/Phil Fortune*, Competition Authority decision No. 9, 14 September 1992.
3. *Nutricia/De Rooij* and *Nutricia/Zuid Hollandse Conservenfabriek* (83/670/EEC, OJ L376, 31 December 1983, p. 22), on appeal *Remia BV and Others v European Commission*, Case 42/84, [1985] ECR 2545.
4. Notification No. CA/57/92—*Scully Tyrrell & Co./Edberg Ltd*, Competition Authority decision No. 12 of 29 January 1993.

Competition Authority Decision No. 29 Carrolls Catering (CA/1136/92) 9 September 1993

Arrangements for the purchase of the entire issued share capital of John D. Carroll Catering Ltd (Carrolls Catering) by Sutcliffe Ireland Ltd (Sutcliffe) from Mr John D. Carroll and Ms Marie Therese Bosco Carroll (the Carrolls), were notified to the Competition Authority on 30 December 1992. The notification requested a certificate, or in the event of a refusal by the Authority to grant a certificate, a licence.

. . .

The arrangements

. . . The agreement notified included in clause 7 a number of non-compete provisions which are summarised below:

Each of the vendors hereby covenants with the purchaser . . . that each of the vendors shall not (without the previous consent in writing of the board of the company, i.e. Sutcliffe):

1. for the period of five years after completion either on their own account or for any other person, firm or company,
(a) transact business dealings with; or
(b) solicit or endeavour to entice away from the company any person, firm, or company who or which within the preceding three years shall have been a customer of or in the habit of dealing with the company.
2. for the period of three years after completion either on their own account or for any other person, firm or company, solicit or endeavour to entice away from the company any person who or which within the preceding one year shall have been an employee of the company.
3. for a period of three years after completion within the Republic of Ireland . . . engage or be concerned or interested whether as principal, director, manager, employee, agent, shareholder, partner, consultant, or otherwise in or provide funds (whether by way of loan, investment, gift or otherwise) to or for any trade or business or body corporate owning or operating such trade or business being carried on at completion by the company.

. . .

Clause 8, as notified, restricted the vendors for an unlimited time from using or disclosing any confidential information used by the company including but not limited to:

(a) information used in the production of goods or the provision of services;
(b) information relating to the programming or using of any computer;
(c) information relating to marketing including customers' names and market surveys

unless the use or disclosure of such information does not cause any damage or injury to the company.

10. As part of the sale agreement Mr John Carroll and Mr K. Carroll entered into employment agreements with the company. Mr John Carroll was to be employed as Deputy Chairman and full-time Executive Director until 12 July 1993 and as Deputy Chairman and part-time Executive Director from then until 6 February 1996. Clause 10 of this agreement contained a number of non-compete provisions. Specifically it provided that for three years after the termination of such employment, Mr John Carroll would not, without the previous written consent of the company:

(i) transact business dealings with or solicit or endeavour to entice away from the company anyone who was a customer within the previous three years;
(ii) solicit or endeavour to entice away from the company anyone who had been an employee within the previous three years;
(iii) engage in or be concerned or interested in any firm engaged in a business being carried on by the company at termination.

The agreement with Mr K. Carroll appoints him as Sales and Operations Director. It also contains a number of non-compete provisions although these are only for six months after termination of employment.

...

Subsequent developments
Following discussions with the Authority the parties indicated by letter dated 9 August 1993, that they would amend a number of the restrictive provisions in the sale agreement by means of a supplemental agreement and that they would amend the provisions of Mr John Carroll's employment contract.

15. Clause 7 (1) of the principal agreement was amended to provide that:

Each of the vendors would not (without the previous consent in writing of the board of the company):
(a) for the period of three years after completion either on their own account or for any other person, firm or company, solicit or endeavour to entice away from the company any person, firm, or company who within two months prior to the date of completion shall have been a customer of or in the habit of dealing with the company.
(b) for the period of two years after completion either on their own account or for any other person, firm or company, transact business dealings with any person, firm, or company who within two months prior to the date of completion shall have been a customer of or in the habit of dealing with the company.

16. The effect of these changes is to reduce the duration of the restriction on the vendors soliciting customers of the business from five years to three, while limiting it to those who were customers during the period immediately prior to completion rather than at any time during the previous three years. The restriction on doing business with such customers is reduced from five years to two. Clause 7.2 was amended so as to reduce the duration of the restriction on the vendors soliciting the employees of the business from three years to two. The restriction was also amended so as to apply only to those who were employees at completion as opposed to anyone employed within

the preceding year. The restriction on being involved in a competing business in clause 7.3 was also reduced from three years to two.

17. Clause 8 relating to confidential information was also amended. In particular clause 8(b) which specified information relating to the programming or use of any computer was deleted, while it was also stated that the amended clause 8 would not apply 'to the extent that a vendor would, by virtue of such provisions, be deemed to be prohibited himself or herself from doing any one or more of the acts matters or things referred to in subclauses (1), (2) or (3) of clause 7 after the expiry of the respective periods of time specified in those subclauses.'

18. In their letter of 9 August 1993 the parties proposed that Mr John Carroll's employment contract would be amended to provide that the restrictions contained therein in respect of (a) transacting business with or soliciting customers, (b) soliciting employees, and (c) being involved in a competing business would apply only for so long as Mr Carroll was employed by the company. In addition it only applies in respect of employees and businesses currently engaged in by the company, and in respect of persons who were or shall have been customers at or at any time since 14 October 1992.

....

Assessment

(b) The undertakings and the agreement

21. S. 3(1) of the Competition Act defines an undertaking as 'a person being an individual, a body corporate or an unincorporated body of persons engaged for gain in the production, supply or distribution of goods or the provision of a service.' The parties to the present agreement are Sutcliffe and the Carrolls. Sutcliffe is a body corporate which has acquired the business of Carrolls Catering with the intention of providing a service for gain. Consequently it is an undertaking within the meaning of s. 3(1).[1] The Carrolls were at the time of the agreement the owners of the business of Carrolls Catering. The Authority has previously stated in identical circumstances that, in its view, the owners of a business are undertakings within the meaning of s. 3(1).[2] The Carrolls are therefore undertakings. The present arrangement is, in the Authority's view, an agreement between undertakings.

(c) Applicability of s. 4(1)

The sale agreement

22. The present arrangements therefore constitute an agreement between undertakings whereby Sutcliffe has purchased Carrolls Catering from the Carrolls. The Authority indicated in *Scully/Tyrrell* that in considering whether an agreement for the sale of business had the effect of preventing, restricting or distorting competition within the State or any part of the State, it would consider its effect on the degree of market concentration. Sutcliffe was not previously active in the market so that arrangement has no impact on the actual number of competitors or their market shares. Consequently the degree of market concentration, however measured, is unaffected by the arrangements.

23. If the definition of the relevant market were limited to the actual provision of catering services to firms and institutions by specialist catering firms, the market could be deemed to be highly concentrated. In the Authority's view it is unlikely that contract catering firms either individually or collectively are in a position to exercise market power. It seems likely that, if they attempted to do so, users of catering services would

respond by providing such services in-house. In the Authority's view the costs of switching to in-house provision of such services would not represent a deterrent. Consequently the Authority believes that self-operated catering services are sufficiently close substitutes for bought-in catering services for them both to be regarded as part of the same market in the context of the present agreement.[3] The Authority believes that the acquisition of Carrolls Catering by Sutcliffe is highly unlikely to have any anti-competitive effects in the relevant market as there is no indication that the level of market concentration after the merger will pose any threat to competition. In its opinion the sale of the business does not offend against s. 4(1).

The non-compete provisions

24. Clause 7 of the agreement, as notified, contained a number of non-compete provisions. Clause 7(4) is a restriction on the vendor using certain trade names associated with the business which is being sold. The Authority has already indicated in previous decisions that it does not consider such provisions offend against s. 4(1).[4]

25. Clause 7(3), as notified, provided that the vendors would not directly or indirectly for a period of three years after completion engage in the business being carried on at completion by the company. The Authority has stated its views on such restrictions in a number of previous decisions, (including that cited by the parties in their submission). Where such a restriction does not exceed what is necessary for the protection of the goodwill in terms of its duration, geographic coverage and subject matter, then it does not, in the Authority's opinion, offend against s. 4(1). In *General Semiconductor*, the Authority indicated that, having had an opportunity to consider a number of such agreements, it would generally consider a non-competition clause exceeding two years in a sale of business agreement to offend against s. 4(1).[5]

26. As clause 7(3) is limited to the business carried on by Carrolls Catering at completion, the restriction does not go beyond what is necessary to protect the goodwill in terms of subject matter. It applies to the whole of the State but, as the business operated on a nationwide basis, this is no more than is necessary to protect the goodwill of the business being sold. The duration of the restriction was three years from the date of completion. A comparison with the position in *Nallen/O'Toole* where the Authority allowed a three year non-compete clause, is relevant. In that instance the Authority indicated that a period of more than two years was justified on the grounds that the business concerned was located in a small town, customers only purchased the products involved infrequently, it involved a fair degree of personal contact with the customers and the vendor remained active in business in the locality. In this instance, although the personal involvement of Mr John Carroll was a factor in the development of the business, the purchaser will be supplying services on a regular basis, (in many cases on a daily basis), for the duration of the outstanding contracts. In such circumstances the Authority considers that customers would be likely to renew their contracts unless they feel that they can obtain a better service at a better price from a competitor.

27. The Authority considered the parties' claim that the duration of the non-compete clause should be sufficiently long to enable them to have an opportunity of renewing all of the business' existing contracts without facing competition from Mr John Carroll. The Authority's view is that the non-compete clause must be limited in duration to what is necessary to enable the purchaser of a business to secure its goodwill. It must therefore be no more than is necessary to enable the purchaser to build up a relationship with the customers of the business. The Authority cannot accept the argument

that a non-compete clause should be for so long as is necessary to enable the renewal of all of the business' existing contracts since in many cases this could represent a period well in excess of two years.

28. In the light of its *General Semiconductor* decision the Authority believes that a restriction of more than two years would offend against s. 4(1), unless there were good reasons to justify a longer restriction. Consequently it will be extremely reluctant to certify that a sale of business agreement with a non-compete clause of more than two years does not offend against s. 4(1), where only a transfer of goodwill is involved. In this instance the Authority considered that the duration of the restriction on the vendors competing with business originally contained in clause 7(3) went beyond what was necessary to secure the complete transfer of the goodwill of the business, and it therefore offended against s. 4(1). The duration of the clause has now been reduced to two years and consequently it no longer offends against s. 4(1).

29. Clause 7(1), as notified, restricted the vendors from transacting business with or soliciting customers of Carrolls Catering for five years from completion. The duration of this provision also went beyond what was necessary to secure the complete transfer of the goodwill of the business and, in the Authority's view, offended against s. 4(1). The duration of clause 7(1) has now been reduced to three years in respect of soliciting customers of the business and two years in respect of doing business with such customers. The Authority remains of the view that a restriction of two years on a vendor competing with a business which he has sold is normally adequate to secure the complete transfer of the goodwill and provide sufficient protection to the purchaser. The Authority considers that a three year restriction applying only to soliciting former customers may be necessary in this case, given the key role played by Mr Carroll in the development of the business, and the fact that his personal contacts in the business constitute an important element of the goodwill of the firm. The limitation of the restriction on doing business with such customers to two years means that Mr Carroll would be free to deal with them after such a time if they were to approach him. He would also be free to advertise his services after two years. The clause as amended does not, in the Authority's opinion offend against s. 4(1).

30. Clause 7(2), as notified, provided that for a period of three years after completion the vendors would not solicit or entice any employee of the company. As the Authority considered that a restriction on the vendor competing with the business for a period of two years was sufficient to secure the transfer of the goodwill of the business, the restriction in clause 7(2) also offended against s. 4(1). As the duration of this clause has been reduced to two years, it does not, in the Authority's opinion offend against s. 4(1).

31. The restrictions in clause 8 relate to the disclosure of know-how and confidential information. The Authority has already considered such restrictions in previous decisions.[6] In ACT/*Kindle* the Authority indicated that it would accept a five year restriction on the vendor using technical know-how. It indicated that: 'To afford the purchaser unlimited protection against the use of technical know-how by the seller would, in the Authority's view, restrict competition since such an unlimited restriction would go beyond what is necessary to secure the complete transfer of the business to the purchaser.' In the Authority's view the information used in the production of goods or the provision of services which is specified in clause 8(a) does not constitute technical know-how. The Authority indicated in ACT/*Kindle* that it would accept the definition of technical know-how contained in the EC Know-How Licensing Regulation. This

provides that 'know-how means a body of technical information that is secret, substantial and identified in the appropriate form'.[7] In this instance the Authority does not consider that information used in the production of goods or the provision of services constitutes technical know-how as defined in the Regulation. The restriction in clause 8 on the use of know-how involved in the production of any goods or provision of a service unless it did not cause any damage or injury to the company, could effectively constitute a restriction on producing such goods or providing such services in competition with the company for an unlimited period of time.

32. In *Budget Travel* the Authority indicated that a restriction on the use of confidential information could not be used to prevent the vendor of a business re-entering the market once a non-competition clause had expired. Clause 8, as notified, could have had this effect, and it therefore offended against s. 4(1). In addition the restriction in clause 8(b) on the use or disclosure of any information relating to the programming or use of any computer also offended against s. 4(1) as it went beyond what was necessary to protect confidential information belonging to the company. Indeed such a restriction could make it extremely difficult, if not impossible, to engage in any form of business, given the importance of computers in modern business. As clause 8 has been amended to provide that it will not be used to prevent the vendor re-entering the market once the non-compete provisions have expired and the reference to programming or use of computers has been dropped, it no longer offends against s. 4(1).

The employment agreements

33. The employment contracts between Carrolls Catering and Mr John Carroll and Mr K. Carroll were entered into as part of the sale agreement. They were expressly included as part of the notified arrangements. Essentially the arrangement involved Sutcliffe buying the business of Carrolls Catering and retaining the services of the Carrolls. If Mr John Carroll had not entered into such an employment agreement the purchase price would have been lower than it was. Consequently, in the Authority's view the agreement between Mr John Carroll and Carrolls Catering was an essential part of the overall agreement and it must be regarded as part of that agreement between undertakings.[8] The agreement between Carrolls Catering and Mr K. Carroll was also entered into as part of the sale. One of the parties to that agreement, however, Mr K. Carroll, was not, and is not now, an undertaking, since he did not own or control the business, and he was not a party to the sale agreement. He was a director of Carrolls Catering but he held no shares in that company. This agreement is not an agreement between undertakings and so does not come within the scope of s. 4(1). This view is consistent with that expressed by the Authority in its notice on employee agreements[9] and its decision in Peter Mark.[10] It is without prejudice to the fact that he might become an undertaking on the cessation of this employment.

34. The Authority has indicated in *Scully/Tyrrell*, where the vendors remained on as shareholders and employees of the business following a merger, that a restriction on the vendors competing with the business for so long as they were employees and/or shareholders and for two years after they disposed of their shareholding did not offend against s. 4(1). It went on to state that:

> In its view a restriction on individuals competing with a business in which they were shareholders would offend against s. 4(1) where such shareholding was purely for investment purposes or was an artificial arrangement whose object or effect was to evade the prohibition contained in that section. It would take a similar view of

an employment contract that was an artificial arrangement whose object or effect was to evade the prohibition contained in that section.

35. In the Authority's view the effect of clause 10 of the employment contract, as notified, was to further extend the duration of the non-competition clause contained in clause 7 of the sale agreement. Specifically, as Mr John Carroll will remain employed under the agreement until February 1996, a non-compete clause for three years from that date would result in a restriction on competition for over six years from the date of completion. The Authority believes that, where the vendor agrees to become an employee of the business, he should not compete with it for so long as he remains an employee, but a restriction on his competing after he has ceased to be an employee is not acceptable. In particular it is concerned that this could simply become a way of extending the duration of non-competition clauses in sale of business agreements far beyond what is necessary to secure the transfer of the goodwill of the business. Consequently, in the Authority's opinion, clause 10 of the employment agreement between Mr John Carroll and Carrolls Catering offended against s. 4(1). As the duration of clause 10 has now been limited to the period during which Mr John Carroll remains an employee it no longer offends against s. 4(1).

36. The Authority wishes to point out that, in its opinion, where restrictions in a sale of business agreement offend against s. 4(1), because they are deemed to go beyond what is necessary to secure the transfer of the goodwill, they cannot be regarded as indispensable to the sale of the business, and, consequently, they would fail to meet the requirements for a licence specified in s. 4(2).

The decision

37. The agreement between Sutcliffe (Ireland) and Mr John D. Carroll and Ms Marie Therese Carroll for the sale of the entire issued share capital of Carrolls Catering is an agreement between undertakings, since the parties to the agreement are undertakings. The employment agreement between Mr John Carroll and Carrolls Catering is also an agreement between undertakings, since it constitutes an integral part of the overall sale agreement. As Mr K. Carroll was not, and is not an undertaking, the employment agreement between him and Carrolls Catering is not an agreement between undertakings and is not, therefore, an agreement of a kind described in s. 4(1). The notified agreement, as amended by the letter of 9 August 1993, does not, in the Authority's opinion offend against s. 4(1).

[1.] In AGF/*Irish Life Holdings*, (Competition Authority decision no. 2, CA/7/92, 14 May 1992), the Authority indicated that, in its view, a holding company was engaged for gain through its subsidiaries and was therefore an undertaking.

[2.] Competition Authority decision no. 8, ACT/*Kindle*, CA/9/91, 4 September 1992.

[3.] The Authority has previously considered that insurance companies could substitute in-house provision of services for those of loss adjusters. See Competition Authority decision no. 12, *Scully/Tyrell*, (CA/57/92), 29 January 1993.

[4.] See, for example, ACT/*Kindle*.

[5.] Competition Authority decision no. 10, GI/*General Semiconductor Industries*, (CA/51/92 and CA/52/92), 23 October 1992.

[6.] The issue of technical know-how was considered in ACT/*Kindle*, while restrictions on disclosure of confidential information were considered in *Budget Travel*.

[7.] Regulation no. 556/89 on the application of article 85(3) of the Treaty to certain categories of know-how licensing agreements, OJ L61/1, 1989.

8. In *Scully/Tyrrell* the Authority indicated that related agreements would be considered as part of a single agreement.
9. Competition Authority Notice on Employee Agreements and the Competition Act, *Iris Oifigiuil*, 18 September 1992, pp 632–3.
10. Competition Authority decision no. 13, *Peter Mark/Majella Stapleton*, (CA/1011/92E), 18 February 1993.

Note

See 'A Significant Shift due to 1991 Act', 3 *Competition* 59 (*Competition Press*).

SECTION TWO—EXCLUSIVE DEALING ARRANGEMENTS INCLUDING SOLUS AGREEMENTS

Esso Petroleum Co. Ltd v Harpers Garage (Stourport) Ltd [1968] AC 269

The respondent company which owned two service stations entered a typical 'solus' agreement with Esso, the appellant. This involved the respondent agreeing to purchase from the appellant the whole of its requirements of motor fuel for resale at its service stations, accepting a resale price maintenance clause, agreeing to operate the relevant service stations in accordance with the Esso dealer co-operation plan, which included a provision that the service station should be kept open at all reasonable hours for the Esso petrol and oil, and finally, agreeing that, before completing any sale or transfer of the relevant service station, the respondent would notify Esso and procure the intended successor to assume the respondent's obligations under the agreement. The agreement in respect of Mustow Green station was for a period of four years and five months and the agreement in respect of Corner station was for twenty one years. The appellant had a mortgage over the latter station to secure a loan made to the respondent. Subsequently the appellant sought injunctions restraining the respondents from buying or selling fuels other than those of the appellants at their stations. The Court of Appeal held that the agreement was in restraint of trade and unenforceable and Esso appealed to the House of Lords.

Lord Reid:

. . .

If a contract is within the class of contracts in restraint of trade the law which applies to it is quite different from the law which applies to contracts generally. In general unless a contract is vitiated by duress, fraud or mistake its terms will be enforced though unreasonable or even harsh and unconscionable, but here a term in restraint of trade will not be enforced unless it is reasonable. And in the ordinary case the court will not remake a contract: unless in the special case where the contract is severable, it will not strike out one provision as unenforceable and enforce the rest. But here the party who has been paid for agreeing to the restraint may be unjustly enriched if the court holds the restraint to be too wide to be enforceable and is unable to adjust the consideration given by the other party.

It is much too late now to say that this rather anomalous doctrine of restraint of trade can be confined to the two classes of case to which it was originally applied. But the cases outside these two classes afford little guidance as to the circumstances in which it should be applied. In some it has been assumed that the doctrine applies and the controversy has been whether the restraint was reasonable. And in others where one might have expected the point to be taken it was not taken, perhaps because counsel thought that there was no chance of the court holding that the restraint was too wide to be reasonable.

. . .

The main argument submitted for the appellant on this matter was that restraint of trade means a personal restraint and does not apply to a restraint on the use of a particular piece of land. Otherwise, it was said, every covenant running with the land which prevents its use for all or for some trading purposes would be a covenant on restraint of trade and therefore unenforceable unless it could be shown to be reasonable and for the protection of some legitimate interest. It was said that the present agreement only prevents the sale of petrol from other suppliers on the site of the Mustow Green garage: It leaves the respondents free to trade anywhere else in any way they choose. But in many cases a trader trading at a particular place does not have the resources to enable him to begin trading elsewhere as well, and if he did he might find it difficult to find another suitable garage for sale or to get planning permission to open a new filling station on another site. As the whole doctrine of restraint of trade is based on public policy its application ought to depend less on legal niceties or theoretical possibilities than on the practical effect of a restraint in hampering that freedom which it is the policy of the law to protect.

It is true that it would be an innovation to hold that ordinary negative covenants preventing the use of a particular site for trading of all kinds or of a particular kind are within the scope of the doctrine of restraint of trade. I do not think they are. Restraint of trade appears to me to imply that a man contracts to give up some freedom which otherwise he would have had. A person buying or leasing land had no previous right to be there at all, let alone trade there, and when he takes possession of that land subject to a negative restrictive covenant he gives up no right or freedom which he previously had. I think that the 'tied house' cases might be explained in this way, apart from *Biggs v Hoddinott*,[1] where the owner of a freehouse had agreed to a tie in favour of a brewer who had lent him money. Restraint of trade was not pleaded. If it had been, the restraint would probably have been held to be reasonable. But there is some difficulty if a restraint in a lease not merely prevents the person who takes possession of the land under the lease from doing certain things there, but also obliges him to act in a particular way. In the present case the respondents before they made this agreement were entitled to use this land in any lawful way they chose, and by making this agreement they agreed to restrict their right by giving up their right to sell there petrol not supplied by the appellants.

In my view this agreement is within the scope of the doctrine of restraint of trade as it had been developed in English law. Not only have the respondents agreed negatively not to sell other petrol but they have agreed positively to keep this garage open for the sale of the appellants' petrol at all reasonable hours throughout the period of the tie. It was argued that this was merely regulating the respondent's trading and rather promoting than restraining his trade. But regulating a person's existing trade may be a greater restraint than prohibiting him from engaging in a new trade. And a contract to take one's whole supply from one source may be much more hampering than a contract to sell one's whole output to one buyer. I would not attempt to define the dividing line between contracts which are and contracts which are not in restraint of trade, but in my view this contract must be held to be in restraint of trade. So it is necessary to consider whether its provisions can be justified.

But before considering this question I must deal briefly with the other agreement tying the Corner Garage for twenty one years. The rebate and other advantages to the respondents were similar to those in the Mustow Green agreement but in addition the appellants made a loan of £7,000 to the respondents to enable them to improve their garage and this loan was to be repaid over the twenty one years of the tie. In security they took a mortgage of this garage. The agreement provided that the loan should not be paid off earlier than at the dates stipulated. But the respondents now tender the unpaid balance of the loan and they say that the appellants have no interest to refuse to accept repayment now, except in order to maintain the tie for the full twenty one years.

The appellants argue that the fact that there is a mortgage excludes any application of the doctrine of restraint of trade. But I agree with your Lordships in rejecting that argument. I am prepared to assume that, if the respondents had not offered to repay the loan so far as it is still outstanding, the appellants would have been entitled to retain the tie. But, as they have tendered repayment, I do not think that the existence of the loan and the mortgage puts the appellants in any stronger position to maintain the tie than they would have been in if the original agreements had permitted repayment at an earlier date. The appellants must show that in the circumstances when the agreement was made a tie for twenty one years was justifiable.

It is now generally accepted that a provision in a contract which is to be regarded as in restraint of trade must be justified if it is to be enforceable, and that the law on this matter was correctly stated by Lord Macnaghten in the *Nordenfelt* case.[2]

. . .

So in every case it is necessary to consider first whether the restraint went farther than to afford adequate protection to the party in whose favour it was granted, secondly whether it can be justified as being in the interests of the party restrained, and, thirdly, whether it must be held contrary to the public interest. I find it difficult to agree with the way in which the court has in some cases treated the interests of the party restrained. Surely it can never be in the interest of a person to agree to suffer a restraint unless he gets some compensating advantage, direct or indirect. And Lord Macnaghten said: ' . . . of course the quantum of consideration may enter into the question of the reasonableness of the contract'.

. . .

The Court of Appeal held that these ties were for unreasonably long periods. They thought that, if for any reason the respondents ceased to sell the appellants' petrol, the appellants could have found other suitable outlets in the neighbourhood within two or three years. I do not think that that is the right test. In the first place there was no evidence about this and I do not think that it would be practicable to apply this test in practice. It might happen that when the respondents ceased to sell their petrol, the appellants would find such an alternative outlet in a very short time. But, looking to the fact that well over ninety per cent of existing filling stations are tied and that there may be great difficulty in opening a new filling station, it might take a very long time to find an alternative. Any estimate of how long it might take to find suitable alternatives for the respondents' filling stations could be little better than guesswork.

I do not think that the appellants' interest can be regarded so narrowly. They are not so much concerned with any particular outlet as with maintaining a stable system of distribution throughout the country so as to enable their business to be run efficiently end economically. In my view there is sufficient material to justify a decision that ties of less than five years were insufficient, in the circumstances of the trade when these agreements were made, to afford adequate protection to the appellants' legitimate interests. And if that is so I cannot find anything in the details of the Mustow Green agreement which would indicate that it is unreasonable. It is true that if some of the provisions were operated by the appellants in a manner which would be commercially unreasonable they might put the respondents in difficulties. But I think that a court must have regard to the fact that the appellants must act in such a way that they will be able to obtain renewals of the great majority of their very numerous ties, some of which will come to an end almost every week. If in such circumstances a garage owner chooses to rely on the commercial probity and good sense of the producer, I do not think that a court should hold his agreement unreasonable because it is legally capable of some misuse. I would therefore allow the appeal as regards the Mustow Green agreement.

But the Corner Garage agreement involves much more difficulty. Taking first the legitimate interests of the appellants, a new argument was submitted to your Lordships that, apart from any question of security for their loan, it would be unfair to the appellants if the respondents, having used the appellants' money to build up their business, were entitled after a comparatively short time to be free to seek better terms from a competing producer. But there is no material on which I can assess the strength of this argument and I do not find myself in a position to determine whether it has any validity. A tie for twenty one years stretches far beyond any period for which developments are reasonably foreseeable. Restrictions on the garage owner which might seem tolerable and reasonable in reasonably foreseeable conditions might come to have a very different effect in quite different conditions: the public interest comes in here more strongly. And, apart from a case where he gets a loan, a garage owner appears to get no greater advantage from a twenty year tie than he gets from a five year tie. So I would think that there must at least be some clearly established advantage to the producing company—something to show that a shorter period would not be adequate—before so long a period could be justified. But in this case there is no evidence to prove anything of the kind. And the other material which I have thought it right to consider does not appear to me to assist the appellant here. I would therefore dismiss the appeal as regards the Corner Garage agreement.

[1.] [1898] 2 Ch. 307; 14 TLR 504, CA.   [2.] [1894] AC 535, 565.

Note

In the above extract from *Esso*, Lord Reid draws a distinction between a clause that fetters a person's existing freedom from one which a person accepts as part of the process by which he will acquire a future freedom; the significance of this is that the doctrine of restraint of trade applies to the former not the latter type of clause. This proposition has been accepted and applied by the Irish courts in *Irish Shell Ltd v Elm Motors Ltd* [1984] IR 200. This is one area where the common law approach has been supplanted. In the case of shopping centre leasing of trading units, prospective lessees commonly agree to confine their trading activities in order to obtain the lease. The Competition Authority regards these leases as within the Act, even though the common law would appear not to regulate them through restraint of trade.

In the case of Irish solus agreements, these were regulated under the old fair trade legislation (Restrictive Practices Act 1972) which struck down restraints that lasted for longer than ten years. However, these agreements are now open to more general scrutiny by the Authority.

Competition Authority Decision No. 4 Esso Solus and Related Agreements (CA/11–13/92) 25 June 1992

Notification was made with a request for a licence under s. 4 of the Competition Act 1991 by Esso Ireland Ltd on 19 December 1991 in respect of the standard Esso solus agreement with independent dealers, and its dealer loan equipment and dealer loan agreements, and its deed of charge/mortgage.

. . .

The facts:

This decision concerns the standard Esso solus agreement, which provides for the exclusive purchase by an independent dealer of Esso motor fuels for resale, for a maximum period of ten years, and the following related agreements:

- the dealer loan equipment agreement, which relates to the provision of service station equipment on loan to the dealer;
- the dealer loan agreement, which is used when an interest-bearing loan is made available to the dealer for redevelopment of the outlet; and
- the deed of charge/mortgage, which is used to provide security for the loan to the dealer.

Each notified agreement is a standard agreement which Esso employs with the dealers in its independent dealer network throughout the State. While each independent dealer is a party to the solus agreement, not all dealers are party to the other three agreements.

. . .

48. In the opinion of the Authority, the solus and related agreements notified by Esso fulfil the conditions provided for in s. 4(2).

49. Solus agreements in the motor fuels sector differ from other exclusive purchase agreements in that the supplier confers on the reseller special commercial or financial advantages by contributing to his financing, granting him a loan on favourable terms, and providing him with equipment, while the reseller enters into a long-term exclusive purchasing obligation which is accompanied by a ban on dealing in competing products and the supplier agrees to supply the reseller's total requirements of motor fuels.

50. The solus agreements produce an appreciable improvement in distribution in which consumers are allowed a fair share of the resulting benefit. The commercial and financial advantages conferred by the supplier on the retailer make it significantly easier to establish, modernise, maintain and operate service stations. A high level of investment is needed to provide adequate facilities and to meet safety standards, and Esso has invested heavily in its company-owned stations. Independent dealers would have insufficient resources for the necessary investment without substantial support from the supplier, otherwise company stations would become dominant. They are able to provide a range of services which they would otherwise be unable to offer. The exclusive purchasing obligation and the ban on dealing in competing products imposed on the reseller encourage the reseller to devote all the resources at his disposal to the sale of motor fuels, while retaining his independence and freedom to run the business as he sees fit. Solus agreements lead to durable co-operation between the parties, allowing them to improve or maintain the quality of the motor fuels and of the services to the customer and the sales efforts of the reseller. The investment by the supplier ensures security of supply by providing assured outlets for its product, and

retailers are guaranteed regular supplies. This allows long-term planning of sales and consequently a cost-effective organisation of production and distribution. The costs of distributing motor fuels to a limited number of exclusive outlets which purchase in large quantities are lower than delivering smaller volumes to a large number of outlets selling two or more brands at the one service station. The pressure of competition between different brands of motor fuel obliges the undertakings involved to determine the number and characteristics of service stations in accordance with the wishes of consumers.

51. The solus agreement includes a clause extending the exclusive purchasing requirements to include the sale of motor fuels by the dealer at any premises within a one mile radius of the designated service station. The Authority accepts that competition in the sale of motor fuels is a fairly localised phenomenon. Motorists do not tend to travel any great distance to buy at a cheaper price, since the cost of so doing would soon eliminate any savings made. The dedication of the dealer to maximising sales of Esso motor fuels at the designated outlet would be likely to be adversely affected if he were permitted to sell another brand at a station owned or operated by himself within one mile of the designated station. Without such a requirement, the improvement in distribution would not be secured. The dealer is free, however, to sell competing motor fuels outside the one mile radius.

52. Consumers benefit from these improvements especially because they are ensured supplies of motor fuel of satisfactory quality while being able to choose between different brands of motor fuel. The solus system leads to more efficient distribution and to better facilities and services at dealer stations, to the benefit of consumers. They have a choice between stations offering differing degrees and types of service. The system should ensure both intra-brand and inter-brand competition, including price competition.

53. The advantages produced by solus agreements cannot be achieved to the same extent and with the same degree of certainty in any other way. The exclusive purchasing obligation on the reseller and the non-competition clause imposed on him are essential components of such agreements and are indispensable for the attainment of these advantages. These obligations are confined to the purchase of motor fuels for resale, and do not extend to other products. The limitation of the period of the exclusive agreement to ten years is sufficient to produce the advantages, while maintaining the reseller's commercial freedom to change supplier and to ensure access to the retail level of distribution on the part of other suppliers. Any shorter period would substantially lessen the incentive for suppliers to invest in dealer outlets, to the detriment of dealers and consumers. This is especially so in the State, where the average throughput in petrol stations is only about one quarter of the EC average.

54. There are large numbers of Esso solus, company and non-solus outlets, and there are many other outlets of these types which sell motor fuels under other brand names. There is a high degree of competition between outlets, both intra-brand and inter-brand, and, with the removal of price control, there is scope for price competition, in particular, since solus and non-solus dealers are free to determine their own selling prices. While the long-term nature of the exclusive supply contracts limits the possibilities for a new entrant to secure outlets, all dealers are free to change their supplier at the expiry of the contract, and this does occur, and agreements are expiring on a continuous basis. In addition, a new supplier entrant would be likely to want the

security offered by long-term solus agreements before making the sizeable investment necessary to enter the market in the first place. There is thus no possibility of the undertakings being afforded the possibility of eliminating competition for a substantial part of the products in question.

55. It will be apparent that, in its assessment, the Authority has had regard to EC Regulation No. 1984/83, which exempts certain exclusive purchasing agreements, including service station agreements, from the prohibition of article 85(1) of the Treaty of Rome.

. . .

The Authority therefore grants a licence under s. 4(2) in respect of each of the notified Esso agreements. . . .

SECTION THREE—RESALE PRICE MAINTENANCE AND RESTRICTIVE COMMERCIAL PRACTICES

Competition Authority Decision No. 336. Net Book Agreement (CA/23–30/92E) 20 June 1994

Arrangements for the imposition by UK publishers of a minimum net price on most of their books sold within the State were notified to the Authority on 20 May 1992. The arrangements comprising eight agreements in total are known as the Net Book Agreement and have operated in their present form since 1957. The notification requested a certificate, or in the event of a refusal by the Authority to grant a certificate, a licence.

. . .

(a) *The subject of the notification*

2. The notification concerns an arrangement known as the Net Book Agreement (NBA). This is a voluntary agreement administered by the Publishers Association (PA), whereby UK book publishers impose a minimum net price on the sale of most of their publications in the UK and the Republic of Ireland. The notification also contains a number of ancillary agreements providing for limited exemptions from the provisions of the NBA for specified groups of book purchasers.

. . .

Assessment

(b) *The undertakings and the agreement*

61. . . . . The parties to the PA agreements are book publishers based in the UK. The majority of these publishers are corporate bodies. The publishers are engaged for gain in the production and publication of books and are therefore undertakings within the meaning of the Act.

62. There are two NBAs, one for members of the PA and the other for non-members. These agreements constitute agreements between undertakings relating to the standard conditions of sale for UK published books within the State. They also constitute decisions of an association of undertakings. In addition to the two versions of the NBA the PA has notified a series of related arrangements. These are:

(a) the book club regulations;
(b) the library licence;
(c) the book agent's licence;
(d) the quantity book buying scheme;
(e) the primary and secondary school licence.

These set out the conditions upon which publishers supply books to different categories of buyer. In addition the association has drawn up a set of conditions for a national book sale. Each of these documents constitutes an agreement between undertakings (the publishers), setting out the terms upon which net books may be sold below the net published price to certain categories of customer. These arrangements also constitute decisions of an association of undertakings within the meaning of s. 4(1).

The Authority also found that the book club regulations, the library licence, the book agent's licence, the quality book buying scheme, the rules for the national book sale and the primary and secondary school licence offended against s. 4 (1).

(c) Applicability of s. 4(1)

Resale Price Maintenance

64. Resale Price Maintenance (RPM) describes a practice whereby a supplier agrees to supply retailers on condition that they sell the goods at a price specified by the supplier. The arrangements notified involve a form of RPM. Such arrangements restrict the ability of retailers to determine their own prices. They also eliminate price competition between retailers for the suppliers' products, assuming that the supplier applies such arrangements to all retailers handling his products.

65. There is some disagreement among economists as to whether or not RPM is an undesirable practice. Over the past twenty five years or so, the so-called 'Chicago school' economists have challenged traditional economic thinking concerning most forms of vertical restrictions[1] including RPM. Essentially their argument is that manufacturers will not impose vertical restraints such as RPM unless they increase output and hence profits. Specifically it is argued that RPM causes the retailer to devote greater efforts to selling the manufacturer's goods through promotional efforts and/or increased service, in the form of information about the product, instruction in its use, the holding of larger stocks and the like. It is argued that retailers would not provide such services in the absence of RPM since consumers would avail of such free services and then purchase the goods in question from lower cost outlets which would effectively 'free ride' on the services provided by others. According to the Chicago approach consumers benefit from increased service levels resulting from RPM and sales are increased resulting in greater output of the goods in question. Consequently RPM should not be seen as anti-competitive, but as a mechanism for increasing distribution efficiency to the benefit of consumers, retailers and suppliers.

66. The Chicago approach is, however, strongly challenged by other economists. Scherer and Ross,[2] for example, argue that relatively few products are susceptible to 'free riding' which RPM is supposed to prevent. Many consumers know what they want and do not need pre-sales service. Similarly consumers will only go to lower priced outlets, having availed of the free pre-sales service provided in the more expensive outlet, in the case of goods which are expensive, and where the cost saving is

significant. They also argue that it is not clear why RPM is necessary to cause retailers to provide a greater level of service anyway. Thus, in response to the Chicago claim that without RPM discount retailers would 'free ride', many would argue that a lot of products are not susceptible to free riding and that free rider arguments can only apply in respect of pre-sale services.

67. Scherer and Ross show that RPM may inhibit competition in a number of ways. It can inhibit the entry of discount outlets and thus prevent retailing innovations. Manufacturers who have relied on RPM in order to encourage product promotion by retailers and increase sales may be unwilling to dispense with such arrangements long after the need to promote new products has ended. Where many manufacturers engage in RPM it may be difficult for one to end the practice since retailers may simply cease stocking the firm's products. They conclude that, on balance, the evidence suggests RPM is likely to restrict competition and result in prices being higher and output lower than would otherwise be the case.

68. While economic theory suggests that there may be circumstances in which RPM may increase overall economic welfare, most goods and services do not appear to satisfy the necessary conditions for such a result. In addition other methods are available to induce greater efforts by retailers to sell the manufacturers' products. On balance therefore, economic arguments indicate that RPM is generally harmful and restricts competition.

69. RPM has been prohibited under the competition laws of most developed countries. Legislation which permitted RPM was repealed in the US in 1976 and the Supreme Court has regarded RPM as a *per se* violation of the antitrust rules.3 Legislation prohibiting RPM was enacted in Canada in 1951, in France in 1953 and in the UK in 1964. The UK Competition Act is generally neutral with respect to most forms of anti-competitive behaviour, in that it only prohibits practices which are shown to be against the public interest, and there is no presumption one way or the other as to whether practices are against the public interest. RPM, however, is specifically prohibited by statute. While the latter legislation allows for exemption, there have only been four requests for such exemption, and in only two instances, one involving the NBA, has such an exemption been granted.

70. The Authority considers that the weight of evidence indicates that RPM is generally restrictive of competition. Consequently, in its view, agreements involving RPM will generally offend against s. 4(1).

NBA—*members' version*

71. Clause (i) provides that, except in specified circumstances, net books cannot be sold at less than the net published price. Such net prices are determined by individual book publishers who must also decide whether or not to classify a particular book as a net book. The agreement provides that in certain circumstances a net book may be sold below the net price. These apply where the book has been in stock for some considerable time and to secondhand copies of net books. In addition the agreement allows net books to be sold below the net published price to certain classes of customer subject to certain conditions, in particular relating to prices.

72. Individual RPM refers to a situation in which an individual supplier sets resale prices for his products. Collective RPM relates to a situation where a number of

suppliers agree to set resale prices for their products. The agreement, according to the PA, is designed to enable publishers to operate a system of individual RPM. Thus it involves a mixture of individual and collective RPM. The NBA eliminates price competition between retailers in respect of every book which has been designated a net book by its publisher. To the extent that each individual book title constitutes a unique product, price competition at the retail level is therefore eliminated in respect of any book designated a net book. The Authority believes that to some degree certain books are substitutes for one another. While some consumers will wish to buy a particular book by a particular author, others are looking for a particular type of book, whether a thriller or one on gardening, and will therefore choose from among the range of titles available in that particular category. As the majority of UK published books are net books, price competition between retailers in respect of different titles is also restricted. It is true that not all books of a particular type retail at a uniform price, but where books which could be considered substitutes are designated net books the possibility of retailers offering discounts on such books is eliminated and so competition is restricted between different titles.

73. Price fixing agreements have been consistently regarded as in breach of article 85(1) of the Treaty of Rome. Bellamy and Child point out that: 'Since price is the main instrument of competition, article 85(1)(a) expressly prohibits agreements, which "directly or indirectly fix purchase or selling prices or any other trading conditions." An agreement to fix prices by its very nature constitutes a restriction on competition within the meaning of article 85(1).'[4]

74. The agreement requires the publisher to apply the standard conditions of sale on their resellers. This restricts price competition between retailers as far as net books are concerned by curtailing the freedom of resellers to depart from the fixed resale price by offering discounts in order to increase their sales. The agreement also restricts competition between publishers as all the publishers who are parties to the agreement must apply uniform terms in respect of the resale of all books designated by them as net books. In addition once a book is designated as a net book by a publisher, the publishers of rival titles can set their prices in the knowledge that the designated book will not be sold below the designated net price. Consequently the agreement reduces the element of uncertainty regarding a competitor's response to a firm's marketing strategy which is an essential feature of competitive markets. Allen and Curwen, for example, argued that:

> In general, given the existence of the NBA, we would expect publishers to price similar products as though they were operating a cartel. The fact that they can fix the price of a specific title at any level they wish is very far from what is meant by 'conditions of free competition'. In conditions of free competition there would be constant downward pressure upon prices in order to clear the market, so that over time prices, on average, would rise more slowly than elsewhere in the economy where free competition did not exist.[5]

While the Authority does not consider that the NBA necessarily amounts to a fully fledged horizontal price fixing arrangement, it nevertheless believes that it does go some considerable way towards reducing uncertainty regarding competitors' pricing decisions in the publishing industry and that such uncertainty is normally an essential part of the competitive process. As the vast bulk of UK published books are net books and these account for the majority of books sold within the State, price competition between retailers and between publishers is restricted in respect of a substantial part of the book market within the State. The NBA therefore has the object and effect of restricting competition in the market for books within the State.

75. The PA in its response to the statement of objections, claimed that:

(a) the Authority had not made any criticism of the operation that is specific to its effects in Ireland but had instead made a general attack on the NBA; and
(b) the sole ground for the Authority asserting jurisdiction in respect of the NBA was that it affects inter-State trade between the UK and Ireland and therefore has effects within Ireland. It argued that the Authority was wrong to assert jurisdiction in this way.

The Authority rejects such claims. It is clear from the preceding paras that the Authority, in finding that the NBA offends against s. 4(1), has based its decision on its assessment of the effects of the NBA on competition within the State. The Authority has never introduced the issue of inter-state trade. S. 4(1) of the Competition Act refers to the agreements which prevent, restrict or distort competition within the State. The PA's claim that the Authority cannot assert jurisdiction over the notified agreement amounts to a claim that the Competition Act does not apply in respect of goods which are imported into the State.

76. The Authority's view that the NBA restricts competition is in accord with that of the EC Commission which stated in the case of the NBA: 'Thus, the agreements and rules have facilitated and contributed to the maintenance or introduction of fixed book prices by a large number of publishers and continue to do so.'[6]

The Commission found that the arrangements had the object and effect of restricting competition within the EC. This view was subsequently upheld by the Court of First Instance following an appeal by the PA.

77. In VBVB/VBBB *v* EC *Commission* the Court of Justice upheld an EC Commission decision that an agreement between two associations of publishers and booksellers, one based in Holland and the other in Belgium, that books could not be sold in Belgium or the Netherlands at prices below those fixed by the Dutch or Belgian publishers infringed article 85(1).

78. Agreements between Dutch and Belgian publishers and booksellers involving RPM in respect of books were also the subject of proceedings in the national courts. The Amsterdam district court made an order on 26 May 1977 which provided that books published in the Netherlands, which had been bought abroad, could be sold at a price below that set by the publisher. This was confirmed by the Dutch Supreme Court on 18 May 1979.[7] The Commercial Court in Brussels by order dated 18 June 1979, in a dispute between the Flemish Association and a department store chain, ordered the association to cease making the sale of Dutch language books conditional on the store being obliged to conform to the retail price fixed by the supplier. The court found that the rules infringed article 85(1) and it had not been shown that there was any great probability that the Commission would grant an exemption.

79. While the NBA does not require that the publishers designate any particular book or even the majority of their books as net books, in practice the publishers involved in the agreement do so designate the vast majority of books published by them. It was conceded that up to seventy five per cent of books published are designated net

books. The publishers are free not to designate any particular book a net book. Having designated a book to be a net book, however, the publisher is bound to apply the standard conditions governing net books including the terms upon which discounts can be granted in respect of such a book i.e. the only circumstances in which a net book may be sold at below the specified net price are those specified in clauses (ii) to (iv) of the agreement. This aspect of the arrangements also restricts competition in the market for books within the State and offends against s. 4(1). It is not sufficient to put the arrangements outside the scope of s. 4(1) that publishers are not compelled to designate every book a net book. The purpose of the NBA, according to the PA, is to enable all book publishers to operate a system of RPM.

80. Again the EC Commission decided in respect of the NBA that:

> Neither the freedom for publishers to decide whether to make a net book or not or to end the net character of the book or not, nor their freedom to determine the level of the net price prevent the agreements and implementing rules from being restrictive. The fact that, if a publisher decides to impose a fixed price for a book, he is then bound to impose almost wholly uniform conditions . . . upon resellers as to the discounts they may give to their customers, is sufficient to make the agreements and implementing rules restrictive.[8]

81. The Authority notes that, in its appeal to the Court of First Instance against the Commission decision that the agreement infringed article 85(1), the PA only sought to show that the agreement did not affect trade between member states and did not challenge the finding that it restricted competition. Indeed it was conceded at the oral hearing by the PA's representative that the arrangements offended against s. 4(1).

82. Under the agreement the publishers have agreed to appoint the PA to act on their behalf in relation to collecting information concerning breaches of contract by persons selling or offering for sale net books, breaches of the agreement and keeping each publisher informed of breaches in respect of such net books as are published by him. This reinforces the extent of the restriction on competition contained in the basic agreement as it is designed to ensure more efficient surveillance of compliance with the agreements and rules.

83. The parties also agree to enforce such contractual rights if called upon to do so by the PA, provided that they are indemnified by the association in respect of any costs of such action incurred by them or by the council of the association on their behalf. Under these provisions the parties agree to take action against any retailer who sells a net book below the net price where he has contractually agreed not to. The purpose of this provision is to ensure effective adherence to the net prices as specified by the publishers. While no individual contractual arrangement with any bookseller in the State has been notified to the Authority, any such agreement which required that the retailer not sell below the net price specified by the publisher would offend against s. 4(1). The enforcement provisions are therefore designed to ensure adherence to arrangements which offend against s. 4(1). For that reason the agreement by the publishers to enforce such agreements also offends against s. 4(1).

84. The parties' submission concedes that the arrangements involve resale price maintenance but argues that such arrangements are beneficial in the case of books. In VBVB/VBBB *v Commission* the European Court of Justice found that:

The special features of the book trade do not permit national associations of publishers and booksellers in two Member States to set up, in their mutual relations, a restrictive system whose effect is to deprive distributors of all freedom of action as regards the fixing of selling price up to the level of the final price to the consumer. Such an arrangement infringes article 85(1)(a) which expressly prohibits all agreements which 'directly or indirectly fix purchase or selling prices'. Furthermore, where the system of resale price maintenance laid down in the agreement allows each of the two associations to control outlets as far as the last stage in the other Member State from the point of view of price-fixing and thus to make impossible the introduction of sales methods capable of allowing consumers to be supplied in economically more favourable conditions, the associations are also brought into conflict with article 85(1)(b).[9]

The parties' claim that RPM is beneficial in the case of books does not, therefore, prevent the agreement from offending against s. 4(1).

85. Clauses (ii), (iii) and (iv) set out circumstances in which a net book may be sold below the net price. Under clause (ii) a net book may be sold below the net price if the bookseller has held it in stock for a period of more than twelve months from the date of purchase and he has offered it to the publisher at either the lower of cost price or the proposed reduced price and such offer has been rejected by the publisher. Clause (iii) allows the bookseller to sell a book below the net price if it is secondhand and more than six months have elapsed since publication. Clause (iv) allows for net books to be sold to libraries, book agents, quantity buyers and other institutions as are from time to time authorised by the council of the association on such conditions as are laid down in the instrument of authorisation.

86. While allowing the bookseller some scope to sell below the net price, these clauses seriously restrict the circumstances in which he may do so and generally set maximum levels of discount. They therefore also have the effect of restricting competition in the market for books within the State. By limiting the circumstances in which net books may be sold below the net price these clauses reinforce the RPM arrangements contained in clause (i). Consequently these clauses also offend against s. 4(1).

Non-members' version

87. As already pointed out the non-members' version of the NBA is the same as the members' version save that there is no provision for indemnifying non-members in respect of the costs of court actions to enforce the terms of the agreement on booksellers. The non-members' version of the NBA also offends against s. 4(1) as its object and effect is to prevent, restrict or distort competition in the market for books within the State. Clauses (i), (ii), (iii) and (iv) which are identical to the corresponding clauses in the members' version all offend against s. 4(1) as their object and effect is to restrict competition in the market for books within the State. The provision whereby publishers who are not members have agreed to appoint the PA to act on their behalf in relation to collecting information concerning breaches of the agreement by booksellers and keeping each publisher informed of breaches in respect of such net books as are published by him reinforces the extent of the restriction on competition contained in the basic agreement. Similarly the provision whereby the publishers have agreed to take action against any retailer who sells a net book below the net price, where he has contractually agreed not to, also offends against s. 4(1).

. . .

98. Under s. 4(2), the Competition Authority may grant a licence in the case of any agreement or category of agreements which offends against s. 4(1) which:

> having regard to all relevant market conditions, contributes to improving the production of goods or provision of services or to promoting technical or economic progress, while allowing consumers a fair share of the resulting benefit and which does not:
> (i) impose on the undertakings concerned terms which are not indispensable to the attainment of those objectives;
> (ii) afford undertakings the possibility of eliminating competition in respect of a substantial part of the products or services in question.

99. The PA claimed that the Authority, in its statement of objections, had argued that because the first requirement was not satisfied the other three were equally not satisfied. In making this argument the PA appear to be misreading the provisions of s. 4(2). Firstly all four tests must be met before a licence can be granted. Secondly, however, the tests are not disjunctive, they are cumulative. Thus an agreement must first of all contribute to improving the production of goods or provision of services or to promoting technical or economic progress. If it does so, it must allow consumers a fair share of the resulting benefit, i.e. a fair share of the benefit which satisfies the first test. Similarly if it meets both of these requirements it must not impose on the undertakings concerned terms which are not indispensable to the attainment of those objectives, and, finally, it must not afford the undertakings the possibility of eliminating competition in respect of a substantial part of the products or services in question. Clearly if an agreement does not satisfy the first test it cannot satisfy the second since there is no resulting benefit. Conversely, however, an agreement which satisfies the first test may well not satisfy the second, third or fourth test.

100. It was submitted by the PA that the various restrictions involved in the NBA and associated arrangements satisfied the requirements for a licence. In particular it argues that the restrictions in the NBA, by preventing discounting, enabled specialist bookshops to provide a comprehensive service to consumers which includes, *inter alia*, services such as ordering particular titles as well as general advice. In addition it was argued that preventing discounting allows bookshops to stock a wide range of less popular titles, thereby providing consumers with a wider choice of book titles.

101. In the absence of the price restrictions contained in the NBA it was submitted that non-specialist shops and some discount booksellers would offer popular titles at reduced prices. This would force specialist booksellers to reduce their prices on such titles. The reduction in margins on popular titles would reduce the ability of specialist booksellers to provide back-up services such as ordering for which they do not charge. In addition they would have to recoup the loss in margin on more popular books by increasing their margins on less popular titles or by reducing their stock of such titles. The effect of this, it was claimed, would be to eliminate a number of smaller booksellers while reducing the range of titles currently available to consumers.

102. It was further argued that in the absence of RPM the risks involved in publishing books would be increased and this in turn would make publishers less willing to publish titles by new or less popular authors and on subjects which were of minority interest. Many of these arguments were advanced by the Association in the 1962

hearing before the UK Restrictive Practices Court and before the EC Commission and the Court of First Instance. In particular the PA has argued that the decision of the UK Restrictive Practices Court indicates that the NBA meets the requirements of s. 4(2). The Authority does not accept this claim. In the first place there is a fundamental difference between Irish and UK legislation. Under the UK legislation it is necessary to establish that restrictive arrangements are not in the public interest. Under the Competition Act the onus is on the parties to establish that the specific requirements of s. 4(2) are satisfied. More fundamentally, however, the Authority does not believe that a decision based on the conditions prevailing in the UK book trade over thirty years ago is applicable to the conditions prevailing in the Irish market today. The PA claimed that the DGFT had re-examined the NBA in 1989 and had found that it was still in the public interest. In fact the DGFT announced in 1993 that the NBA was being re-examined because there had been significant changes in the book trade since 1962 and that the decision not to refer it back to the court in 1989 was prompted, in part, by an expectation that UK legislation would change and that all restrictive agreements would have to be re-assessed in the light of new legislation.

103. Undoubtedly in the absence of RPM the price of some book titles at least would be reduced. The Authority accepts that some stores may well discount the more popular titles in order to increase their sales. It may be also that many non-specialist bookshops will offer such discounts while stocking only a limited range of books. The effect may well be to increase sales of such books. Consequently the abolition of RPM would to this extent benefit consumers, those retailers offering discounts, and authors who would benefit from an increase in sales of their works. The Authority agrees with the views of the EC Commission in the *Dutch Books* case that: 'It would be possible to reach fresh categories of purchaser by liberalising price competition.' The Commission went on to dismiss claims that RPM in the case of books contributed to improvements in distribution or technical or economic progress.

104. The PA's case is that, in the absence of the NBA, there would be limited discounting of the most popular book titles. Shops would have to raise the prices of less popular book titles to counter such discounting. In effect this implies that RPM results in higher prices of popular book titles than would otherwise be the case, but that this permits cross-subsidisation of less popular titles and of back-up services provided by specialist booksellers. It is widely recognised in economic theory that cross-subsidisation results in a misallocation of resources since consumers do not bear the true cost of individual products. A misallocation of resources reduces efficiency and so cannot be claimed to increase technical or economic progress. The PA claim that in the longer run the effect of discounting would be to increase the risks in publishing thereby raising costs and leading to higher overall book prices. The Authority does not accept this argument. The economics of the publishing business have changed significantly due to technological developments over the past thirty years and it is no longer the case that producing shorter print runs will result in much higher book prices.

105. It may be that price discounting of books will result in a loss of business by specialist bookshops to other types of retail outlet, or that larger bookshops will gain at the expense of smaller ones. The purpose of the Competition Act is to protect competition not competitors. The essence of competition is that competitors will seek to take custom away from their rivals. At the heart of the view that competition is desirable is the judgment that such activity benefits consumers and enhances overall economic welfare. Consequently the fact that some competitors may be harmed by

the elimination of a particular restrictive practice cannot justify the continuance of such a practice. To the extent that RPM prevents the emergence of new competitors and of innovative methods of retailing such as discounting, it cannot be said to result in any improvement in the distribution of goods or in the promotion of economic progress. The PA have agreed that, as a result of the NBA, the number of specialist booksellers is greater than it would otherwise be, and that without it, many rural book-shops would close. It pointed to the increase in the number of bookshops between 1977 and 1988 as evidence of the favourable effects of the NBA. While the number of bookshops certainly increased over this period, much of the increase occurred in the larger urban centres. In contrast in the three Ulster counties the number of bookshops fell sharply. It was pointed out at the oral hearing that there was evidence that the abolition of RPM in France led to an increase in the number of rural bookshops there and that many of these subsequently closed following its re-imposition. The PA disputed this.

106. The claim that discounting will cause booksellers to reduce the range of titles covered also appears unrealistic. Rural bookshops are, as was noted earlier, consider-ably smaller than those in Dublin. By definition therefore they carry a far more limited range of stock and presumably concentrate on the more popular titles anyway. Consequently even if the argument regarding stocks was valid, it would only apply to some bookshops in Ireland. The validity of the argument itself is questionable. As the EC Commission noted in the *Dutch Books* case: 'As the holding of stock is the essential characteristic of a bookshop it would be illogical to consider reducing it; bookshops might usefully improve their efficiency by specialising.' The abolition of the NBA may result in the closure of some shops but these are likely to be replaced by new entrants.

107. The Authority does not believe that the abolition of RPM would have serious adverse effects on the availability of minority interest books. The price of such books may well increase reflecting the slower turnover and higher costs of stocking such titles. Those wishing to purchase such books will have to pay higher prices because they are no longer being subsidised by purchasers of more popular titles. The subsidi-sation of a minority of consumers by the majority cannot be regarded as efficiency enhancing or contributing to the promotion of economic or technical progress.

108. It may be that the abolition of RPM will mean that specialist booksellers will have to introduce specific charges to cover the cost of back-up services such as ordering titles which are out of stock. The Authority does not believe that the type of pre-sales services provided by bookshops is conducive to free riding. In simple terms it does not believe that consumers will go into specialist bookshops in order to obtain detailed advice concerning a particular book and then go to a discount outlet to purchase it. Particular services such as ordering out of stock titles are not prone to free riding anyway. Indeed if consumers must pay a charge to order a book they are likely to come back and buy the book. Under the present system consumers may order a book but subsequently obtain it elsewhere in which case the first store has suffered a loss by ordering the book.

109. Nor is the Authority persuaded by the argument that the abolition of RPM in the NBA will lead to fewer books being published. As already stated modern technological developments have greatly altered the economics of the book publishing industry. 'Desk-top publishing' technology has greatly eased the task of publishing books. The Authority notes that as a result of such technological advances many new small scale

specialist book publishers have emerged in the UK in recent years. Many are engaged in publishing books which have a very limited minority appeal and which would not previously have been published by mainstream publishers. Desk-top publishing has also enabled many authors particularly in the academic field to publish their own works. It has been claimed that the cost of producing a book using desk-top publishing techniques may be as low as UK£1. The low cost of desk-top publishing greatly reduces the risk of publishing minority interest books. The fact that new technology has enabled the publication of many titles which would not have been published by established UK publishing firms under the NBA undermines the argument that in the absence of the NBA fewer books would be produced. It is advances in publishing technology rather than the NBA which have enabled an ever growing range of titles to be published.

110. The Authority notes that if an agreement fails to meet any of the requirements specified in s. 4(2), a licence cannot be granted to it. The primary objective of the NBA is to establish a system of RPM in respect of UK published books in Ireland. RPM does not in the Authority's view contribute to improving the production of goods or provision of services or to promoting technical or economic progress. Consumers cannot therefore be said to share in such benefits and the restrictions cannot be regarded as indispensable to the achievement of such objectives. UK published books account for a substantial portion of books sold in Ireland. As most UK books are net books the restrictions contained in the NBA eliminate competition in respect of a substantial part of the relevant market. Consequently the NBA, both members' and non-members' versions, do not satisfy any of the requirements for a licence set out in s. 4(2) of the Competition Act. The primary aim of the remaining agreements is to ensure the effective operation of RPM. Thus they also fail to satisfy the requirements for a licence.

111. The PA argued that the Authority, in deciding that all four requirements for a licence were not met, had taken a view which was directly at odds with the EC Commission. In particular it claimed that the Commission accepted that the NBA produced benefits which were shared with consumers. On the contrary the Commission, as already noted in para. 45, stated that: ' . . . the agreements are not indispensable to the attainment of their objectives. Since an agreement, in order to be exempted from the prohibition contained in article 85(1), has to fulfil all conditions of article 85(3), the agreements cannot be exempted. It is therefore not necessary to examine whether the agreements meet the other conditions of article 85(3).' In the *Dutch Books* case the Commission specifically decided that a system of RPM for books failed all four tests for exemption under article 85(3). These tests are the same as those contained in s. 4(2).

112. The PA also claimed that the Authority was wrong in finding that the NBA failed the fourth test under s. 4(2), arguing that competition was not eliminated by the NBA. The Authority wishes to point out that the specified test is whether the arrangements afford the undertakings concerned the possibility of eliminating competition in respect of a substantial part of the products in question. As UK published books account for the vast bulk of books sold within the State, and, as the overwhelming majority are net books, the Authority believes that net books constitute a substantial part of the products in question, and that price competition, which is particularly important in the case of books, is eliminated by the NBA in the case of the majority of imported books.

1. A vertical restriction is one applied by a firm at one level of the production/distribution chain to one operating at a different level. Generally these apply between manufacturers/suppliers and retailers.

2. F. M. Scherer and D. Ross, *Industrial Market Structure and Economic Performance*, (3rd ed.), New York: Houghton Mifflin 1990, 550.
3. This view was restated in *Sylvania* where the court distinguished between RPM and other forms of vertical restraint.
4. C. Bellamy and G. Child, *Common Market Law of Competition*, (3rd ed.), London: Sweet and Maxwell 1987, at para. 4–002.
5. W. Allen and P. Curwan, *Competition and Choice in the Publishing Industry*, London: Institute for Economic Affairs 1991, 25.
6. Point 62.
7. *Nederlandse Jurisprudentie* 1979, no. 480.
8. Point 52.
9. Point 9.
10. VBVB *and* VBBB *v Commission*, p. 40.
11. At para. 86.

The Authority decided that none of the agreements satisfied the requirements of s. 4 (2) and thus refused to grant a certificate or a licence in respect of the agreements.

Note

In *Kerry Co–operative Creameries Ltd v An Bord Bainne* (1991) ILRM 851 the court held that there must be an express covenant between the parties to restrain trade.

SECTION FOUR—SEVERANCE

Skerry, Wynne and Skerry's College (Ireland) Ltd *v* Moles (1907) 42 ILTR 46

In August 1904, the defendant entered the employment of the plaintiffs, Skerry and Wynne, as a teacher of shorthand, &c. On 12 October 1904, he signed an agreement with them, of which the following was the material clause:

2. In consideration of the said engagement, the said Joseph A. Moles shall not, during a period of three years, to be computed from the date on which the said J. A. Moles shall cease to be employed by the said G. E. Skerry and A. E. Wynne, carry on or engage in the business of teacher of shorthand, typewriting, and general business training, or in any or either of the said businesses, either as principal or assistant, in Dublin, Belfast, or Cork, or within a radius of 7 miles from the academy or place of business of the said G. E. Skerry and A. E. Wynne in any of the said cities. And if the said J. A. Moles shall so carry on or engage in such business, either as principal or assistant, he shall pay to the said G. E. Skerry and A. E. Wynne, or the survivor of them, the sum of £20 for every month during which or any part of which he shall so carry on or engage in the said business as and for liquidated damages.

The plaintiffs claimed: (1) An injunction restraining the defendant from carrying on business in Dublin, Belfast, or Cork, or within a radius of 7 miles from the academy or place of business of the plaintiffs in any of the said cities, in breach of the said agreement. (2) Damages for breach of the said agreement; and in the alternative (3) a declaration that, under the said agreement, the defendant was bound to pay either to the plaintiff company, or to the said Skerry and Wynne, the sum of £20 by way of liquidated damages for each month during which he had carried on business in Dublin, Belfast, &c., for three years from the date on which he left the plaintiffs' employment.

Barton J.:

. . .

The contract of employment was limited to Skerry's Academy in Belfast, but the restrictive clause extended also to Dublin and Cork. I have no difficulty in saying that the clause was unreasonable *qua* Dublin and Cork, but reasonable *qua* Belfast, and that it is a case in which the reasonable part is severable from the unreasonable part.

. . .

I think that the injunction can and ought to be granted so far as the City of Belfast is concerned.

Patrick J. Mulligan *v* Edmund Corr [1925] 1 IR 170

The plaintiff, a solicitor sought an injunction to prevent the defendant, a former clerk, from practising as a solicitor within a radius of 30 miles from the towns of Ballina, and Charlestown or within 20 miles of Ballaghadereen in breach of an agreement entered into by him when taken into employment six years previously. The plaintiff had an office in Ballina and a branch office in Charlestown. The trial judge held that the restriction was severable as regards each area defined, and granted an injunction restraining the defendant from practising as a solicitor within 30 miles of Ballina. The defendant appealed.

Fitzgibbon J.:

. . .

The principles of law applicable to covenants of this description in restraint of trade may be regarded as now finally settled; the only difficulty is to ascertain the facts to which they are to be applied.

The restriction imposed must not be greater than is reasonably required for the protection of the convenantee. If it exceed in area or duration the limits which the court considers reasonable it is void. The question of reasonableness is one of law for the court to decide. A restriction though unlimited as to space may be reasonable if confined to a period of reasonable duration. All these points were settled by the *Nordenfelt* case[1] some thirty years ago, and the converse of the last proposition, *viz.*: that a restriction, though unlimited in point of time, was valid if limited to a reasonable area, was decided by the House of Lords in 1921 in the case of *Fitch v Dewes*,[2] which was, like this, an action brought by a solicitor to restrain a former clerk from practising as a solicitor within a radius of 7 miles of the Town Hall of Tamworth, in breach of an agreement entered into by him, when taken into employment as managing clerk ten years previously. The area in that case was smaller than this, but it included a thickly populated district and portions of four English counties, Stafford, Warwick, Leicester, and Derby.

The first question we have to decide is the true construction of the covenant in the present case. The defendant has contended that it prohibits him from practising within three separate circles, one having Ballina as its centre with a radius of 30 miles, another of like radius having Charlestown as its centre, and a third with a radius of 20 miles and Ballaghadereen as its centre, and maps marked by an engineer with these three circles have been given in evidence, and that this is the true construction has not been disputed by the plaintiff and was decided by Meredith J. It is not clear that this is the true interpretation of the clause, and I think the maps rather support a different construction, based on grammatical considerations, for it will be seen that the Ballaghadereen circle falls entirely within the Charlestown circle, and the prohibition relating to it was therefore wholly unnecessary. In case of ambiguity, a contract should receive an interpretation which will give some effect to every provision in it, if such a construction is reasonably practicable, and by construing the restriction regarding Ballina and Charlestown as prohibiting practice at any place within 30 miles of *both* towns, there will be a considerable area left to be included by the Ballaghadereen circle, comprising such important places as Carrick-on-Shannon, Castlerea, Boyle, and Dromahaire. Assuming the construction placed upon the agreement by the parties to be correct, does the restriction exceed that which was reasonably necessary for the protection of the plaintiff? He had not been long in practice, but he had good connections and might reasonably expect, before the defendant would be out of his indentures, to build up a fair business, which he was entitled to protect against the possibility that his managing clerk, with all the knowledge acquired in the plaintiff's service of the plaintiff's clients and their affairs, might set up, as he has done, in opposition to his former employer.

In my opinion, however, the area which the plaintiff endeavoured to protect was too large. It was certainly so if it included the two 30-mile circles. They covered three county Assize towns, practically the whole of Mayo, more than half of Sligo, a large part of Roscommon, and portions of Galway and Leitrim. That appears to us to go far beyond anything which the plaintiff could reasonably require for his protection. Even the more limited area which I believe to be covered by the clause is, in my opinion, excessive. The plaintiff does not appear to have done much business in Ballaghadereen or its vicinity, and it was suggested at the bar by his counsel that the reason for including Ballaghadereen in the agreement was that if he did not make good in Ballina he might go to the other side of the county and work Ballaghadereen alone or in connection with Charlestown. If this were so, a restriction imposed to protect a business which was not in fact being worked and might never be set up at all was quite unreasonable.

Having come to the conclusion that the agreement cannot in any view of its construction be upheld in its entirety, questions arise whether it can be divided, and, if so, whether any fraction of it can be supported as reasonable.

As to the former, this restrictive covenant falls in our opinion within the principle of decisions such as *Mallan v May,*[3] the case of a dentist's assistant; *Green v Price,*[4] the case of the perfumery business; *Davies v Lowen,*[5] the case of the carrier's clerk; and if, by eliminating part which appears to be void, we can leave a valid and effective contract remaining, such a course is lawful, though the court cannot make a new covenant or mould one which is already complete in itself so as to create a different restriction which would be reasonable in the opinion of the court. I confess that my own opinion has fluctuated during the argument (which was ably conducted on both sides), and since; but after very careful consideration, we have come to the unanimous conclusion that it is not reasonable for the plaintiff, though practising and having offices both in Ballina and Charlestown, to insist that his managing clerk should not practise or set up a business in any place which was within a distance so great as 30 miles from both or either of those towns. Even the more restricted area includes the town of Sligo, and although that part of County Sligo which is served by Ballina or Charlestown, each of which actually touches the county border, might fairly be the subject of a protective clause, we cannot hold that it is necessary for the fair protection of the plaintiff that the defendant should be precluded from practising in the capital of the adjoining county, a restriction which would in effect have debarred him from taking business at the Assizes from any part of the County Sligo, and would exclude him from all that portion of County Sligo which lies outside the 30-mile circle, but whose inhabitants resort to Sligo for legal advice. There is no possible construction of this agreement which would not include the town of Sligo in the prohibited area, and the Ballina circle, which was adopted by Meredith J., would include Westport, as well as Claremorris and Ballyhaunis, none of which is shown to be in any real competition with Ballina for legal affairs so far as the plaintiff is concerned. It is to be regretted that the plaintiff did not give fuller information as to his own business, and, in our opinion, having regard to the fact that, notwithstanding a dictum to the contrary of the Earl of Birkenhead, the onus appears to be upon the plaintiff to establish the reasonableness of the restriction imposed, we have come to the conclusion that it is not reasonable or necessary for the protection of the plaintiff's business that the defendant should be restrained from practising as a solicitor at any place within 30 miles of Ballina and Charlestown or of either of those towns.

1. [1894] AC 535.   3. 11 M & W 652.   5. 64 LT 655.
2. [1921] 2 AC 158.   4. 13 M & W 695; 16 M & W 346.

Note

Although Fitzgibbon J. delivered the judgment of the court, Kennedy C.J. added his observations concerning the defendant's 'inauspicious beginning' to his career. He noted 'every man who appreciates the standards of conduct and of honour which are required of the members of that profession required by its privileges and the great trusts confided to it, must be shocked by the defendant's first invitation of public confidence.'

ECI European Chemical Industries Ltd v Ian Douglas Bell [1981] ILRM 345

McWilliam J.:

The plaintiff manufactures mastic sealants and similar products at Castleblayney, County Monaghan. The defendant, who had previously been in employment as a qualified chemist dealing with somewhat similar products for a period of seven years or so, was employed by the plaintiff from 3 January 1980, under an agreement in writing which provided that his employment could be terminated by either party on giving three months' notice in writing.

By letter dated 27 March 1981, the defendant gave notice of termination of his employment on 26 June 1981. His object in leaving the employment of the plaintiff is to take up employment with ACS Teoranta in County Galway, a firm which manufactures products similar to those of the plaintiff. ACS Teoranta is a subsidiary or an associate of an American company. The plaintiff is a subsidiary or an associate of a German company. It is probable that the parent or associated companies have business interests in various parts of the world.

The contract of employment of the defendant contains the following clauses:

17. Upon the termination of his employment for any cause or by any means whatsoever the employee shall not for a period of two years thereafter:
(b) undertake to carry on alone or in partnership nor be employed or interested directly or indirectly in any capacity whatsoever in any trade or business of a nature

similar to or competing or calculated to compete with any business or businesses carried on by the company or by any of its subsidiaries or associated companies at the date of such termination PROVIDED THAT this restriction shall not extend to any country in which neither the company nor any of its subsidiary or associated companies has or shall have established a place of business or in which neither the company nor any of its subsidiaries or associated companies carried on business at the time of such termination.

18. In the event that any covenant or provision herein shall be determined to be void or unenforceable in whole or in part by reason of the area, duration or type or scope of service covered by the said covenant then the said covenant shall be given effect to in its reduced form as may be decided by any court of competent jurisdiction. The employee hereby acknowledges and agrees that the restriction contained in this agreement is valid and reasonable.

Immediately after his employment with the plaintiff, the defendant was sent to Germany for a period of seven months for training in the plaintiff's processes, products and 'know-how'. The defendant agrees that he there learned the plaintiff's manufacturing techniques, testing techniques, production processes and some trade secrets.

It appears that, until recently, ACS Teoranta purchased supplies of mastik sealants from the plaintiff but that in January of this year, it entered into an agreement with a German company to produce similar material in Galway and has purchased a machine of a kind used by the plaintiff for the production of such material.

. . .

The case presented on behalf of the defendant is that this is a contract in restraint of trade, that the plaintiff has not got a reasonable interest to be protected by the agreement, that the restraint is unreasonable with regard to the geographical area of the restraint and that it is unreasonable with regard to the length of the period of restraint. The argument necessitates the submission that, even on an interlocutory application, there is an onus on the plaintiff to establish the reasonableness of the restraint in each of these respects, that this has not been done and that the plaintiff is, therefore, not entitled to succeed on this application.

Having regard to this approach to the case and the arguments which have been addressed to me I feel I ought to consider the doctrine of restraints of trade and its application by the courts.

The relevant clauses in the agreement are clearly in restraint of trade and this has not been contested on behalf of the plaintiff. A long line of cases from *Nordenfelt v Maxim Nordenfelt Guns and Ammunition Co. Ltd* (1894) AC 535 to *Greig v Insoles* [1978] 1 WLR 303 appears to establish that a contract in restraint of trade is contrary to public policy and void or unenforceable unless the restraint reasonably protects a valid interest of the person in whose favour it is imposed, is not unreasonable with regard to the person restrained and is not unreasonable as being injurious to the public interest.

On the affidavits before me, I am satisfied, notwithstanding the arguments to the contrary on behalf of the defendant, that there is *prima facie*, a valid interest of the plaintiff to be protected, that is to say, the protection of trade secrets, testing techniques and production processes which have come to the knowledge of the defendant. Certainly I cannot accept that there is not, at least, a serious issue to be tried in this respect.

A more substantial objection on behalf of the defendant is that the clause is unreasonable both because it is too wide in the area of its application geographically and as making the period of restraint too long. I was addressed at some length as to the power of the court to modify the agreement should it be considered to be unreasonable in its present form.

The most recent case to which I was referred is that of *Littlewoods Organisation v Harris* [1977] 1 WLR 1472. It has been discussed on behalf of both parties but I find some aspects difficult to follow. It seems to me that the majority of the court of Appeal, Lord Denning M.R. and Megaw L.J., formed the opinion, contrary to the view expressed in the case of *Commercial Plastics v Vincent* [1965] 1 QB 623; [1964] 3 WLR 820, that the court is entitled to ignore the literal meaning of such a covenant and construe it with regard to the surrounding circumstances existing at the time when the covenant was entered into. See Megaw L.J. at 1489, or that the clause should be interpreted as limited to the reasonable objects which the parties to the agreement sought to achieve, see Lord Denning at 1483.

It seems to me that a point to be determined is whether a covenant which can be construed as being too wide in some respects and therefore unreasonable in those respects is wholly void in all respects or whether, although including unreasonable provisions which will not be enforced, reasonable provisions which are contained in it may be enforced. This is an aspect discussed by Lord Denning in a different form at pp 1481–2 of *Littlewoods* case. He said, at 1482, 'It has often been said that a covenant in restraint of trade is not to be rendered invalid simply by putting forward unlikely or improbable contingencies in which it might operate unreasonably . . . If such an unlikely or unusual event should happen, the court would not enforce it so as to work an injustice.' The conclusion of the Court of Appeal in the case of *Commercial Plastics v Vincent* was that the covenant, being too wide, had to be ruled out and declared void although the actual relief sought was held to be reasonable and proper to be granted. See Pearson L.J. at 832 of the WLR. The same view was taken by Browne L.J. in his dissenting judgment in the *Littlewoods* case. He said at p. 1491 'It seems to me that if the clause is read literally it is much too wide and is void and unenforceable.' This was also the view of the Court of Appeal in the case of *Gledhow Autoparts v Delaney* [1965] 1 WLR 1366. Sellers L.J. said at 1371:

> The injunction for which the plaintiffs asked and which they received is admittedly less than clause 6 in its terms would have permitted as regards area, that is, places where the defendant had operated. But when, as is the defendant's contention, the clause is said to be unenforceable because it is in restraint of trade, it must be construed as it stands and not to the extent that the employer seeks to enforce it. The modified request may reveal an apprehension as to the full effect of the clause. Whether this clause is, as the judge held, enforceable and not in restraint of trade, or whether it is too wide and not to be invoked, is a question of law and has to be decided on the authorities.

Diplock L.J., said at 1377

> The defendant was in fact employed for over six years by the plaintiffs and no doubt became a valuable servant and acquired considerable knowledge of and personal relation with the plaintiff's customers. It is natural in these circumstances to tend to look at what in fact happened under the agreement. But the question of the validity of a covenant in restraint of trade has to be determined at the date at which the agreement was entered into and has to be determined in the light of what may happen under the agreement, although what may happen may cover many possibilities which in the event did not happen. A covenant of this kind is invalid *ab initio* or valid *ab initio*. There cannot be some moment at which it passes from the class of invalid to that of valid covenants.

These two statements are very clear and are difficult to reconcile with some of the views expressed in the *Littlewoods* case.

At the same time, doubts have been cast on the correctness of this strict view and it might be considered that a court of equity is entitled to consider the effect of the contract as the circumstances come before it so as to avoid working an injustice. The entire doctrine that contracts in restraints of trade are void or unenforceable is based on the proposition that such contracts are contrary to public policy or, as was said in a very old case, 'against the benefit of the Commonwealth'. Can it be said that it is of any advantage to public policy or refuse relief which is held to be reasonable and proper to be granted, as in the *Commercial Plastics* case?

In the case of *McEllistrim v Ballymacelligott Co-operative Agricultural & Dairy Society* [1919] AC 548; 53 ILTR 121, Viscount Finlay at 128 of ILTR adopted a statement of James V.C. in the case of *Leather Cloth Co. v Lorsont* (1869) LR 9 Eq, 345 at 353. It is:

> All the cases when they come to be examined seem to establish this principle—
> that all restraints upon trade are bad as being in violation of public policy unless
> they are natural, and not unreasonable for the protection of the parties dealing
> legally with some subject matter of contract. The principle is this—public policy
> requires that every man shall be at liberty to work for himself, and shall not be at
> liberty to deprive himself or the State of his labour, skill or talent by any contract
> that he enters into. On the other hand, public policy requires that when a man has,
> by skill or other means, obtained something which he wants to sell, he should be at
> liberty to sell it in the most advantageous way in the market; and in order to enable
> him to sell it advantageously in the market, it is necessary that he should be able to
> preclude himself from entering into competition with the purchaser. In such a case
> the same public policy that enables him to do that does not restrain him from alien-
> ating that which he wants to alienate and, therefore, enables him to enter into any
> stipulation, however restrictive it is, provided that restriction, in the judgment of
> the court, is not unreasonable having regard to the subject matter of the contract.

I have considered these matters at some length because the present application has been met to a large extent on the basis that it should be refused on the ground that the covenant is void and the plaintiff cannot succeed in its action. I am not satisfied about this as there seems to be a number of arguments open to the plaintiff and it would be improper for me on an interlocutory application to decide the main issue in the case without hearing the evidence which may be adduced and having a full argument on the various aspects to which I have referred. All I have to do on an interlocutory application is to decide whether the plaintiff has established a *prima facie* case in the sense that there is a serious question to be tried and, if so, what is the balance of convenience to the parties between granting and refusing an injunction.

From the facts which are before me and the review which I have made of the decisions, I am satisfied that there is a serious issue to be tried. On the question of the balance of convenience, it seems to me that the defendant can be adequately compensated in damages if he is successful in his defence and that an undertaking by the plaintiff to pay such damages will be met, whereas damages would not be an adequate remedy for the plaintiff and it is doubtful whether any damages could be recovered from the defendant if the plaintiff were to be successful. Accordingly, I am of opinion that the *status quo* should be preserved and that I should grant the interlocutory injunction sought.

Note

Severance is provided for under s. 4 (7) and (8) of the Competition Act:

4. (7) The prohibition in sub-s. (1) shall not prevent the court, in exercising any jurisdiction conferred on it by this Act concerning an agreement, decision or concerted practice which contravenes that prohibition and which creates or, but for this Act, would have created legal relations between the parties thereto, from applying, where appropriate, any relevant rules of law as to the *severance* of those terms of that agreement, decision or concerted practice which contravene that prohibition from those which do not.

(8) In respect of an agreement, decision or concerted practice such as is referred to in sub-s. (7) a court of competent jurisdiction may make such order as to recovery, restitution or otherwise between the parties to such agreement, decision or concerted practice as may in all the circumstances seem just, having regard in particular to any consideration or benefit given or received by such parties on foot thereof.

See 'How Severance by Courts might save Offending Articles' 2 *Competition* 153 (*Competition Press*).

Chapter Eighteen

Discharge of Contractual Obligations

SECTION ONE—PERFORMANCE

In order to discharge a contract by performance, exact performance according to the specific terms of the contract must be established.

Cutter v Powell (1795) 6 TR 320

The plaintiff's husband was employed as second mate on a ship to sail from Jamaica to Liverpool for a gross sum of 30 guineas. When he died on route, the plaintiff sued to recover a proportionate part of the wages on a *quantum meruit* basis.

Lord Kenyon C.J.:

. . . That where the parties have come to an express contract none can be implied has prevailed so long as to be reduced to an axiom in the law. Here the defendant expressly promised to pay the intestate 30 guineas, provided he proceeded, continued and did his duty as second mate in the ship from Jamaica to Liverpool; and the accompanying circumstances disclosed in the case are that the common rate of wages is £4 per month, when the party is paid in proportion to the time he serves: and that this voyage is generally performed in two months. Therefore if there had been no contract between these parties, all that the intestate could have recovered on a *quantum meruit* for the voyage would have been £8; whereas here the defendant contracted to pay thirty guineas provided the mate continued to do his duty as mate during the whole voyage, in which case the latter would have received nearly four times as much as if he were paid for the number of months he served. He stipulated to receive the larger sum if the whole duty were performed, and nothing unless the whole of that duty were performed: it was a kind of insurance.

(Ashurst, Grose and Lawrence JJ. concurred.)

Callan v Marum (1871) 5 IRCL 315

The plaintiff sued the defendant for repair work executed on the defendant's house and materials provided. The defendant claimed that the plaintiff failed to execute the work according to the terms of a special contract. He pleaded that 'no work was done or material provided . . . as alleged'.

Whiteside C.J.:

I now come to the argument, which was founded on the common counts. It is not to be forgotten that the contract was to build a house for a specific sum of money to be paid on the completion of the building, if no instalments had, under certificates from the architect, and according to the agreement, been paid during the progress of the work. I take it to be clear that in such a case the contract is entire and indivisible, and that the employer is not bound to pay for half, or quarter of a house; for the court and jury can have no right to apportion that which the parties themselves have treated as entire. If the agreement had been, that the builder was to be paid for work and labour and materials provided by measure and value, he might then have demanded payment from time to time, as the work proceeded and after it had been duly measured; *Williams v Fitzmaurice*;[1] but that would be a different contract to the one relied on by the present plaintiff. And I am of opinion that the principle laid down by Ashurst J. in *Cutter v Powell*,[2] applies to this case. These cases are a complete answer to the argument that the general question of work and labour ought to have been left to the jury, who could have made the necessary deductions on the ground that the work had not been completed conformably to the contract. The question then that arises upon the common counts is this, can the plaintiff, under the common count for work done and materials provided, recover for work done in part performance of a written contract, which, when the action was brought was open, unrescinded, and unperformed? I believe the law is quite settled that he can not: *Hulle v Heightman*.[3] On the same principle proceeded, the decision in *Ellis v Hamlen*,[4] the application of which to the present case cannot be disputed; and no case has been cited in which *Ellis v Hamlen* is impugned or questioned. I have always thought that it was almost an axiom in the law, and the proposition is certainly so stated by the text books, that in order to maintain an action for work and labour the plaintiff must prove a performance of the work according to the terms of the contract; or, if he has deviated from these terms, he must show that the defendant acquiesced in such deviation. See *Add. Cont.*, (6th ed.), 388, where the substance of *Ellis v Hamlen* is stated as an authority, and as binding as if fresh from the legal mint. In the *Books of Evidence* also the case is given as good law; and Mr Starkie, in his excellent work, quotes with approval the well known judgment of Le Blanc J., in *Basten v Butter*,[5] deciding that if a man contracts with another to build him a house for a certain sum, the stipulated work must be done according to the contract. I am, therefore, of opinion that *Ellis v Hamlen* is a well decided case, and that so far as it applies to the facts of the principal case, it is decisive against the plaintiff. The pleadings and arguments in *Munro v Butt*[6] were very similar to those in the principal case, with this important exception, however, that in *Munro v Butt*, the facts were much more favourable for the plaintiff's contention; because, in that case a great deal—the whole as the plaintiff alleged—of the work had been done, and the defendant had actually taken possession of the house. The surveyor, however, refused to give the certificate, the obtaining of which was to be a condition precedent to the plaintiff's right to recover, on the ground that the work had been incompletely or imperfectly performed, yet in this case, also, it was held that the plaintiff could not recover for work and labour generally, because there was a written contract for the work open, and unrescinded, nor on the count upon the contract, because it was not in the terms performed. From the judgment in this case we perceive, with what firmness the principles of the law were applied to the facts of the case before the court. The builder who had contracted to build two houses according to a plan and specification, and who built them not according to the agreement, and of inferior materials, was not allowed to recover one shilling upon his special contract, because he had not performed it according to its terms; and the argument that he might so recover upon the common count for work and labour and material, because he had violated the specific written contract, the only contract assented to by the other party, was refuted and rejected. The decision in *Munro v Butt* I hold to be an excellent precedent, and to

be clearly applicable to one portion of this case. The principle so well laid down in
Munro v Butt, and the case itself, are directly affirmed in the Exchequer Chamber, and
in an instructive judgment delivered by Blackburn J. in *Appleby v Myers*.[7]

[1.] 3 H & N 844.	[5.] 7 East 479.
[2.] 6 TR 320; 2 Sm LCL.	[6.] 8 E & B 738.
[3.] 2 East 145.	[7.] LR 2 CP 651; SC sub. nom.
[4.] 3 Taunt 52.	*Appleby v Myers*, 36 LJN SCP 331.

(The majority of the court decided that a new trial should be ordered due
to the defendant's failure to make a special plea alleging that the work was
done under a special contract.)

A. SUBSTANTIAL PERFORMANCE

Coughlan *v* Moloney and Wife (1905) 39 ILTR 153

The plaintiff agreed to build a house for the defendants for £200, the
house to be completed before Christmas 1902. There was no provision for
payment by instalments but £83 had been so paid prior to the action. The
work was not completed by Christmas and the following October the
defendants asked the plaintiff to estimate a value for the work done so
that the matter could be wound up. In November the defendants took
possession of the site, denying the plaintiff access. The plaintiff sued for
the balance due under the contract or alternatively for *quantum meruit.*

Palles L.C.B. (King's Bench Division):

. . . The jury found that the work was not performed before Christmas 1902; that it was
not performed within a reasonable time; that it was not performed at the time of
action brought, and, therefore, it is impossible for the plaintiff to recover on the special
contract. . . .

. . .

. . . Now, first, I wish to put out of consideration a contract which is plainly implied
by law under the circumstances of this case. Christmas, 1902, was the date of performance. Plainly, after that date the plaintiff continued to perform work, and plainly
either at the request or with the consent of the defendants, so there is ground for
implying a contract to pay for this performance after the date fixed for completion.
There is no evidence as to whether this implied contract was a contract in the terms of
the old contract. It was an implied contract to do the work within a reasonable time.
Taking it that the plaintiff sues on this implied contract under his *indebitatus* count, the
answer to it is that the work was not completed within a reasonable time, or at all,
and, consequently, on this contract he would not be entitled to recover. Ultimately, the
question comes to what were the plaintiff's rights in reference, not to the mere taking
over and entering upon this building by the defendants, but to the circumstances under
which it was so entered. Evidence was given of two letters asking the plaintiff to
furnish particulars of the work that he had done, and for an estimate of its value, in
order that the matter should be finally wound up. I do not say that if the terms of
these letters had been assented to by the plaintiff that there would not have been a
complete contract to pay on a *quantum meruit*. But, then, there was no assent to those
terms by the plaintiff, and, on the contrary, it is clear that from that time and always
he has been insisting on his right to recover on the special contract. The plaintiff's

right to recover upon this *quantum meruit* depended on a state of facts which it would have been impossible for the jury to have found. I am clear that the view of counsel was that they were entitled to recover on a *quantum meruit*, based not upon any contract found by the jury, but upon the fact that possession was taken up of the work by the defendants—that they retained the benefit of it—and that under the circumstances the plaintiff was entitled to recover the full value of his work. That proposition, stated nakedly, is simply that *Munro v Butt* 8 E & B 738, and cases of that description, are not law. It is going upon the principle applicable to chattels, that if a certain thing is done, not in performance of a contract, but under circumstances under which the defendant is able to obtain benefit from it, and if the defendant accepts and avails himself of it, then the plaintiff is able to recover on a *quantum meruit*. The decision in *Munro v Butt* is that this principle does not apply to a house on a man's land, because there is no possibility of rejecting the benefit of what has been done, unless he destroys the house built on it. Again, it was argued that if there was nothing more than the mere taking up of possession—that is, if the possession was availed of, and the house improved, that would render the defendant liable. I am of opinion that it cannot. I do not go into the question of hardship. *Cutter v Powell* 2 SLC 1 is always apt to work hardship, but I think that this application should be refused with costs, . . .

(The Court of Appeal confirmed this principle.)

Walker L.J:

The only question is that of the *quantum meruit*. The defendants were, by the findings of the jury, justified in serving notice and taking up possession. To enable the plaintiff to recover, something more than the defendants merely taking the benefit of the work done upon the land, is necessary, from which a new contract may be inferred. There is no evidence of such a kind here. The most favourable case for the plaintiff would be that possession was taken up on the terms that he should be paid on a *quantum meruit*. But terms mean terms agreed upon on both sides. The acts of the plaintiff show that he never adopted this view. The principle of *Munro v Butt* is quite applicable to this case.

Note

See Anthony Beck 'The Doctrine of Substantial Performance: Conditions and Conditions Precedent' (1975) 38 MLR 413.

Kincora Builders Ltd *v* Patrick A. Cronin (HC) 5 March 1973, unrep.

The plaintiffs, a firm of builders, contracted to build a house for the defendants. Upon visiting the site the defendant noticed that the walls and ceilings were not insulated as stipulated in the contract. The defendant agreed to accept a sum of £350 in satisfaction of the failure of the plaintiffs to complete the insulation work on the walls but claimed to have received no settlement for failure to insulate the ceiling. The plaintiffs sued for the sum of £6,000, the balance due on foot of the contract. The defendant claimed that the house was never completed in accordance with the contract and counterclaimed for damages for breach of contract.

Pringle J.:

. . .

. . . |Counsel for the plaintiffs| submitted that, as the contract had been *substantially* completed, his clients were entitled to insist on the completion of the contract, subject to whatever deductions the defendant was entitled to for defective work (if any). He referred to the case of *Bolton v Mahadeva* |1972| 1 WLR 1009, in which the Court of Appeal in England dealt with the question of the circumstances under which a building contractor who has entered into a lump sum contract, can recover anything on foot thereof, if the contract has not been completely performed. The court reviewed the authorities, and in particular distinguished an earlier decision of the Court of Appeal in the case of H. *Dakin & Co. v Lee* |1916| 1KB 566, which had been followed in the case of *Hoenig v Isaacs* |1952| 2 All ER 176.

In *Dakin's* case the plaintiffs had agreed to carry out certain repairs to the defendant's house for the sum of £264 and the plaintiffs claimed that sum and a sum for extras. The defendant, who had gone back into the house after the plaintiffs' workmen had left, disputed her liability to pay any part of the contract sum on the ground that the contract had not been fulfilled in three respects, (1) the concrete which was to be placed under a part of one of the side walls of the house which was to be underpinned was to be of the depth of 4 feet and it was in fact only done to a depth of 2 feet, (2) columns of hollow iron, 5 inches in diameter were to be used to support a certain bay window, whereas the columns supplied were of solid iron 4 inches in diameter, and (3) the joists over the bay window were to be cleated at the angles and bolted to caps and to each other and this was not done. The official referee found as a fact that the contract had not been fulfilled in the three instances mentioned, and he held that the plaintiffs were therefore not entitled to recover any part of the contract price, or of the amount claimed for extras, but he allowed £70 for the additional work. This decision was reversed by Ridley and Sankey JJ. in the Kings Bench Division and their decision was upheld by the Court of Appeal. The Master of the Rolls, Lord Cozens-Hardy, said in his judgment, after dealing with the deviations from the contract:

> In these circumstances it has been argued before us that, in a contract of this kind to do work for a lump sum, the defect in some of the items of the specification, or the failure to do every item in the specification, puts an end to the whole contract and prevents the builders from making any claim upon it: and therefore, where there is no ground for presuming any fresh contract, he cannot obtain any payment. The matter has been treated in the argument as though the omission to do every item perfectly was an abandonment of the contract. That seems to me, with great respect, to be absolutely and entirely wrong. An illustration of the abandonment of a contract which was given from one of the authorities was that of a builder who, when he had half finished the work, said to the employer 'I cannot finish it because I have no money' and left the job undone at that stage. That is an abandonment of the contract and prevents the builder, therefore from making any claim, unless there be some circumstances leading to a different conclusion. But to say that a builder cannot recover from a building owner merely because some item of the work has been done negligently, or inefficiently, or improperly, is a proposition which I should not listen to, unless compelled by a decision of the House of Lords. Take a contract for a lump sum to decorate a house: the contract provides that there shall be three coats of oil paint, but in one of the rooms only two coats of paint are put on, can anybody seriously say that, under these circumstances, the building owner could go and occupy the house and take the benefit of all the decorations which had been done in the other rooms without paying a penny for all

the work done by the builder just because two coats of paint had been put on in one room where there ought to have been three? I regard the present case as one of negligence and bad workmanship and not as a case where there has been an omission of any one of the items in the specification. The builders thought apparently, as they have sworn, that they had done all that was intended to be done in reference to the contract: and I suppose that the defects are due to carelessness on the part of some of the workmen or of the foreman: but the existence of these defects does not amount to a refusal by them to perform part of the contract: it simply shows negligence in the way they have done the work.

Lord Justice Pickford in his judgment said:

Certainly I have not the slightest wish to differ from the view that, if a man agrees to do a certain amount of work for a lump sum and only does part of it, he cannot sue for the lump sum, but I cannot accept the proposition that, if a man agrees to do a certain amount of work for a lump sum, every breach which he makes of that contract by doing his work badly, or by omitting some small portion of it, is an abandonment of the contract, or is only a performance of part of the contract so that he cannot be paid his lump sum.

Lord Justice Warrington agreed with these judgments.

In *Bolton's* case the plaintiff agreed to install a combined heating and domestic hot water system in the defendant's house at a cost of £560. It was proved that there were certain defects in the work done by the plaintiff, the main being that the heating system did not heat adequately and gave out fumes, and to cure these defects would cost £174. The Court of Appeal, reversing the decision of the County Court Judge, held that the plaintiff had not substantially completed his contract and that he was therefore not entitled to recover the contract price. Lord Justice Cairns in his judgment said, at 1011: 'The main question in the case is whether the defects in workmanship found by the judge to be such as to cost £174 to repair—that is between one third and one quarter of the contract price—were of such a character and amount that the plaintiff could not be said to have substantially performed his contract. That is in my view clearly the legal principle which has to be applied in this case.' Again, at 1013, he said 'In considering whether there was substantial performance, I am of opinion that it is relevant to take into account both the nature of the defects and the proportion between the cost of rectifying them and the contract price. It would be wrong to say that the contractor is only entitled to payment if the defects are so trifling as to be covered by the *de minimis* rule.'

Lord Justice Sachs in his judgment at 1015 said:

So far as the law is concerned, I would merely add that it seems to me to be compactly and accurately stated in *Cheshire and Fifoot's Law of Contract* (7th ed. 1969), 492 in the following terms: . . . 'the present rule is that, so long as there is a substantial performance, the contractor is entitled to the stipulated price, subject only to a cross-action of counterclaim for the omissions or defects in "execution", and to cross action or counterclaim I would of course add "set off".' The converse however is equally correct—if there is not a substantial compliance the contractor cannot recover. It is upon the application of that converse rule that the plaintiff's case here fails. This rule does not now work hardly on a contractor, if only he is prepared to remedy the defects before seeking to resort to litigation to recover the lump sum. It is entirely the fault of the contractor in this instant case that he has placed himself in a difficulty by his refusal on 4 December 1969 to remedy the defects of which complaint was being made.

Applying the principles of law laid down in these cases, with which I agree, to the facts of this case, I am satisfied that, while the cost of installing the insulation in the ceiling of the attic would be a very small figure compared with the contract price, the position is materially different from that which existed in *Dakin's* case in that the plaintiffs, owing no doubt to what I have held to be an erroneous interpretation of what had been agreed in regard to the payment of the £350, have up to the present time refused to do this work which was clearly part of their contract. There has therefore been a refusal by the plaintiffs to carry out part of their contract, and this amounts in law to an abandonment of their contract, which would have disentitled them to payment of the balance of the contract price until they did this work. I should also say that no question arises here as to the defendant having entered into possession and obtained any benefit from the work which has been done, as was the case in *Dakin's* case.

Law Commission Report No. 121 (1983)
(Footnotes abridged.)

. . .

2.25 The principal justification of the present law as it applies to entire contracts is that 'it holds men to their contracts'.[1] The contractor who has agreed to do a job for an all-in price, to be paid when the work is completed, may not then insist on payments on account; much less may he break the contract by leaving the work half-finished and recover payment for what he has done. By refusing him redress except as provided by the contract the law gives him an incentive to complete the job. It may be argued that this incentive would be greatly reduced if he were to be entitled to payment, otherwise than under the contract, in respect of benefits conferred by partial performance.

2.26 The present law may also be justified on the basis that the drastic consequences for the contractor who fails to complete the work to be done under the contract place the other party in a strong bargaining position. It may be argued that this encourages the settlement of disputes in favour of the party not in breach of contract and that in consequence the removal of the hardship that the present law may cause to some could result in more serious and more general hardship to others whom the law now benefits. Finally the present law, whatever its defects, has the merit of being reasonably certain and therefore may be said to have the desirable effect of discouraging litigation.

2.27 However, although both parties may intend that the innocent party should not have to pay any amount in respect of a benefit obtained by him as a result of partial performance of the contract by the party in breach, it is arguable that such a result has a penal flavour and that accordingly it should not lightly be assumed that the parties so intend. The mere postponement of payment of a lump sum by one party until after the other party has completely performed is a normal provision and it is arguable that it should not have such penal overtones.

2.28 In our working paper[2] we considered that this type of provision should not *by itself* preclude the party in breach from recovering an amount which reflects any enrichment which the innocent party has obtained as a result of having had a benefit conferred upon him under the contract by the partial performance. It was this aspect of the present law that in our view constituted a mischief.

. . .

2.29 In considering whether the present law should be retained we have taken into account another factor, namely that in the great majority of contracts, involving substantial sums of money, there will be provision for stage payments. It might therefore be argued that any change in the present law would, in general, only affect contracts between jobbing builders and householders and that in such cases the bargaining position of the parties makes undesirable any such change. However, a number of points may be made in this regard.

2.30 The first point is that, in our view, the mischief we have identified in the present law may arise even in relation to contracts involving substantial sums of money. Not all such contracts will provide for stage payments and even where the parties have made such provision, they will not always have considered or provided for the situation where a stage is not completed. The second point is that many lump sum contracts between householders and jobbing builders involve not insignificant sums—contracts of this type involving several thousand pounds are far from unknown. Accordingly, the mischief which we have identified in the present law may well arise when considerable sums are at stake.

2.31 The final point concerns the bargaining position of the householder and his jobbing builder. Although any alteration in the present law will weaken the bargaining position of the householder, the extent of any such weakening should not be exaggerated. The householder is entitled not only to damages for losses caused by the failure to complete but also to damages for inconvenience.[3] This latter entitlement is a recent development in the law which has occurred since the rule relating to entire contracts was established. In the light of his entitlement to damages in respect of both loss and inconvenience the householder will be in a position where his claim in damages may well exceed whatever the builder is entitled to. Accordingly, any change in the present law which would entitle the builder to make a claim in respect of the work he has done would, in effect, only entitle him to recover money from the householder where the latter has received a significant benefit which exceeds the loss which he has suffered as a result of the breach.

2.32 We considered the justification of the present law but we think that it loses some of its force in view of the fact that the mischief which we have identified is not that the parties can require complete performance before any counter-performance is due, but that under the present law they may, and usually will, be held to have done so merely by providing for postponement of payment. In our view the present law leads to a result which was not necessarily the one which the parties in all cases would have contemplated as flowing from their agreement solely by reason of the postponement of payment.

2.33 Accordingly we consider that our provisional conclusion was correct and recommend that a new remedy should be provided for the party in breach (including, of course, his assignees) where he or a third party acting on his behalf has conferred a benefit on the innocent party by his incomplete or defective performance of an entire contract. We recommend that this new remedy should apply whether the consideration to be furnished by one party for the completion of something to be done by the other consists in promising to pay a sum of money or in promising either to do some other act or to forbear from doing something.

Note of Dissent

I have the misfortune to differ from my colleagues both as regards the principal policy conclusion reached in this report and as to the manner of its implementation. In almost all contracts of any substance today under which one party promises to carry out certain work in return for a consideration to be given by the other, the contract will make provision for stage payments of one sort or another. The facts of modern economic life have demonstrated that payments on account while the work proceeds are a necessity. Both printed and specially prepared contracts will therefore, in almost every case, provide for such payments. Where a written contract does not provide for such payments, the reason may well be that the parties intended that payment would be due if, but only if, the contractor finished the work. The so-called mischief which the report is intended to correct is therefore likely only to exist in relation to small, informal contracts of which the normal example will be a contract between a householder and a jobbing builder to carry out a particular item of work. Experience has shown that it is all too common for such builders not to complete one job of work before moving on to the next. The effect of the report is to remove from the householder almost the only effective sanction he has against the builder not completing the job. In short, he is prevented from saying with any legal effect, 'Unless you come back and finish the job, I shan't pay you a penny'. In my view, the disadvantages in practice of the recommendations contained in the report outweigh the advantages to be gained from the search for theoretically perfect justice between the parties. If the report's recommendations are implemented, the jobbing builder can leave the site and, when the irate and exasperated householder finally brings the contract to an end, send in a bill for the work done up to the time when he abandoned the site. It will then be for the householder to dispute the amount and calculate his counterclaim for damages. To put the burden on the householder in this manner is, in my view, to put him in a disadvantageous position where he negotiates from a position of weakness. It must not be forgotten that it is the builder who has broken the contract, not the householder, and that the contract is one under which the parties agreed that payment would be by lump sum only when the work was done.

(*Signed* Brian Davenport)

1. *Munro v Butt* (1858) E & B 735, 754, per Lord Campbell C.J.
2. Working Paper No. 65, para. 21.
3. *Rawlings v Rentokil Laboratories* [1972] EGD 744.

Note

1. There have been certain statutory modifications of this rule.

Sale of Goods Act 1893 ss 30 and 31

30. (1) Where the seller delivers to the buyer a quantity of goods less than he contracted to sell, the buyer may reject them, but if the buyer accepts the goods so delivered he must pay for them at the contract rate.

(2) Where the seller delivers to the buyer a quantity of goods larger than he contracted to sell, the buyer may accept the goods included in the contract and reject the rest, or he may reject the whole. If the buyer accepts the whole of the goods so delivered he must pay for them at the contract rate.

(3) Where the seller delivers to the buyer the goods he contracted to sell mixed with goods of a different description not included in the contract, the buyer may accept

the goods which are in accordance with the contract and reject the rest, or he may reject the whole.

(4) The provisions of this section are subject to any usage of trade, special agreement, or course of dealing between the parties.

31. (1) Unless otherwise agreed, the buyer of goods is not bound to accept delivery thereof by instalments.

(2) Where there is a contract for the sale of goods to be delivered by stated instalments, which are to be separately paid for, and the seller makes defective deliveries in respect of one or more instalments, or the buyer neglects or refuses to take delivery of or pay for one or more instalments, it is a question in each case depending on the terms of the contract and the circumstances of the case, whether the breach of contract is a repudiation of the whole contract or whether it is a severable breach giving rise to a claim for compensation but not to a right to treat the whole contract as repudiated.

Apportionment Act 1870 ss 2 and 3

2. From and after the passing of this Act all rents, annuities, dividends, and other periodical payments in the nature of income (whether reserved or made payable under an instrument in writing or otherwise) shall, like interest on money lent, be considered as accruing from day to day, and shall be apportionable in respect of time accordingly.
3. The apportioned part of any such rent, annuity, dividend, or other payment shall be payable or recoverable in the case of a continuing rent, annuity, or other such payment when the entire portion of which such apportioned part shall form part shall become due and payable, and not before, and in the case of a rent, annuity, or other such payment determined by re-entry, death, or otherwise when the next entire portion of the same would have been payable if the same had not so determined, and not before.

This Act was applied in the case of *Treacy v Corcoran* (1874) IR 8 CL 40 to award the plaintiff who had resigned from his employment in the middle of a half year, an apportioned part of that half year's salary.

2. Certain contracts may be deemed to be divisible in that they contain separate obligations which may be performed individually. In *Verolme Cork Dockyard Ltd v Shannon Atlantic Fisheries Ltd* 31 July 1978, unrep. Finlay P. in the High Court found that it was a term of a contract made between the plaintiffs and the defendants for the repair of a ship, that a substantial payment on account would be made by the defendants when a reasonably high proportion of the work had been carried out. The judge decided this despite the fact that the request for a payment on account did not precisely comply with the power to make such a request reserved in the printed conditions supplied by the plaintiffs. The defence argument that no payment was due until completion of the entire of the repairs was not accepted.
3. If one party's failure to perform their obligations is caused by some act or default of the other party *quantum meruit* may be available. See *Arterial Drainage Co. Ltd v Rathangan River Drainage Board* (1880) 6 LR (Ir.) 513.

B. Time of Performance

The time of performance may be deemed to be 'of the essence of the contract'. In such a case failure to perform on time may result in a discharge of the contract.

William G. Nolan *v* George Driscoll (HC) 25 April 1978, unrep.

In December 1975 the defendant agreed to sell a house to the plaintiff. Due to registration of title problems the sale was delayed. On 2 March 1977, the defendant's solicitors notified the plaintiff that as the registration difficulties were due to be settled within a few days, completion would be required by 30 March. Time was made of the essence of the contract in this respect. As the sale was not completed by the set date, the defendant purported to rescind the contract and the plaintiff sued for specific performance.

McWilliam J.:

. . . it is unfortunate that the defendant should finally have lost his patience at this stage. I am of opinion, however, that he was entitled to ask the plaintiff to complete on the title he had shown and that the time given was reasonable. . . .

. . . Accordingly, although it is with some hesitation, I will dismiss the claim for specific performance.

Sepia Ltd and Opel Ltd *v* M. & P. Hanlon Ltd and Another (HC) 23 January 1979, unrep.

The defendants agreed to sell two parcels of land to the plaintiffs. Block A was the subject of a contract which expressly fixed the closing date and expressly made time of the essence. The agreement was subject to the plaintiff's obtaining planning permission. In the events which occured the closing date in respect of both contracts became 31 December 1976. By notice of 7 April 1977 the defendants called on the plaintiffs to close both sales within three months, and made time the essence of the contract. As the sales were not closed, the defendants claimed to be entitled to retain the money paid by the plaintiffs on the signing of the two contracts.

Costello J.:

. . .

1. In the first contract the parties had expressly made time of the essence of the contract when they provided that the sale was to be closed on 1 May 1975. Condition 11 relating to planning permission must be interpreted in the light of the necessity strictly to observe the date set for closing. The result is, in my opinion, that if the plaintiffs had failed to obtain planning permission by 1 May 1975 and if the closing date was not extended by mutual agreement then the defendants were entitled to treat the contract as at an end if the plaintiffs refused to complete—the absence of planning permission would not have excused the non-performance by the plaintiffs of the contract.

2. The second contract of 16 May did not make time of the essence of the contract in relation to the sale of Block B and when it amended the closing date of the first contract it did not provide that in respect of the new closing date time was to be of the essence of the contract. In addition it will be observed that the two sales were to be closed simultaneously. It was not, in my opinion, the intention of the parties that time was to be the essence of the first contract but not of the second contract. The result was that two possible closing dates in respect of both sales were agreed to but time was not made the essence of the contract in respect of either sale.

3. The second sale was not made subject to planning permission being obtained but the first sale remained subject to special condition 11. The result of the amendment of the first contract was that if the plaintiffs were in default in closing the sales on either of the dates specified then the vendors could serve a notice making time the essence of the contract and fixing a reasonable time for their completion. If time was made the essence of the contract and the period for completion given a reasonable one then the position at the expiration of the notice would be this. If planning permission had then been obtained the plaintiffs were bound to complete both sales. If planning permission had not been obtained then the plaintiffs could waive this provision of the contract (for reasons given in the next succeeding contract) and complete both sales. If however the plaintiffs did not waive special condition 11 then the first contract would come to an end at the expiration of the notice (the condition relating to planning permission not having been complied with) (see *Smith v Butler* [1900] 1 QB 694; *Aberfoyle Plantation Ltd v Cheng* [1960] AC 115). Alternatively, the plaintiffs' refusal to complete would amount to a repudiation of the contract entitling the defendants to treat it as at an end. In either case, the defendant would be entitled to retain the non-refundable deposit of £30,000. As to the second contract (which was not expressly subject to a condition relating to planning permission) the plaintiffs' failure to complete at the expiration of the notice would entitle the defendants to treat this contract as at an end and to retain the non-refundable deposit of £20,000.

4. The evidence satisfies me that the clause in the first contract relating to planning permission had been inserted for the exclusive benefit of the plaintiffs. This means that it could be waived by them.

The principle that a condition inserted exclusively for the benefit of one party can be waived by that party is referred to in *Heron Garage Properties Ltd v Moss* [1974] 1 WLR 148. The plaintiffs therefore could have waived condition 11 if they wished to close the sale in the absence of planning permission.

5. The two contracts remained separate and independent contracts notwithstanding the provision that they were to be closed simultaneously. In certain events the parties might have been under an obligation to complete one but not the other. In the events that have happened, however, a single notice fixing a date for the simultaneous closing of the two contracts was permissible.

. . .

Reasonableness of the notice

The legal principles to be applied in this case are clear and well established. If a stipulation as to time is not of the essence of a contract then when one party has been guilty of undue delay the other may give notice requiring the contract to be performed within a reasonable time specified in the notice. In considering the reasonableness of the time so limited the court will consider not merely what remains to be done at the date of the notice but all the circumstances of the case, including the previous delay of the purchaser and the attitude of the vendor to it. If the notice is a reasonable one the vendor may at its expiration treat the contract as at an end if the purchaser refuses to complete (see *Stikney v Keeble* |1915| AC 386; and *Ajit v Sammy* |1967| 1 AC 255). In this case there was without any doubt undue delay on the part of the plaintiffs after 31 December 1976. In the previous July the plaintiffs had intimated that they were not prepared to close and on 7 September they had been made aware that their request for an extension of time had been refused. By 7 April 1977 three months had expired from the contractual closing date and the plaintiffs had by this time made it perfectly clear that they were not going to close the sale for an indefinite period (if at all). In these circumstances the defendants became entitled to serve a notice specifying a closing date and making time the essence of the contract. The real issue in the case, however, is whether the length of time given by the notice of 7 April was a reasonable one.

I have come to the conclusion that in all the circumstances of this case, the notice given was in fact a reasonable one. . . .

Daniel Crean *v* David Drinan [1983] ILRM 82

The plaintiff entered into a contract to purchase a public house from the defendant. The closing date was to be 4 May 1979. Clause 2 provided that the contract was subject to the defendant obtaining an assignment of any outstanding third party interest in the property on or before the closing date. In the event of the deed of sale not being executed the deposit was to be returned. As the assignment was not available by the agreed date, the plaintiff decided not to proceed with the sale and sought the return of his deposit.

Barrington J.:
. . .

|Counsel for the plaintiff| relies principally upon the decision in *Aberfoyle Plantations Ltd v Cheng* |1959| 3 All ER 910. In that case, which was a decision of the Privy Council, the court drew a distinction between the flexibility which courts of equity have adopted in the past in relation to the closing date in contracts for the sale of land and the rigidity which courts have adopted toward dates fixed by conditions on which the very existence of the contract depends. The court adopted with approval a passage from the judgment of Maugham J. in *Re Sandwell Park Colliery Co.*; *Field v The Company* |1929| 1 Ch. 277 in which he stated at 282:

> Courts of equity, in dealing with actions for specific performance relating to land, have been accustomed to give effect to the real intention, rather than to the precise words, fixing the date for completion. The effect is that a clause fixing a date for completion is equivalent to a clause stating that completion shall be on that date or within a reasonable time thereafter. But there is no ground for a similar construction in the case of a condition upon which the validity of the contract as one for sale depends. The distinction is obvious. In the first case both parties are bound and a moderate delay in completion is thought not to injure either. In the latter, the very existence of the mutual obligations is dependent upon the performance of the condition. The purchasers do not know in the first instance if their purchase money will ever be required. In general, and in the present case, there is no promise or undertaking by the vendor that the condition will be fulfilled. Equity has, I think

never applied its liberal views as to time to such a condition. If a date is mentioned, the condition must be exactly complied with. If a date is not mentioned, the condition must be fulfilled within a reasonable time; there is no difference between the views of law and equity in considering what is a reasonable time, and the uncertain position of the purchasers must be borne in mind.

In *Aberfoyle Plantations v Cheng* the Privy Council having referred to the overriding rule that the meaning of a contract is to be found in the intention of the parties as expressed in, or to be implied from, the language they have used, went on to adopt 'as warranted by authority and manifestly reasonable in themselves' the following general principles of interpretation:

i. Where a conditional contract of sale fixes the date for the completion of the sale then the condition must be fulfilled by that date;
ii. Where a conditional contract of sale fixes no date for completion of the sale, then the condition must be fulfilled within a reasonable time;
iii. Where a conditional contract of sale fixes (whether specifically or by reference to the date fixed for completion) the date by which the condition is to be fulfilled, then the date so fixed must be strictly adhered to, and the time allowed is not to be extended by reference to equitable principles.

McWilliam J. appears to have adopted this third principle in *Maloney v Elf Investments Ltd* (HC) 1979 No. 295Sp 7 December 1979. The condition under discussion in that case provided that the 'sale is subject to the purchasers getting full planning permission before 31 July 1978'. Discussing this condition McWilliam J. says:

This can only mean that the contract is only to be enforceable if the permission is obtained by that date. Certainly no other meaning has been suggested to me. But it has been argued on behalf of the defendant that time was not, in this respect, made the essence of the contract and that a reasonable time ought to be allowed to obtain the permission by analogy to the principle that time for completing a contract is regarded in equity as the date fixed for completion or a reasonable time thereafter unless time has been made of the essence of the contract in this respect.
I was referred to conditions 4 and 28 of the general conditions in the contract. Condition 4 is the normal condition relating to payment of interest should the purchase not be completed on or before the closing date and condition 28 is the normal condition providing for service of notice to complete within twenty eight days save where the special conditions provide that time should be made of the essence of the contract in respect of the closing date. I do not consider that these conditions give me any assistance and I was not referred to any authority in support of the proposition that a reasonable time ought to be allowed for the performance of the condition. I have however, been referred on behalf of the plaintiff to the case of *Aberfoyle Plantations Ltd v Cheng* [1959] 3 WLR 1011 in which this proposition was rejected and Lord Jenkins said, at 1016: '(iii) Where a conditional contract of sale fixes . . . the date by which the condition is to be fulfilled, then the date so fixed must be strictly adhered to, and the time allowed is not to be extended by reference to any equitable principles.'

I was concerned by the fact that special condition no. 2 in the present case refers in terms not to '4 May 1979' but to 'closing date'.

However this matter appears to be covered by the passage in parenthesis in the third principle set out in the passage quoted above from the decision in *Aberfoyle Plantations v Cheng*. That principle is to the effect that where a conditional contract of sale fixes (whether specifically or by reference to the date fixed for completion) the date by which the condition is to be fulfilled, then the date so fixed must be strictly adhered to. . . .

. . .

[Counsel for the defendant] submitted that special condition no. 2 is not a condition precedent to the validity of the contract as a contract for sale. . . .

. . .

He relied on *Property & Bloodstock Ltd v Emerton* [1967] 2 All ER 839. In that case the clause provided that the sale was subject to the vendor's obtaining the consent of the landlords to the assignment of the lease to the purchaser. The date fixed by the contract for completion of the sale was 24 October 1966. By that date the vendor had not in fact obtained the consent of the landlord but Ungoed-Thomas J., distinguishing *Aberfoyle Plantations Ltd v Cheng* held that the obtaining of the consent of the landlord was not a condition precedent to the validity of the contract but was a matter of title to be attended to before completion.

In a passage of the report Ungoed-Thomas J. states at 848: 'If what the agreement provides for is that title and not the creation of a contract of sale is subject to that consent being obtained, then that consent has to be forthcoming by the date at which title has to be established, normally actual completion.'

It appears to me that the decision in *Property & Bloodstock Ltd v Emerton* turned upon the actual wording of the contract in that case and upon the fact that the matter at issue was one of title only. It may well be in the present case that the matter at issue was also one of title, but it was a matter which [the plaintiff's solicitor], for legitimate reasons of his own, saw fit to make the subject matter of a special condition in the contract. The contract is expressed to be subject to the performance of that condition and in the event of the deed referred to not being executed the special condition itself provides that 'the purchaser shall be refunded his deposit but without interest, costs or compensation of any kind.' . . .

SECTION TWO—AGREEMENT

A contract may be rescinded or varied by subsequent agreement

A. RESCISSION

Rescission involves releasing the parties from their obligations under the contract. For a contract to be terminated by mutual agreement ('accord'), consideration ('satisfaction') must be present. In an executory contract consideration is provided by the parties yielding up their rights against the other. However, if the contract has been executed by one of the parties rescission will be effective only if additional consideration is provided.

B. Variation

A variation involves altering a certain term or terms of the contract. Consideration will be required for a variation to be effective. In *McQuaid v Lynam* |1955| IR 564 (see p. 233 above), Kenny J. discussed the situations in which a variation would have to comply with s. 2 of the Statute of Frauds 1695.

C. Waiver

The term waiver may be used to describe a total rescission of the contract, or a variation supported by consideration, or a forbearance.

McKillop and Another *v* McMullan [1979] NI 85

The defendant entered into a contract to sell land to the plaintiffs. Under this contract the defendant was entitled to a right of way over a road which the plaintiffs were to construct on part of the land. The contract was signed subject to the plaintiffs obtaining planning permission for the construction of the road. The stated completion date of 17 June 1974 passed and the defendant continued to enquire as to the existence of planning permission. He rejected the plaintiffs' suggestions that the planning condition be deleted from the contract. Finally, on 13 November 1975, the defendant without prior warning returned the deposit and notified the plaintiffs that he regarded the contract as no longer binding due to the non-fulfilment of the planning permission condition. Shortly afterwards permission was obtained and the plaintiffs sought specific performance of the contract.

Murray J.:

For the plaintiffs |counsel| put forward two main submissions:

(1) that the planning condition was inserted for the sole and exclusive benefit of the plaintiffs and that they could and did unilaterally waive it; but

(2) in the alternative, that if it could not be treated as waived, time was not of the essence of the contract in relation to the planning condition, and a reasonable period of notice to make it so would have been necessary on the part of the defendant before he became entitled to say that the failure to fulfil the condition had rendered the contract void.

. . .

For the defendant |counsel| submitted:

(1) that a distinction had to be drawn between the effect of a time stipulation in relation to the completion of an unconditional contract of sale, and a time stipulation related to the fulfilment of a condition precedent to the taking effect of a contract of sale;

(2) that whereas equity might treat a provision saying that completion was to take place on a certain date as meaning on the date or within a reasonable time thereafter, it treated a time stipulation in relation to the fulfilment of a condition precedent as absolute, subject only to the operation of the doctrines of waiver and estoppel;

(3) that in the present case it was a condition precedent to the parties being bound respectively to sell and buy, that by the completion date, *viz.* 17 June 1974, the planning condition should be fulfilled and

(4) that at any time after 17 June 1974—the planning condition being then unfulfilled—it was open to the defendant without prior notice to the plaintiffs to declare the contract at an end for non-fulfilment of the condition precedent.

. . .

I now come to my decision in the case.

In my view [counsel's] first submission on behalf of the plaintiffs, *viz.* that the planning condition is a stipulation incorporated in the contract for the exclusive benefit of the plaintiffs—and therefore waivable unilaterally by them—is quite unsustainable. On the face of the contract the defendant is entitled to a right of way with or without vehicles over the access road, and to suggest that it would not be of benefit to him to have a road lawfully and properly constructed in accordance with a valid planning permission does not bear a moment's examination: from the judgment of Brightman J. in *Heron Garage Properties v Moss* [1974] 1 WLR 148, it appears that in determining whether a stipulation is for the exclusive benefit of one party so as to be waivable unilaterally by him, it must be obviously so on the face of the contract.

It is my view that [counsel for the defendant] is correct and [counsel for the plaintiff] not so in the analysis of the legal situation created by the planning condition and the completion date condition. The planning condition created a condition precedent to the coming into existence of an effective and enforceable contract of sale, and on the basis of the principles enunciated in *Aberfoyle Plantations v Cheng* [1960] AC 115 I regard the contract, *as originally made between the parties,* as requiring the fulfilment of that condition by 17 June 1974, the completion date. (In passing I comment that in his opening the plaintiff's counsel suggested that 17 June 1974, was not the correct date for completion, but there was nothing in the evidence to bear this out and in my view that date must be taken as the originally agreed date.) It follows that if on 17 June 1974, the defendant had said to the plaintiffs—'You have now failed to obtain the necessary planning permission in accordance with the planning condition and the contract is therefore null and void' he (the defendant) would have been entitled in law to take up that attitude. In fact, of course, he did nothing of the kind and as late as 17 June 1975—exactly one year later—we find the defendant's solicitors writing: 'Our client insists that the contract be performed as it is written.' The inference is irresistible, and [counsel for the defendant] did not really try to resist it, that the defendant had waived the original failure of the plaintiffs to fulfil the planning condition, but basing himself on *Barclay v Messenger* (1874) 43 LJ Eq 449 [counsel] said it was only a qualified waiver. I think he is right about this. The defendant by not insisting on avoiding the contract on 17 June 1974, did not thereby lose his right to insist on a fulfilment of the planning condition as a condition precedent to the taking effect of the sale contract. However, the crucial question in this: what date was to be substituted for 17 June 1974, as the date by which the condition precedent had to be fulfilled? There was no difficulty about this in *Barclay v Messenger* because another specific date was substituted for the original date in the contract and the substituted date was taken by the court to be the relevant date. In this case no specified date was substituted. What then was the position? [Counsel] says that at any time after 17 June 1974, the defendant was entitled *without warning* to say to the plaintiffs—'I will wait no longer: you have not obtained the planning permission and the contract is void'—as he purported to do by his solicitors' letter of 13 November 1975. My opinion is that such a course of action was not open to the defendant. Clearly he was entitled to fix a new date for the fulfilment of the condition precedent, but in my judgment the principles of equity required him to give the plaintiffs reasonable notice of that date so that they had at least an opportunity of fulfilling the condition in time. I think this reasoning applies with particular force when one considers that even after a year—as I have pointed out—the defendant showed no sign whatever of calling the contract off for the non-fulfilment of the planning condition. I do not overlook the defendant's solicitors' letter of 7 July 1975, in which no doubt the solicitors made a distinctly frosty comment on the delay, but there is not in that letter a word of warning that the defendant is going to rely on the non-fulfilment of the condition precedent.

In the result I hold that the letter of 13 November 1975, was ineffective to avoid the contract and since the plaintiffs fulfilled the planning condition by obtaining the necessary planning permission on or about 26 November 1975, the contract of sale became effective and enforceable on that date. In case there should be any doubt about the matter I must say expressly that in my view the obtaining of the permission dated 25 November 1975, is a complete compliance with the planning condition, notwithstanding that the Roads Act consent—which of course is not referred to in the planning condition—had not, and still has not, been obtained.

Having regard to the basis upon which I have decided the case I will give leave at this late stage to the plaintiffs to amend their reply to plead a waiver by the defendant of the plaintiffs' original failure to fulfil the planning condition. In essence the point is a legal one arising on the correspondence and I am satisfied that no injustice will be done to the defendant by giving the plaintiffs leave to amend.

In the result the plaintiffs succeed in the action and I will decree specific performance of the contract.

Tony Dugdale and David Yates, 'Variation, Waiver and Estoppel—A re-Appraisal' (1976) 39 MLR 680

(Footnotes abridged.)

. . . A post-contractual representation, in this context, means a representation made, either by words or conduct, by one party to the other, after the contract has been made. This may take place whilst the contract is still executory or after a breach has occurred, but the legal effect of the representation will be different depending upon which of these two categories it falls into. There has been considerable confusion as to the possible legal effects of post-contractual representations and as to the requirements necessary before such effects are operative. . . .

. . .

At common law, such a representation may have effect as a simple variation or a rescission of the old contract followed by the making of a new one. The fine distinction between these two concepts is material where written evidence is required for the formal validity of the contract, but is immaterial in so far as both require consideration. In the absence of consideration, such a representation may still have effect at common law as a waiver, although there is a confusion as to whether it then binds both parties or just the representor and as to whether it is absolute or temporary in effect. Equity's attempt to deal with the problem of absence of consideration in such situations has been to develop the doctrine of equitable or promissory estoppel. Neither the precise requirements nor the effect of the doctrine appear to be settled. The overall picture is thus confusing and confused.

There are two main reasons for this confusion. First, no clear distinction seems to have been drawn in the cases between representations made whilst the contract is still executory (termed in this article 'pre-breach representation') and representation made after a breach has occurred (termed in this article 'post-breach representations'). This distinction is vital because the effects of the representation in the two situations are entirely different. In the case of pre-breach representations, their purported effect is to alter the obligations arising under the contract, whilst the effect of a post-breach representation is to alter the already established remedial consequences of the breach. As the effects of the representation are thus different, so too should the requirements necessary before the representations can be said to have any effect be different. The second source of confusion seems to be a terminological one, in that both pre- and post-breach representations seem to go under the generic name of 'waiver'.

The term 'waiver' is a troublesome term in the law of contract. It is used with different meanings and there are, therefore, necessarily conflicting judicial statements as to its requisites. When members of the bench take issue with each other on the correct meaning of the term it is, perhaps, because the different legal effects of a waiver have not been kept clear. It is possible to isolate the following meanings for the term:

1. An agreement for sufficient consideration, made as part of or in substitution for an obligation previously made and still unperformed, which provides for a performance different from or substituted for that to which the parties were bound and entitled by their original obligation. This is sometimes called an accord and has the effect of a variation of the original contract.

2. A promise or permission express or implied, unsupported by consideration, to excuse performance of an obligation not due at the time when the promise is made. This is sometimes called forbearance.

3. A promise or permission express or implied, supported only by action in reliance thereon, to excuse performance in the future of a term of the contract. This is applicable to terms which are still to be performed and the promise may be binding in equity though unsupported by consideration.

4. A promise by each party to a contract to the other, made after *both* parties are in breach, that certain rights or certain obligations are to be varied, or not to be enforced against the other. This 'waiver' is supported by consideration in that each party gives up his rights against the other under the original contract.

5. A promise express or implied, made without consideration, to give up a defence which has already arisen or to be liable in spite of an excuse which has already freed the promisor, and where, therefore, there can be no promissory estoppel of the sort mentioned in 3 above. The effect of this waiver is that the representor is deprived of all remedies or defences (whichever is appropriate) under the contract.

6. An election whereby a party who has a choice of several rights or remedies adopts one and thereby destroys all right to the others. In the event of certain breaches of contract taking place, the innocent party may have a choice of remedies. He may repudiate the contract and sue for damages or he may elect to treat the breach as non-repudiatory, affirm the contract, and content himself with the remedy of damages. Once he has elected for damages rather than repudiation, he cannot normally change his mind. The basis of this rule seems to be that, where a party injured by a breach definitely manifests a choice of a remedy available to him in the place of some other alternative remedy, such a manifestation will bar an action for the latter remedy. The reason for this is the injustice that would result to the party being sued if the representor were allowed so to conduct himself that a particular remedy (e.g. damages) appeared to be the remedy desired so that the party against whom the remedy is sought makes a substantial change of position in reliance on the manifestation of intention, and then another remedy (e.g. repudiation) was in fact asked for.

It will be noted that the first three types of waiver arise *prior* to breach or performance of a contractual obligation; the last three types arise *after* breach or performance. Thus, the first three types of waiver can, in the true sense, be said to effect a variation of the obligations undertaken in the contract. The other three types cannot and will only be material in relation to any remedies that may be sought after breach. The terminological confusion resulting from calling all six types 'waiver' has not only disguised the distinction between pre-breach and post-breach representations but has also contributed to the failure to discuss the extent to which the requirement of consideration can and should be dispensed with in a situation arising from a post-contractual representation. Obviously, the extent to which this is possible will depend upon the purported effect of the representation, which in turn depends upon whether it is made before or after a breach has occurred.

. . .

Pre-breach representations
This type of representation is one made whilst the contract is still wholly or partially executory. The effect of such a representation is to alter the terms of the contract as originally agreed by the parties. In this case, all the requirements of a consensual variation save that of consideration must be present. The problems here were highlighted in a recent decision of the House of Lords, that in Woodhouse A.C. Israel Cocoa Ltd S.A. v Nigerian Produce Marketing Co. Ltd.[1]

In this case, the appellant English buyers had entered into fourteen contracts with the respondent sellers for the purchase of cocoa. The contracts provided for the sale of the cocoa at a price payable in Nigerian pounds, but, shortly before the devaluation of sterling, the parties, by an exchange of letters involving themselves and the Cocoa Association of London, agreed that the price could be paid in sterling in London or Nigerian pounds in Lagos. The sellers subsequently withdrew this arrangement and a new arrangement was reached whereby the sellers consented to the temporary alternative of payment in sterling in Lagos. The buyers claimed that the effect of this arrangement was either that of a contractual variation of the money of account from Nigerian to sterling pounds or of a representation that the sellers had waived Nigerian pounds in favour of pounds sterling as the money of account in such a way as to stop them from asserting otherwise. Therefore, the buyers claimed to discharge the payment of the price by paying one pound sterling for every Nigerian pound in the contract price. The sellers claimed that only the money of payment had been altered and that the buyers must pay so much sterling as was necessary to purchase the quantity of Nigerian pounds expressed in the contract price. The House of Lords unanimously held for the sellers, rejecting the buyers' arguments both as to variation and as to estoppel.

(A) Variation (accord)
Three of their Lordships expressly considered the possibility of a variation both in respect of the first arrangement and the substituted temporary alternative. As for the first arrangement, Viscount Dilhorne found that it varied only the money of payment. Lord Cross found that it varied the money of account but both he and Lord Hailsham L.C. (who did not state whether the money of payment or the money of account was varied) found that there had been a withdrawal of the variation with the acquiescence of the buyers. However, surely consideration must be necessary both for the first variation and also for the withdrawal of that variation since such withdrawal amounts either to a further variation or a rescission. As to the consideration supporting the first variation, only Lord Hailsham L.C. expressly dealt with this point, stating that the attitude of 'a modern court' should be that 'businessmen know their own business best even when they appear to grant an indulgence, and in the present case I do not think that there would have been insuperable difficulty in spelling out consideration from the earlier correspondence.' Perhaps this heralds a new approach to the requirement of consideration in commercial cases but, applying the traditional approach, Chitty suggests that consideration for the variation might be found in the fact that

sterling could have been revalued as against the Nigerian pound and that this variation *could* have been detrimental to the buyers.[2] However, this was not, as a matter of economic actuality, a possibility, nor was it in the contemplation of the parties. Perhaps the most convincing explanation is provided by Lord Salmon who, whilst not expressly discussing variation, remarked that the buyers' agreement to the sellers' conversion would increase the amount of business the sellers would be able to do and hence it might be argued that the buyers did confer a benefit upon the sellers by the variation. As to the consideration necessary to support the withdrawal of the variation, there is no discussion. Lord Hailsham L.C. remarked that the first variation was binding when accepted, at least until the sellers gave reasonable notice to terminate the variation. If this means that on the construction of this particular varied term it could be withdrawn by reasonable notice, then this must be based on a term to be implied into the contract as a result of the variation. If it means, on the other hand, that as a matter of law a variation can be withdrawn by reasonable notice, then this is not in conformity with the existing law and is confusing the concept of variation with the effect of a representation unsupported by consideration, operating as an estoppel. It is, in any event, an open question whether the buyers acquiesced in the withdrawal of the variation but their Lordships seem unanimous in their view that they did.

As for the temporary arrangement, Lord Hailsham L.C. and Viscount Dilhorne found that the correspondence referred to the money of payment. Lord Cross accepted that from the buyers' point of view the correspondence could be taken to refer to the money of account but he held equally that from the sellers' point of view it referred to the money of payment and that as the parties were thus not *ad idem* there was no variation. Viscount Dilhorne agreed that if, contrary to his view already expressed, the correspondence did refer to the money of account, then there was still no variation as the parties were not *ad idem*, since the final letter from the sellers most definitely referred to the money of payment.

With respect it is submitted that the weakness of the approach taken by Viscount Dilhorne and Lord Cross is that although they both concluded that the sellers' letter could not refer to the money of account by virtue of the effect of the first arrangement, there is nevertheless a conflict between their interpretation of the first arrangement and their reasoning consequent upon that interpretation. Lord Cross found that because the first arrangement was concerned with a variation (subsequently withdrawn) of the money of account, the subsequent arrangement must, from the sellers' viewpoint, only be concerned with the money of payment as it was clear that the sellers were no longer concerned with the money of account. Viscount Dilhorne argued that as the first arrangement was concerned with a variation of the money of payment, and that variation had been withdrawn, the subsequent arrangement must, from the sellers' viewpoint, also be concerned with the money of payment because it was clear that the sellers were not prepared to concede more than this. Both views cannot be right, but whichever view is preferred it is difficult to see why those objective criteria of interpretation for resolving ambiguities in relation to the formation of a contract should be jettisoned in favour of a highly subjective approach to terms amounting to a variation.

(B) *Estoppel*

All five Law Lords found that the sellers' representation of their willingness to take sterling in Lagos as a temporary alternative could not give the buyer any right to insist that the money of account should be sterling. Nor could the sellers be estopped from claiming that the money of account was Nigerian pounds, even though the buyers had so interpreted the representation and given evidence that they had relied upon it in this way. The unanimous reasoning was that a representation must be unambiguous in order to found an estoppel and the representation in this case was ambiguous in that it could reasonably carry the meanings put upon it either by the sellers or the buyers. Viscount Dilhorne and Lord Salmon only state the proposition that in order to found an estoppel the representation must be clear and unequivocal. The other three Law Lords reason that, were the law otherwise, it might be possible for an ambiguous representation, which would be insufficient to give rise to a variation, to be effective as a promissory estoppel and thus, for all practical purposes, to have the same effect as a variation.

Lord Cross puts this most clearly by stating that a person who makes a representation in response to a request for indulgence cannot be in a worse position than if the request for indulgence was an offer and the granting of it the acceptance of that offer. Therefore, before a representation can have the effect of varying the terms of a contract through the doctrine of promissory estoppel, the negotiations between the representor and the representee must contain all the elements of a contract save that of consideration. Hence it is necessary that the conduct of the representor and the representee should be capable of analysis into the concepts of offer and acceptance and there must also be evidence that the parties intended to alter their legal relationship.

Logically, this reasoning should apply to all representations purporting to alter the terms of a contract. Unfortunately, none of their Lordships extended his reasoning in this way. In distinguishing those cases in which ambiguous representations by conduct have been held to be effective, their Lordships remained victims of their terminology. The cases were distinguished as being concerned with estoppel by a representation of fact as opposed to promissory estoppel. However, it is recognised that a representation of fact made by the conduct of one party can constitute the acceptance of an offer to enter a contract. Surely, such a representation by conduct can also give rise to an implication that a contract has been varied. Thus, to base the distinction on the difference between representations of fact and intent does not seem to accord with their Lordships' own views that a person who makes a request for an indulgence, which is granted, must be able to show, before the agreement is enforceable, that it is susceptible of analysis into the component parts necessary for contractual formation. Their Lordships should have distinguished the authorities as being cases where the effect of the representation was not intended to alter the legal relations between the parties. It is precisely this failure to distinguish the requirements of a representation according to its effect rather than according to its terminological classification which has produced the conceptual difficulties in this area of law.

Post-breach representations

It has been observed that the true dichotomy is that which arises between representations made before performance or breach and those made afterwards. What is required in both cases is a greater emphasis on the purported effect of a post-contractual representation and less emphasis on the terminology with which its effect is described. It is just such a terminological disagreement with the judge at first instance that led to the somewhat unsatisfactory decision of the Court of Appeal in the case of *Panchaud Frères S.A. v Etablissements General Grain Co.*[3]

This case concerned a contract for the sale of a quantity of maize c.i.f. Antwerp. The contract provided for shipment during June/July 1965 and also provided that the bill of lading should be considered proof of the date of shipment in the absence of evidence to the contrary. The sellers tendered a quantity of maize under a bill of lading dated 31 July 1965. The date of shipment had been incorrectly stated on the bill of lading completed by the shipper engaged by the sellers. The correct date appeared on the quality certificate issued at the time of shipment. So, the sellers had broken the contract by not shipping the goods during the contractual shipment period. This breach would normally have given the buyers a right to repudiate the contract. However, before the goods arrived the buyers accepted the shipping documents from the sellers without examining them with a sufficient degree of care to discover the discrepancy between the dates on the bill of lading and the quality certificate. The buyers only discovered the sellers' breach of contract when trying to reject the goods on other insufficient grounds. The buyers then argued that they were entitled to reject the goods for late shipment. The sellers argued that by accepting the shipping documents the buyers had represented, by their conduct, that they would not reject the goods. The sellers were not claiming that this representation had the effect of altering the terms of the contract, for by then a breach had already occurred. The sellers conceded that the buyers could still claim damages for late shipment. It was the sellers' contention that the buyers' conduct had manifested an election for the remedy of damages sufficient to deprive them of the right to repudiate.

The arbitrator upheld the sellers. However, Roskill J. rejected their claim. He held that the buyers *could not* have been expected to reject the bill of lading with a *prima facie* correct date on it merely because, accompanying it and for a different purpose, was a quality certificate with a different date. Hence the buyers' conduct did not amount to an unambiguous representation that whatever the true facts as to shipment, they would waive their right to reject the goods. The ambiguity lay in the shipping documents being unclear as to whether there had been late shipment, and hence acceptance of the bill of lading was not an unambiguous acceptance of the true state of affairs. Roskill J. gave a further reason for his decision in that the buyers had not waived the right to reject for late shipment because they had not got actual knowledge of the breach. At most they had constructive notice of it and a notion of constructive notice is unknown in commercial law.

The Court of Appeal unanimously reversed Roskill J.'s decision, holding that the crucial factor was the effect of the buyers' conduct upon the sellers. As the buyers had, by their conduct, represented to the sellers that the contract would not be repudiated, it would now be unjust to allow the buyers to depart from this representation. The court was clearly influenced by the view of the arbitrator, representing the opinion of commercial men, that the buyers should have read the shipping documents carefully and realised that shipment had been late and, therefore, must bear the consequences of their fault. It is true that if both the bill of lading and the quality certificate contained statements of the late shipment then the justice of the case would clearly lie against the buyer if he accepted the documents without reading them. However, it is less clear that justice is with the sellers where, as in the instant case, the shipper, engaged by the seller, has deliberately falsified the date of shipment in the bill of lading. Why should the buyers believe the statement in the quality certificate rather than that in the bill of lading, especially since it is an implied condition in every c.i.f. contract that a properly dated bill of lading shall be procured and tendered? Only Cross L.J. seemed to be troubled by the point, but he avoids the issue by stating that the arbitrator must have considered the point and found strong reasons for thinking that the buyers ought to have believed the date in the quality certificate rather than the bill of lading.

A more fundamental criticism of the case relates to the way in which the Court of Appeal dealt with the conclusion drawn by Roskill J. that the representation, to be effective, must have been unambiguous and made with actual knowledge of the facts giving rise to the right to reject. The Court of Appeal disagreed with Roskill J.'s assessment on the ground that the case does not involve 'waiver' strictly so-called. Lord Denning M.R. describes the case as one of 'estoppel by conduct', the basis of which was the unfairness to the representee of any departure from the state of affairs he believed to exist as a result of the representation. Winn L.J., whilst maintaining that this was not a case of traditional estoppel, held that it was an example of an 'inchoate doctrine—a criterion of what is fair conduct between the parties.'

This difference of opinion as to terminology demonstrates the unsatisfactory character of the *Panchaud Frères* decision. There seems little purpose in using different terminology. The old doctrine of waiver as enunciated by Roskill J., and the new 'inchoate doctrine' as enunciated by the Court of Appeal, are both based on the concept of unfairness, or what is just and equitable between the parties. The Court of Appeal's new doctrine will, *ipso facto*, be applicable in all cases where the old doctrine of waiver would have applied, and the legal effect of the new doctrine is the same as the old, although it is, of course, wider in ambit. Since it would appear that the old concept of waiver has been eclipsed by the new, and since the new concept *embraces* the old, why *distinguish* the old concept from the new on the basis of technicalities? The legal *consequences* are exactly the same for both parties whether one requires actual knowledge and terms the situation 'waiver' or looks to the unfairness of the case and terms it 'estoppel by conduct'. This concentration on terminology disguises the real issue in question, which is the effect that the representation is claimed to have and the requirements that must be satisfied by the representation before it can be said to have that proposed effect.

The *purported* effect of the representation in this case is of an election of remedies and whether or not this effect is achieved should be determined by reference to the requirements for a proper election. The crucial question then becomes whether actual knowledge of the breach which has occurred, and an unambiguous representation that one remedy is to be sought to the exclusion of the others, are necessary for an election to take place. The existing authorities seem to indicate that acceptance of the goods without an *actual* knowledge of a breach affecting the goods, amounts to an election and a consequent loss of the right to reject. The rights to reject may be lost by waiver under s. 11 (1) (a) of the Sale of Goods Act 1893, which requires actual knowledge of the facts giving rise to the right to reject or by acceptance under s. 11 (1) (c); but the right to reject may be lost by *acceptance* where there is no such knowledge. Where the right to reject is lost by waiver or acceptance (and in this context waiver really seems to mean an election of remedies) the right to damages normally survives. A buyer under a c.i.f. contract who takes the documents with the knowledge that they are defective loses his right to reject the documents. He is further prevented from rejecting the goods on the ground of defective documents. If he takes up the documents in ignorance of facts giving him the right to reject, he will not be taken to have waived his right to reject the documents or the goods although he may still lose his right to reject the goods by acceptance of them in ignorance of a breach, by virtue of s. 11 (1)(c) of the 1893 Sale of Goods Act.

Although in some cases actual knowledge may not be necessary for an election to take place, the court should look to the broader issue of the justice of the case. This would have several consequences. First, any ambiguity in the representation resulting from the conduct of the representee should entitle the representor to argue that he has not manifested an election whatever the representee thinks or does in reliance on the representation. Secondly, if the representee behaved inequitably, this could be a further reason for not allowing him to hold the representor to his election. Thirdly, the question of knowledge could be a factor, but not necessarily a deciding factor. Had these factors been considered by the Court of Appeal, it would not have reached the same decision. It is therefore unfortunate that the Court of Appeal failed to consider these broader factors relating to the 'justice of the case' when it put forward the new 'inchoate doctrine' and instead thought it sufficient to show that the new concept was independent from the doctrine of waiver when, in truth, it was not.

... post-contractual representations should be dealt with in two categories, those of pre-breach and post-breach representations. The former have the effect of altering the terms of the contract whilst the latter have the effect of barring a remedy, usually repudiation. The essential requirement of the first category is that the conduct of the representor and the representee must be capable of being analysed in consensual terms, i.e. it must be shown that the parties agreed upon an alteration of the terms of the contract. Hence, it must be shown that the representation is unambiguous, that there is an intention to alter the terms of the contract and that this has been accepted by the representee. The essential requirement for the second category is that the representee must reasonably rely upon the representation in continuing to perform the contract. Hence, ambiguity and the intention of the parties are only factors in determining the reasonableness of the reliance. The terminology to be used to describe the two categories is immaterial as long as the distinction is drawn. The importance of this analysis is that it provides a more coherent basis not only for examining such cases as *Alan* and *Panchaud Frères* but also for dealing with such traditional problems raised in the context of promissory estoppel as the necessity of reliance and the revocability of the representation.

In the case of a post-contractual representation operating in a post-breach situation, inevitably the representee will act in reliance on the representation that the contract will not be repudiated by continuing to perform. However, it has been argued that in dealing with the effects of these representations, the courts should look to the broader question of the justice of the case. Questions of reliance then become one factor, along with the questions of knowledge and inequitable conduct by the representee, in determining whether there has been an effective election or whether the representation can be revoked. In the case of pre-breach, post-contractual representation there should logically be no requirement that the representee rely upon the representation, simply a requirement that he accept it, thus making the relationship consensual in nature. In the *Alan* case, Lord Denning M.R. stated that the representee need only act upon the belief induced by the other party rather than having to act to his detriment. But, it is submitted, that even this requirement is unnecessary unless it is used to show acceptance of the representation. The requirement of consensuality should simply be the safeguard against the liberal use of the doctrine.

In the case of a pre-breach representation it should be possible for the representor to revoke the alteration, provided that it is still possible, i.e. that the circumstances provided for in the altered terms have not yet occurred. The possibility of such a revocation is the essential difference between an alteration of the terms of the contract without consideration and an alteration with consideration which amounts to a variation. . . .

[1.] [1972] AC 741; and see (1975) 38 MLR 65 (Atiyah).
[2.] 5th suppl. to the 23rd ed., para. 134.
[3.] [1970] 1 Lloyd's Rep. 53.
[4.] W. J. Alan & Co. Ltd v El Nasr Export & Import Co. [1972] 2 QB 179.

SECTION THREE—BREACH

A. Repudiatory Breach

A repudiatory breach involves one of the parties to a contract unilaterally deciding not to fulfil obligations due under the contract.

Leeson v North British Oil and Candle Co. (1874) 8 IRCL 309

Whiteside C.J.:

. . . A contract is to be regarded in reference to its subject matter. In this instance it was for the sale of a certain quantity of oil which was to be delivered by the defendants to persons named by the plaintiff in the orders sent by him from time to time. For a while the contract was kept, and the orders of the plaintiff were duly executed by the defendants, but after a time the defendants became irregular in the delivery of the oil. The plaintiff thereupon complained to their agent, who advised him to write direct to the manager in Glasgow. He did so, and subsequently the agent to whom he showed the letter he had received in reply pointedly informed him that the defendants had no oil to give him. It has been contended that, notwithstanding this announcement by the agent of the defendants, the plaintiff should have continued as before to send his orders for oil pursuant to the contract, and that having failed to do so, he is not entitled to retain his verdict. We are of opinion that he was quite justified in accepting the statement made by the defendants' agent, and in acting upon it, and that he was not any longer bound by the contract.

It has been argued that although the defendants may have been at the time this statement was made incapable of supplying the oil, yet that their inability might have been merely temporary, and that it might have passed away altogether in a short time. Their contract was, however, to deliver whenever the plaintiff transmitted an order. It does not appear that there was any particular time fixed until the arrival of which they could not be required to deliver, so that the argument which has been suggested does not apply. . . .

Athlone (No. 2) Rural District Council v A.G. Campbell & Son (1912) 47 ILTR 142

Viscount Haldane L.C.:

My Lords, the litigation out of which this appeal and cross-appeal arise relates to a matter connected with two artesian wells which were made in the district of the appellants, who are a district council. The wells were constructed by contractors who had experience in making such wells, and the question is whether the contractors are now entitled to payment. . . .

. . .

. . . the contract contains a clause on which this question arises—'In consideration of the sums in the said tender and supplemental tender mentioned the contractors (that is to say, the respondents in this appeal) will upon and subject to the conditions hereinafter contained do all things necessary and execute and complete all work necessary to put down artesian wells and erect pumps in the said townlands of Famore, Kilmore, Ballyforan, Ballybrogan, and Bredagh, until a copious supply of water shall have been obtained to the satisfaction of the engineer to the council.' Then there are clauses which provide that 'immediately on the perfection of this agreement the contractors shall begin the works at the places in the townlands where pointed out by the engineer of the council, and shall regularly proceed with the said works, and shall complete' them within eight months from the date of the agreement subject to certain provisions for extension of time. No question turns here upon time being of the essence of the contract. The general view taken in the courts below was that time was not of the essence of the contract, and I see no reason to dissent from that view. Then there are other stipulations which enable the engineer to make an extension of time, and which provide that 'the works shall be completed to the satisfaction of t' ~ engineer to the council, and in accordance with the said tender and supplemental tender and these conditions, and the contractors shall be entitled to payment under the certificate of the engineer that the said works have been so completed.' I need read no more of the contract for the present purpose. My Lords, the respondents, who are contractors, set to work, and proceeded to bore at the well at Bredagh. The correspondence shows that they made progress, and that they got certain results which in their early stages were encouraging. The first document to which I wish to refer is a telegram of 21 April, which is from Carlton, the foreman of the respondents, to the respondents themselves. It appears from that telegram, and from a previous telegram, that the supply of water, which at first had promised well, had begun to run short. Then the respondents telegraphed to the appellants for 'engineer's instructions'. On that the engineer wrote a letter of 24 April to the clerk of the appellant council, in which he says: 'I went twice to Bredagh, where they said a sufficient supply was got, and on both occasions well gave out.' Then there is a meeting of the council of 8 May, at which a report was read from the engineer, stating the depth of various wells, and 'that the men have left Rackins and Bredagh as if they had given up hopes of finding water, and that he thought the safest thing the council could do would be to stop them going any further.' Then there is an order of the council, at a subsequent meeting on 22 May. The council orders 'that the engineer be instructed to stop the contractors at wells when he considers that a sufficient supply of water has been obtained for the needs of the district, and that the time of testing do not exceed twelve hours.'

Then on 23 May the engineer gives to the contractors certain instructions. My Lords, before I read those instructions, upon which a good deal turns, I wish to state what, in my view, was the position of the contractors. The contractors were mere licensees; they had no title to go upon the land, they had no right to continue to bore excepting by the permission of the appellants. No doubt, if the appellants had improperly withheld their permission it might have amounted to a breach of the contract, as preventing the respondents from earning money due to them, and they might have sued upon the contract for damages, but they had no right or title of any kind to bore except so far as the appellants gave them permission, accordingly the letter of 23 May, which I am now about to read, must be construed in that light. It is said that it was not a letter written by the engineer as such. That does not matter; it purports to have been written, and was written, on behalf of the council, and it affects very materially the right to bore. The letter says: 'Please send on two permanent pumps—one for Cornaseer and one for Bredagh—as I am satisfied there is a sufficient supply of water at both places.' Now, my Lords, that meant, and could only have meant, and it was taken to mean, that they were not to dig any deeper, but were to put in pumps for the well as dug to that depth.

Now, before I pass to the next material document, I will refer to what happened in the meantime. The appellants, being apparently satisfied with what they had done, the respondents put in the pumps—and the pumps were put in by 27 July. The respondents were uneasy about the money which was due to them, and they issued their writ the next day. My Lords, the action which they then commenced turned out most unfortunately for the respondents. It was decided against them on the ground that they had not got the engineer's certificate. The court said that without the engineer's certificate they were entitled to nothing, and their action was dismissed on the simple ground that they had not made out any case for payment.

That action was commenced, as I have said, on 28 July, and it proceeded, and judgment was given in it considerably later—in January. Meantime, of course, very little was done. There was a meeting of the appellant council on 21 August, at which the engineer reported as to Bredagh: 'There being no water, I cannot certify till a supply is obtained' apparently regarding the matter as to Bredagh as still continuing. Again, on 21 September, the clerk of the council writes to the contractors: 'The engineer reports that the supply of water at Bredagh pump has given out.'

My Lords, I only refer to these documents because they bear upon the contention which has been pressed upon us. It has been said that the issue of the writ in July by the contractors put an end to the contract, and that it became impossible to regard the contract as being a subsisting contract after that time.

With that contention, my Lords, I am quite unable to agree. The position when the writ was issued on 28 July was this—that the contract was still a subsisting contract in so far as the certificate had yet to be given (or withheld) under it, and payment had to be made to the contractors. The contractors had been told that they were to dig no further, and were to put in pumps on the well as sunk to that depth, and they had done so, and, for the time at any rate they had done all that they had to do under the contract. It might be that the result of further tests would involve their doing something more; but as matters stood there was for the moment nothing for the contractors to do. The next step remained to be taken by the appellants. It may be that the action was a totally misconceived action. That could not, in my opinion, affect the rights of the respondents under the contract. I see no ground at all for the contention, or for the view which has been taken in the King's Bench Division, that the action put an end to the contract, and made it impossible to say that the contract was any longer subsisting.

My Lords, in that state of things, the judgment of Mr Justice Wright in the first action was given, as I have said, in January, and the effect of it was that the respondents failed to obtain their money. Then they appear to have considered what they ought to do, and in February—obviously acting upon advice—they wrote, through their solicitors, to the appellants to say that they 'were willing to do all things necessary under the contract, . . . to complete the work at the defendants' expense, and to obtain the certificate necessary to entitle them to payment'; and they asked for definite instructions in writing as to what the council required them to do. The reply to that letter from the appellants was: 'The plaintiffs have utterly failed to carry out their contract, and at a time nearly five months after the time limited they have done no more than sink a well which is not in accordance with their tender, and which is producing no water, and no work has been done at it since the late action was brought. Under these circumstances, the defendants are advised that they are entitled to regard the contract as at an end, and will so treat it.' Thereupon the writ in the present action was issued.

Now, my Lords, the course of the second and present action, brought after that letter has been this: It was tried before Mr Justice Wright, sitting without a jury, who took evidence. Then his judgment, which was a judgment for the appellants, went to the King's Bench Division, and there Mr Justice Gibson and the Chief Baron gave judgment, affirming the judgment of Mr Justice Wright, and they did so on the ground which I have indicated, and which has been the main basis of the argument here. I have already stated that I cannot agree with the view which they took. The different view which I have indicated as being my own was taken by the Court of Appeal, which consisted of the Lord Chancellor, Lord Justice Holmes, and Lord Justice Cherry. The judgment of the Court of Appeal was delivered by Lord Justice Holmes. That learned judge held that the first action did not amount to a repudiation, or, rather, he dealt very little with that action, but he held that what took place in July and May, in the summer of 1909, did not put an end to the contract or amount to a repudiation on the part of the respondents; that the letter which I have read directing the putting in of the pumps when a certain depth had been sunk, amounted to a direction to the respondents to stop digging any deeper, and that, consequently, they were in a position in which, although they had failed in the first action for want of the certificate, they got entirely new rights when the repudiation by the appellants took place in February; and he held that that repudiation was a repudiation which was, under the circumstances, improper and unjustified, and entitled the respondents to sue either upon the contract for damages, which he measured, and there is no question raised as to the measure which he laid down, by their expenditure, amounting to £256, upon the works, or on a *quantum meruit*, which would have come to the same thing.

My Lords, that being the judgment of the Court of Appeal, I find myself in substantial agreement with it, . . .

(Lord Atkinson and Lord Shaw of Dunfermaline agreed; Lord Ashbourne dissented.)

Continental Oil Co. of Ireland Ltd v Thomas Moynihan (Trading as Cobh Motor Works) and National Oil Co. of Ireland Ltd (1977) 111 ILTR 5

Kenny J.:

. . .

. . . In November 1972 the Minister for Industry and Commerce allowed the petrol companies to increase their wholesale price to dealers by a halfpenny. There is price control of the wholesale price at which petrol may be sold to dealers but there is none on the retail price. When the minister gave this permission, the plaintiffs offered their dealers a choice of either increasing their price to the public by a $\frac{1}{2}$p a gallon and then the plaintiffs would charge them this extra amount on the wholesale price or keeping their price to the public at the amount it was before and, in that event, the plaintiffs would pay them a publicity allowance of $\frac{1}{4}$p per gallon which was to be deducted from the price of the petrol paid by the dealer. Though called a publicity allowance, the effect of this offer was that the dealers who did not increase their price to the public would be getting their petrol at $\frac{1}{4}$p per gallon less than those who did. The result for those who decided that they would not increase the price to the public was a further reduction in the profit margin. Mr Moynihan was determined that he would not accept this reduction and that he would continue to sell petrol at the former price and so, when he received his bills after 27 November, he deducted $\frac{1}{2}$p per gallon from the price. Mr Moynihan was then interviewed by Mr Morgan, the dealer representative of the plaintiff company. Mr Morgan told him that as he had not increased his price to the public, the price to him of petrol supplied by the plaintiffs would be increased by $\frac{1}{4}$p per gallon and that this would be carried out by giving him a credit note for the excess charged. Mr Moynihan was not prepared to accept this suggestion: he wanted petrol supplied to him at the price which was in force before 27 November and was not prepared to pay more. The plaintiffs therefore discontinued supplies to Mr Moynihan. . . .

. . .

The next argument was that the plaintiffs had committed a fundamental breach of contract because they sold petrol to Mr Moynihan at the higher price after 27 November and it was said that the breach was so fundamental that it entitled Mr Moynihan to repudiate the contract. In the invoices which were sent to Mr Moynihan after 27 November he was charged an additional $\frac{1}{2}$p per gallon but I accept the evidence of Mr Morgan that he offered Mr Moynihan a credit note for petrol supplied after 27 November in respect of $\frac{1}{4}$p of a gallon and that the plaintiffs are prepared to supply Mr Moynihan with petrol at the lower price if he does not increase the price which he charged to the public before 27 November. The plaintiffs call the ¼p per gallon a pub-licity allowance but I think it is in fact a reduction in price. They may be committing a breach of the order of 1961 but Mr Moynihan cannot call this in aid when they are prepared to supply him at the lower price. Even if the charging of two prices was a breach of the agreement of 1970, it is not so fundamental that it would entitle Mr Moynihan to repudiate the contract. A person who relies on fundamental breach as a ground for discharging him from a contract must establish that the breach shows that the other party does not intend to be bound by the contract.

Note

In *House of Spring Gardens Ltd and Others v Point Blank Ltd and Others* [1985] IR 611 the defendants entered a licensing agreement with the plaintiffs to manufacture bullet proof vests designed by the latter. Subsequently the defendants commenced to manufacture a similar product and the plaintiffs sued for infringement of copyright and breach of contract. The Supreme Court affirmed the High Court's finding that a repudiatory breach of contract had occured. Evidence indicated that the defendants had attempted to defraud the plaintiffs by suppressing information and dissimilating the origins of their product.

B. FUNDAMENTAL BREACH

A fundamental breach is 'a breach which goes to the root of a contract' (Per Lord Denning in *Karsales (Harrow) Ltd v Wallis* [1956] 1 WLR 936).

Robb & Co. v James and Clarke & Son (1881) 15 ILTR 59

The defendants auctioned certain drapery goods. The terms of the sale required that the goods purchased be removed within twenty four hours of the auction, and paid for prior to removal. The plaintiffs were declared the purchasers but they refused to pay the full price or to remove the goods within the set time. The defendants rescinded the contract and resold the goods to another person. The plaintiffs sued for breach of contract. The trial judge directed a verdict for the defendants.

May C.J.:

We are unanimously of opinion that the verdict for the defendants should stand, and that their demurrer should be allowed. With respect to the demurrer, the defendants, by the second paragraph of their defence, alleged that it was a term of the contract of sale that the goods bought should be paid for and removed within twenty four hours from the sale; that the price of the goods was £178 5s 1d; that the plaintiffs wholly refused to pay any greater sum than £173 10s 6d, or to remove the goods within the period of twenty four hours; whereupon the defendants rescinded the contract of sale, and kept, and afterwards sold the goods. To this plea the plaintiffs reply that there was no provision in the contract of sale empowering the defendants to rescind the contract of sale, without the consent of the plaintiffs, and that they never did consent to such rescission. To this replication the defendants demurred. On their pleadings it is admitted that the plaintiffs absolutely refused to perform the most essential term of the contract, *viz.* to pay for and remove the goods of which they had been declared the purchasers. It is well established that, under such circumstances, the seller may treat the contract as abandoned by the purchaser, and may detain and resell the goods.[1] The law confers this right on the seller wholly independently of any consent of the purchaser.[2] And we, therefore, think that the replication affords no answer to the plea, and that the demurrer must be sustained.

[1.] See Ex *parte Hunter*, 6 Ves. jun. 94; *Bowles v Rogers*, ibid. 954, n. (a), Cook's BL 146; *Ex parte Lord Seaforth*, 19 Ves. 235, 1 Rose, 106; *Ex parte Gyde*, 1 Glyn & Jam. 323; *Hope v Booth*, 1 B & Ad 498

[2.] And it seems that, even in the absence of express stipulation, the first purchaser would be responsible for loss occurring, although he did not consent to the second sale: *M'Clean v Dunn*, 1 M & P 761, 4 Bing. 722.

Note

Is this approach consistent with that of Kenny J. in *Continental Oil Co. v Moynihan* (see p. 880 above)?

Dundalk Shopping Centre Ltd v Roof Spray Ltd (HC) 21 March 1979, unrep.

The defendants contracted to supply and execute a waterproof application and finish to the roof of the plaintiff's shopping centre. Work commenced in late September and despite the fact that the estimate suggested completion in under four weeks, by mid-November the roof was still unfinished. The spraying which had taken place proved totally useless and damaged the roof. The plaintiffs thus repudiated the contract, claiming damages on the basis that the work was not carried out in a professional manner and was not of merchantable quality.

Finlay P.:

. . .

Work was commenced by the defendants on the provision of this system on 24 September 1974 at which time the estimate for the completion of the work was just under four weeks. The defendants continued to work from that time, though not continuously, until 13 November 1974 on which date the plaintiffs purported to repudiate their contract and engaged the services of another contractor who laid an alternative type of roof, namely an asphalt roof.

. . .

I am satisfied that this repudiation of the contract was justified and that the defendants had by that time failed in a fundamental term of the contract namely to provide an effective waterproofing of this roof within a reasonable time. On the evidence before me that failure was, it is clear, due to the fact that they never succeeded in applying the spray in appropriate weather conditions and was probably also contributed to by the manner in which the spray was applied. There is considerable evidence that it must have been applied in a loose and almost scattered fashion whereas the system required careful close spraying. Evidence of the meteorological conditions applicable during the period from about 20 October to the first week in November was made available to me during the hearing and it is clear that had the defendants been there with sufficient number of men and in sufficient time on each day that there were conditions which, according to their own specifications, would have led to a successful application of the spray and its setting before further weather intervened to spoil it. I therefore conclude that the plaintiffs are entitled to damages for breach of the contract by the defendants and that the defendants are not entitled to any damages by way of counterclaim for any breach by the plaintiffs of their contract with them the plaintiffs being entitled, in my view of the facts, to repudiate the contract when they did.

Sidney Taylor v Philip Smyth, Kape Investments Ltd, Calla Associates Ltd and Northern Bank Ltd [1990] ILRM 377

As part of an agreement to compromise a legal dispute the plaintiff, an owner and lessor of premises agreed to sell his fee simple interest to the first defendant. The contract provided that the plaintiff would consent as lessor to the assignment of the leasehold interest and would waive all claims to arrears of rent. The sale was to be completed before 15 July 1980. On 16 September 1980 the first defendant purported to rescind the contract for sale and the plaintiff sued for breach of contract.

Lardner J.:

. . .

The question I must consider is whether in regard to an agreement to compromise of this extensive scope [counsel for the defendant] is correct when he contends that unreasonable delay by Mr Taylor in completing the sale of the freehold occurred which entitled the parties to treat that part of the consent, which provided for the sale of the freehold, as having been repudiated.

Firstly, was there unreasonable delay by Mr Taylor? Before he was in a position to complete there were at least two matters to be resolved, namely securing a withdrawal by his brother Thomas Taylor of his claim to an interest in the property and of the *lis pendens* he had registered against it and securing a settlement of Barclays Bank's claim as judgment mortgagee against the property. I think as a matter of probability that Mr Taylor was not in a position to complete until the beginning of December 1980. I conclude that having regard to what was required to be done after 20 June 1980 to effect performance of the contract for sale this was an unreasonable delay in all the circumstances.

The next question is whether this unreasonable delay in regard to the completion of the sale of the freehold entitled Mr Smyth, Kape Investments Ltd and Calder Investments Ltd to treat the agreement for sale as repudiated. . . .

. . . In my judgment the agreement for sale of the freehold is not severable from the other terms of the consent.

It was not contended by any of the defendants that the unreasonable delay of the plaintiff in completing the sale of the freehold should by itself properly be regarded as a repudiation of the entire consent. The first and second defendants have indeed asserted the continued existence of other terms of the settlement. So the question of the repudiation of the consent considered as an entire agreement does not arise. Nonetheless perhaps I should state my view in relation to the effect which the plaintiff's delay could be regarded as having. It seems to me that the correct principle to be applied in determining whether delay by one party in performing an obligation under a contract, where, as in this case, the contract must be considered entire but there are a number of heterogeneous obligations to be performed, entitles another party to treat it as a repudiation, is to consider the effect of the breach upon the contract as a whole and whether the effect of the delay (here in completing the sale of the freehold) deprived the innocent parties of substantially the whole benefit of the contract. See the observations of Diplock L.J. in *Hong Kong Fir Shipping Co. Ltd v Kawasaki Kisen Kaisha Ltd*

[1962] 2 QB 26. If it has this effect the innocent parties in addition to any remedy in damages would be entitled to be discharged from any further obligation. But if the breach does not have this effect, its consequences can be remedied only by an award of damages. One of the matters urged on behalf of Kape Investments Ltd was that in September and October 1980 the delay in completing the sale of the freehold had put the licence attached to the hotel at risk and that this threatened the value of Kape's security. I am not satisfied that during these two months the position in regard to the licence had significantly deteriorated from what it had been since 1975. It certainly does not seem to me to justify Mr Smyth or Kape Investments Ltd treating the contract for sale as repudiated.

Having regard to the nature of the consent, that it was intended to settle the 1975 action and all other pending proceedings between the parties, that there were a number of terms whose performance was effected and achieved by the agreement to them of the relevant parties, (e.g. the plaintiff's agreement to waive all claims for arrears of rent), that there was at least one other term—the plaintiff giving his consent as lessor to the assignment of the leasehold interest—which was separately performed by the plaintiff, I am unable to conclude that the defendants were, as a result of the plaintiff's delay in completing the sale of the freehold, deprived of substantially the entire benefit of the consent agreement. Consequently they were not entitled to treat the consent agreement as having been repudiated.

The same principles will apply to a fundamental breach of an employment contract.

Industrial Yarns Ltd *v* Leo Greene and Arthur Manley [1984] ILRM 15

Costello J.:

. . . A number of former employees of Industrial Yarns Ltd, a company carrying on a textile business in Bray, County Wicklow, made claims to the Employment Appeals Tribunal that, pursuant to the provisions of the Minimum Notice and Terms of Employment Act 1973, they were entitled to compensation for loss which they had suffered arising from the failure of the company to give them notice of intention to terminate their contracts of employment to which they claimed they were entitled under the Act. Having heard submission on behalf of the parties the tribunal in a decision of 5 May 1981 decided that in respect of forty six cases named in the first schedule to its order compensation was payable by the company. . . . The company, however, appealed the tribunal's decision pursuant to s. 11 of the Act and challenged its legal validity. The dispute before the tribunal and now before the court turns on the legal effect of events which happened in the middle of July 1980; the company says that as a matter of law it did not terminate its employees' contracts of employment (as the tribunal decided that it had done), and so it is submitted that the company was not required to give the notices referred to in the Act of 1973.
. . .

A strike took place at the company's Bray premises on 26 February 1980 which lasted until 19 July 1980. It was settled following discussions which took place at the Labour Court on 17 July between representatives of the company and representatives of the employees' union. As a result of these discussions a letter was written by Mr Egan, the company's secretary, to Mr Gannon, the national group secretary of the Irish Transport and General Workers' Union, and this letter was the basis on which the employees voted to end their strike and return to work. . . .

. . .

When work at the factory resumed on 19 July only a small number of the pre-strike labour force of 188 employees were employed, the remainder, including the present claimants, being 'laid off'. . . .

The proposal in the letter of 17 July was that (a) the union would forward to the company a list of those of its members who would prefer to be made redundant rather than work for the rates the company was able to offer and (b) that the company would lay off those employees who were on the list and they could subsequently apply to be made redundant. This proposal was accepted and a list of approximately sixty employees was sent to the company on 26 July, a list headed 'list of people who do not wish to return'. All these employees were laid off by the company and subsequently after a four week period of lay-off made claims for redundancy payments. Each subsequently received redundancy payments under the Redundancy Acts 1967–1979.

. . .

It will be noted that the employer is only allowed to avail of the statutory lay-off procedures when it is reasonable in the circumstances for that employer to believe that the 'cessation of employment will not be permanent' (s. 11(1)(a)) and he gives notice to that effect. But what are the legal consequences if, objectively, it could be shown that when the employer served the notice of lay-off he could not reasonably have held the belief he expressed in the notice? That was the situation which the tribunal concluded existed in the present case. It held that the company did not expect to re-employ the full work force of 188 when the letter of 17 July was sent; that it was given a list of sixty persons who were willing to be made redundant; that it was not reasonable for it to believe that the cessation of the employment of those on the list would not be permanent. The tribunal concluded:

> We consider from a recognition of the reality of the situation that the appellants who were willing to be made redundant and whose names were on the list given to the company were dismissed when or at the time the respondents purported to lay them off, namely 22 July 1982. We take this view from our belief that the lay-off had no basis in reality but was merely the means used by the respondents to implement a redundancy situation. The respondents had by letter of 17 July made it clear that they accepted the redundancy situation, and had agreed that these people would be made redundant though they used the lay-off procedure to implement the redundancies.

. . .

. . . This means that the employer was not entitled to avail of the special statutory lay-off procedures contained in ss 11 to 13. But obviously the Oireachtas could not have intended that an employee should be deprived of his right to redundancy payment by an erroneous use by the employer of the lay-off procedures, and so it seems to me that the resulting legal position is as follows. If there is no contractual power (express or implied) in the contract of employment to suspend the operation of the contract for a limited period then by ceasing to employ an employee and refusing to pay him wages the employer has been guilty of a serious breach of contract amounting to a repudiation of it. At common law that repudiation would not automatically bring the contract of employment to an end; the employee is free to accept that the repudiation has terminated the contract or not to do so (see: *Gunton v Richmond-upon-Thames London Borough Council* [1980] 3 WLR 714 for a recent view on the effect of an employer's repudiation of the contract of employment). If he accepts the repudiation of the contract then there has been a constructive dismissal of the employee at common law and the contract has been terminated by the employer. But if the employee responds to the employers' lay-off notice and adopts the lay-off procedures (instead of immediately accepting the employer's repudiation of the contract) and it is shown that the statutory condition for their initiation by the employer did not exist, then it seems, the employee is entitled to treat the repudiation of the contract (which occurred when the cesser of employment began) as having terminated the contract of employment, and to base his claim for redundancy payment on that fact. The tribunal was, therefore, in my view correct in its opinion that an employee can properly assert that an employer who ceases to employ him, and who cannot show that the cesser will not be permanent has terminated his contract of employment even though previously the employee had served an RP 9 Form.

C. Breach of a Condition

Breach of a condition will entitle the injured party to repudiate the contract. (See Chapter 6, p. 253.)

This right may however be waived by the injured party or in certain circumstances lost.

Sale of Goods Act 1893 s. 11:

11. (1) Where a contract of sale is subject to any condition to be fulfilled by the seller, the buyer may waive the condition, or may elect to treat the breach of such condition as a breach of warranty, and not as a ground for treating the contract as repudiated.

(2) Whether a stipulation in a contract of sale is a condition, the breach of which may give rise to a right to treat the contract as repudiated, or a warranty, the breach of which may give rise to a claim for damages but not to a right to reject the goods and treat the contract as repudiated depends in each case on the construction of the contract. A stipulation may be a condition, though called a warranty in the contract.

(3) Where a contract of sale is not severable, and the buyer has accepted the goods, or part thereof, the breach of any condition to be fulfilled by the seller can only be treated as a breach of warranty, and not as a ground for rejecting the goods and treating the contract as repudiated, unless, there be a term of the contract, express or implied, to that effect.

(4) Nothing in this section shall affect the case of any condition or warranty, fulfilment of which is excused by law by reason of impossibility or otherwise.

D. Effects of a Breach

An Bord Iascaigh Mhara *v* Stephen Scallan (HC) 8 May 1973, unrep.

Pringle J.:

The plaintiffs' claim, as amended, falls under two headings. *First* they claim the sum of £1,246 1s 3d for arrears of hire purchase instalments and insurance payments from 1 May 1967 to 3 July 1969, and *secondly*, they claim the sum of £1,881 3s for damages for breach of contract by the defendant in failing to keep the vessel, gear, and equipment, the subject matter of the hire-purchase agreement, hereinafter referred to, in good order repair and condition. The defendant in his amended defence denies liability on foot of both these claims and counterclaims for the sum of £2,658 damages for breach of contract and he also claims to set off so much of such damages as may be necessary to satisfy the plaintiffs' claim, if any.

The plaintiffs are a statutory body and they carry on (*inter alia*) the business of hiring out fishing vessels. The defendant is a fisherman carrying on that business at Kilmore Quay County Wexford and on 13 August 1965 he applied to the plaintiffs for credit facilities under their Marine Credit Plan in order to purchase, by means of a hire-purchase agreement from the plaintiffs, a motor fishing vessel for the purposes, as he specified, of lobster fishing, lining, and trawling. The necessary credit facilities having been granted, the plaintiffs on 15 September 1965 forwarded to the defendant a copy of a quotation for the building of the boat which they had obtained from Messrs John Tyrrell and Sons Ltd, Boat Builders Arklow, and which contained two alternative proposals, called 'Proposal A' and 'Proposal B', and the defendant chose 'Proposal A' which included the following, under the heading of 'Engine': 'Power take-off on fore-end of engine with dog clutch fitted for winch hydraulic pump drive.' The defendant paid a deposit of £250 to the plaintiffs and Messrs Tyrrell proceeded to build the boat, which was delivered to the defendant on 10 March 1967, on which date he entered into a hire-purchase agreement with the plaintiffs. . . .

The boat is described in this agreement as having a Fifer hydraulic trawl winch, but there is no mention of a dog clutch which had been specified by Messrs Tyrrell. Also on 10 March 1967, the defendant signed a delivery receipt in which the boat was described in the same terms as in the hire-purchase agreement and this receipt contained the words 'I hereby confirm having examined and this day taken delivery of the goods as described in the following schedule and am satisfied as to their condition and fitness'. In fact the hydraulic trawl winch on the boat delivered to the defendant had no dog clutch, or indeed a clutch of any kind, but the defendant admits that he knew this when he took delivery and was told by Mr William Tyrrell that a dog clutch was not necessary, and, as the defendant said in his evidence, 'I accepted it. I knew no better'. I do not consider that the fact that the defendant was made aware that the boat had in fact no dog clutch precludes him from making the case that the absence of either a dog clutch or a clutch of some kind was one of the reasons that, as he alleged, the boat was not reasonably fit for the purposes for which it was required.

The history of the boat after it was delivered to the defendant was, I am satisfied on the evidence, one of continuous trouble and misfortune in respect of the hydraulic winch which was a very important part of the boat, so far as the defendant's fishing activities, for which of course it had been hired, were concerned. . . .

. . .

He continued to use the boat up to October 1968 when he decided to 'go to the top', as he said, with the plaintiffs and when he failed to succeed in obtaining an interview to complain about the boat with a Mr Kelly, through Mr Howlin, the plaintiffs' local representative, he tied the boat up in Wexford Harbour and told Mr Howlin that he could do what he liked with it, as he was not going to fish it any more. . . . the boat remained tied up in Wexford until 3 July 1969 (a period of about nine months), when it was eventually repossessed by the plaintiffs. . . .

When the plaintiffs eventually took possession of the boat it was found to be in a very bad state, to a large extent owing to the place and manner in which it had been left, . . .

. . .

The first question which arises is as to whether the plaintiffs were guilty of a breach of either of the implied conditions under s. 9 of the Hire-Purchase Act 1946 upon which the defendant relies, that is to say the condition that the goods shall be of merchantable quality contained in s. 9 (1)(d), and the condition as to suitability for a particular purpose contained in s. 9 (2). In my opinion the defendant has not established that the boat was of unmerchantable quality. It was perfectly seaworthy and could be used for all purposes other than those involving the use of the winch. On the other hand I am satisfied that the defendant *has* established that there was a breach by the plaintiffs of the implied condition under s. 9 (2) of the Act. That the particular purpose for which the boat was required was made known to the plaintiffs is quite clear, that is to say for lobster fishing, lining, and trawling. . . . The evidence satisfies me that, for the purpose of efficient lobster fishing and trawling, the hydraulic winch was the most important part of the equipment, and I am also satisfied that at no time did the winch on this boat operate satisfactorily and the boat was not therefore reasonably fit for the purpose for which it was hired and the plaintiffs were guilty of a breach of the statutory condition under s. 9 (2) of the Act. The effect of a breach of this condition was dealt with by Mr Justice Davitt, the then President of the High Court, in the case of *Butterly v United Dominions Trust (Commercial) Ltd* [1963] IR 56, at 62, where he said:

> The only question remaining is the main one, whether the plaintiff was entitled to repudiate the contract. He was always of course entitled to terminate the hiring under the provisions of clause 8, but, quite apart from that, he would be entitled to repudiate, as soon as he discovered that the car was useless for the purpose for which he required it, and that the condition implied in s. 9 (2) had been broken. The principles which apply to the matter of repudiation under the Sale of Goods Act have no application in the case of a contract under the Hire-Purchase Act. In the case of the Sale of Goods Act, once the goods have been accepted and the property has passed to the buyer, he cannot repudiate and he is confined to the remedy by way of action for damages. The Hire-Purchase Act is entirely different and, having regard to the submissions on the point made by [counsel] on behalf of the defendants and by [counsel] on behalf of the plaintiff, it would appear to be common case that the hirer can repudiate within a reasonable time of becoming aware of a breach of a condition which would entitle him to repudiate.

In the present case therefore the defendant was entitled to repudiate the contract within a reasonable time of becoming aware that the boat was not reasonably fit for the purposes for which it was required. In the early stages, when attempts were being made by the plaintiffs to remedy the defects in the winch, and even though these attempts were unsuccessful, it was reasonable, in my opinion, for the defendant to delay repudiating the contract, but after about November 1967, when it was clear that the winch had still not sufficient power, the defendant not only did not repudiate the contract, but went on using the boat for another year and it was not until October 1968, that he notified the plaintiffs, through Mr Howlin, that he was abandoning the boat and that the plaintiffs could do what they liked with it. It was then in my opinion too late for him to repudiate the contract and require the plaintiffs to return the deposit, as claimed. He had clearly approbated the contract and could only rely on his claim for damages for breach of contract. . . .

Lutton *v* Saville Tractors (Belfast) Ltd and Another [1986] NI 327

The plaintiff purchased a secondhand car from the first defendant. The sales representative assured him that the car was in good repair and had not sustained any accidental damage. A full service and three month warranty was provided. The plaintiff never found the car satisfactory and returned it constantly with lists of complaints. Finally, two months after purchase, after the plaintiff had done between 3,000 and 4,000 miles, the plaintiff notified the first defendant of his desire to return the car and obtain a refund. When the first defendant refused, the plaintiff sought to rescind the contract and sued for damages.

Carswell J.:

. . .

. . . it has not been proved that the salesman Sinclair knew of the untruth of his representation that the car had not been in an accident. The sales manager knew of the accident, but it was not suggested that he authorised the making of the representation. The misrepresentation—for such it obviously was—was made in the course of Sinclair's employment and apparently on behalf of his employers, and therefore Saville Motors must be held to have made an innocent misrepresentation. . . .

. . .

A person who has been induced to enter into a contract by a misrepresentation is entitled to the equitable remedy of rescission, but that right is lost if he has affirmed the contract, in certain cases by lapse of time, or if *restitutio in integrum* is no longer possible. I do not think that the latter two defences are in point, but the question of affirmation may well be. I shall have to consider it further after deciding the issue of breach of contract, but so far as the misrepresentation about accident damage is concerned there is no evidence that the plaintiff knew its untruth at any time before the proceedings were brought, and in the absence of knowledge he cannot be held to have affirmed the contract despite the misrepresentation: see *Farnworth Finance Facilities Ltd v Attryde* [1970] 2 All ER 774, 778, per Lord Denning M.R., and cf. *Peyman v Lanjani* [1984] 3 All ER 703. The fact that the plaintiff did not know of the untruth of the accident damage misrepresentation when he repudiated the contract in November 1984 is not an obstacle to his relying upon it now as legitimate ground for the repudiation. It is a well established principle of the law of contract that a person who refuses to perform a contract on one ground may, if that is inadequate, subsequently rely upon another ground which justifies his refusal to perform, provided it in fact existed at the time of the refusal: *Benjamin's Sale of Goods*, (2nd ed.), para. 1725. . . .

. . .

In my judgment the number and seriousness of the faults which were present or developed in the car the subject of this case were such that it was not of merchantable quality. I consider that the plaintiff was entitled to expect that it would be in much better condition on the purchase of a car of this age, type and mileage at the price he agreed. . . .

. . .

It is not established that Mr Lutton knew of the accident damage at any time up to his final attempt to get rid of the car. He accordingly cannot be said to have affirmed the contract with knowledge of the facts which gave him a right to rescind because of the misrepresentation that the car had not sustained any accident damage.

On the issue of the misrepresentation about the condition of the car the defendants point to the fact that the plaintiff kept the car for a period approaching two months and drove some 3,000 to 4,000 miles before finally attempting to return it. In *Farnworth Finance Facilities Ltd v Attryde* it was held that the purchaser of a new motor cycle which developed a number of serious defects had not affirmed the contract, which in that case was one of hire-purchase, by attempting over a period of over four months to have the defects put right, using the machine a good deal in the process. He did not elect to accept it until the defects were remedied, which they never were, and the final breakdown showed the plaintiff conclusively that it could not be relied on. The plaintiff relies upon this case in support of the proposition that his use of the car for a period did not amount to affirmation.

Before I reach a conclusion on the issue of affirmation, I should for the sake of completeness look at that of acceptance under the Sale of Goods Act 1979. By virtue of s. 11(4), where the buyer has accepted the goods, the breach of a condition to be fulfilled by the seller can only be treated as a breach of warranty, and not as a ground for rejecting the goods and treating the contract as repudiated. This express statutory provision accordingly dispenses with the need to consider affirmation in the case of breach of condition, for that issue is replaced by that of acceptance. The circumstances in which a buyer is regarded as having accepted the goods are set out in s. 35(1) of the 1979 Act: 'The buyer is deemed to have accepted the goods when he intimates to the seller that he has accepted them, or (except where s. 34 above otherwise provides) when the goods have been delivered to him and he does any act in relation to them which is inconsistent with the ownership of the seller, or when after the lapse of a reasonable time he retains the goods without intimating to the seller that he has rejected them.' The third part of the subsection is the material one here, and the issue is whether after the lapse of a reasonable time the plaintiff retained the car without intimating to Saville Motors that he had rejected it.

Reported decisions have varied to a marked extent in their approach to deciding on acceptance by a buyer. In some of them courts have held that the right of rejection is lost speedily where goods are in daily use, and this normally means days rather than months: see Atiyah, *The Sale of Goods*, (5th ed.), 402. On the other hand, there is a trend of thought, accepted by the Law Commission in its Working Paper No. 85, that time taken up while goods are being repaired should not count as part of the reasonable time during which the buyer must reject the goods. A possible avenue of approach is by the concept that the seller's attempts to cure defects constitutes acquiescence in the buyer's holding off final acceptance: see *Benjamin's Sale of Goods*, (2nd ed.), para. 925.

Some support for this type of approach may be found in the Canadian case-law. In *Burroughs Business Machines Ltd v Feed-Rite Mills* (1962) Ltd [1973] 42 DLR 3d 303, affd. on appeal 64 DLR 3d 767, an accounting machine supplied by the plaintiff proved defective. It was held that the defendant's efforts in co-operating with the plaintiff in an attempt to make the equipment work could not be used to negate the absence of acceptance as a matter of law. A *fortiori*, they would hardly constitute affirmation of the contract. In two cases concerning the sale of new cars, *Lightburn v Belmont Sales Ltd* [1969] 6 DLR 3d 692 and *Finlay v Metro Toyota Ltd* [1977] 82 DLR 3d 440, the purchasers used them for several months each and drove them for several thousand miles. In each case it was held that the buyer had not accepted the car within the meaning of a provision similar to that contained in our Sale of Goods Act. In the former case Ruttan J. said: 'He was endeavouring to give it a reasonable chance to perform, and I do not agree that delay in finally repudiating his contract can be attributed to that period of time or the mileage that was covered. He was not acting as a capricious buyer who had repented the purchase and sought to get out of his contract at an early time on a frivolous basis.'

This description would in my view apply aptly to Mr Lutton. He sensibly enough took the car back several times to try to have the defects cured, but eventually, in his own words, he was 'sick of having problems with the car'. He attempted to return the car, but the service manager would not accept it. His solicitors sent a letter of repudiation, and when the car broke down again the plaintiff washed his hands of it and attempted to return the keys and tax book to Saville Motors. On these facts I consider that the plaintiff did not at any time so act that he must be taken to have accepted the goods. I also hold that he did not by keeping the car for a period affirm the contract and lose his right of rescission.

Note

See also *Thomas Dillon-Leetch v Maxwell Motors Ltd* [1984] ILRM 624.

SECTION FOUR—FRUSTRATION

The traditional view was that contractual obligations were absolute, and the fact that performance may be difficult or even impossible was no excuse at common law. This traditional view was questioned in *Taylor v Caldwell* (1863) 3 B & S 826.

Gamble v The Accident Assurance Co. (1869) 4 IR CL 204

The plaintiff was the executor of the estate of a person insured under a contract with the defendant assurance company. The contract made it a condition precedent to the right of recovery that a notice containing the details of the accident should be delivered to the defendant's head office within seven days from the occurrence of the accident. When John Gamble was drowned in a boating accident, the plaintiff claimed that due to the sudden and fatal nature of the accident notification was impossible.

Pigot C.B.:

...

. . . The notice is addressed to insurers, because it is with them that the company deals. They are 'informed' of what the company requires, because they are the persons who are interested in measures being taken for the doing of that which the company so requires. And, although a man cannot serve a notice after he has ceased to live, it is perfectly practicable for him so to arrange that what is required by the company shall be done by a survivor. The terms of the sixth condition, and of the notice, specify two classes of requirements: first, what is to be done 'in the event of *any* accident, whether fatal or not, occurring to the insured;' secondly, what is to be done 'in case the accident shall not prove fatal.' In the latter case, *the insurer* is required, within seven days from the accident, to furnish a full written report by a medical practitioner of the facts of the case; and the insurer is to furnish further information, and to submit himself to examination, in the manner described in the sixth condition. But the former provision, which is expressly applied to *any* accident, whether *fatal or not*, does not specify by whom the notice shall be given, but peremptorily requires that the notice shall be given within seven days. The matters of which such notice is required are not matters lying within the knowledge of the insured alone. They can be learned by any surviving member of his family, by any surviving friend, or by any person having means of inquiring into the facts. . . .

. . .

If the contract was, as I conceive it was, that the required notice *should* be given by *some* one, the instantaneous death of the insured did not render it impossible to do what the condition required, since it could have been done by a survivor. The plaintiff's counsel relied on the averment in the summons and plaint, that 'no other person having knowledge of the existence of the said policy, or of its having been executed, or of the aforesaid contract of assurance, had, within such seven days, any knowledge or notice of such occurrence, or could give the defendants any notice thereof.' That averment only shows that the insured did not take the necessary means of enabling some one who was likely to survive him, if he should meet immediate death by a sudden accident, to give the necessary notice, by apprising some of his family or friends of the policy, and of the strict condition contained in it. The dispensation of providence, in his instantaneous death, would not have occasioned the omission to give the necessary notice, but for his own neglect in not providing for that contingency. The case is, therefore, entirely without the range of those exceptions to the rule laid down in *Paradine v Jane*,[1] and in the class of authorities of which several are cited in the note to *Walton v Waterhouse*,[2] of which exceptions *Taylor v Caldwell*[3] is one of the latest examples. In those cases it was held that, in the nature and import of the contract itself, there was that which involved an implied condition, that the destruction of the person, or the thing, with which the contract dealt, should absolve from its performance—which was the case of *Taylor v Caldwell*. There, A agreed with B to give him the use of a music hall on certain specified days, for the purpose of holding concerts, with no express stipulation for the event of the destruction of the music hall by fire. It was held that both parties were excused from the performance of the contract. 'In none of those contracts,' says Mr Justice Blackburn in his judgment:

> is the promise in words other than positive, nor is there any express stipulation that the destruction of the person or thing shall excuse the performance; but that excuse is by law implied, because, from the nature of the contract, it is apparent that the parties contracted upon the basis of the continued existence of the particular person or chattel. In the present case . . . looking at the whole case, we find that the parties contracted on the basis of the continued existence of the music hall at the time when the concerts were to be given; that being essential to their performance.

In this case of *Gamble v The Accident Assurance Co.*, now before us, the distinction, to which I have already adverted, between the language of the sixth condition, where it deals with accidents which do *not* prove fatal, and its language where it deals with *all* accidents, whether fatal or not, appears to me to exempt this case from the application of the class of authorities to which *Taylor v Caldwell* belongs. There is nothing stipulated for in the sixth condition, which, in the case of a casualty fatal to the insured, could not have been done by a survivor, whom the insured had taken the precaution of making acquainted with the policy.

[1.] Aleyn, 26.   [2.] 2 Wms Saund. 422, a.   [3.] 3 B & S 826.

Cummings v Stewart (No. 2) [1913] 1 IR 95

The plaintiff, a patentee of improvements for making reinforced concrete, granted the right to work the patents to the defendant licensee in return for royalty payments. When the patents lapsed due to the plaintiff's non-payment of the renewal fees, the defendant refused to pay the plaintiff royalties.

O'Connor M.R.:

. . .

. . . It is manifest that the parties contracted on the basis that at least three patents should continue to be existing patents during the whole term of the licence. Owing to the conduct of the plaintiff, two, or at least one, of the patents were lost, with the result that a substantial part of the subject matter of the contract was destroyed, and the contract, in a substantial part, became impossible of performance, and ceased to be binding.

There is ample authority for this. In the *Panama and South Pacific Telegraph Co. v India Rubber, Gutta-Percha, and Telegraph Works Co.*,[1] Lord Justice Mellish, at 532, says: 'No doubt it is a clear principle of law that if, by any act of one of the parties, the performance of a contract is rendered impossible, then the other side may, if they choose, rescind the contract, and certainly, according to the case of *Planchè v Colburn*[2] and other cases, it appears sufficient, if the contract cannot be performed in the manner stipulated, though it may be performed in some other manner not very different.' The principle so laid down is strikingly applicable to the present case. It is put in another way by Blackburn J. in *Taylor v Caldwell*[3]:

> When from the nature of the contract it appears that the parties must from the beginning have known that it could not be fulfilled, unless when the time for the fulfilment of the contract arrived some particular specified thing continues to exist, so that when entering into the contract they must have contemplated such continued existence, as the foundation of what was to be done, then, in the absence of any express or implied warranty that the thing shall exist, the contract is not to be considered a positive contract, but subject to the implied condition that the parties shall be excused, in case, before breach, performance becomes impossible, from the perishing of the thing without the default of the contractor.

This statement of the law covers the situation; and applies with all the more force when the disappearance of the subject matter of the contract is owing to the default of the plaintiff.

Further down in his judgment, after reviewing several cases where the condition of performance was implied, he says, at 859: 'In none of these cases is the promise in words other than positive; nor is there any express stipulation that the destruction of the person or thing shall excuse the performance; but that excuse is, by law, implied, because from the nature of the contract it is apparent that the parties contracted on the basis of the continued existence of the particular person or chattel.'

[1] LR 10 Ch App 515.   [2] 8 Bing. 14.   [3] 3 B & S 833.

Note

The idea of an implied term that the promisor's obligation will be capable of performance without alterations which frustrate the contract is no longer in favour. Since *Davis Contractors Ltd v Fareham UDC* [1956] 2 All ER 145 the procedure has been to construe the contract and then determine whether a literal enforcement would yield a radically different result from that contemplated by the contract. Lord Radcliffe in the House of Lords stated:

> . . . there is something of a logical difficulty in seeing how the parties could even impliedly have provided for something which *ex hypothesi* they neither expected nor foresaw; and the ascription of frustration to an implied term of the contract has been criticised as obscuring the true action of the court which consists in applying an objective rule of the law of contract to the contractual obligations that the parties have imposed upon themselves. . . .
>
> . . . So perhaps it would be simpler to say at the outset that frustration occurs whenever the law recognises that without default of either party a contractual obligation has become incapable of being performed because the circumstances in which performance is called for would render it a thing radically different from that which was undertaken by the contract. . .

A. FRUSTRATION OF THE BUSINESS VENTURE

Enda McGuill v Aer Lingus Teoranta and United Airlines Incorporated (HC) 3 October 1983, unrep.

McWilliam J.:

This action is brought by the plaintiff for damages alleged to have been sustained by him by reason of the breach of a contract whereby United Airlines Incorporated (hereinafter called United) agreed to carry 234 passengers, members of the Vintners Federation of Ireland, from New York to San Francisco and from there to Hawaii and back from Hawaii to New York via Los Angeles and Las Vegas.

. . .

Due to labour disputes with its employees, United was unable to carry the group and alternative arrangements were made whereby the group was taken to Hawaii by alternative air companies but at a considerably increased expenditure and without completing the itinerary originally arranged.

. . .

The negotiations with United for the tour commenced in the summer of 1978 and, by autumn, terms had been arranged.

. . .

On 16 November 1978, United confirmed flights to New York, San Francisco, Honolulu, Los Angeles, Las Vegas, New York.

. . .

A strike by United employees commenced on 31 March 1979 and a message was sent to United's managers at most principal centres, including London, directing them to notify all airlines in their areas that, due to suspension of services, all carriers were requested not to issue tickets on United airlines until advised of resumption of service and that pre-paid ticket authorities would not be accepted for ticket insurance by United after 30 March and until further notice. It has not been established that Aer Lingus was officially notified but it is agreed by its representatives that they became aware of the strike within a couple of days. Notwithstanding this, Aer Lingus went ahead with the preparation of the tickets for the group and these were issued on 6 April.

. . .

. . . the plaintiff claims that there was an unconditional contract by United to carry the group on the tour and that United must bear the additional costs occasioned by the strike. . . .

. . .

As presented to the court, the defence of United was made on two main grounds. First, that, on being informed of the strike, the plaintiff took a calculated risk that United would be able to carry the group and that he should have cancelled the tour immediately. Secondly, that the contract was frustrated by the outbreak of the strike.

For the plaintiff it was argued with regard to frustration that the strike was caused by the employees of United, that the refusal of the employees to operate the planes is a refusal by United and therefore United is liable. It was also argued that United did not, at any time during the alternative arrangements to have the group carried, claim that the contract had been frustrated but was holding on in the hope that the strike would be settled.

I was referred to a number of authorities on the question of frustration. They were: *Davis Contractors Ltd v Fareham* UDC (1956) 3 WLR 37; *Pioneer Shipping Ltd v B.T.P. Tioxide Ltd* (1981) 3 WLR 292; *Paradine v Jane* (1647) Aleyn 26; *The Penelope* (1928) p. 180. I was also referred to *Halsbury*, (4th ed.), vol. 9 and to *Chitty on Contracts* ch. 23. Although it was not referred to during the hearing I note the following passage in *Chitty*, (24th ed.) para. 1417. 'If one party foresaw the risk but the other did not, it will be difficult for the former to claim that the occurrence of that risk frustrates the contract.' The reference given is to *Walton Harvey Ltd v Walker & Homfrays* |1931| 1 Ch. 274. I have also considered this report.

From these authorities, the following principles appear to apply when considering a claim that a contract has been frustrated.

1. A party may bind himself by an absolute contract to perform something which subsequently becomes impossible.
2. Frustration occurs when, without default of either party, a contractual obligation has become incapable of being performed.
3. The circumstances alleged to occasion frustration should be strictly scrutinised and the doctrine is not to be lightly applied.
4. Where the circumstances alleged to cause the frustration have arisen from the act or default of one of the parties, that party cannot rely on the doctrine.
5. All the circumstances of the contract should also be strictly scrutinised.
6. The event must be an unexpected event.
7. If one party anticipated or should have anticipated the possibility of the event which is alleged to cause the frustration and did not incorporate a clause in the contract to deal with it, he should not be permitted to rely on the happening of the event as causing frustration.

It does not appear, from the authorities to which I have been referred, what principle is to apply in considering frustration of a contract in circumstances such as the present so as to establish when a contract comes to an end. No evidence was tendered on behalf of United to indicate that United claimed at any particular time that the contract had come to an end and no submission was made as to the time of the termination of the contract. The suggestion on behalf of United seems to be that, once the parties became aware of the strike, a new agreement must be implied that the contract would continue until it was clear that the strike would not be settled in time to enable United to carry the group. Although the decision in the *Pioneer Shipping* case appears to support this proposition to some extent, I am not satisfied that such a proposition should be extended to the circumstances of the present case.

A significant circumstance in the present case is the fact, stated by two witnesses for United, that there had been a 'cooling-off' period of sixty days in operation prior to the strike being declared and taking effect. This must have been within the knowledge of United at all times during that period, that is to say, from 30 January 1979. It can hardly be suggested that there had not been some threat of industrial action before the 'cooling-off' period started to run and that, whatever the dispute was about, there had not previously been negotiations in progress between United and their employees. At no time was any communication about these circumstances made to the plaintiff and I conclude that this was because United felt that, if the plaintiff were made aware of the possibility of a strike, he might try to get another airline to carry the group. In my opinion this means that United, being aware of the threat or possibility of a strike, and the evidence is that United had had a somewhat similar strike a few years previously, but being anxious to obtain the business, took the risk of entering into the contract without including a provision to safeguard its position in the event of a strike taking place.

Under these circumstances I am of opinion that United is not entitled to succeed on its defence that the contract was frustrated.

I do not accept the argument made on behalf of the plaintiff that a strike by the employees of a party cannot cause frustration of a contract. In my opinion it depends entirely on the circumstances whether it does or not, but, on the view I have formed as to the position of United, it is not necessary for me to deal with this further.

(Damages were awarded against United Airlines. The plaintiff's claim against Aer Lingus for misrepresentation was dismissed, McWilliam J. holding that as Aer Lingus was acting as an agent for a disclosed principal it was not liable in contract.)

Note

The doctrine of frustration will not normally operate to discharge a contract where the event which is alleged to give rise to the frustration is provided for by a term of the contract.

William Neville and Sons Ltd *v* Guardian Builders Ltd [1990] ILRM 601

The defendants owned a plot of land at Stillorgan, County Dublin for which they sought planning permission. In order to gain access to develop the site a new roadway would have to be constructed part of which would traverse a strip of land owned by Dublin County Council. The defendants negotiated the purchase of this strip from the county council. The plaintiffs and the defendants entered into a licence agreement whereby, *inter alia*, the plaintiffs agreed to erect houses on the site. Later when the sale fell through the plaintiffs sought specific performance of the agreement together with damages for breach of contract.

Murphy J.:

Counsel on behalf of Guardian referred to three authorities, namely *Parkinson (Sir Lindsay) & Co. Ltd v Commissioners of Works* |1949| 2 KB 632; *Davis Contractors Ltd v Fareham Urban District Council* |1956| AC 696 and *National Carriers Ltd v Panalpina (Northern) Ltd* |1981| AC 675. These authorities were referred to largely for the purpose of demonstrating how far the courts in England, at any rate, had moved from the implied term as the basis for the doctrine of frustration to an objective test based on the construction of the contract. On behalf of the defendants it was contended that the correct test was that laid down by Lord Radcliffe in the *Davis Contractors* case at 728 in the following terms: 'So perhaps it would be simpler to say at the outset that frustration occurs whenever the law recognises that without default of either party a contractual obligation has become incapable of being performed because the circumstances in which performance is called for would render it a thing radically different from that which was undertaken by the contract. *Non haec in foedera veni.* It was not this that I promised to do.'

Attention was directed to a further quotation from Lord Radcliffe in the same case at 729 as follows:

> The court must act upon a general impression of what its rule requires. It is for that reason that special importance is necessarily attached to the occurrence of any unexpected event that, as it were, changes the face of things. But, even so, it is not hardship or inconvenience or material loss itself which calls the principle of frustration into play. There must be as well such a change in the significance of the obligation that the thing undertaken would, if performed, be a different thing from that contracted for.

What an analysis of the agreement and the circumstances in which it was executed shows is that the site which the parties agreed to develop was at the date of the contract effectively landlocked, that is to say, that the site was surrounded by land over which neither the plaintiffs nor the defendants had the right to pass and repass for the purpose of developing the site or granting similar rights-of-way to purchasers of the houses erected by them. No change took place in that objective situation between the date of the contract and the institution of the proceedings. However it seems to me clear beyond debate that both parties recognising this objective fact necessarily believed or assumed that the Dublin County Council as the owners of the crucial strip of land would facilitate the development and in that way enable the contract to be performed. The change that took place between the date of the contract and the time for its performance was the frustration of this expectation. In that sense the present case has something in common with the coronation cases and particularly *Krell v Henry* |1903| 2 KB 740. When the courts were satisfied that the foundation of the contract was the intention of the hirer to view the coronation procession and that the contract of hiring was entered into in the common expectation that the procession would take place on the date fixed for the hiring the cancellation of the procession was held to frustrate the contract. Of course it has long been recognised that care must be taken to ensure that a particular event was the purpose of the contract otherwise the alteration of a programme would not strike at the foundation of the contract (see *Herne Bay Steam Boat Co. v Hutton* |1903| 2 KB 683).

The argument for frustration in the present case is in many respects far stronger than that which succeeded in *Krell v Henry* because here the change in expectation did not defeat the purpose of the agreement but effectively the only means of performing it short of requiring one or other of the parties to do something not merely different from what he had agreed to do but something which he had not agreed to do at all.

It seems to me that the only factor which casts doubt upon the argument in favour of frustration is the continuing insistence of Nevilles even at this stage that the contract should be performed and an order for specific performance made. Counsel on behalf of Nevilles have urged that the doctrine of frustration applies only at common law and has no application where equitable relief is sought. I do not see how such a distinction could be maintained. If a contract is discharged by impossibility then clearly no court could compel its performance. Again, however, it was urged that the plaintiffs were entitled to obtain an order for specific performance of so much of the agreement as could be performed and either to waive performance of the remaining terms or to be compensated for their breach. In an appropriate case I do not doubt the correctness of that contention. However it has no application in the present case. The problem in performing the contract as a whole is not due to any breach of any of its terms by the defendants. The defendants did not agree to secure access to the site. If they had done so or if the unwillingness of the county council was due to the default of the defendants then indeed a claim—at least a claim for damages—would lie and the defendants could not rely on the doctrine of frustration.

However it is not so much the legal argument made on behalf of the plaintiffs which gives me pause. It is the apparent contradiction which this attitude illustrates. I must hesitate to conclude that it is impossible to perform a contract which a party directly concerned with its performance wishes to enforce. It does seem an impertinence to say to Nevilles 'You are mistaken in seeking to implement this contract. You cannot gain access to the site as matters stand and accordingly it cannot be performed by you.'

It seems to me that this apparent contradiction is due to the fact that Mr Neville believes—perhaps correctly—that alternative arrangements could be made; that the corporation or Parkes Hotel could be persuaded to relocate the access to the proposed new road. Indeed it may be that this objective could be achieved by providing the county council with a suitable if unspecified bond to secure them from any claim made by Parkes Hotel as a result of that relocation. However to proceed on that footing would be to impose entirely new terms on one or other of the parties. I think that the real extent of the problem could best be seen by considering what would happen if it was Nevilles and not Guardian who were seeking the declaration that the agreement had been frustrated. Could any court compel Nevilles to build houses on land to which they could not gain access as a matter of right? The answer must be in the negative. Accordingly it seems to me that performance of the contract has been frustrated.

In these circumstances I have concluded somewhat regretfully that the plaintiffs' claim must be dismissed.

Note

Murphy J.'s decision has been revised on the issue of frustration by the Supreme Court in a judgment delivered on 13 July 1994.

In the *Herne Bay Steam Boat Co. v Hutton* [1903] 2 KB 683 a contract to hire a boat to view a naval review was not frustrated when the review was cancelled. Vaughan Williams L.J. noted that although the purposes of the hirer became impossible, it could not be inferred that the review was contemplated by both parties as 'the foundation of the contract'.

John A. Browne *v* Patrick Mulligan, Francis Gallagher and Others (SC) 23 November 1977, unrep.

In August 1958, the governors of a hospital in Donegal appointed the plaintiff as physician to the hospital. The appointment was stated to be terminable if insufficient funds were available to enable the hospital to continue in operation. In February 1974, the hospital closed due to lack of funds and the plaintiff's employment was terminated by the governors. The plaintiff sought compensation.

Kenny J.:

. . .

On 9 December 1974 the High Court ordered that an issue be tried before the court whether any sum of money was payable to the plaintiff and, if so, the amount of it in respect of his claim for compensation arising out of the termination of his 'employment' under the governors of Sheil Hospital.

This issue was tried by Mr Justice Gannon in June 1976. He held that the plaintiff's employment had been effectively terminated in circumstances under which the governors of the hospital were discharged from the obligations of the agreement of 28 August 1958, because the agreement was no longer capable of being performed by either of the parties. He awarded the plaintiff £743, the amount tendered to him for three months salary less income tax under the Pay As You Earn scheme and £1,000 for loss of earnings from private practice during that period.

. . .

The plaintiff has now appealed against the amount awarded to him . . . .

. .

[His counsel] contended that the circumstances which were required to justify the termination of the contract of 28 August 1958 had not arisen and that the plaintiff was entitled to much more than the trial judge had awarded him. Counsel for the defendants, argued that the contract of 28 August 1958 had been frustrated by the order of 11 February 1974 so that nothing was payable to the plaintiff and if he was incorrect in this, that the sum payable was at most three months salary and three months loss of earnings.

The doctrine of frustration of a contract has been considered in one Irish case only (*Byrne v Limerick S.S. Co.* [1946] IR 138) where it was dealt with very briefly. During the past seventy years it has however been developed and refined by many decisions of the House of Lords and the Privy Council. The expression 'the contract is frustrated' so commonly used today is misleading: the doctrine relates, not to the contract but to the events or transactions which are the basis of the contract. It is these which make performance of the contracts impossible. This aspect of the doctrine was explained by Lord Wright in the *Constantine Line v Imperial Smelting Corp.* [1942] AC 154:

> In more recent days, the phrase more commonly used is 'frustration of the contract' or more shortly 'frustration'. 'Frustration of the contract' however is an elliptical expression. The fuller and more accurate phrase is 'frustration of the adventure or of the commercial or practical purpose of the contract'. The change in language corresponds to a wider conception of impossibility, which has extended the rule beyond contracts which depend on the existence, at the relevant time of a specific object. . . . to cases when the essential object does indeed exist, but its condition has by some casualty been so changed as to be not available for the purposes of the contract, either at the contract date or if no date is fixed, within any time consistent with the commercial or practical adventure.

There has been considerable judicial controversy as to its foundation. At least three possible bases for it have been suggested each of which can claim eminent judicial support. The first is that it depends upon an implied term in the contract (Viscount Simon in *Constantine Line v Imperial Smelting Corp.* [1942] AC 154) or upon 'the presumed common intention of the parties' (Viscount Maugham in the same case). The second rejects wholly the implied term theory and rests the doctrine on the true construction of the contract (Lord Reid in *Davis Contractors v Farnham* UDC (1956) AC 696 [and] Lord Radcliffe in the same case). The third theory—associated with Lord Wright—is that where the dispute between the parties arises from an event which they never thought of, the court imposes the solution that in the circumstances is just and reasonable (Lord Wright's *Legal Essays and Addresses*, 258 and *Denny Mott and Dickson Ltd v Fraser and Co. Ltd* [1944] AC 265 at 275).

I do not think it necessary to decide which theory we should adopt because, in my opinion, the doctrine does not apply to this case. The event on which reliance is placed as terminating the contract must be unanticipated by the parties and so not mentioned in the contract. If it is dealt with in the contract, then it was within the contemplation of the parties and the doctrine cannot apply. 'Equally, if the terms of the agreement show that the parties contemplated the possibility of such an intervening circumstance arising, frustration does not occur' (per Viscount Simon in *Cricklewood Pty Trust Ltd v Leightons Investment Trust Ltd* [1945] 1 All ER 252 at 255). The contract dealt with the closing down of the hospital when there were not sufficient funds available to allow it to continue in operation. This is the event which happened and the parties provided in the contract for its effect on the plaintiff's position. The order of 11 February 1974 was a recognition of the impossibility of carrying on the hospital.

(Kenny J. awarded the plaintiff a sum of £2,243 to compensate for loss of three months salary plus loss of private fees.)

Note

In the High Court, Gannon J. noted that a continuation of the operation of the hospital by the trustees would amount to a breach of their legal duties as trustees.

Patrick Sullivan v Southern Health Board (HC) 29 July 1993, unrep.

The plaintiff, a consultant physician in the defendants' hospital, sued for breach of his contract of employment. He claimed that the defendants had failed to make reasonable resources or staff available to him requiring him to work excess hours for lower remuneration than agreed. The defendants claimed *inter alia* that the contract was rendered frustated and impossible to perform due to the refusal of the Minister for Health and the Comhairle na hOispideal to provide them with the necessary funds or necessary staff.

Keane J.:

. . .

It is clear, in my view, that a body such as the defendants cannot enter into contractual obligations with another person in the knowledge that they are dependent on the co-operation of a third party—in this case the minister and the comhairle—in implementing them and then repudiate responsibility for the consequences to the other contracting party because of the refusal of the third party to co-operate. That was also the view taken by Lardner J. in *Staunton v St Laurence's Hospital and Others* with which I respectfully agree.

Nor can the defendants escape liability by relying on the doctrines of frustration of contract and impossibility of performance. It is, of course, always open to a defendant to plead that the contract for the breach of which he is now asked to pay damages is not the contract into which he originally entered.

[Referring to Lord Radcliffe in *Davis Contractors Ltd v Fareham* UDC ([1956] AC 696) he continued:]

That is not this case. Here the contract, its underlying basis and the legal context in which it was entered into all remained the same. There is thus no ground which relieves the defendants from the legal consequences of their breach of the contract.

B. SELF-INDUCED FRUSTRATION

Parties to a contract may not rely on frustration which is self-induced as a ground for discharging their obligations under the contract.

Achilles Herman and Others v The Owners and Master of the S.S. 'Vicia' [1942] IR 305

The plaintiffs were hired for a voyage from the US to Britain and back again. The ship's Finnish owners obtained a British ship's permit for the period from August 1940 to February 1941. This permit protected the vessel from British seizure. Although the permit had expired at the time the plaintiffs were hired it was not renewed. The British Ministry of Shipping assured the defendants that all facilities required would be provided. When the ship arrived in Dublin the plaintiffs were informed that the ship had no papers to proceed in Britain. They were discharged and subsequently they sued for breach of contract. The defendants pleaded frustration.

Hanna J.:

. . .

Now, on these facts can I come to the conclusion that there was what is known in law as frustration of the seamen's contract, and, if there was frustration, are the seamen still entitled to the cost of repatriation? These are difficult and unusual questions to be decided.

What is frustration? In the case of *Joseph Constantine S.S. Line Ltd v Imperial Smelting Corp. Ltd*[1] various definitions are given of frustration—incidental to the main question involved in that case—namely, upon whom the burden of proof lies. In that case, the ship in question, the 'Kingswood', was chartered to agents of the respondents in a voyage with ores from Port Pirie in South Australia to Europe. Before she became an 'arrived ship' at Port Pirie, there was a severe explosion in the neighbourhood of her auxiliary boiler, causing such damage that she could not perform her charterparty. As the headnote says, that was 'a destruction of the essential subject matter of the contract so as to frustrate the commercial object of the adventure.' In that respect the case differs from the one under consideration. As there was no negligence or default found with either party, it was held to discharge all liability under the charter. At 29, Viscount Simon L.C. says that 'when "frustration" in the legal sense occurs, it does not merely provide one party with a defence in an action brought by the other. It kills the contract itself and discharges both parties automatically. The plaintiff sues for breach at a past date and the defendant pleads that at that date no contract existed.' He further says that frustration depends on the terms of the contract and the surrounding circumstances of each case, as some kinds of impossibility may not discharge the contract at all.

Lord Maugham says, at 31, that 'frustration is based on the presumed common intention of the parties,' and he also states that the legal rights already accrued are unaffected.

At 35–36, Lord Wright, while recognising frustration by the destruction of the subject matter, gives a wider conception of impossibility and says:

> Another illustration is where the actual object still exists and is available, but the object of the contract as contemplated by both parties was its employment for a particular purpose, which has become impossible, as in the coronation cases. In these and similar cases, where there is not in the strict sense impossibility by some casual happening, there has been so vital a change in the circumstances as to defeat the contract. . . . The common object of the parties is frustrated. The contract has perished, *quoad* any rights or liabilities subsequent to the change.

He then cites passages from the judgment in *Paradine v Jane;*[2] and from the judgments in *Hirji Mulji v Cheong Yue S.S. Co.;*[3] *Couturier v Hastie;*[4] and *Dahl v Nelson, Donkin & Co.,*[5] and then he says: 'I have quoted these statements of law to emphasise that the court is exercising its powers, when it decides that a contract is frustrated, in order to achieve a result which is just and reasonable.'

The converse proposition is that it is not to be held to be frustrated unless it is just and reasonable.

Lord Porter, in the same case, seems to give a larger interpretation to frustration, where he says, at 40: 'Frustration is the term now in common use in cases in which the performance of a contract becomes impossible because its subject matter has ceased to be available for the purpose for which both parties intended it to be used.' He points out that in that case no question arises as to the extension of the doctrine to a case where the subject matter of the contract is not itself destroyed but the underlying purpose alone has been frustrated.

On these principles I am of opinion that the evidence on the part of the owners is not sufficient to justify a finding of frustration of the seamen's contracts. Adopting the words of Lord Wright, I decline to hold that it would be just and reasonable under the circumstances to decide that the seaman's contracts had been frustrated. The vessel had gone from Lisbon to Tampa without a convoy and was not interfered with. She sailed for thirteen days alone in the Atlantic without a convoy and without a proper warrant. I can find no case similar in facts to this, where it has been alleged, or held to be, a frustration for the owners of the vessel, apart from any hostile act of an enemy, to be unwilling to send her to sea on account of the risks and perils of war, with possible interception or seizure. It seems to me that the vessel could have reasonably reached Cardiff to obtain bunkers as she had the undertaking of the British Ministry of Shipping to give her facilities to a port in the UK. As Lord Sumner described the rule in *Hirji Mulji v Cheong Yue S.S. Co.* at 510: 'The rule as to frustration is to reconcile justice with the absolute contract. The seamen's contract was in this case an absolute contract. If the contingency was known to the parties as something which might happen and they did not provide for it, the contract ought to stand.'

Upon this point of the implied term in the contract, in the case of *Emanuel v La Compagnie Fermière*,[6] Lord Esher says: 'A term which was not actually contained in a written contract could not be implied unless the court came to a clear conclusion that both parties must have intended that term to be implied. It was not enough that both parties should have contemplated that a certain state of circumstances would exist. The court must be satisfied that the party against whom the implied term was to be enforced intended to bind himself that that state of circumstances should exist.' A similar principle is stated by Viscount Simon L.C. in the case of *Luxor Ltd v Cooper*,[7] and in *Jacob Marcus & Co. v Crédit Lyonnais*[8] Bowen L.J. said: 'One of the incidents which the English law attaches to a contract is that . . . a person who expressly contracts absolutely to do a thing not naturally impossible, is not excused for non-performance because of being prevented by *vis major*.' And in the case of *Larrinaga & Co. v Société Franco-Américaine des Phosphates*,[9] Lord Sumner said: 'If the appellants' own ships were under requisition, they could have fulfilled their contract with other ships, of which they might be able to obtain the disposition.' Applying that principle to this case the agents here might have made arrangements to take the seamen back to America in other vessels, but they did not do so and relied upon frustration.

This case is obviously different on the facts from any other, and the critical point is the British shipping warrant. I am not satisfied that all the four plaintiffs had information as to the British shipping warrant having expired, or that the captain did not renew it. The captain knew, and it would have been his duty to anticipate, that if he did not get it renewed to the UK while in Charleston, or Halifax, or Sydney, there might be some difficulty in Dublin, and, therefore, he should have included in the conditions of the contract the rights of the crew on the kind of frustration which actually occurred as well as frustration by 'torpedo, mine or loss'. As he did not, I find as a fact that the alleged frustration in Dublin, if the British shipping warrant was necessary and the letter from the British Ministry of Shipping insufficient, was due to the neglect of the captain who was responsible to the owners. If the full British warrant was not absolutely necessary and the letter from the British Ministry of Shipping sufficient, then there was no frustration in the Port of Dublin as it would have carried the vessel to Cardiff.

For these reasons I am of opinion, when the case is carefully analysed, that in the Port of Dublin there was no ground for concluding that there was impossibility of performance. . . .

1. 165 LTR 27; [1942] AC 154.   4. 5 HLC 673, at 681.   7. [1941] 1 All ER 33, at 40.
2. Aleyn, 26, at 27.   5. 6 AC 38, at 59.   8. 12 QBD 589, at 603
3. [1926] AC 497, at 510.   6. [1889] WN 151.   9. 92 LJKB 455, at 463.

Edward Byrne v The Limerick Steamship Co. Ltd [1946] IR 138

On 3 February the plaintiff was hired as part of a crew for one of the defendant's ships. As the ship was to call at a British port the crew list had to be approved by the British Permit Office in Dublin. When the plaintiff's permit was refused, he was discharged and a substitute hired. The plaintiff sued for breach of contract.

Overend J.:

. . .

The defendants pleaded that, by reason of the refusal of the permit, performance of the contract was frustrated and the contract was determined. . . .

Now, assuming, as I do, that it was impossible, from a practical point of view to undertake this voyage save under the aegis and with the facilities afforded by the British, yet the defendants have proved nothing amounting to frustration on 3 February, as of which date the rights of the parties must be determined. Where an essential licence or permission is refused, the defendants must prove that they have taken all reasonable steps to have such refusal withdrawn: *Bakubhai & Ambalal v South Australian Farmers' Co-operative Union of Adelaide*.[1]

Byrne has been given an excellent character and there is no evidence that the refusal of a permit would have been continued had it been questioned, or that he would have been refused permission to sail on any of the subsequent voyages contemplated by the Articles. . . .

In F. A. *Tamplin Steamship Co. Ltd v Anglo-Mexican Petroleum Products Co. Ltd*,[2] the ship—a tanker—was chartered by the respondents on a time charter for sixty months from 4 December 1912 to 4 December 1917. The ship was requisitioned by the British government early in December 1914, and before her release was again requisitioned in February 1915. She was still under requisition at the date of the hearing in July 1916, having meantime been structurally altered to carry troops. The owners claimed that the charter had been determined. The judge of first instance, the Court of Appeal, and the majority of the House of Lords all held there had been no frustration. Lord Parker in his speech (pp 425–8) emphasises the difficulty of applying this principle of frustration in the case of a time charter in which no definite commercial adventure is contemplated, and especially where the contract is already partly performed.

In *Barras v Aberdeen Steam Trawling and Fishing Co.*[3] a seaman was employed on a running agreement for six months fishing in the North Sea. On the trawler's first return she collided with another and had to be docked for some days for repairs, the seaman being paid off. Four members of the court (Viscount Buckmaster L.C. and Lords Warrington, Russell, and Macmillan) clearly expressed the view that there was no frustration of the contract. The reasoning mentioned seems to me to apply with equal force in the present case.

It has been frequently stressed that frustration operates automatically to determine the entire contract and does not depend on the volition, or even the knowledge, of the parties: *Joseph Constantine Steamship Line Ltd v Imperial Smelting Corp. Ltd*;[4] *Hirji Mulji v Cheong Yue Steamship Co. Ltd*;[5] *Cricklewood Pty and Investment Trust Ltd v Leighton's Investment Trust Ltd*;[6] *Maritime National Fish Ltd v Ocean Trawlers Ltd*.[7]

In my opinion Byrne's contract with the defendant company was not determined by frustration, but by his discharge by the captain on 3 February.

1. 69 Lloyd's Rep. 138.
2. [1916] 2 AC 397.
3. [1933] AC 402, at 413, 439, 443, 448.
4. [1942] AC 154.
5. [1926] AC 497.
6. [1945] AC 221.
7. [1935] AC 524.

(The plaintiff was deemed to be entitled to one month's wages as compensation for the discharge.)

F.C. Sheppard & Co. Ltd v Jerrom [1986] 3 All ER 589

An apprentice under a four year training service agreement, was convicted of affray and sentenced to borstal training, while less than half way through his apprenticeship. He was sentenced for an indeterminate period of between six months and two years. Upon his release six months later his employer refused to re-hire him. His employer appealed from the decisions of an industrial tribunal and the Employment Appeal Tribunal that they had repudiated his contract and that the dismissal was thus unfair.

Lawton L.J.:

. . .

. . . The first question is whether what happened was capable in law of frustrating the contract. The second is whether it did frustrate it; this is a question of fact (see *Pioneer Shipping Ltd v B.T.P. Tioxide Ltd, The Nema* [1981] 2 All ER 1030 at 1047, [1982] AC 724 at 752 per Lord Roskill)

. . .

As to the first of these questions, there was an event, namely the sentence of borstal training, which was not foreseen or provided for by the parties at the time of contracting. It was a question of fact, to which I shall return later, whether it rendered the performance of the contract radically different from what the parties had contemplated when they entered into it. What has to be decided is whether the outside event and its consequences in relation to the performance of the contract occurred without either the fault or default of either party to it. I have based this dissection of the problem on the speech of Lord Barandon in *Paal Wilson & Co A/S v Partenreederei Hannah Blumenthal, The Hannah Blumenthal* [1983] 1 All ER 34 at 44, [1983] 1 AC 854 at 909.

There was no fault or default on the part of the employers. They were alleging that because of the unforeseen outside event the contract had been frustrated. If it had been, there had been no dismissal as defined in s. 55 of the 1978 Act. The oddity of this case is that the apprentice, for his own purposes, is seeking to allege that he was in default so as to keep in being a contract which the employers would otherwise have been able to say had been terminated by operation of law. Through his counsel he has submitted, relying on *Universal Cargo Carriers Corp. v Citati* [1957] 2 All ER 70, [1957] 2 QB 401, that his conduct, resulting as it did in a sentence of borstal training, amounted to a repudiation of the contract which the employers did not accept until January 1982. It seems to me that the apprentice is seeking to rely on his own default, if in law it should be regarded as such, to establish his right to claim for unfair dismissal.

This is the opposite of what happened in two of the leading cases dealing with the consequences of default in relation to the frustration of contracts, namely *Maritime National Fish Ltd v Ocean Trawlers Ltd* [1935] AC 524, [1935] All ER Rep 86 and *Mertens v*

Home Freeholds Co. |1921| 2 KB 526, |1921| All ER Rep 372. In each of these cases the plaintiff had sought to enforce the contract and the defendants had pleaded frustration because of change of circumstances. It was adjudged in both cases that these pleas failed because the defendants' own acts had caused or contributed to what had made performance impossible. The frustration which the two defendants had sought to rely on were self-induced and in consequence in law there had been no frustrations. In the *Maritime National Fish Ltd* case the act had been an election; in the *Mertens* case, reprehensible conduct which could fairly be described as a default. As Lord Brandon commented in the *Paal Wilson & Co.* case ' . . . the courts have never defined with precision the meaning of the expression "default" in this context.' This case does call for this court to decide whether the apprentice's conduct resulting in a sentence of borstal training was a default which prevented the contract from being frustrated.

The classic formulation of the concept of 'self-induced frustration' is to be found in the speech of Lord Sumner in *Bank Line Ltd v Arthur Capel & Co.* |1919| AC 435 at 452 when he said: 'I think it is now well settled that the principle of frustration of an adventure assumes that the frustration arises without blame or fault on either side. Reliance cannot be placed on a self-induced frustration; indeed, such conduct might give the other party the option to treat the contract as repudiated.'

In *Joseph Constantine Steamship Line Ltd v Imperial Smelting Corp. Ltd, The Kingswood* |1941| 2 All ER 165, |1942| AC 154 the House of Lords had to adjudge whether in a claim by charterers against shipowners for damages for failure to load a cargo when the shipowners pleaded that the contract had been frustrated by an explosion, for which no cause was ascertained, they had to prove that it had not been caused by their act or default. Their Lordships adjudged that they did not have to do so. At the end of his speech 'For purposes of clearness, and to avoid possible misunderstanding hereafter' Viscount Simon L.C. said:

> . . . I do not think that the ambit of 'default' as an element disabling the plea of frustration to prevail has as yet been precisely and finally determined. 'Self-induced' frustration, as illustrated by the two decided cases already quoted |that is the *Maritime National Fish Ltd* and *Mertens* cases|, involves deliberate choice, and those cases amount to saying that a man cannot ask to be excused by reason of frustration if he has purposely so acted as to bring it about. 'Default' is a much wider term, and in many commercial cases dealing with frustration is treated as equivalent to negligence. Yet in cases of frustration of another class, arising in connection with a contract for personal performance, it has not, I think, been laid down that, if the personal incapacity is due to want or care, the plea fails. Some day it may have to be finally determined whether a *prima donna* is excused by complete loss of voice from an executory contract to sing if it is proved that her condition was caused by her carelessness in not changing her wet clothes after being out in the rain. The implied term in such a case may turn out to be that the fact of supervening physical incapacity dissolves the contract without inquiring further into its cause, provided, of course, that it has not been deliberately induced in order to get out of the engagement.

The apprentice's criminal conduct was deliberate but it did not by itself have any consequences on the performance of his contract. What affected performance was his sentence of borstal training, which was the act of the judge and which he would have avoided if he could have done so. It cannot be said, I think, that the concept of 'self-induced frustration' can be applied to this case. What can be said, however, is that when the apprentice acted in the criminal way he did he was recklessly putting at risk his ability to perform his contract. He should have appreciated that if he joined in an affray he might lose his liberty. I doubt, however, whether as a matter of contract he had impliedly agreed with his employers that outside working hours he would never behave in a way which might interrupt for a substantial period his ability to go to work.

Lord Wright, in the same case [*Constantine*], after having referred to some of the undecided aspects of the law relating to frustration, said:

> The appeal can, I think, be decided according to the generally accepted view that frustration involves as one of its elements absence of fault, by applying the ordinary rules as to onus of proof. If frustration is viewed, as I think it can be, as analogous to an exception, since it is generally relied upon as a defence to a claim for failure to perform a contract, the same rule will properly be applied to it as to the ordinary type of exceptions. The defence may be rebutted by proof of fault, but the onus of proving fault will rest on the plaintiff. This is merely to apply the familiar rule which is applied, for instance, where a carrier by sea relies on the exception of perils of the seas. If the goods owner then desires to rebut that *prima facie* defence on the ground of negligence or other fault on the part of the shipowner, it rests on the goods owner to establish the negligence or fault.

This line of reasoning was discussed by Lord Porter. He queried whether an accidental injury to a contractor preventing performance would be regarded as caused by his default.

In the absence of any binding, or even persuasive, authority dealing with this problem I approach it in this way. The employers wanted to establish that the contract had been frustrated. They had to prove that there had been some outside event which rendered performance of the contract radically different from what the parties had contemplated when they made it. They proved an outside event which had occurred because of the sentence which the judge had imposed. They claimed that performance would have been radically different. The apprentice did not suggest that they had been at fault. In my judgment the apprentice should not be allowed to plead his own 'default' in order to establish his right to claim compensation for unfair dismissal.

In my judgment the principle of law is that he who asserts that the performance of a contract had been frustrated must prove not only the two essential elements to which Lord Brandon referred but that the outside event or extraneous change of situation was not caused by any default on his part. If the party against whom frustration is asserted can by way of answer rely on his own misconduct, injustice results, as is shown by the following example which was discussed in argument. A butler is convicted of stealing his employer's silver and is sentenced to two years' imprisonment. If this is no more than repudiatory conduct on his part and his employer does not tell him either expressly or by implication (see *London Transport Executive v Clarke* [1981] ICR 355) that he has been dismissed, he could claim on release from prison that he was still employed as a butler. Such a contention would surprise the employer, but perhaps not his solicitors.

The only decision of this court which deals with the effect of a custodial sentence on a contract of employment, *Hare v Murphy Bros Ltd* [1974] 3 All ER 940, was decided before the decision of this court in *London Transport Executive v Clarke*. In *Hare*'s case [1973] ICR 331 the National Industrial Relations Court had adjudged that the employee's criminal conduct which had resulted in his being sentenced to twelve months' imprisonment amounted to a breach of his contract of employment of so serious a nature that it constituted a unilateral repudiation of that contract at the date when he was convicted and sentenced. That made it impossible for him to claim unfair dismissal because at that date the Industrial Relations Act 1971 was not in force. The National Industrial Relations Court has said that the sentence was not an event frustrating the contract of employment because it had been brought about by the employee's own conduct. In this court the employee submitted that the contract had not been determined until his repudiatory conduct by being sent to prison had been accepted by his employers, which, he submitted, was within time for the purpose of claiming that he had been unfairly dismissed. Lord Denning M.R., who delivered the leading judgment, said that he could not accept that by becoming involved in a brawl the employee had been in breach of contract. He thought that the sentence of imprisonment was a frustrating event which brought his contract of employment to an end. Stephenson L.J. thought that the contract had been brought to an end in one of four ways, but he did not find it necessary to say which was the appropriate label to apply. I was a member of the court. I agreed that the appeal should be dismissed on what I called the 'common sense of the situation', which was not an example of sound legal reasoning. Since it is not clear on what grounds the court as such decided Hare's case I do not regard it as a binding authority. In my opinion this court can reconsider the problem of the effect of a custodial sentence on a contract of employment. In my judgment such a sentence is capable in law of frustrating the contract.

The next question is whether on the facts of this case the sentence of borstal training did frustrate the contract. In my judgment it did. The parties must have contemplated that four years' training was necessary for producing a qualified plumber. The passing of the sentence meant that there was going to be a substantial break in the period of training, probably thirty nine weeks, possibly six months but also possibly more than thirty nine weeks. At the end of the contract period the apprentice was not going to be as well trained as the parties had contemplated he would be.

Much time was spent in this court discussing whether the apprentice's conduct, resulting as it did in his being sentenced to borstal training, was repudiatory of the contract. He broke no term of it. His conduct can only be said to be repudiatory on the grounds set out by Devlin J. in *Universal Cargo Carriers Corp. v Citati* [1957] 2 All ER 70 at 84, [1957] 2 QB 401 at 436. Even if that case states the law relating to commercial contracts correctly (and I make no comment on that) I doubt whether the principle it establishes applies to contracts of personal service. The apprentice's criminal conduct itself would have had no effect on his performance of it had he not been arrested, convicted and sentenced. The sentence was a consequence of the disorderly conduct; probably a foreseeable one; but not an inevitable one. . . .

I would allow the appeal.

(Mustill and Balcombe L.JJ. agreed.)

C. EMPLOYMENT CONTRACTS

Frustration may operate to discharge a party's obligations under a contract of employment.

Frank Flynn v Great Northern Rly Co. (Ireland) Ltd (1953) 89 ILTR 46

The plaintiff, an employee of the defendant company was injured as a result of an accident at work on 30 July 1947. The court had to decide *inter alia* whether the plaintiff's contract of services was frustrated due to his incapacity.

Budd J.:

....

The first ground relied on is that, whether properly dismissed or not, Flynn's contract of service is in any event at an end because of the nature of his incapacity, which it is alleged was such as to frustrate the contract.

Dr Bouchier Hayes said that he formed the opinion in October 1947, that Flynn was not then fit for work on the foot-plate. He made a report to that effect dated 16 October 1947. From 1947 to the present date he said there was no prospect of Flynn being able to work as a fireman on the foot-plate and that he had formed the opinion that it was undesirable that he should ever work on the foot-plate again. Dr Bouchier Hayes' view is that there was no period between 1947 and the present time when Flynn was fit for work on the foot-plate and he has in fact done no work since 30 July 1947, a period of nearly six years. He has suffered during that period from a number of serious complaints, and, from what Dr Bouchier Hayes said, and having regard to the nature of his condition and the record of his incapacity, my view is that in all human probability Flynn will not be fit to work on the foot-plate again and that he is permanently incapacitated for such service. Having regard to Flynn's history and condition my view is that prior to 16 October 1947, Flynn had become permanently incapacitated in the physical sense from performing his duties on the foot-plate.

The precise result of the illness of a servant on a contract of service is not always easy to determine. From a perusal of the cases it would seem that in law the illness or physical incapacity of the servant will determine the contract if it is of such a nature as to frustrate the business object of the engagement. In *Poussard v Spiers* 1 QBD 410, an opera singer was engaged to sing in an opera for three months, provided the opera ran so long. The plaintiff was unable to sing on the first night through illness, which was serious and of uncertain duration. It was held that the failure on the plaintiff's part went to the root of the matter and discharged the contract. The result was different in *Storey v Fulham Steel Works* 24 TLR 89, where six months illness, after two years service in a five years engagement, was held not to determine the contract. Lord Alverstone, however, in that case adopted what was said in *Jenkinson v Union Marine Insurance Co.* by Baron Bramwell as a correct statement of the law, namely, that if the illness was such as to put an end in the business sense to their business engagement and would frustrate the object of that engagement, then the employer could dismiss its servant and no action would lie against him. What Lord Alverstone said seems to indicate the necessity of the master giving notice before the contract is terminated, but that point was not at issue in the case. Lord Campbell used words in *Cuckson v Stone* 1 E & E 248 which would also seem to indicate that notice would be necessary where he says at 257 that, if the plaintiff in that case had by illness become permanently incapacitated to act in the capacity of a brewer, the defendant might in the view of the court have determined the contract. Again, Lord Atkinson in *Price v Guest Keen and Nettlefolds* |1918| AC 760 said that illness might be of such a permanent character that it would justify dismissal, thereby implying that notice was necessary, but again in neither of these cases was that precise point in issue. On the other hand, Scrutton L.J., in *Warburton v Co-operative Wholesale Society, Ltd* |1917| 1 KB 663, said that under the decided cases a servant incapacitated by illness and in the absence of notice does not cease to be employed unless the illness is such as seriously to interfere with or frustrate the business purpose of the contract, thereby implying that in such case notice is unnecessary. From the words used by Blackburn J., delivering the judgment of the court in *Poussard v Spiers* 'that the failure on the plaintiff's part went to the root of the matter and discharged the defendant' and from the nature of the decision it would appear that the court in that case did not regard notice as necessary, but it is right to bear in mind that the engagement was to commence on a specific date and was of a very particular nature. Of recent years as a result, no doubt, of cases arising from war conditions, the doctrine of frustration has received more detailed consideration. In *Denny Mott and Dickson Ltd v Fraser* |1944| AC 265, Lord Wright at 274 points out that where there is frustration a dissolution of the contract occurs automatically. Overend J., in *Byrne v Limerick Steamship Co. Ltd* |1946| IR 138, 80 ILTR 142, also accepted the view that frustration operates automatically to determine the entire contract and does not depend upon the volition of the parties or even on their knowledge. It is right to add that he decided that the contract in that case had not been determined by frustration. If frustration is the test, there does not in principle seem to be any reason why a master should have to give notice to terminate a contract, already frustrated, and my view, therefore, is that notice is unnecessary.

It would seem to be a question of fact to be determined in each case as to whether or not the illness is of such a kind and duration, or likely duration, as to frustrate the business object of the contract, and I must consider what the true position is in this case, having regard to the nature of Flynn's illness or incapacity, and the nature of his contract. I have determined that he was a weekly wage earner whose contract was subject to be determined by a week's notice. He is a manual worker but without him and men of his grade the engines of the company cannot be properly manned and the service maintained. His incapacity is, I am satisfied, now permanent for work as a fireman. His incapacity on 16 October 1947, was such that it was the doctor's view, communicated to the company, that it would be undesirable that he should ever again resume duty as a fireman on the foot-plate, a view that has been amply substantiated by subsequent events. I am satisfied that in all the circumstances his incapacity was such at that time as to frustrate the business object of the engagement. I have come to the conclusion, therefore, that I ought to find in accordance with the defendant's alternative plea that Flynn was permanently incapacitated on 16 October 1947, to perform his duties as a fireman on the foot-plate and, his incapacity being such at the time as to frustrate the business object of the engagement, his contract, accordingly, then terminated. . . .

Donegal County Council v Daniel Langan. Employment Appeals Tribunal Case No. UD143/89

The determination of the tribunal was as follows:

The employer is appealing the recommendation of the Rights Commissioner, who found that the employee was unfairly dismissed.

The employee, a general operative, commenced employment with the employer in May 1974. On 27 June 1985, he became incapacitated for work, certified as suffering from lumbar pain.

He was still absent on sick leave and submitting medical certificates when he was informed by the employer in a letter dated 21 April 1988 that 'the council does not intend to re-employ you and it will therefore, not be necessary for you to submit any further medical certificates'.

The employee accepted this letter as a dismissal and we hold that he was entitled to do so. In July 1988, he was medically certified as fit to resume his employment by his own medical adviser. After he had served a claim for unfair claim dismissal on the employer he was requested to attend Dr David St C. Baird FRCS, Consultant Orthopaedic Surgeon in Derry, for medical examination. This he duly did and Dr Baird, in his report, stated 'I would feel that he is fit enough to carry out manual work'.

The employer is contesting that his contract of employment had become frustrated by illness.

The doctrine of frustration has been used very selectively and only in cases where the event relied on, renders all further performance of an employment contract impossible. In most cases a defence of fair dismissal because of sickness is entered. Such is not the case here. The general 'impossible to perform' test applies. There may be an event (e.g. a crippling accident) so dramatic and shattering that everyone concerned will realise immediately that to all intents and purposes the contract must be regarded as at an end. Or there may be an event, where an employee becomes incapacitated by an incurable disease, or an illness or accident, the course and outcome of which, is uncertain. It may be a long process before one is able to say whether the event is such as to bring about the frustration of the contract and that it is no longer possible to regard the contract as still subsisting. Among the matters to be taken into account in deciding whether the contract is frustrated are:

   (i) the length of the previous employment.
  (ii) how long it has been expected that the employment would last.
 (iii) the nature of the job.
 (iv) the nature, length and effect of the illness or disabling event.
  (v) the need of the employer for the work to be done.
 (vi) whether wages have continued to be paid.
(vii) the actions of the employer in relation to the employment.
(viii) whether consideration was given to retaining the employee on the books if not in employment.
 (ix) whether the employer discussed with the employee and his trade union the employee's problems and prospects.
  (x) whether adequate medical investigation was carried out, (e.g. employers should ask their own or their employee's doctor for reports to establish the real medical facts and if there is conflicting medical evidence, to seek an independent source).
 (xi) whether, in all the circumstances a reasonable employer could be expected to wait any longer.

It was clear from the evidence that the employee was not a key worker. Apart from the initial twelve weeks of his absence he was not paid during his period of absence. There was no consultation with either the employee or his trade union and no medical investigation was carried out prior to termination of his employment. We are at a loss to know why the employer waited until some eleven months after the termination of the employment before requesting the employee to attend for medical examination. His own medical adviser had certified him fit for full duties, some three months after the termination of his employment. In a case of frustration it is not necessary that the employers should take steps to end the employment for the whole point of frustration is that it operates automatically to discharge the contract as a result of the event bringing it about. Proving frustration can be a difficult task and employers are more likely to succeed when there is clear evidence that there is little prospect of recovery. Where there is prospect of recovery, a lengthy absence does not necessarily frustrate the contract.

We find, that the employer has failed to prove that the employee's contract was frustrated by illness and the fact that he was medically certified as fit to resume his employment within some three months after the termination of his employment was not a factor in our finding. Even if the employer had contended that the employee was fairly dismissed because of his prolonged absence, we would find that the dismissal was unfair on procedural grounds. Accordingly we uphold the recommendation of the Rights Commissioner that the employee was unfairly dismissed.

   Accordingly we determine that the employee should be reinstated in accordance with s. 7 (1)(a) of the Unfair Dismissals Act 1977.

Chapter Nineteen

Damages

INTRODUCTION

A contracting party who is confronted by an actual or threatened breach of contract may seek a number of remedies, often in pleadings which stress that it is for the judge to select the most appropriate relief in the instant case. These remedies include a declaratory judgment in which the rights of the parties are clarified by the court, an injunction of some kind, specific performance of the contract, or an order that any profits made as a result of wrongdoing be estimated and paid to the victim of the breach of contract. However, many of these remedies may not be available for any number of reasons, and in such a case damages may be awarded as an alternative remedy. It is necessary to emphasise that in most cases the plaintiff's only realistic remedy will be damages and that the plaintiff may actually only seek this remedy. It is possible however for the plaintiff to use the rules which determine the way in which damages will be assessed, in order to maximise the plaintiff's prospects of obtaining compensation, so a clear understanding of the principles and rules which govern the assessment of damages is an important skill for any lawyer to acquire.

SECTION ONE—REASONS FOR THE AWARD OF DAMAGES FOLLOWING ON A BREACH OF CONTRACT

Robinson v Harman (1848) 1 Ex 850

This was an action which arose out of an agreement to grant a lease in favour of the plaintiff, for an annual rent of £110, the lease to run for twenty years. The plaintiff had entered into a good bargain, the leased premises being worth more than £110 per year. When the defendant failed to execute the lease the plaintiff sued. His costs in wasted solicitor's fees were £15 12s 8d but the jury awarded the plaintiff £200 damages. The defendant appealed against this award.

Parke B.:

. . .

. . . what damages is the plaintiff entitled to recover? The rule of the common law is, that where a party sustains a loss by reason of a breach of contract, he is, so far as money can do it, to be placed in the same situation, with respect to damages, as if the contract had been performed. The case of *Flureau v Thornhill*[1] qualified that rule of the common law. It was there held, that contracts for the sale of real estate are merely on

911

condition that the vendor has a good title; so that, when a person contracts to sell real property, there is an implied understanding that, if he fail to make a good title, the only damages recoverable are the expenses which the vendee may be put to in investigating the title. The present case comes within the rule of the common law, and I am unable to distinguish it from *Hopkins v Grazebrook*.[2]

Alderson B.:

I am of the same opinion. The damages have been assessed according to the general rule of law, that where a person makes a contract and breaks it, he must pay the whole damage sustained. Upon that general rule an exception was engrafted by the case of *Flureau v Thornhill*, and upon that exception the case of *Hopkins v Grazebrook* engrafted another exception. This case comes within the latter, by which the old common law rule has been restored. Therefore the defendant, having undertaken to grant a valid lease, not having any colour of title, must pay the loss which the plaintiff has sustained by not having that for which he contracted.

Platt B.:

Upon general principle I cannot distinguish this case from *Hopkins v Grazebrook*.

[1]. 2 Wm. Bl. 1078.   [2]. 6 B. & C. 31.

Note

It is necessary to stress that the compensatory principle does not of itself identify the basic measure of damages. As we shall see both contract and tort damages are compensatory but different results follow depending on the cause of action. It is essential to distinguish possible measures of compensation from specific heads of loss. The 'exception' referred to in *Robinson v Harman* is considered below, the rule in *Bain v Fothergill* on p. 975.

A. THE RELIANCE INTEREST IN CONTRACT DAMAGES

Fuller & Purdue (1936) 46 Yale LJ 52, 53–7 (Footnotes omitted.)

The Purposes Pursued in Awarding Contract Damages

It is convenient to distinguish three principal purposes which may be pursued in awarding contract damages. These purposes, and the situations in which they become appropriate, may be stated briefly as follows:

First, the plaintiff has in reliance on the promise of the defendant conferred some value on the defendant. The defendant fails to perform his promise. The court may force the defendant to disgorge the value he received from the plaintiff. The object here may be termed the prevention of gain by the defaulting promisor at the expense of the promisee, more briefly, the prevention of unjust enrichment. The interest protected may be called the *restitution interest*. For our present purposes it is quite immaterial how the suit in such a case be classified, whether as contractual or quasi-contractual, whether as a suit to enforce the contract or as a suit based upon a rescission of the contract. These questions relate to the superstructure of the law, not to the basic policies with which we are concerned.

Secondly, the plaintiff has in reliance on the promise of the defendant changed his position. For example, the buyer under a contract for the sale of land has incurred expense in the investigation of the seller's title, or has neglected the opportunity to enter other contracts. We may award damages to the plaintiff for the purpose of undoing the harm which his reliance on the defendant's promise has caused him. Our object is to put him in as good a position as he was in before the promise was made. The interest protected in this case may be called the *reliance interest*.

Thirdly, without insisting on reliance by the promisee or enrichment of the promisor, we may seek to give the promisee the value of the expectancy which the promise created. We may in a suit for specific performance actually compel the defendant to render the promised performance to the plaintiff, or, in a suit for damages, we may make the defendant pay the money value of this performance. Here our object is to put the plaintiff in as good a position as he would have occupied had the defendant performed his promise. The interest protected in this case we may call the *expectation interest*.

It will be observed that what we have called the *restitution interest* unites two elements: (1) reliance by the promisee, (2) a resultant gain to the promisor. It may for some purposes be necessary to separate these elements. In some cases a defaulting promisor may after his breach be left with an unjust gain which was not taken from the promisee (a third party furnished the consideration), or which was not the result of reliance by the promisee (the promisor violated a promise not to appropriate the promisee's goods). Even in those cases where the promisor's gain results from the promisee's reliance it may happen that damages will be assessed somewhat differently, depending on whether we take the promisor's gain or the promisee's loss as the standard of measurement. Generally, however, . . . gain by the promisor will be accompanied by a corresponding and, so far as its legal measurement is concerned, identical loss to the promisee, so that for our purposes the most workable classification is one which presupposes in the restitution interest a correlation of promisor's gain and promisee's loss. If, as we shall assume, the gain involved in the restitution interest results from and is identical with the plaintiff's loss through reliance, then the restitution interest is merely a special case of the reliance interest; all of the cases coming under the restitution interest will be covered by the reliance interest, and the reliance interest will be broader than the restitution interest only to the extent that it includes cases where the plaintiff has relied on the defendant's promise without enriching the defendant.

B. THE PLAINTIFF'S LOSS

British Westinghouse Electric and Manufacturing Co. Ltd v Underground Electric Rlys of London Ltd [1912] AC 673

The appellants, British Westinghouse, supplied turbines to the respondents. The turbines failed to perform to the standard set by the contract and the respondents replaced these turbines with a rival product that proved much more efficient than the British Westinghouse turbines. Indeed, in an arbitr--ation the arbitrator found, (1) that purchase of the replacement turbines was a reasonable and prudent course for the respondents to take in mitigating their losses, and (2) that even if the original turbines had complied with the contract, there would have still been a pecuniary advantage to the respondent in replacing the British Westinghouse machines. The arbitrator, the Divisional Court, the High Court and the Court of Appeal nevertheless held that the respondents could recover the cost of the substituted turbines as part of their damages. British Westinghouse appealed to the House of Lords.

Viscount Haldane:

. . .

. . . I think that there are certain broad principles which are quite well settled. The first is that, as far as possible, he who has proved a breach of a bargain to supply what he contracted to get is to be placed, as far as money can do it, in as good a situation as if the contract had been performed.

The fundamental basis is thus compensation for pecuniary loss naturally flowing from the breach; but this first principle is qualified by a second, which imposes on a plaintiff the duty of taking all reasonable steps to mitigate the loss consequent on the breach, and debars him from claiming any part of the damage which is due to his neglect to take such steps. In the words of James L.J. in *Dunkirk Colliery Co. v Lever*,[1] 'The person who has broken the contract is not to be exposed to additional cost by reason of the plaintiffs not doing what they ought to have done as reasonable men, and the plaintiffs not being under any obligation to do anything otherwise than in the ordinary course of business.'

As James L.J. indicates, this second principle does not impose on the plaintiff an obligation to take any step which a reasonable and prudent man would not ordinarily take in the course of his business. But when in the course of his business he has taken action arising out of the transaction, which action has diminished his loss, the effect in actual diminution of the loss he has suffered may be taken into account even though there was no duty on him to act.

Staniforth v Lyall[2] illustrates this rule. In that case the defendants had chartered a ship to New Zealand, where they were to load her, or by an agent there to give the plaintiff, the owner, notice that they abandoned the adventure, in which case they were to pay £500. The ship went to New Zealand, but found neither agent nor cargo there, and the captain chose to make a circuitous voyage home by way of Batavia. This voyage, after making every allowance for increased expense and loss of time, was more profitable than the original venture to New Zealand would have been. The Court of Common Pleas decided that the action was to be viewed as one for a breach of contract to put the cargo on board the plaintiff's vessel for which the plaintiff was entitled to recover all the damages he had incurred, but that he was bound to bring into account, in ascertaining the damages arising from the breach, the advantages which had accrued to him because of the course which he had chosen to adopt.

I think that this decision illustrates a principle which has been recognized in other cases, that, provided the course taken to protect himself by the plaintiff in such an action was one which a reasonable and prudent person might in the ordinary conduct of business properly have taken, and in fact did take whether bound to or not, a jury or an arbitrator may properly look at the whole of the facts and ascertain the result in estimating the quantum of damage.

Recent illustrations of the way in which this principle has been applied, and the facts have been allowed to speak for themselves, are to be found in the decisions of the Judicial Committee of the Privy Council in *Eric County Natural Gas and Fuel Co. v Carroll*[3] and *Wertheim v Chicoutimi Pulp Co.*[4] The subsequent transaction, if to be taken into account, must be one arising out of the consequences of the breach and in the ordinary course of business. This distinguishes such cases from a quite different class illustrated by *Bradburn v Great Western Rly Co.*,[5] where it was held that, in an action for injuries caused by the defendants' negligence, a sum received by the plaintiff on a policy for insurance against accident could not be taken into account in reduction of damages. The reason of the decision was that it was not the accident, but a contract wholly independent of the relation between the plaintiff and the defendant, which gave the plaintiff his advantage. Again, it has been held that, in an action for delay in discharging a ship of the plaintiffs' whereby they lost their passengers whom they had contracted to carry, the damages ought not to be reduced by reason of the same persons taking passage in another vessel belonging to the plaintiffs: *Jebsen v East and West India Dock Co.*,[6] a case in which what was relied on as mitigation did not arise out of the transactions the subject matter of the contract.

The cases as to the measure of damages for breach of a covenant by a lessee to deliver up the demised premises in repair illustrate yet another class of authorities in which the qualifying rule has been excluded. In *Joyner v Weeks*[7] the lessor had made a lease to another lessee by way of anticipation, to commence from the expiration of the term of this lease, and the new lessee had made no claim to be reimbursed the cost which he had incurred in repairing after the expiration of the demised lease. Wright J. held that the true test was the amount of diminution in value to the lessor, not exceeding the cost of doing the repairs. The Court of Appeal, including Lord Esher and Fry L.J., took a different view. They thought that there had been a constant practice of laying down the measure of damages as being the cost of putting into repair, and that in the particular class of cases with which they were dealing it was a highly convenient rule which ought not to be disturbed. Any other measure appeared to involve complicated inquiries. Moreover, the arrangement between the lessor and the new lessee was *res inter alios acta* with which the original lessee had nothing to do and which he was not entitled to set up.

I think the principle which applies here is that which makes it right for the jury or arbitrator to look at what actually happened, and to balance loss and gain. The transaction was not *res inter alios acta*, but one in which the person whose contract was broken took a reasonable and prudent course quite naturally arising out of the circumstances in which he was placed by the breach. Apart from the breach of contract, the lapse of time had rendered the appellants' machines obsolete, and men of business would be doing the only thing they could properly do in replacing them with new and up-to-date machines.

1. (1878) 9 ChD 20, at p. 25.
2. 7 Bing. 169.
3. |1911| AC 105.
4. |1911| AC 301.

5. LR 10 Ex 1.
6. LR 10 CP 300.
7. |1891| 2 QB 31.

(Ashbourne, Macnaghten and Atkinson L.JJ. concurred.)

Hussey and Another v Eels [1990] 1 All ER 449

Mustill L.J.:

...

For many years until the beginning of 1984 the defendants had lived in a bungalow in Farnham, Surrey. The nature of the underlying ground was such that the building suffered from subsidence. At the end of 1983 the defendants commenced negotiations for the sale of the bungalow to the plaintiffs, whose solicitor served the customary inquiries before contract. Additional inquiry 5 read as follows: 'Please confirm to the vendor's knowledge that the property has not been subject to the following matters . . . (c) subsidence.' The response was: 'Confirmed'. In due course the transaction went ahead, and on 7 February 1984 the purchase and sale was completed at a price of £53,250.

The judge has found that the untrue statement given on the defendants' behalf in the response to additional inquiry 5 was made negligently, and that the plaintiffs relied on this statement when deciding to purchase the bungalow.

Resuming the story, it was not long before the plaintiffs discovered that there was something badly wrong with the house. They had wanted to carry out a roof conversion but their builder advised them of the subsidence, and they formed the view that they could not live there without measures to stabilise the foundations. This would have required them to vacate the house for two or three months, and to pay a sum estimated at £17,000 as the cost of necessary work. They did not have sufficient money to permit this to be done, so they decided to build another residence in the existing garden. Accordingly, within a few months of the purchase they made a planning application to erect another building. This was refused on 9 August 1984, essentially on the ground that this would lead to overcrowding. A second application was refused five months later. The plaintiffs then reformulated their application, so as to permit the erection of one new bungalow and one new chalet bungalow, after the demolition of the existing bungalow. This time the application was successful, permission being granted on 18 August 1986. The plaintiffs then set about finding buyers for the land with planning permission, and by October 1986 they had sold it to developers for a price of £76,094.47. The purchasers were going to pull down the bungalow and build on the land, so the question of repair was no longer relevant.

Meanwhile in January 1986 the plaintiffs had commenced their action in the High Court; it was subsequently transferred to the County Court. In its original and amended form that statement of claim contained no particulars of damage. These were, however, requested and in response the plaintiffs pleaded as follows:

> The value of the freehold land and bungalow known as Oakwood had it not suffered from subsidence is £80,000. The plaintiffs in an attempt to mitigate their loss have managed to sell the bungalow and land for a gross sale price of £78,500.
>
> The cost of the sale is £1,905.53. The cost of removal from the premises is £500. The net price obtainable for the bungalow and land by the plaintiffs is therefore £76,094.47. The net loss in value of the land to the plaintiffs is therefore £3,905.53.

> The plaintiffs have adopted this course of action in preference to having remedial work carried out on the premises to remedy the damage caused by the said subsidence which would have cost in excess of £17,000.

Seventeen months later, on 12 July 1988, the plaintiffs amended the particulars to increase the sound value of the land and bungalow to £90,000 and hence the 'net loss in value' to £13,905.53. All this happened before the grant of planning permission and the sale to the developers.

The trial began on 7 November 1988. On the first day the plaintiffs' counsel (who had not pleaded either the first or the amended set of particulars) applied to reamend so as to add the following paragraph: 'Alternatively the plaintiffs' claim is for the difference between the price paid of £53,250 and the actual market value of the property at the date of completion namely £36,250, the difference representing the cost of carrying out repairs to the property to remedy the subsidence.' In addition, the amendment deleted the second of the paragraphs from which I have quoted. There is an unfortunate difference of recollection about whether the amendment also involved the deletion of the first paragraph. The appeal bundle prepared on behalf of the plaintiffs contains a document purporting to be the reamended particulars, which the judge gave leave to serve on the second day of the trial; these do not show any deletion of the first paragraph, but counsel maintained that this is a later copying error. On the other hand, counsel for the defendants recalls that the reamended pleading never showed this paragraph as deleted. We cannot resolve this dispute. Three things are however clear. (1) For the eighteen months leading up to the trial the plaintiffs had been advancing a case based on the proposition that they had sold to developers in mitigation of damage. (2) By the end of the trial (as the judge's notes disclose) the plaintiffs were contending that the proper measure of damage was '£17,000, being the difference between the sound value of the property, less the price paid'. (3) Counsel were agreed that this would indeed have been the proper measure of damage on the hypothesis that the plaintiffs had remained in occupation. The sole question on damages was whether the effect of the resale at a price much greater than had been paid was to nullify this *prima facie* right of recovery. The judge answered this question in the affirmative. After concluding in favour of the plaintiffs on damages he continued (according to counsel's agreed note):

> However the matter does not end there due to a vitally important mitigation point. I am persuaded by counsel for the defendants that this is a classic *Westinghouse* case. |Counsel| also referred me to the case of *Bellingham v Dhillon* |1973| 1 All ER 20, |1973| QB 304. Damages accrue on the date of completion: the tortious measure applies. I do not think, having considered Lord Denning M.R.'s judgment in *Perry v Sidney Phillips & Son* (a firm) |1982| 3 All ER 705, |1982| 1 WLR 1297, that these principles are affected or excluded. I am bound to hold that the windfall accruing to the plaintiffs wipes out by far the loss that follows. Thus, despite what I have found about the subsidence, the defendants succeed.

In the course of his argument in support of the notion thus briefly conveyed by the judge, counsel for the defendants advanced two distinct propositions. (1) The plaintiffs owed a duty towards the defendants to mitigate the loss resulting from their purchase of the house in reliance on the misrepresentation; the sale to the developers was a performance of this duty; the result of this mitigation was to be taken into account in computing the loss. (2) Whether the resale was a mitigation or not, the fact is that when the plaintiffs' dealings are regarded as a whole it can be seen that they have suffered no loss. Very often it happens that no distinction need be drawn between these two ways of approaching the problem: they raise the same issues of fact and lead to the same conclusion, and are often treated together under the same heading of 'mitigation'. Nevertheless, I believe that counsel for the defendants was right to recognise the distinction when advancing his clients' case.

The first argument depends on proof that the plaintiffs were under a duty to resell the house in mitigation. Counsel for the plaintiffs takes the initial point that there can never be a question of mitigating a loss which has already crystallised, and that the loss has crystallised here in terms of the conventional measure of damage for an unsatisfactory purchase made in reliance on an actionable misrepresentation by the vendor. I feel some reservations about this proposition. It is true that the question of a duty to mitigate tends most often to arise in the context of a continuing loss. Thus, for example, where a plaintiff is suffering a loss of business profits which will go on until he does something to stop it, then if there is something which he could reasonably do, and yet he fails to do it, the damages are computed as if the loss had come to an end; conversely, if he does take action to prevent further loss, all the consequences of his act are brought into account. It is also true that superficially the proposition of counsel for the plaintiffs does appear at first sight to gain support from the cases on failure to perform contracts for the supply of goods or services for which there is an available market, where the courts have tended to proceed directly to a conventional measure of damage without investigating what the injured party has actually done after the breach. (I say 'at first sight' because these conventional measures of damages depend on the fiction that the innocent party has gone into the market to sell against the defaulting buyer, or to buy in against the defaulting seller. The loss is therefore crystallised, not in terms of the immediate consequences of the breach, but of a deemed mitigation.) Nevertheless, I would not be prepared without a very full review of the authorities to underwrite a generalisation such as counsel for the plaintiffs proposes, especially in the field of damages, where broad statements of principle tend to be unreliable. (Indeed I believe that R. _Pagnan & Flli v Corbisa Industrial Agropacuaria Ltd_ [1971] 1 All ER 165, [1970] 1 WLR 1306 shows the generalisation to be unsound.) This is of no moment here, however, because whatever the true state of the law it is to my mind clear that the defendants' first argument fails at the outset. The breach compelled the plaintiffs to choose between (a) continuing to live in the bungalow despite its serious faults, (b) repairing the bungalow or (c) selling the bungalow and land and going to live elsewhere. If the plaintiffs had chosen to pursue either of the first two options it is inconceivable that they would have been held to be in breach of any obligations towards the defendants; their recovery of the estimated or actual cost of repair (as reflecting the difference between the true market value and the price) would have followed as a matter of course. Given therefore that alternatives (a) and (b) were legitimate, the proposition that the plaintiffs were under a duty to spend more than two years in applications for planning permission, and that having obtained it were under a further duty to move out of the house in which they had hoped to live and to buy somewhere else, all for the benefit of the defendants who had by their actionable wrong put them into this dilemma need only be stated to be rejected, and the rest of the argument falls with it.

The alternative proposition is more formidable. Before considering its legal aspects the assertion that the plaintiffs made a profit out of the transaction needs to be examined. In one sense of course it is right, since the plaintiffs ultimately sold the property for twice what they had paid for it. This is however misleading, for it ignores the general rise in the housing market in the interval between purchase and resale, and it also terminates the analysis halfway through. The plaintiffs were not property speculators but residents; their object in reselling was not to realise a profit, but to rid themselves of an uninhabitable house so that they could acquire another. What they actually did do after the sale to the developers was never explored at the trial, nor is it possible on the judge's findings to arrive at an assessment of the cost of buying a comparable bungalow into which they could have moved after the resale. If one of the experts was right, and the comparator would have cost about £80,000 then over the whole run of transactions the plaintiffs would have broken even. But if the other expert's figure of £90,000 is preferred the plaintiffs would have made a substantial loss, for which on any view they ought to be compensated.

Thus, if the right approach in law is to look at the plaintiffs' position at the end of a chain of transactions consisting of purchase, resale and fresh purchase, the case will have to be returned to the County Court for a further investigation of the figures.

Is this the right approach in law? Undoubtedly, the starting point is _British Westinghouse Electric and Manufacturing Co. Ltd v Underground Electric Rlys Co. of London Ltd_ [1912] AC 673, [1911–13] All ER Rep 63. The respondents agreed to purchase from the appellants a series of turbo-alternator sets intended to deliver electric power to the respondents' railway. The sets were deficient in output and the fuel consumption exceeded the guaranteed rate. The respondents nevertheless kept the machines in use for a considerable time while efforts were made to improve them, but on this proving fruitless they replaced them with Parsons machines, which had a greater output and lower consumption than those purchased from the appellants. In the resulting arbitration the respondents claimed two items of damages: the cost of obtaining and installing the Parsons machines and the loss caused by the excess in consumption while the appellants' machines were in use. As to the latter claim there was no dispute in principle. As to the former the arbitrator found that the purchase of the Parsons machines was a reasonable and prudent course and that it mitigated the loss and damage which would have been recoverable if the respondents had continued to use the defective machines; he went on to find that even if the machines supplied by the appellants had been up to contract the Parsons machines would still have been superior in efficiency and economy, so that it was to the respondents' pecuniary advantage to have made the replacement. In the House of Lords it was held that the arbitrator should be directed to take the advantages of the new machines into account when assessing the damages. Since the speech of Viscount Haldane L.C. (with which the other members of the Appellate Committee agreed) is generally regarded as the leading source of authority on this topic I must quote from it at a little length, but it may be useful first to record the argument addressed for the appellants, which, after citing *Joyner v Weeks* |1891| 2 QB 31, proceeded (|1912| AC 673 at 679): 'When once the court has arrived at the conclusion that the measure of damages is x, which in that particular class of case was the cost of putting the premises into repair, no outside circumstances will be taken into consideration for the purpose of reducing x to $x-a$. But here the measure of damages never was x, but was $x-a$, that is to say, the price of the new machines less the value of the additional advantages derived from their use.' This I take to be an epitome of the argument which was accepted by the House of Lords. It is also to be observed that the arbitrator did not make any finding about the possibility that the respondents could have purchased machines of equal output to those which the appellants should have supplied, an omission which Viscount Haldane L.C., differing from Buckley L.J. in the Court of Appeal (|1912| 3 KB 128), regarded as of no moment.

The following extracts from the speech of Viscount Haldane L.C. serve to illustrate the grounds on which the House of Lords remitted the dispute to the arbitrator. He said (|1912| AC 673 at 689, |1911–13| All ER Rep 63 at 69):

> . . . I think that there are certain broad principles which are quite well settled. The first is that, as far as possible, he who has proved a breach of a bargain to supply what he contracted to get is to be placed, as far as money can do it, in as good a situation as if the contract had been performed. The fundamental basis is thus compensation for pecuniary loss naturally flowing from the breach; but this first principle is qualified by a second, which imposes on a plaintiff the duty of taking all reasonable steps to mitigate the loss consequent on the breach, and debars him from claiming any part of the damage which is due to his neglect to take such steps. In the words of James L.J. in *Dunkirk Colliery Co. v Lever* ((1878) 9 ChD 20 at 25), 'The person who has broken the contract is not to be exposed to additional cost by reason of the plaintiffs not doing what they ought to have done as reasonable men, and the plaintiffs not being under any obligation to do anything otherwise than in the ordinary course of business.' As James L.J. indicates, this second principle does not impose on the plaintiff an obligation to take any step which a reasonable and prudent man would not ordinarily take in the course of his business. But when in the course of his business he has taken action arising out of the transaction, which action has diminished his loss, the effect in actual diminution of the loss he has suffered may be taken into account even though there was no duty on him to act.

Then, after citing *Staniforth v Lyall* (1830) 7 Bing. 169, 131 ER 65. Viscount Haldane L.C. continued (|1912| AC 673 at 690–692, |1911–13| All ER Rep 63 at 70–71):

I think that this decision illustrates a principle which has been recognised in other cases, that, provided the course taken to protect himself by the plaintiff in such an action was one which a reasonable and prudent person might in the ordinary conduct of business properly have taken, and in fact did take whether bound to or not, a jury or an arbitrator may properly look at the whole of the facts and ascertain the result in estimating the quantum of damage . . . I think the principle which applies here is that which makes it right for the jury or arbitrator to look at what actually happened, and to balance loss and gain. The transaction was not *res inter alios acta*, but one in which the person whose contract was broken took a reasonable and prudent course quite naturally arising out of the circumstances in which he was placed by the breach. Apart from the breach of contract, the lapse of time had rendered the appellants' machines obsolete, and men of business would be doing the only thing they could properly do in replacing them with new and up-to-date machines. The arbitrator does not in his finding of fact lay any stress on the increase in kilowatt power of the new machines, and I think that the proper inference is that such increase was regarded by him as a natural and prudent course followed by those whose object was to avoid further loss, and that it formed part of a continuous dealing with the situation in which they found themselves, and was not an independent or disconnected transaction.

It will be seen that the decision in the *Westinghouse* case had two aspects. First, the conclusion that the benefits derived from the purchase of superior machinery should be set against the two elements of loss. In retrospect it is hard to see how the contrary could have been maintained. The purchase amounted to mitigation in the narrower sense, designed to put a stop to the continuing loss. To compensate the respondents for the cost of replacement while ignoring the additional benefits which this replacement had brought would have been a palpable injustice.

The second aspect of the decision concerned the element of over-mitigation introduced by the fact that the respondents had bought equipment with a greater output than before, presumably at greater cost than if exactly equivalent replacements had been obtained. Again, once it was found that the purchase had been reasonably made the conclusion in favour of the appellants now seems inevitable, given that the act which constituted the mitigation and the act which was said to constitute the over-mitigation were in the event the same. Thus, there was no question of the case being concerned with a chain of disconnected transactions, and so I cannot follow the judge in treating the present case as directly governed by the *Westinghouse* case.

. . .

I have dealt with the authorities at some length, because it was said that in one direction or another they provided a direct solution to the present problem. For the reasons already stated, I do not see them in this light. Ultimately, as with so many disputes about damages, the issue is primarily one of fact. Did the negligence which caused the damage also cause the profit, if profit there was? I do not think so. It is true that in one sense there was a causal link between the inducement of the purchase by misrepresentation and the sale two and a half years later, for the sale represented a choice of one of the options with which the plaintiffs had been presented by the defendants' wrongful act. But only in that sense. To my mind the reality of the situation is that the plaintiffs bought the house to live in, and did live in it for a substantial period. It was only after two years that the possibility of selling the land and moving elsewhere was explored, and six months later still that this possibility came to fruition. It seems to me that when the plaintiffs unlocked the development value of their land they did so for their own benefit, and not as part of a continuous transaction of which the purchase of land and bungalow was the inception.

Accordingly, although I acknowledge that the plaintiffs had until the start of the trial persisted in a claim which was inconsistent with the one which they introduced by reamendment, I consider that in fact and law their second thoughts were correct, and that the proper measure of damages here is the difference between the contract price and the market value of the property in its unsound condition. I would therefore allow the appeal.

(Farquharson L.J. and Sir Michael Kerr agreed.)

Note

If no loss is shown then damages may be nominal.

Baker Perkins Ltd and C. J. O'Dowd Ltd (HC) 13 April 1989, unrep.

Blayney J.:

This case involves a claim and counterclaim arising out of two contracts for the supply of bakery equipment entered into on the 13 September 1982.

The plaintiffs are an English company specialising in the manufacture of plant for bakeries. The defendant is a company carrying on a bakery business in Kinsale, County Cork. In March 1982 the defendant ordered orally from the plaintiffs certain plant of which the main item was a convertoradiant (CVR) oven. The price was UK£250,000. The plant was to be manufactured and ready for dispatch in October 1982. The terms of the contract were formalised on 13 September 1982 when both parties signed a document entitled an 'Order Confirmation' which was the standard form of contract used by the plaintiffs. The substantive part of this document provided as follows: 'This contract is subject to the seller's general conditions of sale which are printed overleaf. The seller shall sell and the customer shall purchase the goods described in the order confirmation on the terms and conditions stated therein'.

The plant was ready for dispatch in October 1982 but was not sent as the defendant had not been able to arrange finance. This continued to be the position in the following year. At a meeting between representatives of the parties in Peterborough on 17 February 1984 the price of £250,000 was by agreement increased to £300,000 to compensate the plaintiffs for interest and storage charges which had been incurred, and on 26 March 1984 the plaintiffs wrote to the defendant suggesting *inter alia* that they should agree to the contract being subject to cancellation if the £300,000 sterling was not received by 9 April. The defendant agreed to this. The money was not received by the date mentioned, and finally by letter dated 10 July 1984 the plaintiffs wrote saying they had to accept that the contract was cancelled. Their solicitor then wrote claiming cancellation charges and on 10 January 1985 these proceedings were issued.

The defendant claimed in its defence that the contract had been conditional on its being able to obtain finance and that, as this condition had not been satisfied, the contract automatically came to an end. In the course of the hearing, however, counsel for the defendant abandoned this defence so that insofar as the plaintiffs' claim is concerned the sole issue is what damages, if any, the plaintiffs are entitled to recover. As this issue is wholly separate from the defendant's counterclaim I propose to deal with it before taking up the latter.

In their statement of claim the plaintiffs claimed the following heads of damage:

1. Interest charges pursuant to clause 10 of the general conditions of sale which form part of the contract.

2. Loss of profits.
3. Storage charges.

. . .

The clause which is applicable in assessing the plaintiffs' damages is in my opinion subclause (iv) of clause 10: 'The measure of damages shall be any loss or expense of any nature incurred by seller arising out of disposal of the goods.'

I accept the submission of counsel for the defendant that it is the measure of damages specified in the contract that is to be applied rather than that set out in s. 50(3) of the English Sale of Goods Act 1979—this being the relevant Act, as the general conditions provide in clause 15 that 'the contract shall in all respects operate and be construed in accordance with English law.' There was no real dispute in regard to this. Counsel for the plaintiffs accepted that where the parties had agreed on the measure of damages he could not contend for a different measure.

Damages may only be given, accordingly, in respect of any loss or expense of which it can be said that it arose 'out of the disposal of the goods'. The question is whether the loss of profits and the storage charges up to the date of the termination of the contract fall into this category.

In my opinion they do not. The loss of profit claimed is the profit that the plaintiffs would have made if the defendant had completed the contract. It seems to me that this loss resulted from the defendant's refusal to pay for the goods and did not arise out of the disposal of the goods. In refusing to pay for the goods, the defendant deprived the plaintiffs of their profit. So the plaintiffs' loss was suffered at that stage which at the latest occurred on 10 July 1984 when the plaintiffs terminated the contract by reason of the defendant's breach. And it was only then that the question of the disposal of the goods arose. But the loss of profit, having already been suffered, could not have arisen out of that disposal. It preceded it and was caused by the plaintiffs' breach of contract.

As regards the storage charges, what are in question here are the charges up to 10 July 1984, when the contract was terminated. I will deal later with charges which arose after that date. It seems to me that those which arose before it were incurred in connection with the performance of the contract by the plaintiffs and did not arise out of the contract by the plaintiffs and did not arise out of the disposal of the plant. The plant had to be stored by the plaintiffs so that it would be available to be dispatched to the defendant when the latter had procured the necessary finance to pay for it. So the storage was necessitated by the plaintiffs' obligation to perform its part of the contract. The charges arose out of this obligation and were unconnected with the disposal of the plant after the contract had come to an end. Accordingly they did not arise out of that disposal.

Counsel for the defendant submitted that the plaintiffs had suffered no loss or expense whatsoever arising out of the disposal of the plant. In particular he submitted that on the resale to East Midlands Co-Op the plaintiffs had made a profit and so there was no question of their having suffered a loss in respect of which they would be entitled to damages. It seems to me that this latter submission is correct. The evidence in regard to the disposal of the plant which was the subject matter of the contract was that it was sold to the East-Midlands Co-Op together with other plant on 5 October 1984 for a total consideration of UK£585,900. The part of the consideration referable to the defendant's plant exceeded by £60,359 the original purchase price of £250,000 which the defendant had agreed to pay. Whether or not there was a loss on the resale hinges on what the defendant would have had to pay to complete the purchase in July 1984, in other words, on what the price would have been at that time. This is the figure which has to be compared with what the plaintiffs obtained from the East Midlands Co-Op.

While the original purchase price was £250,000, this was, by agreement, increased to £300,000 at a meeting in Peterborough between Mr Harold Jackson, the plaintiffs' sales manager, and Mr Charles O'Dowd, the defendant's managing director. This agreement was referred to by Mr Jackson in a letter to the defendant of 26 March 1984 and was confirmed by a telex of 4 April 1984 from Mr O'Dowd to Mr Jackson. In that letter Mr Jackson suggested 'that we agree to regard this contract as being subject to cancellation should we not receive the UK£300,000 payment by 9 April 1984—in other words should your current financing investigations prove to be unsuccessful'. It is clear from this that had Mr O'Dowd been able to obtain the finance in time, the amount he would have needed to complete the contract before 9 April 1984 would have been £300,000. So the figure for the purchase price would have been the same then as was agreed on 17 February 1984. Would this still have been the position in July? This depends upon whether the plaintiffs would have claimed interest on the purchase money between April and July.

Clause 11 of the general conditions in the contract, provides that interest at the rate of two per cent per month shall be payable by the buyer on the written demand of the seller where any payment is not made on the due date. On 11 May 1984, Mr J. M. Hicks, the plaintiffs' bakery division accountant, wrote to Mr Kidney, who was the defendant's financial adviser at the time, and amongst other things he pointed out 'that further storage and interest costs are accruing since our meeting in Peterborough when we agreed that the sterling payment should be made on 9 April 1984'. That put the defendant on notice that the plaintiffs might exercise their right to demand interest if the defendant succeeded in getting the necessary finance to complete. But it is still an open question as to whether they would have exercised their right in this respect. There was no evidence that further interest would in fact have been demanded so there is nothing to support a finding that it is probable that this would have been done. Furthermore, since the plaintiffs had been waiting since December 1982 for payment I think it very likely that if the defendant had been able to come up with £300,000 at any time between May and July 1984 the plaintiffs would have been prepared to accept that sum in full discharge and would not have insisted on interest. And in that case the deal would have been concluded at the figure of £300,000. It follows that since the plaintiffs were able to dispose of the plant to East Midlands Co-Op at a figure in excess of this they did not, insofar as the resale price was concerned, suffer any loss arising out of the disposal of the plant.

The position in regard to the storage charges is different. The plant clearly had to be stored pending its disposal. So the storage charges after 10 July 1984 did arise out of the disposal. But in my opinion such charges must be confined to the warehousing charges. They could not include the hire of the six trailers on which the plant had been loaded in July 1983 in expectation of its being delivered to the defendant and on which it had remained up to July 1984. It was not necessary to keep it loaded on trailers while awaiting resale. All that was required was that it should be warehoused. The evidence was that the cost of warehousing was £16 per trailer per week. There were six trailers, so the weekly cost was UK£96. The sale to East Midlands Co-Op was on 5 October 1984, so the plant would have had to be warehoused for approximately thirteen weeks. This gives a total charge of UK£1,248. To this must be added interest at eleven per cent from the middle of October 1984 to 21 January 1989 and at eight per cent from that date to 10 March 1989 which I calculate comes to £597. So the total due for principal and interest is UK£1,845.

To this must be added the cost of the circulating table which was delivered to the defendant and not paid for. It cost UK£5,234. And interest under the Courts Act up to 7 March 1989 comes to £2,660.84 giving a total of £7,894.84.

When this is added to the amount due for the storage charges, the final figure to which the plaintiffs are entitled on their claim is £9,739.84 and there will be judgment for them for this amount.

(The defendants' counterclaim was dismissed.)

C. WHICH HEAD OF LOSS?

It is generally accepted that the plaintiff may select which head of loss the plaintiff is to be compensated for. If the contract was breached at a preliminary stage, or the venture never came to fruition, this may give the plaintiff the opportunity to recover all costs incurred following on from the breach. The question, what follows from the breach, is an interesting one.

Anglia Television Ltd v Reed [1972] 1 QB 60

Lord Denning M.R.:

Anglia Television Ltd, the plaintiffs, were minded in 1968 to make a film of a play for television entitled 'The Man in the Wood'. It portrayed an American man married to an English woman. The American has an adventure in an English wood. The film was to last for ninety minutes. Anglia Television made many arrangements in advance. They arranged for a place where the play was to be filmed. They employed a director, a designer and a stage manager, and so forth. They involved themselves in much expense. All this was done before they got the leading man. They required a strong actor capable of holding the play together. He was to be on the scene the whole time. Anglia Television eventually found the man. He was Mr Robert Reed, the defendant, an American who has a very high reputation as an actor. He was very suitable for this part. By telephone conversation on 30 August 1968, it was agreed by Mr Reed through his agent that he would come to England and be available between 9 September and 11 October 1968, to rehearse and play in this film. He was to get a performance fee of £1,050, living expenses of £100 a week, his first class fares to and from the US and so forth. It was all subject to the permit of the Ministry of Labour for him to come here. That was duly given on 12 September 1968. So the contract was concluded. But unfortunately there was some muddle with the bookings. It appears that Mr Reed's agents had already booked him in America for some other play. So on 3 September 1968, the agent said that Mr Reed would not come to England to perform in this play. He repudiated his contract. Anglia Television tried hard to find a substitute but could not do so. So on 11 September they accepted his repudiation. They abandoned the proposed film. They gave notice to the people whom they had engaged and so forth.

Anglia Television then sued Mr Reed for damages. He did not dispute his liability, but a question arose as to the damages. Anglia Television do not claim their profit. They cannot say what their profit would have been on this contract if Mr Reed had come here and performed it. So, instead of claim for loss of profits, they claim for the wasted expenditure. They had incurred the director's fees, the designer's fees, the stage manager's and assistant manager's fees, and so on. It comes in all to £2,750. Anglia Television say that all that money was wasted because Mr Reed did not perform his contract.

Mr Reed's advisers take a point of law. They submit that Anglia Television cannot recover for expenditure incurred *before* the contract was concluded with Mr Reed. They can only recover the expenditure *after* the contract was concluded. They say that the expenditure *after* the contract was only £854.65, and that is all that Anglia Television can recover.

The master rejected that contention: he held that Anglia Television could recover the whole £2,750; and now Mr Reed appeals to this court.

[Counsel], for Mr Reed, has referred us to the recent case of *Perestrello & Companhia Limitada v United Paint Co. Ltd, The Times*, 16 April 1969, in which Thesiger J. quoted the words of Tindal C.J. in *Hodges v Earl of Litchfield* (1835) 1 Bing. NC 492, at 498: 'The expenses preliminary to the contract ought not to be allowed. The party enters into them for his own benefit at a time when it is uncertain whether there will be any contract or not.' Thesiger J. applied those words, saying: 'In my judgment pre-contract expenditure, though thrown away, is not recoverable.'

I cannot accept the proposition as stated. It seems to me that a plaintiff in such a case as this has an election: he can either claim for loss of profits; or for his wasted expenditure. But he must elect between them. He cannot claim both. If he has not suffered any loss of profits—or if he cannot prove what his profits would have been—he can claim in the alternative the expenditure which has been thrown away, that is, wasted, by reason of the breach. That is shown by *Cullinane v British 'Rema' Manufacturing Co. Ltd* [1954] 1 QB 292, 303, 308.

If the plaintiff claims the wasted expenditure, he is not limited to the expenditure incurred *after* the contract was concluded. He can claim also the expenditure incurred *before* the contract, provided that it was such as would reasonably be in the contemplation of the parties as likely to be wasted if the contract was broken. Applying that principle here, it is plain that, when Mr Reed entered into this contract, he must have known perfectly well that much expenditure had already been incurred on director's fees and the like. He must have contemplated—or, at any rate, it is reasonably to be imputed to him—that if he broke his contract, all that expenditure would be wasted, whether or not it was incurred before or after the contract. He must pay damages for all the expenditure so wasted and thrown away. This view is supported by the recent decision of Brightman J. in *Lloyd v Stanbury* [1971] 1 WLR 535. There was a contract for the sale of land. In anticipation of the contract—and before it was concluded—the purchaser went to much expense in moving a caravan to the site and in getting his furniture there. The seller afterwards entered into a contract to sell the land to the purchaser, but afterwards broke his contract. The land had not increased in value, so the purchaser could not claim for any loss of profit. But Brightman J. held, at 547, that he could recover the cost of moving the caravan and furniture, because it was 'within the contemplation of the parties when the contract was signed.' That decision is in accord with the correct principle, namely, that wasted expenditure can be recovered when it is wasted by reason of the defendant's breach of contract. It is true that, if the defendant had never entered into the contract, he would not be liable, and the expenditure would have been incurred by the plaintiff without redress; but, the defendant having made his contract and broken it, it does not lie in his mouth to say he is not liable, when it was because of his breach that the expenditure has been wasted.

I think the master was quite right and this appeal should be dismissed.

(Phillimore and Megaw L.JJ. agreed.)

Note

However, this principle of choice is subject to the overriding requirement that the breach of contract must occasion the plaintiff's loss.

Bowlay Logging *v* Domtar Ltd (1978) 87 DLR (3d) 325

Domtar Ltd were under a contractual obligation to provide logging trucks to allow Bowlay Logging transport the logs it felled to its sawmill. Eventually the Bowlay Logging operation closed down. Bowlay Logging sought damages for breach of contract by Domtar Ltd in failing to provide a sufficient number of trucks.

Berger J.:

. . .

This brings me to the issue of damages. Bowlay's claim is not for loss of profits, but for compensation for expenditures made in part performance. Bowlay is not in a position to claim damages for loss of profits, because it cannot prove that if it had gone on to complete the contract it would have made any money. Bowlay, since it cannot prove any loss of profits, is seeking to recover its losses for actual outlay. These came to $232,905. The payments received from Domtar for deliveries of logs came to $108,128.57. Bowlay's claim is for the balance, $124,776.43.

While it is true that the parties contemplated that the contract might be renewed on an annual basis, I think Bowlay's claim for damages must be limited to damages in respect of Bowlay's losses on Timber Sale No. A03518. Any claim based on the loss of expected profits on future timber sales would be too uncertain and remote. In any event, Bowlay has limited its claim to compensation for expenditures made in part performance. It has not advanced any claim for loss of profits.

The cases say that a plaintiff can sue for expenses incurred in part performance of a contract when the contract has been ended by breach. In *Cullinane v British 'Rema' Manufacturing Co. Ltd* [1954] 1 QB 292, Lord Evershed said at 303:

> As a matter of principle also, it seems to me that a person who has obtained a machine, such as the plaintiff obtained, being a machine which was mechanically in exact accordance with the order given but which was unable to perform a particular function which it was warranted to perform, may adopt one of two courses. He may say, when he discovers its incapacity, that it was not what he wanted, that it is quite useless to him, and he may claim to recover the capital cost he has incurred, deducting anything he can obtain by disposing of the material that he got. A claim of that kind puts the plaintiff in the same position as though he had never made the contract at all. In other words, he is back where he started; and, if it were shown that the profit-earning capacity was in fact very small, the plaintiff would probably elect so to base his claim. But, alternatively, where the warranty in question relates to performance, he may, in my judgment, make his claim on the basis of the profit which he has lost because the machine as delivered fell short in its performance of that which it was warranted to do.

See also *McRae et al. v Commonwealth Disposals Com'n et al.* (1951) 84 CLR 377.

In *Anglia Television Ltd v Reed* [1972] 1 QB 60, Lord Denning M.R., held that a plaintiff had the right to sue for expenditures made in part performance. He said, at 64: 'If he has not suffered any loss of profits—or if he cannot prove what his profits would have been—he can claim in the alternative the expenditure which has been thrown away, that is, wasted, by reason of the breach. That is shown by *Cullinane v British 'Rema' Manufacturing Co. Ltd* [1954] 1 QB 292, 303, 308.'

But Domtar has raised an issue not reached by these cases. [Counsel for the defendant] says that even if there was a breach of contract Domtar is not bound to compensate Bowlay for its expenses—at any rate certainly not the full measure of those expenses—because the operation was losing money. If it had continued it would have lost more money. Domtar says that in fact Bowlay's losses on full performance would have exceeded its losses in expenses 'thrown away'. It is said that in these circumstances Bowlay cannot recover any damages.

May a claim for expenses made in part performance be sustained where the defendant shows that the plaintiff was engaged in a losing operation and, even if there had been no breach and the contract had been fully performed, would inevitably have suffered a loss on the contract? Should the defendant be entitled to have the losses that would have been incurred deducted from the plaintiff's claim for compensation for expenses made in part performance? What if the plaintiff's losses, in the event the contract had been fully performed, would have exceeded the claim for expenses? To what extent should the plaintiff be entitled to recover in such a case?

McGregor on Damages, (13th ed., 1972), 28–9, commenting on the *Anglia* case, said:

This decision however does not cover the case where the plaintiff has made a bad bargain, and it is still an open question whether in such circumstances he should be allowed to opt for the alternative measure. The argument on the one side is that he should not be entitled to more than the normal measure would give him; the argument on the other is that a defendant in breach should not be entitled to object to a claim for the alternative measure even though not dictated by law or by the difficulties of proof.

Mr Shaw says that the plaintiff should be entitled to recover all of its expenses by way of outlay, and that no deduction should be made even if the plaintiff would have suffered a net loss if the contract had been fully performed. He relies on a judgment of the US Supreme Court: *United States v Behan* (1884) 110 US 338. Mr Justice Bradley, speaking for the court, said, at 345–6:

When a party injured by the stoppage of a contract elects to rescind it, then, it is true, he cannot recover any damages for a breach of the contract, either for outlay or for loss of profits; he recovers the value of his services actually performed as upon a *quantum meruit*. There is then no question of losses or profits. But when he elects to go for damages for the breach of the contract, the first and most obvious damage to be shown is, the amount which he has been induced to expend on the faith of the contract, including a fair allowance for his own time and services. If he chooses to go further and claims for the loss of anticipated profits, he may do so, subject to the rules of law as to the character of profits which may be thus claimed. It does not lie, however, in the mouth of the party who has voluntarily and wrongfully put an end to the contract, to say that the party injured has not been damaged at least to the amount of what he has been induced fairly and in good faith to lay out and expend (including his own services), after making allowance for the value of materials on hand; at least it does not lie in the mouth of the party in fault to say this, unless he can show that the expenses of the party injured have been extravagant, and unnecessary for the purposes of carrying out the contract.

If it is only 'extravagant and unnecessary expenses' that the defendant may insist be deducted from the plaintiff's claim, then what about expenses legitimately incurred, but in an unprofitable venture? The implication in the *Behan* case is that the defendant may not have them deducted from the plaintiff's claim for compensation for expenses. Mr Justice Bradley went on at 346–7: '. . . the party who voluntarily and wrongfully put an end to a contract and prevents the other party from performing it, is estopped from denying that the injured party has not been damaged to the extent of his actual loss and outlay fairly incurred.' The *Behan* case was decided in the last century. It has been rejected in the US in this century.

Professor L. L. Fuller and W. R. Perdue Jr., writing in 'Reliance Interest in Contract Damages', 46 Yale LJ 52 (1937), concluded that the principle enunciated in the *Behan* case compromised the basic notion of *restitutio in integrum*. They urged, at 79, that the law ought to reflect the following proposition: 'We will not in a suit for reimbursement for losses incurred in reliance on a contract knowingly put the plaintiff in a better position than he would have occupied had the contract been fully performed.' In L. *Albert & Son v Armstrong Rubber Co.* (1949) 178 F. 2d 182 (USCA, 2nd Cir.), Chief Justice Learned Hand, speaking for the Court of Appeals, Second Circuit, held that on a claim for compensation for expenses in part performance the defendant was entitled to deduct whatever he can prove the plaintiff would have lost if the contract had been fully performed. Chief Justice Learned Hand expressed his concurrence with the formula laid down by Professor Fuller: see also *Re Yeager Co.* (1963) 227 F. Supp. 92 (DC Ohio).

It has been said by the US Circuit Court of Appeals in *Dade County, Florida v Palmer & Baker Engineers Inc.* (1965) 339 F. 2d 208 (USCA, 5th Cir.), that where the defendant alleges that full performance by the plaintiff would have resulted in a net loss to the plaintiff, the burden of proof is on the defendant. Accepting then that the onus is on the defendant, what has the defendant been able to prove in the case at bar?

Mr Dunn, a chartered accountant called by Domtar, prepared a list of expenses of the Bowlay logging operation. The list is not complete. But Mr Dunn says that when the revenues of the operation are measured against the expenses, whether on a cash basis or an accrual basis, there is no footing on which the operation could have been regarded as a profitable one. I think he is right about this. The losses would have been very high. Bowlay was entitled to $15 per cunit from Domtar. Mr Dunn said that expenses stood at $114,000 on 31 July 1972; On 15 October 1972, they came to $186,434.79. Given that the actual cut by Bowlay came to 8,029.56 cunits, Bowlay's actual cost of production per cunit came to $22.94.

Then there is the evidence of Greg Lay. On 26 July he made an analysis of Bowlay's costs. His diary reveals that Bowlay's costs were running at $19 per cunit. Lay said that to operate at a profit Bowlay had to deliver fifteen loads of hot and cold wood a day. He said that they would have to keep hauling fifteen loads a day until 30 November (hauling could continue until then) to supply 10,000 cunits as required by the contract. Of course they never did haul fifteen loads a day, even before the diminution in the supply of trucks. And Bowlay says that its total outlay came to $232,905.

The law of contract compensates a plaintiff for damages resulting from the defendant's breach; it does not compensate a plaintiff for damages resulting from his making a bad bargain. Where it can be seen that the plaintiff would have incurred a loss on the contract as a whole, the expenses he has incurred are losses flowing from entering into the contract, not losses flowing from the defendant's breach. In these circumstances, the true consequence of the defendant's breach is that the plaintiff is released from his obligation to complete the contract—or in other words, he is saved from incurring further losses.

If the law of contract were to move from compensating for the consequences of breach to compensating for the consequences of entering into contracts, the law would run contrary to the normal expectations of the world of commerce. The burden of risk would be shifted from the plaintiff to the defendant. The defendant would become the insurer of the plaintiff's enterprise. Moreover, the amount of the damages would increase not in relation to the gravity or consequences of the breach but in relation to the inefficiency with which the plaintiff carried out the contract. The greater his expenses owing to inefficiency, the greater the damages.

The fundamental principle upon which damages are measured under the law of contract is *restitutio in integrum*. The principle contended for here by the plaintiff would entail the award of damages not to compensate the plaintiff but to punish the defendant. So it has been argued that a defendant ought to be able to insist that the plaintiff's damages should not include any losses that would have been incurred if the contract had been fully performed. According to Treitel, *Law of Contract*, (3rd ed., 1970), at 798: 'It is uncertain whether the plaintiff can recover his entire expenses if those exceed the benefit which he would have derived from the contract, had there been no breach.' Ogus, in *The Law of Damages* (1973), has said at 347 that, 'it is not yet clear whether English law imposes this limitation'.

The tendency in American law is to impose such a limitation. And I think Canadian law ought to impose it too.

The onus is on the defendant. But the onus has been met. The only conclusion that I can reach on the evidence is that if the plaintiff had fully performed the contract its losses would have continued at the rate that the figures show they were running at up to the time when the logging operation was closed down.

The case at bar takes the matter farther than any of the cases cited, because here the defendant has shown that the losses the plaintiff would have incurred on full performance exceed the expenditures actually made in part performance. No award for loss of outlay can therefore be made. There is no escaping the logic of this: see *Corbin on Contracts* (1964), 205–6: 'If, on the other hand, it is proved that full performance would have resulted in a net loss to the plaintiff, the recoverable damages should not include the amount of this loss. *If the amount of his expenditure at the date of breach is less than the expected net loss, he should be given judgment for nominal damages only.* If the expenditures exceed this loss, he should be given judgment for the excess.' (Emphasis added.)

On a conservative view of the evidence as a whole, the notional loss (had there been full performance) may be said to be in the amount of $124,653.60 calculated as follows:

A. *Plaintiff's claim*	$ 232,905.00
Less:	108,128.57
	124,776.43
Less: March 28/72 payment: see ex. 39, Schedule I	179.34
	$124,597.09
B. *Full Contract Price*—(See ex. 38, Schedule IV)	$120,443.40
Less:	2,793.24
	$117,650.16
C. *Probable Loss on Full Performance of Contract:*	
Expenses on partial completion, i.e. incurred by Bowlay	$232,905.00
Rate of $3.50/ccf (W.C. Bowles' rate) applied to 2.283.23 ccf	
left cut but not skidded (2685.39 ccf × $3.50)	9,398.76
	$242,303.76
Less: Full contract price	117,650.16
Loss there would have been on full performance	$124,653.60
D. *Deduct Loss on Full Performance from Plaintiff's Claim for Part Performance*	
Plaintiff's claim (A)	$124,597.09
Less: Loss (C)	124,653.60
Amount Recoverable	$ – 56.51

The plaintiff is entitled nevertheless to nominal damages for the breach of contract in the sum of $250.

Note

1. *Bowlay Logging v Domtar Ltd* was followed by the English Court of Appeal in *C & P Haulage (a firm) v Middleton* [1983] 3 All ER 94. Here, a tenant who had been unlawfully evicted from commercial premises by his landlord unsuccessfully sued for expenditure incurred in improving those premises. In fact, following his unlawful eviction his local council allowed him to run his business from his own residential garage, thus saving him the rental due if the leased premises had been available to him. In awarding nominal damages of £10 Ackner L.J. said of *Bowlay Logging*:

... In my judgment, the approach of Berger J. is the correct one. It is not the function of the courts where there is a breach of contract knowingly, as this would be the case, to put the plaintiff in a better financial position than if the contract had been properly performed. In this case the appellant, if he was right in his claim, would indeed be in a better position because, as I have already indicated, had the contract been lawfully determined, as it could have been in the middle of December, there would have been no question of his recovering these expenses.

2. The onus of proof lies upon the defendant to show that the plaintiff's business venture was such that the plaintiff would not have led to recovery of the expenditure incurred by the plaintiff. If the defendant does not satisfy the court of this the plaintiff will be able to recover wasted expenditure: *CCC Films (London) Ltd v Impact Quadrant Films Ltd* [1984] 3 WLR 245.

SECTION TWO—ASSESSMENT OF DAMAGES AS GUESSWORK

In some instances the plaintiff may not have incurred any wasted expenditure, or the plaintiff may not wish to return the property purchased and seek the return of the price. If there is a breach of contract which results in a loss of expectation the assessment of damages may be intuitive rather than a precise arithmetical exercise.

Hawkins *v* Rodgers (1950) 85 ILTR 1L8

Dixon J.:
...

The plaintiff was a person interested in horse-racing and the breeding of racehorses, while the defendant was, and had been for a good many years, a breeder and trainer of racehorses. The partnership between them commenced about 1943 and continued until 1949, when, by a letter from his solicitor, dated 28 May 1949, the plaintiff purported to terminate the partnership. For some weeks previously there had been what each party described as a 'coolness' between them. The evidence made it clear that the partnership was considered and treated as having been dissolved in or about the date of receipt of the letter referred to. There was never any written partnership agreement nor any arrangement as to the length of notice of dissolution necessary, and accordingly, his Lordship would be prepared, if necessary, to hold the letter effectual for its declared purposes.

By the time the partnership came to be dissolved, its assets comprised a considerable number of horses, including foals, yearlings, racehorses in training, brood mares and one stallion. During its currency the activities of the partnership included the buying and selling of horses, and their breeding, training and racing. So far as the training and racing of horses were concerned the defendant was the active partner. He trained the horses, and made the entries and other arrangements with regard to racing them; he had authority to act on behalf of the plaintiff in these matters. Horses were generally entered in the defendant's name as owner. The partnership was never registered with the racing authorities. The expenses in respect of all partnership horses were borne equally, while the profits were also equally divided.

In the letter of 28 May 1949, already referred to, the plaintiff withdrew from the defendant all authority to act on his behalf in connection with partnership property, and requested an agreement that the horses be sold by public auction. Subsequently there were conversations between the defendant and the plaintiff's solicitor, Mr Dunne; these were mainly concerned with the time, place and mode of sale of the horses. The accounts of those conversations given in evidence to his Lordship differed substantially in only one important matter, a finding on which was necessary for the purpose of his Lordship's decision between the parties.

It was with the sale of one particular horse, belonging to the partnership, that his Lordship was concerned. The animal in question was a thoroughbred filly, foaled in 1947, to a mare bought that year, in foal, as partnership property; and it was not disputed that the filly was partnership property. She was registered with the Turf Club in the name of 'Lonely Maid'. The importance of this animal, and the source of the present dispute, lay in the fact that, at the time of the sale, she had been entered for three important races, known in racing phraseology as 'classics'. In the same phraseology entries for races are known as 'engagements' and his Lordship would so refer to them. The three classics were the Curragh Foal Plate, to be run in July 1949, the Irish 1,000 Guineas to be run in May 1950, and the Irish Oaks to be run in July 1950. The value of those engagements would, of course, depend on whether the horse had a reasonable prospect of winning, or doing well in, any or all of the races. The prize money involved in those three races was very substantial. The entries were all made by the defendant in his own name, the plaintiff being debited in accounts between them with half the entry fees that had been paid. In the case of each of the races, there were dates subsequent to the original entry at each of which, under the condition of the race, further fees (called 'forfeits') became payable if the entry of the horse for the particular race was not cancelled or struck out of that race.

At the auction which took place at the Phoenix Park on 25 June, the plaintiff became the purchaser of 'Lonely Maid'. He bid for and bought her through Mr Prendergast who had become the trainer for horses of the plaintiff which had previously been with the defendant, and whom the plaintiff had also appointed his agent in racing matters. The defendant also bid at the auction through an agent; and these two agents appeared to have been the only bidders. Both parties were present but took no part in the auction, although each had had a conversation with the auctioneer prior to the auction.

The foundation of the plaintiff's claim was that he bought the horse with its engagements. A few days after the sale, on 29 June 1949, the defendant, without consulting either the plaintiff or Mr Prendergast, struck the horse out of all engagements in his name. That action prevented the plaintiff from running the horse in any of the important races already mentioned, and he claimed that he thereby lost a reasonable chance of securing prize money in any of those races, and in addition the enhanced value that a good performance in any of those races would have given her. He claimed that the defendant's action in striking the horse out of the engagements was a breach of contract or a breach of trust on his part, and was also malicious, in the sense not merely of ill-will, but also of being deliberately intended to injure him.

The defendant disputed that the sale was with engagements, but the plaintiff countered that contention with the argument that, even if the sale were without engagements, the latter then remained partnership property and that the defendant's complaint was then a breach of trust, which, if malice were established, gave the plaintiff a cause of action.

. . .

His Lordship referred in detail to the evidence adduced to establish whether or not the engagements were sold with the horse. The sale by auction was advertised beforehand in the Irish Racing Calendar, Irish Field and Irish Times. These notices, and also the notification of sale on the racecard for the meeting at which the filly was to be sold, contained no reference to engagements and merely stated that the sale was 'to dissolve a partnership'. The contents of those notices followed the instructions in writing given in each case by Mr Dunne. It was common case that at the auction the auctioneer made no reference to engagements. He notified the result of the sale to the Turf Club in the manner acceptable by that body, namely, by a note on his own official copy of the racecard, which merely gave the name of the purchaser and the price paid for the horse. In the absence of any notification as to engagements, the Turf Club did, and could only, under their rules, treat the sale as not having been with engagements. Their view of the matter, of course, did not conclude the issue as between the parties.

His Lordship reviewed in detail the evidence given of the conversations that took place between the defendant and the plaintiff's solicitor, prior to the auction, concerning the mode of sale of the partnership horses. He had no hesitation in accepting Mr Dunne's account as not only probable but accurate. The position, therefore, was that he was satisfied that there was an agreement between the partners to sell 'Lonely Maid' with her engagements, a list of such engagements to be supplied to the auctioneer at the auctions; and he thought that the letter from Mr Dunne to the Phoenix Park authority should have conveyed that the intention was to sell the horse with her engagements. The auctioneer was furnished with the relevant correspondence but one could readily understand his silence on the question of the engagements at the auction when, although he spoke to each partner shortly before the auction, neither made any reference to engagements and nobody at any time tendered him a list of the engagements. From the point of view of the actual purchaser, the plaintiff, his Lordship was satisfied that there was no doubt in his mind but that he was buying the engagements with the horse; and he was also satisfied that that was the state of mind of the plaintiff's agent.

The parties to the sale were therefore *ad idem* as to the engagements and if the sale had been by private treaty there would have been no difficulty about the matter. It was objected, however, by counsel for the defendant, that, the sale being by auction, the special knowledge or state of mind of any individual prospective purchaser was irrelevant and the property sold was limited to that advertised or announced by the auctioneer. In that view, said his Lordship, the engagements were not sold, and there was considerable force in the argument. It seemed to him, however, that the better view was that the auctioneer, who was only an agent, and primarily an agent for the vendor, sold what the vendor intended to sell, in the absence of anything to the contrary. Thus, a purchaser at the auction, other than one of the partners, who had become aware of the intention to include the engagements, could, in his Lordship's view, succeed in a claim that they had been sold to him. On the other hand, if there had been any advertisement, or any statement by the auctioneer, that the horse was being sold without engagements, even though that were contrary to the intention or the instructions, that might have been sufficient to preclude such a claim.

Even if his Lordship were wrong in that view, he was of opinion that the same result would be arrived at, as between the parties, in the case before him, by applying the doctrine of estoppel based on a representation by the defendant, in his agreement with Mr Dunne in the matter, that the engagements were being sold.

His Lordship had arrived therefore at the conclusion that there was a sale of the horse with her engagements by the partnership to the plaintiff. The dual position of the plaintiff as the purchaser and also one of the vendors raised the legal difficulty that he could not sue the partnership, as by so doing he would be the plaintiff and also a defendant in the same action. That legal disability, however, did not prevent him becoming the purchaser of partnership property. Before considering the form of the present action, it might be convenient to refer to the events subsequent to the auction sale.

The outstanding event was, that a few days after the sale 'Lonely Maid' was struck out of all engagements in the name of the defendant, which, in effect, put her out of all her engagements. This was done by the defendant on a form known as a 'Nomination circular' dealing with the entry and striking out of horses, used by trainers and owners and sent periodically to the Turf Club. The defendant explained in evidence that he was completing that form for that particular week on the day previous to the twenty ninth and, having looked up a publication known as 'Races to come', to see if any forfeits were falling due, he saw that 'Lonely Maid' was entered for the Curragh Foal Plate and that it then came to his mind that she might be entered for other races and he looked this up and found it was so. Thereupon he decided to strike her out of all engagements in his name, and did so. The explanation offered by the defendant for his action was that in so doing he was merely following his invariable practice of striking out every horse he sold, lest he should become liable for forfeits in respect of animals in which he had ceased to have any interest.

Commenting on that suggestion his Lordship stated that the question was whether or not the occasion in question was an example of the general practice. The proposition could only apply where it was clear that the horse had been sold without engagements, or, if not, where the striking out was in accordance with the new owner's wishes.

. . .

His Lordship said that on the evidence before him he did not accept the defendant's explanation of his action in striking out 'Lonely Maid's' engagements. He referred to the fact that the total extent of the forfeits that could have become payable after the sale to the plaintiff was £39 in respect of all the engagements; he found it impossible to believe that the defendant was seriously perturbed by that liability, either immediate or prospective, or that the more rational alternative of ascertaining the views of his partner or of Mr Prendergast to whom at least he knew the horse had been knocked down, did not occur to him. If it occurred to him, as his Lordship felt sure it must have, why did he reject it?

In the light of all the circumstances already detailed, his Lordship could find only one answer to that question. It was, and he so held, that the defendant's suggested justification was not genuine nor the real reason of his conduct. He felt satisfied that the defendant in acting as he did was actuated by some ill-will towards the plaintiff, and his motive was deliberately to injure the plaintiff, in other words, that he was actuated by what is known in law as malice.

That view of the matter had an important bearing, in his opinion, on the plaintiff's claim. That claim was partly based on breach of contract and the only contract involved was a sale of the horse with her engagements by the partnership to the plaintiff. The plaintiff's status as a partner prevented him suing the partnership and neither could he sue the defendant, who was only one partner, in respect of a partnership liability. Nevertheless, he acquired, as his Lordship had held, the legal right to, and ownership of, the engagements, but was deprived of any benefit therefrom by the deliberate and malicious act of the defendant. His Lordship felt that the law might justly be accused of futility if the plaintiff were in such circumstances left without any legal remedy. It was contended on behalf of the defendant, not that he was without any remedy, but that his remedy was by way of a partnership action involving an accounting between the parties and the ascertainment of the ultimate balance due by each to the other. That view, however, depended for its validity on the matter being a partnership one. The gist of the plaintiff's complaint was an interference by the defendant in his personal capacity, and not as a partner, with the property of the plaintiff. Could it be contended, if the defendant had deliberately injured or destroyed the horse after the sale, that such an interference with the property of the plaintiff was simply a partnership matter? Yet, the engagements had, in his Lordship's view, equally become the property of the plaintiff.

. . .

That there was loss to the plaintiff he had no doubt, but the assessment of its amount was a matter of difficulty for the reason that it was not a matter of certainty but of probability. The damage was alleged to consist in the loss of one or more of the amounts payable as prize money in the three engagements, with the further loss of the enhanced value of the animal if it had done well in any of those races. Such loss clearly depended on a contingency, the second branch of it on a double contingency. The case of *Chaplin v Hicks* |1911| 2 KB 786, seemed to be authority for the view that the fact of such loss depending on such contingencies did not disentitle the plaintiff to damages, but only rendered their assessment more difficult.

On all the evidence, and having regard to the value of the stakes in the three races in question, and to the ability of the filly as proved by her subsequent performances, his Lordship assessed damages at £750 and gave judgment for that amount.

McGregor on Damages (15th ed.) London: Sweet & Maxwell, 1988, 469–70 (Footnotes omitted.)

Is the measure of damages in contract and tort the same? This is a question frequently posed. Sometimes it is said that it is, sometimes that it is not. Before any clear answer can be found it is necessary to break down this omnibus question, for the term 'measure of damages' may refer to a number of things.

The clearest and undoubted distinctions between contract and tort lie in the exceptional cases where damages are not given strictly on the principle of awarding compensation. On the one hand since liquidated damages can only result from agreement, they apply to contract and cannot in the nature of things refer to tort. On the other hand exemplary damages, though now explicitly confined to three categories of case, continue to be awarded only in tort and have not spread to contract. Further, nominal damages have application to all contracts but only to some torts.

Turning to the case of compensatory damages, which is much more important because it represents the norm, there is at the very start a basic, though somewhat latent, distinction between contract and tort. This distinction is in the general rule which is the starting point for resolving all problems as to measure of damages. The distinction is latent because the leading formulation of the general rule is sufficiently wide to cover contract and tort equally: this formulation is that the plaintiff is entitled to be put into the same position, as far as money can do it, as he would have been in had the wrong not been committed. In contract, however, the wrong consists not in the making but in the breaking of the contract and therefore the plaintiff is entitled to be put into the position he would have been in if the contract had never been broken, or in other words, if the contract had been performed. The plaintiff is entitled to recover damages for the loss of his bargain. In tort, on the other hand, no question of loss of bargain can arise: the plaintiff is not complaining of failure to implement a promise but of failure to leave him alone. The measure of damages in tort is therefore to be assessed on the basis of restoring as far as possible the *status quo ante*. This distinction does not stand out in the great majority of cases since contract and tort have such widely different areas of application, but in cases involving misrepresentations there is an overlap of contract and tort which is instructive in this connection. Where the plaintiff has been induced to enter into a contract by a misrepresentation of fact on the defendant's part, then if the representation constitutes a term of the contract, whether condition or warranty, he can sue for breach of contract and, in claiming for loss of his bargain, is entitled to such damages as will put him into the position he would have been in had the misrepresentation been true. If, however, the representation does not constitute a term of the contract, then, although the plaintiff may be entitled to rescind on the ground of misrepresentation, there is no breach of contract for which he can get damages, and his only common law action for damages can be in tort, in deceit if the misrepresentation has been fraudulently made, in negligence where it has been carelessly made. It is sometimes assumed that if the plaintiff can show fraud he is in as good a position as far as damages are concerned as if he had been able to sue for breach of contract on the ground that the representation was a term of the contract. This is fallacious, for the proper measure of damages in deceit—a measure adopted in the late nineteenth century and now firmly established by the Court of Appeal in *Doyle v Olby (Ironmongers)*—is to put the plaintiff in the position he would have been in, not if the representation had been true, but if the representation had never been made. This is a more restrictive rule: the action in tort does not take into account the loss of a bargain. Conversely, cases of breach of warranty of authority are sometimes regarded as in effect giving damages for innocent misrepresentation. That this is not the proper view is shown by the fact that it has been consistently decided in the cases, of which *Re National Coffee Palace Co., ex p. Panmure* is perhaps the most important, that the measure of damages is based upon putting the plaintiff in the position he would have been in, not if the representation had never been made, but if the representation had been true.

A. Measures of Compensation

Sale of Goods Act 1893 ss 50 and 51

Part V. Actions for Breach of the Contract

Remedies of the Seller

50. (1) Where the buyer wrongfully neglects or refuses to accept and pay for the goods, the seller may maintain an action against him for damages for non-acceptance.

(2) The measure of damages is the estimated loss directly and naturally resulting, in the ordinary course of events, from the buyer's breach of contract.

(3) Where there is an available market for the goods in question the measure of damages is *prima facie* to be ascertained by the difference between the contract price

and the market or current price at the time or times when the goods ought to have been accepted or, if no time was fixed for acceptance, then at the time of the refusal to accept.

Remedies of the Buyer

51. (1) Where the seller wrongfully neglects or refuses to deliver the goods to the buyer, the buyer may maintain an action against the seller for damages for non-delivery.

(2) The measure of damages is the estimated loss directly and naturally resulting, in the ordinary course of events, from the seller's breach of contract.

(3) Where there is an available market for the goods in question the measure of damages is *prima facie* to be ascertained by the difference between the contract price and the market or current price of the goods at the time or times when they ought to have been delivered, or, if no time was fixed, then at the time of the refusal to deliver.

Macauley & Cullen v Horgan [1925] 2 IR 6

In this case the defendant was held to be in breach of a contract to deliver wool, the contract being concluded by correspondence on 26 October 1923.

Sullivan P.:

. . .

I hold that a reasonable time for delivery had elapsed by 5 December, and that the wool should have been delivered on or before that date. I further hold that the refusal or neglect of defendant to answer the plaintiffs' letters of 5 December and 18 December amounted to a refusal by the defendant to perform his contract, one month prior to his receipt of the letter of 18 January 1924, from the plaintiffs' solicitors.

The measure of damages is prescribed by s. 51 of the Sale of Goods Act 1893. That section provides that where the seller wrongfully neglects or refuses to deliver the goods to the buyer, the buyer may maintain an action against the seller for damages for non-delivery (sub-s. (1)). The measure of damages is the estimated loss directly and naturally resulting, in the ordinary course of events, from the seller's breach of contract (sub-s. (2)). And then sub-s. (3) provides: 'Where there is an available market for the goods in question the measure of damages is *prima facie* to be ascertained by the difference between the contract price and the market or current price of the goods at the time or times when they ought to have been delivered, or, if no time was fixed, then at the time of the refusal to deliver.' The section, it will be seen, states two alternative dates for ascertaining the measure of damages, namely, 'when the goods ought to have been delivered,' or, if no time was fixed, then 'the time of the refusal to deliver.'

I have held that the conduct of the defendant in not answering the letters of the plaintiffs amounted to a refusal to deliver, that before the end of December there had been a refusal by the defendant to deliver the wool to the plaintiffs, and that the plaintiffs were not entitled to wait until the end of January before accepting such refusal. Accordingly, the next question is, was there an available market for the goods in question, and, if so, what was the difference between the market price and the contract price at that time? There was no evidence as to the existence of an available market for wool at Cahirciveen where delivery was contracted for, but, having regard to the previous dealings between the parties and the inter-communication between Cahirciveen and Dublin, I think that the market price at Cahirciveen may, for the purposes of the measure of damages, be taken to be the market price at Dublin, less the cost of carriage, and, accordingly, I hold that the plaintiffs can rely on the market price in Dublin. I think that *Wertheim v Chicoutimi Pulp Co.*[1] justifies me in so holding and in accepting evidence of the Dublin price.

Accordingly, the next question is, what was the Dublin price at the end of December? |His Lordship then dealt with the figures given in evidence as to the price of such wool in Dublin at the end of December, and held that the price then was £100 in excess of the price contracted for, and continued:|

Accordingly, I hold that the price of wool in Dublin at the end of December was £100 over that contracted for, and from this I deduct £50 for the cost of carriage to Dublin, and I therefore assess damages at £50.

1. |1911| AC 301.

B. So-called 'Lost Volume Sales' Cases

W. L. Thompson Ltd v Robinson (Gunmakers) Ltd [1955] Ch. 177

The defendant company refused to accept delivery of a Vanguard motor car which they had contracted to buy from the plaintiffs, who were dealers in motor cars. The Vanguard motor car was readily available and the retail selling price was fixed by the manufacturers.

The plaintiffs mitigated their damage by returning the vehicle to their suppliers, who took it back, but the plaintiffs contended that they were nevertheless entitled to damages amounting to £61, the loss of profit on the repudiated sale. The defendants, relying on s. 50 (3) of the Sale of Goods Act 1893, contended that the plaintiffs' loss was only nominal:

Upjohn J. held for the plaintiffs:

Apart altogether from authority and statute it would seem to me on the facts which I have to consider to be quite plain that the plaintiffs' loss in this case is the loss of their bargain. They have sold one Vanguard less than they otherwise would. The plaintiffs, as the defendants must have known, are in business as dealers in motor cars and make their profit in buying and selling motor cars, and what they have lost is their profit on the sale of this Vanguard. There is no authority exactly in point in this country, although it seems to me that the principle to be applied is a clear one. It is to be found in In re Vic Mill Ltd.[1]

1. |1913| 1 Ch. 465.

Further discussion on this issue arose two years later in the Court of Appeal.

Charter v Sullivan [1957] 2 QB 117

The facts:

The defendant refused to accept delivery of a Hillman Minx motor car which he contracted to buy from the plaintiff, a motor car dealer, at the retail price fixed by the manufacturers. Within ten days the plaintiff resold the car to another purchaser. In an action by the plaintiff for breach of contract, the County Court Judge awarded the plaintiff £97 15s, the loss of profit on the repudiated sale. The defendant appealed on the grounds that the true measure of damages was the difference between the market value and the contract price and that the plaintiff had not suffered any damage since he had subsequently resold the car for the agreed price.

Jenkins L.J.:

. . . the plaintiff is a motor car dealer whose trade for the present purpose can be described as consisting in the purchase of recurrent supplies of cars of the relevant description from the manufacturers, and selling the cars so obtained, or as many of them as he can, at the fixed retail price. He thus receives on each sale he is able to effect, the predetermined profit allowed by the fixed retail price, and it is obviously in his interest to sell as many cars as he can obtain from the manufacturers. The number of sales he can effect, and consequently the amount of profit he makes, will be governed, according to the state of trade, either by the number of cars he is able to obtain from the manufacturers, or by the number of purchasers he is able to find. In the former case demand exceeds supply, so that the default of one purchaser involves him in no loss, for he sells the same number of cars as he would have sold if that purchaser had not defaulted. In the latter case supply exceeds demand, so that the default of one purchaser may be said to have lost him one sale.

Accordingly, it seems to me that even if there was within the meaning of s. 50 (3) an available market for cars of the description in question, and even if the fixed retail price was the market or current price within the meaning of the same subsection, the *prima facie* rule which it prescribes should be rejected in favour of the general rule laid down by sub-s. (2); for it does not by any means necessarily follow that, because the plaintiff sold at the fixed retail price to Wigley the car which the defendant had agreed to buy at the selfsame fixed retail price, but refused to take, therefore the plaintiff suffered no 'loss directly and naturally resulting, in the ordinary course of events' from the defendant's breach of contract.

This makes it strictly unnecessary to decide whether there was in the present case an available market for cars of the description in question within the meaning of s. 50 (3). But I would find it difficult to hold that there was. Given default by some purchaser of one of his cars of the relevant description, the plaintiff's only alternative mode of disposal would be to sell it at the fixed retail price to some other purchaser. He could endeavour to find another purchaser by displaying the car in his saleroom, circularising or canvassing old customers or the public at large, and advertising by posters or in newspapers. The car would obviously be of interest to retail customers only (i.e. the car-using public as distinct from the trade) and any purchaser he might succeed in finding would necessarily have to be a purchaser at the fixed retail price. At that price there might be no takers, in which case the plaintiff would be left with the car on his hands. S. 50 (3) seems to me to postulate a market in which there is a market or current price, i.e. a price fixed by supply and demand at which (be it more or less than the contract price) a purchaser can be found. If the only price at which a car can be sold is the fixed retail price and no purchaser can be found at that price, I do not think it can reasonably be said that there is a market or current price or that there is an available market. If the state of the trade were such that the plaintiff could sell at the fixed retail price all the cars he could get, so that the defendant's default did not result in the plaintiff effecting one sale less than he would otherwise have effected, it may well be that the plaintiff could not make out his claim to anything more than nominal damages. I am, however, inclined to think that this would not be on account of the necessary equality of the contract price and the fixed retail price at which alone the car could be sold, taken for the present purpose as the market or current price within the meaning of s. 50 (3), but because on an application of the general principle laid down by s. 50 (2) the plaintiff would be found to have suffered no damage.

In *Thompson* (W.L.) *Ltd v Robinson* (*Gunmakers*) *Ltd*[1] Upjohn J. had before him a claim for damages in a case resembling the present case to the extent that the damages were claimed in respect of the defendants' refusal to perform a contract with the plaintiffs for the purchase from the plaintiffs of a car (in that instance a Standard Vanguard car) which, like the car in the present case, could only be sold by the plaintiffs at a fixed retail price. It is, however, important to note that the case to which I am now referring proceeded on certain admissions, including an admission to the effect that in the relevant district at the date of the contract (which was also the date of the breach) 'there was no shortage of Vanguard models to meet all immediate demands in the locality,' which I take to mean, in effect, that the supply of such cars exceeded the demand. In these circumstances the plaintiffs by agreement with their suppliers rescinded their contract with them, and returned the car. In the ensuing action the plaintiffs claimed from the defendants damages amounting to the profit the plaintiffs would have made on the sale of the car to the defendants if the defendants had duly completed their purchase of it, and the judge held them entitled to those damages. The defendants raised the same argument as has been raised by the defendant in the present case, namely, that there was an available market for a car of the kind in question, within the meaning of s. 50 (3), that there was a market or current price in the shape of the fixed retail price, and that as the fixed retail price was the same as the contract price the plaintiffs had suffered no damage. In the course of his judgment Upjohn J. referred to James L.J.'s definition of a market in Dunkirk Colliery Co. v Lever[2] James L.J. said this:

> Under those circumstances the only thing that we can do is to send it back to the referee with an intimation that we are of opinion upon the facts (agreeing with the Master of the Rolls in that respect), that the facts do not warrant the application of the principle mentioned in the award, namely, that there was what may be properly called a market. What I understand by a market in such a case as this is, that when the defendant refused to take the 300 tons the first week or the first month, the plaintiffs might have sent it in waggons somewhere else, where they could sell it, just as they sell corn on the Exchange, or cotton at Liverpool: that is to say, that there was a fair market where they could have found a purchaser either by themselves or through some agent at some particular place. That is my notion of the meaning of a market under those circumstances.

Upjohn J. also referred to the Scottish case of Marshall & Co. v Nicoll & Son,[3] where it was held in the Court in Session that there was an available market within the meaning of s. 51 (3) of the Sale of Goods Act 1893, for annealed steel sheets although they were not kept in stock and were not purchasable in the open market. In the House of Lords the decision was affirmed, but their Lordships would seem to have been equally divided on the question whether there was an available market for the goods. In this state of the authorities, the judge felt himself bound by Dunkirk Colliery Co. v Lever, and held, in effect, that James L.J.'s definition in that case prevented him from holding that in the case then before him there was an available market within the meaning of s. 50 (3).

Upjohn J. went on to propound a more extended meaning for the phrase 'available market' in these terms: 'Had the matter been res integra I think that I should have found that an "available market" merely means that the situation in the particular trade in the particular area was such that the particular goods could freely be sold, and that there was a demand sufficient to absorb readily all the goods that were thrust on it, so that if a purchaser defaulted, the goods in question could readily be disposed of.' He went on to say, in effect, that in the case then before him there was no available market because the supply of Vanguard cars at the material time exceeded the demand.

I doubt if James L.J.'s observations in Dunkirk Colliery Co. v Lever should be literally applied as an exhaustive definition of an available market in all cases. On the other hand, I do not find Upjohn J.'s definition entirely satisfactory. I will not, however, attempt to improve upon it, but will content myself with the negative proposition that I doubt if there can be an available market for particular goods in any sense relevant to s. 50 (3) of the Sale of Goods Act 1893, unless those goods are available for sale in the market at the market or current price in the sense of the price, whatever it may be, fixed by reference to supply and demand as the price at which a purchaser for the goods in question can be found, be it greater or less than or equal to the contract price. The language of s. 50 (3) seems to me to postulate that in the cases to which it applies there will, or may, be a difference between the contract price and the market or current price, which cannot be so where the goods can only be sold at a fixed retail price.

Accordingly, I am of opinion that whether there was in this case 'an available market' within the meaning of s. 50 (3) or not, it is a case in which s. 50 (2) should be applied to the exclusion of s. 50 (3).

It remains, therefore, to ascertain the loss (if any) 'naturally resulting, in the ordinary course of events' from the defendant's breach of contract, and the measure of that loss must, in my opinion, be the amount, if any, of the profit the plaintiff has lost by reason of the defendant's failure to take and pay for the car he agreed to buy. This accords with the view taken by Upjohn J. in *Thompson* (W. L.) *Ltd v Robinson* (*Gunmakers*) *Ltd*, and also with the principle stated in In re *Vic Mill Ltd*[4] which Upjohn J. applied.

I should next refer to evidence of which I have deferred consideration earlier in this judgment.

The plaintiff's sales manager, Winter, gave evidence, from the judge's abbreviated note of which I extract the following. From examination-in-chief: 'I'm certain we would have sold this purchaser' [Wigley] 'another Hillman Minx if not this one' [the one the defendant had rejected]. From cross-examination: 'No other Hillman Minx in stock I think. If defendant had taken car we would have ordered one from stock' [I think this must mean from the manufacturers' stock] 'it would have taken a week to ten days to get one. Can sell all Hillman Minx we can get. We are Rootes Group area dealers for this area. We have lost the sale of a car—sold same price to Wigley.'

In the brief record of his judgment with which we have been provided, the judge in terms expressed his acceptance of Winter's evidence as to selling Wigley 'another Hillman Minx if not this one', and as to being able to order one from stock and obtain it in seven to ten days; but he made no reference to what appears to me to be the vital passage in Winter's evidence: 'Can sell all the Hillman Minx we can get.'

Notwithstanding [counsel's] submission to the contrary on the plaintiff's behalf, I think we should assume that the judge accepted as accurate the plaintiff's sales manager's own description of the state of the plaintiff's business in Hillman Minx cars. Moreover, I think we should take that description as signifying, according to the ordinary meaning of the language used, that the plaintiff could always find purchasers for all the Hillman Minx cars he was able to get.

[Counsel for the defendant] objected to Winter's statement to the effect that he was certain that he could have sold another Hillman Minx to Wigley if Wigley had not bought the one which the defendant had rejected. [Counsel] said that this was mere hearsay and opinion and inadmissible as evidence, and that Wigley should have been called to prove his intention. I think this is hypercritical. The judge described Winter as a very experienced salesman and expressly accepted this part of his evidence. I therefore see no reason to doubt the correctness of Winter's assessment of Wigley's intention, and I accept it accordingly.

I have not overlooked the evidence given by the plaintiff's storeman Harold Charles Charter, and noted by the judge as 'Delivery Hillman Minx not easy at this time— might have to wait some time', but I attach no importance to it because, as will here- after appear, the judge preferred the evidence of Winter.

The matter therefore stands thus. If the defendant had duly performed his bargain the plaintiff would have made on that transaction a profit of £97 15s. The calculation accordingly starts with a loss of profit, through the defendant's default, of £97 15s. That loss was not cancelled or reduced by the sale of the same car to Wigley, for if the defendant had duly taken and paid for the car he agreed to buy, the plaintiff could have sold another car to Wigley, in which case there would have been two sales and two profits: see In re Vic Mill Ltd, and particularly per Hamilton L.J. and Buckley L.J. But the matter does not rest there. The plaintiff must further show that the sum representing the profit he would have made if the defendant had performed his contract has in fact been lost. Here I think he fails, in view of Winter's evidence to the effect that the plaintiff could sell all the Hillman Minx cars he could get.

I have already expressed my opinion as to the meaning of this statement. It comes, I think, to this, that according to the plaintiff's own sales manager the state of trade was such that the plaintiff could always find a purchaser for every Hillman Minx car he could get from the manufacturers; and if that is right it inevitably follows that he sold the same number of cars and made the same number of fixed profits as he would have sold and made if the defendant had duly carried out his bargain.

Upjohn J.'s decision in favour of the plaintiff dealers in Thompson's case was essentially based on the admitted fact that the supply of the cars in question exceeded the demand, and his judgment leaves no room for doubt that if the demand had exceeded the supply his decision would have been the other way.

In dealing with the present case we were put in some difficulty by the appellant's failure to perform the duty laid upon him by the RSC, Ord. 58, r. 20 (4), of obtaining from the judge and furnishing to this court a copy of the judge's note made under s. 108 of the County Courts Act 1934, of the question of law involved in the present appeal. We accepted as the best available substitute a short note of the arguments and judgment taken by the plaintiff's solicitor and submitted by him to the judge, who signed it on 9 November 1956, with the note 'This appears to me accurately to represent my findings.' The relevant part of this note reads thus:

It was Mr Jaye's contention [Mr Jaye was the defendant's solicitor] that because the car had been sold to Mr Wigley within seven to ten days the plaintiff had lost no profit. He further submitted 'that the plaintiff had not shown that there was no [the note here says 'an' but clearly 'no' was intended] available market to bring the case within Thompson (W. L.) Ltd v Robinson (Gunmakers) Ltd. Mr Winter has said it would have taken a week to ten days to obtain another and Mr Charter had said delivery of Hillman Minx not easy at that time. Mr Jaye stated further that the plaintiff had pleaded that he has lost the profit on this particular car but in fact the car had been sold. I applied for leave to amend the particulars of claim by deleting the words 'the said' and adding 'a second'. Mr Jaye raised no objection to the amendment and the judge granted leave. I was not called upon by the judge to reply. In a very short judgment His Honour stated he was satisfied the plaintiff had made out his case, and that the case came within the decision in Thompson (W. L) Ltd v Robinson (Gunmakers) Ltd. . . . He accepted the evidence of Mr Winter whom he considered to be a very experienced salesman when he said he had some difficulty in getting Mr Wigley to take the car, because it had already been registered, and that if he had not sold this car to Mr Wigley, he would have sold another one to him. Mr Charter did say that delivery of Hillman Minx was not easy at this time but he was only a storeman employed by the plaintiff and the delivery position of cars was not within his knowledge—he accepted what Mr Winter had said that he could have ordered one from stock and obtained it in a week to ten days.

It will be seen that this note of the judgment contains no reference to Winter's statement 'Can sell all Hillman Minx we can get.'

. . .

The materials before the court leave a good deal to be desired. The parties were no doubt preoccupied with the issue of contract or no contract, and the argument in regard to damages based on *Thompson's* case was perhaps something of an afterthought, as is suggested by the belated (and as I think unnecessary) amendment of the points of claim by substituting 'a second motor car' for 'the said motor car' in the first item of damage claimed.

But it was for the plaintiff to prove that he did in fact sustain the loss of profit claimed, and this to my mind he wholly failed to do. The mere assertion by Winter 'We have lost sale of a car' is clearly not enough, particularly when read in conjunction with his 'Can sell all Hillman Minx we can get.' Accordingly there was in my view no evidence on which the judge could properly hold that the plaintiff had suffered the damage claimed, and I would allow this appeal.

1. |1955| Ch. 177.
2. (1878) 9 ChD 20.
3. 1919 SC 120.
4. |1913| 1 Ch. 465.

(Lords Hodson and Sellers agreed.)

SECTION THREE—NON-COMPENSATORY DAMAGES

A. EXEMPLARY DAMAGES

In *Rookes v Barnard* |1964| 2 WLR 269 the House of Lords indicated that an award of damages should not in general be utilised to punish a wrongdoer. The Supreme Court in subsequent cases has endorsed *Rookes v Barnard*.

Garvey v Ireland An Taoiseach and Others (HC) 19 December 1980, unrep.

McWilliam J.:

The plaintiff became a member of the Garda Siochana in 1939 and rose through the ranks until he was appointed Commissioner of the force on 1 September 1975. He then had the expectation of continuing as Commissioner until his retirement in February 1980. The government purported to remove him from office on 19 January 1978. It has been held by the Supreme Court that the circumstances of his purported removal from office, with which I am not now concerned, were such that his appointment was not validly terminated.

He resigned his position in May 1979, having then only about nine months to go before reaching the retiring age. Although he was deprived of all his functions and ceased to have any authority in the force, it is accepted by the defendants that he was entitled to his salary as Commissioner from 20 January 1978, until 15 May 1979, and the sum of £11,309, the accumulated arrears of salary, was paid to him on 23 May 1979, in respect of this period.

The matter comes before me now to decide whether the plaintiff is entitled to damages for his wrongful removal from office and, if so, what is the measure of those damages.

Damages appear to me to be conveniently grouped under three headings: (1) Special damage, which includes all pecuniary loss caused by a wrongful act. (2) General damages, which, where appropriate include recompense for such things as physical suffering, injury to reputation, consequential loss, etc. (3) Exemplary damages, which may, in certain circumstances, be awarded for the aggravated nature of the wrongful act. The plaintiff makes his claim under each head.

Although the appointment of the plaintiff as Commissioner did not create the relationship of master and servant between the government and the plaintiff, it seems to me that the offer and acceptance of the appointment must have been accompanied by some form of implied agreement that the plaintiff would receive pay in accordance with the provisions of s. 12 of the Police Forces Amalgamation Act 1925, for so long as he should hold his appointment. The relevant orders made under this section have not been opened to me but it appears to be accepted that the plaintiff was entitled to be paid fortnightly. After his purported removal from office the plaintiff was not paid anything until 23 May 1979. It seems to me that the plaintiff did suffer loss by not receiving his salary at the proper times because either he had to borrow money at interest to replace his salary or he was deprived of the opportunity of using the money by investment or otherwise so as to make a profit. The only evidence as to this was given by an accountant who gave evidence on behalf of the plaintiff and calculated this loss at the sum of £1,298.11. I am of opinion that the plaintiff is entitled to recover this sum under this heading.

Under the second heading, the plaintiff claims general damages for loss of job satisfaction, loss of opportunity for preparing for his retirement, invasion of privacy due to the public interest in his removal from office, injury to his health and general distress aggravated by the effect the events had upon his family.

The case of Cox v Phillips Industries Ltd [1976] 1 WLR 638 is very strongly relied upon on behalf of the plaintiff. In this case it was held that vexation, frustration and distress caused by being relegated to a position of lesser responsibility in his firm in breach of his contract of employment which led to a plaintiff's ill-health was a matter which could be compensated in damages where the effects of the wrongful conduct by the employers must have been within the contemplation of the parties.

The case of Addis v Gramophone Co. Ltd [1909] AC 488 was equally strongly relied upon on behalf of the defendants. This case was somewhat similar to the present in that the plaintiff was given six months notice but was not permitted to discharge his duties as manager during that period. Lord Loreburn said, at 490, 'To my mind it signifies nothing in the present case whether the claim is to be treated as for wrongful dismissal or not. In any case there was a breach of contract in not allowing the plaintiff to discharge his duties as manager, and the damages are exactly the same in either view.' At 491 he said 'If there be a dismissal without notice the employer must pay an indemnity; but that indemnity cannot include compensation either for the injured feelings of the servant, or for the loss he may sustain from the fact that his having been dismissed itself makes it more difficult to obtain employment.' It is right to point out that in the Addis case, no question of a breakdown in health was alleged and the distinction drawn in the judgments was between what I have called special damage and exemplary damages. It was held that a claim for exemplary damages could not be sustained but it was emphasised that, where a claim is made for breach of contract whether of a contract of employment or otherwise, circumstances of malice, fraud, defamation or violence which might sustain an action of tort cannot be taken into consideration.

I accept the decision in this case. Accordingly, unless some injury was occasioned to the plaintiff as a result of the wrongful removal from office of the plaintiff which could reasonably have been foreseen by the defendants, I am of opinion that he is not entitled to any general damages under this heading. In this connection I am not satisfied that there was any injury to the health of the plaintiff in the normally accepted sense. In addition all the other matters of which he complains would have been applicable to a greater or lesser extent had he been lawfully removed from office and cannot be solely attributable to the unlawful nature of his removal.

Finally, the plaintiff claims to be entitled to exemplary damages and the statement of Lord Devlin in *Rookes v Barnard* |1964| 2 WLR 269 at 328 is relied upon. This statement is 'that there are certain categories of cases in which an award of exemplary damages can serve a useful purpose in vindicating the strength of the law and thus affording a practical justification for admitting into the civil law a principle which logically ought to belong to the criminal. The first category is oppressive, arbitrary or unconstitutional action by the servants of government.' As that case was not dealing with actions by servants of government, this statement was not elaborated. It was, however, very fully discussed in the case of *Broome v Cassell & Co.* |1972| 2 WLR 645 and I am satisfied from the judgments in that case that I should award what I have described as exemplary damages to the plaintiff but that these must be related to the injury which the plaintiff has suffered by reason of the arbitrary and oppressive conduct of the government. Having regard to my view that similar injury would, to a large extent, have been sustained by the plaintiff had he been lawfully removed from office I will award £500 on this part of the claim.

Note

In *Conway v* INTO |1991| ILRM 497 the Supreme Court ruled that exemplary and punitive damages are to be considered as the same thing. Such damages are properly awardable in the case of a breach of a constitutional right. However, such damages are not automatically awarded. The relationship between various civil law causes of action and exemplary damages has recently been considered by the English Court of Appeal (see |1993| 1 All ER 609). Law Commission Working Paper No. 132 (1993) has canvassed extensive reform of the law relating to exemplary damages in England.

R. Clark 'Unjust enrichment as a non-compensatory principle justifying the award of damages' (1978) 29 NILQ 129

Damages and Unjust Enrichment

As is well known the House of Lords in *Rookes v Barnard*[1] considered those situations in which the award of punitive or exemplary damages may be permissible as a means of punishing a wrongdoer or depriving him of any pecuniary advantage he may obtain from his misconduct. Lord Devlin outlined three such categories: firstly, instances of arbitrary or unconstitutional action by servants of the government; secondly, instances where the defendant has calculated that a profit he may make by an act of wrongdoing will exceed the compensation payable to any person injured by that unlawful act; and thirdly, where statutory authority exists for such an award. The Law Lords asserted that apart from such cases damages should be assessed on compensatory principles. This cardinal principle of law is necessary lest the fundamental distinction between the functions of the criminal and civil law becomes confused.

In a recent decision the President of the Irish High Court, Mr Justice Finlay, has indicated that those guidelines are not authoritative within the Republic of Ireland. While the present writer concedes that the fact that English precedents run contrary to such a stance is not sufficient reason to doubt the soundness of Mr Justice Finlay's reasoning in this case, it is submitted that general aspects of the judgment in *Hickey and Co. Ltd v Roches Stores (Dublin) Ltd*[2] are difficult to reconcile with both legal principle and current authority.

The defendants, Roches Stores (Dublin) Ltd, owned a large drapery shop in Dublin and were in association with other Roches Stores in Limerick and Cork. In 1969 they entered into an agreement with Hickeys, a drapery company, under the terms of which Hickeys were to be allowed to sell fashion fabrics in the defendant company's Dublin store. The agreement provided certain procedures to be applicable when either party sought to terminate it. If either party terminated with good cause no compensation was to be payable. However, where one party unilaterally terminated the agreement, whilst it was functioning satisfactorily, compensation was to be payable by the party terminating. A proviso to the clause gave Roches Stores in such a situation the power to terminate the agreement and avoid the obligation to pay compensation, provided they tendered six months' notice to Hickeys and gave an undertaking that Roches Stores would not sell fashion fabrics for a further period of twelve months following expiry of that notice.

Although the commercial venture was successful and profitable to both parties, Roches Stores, some two years later, terminated the agreement in circumstances which an arbitrator later found to be unjustifiable. Further, the notice given, less than two months, clearly did not satisfy the proviso therefore rendering it incumbent upon Roches Stores to pay compensation for termination. More seriously, perhaps, Roches Stores began immediately to sell fashion fabrics in all three of their stores. The Dublin store was thus in direct competition with Hickeys who had left the Dublin premises and found an alternative location nearby.

The sole issue before Finlay P. in the High Court related to the principles that were to apply in calculating the damages payable by Roches to Hickeys. Roches Stores conceded that they were in breach of the obligation to give six months' notice of intention to terminate, and that they had failed to give an undertaking not to sell fashion fabrics for a further twelve months but submitted that damages were to be estimated solely by reference to profits Hickeys would have made had the contract not been terminated in breach of the agreed procedure and to any loss to Hickeys caused by Roches Stores competing in fashion drapery until the date upon which the restraint covenant, had notice been given, would have expired.

Hickeys, however, contended that they were entitled to recover damages not simply for their own loss of profit but were also to be awarded the value of the business carried on by Roches Stores during the post-breach period. In addition, a sum in accordance with the goodwill built up by Roches Stores, with the assistance of the plaintiffs, was to be recoverable. In short, Hickeys were contending that two factors other than their own economic loss were relevant: the profits made by the wrongdoer subsequent to breach that were only possible because of his breach and also the benefits accruing to the defendants from performance by the plaintiffs. The task of Finlay P. was to determine which, if either, of these rival modes of assessment was to be applicable and, in particular, whether the conduct of a party in breach and the benefits he obtains from the contract broken are relevant in assessing damages. Put in these terms the judgment of Finlay P. is of great importance for Irish commercial lawyers and of interest in other jurisdictions.

After examining the facts Finlay P. found that the defendants had broken the agreement because of a decision taken at executive level that the defendants should develop their own retail business in fashion drapery. Finlay P. advanced the following propositions that were to determine the issues before him.

Firstly, 'assessment of damages in tort and in breach of contract should have as its purpose the putting back of the injured party, insofar as money can do so, to the position in which he would have been had the wrong not been committed.' With the greatest respect to the learned judge, such a proposition seems inaccurate. The courts have long recognised that damages in contract have a different function, that is, to put the party in the position he would have been in but for the breach, rather than to restore him to the *status quo ante*, which is the function of an award of damages in tort. These alternative theoretical starting points can have important practical consequences. Finlay P. continued: 'There are exceptions both in cases of tort and in cases of breach of contract some of which may be different for each particular cause of action and some of which are the same.'

However, 'Where a wrongdoer calculated and intended by his wrongdoing to achieve and has in that way acted *male fide* then irrespective of whether the form of his wrong-doing constitutes a tort or a breach of contract the court should, in assessing damages, look not only at the loss suffered by the injured party but also to the profit or gain unjustly or wrongfully obtained by the wrongdoer.'

If, after considering the quantum of the damages calculated by reference to the innocent party's loss, the wrongdoer would still obtain a profit then damages should be assessed so as to deprive him of that profit. On the facts before him Finlay P. was unable to apply the principle outlined above because no allegation of *mala fides* had been made against the defendants. This suggests that *mala fides* should be expressly pleaded for it is clear that Roches deliberately acted in bad faith by terminating the agreement and therefore would have satisfied such a test.

Nevertheless, the court did not accept the defendants' submissions on the extent of their liability. An additional head of damage, the loss the plaintiffs must have suffered because of the competition presented by the defendants operating a business which the plaintiffs had helped develop, was to be considered and compensated for by an award of aggravated damages. This dictum of Finlay P. is not (as would appear at first sight) an application of Lord Devlin's second category mentioned at the beginning of this article. Lord Devlin indicated that exemplary damages are the result of a calculation on the part of the wrongdoer that he will make a profit in excess of compensation payable to the plaintiff. Finlay P.'s judgment is based upon a wider calculation by the wrongdoer. The difference between the two approaches can be illustrated by reference to a situation where a party to a contract calculates that he will profit by breaking an existing contract with A and negotiating a similar contract with B. Falling market prices may render this an attractive economic proposition.

If the anticipated profit does not materialise, according to Finlay P., non-compens-atory damages are irrecoverable and, presumably, damages in excess of any profit made cannot be awarded. Under Lord Devlin's second category (assuming that such a calculation is permissible in an action in contract) exemplary damages are recoverable because the essential issue is the calculation made at the time of breach rather than profits actually made. It, therefore, appears that in *Hickey* the assessment is based upon principles of unjust enrichment rather than exemplary or punitive damages, which seems curious given that *Rookes v Barnard*, heavily relied on by Finlay P., is an authority on the award of punitive or exemplary damages in tort.

Finlay P. acknowledged that he was well aware that he was extending non-compens-atory principles of assessment into areas of contract when the scope of such factors in the law of tort is uncertain within the Irish Republic. This principle of unjust enrichment was immediately qualified by the learned judge, reflecting the essential difference between contract and tort, that is, the possibility of contractual obligations being created and limited by agreement. In a passage not free from ambiguity he stated that: '. . . where an action lies in contract only, the necessity to create certainty as to the obligations which may arise from the contract and from breach thereof make it necessary to confine, in cases where the element of *male fides* has not occurred, damages to the loss suffered by the injured party even though such restriction may result in a profit to the wrongdoer.'

Finlay P. left open the possibility that the parties to a contract may covenant to the effect that if one breaches the contract damages are to be assessed by reference to both the loss of the injured party and the profits made by the other. This, of course, is simply another application of the principle of freedom of contract. Nevertheless, the possibility of contracting parties drafting such a clause seems to be both unlikely and fraught with difficulty; may not a court faced with such a provision strike it down as a penalty clause, for, by definition, such a term would not be a genuine pre-estimate of the loss suffered by one party.

A further difficulty caused by the conceptual differences between the law of torts and contract, may attach to the converse position to that considered by the court. How would a court deal with the situation where one party wilfully breaks a contract because he calculates that he may profit from such a breach and that contract contains a clause which, on its true construction, limits the damages that are to be recoverable even in cases where one party deliberately and cynically breaks the agreement? Would a substantive rule of law apply so as to defeat such a clause? The courts would be faced with the clear intent of the parties and to award damages greater than those expressly provided for would once again flout freedom of contract as a means of allocating risk between parties contracting at arm's length.

The decision in Hickey itself indicates that the principles advanced therein will be largely superfluous. Exemplary damages and the principle of unjust enrichment may well be necessary in limited instances in order to display to a *tortfeasor* that his conduct is socially unacceptable. Where, however, an action in contract lies and the loss is entirely economic—a head of damage not extensively covered in tort—then ordinary principles of assessment may be able to produce a satisfactory result. In most situations (and the eventual result in the Hickey case bears this out) a breach of contract will have some effect upon the other contracting party. By concentrating on assessing the loss suffered by the innocent party and awarding aggravated damages accordingly, the plaintiff will be compensated and the defendant forced to disgorge his ill-gotten gains without having to extend what amount to quasi-criminal remedies into the law of contract.

1. [1964] AC 1129.   2. (HC) 14 July 1976, unrep.

Surrey County Council v Bredero Homes Ltd [1993] 3 All ER 705

Dillon L.J.:

This is an appeal by the plaintiffs, the Surrey County Council and the Mole Valley District Council, against a decision of Ferris J. given on 21 November 1991, after the hearing of issues directed by an earlier order. By his decision the learned judge awarded the plaintiffs nominal damages only against the defendant, Bredero Homes Ltd, for breaches of virtually identical positive covenants contained in transfers by the plaintiffs to the defendant of certain land in Surrey in 1981.

The facts are straightforward and not in dispute. I can take them from the judgment of the learned judge.

In 1980 the Surrey County Council and the Mole Valley District Council were respectively the registered proprietors with absolute title of two adjoining parcels of land lying to the west of The Ridgeway, Fetcham at Leatherhead in Surrey. The total areas of the two parcels was some 12.33 acres. The land had originally been acquired by the councils or their predecessors for road purposes but, by 1980, it was no longer required for these purposes and the two councils decided to act together in offering the entire site for development as a housing estate.

The defendant made an offer which included a purchase price of £1.52m. This led to a contract, dated 28 November 1980, between the two plaintiffs as vendors and the defendant as purchaser. This contract was completed by two transfers both dated 22 January 1981—one being by the Mole Valley District Council and the other by the Surrey County Council. The transfer made by the Mole Valley District Council contained a covenant by the defendant with that council: 'To commence the development of the land hereby transferred in accordance with the planning permission issued by Mole Valley District Council reference number MO/80/1214 and dated 11 December 1980 within six months from the date hereof and thereafter to diligently pursue the development of the land hereby transferred to its completion complying with the said planning permission . . .'

The transfer by the Surrey County Council was in substantially the same terms. The planning permission MO/80/1214 there referred to, 'the first planning permission', was granted on the application of the defendant. It provided for the development of the land, i.e. both parcels taken together, by the erection of seventy two detached bungalows and houses in six different designs according to a layout as shown in certain drawings.

The defendant started work on the development in accordance with the first planning permission. There were certain minor alterations by way of modification of that planning permission but these do not matter.

A bit later, however, the defendant applied for and obtained, on 29 June 1983, from the Mole Valley District Council as the planning authority, a planning permission which had the effect of raising the total number of dwellings to be built on the estate from seventy two to seventy seven, the main changes being a reduction in the number of four-bedroom houses and an increase in the number of three-bedroom houses—the size and arrangement of plots being amended, but the layout of roads and verges remaining unchanged. This planning permission, the 'later planning permission', was given the reference number MO/83/0368 and it related to 3.64 acres of the land.

The defendant then completed the development of those final 3.64 acres in accordance with the later planning permission and not, as had been covenanted, in accordance with the first planning permission.

The plaintiffs object to the development of the final 3.64 acres, in accordance with the later planning permission, not on planning grounds, but on the grounds that the later permission enabled the defendant to build seventy seven rather than seventy two houses and bungalows on the two adjoining parcels. There is no objection on planning grounds, not surprisingly, since it was the Mole Valley District Council which granted the later planning permission.

The objection is on the ground that it was a more profitable planning permission for the defendant than the first planning permission because more houses were built. As a legal basis it is said by the plaintiffs and conceded by the defendant that in building seventy seven houses in all under the later planning permission, rather than seventy two under the first planning permission, the defendant has acted in breach of the covenants in the transfers.

The plaintiffs therefore seek damages. They have never sought an interim injunction to restrain the defendant from developing the land otherwise than in accordance with the first planning permission. They never sought an injunction at the trial requiring the defendant to pull down the completed houses. They recognised that there was never any practical possibility of such an injunction being granted. There was a formal amendment of the relief sought at the trial to raise in form a claim for an injunction, but that was not pursued. The plaintiffs have merely sought damages which have been described as 'damages at common law', as opposed to 'damages in equity under Lord Cairns' Act' (the Chancery Amendment Act 1858). The plaintiffs accept that they have not suffered any damage at all of the nature of damage to adjoining property owned or occupied by them. What they claim as damages is essentially the profit made by the defendant by breaking the covenants and building seventy seven houses and not just seventy two—or, since the defendant wishes to be modest in its demands in putting forward a somewhat revolutionary development of the law of damages, such a part of the profit as would reflect the reasonable premium that the defendant should have paid them for contractual permission by way of relaxation of the covenants to build the seventy seven houses rather than seventy two.

Indeed, the plaintiffs say, and I have no reason to doubt, that their sole purpose in imposing the covenants at all—to commence and pursue the development to its completion in accordance with the first planning permission—was that the defendant would have to apply for and pay for a relaxation if it wanted to build anything more.

It is of course clear that had the contracts been worded otherwise there could have been provision for the payment by the defendant of an additional price of a specified amount or fixed by an appropriate formula for each extra house or bungalow, if they or their successors in title built more than seventy two houses or bungalows on the land within a specified period, but that is not the contract that was made.

In putting forward the claim for damages with which we are concerned, the plaintiffs rely very strongly on the decision of Brightman J., in *Wrotham Park Estate Co. v Parkside Homes Ltd* |1974| 2 All ER 321, |1974| 1 WLR 798, to which I shall have to come.

The starting point, however, in my judgment is that the remedy at common law for a breach of contract is an award of damages and damages at common law are intended to compensate the victim for his loss, not to transfer to the victim, if he has suffered no loss, the benefit which the wrongdoer has gained by his breach of contract. Thus it is stated in *Chitty on Contracts* (26th ed., 1989) vol 1, para. 1771: 'Damages for a breach of contract committed by the defendant are a compensation to the plaintiff for the damage, loss or injury he has suffered through that breach.'

Similarly in *British Westinghouse Electric and Manufacturing Co. Ltd v Underground Electric Rlys Co. of London Ltd* |1912| AC 673 at 689, |1911–13| All ER Rep 63 at 69 Viscount Haldane L.C. said: 'The fundamental basis is thus compensation for pecuniary loss naturally flowing from the breach . . . '

In *Johnson v Agnew* |1979| 1 All ER 883 at 896, |1980| AC 367 at 400 Lord Wilberforce said: 'The general principle for the assessment of damages is compensatory . . . ' Each of these three statements is accompanied by a statement to the effect that the innocent party is to be placed, so far as money can do so, in the same position as if the contract had been performed. That follows the wording of the statement of the rule of the common law by Parke B. in *Robinson v Harman* (1848) 1 Ex 850 at 855, |1843–60| All ER Rep 383 at 385. That rule has been referred to in argument in the present case as the 'conventional' rule.

|Counsel| for the plaintiffs has pointed out that the conventional rule is not of universal application in that there are cases in which the plaintiff is awarded not what is required to place him in the same situation as if the contract had been performed, but what is required to recoup to him the expenditure which he has incurred which has been wasted because the contract has not been performed: see, for instance,

Wallington v Townsend |1939| 2 All ER 225, |1939| Ch. 588 and *Anglia Television Ltd v Reed* |1971| 3 All ER 690, |1972| 1 QB 60.

The principle is still compensation for loss. The difference is merely that there are cases where the contract has so palpably not been performed at all that it would be unreal to assume that it had been performed and impossible to calculate damages on such an unreal assumption.

Every student is taught that the basis of assessing damages for breach of contract is the rule in *Hadley v Baxendale* (1854) 9 Ex 341, |1843–60| All ER Rep 461, which is wholly concerned with the losses which can be compensated by damages. Such damages may, in an appropriate case, cover profit which the injured plaintiff has lost, but they do not cover an award to a plaintiff who has himself suffered no loss, of the profit which the defendant has gained for himself by his breach of contract.

In the field of tort there are areas where the law is different and the plaintiff can recover in respect of the defendant's gain. Thus in the field of trespass it is well established that if one person has, without leave of another, been using that other's land for his own purposes he ought to pay for such use. Thus even if he had done no actual harm to the land he was charged for the user of the land. This was applied originally in wayleave cases where a person had without authority used his neighbour's land for passage: see, for instance, *Jegon v Vivian* (1871) LR 6 Ch App 742 and *Phillips v Homfray, Fothergill v Phillips* (1871) LR 6 Ch App 770.

The same principle was applied where the defendant had trespassed by tipping spoil on the plaintiff's land: see *Whitwham v Westminster Brymbo Coal and Coke Co.* |1896| 2 Ch. 538.

The same principle was applied to patent infringement by the House of Lords in *Watson Laidlaw & Co. Ltd v Pott Cassels and Williamson* (1914) 31 RPC 104. The infringer was ordered to pay by way of damages a royalty for every infringing article because the infringement damaged the plaintiff's property right, that is to say his patent monopoly. So in a case of detinue the defendant was ordered to pay a hire for chattels he had detained: see *Strand Electric and Engineering Co. Ltd v Brisford Entertainments Ltd* |1952| 1 All ER 796, |1952| 2 QB 246.

Those cases do not apply in the present case as the defendant has made no use of any property of either plaintiff.

The cases have been taken still further in some fields of tort, particularly concerned with intellectual property, where it is well established that the plaintiff can choose to have either damages or an account of profits made by the defendant by his wrongful acts: see, for instance, *Lever v Goodwin* (1887) 36 ChD 1 at 7, |1886–90| All ER Rep 427 at 429–30 per Cotton L.J. This is in line with the long established common law doctrine of waiving the tort.

The liability in the present case is solely in contract and not in tort.

I come then to the *Wrotham Park* case. In that case the predecessor in title of the plaintiffs had, in 1935, sold some land to a predecessor in title of the defendants, subject to a restrictive covenant restricting building to a particular layout. That covenant was duly registered under the Land Charges Act 1925. In 1971 the land was sold to the defendant, who had no actual knowledge of the restrictive covenant and proceeded to build fourteen houses on the land in breach of the covenant. In early 1972 the plaintiffs, as successors in title to the benefit of the covenant, issued their writ against the defendant claiming an injunction to restrain building in breach of the covenant, and demolition of anything built in breach. The plaintiffs made no application for an interim injunction. By the time the action came on for trial in July 1973, the fourteen houses had all been completed and sold to purchasers with the benefit of indemnity insurance policies. At the trial Brightman J. held that the plaintiffs were indeed entitled to the benefit of the covenant and the defendant was bound by it.

For obvious reasons however—that he could not shut his eyes to the fact that the houses existed and it would be an unpardonable waste of much needed houses to direct that they be pulled down—he refused to grant a mandatory injunction. He commented that no damage of a financial nature had been done to the plaintiffs by the breach of the covenant and proceeded to consider what damages, if any, he should award under the jurisdiction which had originated under Lord Cairns' Act to award damages in substitution for an injunction.

It was submitted to him that the damages should be nil or purely nominal because the value of the Wrotham Park estate was not diminished by one farthing in consequence of the breach of covenant.

But Brightman J. concluded that such a result would be of questionable fairness. He said ([1974] 2 All ER 321 at 339, [1974] 1 WLR 798 at 812): 'If, for social and economic reasons, the court does not see fit in the exercise of its discretion, to order demolition of the fourteen houses, is it just that the plaintiffs should receive no compensation and that the defendants should be left in undisturbed possession of the fruits of their wrongdoing?' He then referred to the wayleave cases and Whitwham v Westminster Brymbo Coal and Coke Co., and the other cases which I have mentioned where the same principle has been applied.

He concluded that the appropriate course was that the defendant should pay by way of damages the sum which the plaintiffs might hypothetically have been willing to pay—though actually they would never have been willing to relax the covenant to permit the defendant to do what it wanted to do on the land. He fixed that at a small percentage of the defendant's anticipated profit from building the fourteen houses on the land.

The difficulty about the decision in the Wrotham Park case is that in Johnson v Agnew Lord Wilberforce, after citing certain decisions on the scope and basis of Lord Cairns' Act, which were not cited to Brightman J., stated in the clearest terms that on the balance of those authorities, and on principle, he found in the Act no warrant for the court awarding damages differently from common law damages (see [1979] 1 All ER 883 at 896, [1980] AC 367 at 400).

[Counsel for the plaintiffs] submits that it follows from that analysis by Lord Wilberforce in Johnson v Agnew that the damages awarded by Brightman J. in the Wrotham Park case were indeed damages assessed on recognised common law principles which should, so he says, be applied in the present case.

I doubt, however, whether that does follow from Lord Wilberforce's analysis in Johnson v Agnew. As I read his judgment Brightman J. was not seeking to analyse the scope or basis of the court's jurisdiction under Lord Cairns' Act. He merely concluded that, as Parliament had expressly empowered the court to grant damages in lieu of an injunction, Parliament must have intended that in every case the court must be able to award such damages as would achieve a fair result between the parties and would not be limited to awarding nominal damage only. He sought to apply that conclusion.

That involves a conclusion by the judge that Lord Cairns' Act effected a substantive change in the law of damages and was not a merely procedural statute as Johnson v Agnew has held. It is unnecessary to refer further in this judgment to the Wrotham Park case since that was under Lord Cairns' Act and stands or falls by that; whereas, the present case is not, and makes no pretence of being, under that Act. I should however mention in passing that we were referred to a number of cases where the measure of damages chosen by Brightman J. in the Wrotham Park case was applied by other judges. For instance Bracewell v Appleby [1975] 1 All ER 993, [1975] Ch. 408, Carr-Saunders v Dick McNeil Associates Ltd [1986] 2 All ER 888, [1986] 1 WLR 922 and Griffiths v Kingsley-Stubbs [1986] CA Transcript 506 decided by this court on 3 June 1986, but unreported. All those were cases where the plaintiff's cause of action lay in tort, either trespass or nuisance, where the defendant had interfered with the plaintiff's property rights. The decisions and awards of damages are amply justified by the common law principles in tort of the wayleave cases and *Whitwham's* case, already mentioned.

Given that the established basis of an award of damages in contract is compensation for the plaintiff's loss, as indicated above, I have difficulty in seeing how [counsel's] suggested common law principle of awarding the plaintiff, who has suffered no loss, the gain which the defendant has made by the breach of contract, is intended to go. Is it to apply, for instance, to shipping contracts or contracts of employment or contracts for building works?

[Counsel] suggested, in his skeleton argument, that the conventional measure fails to do justice and a different measure should be applied where the following conditions are satisfied: (a) the breach is deliberate, in the sense that the defendant is deliberately doing an act which he knows or should know is plainly or arguably in breach of contract; (b) the defendant, as a result of the breach, has profited by making a gain or reducing a loss; (c) at the date of the breach it is clear or probable that damages under the conventional measure will either be nominal or much smaller than the profit to the defendant from the breach; and (d) if the profit results from the avoidance of expenditure, the expenditure would not have been economically wasteful or grossly disproportionate to the benefit which would have resulted from it.

He suggested in that paragraph in the skeleton argument that the underlying principle might be that the conventional measure of damages might be overridden 'in certain circumstances' by the rule that no-one should benefit from his deliberate wrongdoing. In the course of his submissions Sir William limited his formulation and while retaining conditions (a), (b) and (c), substituted for condition (d) the following:

> Damages for loss of bargaining power can be awarded if—but only if—the party in breach could have been restrained by injunction from committing the breach of contract or compelled by specific performance to perform the contract. Where no such possibility existed, there was no bargaining power in reality and no right to damages for loss of it. Hence, damages for loss of bargaining power cannot be awarded where there is (for example) a contract for the sale of goods or (generally) a contract of employment.

I find difficulty with that because in theory every time there is a breach of contract the injured party is deprived of his 'bargaining power' to negotiate for a financial consideration a variation of the contract which would enable the party who wants to depart from its terms to do what he wants to do. In addition it has been held in *Walford v Miles* [1992] 1 All ER 453, [1992] 2 AC 128 that an agreement to negotiate is not an animal known to the law and a duty to negotiate in good faith is unworkable in practice—and so I find it difficult to see why loss of bargaining or negotiating power should become an established factor in the assessment of damages for breach of contract.

Beyond that, since we are looking for the measure of damages at common law for breach of contract, apart from Lord Cairns' Act, I do not see why that should vary depending on whether the party in breach could or could not have been restrained by injunction from committing the breach or compelled by specific performance to perform the contract. Injunctions and specific performance were not remedies in the common law courts and were granted by the Court of Chancery, which, before Lord Cairns' Act, had no power to award damages, just because the common law remedy of damages was not an adequate remedy.

We were referred, in the course of |counsel's| argument, to a number of other cases and, in particular, to passages in the judgment of Megarry V.C. in *Tito v Waddell* (No. 2) |1977| 3 All ER 129, |1977| Ch. 106 and to the decision of this court in *Stoke-on-Trent City Council v W & J Wass Ltd* |1988| 3 All ER 394, |1988| 1 WLR 1406. In the latter case this court upheld the general principle that in tort a plaintiff recovered damages equivalent to the loss he had suffered and held also that the 'user' principle in the wayleave cases and *Whitwham v Westminster Brymbo Coal and Coke Co.* should not be extended to cover infringement of a market right of the plaintiff council by the holding by the defendant of an unauthorised market where the plaintiff could not show he had suffered any actual loss by the infringement. What was sought in that case was damages calculated by reference to a notional licence fee that the plaintiff council might have charged for permitting the defendant's infringement but that was refused. I need not refer to the cases further.

As I see it, therefore, there never was in the present case, even before the writ was issued, any possibility of the court granting an injunction to restrain the defendant from implementing the later planning permission. The plaintiff's only possible claim from the outset was for damages only, damages are common law.

The plaintiffs have suffered no damage. Therefore on basic principles, as damages are awarded to compensate loss, the damages must be merely nominal.

For these reasons, which substantially accord with those of Ferry J., I would dismiss the appeal.

(Steyn and Rose L.JJ. concurred.)

SECTION FOUR—REMOTENESS OF DAMAGE

Hadley v Baxendale (1854) 9 Ex 341

The plaintiffs were millers in the city of Gloucester. The crank shaft of the steam engine that operated the mill broke and the plaintiffs engaged the defendants to transport the broken shaft to Greenwich to have a replacement made. However, the defendants negligently failed to deliver the shaft expeditiously and the mill was stopped for five days more than would have been the case if delivery had taken place in accordance with the contract.

One crucial issue of fact that was resolved at the trial was whether the plaintiffs had told the defendants that the mill had ceased to function because of the broken crank shaft. The headnote states that before Crampton J. the plaintiffs proved that their employee had told the defendants that the mill was stopped. The jury awarded damages of £50. The defendants appealed and while a new trial was ordered Alderson B. indicated the principles that should govern remoteness of damages in contract.

Alderson B.:

. . .

Now we think the proper rule in such a case as the present is this: Where two parties have made a contract which one of them has broken, the damages which the other party ought to receive in respect of such breach of contract should be such as may fairly and reasonably be considered either arising naturally, i.e. according to the usual course of things, from such breach of contract itself, or such as may reasonably be supposed to have been in the contemplation of both parties, at the time they made the contract, as the probable result of the breach of it. Now, if the special circumstances under which the contract was actually made were communicated by the plaintiffs to the defendants, and thus known to both parties, the damages resulting from the breach of such a contract, which they would reasonably contemplate, would be the amount of injury which would ordinarily follow from a breach of contract under these special circumstances so known and communicated. But, on the other hand, if these special circumstances were wholly unknown to the party breaking the contract, he, at the most, could only be supposed to have had in his contemplation the amount of injury which would arise generally, and in the great multitude of cases not affected by any special circumstances, from such a breach of contract. For, had the special circumstances been known, the parties might have specially provided for the breach of contract by special terms as to the damages in that case; and of this advantage it would be very unjust to deprive them. Now the above principles are those by which we think the jury ought to be guided in estimating the damages arising out of any breach of contract. It is said, that other cases such as breaches of contract in the non-payment of money, or in the not making a good title to land, are to be treated as exceptions from this, and as governed by a conventional rule. But as, in such cases, both parties must be supposed to be cognisant of that well known rule, these cases may, we think, be more properly classed under the rule above enunciated as to cases under known special circumstances, because there both parties may reasonably be presumed to contemplate the estimation of the amount of damages according to the conventional rule. Now, in the present case, if we are to apply the principles above laid down, we find that the only circumstances here communicated by the plaintiffs to the defendants at the time the contract was made, were, that the article to be carried was the broken shaft of a mill, and that the plaintiffs were the millers of that mill. But how do these circumstances shew reasonably that the profits of the mill must be stopped by an unreasonable delay in the delivery of the broken shaft by the carrier to the third person? Suppose the plaintiffs had another shaft in their possession put up or putting up at the time, and that they only wished to send back the broken shaft to the engineer who made it; it is clear that this would be quite consistent with the above circumstances, and yet the unreasonable delay in the delivery would have no effect upon the intermediate profits of the mill. Or, again, suppose that, at the time of the delivery to the carrier, the machinery of the mill had been in other respects defective, then, also, the same results would follow. Here it is true that the shaft was actually sent back to serve as a model for a new one, and that the want of a new one was the only cause of the stoppage of the mill, and that the loss of profits really arose from not sending down the new shaft in proper time, and that this arose from the delay in delivering the broken one to serve as a model. But it is obvious that, in the great multitude of cases of millers sending off broken shafts to third persons by a carrier under ordinary circumstances, such consequences would not, in all probability, have occurred; and these special circumstances were here never communicated by the plaintiffs to the defendants. It follows, therefore, that the loss of profits here cannot reasonably be considered such a consequence of the breach of contract as could have been fairly and reasonably contemplated by both the parties when they made this contract. For such loss would neither have flowed naturally from the breach of this contract in the great multitude of such cases occurring under ordinary circumstances, nor were the special circumstances, which, perhaps, would have made it a reasonable and natural consequence of such breach of contract, communicated to or known by the defendants. The judge ought, therefore, to have told the jury, that, upon the facts then before them, they ought not to take the loss of profits into consideration at all in estimating the damages. There must therefore be a new trial in this case.

Note

On the factual issue of whether the stoppage of the mill had been communicated see *Danzig* (1975) 4 JLS 249 and the judgment of the Court of Appeal in *Victoria Laundry (Windsor) Ltd v Newman Industries Ltd* |1949| 2 KB 528 (see p. 960 below).

The application of Hadley v Baxendale

A. THE FIRST LIMB OF THE REMOTENESS TEST

Wilson *v* Dunville (1879) 6 LR (Ir.) 210

Palles C.B.:

This is an action for damages for breach of a contract for the sale of distillery grains. We held on a former argument,[1] that under the circumstances of the sale, the contract implied was (not that the grains were fit for cattle-feeding, but) that the thing sold reasonably answered the description of grains. The plaintiff bought the substance in question for the purpose, known to the defendants, of applying it to a use which was proved to be *an* ordinary (if it were not its *only* ordinary) use, cattle-feeding. This substance, but not to the knowledge of the defendants, contained an admixture of fine particles of lead to such an extent that (according to the finding of the jury, which is not in this respect quarrelled with), it did not reasonably answer the description of grains. It was used in feeding the plaintiff's cattle, several of which were poisoned by the lead and died. The question is, was the value of the cattle an element which the jury were entitled to take into consideration in assessing damages?

Now, the breach of contract was, that the grains contained an admixture of lead to an extent which prevented them answering the description. The usual course was, that this substance which was sold as grains should be used for feeding cattle; it was so used, and the natural result of that use was that the cattle were poisoned. Under such circumstances I confess that, from the moment I heard the case opened, I thought it essentially unarguable. The circumstances demonstrated that the loss of the cattle might fairly and reasonably be considered as arising, according to the usual course of things, from the breach of contract itself: *Hadley v Baxendale.*[2]

The argument of |counsel|, as I understood it, was this: The breach alleged was, that the thing sold did not reasonably answer the description of grains. That might be true, and still the grains might not contain an admixture of lead, or be otherwise poisonous; therefore, the death of the cattle could not have been in the contemplation of the parties at the time of the contract as the probable result of the breach of it.

It is admitted that, if the contract were particular instead of general, if it had been that the substance did not contain lead or poisonous matter the result would have been different; but it is argued that, in such a case any breach would have involved the existence of poison, and that injury by poison should, therefore, be taken to have been within the contemplation of the parties. This reasoning, it is suggested, was the *ratio decidendi* of *Smith v Green.*[3] It might be sufficient in answer to this argument to say, that in the present case there is evidence that those acting for the defendants knew there were some unusual substances in the thing sold; and that there might be risk in its use for cattle-feeding unless caution were used.

But, for myself, I desire to base my judgment upon broader grounds. I think that the mode in which the case was left to the jury was right, irrespective of the evidence that the defendants contemplated risk. In my opinion the defendants' argument applies to the breach of contract considerations applicable only to the consequences of the breach, not to the breach itself. For the purpose of rendering a defendant responsible for damages which in the ordinary course of things flow from a particular breach, it is unnecessary that the actual breach of contract which ensued should have been within the contemplation of the parties. For anything which amounts to a breach of contract, whether foreseen or unforeseen, the party who breaks the contract is responsible. In the present case the delivery of poison as food did not cease to be the defendants' act because of any want of knowledge in them of the nature of the thing delivered. Nor was the plaintiff by reason of the absence of knowledge in them the less entitled to act upon their contract that the thing sold was grains, or the less damnified by its being in fact poison. It is because the consequences of the defendants' acts are not themselves necessarily the acts of the defendants, that the liability for consequences is limited. If those consequences result solely from the act in question, and an usual state of things, they are the ordinary and usual consequences of that act, and the defendants are liable.

If the consequences flow not from the defendants' act alone, or from the defendants' act operating upon an usual state of things, but from that act and an exceptional state of circumstances, then a question of much difficulty (and one as to which the cases are not wholly consistent) would arise as to the effect on the defendants' liability of their knowledge, at the time of the contract, of such exceptional circumstances. Upon the discussion of this latter question, as to which alone many of the cases cited were material, I do not propose to enter. It has no application here. The loss of the cattle did not arise from exceptional circumstances, but was a natural result of the ordinary use of the substance sold to the plaintiff as grains. The motion to reduce the damages must be refused with costs.

[1.] *Wilson v Dunville* 4 LR (Ir) 249.   [2.] 9 Ex 341.   [3.] 1 CP Div 92.

(Fitzgerald and Dowse BB. concurred.)

Stock *v* Urey [1951] NI 71

The plaintiff purchased a motor car from the defendant for £35 and later sold it to one Eakin for £58 10s. While the car was in the possession of Eakin it was seized by the customs authorities as having been illegally imported into Northern Ireland. Eakin paid to the customs authorities the sum of £68 3s 2d, the amount due in respect of duty and tax, in order to regain possession of the car. Eakin sued the plaintiff for the sum of £68 3s 2d as damages for breach of the implied warranty for quiet possession and of the implied condition, treated as a warranty, that the seller had the right to sell the car. Eakin was awarded the full amount claimed and costs, and the plaintiff paid £86 13s 10d on foot of the decree. The plaintiff then sued the defendant to recover that sum from the defendants as damages for the breach of the implied warranty and condition on the sale of the car to the plaintiff. The defendant contended that since Eakin might have abandoned the car and then sued for the purchase price which he had paid for it, the sum of £68 3s 2d, being in excess of that price, could not be regarded as the reasonable measure of the damage 'directly and naturally resulting' from the breaches alleged. The acting County Court Judge gave a decree for the full amount claimed and the defendant now appealed.

Curran J.:

The claim by Eakin against Stock was based upon breach of warranty and breach of condition. The claim by Stock against Urey is on the same basis. The legal basis for the claim is to be found in ss 12 and 53 of the Sale of Goods Act 1893. S. 12(1) provides for an implied *condition* on the part of the seller that he has a right to sell the goods. Since Eakin retained the motor car and sued for damages it would appear that the implied condition has been treated as a warranty. Accordingly, the claim is, in substance, for damages for breach of warranty under two heads, (1) breach of condition (treated as a warranty) that the seller had a right to sell, and (2) breach of warranty under s. 12 (2) of the Sale of Goods Act 1893, that the buyer shall have and enjoy quiet possession of the goods. Mr Agnew contends that Eakin need not have paid the £68 3s 2d to the customs authorities. He might have let the car go and have sued Stock for the price he paid him, namely, £58 10s 0d. S. 53(2) provides that the measure of damages for breach of warranty is the estimated loss directly and naturally resulting, in the ordinary course of events, from the breach of warranty.

As I see it, the purchaser was warranted quiet enjoyment—in order to secure that quiet enjoyment he had to pay the duty to the customs authorities. That payment, in my view, directly and naturally resulted from the breach of warranty.

Mr Agnew has contended that the payment to the customs authorities was in excess of the actual value of the car and was not 'reasonable and natural'. Undoubtedly, the seizure of the car was an unusual occurrence and there is substance in the contention that it was not reasonably foreseeable by the defendant—assuming that he had no knowledge of the illegal importation of the car from Eire. The substance of the breach of warranty is, however, that the car had been illegally imported and was liable to seizure. Accordingly, s. 53(2), in my opinion, must be read in this way, 'the estimated loss directly and naturally resulting in the ordinary course of events'—from a breach of warranty for quiet enjoyment, such breach being based upon a liability to seizure for illegal importation. What 'directly and naturally results in the ordinary course of events' from a breach of warranty must depend, in my view, on the nature of the grounds upon which the warranty for quiet enjoyment is impeached—in this case liability to seizure for illegal importation. From the breach of warranty, based upon this liability to seizure, the payment made to prevent such seizure and to protect the purchaser's quiet enjoyment, in my opinion, was reasonable and natural, and directly and naturally resulted, in the ordinary course of events, from the breach of warranty. Whether the amount paid was greater or less than the actual value of the car cannot, in my view affect the matter. I accordingly affirm the decree.

B. THE SECOND LIMB OF THE REMOTENESS TEST

Waller *v* Midland Great Western Rly (1879) 4 LR (Ir.) 376

The plaintiff wished to send some horses to an auction sale. The railway company failed to provide horse-boxes, thereby requiring the plaintiff to send the horses by road. The horses arrived at the sale in a distressed state and were sold for less than they would have fetched if they had made the journey without mishap. Damages were awarded to the plaintiff: the railway company appealed.

Morris C.J.:

The damages awarded by the jury on the reference to the Master of the Queen's Bench Division were the entire amount claimed by the plaintiff, *viz.* £200, and were awarded as damages for the lameness and injury of the horses, as appears by the Master's notes. The defendants have contended that the damages should be nominal, or in the alternative that the inquiry had should be set aside and a new inquiry directed.

Adopting as a principle the rule as to damages laid down in *Hadley v Baxendale*,[1] *viz.* that the damages should be such as arose, according to the usual course of things, from the breach of contract, or such as reasonably might be supposed to have been in the contemplation of the parties at the time they made the contract, how does it apply to this case?

The plaintiff, I assume, adopted a reasonable alternative in sending his horses by road, when the defendants could not supply horse-boxes, nor undertake to do so in time, as he wanted his horses to reach Sewell's on the Wednesday night, in order to show them, as is usual, on the day prior to the auction. His manager, Patrick Johnston, who was in charge of the horses, and who made the decision to go to Dublin by road, states in his evidence that he did not expect lameness or injury to the horses there-from, and that he did not expect they would be unfit for the journey, and attributes their injury to their being in soft condition, as it turned out they were; that one of the horses became lame, and the rest were injured, by the journey; and that they were unfit to make the journey—why? because they had been from 6 April, the end of the hunting season, or eighteen days, in soft condition as to feeding, *viz.* fed on oats, bran, linseed cake and seed cake. Now, applying any reasonable principle, why should the defendants be amerced in damages to the amount of the loss accruing to the plaintiff by reason of the mistaken conclusion of the plaintiff's manager, that the horses could make the journey by road to Dublin without injury? Would that be usual or natural damage; or would it be in the contemplation of the parties at the time they made the contract? The plaintiff appears to me to be in a dilemma: either his horses were fit to make the journey or they were not. If they were fit, nothing to the extent of these con-sequences of lameness and injuries could have occurred to them; if these consequences did occur, why then they must have been in an unfit and exceptional condition, and susceptible to injury to an extraordinary degree—when for such exceptional suscep-tibility the defendants would not be liable in damages.

I am of opinion that the damages, the natural or direct result of the breach of con-tract, or which the parties could have ever contemplated at the time of the contract, or that any reasonable rule on the subject could support, would be the deterioration that horses that were fit to make the journey would experience in doing so. That might be, and I should say would be, more than nominal damages, and would be analogous to the damages for inconvenience to which the plaintiff was held entitled in *Hobbs v The London & South Western Rly Co.*[2]

The result is that we reverse the judgment of the Queen's Bench Division, which decides that the plaintiff should retain his verdict for £200, and we direct that the inquiry had should be set aside, and a new inquiry had; and as neither party has succeeded to the full extent contended for, the plaintiff is seeking to retain his full verdict, and the defendants in seeking to enter the verdict for nominal damages only, let each party abide his own costs of this appeal and of the motion in the Queen's Bench Division.

Fitzgibbon L.J.:

The injuries resulting from breaches of contract may be of infinite variety, and con-nected in infinite degrees and closeness or remoteness with the breaches from which they spring.

It is impossible to hold those who break contracts answerable for all consequences, however remote, unexpected or serious; and hence, in each case it must be decided whether the damage which has arisen is so closely connected with the breach as to make it just and reasonable to hold the person in default liable to make compensation for it. This question of remoteness of damage should be decided by the court, and not by the jury; and, though the general principle of decision may be easily stated, its application must depend upon the special circumstances of the particular case. Where the principle has been applied it is for the jury to measure the amount. The general principle is, that the person breaking his contract must answer for the necessary, natural, or probable consequences of his default, and for those which ought to have been within the reasonable contemplation of both parties when making their contract, as likely to arise from its breach. These are not separate definitions: it is presumed that every necessary natural and probable result was contemplated by the parties. But if the injured party wishes to go beyond presumption, he may prove that any specified result was, in fact, contemplated as likely to arise from a breach of the particular contract.

To recover compensation, however, for extraordinary damage, he must show that the defendant ought to have contemplated, or did in fact contemplate it, as likely to arise, and undertook, expressly or by implication, in case of breach, to answer for it.

The Court of Queen's Bench held that the injury sustained in this case was a natural and probable consequence of the breach, and also was, or ought to have been, contemplated by the parties as likely to arise.

I am quite unable to agree with this decision; it seems to me to rest on a confusion of the enforced journey which the horses took, and which was a probable or perhaps a necessary consequence of the failure to send them by train, with the lameness and other serious injury, and the depreciation at a particular sale, which followed from that journey, and for which it is conceded that the jury have compensated the plaintiff.

That these serious injuries were not in fact contemplated is proved by the plaintiff's steward, who was in charge of the horses, and who swore that he did not expect that they would be injured, and, therefore, we have only to consider whether damage to the amount of £200 was the natural necessary or probable consequence of the journey which was undertaken.

Common experience and common sense are opposed to the conclusion that such an amount of injury is the natural or probable consequence of sending ordinary horses such a distance; and if, with a view to an immediate sale, or from the condition of the animals, or from any other circumstances, it was impossible to bring these horses to Dublin by road on the evening in question, without such serious injury, the plaintiff was bound either to have adopted some other mode of transit, or to have taken more time or greater precautions; and not having done so, he cannot look to the defendants to compensate him for the unexpected and exceptional loss which he sustained. I can see no escape from the dilemma pointed out by my Lord Chief Justice, that if lameness, and injury, and depreciation to the extent of £200, was the natural or probable consequence of taking these fifteen horses, in their then condition, 26 miles by road, it was not reasonable so to take them. But if the injury sustained was not the natural or probable consequence of the journey, it was not within the scope of the defendants' liability.

I agree with [counsel] that the question resolves itself into this: 'Was it reasonable, under the circumstances, to take the horses to Dublin by road?' The answer is, 'It was not, if such serious injury was the natural or probable result of so taking them.' If we were to allow the plaintiff to recover damages to the average amount of £13 6s 8d, or 10s per mile for each horse, as compensation for having to send his horses a journey of 26 miles, we should either compel the defendants to pay for an unexpected, unnecessary, and improbable amount of injury, or we should disregard the limitation well expressed in Le Blanche v London & North Western Rly Co.,[3] and hold the plaintiff entitled to fulfil the broken contract for himself unreasonably, extravagantly, and oppressively.

The assessment made cannot stand, but it does not follow by any means that the measure of damages is nominal. Nor do I think they are to be measured by hypothetical expenses or damages consequential on other possible courses of action which the plaintiff did not adopt, and was, in my judgment, not bound to adopt. Where a defendant, by his breach of contract, forces a plaintiff to select some one course of several, I think he must answer for the natural and probable consequences of the course chosen, if the choice be a reasonable one, though some other might possibly have turned out more fortunately; and, just as Mr and Mrs Hobbs were held entitled to recover compensation for their fatigue and inconvenience, but not for the exceptionally injurious consequences of their walk, I think the plaintiff here is entitled to recover compensation for the time and labour of both men and horses expended upon the road, with reasonable compensation for the fatigue, inconvenience, and depreciation which would naturally arise from such a journey when undertaken by horses in ordinary condition; but not for lameness or extraordinary injury caused by the exceptional state of the horses, nor for depreciation, measured not by any alteration in their permanent intrinsic value, but by offering them for sale while footsore and temporarily out of condition. A jury alone can fix the amount to be assessed on this principle; and if the railway company, who very unjustifiably broke their contract, and undoubtedly thereby caused very serious loss to the plaintiff, will not now agree to name a reasonable sum, which they may measure more liberally on escaping further litigation, we can only reverse the decision of the Queen's Bench Division, and direct a new inquiry.

[1] 1 CP Div. 286.   [2] 9 Ex 341.   [3] LR 10 QB 111.

C. REMOTENESS OF DAMAGE—TERMINOLOGY

Victoria Laundry (Windsor) Ltd v Newman Industries Ltd [1949] 2 KB 528

The plaintiffs, a limited company, carrying on a business as launderers and dyers at Windsor, were in January 1946, minded to expand their business, and to that end required a boiler of much greater capacity than the one they then possessed, which was of a capacity of 1,500–1,600 lbs evaporation per hour. Seeing an advertisement by the defendants on 17 January 1946, of two 'vertical Cochran boilers of 8,000 lb per hour capacity heavy steaming', the plaintiffs negotiated for the purchase of one of them, and by 26 April had concluded a contract for its purchase at a price of £2,150, loaded free on transport at Harpenden, where it was installed in the premises of the defendants. The defendants knew that the plaintiffs were launderers and dyers, and wanted the boiler for use in their business. Also, during the negotiations the plaintiffs by letter expressed their intention to 'put it into use in the shortest possible space of time.' Arrangements were made by the plaintiffs with the defendants to take delivery at Harpenden on 5 June, and the plaintiffs on that date sent a lorry to Harpenden to take delivery, but it was then ascertained that four days earlier the third parties, who had been employed by the defendants to dismantle the boiler, had allowed it to fall on its side and sustain damage. The plaintiffs refused to take delivery unless the damage was made good and ultimately the defendants agreed to arrange for the necessary repairs. The plaintiffs did not receive delivery of the boiler until 8 November 1946, and in the present action they claimed damages for breach of contract and sought to include in the damages loss of business profits during the period from 5 June to 8 November 1946.

Streatfeild J. gave judgment for the plaintiffs against the defendants for £110 damages under certain minor heads, but held that they were not entitled to include in their measure of damages loss of business profits during the period of delay. The boiler, he said, was not a whole plant capable of being used by itself as a profit-making machine. Only the entire plant, including the vats, was a profit-making machine. The defendants were supplying the plaintiffs with only a part, the function of which they did not know, of that plant. The case fell, in his opinion, within the second rule in Hadley v Baxendale[1] and the defendants were not liable for the loss of profits because the special object for which the plaintiffs were acquiring the boiler had not been drawn to the defendants' attention.

Asquith L.J.:

. . .

The ground of the learned judge's decision, which we consider more fully later, may be summarised as follows: He took the view that the loss of profit claimed was due to special circumstances and therefore recoverable, if at all, only under the second rule in Hadley v Baxendale and not recoverable in this case because such special circumstances were not at the time of the contract communicated to the defendants. He also attached much significance to the fact that the object supplied was not a self-sufficient profit-making article, but part of a larger profit-making whole, and cited in this connexion the cases of Portman v Middleton[2] and British Columbia Sawmills v Nettleship.[3] Before commenting on the learned judge's reasoning, we must refer to some of the authorities.

The authorities on recovery of loss of profits as a head of damage are not easy to reconcile. At one end of the scale stand cases where there has been non-delivery or delayed delivery of what is on the face of it obviously a profit-earning chattel: for instance, a merchant or passenger ship: see Fletcher v Tayleur,[4] In re Trent and Humber Co., ex parte Cambrian Steam Packet Co.;[5] or some essential part of such a ship; for instance, a propeller in Wilson v General Ironscrew Co.,[6] or engines, Saint Line v Richardson.[7] In such cases loss of profit has rarely been refused. A second and intermediate class of case in which loss of profit has often been awarded is where ordinary mercantile goods have been sold to a merchant with knowledge by the vendor that the purchaser wanted them for resale; at all events, where there was no market in which the purchaser could buy similar goods against the contract on the seller's default, see, for instance, Borries v Hutchinson.[8] At the other end of the scale are cases where the defendant is not a vendor of the goods, but a carrier, see, for instance, Hadley v Baxendale and Gee v Lancashire and Yorkshire Rly.[9] In such cases the courts have been slow to allow loss of profit as an item of damage. This was not, it would seem, because a different principle applies in such cases, but because the application of the same principle leads to different results. A carrier commonly knows less than a seller about the purposes for which the buyer or consignee needs the goods, or about other 'special circumstances' which may cause exceptional loss if due delivery is withheld.

Three of the authorities call for more detailed examination. First comes Hadley v Baxendale itself. Familiar though it is, we should first recall the memorable sentence in which the main principles laid down in this case are enshrined:

> Where two parties have made a contract which one of them has broken, the damages which the other party ought to receive in respect of such breach of contract should be such as may fairly and reasonably be considered as either arising naturally, i.e. according to the usual course of things, from such breach of contract itself, or such as may reasonably be supposed to have been in the contemplation of both parties, at the time they made the contract, as the probable result of the breach of it.

The limb of this sentence prefaced by 'either' embodies the so-called 'first' rule; that prefaced by 'or' the 'second'. In considering the meaning and application of these

rules, it is essential to bear clearly in mind the facts on which Hadley v Baxendale proceeded. The head-note is definitely misleading in so far as it says that the defendant's
clerk, who attended at the office, was told that the mill was stopped and that the shaft
must be delivered immediately. The same allegation figures in the statement of facts
which are said on p. 344 to have 'appeared' at the trial before Crompton J. If the Court
of Exchequer had accepted these facts as established, the court must, one would
suppose, have decided the case the other way round; must, that is, have held the
damage claimed was recoverable under the second rule. But it is reasonably plain
from Alderson B.'s judgment that the court rejected this evidence, for on p. 355 he
says: 'We find that the only circumstances here communicated by the plaintiffs to the
defendants at the time when the contract was made were that the article to be carried
was the broken shaft of a mill and that the plaintiffs were the millers of that mill,' and
it is on this basis of fact that he proceeds to ask, 'How do these circumstances show
reasonably that the profits of the mill must be stopped by an unreasonable delay in
the delivery of the broken shaft by the carrier to the third person?'

British Columbia Sawmills v Nettleship annexes to the principle laid down in Hadley v
Baxendale a rider to the effect that where knowledge of special circumstances is relied
on as enhancing the damage recoverable that knowledge must have been brought
home to the defendant at the time of the contract and in such circumstances that the
defendant impliedly undertook to bear any special loss referable to a breach in those
special circumstances. The knowledge which was lacking in that case on the part of the
defendant was knowledge that the particular box of machinery negligently lost by the
defendants was one without which the rest of the machinery could not be put together
and would therefore be useless.

Cory v Thames Ironworks Co.[10]—a case strongly relied on by the plaintiffs—presented
the peculiarity that the parties contemplated respectively different profit-making uses
of the chattel sold by the defendant to the plaintiff. It was the hull of a boom derrick,
and was delivered late. The plaintiffs were coal merchants, and the obvious use, and
that to which the defendants believed it was to be put, was that of a coal store. The
plaintiffs, on the other hand, the buyers, in fact intended to use it for transhipping
coals from colliers to barges, a quite unprecedented use for a chattel of this kind, one
quite unsuspected by the sellers and one calculated to yield much higher profits. The
case accordingly decides, *inter alia*, what is the measure of damage recoverable when
the parties are not *ad idem* in their contemplation of the use for which the article is
needed. It was decided that in such a case no loss was recoverable beyond what would
have resulted if the intended use had been that reasonably within the contemplation
of the defendants, which in that case was the 'obvious' use. This special complicating
factor, the divergence between the knowledge and contemplation of the parties
respectively, has somewhat obscured that general importance of the decision, which is
in effect that the facts of the case brought it within the first rule of Hadley v Baxendale
and enabled the plaintiff to recover loss of such profits as would have arisen from the
normal and obvious use of the article. The 'natural consequence', said Blackburn J., of
not delivering the derrick was that £420 representing those normal profits was lost.
Cockburn C.J., interposing during the argument, made the significant observation: 'No
doubt in order to recover damage arising from a special purpose the buyer must have
communicated the special purpose to the seller; but there is one thing which must
always be in the knowledge of both parties, which is that the thing is bought for the
purpose of being in some way or other profitably applied.' This observation is apposite
to the present case. These three cases have on many occasions been approved by the
House of Lords without any material qualification.

What propositions applicable to the present case emerge from the authorities as a whole, including those analysed above? We think they include the following:

(1) It is well settled that the governing purpose of damages is to put the party whose rights have been violated in the same position, so far as money can do so, as if his rights had been observed: (*Sally Wertheim v Chicoutimi Pulp Co.*[11]). This purpose, if relentlessly pursued, would provide him with a complete indemnity for all loss *de facto* resulting from a particular breach, however improbable, however unpredictable. This, in contract at least, is recognised as too harsh a rule. Hence,

(2) In cases of breach of contract the aggrieved party is only entitled to recover such part of the loss actually resulting as was at the time of the contract reasonably foreseeable as liable to result from the breach.

(3) What was at that time reasonably so foreseeable depends on the knowledge then possessed by the parties or, at all events, by the party who later commits the breach.

(4) For this purpose, knowledge 'possessed' is of two kinds; one imputed, the other actual. Everyone, as a reasonable person, is taken to know the 'ordinary course of things' and consequently what loss is liable to result from a breach of contract in that ordinary course. This is the subject matter of the 'first rule' in *Hadley v Baxendale*. But to this knowledge, which a contract breaker is assumed to possess whether he actually possesses it or not, there may have to be added in a particular case knowledge which he actually possesses, of special circumstances outside the 'ordinary course of things', of such a kind that a breach in those special circumstances would be liable to cause more loss. Such a case attracts the operation of the 'second rule' so as to make additional loss also recoverable.

(5) In order to make the contract breaker liable under either rule it is not necessary that he should actually have asked himself what loss is liable to result from a breach. As has often been pointed out, parties at the time of contracting contemplate not the breach of the contract, but its performance. It suffices that, if he had considered the question, he would as a reasonable man have concluded that the loss in question was liable to result (see certain observations of Lord du Parcq in the recent case of *A/B Karlshamns Oljefabriker v Monarch Steamship Co. Ltd*[12]).

(6) Nor, finally, to make a particular loss recoverable, need it be proved that upon a given state of knowledge the defendant could, as a reasonable man, foresee that a breach must necessarily result in that loss. It is enough if he could foresee it was likely so to result. It is indeed enough, to borrow from the language of Lord du Parcq in the same case, at 158, if the loss (or some factor without which it would not have occurred) is a 'serious possibility' or a 'real danger'. For short, we have used the word 'liable' to result. Possibly the colloquialism 'on the cards' indicates the shade of meaning with some approach to accuracy.

If these, indeed, are the principles applicable, what is the effect of their application to the facts of this case? We have, at the beginning of this judgment, summarised the main relevant facts. The defendants were an engineering company supplying a boiler to a laundry. We reject the submission for the defendants that an engineering company knows no more than the plain man about boilers or the purposes to which they are commonly put by different classes of purchasers, including laundries. The defendant company were not, it is true, manufacturers of this boiler or dealers in boilers, but they gave a highly technical and comprehensive description of this boiler to the plaintiffs by letter of 19 January 1946, and offered both to dismantle the boiler at Harpenden and to re-erect it on the plaintiffs' premises. Of the uses or purposes to which boilers are put, they would clearly know more than the uninstructed layman.

Again, they knew they were supplying the boiler to a company carrying on the business of laundrymen and dyers, for use in that business. The obvious use of a boiler, in such a business, is surely to boil water for the purpose of washing or dyeing. A laundry might conceivably buy a boiler for some other purpose; for instance, to work radiators or warm bath water for the comfort of its employees or directors, or to use for research, or to exhibit in a museum. All these purposes are possible, but the first is the obvious purpose which, in the case of a laundry, leaps to the average eye. If the purpose then be to wash or dye, why does the company want to wash or dye, unless for purposes of business advantage, in which term we, for the purposes of the rest of this judgment, include maintenance or increase of profit, or reduction of loss? (We shall speak henceforward not of loss of profit, but of 'loss of business'.) No commercial concern commonly purchases for the purposes of its business a very large and expensive structure like this—a boiler 19 feet high and costing over £2,000—with any other motive, and no supplier, let alone an engineering company, which has promised delivery of such an article by a particular date, with knowledge that it was to be put into use immediately on delivery, can reasonably contend that it could not foresee that loss of business (in the sense indicated above) would be liable to result to the purchaser from a long delay in the delivery thereof. The suggestion that, for all the supplier knew, the boiler might have been needed simply as a 'stand-by', to be used in a possibly distant future, is gratuitous and was plainly negatived by the terms of the letter of 26 April 1946.

Since we are differing from a carefully reasoned judgment, we think it due to the learned judge to indicate the grounds of our dissent. In that judgment, after stressing the fact that the defendants were not manufacturers of this boiler or of any boiler (a fact which is indisputable), nor (what is disputable) people possessing any special knowledge not common to the general public of boilers or laundries as possible users thereof, he goes on to say:

> That is the general principle and I think that the principle running through the cases is this—and to this extent I agree with [counsel for the plaintiffs]—that if there is nothing unusual, if it is a normal user of the plant, then it may well be that the parties must be taken to contemplate that the loss of profits may result from non-delivery, or the delay in delivery, of the particular article. On the other hand, if there are, as I think there are here, special circumstances, I do not think that the defendants are liable for loss of profits unless these special circumstances were drawn to their notice. In looking at the cases, I think there is a distinction as [counsel for the defendants] has pointed out and insists upon, between the supply of the part of the profit-making machine, as against the profit-making machine itself.

Then, after referring to *Portman v Middleton*, he continues:

> It is to be observed that not only must the circumstances be known to the supplier, but they must be such that the object must be taken to have been within the contemplation of both parties. I do not think that on the facts of the case as I have heard them, and upon the admissions, it can be said that it was within the contemplation of the supplier, namely, the defendants, that any delay in the delivery of this boiler was going to lead necessarily to loss of profits. There was nothing that I know of in the evidence to indicate how it was to be used or whether delivery of it by a particular day would necessarily be vital to the earning of these profits. I agree with the propositions of [counsel for the defendants] that it was no part of the contract, and it cannot be taken to have been the basis of the contract, that the

laundry would be unable to work if there was a delay in the delivery of the boiler, or that the laundry was extending its business, or that it had any special contracts which they could fulfil only by getting delivery of this boiler. In my view, therefore, this case falls within the second rule of Hadley v Baxendale under which they are not liable for the payment of damages for loss of profits unless there is evidence before the court—which there is not—that the special object of this boiler was drawn to their attention and that they contracted upon the basis that delay in the delivery of the boiler would make them liable to payment of loss of profits.

The answer to this reasoning has largely been anticipated in what has been said above, but we would wish to add: First, that the learned judge appears to infer that because certain 'special circumstances' were, in his view, not 'drawn to the notice of' the defendants and therefore, in his view, the operation of the 'second rule' was excluded, ergo nothing in respect of loss of business can be recovered under the 'first rule'. This inference is, in our view, no more justified in the present case than it was in the case of Cory v Thames Ironworks Co. Secondly, that while it is not wholly clear what were the 'special circumstances' on the non-communication of which the learned judge relied, it would seem that they were, or included, the following: (a) the 'circumstance' that delay in delivering the boiler was going to lead 'necessarily' to loss of profits. But the true criterion is surely not what was bound 'necessarily' to result, but what was likely or liable to do so, and we think that it was amply conveyed to the defendants by what was communicated to them (plus what was patent without express communication) that delay in delivery was likely to lead to 'loss of business'; (b) the 'circumstance' that the plaintiffs needed the boiler 'to extend their business'. It was surely not necessary for the defendants to be specifically informed of this, as a pre-condition of being liable for loss of business. Reasonable persons in the shoes of the defendants must be taken to foresee without any express intimation, that a laundry which, at a time when there was a famine of laundry facilities, was paying £2,000 odd for plant and intended at such a time to put such plant 'into use' immediately, would be likely to suffer in pocket from five months' delay in delivery of the plant in question, whether they intended by means of it to extend their business, or merely to maintain it, or to reduce a loss; (c) the 'circumstance' that the plaintiffs had the assured expect-ation of special contracts, which they could only fulfil by securing punctual delivery of the boiler. Here, no doubt, the learned judge had in mind the particularly lucrative dyeing contracts to which the plaintiffs looked forward and which they mention in para. 10 of the statement of claim. We agree that in order that the plaintiffs should recover specifically and as such the profits expected on these contracts, the defendants would have had to know, at the time of their agreement with the plaintiffs, of the prospect and terms of such contracts. We also agree that they did not in fact know these things. It does not, however, follow that the plaintiffs are precluded from recovering some general (and perhaps conjectural) sum for loss of business in respect of dyeing contracts to be reasonably expected, any more than in respect of laundering contracts to be reason-ably expected.

Thirdly, the other point on which Streatfeild J. largely based his judgment was that there is a critical difference between the measure of damages applicable when the defendant defaults in supplying a self-contained profit-earning whole and when he defaults in supplying a part of that whole. In our view, there is no intrinsic magic, in this connection, in the whole as against a part. The fact that a part only is involved is only significant in so far as it bears on the capacity of the supplier to foresee the consequences of non-delivery. If it is clear from the nature of the part (or the supplier of it is informed) that its non-delivery will have the same effect as non-delivery of the whole, his liability will be the same as if he had defaulted in delivering the whole. The cases of *Hadley v Baxendale*, *British Columbia Sawmills v Nettleship* and *Portman v Middleton*, which were so strongly relied on for the defence and by the learned judge, were all cases in which, through want of a part, catastrophic results ensued, in that a whole concern was paralysed or sterilised; a mill stopped, a complex of machinery unable to be assembled, a threshing machine unable to be delivered in time for the harvest and therefore useless. In all three cases the defendants were absolved from liability to compensate the plaintiffs for the resulting loss of business, not because what they had failed to deliver was a part, but because there had been nothing to convey to them that want of that part would stultify the whole business of the person for whose benefit the part was contracted for. There is no resemblance between these cases and the present, in which, while there was no question of a total stoppage resulting from non-delivery, yet there was ample means of knowledge on the part of the defendants that business loss of some sort would be likely to result to the plaintiffs from the defendants' default in performing their contract.

We are therefore of opinion that the appeal should be allowed and the issue referred to an official referee as to what damage, if any, is recoverable in addition to the £110 awarded by the learned trial judge. The official referee would assess those damages in consonance with the findings in this judgment as to what the defendants knew or must be taken to have known at the material time, either party to be at liberty to call evidence as to the quantum of the damage in dispute.

1. (1854) 9 Ex 341
2. 4 CB (NS) 322.
3. LR 3 CP 499.
4. (1855) 17 CB 21.
5. (1868) LR 6 Eq 396.
6. (1878) 47 LJ (QB) 23.
7. [1940] 2 KB 99.
8. (1865) 18 CB (NS) 445.
9. 6 H & N 211.
10. LR 3 QB 181, 187.
11. [1911] AC 301.
12. [1949] AC 196.

Note

In *Koufos v Czarnikow (The Heron II)* [1969] 1 AC 350 at 388–9. Lord Reid had this to say about Asquith L.J.'s judgment in *Victoria Laundry*:

. . . The plaintiffs bought a large boiler from the defendants and the defendants were aware of the general nature of the plaintiffs' business and of the plaintiffs' intention to put the boiler into use as soon as possible. Delivery of the boiler was delayed in breach of contract and the plaintiffs claimed as damages loss of profit caused by the delay. A large part of the profits claimed would have resulted from some specially lucrative contracts which the plaintiffs could have completed if they had had the boiler: that was rightly disallowed because the defendants had no knowledge of these contracts. But Asquith L.J. then said: 'It does not, however, follow that the plaintiffs are precluded from recovering some general (and perhaps conjectural) sum for loss of business in respect of dyeing contracts to be reasonably expected, any more than in respect of laundering contracts to be reasonably expected.'[1]

It appears to me that this was well justified on the earlier authorities. It was certainly not unlikely on the information which the defendants had when making the contract that delay in delivering the boiler would result in loss of business: indeed it would seem that that was more than an even chance. And there was nothing new in holding that damages should be estimated on a conjectural basis. This House had approved of that as early as 1813 in *Hall v Ross*.[2]

But what is said to create a 'landmark' is the statement of principles by Asquith L.J.[3] This does to some extent go beyond the older authorities and insofar as it does so I do not agree with it. In para. (2) it is said that the plaintiff is entitled to recover 'such part of the loss actually resulting as was at the time of the contract reasonably foreseeable as liable to result from the breach.' To bring in reasonable foreseeability appears to me to be confusing measure of damages in contract with measure of damages in tort. A great many extremely unlikely results are reasonably foreseeable: it is true that Lord Asquith may have meant foreseeable as a likely result, and if that is all he meant I would not object further than to say that I think that the phrase is liable to be misunderstood. For the same reason I would take exception to the phrase 'liable to result' in para. (5). Liable is a very vague word but I think that one would usually say that when a person foresees a very improbable result he foresees that it is liable to happen.

[1] [1949] 2 KB 528, 543.   [2] (1813) 1 Dow. 201, HL.   [3] [1949] 2 KB 528, 539, 540.

Lee and Donoghoe *v* Rowan (HC) 17 November 1981, unrep.

The plaintiffs agreed to construct a drying shed for the defendant, a farmer, for £10,500. The work was not carried out satisfactorily and the defendant resisted the plaintiff's *quantum meruit* claim and counterclaimed for £2,000, being the cost of getting another contractor to provide similar facilities over and above the (unpaid) contract price of £10,500. The defendant also sought compensation for loss of profit resulting from the entire loss of the potato harvest due to non-completion of the drying shed. Costello J. held the plaintiffs entitled to £1,291.63 being the value of work completed and accepted by the defendant. The learned judge went on to consider the defendant's counterclaim.

Costello J.:

. . .

The rule relating to damages for breach of contract has been stated in the well known case of *Hadley v Baxendale* (9 Ex at 354) as follows:

> Where two parties have made a contract which one of them has broken, the damages which the other party ought to receive in respect of such breach of contract should be such as may fairly and reasonably be considered either arising naturally, i.e according to the usual course of things from such breach of contract itself, or such as may reasonably be supposed to have been in the contemplation of the parties, at the time they made the contract, as the probable result of the breach of it.

It seems to me that under the first branch of this rule will fall the defendant's claim arising from the extra building costs amounting to £2,000. Such loss, in my opinion, may fairly and reasonably be considered as arising according to the usual course of things from the plaintiffs' breach of contract. The remainder of the defendant's loss is sustainable, if at all, under the second branch of the rule. Under this branch I must decide what damages may reasonably be supposed to have been in the contemplation of the parties at the time they made the contract as the probable result of its breach. In this connection, the plaintiffs of course knew that the defendant was growing a substantial amount of vegetables for drying and storage in the building they were erecting for him. They were not, however, aware of the exact acreage sown by the defendant but this does not, I think, affect their liability. In view of their knowledge of the trade I think the plaintiffs would have known that if they broke their contract in

May 1977 so that the defendant would have to erect a new building in place of the plaintiffs' unfinished one it would have been highly probable that the new building would not be completed in time to take the produce of the 1977 harvest. But I do not think that either party could have contemplated that the effect of a breach of contract would have been the loss of the defendant's entire crop. This unfortunate result arose not only because of the defendant's inability to have the work completed in time by a new contractor but also because of the shortage in the country of adequate storage and drying facilities. The defendant has not established to my satisfaction that at the time the contract was made the plaintiffs were aware that such a shortage would arise in 1977 and that as a result the defendant would be unable to dry and store his crop. The plaintiffs could not have contemplated that all the defendant's sowing and cultivating costs would be thrown away and so I do not think that the claim for this loss is sustainable. But the plaintiffs would have contemplated that some loss of profits would result in a breach of contract on their behalf as the defendant would be put to expense in hiring alternative storage and extra transport charges in putting his crop into store. The defendant was not able to help me as to the storage charges which he would have incurred in 1977/78 and I have not been supplied with any figures as to what the possible transport charges would be. The assessment of damages, therefore, must be to a considerable extent conjecture. Based on the total marketing costs which have been proved I think that a figure of £10 per ton would be a reasonable estimate of the extra cost to which I have referred. It seems to me, therefore, that the claim for loss of profits should be limited to the sum of £9,240 being the extra transport and storage costs of 300 tons of onions and 644 tons of potatoes, costs which the parties would have contemplated as arising from the breach by the plaintiffs in May 1977, of their contract.

The total damages to which the defendant is entitled are £11,240. He is entitled to set off this sum against the plaintiffs' claim of £1,291 and recover on the counterclaims the balance, namely, the sum of £9,949.

The plaintiffs' claim will therefore be dismissed with no order as to costs. There will be judgment on the counterclaim amounting to £9,949 with costs.

Kemp *v* Intasun (1987) 2 FTLR 234

Kerr L.J.:

On 2 February 1984 Mrs Kemp and her daughter called at Thomas Cook to choose a summer holiday.

There was a conversation with one of the assistants in which Mrs Kemp referred to the fact that her husband suffered from asthma. She said he could not be there because he was ill, and that because of his health special insurance was required.

It was decided they should choose a holiday at a hotel called America 1 at Calas de Mallorca. The relevant booking form and an insurance proposal form were taken away by Mrs Kemp.

By 29 February the Kemps had completed the booking form and returned it, and it was accepted by Intasun. Accordingly by that date the contract was concluded between the Kemps and Intasun on the terms of the booking note.

The booking note had a space for 'special requests', but nothing was inserted in it.

The first thirty hours of the holiday proved disastrous. The America 1 was full up, and the family was taken to a Spanish hotel called Las Chihuahuas, which was of nothing like the same quality.

They were taken to a room in the staff quarters. It had a broken window filled with bricks, glass on the floor, and it was filthy and very dusty. The toilet had no door and the shower did not work. There were two single beds, and a portable bed which they could not operate.

The room's dusty and dirty condition had a particular effect on Mr Kemp's asthma. He had an attack which caused him and his family considerable distress. He suffered from it throughout the thirty hours spent in that insalubrious room, and continued to be affected for several days.

Mr Kemp sued Intasun on behalf of himself and his family.

Judge Lee awarded £1,000 for breach of Intasun's contractual obligations. He divided the award into two parts. The first part was £400 for inconvenience, discomfort, loss of enjoyment and disappointment. That was not appealed.

The second part was £800 for the consequences of Mr Kemp's having suffered an asthma attack due to the state of the alternative accommodation. Intasun challenged that as a consequence which was too remote to be recoverable.

The judge had said that to succeed on this point Mr Kemp must prove that Intasun 'had knowledge of his asthma and associated problems.' He found that asthma was sufficiently uncommon to be not normally in the contemplation of Intasun—'it would, however, be sufficient if the defendant's agent was told.'

Once Intasun had knowledge, he said, the circumstances in which it came to know were irrelevant, as was the purpose for which the information was given.

He held that knowledge was attributable to Intasun.

The relevant test was not formulated entirely accurately or completely when the judge said that Mr Kemp must prove that Intasun 'had knowledge of his asthma and associated problems.'

Intasun was responsible for all the consequences which it could reasonably have contemplated as liable to flow from its breach of contract (see *Koufos v Czarnikow* [1969] 1 AC 350).

It was clear that the foreseeable consequences of a breach of contract of this kind would always include distress, discomfort, disappointment. For that the £400 was awarded.

But the responsibility of a tour operator did not necessarily stop there. He must also accept liability for any other consequences which should have been in the reasonable contemplation of the parties if they flowed naturally from his breach and caused additional foreseeable loss or damage.

The issue really was whether Intasun should have reasonably contemplated that the conditions in a room provided by way of alternative accommodation, might foreseeably be injurious to Mr Kemp's health.

The answer was in the negative. Mrs Kemp answered the question frankly in evidence when she said that had her husband not been susceptible 'we'd have had an unpleasant thirty hours or so, but no more.'

That must be read in the context of the judge's unchallenged finding that asthma was not sufficiently common to be in Intasun's reasonable contemplation and foreseeable.

Mrs Kemp's evidence was that her conversation in Cook's was casual and not part of the booking arrangements. The judge was in error in attributing any contractual consequences to that casual conversation.

At the time of the conversation Thomas Cook was not the agent of Intasun, let alone for the purpose of receiving or passing on the content of the conversation. Whether it became its agent at a later stage and for what purpose it was unnecessary to decide.

The circumstances in which Mrs Kemp's remarks were made and the position which Thomas Cook then occupied entirely precluded the court from holding that the limited knowledge about Mr Kemp's state of health which a Thomas Cook assistant happened to acquire casually, had any consequence for Intasun's contractual obligations.

The £800 was not awarded for any consequence which flowed in the ordinary course of events from Intasun's breach.

The appeal would be allowed and the award of £800 struck out.

Lord Justice Parker agreeing said that he could not accept that a casual conversation in February was sufficient to bring the asthma attack within the contemplation of the parties, even if knowledge of it were imputed to Intasun.

Seven Seas Properties Ltd *v* El Assa and Another (No. 2) [1993] 3 All ER 577

Gavin Lightman Q.C.:

I have before me an inquiry as to damages directed by Master Cholmondeley Clarke on 17 February 1988 which raises a question of law of some interest. The defendants were the owners of two leasehold properties known as 27 and 29 Sloane Garden, London SW1. The properties comprised two adjoining houses which had been converted into a number of self-contained flats. In 1987 all the flats, save one occupied by the first defendant, were vacant. The properties themselves required renovation or refurbishment to achieve a proper return, whether in the form of lettings or a sale of the flats on long leases. The defendants retained Messrs William Willetts, estate agents (whom I shall call 'Willetts') to offer the properties for sale at the price of £1.5m. and after full extensive marketing, including an advertisement in the Estates Gazette on 30 May 1987, Willetts found the plaintiffs as prospective purchasers. Mr Sharram Sabagi and Mr Basham Danishand of the plaintiffs were interested in purchasing for the purpose of a quick resale at a profit. They could not afford the cost of the purchase out of their own pockets, let alone the costs of refurbishment and renovation. Nonetheless, they kept their intentions to themselves and told Willetts that they intended to refurbish and then sell the refurbished flats and discussed with the agents the probable prices obtainable for the refurbished flats on such sale. They naturally kept to themselves any hopes for a quick return, for any such intimation might have put the defendants on notice of the potential availability of a purchaser at a higher price, and indeed it is clear that, if the defendants had received any such intimation, the defendants would not have sold to the plaintiffs.

The plaintiffs found such a sub-purchaser in a company called Grangeville Marketing Inc. (which I shall refer to as 'Grangeville') who were willing to buy for £1,635,000. In the course of the arrangements made for such sub-sale Mr Sabagi and Mr Danishand agreed that one third of any profit of such resale should be paid by the plaintiffs to a Mr Ismael Gandoor. The contract for sale by the plaintiffs to the defendants (which I shall call 'the plaintiffs' contract') and the contract for resale (which I shall call 'the first Grangeville contract') were both signed on 26 June 1987. Thereafter the defendants learned of the first Grangeville contract and because they considered that they were being underpaid the difference between the prices payable under the two contracts they refused to proceed or complete.

On 22 October 1987 the plaintiffs served notice to complete the plaintiffs' contract and Grangeville served notice to complete the first Grangeville contract, both notices expiring on 13 November 1987. Since the defendants persisted in their refusal to proceed and the plaintiffs were unable to complete the first Grangeville contract, on 13 November 1987 Grangeville accepted the failure of the plaintiffs to complete as a breach discharging them from further performance of that contract.

On 16 November 1987 Grangeville wrote an open letter to the plaintiffs threatening proceedings for damages for loss of bargain totalling some £700,000, and in a without prejudice letter of the same date offered in settlement of all claims against the plaintiffs to enter into a new contract of sub-purchase at the price of £1,325,000. This offer was not accepted. On 1 December 1987 Grangeville commenced proceedings against the plaintiffs claiming damages along the lines intimated in the open letter and on 2 December 1987 the plaintiffs commenced proceedings against the defendants for specific performance of the plaintiffs' contract. On 17 February 1988 in the plaintiffs' action Master Cholmondeley Clarke made an order for specific performance of the plaintiffs' contract, directed this inquiry as to damages and ordered a retention of £650,000 from the purchase price pending the outcome of this inquiry. On 29 March 1988 Master Cholmondeley Clarke fixed the completion date for 12 April 1988, and the sale by the defendants to the plaintiffs subject to the retention was in fact completed on 21 April 1988.

On the same day, pursuant to a contract made in March (which I refer to as 'the second Grangeville contract'), the plaintiffs competed a sale to Grangeville for £1,375,000. The sale at this price contained no provision precluding enforcement of the claims by Grangeville against the plaintiffs for breach of the first Grangeville contract.

On 27 May 1988 an appeal came before Hoffmann J. ([1989] 1 All ER 164, [1988] 1 WLR 1272) against the order of Master Cholmondeley Clarke so far as he ordered a retention of £650,000. Hoffmann J. made clear his view that, so far as the retention was intended to protect the plaintiffs against any entitlement on the part of the plaintiffs to an indemnity in respect of any claim by Grangeville for damages for breach of the first Grangeville contract, the ordered retention was far too high because any claim by Grangeville must, in view of the rule in Bain v Fothergill (1874) LR 7 HL 158, [1874–80] All ER Rep 83, be limited to wasted conveyancing expenses and costs and possibly wasted bank facility charges, architects' and surveyors' costs. He reduced the figure to £275,000.

On 28 June 1989 Master Cholmondeley Clarke ordered a trial as a preliminary issue whether the rule in Bain v Fothergill applied to limit Grangeville's claim against the plaintiffs to such wasted costs and expenses.

Meanwhile, on 27 September 1989 s. 3 of the Law of Property (Miscellaneous Provisions) Act 1989 came into law abolishing the rule in Bain v Fothergill in respect of contracts made after that date but not before.

On 28 February 1990 the preliminary issue was determined by Hirst J. who held that the rule applied. He granted a certificate under s. 12 of the Administration of Justice Act 1969 enabling an application to be made to the House of Lords for a leapfrog appeal to the House of Lords. On 23 March 1990 Grangeville petitioned the House of Lords for leave to appeal and this petition was dismissed on 20 June 1990. Baulked by that decision, in July 1990 Grangeville served notice of appeal to the Court of Appeal intending to reach the House of Lords by this alternative route. On 31 January 1991 the appeal and the Grangeville action were compromised on terms providing for repayment of £60,000 to Grangeville within twenty eight days after determination of this, the plaintiffs' action.

On this inquiry as to damages the plaintiffs claim as follows. They claim, first of all, £135,000 as loss of profits under the first Grangeville contract. This figure has however in the course of the hearing been reduced. First of all, it is agreed that the sum of £5,000 must be deducted from this sum to reflect certain legal costs and the net figure is to be reduced by a further one third to reflect the entitlement of Mr Ismael Gandoor to one third of the total net profit. Secondly, there was a claim for £125,000 as loss arising under the sale under the second Grangeville contract. Thirdly, there is a claim for £60,000 as a sum agreed to be paid to Grangeville in the compromise of its claims. Fourthly, there is a sum of £5,750 as the costs paid to their solicitors in respect of the defence of the Grangeville action. It is to be observed that all these claims represent losses arising by reason of the inability of the plaintiffs to complete the first Grangeville contract, an inability entirely attributable to the defendants' breach of their contract with the plaintiffs.

The decision on this application whether these claims should be upheld turns on the application to the facts of this case of the rule in *Hadley v Baxendale* (1854) 9 Ex 341, [1843–60] All ER Rep 461. The two branches of this rule were stated by Lord Upjohn in *Koufos v Czarnikow Ltd* (*The Heron II*) [1967] 3 All ER 686 at 715, [1969] 1 AC 350 at 421 as follows: '1. Damages should be such as may naturally and usually arise from the breach, or 2. Damages should be such as in the special circumstances of the case known to both parties may be reasonably supposed to have been in the contemplation of the parties, as the result of a breach, assuming the parties to have applied their minds to the contingency of there being such a breach.'

The plaintiffs do not in their pleadings claim that the damages sought fall within the first branch. Indeed, I invited [counsel for the plaintiffs], if he so wished, to apply to amend to invoke this head but he declined. He has, no doubt quite properly, nailed his flag to the second branch. [Counsel] does not contend that at the date of the plaintiffs' contract the defendants actually knew of any intention on the part of the plaintiffs to enter into a contract of resale, but he contends that in the special circumstances of this case known to the defendants there may reasonably be supposed to have been in their contemplation that the plaintiffs would or might enter into such a contract and that if they did so the result of the defendants' breach of contract was liable, indeed likely, to put the plaintiffs in breach of such contract of resale and would occasion to the plaintiffs such damages as were indeed occasioned in this case. The special circumstances relied on are, first of all, the character of the premises, namely a block of flats ripe for refurbishment; secondly, the character of likely interested purchasers who have been called by at least one witness 'property professionals', persons who may be expected to buy in order to turn the property to account as opportunity might arise and to resell quickly if the price available was right; thirdly, the buoyant state of the property market for this kind of property at the time of the contract with both rising property prices and in many cases rapid returns and resales.

I accept that the evidence establishes these special circumstances. Indeed, they are not materially, if at all, in dispute. A more contentious issue relates to the probability or likely quick return or resale by the purchasers of this property after the marketing by Willetts at the price of £1.5m. It was common ground that the purchaser should be expected to purchase for the purpose of refurbishment and subsequent sale of the flats after refurbishment. Mr Duncan, the plaintiffs' expert, expressed the view that nonetheless there was a chance, which he estimated at ten per cent, that such a purchaser might yet seek and achieve such a quick return as the plaintiffs in fact achieved. On the other hand, the defendants' expert, Mr Hutchinson, firmly expressed the view that after the extensive marketing by Willetts and the achievement of the optimum price a resale by the plaintiffs within the ten week completion period was highly unlikely and the shortest period within which a resale could reasonably be expected was six to nine months. [Counsel for the plaintiffs], in his address to me, cautioned me about accepting Mr Duncan's (his own expert's) opinion on the percentage chance as a spot assessment off the cuff in his oral evidence rather than a careful, considered judgment. His purpose was to persuade me to treat his expert's assessment as too low. Mr Duncan on at least two occasions in his oral evidence gave this percentage assessment and I cannot see how in particular in the light of the careful and considered evidence of Mr Hutchinson, who plainly thought the assessment of ten per cent was over-generous, I can evaluate the odds above ten per cent. Indeed, in the light of the caution with which perhaps I should view Mr Duncan's spot assessment and the unequivocal considered views of Mr Hutchinson, I think I should conclude that a reasonable assessment of the prospects of an early resale contract, and certainly prior to the contractual completion date, were somewhat below ten per cent.

I turn now to the law. The relevant legal principles appear to me to be as follows. First of all, under the first head of the rule in *Hadley v Baxendale* a plaintiff is entitled to recover all damages which may fairly and reasonably be considered as arising naturally, i.e. according to the usual course of things, from the breach of contract. In the case of a breach by a vendor under a contract for sale, losses occasioned to the purchaser under and by reason of the existence of a sub-contract entered into by him will not without more fall within this head. The court will not take into account the existence of such sub-contract whether to increase or decrease the award of damages and the same principle applies whether the contract is for the sale of goods or the sale of land: see *Brading v McNeill* |1946| Ch. 145. No doubt it is for this reason that the plaintiffs in this case quite properly disavow any reliance on the first head and rely solely on the second head of the rule.

Secondly, a plaintiff is entitled to recover by way of damages all loss which at the date of contract the defaulting party was on notice might be occasioned by the breach such that he may fairly be held, in entering into his contract, to have accepted the risk. A party of this purpose is on notice of facts (i) which were actually known by him, (ii) which were known by his agent and which it was his agent's duty to communicate to him, and (iii) which he should reasonably have deduced from (i) and (ii). He will only be held to have accepted the risk if he was on notice of the purpose and intent of the plaintiff in entering into the contract with him and the consequent exposure of the plaintiff to the risk of damage of the character in question in the event of the defendant's breach: see *Treitel on Contract* (8th ed., 1991), 860–862 and the cases cited and in particular *Finlay & Co. Ltd v NV Kwik Hoo Tong HM* |1929| 1 KB 400, |1928| All ER Rep 110. This is only just, for a party to a contract should not be exposed to risks of liability going beyond the first branch of the rule but arising out of the special susceptibility to damage of the plaintiff unless he has had the opportunity to make an informed decision whether or not by entering into the contract to accept such risk, and whether to negotiate some exclusion from such liability.

Third, applying these principles to a claim by a plaintiff to recover from a defendant vendor losses arising under a sub-contract, the plaintiff must establish that the defendant was on notice of the existence at the date of the contract of the purpose and intent on the part of the vendor to enter into the sub-contract and that its fulfilment depended on the performance by the defendant of his contractual obligations to the plaintiff. It is not sufficient for the plaintiff to establish that the conclusion of a sub-contract was an available option: consider *Diamond v Campbell-Jones* |1960| 1 All ER 583, |1961| Ch. 22. He must show that he or the circumstances 'signalised' (in the language of *Cheshire and Fifoot on Contract* (11th ed., 1986), 588 such to be his purpose or intent in entering into the contract with the defendant. If such notice or acceptance of risk is established, the plaintiff is entitled to recover loss of profit in respect of such sub-contract and an indemnity in respect of liabilities arising from breach: see *Household Machines Ltd v Cosmos Exporters* |1946| 2 All ER 622, |1947| KB 217.

Applying those principles to the facts of this case, it is quite clear that neither the defendants nor their agent knew of any intention on the part of the plaintiffs to enter into any such contract as the first Grangeville contract. Indeed, quite deliberately the plaintiffs kept this from them and encouraged their naturally held view that their intent was refurbishment. Nor can I see how the special circumstances relied on signalised any such intent or purpose. At best such circumstances indicated that such an early sale was a possibility, but even then only a somewhat remote possibility, a possibility not greater than, and in my view, probably somewhat short of ten per cent.

In these circumstances the plaintiffs' claim based on the second limb of *Hadley v Baxendale* must fail. The defendants were not on notice of the first Grangeville contract and accordingly any loss in respect of such contract arising from the defendants' default under the plaintiffs' contract was not within their contemplation as required by the second limb. I should add that even if, contrary to my view, it was not necessary for the plaintiffs to establish that the defendants were on notice and it was sufficient that objectively the losses in question were liable to occur, the likelihood of such occurrence on the facts of this case were very limited indeed and certainly beyond any reasonable contemplation of the defendants: consider *Transworld Oil Ltd v North Bay Shipping Corp., The Rio Claro* [1987] 2 Lloyd's Rep. 173. Reaching this conclusion, as [counsel for the plaintiffs] conceded in argument, all his claims must fail. I should perhaps add that if I had held that the first Grangeville contract fell within the contemplation of the defendants at the date of the plaintiffs' contract, whilst I would have awarded the plaintiffs the sum claimed for loss of profit I would have awarded nothing more. The alleged losses on resale would have been irrecoverable in the absence of any allegation in the pleadings and evidence that the price on resale was the best price reasonably obtainable. Indeed, there are reasons to doubt whether this was the case and whether the sale at this price may have been designed to appease Grangeville. The sum claimed in respect of the compromise likewise I would have rejected, for it is neither pleaded nor proved that the settlement was a reasonable one to enter into. The onus was on the plaintiffs to do this if they were to seek to recover this sum from the defendants: see *Biggin Co. Ltd v Permanite Ltd* [1951] 2 All ER 191, [1951] 2 KB 314. It is not sufficient for the plaintiffs merely to plead the compromise without any explanation as to how the figure was made up or arrived at or any evidence as to how or why or on what advice it was entered into. The settlement appears to me on its face to place far too high a premium on the possible claim by Grangeville for damages for loss of bargain, a claim which could only succeed if the House of Lords were persuaded to overrule the rule in *Bain v Fothergill*. Whatever the prospects at the time of the case of *Sharneyford Supplies Ltd v Edge (Barrington Black Austin & Co. (a firm), third party)* [1987] 1 All ER 588, [1987] Ch. 305, that is to say 14 October 1986, when the Court of Appeal attacked the injustice of the rule and gave leave to appeal to the House of Lords to enable the House of Lords to review that decision, the situation had critically changed after the passing of the 1989 Act. The possibility that the House of Lords would grant leave to appeal after the new legislation, which is deliberately not retrospective, and after the refusal to leave to appeal on the leap-frog application, appear to me to have been remote indeed. My doubts about the compromise are reinforced by the apparent deliberate choice not to involve the defendants in the decision despite the apparent intent to claim an indemnity from them. As to the claim for recovery of the legal costs, assuming that it could be established that the costs of defending the Grangeville action were paid, I would have felt the need for evidence explaining the course taken in respect of that action and in particular the advice (if any) taken regarding whether there should be a payment into court. In respect of the compromise, involving as it did the plaintiffs forgoing any prospect of recovery of the costs of the action, I would wish to have known how much was due in reimbursement to the plaintiffs under orders for costs against Grangeville (for example in respect of the hearing before Hirst J.). I am given no details. I cannot think that a bare claim to have paid a figure in respect of costs is enough to found any claim.

For the reasons which I have given, I hold therefore that the claims made by the plaintiffs should be dismissed and I so direct.

D. THE RULE IN BAIN V FOTHERGILL

J. O'Driscoll 'A Note on the Rule in *Bain v Fothergill*' (1975) 10 Ir Jur (NS) 203 (Footnotes abridged.)

Where a party fails to perform his contract, the injured party is to be placed, so far as money can do it, in the same position as he would have been in had the contract been performed. This is the principle established in the case of *Robinson v Harman*.[1]

The damages which the injured party ought to receive in respect of the breach of contract should be such as may fairly and reasonably be considered to arise naturally, i.e. according to the usual course of things, from such breach of contract itself, or such as may reasonably be supposed to have been in the contemplation of both parties, at the time they made the contract, as the probable result of the breach of it. This is the now well established rule in *Hadley v Baxendale*, a decision of the Court of Exchequer in 1854.[2]

Where a seller or lessor of land fails to complete the contract through a defect in his title, the purchaser cannot claim damages for the loss of his bargain, but is restricted to recovery of his deposit and his expenses in investigating title. This, broadly, is the rule in *Bain v Fothergill*, a decision of the House of Lords in 1874.[3] The decision, consequently, came after both *Hadley v Baxendale* and *Robinson v Harman*.

Whilst the principle of law is now known as the rule in *Bain v Fothergill*, an examination of the judgments in the case make it clear, however, that the House of Lords was following what it considered to have been decided by *Flureau v Thornhill*[4] in 1776. As is pointed out later, the judgment in *Flureau v Thornhill* is unsatisfactory in that no attempt to provide a rationale for the rule was provided. Further, the question of the principles behind the proper measure of damages does not appear to have been properly tackled until *Hadley v Baxendale*, some eighty years after *Flureau v Thornhill*.

It is now well settled that the rule in *Hadley v Baxendale* failed to remove the principle that was understood to have been laid down in *Flureau v Thornhill*. As we will see later, the rationale of *Bain v Fothergill* and what is considered to have been the true rationale of *Flureau v Thornhill* was the difficulty which existed at that time of showing title to land in England.

The facts in *Bain v Fothergill* were as follows. Fothergill having contracted for the purchase of a mine, held under an agreement for a lease with a clause against assignment without licence, entered into possession, and, without taking any assignment, agreed to sell to Bain. At the date of this sub-contract, Fothergill was aware that the assent of the lessors was necessary to complete his title but did not anticipate any difficulty in obtaining it and treated the matter as unimportant, and did not mention it to Bain. Subsequently, the lessors, having first verbally promised their assent, withdrew it and the sale to Bain fell through. In an action by Bain for non-performance of the contract, the House of Lords, affirming the decision of the Court of Exchequer, held that Bain could only recover the expenses which he had incurred, not damages for the loss of his bargain.

The extracts from the judgments set out in the headnote impart the sense of the decision. There appears first this extract from the speech of Lord Chelmsford:

> The rule laid down in *Flureau v Thornhill* as to the limits within which damages may be recovered upon the breach of a contract for the sale of real estate must be taken to be without exception. If the person enters into a contract for the sale of real estate, knowing that he has no title to it, nor any means of acquiring it, the purchaser cannot, in an action for breach of the contract, recover damages beyond the expenses he has incurred. Any other damages must be the subject of an action for deceit.

The law report editor then adds this extract from the speech of Lord Hatherley: 'A contract for sale of real estate is very different from a contract for the sale of a chattel. In the former the purchaser knows that there must, with all the complications of our law, be an uncertainty as to making out a good title; in the latter the vendor must know what his right to the chattel is.'

The judges in *Bain v Fothergill* clearly considered that the principle enunciated in *Flureau v Thornhill* was now well established in law, but were critical of both the reasoning or lack of reasoning and the report itself. Mr Justice Denman was among the judges summoned to advise the House of Lords, and he stated:

> It may be admitted that the case of *Flureau v Thornhill* is not a wholly satisfactory case. The report is meagre, and the judgments unargumentative; but the case cannot truly be said to be founded on no principle. . . . For example, in *Robinson v Harman*, Parke B., in speaking of *Flureau v Thornhill*, says, 'It was there held that contracts for the sale of real estate are merely on condition that the vendor has a good title' (adopting the judgment of Blackstone J.), and then adds, 'so that when a person contracts to sell real property there is an implied understanding that if he fails to make good title the only damages recoverable are the expenses which the vendor may be put to in investigating the title.

Lord Chelmsford, in referring to the decision in *Flureau v Thornhill*, stated: 'Lord Chief Justice De Grey merely laid down the rule, without giving any reason for it. But Mr Justice Blackstone said this: "These contracts are merely upon condition frequently expressed, but always implied, that the vendor had a good title."'

Later in his speech, Lord Chelmsford continued:

> There is, perhaps, some difficulty in ascertaining the exact grounds of the judgment in *Flureau v Thornhill*; but, in addition to those which have been previously assigned, it seems to me that the following consideration may be suggested as in some degree supporting the correctness of the decision: 'The fancied goodness of the bargain' must be a matter of a purely speculative character, and in most cases would probably be very difficult to determine, in consequence of the conflicting opinions likely to be formed upon the subject; and even if it could be proved to have been a beneficial purchase, the loss of the pecuniary advantage to be derived from a resale appears to me to be a consequence too remote from the breach of the contract.

To describe 'the fancied goodness of the bargain' as of a purely speculative character and difficult to determine would clearly not be accepted in modern times. Neither, is it submitted, would the proposition that the loss of the pecuniary advantage to be derived from a resale was too remote. Indeed, the pecuniary advantage is very frequently a primary consideration when parties have entered into an agreement for the sale of lands.

Some Irish cases

In *Kelly v Duffy*[5] the vendor agreed with the purchaser for the sale of certain leasehold premises and the purchaser paid a deposit on his purchase money. At the date of the agreement, the vendor had no interest in the premises agreed to be sold. The vendor died without having completed his contract. The purchaser sued the vendor's personal representative for specific performance and damages, and it was held that the action, being founded upon breach of contract and not upon fraud or deceit, the damages award in lieu of specific performance must be confined to the loss occasioned to the purchaser by the vendor's failure to complete; the rule in *Bain v Fothergill* applied.

O'Connor M.R., in his judgment, commented on the unsatisfactory nature of the report of *Flureau v Thornhill*. Yet, he continued, unsatisfactory as the decision might be, it was then too late to question it; it was settled law. Mr Justice Denman had described it in *Bain v Fothergill* 'as a part of the law of the land binding upon all Courts of Justice, and only to be altered, if at all, by legislation'. The concern of O'Connor M.R. was solely as to whether the facts in the case came within the rule in *Bain v Fothergill*, and he held that they did. The Master of the Rolls next considered a celebrated passage in the judgment of Lindley M.R. in *Day v Singleton*:[6] 'The only reason which can be assigned for deciding that he [Day] is entitled to more is that the rule which limits his damages in the first case, is itself an anomalous rule based upon and justified by difficulties in shewing a good title to real property in this country, but one which ought not to be extended to cases in which the reasons on which it is based do not apply.'

Of this, O'Connor M.R. remarked: 'I do not know what is meant by an anomalous rule of law. A rule is either good or bad. If it is good, as founded on some principles, it can't be called anomalous. If it is bad, it ought not to be followed.'

It seems to this writer that O'Connor M.R. failed to grasp the essential nature of the rule and certainly failed to grasp the argument of Lindley M.R. referred to, and decided *Kelly v Duffy* in blinkers, once he had established that the fact fitted the rule. He did not consider the rationale for the rule itself.

In *McDonnell v McGuinness*[7] it was held by the Supreme Court, where a right of dower was subsisting in the lands, that the vendor had, without fraud, been unable to make title; in consequence, the purchaser was entitled only to interest on his deposit, together with the costs and expenses actually incurred by him in investigating title, and was not entitled to damages for the loss of his bargain. The court specifically applied the rule in *Bain v Fothergill*, adding that, if wilful default had been proved, it would not have been. Again, it appears that the Supreme Court, once they established that the vendor acted without fraud or wilful default, simply applied the rule. The defect in the judgment, in the writer's opinion, is that once more the rule itself was not seriously considered or analysed. Sullivan C.J., in the course of his judgment, stated: 'Unquestionably if Dr McCann [the principal of the defendant] was, without fraud, incapable of making a good title the plaintiff would not be entitled to recover more than his deposit with interest and his costs, he would not be entitled to damages for the loss of his bargain.'

Meredith J. in the same case expressly dissented from the view propounded by Gavan Duffy J. in the High Court to the effect that on a claim for damages for breach of a contract for the sale of land a purchaser could not recover damages for loss of bargain if he alleged and proved wilful default. 'Such proof', Meredith J. continued, 'would simply prevent the special rule affirmed in *Bain v Fothergill* from applying'.

1. (1848) 1 Ex 850, at 855.
2. (1854) 9 Ex 341.
3. (1874) LR 7 HL 158.
4. (1776) 2 Wm. Bl. 1078.
5. [1922] 1 IR 62.
6. [1899] 2 Ch. 320.
7. [1939] IR 223.

Note

The rule in *Bain v Fothergill* is seen as anachronistic and Irish courts have been careful to limit its scope: See Clark, R. *Contract Law in Ireland* (op. cit.), 461–2.

For the current English position see the *Seven Seas* case, p. 970 above.

SECTION FIVE—BANKER AND CUSTOMER CASES

Kinlen *v* Ulster Bank [1928] IR 171

In this case the plaintiff had a current account credit balance with the defendant bank. He tried to withdraw moneys within this balance but the bank manager refused to allow the plaintiff to do this. The plaintiff even resorted to drawing cheques on the account but these cheques were refused. At trial of the action substantial damages of £250 were awarded. The bank appealed.

Kennedy C.J.:

...

The questions for consideration arise out of the relationship of banker and customer in respect of what we all know as a 'current account'. The principles governing that relationship have been gradually defined during the past century in a series of judicial decisions in England. We have not been referred to any decision of the courts in Ireland touching the subject. No difference, however, in banking usage and practice as to current accounts in the two countries has been brought to our notice, and we may take it that the same governing legal principles apply to current accounts in both countries in the existing state of the law. They may be collected, so far as they have been stated up to the present time, in a group of early cases, namely: *Marzetti v Williams;*[1] *Pott v Clegg;*[2] *Foley v Hill;*[3] and *Rolin v Steward;*[4] and in a recent review of the authorities by the English Court of Appeal in *Joachimson v Swiss Bank Corp.*[5]

When a person desires to open a current account at a bank he pays a sum of money into the bank. The common expression that he *'lodges money* in bank' is somewhat misleading as to the nature of the transaction. The legal relation which thereupon arises is that of debtor or creditor. It is not the fiduciary relation of *cestui que trust* and trustee, nor the relation of principal and agent. The money paid in is no longer the money of the customer. It has been, as it were, lent to the bank, and the customer has, in lieu of it, a common law debt due to him by the bank, and recoverable by an action for money lent. But it is not merely a simple loan. Certain terms as to repayment are (apart from any special contract) implied from the relationship of customer and banker. These include, on the part of the banker, a promise to repay the money on demand made during banking hours at the branch of the bank at which the account is standing, and a promise to repay the money against the cheque or written order of the customer presented at the branch during business hours.

It follows that if the customer's account be in funds, the failure of the banker to comply with the customer's own demand for repayment or to honour his cheques, in either case up to the amount standing to credit of the account, entitles the customer to at least nominal damages for breach of contract. The matter is carried a stage further by the authorities, for it has long been settled law that if a banker wrongfully dishonours the cheque of a customer who is a trader, the customer is entitled to substantial, and not merely nominal, damages, without proof of special damage. There does not appear to be any positive decision directly negativing the like right of a non-trader in the same circumstances. Nor have we been referred to, and I do not know of, any decision directly on the question which precisely defines the damages to which a customer is entitled for non-compliance with his demand for repayment of his balance to himself.

. . .

The real position, then, may be shortly stated, and it is right to say that it is fully covered by the statement of claim as pleaded. The plaintiff had a current account with the defendant bank, with a balance standing to his credit. Admittedly now (for the attempt to make another case failed at the trial, and was not pursued here) there was no special contract affecting the credit balance. It was, therefore, subject to the ordinary contract of banker and customer. Admittedly, the customer on several occasions personally, in business hours, at the branch where the account was kept, demanded payment of sums within the limits of the amount of his credit balance, and, as found by the jury, tendered on three occasions cheque forms filled up in writing answering the purpose of demands in writing and receipts. Admittedly, his demands were wrongfully refused, and wholly untenable grounds of excuse were put forward by the bank through their manager. The plaintiff is clearly entitled to nominal damages, at least, in respect of each of these several breaches of contract. The question is whether he is entitled to substantial damages (apart from special damage), as the learned trial judge directed the jury, or to special damages.

The rule as to damages in the case of the dishonouring of a trader's cheque, to which I have referred, was invoked by plaintiff's counsel. Now the right of a trader to substantial damages, without proof of special damage for the wrongful dishonouring of his cheque, is really founded upon the implication of defamation—of slander of the trader in the way of his trade and credit. The bank represents him to the holder, payee, or indorsee of the cheque, as having committed a fraud in drawing upon a bank where he has no assets, or as having made a false statement as to a fact within his own knowledge, or the bank may be taken as conveying an imputation of the trader-customer's insolvency. Hence, in such cases the jury is properly directed not to limit their verdict to nominal damages, but to give substantial, though temperate and reasonable, damages for the injury caused to the plaintiff: *Rolin v Steward*. This is one of the anomalous cases of damages for breach of contract analogous to the case of breach of promise of marriage. The learned trial judge in his direction to the jury on the question of damages was certainly following the lines of the trader's cheque cases. His emphasis on the defamatory element demonstrates this.

In my opinion, the principle applied to cases of dishonoured traders' cheques has no application to the facts of the present case. A demand made personally by a customer upon his banker for payment is a two-party transaction. The refusal of payment cannot give rise to the implication of defamation of the customer to a third party, which necessarily arises when a trader's cheque, drawn or endorsed in favour of a third party, is presented by the holder and dishonoured by the banker.

. . .

The plaintiff has relied on two matters for the purpose of aggravating the damages to which he is entitled. In the first place, he said that the bank manager not only refused him the money to which he was entitled, but refused it contemptuously, and with contumely. Indeed, I have no doubt that the plaintiff was very badly treated indeed by the bank. In the second place, he urged that by reason of the first refusal he was subjected to great humiliation in raising money to pay his workmen. He had to pawn some of his personal belongings to raise part of the money, and he had to borrow part of it from a friend. These matters were greatly pressed upon us, and they evoke much sympathy with the plaintiff, but they are not matters which can be considered as elements of damages. It is very clearly settled, both in this country and in England, and affirmed in many cases, that in actions for breach of contract damages may not be given for such matters as disappointment of mind, humiliation, vexation, or the like, nor may exemplary or vindictive damages be awarded. See *Breen v Cooper*;[6] *Hamlin v*

Great Northern Rly;[7] *Addis v Gramophone Co. Ltd.*[8] I am not now, of course, referring to the three recognised anomalies—actions for breaches of promise of marriage, actions for dishonouring traders' cheques, and a special class of actions for failure by a vendor to make title.

In the case of a breach of a simple contract to pay money, the law in this country, settled by a long line of authorities, is that the measure of damages is a reasonable compensation for non-performance of the contract, and that the amount of such compensation is to be arrived at by allowing interest on the money (which may vary in amount). See *Fletcher v Tayleur;*[9] *British Columbia Sawmill Co. v Nettleship;*[10] *Prehn v Royal Bank of Liverpool;*[11] *Wallis v Smith;*[12] *In re English Bank of the River Plate, ex parte Bank of Brazil;*[13] *South African Territories v Wallington;*[14] *Parker v Dickie.*[15]

I think, however, that there is no doubt that the courts are not bound to apply the measure I have just stated to the case of a special contract; as, for instance, where the money is to be paid for a special purpose known to the debtor, and injurious consequences of a particular character flow naturally from the non-payment: *Mackenzie v Corballis.*[16]

Now the relation of banker and customer in respect of a current account rests upon a special contract, to the special terms of which I have already referred. The due and unfailing performance of that contract on the part of the banker is, as he knows, vital to the ordinary daily life of his customers in our modern social organisation. The customer relies on his credit balance being at his instant call for innumerable purposes—commercial, domestic, social—constantly pressing upon him. The banker knows that if the credit balance is withheld from the customer when he demands payment, inevitably the customer must immediately procure an equivalent amount of money from some other source—probably by borrowing at interest. But the customer may fail to obtain a loan, or the delay may be such that injurious consequences naturally flow from the banker's default—a judgment may be marked against the customer, he may be evicted, his goods may be taken in execution, he may lose the benefit of a valuable contract, in a variety of ways he may suffer grievous loss and damage as the direct result of the banker's refusing him payment of his credit balance on his demand, a result which in the nature of things cannot but be within the banker's contemplation.

In my opinion, a customer is entitled to recover from his banker by way of damages for wrongfully refusing payment of a demand not exceeding the amount of the customer's credit balance on his current account—in the first place, the amount which he must pay for interest upon a loan of the amount of his demand during such time as payment is withheld by the banker. In the second place, the customer is, in my opinion, entitled, if he pleads and proves that he has suffered special damage flowing naturally in the circumstances from the banker's breach of contract, to recover special damages.
. . .

The measure of damages then to which the plaintiff is in my opinion entitled is only the amount of the interest which he should pay to procure the loan of a sum equivalent to his demand, payment whereof was wrongfully refused, during the period while payment was so withheld. The rate of such interest would necessarily be larger in the case of a poor man, without security, such as the plaintiff is. Strictly speaking, it should I think be calculated only on the first demand of £25. He would be entitled to nominal damages, and no more, for the dishonouring of the fourth, the test, cheque.

[1.] 1 B & Ad 415.   [2.] 16 M & W 321.

3. 2 H of L Cas 28.
4. 14 CB 595.
5. |1921| 3 KB 110.
6. IR 3 CL 621.
7. 1 H & N 408.
8. |1909| AC 488, per Lord Atkinson, at 495, 496.
9. 17 CB 21, per Willes J., at 29.
10. LR 3 CP 499 per Bovill C.J., at 506.
11. LR 5 Ex 92.
12. 21 ChD 243, per Jessel M.R., at 257.
13. |1893| 2 Ch. 438, per Chitty J., at 446.
14. |1897| 1 QB 692, per Chitty L.J., at 696.
15. 4 LR (Ir) 244, per Lawson J., at 248.
16. 40 ILTR 28.

SECTION SIX—DAMAGES FOR PHYSICAL DISCOMFORT AND INCONVENIENCE CAUSED BY BREACH OF CONTRACT

Hobbs v London and South Western Rly (1875) 10 QBD 111

Cockburn C.J.:

...

The facts are simple, The plaintiffs took tickets to be conveyed from the Wimbledon station of the defendants' railway to Hampton Court. It so happened that the train did not go to Hampton Court, and the plaintiffs were taken on to Esher Station, which increased the distance which they would have to go from the railway station to their home by two or three miles.

Damages were asked for upon two grounds: first, for the inconvenience that the husband and wife, with their two children, sustained by having to go this distance, the night happening to be a wet night; in the second place, damages were asked by reason of the wife, from her exposure to the wet on that night, getting a bad cold and being ill in health, the consequence of which was that some expense was incurred in medical attendance upon her. We think these two heads of damage must be kept distinct, and I propose to deal with them as distinct subjects.

With regard to the first, there can be no doubt whatever upon the facts that the plaintiffs were put to personal inconvenience: they had to walk late at night, after twelve o'clock, a considerable distance, the wife suffered fatigue from it, and they had to carry their children, or to get them along with great difficulty the children being fatigued and exhausted; and there is no doubt that there was personal inconvenience suffered by the party on that occasion, and that inconvenience was the immediate consequence and result of the breach of contract on the part of the defendants. The plaintiffs did their best to diminish the inconvenience to themselves by having recourse to such means as they hoped to find at hand; they tried to get into an inn, which they were unable to do; they tried to get a conveyance; they were informed none was to be had; and they had no alternative but to walk; and therefore it was from no default of their part, and it cannot be doubted that the inconvenience was the immediate and necessary consequence of the breach of the defendants' contract to convey them to Hampton Court. Now inasmuch as there was manifest personal inconvenience, I am at a loss to see why that inconvenience should not be compensated by damages in such an action as this. It has been endeavoured to be argued, upon principle and upon authority, that this was a kind of damage which could not be supported; and attempts were also made to satisfy us that this supposed inconvenience was more or less imaginary, and would depend upon the strength and constitution of the parties, and various other circumstances; and that it is not to be taken that a walk of so many additional miles would be a thing that a person would dislike or suffer inconvenience from; and that there may be circumstances under which a walk of several miles, so far from being matter of inconvenience, would be just the contrary. All that depends on the actual facts of each individual case; and if the jury are satisfied that in the particular instance personal inconvenience or suffering has been occasioned, and that it had been occasioned as the immediate effect of the breach of the contract, I can see no reasonable principle why that should not be compensated for. The case of *Hamlin v Great Northern Rly Co.*[1] was cited as an authority to shew that for personal inconvenience damages ought not to be awarded. That case appears to me to fall far short of any such proposition. It merely seems to amount to this: that where a party, by not being able to get to a place which he would otherwise have arrived at in time to meet persons with whom he had appointments, has sustained pecuniary loss, that is too remote to be made the subject of damages in an action upon a breach of contract. That may be perfectly true, because, as in every one of the instances cited, you would have to go into the question whether there was a loss arising from the breach of contract, before you could assess that loss. And, after all, if the true principle be laid down in *Hadley v Baxendale*,[2] the damage must be something which is in the contemplation of the parties as likely to result from a breach of contract; and it is impossible that a company who undertake to carry a passenger to a place of destination can have in their minds all the circumstances which may result from the passenger being detained on the journey. As far as the case of *Hamlin v Great Northern Rly Co.* goes, I am far from saying it was a wrong decision; but it did not decide that personal inconvenience, however serious, was not to be taken into account as a subject matter of damage in a breach of contract of a carrier to convey a person to a particular destination. If it did, I should not follow that authority; but I do not think it applicable to this case at all. I think there is no authority that personal inconvenience, where it is sufficiently serious, should not be the subject of damages to be recovered in an action of this kind. Therefore, on the first head, the £8, I think the verdict ought to stand.

With regard to the second head of damage, the case assumes a very different aspect. I see very great difficulty indeed in coming to any other conclusion than that the £20 is not recoverable; and when we are asked to lay down some principle as a guiding rule in all such cases, I quite agree with my brother Blackburn in the infinite difficulty there would be in attempting to lay down any principle or rule which shall cover all such cases; but I think that the nearest approach to anything like a fixed rule is this: That to entitle a person to damages by reason of a breach of contract, the injury for which compensation is asked should be one that may be fairly taken to have been contemplated by the parties as the possible result of the breach of contract. Therefore you must have something immediately flowing out of the breach of contract complained of, something immediately connected with it, and not merely connected with it through a series of causes intervening between the immediate consequence of the breach of contract and the damage or injury complained of. To illustrate that I cannot take a better case than the one now before us: Suppose that a passenger is put out at a wrong station on a wet night and obliged to walk a considerable distance in the rain, catching a violent cold which ends in a fever, and the passenger is laid up for a couple of months, and loses through this illness the offer of an employment which would have brought him a handsome salary. No one, I think, who understood the law, would say that the loss so occasioned is so connected with the breach of contract as that the carrier breaking the contract could be held liable. Here, I think, it cannot be said the catching cold by the plaintiff's wife is the immediate and necessary effect of the breach of contract, or was one which could be fairly said to have been in the contemplation of the parties. As my brother Blackburn points out, so far as the inconvenience of the walk home is concerned, that must be taken to be reasonably within the contemplation of the parties; because, if a carrier engages to put a person down at a given place, and does not put him down there, but puts him down somewhere else, it must be in the contemplation of everybody that the passenger put down at the wrong place must get to the place of his destination somehow or other. If there are means of conveyance for getting there, he may take those means and make the company responsible for the expense; but if there are no means, I take it to be law that the carrier must compensate him for the personal inconvenience which the absence of those means has necessitated. That flows out of the breach of contract so immediately that the damage resulting must be admitted to be fair subject matter of damages. But in this case the wife's cold and its consequences cannot stand upon the same footing as the personal inconvenience arising from the additional distance which the plaintiffs had to go. It is an effect of the breach of contract in a certain sense, but removed one stage; it is not the primary but the secondary consequence of it; and if in such a case the party recovered damages by reason of the cold caught incidentally on that foot journey, it would be necessary, on the principle so applied, to hold that in the two cases which have been put in the course of the discussion, the party aggrieved would be equally entitled to recover. And yet the moment the cases are stated, everybody would agree that, according to our law, the parties are not entitled to recover.

(Blackburn J. concurred.)

Mellor J.:

I am entirely of the same opinion. I quite agree with my brother Parry, that for the mere inconvenience, such as annoyance and loss of temper, or vexation, or for being disappointed in a particular thing which you have set your mind upon, without real physical inconvenience resulting, you cannot recover damages. That is purely sentimental, and not a case where the word inconvenience, as I here use it, would apply. But I must say, if it is a fact that you arrived at a place where you did not intend to go to, where you are placed, by reason of the breach of contract of the carriers, at a considerable distance from your destination, the case may be otherwise. It is admitted that if there be a carriage you may hire it and ride home and charge the expense to the defendants. The reason why you may hire a carriage and charge the expense to the company is with the view simply of mitigating the inconvenience to which you would otherwise be subject; so that where the inconvenience is real and substantial arising from being obliged to walk home, I cannot see why that should not be capable of being assessed as damages in respect of inconvenience.

1. 1 H & N 408; 26 LJ (Ex) 20.   2. 9 Ex 341; 23 LJ (Ex) 179.

Note

The rule about physical discomfort also applies in sale of real property or house construction contracts. *Murphy v Quality Homes* (HC) 22 June 1976, unrep.

Contracts for the carriage of persons to places of entertainment are also covered: *French v West Clare Rly Co.* (1897) 31 ILT 140. The plaintiff recovered £10 damages when a train transporting him to a concert failed to arrive on time, thereby causing him to miss the event.

In relation to the possibility of damages for distress caused by breach of a commercial contract see *Lennon and Others v Talbot Ireland* (see p. 994 below).

Jarvis v Swans Tours [1973] 1 All ER 71

Lord Denning M.R.:

The plaintiff, Mr Jarvis, is a solicitor employed by a local authority at Barking. In 1969 he was minded to go for Christmas to Switzerland. He was looking forward to a ski-ing holiday. It is his one fortnight's holiday in the year. He prefers it in the winter rather than in the summer.

Mr Jarvis read a brochure issued by Swans Tours Ltd. He was much attracted by the description of Mörlialp, Giswil, Central Switzerland. I will not read the whole of it, but just pick out some of the principal attractions:

> House Party Centre with special resident host . . . Mörlialp is a most wonderful little resort on a sunny plateau . . . Up there you will find yourself in the midst of beautiful alpine scenery, which in winter becomes a wonderland of sun, snow and ice, with a wide variety of fine ski-runs, a skating-rink and an exhilarating toboggan run . . . Why did we choose the Hotel Krone . . . mainly and most of all, because of the *Gemütlichkeit* and friendly welcome you will receive from Herr and Frau Weibel . . . The Hotel Krone has its own Alphütte Bar which will be open several evenings a week . . . No doubt you will be in for a great time, when you book this houseparty holiday . . . Mr Weibel, the charming owner, speaks English.

On the same page, in a special yellow box, it was said: 'Swans Houseparty in Mörlialp. All these Houseparty arrangements are included in the price of your holiday. Welcome party on arrival. Afternoon tea and cake for seven days. Swiss Dinner by candlelight. Fondue-party. Yodler evening. Chali farewell party in the Alphütte Bar. Service of representative.' Alongside on the same page there was a special note about ski-packs: 'Hire of Skis, Sticks and Boots . . . twelve days £11.10.'

In August 1969, on the faith of that brochure, Mr Jarvis booked a fifteen day holiday, with ski-pack. The total charge was £63.45, including Christmas supplement. He was to fly from Gatwick to Zurich on 20 December 1969 and return on 3 January 1970.

The plaintiff went on the holiday, but he was very disappointed. He was a man of about thirty five and he expected to be one of a houseparty of some thirty or so people. Instead, he found there were only thirteen during the first week. In the second week there was no houseparty at all. He was the only person there. Mr Weibel could not speak English. So there was Mr Jarvis, in the second week, in this hotel with no houseparty at all, and no one could speak English, except himself. He was very disappointed, too, with the ski-ing. It was some distance away at Giswil. There were no ordinary length skis. There were only mini-skis, about 3 feet long. So he did not get his ski-ing as he wanted to. In the second week he did get some longer skis for a couple of days, but then, because of the boots, his feet got rubbed and he could not continue even with the long skis. So his ski-ing holiday, from his point of view, was pretty well ruined.

There were many other matters, too. They appear trivial when they are set down in writing, but I have no doubt they loomed large in Mr Jarvis' mind, when coupled with the other disappointments. He did not have the nice Swiss cakes which he was hoping for. The only cakes for tea were potato crisps and little dry nutcakes. The yodler evening consisted of one man from the locality who came in his working clothes for a little while, and sang four or five songs very quickly. The Alphütte Bar was an unoccupied annex which was only open one evening. There was a representative, Mrs Storr, there during the first week, but she was not there during the second week. The matter was summed up by the learned judge: ' . . . during the first week he got a holiday in Switzerland which was to some extent inferior . . . and, as to the second week he got a holiday which was very largely inferior [to what he was led to expect].'

What is the legal position? I think that the statements in the brochure were representations or warranties. The breaches of them give Mr Jarvis a right to damages. It is not necessary to decide whether they were representations or warranties; because, since the Misrepresentation Act 1967, there is a remedy in damages for misrepresentation as well as for breach of warranty.

The one question in the case is: what is the amount of damages? The judge seems to have taken the difference in value between what he paid for and what he got. He said that he intended to give 'the difference between the two values and no other damages' under any other head. He thought that Mr Jarvis had got half of what he paid for. So the judge gave him half the amount which he had paid, namely, £31.72. Mr Jarvis appeals to this court. He says that the damages ought to have been much more.

There is one point I must mention first. Counsel together made a very good note of the judge's judgment. They agreed it. It is very clear and intelligible. It shows plainly enough the ground of the judge's decision; but, by an oversight, it was not submitted to the judge, as it should have been; see *Bruen v Bruce*.[1] In some circumstances we should send it back to the judge for his comments. But I do not think we need do so here. The judge received the notice of appeal and made notes for our consideration. I do not think he would have wished to add to them. We will, therefore, decide the case on the material before us.

What is the right way of assessing damages? It has often been said that on a breach of contract damages cannot be given for mental distress. Thus in *Hamlin v Great Northern Rly Co*.[2] Pollock C.B. said that damages cannot be given 'for the disappointment of mind occasioned by the breach of contract'. And in *Hobbs v London & South Western Rly Co*.[3] Mellor J. said that: ' . . . for the mere inconvenience, such as annoyance and loss of temper, or vexation, or for being disappointed in a particular thing which you have set your mind upon, without real physical inconvenience resulting, you cannot recover damages.' The courts in those days only allowed the plaintiff to recover damages if he suffered physical inconvenience, such as, having to walk five miles home, as in *Hobbs'* case; or to live in an overcrowded house: see *Bailey v Bullock*.[4]

I think that those limitations are out of date. In a proper case damages for mental distress can be recovered in contract, just as damages for shock can be recovered in tort. One such case is a contract for a holiday, or any other contract to provide entertainment and enjoyment. If the contracting party breaks his contract, damages can be given for the disappointment, the distress, the upset and frustration caused by the breach. I know that it is difficult to assess in terms of money, but it is more difficult than the assessment which the courts have to make every day in personal injury cases for loss of amenities. Take the present case. Mr Jarvis has only a fortnight's holiday in the year. He books it far ahead, and looks forward to it all that time. He ought to be compensated for the loss of it.

A good illustration was given by Edmund Davies L.J. in the course of the argument. He put the case of a man who has taken a ticket for Glyndbourne. It is the only night on which he can get there. He hires a car to take him. The car does not turn up. His damages are not limited to the mere cost of the ticket. He is entitled to general damages for the disappointment he has suffered and the loss of the entertainment which he should have had. Here, Mr Jarvis's fortnight's winter holiday has been a grave disappointment. It is true that he was conveyed to Switzerland and back and had meals and bed in the hotel. But that is not what he went for. He went to enjoy himself with all the facilities which the defendants said he would have. He is entitled to damages for the lack of those facilities, and for his loss of enjoyment.

A similar case occurred in 1951. It was *Stedman v Swan's Tours*.[5] A holidaymaker was awarded damages because he did not get the bedroom and the accommodation which he was promised. The County Court Judge awarded him £13 15s. This court increased it to £50.

I think the judge was in error in taking the sum paid for the holiday, £63.45, and halving it. The right measure of damages is to compensate him for the loss of entertainment and enjoyment which he was promised, and which he did not get. Looking at the matter quite broadly, I think the damages in this case should be the sum of £125. I would allow the appeal accordingly.

(Stephenson L.J. agreed.)

Edmund Davies L.J.:

Some of the observations of Mellor J. in the 100 year old case of *Hobbs v London & South Western Rly Co.* call today for reconsideration. I must not be taken to accept that, under modern conditions and having regard to the developments which have taken place in the law of contract since that decision was given, it is right to say, as the learned judge did, that: ' . . . for the mere inconvenience, such as annoyance and loss of temper, or vexation, or for being disappointed in a particular thing which you have set your mind upon, without real physical inconvenience resulting, you cannot recover damages. That is purely sentimental, and not a case where the word inconvenience, as I here use it, would apply.' On the contrary, there is authority for saying that even inconvenience that is not strictly physical may be a proper element in the assessment of damages. In *Griffiths v Evans*,[6] in the course of a dissenting judgment where a solicitor was being sued for negligence in wrongly advising a plaintiff as to his right to sue his employers at common law, Denning L.J. said that the damages should be assessed: 'by taking into account the inconvenience and expense to which |the plaintiff| will be put in suing the employers and the risk of failure.'

Be that as it may, Mellor J. was dealing with a contract of carriage and the undertaking of the railway company was entirely different from that of the defendants in the present case. These travel agents made clear by their lavishly illustrated brochure with its ecstatic text that what they were contracting to provide was not merely air, travel, hotel accommodation and meals of a certain standard. To quote the assurance which they gave regarding the Mörlialp House Party Centre, 'No doubt you will be in for a great time, when you book this houseparty holiday'. The result was that they did not limit themselves to the obligation to ensure that an air passage was booked, that hotel accommodation was reserved, that food was provided and that these items would measure up to the standards they themselves set up. They went further than that. They assured and undertook to provide a holiday of a certain quality, with *Gemütlichkeit* (that is to say, geniality, comfort and cosiness) as its overall characteristics, and 'a great time', the enjoyable outcome which would surely result to all but the most determined misanthrope.

If in such circumstances travel agents fail to provide a holiday of the contracted quality, they are liable in damages. In assessing those damages the court is not, in my judgment, restricted by the £63.45 paid by the client for his holiday. Nor is it confined to matters of physical inconvenience and discomfort.

1. [1959] 2 All ER 375, [1959] 1 WLR 684
2. (1856) 1 H & N 408 at 411
3. (1875) LR 10 QB 111 at 122,
   [1874–80] All ER Rep 458 at 463
4. [1950] 2 All ER 1167
5. (1951) 95 Sol J 727
6. [1953] 2 All ER 1364, [1953] 1 WLR 1424

Note

This line of authority has taken root in Ireland also, as this extract from *The Irish Independent* 28 February 1985 illustrates.

A Dublin housewife was hospitalised suffering from food poisoning and exhaustion after she returned from a Spanish holiday, the Dublin District Court heard yesterday.

Mrs Patricia Hynes and her husband Michael, of Blanchardstown, were awarded £300 plus costs after they sued Happy Holidays Ltd, Blanchardstown.

They claimed that facilities and accommodation in Malaga were 'deplorably inadequate' and that they suffered severe inconvenience and disruption.

Mrs Hynes said she wanted to come home a few days after she arrived. The blankets were dirty and the floors full of dust. She added that she was hospitalised suffering from food poisoning and exhaustion after she returned.

Mr Hynes said he booked the holiday last April. He paid £650.

During the holiday in May, his son had to sleep on a mattress on the floor, while he and his wife slept in two single beds. They made a bed for their daughter out of cushions. He gave examples of facilities which were not as described in the brochure.

Mr Freddie Greehan of Happy Holidays said the family had only paid for three people. Their youngest child, an infant, had travelled free. The apartment block was used every week by about fifty people and he had few complaints.

Awarding damages and costs, Justice Liam McMenamin said any reasonable person reading the brochure would assume they were entitled to fourteen days' comfort in hygienic surroundings. This was not so, he said. He added that the courts must protect consumers.

SECTION SEVEN—LOSS OF BARGAIN—THE IMPORTANCE OF FREEDOM TO SUE IN CONTRACT

McAnarney & McAnarney v Hanrahan and T. E. Potterton Ltd [1994] 1 ILRM 210

Costello J.:

The facts

Nearly nine years ago, on 4 December 1984 and again on 21 December 1984, conversations took place between the plaintiffs and Mr Hanrahan (the first-named defendant). At that time Mr Hanrahan was an auctioneer in the employment of the second-named defendant. The conversation related to the possibility that the plaintiffs might purchase a residential licensed premises in Athboy, County Meath. Not surprisingly recollections are infirm about what was said and a clash of evidence has resulted. Liability in this case depends entirely on which version of the evidence I accept and I should begin this judgment by giving my conclusions on this point.

I think that the recollections of the plaintiffs and their solicitor, Mr Binchy, are more accurate than that of Mr Hanrahan and Mr Potterton (the principal in the defendant firm) and their version of events finds support in the contemporary correspondence. My conclusions on the evidence are therefore as follows:

1. In December 1984 the defendant firm held an auction for the sale of a licensed premises situated in Athboy, County Meath which was then known as 'Farrells' or 'the Central Bar'. It was a small two-storey premises with living accommodation. The premises were held under a lease dated 31 July 1959 for a term of thirty one years from 13 November 1958 at a yearly rent of £80. Thus there was a serious infirmity in the title—the lease would expire within about five years, but under the existing law the lessee would have been entitled to a renewal on expiration, but at the market (and therefore greatly increased) rent then prevailing.

2. The plaintiffs were most anxious to buy the premises, partly as a residence for their family, (for they were then living with Mrs McAnarney's mother at the time with their four young children) and partly as a business venture. The premises were offered for sale without any accounts as to turnover or profitability. Before attending the auction the plaintiffs had obtained particulars of the premises and a promise of financial accommodation for £35,000 from a financial institution. They also had approximately £8,000–£10,000 available to add from property in Northern Ireland.

3. The plaintiffs were late for the auction on 4 December 1984, arriving with their solicitor, Mr Binchy, at the offices of the defendant firm when the auction was over. They were brought into the offices by Mr Hanrahan who told them that there had been a bid at the auction of £54,000 and that the property had then been withdrawn. In fact this information was not true—there had been no such bid at the auction. He asked them to bid £55,000. The plaintiffs said that they would be prepared to make an offer of £55,000 if they could get an increase in their loan facilities. In the course of conversation leading up to this offer Mr Hanrahan referred to the short remaining term of the lease. He informed them that there had been negotiations with the ground landlords about the purchase of the freehold and he told the plaintiffs and Mr Binchy not to worry as the freehold could be purchased for £3,000 or perhaps less. This was not true— there had been no negotiations about the purchase of the freehold and the landlords had not at that time or any time previously been asked to indicate the price at which the freehold could be purchased. Mr Hanrahan was basing his statements on the fact that the principal of the firm, Mr Potterton, had previously negotiated with the landlords in respect of other premises and had done so on terms he considered favourable.

4. The representations were made by Mr Hanrahan, and not by Mr Potterton. He made them for the purpose of inducing the plaintiffs to purchase the premises. Whilst the plaintiffs undoubtedly were anxious to purchase the premises I think that the information concerning the purchase of the freehold materially induced their final decision to purchase at a price higher than that which they originally were prepared to bid.

5. The plaintiffs failed to obtain an increase in their financial accommodation. They could only make an offer of £50,000, which the defendant firm accepted. On 21 December 1984 the plaintiffs again returned to Athboy and signed a proposal to purchase. The agreed price for the premises was £45,000 and £5,000 for the furniture and fittings. Prior to signing the proposal form Mr Hanrahan again assured the plaintiffs that they could probably purchase the freehold for £3,000.

6. The contract for sale is dated 8 January 1985. It contained no contractual obligation on the vendor in relation to the freehold.

7. The plaintiffs duly went into occupation. They paid the contract price of £45,000 but not the sum of £5,000 (which was left outstanding on a promissory note). They

made no effort to purchase the freehold as they were not in a financial position to do so. They got into serious financial difficulties after about eighteen months and in 1986 they then decided to attempt to sell the property. For this purpose they were advised to purchase the freehold. They then discovered that the landlords' price for the freehold was £40,000. In 1988 they instructed their solicitors to write claiming damages against the defendants. Shortly afterwards these proceedings were instituted.

The law

The plaintiffs do not maintain a claim for damages for deceit—their claim is for damages for negligence. It is claimed that Mr Hanrahan owed a duty of care to them and that this duty was breached and in support they rely on the principle established in *Hedley Byrne and Co. Ltd v Heller & Partners Ltd* |1964| AC 465. It is important to bear in mind that this is not a case in which a party to a contract (or his agent) has made a negligent misstatement to another—it is a case of an auctioneer acting for a vendor making a statement to a proposed purchaser. The question for determination is whether in the particular circumstances the auctioneer owed a duty of care to the purchasers. As pointed out in *Hedley Byrne* by Lord Morris at 502–3: 'If, in a sphere in which a person is so placed that others could reasonably rely upon his judgment or his skill or upon his ability to make careful enquiry, a person takes it upon himself to give information or advice to, or allows his information or advice to be passed on to, another person who, as he knows or should know, would place reliance upon it, then a duty of care will arise.'

Here Mr Hanrahan took upon himself responsibility for giving his opinion about the purchase of the freehold. He should have known that the plaintiffs would place reliance on what he told them, particularly as he expressly stated that negotiations had already taken place with the landlords. In my opinion a special relationship thus arose between Mr Hanrahan and the plaintiffs which imposed on him the duty of care in giving the information. He breached that duty in that before making the statement he took no care to see what price the landlords would require for their interest. This case is different to that of *Bank of Ireland v Smith* |1966| IR 646 in which Kenny J. held that no duty of care towards prospective purchasers was imposed on an auctioneer when placing an advertisement which contained misleading information. In this case the particular circumstances of the negotiations and the express assumption of responsibility to which I have referred created a special relationship which was absent in the circumstances which Kenny J. was considering.

It follows, therefore, that if the plaintiffs can establish loss arising from the negligent misstatement that damages are recoverable against Mr Hanrahan personally and against his employers, the second-named defendants, who are vicariously liable for his negligence.

Damages

The plaintiff claims damages under three headings (a) £27,000 being the difference between the represented price of the freehold and its eventual cost, (b) £15,000 spent on refurbishing the premises and (c) general damages for mental distress.

As to (a) the facts relevant to this claim are as follows. The plaintiffs took no step to purchase the freehold after they obtained the assignment of the lease because they were in no financial position to do so. Out of the business takings they raised £15,000 needed for refurbishing the premises but they had not enough cash available to meet the commitment to pay the £5,000 due on the promissory note (this sum was never, in fact, paid). The business was carried on successfully only for a limited period of about eighteen months—thereafter it failed virtually completely and in 1986 the plaintiffs decided to sell the premises. When enquiries were made they found that the landlords were looking for £40,000 for their interest in the premises, a sum which the plaintiffs had no possibility of paying. They remained in the premises and paid no rent after the lease expired and were unable to make any payments to their bankers and eventually they owed them £61,000 approximately. After these proceedings were instituted in 1988 the plaintiffs remained in possession but by 1991 their fortunes changed. The bankers agreed to write down their debt to £21,000, and the plaintiffs were able to negotiate the purchase of the freehold in May 1991 for £30,000 and able to sell the premises with the benefit of the freehold in October 1991 for £80,000. Thus they were able eventually to make a substantial profit on the transaction.

What now falls for consideration is the correct way in which damages should be assessed in a case of negligent misrepresentation.

Damages in such cases are assessed by analogy with claims for damages for deceit. Where damages are claimed for fraudulent misrepresentation then they are assessed so as to put the plaintiff in the position he would have been in if the representation had not been made to him. This is different to the case where damages are being assessed in the case of a claim based on breach of warranty—then damages are assessed on the basis that the warranty was true. So, in the case of a sale of shares induced by fraudulent misrepresentation the normal measure of damages is the purchase price of the shares less their actual value at the time of acquisition (see *McGregor on Damages*, (15th ed.) paras 1718, 1724 and 1939) and in a case like the present one, where a plaintiff has been induced to enter into a contract for the purchase of land by a misrepresentation negligently made the normal measure of damages is the price paid for the land less its actual value at the time of sale. This means that damages are not assessed on the basis as urged on the plaintiff's behalf that he lost a bargain for the purchase of the freehold at £3,000 and should be compensated by a payment of £27,000, being the difference between the price of the freehold (£30,000) and the sum referred to in the misrepresentation. Instead, damages must be assessed on the difference between the price actually paid for the premises (£45,000) and the actual market value of the premises (that is the premises with the infirm title to which I have referred) at the time of sale.

In cases where a client sues his own solicitor or valuer for damages for advice negligently given in relation to the purchase of property the principle which I am applying in this case is also applied. *Ford v White & Co.* [1964] 1 WLR 885 is an example of the operation of this measure of damages. That was a case in which the plaintiff had negotiated for the purchase of land. The land was subject to a restriction on its development and the offered price reflected this fact. The plaintiff's solicitors, however, negligently advised the plaintiffs that the land was not so restricted and acting on that advice the plaintiffs purchased it at the price originally asked. In an action for damages for negligence against his solicitors the plaintiffs contended that the plaintiffs were entitled to be placed in the same position as if the property were indeed free from building restrictions and claimed that the measure of damages was the difference between the market value at the date of the sale subject to restrictions and its market value free from those restrictions. This argument was rejected and the court held that the proper measure of damages was the difference between the market value and the price actually paid. In that case, as the plaintiff had acquired property equal in value to the price paid for it, they had suffered no damage.

The onus is on the plaintiffs to prove their loss. They have adduced no expert evidence of the market value of the premises at the date of sale and the evidence of the auctioneer, Mr Heffernan called on their behalf, was directed to a different aspect of the case. As I do not accept that there were any genuine bids at the auction I cannot rely on the evidence of what happened at the auction to establish the market value of the premises. There was, however, some evidence on which this fact could be established with reasonable accuracy. Before the auction and before any misrepresentation had been made a financial institution was prepared to lend £35,000 to the plaintiffs on the existing (defective) title. It is notorious that financial institutions do not lend 100 per cent of the value of premises in circumstances like the present case and so it follows that the value placed on the premises by the financial institution must have been in excess of the sum to be lent. The plaintiffs' evidence was to the effect that they had out of their own resources a limited sum available to add to the money to be borrowed. Whilst precise evidence of their intended offer has not been forthcoming it appears to me to have been in the region of £45,000 all-in as this was the limit of the finances available to them when the sale actually took place. In this case, I think I can reasonably take the price the plaintiffs were prepared to pay before the misrepresentation as representing the market value. This was a sum of £45,000 which included fixtures and fittings and as these were valued at £5,000 it seems to me that the market value of the premises was approximately £40,000. The plaintiffs' loss under this heading is therefore £5,000, being the difference between the market value of the premises at the date of sale and the sum they actually paid for it.

In addition the plaintiffs have claimed £15,000 special damages being the cost of refurbishing the premises after they took possession of them. This sum was certainly spent but I do not think that it is recoverable as damages from the defendants as it was a sum which would have been spent in any event on the premises and is not a loss which had flowed from the negligent act complained of.

Finally, general damages for mental distress have also been claimed. Compensation for injury to feelings may be included in cases of fraud (see *Doyle v Olby (Ironmongers) Ltd* [1969] 1 QB 158, 170) and in principle in suitable cases I think that damages for negligent misrepresentation in respect of mental distress caused to the plaintiff could be assessed. In the present case, however, I do not think that the distress caused by the defendants' wrongdoing can be measured in any meaningful way and I do not think that the justice of the case requires damages to be increased under this heading.

There will therefore be a decree for £5,000.

SECTION EIGHT—MITIGATION OF DAMAGE

McGregor on Damages (15th ed.) ch. 7

Various Meanings of the Term 'Mitigation'

The expression 'mitigation of damage' is an umbrella term applied, in the books and in the cases, to a number of matters, some of which are related and some of which are completely unconnected. Surprisingly, in view of the importance of the subject these differences have not been fully analysed in English law; yet it is vital to an understanding of the issues to separate the various meanings of the term.

(1) Principal meaning: the three rules as to the avoiding of the consequences of a wrong

The principal meaning of the term 'mitigation', with which alone this chapter deals, concerns the avoiding of the consequences of a wrong, whether tort or breach of contract, and forms probably the only exact use of the term. Even if the subsidiary or residual meanings enumerated below cannot strictly be called incorrect, it would be well if the use of the term 'mitigation' in connection with them was qualified, if not completely discarded, as matters are only confused by employing one term to describe disparate concepts.

The principal meaning itself comprises three different, although closely inter-related, rules. This analysis into three rules, although clearly implicit in the cases, is one which has not formerly been given explicit statement in English law. It is sub-mitted that such a division lends clarity to a difficult topic. The three rules are these.

(1) The first and most important rule is that the plaintiff must take all reasonable steps to mitigate the loss to him consequent upon the defendant's wrong and cannot recover damages for any such loss which he could thus have avoided but has failed, through unreasonable action or inaction, to avoid. Put shortly, the plaintiff cannot recover for avoidable loss.

(2) The second rule is the corollary of the first and is that, where the plaintiff does take reasonable steps to mitigate the loss to him consequent upon the defendant's wrong, he can recover for loss incurred in so doing; this is so even though the resulting damage is in the event greater than it would have been had the mitigating steps not been taken. Put shortly, the plaintiff can recover for loss incurred in reasonable attempts to avoid loss.

(3) The third rule is that, where the plaintiff does take steps to mitigate the loss to him consequent upon the defendant's wrong and these steps are successful, the defendant is entitled to the benefit accruing from the plaintiff's action and is liable only for the loss as lessened; this is so even though the plaintiff would not have been debarred under the first rule from recovering the whole loss, which would have accrued in the absence of his successful mitigating steps, by reason of these steps not being ones which were required of him under the first rule. Put shortly, the plaintiff cannot recover for avoided loss.

Note

Sometimes the opportunity to mitigate loss occasioned by breach of contract may result from an offer made by the party in breach.

Payzu Ltd *v* Saunders [1919] 2 KB 580

McCardie J.:

By a contract in writing dated 9 November 1917, the defendant, who was a dealer in silk, agreed to sell to the plaintiffs 200 pieces of crêpe de chine at 4s 6d a yard and 200 pieces at 5s 11d a yard, 'delivery as required January to September 1918; conditions 2.5 per cent. One month,' which meant that payment for goods delivered up to the twentieth day of any month should be made on the twentieth day of the following month, subject to 2.5 per cent discount. At the request of the plaintiffs the defendant delivered, in November 1917, a certain quantity of the goods under the contract, the price of which amounted to £76, less 2.5 per cent discount. On 21 December the plaintiffs drew a cheque in favour of the defendant in payment of these goods, but the cheque was never received by the defendant. Early in January 1918, the defendant telephoned to the plaintiffs asking why she had not received a cheque. The plaintiffs then drew another cheque, but owing to a delay in obtaining the signature of one of the plaintiffs' directors, this cheque was not sent to the defendant until 16 January. On that day the plaintiffs gave an order by telephone for further deliveries under the contract. The defendant in the belief, which was in fact erroneous, that the plaintiffs' financial position was such that they could not have met the cheque which they alleged had been drawn in December, wrote to the plaintiffs on 16 January refusing to make any further deliveries under the contract unless the plaintiffs paid cash with each order. The plaintiffs refused to do this, and after some further correspondence brought this action claiming damages for breach of contract. The damages claimed were the difference between the market prices in the middle of February 1918, and the contract prices of the two classes of goods, the difference alleged being respectively 1s 3d and 1s 4d a yard.

. . .

Bankes L.J.:

At the trial of this case the defendant, the present respondent, raised two points: first, that she had committed no breach of the contract of sale, and secondly that, if there was a breach, yet she had offered and was always ready and willing to supply the pieces of silk, the subject of the contract, at the contract price for cash; that it was unreasonable on the part of the appellants not to accept that offer, and that therefore they cannot claim damages beyond what they would have lost by paying cash with each order instead of having a month's credit and a discount of 2.5 per cent. We must take it that this was the offer made by the respondent. The case was fought and the learned judge has given judgment upon that footing. It is true that the correspondence suggests that the respondent was at one time claiming an increased price. But in this court it must be taken that the offer was to supply the contract goods at the contract price except that payment was to be by cash instead of being on credit.

In these circumstances the only question is whether the appellants can establish that as matter of law they were not bound to consider any offer made by the respondent because of the attitude she had taken up. Upon this point McCardie J. referred to British *Westinghouse Electric and Manufacturing Co. v Underground Electric Rlys Co. of London*,[1] where Lord Haldane L.C. said:

> The fundamental basis is thus compensation for pecuniary loss naturally flowing from the breach; but this first principle is qualified by a second, which imposes on a plaintiff the duty of taking all reasonable steps to mitigate the loss consequent on the breach, and debars him from claiming any part of the damage which is due to his neglect to take such steps. In the words of James L.J. in *Dunkirk Colliery Co. v Lever*[2]: 'What the plaintiffs are entitled to is the full amount of the damage which they have really sustained by a breach of the contract. The person who has broken the contract not being exposed to additional cost by reason of the plaintiffs not doing what they ought to have done as reasonable men, and the plaintiffs not being under any obligation to do anything otherwise than in the ordinary course of business.

It is plain that the question what is reasonable for a person to do in mitigation of his damages cannot be a question of law but must be one of fact in the circumstances of each particular case. There may be cases where as matter of fact it would be unreasonable to expect a plaintiff to consider any offer made in view of the treatment he has received from the defendant. If he had been rendering personal services and had been dismissed after being accused in presence of others of being a thief, and if after that his employer had offered to take him back into his service, most persons would think he was justified in refusing the offer, and that it would be unreasonable to ask him in this way to mitigate the damages in an action of wrongful dismissal. But that is not to state a principle of law, but a conclusion of fact to be arrived at on a consideration of all the circumstances of the case. [Counsel for the plaintiffs] complained that the respondent had treated his clients so badly that it would be unreasonable to expect them to listen to any proposition she might make. I do not agree. In my view each party was ready to accuse the other of conduct unworthy of a high commercial reputation, and there was nothing to justify the appellants in refusing to consider the respondent's offer. I think the learned judge came to a proper conclusion on the facts, and that the appeal must be dismissed.

Scrutton L.J.:

I am of the same opinion. Whether it be more correct to say that a plaintiff must minimise his damages, or to say that he can recover no more than he would have suffered if he had acted reasonably, because any further damages do not reasonably follow from the defendant's breach, the result is the same. The plaintiff must take 'all reasonable steps to mitigate the loss consequent on the breach', and this principle 'debars him from claiming any part of the damage which is due to his neglect to take such steps': *British Westinghouse Electric and Manufacturing Co. v Underground Electric Rlys Co. of London*, per Lord Haldane L.C. [counsel for the plaintiffs] has contended that in considering what steps should be taken to mitigate the damage all contractual relations with the party in default must be excluded. That is contrary to my experience. In certain cases of personal service it may be unreasonable to expect a plaintiff to consider an offer from the other party who has grossly injured him; but in commercial contracts it is generally reasonable to accept an offer from the party in default. However, it is always a question of fact. About the law there is no difficulty.

^{1.} [1912] AC 673, 689. ^{2.} (1878) 9 ChD 20, 25.

(Eve J. agreed.)

Lennon and Others *v* Talbot Ireland Ltd (HC), 20 December 1985, unrep.

Keane J.:

In these proceedings, the plaintiffs claim damages in respect of what they say was the wrongful termination by the defendants of certain agreements entered into by the plaintiffs with the defendants.

The background to the dispute is as follows. Each of the plaintiffs had entered into main dealership agreements at various times with the defendants in respect of private and commercial vehicles imported by them and distributed throughout the Republic of Ireland. The defendants notified the plaintiffs by letter dated 5 October 1984, that with effect from 2 November 1984 the Talbot range would be distributed in the Republic of Ireland by the Gowan Group. The plaintiffs contend in these proceedings that this letter constituted an unlawful termination by the defendants of the agreements and claim compensation for damage which they allege they have sustained as a result. While a defence was delivered in the proceedings denying liability, it was conceded shortly before the case came on for hearing that the agreements had been wrongfully terminated by the defendants. This concession was, however, withdrawn almost immediately before the hearing in respect of the sixth-named defendants, Gleeson Brothers Motor Engineers Ltd (who are referred to in this judgment as 'Gleesons'). None of the agreements contained any provision for termination, but it was agreed by the parties that six months' notice would have been reasonable in the case of an agreement such as this. In respect of the plaintiffs other than Gleesons, the case accordingly became an assessment of damages only.

Gleesons wrote to the defendants on 29 November 1984 saying that they thought it was essential for them to continue getting supplies from the Gowan Group, as it was not possible for them to suspend operations in mid-stream. [Counsel for the defendants] submitted that in writing such a letter, Gleesons had acquiesced in the assignment by Talbot of their liability under the dealership agreements to the Gowan Group. This letter was, however, written after the defendants had by their letter of 5 October wrongfully terminated each of the dealership agreements and represented no more than an attempt by Gleesons to mitigate the loss arising from that wrongful termination. It follows, in my view, that they also are entitled to damages for the wrongful termination of the agreement.

While it will be necessary at a later stage to consider the position of the plaintiffs individually, since their circumstances differed significantly from one another, there are also features common to all the claims which can be conveniently considered at the outset.

All the plaintiffs claimed that, as a result of the wrongful termination by the defendants of the dealership agreements, they had lost profits that they would other-wise have earned on the sale of vehicles and spare parts, the carrying out of repair work and the provision of spare parts and repair work to which the customers were entitled under 'warranties'. The defendants contended that, even if such losses had been established, they were effectively the result of the plaintiffs' negligent failure to mitigate their loss by entering into new dealership arrangements with the Gowan Group under which they would have been entitled to a continued supply of Talbot vehicles and spare parts. The plaintiffs for their part said that it was unreasonable to expect them to enter into new agreements with the Gowan Group in order to ensure themselves a continuing supply of Talbot vehicles and parts. They claimed that the arrangements with the Gowan Group would be significantly different in the following respects:

(1) The defendants were manufacturers, whereas the Gowan Group were not. It was said that this would put the plaintiffs in the invidious position of depending for their supplies of vehicles and spare parts on a firm which was in direct competition with them rather than a manufacturer such as the defendants who could be relied on not to discriminate between the individual dealers and had never done so in the past.

(2) The plaintiffs had established a relationship of trust and confidence with the defendants, which did not exist between them and the Gowan Group.

(3) The plaintiffs were afforded the valuable facility by the defendants of free stocking of vehicles until they were sold. It was said that the Gowan Group, by contrast, required to be paid cash for vehicles as they were supplied to the dealer except in the case of models which were not selling particularly well.

(4) In the case of those dealers who were limited companies, the Gowan Group required the directors to enter into personal guarantees, whereas no such requirement had been imposed upon the dealers by the defendants.

(5) The Gowan Group were engaged in the export of vehicles from the Republic of Ireland in competition with some of the plaintiffs.

While some of these matters were in dispute during the hearing, there was and could be no dispute as to the first. It was beyond controversy that the Gowan Group were in a different position from the defendants: they were distributors of vehicles and not manufacturers. It is obvious that their interests as distributors would not necessarily coincide with those of the plaintiffs and it is not surprising that the plaintiffs were concerned that their interests might suffer under the new dispensation.

[Counsel for the defendants] relied on the decisions in *Payzu v Saunders* [1919] 2 KB 581 and *Houndsditch Warehouse Co. Ltd v Waltex* [1944] KB 579 as establishing that where the defendant is in breach of contract but gives the plaintiff an opportunity to mitigate his loss, the plaintiff refuses that offer at his peril, because if the court should subsequently determine that it was a reasonable offer the plaintiff is then confined to such losses as he suffered up to the date of the offer. But these decisions do not assist the defendants in circumstances such as arose in the present case where the new arrangement proposed was significantly different from the existing arrangement in a way which could only be detrimental to the plaintiffs. In the words of Lord Macmillan in *Banco de Portugal v Waterlow & Sons Ltd* [1932] AC 452 at 506:

> Where the sufferer from a breach of contract finds himself in consequence of that breach placed in a position of embarrassment, the measures which he may be driven to adopt in order to extricate himself ought not to be weighed in nice scales at the instance of the party whose breach of contract has occasioned the difficulty. It is often easy after an emergency has passed to criticise the steps which have been taken to meet it, but such criticism does not come well from those who have themselves created the emergency. The law is satisfied if the party placed in a difficult situation by reason of the breach of a duty owed to him has acted reasonably in the adoption of remedial measures, and he will not be held disentitled to recover the cost of such measures merely because the party in breach can suggest that other measures less burdensome to him might have been taken.

I am satisfied that the refusal of the plaintiffs, other than the sixth-named plaintiffs, to enter into arrangements with the Gowan Group did not constitute an unreasonable refusal by the plaintiffs to mitigate the loss flowing from the defendants' admitted breach.

The plaintiffs are entitled to the damages which might fairly and reasonably be considered as arising naturally from the breach or might reasonably be supposed to have been in the contemplation of both parties at the time of the agreements as the probable result of the breach. It was agreed that in the present case this meant that the plaintiffs were entitled to such damages as would restore them to the position that they would have been in had the appropriate length of notice been given.

Each of the plaintiffs claimed damages under a number of different headings which must be considered individually.

Loss of profit on sales of private cars and commercial vehicles

Each of the plaintiffs claim damages under this heading. In each case the method adopted of calculating the amount of the loss was broadly the same. The number of cars and vans sold in a period of up to two years preceding the breach was divided by an appropriate figure in order to arrive at the probable sales of vehicles during the six months' period had the dealership agreements remained in force. The average gross profit on the sales of such vehicles during the relevant period was then calculated and multiplied by the number of estimated sales during the six months' period.

The validity of this approach was questioned by the defendants on a number of grounds. First, it was said that taking a period of up to two years gave a necessarily distorted result, having regard to the overall decline in motor car sales in the Republic during the relevant period and the relative decline in the defendants' share of the market during that period. In the second place, it was said that this approach had no regard to the actual stocks of cars which the plaintiffs had on hands as of 1 January 1985, i.e. during the six months' period following termination. In the third place, it was argued that the actual sales by the dealers who accepted the new dispensation provided a more reliable guide to the projected losses than the sales in the period preceding termination. In the fourth place, it was said that the estimate of loss was distorted by taking the gross profit rather than the net and that the calculations of the plaintiffs also failed to take into account the incidence of the Value Added Tax [VAT] on each transaction. I will consider each of these contentions in turn.

It is quite clear that the overall volume of car sales in the Republic was declining in the years immediately preceding the withdrawal by the defendants and that their relative share of the market was also declining. The figures set out below, demonstrate this quite clearly.

Year	Talbot Sales	Total Sales	Talbot percentage of Sales
1984	542	56,451	1%
1983	944	60,769	1.6%
1982	1,063	72,811	1.5%
1981	2,065	106,070	1.9%
1980	2,630	93,604	2.8%
1979	3,951	97,886	4%

The only inference which can be reasonably drawn from these figures is that there was a significant decline in the total volume of car sales in the Republic during the two years preceding the termination of the agreement and that during the same period there was also a significant decline in the defendants' share of the market. I think that the evidence of the many witnesses concerned in the motor industry who were called by both sides confirms that this was, on the whole, the general picture, although the circumstances of individual dealers naturally differed. I have come to the conclusion that, in these circumstances, the safer guide to the profits which would actually have been earned by each of the plaintiffs during the six months' period had proper notice of termination been given is the six months' period immediately preceding such termination. I am not satisfied that the sales of the dealers who accepted the new dispensation during the six months' period provide a reliable guide to the projected sales of the plaintiffs, since the circumstances of individual dealers will obviously vary greatly depending on their area of operation and other factors.

The evidence also established that some of the plaintiffs had stocks on hand at 1 January 1985. The relevant figures are: the second-named plaintiff (1), the third-named plaintiff (6), the fifth-named plaintiff (3), the seventh-named plaintiff (5) and the eight-named plaintiff (3). The plaintiffs contend that their failure to dispose of these units (some of which might of course have been subsequently sold prior to the expiration of the six months' period) was due to the lack of confidence in the defendants' products following their abrupt withdrawal from the Irish market. I have come to the conclusion that while there is some substance in the plaintiffs' contention one cannot fairly disregard the actual units unsold in arriving at the damages to which the plaintiffs are entitled.

The defendants' claim that the loss of profits should be quantified in terms of net rather than gross profits was based on the contention that the plaintiffs' approach ignored the savings that were effected by losing the sales in question. While the evidence undoubtedly established that there were direct costs associated with the sales which should be taken into account in arriving at the appropriate profit figure, it is also clear that the fixed overheads, consisting in the main of charges associated with the premises and wages and salaries, should not be taken into account. None of the plaintiffs actually ceased business as a result of the notice of termination and the situation would have been no different had the appropriate notice been given. Accordingly, the plaintiffs, if they wished to remain in business, had to continue paying these fixed overheads and they are not an appropriate deduction, in my view, in arriving at the actual loss which they sustained.

While again the circumstances of the plaintiffs differed substantially, the direct costs associated with the sales of vehicles which constituted an appropriate deduction in order to arrive at the loss of profits figure were in many instances the same. The principal items were:

First service and pre-delivery inspection:	£40.00
Petrol:	£5.00
Collection cost:	£10.00
Wax polishing:	£12.00
*Commission:	£30.00
Advertising:	£20.00
Used vehicle service	£38.00
TOTAL	£155.00

* (It should be noted that some of the plaintiffs did not pay any commission to a salesman.)

The difficulty as to the effect of VAT on the profit figure can best be illustrated by reference to an example which the accountants and other financial experts on both sides used. In the case of a sale by Traynor Motors Ltd (Invoice No. 002581), a Talbot Solara was sold at a price of £9,015 (including VAT). Since the customer traded in a car against the new car, he was allowed £4,740 on his old car. The amount of VAT actually paid by the garage, however, in respect of this deal was £799.39. When the old car was in due course sold, there was again a trade-in, the allowance this time being £3,250. The cost to the customer (including VAT) was £4,950, so that there was an amount due by the customer of £1,700. The garage remitted £317.89 in respect of VAT. There was then a third sale, the cost this time to the customer being £3,000 (including VAT) and the trade-in allowance £1,650, leaving an amount due from the customer of £1,350. The sum of £252.44 was remitted by the garage in respect of VAT. Finally the traded-in car on this last transaction was sold for cash, the price being £650 including VAT. The amount of VAT remitted on this occasion was £121.54. The cost of the vehicle to Traynor Motors Ltd as invoiced by the defendants was £6,814 which included a sum of £1,274.43 in respect of VAT. These figures when analysed and when allowance is made for internal costs of £170.73 show a net profit to the dealer of £773.44. The total of VAT payments by the garage in respect of the four sales was £1,491.26. They would, however, be entitled to a refund of the VAT which they had paid to the defendants initially, i.e. £1,274.43. It follows that, to arrive at the actual net profit, one should deduct the difference between the VAT remitted by the garage and the amount refunded to them. When this figure of £216.83 is deducted from the net profit, it results in a true net profit figure of £556.61. This example also illustrates, incidentally, the normal method by which the profit is calculated in retail car sales, assuming, of course, as is frequently the case, that there are a series of trade-ins, the final profit figure being known in the trade as the 'wash out' figure.

The evidence as to the gross profits actually earned varied considerably as between the various plaintiffs. I am satisfied that these variations are due to a number of factors. In the first place, the discounts available to the dealers were obviously affected by the actual volume of business which they put through. In the second place, the absence of documentation made it difficult to establish with precision what deductions, if any, were being made in certain cases in respect of direct costs attributable to the sales and the incidence of VAT. In the third place, in the case of some dealers one at least of the direct costs was not relevant since commission was not paid to a salesman in respect of relevant sales.

The evidence given by the different plaintiffs in respect of gross profits is dealt with hereunder individually. Evidence was given on behalf of the defendants by Mr Ian McNeil, the general manager of Gowan Merrion Ltd, to the effect that the gross profit in respect of his garage on the sale of Talbot Motor Cars for the twelve month period ending in October, 1984 was £302. After making the deductions already referred to this left a gross profit figure of £147.

(1) The first-named plaintiff

The number of vehicles sold by the first-named plaintiff in the six month period to October 1984 was 9, but the claim is based on a projected sale of 6 for the relevant period. The average gross profit is claimed in the sum of £530, but the evidence did not establish with any degree of precision how this figure had been arrived at. If one assumes that the figure should be reduced by approximately 25 per cent in order to allow for the difference between VAT remitted by the garage and ultimately refunded, the figure is reduced to approximately £400 in the case of motor cars and £450 in the case of vans. It seems probable that the amount of the direct costs attributable to each sale would have been less than in other cases and, making a deduction of £100 in the case of each category, this leaves one with a gross profit of £300 in the cases of the motor vehicles and £350 in the case of vans. In this case, accordingly, the recoverable figure for loss of profit on the sale of cars is £1,200 and on the sale of vans £700.

(2) The second-named plaintiff

In this case, the evidence established that there had been only one sale in the six months' period prior to October 1984 as contrasted with the figure of three in the plaintiff's claim. The plaintiff had one unit in stock during the six month period and I am not satisfied that he has established as a matter of probability that he lost any sales in respect of the breach.

(3) The third-named plaintiff and fourth-named plaintiff

These two companies can conveniently be taken together, although they are of course separate legal entities. The figures in this case show the greatest disparity between the sales in the six months' period prior to October 1984 and the projected sales for the six months' period thereafter. The significant discrepancy is in the case of the Dublin-based company which sold only one vehicle in the six months' period prior to termination, although the estimated loss of sales is 31.

Taking the third-named plaintiff first, the evidence established that 34 cars and 9 vans were sold during the relevant periods. The gross profit claimed in the case of the sale of cars was £332.72 and in the case of vans £577.21. I am satisfied that in each of these cases the figures are adequately supported by the evidence. There were, however, 6 cars still in stock and accordingly the appropriate multiplier is 28. In the result the third-named plaintiff is entitled to £7,319 in respect of loss of profit on the sale of cars and £5,194 in respect of loss of profit on the sale of vans. The fourth-named plaintiff is, however, entitled to £332.72 only in respect of the loss of profit on the sale of cars.

(4) *The fifth-named plaintiff*

In this case the evidence established that 12 vehicles had been sold in the six month period prior to October 1984. The estimated figure for the six months' period after termination was 19. The estimated gross profit on the sale of cars was £500, but again I am not satisfied that this figure was established by evidence. After making an allowance for the VAT element I think that a further deduction of £100 in respect of direct costs would be reasonable. This would give a gross profit figure of £275 and the multiplier after allowing for the 3 cars in stock is 9. This gives a total loss of profits of £2,475.

(5) *The sixth-named plaintiff*

In this case, the sales of cars for the six months' period prior to termination were 27, as opposed to the estimated figure of 22 for the six months' period after termination. The evidence established a gross profit figure of £489 but again I am satisfied that in order to allow for the incidence of VAT this must be reduced by 25 per cent, giving a gross profit figure of £368 in respect of each car. This gives a total of £8,096 in respect of the claim for loss of profits on the sale of cars.

(6) *The seventh-named plaintiff*

The figure on which the claim was based in this case is the same (41) as the figure for sales in the six months' period prior to termination. Making an allowance for the vehicles in stock, the appropriate multiplier is 36. The gross profit figure proved is £536.71. The recoverable amount is accordingly £19,317.96.

(7) *The eighth-named plaintiff*

The evidence established in this case that only 5 cars had been sold during the six months' period prior to termination although the claim was on the basis of projected sales of 24 in the six months' period after termination. A gross profit figure of £750 was claimed, but again it was not supported satisfactorily by evidence. I think that the actual gross profits achieved are unlikely to have been higher than in the case of the first- or second-named plaintiffs and this would suggest a gross profit figure of £275. Allowing for the 3 cars in stock this results in a total established loss of £550.

Loss of profits on sales of spare parts

Again there were variations in the circumstances affecting the individual plaintiffs. Obviously the discount allowed to the dealer depended on the volume of business being done and, in particular, stock orders attracted a larger rate of discount than individual orders.

The principal area of controversy again, however, was whether the appropriate figure to take in calculating a loss of profit was the gross profit or the net profit after deducting overheads. For the reasons I have already given when dealing with the car sales, I am satisfied that the appropriate figure for the purpose of ascertaining the plaintiffs' loss is the gross profit.

There were some discrepancies between the figures produced by the plaintiffs in respect of the gross profits on sales of spare parts and the figures produced by Mr Michael Davenport, who had been the parts manager for the defendants. This is explained in part by the fact that Mr Davenport was taking the six months' period only from April to September, 1984. However, while the plaintiffs' use of the gross profit figure was contested by the defendants, the accuracy in general of their records as to purchases of spare parts from the defendants and their retail sales was not seriously questioned. With some modifications, accordingly, I have taken these figures as the basis of calculation so far as this heading of claim is concerned.

In the case of the second-named plaintiff, I think that the figure of 33$\frac{1}{3}$ per cent profit is not established by the evidence and that a figure of 25 per cent would be more realistic. In the case of the sixth-named plaintiff, the sum of £10,757 claimed was amended in the course of the hearing to the sum of £6,961.

The defendants also contended that in determining the amount of any loss sustained by the plaintiffs in respect of the sale of spare parts, one had to have regard to the fact that the plaintiffs retained stocks of spare parts after the notice of termination which should have been taken into account in assessing their possible sales. The evidence, however, on this matter was not sufficiently exact to permit of any accurate estimate being made and accordingly I have not taken this into account in assessing the damages to which the plaintiffs are entitled under this heading.

Loss of profit on future repairs

This claim is based on the assumption that in the case of each vehicle sold a profit figure of £100 in respect of repairs in the future to that vehicle would have been realised by the plaintiffs. I am prepared to accept this as an appropriate figure. It is, however, necessary to adjust the figures claimed having regard to the findings I have already made in relation to the loss of sales of cars.

Loss of profit on future warranty work

In the case of what is described in the trade as 'warranty work', the customer is not charged. Accordingly, the dealer is recouped the sums he paid for the parts involved. In respect of the labour, however, he is normally allowed a rate per hour which is significantly higher than the actual cost to him of the labour and this, which is the only profit element in the 'warranty' work appears on average, from the evidence, to have amounted to £100 per vehicle. This amount is also clearly recoverable, subject again to adjustments as to the number of car sales of vehicles that would have been affected.

Other heads of claim

A number of other claims were also advanced. Some of the plaintiffs alleged that they had been put to expense in removing signs associated with the sale of the defendants' products by them. No reason was suggested as to why these signs would not in any event have been removed at the end of the six months' period had the proper notice been given and, accordingly, it appears to me that the plaintiffs are not entitled to any damages under this heading. Similarly, the first-named plaintiff claimed the cost of erecting a concrete shed which he said he had been encouraged to put up by the defendants and which he said was unnecessary for his business and only involved him in additional rates, now that the franchise had been withdrawn. This would have been the consequence whether or not the appropriate length of notice had been given, and, accordingly, in my view no damages are recoverable in respect of this item.

The dealership agreement in each case contained a provision that on the termination of the agreement the defendants would buy back from the plaintiffs on the terms specified in the agreement unused vehicle parts. Following the termination of the agreements, the plaintiffs formulated claims under this clause in respect of the re-purchase of the parts in question by the defendants. The plaintiffs claimed to be entitled to a sum in respect of the expense of preparing this claim. It is clear, however, that the claim under this clause does not arise out of the wrongful termination by the defendants of the agreement. Had the proper length of notice been given, the relevant clause in the dealership agreements would still have been operative and in order to make a claim on foot of it the plaintiffs would have been put to precisely the same expense. I am satisfied, however, that each of the plaintiffs was occasioned additional travelling and other expenses as a result of the wrongful termination and that these items of loss are properly recoverable. I will accordingly allow a sum of £500 in respect of each plaintiff under this heading.

Some of the plaintiffs also claim to be entitled to damages for what is described as an 'anticipated loss' on trade-in guarantees. This arose because with a view to increasing sales the defendants introduced a scheme under which a dealer could guarantee a customer a minimum trade-in price on a new car within a specified period. The defendants agreed to indemnify the dealers against any loss they might sustain as a result of giving such guarantees. There was no evidence that any of the plaintiffs had been required to pay any sums in respect of these guarantees and it follows that the defendants have never been asked to implement their indemnity. I am satisfied that the claim in respect of this item of alleged loss is premature and unfounded.

Each of the plaintiffs also claimed damages in respect of the increase in bank overdraft interest due to loss of cash flow which they claimed resulted from the defendants' wrongful termination of the agreement. In a period of severe recession it was inevitable that the businesses of each of the plaintiffs would have been affected by the overall decline in business and it is not surprising that in such circumstances they should have found it necessary to obtain increased accommodation from their banks. It is quite another matter, however, to attribute this to the defendants' premature termination of their dealership agreements and in my view the evidence falls far short of establishing that it was the consequence of that breach. In any event, had the appropriate six months' notice been given, the plaintiffs would have inevitably sustained a reduction in their cash flow as a result of the loss of the dealership and, although in some cases other dealerships were obtained to replace the lost Talbot franchise, it seems reasonable to assume that, even had the appropriate notice been given, a period would have elapsed before the franchise was replaced during which the cash flow would inevitably have been diminished. It seems to me that the attribution of the increased bank interest to the premature termination of the dealership agreements is too conjectural and accordingly the plaintiffs are not entitled to this item of claim.

In the case of the plaintiffs who are not limited companies the first, second and fifth—a claim has been made for damages for the distress and anxiety caused to them by the defendants' breach of contract. I accept the evidence of the individual plaintiffs that the action of the defendants caused them considerable anxiety resulting in at least two cases in their seeking medical assistance. Again, however, two features of this claim must be borne in mind. The individual plaintiffs would in any event have undoubtedly experienced stress and anxiety as a result of the adverse trading conditions in the motor industry in recent years which have been abundantly demonstrated in the evidence. In the second place, in the case of a relatively small business the withdrawal of the franchise was obviously a far more serious matter to the entrepreneur than in the case of the large scale businesses which in any event enjoyed the protection of limited liability. The withdrawal of the franchise in a peremptory manner rather than in accordance with the six months' notice of termination may well have been a factor in the ill health experienced by the plaintiffs concerned, but it is only one element in a larger picture. In the result, while I am satisfied the plaintiffs are entitled to some compensation in respect of this claim, it must inevitably be of a modest order. I will accordingly award £750 general damages in respect of the three individual plaintiffs for the general anxiety and inconvenience caused to them by the defendants' action.

Finally, in the case of the sixth-named plaintiff there is a claim which is peculiar to it, i.e. a 'loss on volume bonus'. This provided that, in the event of the dealer's sales reaching a particular level in a specified period, the dealer would be entitled to a bonus in respect of each car sold. The evidence established, however, that the bonus scheme as such had been replaced in 1983 by other incentive schemes such as volume discounts which would inevitably have been reflected in the gross profits. I am accordingly satisfied that this item is not recoverable.

SECTION NINE—PENALTY CLAUSES AND LIQUIDATED DAMAGES

Treitel, G. H. Remedies for Breach of Contract, Oxford: Clarendon, 1988, 212–3. (Footnotes omitted.)

Purposes of penalty clauses

One purpose of penalty clauses is to fix in advance the damages payable in the event of default. That is in itself a perfectly legitimate and indeed laudable purpose. It obviates the often difficult tasks of assessing the aggrieved party's loss and of determining how much of that loss is legally recoverable. A clause which serves this purpose may even be advantageous from the point of view of the defaulting party in enabling him with some degree of certainty to know in advance what his liability will be in the event of default.

A second object of penalty clauses is precisely to limit a defaulting party's liability; and this is true in spite of the fact that penalty clauses are distinct in their legal nature from limitation clauses. This second object of penalty clauses is not always achieved; we shall see that in many legal systems liability is not necessarily limited to the amount of the payment stipulated.

A third object of penalty clauses is to provide a means of pressure on the debtor so as to coerce him into performing his principal undertaking. Indeed, in France penalty clauses have been described as a sort of *astreinte*, an analogy which is particularly apt where the penalty clause provides for a series of payments for each designated period of delay. It is obvious that the use of penalty clauses for this purpose is a potential source of abuse in that it may enable the creditor to exert an amount of pressure on the debtor which a particular legal system regards as excessive. It may at the same time enable the creditor to recover a sum of money which manifestly and very considerably exceeds the amount of his loss; and there is a natural reluctance on the part of the courts to make awards which drastically cut across the rules of law which determine the assessment of damages.

Such considerations have led to restrictions on the enforceability of penalty clauses in many legal systems: as a Scottish judge has said, 'the law will not let people punish each other.' This represents the attitude of Anglo-American law in which certain kinds of penalty clauses are wholly invalid, and indeed are sometimes said to be contrary to 'public policy' or to be 'unlawful' contracts; it is also the basis of the rule adopted in German law, in French law (since 1975) and in certain other systems by which the courts have power to reduce the amount of a disproportionately high penalty. These solutions are of course open to the objection that they tend to subvert the first and legitimate purpose of penalty clauses; and this purpose is best served by the general principle (which formerly prevailed in France and is still found in Belgium) of giving literal effect to penalty clauses. What is at stake here is the perennial conflict between certainty and justice; and in fact some degree of compromise is to be found in all the legal systems under consideration.

A. AGREED DAMAGES AND PENALTY CLAUSES

Dunlop Pneumatic Tyre Co. *v* New Garage and Motor Co. [1915] AC 79

Lord Dunedin:

My Lords, the appellants, through an agent, entered into a contract with the respondents under which they supplied them with their goods, which consisted mainly of motor tyre covers and tubes. By this contract, in respect of certain concessions as to discounts, the respondents bound themselves not to do several things, which may be shortly set forth as follows: not to tamper with the manufacturers' marks; not to sell to any private customer or co-operative society at prices less than the current price list issued by the Dunlop company; not to supply to persons whose supplies the Dunlop company had decided to suspend; not to exhibit or to export without the Dunlop company's assent. Finally, the agreement concluded (clause 5), 'We agree to pay the Dunlop Pneumatic Tyre Co. Ltd the sum of £5 for each and every tyre, cover or tube sold or offered in breach of this agreement, as and by way of liquidated damages and not as a penalty.'

The appellants, having discovered that the respondents had sold covers and tubes at under the current list price, raised action and demanded damages. The case was tried and the breach in fact held proved. An inquiry was directed before the master as to damages. The master inquired, and assessed the damages at £250, adding this explanation: 'I find that it was left open to me to decide whether the £5 fixed in the agreement was penalty or liquidated damages. I find that it was liquidated damages.'

The respondents appealed to the Court of Appeal, when the majority of that court, Vaughan Williams and Swinfen Eady L.JJ., held, Kennedy L.J. dissenting, that the said sum of £5 was a penalty, and entered judgment for the plaintiffs the sum of £2 as nominal damages. Appeal from that decision is now before your Lordships' House.

My Lords, we had the benefit of a full and satisfactory argument, and a citation of the very numerous cases which have been decided on this branch of the law. The matter has been handled, and at no distant date, in the courts of highest resort. I particularly refer to the *Clydebank* case[1] in your Lordships' House and the cases of *Public Works Commissioner v Hills*[2] and *Webster v Bosanquet*[3] in the Privy Council. In both of these cases many of the previous cases were considered. In view of that fact, and of the number of the authorities available, I do not think it advisable to attempt any detailed review of the various cases, but I shall content myself with stating succinctly the various propositions which I think are deducible from the decisions which rank as authoritative:

1. Though the parties to a contract who use the words 'penalty' or 'liquidated damages' may *prima facie* be supposed to mean what they say, yet the expression used is not conclusive. The court must find out whether the payment stipulated is in truth a penalty or liquidated damages. This doctrine may be said to be found *passim* in nearly every case.

2. The essence of a penalty is a payment of money stipulated as *in terrorem* of the offending party; the essence of liquidated damages is a genuine covenanted pre-estimate of damage (*Clydebank Engineering and Shipbuilding Co. v Don Jose Ramos Yzquierdo y Castaneda*).

3. The question whether a sum stipulated is penalty or liquidated damages is a question of construction to be decided upon the terms and inherent circumstances of

each particular contract, judged of as at the time of the making of the contract, not as at the time of the breach (*Public Works Commissioner v Hills* and *Webster v Bosanquet*).

4. To assist this task of construction various tests have been suggested, which if applicable to the case under consideration may prove helpful, or even conclusive. Such are:

(a) It will be held to be penalty if the sum stipulated for is extravagant and unconscionable in amount in comparison with the greatest loss that could conceivably be proved to have followed from the breach. (Illustration given by Lord Halsbury in *Clydebank* case.)

(b) It will be held to be a penalty if the breach consists only in not paying a sum of money, and the sum stipulated is a sum greater than the sum which ought to have been paid (*Kemble v Farren*[4]). This though one of the most ancient instances is truly a corollary to the last test. Whether it had its historical origin in the doctrine of the common law that when A promised to pay B a sum of money on a certain day and did not do so, B could only recover the sum with, in certain cases, interest, but could never recover further damages for non-timeous payment, or whether it was a survival of the time when equity reformed unconscionable bargains merely because they were unconscionable,—a subject which much exercised Jessel M.R. in *Wallis v Smith*[5]—is probably more interesting than material.

(c) There is a presumption (but no more) that it is penalty when 'a single lump sum is made payable by way of compensation, on the occurrence of one or more or all of several events, some of which may occasion serious and others but trifling damage' (Lord Watson in *Lord Elphinstone v Monkland Iron and Coal Co.*[6]).

On the other hand:

(d) It is no obstacle to the sum stipulated being a genuine pre-estimate of damage, that the consequences of the breach are such as to make precise pre-estimation almost an impossibility. On the contrary, that is just the situation when it is probable that pre-estimated damage was the true bargain between the parties (*Clydebank* case, Lord Halsbury; *Webster v Bosanquet*, Lord Mersey).

Turning now to the facts of the case, it is evident that the damage apprehended by the appellants owing to the breaking of the agreement was an indirect and not a direct damage. So long as they got their price from the respondents for each article sold, it could not matter to them directly what the respondents did with it. Indirectly it did. Accordingly, the agreement is headed 'Price Maintenance Agreement', and the way in which the appellants would be damaged if prices were cut is clearly explained in evidence by Mr Baisley, and no successful attempt is made to controvert that evidence. But though damage as a whole from such a practice would be certain, yet damage from any one sale would be impossible to forecast. It is just, therefore, one of those cases where it seems quite reasonable for parties to contract that they should estimate that damage at a certain figure, and provided that figure is not extravagant there would seem no reason to suspect that it is not truly a bargain to assess damages, but rather a penalty to be held *in terrorem*.

The argument of the respondents was really based on two heads. They overpressed, in my judgment, the dictum of Lord Watson in *Lord Elphinstone's* case, reading it as if he had said that the matter was conclusive, instead of saying, as he did, that it raised a presumption, and they relied strongly on the case of *Willson v Love*.[7]

Now, in the first place, I have considerable doubt whether the stipulated payment here can fairly be said to deal with breaches, 'some of which'—I am quoting Lord Watson's words—'may occasion serious and others but trifling damage.' As a mere matter of construction, I doubt whether clause 5 applies to anything but sales below price. But I will assume that it does. Nonetheless the mischief, as I have already pointed out, is an indirect mischief, and I see no data on which, as a matter of construction, I could settle in my own mind that the indirect damage from selling a cover would differ in magnitude from the indirect damage from selling a tube; or that the indirect damage from a cutting-price sale would differ from the indirect damage from supply at a full price to a hostile, because prohibited, agent. You cannot weigh such things in a chemical balance. The character of the agricultural land which was ruined by slag heaps in *Elphinstone's* case was not all the same, but no objection was raised by Lord Watson to applying an overhead rate per acre, the sum not being in itself unconscionable.

I think *Elphinstone's* case, or rather the dicta in it, do go this length, that if there are various breaches to which one indiscriminate sum to be paid in breach is applied, then the strength of the chain must be taken at its weakest link. If you can clearly see that the loss on one particular breach could never amount to the stipulated sum, then you may come to the conclusion that the sum is penalty. But further than this it does not go; so, for the reasons already stated, I do not think the present case forms an instance of what I have just expressed.

As regards *Willson's* case, I do not think it material to consider whether it was well decided on the facts. For it was decided on the view of the facts that the manurial value of straw and of hay were known ascertainable quantities as at the time of the bargain, and radically different, so that the damage resulting from the want of one could never be the same as the damage resulting from the want of the other.

Added to that, the parties there had said 'penalty', and the effort was to make out that that really meant liquidated damages; and lastly, if my view of the facts in the present case is correct, then Rigby L.J. would have agreed with me, for the last words of his judgment are as follows:

On the other hand it is stated that, when the damages caused by a breach of contract are incapable of being ascertained, the sum made by the contract payable on such a breach is to be regarded as liquidated damages. The question arises, What is meant in this statement by the expression 'incapable of being ascertained'? In their proper sense the words appear to refer to a case where no rule or measure of damages is available for the guidance of a jury as to the amount of the damages, and a judge would have to tell them they must fix the amount as best they can.

To arrive at the indirect damage in this case, supposing no sum had been stipulated, that is just what a judge would, in my opinion, have had to do.

I move your Lordships that the appeal be allowed.

1. [1905] AC 6.
2. [1906] AC 368.
3. [1912] AC 394.
4. 6 Bing. 141.
5. 21 ChD 243.
6. (1886) 11 App Cas 332.
7. [1896] 1 QB 626.

Bradshaw v Lemon [1929] NI 159

Andrews L.J.:

In this case the plaintiff appeals from that portion of an order of the Lord Chief Justice made on 30 January 1929, by which he held that a rent of £50 sued for in paras 5 and 6 of the statement of claim was in the nature of a penalty, and that the plaintiff was therefore only entitled to such damages as he could prove. These damages the Lord

Chief Justice measured at the sum of one shilling, and for this sum he, accordingly, gave judgment with costs of suit. The plaintiff asks that the judgment be set aside, and that judgment be entered for him for the sum of £369 15s, or, alternatively, that a new trial be ordered.

The only questions argued before us were whether the learned Lord Chief Justice was right in holding that the said rent of £50 was in the nature of a penalty; and, if he was correct in so holding, whether the damages of one shilling which he awarded were inadequate.

By lease, dated 9 September 1919, the plaintiff demised to the defendants certain premises situate in the town of Enniskillen consisting of a shop, dwelling house, yard and out offices, which were then in the occupation of the defendants for the term of twelve years from 1 November 1918, at the rent of £100, payable quarterly in every year. The lease contained the usual provisions for distress and re-entry, and a covenant by the defendants for payment of the rent, rates and taxes. Then followed a further covenant by the defendants that, owing to dilapidations caused during the defendants' present tenancy, they would within two years put the demised premises into a state of thorough repair according to the estimate of Mr Harvey at a cost of at least £420 16s 9d; and a proviso that if the works included in the estimate should not be completely finished within two years the said rent of £100 should be increased by the annual sum of £50, and during the residue of the term or so long as the said works should be unfinished the annual sum of £150 should be the rent reserved. Next followed covenants by the defendants for insurance, for the execution of sanitary works, for painting the cement on the front and gable of the premises, for keeping the premises in repair, and also against using any part of the front of the house as a bill posting hoarding, and against carrying on offensive trades in the premises. These covenants and provisions are followed by the clause with which alone we are directly concerned in this appeal, and which, by reason of its importance, I shall set out verbatim, namely:

> ... that on breach of any of these covenants or any part thereof this present demise shall be utterly null and void to all intents and purposes as if the same had never been made or that otherwise at the election of the lessor the lessees shall forfeit and pay unto the lessor from the time of the breach of any of these covenants or any part thereof a further additional yearly rent or sum of £50 sterling, to be paid quarterly as the said other rent and to be recovered by action of debt, distress or otherwise as the said hereby reserved yearly rent is recoverable anything herein contained to the contrary in anywise notwithstanding.

The construction of this covenant is a matter of some difficulty. I agree with [counsel for the plaintiff] that this additional rent of £50 is payable quarterly, as this is expressly provided, but I look in vain for any words similar to those contained in the covenant for payment of the first mentioned rent of £50, which would make the liability for this rent terminate if and when the breach of covenant were remedied; and it is difficult to imply words of limited duration in regard to the second rent which are expressed in regard to the first. Were it necessary, therefore, to decide the point I would not, as at present advised, be prepared to hold with [counsel's] contention that liability for this second rent of £50 could be determined at any time by remedying the breach and paying the sum of £12 10s as the then current quarter's instalment of such additional rent. It is unnecessary, however, to express any concluded opinion on the point, as there are other features of the liability for this rent which satisfy me that the Lord Chief Justice was perfectly right in holding that it was penal in character, and that the £50 must not be regarded as in the nature of liquidated damages.

In the first place, it is to be observed that on breach of any covenant the lessor is given an alternative remedy. He is entitled to elect whether the demise should be 'utterly null and void to all intents and purposes'—a right against which, no doubt, a court of equity would in a proper case grant relief under s. 14 of the Conveyancing Act 1881, yet one which is obviously penal in character. In these circumstances it would not be unreasonable to suppose that the alternative right—the additional rent of £50— was likewise penal. The view that it is such is in my opinion also supported, though not determined, by the expression that the lessees should 'forfeit and pay' this rent to the lessor—the significance of the use of this word *'forfeit'* is referred to by Lord Dunedin in *Public Works Commissioner v Hills*,[1] in which (at 375) he says that the word 'forfeited' is 'peculiarly appropriate to penalty, and not to liquidated damages.'

It is necessary, however, to consider briefly, so far as applicable, the general principles upon which the courts act in determining whether a named sum is to be regarded as a penalty or as liquidated damages. These principles have been enunciated so frequently during the last quarter of a century in both the House of Lords and the Privy Council that there can be no longer any doubt in regard to them. Amongst these cases may be cited *Clydebank Engineering & Shipbuilding Co. Ltd v Don Jose Ramos Yzquierdo y Castaneda*,[2] *Public Works Commissioner v Hills*, *Webster v Bosanquet*,[3] and *Dunlop Pneumatic Tyre Co. Ltd v New Garage & Motor Co. Ltd*.[4] From these cases it is clear that the essence of a penalty is a payment *in terrorem*, whilst the essence of liquidated damages is a genuine covenanted pre-estimate of damage. Hence if the sum stipulated for is extravagant and unconscionable in amount in comparison with the greatest amount of damage which could have possibly been in the contemplation of the parties when they made the contract, it is a penalty. The mere fact, however, that precise pre-estimation of damage is almost an impossibility is not a reason for a named sum being regarded as a penalty. On the contrary, it is just in such a case, where precise proof of damage would be difficult or complex, that the parties may reasonably be said to have intended the sum which they named to be a pre-estimate which would avoid all such difficulties of proof. Again, there is a presumption (though one which is rebuttable) that when a single indiscriminate lump sum is made payable by way of compensation on the occurrence of one or more or all of several events, some of which may occasion serious and others but trifling damage, such sum is a penalty; and the strength of the chain must be tested on its weakest link, so that if it be clearly established that the loss on one particular breach could never possibly amount to the stipulated sum, it must be regarded as a penalty. On the other hand, if, though there be several stipulations of varying degrees of importance, the damage likely to accrue from each is the same in kind, and the same agreed sum could be properly construed as a fair and reasonable pre-estimate of probable damage, the named sum would be held to be in the nature of liquidated damages. Enormous disparity of the sum to any conceivable loss will point one way; while the fact of the payment being in terms proportionate to the loss will point the other.

When I apply these principles to the facts of the present case I have no hesitation in holding that this additional rent of £50, imposed in respect of breaches of covenant of varying importance and different in kind, must be regarded as fixed *in terrorem* to compel the lessee's obedience to the covenants in the lease, and, therefore, in the nature of a penalty; for such a sum would in my opinion be 'disproportionate to', and 'wholly extravagant and unconscionable' in comparison with any damage which the parties could possibly have contemplated as resulting from the breach of such covenants, as, for example, the covenants to paint the cement, or not to use any part of the front of the house as a bill-posting hoarding.

In these circumstances it was in my opinion the duty of the learned Lord Chief Justice to assess as damages the actual loss which in his opinion the plaintiff sustained by the breach of covenant established by the evidence. The plaintiff endeavoured to prove substantial dilapidations and serious disrepair in these old premises, but this was denied by the defendants' witnesses; and in this conflict of testimony the Lord Chief Justice held that the defendants were only in default in what he calls two minor respects:—(a) the state of 'disrepair' or 'disappearance of the bird cage', which is referred to by the defendants' engineers as a wooden structure, and is described by the Lord Chief Justice as a plank on an outside wall under which pigeons used to sit; and (b) allowing the drains in the yard to get clogged up for a period of roughly two years, by reason of which the yard became waterlogged. These findings of fact, it is admitted, cannot be successfully challenged as there is evidence to support them; but |counsel| argues for the plaintiff that even if these facts be accepted the finding of the Lord Chief Justice of merely nominal damages cannot be sustained, as the defendants' engineer admitted that it would cost £5 to re-erect the bird cage. The fallacy underlying this argument is that the measure of the plaintiff's damages is not, as is assumed, the present cost of re-erection. The plaintiff is merely a reversioner, who at the time of the trial was not entitled to possession of the premises for a period of almost two years. It is as such reversioner only that he is entitled to compensation for his loss. In *Doe d. Worcester Trustees v Rowlands*,[5] Coleridge J. said that in such a case 'the true question is to what extent is the reversion injured by the non-repair of the premises?' In *Conquest v Ebbetts*[6] Lord Herschell, whilst stating that damages must be assessed at such a sum as reasonably represents the damage which the covenantee has sustained, applied the test 'of inquiring how much the value of the respondents' reversion has been diminished by the breach of covenant.' The question was also considered and determined in the well known Irish case of *Metae v Kavanagh*,[7] in which the Court of Exchequer held that the damages in such case may, but need not necessarily, be the present value of a sum equal to the cost of repair, that sum being payable at the end of the term, or they may, but need not necessarily, be the injury caused by the want of repair to the saleable value of the reversion. It was further held that save in very extreme cases it was the province of the jury to decide which of these modes was, in the particular case, the appropriate one.

In my opinion there was nothing in the facts and circumstances of the present case which would justify this court in holding that the learned Lord Chief Justice acted on an erroneous principle in adopting one of the two recognised modes and in taking, as he did, the measure of damages as 'the injury to the reversion'. So acting he thought nominal damages constituted adequate compensation for what he described as a technical breach. With this finding we cannot in my opinion interfere; for it may well be that neither of the trivial matters referred to would cause the slightest depreciation in the saleable value of the reversion.

For these reasons the plaintiff's motion must be dismissed with costs.

1. |1906| AC 368.   4. |1915| AC 79.   6. |1896| AC 490.
2. |1905| AC 6.   5. 9 C & P 734.   7. IR 11 CL 431.
3. |1912| AC 394.

(Best L.J. agreed.)

Irish Telephone Rentals Ltd *v* Irish Civil Service Building Society [1992] 2 IR 525

The plaintiff rented out to the defendant a telephone installation for use in its head office. The system proved unfit for its purpose and was replaced by another system. This system, while far from problem free, was held by

Costello J. not to be such as to justify repudiation of the contract by the defendant. The plaintiff sought damages for wrongful termination under clause 11 of the contract.

Costello J.:

. . .

What falls therefore now for consideration is whether the plaintiff is entitled to an award under clause 11 or whether this clause, as the defendant contends, is a penalty clause and therefore unenforceable. If it is then I must assess damages according to common law principles.

Clause 11 provides as follows:

> If the subscriber [that is, the defendant] shall repudiate this contract and the company [that is, the plaintiff] shall accept such repudiation so as to terminate this contract the company may thereupon remove the installation and the subscriber shall pay to the company all payments then accrued and also a sum equal to the present value on a 5 per cent basis of the remaining rentals that would have been payable under this contract if not so terminated less allowance of 25 per cent to cover the estimated cost of maintenance and value of recovered material. The said sums shall be payable as liquidated damages it being an agreed estimate of the loss the company would suffer.

I have the following comments to make on this clause.

(1) The estimate of the plaintiff's loss arising from premature termination is based on the gross rents outstanding for the unexpired term of the contract. However, the clause accepts, and correctly accepts, that the plaintiff is not entitled to the full amount of these rents. It also accepts that whatever may be the figure for the agreed loss which the plaintiff may suffer that figure should be discounted because instead of receiving the balance of the rents in instalments over the years an accelerated payment of the rent will be made to the plaintiffs. The discount in clause 11 is 5 per cent. Whilst the defendant readily accepts the principle of discounting it is urged that the sum estimated for the plaintiff's loss should be discounted at a higher rate.

(2) The figure for the gross rent is to be reduced, according to clause 11, by a further 25 per cent of the discounted rent because (a) the plaintiff will have been saved maintenance costs during the unexpired term and (b) an allowance should be given for the value of the installations recovered. The plaintiff's evidence is that the 25 per cent deduction was calculated by allowing a figure of 5 per cent of the discounted gross rent as the percentage attributable to maintenance charges and 20 per cent of the discounted gross rent as the percentage attributable to the value of the returned installations.

(3) It will be observed that the formula is based on a deduction from the gross amount of the outstanding rent of a sum equivalent to 28.7 per cent of the gross rent (25 per cent of 5 per cent of the gross rents) in respect of the estimated cost of maintenance and the estimated value of the recovered installations. The clause was attempting to make an estimate of what the plaintiff would lose by the contract's premature termination. As the correct measure of the plaintiff's loss on premature termination at any point of time during the life of the contract is the profit it would have earned in the outstanding period of the contract's life the formula in clause 11 can only be correct if it produces a figure which approximates

to that profit. It follows, therefore that this clause can be shown to be a correct estimate of the plaintiff's loss if in every case of premature termination the profit thereby lost is 71.25 per cent of the gross rental then outstanding.

(4) Clause 11 is a standard clause. All the plaintiff's hiring contracts contain this estimate of the loss suffered on each of the plaintiff's contracts should they be prematurely terminated. The defendant has submitted that the sum calculated in accordance with the condition does not represent a genuine pre-estimate of the actual loss which the plaintiff sustained as a result of the wrongful repudiation of the hiring agreement but is a penalty clause which the court should not enforce. The courts have evolved various rules for considering whether a stipulated sum is a penalty or a genuine pre-estimate. That which is relevant to the present case is that stated by Lord Dunedin in *Dunlop Pneumatic Tyre Co. Ltd v New Garage and Motor Co. Ltd* |1915| AC 79 at 87: 'It will be held to be a penalty if the sum stipulated for is extravagant and unconscionable in amount in comparison with the greatest loss that could conceivably be proved to have followed from the breach.'

The application of this principle is to be seen in the majority decision of the Court of Appeal in England in *Robophone Facilities Ltd v Blank* |1966| 1 WLR 1428 in which the court considered a contract for the hiring of a telephone-answering machine for a seven year period which was repudiated before the hiring began. The hiring agreement contained a clause which made provision in the event of premature termination for the payment of agreed liquidated damages equal to 50 per cent of the total of the rentals due. In deciding that the sum of 50 per cent was a genuine pre-estimate of loss and not a penalty Lord Diplock examined what would be recoverable by way of damage assessed on common law principles and concluded that because 50 per cent of the gross rent would not produce a figure which was 'extravagantly greater' than those damages the clause was enforceable.

Before considering in greater detail the operation in this case of clause 11 I should give some more detail of how the plaintiff's claim is made up.

The plaintiff has calculated that there were nine full years of the agreement to run from the date of termination. The annual rent at that time (which had been increased over the years pursuant to the rent revision clause) was then £1,438.16. This annual rent was discounted over a nine year period by 5 per cent giving a discounted figure of £10,222.15. There was added to this one quarter's rent unpaid in 1988 (that is, £359.51) giving a total of £10,581.69. A figure of 25 per cent of this sum was then calculated, that is a sum of £2,645.42. This was deducted from the sum of £10,581.69 giving a figure of £7,936.27. It is to be noted that the gross rent for the unexpired nine year period of the hiring was £13,043.62 according to these calculations.

I have come to the conclusion that the formula contained in clause 11 does not produce a liquidated sum that can properly be regarded as a genuine pre-estimate made at the date of the contract of the loss which the plaintiff would suffer should the contract be prematurely determined and that it is in reality a penalty and therefore unenforceable. My reasons are as follows:

(a) In estimating the plaintiff's loss clause 11 correctly allows a deduction from the gross rents of the sums saved in maintenance charges. But the evidence establishes that the 5 per cent figure is an estimate not of all the maintenance charges which would have been incurred had the contract run its course but only an estimate of the cost of materials used in maintenance and expenses such as daily allowance, petrol and the travelling expenses of maintenance staff. The wages of the maintainence staff are excluded. Support for this approach is claimed by the plaintiff from an unreported judgment of the High Court in England (the transcript of which was made available) in *Telephone Rentals Ltd* (the plaintiff's English parent company) *v Photophone Ltd* delivered 8 February 1957. I do not think that this approach is correct and, with respect, I cannot follow that judgment to which I was referred. In estimating the loss which the plaintiff would suffer the draftsman of clause 11 should have attempted to estimate the net profit which the plaintiff would have earned had the contract been performed. This net profit should have been calculated by deducting the actual total costs of maintenance and not only a proportion of those costs. It seems to me that this error produces an estimate very much in excess of the plaintiff's actual loss and cannot be regarded as a genuine pre-estimate of that loss.

(b) The clause makes no allowance for other deductions which in my judgment should have been made from the gross rent figure. The evidence establishes that when originally fixing the rent under the contract the plaintiff took into account not only the likely maintenance charges but also finance charges, administrative costs and engineering costs. Any genuine calculation of the actual loss likely to be suffered from premature termination should make an allowance for these charges as otherwise the plaintiff would receive more than the profit it would have made had the contract run its course. As I will show later it would have been a simple enough matter to estimate what that profit would have been. But by only deducting maintenance charges (and only a portion of such charges at that) the clause seriously overestimates the profit which the plaintiff would have made on the hiring.

(c) Part of the 25 per cent deduction is based on an estimate of the value of the materials obtained at the date of premature termination. The evidence established that the clause was based on the assumption that this value would be 20 per cent of the discounted gross rents. This, in my view, is an entirely arbitrary figure and cannot be regarded as a genuine pre-estimate of the value of the recovered installations. It is to be borne in mind that the hiring was to last for twelve years and that there was a rent variation clause. Perhaps by a coincidence 20 per cent of the discounted rent might at some point during that period approximate to the depreciated value of the installations. But this would be mere coincidence; there is no real connection between the figures produced by these calculations. The facts of this case illustrate the point. Twenty per cent of the discounted rent at the date of termination of the broadcasting contracts was £2,116. But in fact the installations when returned were valueless. Twenty per cent of the discounted value of the outstanding rents under the telephone contracts was £16,789. In fact their value was only £7,500 (only the switchboard being marketable). It seems to me that the relationship between discounted value of outstanding rents due at any point of time during the contract and the then value of the installations at that point of time is so tenuous that an estimate of the plaintiff's loss based on this connection cannot be a genuine one.

(d) The result of the operation of the formula is to award a liquidated sum equal to 71.25 per cent of the gross rent, less 5 per cent for accelerated payment. This predicates a net profit of 71.25 per cent had the contract not been terminated. This is quite an enormous net profit. Whilst the onus is on the party who alleges that a clause in a contract is a penalty and not a genuine pre-estimate of the loss which would be suffered by premature termination I think the onus is discharged once the clause in question is based on the assumption that this is an estimate of the profit the plaintiff lost. The plaintiff is engaged in the business of letting goods on hire. Its turnover in its profit and loss account would therefore (apart from an occasional and small sum received for goods recovered prematurely and sold) represent its annual rents received under all its contracts. Its profit and loss account would show the net profit (after deducting all maintenance charges administrative and financial charges and depreciation). This would indicate the average net profit on each of its hiring contracts. If clause 11 (which is a standard clause in all its contracts) is a correct estimate of the net profit made on each of its hiring contracts this would mean that the net profit figure in its profit and loss account would be about 71.25 per cent of its turnover.

The plaintiff has not produced its profit and loss account and so I do not know what it shows. But I am entitled to apply the knowledge of financial affairs which is available to every reader of the daily press from which companies' net profits as a percentage of their turnover is shown for an extensive range of different classes of businesses. These, of course, vary widely. In the retail trade a net profit of 10 per cent of turnover is an average figure. In some manufacturing companies it may be considerably less or considerably more. A net profit of 71 per cent of turnover would be a staggeringly large one in any business and in the absence of proof that this is what the plaintiff earned I am driven to the conclusion that the estimate of loss contained in clause 11 is not a genuine pre-estimate but is a penalty.

I cannot therefore allow the plaintiff's claim based on clause 11 and must assess damages based on the actual loss I think the plaintiff suffered.

The plaintiff recovered back the equipment let under the contracts but was unable to re-let or sell them. The plaintiff's damages will therefore be an estimate of the profit lost on the transaction, appropriately discounted for accelerated payment. The gross rent which would have been received for the nine year balance of the contract was £13,043.62 (assuming no increase, in the rent, an assumption the plaintiff has made in its calculations). I have been given no information as to what the plaintiff's average net profit is, but bearing in mind that the evidence establishes that the plaintiff's business is a competitive one (which would oblige them to keep their hiring charges at a reasonable competitive level) and that the plaintiff is a long established firm (which would give it the benefit of a considerable goodwill) I would consider it probable that a net profit of 20 per cent of gross rents is what the plaintiff would have earned on average. There is nothing to suggest that there are any special circumstances which would justify an award for breach of this particular contract on a basis higher than average net profit and so the plaintiff's loss of profit for the last nine years of this transaction is £2,608.72 (20 per cent of £13,043.62). I have very little evidence to help me on how this sum should be discounted and I will, in the absence of evidence, accept the 5 per cent figure contained in clause 11. This means that there should be a deduction of £130.47, giving an award for the loss the plaintiff has suffered for this period of £2,478.29. To this is to be added the loss in relation to one quarter of the 1988 rent, namely, £359.51. Twenty per cent of this sum, discounted by 5 per cent is £68.04. This gives a total figure for damages of £2,546.69. The plaintiff is entitled to an award of this sum.

Note

In *Philips Hong Kong v AG of Hong Kong* (1993) 61 BLR 41 the Privy Council held that a clause is not a penalty if it seeks to impose different penalties for breach, even if such a clause contains a minimum amount by way of liquidated and ascertained damages, regardless of the extent to which the actual performance falls short of the contracted standard.

B. THE RULE IN RELATION TO PENALTIES CAN BE AVOIDED BY CAREFUL DRAFTING

Lombard North Central plc *v* Butterworth [1987] 1 All ER 267

Mustill L.J.:

The respondent plaintiffs are a finance company. The defendant appellant is an accountant. The defendant wished to buy a computer to improve his business, and enlisted the help of the plaintiffs. They purchased a particular model, and then entered into an agreement of hiring whereby they agreed to lease the computer to the defendant for a period of five years. There was to be an initial payment of £584.05 and nineteen subsequent instalments of the same amount, payable at intervals of three months. In addition, VAT was to be paid.

The hiring agreement contained the following material provisions:

The lessee . . . agrees . . .

2. (a) to pay to the lessor: (i) punctually and without previous demand the rentals set out in part 3 of the schedule together with VAT thereon punctual payment of each which shall be of the essence of this lease . . .

5. *In the event that* (a) the lessee shall (i) make default in the due and punctual payment of any of the rentals or of any sum of money payable to the lessor hereunder or any part thereof . . . then upon the happening of such event . . . the lessor's consent to the lessee's possession of the goods shall determine forthwith without any notice being given by the lessor, and the lessor may terminate this lease either by notice in writing, or by taking possession of the goods . . .

6. *In the event* that the lessor's consent to the lessee's possession of the goods shall be determined under clause 5 hereof (a) the lessee shall pay forthwith to the lessor: (1) all arrears of rentals; and (ii) all further rental which would but for the determination of the lessor's consent to the lessee's possession of the goods have fallen due to the end of the fixed period of this lease less a discount thereon for accelerated payment at the rate of 5 per cent per annum; and (iii) damages for any breach of this lease and all expenses and costs incurred by the lessor in retaking possession of the goods and/or enforcing the lessor's rights under this lease together with such VAT as shall be legally payable thereon; (b) the lessor shall be entitled to exercise any one or more of the rights and remedies provided for in clause 5 and sub-clause (a) of this clause and the determination of the lessor's consent to the lessee's possession of the goods shall not affect or prejudice such rights and remedies and the lessee shall be and remain liable to perform all outstanding liabilities under this lease notwithstanding that the lessor may have taken possession of the goods and/or exercised one or more of the rights and remedies of the lessor. (c) Any right or remedy to which the lessor is or may become entitled under this lease or in consequence of the lessee's conduct may be enforced from time to time separately or concurrently with any other right or remedy given by this lease or now or hereafter provided for or arising by operation of law so that such rights and remedies are not exclusive of the other or others of them but are cumulative.

The letting under this agreement did not go well. The instalments were due to be paid by direct debit. The first two were effected satisfactorily but the third was twice recalled by the bank and remained unpaid for a period of four months. The fourth was paid two weeks late. The fifth was two months late. The sixth was paid on time, but was recalled by the bank. It was paid again one month later, and again recalled by the bank. Two weeks later the plaintiffs lost patience and sent to the defendant a letter in the following terms:

> We regret that in spite of our previous reminders you are still in arrear with your payments. Please take notice that pursuant to the terms of the lease our consent to your possession of the goods is now withdrawn and you are required to make them available for collection. Your liability under the terms of the lease will not cease upon the return of these goods as we are entitled to call upon you to make payment of the balance of the rentals due under the remaining period of the lease. If payment of the arrears has been made within the last seven days please ignore this notice.

Subsequently, the plaintiffs recovered possession of the computer and sold it. The instrument fetched very little by comparison with its purchase price, and the net proceeds of sale were only £172.85.

On 18 May 1984 the plaintiffs commenced the present action by specially indorsed writ. The material parts read:

> 4. Pursuant to clause 5 of the said lease agreement the plaintiff terminated its consent to the defendant's possession of the said computer and printer by a notice in writing dated the 20th day of December 1982 and by virtue of the defendant's default under the said lease agreement the same has been determined.
>
> 5. Pursuant to clause 6 of the said lease agreement and by virtue of the determination of consent to possession pursuant to clause 5 thereof the plaintiff is entitled to claim (a) all of his rentals (b) all further rentals which would have been payable had the lease agreement continued for the full period and (c) damages for breach of the lease agreement.
>
> 6. The plaintiff has recovered possession of the said computer and printer in accordance with its entitlement to do so under clause 5 of the said lease agreement and the net proceeds of sale amounted to £172.85. Calculating the amounts due to the plaintiff the defendant will be given credit for this sum and an allowance will be made for accelerated receipt of the payment due under the said lease agreement as provided in clause 6 thereof.
>
> 7. The defendant has failed to pay the sums referred to in para. 5 hereof and the plaintiff is entitled under the lease of alternatively as damages for breach of the lease, the sum of £6,869.97.

The sum of £6,869.97 was arrived at by adding the amount of the unpaid instalment and VAT, and the thirteen rentals due after termination, and then giving credit for the net proceeds of sale and an allowance of £1,221.49 for accelerated receipt. The pleading concluded with claims of £6,869.97 under para. 7, interest and 'damages for breach of contract'.

The plaintiffs then issued an application for summary judgment under RSC Ord. 14. An affidavit in reply was sworn on behalf of the defendant. This did not put in issue the plaintiffs' right to terminate the contract, or to recover a sum attributable to the future instalments, but complaint was made about the low price obtained on the resale. The affidavit concluded by asserting that the defendant had a partial defence on the merits, and asking that he should have leave to defend sufficient to enable him to dispute the calculations in the statement of claim.

Precisely what happened thereafter is not clear, but it appears that the plaintiffs did not go to judgment for their claim in debt under clause 6 of the agreement, but instead obtained a judgment for damages to be assessed. The matter was then referred to Master Lubbock, who heard evidence on the resale value of the computer. He decided this issue in favour of the plaintiffs. Argument was also addressed on the measure of recovery. Notwithstanding that the plaintiffs had recovered judgment for damages to be assessed, they continued to rely on clause 6. The defendant replied that this was a penalty. In the event, the master found it unnecessary to reach a conclusion on this question, since he found that the defendant had repudiated the contract, and that accordingly damages were recoverable in respect of the future instalments, subject to the credits allowed in the statement of claim. He gave judgment accordingly. The defendant now appeals, maintaining that he should not be held liable for more than the amount due and unpaid at the date of termination.

Three issues were canvassed before us. (1) Is clause 6 of the agreement to be disregarded, on the ground that it creates a penalty? (Strictly speaking, this issue does not arise, since the judgment was for damages to be assessed, but clause 6 was relied on by the plaintiffs before the master and in this court, without objection.) (2) Apart from clause 2(a) of the agreement, was the master correct in holding that the conduct of the defendant amounted to a wrongful repudiation of the contract, and that the sum claimed was recoverable in damages? (2) Does the provision in clause 2(a) of the agreement that time for payment of the instalments was of the essence have the effect of making the defendant's late payment of the outstanding instalment a repudiatory breach?

As to the first two issues, I need say only that I have had the advantage of reading in draft the judgment to be delivered by Nicholls L.J. and that I am in such entire agreement with his conclusions and reasons that it is unnecessary to add any observations of my own.

I would, however, wish to deal with the third point. Important as it is, this point has played only a minor part in the proceedings. There is no explicit reference to it in the pleadings, although it is just open to the plaintiffs through their claim for damages. We are told that it was argued before the master, yet there is no reference to it in his judgment. The matter received little prominence during the argument before us, nor were submissions directed at any stage to the possibility that the plaintiffs had by their prior conduct waived their right to insist on the stipulation that time was of the essence.

The reason why I am impelled to hold that the plaintiffs' contentions are well founded can most conveniently be set out in a series of propositions. (1) Where a breach goes to the root of the contract, the injured party may elect to put an end to the contract. Thereupon both sides are relieved from those obligations which remain unperformed. (2) If he does so elect, the injured party is entitled to compensation for (a) any breaches which occurred before the contract was terminated and (b) the loss of his opportunity to receive performance of the promisor's outstanding obligations. (3) Certain categories of obligation, often called conditions, have the property that any breach of them is treated as going to the root of the contract. On the occurrence of any breach of condition, the injured party can elect to terminate and claim damages, whatever the gravity of the breach. (4) It is possible to express provision in the contract to make a term a condition, even if it would not be so in the absence of such a provision. (5) A stipulation that time is of the essence, in relation to a particular contractual term, denotes that timely performance is a condition of the contract. The consequence is that delay in performance is treated as going to the root of the contract, without regard to the magnitude of the breach. (6) It follows that where a promisor fails to give timely performance of an obligation in respect of which time is expressly stated to be of the essence, the injured party may elect to terminate and recover damages in

respect of the promisor's outstanding obligations, without regard to the magnitude of the breach. (7) A term of the contract prescribing what damages are to be recoverable when a contract is terminated for a breach of condition is open to being struck down as a penalty, if it is not a genuine covenanted pre-estimate of the damage, in the same way as a clause which prescribes the measure for any other type of breach. No doubt the position is the same where the clause is ranked as a condition by virtue of an express provision in the contract. (8) A clause expressly assigning a particular obligation to the category of condition is not a clause which purports to fix the damages for breaches of the obligation, and is not subject to the law governing penalty clauses. (9) Thus, although in the present case clause 6 is to be struck down as a penalty, clause 2(a)(i) remains enforceable. The plaintiffs were entitled to terminate the contract independently of clause 5, and to recover damages for loss of the future instalments. This loss was correctly computed by the master. These bare propositions call for comment. . .
. . .

. . . The seventh is uncontroversial, and I would add only the rider that when deciding on the penal nature of a clause which prescribes a measure of recovery for damages resulting from a termination founded on a breach of condition, the comparison should be with the common law measure, namely with the loss to the promisee resulting from the loss of his bargain. If the contract permits him to treat the contract as repudiated, the fact that the breach is comparatively minor should in my view play no part in the equation.

I believe that the real controversy in the present case centres on the eighth proposition. I will repeat it. A clause expressly assigning a particular obligation to the category of condition is not a clause which purports to fix the damages for breach of the obligation, and is not subject to the law governing penalty clauses. I acknowledge, of course, that by promoting a term into the category where all breaches are ranked as breaches of condition, the parties indirectly bring about a situation where, for breaches which are relatively small, the injured party is enabled to recover damages as on the loss of the bargain, whereas without the stipulation his measure of recovery would be different. But I am unable to accept that this permits the court to strike down as a penalty the clause which brings about this promotion. To do so would be to reverse the current of more than 100 years' doctrine, which permits the parties to treat as a condition something which would not otherwise be so. I am not prepared to take this step.

It remains to mention two reported cases. The first is *Steedman v Drinkle* [1916] 1 AC 275, [1914–15] All ER Rep 298. Land in Canada was purchased under an agreement, whereby the price was payable by one initial payment followed by annual instalments. The agreement stipulated that if the purchaser should make default in any of the payments, the vendor should be at liberty to cancel the agreement and to retain, as liquidated damages, the payments already made. It was also provided that time was to be considered as of the essence of the contract. The first deferred payment was not made on the due date. The vendor gave notice cancelling the agreement. Three weeks after the due date the purchaser tendered the amount due, which was refused. He thereupon brought an action claiming specific performance and relief from forfeiture of the amount already paid. The Judicial Committee of the Privy Council upheld the decision of the Canadian court, that the stipulation as to the retention of the sums already paid was a penalty. But the board declined to grant specific performance. Viscount Haldane said ([1916] 1 AC 275 at 279, [1914–15] All ER Rep 298 at 300):

Courts of equity, which look at the substance as distinguished from the letter of agreements, no doubt exercise an extensive jurisdiction which enables them to decree specific performance in cases where justice requires it, even though literal terms of stipulations as to time have not been observed. But they never exercise this jurisdiction where the parties have expressly intimated in their agreement that it is not to apply by providing that time is to be of the essence of their bargain.

This authority would, of course, have been decisive of the present case if the vendor had gone on to claim damages for loss of the contract. He did not do so. Nevertheless, it does, in my view, show quite clearly that a clause making time of the essence, and hence making prompt performance a condition, is not to be struck down merely because a breach of the obligation is not sufficient on its own to constitute a repudiation.

Secondly, there is *Photo Production Ltd v Securicor Transport Ltd* |1980| 1 All ER 556, |1980| AC 827. This case is of great importance, for giving the *quietus* to the doctrine of fundamental breach. Its significance in the present instance lies in a passage from the speech of Lord Diplock. In order to place this in context, I must first quote from that part of the speech in which Lord Diplock develops a system of primary and secondary obligations, foreshadowed in earlier pronouncements (|1980| 1 All ER 556 at 566–7, |1980| AC 827 at 849):

> Every failure to perform a primary obligation is a breach of contract. The secondary obligation on the part of the contract breaker to which it gives rise by implication of the common law is to pay monetary compensation to the other party for the loss sustained by him in consequence of the breach; but, with two exceptions, the primary obligations of both parties so far as they have not yet been fully performed remain unchanged. This secondary obligation to pay compensation (damages) for non-performance of primary obligations I will call the 'general secondary obligation'. It applies in the cases of the two exceptions as well. The exceptions are: (1) where the event resulting from the failure by one party to perform a primary obligation has the effect of depriving the other party of substantially the whole benefit which it was the intention of the parties that he should obtain from the contract, the party not in default may elect to put an end to all primary obligations of both parties remaining unperformed (if the expression 'fundamental breach' is to be retained, it should, in the interests of clarity, be confined to this exception); (2) where the contracting parties have agreed, whether by express words or by implication of law, that any failure by one party to perform a particular primary obligation ('condition' in the nomenclature of the Sale of Goods Act 1893), irrespective of the gravity of the event that has in fact resulted from the breach, shall entitle the other party to elect to put an end to all primary obligations of both parties remaining unperformed (in the interest of clarity, the nomenclature of the Sale of Goods Act 1893, 'breach of conditions', should be reserved for this exception). Where such an election is made (a) there is substituted by implication of law for the primary obligations of the party in default which remain unperformed a secondary obligation to pay monetary compensation to the other party for the loss sustained by him in consequence of their non-performance in the future and (b) the unperformed primary obligations of that other party are discharged. This secondary obligation is additional to the general secondary obligation; I will call it 'the anticipatory secondary obligation'. (Lord Diplock's emphasis).

A little later comes the passage relied on (|1980| 1 All ER 556 at 567, |1980| AC 827 at 850):

> Parties are free to agree to whatever exclusion or modification of all types of obligations as they please within the limits that the agreement must retain the legal characteristics of a contract and must not offend against the equitable rule

against penalties, that is to say, it must not impose on the breaker of a primary obligation a general secondary obligation to pay to the other party a sum of money that is manifestly intended to be in excess of the amount which would fully compensate the other party for the loss sustained by him in consequence of the breach of the primary obligation.

I do not read this passage as being concerned with anything other than penalty clauses in their ordinary sense, *viz.* clauses which purport to fix the damages recoverable for breach of a primary obligation in a manner which does not reflect those which would be recovered at common law. The reference is to clauses which, in the terminology established by Lord Diplock, fix the extent of the general secondary obligation (not, it may be noted, the 'anticipatory secondary obligation') to pay damages for breach of the primary obligation. I cannot see anything to suggest that Lord Diplock was putting in question the right of the parties to decide on the character of the primary obligation. Put in language perhaps more familiar, Lord Diplock was speaking of clauses which restrict the rights of the parties to recover the appropriate measure of damages; he was not concerned with the right of the parties to decide that all breaches of contract should be treated as breaches of condition. Nor am I able to accept that Lord Diplock, who had been concerned for nearly twenty years with explaining the consequences of a breach of contract, should at this very late stage introduce the law of penalties so as to produce a result quite different from anything which he had said before.

For these reasons I conclude that the plaintiffs are entitled to retain the damages which the master has awarded. This is not a result which I view with much satisfaction, partly because the plaintiffs have achieved by one means a result which the law of penalties might have prevented them from achieving by another and partly because if the line of argument under clause 2 had been developed from the outset, the defendant might have found an answer based on waiver which the court is now precluded from assessing, for want of the necessary facts. Nevertheless, it is the answer to which, in my view, the authorities clearly point. Accordingly, I would dismiss the appeal.

(Nicholls and Lawton, L.JJ. gave judgments to like effect.)

Chapter Twenty

Equitable Remedies and Breach of Contract

SECTION ONE—THE INJUNCTION

Courts of equity developed specific remedies that were not generally available in the common law courts until the Common Law Procedure Act 1854 made it possible for common law courts to grant injunctions in certain cases. The statutory basis for the awarding of an injunction is found in s. 28 (8) of the Supreme Court of Judicature (Ireland) Act 1877 which provides:

an injunction may be granted . . . by an interlocutory order of the court in all cases in which it shall appear to the court to be just or convenient that such order shall be made, and any such order shall be made either unconditionally or upon such terms and conditions as the court shall think just . . .

Interlocutory injunctions are injunctions in which the party seeking such an injunction fears that an actual or anticipated wrong, such as a breach or future breach of contract, will cause irreparable loss to that person's interests. That person may seek an order which directs the other party not to carry out, or to abstain from carrying out, these prejudicial acts, pending the trial of the underlying dispute as between the parties.

Interlocutory injunctions are a common feature of restraint of trade disputes and certain types of contract which involve the parties in long term or repetitive acts of performance, such as distributorship agreements, and in such litigation the award of the interlocutory agreement may in practical terms decide the outcome of the dispute; indeed the parties are free to elect to allow the outcome of the injunction to be regarded as trial of the action itself.

A perpetual injunction however will normally be awarded at the hearing of the action itself, whether an interlocutory injunction has been awarded or not. The perpetual injunction is intended to resolve the underlying dispute as between the parties.

Irish Shell v Elm Motors Ltd [1984] IR 200

Irish Shell granted a lease to Elm Motors which allowed Elm Motors to develop a filling station on this and their adjoining property. The lease contained a clause obliging Elm Motors to take petroleum products only from Irish Shell. The defendants ceased to trade with the plaintiffs, taking their products from a rival petroleum wholesaler. Irish Shell obtained mandatory and prohibitory interlocutory injunctions in the High Court, Costello J. holding the defendants to be in clear breach of the covenants in the lease.

In the Supreme Court, McCarthy J. examined the basis upon which interlocutory injunctions are awarded in Irish law.

McCarthy J.:

. . .

In *Educational Co. of Ireland Ltd v Fitzpatrick*[1] the former Supreme Court laid down certain principles applicable on applications for interlocutory injunctions. The exact nature of the decision must be determined by an examination of the judgments of the majority but, at first sight, it appears to me that the headnote of the report is incorrect insofar as it states that the issue of the balance of convenience was determined as follows: ' . . . as it was not agreed between the parties that all the facts necessary to decide the issue in the case were properly established or admitted before the court.' Teevan J. in the High Court, had expressed the opinion (p. 325) that there were certain matters that could be made the basis of contentious issues in the case. Maguire C.J., who dissented from the majority of the Supreme Court on a different issue, concluded (p. 333) that ' . . . all the facts which the plaintiffs think necessary to secure the interlocutory injunction are to be found in the affidavits and in my view a vague hope that other facts essential to a decision may emerge at the trial is not sufficient to bring this case within the judgment relied upon.' Lavery J., to whose judgment I shall revert, expressed (p. 338) the view: 'In this case there may well be further facts elicited at the trial, *but there can be no doubt that a serious question of law arises.*' (The emphasis is mine.)

At 342 of the report Kingsmill Moore J. said:

> [Counsel for the defendants] counters by saying that, even if this is so, the facts are not in dispute and the court should decide the question of law here and now. I am not convinced that all relevant facts are established or admitted, though it seems to me likely that they are. [Counsel] for the plaintiffs does not accept that all relevant facts have been established and says that there are further facts which he hopes to establish if the case goes to a full hearing, and if he can avail himself of discovery, interrogatories, and cross-examination to elicit them. I am of opinion that a plaintiff is entitled to have his case fully investigated in the ordinary course of legal procedure and that it would be undesirable in the absence of consent to decide a legal question of this magnitude merely on the affidavits filed for the purpose of the interlocutory motion. In *Smith and Another v Beirne and Another*[2] the defendants (who were the picketers) resisted the motion for an interlocutory injunction on the grounds that they did not agree that all facts necessary to decide the issue were established or admitted, and the court, while granting an interlocutory injunction, did not make any attempt then and there to decide the question of law. I think similar weight must be given to the refusal of the plaintiff to agree that all necessary facts are established or admitted. [Counsel for the plaintiffs] seeks to raise a question of *bona fides* on the part of the union. He is entitled to a full investigation of the facts.

This quotation might appear to lend support to that part of the headnote of the report that I have cited but it is taken out of context in a case where Kingsmill Moore J. held (p. 342) that ' . . . a very important and difficult question of law is involved and one which requires the most careful consideration.' Ó Dálaigh J., as he then was, makes no reference (p. 342) to there being any issue as to facts or any need to refer to the facts in any detail. Martin Maguire J. fully endorsed the judgment of Lavery J. and also agreed with those of Kingsmill Moore and Ó Dálaigh JJ.

In *Esso Petroleum Co. (Ireland) Ltd v Fogarty*,[3] Ó Dálaigh C.J. and Lavery J. (Walsh J. not expressly citing the case) affirmed the principles of law to be applied by this court on the hearing of an appeal to justify an order granting an interlocutory injunction as set out in the judgment of Lavery J. in the *Educational Co.* case. With great respect to the late Chief Justice, it appears to me that the principles of law set out by Lavery J. were not confined to the hearing of an appeal to set aside an order granting an interlocutory injunction but were, and are, to be applied by the High Court or, on appeal, by this court to any case concerning an interlocutory injunction, unless it is clear these principles of law cannot be applied. Ó Dálaigh C.J. cited (p. 538) two passages from the judgment of Lavery J. quoting from *Kerr on Injunctions* and the second edition of the *Laws of England*. The quotation from *Kerr on Injunctions* (6th ed.), 15–16 is as follows:

> The office of the court to interfere being founded on the existence of the legal right, a man who seeks the aid of the court must be able to show a fair *prima facie* case in support of the title which he asserts. He is not required to make out a clear legal title, but he must satisfy the court that he has a fair question to raise as to the existence of the legal right which he sets up, and that there are substantial grounds for doubting the existence of the alleged legal right, the exercise of which he seeks to prevent. The court must, before disturbing any man's legal right, or stripping him of any of the rights with which the law has clothed him, be satisfied that the probability is in favour of his case ultimately failing in the final issue of the suit. The mere existence of a doubt as to the plaintiff's right to the property, interference with which he seeks to restrain, does not of itself constitute a sufficient ground for refusing an injunction, though it is always a circumstance which calls for the attention of the court.

Further, Ó Dálaigh C.J. quoted (p. 539), as Lavery J. did, the following passage from *Halsbury's Laws of England* (2nd ed.), 33, paras 48 and 49; the observations of the learned author are repeated in the fourth edition of that work (vol. 24, para. 956):

> Where any doubt exists as to the plaintiff's right, or if his right is not disputed, but its violation is denied, the court, in determining whether an interlocutory injunction should be granted, takes into consideration the balance of convenience to the parties and the nature of the injury which the defendant, on the one hand, would suffer if the injunction was granted and he should ultimately turn out to be right, and that which the plaintiff, on the other hand, might sustain if the injunction was refused and he should ultimately turn out to be right. The burden of proof that the inconvenience which the plaintiff will suffer by the refusal of the injunction is greater than that which the defendant will suffer, if it is granted, lies on the plaintiff.

The equivalent passage in *Halsbury's Laws of England* (4th ed.) vol. 24, 539, para. 956 ends with this sentence: 'Where there is a clear breach the question of balance of convenience does not arise.'

I would respectfully adopt that statement of the law and add to it the observations of Lord Diplock in *American Cyanamid v Ethicon Ltd*[4] at 407–8 of the report:

> It is no part of the court's function at this stage of the litigation to try to resolve conflicts of evidence on affidavit as to facts on which the claims of either party may

ultimately depend nor to decide difficult questions of law which call for detailed argument and mature considerations. *These are matters to be dealt with at the trial.* One of the reasons for the introduction of the practice of requiring an undertaking as to damages upon the grant of an interlocutory injunction was that 'it aided the court in doing that which was its great object, *viz.* abstaining from expressing any opinion upon the merits of the case until the hearing': *Wakefield v Duke of Buccleugh.*[5] So unless the material available to the court at the hearing of the application for an interlocutory injunction fails to disclose that the plaintiff has any real prospect of succeeding in his claim for a permanent injunction at the trial, the court should go on to consider whether the balance of convenience lies in favour of granting or refusing the interlocutory relief that is sought. (I have added the emphasis.)

The converse must also be true. Unless the material available to the court at the hearing of the application for an interlocutory injunction fails to disclose that the defendant has any real prospect of succeeding in his defence to a claim for a permanent injunction at the trial, the court should go on to consider the balance of convenience. If it were otherwise, it appears to me that an interlocutory injunction, however detailed the argument and mature the consideration, in effect, determines the issue and a trial becomes superfluous.

In the instant appeal, the learned trial judge clearly took a very decided view on the complex legal issues which had been raised; the very positive nature of his decision and its finality is marked by the absence from the order of any undertaking as to damages and the awarding of costs to the plaintiffs at the interlocutory stage. In my judgment, whilst reserving the question as to whether or not there are cases in which it is proper for a court to express a concluded view as to factual or legal issues arising at the interlocutory stage, ordinarily, the determination of whether or not to grant an interlocutory injunction lies, and lies only, in answers to the two material questions as to there being a fair case to be made and where the balance of convenience lies.

Since writing this judgment I have had the opportunity of reading the judgments of the Chief Justice and Mr Justice Griffin in *Campus Oil v Minister for Industry* (No. 2);[6] they appear to confirm the views I have expressed.

Foreign precedents

In referring to the observations cited from *Kerr on Injunctions, Halsbury's Laws of England* and the *American Cyanamid* case, I pause to draw attention to the observations of the learned trial judge in his relatively lengthy judgment after his analysis of the English case law in *Esso Petroleum Co. Ltd v Harper's Garage (Stourport) Ltd;*[7] *Cleveland Petroleum Co. Ltd v Dartstone Ltd*[8] and *Amoco Australia v Rocca Bros*[9]—the latter being a decision of the Judicial Committee of the Privy Council. I do not necessarily agree or disagree with the analysis made by the learned trial judge but I deem it proper to comment on his observation that 'The High Court is not bound to follow the decisions and judgments to which I have referred if there are compelling reasons for rejecting them.' I do not believe that the true inference from this observation is that, in the absence of compelling reasons for rejection, the High Court is bound to follow decisions and judgments of the House of Lords, the Court of Appeal in England, or the Judicial Committee of the British Privy Council; but, lest any such view should be entertained, I would unequivocally deny the existence of any such principle or the propriety of any such practice. Of the decisions of those courts decided prior to 1922, it is proper to say that they are part of the corpus of jurisprudence and law that was taken over on the foundation of Saorstát Éireann, being the laws in force in Saorstát Éireann at the date of the coming into operation of the Constitution of the Irish Free State (Saorstát Éireann), subject to that Constitution and to the extent to which they were not inconsistent therewith. Similarly Article 50 of the Constitution provides:

1. Subject to this Constitution and to the extent to which they are not inconsistent therewith, the laws in force in Saorstát Éireann immediately prior to the date of the coming into operation of this Constitution shall continue to be of full force and effect until the same or any of them shall have been repealed or amended by enactment of the Oireachtas.

2. Laws enacted before, but expressed to come into force after, the coming into operation of this Constitution, shall, unless otherwise enacted by the Oireachtas come into force in accordance with the terms thereof.

Article 50 was stated (p. 345) by Kingsmill Moore J. in *Educational Co. of Ireland Ltd v Fitzpatrick* (No. 2)[10] as relating to 'statutes or law carried forward into our *corpus juris*'; but that view has been questioned by Mr Justice Walsh (with whom the Chief Justice agreed) in *Gaffney v Gaffney*[11] where he said at 151 of the report: 'Contrary to what appears to have been the view of Kingsmill Moore J., I do not think that Article 50 of the Constitution refers to any law other than statute law, and in my view the text of Article 50 makes that clear.'

Mr Justice Walsh may well have been echoing the observations of Gavan Duffy J. (as he then was) in *Exham v Beamish*[12] where at 348–9 of the report, he stated:

As a matter of practice, we constantly refer to judgments in the English courts and such judgments, as every lawyer will recognise, have often proved to be of great service to us; but let us be clear. In my opinion, when Saorstát Éireann, and afterwards Éire, continued the laws in force, they did not make binding on their courts anything short of law. In my opinion, judicial decisions in Ireland before the Treaty, and English decisions which were followed here, are binding upon this court only when they represent a law so well settled or pronounced by so weighty a juristic authority that they may fairly be regarded, in a system built up upon the principle of *stare decisis*, as having become established as part of the law of the land before the Treaty; and to bind, they must, of course, not be inconsistent with the Constitution . . . In my opinion, this court cannot be fettered in the exercise of the judicial power by opinions of very different courts under the old régime, unless those opinions must reasonably be considered to have had the force of law in Ireland, so that they formed part of the code expressly retained . . . If, before the Treaty, a particular law was administered in a way so repugnant to the common sense of our citizens as to make the law look ridiculous, it is not in the public interest that we should repeat the mistake. Our new High Court must mould its own *cursus curiae*; in so doing I hold that it is free, indeed bound, to decline to treat any such absurdity in the machinery of administration as having been imposed on it as part of the law of the land; nothing is law here which is inconsistent with derivation from the people.

Whilst observations of judges of the former Supreme Court in *Boylan v Dublin Corporation*[13] and in *Minister for Finance v O'Brien*[14] appear to support the view that decisions of the House of Lords upon law common to England and Ireland, given before the coming into operation of the Constitution of 1922, are a binding force in our courts, in my view the decision of this court in *Attorney General v Ryan's Car Hire Ltd*[15] and *The State (Quinn) v Ryan*[16] (wherein the rigidity of the principle of *stare decisis* was denied) must now call into question the binding force of any such pre–1922 decision. Since 26 July 1966, the House of Lords has recognised that too rigid an adherence to precedent may lead to injustice in a particular case and also unduly restrict the proper development of the law. It stated its right, while treating former decisions of the House as normally binding, to depart from a previous decision when it appears right to do so: see the practice note published in |1966| 3 All ER 77. Such a statement of principle by the House of Lords inevitably makes even weaker any case for following the decisions of that House whether they are decisions made before or after the year 1922. There are many other jurisdictions like our own where the *corpus juris* includes the common law, such as the US, Canada, Australia and New Zealand. These are nations where, in addition, there are written and, consequently, rigid Constitutions unlike that of the UK. Whilst the judgments in cases decided in the English courts at all levels will, on a great many occasions, provide convenient and, indeed, convincing statements of principle and attractive arguments in favour of such principles, they are no more than that and must be examined and questioned in the light of a jurisprudence whose fundamental law is radically different in its denial of a supremacy of parliament and its upholding of three co-equal organs of government in the Legislature, the Executive, and the Judiciary.

In no sense are our courts a continuation of, or successors to, the British courts. They derive their powers from a Constitution enacted by the people and would, in my view, find more appropriate guidance in the decisions of courts in other countries based upon a similar constitutional framework than in what, at times, appears to be an uncritical adherence to English precedent which, itself, appears difficult to reconcile from time to time: see *Pirelli v Oscar Faber & Partners*.[17] Within the relatively narrow confines of the instant appeal, it is to be noted that the *American Cyanamid* case appears to have departed from an existing requirement of 'probable success' and to substitute for it that of there being a serious issue to be tried.

In my view, it is unnecessary to enter upon an examination of the conclusions to which the learned trial judge came on the hearing of the interlocutory application, and the reasons for them. I am satisfied that it was unnecessary and, in an interlocutory application, undesirable that he should have come to the firm conclusion set out in his judgment. It may well be that his conclusion was correct; I express no view upon it save to state that an examination of the judgment itself demonstrates the complexity of the legal issue that arose and the certain need that all the facts, including the exact nature and location of the development that took place, should be established before any view of the legal position is formed. The difficult legal issues raised by this undisputed fact, for instance, that the covenants are in form affirmatory rather than negative indicate the wide range of the problem; indeed the learned trial judge's own analysis of the alleged anomalies originally suggested as arising out of the *Esso* case in an article in the *Law Quarterly Review* vol. 8, 229 adds force to this view. If the covenants are, in fact, negative, it is contended that the balance of convenience need not be taken into consideration upon the principle allegedly founding the decision in *Doherty v Allman*.[18] That case was the subject of comment by Ó Dálaigh C.J. in *Dublin Port & Docks Board v Brittania Dredging Co. Ltd*,[19] which decision was considered by Mr Justice Keane in *TMG Group v Al Babtain*.[20] In referring to the *Brittania* case, Mr Justice Keane said at 353–4 of the report:

> The defendants in that case were proposing to repudiate the contract in its entirety in circumstances where the court was satisfied that they were not entitled so to do. The circumstances of the present case are wholly different: the defendants strenuously contend that neither of the transactions which the company proposes to enter into will constitute a breach of their contractual obligations under the shareholders' agreement. I do not think that Ó Dálaigh C.J. in the passages to which I have referred, was laying down any general principle that, in all cases where the plaintiff establishes a *prima facie* case of a breach of a negative stipulation in a contract, the court

could disregard any question of the balance of convenience as between the parties. His observations were clearly confined to a case where one party to a contract was proposing to act in breach of a negative contract (and indeed to repudiate the whole contract) in circumstances where the court was not satisfied on the evidence that they were entitled so to do. I do not think that the passage lends any support to the proposition that even where the violation of the plaintiff's right is denied, as it unquestionably is in the present case, the court can disregard the balance of convenience to the parties.

It is right to point out that it does not appear that the learned judge in the High Court was referred to the decision of Mr Justice Keane in the TMG case; that case was appealed to this court but this point was not canvassed. I would endorse the views expressed by Mr Justice Keane, as cited above, and I repeat my firm view that, save in the most exceptional circumstances (which it would be invidious to attempt to detail or delimit), the determination of an application for an interlocutory injunction lies, and lies only, in the answers to the two material questions as to there being a fair case to be made and where the balance of convenience lies.

In the result, whilst, due to the passage of time and the events that have taken place in the interval, it is clear that the balance of convenience lies in the continuance of the injunction and that, save as already indicated, the order of the High Court should stand, in principle, I would allow this appeal.

Griffin J.:

I agree with the judgment delivered by Mr Justice McCarthy, save and except in respect of that portion of his judgment which deals with the effect of decisions of the House of Lords, the English Court of Appeal, or the Judicial Committee of the Privy Council, and of the effect of Article 50 of the Constitution. In respect of these matters I neither agree nor disagree, as they were not argued or discussed on the hearing of this appeal. I would express no opinion on them, and would reserve any such opinion until such questions arise and are argued in an appropriate case.

O'Higgins C.J.:

I also agree and add the same reservations as are expressed in the judgment of Mr Justice Griffin.

[By its order the Supreme Court ordered 'that this appeal to stand dismissed and that the said order of the High Court do stand affirmed save that the provision therein contained as to costs do stand discharged and in lieu thereof it is ordered that the question of the costs of the said motion in the High Court be reserved to the trial judge and it is ordered that the plaintiffs do pay to the defendants their costs of this appeal when taxed and ascertained.']

1. [1961] IR 323.
2. (SC) 29 January 1953, unrep.
3. [1965] IR 531.
4. [1975] AC 396.
5. (1865) 12 LT 628.
6. [1983] IR 88.
7. [1968] AC 269.
8. [1969] 1 WLR 116.
9. [1975] AC 562.
10. [1961] IR 345.
11. [1975] IR 133.
12. [1939] IR 336.
13. [1949] IR 60.
14. [1949] IR 91.
15. [1965] IR 642.
16. [1965] IR 70.
17. [1983] 2 AC 1.
18. (1878) 3 App Cas 709.
19. [1968] IR 136.
20. [1982] ILRM 349.

Note

In this case Costello J. in the High Court did not consider the balance of convenience issue, given the blatant nature of the defendants' breach of contract. McCarthy J. said, *obiter*, that had he to decide the point, the balance of convenience would lie in favour of the plaintiffs.

One of the most important matters to be taken into account in testing the balance of convenience is whether damages will prove to be an inadequate remedy if the party seeking the injunction is successful in the trial of the action.

Curust Financial Services Ltd *v* Loewe-Lackwerke Otto Loewe GmbH & Co. and Others [1993] ILRM 723

Finlay C.J.:

These are two appeals brought by the first- and second-named defendants against an order made in the High Court by Barron J. on 3 June 1992, by way of interlocutory injunction.

The proceedings arise out of a dispute originating between the plaintiffs (which I will jointly refer to as Curust), and the first-named defendant (which I will refer to as Loewe) concerning what Curust allege to be a breach by Loewe of an agreement dated 27 November 1986 made between them and Loewe, whereby Loewe granted to Curust the sole and exclusive licence to manufacture, market, sell and distribute the goods manufactured or distributed by them from time to time, in certain areas, including Ireland. The second-named defendant (which I will refer to as Sales Ltd) became involved in the action by reason of accepting appointment as a distributor from Loewe. The particular product with which this case is concerned is a product known as Loewe Rust Primer, a paint sold under the trademark of Loewe in Ireland, being a paint for application to prevent rust on objects to which it is applied. It is stated by all the parties to this action to be the major rust primer sold on the Irish market in the retail shops and in what is described as the DIY trade.

The commercial relationship between Curust and Loewe has existed for over thirty years, and prior to November 1986 it is agreed that Curust manufactured and distributed Loewe Rust Primer in Ireland, using the trade mark of Loewe under a series of licences or agreements.

The plenary summons was issued on 17 June 1992, and claimed a declaration that Loewe was bound by the terms of the agreement of 27 November 1986 and claimed a series of injunctions restraining Loewe, its servants and agents from what were claimed were breaches of that agreement. Further injunctions were sought restraining Sales Ltd from carrying out activities which would, in effect, constitute a breach of the agreement and an invasion of what is alleged to be the sole right of Curust to manufacture, sell and distribute these products. The hearing of the application for an interlocutory injunction was on affidavit, and by his order, Barron J. restrained Loewe, pending the trial of the action, from appointing or purporting to appoint Sales Ltd, or any other person as a licensee for the manufacture, distribution or sale in Ireland and in other territories of all or any of the products manufactured by Loewe and from supplying Loewe Rust Primer or any other product manufactured or distributed by them to Sales Ltd or to any other person for distribution or sale within the territory. The order further restrained Sales Ltd, pending the trial of the action, without permission of Curust, from manufacturing, distributing, selling or offering for sale in Ireland or in the UK all or any of the products manufactured or distributed by Loewe, including Loewe Rust Primer.

In the order it was provided that the relief granted to Curust was subject to their applying for consent in accordance with the exclusive manufacturing and distribution agreement of 27 November 1985, of Loewe in relation to the manufacture of the product the subject matter of the proceedings, by an agent on behalf of Curust. This condition and the issues arising in it do not form part of the subject matter of this appeal.

Whilst on the affidavits filed and on the submissions made both in the High Court and on this appeal there are a number of disputed issues of both law and fact, it is possible to trace an uncontroversial broad history of the matters arising in this appeal.

From the early 1960s Curust had a sole manufacturing and distribution agreement from Loewe which covered Loewe Rust Primer.

Up to the end of the year 1988, Curust manufactured and put into tins the Loewe rust Primer in Ireland from formulae provided to them and in accordance with processes of which they were informed and instructed by Loewe, with a raw material sold to them by Loewe at cost price. Curust then paid to Loewe a commission on the products sold by them. At the end of 1988 Curust ceased the manufacture of the primer by reason of the fact that a change in the specification required different methods of production, and it was necessary for them to reorganise their manufacturing process in order to comply with that.

An agreement was then entered into for the supply by Loewe to Curust of the finished product of Loewe Rust Primer to be put into tins and sold and distributed in Ireland. This agreement contained terms with regard to price and with regard to credit, and disputes have arisen with regard to those precise terms. It was expressed, or appears to have been expressed to conclude at the end of the year 1991 when it was anticipated that Curust would have returned to manufacturing of the Loewe Rust Primer.

During the currency of that agreement and in the years 1990 and 1991, disputes arose between the parties concerning the payments, the amount of credit to be allowed and the date of payments, and eventually Loewe purported to repudiate all agreements, including the agreement of November 1986, and stated that all agreements were at an end between the parties, and that they would, after the expiry of the agreement for the supply of the finished product at the conclusion of 1991, cease to supply any further products or raw materials to Curust.

At some time which is not identified in the affidavits Loewe entered into an agreement with Sales Ltd for the sale and distribution by them of Loewe's product in Ireland, and this was put on the market at the end of May and beginning of June of this year by Sales Ltd, under the name Durabond, in a tin similar to that used by Curust. What is in that tin is, undoubtedly, the Loewe Rust Primer and, on the evidence, it is being sold as such by the retailers to whom it has been distributed.

It was provided by clause 9 of the agreement of November 1986 that either party might assign, sub-license or sub-contract all or part of its obligations or benefits under the agreement, subject to the prior, written consent of the other party. In addition, Curust undertook, by virtue of the agreement that they would not, at any time otherwise than for the purpose of the rights given to them, including, of course, the right of sub-contracting, divulge any information in relation to the goods, methods of manufacture, price structure or the affairs, business or methods of carrying on business of Loewe without written consent of Loewe.

On the evidence before the learned trial judge, which he accepted and which is not disputed on the affidavits, in March 1992, at an interview between Mr Brocklesby representing Curust and Mr Schoening representing Loewe, Mr Brocklesby informed Mr Schoening that it was the intention of Curust, if possible, to enter into an arrangement with a third party involving the resumption of the manufacture in Ireland of the Loewe prime rust product, and he asked (according to his affidavit) Mr Schoening to give him an assurance that if he informed him of the identity of that party that he, Mr Schoening and his company, would not try and intimidate that person from entering into an arrangement. This conversation was in the light of an assertion then being made, and still being made, by Loewe that all contractual relationships between the two companies had ceased, and that Curust had no right to sell, distribute or manufacture the product of Loewe. Mr Schoening refused to give any such assurance, and, accordingly, he was not informed of the identity. Apparently, subsequent to that, an arrangement was entered into between Curust and a company known as International Coating Ltd for the manufacture of the product Loewe Rust Primer in Ireland, and that has been done and Curust has put that on the market in tins clearly marked Loewe Rust Primer.

On these broad facts, Loewe sought in the High Court to resist the making of an interlocutory injunction on a number of grounds.

1. They asserted that an agreement had not been concluded between the parties in November 1986, and in the absence of the production by Curust of the original of that agreement which they say has been mislaid, they challenged the validity of a produced copy of it.

2. They asserted that if the agreement was concluded it was void, having regard to the provisions of article 85 (1) of the Treaty of Rome, and, in the alternative, that Curust had not established a triable issue that the agreement did not have an appreciable effect upon trade and competition in the product the subject matter of the agreement so as to bring it outside the invalidity arising from the said article of the treaty.

3. That damages would be an adequate remedy for Curust, and that, therefore, they should not be entitled to an injunction.

4. That Curust, by reason of their delay in seeking relief, were disentitled to an injunction.

5. That the admitted breach by Curust of the agreement of 1986, consisting of their entering into arrangements with a third party for the manufacture and supply of Loewe Rust Primer in Ireland without the prior written consent of Loewe, disentitled them to an injunction.

6. That if damages were not an adequate remedy, then the balance of convenience did not favour the granting of relief.

Judgment of the High Court

In deciding to grant the injunction Barron J. reached the following conclusions concerning the issues which had been raised before him.

Dealing with the question of the conclusion of the agreement in November 1986, he held that, on the facts, there was a triable issue concerning that. Although in the notice of appeal filed by Loewe a ground was inserted appealing against that decision, this was not pursued on the hearing of the appeal before us.

With regard to the issue arising under the Treaty of Rome, the learned trial judge found as follows: 'In my view the provisions of the treaty are a matter of defence but once raised as a matter of defence the onus reverts to the plaintiffs to establish that they can bring themselves outside the terms of the treaty. On the evidence before me which is slight, it does seem to me that the amount of trade involved is small and that accordingly the plaintiffs have established a triable issue on this point.'

Loewe on the hearing of this appeal did not pursue a contention that this court could or should at this stage hold that the agreement of November 1986 was void, having regard to the provisions of article 85(1) of the treaty, but did contend that the learned trial judge's finding that there was a triable issue as to the avoidance of that invalidity, by reason of the smallness of the trade, was not supported by the evidence.

The learned trial judge in holding that damages would not be an adequate remedy for the plaintiffs stated as follows:

> The next issue is whether or not damages would be an adequate remedy. Damages are clearly an adequate remedy if they are liquidated in circumstances where there is no particular interest in the plaintiff to maintain the right save to obtain such damages. Save in the situation envisaged by the Lord Cairns' Act where the damage is small, damages which are not readily susceptible to accurate measurements are not usually an appropriate remedy. A rich man has never been entitled to buy out the rights of a poor man just because he wishes to do so. For example the owner of a premises which would be devalued by a readily ascertainable amount cannot be forced to accept that sum in lieu of an injunction to restrain a defendant from infringing that right. In my view that in essence is what the defendants are saying here: if there is a breach of the 1986 agreement, then the first-named defendant can pay the plaintiffs the value of the business which they will lose as a result. I do not accept such a proposition.

Dealing further with the question of adequacy, the learned trial judge stated as follows:

> Where trade is involved as in this case it is always difficult to determine whether trade has been lost by reason of the failure to obtain the injunction, or whether it has been lost through other causes and equally it is difficult if the injunction is ultimately given to establish whether or not all the trade which was lost has come back and if it has not why it has not. In such cases it is also fairly notorious that people once they change over from a product which they have been using do not always return to that product when they are free to do so. Having regard to these views and to what I regard to be the general principles as to the adequacy of damages it seems to me that damages would not be an adequate remedy in the present case.

Dealing with the position of Sales Ltd, who are also appellants and who pursue most of the grounds of appeal pursued by Loewe, the learned trial judge on this issue came to the following conclusion:

> However, as I have indicated I do not regard damages as being an adequate remedy and this would apply as much to the second-named defendant as to the plaintiffs. In the circumstances the issue seems to me as to whether or not I should preserve the *status quo ante* rather than to permit these defendants and the plaintiffs to sell the product in competition. It seems to me that it would be more reasonable to require the maintenance of the *status quo ante*.

The learned trial judge rejected the contention made in the High Court that Curust had delayed too long and would be, therefore, disentitled to the relief claimed. This ground was not pursued as a separate ground of appeal, but it was contended that it was the date of the issue of the summons, at which date they had already placed the Loewe Rust Primer under the name of Durabond on the market, that was the material date if the court came to the question of the balance of convenience, and, in particular, if the court was viewing it in the light of trying to deal with the *status quo ante*.

The learned trial judge rejected the contention that Curust by its action in sub-contracting the manufacture of the rust primer in March 1992 were disentitled to an injunction.

The decision

Since Sales Ltd, in essence, supported the grounds of appeal put forward by Loewe, merely adding the factual assertion that it was unaware of any difficulty or problem arising from accepting the agreement for the distribution of the rust primer concerned, and was unaware of any subsisting licence to Curust, I deal with all the issues raised by both appellants in a single series of decisions.

(1) *Is there a triable issue concerning the exemption of the agreement of 1986 from the prohibition contained in article 85(1) of the Treaty of Rome?*

No cross-appeal has been entered against the ruling by the learned trial judge in the High Court that once Loewe had raised the question of the prohibition contained in article 85(1) as a defence (and presumably had shown *prima facie* that the article applied to the agreement) the onus of establishing an exemption or avoidance of that prohibition rested on Curust. That being so, without making any decision on the question, I proceed on the basis that the onus is on Curust to establish a triable issue as to whether, by reason of the smallness of the market in Ireland for the product concerned, the agreement relating to it is outside Article 85(1). Dealing with this issue which was raised in the affidavit of Mr Schoening, Mr Brocklesby in a supplemental affidavit, at para. 6, stated as follows:

> With regard to para. 11 of Mr Schoening's affidavit, I do not accept that the 1986 agreement is void, having regard to the provisions of article 85 of the Treaty of Rome. It is my belief that the agreement is one of minor importance which does not have any material effect on inter-community trade. The plaintiffs have only a tiny share of the sales of metal primer paint and rust paint in the relevant part of the territory in the community, that is, Ireland and the UK. The plaintiffs even have a very small and minor share of that part of the patent market concerned with metal priming and rust protection, being largely confined to the DIY market, rather than the steel industry. In industry generally and in transport, there are significant sales of comparable products. I am unaware of the precise turnover of the first-named defendant, but even by Irish standards, and certainly by European standards, the plaintiff companies are extremely small.

I would accept the learned trial judge's classification of these averments as being slight evidence, but at the same time I would also accept his conclusion that they do establish a triable issue which, undoubtedly, at the hearing of the action would have to be gone into in much greater detail. In those circumstances I am satisfied that he was correct in rejecting that ground as a ground for refusing to grant an injunction.

(2) *Does a breach by Curust of the agreement of 1986, consisting of their sub-contracting the manufacture of the product without the prior written consent of Loewe, disentitle them to an injunction?*

On this issue I have come to the following conclusions. I accept that, the granting of an injunction being an equitable remedy, the court has a discretion, where it is satisfied that a person has come to the court, as it is so frequently expressed, otherwise than 'with clean hands' by that fact alone to refuse an equitable relief of injunction. It seems to me, however, that this phrase must of necessity involve an element of turpitude and cannot necessarily be equated with a mere breach of contract.

If Curust are correct in the contention which they are making, Loewe in March 1992 was still bound by the agreement of November 1986 and was prohibited by the terms of that agreement from entering into any arrangement with any other supplier to manufacture or distribute these products in Ireland, and was furthermore obliged not unreasonably to withhold its consent to the sub-contracting by Curust of any part of their rights or obligations under that agreement. It must be on the basis that Curust may succeed in establishing such a case finally at the hearing that the question of an interlocutory injunction must be viewed. If they do, then, obviously Loewe in March 1992 was quite wrong in asserting that it had no obligation to Curust, and quite wrong in proceeding, as it obviously was proceeding, to enter into arrangements with another party to sell this product in Ireland. Having regard to those facts, it seems to me that it was entirely justifiable for the representative of Curust to seek an assurance from the representative of Loewe that he would not interfere with or, presumably, intimidate any person with whom Curust were negotiating in order to sub-contract the manufacturing of this product. Having regard to that view, I conclude that it would be unreasonable to say that what may be established as a breach by Curust of the agreement not to sub-contract without prior consent, which may also be established as having been provoked by a repudiation which was wrongful on the part of Loewe, of the existence of contractual obligations subsisting under the 1986 agreement, and a refusal which would also have been wrongful to undertake not to interfere with what would appear to be almost certainly a right on the part of Curust at least to negotiate in general terms with other parties, should disentitle them to an injunction if they were otherwise entitled to it. I would, therefore, agree with the view of the learned trial judge that this did not constitute a ground for rejecting the claim for an injunction.

(3) *Are damages an adequate remedy for Curust?*

I am satisfied the following considerations apply to this issue which, in my view, is the most difficult issue arising on this appeal.

(a) No suggestion has been made that if Curust were to obtain a decree for damages arising out of Loewe's breach of contract, that Loewe would not be in a position to pay the amount of such damages.

(b) Whilst the loss likely to be sustained by Curust in the event of an injunction not being granted, is purely and simply a commercial loss arising from a diminution in trade and, therefore, ostensibly capable of quantification and assessment, they assert that there would be considerable difficulty in such quantification and a real risk that damages assessed in accordance with the evidence would not be adequate. This assertion largely consists of an assertion that whilst it might be possible to calculate between the time of the advent into the market of Sales Ltd up to the time of the successful conclusion by Curust of their action and the obtaining of a permanent injunction, the loss of trade and, therefore, the loss of profits sustained by Curust, that it would be extremely difficult, if not impossible to quantify into the future the loss of profits which would continue to be sustained until such time as Curust recovered their pre-1992 share of the market.

(c) It is asserted on behalf of Curust that if they lose the substantial market in these products, which they had up to the end of 1991 and continue to suffer that loss up to the date of the determination of the action, that having regard to the proportion which the sales of this product constituted of both their turnover and gross profits, that they might not survive as a solvent, trading unit.

To these issues the following general principles apply, The loss to be incurred by Curust if they succeed in the action and no interlocutory injunction is granted to them, is clearly and exclusively a commercial loss, in what had been, apparently, a stable and well established market. In those circumstances, *prima facie* it is a loss which should be capable of being assessed in damages both under the heading of loss actually suffered up to the date when such damages would fall to be assessed and also under the heading of probable future loss. Difficulty, as distinct from complete impossibility, in the assessment of such damages should not, in my view, be a ground for characterising the awarding of damages as an inadequate remedy.

With regard to the particular question of the assessment of damages in respect of any period after the granting of a permanent injunction to Curust while their share of the market is being recovered, it does not seem to me that insuperable difficulties of quantification could arise. The extent of the market to which Curust were accustomed before an interruption in their exclusive rights of sale and distribution is ascertainable, the quantity sold by Sales from April 1992 until the conclusion of the action would also be ascertainable, as would its value. Evidence in such a situation could surely be adduced which would permit a judge to make a reasonable forecast of the period during which Curust may suffer a continued diminution of trade and the approximate extent of that. In those circumstances, I do not see, by reason of difficulties in quantification, any ground for holding that damages are not an adequate remedy. So much of the learned trial judge's judgment on this issue as refers to Lord Cairns' Act and the question of an injunction being in many ways preferable to the awarding of damages, except in cases where damages are very small, relates more correctly, in my view, to the final decision as to whether relief being claimed for breach of contract which is continuing, should be in the form of a permanent injunction or in the form of an assessment of damages, but is not strictly relevant to the issues which arise with regard to an interlocutory injunction.

There remains the question as to whether on the evidence which was before the learned trial judge it was open to him to conclude that damages would not constitute an adequate remedy by reason of a real risk that the postponement of their payment necessarily involved until after the determination of the action, would lead to the collapse, from a financial point of view, of Curust. Although this issue was submitted in the High Court and is the subject matter of certain averments in the affidavits, it was not decided by the learned trial judge because, for other reasons, he concluded that damages would not be an adequate remedy and proceeded on to consider the balance of convenience.

The factual information contained in the affidavits which is relevant to this issue is as follows. Mr Brocklesby in his affidavit of 15 June 1992 stated as follows:

> 31. Further, although Curust sells a range of hardware products, including turpentine, brush cleaner, teak oil, penetrating oil and a range of branded locks and door catches, Curust's principal business is with Loewe Rust Primer and with white spirits. The rust primer not only gives the best margin but sales of rust primer also tend to lead to sales of all other products.
>
> 32. In the circumstances, I am extremely concerned that if R. S. Sales is allowed to continue sales of rust primer pending the hearing of the action, there will not only be very serious direct results as a result of loss of sales of Loewe Rust Primer, but there will be consequential reduction in turnover of other products. This would be likely to prejudice the viability of both Curust Industries and Curust Financial Services. Loewe Rust Primer has been a mainstay of Curust's business since the early 1960s and considerable advance planning would be required to build up other aspects of the business or introduce new products to replace without doing very great long term damage to the viability of both the plaintiff companies. Further, the paint market is seasonal, and the prime selling period is April to October.

In the same affidavit Mr Brocklesby stated a turnover figure for the plaintiff companies of £650,000 *per annum*.

In para. 20 of Mr Schoening's affidavit, dated 25 June 1992, he stated as follows:

> I beg to refer to para. 32 of Mr Brocklesby's said affidavit wherein he avers that the loss of sale of Loewe Rust Primer 'would be likely to prejudice the viability of both Curust Industries and Curust Financial Services'. Having regard to both the turnover figure of £650, 000 *per annum* given at para. 4 of Mr Brocklesby's said affidavit and the sales figures in relation to the supply of primer by the first-named defendant to the plaintiffs for the past three years I am at a loss to understand this averment.

The deponent then went on, in the form of Deutsch marks converted to Irish pounds, to give the figure for supply of primer for the three years as follows:

    1989   DM 104,828 = IR £39,155.83
    1990   DM 61,814 = IR £23,089.04
    1991   DM 157,920 = IR £58,987.01

He further explained that the figures were somewhat deceptive in that those for 1991 included both an item which would ordinarily have been costed into the 1990 year, and an item which would have been costed into the 1992 year. The average for the three years would appear to be slightly more than £40,000. In the supplemental affidavit of Mr Brocklesby, dated 26 June 1992, he dealt with this issue at para. 12, in the following terms:

> With regard to para. 20, I have not had time to check the figures which are given by Mr Schoening in respect of the value to Loewe of sales for the years 1989 to 1991, but I am able to say that in 1988 Curust's turnover was £575,000 of which £145,000 was attributable to Loewe Rust Primer. In 1989 the turnover was £632,000 of which £153,700 was attributable to Loewe Rust Primer. In the same year the total gross profit of Curust was £295,000 of which £88,000 (more than a quarter) is attributable to Loewe Rust Primer. In 1990 the proportion was even higher. The total gross profit was £200,606, of which £92,000 was attributable to Loewe. In 1991 the total gross profit was £220,000, of which £99,000 was attributable to Loewe.

Considering these facts, it is necessary to add in as a relevant factor that it is anticipated that the substantive action in which a statement of claim has been filed and in which, we are informed, a defence is almost ready, is likely to be heard, on the state of the High Court list, some time in the Spring of 1993. If the injunction were now set aside Curust would not be deprived of access to the market in rust primer, but rather would be obliged to share it in competition with Sales Ltd.

Since this issue on affidavit and the inferences to be drawn from it was not decided in the High Court, by reason of the learned trial judge's view that damages were for other reasons not an adequate remedy, and since I find myself in disagreement with that view, it is necessary that I should reach a conclusion on the affidavit evidence as to whether it has, as a matter of probability been established at this stage for the purpose of the interlocutory injunction that damages would not be an adequate remedy, by reason of the real risk of the financial collapse of the Curust companies. In my view, having regard to all the factors which I have outlined, there has not been established such a case as a matter of probability. No information is forthcoming about the general position of the companies with regard to their indebtedness or net assets situation. No attempt has been made to assess the probable result of competition between Curust and Sales Ltd in relation to this market for rust primer, except an averment in affidavit that Sales Ltd is underselling Curust with regard to the cost of the rust primer being offered for sale. In these circumstances, where damages can be quantified and where the loss is quite clearly a commercial loss and there is no doubt about the capacity of the defendants to pay any damages awarded against them and where there is no element of new or expanding business which may make quantification particularly difficult, as a matter of principle, I conclude that damages must be deemed to be an adequate remedy in this case, and I would therefore allow the appeal and set aside the order made in the High Court. In so doing, however, I have as a factor taken into consideration an estimate of the probable date on which this case will come on for hearing and, having regard to that fact, would request that all parties should inform the High Court of a request emanating from this court that the proceedings should be given a speedy trial, and that both parties should expedite the completion of pleadings to facilitate such an event.

(Egan J. concurred.)

O'Flaherty J.:

It was found by the learned High Court Judge and not disputed before us that Curust had made out a fair case to be tried concerning the binding effect of the 1986 agreement. Further evidence, slight though the learned trial judge held it to be at this stage of the case, went to show that there was no breach of Article 85 of the Treaty of Rome.

In general, the court's function at the hearing of the application of an interlocutory injunction is to determine whether there is a fair question to be tried and, if there is, where the balance of convenience lies. In my judgment, there are cases, however, where the breach of contract, which is the matter in issue in this case, is so clear or the party attempting to resist the application for an injunction so devoid of merits that the court should immediately provide a remedy by way of injunction: *Doherty v Allman* (1873) 3 App Cas 709; *Dublin Port & Docks Board v Brittania Dredging Co. Ltd* [1968] IR 136 and *Irish Shell Ltd v Elm Motors Ltd* [1984] IR 200 at 225.

As I understand the submissions made to us it is not asserted that this is such a case. It seems to be agreed by both sides that complex questions of law and fact remain outstanding. Perhaps that is so and, therefore, I must abstain from offering any view on the strength of the case for the enforcement by Curust of the 1986 agreement.

I then turn to the question of the balance of convenience. That involves as a first inquiry whether damages would be an adequate remedy for Curust should Curust ultimately succeed at the plenary hearing. I agree with the Chief Justice's reasoning that it would be in the circumstances of this case. The crucial matter, in my judgment, is that Curust are not to be deprived of access to the market in rust primer, but rather would be obliged to share it in competition with Sales Ltd.

Were it not for that factor I would hold that the matter was so finely balanced as to require a further inquiry as to where the balance of convenience lay. I would not, except for that circumstance, regard damages as an adequate remedy. Then I would look to the *status quo ante* which I would regard as comprising the long trading relationship that existed between the parties and the equilibrium of which was affected not by any direct default by Curust in relation to the 1986 agreement (on which agreement Curust rely) but on alleged tardiness in making payments in relation to a subsidiary agreement or agreements. In that situation I would have upheld the order of the High Court. However, in the conclusion that I have reached, in concurring with the Chief Justice on the matter of the adequacy of damages, I would allow the appeal and I would join with the Chief Justice in the proposal that he has made in relation to the early disposal of the substantive case.

A. MANDATORY AND PROHIBITORY INJUNCTIONS

A mandatory injunction seeks either to compel a wrongdoer to restore the parties to their previous position or perform some positive duty or obligation. These injunctions are less common than prohibitory injunctions and they are generally more difficult to obtain because of difficulties of ensuring performance. Indeed order 42, rule 31 of the Rules of the Superior Courts makes provision allowing for an injunction of this kind to be carried into effect by the party obtaining the injunction, the cost to be borne by the disobedient party.

Bula Ltd *v* Tara Mines Ltd (No. 2) [1987] IR 95

The State had leased mineral rights to Tara Mines. Under the lease the defendant was obliged to co-operate in the exploitation of these mineral rights and act reasonably in all negotiations intended to exploit this resource. The plaintiffs, owners of an adjoining orebody under a similar lease from the State, claimed that they could not adequately exploit their resource because of improper behaviour by Tara Mines and the plaintiffs sought injunctive relief requiring the State and Tara Mines to implement the relevant clause of the Tara Mines lease, alleging that non-implementation was wrongful interference in the economic interests of the plaintiffs under their lease with the State.

Murphy J.:

. . .

The plaintiffs assert that damages would be an inadequate remedy for them. First they say that the sums involved would be enormous. Secondly it is pointed out that there would be extraordinary difficulties in calculating the loss. Thirdly it is submitted that the recovery of damages would not compensate the individual plaintiffs for the embarrassment and ignominy of their bankruptcy which may result from the alleged breach of the contracts by the defendants in circumstances in which the plaintiffs have guaranteed very substantial sums of money which have now been called in.

In opposing the application the defendants relied on a number of propositions. First, it was said that a mandatory injunction would be granted at the interlocutory stage only in a very strong case. This proposition was supported by the decision in *Shepherd Homes Ltd v Sandham* [1971] Ch. 340. In his judgment Megarry J. at 349 commented as follows: 'At the trial of the action, the court will, of course, grant such injunctions as the justice of the case requires; but at the interlocutory stage, when the final result of the case cannot be known and the court has to do the best it can, I think the case has to be unusually strong and clear before a mandatory injunction will be granted, even if it is sought in order to enforce a contractual obligation.'

Whilst I would respectfully agree with much of what the learned judge said in the *Shepherd Homes* case about the important differences between prohibitory and mandatory injunctions I would be reluctant to accept the proposition, if that is what it is, that the granting or withholding of a mandatory injunction on an interlocutory application should be related to or depend upon the strength of the applicant's case. As has been pointed out in a number of cases in recent years there are grave difficulties in evaluating the strength of an applicant's case on fact or even in law at any time before a full hearing has taken place.

The defendants also referred to the decision of the Supreme Court in *Campus Oil Ltd v Minister for Industry* (No. 2) [1983] IR 88 and in particular a passage from the decision of O'Higgins C.J. at 107 thereof in the following terms: 'The plaintiffs also argue that, insofar as the relief which was granted was mandatory in nature, such should not have been given by way of interlocutory relief. It is correct to say that a mandatory injunction does not usually issue prior to the trial of an action. However, there are exceptions and, in my view, this case is one of them.' The then Chief Justice went on to consider the exceptional nature of the issue before the court.

In the course of his judgment he had also commented upon the general nature of interlocutory relief (at 106) in the following terms: 'As I have already mentioned, interlocutory relief is intended to keep matters in *status quo* until the trial, and to do no more. No rights are determined nor are issues decided.'

The third matter of principle on which the defendants placed reliance was the need for certainty in a mandatory order. In this connection reference was made to *Redland Bricks Ltd v Morris* [1970] AC 652. In delivering the unanimous opinion of the House of Lords Lord Upjohn adopted at 667 of the report the principle enunciated by Maugham L.J. in *Fishenden v Higgs & Hill Ltd* (1935) 153 LT 128 at 142 in the following terms: 'I should like to observe, in the first place, that I think a mandatory injunction, except in very exceptional circumstances, ought to be granted in such terms that the person against whom it is granted ought to know exactly what he had to do.' It should be emphasised that the *Redland Brick* case concerned a mandatory order granted after a plenary hearing. It does seem to me, however, that the same principle is at least equally applicable to the granting of a mandatory order at the interlocutory stage.

If one then reverts to the notice of motion and examines the terms of the relief sought, not with a view to raising procedural or technical difficulties but for the purpose of understanding what is involved in the interlocutory relief sought, one finds that the plaintiffs require an order directing:

> The first-named defendant, its servants or agents, to meet with the plaintiffs, their servants or agents at such times and with such frequency as may be necessary for the purpose of discussing what arrangements may be made between the first-named plaintiff and the first-named defendant as regard the use of the first-named defendant's facilities in the exploitation of the mineral assets of the first-named plaintiff and for the purpose of discussing such other proposals as may be put forward by any party with a view to ensuring that the said mineral assets and the mineral assets the subject matter of the lease dated 19 September 1975, between the last-named defendant's predecessor in title of the first part, the Minister for Finance of the second part and the first-named defendant of the third part, are exploited in the most efficient and most economical manner with consequent benefit to all concerned.

What would the defendants have to do to comply with an order in those terms? Would attendance at one or two meetings suffice? Must they actively participate in discussions at such meetings? Would they be entitled to adopt negotiating positions in which they would not, in the first instance at any rate, put forward their best proposals? Above all could it happen that the court would be required to test the sincerity of the defendants in their purported compliance with the order?

The plaintiffs of course were fully conscious of these problems. Counsel on their behalf was not prepared to accept that the mere physical presence of representatives of Tara at a meeting would be adequate to resolve the plaintiffs' immediate problems. On behalf of the plaintiffs it was clearly and fairly said that the meeting to be directed was a meeting under and for the purposes of clause f of the State mining lease and that being so, it was contended that the arbitration clause in the State mining lease could be invoked to test whether Tara had complied with its undertaking 'to act reasonably in all negotiations'. It seems to me that this line of reasoning does not in fact provide a solution to the problem. Whether or not there has been compliance with an order of the court is a matter which the court itself must be in a position to determine and it seems to me that it would be wrong in principle and unhelpful in practice if the court were to make an order in the very general terms of the notice of motion on the basis that any uncertainty would be corrected by the intervention of a third party whose decision was in no way dependent upon or related to the decision of the court. The plaintiffs' argument involves a further problem. To direct that the meeting should be held for the purposes of clause f in my view involves prejudging one of the crucial issues in the action. So far from maintaining the *status quo* it would compel the parties not merely to take certain actions but also to decide, at least on some temporary or conditional basis, the legal framework within which those actions were to be taken. In my view it would be quite wrong for the court to adopt that course at an interlocutory stage.

Finally, I think it is proper, particularly in the interest of the Minister of Energy, to recall the factual position with regard to the negotiations between the parties. On behalf of Bula it has been suggested that the appropriate method of exploiting the Bula orebody would be by means of a 'tolling arrangement' between Tara and Bula and a proposal to the effect in general terms was made by Bula in the months of September and October of last year. It was in that background that the Chief State Solicitor wrote to the solicitors on behalf of the plaintiffs on 18 November 1986, in the following terms:

I act for the Minister of Energy.
I wish to inform you
(1) that the minister is and always has been willing to see discussions between Tara and Bula about a tolling arrangement;
(2) that the legal advice available to the minister is that there are no further steps the minister could take to require Tara to give any further consideration to the tolling arrangement than they have already done; and
(3) that if your clients wish to make further or more detailed proposals concerning a tolling arrangement they will be communicated to Tara who will be requested to consider them in the light of their obligations under the agreement.

In these circumstances it seems clear that the minister is not refusing his co-operation though there may well be a considerable difference between him and the plaintiffs as to the precise extent of his obligations or the nature of the intervention which he could make.

In all of the circumstances it seems to me that this is not a case in which it would be proper to grant a mandatory order in the terms sought or any other mandatory injunction to a like effect.

Note

The court must consider, before regarding any question as to the balance of convenience: is there a serious issue to be tried?

Oblique Financial Services Ltd *v* The Promise Production Co. and Others (1994) 1 ILRM 74

Keane J.:

This is an application under s. 11 of the Jurisdiction of Courts and Enforcement of Judgments (European Communities) Act 1988 which provides:

(1) Where:

(a) proceedings have been commenced or are to be commenced in a contracting state other than the state, and

(b) they are or will be proceedings whose subject matter is within the scope of the 1968 Convention as determined by article 1 (whether or not the 1968 Convention has effect in relation to the proceedings),

the High Court may, on application to it pursuant to article 24, grant provisional, including protective, measures of any kind that the court has power to grant in proceedings that, apart from this Act, are within its jurisdiction.

(2) On an application under subs. (1) of this section, the High Court may refuse to grant the measures sought if, in the opinion of the court, the fact that the court has no jurisdiction, apart from this section, in relation to the subject matter of the proceedings in question makes it inexpedient for that court to grant such measures.

The background to the present case is as follows. The plaintiff is a company, incorporated in the UK, which according to the affidavit filed on its behalf in these proceedings, is essentially engaged in marrying financial sources with production sources and is thereby earning for the company fees from investment clients, particularly from film revenues. The plaintiff company entered into a contract with the first-named defendant in these proceedings relating to the financing of a film, to be called 'The Promise'. The plaintiffs say that the terms of that agreement are that what was described as 'absolute and total confidentiality' would be maintained by the parties to that agreement in relation to any information as to the transaction which they acquired as a result of entering into the agreement.

The plaintiffs say that the first- and second-named defendants are in breach of that agreement by disclosing certain information, which they acquired as the result of having entered into the agreement or in the negotiations preliminary thereto, to other persons, and the matter, which they say, that particularly concerns them is that the identity of an investor in this country was disclosed by the first- and second-named defendants to other parties. This, they say, is in clear breach of the agreement by the first- and second-named defendants to preserve absolutely confidentiality in relation to these matters.

The application for interim protective measures, under the section, to which I have referred, is brought solely against the third- and fourth-named defendants, who are publishers and editor, respectively, of the *Phoenix Magazine*, and who have indicated their intention to publish in a forthcoming issue, information disclosed to them, including the name of the investor, the identity of the investor in question.

On Friday last, Geoghegan J. granted an interim injunction to the plaintiffs in these proceedings, which they indicated they intended to issue in the Queen's Bench Division of the High Court of Justice of England and Wales, as against all the defendants. The application for the interim injunction was brought solely against the third- and fourth-named defendants, under the section of the Judgments Act to which I have already referred.

It is accepted by counsel for both the applicant and the respondent that [in] the substantive case, the substantive proceedings are being instituted in an English court, and it will fall to be decided by that court in accordance with English law. However, the application, as envisaged by s. 11, and it is also accepted by counsel, must fall to be determined by this court, in accordance with the principles of Irish law applicable to granting or withholding of an interlocutory injunction. As it happens, there is no significant difference in the law in this country and the law in England and Wales as to the principles that should be applied by the court in granting or withholding an interlocutory injunction, with one important proviso, and that is, but again, it has been agreed by counsel, that the court cannot by its order, in an application of this nature, abridge the constitutional rights, the rights enjoyed under the Irish Constitution, by any of the parties to the action.

The plaintiffs instituted the proceedings, joining the third- and fourth-named defendants, relying on the doctrine of confidentiality laid down in a number of decisions both in this country and in England. The respondents to this application do not dispute the factual or legal basis of the claim against the first- and second-named defendants, but they make their own defence to the application on the straightforward grounds that they make the distinction between their situation and what they see as the situation which may or may not be the position in relation to the first- or second-named defendants. They say they owe no duty, contractual or otherwise, of confidentiality, to the plaintiffs. They also submit that their constitutional rights to freedom of expression would be infringed by the granting of an interlocutory injunction sought by or on behalf of the plaintiffs, under Article 40.6.1° of the Irish Constitution.

Now, the first issue that has to be determined is whether or not the plaintiff has established a serious question to be tried as against the third- and fourth-named defendants. I have no doubt but that it has established a serious question; and it is sufficient in this context to refer to the decision of the Supreme Court, upholding a decision of the High Court in the case of *House of Spring Garden Ltd v Point Blank Ltd* [1984] IR 611 in which the statement of the law by Costello J. was upheld by the Supreme Court. In the Supreme Court, O'Higgins C.J. cited his approval of the statement of the law by Lord Greene M.R. in *Saltman Engineering Co. Ltd v Campbell Engineering Co. Ltd* (1948) RPC 203. He stated as follows at 695: 'If a defendant is proved to have used confidential information, directly or indirectly obtained from a plaintiff, without the consent, expressed or implied of the plaintiff, he will be guilty of an infringement of the plaintiff's rights.' Now, it is also obvious from the passages in a number of the cases referred to in that case and also cited in the course of the arguments here before me, that the obligation of confidentiality which is enforced by the courts, is not merely applicable to the parties to the contract, but also in relation to third parties who may also come into possession of that information. In this case a similar obligation arises, whether by reason of some contractual obligation or some moral obligation. It is obvious from the cases, and indeed it is a matter of common sense that the right to confidentiality, which the law recognises in these cases, would be of little value, if the third parties to whom this information has been communicated were at liberty to publish it to another party, or in this case, to publish it to the general public, without the court being in a position to intervene.

So, that being the statement of the law, both here in Ireland and in the UK, it is quite clear that the legal position would appear to be that the obligation of confidentiality of a company can be enforced as against third parties. It is again necessary to point out that this is a preliminary application interlocutory in its nature and it is, therefore, not for this court to express a final view on any of the matters which might be mentioned by any of the parties to this preliminary application. They will ultimately be determined by an English court in the substantive proceedings; but it is sufficient, for the purposes of this application by the plaintiffs, that a serious question is to be tried as to whether or not the third- or fourth-named respondents are also bound not to engage in publishing matters of confidentiality arising from the agreement between the plaintiffs and the other defendants.

. . .

The next question is whether or not more damage would be caused by granting the injunction than by its being withheld. It has been submitted on behalf of the respondents, and it is recognised of course, that the damage they would sustain, by reason of non-publication, is necessarily hard to quantify; and it is said on behalf of the respondents that the undertaking is not of any great value to them. That may well be so, and if that were to be the grounds for the withholding of the relief, the inter-locutory relief, then it would apply to virtually every application of this nature where the respondents, if they were in the position, as the present respondents say they are, that as they were publishing newspapers or periodicals of any sort in which a consid-erable amount of material and information is regularly published, so it would be difficult for the respondents to quantify the position, if an injunction was wrongly granted, of the amount of any loss sustained by them. If that proposition were correct, then it would follow that in cases where breach of confidentiality arises it would in effect, be impossible for the courts to grant interlocutory relief, however unjust the consequences, if the respondents, were, as in the present case, publishers in magazines or periodicals, of a large volume of information and comment other than the impugned material. By contrast, it appears that the plaintiffs, quite clearly, by the very nature of their enter-prise, and the importance that they attach to the confidentiality of the information arising in the course of such transactions, it is obvious that the plaintiff, if the case was well founded, would indeed, suffer serious, and perhaps, irreparable damage, by the publication of material of this nature.

That would be sufficient to indicate that this is a case where interlocutory relief should issue, without considering where the balance of convenience lies. If I were to consider where the balance of convenience lies, the whole point of a case like this is to preserve the *status quo* pending the resolution of the action; and the *status quo* would be the non-publication of the material pending a decision by the English courts as to whether indeed the question of confidentiality arises. I will, accordingly accede to the granting of an interlocutory injunction, in the same terms granted by Geoghegan J. on the application for an interim injunction, that will of course, be subject to the under-taking to the court, pending the resolution by the courts in England of the substantive issues.

SECTION TWO—SPECIFIC PERFORMANCE

An order for specific performance is made on a discretionary basis, but the exercise of the discretion is made within certain well established principles. For instance, in a contract for the sale of land, specific performance is the general or primary remedy, while, in relation to contracts for services of a personal nature, the relief will not be generally available.

The plaintiff must prove the agreement.

Howe v Hall (1870) 4 Ir R Eq 242

Sullivan M.R.:

The bill in this case has been filed on 16 June 1868, by James Howe, praying the specific performance of an agreement for a lease of a farm of about 26.5 acres, in County Fermanagh. This agreement is stated by the bill to have been made by parol, and under the following circumstances. . . . The bill further states that the plaintiff, relying on the agreement, paid on 23 October 1858, £19 17s 6d, for half a year's rent, ending 1 May 1858, in lieu of his former rent, £16 10s 0d, and that the increased rent was paid to Mr Clarke during his life. This bill then states. . . . And further alleges that the plaintiff 'spent large sums of money, to wit, £100, in draining and improving said lands, and planting a portion of the same;' and that he 'also drained and reclaimed said bog lands, to the extent of 3 acres and upwards, at considerable expense;' and then the bill states that these sums of money were expended under the advice, directions, and special supervision of the said James Clarke.

James Clarke died in November 1864, having devised the lands to Sarah Jane Clarke, his daughter, for life, with remainder to her eldest son (who is the minor defendant), and his heirs. Miss Clarke appointed Mr Patrick Hall her agent; and the bill states that the plaintiff apprised Mr Hall of his right to the lease, and that he afterwards paid the increased rent. Miss Clarke married the defendant, William Hall, on 29 May 1865, and these lands were conveyed to trustees, to her separate use. On the 29 April 1867, the plaintiff was served with a notice to quit; and the bill states (para. 35), 'that the plaintiff then addressed a letter to the said Sarah Jane Hall, and enclosed the original receipt given by James Clarke to the plaintiff, for the half-year's rent due 1 November 1857, and stated to her the terms of said agreement, but received no reply.' A Civil Bill eject-ment was brought, and the chairman adjourned the hearing of it to allow the plaintiff to file this bill, which he accordingly has done. The bill prays, 'that the said agreement may be specifically performed and carried into execution; and the defendants, or some or one of them, may be decreed to execute a lease of the lands to the plaintiff for the life of himself and his wife, and upon the terms of the aforesaid agreement.'

Now, it will be observed that the bill states, with very great precision, the parol agreement which is stated to have been entered into; and the case of the plaintiff is, that he has proved that agreement, and that he has given such evidence of part performance of it that the court ought to specifically direct its being carried out.

The answer of Sarah Jane Hall and her husband denies that any such agreement as alleged was entered into. It suggests that the plaintiff got a few acres of bog added to his letting in 1858, when the rent was increased; and it states that the rents of all the other tenants on the estate were increased at the time of the agreement which is put forward, and that the alleged improvements in draining and planting were of no real or substantial value; and, in particular, that the bog was cut-out bog, and required very little to be done to make it yield a good crop; and that the subsequent yield of crops has amply repaid the plaintiff's expenditure.

They admit that the plaintiff did, as they were informed, they say, by Patrick Hall, the agent, since the institution of the suit, say something about his having been promised a lease, but without saying anything of its terms and conditions.

They then say that in June 1867, Sarah Jane Hall received a memorial, dated 11 June 1867, from the plaintiff, in relation to the notice to quit (which is plainly what is referred to in para. 35 of the bill), and they rely on it. On this memorial I shall have occasion hereafter to observe.

A considerable amount of evidence has been gone into, on both sides, as to the nature of the improvements stated to have been made by the plaintiff on the lands. I must say that, on the most careful consideration of this evidence, I am forced to the conclusion that these improvements were of no substantial value, nor such as would induce me to think that they were only made in reliance on the promise of the lease which is averred by the plaintiff; and, as an instance of the danger of resting on loose or vague statements as to improvements, I need only refer to the circumstance that the cost of the planting, which is made a component part of the £100 stated to have been expended by the plaintiff, is clearly shown, on the evidence of the defendants, which is not attempted to be contradicted by the plaintiff, to have been capable of being done for a sum of 10s.

However, in respect of these alleged improvements, one of the most remarkable features of the case is that the general improvements by draining stated to have been done on the farm outside the bog is nowhere even stated in the bill to have been done under the agreement for the lease, which agreement, as stated in the bill, is entirely confined to the drainage and improving the waste bog.

Several cases have been cited in the course of the argument, showing that this court will not hesitate to enforce specific performance of a parol agreement where there is part performance of it; and *Nunn v Fabian*[1] is especially relied on as a precise authority in the plaintiff's favour. *Nunn v Fabian* is a case of high authority, and, of course, I would implicitly follow it in this court; but, in the view I take of the case before me, I regard it as inapplicable, inasmuch as the very foundation of that decision was, that the court, on the evidence adduced, saw its way to determining that there was a *concluded agreement* to the effect relied on, while I am of opinion that I cannot hold here that there was any concluded agreement.

In *Nunn v Fabian*, and, indeed, in *Mundy v Jolliffe*,[2] there were written instruments of a very strong character adduced in evidence, fully corroborating the parol agreement relied on. I am far from saying that *Nunn v Fabian* is to be considered (as has been urged in argument for the plaintiff) as overruling the opinion of Lord St. Leonards in *Brennan v Bolton*, on the state of facts there before him. I do not say that a written instrument of such a character as appeared in *Nunn v Fabian* is essential, as this court ought not to be deterred from giving effect to a clearly proved verbal contract, when part performance is plainly referable to it. But, when no such written instrument exists, I do think that the utmost caution must be observed in fastening on a man in his grave a contract binding his estate, such as is here attempted to be enforced; and that the proof in support of such a contract must be clear beyond all reasonable doubt. In *Nunn v Fabian*, Lord Cranworth, although differing from the Master of the Rolls in the decree to be pronounced, says (p. 39): 'But I agree with the Master of the Rolls that, in such a case, the facts must be watched carefully, to see what confirmation there is of the plaintiff's assertion. And, in looking through the evidence with this view, the court is particularly careful to see if there are any documents which confirm it.'

Now, how stands the case here as to proof of the agreement relied on by the bill? The only witnesses to sustain it are the plaintiff and his wife, in addition to which there is the evidence of Mr Collum, such as it is. The bill, as appears from what I have already stated, avers in very clear terms the consideration for the agreement, *viz.* the increase of rent, and the draining and improving of the waste bog. The plaintiff and his wife have been cross-examined, and, so far as I can see, the substance of their testimony is as follows: The plaintiff, after detailing the circumstances which led to the interview stated in the bill, deposes, 'Mr Clarke said he would give me a lease, and to improve the bog and drain some of the land. He said he would give leases for her life and mine. I said I was not satisfied with the survey, and he said he would satisfy me with a survey. I agreed to this, and spent my money.' In answer to a question by myself, he said that he had sent the memorial; that he told the schoolmaster who drew it up the agreement, but that he himself did not read it.

The plaintiff's wife deposed: 'Mr Clarke said he would get it surveyed, and give a lease for his life and mine. He was talking if he would improve the bog, and drain some of the land. They were talking. I did not give much ear to them.'

All this evidence seems to my mind very loose and vague. The dropping of a single word, the alteration of the slightest expression, as has been observed in the argument, would alter the meaning of the whole conversation.

[Solicitor for the plaintiff's] evidence, which is much relied on as corroborating the plaintiff's, is very much of the same character. Being at business at sessions in the same room with Mr Clarke, some time after the alleged agreement is stated to have been entered into, the plaintiff Howe paying his rent, he says: 'Mr Clarke came over to where I was, and said that, when he had a survey made, he would give me [solicitor for the plaintiff] the necessary instructions for a lease.' And he added, that his attention was never called to this conversation till the Civil Bill ejectment was brought.

Leaving the direct evidence in support of the agreement, and looking to the probabilities of the case, I do not see that the occasion of the alleged agreement affords much reason to think that it was entered into, as at that time most, if not all, the tenants' rents on the estate were increased, and the present appears to be the single instance in which the promise of a lease has been put forward. I cannot hold, on the evidence before me, that there was any concluded agreement for a lease. I believe that there was some talk about a lease, but nothing more.

The conclusion I have arrived at is, I think, much strengthened by the circumstance that several different agreements have been from time to time alleged by the plaintiff. The bill states one agreement—namely, that the lease was to be given in consideration of the increased rent, and draining and improving the waste bog. The memorial to Mrs Hall states the agreement for the lease to have been in consideration of the increased rent alone, and the expenditure on the bog is therein put forward without being at all connected with the agreement for the lease; while the affidavit of the plaintiff of 26 January 1869 (para. 5) adds on an additional term—namely, the draining of the upland of the farm, and it actually relies on the drainage of this to the extent of 6 acres as part performance of the agreement.

As to the motives which induced the notice to quit in this case, I will not enter on them. I think they are entirely beside the question which I have to decide; and, however I may regard them, it appears to me that they should have as little weight with me in ruling the true point in this case as the violent conduct of the plaintiff in preventing the agent, Mr Patrick Hall, and Messrs M'Vitty and Neilson, in viewing the lands in February, 1869.

I must dismiss this bill; but, on the fullest consideration, I will do so without costs.

1. LR 1 Ch. 35.   2. 5 M & Cr. 167.

Is there an adequate remedy at common law?

Bagnell v Edwards (1876) 10 IR Eq 215

The facts

In May 1875, the plaintiff and defendant agreed with the Midland Great Western Rly Co. to make a branch line of railway from Enfield to Edenderry for £20,500, and that it should be completed and delivered up to the company on or before 1 September 1876.

By agreement of 22 July 1875, the plaintiff and defendant agreed to carry out the contract in partnership, and clause 1 of the agreement provided that a sum of £2,000 should be lodged in the Ulster Bank, Edenderry, in the names of the plaintiff and defendant, one half of that sum to be advanced by one, and the other half by the other. It was also provided that all salaries and wages and expenses in carrying out the contract should be paid out of the money so lodged in bank, or, in case the same should be deficient, by the plaintiff and defendant in equal shares; and that, in the event of the capital of £2,000 being insufficient, the additional capital should be furnished by the plaintiff and defendant in equal shares; and, in the event of either providing a larger share of the original capital of £2,000, or such additional capital, the person so advancing the same should be entitled to be repaid the amount of such additional sums so advanced by the defaulting person with interest at ten per cent from the time of such advance until the repayment thereof.

The plaintiff and defendant commenced to carry on the works under the contract. The sum of £2,000 was not lodged in the bank pursuant to the agreement, but the funds and necessaries required for carrying on the works were supplied by the plaintiff and by the monthly payments made by the company, being twenty per cent, of the amount due for the works executed and certified by the company's engineer. These monthly amounts were paid by cheques drawn by the company in favour of the plaintiff and defendant jointly. The bill charged that the plaintiff had in the beginning of January 1875, advanced out of his own moneys about £800, after giving credit for what he had received from the company. On 4 January 1876, the defendant received a cheque for £898 0s 10d, drawn by the company in favour of the plaintiff and defendant, and the defendant refused to endorse this cheque to the plaintiff unless he lodged it to their joint credit. This the plaintiff refused to do, as he had advanced the £800, and no part of the £2,000 had ever been lodged in the bank.

The bill charged that the plaintiff had frequently applied to the defendant to lodge the said sum of £1,000, and to provide his share of the capital and in all respects to perform the said agreement, the plaintiff offering to lodge his share of the capital, but that the defendant had refused to lodge the said sum, and had neglected to perform the said agreement.

Chatterton V.C.:

I am of opinion that this suit cannot be maintained. It does not pray a dissolution of the partnership, but asks for a decree for the specific performance of the partnership contract in general terms. The only breach of that contract proved against the defendant is that he has not paid up his one half of the presented capital, in which respect, I may observe the plaintiff is admittedly in the same position, not having paid his half of the £2,000 into the bank. The plaintiff has, in consequence of this default, been obliged to advance sums out of his own moneys to pay the current expenses of the concerns, while the defendant has not paid anything. Such an event is contemplated by the partnership agreement, which by its ninth clause provides that a partner providing a larger share of the capital than his own moiety shall be repaid his advances by the defaulter with interest at ten per cent *per annum*. The relief actually sought is nothing but the payment of money, for which an action at law can be maintained by one partner against the other, and clause 9 measures the damages so to be recovered. The principle of this court is not to decree specific performance in such a case. The allegations made about the refusal of the defendant to sign cheques show that these were only temporary objections yielded by the defendant soon after they were made, and no such default existed when the bill was filed.

I must, therefore, dismiss the bill, but as the defendant is by his own admissions in default, I shall do so without costs.

Note

If damages constitute an adequate remedy then specific performance will be denied: see *Todd v Midland Great Western Rly* (1881) 9 IR Eq 85 and contrast this with *Rushbrooke v O'Sullivan* [1908] 1 IR 232.

If damages will be nominal then specific performance will be available: *Beswick v Beswick* [1968] AC 58 (see p. 669 above).

A. Difficulties in Specific Performance

(i) Partial Performance with Compensation

Connor v Potts [1897] 1 IR 534

Chatterton V.C.:

This action is brought by a purchaser for specific performance of a contract for a sale by the defendant to him of 443 acres of the lands of Knockcairn and Fourscore for the sum of £5,500, or in the alternative for performance of this contract to the extent of 376 acres, part of the 443 acres, and damages or compensation for the remaining 67a 3r 0p.

The material facts of the case are as follows: The defendant was the tenant of several farms on the Wallace Estate, including the farms in question. He employed Messrs Ferguson & Harvey estate agents, to obtain purchasers and receive proposals for the farms. The plaintiff is a farmer residing in the locality, and he desired to purchase the farms in question. In the beginning of November 1895, he applied to Ferguson & Harvey on the subject, and informed them that he wished to buy the farms of Knockcairn and Fourscore, and named a sum of £5,000 as the price; but nothing material was done on that occasion. On 22 November plaintiff received from them the following letter. . . . This is a very important letter, as it shows that the defendant required an exact statement of the quantity plaintiff desired to buy, and that the quantity the defendant had to sell in Knockcairn was 316 acres, subject to the rent of £155 8s 11d.

The plaintiff, on the following Tuesday, which was the twenty sixth, went to the office of Ferguson & Harvey, and had a conversation with them on the subject. He swears that he then offered £5,000 for the two farms, and that Harvey asked if he was aware there were more than 400 acres in the lands mentioned in the letter, and that plaintiff said he had their letter to that effect, and that he would give £12 an acre for the whole lands, which would amount to close on the £5,000, and that they stated they would lay his offer before the defendant. On 11 December Ferguson & Harvey wrote to the plaintiff, stating that they had had a further interview with the defendant, and asking him to call on them. He did call, and as Mr Ferguson stated in his evidence, they had some conversation, in which Ferguson stated that the defendant had not named any price, but that plaintiff had better make an offer, and they would submit it to him; that after some further conversation, which he did not state, the plaintiff eventually offered £5,500, which Ferguson said he would submit to the defendant. The plaintiff swears that on that occasion Ferguson told him that the defendant had called on them and that they had gone through the figures of the farms, and calculated what plaintiff could afford to give for them, and that plaintiff had better increase his offer of £5,000, and that Ferguson produced a list of all the farms of the defendant which they had to sell, and which was given in evidence. It contains figures in pencil, made by Ferguson, which show that Knockcairn contained 316a 1r 19p, and Fourscore 126a 2r 10p, making together 442a 3r 29p, and that the rents were £155 8s 11d and £80 respectively. Plaintiff swore that Ferguson thereupon multiplied the acreage by £12 10s, and brought out £5,500 and a few pounds over, and that they were both acting on the 442 acres, and thereupon plaintiff offered him £5,500. Now Ferguson admitted, on cross-examination, that he was himself then under the impression that the acreage was 442 acres, and that there was a talk about selling by the acre, and that plaintiff asked him how much £12 10s an acre would make, and that he Ferguson made a rough calculation that made it something a little under or over £5,500, and that when he saw it came so close he said to the plaintiff that he should make an offer of £5,500. Mr Harvey, who was also examined, admitted on cross-examination that he also believed that there were 442 acres in the farms, and that plaintiff was buying and defendant was selling 442 acres. Both Ferguson & Harvey attributed their mistake to some incorrect memorandum they had obtained from the Wallace estate office. However that may be, it is plain that all these three persons, plaintiff, Ferguson, and Harvey, entertained at the time the belief that the lands did contain 442 acres, and the negotiation was carried on and closed in this mistaken belief. But if there was a doubt on this it is wholly removed by the very important letter written by Ferguson & Harvey to the defendant, dated 18 December 1895. . . .

On this evidence I have no doubt that the plaintiff offered the sum of £5,500 on the representation by the defendant through his agents that the lands contained 442 acres.

Messrs Ferguson & Harvey stated that they did not sell by the acre, and had no authority to do so. If it were to be dealt with as a matter of credit between the plaintiff and Ferguson & Harvey, I cannot leave out of consideration that Ferguson & Harvey have a very material interest in endeavouring to excuse themselves for their part of this mistake. But it may be true that they did not sell or profess to sell these lands by the acre; but that is a different thing from representing to the plaintiff, with a view to inducing him to purchase at £5,500, that they did contain 442 acres. It may not have been a sale by the acre, but it was a sale at a bulk price, which they knew the plaintiff calculated, and which they helped him to calculate, on the mistaken basis of the supposed acreage. There was no fraud on their part in this, for they swear, and I believe it, that they themselves believed the lands did contain 442 acres. Fraudulent misrepresentation is not necessary for the plaintiff to establish, for a mistaken representation by the defendant of a matter that it was his duty to state correctly, and on the faith of which he knew the plaintiff acted, is sufficient, though he may himself have believed it to be true.

The defendant accepted the offer of £5,500, and the agreement set out in the statement of claim bearing the date 21 December 1895, was prepared, except the addition as to £3,000 remaining out on mortgage. It was taken by Mr Harvey to plaintiff's house for signature. He stated that the addition was then made by him as to the £3,000 being left outstanding; that he told plaintiff before he signed that defendant would not guarantee the acreage: and that the plaintiff brought an old book or something with the acreages in it and made up that of Knockcairn at 315 acres, which he (Harvey) put down in his book, and stated that defendant would not let him say anything about acreage. It was sought to rely on this as showing that plaintiff possessed independent means of knowledge. I do not so regard it. The plaintiff swore, and I believe him, that on that occasion Harvey produced a slip of paper with the acreages and rents of the farms, the acreages being 316a 1r 19p and 126a 2r 10p; and the rents £155 8s 11d and £80; and said that it was a copy of the statement he sent to the defendant on the Wednesday before. This shows that the same representation was repeated on the occasion of the signing of the agreement. It also shows that the defendant was again informed of the making of this representation to the plaintiff by his agents. If he knew that this was not the true acreage he was guilty of a fraud. If he did not know this, he took upon himself to make a material misrepresentation of a fact which he ought to have known and as to which he should have satisfied himself before making the representation.

The general principle applicable to this case is well established that where a misrepresentation is made by a vendor as to a matter within his knowledge even though it may be founded upon an honest belief in the truth of what he states, and the purchaser has been misled by such misrepresentation, the purchaser is entitled to have the contract specifically performed so far as the vendor is able to do so, and to have compensation for the deficiency.

The defendant disputed the application of this rule to the present case on the ground that here the representation was not as to the contract itself but as to a separate and distinct matter collateral to the contract which cannot give the purchaser a right to compensation. But I am at a loss to understand how a representation as to the contents of the lands, the subject matter of the contract, can be treated as collateral to the contract. The plaintiff was led by the defendant to believe that the defendant was selling 442 acres of land when he had no title to 67 acres of that quantity.

It was also contended that so large a deficiency of the estimated acreage prevents this court from dealing with the case as one for specific performance so far as the defendant can perform the contract with compensation for the deficiency. But that is not the rule on which the court proceeds, and it is only necessary to refer to *McKenzie v Hesketh*[1] to show that the court will grant partial performance with compensation in such cases. There is no difficulty here in ascertaining the amount of the compensation, as it is a mere calculation of 67 acres at £12 10s an acre which is to be deducted from the amount of the purchase money. The case of *The Earl of Durham v Legard*[2] was relied on by the defendant in support of this contention, but that case must, in my opinion, be treated as an exception to the general rule, and was decided by Lord Romilly on the ground of the unfair and unreasonable result that would occur in applying the rule to a case where the portion of the estate to which the vendor could not show title was so very large, being over 10,000 acres out of 21,000.

On the whole case I am of opinion that the plaintiff is entitled to judgment for the specific performance of the contract as to the portion of Knockcairn to which the defendant can show title, being 249 acres and the entire of Fourscore 126a 2r 10p, and that he is entitled to compensation for the 67 acres deficiency of the acreage of Knockcairn, at the rate of £12 10s per acre to be deducted from his purchase money of £5,500.

The defendant must pay the plaintiff's costs of the action.

[1] 7 ChD 675.   [2] 34 Beav. 611.

(ii) *Where the contractual standard is imprecise*

Lonergan *v* McCartney [1983] NI 129

Gibson L.J.:

This is an action for specific performance of an agreement under which the defendant is alleged to have given the plaintiff an enforceable option to purchase premises situate at 36 Rossmore Avenue, Belfast. The question whether that is so was raised as a preliminary issue upon agreed facts.

The history of the matter is that by agreement dated 12 May 1975 the defendant let to the plaintiff the premises in question for use only as a builder's yard. The lease was due to expire on 30 April 1981. The annual rent reserved was £1,250, but was stated to be subject to revision on 1 May 1978. It was a full repairing lease with a prohibition against alterations or improvements without the lessor's consent. There are two further terms to which I must refer. By clause (viii) it was provided 'this agreement shall incorporate the additional clauses endorsed hereon'; and by clause (xi) any dispute 'in relation to the interpretation application effect or otherwise arising on foot of the provisions hereof' was to be determined by an independent person nominated by the parties or in default by the chairman of the Northern Ireland branch of the Royal Institution of Chartered Surveyors.

The document was on a printed form in which the blanks had been filled in and certain alterations and deletions made. The 'additional clauses' printed in the form lettered (a) and (b) respectively had been deleted. Following that deletion and immediately above the signatures to the lease was the following typed addendum: 'It is further agreed between the two parties that the tenant shall have the option to purchase the premises 1 May 1978 at the then current market value. Such price to be mutually agreed between the tenant and the landlord's agent.'

A letter dated 17 October 1977 to the defendant's agents, Messrs Blessington Fair & Co., was in the following terms:

Builders yard, 36 Rossmore Avenue.

With reference to my rental agreement on the above property which is due for revision on 1 May 1978, I would like to exercise my option to purchase the above property as agreed.

I look forward to hearing from you in due course.

Yours faithfully,
For Deramore Developments Ltd
E. A. Lonergan

The reply from the landlord's agents dated 24 October 1977 addressed to the plaintiff noted that he wished to exercise the option and indicated that this had been communicated to the defendant. Since then no relevant step has been taken apart from the issue of these proceedings.

Clause (vii) of the lease provided: 'This agreement shall be binding upon the heirs executors administrators and permitted assigns or other successors in title of the landlord and tenant respectively.'

Clause (xiv) prohibited the lessee from assigning or parting with possession of the premises without consent not to be unreasonably withheld.

Clearly Deramore Developments Ltd were assigns of the plaintiff and I have not been told of any consent to that assignment. But no point has been taken about this and the reply referred to indicates that the defendant's agents regarded the plaintiff and his company as one. Though clause (vii) only purports to bind assigns of the parties and not to confer rights on them, I propose to deal with the matter as though the right to exercise the option did pass to the company as if it was an assignee of the plaintiff. Further I treat the words 'I would like to exercise my option' as amounting to an actual exercise of the option and not as a mere expression of the plaintiff's state of mind. The option did not specify when the right was to be exercised or in what manner and the letter exercising the option did not indicate the date when the purchase should apply. Though it is a well established rule that the exercise of options is to be strictly and narrowly construed, I see no ground for questioning the competence of the letter on any such account as I have mentioned.

I turn now to the arbitration clause with a view to deciding whether it is to be regarded as applicable to resolution of the price on exercise of the option followed by lack of agreement as to price. I note that it is limited to cases where 'any dispute exists and cannot be resolved between the parties'. The failure of two persons to agree does not always connote a dispute. There may be a dispute; or, short of that, there may be a difference of opinion; or short of that again there may merely be a lack of agreement. This last state of affairs was the position when the letter of 24 October 1977 was written; but for the present purposes I assume that, as the matter has advanced to the stage of litigation, there is a dispute. Moreover the dispute, if it is to be referable to arbitration under clause (xi), must be a dispute 'arising on foot of the provisions hereof'. Does 'hereof' refer only to the lease or the printed document, or does it extend also to the typed addition? Again, in favour of the plaintiff, I would accept that it applies to the option.

Having decided or assumed all these matters in favour of the plaintiff, the way is now prepared to enable me to deal with the crunch question which is whether the option clause in that context is a contract which is enforceable by the court with or without amendment. The whole history of the litigation on the topic has been so fully examined in the recent case of *Sudbrook Trading Estate Ltd v Eggleton* that I do not consider it is necessary to embark on an independent review of the earlier authorities. The judgment of the Court of Appeal reported at |1981| 3 All ER 105 analysed all the relevant decisions from 1807 to the present day and deduced and applied the consistent judicial opinion that if in an agreement one term (in this case the price) is left to be determined either by agreement of the parties, which is not forthcoming, or by determination of some other person or persons, and the procedure designated has failed or the persons designated have failed to reach a conclusion, the agreement is not enforceable. As against that long accepted view the majority of the House of Lords decided that though the machinery for fixing the price had proved inoperable it was in the circumstances of the case to be disregarded, thus enabling the court to give effect to the intention of the parties which was that the sale should be carried out at a fair and reasonable price. The question which I have to answer is whether the decision in the House of Lords reported at |1982| 3 All ER 1 has swept away the accumulation of centuries at one fell swoop and imposed a new criterion for deciding such cases; and, if so, what is the test now to be accepted.

In order to appreciate the scope and effect of the decision of the House of Lords it is necessary to set out the important facts. By various leases between the parties the lessee was given a right after part of the term had expired to exercise an option to purchase the lessor's reversion 'at such price as may be agreed upon by two valuers one to be nominated by the lessor and the other by the lessees or in default of such agreement by an umpire appointed by the said valuers' subject to certain conditions which specified precisely the terms and conditions upon which the sale was to be carried out. The option was duly exercised but the lessor refused to nominate a valuer and resisted a suit for specific performance.

The general legal principles applicable prior to the decision of the House of Lords were correctly summarised by Templeman L.J. at 1141 as follows:

> The principles which emerge from the authorities may be summarised thus. First, in ascertaining the essential terms of a contract, the court will not substitute machinery of its own for machinery provided by the parties, however defective that machinery may prove to be. Second, where machinery is agreed for the ascertainment of an essential term, then until the agreed machinery has operated successfully, the court will not decree specific performance, since there is not yet any contract to perform. Third, where the operation of the machinery is stultified by the refusal of one of the parties to appoint a valuer or an arbitrator, the court will not by way of partial specific performance, compel him to make an appointment.
>
> All three of these principles stem from one central proposition that where the agreement on the face of it is incomplete until something else has been done, whether by further agreement between the parties or by the decision of an arbitrator or valuer, the court is powerless because there is no complete agreement to enforce.

That is to say, the traditional view was that where the parties had taken the trouble to write into the contract a specifically designated way of reaching the purchase price and that method had failed to achieve its purpose, the court could not strike out the machinery provided and direct another way of reaching a conclusion as to the proper price, for this would be to write a new contract for the parties which was not in accordance with their agreement. This refusal to interfere with the agreed terms applied to the exercise of an option contained in a lease as well as to an agreement for sale where there had been no pre-existing relationship between the parties. It applied also even though the failure of the machinery was due to the default of one of the parties, and even though that default amounted to a breach of contract on his part (unless the breach could be remedied by an injunction, as where the owner of the property had refused right of entry to a valuer). It also applied whether or not the contract provided that the price was to be the market value or any similar standard. The designated machinery for reaching that value was treated as incapable of achievement by order of the court save in the manner stipulated.

If the law had stood, therefore, where it did when the Court of Appeal in the *Sudbrook* case delivered its judgment, the plaintiff in this action would clearly have no case, for the price has not been determined by the persons indicated in the contract.

I now turn to the decision of the House of Lords to see how far it has eroded those long-standing rules which, it would appear, had been widely accepted throughout that part of the world which is governed by the English system of law. I cannot say the common law, for this is a matter of equity; but the established rules which I have set out seem to have been universally accepted not only in the UK but also in the US and Canada and also in Australia and New Zealand. However that may be, I would, of course, regard myself as bound by the reasoning of the House of Lords.

Lord Diplock started from the proposition that a just and rational system of law ought not to countenance a situation where in the case of such an option clause the grantee's legal rights could be frustrated by the simple expedient of the grantor refusing to appoint a valuer. He pointed to the very detailed provisions in the agreement as to the period during which the option could be exercised, the manner in which it was to be exercised and the other elaborate and carefully drafted provisions which showed clearly that both parties intended the clause to have legal effect. He emphasised that the option when exercised created rights and imposed duties on both parties. There was the immediate obligation to appoint a valuer, and, when appointed, the obligation to instruct him in his duties. By refusing to appoint a valuer the lessor was regarded as having waived his contractual right to have the price assessed by the machinery provided in the lease; and as the lessees had agreed to waive their rights in the matter, the way was open to the court to lay down an alternative procedure for ascertaining the fair and reasonable price, which was the implied purpose of the clause. The intention of the clause was deemed to be to indicate a procedure whereby a fair and reasonable price could be determined and that very end could be accomplished by the appropriate officer of the court fixing the price. Lord Diplock expressed himself as being in agreement with the reasons given by Lord Fraser. Briefly these reasons were that all earlier decisions had erred in invariably treating the machinery for ascertaining the price as an essential part of the agreement. He regarded the valuation of property as nowadays much nearer to a science than heretofore, so that the same result is likely to be achieved regardless of who performs the function of valuing. The proper method for determining in any case whether the agreed machinery could be abandoned was stated at 10e (and in this Lord Scarman agreed at 13f) to be whether the mode of ascertaining the price is an essential term of the contract or whether the mode of ascertainment, though indicated in the contract, is subsidiary and non-essential.

How then does the present situation measure up to the standards indicated and the reasons which induced their Lordships to come down against the lessor? I am not sure whether this is a case of any default by the lessor. The letter of 24 October 1977 is indeterminate on the matter; but at least it is clear that the failure to operate the option clause rests either with the defendant or his agent. Unlike the clause in the

Sudbrook case the present option is bare in the extreme. The only things which are specified are the date when the option is to take effect; the price is to be current market value, and it is to be determined by two designated persons, namely the tenant and the landord's agent. What is to happen if, as would be not unlikely, they were to disagree is not suggested unless one can call in aid the arbitration clause which when printed was not intended to cover such an addendum? The fact that the price is to be current market value would suggest an objective test; but the choice of the lessee and the lessor's agent would point the other way. One of the important considerations in *Sudbrook's* case was that the valuers and the umpire were not named and were not indicated as having any association with either party. Thus it could be said that they would all be approaching the matter from the same detached, professional point of view applying the objective standards used by valuers. While the lessor's agent would have that professional knowledge and experience he would be appointed not as an independent person but as the lessor's representative. On the other side would be the lessee who would be unencumbered by either professional skill or knowledge and would be approaching the matter solely with his own interest in view. In *Sudbrook's* case it was largely the fact that the valuers who were not named would be actuated by no personal motives and guided only by professional, objective standards which enabled the house to say that any other objective method of valuing would be likely to achieve the same result. On this point I would refer to the speech of Lord Diplock at 6h.

Another factor which helped the members of the House of Lords to reach their conclusion was, as I have indicated, that there were immediately imposed on each party, once the option was exercised, primary obligations to appoint a valuer and to instruct him, so that the option clause did have immediate legal consequence. Not so in this case, for the persons to perform the task are already appointed by the lease and if there should be a failure on their part to discuss price or to agree it, the fault cannot in the absence of evidence be attributed to the defendant. So that may be another distinction between this case and *Sudbrook's*.

Turning to more general aspects of the case, I confess that a valuer would be faced with considerable problems as to what he was expected to value. The subject of the valuation is stated to be 'the premises' which means the builder's yard. It is not, as, for instance, in *Sudbrook's* case the reversion of the lease. So is the price to be the full value of the premises or only of the landlord's interest? One would think as that is all the landlord could sell that the reversion was what ought to have been intended, but it is not what was stated. Again, assuming it is the reversion only which is to be valued, is one to look at the tenant's interest as being only the residue of his contractual term, or is one to take into account the fact that, as it is a business tenancy, he would have a statutory right to successive renewals? And what about improvements which the plaintiff may have made? Are they to be taken into reckoning in every case or only where made with the lessor's consent, there being a covenant not to make alterations without consent? And in valuing the reversion, what is the rent which the tenant is deemed to be liable to pay, because, as I have pointed out, there was to be a rent revision operative as from the very day when the option to purchase is claimed to apply? And, assuming that the reversion is to be subjected to an extended lease under the Business Tenancies Act, at what rent are the premises to be regarded as subject during the period after expiry of the lease at the fixed rent and any revised rent which would cease to be applicable when the term of the contractual lease expired? For the greater the rent receivable by the lessor the greater will be the value of the reversion; but presumably the longer the term of the tenancy the less will be the value of the reversion.

The conclusion which I have reached is that the present option clause does not, for the reasons I have indicated, fall within the reasoning enunciated in *Sudbrook's* case and so justify me in saying that the choice of negotiators in this case was not essential to the acceptance of the clause by both parties. Moreover, the whole question of valuation would be so shrouded in doubt and ambiguities that it would be quite inappropriate for the court to seek to enforce the contract which the parties have left so vague. Clearly they had not thought the matter out even in the most fundamental matters as instanced by the fact that there was no agreement between counsel as to whether the clause contemplated sale of the premises with vacant possession or only a sale of the lessor's interest.

I, therefore, give judgment for the defendant, as it was agreed by counsel that my determination of this matter would inevitably resolve the action one way or the other.

(iii) Where the contract involves personal services to be performed

Contrast *Lumley v Wagner* (1852) 1 De G. M. & G. 604 with *Giles* (C.H.) & *Co. v Morris* [1972] 1 WLR 307.

SECTION THREE—DEFENCES TO SPECIFIC PERFORMANCE

A. DELAY OR LACHES

In equity, time is not generally of the essence (Supreme Court of Judicature (Ireland) Act 1887, s. 28(7), but a party who fails to bring an action has, historically, sometimes been unable to proceed with a claim. While modern judges doubt the usefulness of such a rule (see Megarry V.C. in *Lazard Bros & Co. v Fairfield Properties (Mayfair) Ltd* (1977) 121 SJ 793) delay and acquiescence may defeat a plaintiff.

Guerin *v* Heffernan [1925] 1 IR 57

Kennedy C.J.:

This was a vendor's action for the specific performance of a contract for the sale of land. The lands, which comprised a holding in the County Tipperary, bought out under the Land Purchase Acts, and duly registered, were offered by the plaintiff for sale by public auction on 18 March 1922, subject to conditions of sale, which, amongst other things, appointed 8 April 1922, as the date for completion.

The highest bid at the auction did not reach the reserve price, and the property was withdrawn. Later, however, on the same day, the defendant, who had been one of the bidders, as a result of private negotiations, made an enhanced offer which was accepted on the part of the plaintiff. The defendant signed the contract at foot of the conditions of sale agreeing to purchase the holding for the sum of £3,350, and to pay the auctioneer's commission of £167 10s, and the sum of £837 10s by way of deposit and in part payment of the purchase money. The contract was also signed by Mr Patrick J. Maher, the auctioneer, confirming the sale on behalf of the vendor.

The conditions of sale provided that the vendor should, within four days from the date of sale, deliver to the purchaser, or his solicitor, an abstract of title consisting of two documents, *viz.* a certain deed of family settlement dated 4 July 1904, and a copy of the land certificate. The time for making requisitions on the title was limited to four days from the delivery of the said abstract. It was further provided that the purchaser should leave a draft of the assurance of the property to him at the office of the vendor's solicitor, Mr Nicholas E. Maher, for approval, not less than six days before 8 April 1922.

The conditions of sale also contained the following provision:

> The lands are sold subject to a right-of-way of said Lizzie Guerin for all purposes in connection with the adjoining holding of said Lizzie Guerin (otherwise Eliza Guerin) and due provisions reserving this right-of-way to the said Lizzie Guerin (otherwise Eliza Guerin) will have to be embodied in the deed of transfer to the purchaser. The nature and extent of this right-of-way will be pointed out to the purchaser and explained to him at any time previous to the sale, and, whether the purchaser avails of such opportunity, or otherwise, he shall be deemed to have purchased with a full knowledge of its nature and extent, and shall not afterwards be free to make any objection or requisition in respect thereof.

It is important to observe that the particulars of sale did not disclose that the sale was to be subject to any such right-of-way, nor did they refer proposing purchasers to the conditions of sale.

The plaintiff claimed specific performance of this contract and payment of the purchase money, or, alternatively, damages for non-completion. He relies in his statement of claim on a letter of the defendant dated 22 March 1922, as a renunciation of and refusal to perform the said contract, and on a letter of 19 April 1922, stated to be from the defendant's then solicitor, as repeating such renunciation and refusal. The plaintiff expressly pleads that he has always been ready and willing to perform the said contract on his part, and to do all necessary acts and deed for vesting the lands in the defendant.

Upon the pleadings, the principal defence appears to be that the defendant was induced to enter into the contract on the faith of representations and assurances by the plaintiff 'that he, the defendant, would be allowed to enter peaceably upon the said lands and enjoy the same without claims, molestations, or threats by members of the plaintiff's family or other persons.' But it is alleged that 'immediately after and upon several occasions since the making of the said contract, the defendant has been subjected to violence, and threats by the sisters of the plaintiff and other persons,' and it is submitted therefore that the enforcement of the said contract would be inequitable and would impose undue hardship upon the defendant. It is also pleaded that the plaintiff has never been ready, willing, or *able* to deliver clear possession of the lands to the defendant.

The defendant counterclaims for rescission of the contract and a return of his deposit. The amount of the deposit is stated in the counterclaim to be £10.

The plaintiff delivered a reply in which he deals specially with the deposit. He alleges that the deposit paid by the defendant amounted altogether to the sum of £837 10s, and that it was made up of two promissory notes, one for £800, the other £27 10s, and a cash payment of £10. This statement was proved in evidence, and is not denied. The pleading continues: 'After the repudiation by the defendant of the said contract . . . a number of armed men broke and entered the residence of the said auctioneers in whose possession and custody, pending the completion of the contract, the said notes had remained, and took and carried away the said notes.' The taking away of the notes in the circumstances alleged was proved in evidence, but there was no evidence as to the person by whom, or the motive with which, they were taken. The plaintiff's suggestion was that it was done by friends of the defendant in his supposed interest. The defendant's suggestion, on the other hand, was that it was done in furtherance of the alleged desire of the plaintiff's sisters to break the sale. We have not sufficient materials upon which to form an opinion one way or the other on the matter, and therefore this foolish outrage cannot affect our decision in the case.

Such was the position of the case on the pleadings when the action came to trial before Pim J., sitting as Chancery Judge, on 23 May, in the present year. The pleadings and the issues knit upon them appear to have been overlooked in the conduct of the trial. All sorts of evidence were offered and received without reference to them; and, without amendment, every possible issue which could be raised by evidence, untrammelled by pleadings, was treated as open to the parties on the hearing of the action, and so admitted on both sides here. The result is that we are confronted with a very large transcript of disorderly testimony which does not lend itself to systematic review in relation to any clear issues to be determined.

The principal matter which, as I read the evidence, undoubtedly affected the defendant's mind all through was his anxiety to buy the farm with the assent of the plaintiff's family. A man who buys what may be called a 'family holding' in this country almost invariably has to consider the attitude of the vendor's family towards the sale. Few will venture the hostility of a vendor's brothers and sisters who think they have moral claims, even when they have no legal rights. Hence, one so often hears of a purchaser of a family holding having got, or not having got, 'the goodwill' of the holding. It is not uncommon to hear that a purchaser has, in addition to the price paid to a vendor, paid something more to members of his family for 'the goodwill'. It is a reality of our social life, though it may not have legal recognition, and it cannot be ignored as a factor in these transactions.

The defendant is a farmer whose land is scattered, but he resides on land immediately adjoining the land in question. His motive in buying appears to have been to concentrate his farming round his residence and give up his outlying lands. But he knew the plaintiff and his sisters, and he knew that there had been some disagreement among them, especially upon the marriage of the plaintiff, an elderly man. I am satisfied that the defendant had some uneasiness on this score, and, after the auction had fallen through, when he was being urged to advance his offer, he decided to assure himself that, if he bought, he would buy with 'the goodwill'. That was the real object of his inquiries of Mr Maher. He was informed that a deed had been executed settling the sisters' claims—and that was the case—but a legal settlement will not always dispose of the non-legal matter of goodwill. He signed the contract. Almost immediately after the contract was signed he began to experience hostility on the part of the plaintiff's sisters. The details of the manner in which that hostility was displayed are the subject of conflicting evidence, but are really immaterial. It is sufficient that there were, as I am satisfied, demonstrations of ill will towards him by these ladies, one of whom could not conceal her hostile sentiments in the witness box.

On 21 March the vendor's solicitor, Mr Maher, wrote to the defendant asking him what solicitor he wished to act for him, so that he, Mr Maher, might furnish an abstract of title. Under the conditions of sale the abstract was to be delivered within four days from the sale, but it might have been delivered to the purchaser personally, and should have been so delivered, failing the nomination of a solicitor to receive it.

On 22 March the defendant wrote to Mr Maher saying: 'I have withdrawn from the purchase . . . I do not wish to be interfering in family affairs. His sisters threatened me several times since, and they wish that anybody would have it besides me, so I am not going to have hand, act, or part in it.' This is the letter relied on in the statement of claim as a renunciation of the contract by the defendant. It was originally relied on here in the same way, but the plaintiff's counsel subsequently admitted he could not, having regard to what occurred afterwards, continue to rely upon it as a repudiation of the contract.

On 23 March Mr Maher wrote to the defendant assuring him that the plaintiff's sisters had no conflicting interest, and requiring him to complete. On 25 March the defendant visited Mr Maher, and gave him particulars of his two outlying farms so that he might arrange for their sale on 8 April, the day fixed for completing the purchase from the plaintiff. The two farms were, in fact, put up for sale. The sale of one was abortive, the reserve not being reached, while a purchaser was found for the other.

On 27 March the defendant again visited Mr Maher to complain of attacks by the plaintiff's sisters, made both on himself personally and at the house on the plaintiff's holding. Mr Maher thereupon wrote to the late Mr John O'Dwyer, who had been acting as solicitor for the plaintiff's sisters, complaining of the ladies' conduct towards the defendant—to whom Mr Maher referred as 'my client'.

On 8 April the defendant again saw Mr Maher and complained of the attitude of the Misses Guerin. Mr Maher says he appeared to be very nervous, so he [Mr Maher] gave him an old revolver he happened to have in the office, and this Mr Maher describes as one of the steps he took for reconciling the defendant to his bargain.

In the meantime, when the defendant was in Mr Maher's office on 25 March, Maher's clerk asked him had he a solicitor, and he said he had Mr D'Arcy. The clerk thereupon advised him to go down to Mr John O'Dwyer, as, he said, 'he is the only man that can quieten these women, and he will make it all right.' The defendant then went with Maher's clerk to Mr O'Dwyer, and, presumably, instructed him to act for him in the purchase from the plaintiff.

On 10 April Mr Maher, solicitor, wrote to Mr O'Dwyer, solicitor: 'Will you please let me have engrossment of deed in this case for signature by my client, and let me know when you will be prepared to close the sale,' to which Mr O'Dwyer replied on 19 April, 'My client called on me some days ago and informed me that owing to a threatening notice, which he said he had showed you, he could not complete. This was in addition to several verbal threats.' This is the repudiation of the contract now relied upon.

Here it is important to observe that Mr O'Dwyer was the solicitor for the plaintiff's sisters. He had acted for them in drawing up the deed of 1904 and an agreement of 14 March 1922, which purported to solve the outstanding disputes between them and the plaintiff. Under these instruments they had charges to be released on a sale of the land. Yet no attempt seems to have been made to prepare draft releases of the charges for approval. Further, a right-of-way was agreed to be given to Lizzie Guerin over the lands sold, which was the right-of-way mentioned in the conditions of sale, and which was to be defined, both under the agreement of 14 March 1922, and under the conditions of sale. Yet no attempt was made to define it. It was the plaintiff's duty to procure releases of the charges and to define the right-of-way to the satisfaction of Lizzie Guerin. His solicitor, Mr Maher, should have taken the initiative in both these matters; and when Mr Maher, without having taken these steps, called for an engrossment of the assurance to the purchaser, it was for Mr Dwyer, whether as solicitor for the purchaser or as solicitor for the plaintiff's sisters, to have pointed out to him that these were necessary preliminaries to carrying out the sale.

Moreover, there were cattle all this time on the lands, some of which were the property of the plaintiff and some belonged to Lizzie Guerin. The defendant complained of this stock remaining on the lands, but owing to the failure of the plaintiff to agree with his sister as to which cattle were their respective properties, the lands were not cleared. Indeed, an attempt was made to induce the defendant to take the risk of clearing the lands himself, which he properly refused to do.

The defendant was persuaded to transfer his business in relation to the sale to Mr O'Dwyer on the ground that Mr O'Dwyer alone could quieten these women. It is a remarkable fact that there is no trace of Mr O'Dwyer ever having been able to reassure the defendant that he had nothing to fear from them, neither does it appear that Mr O'Dwyer ever informed Mr Maher, either before or after he acquired the defendant as a client, that he was in a position to concur in carrying the matter through on behalf of his female clients.

Finally, it does not appear that Mr Maher ever furnished Mr O'Dwyer with the abstract of title according to the conditions of sale, without which he could neither make requisitions nor draft the assurance to the defendant.

I am of opinion, in the first place, that the defence of representations, inducing the defendant to enter into the contract, is a real defence. I think the defendant did make it clear that he must get the goodwill of the family in the sense I have mentioned, and that the plaintiff never was in a position to give him the lands with such goodwill.

In the second place, I cannot find that the plaintiff, or his solicitor, did anything towards carrying out the contract, and, in my opinion, the plaintiff's solicitor was not entitled to write the letter of 10 April 1922, calling for an engrossment of the deed of conveyance, to which the letter of 19 April, relied on by the plaintiff, was a reply.

In these circumstances I would hold that specific performance should be refused.

But then we have the further facts of lapse of time and acquiescence in the repudiation of the contract.

Not until 13 June 1923, was the writ in this action issued, and, in the meantime, we have acts showing that both parties believed the whole transaction to be at an end. The plaintiff attempted to auction the meadow on the land. The defendant, who had agreed to sell one of his farms preparatory to completing this purchase, released the purchaser and was released by him. It would, in my opinion, be a hardship, and it would be inequitable for the court now to say that this is still a living contract which the defendant must perform.

There is one matter on which I wish to add a word. It is my opinion that the defendant has suffered from acting upon the advice given him to leave his independent solicitor. We find him as client, first of one and then of another solicitor representing clients with interests adverse to his. If he had been quite independently advised, this case would have probably reached an earlier solution, and he would have been saved much trouble.

In my opinion the appeal should be dismissed with costs.

O'Connor J.:

On the pleadings in this action, apart from formal traverses, the only issue raised is that the contract for sale of the lands was induced by a misrepresentation made by the plaintiff to the defendant that the latter would be allowed to enter peaceably upon the lands without claims, molestations, or threats by the plaintiff's family or other persons.

The trial of the action lasted three days, and the transcript of the very voluminous evidence shows that every conceivable topic was dealt with—so much so, that it is difficult to gather from the evidence what were the issues to which it was directed. It certainly was not confined to the only issue which was raised by the pleadings. An explanation is to be found in the way in which the trial, with the assent of both parties, was conducted. The pleadings were disregarded, and plaintiff and defendant were left at large without being called upon to formulate the issues by amended pleadings. The result seems to have been that no one at the trial seems to have had a clear conception of the material issues, and much time was wasted and the whole case obscured by evidence of the most rambling and confusing character. I consider this case to be a glaring example of the inconvenience resulting from the absence of proper pleadings raising the real issues to be tried. I do not wish to be taken as an advocate of rigid adherence to pleadings on which an action is brought to trial. Very frequently it appears at the trial that material issues have not been raised by the pleadings, and that it would be unjust to shut out the parties from raising them, but I do maintain that, when the proper issues become manifest, the parties should be called upon to formulate them by proper amendments. This is by no means a matter of merely formal compliance with rules. I know nothing which is more conducive to clear thinking, whether on the bench or at the bar, than the proper formulation of a legal claim or a legal defence, while there is nothing more calculated to lead to confusion and waste of time with consequent expense than to allow a case to drag along without exact knowledge of the issues which are raised.

Reading the evidence I am able to extract from it three grounds of defence which may easily be brought under well defined heads: 1. delay and laches on the plaintiff's part in bringing his action; 2. repudiation by the defendant and acquiescence by the plaintiff in such repudiation; 3. a change of position to the prejudice of the defendant caused by the plaintiff's conduct—a defence closely associated with defence No. 1. These do not exhaust the issues to be extracted from the evidence, but I will confine myself to them, as sufficient for the purpose of my judgment.

A contract for the sale of a farm is one which ought to be expeditiously carried out. A farm is a property which requires immediate attention and treatment. The times for doing things on a farm wait not for the farmer. He must always be up and doing. When he buys his farm he ought to get immediate possession. If he is delayed he may miss a sowing, or a reaping, or a market. Consequently, if there is a dispute between a vendor and purchaser of a farm, the purchaser should know at once whether he is to be on or off with his contract. He ought not to be kept in suspense.

In this case the contract was made on 18 March 1922. The date fixed for completion was 8 April 1922. Everyone knows that this is the time of year at which it is important for a farmer to get immediate possession. Immediately after the making of the contract the defendant had reasons for regretting it. It is not necessary to go into particulars. He repudiated it. he may at one time have withdrawn his repudiation, but it is certain that he finally, and in the clearest manner, repudiated it on 19 April 1922. This repudiation was met by a notice from the plaintiff that he would at once institute legal proceedings. I will assume that the plaintiff had then a good cause of action for damages for breach of contract or for specific performance. He might have rested on his claim for damages until it was barred by the Statute of Limitations; but, if he intended to seek the equitable relief of specific performance he was bound to proceed without delay. A man who sleeps on his rights does not find favour in a court of equity.

The plaintiff, instead of proceeding as he had threatened the defendant that he would, did nothing to assert his rights until 13 June 1923, when he issued his writ. During the intervening period the defendant might very well have assumed that the plaintiff had abandoned his rights under the contract and had accepted the defendant's repudiation. It would certainly be a hardship on the defendant to have his fear of liability lulled, while in the meantime the plaintiff would have the option of selling the farm to advantage and, that failing, of enforcing the contract. On the ground of delay alone I think that the plaintiff is not entitled to equitable relief. There is ample authority to support this view: see *Fry on Specific Performance*, (6th ed.), paras 1071, 1072 and 1073. The length of the delay depends on the circumstances of each case, and, having regard to the nature of the property now in question, I am of opinion that the delay was altogether unreasonable. But the plaintiff's delay was accompanied by acts which are only consistent with his acquiescence in the repudiation and his election to treat the contract as at an end. A considerable time after the day fixed for completion of the contract the plaintiff advertised the meadows on the lands. That was wholly inconsistent with the defendant's rights under the contract if it were to be enforced against him. The letting of the meadows would have incapacitated the plaintiff from giving up clear possession.

Further, I am satisfied on the evidence that the defendant, acting under the belief that the contract was abandoned by the plaintiff, released a purchaser of one of his own farms, which he had agreed to sell, in consequence of the purchase of the plaintiff's farm—whether the defendant has suffered actual loss from this I do not know—but it was a change in position, which, with the other elements in the case, should be taken into consideration.

On these grounds alone I am of opinion that the plaintiff lost the right which may have been vested in him originally of getting a decree for specific performance, and I do not consider it necessary to give any decision on the defence of misrepresentation.

In my judgment the appeal should be dismissed with costs.

B. Mistake or Misrepresentation

Many of the leading Irish authorities are considered in Chapter 11; see in particular *Ferguson v Merchant Banking Ltd* (p. 428) and *Smyth v Lynn* (p. 446).

C. The Conduct of the Parties, particularly the Plaintiff.

Where the plaintiff has perpetrated an equitable fraud or the agreement is unconscionable or procured by undue influence.

Devine v Fields [1920] 54 ILTR 101

The facts
...

The plaintiff and defendant were grazing tenants of different portions of the same holding for a considerable period. The owner of the holding offered it for sale in one lot, and the plaintiff purchased the holding, and, having paid for same, got the usual transfer of registered land, and became registered owner. The defendant alleged an oral agreement prior to the auction, that he should not bid thereat, and that the plaintiff should buy the entire holding and convey defendant's portion afterwards to defendant.

The plaintiff applied for an interlocutory injunction restraining the defendant, pending the trial of the action, from entering upon or being or remaining in or otherwise trespassing upon, and from putting or keeping cattle or sheep in or upon land said to be the plaintiff's. When the motion was called for hearing, on 8 February 1920, counsel for plaintiff and defendant stated that the parties had agreed to the following terms:

> The further hearing of the motion was to stand over until the trial of the action, upon *viva voce* evidence without pleadings; and that the defendant be taken as counterclaiming for a declaration that the plaintiff purchased 22 acres or thereabouts of the lands in dispute as trustee for the defendant, and for consequential relief, and that the plaintiff be taken as having pleaded the Statute of Frauds, &c.

O'Connor M.R.:

I have no doubt as to the law, and I prefer to give judgment while the facts are fresh in my mind. The affidavit of the plaintiff would lead to the conclusion that the defendant was guilty of wanton acts. The plaintiff, however, has not been as open with the court as he should have been. The time at which the plaintiff first saw the advertisement is of little importance. The defendant wrote at once to Potterton, the auctioneer, and got replies. The plaintiff allowed the defendant to negotiate. The defendant did not stop with writing to Potterton. He saw the difficulty about the entire property being sold in only one lot. He wrote to Messrs White & White, solicitors, asking would the Land Commission divide the property. A sentence from the letter of 4 June 1919, written by the defendant to Messrs White & White is as follows: 'I don't want to let my part go if I can help it, nor does Devine want to let his part go.' Fields asked White & White if he and Devine agreed for one of them to buy the property would the Commissioners take him as tenant for the field which he and his father before him had held for a considerable number of years. He swears he showed this letter to Devine. Clearly, the idea behind such a letter was that one should buy for the two and each get his own part, and arrange as to the division of the purchase money and the subsequent annuity payable to the Land Commission. The defendant saw the advertisement the first week in June. He came to see the plaintiff, and discussed buying the property. He says they discussed the possibility of its being sold in one or two lots to enable each of them to purchase their portion. The defendant was anxious for a sale in two lots. About ten days before the sale there was a conversation between the plaintiff and the defendant, when the plaintiff's nephew was present. The plaintiff says he introduced the subject of getting a solicitor to arrange matters, but the defendant strongly objected to the employment of a solicitor, fearing that it would only increase the cost. The plaintiff also deposed that defendant said if plaintiff did not buy it would not be bought at all. The plaintiff replied: 'I'll buy at any price,' and states that defendant said: 'You can; I will not burn my fingers.' If all this be so, the plaintiff cannot be held a trustee for the defendant. But there is a strong conflict of evidence. The defendant swears that the plaintiff said: 'No matter what happens we will buy between us.' He wrote to his solicitors with reference to the sale in one or two lots. When he got their reply he showed it to the plaintiff, and said that they should offer the £4,000 which Potterton, the auctioneer, mentioned. He suggested that they should get a motor car and see about the matter at once, but the plaintiff then refused to employ a solicitor. The plaintiff also said he would have no communication with Potterton. The defendant said he would write to White & White, and to that plaintiff raised no objection. The defendant said that one of them could bid and buy, and afterwards each could get his part. The defendant says he went to Dublin; went to White & White's. He saw the plaintiff afterwards, and told him of his business with White & White. Attention was called by White & White to the fact that the two portions of the holding were not similar in area. The defendant says, regarding this, that he told the plaintiff that an arbitrator should be appointed to fix their respective portions of the purchase money. He says the plaintiff replied that there would not be any dispute; that all he wanted was his own part, and that he did not know any solicitor. The defendant's story is more likely than that of the plaintiff, and is quite consistent with what happened contemporaneously and afterwards. If the defendant's story is the true account, there is a sufficient agreement to enforce. There was a sufficient inducement to prevent the defendant from bidding. The auction was advertised for 26 June 1919. Both parties went to the auction together, in the same train and in the same carriage. What did the defendant go to Dublin for? It seems to me they went on a joint venture. The plaintiff says there was no talk in the train about the sale. It is most unlikely that they did not talk in the train about the sale. The defendant says they did talk, and commented upon the possibility of outside competition. The plaintiff bid for the farm. It was knocked down to him at £3,400. The plaintiff paid the deposit. The defendant says they adjourned to Keogh's publichouse in Queen Street. I believe the story about Keogh's, and that they had drinks—a return of compliments there—though plaintiff does not recollect it. Messrs White & White were selected as solicitors by the defendant with the knowledge of the plaintiff. This shows that defendant was interested in the matter. White & White were the defendant's family solicitors. It shows that the plaintiff must have known that the defendant was interested in the matter, and voiced his interest by his selection of the solicitors whom he had employed on former occasions. The plaintiff denies any offer by the defendant in White & White's office to contribute a portion of the deposit money, but Mr Grove White has a hazy recollection about a conversation concerning the apportionment of the deposit. He also says that he paid no particular attention to the conversation, because the deposit was to bear interest. Mr Blair White clearly recollects that defendant produced a cheque book and offered to pay a portion of the deposit, and that plaintiff said it was no inconvenience to him, and perhaps it would be inconvenient for the defendant, and that, apart from this, it would bear interest. Such conduct is inconsistent with purchase by Devine on his own account. The defendant's evidence harmonises with the rest of the case. Considering that the deposit was to bear interest, perhaps it was actually a gain to the plaintiff if he had the money lying idle. All this can only have one possible explanation—the liability of the defendant to pay a portion of the purchase money. That being so, if the plaintiff purchased entirely for his own benefit, why did he not say to the defendant when the foregoing conversation was going on: 'What interest have you in this matter?' 'Why are you interfering?' 'You have no right to interfere.' There is documentary evidence, if documentary evidence be necessary, in support of the evidence of White & White. There is a letter of 28 June 1919, from White & White to the plaintiff: 'Dear Sir,— We have now received copy of the conditions of sale, as signed by you, for the purchase of the lands of Newtownmoyghy. The contract differs from the copy of the conditions we had as regards the payment of the balance of the purchase money, and the condition mentioned by you regarding interest on deposit as set forth, &c.' It is perfectly plain that the plaintiff was keenly alive to the fact that he was not at any loss by paying the entire deposit. He was to receive interest upon same. On 30 September 1919, defendant wrote to Messrs White & White: 'Dear Sir,—I shall call to see you at the end of this week or early next, as it is time to make final arrangements about the brick-field, and I would like to have it arranged as soon as possible.' The plaintiff relies on that to support his contention that there was no previous agreement, but it was for 'final arrangements', and, therefore, consistent with defendant's case—that he had arranged the joint purchase, but that the apportionment of the purchase money had not been fixed. It also appears that plaintiff called at Messrs White & White's office on 2 October 1919, and there was some conversation regarding the right of the defendant to participate in the sale. But the plaintiff's version is that when he came on 2 October Mr White told him defendant was looking for his part of the field. Plaintiff said: 'That can't be; I bought it for myself.' Mr Grove White gives an account of that interview. He says Devine came into the office to see himself and his partner with reference to the purchase. He told them he was anxious to obtain the entire holding, and asked them to use their influence with the defendant to allow him to do so. He said he would prefer not to buy any of the property rather than to buy only the part which was in his occupation as a grazing tenant. Mr Grove White told him that when the purchase was first discussed he tried to persuade the defendant not to purchase, but without success, and that he would convey plaintiff's wishes to defendant on the next opportunity. He did tell the defendant on a subsequent date, but without any effect, and as a consequence wrote to the plaintiff telling him that defendant had never wavered in his decision to buy the part of the lands in his occupation as grazing tenant known as the 'brick-field', and had counted on taking this over from him as soon as he had completed the purchase with Miss Wade, the vendor. Upon hearing that, the plaintiff stated he would rather not purchase any if he did not get the entire property; the defendant said he was willing to release the plaintiff, and purchase the entire lot for himself. The plaintiff called again on 16 October 1919, at the office of White & White, and informed them that he was going to complete the sale for his own benefit; that he had purchased for self, and self only, Messrs White & White then refused to act for him further. Looking at the correspondence and evidence of both parties, I think the defendant's story is to be credited rather than the plaintiff's. It justifies the inference that there was a common object—a joint acquisition. Both parties were active at every step. If it was not a joint venture, how can the actions of both parties be explained? Defendant had no intention of abandoning without a struggle the land which he required for grazing his dairy cows. The acquisition of the land was essential to his business, essential for the welfare of his family, and it was land which was occupied by his father. I am of opinion there was agreement between plaintiff and defendant and that plaintiff agreed with defendant to purchase on trust for both—*viz.* to purchase the 22 acres for the defendant and to purchase the remainder for himself. Further, it was arranged between them that the annuity as to their respective portions and the purchase money should be paid according to their respective areas. There need not be any uncertainty as to the rent. There need not be any uncertainty as to the adjustment of the purchase money. Any difficulty can be overcome by an adjustment upon inquiry. This is only one of many cases where ambiguity can be overcome by an inquiry. The apportionment will be no more difficult than if it were a common rent charge. The apportionment of the annuity is easy. The apportionment of the purchase money is also made easy by ascertainment of the respective values of the plaintiff's and defendant's portions (*Chattock v Muller* (1878) 8 ChD 177). It is the duty of a court of equity to overcome all technicalities in order to defeat a fraud. The action of the plaintiff in the present case was a fraud. The defendant was lured into making no offer for the property. There is no uncertainty as to the subject matter, such as there was in above case. Specific performance can be obtained, even where the price has to be settled by arbitrators. The plaintiff's action must be dismissed. I make a declaration on the counterclaim that the plaintiff purchased and holds in trust for defendant as to defendant's 22 acres, the defendant being liable for an apportioned part of the annuity and also an apportioned part of the purchase money.

Conlon v Murray [1958] NI 17

Black L.J.:

This is an appeal by the plaintiff Patrick Conlon from the dismissal by Curran J. on 30 July 1956, of an action in which the plaintiff claimed specific performance of an agreement in writing dated 26 May 1954, by which one Mary Sheridan agreed to sell to the plaintiff for the sum of £2,000 the farm on which she lived situated at Ballinarea in the southern part of County Armagh. Mary Sheridan died on 22 September 1955, and the action was continued against James Murray and Peter Murray her executors.

At the time of signing the agreement Mary Sheridan was about sixty nine years of age. According to the evidence of her medical attendant Dr O'Reilly, which was not challenged, her eyesight had been troubling her. She had had an operation on her left eye which necessitated the use of glasses and in her right eye she had no sight at all owing to glaucoma which is associated with increasing pressure of fluid in the eye. This condition was acute and according to Dr O'Reilly was probably quite painful. Dr O'Reilly saw her on 24 May 1954. She then also complained of bleeding from the womb. That suggested to Dr O'Reilly the probability of something malignant and he arranged for her to be treated by a specialist gynaecologist. She was seen by the specialist at Newry Hospital on 1 June, she was admitted to the hospital on 7 June, and her womb was removed on 18 June. She was discharged from hospital on 14 July, and readmitted on 18 July, with an acute urinary infection. She was allowed home on 1 or 2 August, but entered a nursing home on 6 August, where she remained until her death on 22 September 1955. Dr O'Reilly says that in May 1954 her uterus trouble was fairly advanced and that it would be distressing with constant bleeding and general weakness due to carcinoma. She was ill and was generally weak but was mentally alert at any time he saw her apart from the effect of drugs given to relieve her pain.

Mrs Sheridan had a brother called Patrick Toner who had sold his own farm in 1953 and had come to live with her in the house on her farm. He was a man somewhat addicted to drink and had become rather a trial to Mrs Sheridan. It appears that on 24 May 1954, the same day as she had been seen by Dr O'Reilly, Mrs Sheridan arrived sometime between 4.30 p.m and 6 p.m at the house of a Mr Michael Sheridan. She had had a row that day with her brother and according to Michael Sheridan's daughter Miss Mary Sheridan, a trained nurse, she was not terribly distressed, but when she arrived she was slightly distressed but settled down. Mrs Sheridan asked Miss Mary Sheridan would she go when it got dark to Cullyhanna and get her brother's car and take Mrs Sheridan to the house of her sister Mrs Murray. Miss Mary Sheridan cycled over to Cullyhanna but was unable to get her brother's car as he had the engine down cleaning it. She then went to Mrs Murray's house and they both came over to Mr Michael Sheridan's house on their bicycles. When they arrived there about 10.30 p.m. Mrs Sheridan was missing and Mrs Murray went out to look for her. Mrs Murray found Mrs Sheridan in one of her own fields going in the direction of her own home with no coat or hat. They came up to the road where they met a man called Bernard Collins who plays a not unimportant part in the case and had a conversation with him. Eventually Mrs Sheridan agreed to go back home to Mrs Murray's house—a distance of 3 miles away—where they arrived about 1.30 a.m. Collins agreed that Mrs Sheridan was worried that night and that although it was late she had no coat on.

The details of the conversation with Collins on the road on the night of Monday 24 May, are in dispute. According to Collins' own story Mrs Sheridan said that she had had a dispute with her brother Paddy and that he had thrown a bucket of water round her. Collins then, according to his story, advised her to go and live with Mrs Murray and to put up the farm for sale and asked her if she would be willing to take £2,000 for the farm and, if so, he would try to get her a customer. Mrs Sheridan, according to Collins, said that she would indeed be willing to take £2,000 and would give Collins a good shake-hand and the purchaser a good luckpenny. Collins said that he himself meant to be the customer for the farm but when he saw his wife he decided not to buy and then thought of the plaintiff Patrick Conlon as a possible purchaser. Accordingly, Collins sought to get in touch with the plaintiff next day (Tuesday 25 May). The plaintiff, however, was at Ardee Fair but Collins left a message for him and the plaintiff went over to Collins' house about 7 p.m. As a result they went over to Mrs Murray's house to interview Mrs Sheridan. This was quite late at night. Collins says about 11 p.m. Collins apparently got there first and went up to see Mrs Sheridan who was in bed. According to his account Mrs Sheridan was at first averse to selling to Conlon on personal grounds but ultimately said that Conlon's money was as good as any other man's, that she was getting a good price and it was no odds who got it. Conlon was then brought up to the bedroom and according to him Mrs Sheridan and he agreed to the sale of the farm for £2,000. There was then some discussion about getting a solicitor to draw up the agreement. Mrs Sheridan stipulated that she wanted her own solicitor Mr O'Connor of Crossmaglen. It is agreed that on the night of 25 May there was no talk of Conlon getting vacant possession of the lands or what was to be done about Mrs Sheridan's brother being in the house.

No time was wasted about getting the agreement reduced to writing. On the morning of Wednesday 26 May, Gerard Conlon a brother of the plaintiff, went into Crossmaglen for Mr O'Connor. Unfortunately Mr O'Connor was in Dublin that day but his managing clerk Mr Carahar was in the office and was apprised that his services were required for the purpose of drawing an agreement for the sale of a farm. Apparently there was no question of waiting until Mr O'Connor himself should be available. Gerard Conlon got a taxi and drove out with Mr Carahar to Mrs Murray's at Cullyhanna, stopping by arrangement about 20 yards past the house. The plaintiff was already there in the kitchen of Mrs Murray's house. Mr Carahar was shown up to Mrs Sheridan's bedroom. Up till then Mr Carahar had not seen the plaintiff although apparently even up to the trial he was under the impression that the man who called for him and had taken him out in the taxi was not a brother of the plaintiff but the plaintiff himself. At Mrs Sheridan's bedside Mr Carahar proceeded to draft the agreement upon the information given to him by Mrs Sheridan who was sitting up in bed propped up by pillows. Carahar says that he pointed out to Mrs Sheridan what was to happen her when she had disposed of her home and she replied that she could live anywhere. Mr Carahar did not appear clear for whom he was supposed to be acting when he was drafting the agreement. He had been brought out to Mrs Murray's house by an emissary of the plaintiff's and although Mrs Sheridan in the past had been a client of Mr O'Connor's Mr Carahar had not been informed that he was to be regarded as acting on her behalf. There would seem little doubt, however, but that Mrs Sheridan regarded Mr O'Connor as her solicitor and had asked for him for that reason and accordingly would consider Carahar as looking after her interests in the matter. Mr Carahar says that Mrs Sheridan did not ask for any advice, that he pointed out she was disposing of her home, that she told him she had got a good price for it and that he did not suggest that an auction might bring a better price. Mr Carahar says his state of mind was that he might be acting for both parties and thought it his duty to look after both Conlon's and Mrs Sheridan's interests. Conlon conveyed to Mr Carahar that he wanted the contract signed there and then. And Conlon paid for the taxi.

The real difficulty in drafting the agreement was in regard to giving possession of the farm. What was to be done about Toner? Mr Carahar says that he told Mrs Sheridan that she should get her brother to leave as it was her duty to give clear possession and that she did not dispute that but said that she had rather not take proceedings against him. Mr Carahar says she meant that she would rather the purchaser did it and that she said there would be no trouble with her brother. She believed he would leave when asked and she instructed Mr Carahar to write him immediately informing him of the sale and asking him to leave. Mr Carahar then apparently added clause 9 of the agreement which reads: 'The said Mary Sheridan agrees to take all steps necessary to evict said Patrick Toner if he refuses to leave said dwelling house and to pay costs of same.' Mr Carahar says that he did not speak to Conlon before he put in this clause and that he put it in to protect Conlon. In so doing Mr Carahar was, of course, acting in Conlon's interest though it is tolerably clear that Mrs Sheridan was looking upon him as acting on her behalf. In view of the circumstances and of what were obviously Mrs Sheridan's strong feelings in the matter I think that if an independent solicitor had been acting upon behalf of Mrs Sheridan he would have struggled hard to negotiate a modification of this clause. Mr O'Connor himself frankly says that he would agree that in this aspect of the matter she would require independent legal advice and says that he would have taken proper instructions and advised her and such advice would be independent of any obligation to the purchaser.

Mr Carahar says that he read the agreement to Mrs Sheridan and she approved it. He then brought Conlon into the room and read it over again in his presence and he approved and said he was paying £500 deposit which he paid then and there in cash.

Conlon's account of the transaction is substantially different. He says that Mr Carahar called him up to Mrs Sheridan's bedroom after he had part of an agreement drawn up, that the clause about possession had not yet been inserted, that next they talked about possession of the house and Carahar asked him would he take it on him to put Toner out of the house, Conlon says he said 'No' as he earned the first shilling he ever earned with Paddy Toner and he would not be the man to put him out, that Mr Carahar then said to Mrs Sheridan 'You see the situation now?' and that he, Conlon, then said he wasn't putting him out and the deal was off. Conlon says that Mrs Sheridan then said: 'Seeing you won't put him out Paddy, I'll have to put him out,' and she proposed that if Conlon put him out she would bear the expenses. Conlon says he would not agree, so she agreed she would put him out in her own name.

Whether Carahar's account of this matter or the plaintiff's is the true one I have no means of knowing. Both were called as witnesses for the plaintiffs. On another point, where the plaintiff's evidence differed from Carahar's, Curran J., who had the advantage of seeing the witnesses, roundly held that he was satisfied that the plaintiff was not telling the truth. But he did not find it necessary in his judgment to assess where the truth lies on any other particular point.

It is obvious from Mr O'Connor's evidence as regards his visit to Mrs Sheridan on 31 May that Mrs Sheridan fully appreciated that she had entered into an agreement to sell the farm to Conlon and that she was to put her brother out. This was apparently the term of the agreement that she particularly objected to and the term which on 31 May she felt to impose particular hardship on her.

The remedy of specific performance still retains the character of an equitable remedy. It is not granted as of right but is a discretionary remedy which may be withheld in cases of a type where the court, having regard to the conduct of the parties and all the circumstances of the case, considers in its discretion that the remedy ought not to be granted. This discretion is not, of course, the arbitrary discretion of the individual judge but is a discretion to be exercised on the principles which have been worked out in a multitude of decided cases. And it is well established that there is a class of cases in which a contract may be such and entered into in such conditions that the court will not order it to be rescinded but, at the same time, looking to the substantial justice of the case, will not order it to be specifically performed. It follows naturally, as observed in *Kerr on Fraud and Mistake*, (7th ed. 1952), 568 that when the aid of a court is sought by way of specific performance of a contract the principles of ethics have a more extensive sway than when a contract is sought to be rescinded.

(Lord MacDermott L.C.J. agreed.)

The Court of Appeal upheld Curran J.'s decision not to grant specific performance.

Note

Improper pressure is also relevant (see pp 542–5 and 609–618 below).

D. WHERE THE DEFENDANT HAS NO TITLE OR A DUBIOUS TITLE

See for example *Carthy v O'Neill* [1981] ILRM 443.

E. Hardship to the Defendant

Roberts v O'Neill [1983] IR 47

McCarthy J.:

This is an action for specific performance of a contract dated 17 January 1978, and made between the plaintiff (in trust) and the defendants for the sale by the defendants to the plaintiff of the Silver Tassie, being licensed premises at Loughlinstown in County Dublin. In the High Court Mr Justice McWilliam granted the order sought by the plaintiff and also awarded damages which were measured at bank interest on the sum of £30,000 (paid as a deposit on the signing of the contract) up to the date of judgment. The first defendant, who is the husband of the second defendant, appeals against the order for specific performance and seeks, in effect, an order that the plaintiff be compensated in damages only, so that the first defendant and his wife may retain the licensed premises. For the reasons that I shall state, in my judgment, the appeal fails.

The facts

It is desirable to set out the sequence of events in some detail. In the year 1973, the defendants bought the Silver Tassie, for an undisclosed sum and, thereafter, remained joint owners. In November 1977, their daughter was 'coshed' in a burglary at their home, which is a bungalow adjoining the Silver Tassie. Because of that incident, the first defendant became increasingly worried and thought it might be better to sell the premises—a view which was not shared by his wife, who wanted their son, then aged thirteen, to continue in the business. What one might call the defendants' experience in the public house business only began in the year 1973.

During the weekend before 16 January 1978, discussions took place between Corry Buckley (acting on behalf of Mr Gerard Carthy), the defendants, and Gerard Black, who was their solicitor. It was subsequently maintained by Mr Carthy that, arising from those discussions, there was an enforceable contract for the purchase by him of the premises for £190,000.

The plaintiff is a nominee for the Madigan Group, owners of a chain of public houses. On 16 January the plaintiff learnt of the possibility that the premises might be on the market and he called there on that night. The plaintiff's son-in-law, Mr Madigan, contacted Mr Moore who is the agent for the defendants. On the next day a formal contract, in the printed form authorised and issued by the Incorporated Law Society of Ireland, suitably completed as to amount, closing date, deposit and details of title, was executed by the plaintiff personally and by Mr Black, solicitor, as agent for the defendants. The closing date was fixed for 17 February, upon which date the plaintiff's solicitors sent a draft conveyance to the defendants' solicitors.

On 21 February, in a letter to the plaintiff's solicitors, Mr Black stated: '6. Since formally replying to your requisitions on title herein we have been notified by another firm of solicitors that a client of theirs may institute proceedings against the vendor. Such proceedings were in fact issued against the wrong party (not our client) about three weeks ago but we returned same to the said solicitors indicating that the proceedings were not in order. To date neither we nor our clients have received any amended or new summonses.' On 28 February, Mr Black wrote to the plaintiff's solicitors enclosing:

. . . herewith memorandum and index relating this matter'. On 6 March, the plaintiff's solicitors wrote to Mr Black in these terms: 'In order to protect our client's interests, we have registered the contract for sale dated 17 January 1978 and in order to protect our client's interest further, we feel that a *lis pendens* must be registered. This means that proceedings must be commenced and we will be issuing plenary summons in this regard tomorrow. Please let us know what steps your clients intend to take to have the *lis pendens* in the *Carthy* action removed as obviously while this is still on the record we cannot advise our client to complete.

On 7 March 1978, a plenary summons was issued by the plaintiff but no reply to the observation about the *lis pendens* appears to have been received at any time. On 7 June a statement of claim was delivered claiming an order for specific performance of the agreement and damages. On 19 July a joint defence and counterclaim was delivered on behalf of the defendants in which they pleaded, essentially, that because of the *Carthy* action, they were unable to complete the sale. In particular, they pleaded at para. 4:

> If, contrary to the defendant's contention, the contract for sale was not conditional upon the said Gerard Carthy not succeeding in claiming that he had entered into a binding contract for the sale of the said premises to him, the contract is in any event impossible of performance until the determination of the said proceedings, *and, in the event of the said proceedings being determined in favour of the defendants, they are ready and willing to complete the sale to the plaintiff.* (I have added the emphasis.)

The action by Mr Carthy against Mr O'Neill was heard on 4 and 5 July 1979, by Mr Justice Gannon, who delivered judgment in October. The learned judge held that the Carthy contract was legally enforceable and he joined Mrs O'Neill as a defendant to that action. The O'Neills appealed and the Supreme Court, in its judgment of 30 January 1981, allowed that appeal and dismissed Mr Carthy's action.

On 2 March 1981, the plaintiff's solicitors called upon the defendants, through their solicitors, to complete the sale forthwith and indicated a claim for damages for delay. On 19 March, Mr Black informed the plaintiff's solicitors that 'we will be applying on behalf of the first-named defendant to amend the defence as it is the first-named defendant's contention that this is not a proper case for specific performance.' Mr Black had ceased to act on behalf of the second defendant. The terms of the amended defence of the first defendant were sent sometime towards the end of March 1981, to the plaintiff's solicitors, and the amended defence of the second defendant, in which she denied Mr Black's authority, was filed on 5 May 1981. This contention of the second defendant was rejected by the trial judge, and no appeal has been brought against that finding.

On 6 May 1981, an amended defence and counterclaim was filed on behalf of the first defendant, and the material portion of this was to strike out the words (to which I have added emphasis) in the original defence and counterclaim at para. 4 and to add a plea to this effect:

> In the period between the making of the contract for sale to the plaintiff in these proceedings and the delivery of the judgment [of the Supreme Court in *Carthy v O'Neill*[1]] the value of the said premises had greatly increased as has the value of licensed premises generally. The first-named defendant is a publican and it would be grossly unjust if the defendants were obliged to sell said premises to the plaintiff at the contract price, which would now be a gross undervalue and whereby the plaintiff would be unjustly enriched. Accordingly, the court in its discretion should refuse to grant an order of specific performance.

Up to that date, from the delivery of the original joint defence and counterclaim on 19 July 1978, the attitude expressly maintained on behalf of both defendants insofar as an examination of the court record would disclose was that the sole bar to the closing of the sale to the plaintiff was the existence of the *Carthy* action.

The adjourned hearing of this action took place before Mr Justice McWilliam on 4 and 5 June 1981. On 3 July 1981, the delivered judgment in which he rejected the defendants' contention that specific performance should not be granted and that damages in lieu thereof was the appropriate remedy.

The appeal

The first defendant has appealed, by a notice of appeal dated 5 August 1981, against the order for specific performance but without stating in the notice of appeal what he suggests is the alternative order. On the hearing of this appeal, counsel for the first defendant has limited the appeal to seeking a finding that the order of specific performance would cause excessive hardship to the defendants and should, therefore, be refused; and that, in lieu thereof, damages (to be assessed in the High Court) should be awarded to the plaintiff in accordance with Lord Cairns' Act. It is fair to say that the sixth ground of appeal contains this essential matter and that no argument was advanced on any other of the grounds of appeal.

During the course of the agreement, Mr Justice Hederman drew attention to the absence of any appeal by the second defendant and postulated the question as to what the situation would be if the court were to allow the first defendant's appeal whilst an order for specific performance remained in existence against the second defendant. It was indicated that the second defendant was prepared to join in the appeal, if necessary. Having regard, however, to my view on the substantial matter raised in the appeal, it is unnecessary to consider this aspect of the case further. There would appear to be adequate powers under order 58, r. 8, to deal with such a situation.

The argument

As I understand the argument advanced on behalf of the first defendant, and which I accept as being appropriate to be considered as if advanced on behalf of the second defendant, his case may be stated as follows:

1. An order of specific performance is an equitable remedy and, accordingly, discretionary in all cases.

2. There may be cases of real hardship caused by the grant of an order for specific performance.

3. The time to test or measure the degree of hardship is not at the date of the contract which is sought to be specifically performed, but rather at the date of trial.

4. In the instant case, there exists a circumstance over which neither plaintiff nor defendant had control and it prevented the closing of the sale until after the judgment of this court in the *Carthy* case was delivered on 30 January 1981, by which time the original purchase price was but half of the then current value of the property because of the huge nationwide increase in the value of licensed premises due to the high inflationary trends at the time.

5. That is a circumstance over which none of the parties had any control; it effects a great hardship on the defendants because they cannot now afford to buy an alternative public house such as would cater for their plans to have their son continue in that business. The only hardship on the plaintiff (and it, perhaps, a nominal one only, since he appears to have been buying in trust) is the very fact of not obtaining specific performance and having to settle for damages.

The plaintiff's answer is a short one. He says that any hardship that exists has arisen after the date of the contract and after the date for its completion; and that he has not caused or added to that hardship. In addition, it might be added that the defendants have been in receipt of all the profits of the business since the original intended date for closing. A further comment is made that the first defendant wanted initially, at least, to get out of the public house business because of the unhappy burglary incident. Neither the High Court nor this court was given any information about the purchase price paid by the defendants in 1973 and, consequently, the degree of hardship necessitated by them having to pay capital gains tax cannot be assessed.

The law

[Counsel for the defendant] has argued that the correct approach is to measure the hardship existing at the date of the hearing. That argument is unsupported by authority and is, indeed, contradicted by *Lavan v Walsh*[1] in which Budd J. said at 102–3 of the report:

> The defendant in this case also relies on the plea that enforcement of the contract in this case would cause great hardship on her. It is pointed out that the order is a discretionary one and it is strongly urged that the court in the exercise of a proper judicial discretion should not grant the relief of specific performance because of the special facts of the case which I will deal with later. Again, however, I must first refer to a matter of law. The court, it is well established, will not enforce the specific performance of a contract the result of which would be to impose great hardship on either of the parties to it. It is conceded, however, that the question of the hardship of a contract is generally to be judged at the time it is entered into. Change of circumstances taking place later, making the contract less beneficial to one party, are immaterial as a rule unless brought about by the action of the other party. It is stated, however, in *Fry on Specific Performance* (6th ed.), 200: 'It cannot, however, be denied that there are cases in which the court has refused its interference by reason of events subsequent to the contract.' From an examination of the cases of *The City of London v Nash*[2] and *Costigan v Hastler*[3] it appears that this is so, but exceptions to the general rule appear very rare. . . . I must, however, approach the consideration of these matters dispassionately and exercise what I conceive to be the proper judicial discretion. In the first place, as I have pointed out, it is undoubtedly the position in law that save in exceptional cases only a matter of hardship existing at the time of the contract can be taken into consideration. Hardship existing at the time of the contract is out of the case. It thus requires a strong case to be made out before one should accede to a plea for the exercise of judicial discretion in a quite unusual way, that is, by reason of hardship arising subsequently to the contract, and, the onus being on the defendant to satisfy me of the existence and genuineness of the alleged hardship on her, the proof of it should be strong and above suspicion.

Whilst, as Budd J. said, the relevant time issue appears to have been conceded, I do not overlook the quite exceptional standing as a lawyer in which (the counsel who made the concession) was held by bench and bar alike. Further, although Budd J. referred to the matter as being conceded, he expressed his own view in the most positive terms without reference to such concession. [Counsel for the defendant] has suggested that there is an illogicality in taking the date of the contract as the relevant one, since it is unlikely that there would have been any contract if the hardship had been known then. This very argument perhaps answers the problem. Hardship is permitted to defeat specific performance where an existing hardship was not known at the relevant time, being the date of the contract. While recognising that there may be cases in which hardship arising after the date of the contract is such that to decree specific performance would result in great injury, there must be few such cases and, in my view, they should not include ordinarily cases of hardship resulting from inflation alone. To permit, as an ordinary rule, a defence of subsequent hardship, would be to add a further hazard to the already trouble-strewn area of the law of contracts for the sale of land.

The application of the law

An examination of the evidence, including the summary at the commencement of this judgment, throws doubt upon the reality of the alleged claim of hardship. At all material times the defendants knew that they would have to complete a sale of the premises either to Mr Carthy or to the plaintiff. The plaintiff's advisers took meticulous care to make the plaintiff's position clear and, indeed, readily accepted that they could not press for completion until the *Carthy* case was resolved. The original motivation to leave the particular type of business was because of personal hazards; at no time from February 1978 to March 1981, was it ever suggested to the plaintiff or his advisers that there was any doubt about the eventual completion, assuming a satisfactory result to the first action. At no time did the defendants embark on any inquiry about a substitute public house in order that their son might pursue what was alleged to be their wish for his career.

The second defendant, having dispensed with the services of her original solicitor, embarked upon a spurious defence based on an alleged absence of authority; she now seeks to join her husband in criticising the plaintiff (who is a vehicle builder aged seventy six years, without any other connection with the licensed trade save that his daughter is married to one of the Madigans) because he assented in evidence to an extract from a letter dated 29 July 1979, written by his solicitors to Mr Black, specifying four items of alleged damages of which the fourth was 'the difference in value between the premises as they are valued at the date of the hearing and their value at which we purchased them.' It is to be noted that this letter, to which there appears to have been no reply, was written after the hearing of the *Carthy* case before Mr Justice Gannon and before judgment was delivered in that case. I know little of what transpired at that hearing save for some extracts from the transcript of it which were used in evidence in the trial of this case, but it does appear that the second defendant did not give evidence at that hearing, apparently because she would have supported Mr Carthy's claim.

The result

It may be that there are other circumstances surrounding the alleged hardship but I think that I have cited the salient ones. In my judgment, they fall far short of establishing the type of case in which the court should intervene to deny the ordinary remedy to one of the contracting parties in what was, at the time, a perfectly fair and proper transaction. There may be cases in which the court should intervene or, to put it more crudely, interfere with the express wording of a contract, and in which the duty to do justice may override strictly legal principles and the well recognised procedures of the courts of equity. Such is not the case here; indeed, justice here demands that the contract be specifically performed.

I have not overlooked the observations of the learned trial judge in respect of the balancing of the hardship to the defendants themselves whether or not an order of specific performance is granted. I do not dissent from his views as so expressed, but I prefer to rest my judgment as I have endeavoured to explain.

[1.] [1964] IR 87.   [2.] (1747) 1 Ves. Sen. 12.   [3.] (1804) 2 Sch. & Lef. 160.

(O'Higgins C.J. and Hederman J. agreed.)

F. Where the Plaintiff is Unwilling to Perform the Contract

Morrow v Carty [1957] NI 174

The plaintiff was the successful bidder at an auction held to sell a bungalow. The conditions of contract required immediate payment of a cash deposit. The plaintiff could not pay immediately and was given one hour to find the deposit. At the end of the hour the plaintiff had not returned and the property was resold. The plaintiff thereafter returned and tendered a cheque, which was not accepted. The plaintiff brought an action for specific performance.

McVeigh J.:

There can be little doubt that the payment of a deposit is a most important matter in the sale of land, and everybody knows this. As Lord Macnaghten says in *Soper v Arnold*,[1] 'The deposit serves two purposes—if the purchase is carried out it goes against the purchase money—but its primary purpose is this, it is a guarantee that the purchaser means business; and if there is a case in which a deposit is rightly and properly forfeited it is, I think, when a man enters into a contract to buy real property without taking the trouble to consider whether he can pay for it or not.' My view is that the words 'immediately after the sale' in condition 4 meant 'without any delay': see *Shorter Oxford English Dictionary* (2nd ed.); and see *Stroud's Judicial Dictionary* (3rd ed.), vol. 2. I think it means that the purchaser must place himself at the disposal of the vendor or his agent so that it may be ensured that payment of the deposit takes place as soon as it is convenient to bring that about after the sale.

In the construction of this phrase the case of *Johnston v Boyes*,[2] is in point where it was held that what is required is payment in *cash* (not cheque) and that the vendor is not obliged to wait until the next day to enable the purchaser to produce cash even where the purchaser is a person of credit.

As will be seen later the plaintiff, even after he went away and returned, did not produce cash, but only a cheque drawn in favour of his stepfather, which he, the plaintiff, had endorsed, claiming that he had authority to do so. This in itself raises a point, namely, whether the eventual offer of a cheque is a sufficient compliance with the condition that any one seeking performance must have been ready and willing to perform the contract according to its terms. Now, I hold on the authority of *Johnston v Boyes* that condition 4 required payment of cash, and I hold also that this condition was not waived at any time. The position was that at the time this cheque was offered the property had been resold and no question accordingly arose as to whether the cheque was an adequate method of payment. The plaintiff now contends in para. 3 of the statement of claim that he was then and is now ready and willing to perform his obligations under the agreement, but as I hold that the obligation under condition 4 was not waived, and was not complied with because cash was not offered, the question arises as to whether the plaintiff was 'ready' to comply with the contract. It is necessary for the plaintiff to plead that he is ready and willing to carry out the contract. See *Halsbury's Laws of England*, (2nd ed.) vol. 31, 421, and *Ellis v Rogers*.[3] In the case of *Cort v Ambergate Rly*[4] Campbell C.J. said: 'In common sense the meaning of such an averment of readiness and willingness (by plaintiffs) must be that the non-completion of the contract was not the fault of the plaintiffs, and that they were disposed and able to complete it if it had not been renounced by the defendants.'

The plaintiff in this case was not, in my opinion, 'ready', even within the time which he alleges was given to him to get the deposit, to perform his obligation to pay the deposit in cash. This obligation was, in my view, an essential term of the contract, and indeed the words of Lord Macnaghten already quoted in *Soper v Arnold* recognise it as such, and condition 18 providing for forfeiture of deposit and resale in default of compliance with conditions lends weight to this being considered an essential term: see *Harold Wood Brick Co. v Ferris*.[5]

I accordingly hold that his failure to perform this obligation or show that he was ready to perform it at the critical time disentitles him to specific performance. The repudiation of the contract by the defendant did not, in my view, excuse the plaintiff from showing performance or readiness to perform at the material time: see *Halsbury's Laws of England*, (2nd ed.) vol. 31, 384; *Chitty on Contract*, (20th ed.) 399; *Dyster v Randall*;[6] *Fry on Specific Performance*, (6th ed.) 436. I do not think that the plaintiff could have any legitimate ground of complaint if the case was decided against him on this ground for in my view it was somewhat audacious of him, in the way he was placed, to bid for this bungalow; he had not the money to pay the deposit, or any means, so far as the evidence goes, of obtaining any of his own credit, he was not in a position to draw a cheque as he had no bank account, he was not entitled to assume that a cheque would be accepted and as the banks were closed he must have known that no facilities were available for cashing one.

1. (1889) 14 App Cas 429.
2. [1899] 2 Ch. 73.
3. (1884) 29 ChD 661, 667.

4. (1851) 17 QB 127, 144.
5. [1935] 2 KB 198, 205.
6. [1926] Ch. 932, 934.

Bibliography

CHAPTER ONE

Corbin, 'Conditions in the law of contract' (1919) 28 Yale LJ 739
Holdsworth, *History of English Law* vol. III
Jackson (1937) 53 LQR 525
Kennedy, D., 'Form and Substance in the Law of Contract' (1975) 89 Harv L Rev 1685
Kronman and Posner, *The Economics of Contract Law*, Boston: Little Brown & Co. 1979
McLeod, N., *Early Irish Contract Law*, Sydney: Centre for Celtic Studies 1993
Maine, H., *Ancient Law*, Boston: Beacon 1864, 1963
Simpson, A *History of the Common Law of Contract*, OUP 1975
Terry, 'Unconscionable Contracts in NSW' (1982) 10 Aust BL Rev 311
Weber, M., *On Law in Economics and Society*, ed. by Rheinstein, New York: Clarion 1954

CHAPTER TWO

Clark, R., *Contract Law in Ireland*, 3rd ed., London: Sweet & Maxwell 1992
Davenport, 'Lockout Agreements' vol. 107 LQR 366
Neill, 'A Key to Lockout Agreements' vol 108 LQR 405

CHAPTER THREE

Adams and Brownsword, 'Contract Consideration and the Critical Path' (1990) vol. 53 MLR 536
Atiyah, P. S., 'Consideration; A Restatement', *Essays on Contract*, Oxford Clarendon Press 1986
Delaney, H., 'The Doctrine of Legitimate Expectation in Irish Law' [1990] 12 DULJ 1
Fried, C., *Contract as Promise*, Boston: Harvard UP 1981
Law Revision Committee Sixth Interim Report (Cmd. 5449)
Phang, A., 'Consideration at the Crossroads' (1991) 107 LQR 21
Sutton, K. C. T., *Consideration Reconsidered*, University of Queensland Press 1974

CHAPTER FOUR

Reynolds (1988) 104 LQR 353
Stoljer 19 MLR 237

CHAPTER SIX

Law Commission (UK) No. 154 Parol Evidence Rule
Wedderburn, 'Collected Contracts' (1959) 17 CLJ 58

CHAPTER SEVEN

Phang, A., 'Implied Terms revisited' [1990] JBL 39
Treitel, G. H., *The Law of Contract*, 8th ed., London: Sweet & Maxwell 1991

CHAPTER EIGHT

'Bord Telecom's Powers almost draconian—Judge' *Irish Times* 26 February 1985
Calamari, I., 'Duty to Read—A Changing Concept' |1974| 43 Fordham L Rev 1 341
Clark, R., op. cit.
Dean (1993) 56 MLR 581
Ellinghaus (1969) 78 Yale LJ 757
Kessler, F., 'The Contract of Adhesion' (1943) Col L Rev 629
Leff (1967) 115 U. Pa. L Rev 485
Llewellyn, K., 'Review of Prausnitz O., *The Standardization of Commercial Contracts in English and Continental Law* (1937)' in (1939) 52 Harv L Rev 700
Sales, H. B., 'Standard Form Contracts' (1953) 16 MLR 318
Yates, D., *Exemption Clauses*, 2nd ed., London: Sweet & Maxwell 1982

CHAPTER NINE

Anson's Law of Contract (26th ed.)
Clark, R., 'Of Potatoes and Pariahs', Ir Jur (n.s.) xix (1984) 101

CHAPTER ELEVEN

Clark, R.,'Contract Property Insurance—A Return to Utmost Good Faith by Both Sides' (1987) 9 DULJ 117

CHAPTER TWELVE

Binchy, Irish Current Law Statutes Annotated at 82/2–11
Law Reform Commission Report on Minors' contracts (1985) LRC 15
Treitel, G. H., 'The Infants Relief Act 1874' 73 LQR 194

CHAPTER THIRTEEN

Atiyah, 'Economic Duress and "the Overborne Will"' (1982) 98 LQR 197
Ogilvie, 'Economic Duress, Inequality of Bargaining Power and Threatened Breach of Contract' (1981) 2/McGill LJ 289
Wedderburn (1982) 45 MLR 556

CHAPTER FIFTEEN

Beatson |1992| CLP 1
Coote, B., *Consideration and the Joint Promisee* |1978| CLJ 301
Davies, P. J. and Palmer, N. E., 'The Eurymedon, Five Years On' 1979 JBL 334
Flannigan, R., 'Privity—The End of an Era' (1987) 103 LQR 565
Furmston, M. P., 'Return to *Dunlop v Selfridge*?' (1960) 23 MLR 373
Law Commission (UK) Consultation Paper No. 21, 'Privity of Contract; Contracts for the Benefit of Third Parties'
Treitel, G. H., 'Specific Performance and Third Parties' (1967) 23 MLR 373

CHAPTER SEVENTEEN

'A significant Shift due to 1991 Act' 3 *Competition* 59
'How Severance by Courts might save Offending Articles' 2 *Competition* 153
Van Bael, I. & Bellis, J. F., *Competition Law of the EEC*, 2nd ed., CCH Editions Ltd 1990

CHAPTER EIGHTEEN

Beck, A., 'The Doctrine of Substantial Performance: Conditions and Conditions Precedent' (1975) 38 MLR 413

Dugdale, T. and Yates, D. 'Variation Waiver and Estoppel—a Re-appraisal' (1976) 39 MLR 680

Law Commission Report No. 121 (1983)

CHAPTER NINETEEN

Clark, R., 'Unjust enrichment as a non-compensatory principle justifying the award of damages' (1978) 29 NLQ 129

Fuller & Purdue (1936) 46 Yale LJ 52

Irish Independent 28 February 1985

Law Commission Working Paper No. 132 (1993)

McGregor on Damages

O'Driscoll, J., 'A Note on the rule in *Bain v Fothergill*' (1975) 10 Ir Jur (N.S.) 203

Treitel, G.H., *Remedies for Breach of Contract*, Oxford: Clarendon Press 1988